OXFORD READER'S COMPANION TO TROLLOPE

Trollope is seldom seen in a photograph with pad and pencil, although he made no secret of writing in public as he travelled. In a train compartment he had a tablet readily available, and for his travel books he must have recorded facts and impressions on the spot. In this picture, probably taken in the 1870s, despite the elegant top hat he looks his usual dishevelled self with heavily creased frock coat and trousers.

OXFORD READER'S COMPANION TO

Trollope

Edited by R. C. Terry

OXFORD

UNIVERSITY PRESS

OXFORD

UNIVERSITY PRESS

Great Clarendon Street, Oxford OX2 6DP

Oxford University Press is a department of the University of Oxford.
It furthers the University's objective of excellence in research, scholarship,
and education by publishing worldwide in

Oxford New York

Athens Auckland Bangkok Bogotá Buenos Aires Calcutta
Cape Town Chennai Dar es Salaam Delhi Florence Hong Kong Istanbul
Karachi Kuala Lumpur Madrid Melbourne Mexico City Mumbai
Nairobi Paris São Paulo Singapore Taipei Tokyo Toronto Warsaw

and associated companies in Berlin Ibadan

Oxford is a registered trade mark of Oxford University Press
in the UK and in certain other countries

Published in the United States
by Oxford University Press Inc., New York

British Library Cataloguing in Publication Data

Data available

Library of Congress Cataloging in Publication Data

Data available

ISBN 0–19–866210–6

1 3 5 7 9 10 8 6 4 2

Typeset by Interactive Sciences Ltd, Gloucester
Printed in Great Britain
on acid-free paper by
Biddles Ltd
Guildford and King's Lynn

For Kathleen Tillotson

I feel that Trollope and I are living here together, for I seem to spend so much of my time with him, especially in the long hours after midnight. We then wander about Barsetshire in a heavyish carriage drawn by two slow horses with long tails and the motors whiz by us, but with Anthony on the box we do reach our destination which they perhaps don't.

J. M. Barrie

PREFACE

FIRST-TIME readers often get their introduction to Trollope, as Barrie suggests, wandering about Barsetshire, but there is much to attract them to venture beyond that pleasant territory among his vast output of novels, short stories, and travel books. And it comes as a surprise to encounter such a feast of reading. Trollope was the most prolific of the great Victorian novelists and has been described as the busiest man of letters. For a writer of such prodigious output, a volume such as this must be an invaluable resource. The *Companion* therefore addresses as fully as possible the range and diversity of Trollope's life as a man of letters, in the literal sense as well as the metaphorical. Information about him as a civil servant, who served with distinction in the General Post Office, has its place with articles about his twin career as novelist. And since his novels are so thorough an expression of the mid-Victorian times in which he lived, the social context is also addressed. Trollope's milieu is not, however, confined to the shires and cities of England: his work has a unique geographical reach. Thus the seismograph of Victorian life, as he was once called, is shown in relation to a wide range of individuals, locations, and historical events, international as well as national.

Trollope craved friendship, acknowledgement, a position in society. Accordingly, the volume gives brief accounts of many individuals associated with the writer's private, professional, and social life: his love of London and its clubs, the hunting fraternities and house parties up and down the country, his contacts on both sides of the Atlantic and in Australia, and his connections with the arts and public affairs. Because of the colossal *œuvre*, it has been a guiding principle to cover characters and locations in the fiction, so as to help readers find or recall vital landmarks and details. Interconnections of characters, threads from one novel to another, from one journey to the next, a cardinal element in the author's writing, are reflected by the linkage of biographical, historical, and literary commentary in the *Companion*. In this respect the volume strives to be the most extensive reference book devoted to Trollope.

Comprehensiveness has been one criterion for this *Companion*, but this has been achieved without compromising literary judgements and materials required by the serious reader and scholar. Essays on each of the forty-seven novels, which are the focus of the book, draw attention to their thematic concerns and artistry, supplemented by details of publishing, criticism, contemporary reception, and general bibliography. The volume also explores ways in which the novelist, now acknowledged among the greatest Victorian writers, is being read in the light of new interpretation and theory. The chronicler of a pleasantly old-fashioned world of leisured gentry, acquiescing in the values of a bygone age, is now also appreciated for original and often subversive ideas about the fabric of private and public life of the Victorian period. His presentation of controversial ideas about marriage, sexuality, parenting, feminism, racism, and colonialism is covered in this volume.

Trollope concluded *An Autobiography* by saying, 'That I can read and be happy while I am reading, is a great blessing. Could I have remembered, as some men do, what I read,

Preface

I should have been able to call myself an educated man.' Helping all those readers to know Trollope a little better, enjoy him with a little more insight—and remember him—is the object of this book.

ACKNOWLEDGEMENTS

COMPILING the *Oxford Reader's Companion to Trollope* provided an opportunity to reacquaint myself with his books and pick up along the way a mass of new information about him. But the happiest part of the process has been to renew old friendships and to make new ones in what has proved a most satisfying occupation over several years. At the time of Trollope's centenary conference, held at University College, London, in June 1982, we were, relative to Dickensians or Janeites, a small band of *aficionados*. The standard biographies and collections of letters were still those of Sadleir and Booth respectively. Now there are four biographies and N. John Hall's outstanding two-volume edition of the letters. Each year sees a number of essays and articles devoted to individual novels and non-fiction, and there is now a Trollope Society in London and New York. Trollope has at last his plaque in Westminster Abbey.

It is hardly surprising, then, that many friends and colleagues came to my aid when the idea for this *Companion* was proposed, and I must here record my gratitude for all the help they have given me. My advisers, N. John Hall and John Sutherland, not only gave meticulous attention at the outset when I was planning the work, and answered my often frantic e-mails as the work progressed, but also contributed essays. To them and to all those contributors listed by name below I offer congratulations and warmest appreciation. Sadly, one of our number, Walter Kendrick, died in October 1998.

Of equally valued service is the huge team involved in the preparation and production of the text, starting with my two research assistants and ending with the experts who saw the book onto the shelves. My patient, tireless, overworked assistants were Sheila Burgar and Monika Rydygier-Smith, whose presence close at hand as colleagues in the Department of English, University of Victoria, meant that they had nowhere to hide from my constant questions and requests. I acknowledge the co-operation received from Evelyn Cobley, chair of the English Department, and from Puri Pazo-Torres, secretary. When it came to recording, collating and reproducing a vast amount of information, I had the generous secretarial skill of Darlene Hollingsworth, who brought, along with professionalism of the highest order, a discriminating and critical eye to the material in her care. Secretarial assistance was also received from Lisa Powers and Diana Rutherford. I wish to thank colleagues in the English Department, and acknowledge the resources of the University Library's Special Collections, Reference, Inter-Library Loans, and Microforms divisions. A further debt is acknowledged to Sheila Burgar for help with the Chronology, to Graham Handley and Judith Terry for the maps, and to Anthony Jenkins for the Family Tree.

Within Oxford University Press I have been fortunate to have the help of Michael Cox, Pam Coote, Alison Jones, and Wendy Tuckey, and with them an assiduous copy-editor, Jackie Pritchard, whose meticulous reading produced helpful additions to the text, and others in the team, Elizabeth Stratford (desk editing), John Mackrell (production) and Nick Clarke (design). An editor/author working so many thousands of

Acknowledgements

miles away from his advisers presents extra problems in keeping such a project on time and on track, and I thank them for their patience and advice.

My work was generously funded by the Social Science and Humanities Research Council of Canada and I am most grateful for its support.

To all those who offered advice and answered my questions also my thanks. They include Isobel Armstrong, William Baker, Michael Booth, William Clarke, Peter Edwards, R. J. Hall, Graham Handley, John Letts and the Trollope Society, Deborah Morse, Alan Powell, W. G. Shelton, W. G. Streeten, David Skilton, and Peter Smith.

Of assistance from my wife, Judith, I borrow Trollope's own words in acknowledging her role throughout this project. 'She, I think, has so read almost everything, to my very great advantage in matters of taste', accuracy and clarity.

R.C.T

Victoria, British Columbia
October 1998.

CONTENTS

HOW TO USE THIS BOOK

T HE volume is organized in strict alphabetical order with headwords for each entry. Most headwords cover specific single topics, such as the account of Trollope's life (a good starting point for the general reader). Others are intended to cover all the relevant material under an inclusive title such as 'homes of Trollope', so that the reader does not need to search for several different headwords such as 'Keppel Street' or 'Waltham House'.

Cross-references are used to direct the reader to relevant information on an entry. They are indicated by an asterisk, or by 'see' or 'see also' followed by a headword, in small capitals. Suggestions for additional reading on a topic, particularly in the case of novels, follow an entry. Articles on the fiction use a basic framework of factual information about plot, theme, style, reception, and bibliographic details, but allowance has been made for a contributor's choice of what to highlight or illustrate in a particular text. The texts used are the latest World's Classics editions, and references from them are given in roman capitals for chapters, not page numbers. Sources for short stories are indicated from collections, such as *An Editor's Tales*. Each entry concerning Trollope's multifarious journalism consists of a digest of the article, with dates and source in periodicals such as *Saint Pauls Magazine* or the *Fortnightly Review*. A feature of the *Companion* is an exhaustive recording of Characters and Locations with their sources at the end of each entry in abbreviated form. These augment information on individual novels and short stories.

For a writer of such quantity as Trollope, use of abbreviations is unavoidable. A List of Abbreviations for works of fiction and often cited other books is on p. xxiii. *An Autobiography* is shown throughout by abbreviated title and chapter, as in *Auto* IV. Letters are cited by volume number and page, as in *Letters* 2, 747.

The reader may find it helpful first of all to read through the Thematic Overview on p. xiii to get a general idea of what the *Companion* contains. There are eight subject areas: Private Life, Public Life, Trollope the Writer, Characters in Fiction, Locations in Fiction, Individuals Associated with Trollope, Literary Contexts, and Social Contexts (the latter including a section on London). The Overview can be used to track down particular interests, or to make connections with related topics, as, for example, those under headings such as 'Education' or 'Criticisms and reviews on literary themes'.

The *Companion* includes a Chronology on p. 599, Family Trees (pp. 609–12), and Maps of significant places (pp. 615–21). A Select Bibliography on p. 623 lists works frequently cited in the text and other useful reference works relevant to Trollope studies.

Entries conclude with the contributor's initials, for which the key and biographies appear on p. xix.

THEMATIC OVERVIEW

[entries are arranged alphabetically by headword with categories]

Private life of Trollope

appearance, personality, character
card-playing
cartoons and parodies
food and drink
holidays abroad
homes of Trollope
house parties
hunting
library
London: clubs
portraits and photographs
smoking
transportation and travel
Trollope, Anthony
wine

Family

ancestry of Trollope family
brothers and sisters of Trollope
descendants and relatives of Trollope
grandparents of Trollope
Heseltine family
Trollope, Frances (née Milton, mother)
Trollope, Frederic James Anthony (son)
Trollope, Henry Merivale (son)
Trollope, Rose (née Heseltine, wife)
Trollope, Thomas Adolphus (brother)
Trollope, Thomas Anthony (father)

Public life of Trollope

Civil Service, Trollope and the
Copyright, Royal Commission on
politics, Trollope and
Postal Museum, National
public service of Anthony Trollope
Royal Literary Fund

Trollope the writer

Barsetshire series
comedy in Trollope's work
editor, Trollope as
heroes and heroines
journalist, Trollope as
language and style
morality and fiction
Palliser series
political issues in Trollope's fiction
projected or unpublished works

working habits

Adaptations and successors

adaptations
anthologies
guidebooks
Knox, Father Ronald Arbuthnott
Oliphant, Mrs Margaret
Thirkell, Angela Mackail
Trollope, Joanna

Allusions in Trollope's writing

Bible
classical literature
Milton, John
Shakespeare, William

Criticism and collections

bibliographies
biographies
cartoons and parodies
critical opinions of Trollope: contemporary
critical opinions of Trollope: 1882–1920
critical opinions of Trollope: 1921–50
critical opinions of Trollope: 1951–80
critical opinions of Trollope: since 1980
lectures and speeches
letters
manuscripts and editions
obituaries
short stories, Trollope's

Organizations associated with Trollope

Trollope Society

Works

Journalism

America

'American Affairs'
'American Conflict, The' (two articles)
'American Question, The'
'American Reconstruction'
'*Civil War in America, The*, by Goldwyn Smith'
'England and America'
'England and the United States'
'English View of the President's Impeachment, An'
Letter from Anthony Trollope, A'
'Present Condition of the Northern States of the American Union, The'
'President Johnson's Last Message'
'President Lincoln'
'Right of Secession, The'
'St Albans Raiders, The'

Thematic Overview

Thematic Overview

Thematic Overview

'Last Austrian Who Left Venice, The'
'Lotta Schmidt'
Lotta Schmidt and Other Stories
'Malachi's Cove'
'Man Who Kept his Money in a Box, The'
'Mary Gresley'
'Miss Ophelia Gledd'
'Miss Sarah Jack, of Spanish Town, Jamaica'
'Mistletoe Bough, The'
'Mrs Brumby'
'Mrs General Talboys'
'Never, Never—Never, Never'
'Not if I Know It'
'O'Conors of Castle Conor, The'
'Panjandrum, The'
'Parson's Daughter of Oxney Colne, The'
'Relics of General Chassé: A Tale of Antwerp'
'Returning Home'
'Ride across Palestine, A'
'Spotted Dog, The'
Tales of All Countries: First Series
Tales of All Countries: Second Series
'Telegraph Girl, The'
'Turkish Bath, The'
'Two Generals, The'
'Two Heroines of Plumplington, The'
'Unprotected Female at the Pyramids, An'
'Why Frau Frohmann Raised her Prices'
Why Frau Frohmann Raised her Prices and Other Stories
'Widow's Mite, The'
Unpublished writings
 Commonplace Book
 'History of English Prose Fiction'
 'History of World Literature'

Characters

American characters
business entrepreneurs
clergymen as characters
clubs in the novels
doctors as characters
election scenes
farmers as characters
government officials as characters
hunting and horse racing
journalists as characters
lawyers as characters
military characters
moneylenders as characters
politicians as characters
servants as characters
tradesmen as characters

Literary contexts

Drama
 acting and actors
 drama, Elizabethan and Jacobean
 theatre, Victorian
Essay
 essay, contemporary
Novel
 novel, contemporary British
 novel, 18th-century British
Poetry
 poetry, contemporary
 poetry, early 19th-century
 poetry, Elizabethan
 poetry, 17th-century
Genres and kinds of writing
 American literature
 annuals and keepsakes
 Burke's and Debrett's
 comedy of manners
 Dictionary of National Biography
 European literature
 historical fiction
 regional novels
 roman-à-clef
 Russian literature
 sensation fiction
 silver fork fiction
 women writers
Periodicals
 All the Year Round
 Athenaeum
 Blackwood's Magazine
 Chambers's Edinburgh Journal
 Contemporary Review
 Cornhill Magazine
 Dublin Review
 Dublin University Magazine
 Edinburgh Review
 Fortnightly Review
 Good Words
 Graphic
 Harper's New Monthly Magazine
 Macmillan's Magazine
 Punch
 Saint Pauls Magazine
 Saturday Review
 Spectator
 Temple Bar
 Time
 Whitehall Review
Publishing, production, promotion
 copyrights, half-profits, royalties
 illustrators and illustrating
 Mudie's Library
 periodicals
 publishers and publishing
 railway bookstalls

serialization
yellowbacks

Social contexts

Issues of public debate, national
Bribery Commissions
charity and philanthropy
Conservative and Liberal administrations
education
emigration
government
health and medical practice
House of Commons
House of Lords
Hyde Park riots
Ireland
poverty
race and racism
radicalism
Reform Act
Scotland
suffrage
Tichborne case
transportation and travel
urbanization and population
women's issues
Issues of public debate, international
American Civil War
Australia and New Zealand
British imperialism
Canada
Europe, eastern
Europe, western
India and Ceylon
Middle East
Russia
Scandinavia and Iceland
South America
West Indies
Religion
agnosticism, atheism
Church of England
evangelicalism
Judaism and the Jews
Nonconformism
religious faith and worship
Roman Catholic Church
Sabbatarianism
Law
courts of justice
Inns of Court
law and society
legal system and officials

Finance and business
banks and currency
business entrepreneurs
moneylending
Press
Daily Telegraph
Pall Mall Gazette
Times, The
Social issues and culture
aristocracy
art and artists
Christmas
class structure
country houses and estates
courtship
cricket
croquet
dancing
fashion
genre painting
household management
landed gentry, old
lawn tennis
London season
marriage and divorce
middle class, new
monarchy
museums and exhibitions
music-making
National Gallery
old age
parents and children
Pre-Raphaelites
property and inheritance
Royal Academy of Arts
scientific enquiry
sea-bathing
self-help
sexuality
shooting season
spas
street musicians
working class
London
London: assembly rooms
London: churches
London: clubs
London: hotels and inns
London: houses of friends and associates
London: landmarks
London: streets and squares
London: theatres

CONTRIBUTORS

General Editor

R. C. TERRY (RCT). Professor Emeritus of English, University of Victoria, British Columbia. Since publishing *Anthony Trollope: The Artist in Hiding* (1977) he has produced two more books on Trollope, and *Victorian Popular Fiction 1860–1880* (1983). He has edited books on Robert Louis Stevenson and (with Nelson Smith) on Wilkie Collins.

Consultant Editors

N. JOHN HALL (NJH). Distinguished Professor of English, Bronx Community College and the Graduate School, City University of New York. Twice a Guggenheim fellow, his publications include *Trollope and his Illustrators* (1980), *The Trollope Critics* (1981), *The Letters of Anthony Trollope* (1983), *Trollope: A Biography* (1991), and four books on Max Beerbohm.

JOHN SUTHERLAND (JS). Lord Northcliffe Professor of Modern English Literature, University College, London. Author of *Victorian Novelists and Publishers* (1976) and *The Longman Companion to Victorian Fiction* (1989). He has also edited a number of Trollope titles for the Oxford World's Classics and the Penguin Classics series.

Contributors

RUTH apROBERTS (R apR). Professor Emeritus of English, University of California, Riverside. Since publishing *Trollope: Artist and Moralist* (in the USA, *The Moral Trollope*) in 1971, she has published books on Matthew Arnold, Thomas Carlyle, and—most recently—*The Biblical Web* (1994), studies in the influence of the Bible on anglophone culture.

TONY BAREHAM (TB). Professor of English at the University of Ulster at Coleraine. He has published books on Crabbe, Trollope, Lever, Stoppard, and Malcolm Lowry. His articles range in subject matter from Shakespeare to T. S. Eliot. Work in progress includes a definitive bibliography of Charles Lever.

SHEILA BURGAR (SRB). Sessional Lecturer in English at the University of Victoria. She is also working on her doctorate in Victorian literature. Her dissertation will explore Anthony Trollope's treatment of British attitudes towards imperialism, colonization, tourism, and travel.

GEORGE BUTTE (GB). Professor of English, Colorado College. He has published scholarly articles on Austen, Trollope, Conrad, and Hitchcock, and is currently finishing a book-length manuscript on intersubjectivity and narrative. He teaches the English novel, narrative and comic theory, and film studies.

RANDALL CRAIG (RC). Associate Professor at the State University of New York at Albany. He is the author of *The Tragicomic Novel: Studies in a Fictional Mode from Meredith to Joyce* (1989), *Promising Language: Betrothal in Victorian Law and Fiction* (forthcoming), and numerous articles on British fiction.

PETER EDWARDS (PE). Professor Emeritus of English, University of Queensland. He is the author of *Anthony Trollope: His Art and Scope* (1977), *Anthony Trollope's Son in Australia* (1982), and *Dickens's 'Young Men': George Augustus Sala and Edmund Yates* (1997).

MICKIE GROVER (MG). Studied at the Graduate Center, City University of New York. In addition to the Victorians she has written on science fiction and fantasy, recently completing a study of the witch in history and the novel. She is currently writing a dark fantasy with nary a witch in sight.

MARY HAMER (MH). Taught at Cambridge before becoming a fellow of the W. E. B. DuBois Institute, Harvard University. A cultural historian, her publications include: *Writing by Numbers: Trollope's Serial Fiction* (1987); *Signs of Cleopatra: History, Politics, Representation* (1993), and *Julius Caesar* (1998). She

Contributors

has edited *Castle Richmond* and *The Landleaguers* for World's Classics.

GRAHAM HANDLEY (GRH). Has taught and lectured for fifty years. He has specialized in nineteenth-century fiction, writing on George Eliot, Trollope, Mrs Gaskell, Hardy, Thackeray, and Dickens, and editing texts by the first three. He has written books on Eliot and Jane Austen and edited an anthology, *Trollope, the Traveller* (1993).

GEOFFREY HARVEY (GH). Senior Lecturer in English at the University of Reading. His publications include *The Art of Anthony Trollope* (1980) and *The Romantic Tradition in Modern English Poetry* (1986). Among his editions in the Oxford World's Classics series are three Trollope novels: *Mr Scarborough's Family*, *The Bertrams*, and *Marion Fay*.

ANTHONY JENKINS (AWJ). Professor Emeritus of English at the University of Victoria, British Columbia. A specialist in British theatre: among his books are *The Theatre of Tom Stoppard* (1989) and *The Making of Victorian Drama* (1991). He is particularly interested in Trollope's ambitions as a playwright and, having worked with Robert Tracy at Berkeley, in Trollope's later novels.

WALTER KENDRICK (WK). Professor of English at Fordham University and the author of *The Novel Machine: The Theory and Fiction of Anthony Trollope* (1980). He has written or co-edited five other books and contributed frequently to professional and popular journals.

CHRISTOPHER KENT (CK). Professor of Modern British History at the University of Saskatchewan, Saskatoon, Canada, a former editor of the *Canadian Journal of History*, and an editorial advisory board member of *Victorian Studies*. He has published numerous articles on Victorian cultural history and is completing a book on Victorian Bohemia.

JAMES R. KINCAID (JRK). Aerol Arnold Professor of English at the University of Southern California. He is author of a book and several essays on Trollope and, most recently, of *Child-Loving: The Erotic Child and Victorian Culture* (1992), *Annoying the Victorians* (1995), and *Erotic Innocence: The Culture of Child-Molesting* (1998).

LAURENCE KITZAN (LK). Associate Professor, Department of History, University of Saskatchewan. A specialist in British Imperial History, his research and publications are on missionaries in India and China, and on the First Burmese War. He has completed a manuscript on the Victorian literature of imperialism, and is currently working on explorers and travellers.

JUDITH KNELMAN (JK). An Associate Professor in the Faculty of Information and Media Studies at the University of Western Ontario. A historian of journalism, she is the author of *Twisting in the Wind: The Murderess and the English Press* (1998).

ANNE K. LYONS (AKL). Lives in Boulder, Colorado, where she is an occasional instructor. She has degrees from St Louis University and the University of Colorado. Her publications include *Anthony Trollope: An Annotated Bibliography of Periodical Works . . . to 1900* (1985).

JULIET MCMASTER (JM). Professor of English at the University of Alberta. She is the author of *Trollope's Palliser Novels* (1978), *Thackeray: The Major Novels* (1971), *Jane Austen on Love* (1978), *Dickens the Designer* (1987), and *Jane Austen the Novelist* (1996), and co-editor with Edward Copeland of the recent *Cambridge Companion to Jane Austen* (1997).

ROWLAND MCMASTER (RDM). Professor Emeritus at the University of Alberta. He has published *Trollope and the Law* (1986), *Thackeray's Cultural Frame of Reference: Allusion in the Newcomes* (1991), and many articles on Victorian literature. A former editor of *English Studies in Canada*, he is a fellow of the Royal Society of Canada.

JUDITH WITTOSCH MALCOLM (JWM). Director of Development Communications at the University of Michigan, she has an MA and Ph.D. in English Language and Literature from the University of Michigan. Her research has focused on Trollope and *Saint Pauls Magazine*.

MARGARET MARKWICK (MM). Has written *Trollope and Women* (1997), a gender-specific exploration of Trollope's female characters, and the introduction to the Trollope Society's edition of *The Small House at Allington*. A mature student at Exeter University, she expects a further book, *Trollope and Men*, to come out of her doctoral research.

Contributors

JANE NARDIN (JN). Professor of English at the University of Wisconsin-Milwaukee. She has written two studies of Trollope: *He Knew She Was Right: The Independent Woman in the Novels of Anthony Trollope* (1989) and *Trollope and Victorian Moral Philosophy* (1996). Her publications also include books on Jane Austen and Barbara Pym.

HUGH OSBORNE (HO). Lecturer in English at Cardiff University. He has edited numerous Trollope novels for publication, and is currently writing a book on Victorian literary autobiography.

JULIA MIELE RODAS (JMR). Teaching fellow in English at Hunter College. She is currently working on a study of 'scoundrel' and 'interloper' characters in a series of nineteenth-century novels.

ANDREW SANDERS (ALS). Professor of English at the University of Durham. He is the author of *The Victorian Historical Novel 1840–1880* (1978), *Charles Dickens: Resurrectionist* (1982), the Companion to *A Tale of Two Cities* (1988) and *The Short Oxford History of English Literature* (1994). He has edited novels by Dickens, Eliot, Gaskell, Thomas Hughes, and Thackeray. His *Anthony Trollope* in the new 'Writers and their Work' series will be published in 1998 and his study *Dickens and the Spirit of the Age* in 1999.

DAVID SKILTON (DS). Head of the School of English, Communication, and Philosophy at Cardiff University. He is Literary Adviser to the Trollope Society and General Editor of the Trollope Society/Folio Society edition of the novels. His books include *Anthony Trollope and his Contemporaries* (1972), *Defoe to the Victorians* (1985), *The Early and Mid-Victorian Novel* (1993), and numerous editions of Victorian works, including many of Trollope's novels, and *An Autobiography* (1996).

MONIKA RYDYGIER SMITH (MRS). Sessional Instructor at the University of Victoria, British Columbia, where she is also a Doctoral Candidate. She has published on domestic violence in Trollope's *The Way We Live Now* in *Victorian Review*, and is currently working on Dickens's 'grotesque bodies' in relation to nineteenth-century concerns over class and gender.

NELSON C. SMITH (NCS). Associate Professor of English at the University of Victoria, Canada, where he teaches Victorian, American, and Canadian fiction. Author of *James Hogg* (1980) and *Anne Radcliffe: The Art of Gothic* (1980); co-editor, with R. C. Terry, of *Wilkie Collins to the Forefront: Some Reassessments* (1995).

PATRICIA SREBRNIK (PTS). Teaches at the University of Calgary. She is the author of *Alexander Strahan, Victorian Publisher* (1986).

DONALD D. STONE (DDS). Professor of English at Queens College and the Graduate Center, City University of New York. He is the author of *Novelists in a Changing World: Meredith, James, and the Transformation of English Fiction in the 1880s* (1972), *The Romantic Impulse in Victorian Fiction* (1980), *Communications with the Future: Matthew Arnold in Dialogue* (1997), among other works. His awards include a John Simon Guggenheim Fellowship.

JULIAN THOMPSON (PJT). Teaches English at Regent's Park College, Oxford. He has edited Trollope's *Ayala's Angel* and *Cousin Henry* for Oxford World's Classics and *The Small House at Allington* for Penguin, and the *Collected Shorter Fiction* of both Anthony Trollope and Wilkie Collins.

ROBERT TRACY (RT). Professor of English and of Celtic Studies at the University of California, Berkeley. He is the author of *Trollope's Later Novels* (1978) and *The Unappeasable Host: Studies in Irish Identities* (1998). He has edited Trollope's *The Way We Live Now* for Library of Literature, Macmillan, *The Macdermots of Ballycloran*, *Nina Balatka*, and *Linda Tressel* for Oxford World's Classics. He has translated *Kamen'* (as *Stone*, 1981) from the Russian of Osip Mandelstam.

MARK W. TURNER (MT). Lecturer in English at Roehampton Institute, London. He is the author of *Trollope and the Magazines* (forthcoming from Macmillan and St Martin's Press) and has written several articles on Trollope and serialization. He is currently working on the construction of urban, metropolitan masculinity in Trollope's fiction.

LIST OF ABBREVIATIONS

Novels

AA	Ayala's Angel
AS	The American Senator
B	The Bertrams
BE	The Belton Estate
BT	Barchester Towers
C	The Claverings
CH	Cousin Henry
CR	Castle Richmond
CYFH	Can You Forgive Her?
DC	The Duke's Children
DT	Doctor Thorne
DWS	Dr Wortle's School
ED	The Eustace Diamonds
EE	An Eye for an Eye
FixP	The Fixed Period
FP	Framley Parsonage
GLG	The Golden Lion of Granpère
HHG	Harry Heathcote of Gangoil
HKWR	He Knew He Was Right
IHP	Is He Popenjoy?
JC	John Caldigate
KD	Kept in the Dark
KOK	The Kellys and the O'Kellys
L	The Landleaguers
LA	Lady Anna
LCB	The Last Chronicle of Barset
LT	Linda Tressel
LV	La Vendée
MB	The Macdermots of Ballycloran
MF	Marion Fay
MM	Miss Mackenzie
MSF	Mr Scarborough's Family
NB	Nina Balatka
OF	Orley Farm
OML	An Old Man's Love
PF	Phineas Finn
PM	The Prime Minister
PR	Phineas Redux
RH	Ralph the Heir
RR	Rachel Ray
SBJR	The Struggles of Brown, Jones, and Robinson
SHA	The Small House at Allington
SHH	Sir Harry Hotspur of Humblethwaite
TC	The Three Clerks
VB	The Vicar of Bullhampton
W	The Warden
WWLN	The Way We Live Now

Short story collections

ET	An Editor's Tales
LS	Lotta Schmidt and Other Stories
TAC1	Tales of All Countries First Series
TAC2	Tales of All Countries Second Series
WFF	Why Frau Frohmann Raised her Prices and Other Stories

Short stories

'Bath'	'Turkish Bath'
'Bauche'	'La Mère Bauche'
'Bell'	'The Courtship of Susan Bell'
'Brumby'	'Mrs Brumby'
'Bull'	'John Bull on the Guadalquivir'
'Carmichael'	'Catherine Carmichael'
'Chassé'	'The Relics of General Chassé: A Tale of Antwerp'
'Colne'	'The Parson's Daughter of Oxney Colne'
'Dog'	'The Spotted Dog'
'Dugdale'	'Alice Dugdale'
'Euphemia'	'The Gentle Euphemia, or Love Shall Still Be Lord of All'
'Frohmann'	'Why Frau Frohmann Raised her Prices'
'Generals'	'The Two Generals'
'Giles'	'Father Giles of Ballymoy'
'Gledd'	'Miss Ophelia Gledd'
'Gresley'	'Mary Gresley'
'Heine'	'The House of Heine Brothers, in Munich'
'Jack'	'Miss Sarah Jack, of Spanish Town, Jamaica'
'Kirkby'	'Christmas Day at Kirkby Cottage'
'Launay'	'The Lady of Launay'
'Malachi'	'Malachi's Cove'
'Mistletoe'	'The Mistletoe Bough'
'Money'	'The Man Who Kept his Money in a Box'
'Montmorenci'	'Josephine de Montmorenci'
'Never'	'Never, Never—Never, Never'
'Not if'	'Not if I Know It'

List of Abbreviations

'O'Conors' 'The O'Conors of Castle Conor'
'Palestine' 'A Ride across Palestine'
'Panama' 'A Journey to Panama'
'Panjandrum' 'The Panjandrum'
'Pickering' 'The Adventures of Fred Pickering'
'Plumplington' 'The Two Heroines of Plumplington'
'Polignac' 'The Chateau of Prince Polignac'
'Pyramids' 'An Unprotected Female at the Pyramids'
'Returning' 'Returning Home'
'Schmidt' 'Lotta Schmidt'
'Talboys' 'Mrs General Talboys'
'Telegraph' 'The Telegraph Girl'
'Thompson' 'Christmas at Thompson Hall'
'Trow' 'Aaron Trow'
'Venice' 'The Last Austrian Who Left Venice'
'Walker' 'George Walker at Suez'
'Widow' 'The Widow's Mite'

Plays

DHSI   *Did He Steal It?*
NJ   *The Noble Jilt*

Travels

ANZ   *Australia and New Zealand*
HMWI   *How the 'Mastiffs' Went to Iceland*
NA   *North America*
SA   *South America*
WISM   *The West Indies and the Spanish Main*

Biography

LC   *The Life of Cicero*

LP   *Lord Palmerston*
T   *Thackeray*

Social commentary

NZ   *The New Zealander*

Translation

CC   *The Commentaries of Caesar*

Secondary sources

Auto   *An Autobiography* (1883)
Chron   R. C. Terry, *A Trollope Chronology* (1989)
Glendinning   Victoria Glendinning, *Anthony Trollope* (1993)
Hall   N. John Hall, *Trollope: A Biography* (1991)
I & R   R. C. Terry, *Anthony Trollope: Interviews and Recollections* (1987)
Letters   *The Letters of Anthony Trollope*, ed. N. John Hall, 2 vols. (1983)
Mullen   Richard Mullen, *Anthony Trollope: A Victorian in his World* (1990)
NCF   *Nineteenth Century Fiction*
Sadleir   Michael Sadleir, *Trollope: A Commentary* (1927)
Sadleir, *Biblio*   Michael Sadleir, *Trollope: A Bibliography* (1928)
Smalley   Donald Smalley (ed.), *Trollope: The Critical Heritage* (1969)
Super   R. H. Super, *The Chronicler of Barsetshire: A Life of Anthony Trollope* (1988)

'Aaron Trow' was first serialized in *Public Opinion*, 14 and 21 December 1861 (reprinted in *TAC2*). A savagely realistic convict tale, set in the British penal colony in Bermuda. Trow escapes from prison and breaks into the house of a young woman, Anastasia Bergen. He threatens to do 'worse than murder'. Her screams are heard by neighbours, who summon Anastasia's lover, the Presbyterian minister Caleb Morton. He discovers Anastasia bloody, but still alive, and organizes a party to hunt Trow down. They track the convict to a rocky cove where he and Caleb fight hand to hand in the water. Trow is drowned. JS

'About Hunting' (two-part article). Fox-hunting is a most thoroughly English pastime, open to lords, tenants, and tradesmen alike and conducive to goodwill among them. Railway access for city-dwellers is easy. Hunting is not cheap but can be reasonable. Masters' expenses are considerable; all hunters should pay fair subscriptions. Success is measured by pleasure, not a score. It is a wholesome recreation (wild behaviour and excessive drinking are not part of the sport) for all, including clergy. Horses need proper care, landowners deserve courtesy from hunters, and the master of hounds must be respected. *Saint Pauls* (October 1867), 206–19; (March 1868), 675–90. AKL

'Accusations against Lord Brougham, The' (letter). Lord Brougham, now elderly, known for public service over 50 years, stands accused of selling patronage. His faults do not include personal venality. The facts will surely exonerate him; all should wait for evidence. *Pall Mall Gazette* (20 March 1865), 3. AKL

Acorn, Lawrence, young ne'er-do-well and horse thief, known for his scrapes with the law, including two years' imprisonment with hard labour. He is associated with Jack the Grinder in the murder of Farmer Trumbull but is acquitted despite evidence against him by his former fiancée Carry Brattle. *VB* SRB

acting and actors. As a student of drama, Trollope encouraged G. H. *Lewes to publish his theatre critiques in more permanent form. Thus, in 1875, Trollope found himself addressed in a dedicatory 'Epistle' that acknowledged the genesis of *On Actors and the Art of Acting*, Lewes's authoritative account of stage performances from Edmund Kean to Tommaso Salvini. Trollope was 'pleased' by the book and his friend's 'compliment' but begged to differ 'as to trifles, in regard to character', particularly Hamlet's madness (*Letters* 2, 664–5). He concluded with a list of 'The greatest actors I ever saw': 'E. Kean, Rachel,

Mars, Got, Lemaitre . . . Mrs Yates . . . Robson', and two French actors who impressed him so faintly that he could only remember the initial of their surnames. Trollope must have been still at Harrow when he saw Kean, who drank himself to death in 1833; Rachel (Élisa Félix) had a triumphant London season in 1841 (just before Trollope left for Ireland), though he might have seen later performances. The preponderance of French names reflects the decadence of British acting. The list also suggests an affection for comedy and farce: Elizabeth Yates was a major comedienne (1799–1860) and Frederick Robson (1821–64) an expert farceur whose performance in *The Yellow Dwarf* was famous in the 1850s.

Trollope could not share Lewes's discriminating 'admiration for [Charles] Fechter', whose Hamlet, Iago, Claude Melnotte (in *The Lady of Lyons*) were the rage in the 1860s. As he told Kate Field, 'I myself hate Fechter as an actor' (*Letters* 1, 509). He also disagreed with Lewes about William Charles *Macready, who 'never moved me to tears'. Yet he admired him as 'a man of supreme intelligence' who sought to elevate drama, past and present, and bought the actor's prompt-copy of Congreve's *Love for Love* (now in the Folger Library). After seeing W. G. Wills's *Charles I* at the Lyceum, he described Isabel Bateman as 'very lovely, and perfectly dignified . . . when passionate as well as when angry and playful' (*Letters* 2, 577). As the King, Henry Irving, whom Trollope had already seen in Boucicault's *Formosa*, 'was better than I had expected,—very good occasionally, but with some terrible lapses'. Irving had yet to turn the Lyceum into a temple of art, persuading worshippers to overlook his physical and vocal eccentricities.

Trollope disliked the vanities of actors. After reading Macready's *Reminiscences*, he thought it 'disgusting to see the self-consciousness and irritated craving for applause' (*Letters* 2, 671); finding him 'envious, carping, spiteful', he deplored 'his want of manliness' (*Letters* 2, 691–2). Though he claimed to know 'nothing of theatres and very few actors' (*Letters* 2, 612), he did have connections through business or, once actors became respectable, camaraderie. In November 1860, Fanny Stirling, an actress of some repute, wished to dramatize *Framley Parsonage*, but those negotiations came to nothing (*Letters* 1, 125–6). In April 1873, when he discovered Irving had not been accepted by the Garrick Club, Trollope expressed regret and, though he did not then know him personally, wrote offering to sponsor a second application. He did know Squire Bancroft of the Prince of Wales's and, since it normally took twenty years to become a member of the Athenaeum, jocularly volunteered (January 1878) to 'come down,—or up—and give . . . ghostly assistance' at that future date (*Letters* 2, 756).

But if male actors had become clubbable (thirteen belonged to the Garrick by 1880), women who appeared in public had a more precarious hold on social acceptance. Kate Terry gave up the stage (1867) when she married Arthur *Lewis, a silk-merchant and founder of the Arts Club. When *Truth* accused Lewis of paying his employees to cheer the performances of Marion and Ellen Terry, Trollope wrote (January 1877) to say that opinion in 'various circles' was unanimous 'as to the low rascality' of that attack. Even Kate Field, in all her American liberty, felt apprehensive when she extended her journalist's career onto the lecture platform. To emphasize her social eminence, she dressed as though she were receiving her audience 'at home' and spoke conversationally in cultivated tones. Trollope felt sure her lecture-fees were 'honest and honourable', but thought 'writing nicer for either man or woman' (since it paid better). However, he advised her not to let 'an idea of personal independence . . . operate . . . against the idea of marriage' (*Letters* 1, 508–9). Success as a public speaker could not hide her inexperience when she took to the New York stage in 1874. Determined to persevere, since her parents had been successful actors, she appeared in London under her other name, Mary Keemle, in a series of musical monologues, and Trollope gave his friendly support.

Rachel O'Mahony, the American singer of *The Landleaguers*, is not Kate Field but she does reflect Trollope's feelings about his friend's career

as a performer. To stress Rachel's femininity and purity, Trollope makes her exceptionally petite and frail, though she minces no words in defending her honour. However, to reach the heights of Covent Garden Opera House, she must battle the ungentlemanly behaviour of her manager, Mahomet M. Moss, and the treachery of his partner, the mysterious Mme Socani, and, when she asks for a retainer until her new contract begins, she makes herself vulnerable to the advances of Lord Castlewell, who has a reputation with 'singing girls'. Her adventures have the tuppence-coloured melodrama of libretti she enacts at the Embankment Theatre. As if to suggest a performer's life is as fantastical off stage as on, Trollope shows Rachel quarrelling in the wings with Mme Socani before the latter makes a charming entrance, singing 'O, mio tresor' (XVIII). Similarly, Rachel plays the stage lover while thinking what a beast Moss really is. As for her meteoric rise to fame, Trollope merely describes two hours of daily practice. But at the heart of this portrait lies the suspicion that a woman who appears publicly before the gaze of strangers, and earns money for doing so, risks losing her womanliness. Rachel's fiancé Frank Jones is too much a gentleman to accept her earnings, although his father's Irish estate is ruined; so he breaks their engagement, and Rachel loves him 'because he was absolutely unlike an American' (VI). To effect a happy reunion, Trollope takes away Rachel's singing voice and financial independence: she must abandon the theatre—which, 'so unlike the ways of ordinary life, does gratify one's vanity' (VIII)—for down-to-earth matrimony. See also ADAPTATIONS; THEATRE, VICTORIAN.　　AWJ

Acton, Lord John Emerich Edward Dalberg (1834–1902), distinguished English historian, Regius Professor of History at Cambridge (1895); involved in founding the *English Historical Review*; Baron Acton of Aldenham (1869). Meeting Browning soon after *The Prime Minister* appeared, he referred to 'a strange blunder of . . . Trollope's "in having a wolf rather than a fox bite the Spartan boy"' (LXXIII). In 1881 Lord Acton wrote to Mary Gladstone, the Prime Minister's daughter, having talked with Gladstone about bringing in Trollope and Morley as potential candidates for the peerage, only to find that Trollope was condemned as too noisy.　　RCT

Adams, Henry (1838–1918), American historian best known for *The History of the United States during the Administration of Thomas Jefferson and James Madison*, 9 vols. (1889–91); taught history at Harvard 1870–7, editing the *North American Review* for most of this period. Adams was the author of *Democracy: An American Novel* (1880) and *Esther: A Novel* (1884), as well as works of history, biography, and social philosophy. When Trollope's *An Autobiography* was published in 1883, Adams confided to a friend, 'Trollope has amused me for two evenings . . . I mean to do my [autobiography]. After seeing how coolly and neatly a man like Trollope can destroy the last vestige of heroism in his own life, I object to allowing mine to be murdered by any one except myself' (Super 435). RCT

Adamson, Jack, one of the four disreputable conspirators who accuse John Caldigate of bigamy in order to receive money from him as a previous gold-mining partner in Australia. He later admits his perjury. *JC* SRB

adaptations. The Victorian stage regularly plundered Scott and Dickens, whose magnified characters and action-filled plots had an intrinsic theatricality. Trollope was less attractive. Though the popular success of *Framley Parsonage* led to plans for a Christmastide adaptation at Drury Lane while the novel was still being serialized (1860), that idea was soon abandoned. When the theatre became more subtle and intimate in the late 1860s, its boxed-in realism could not convey Trollope's vision temporally or spatially. The invisible fourth wall framed on-stage action in an intensively present tense, and the other three walls isolated those events from a world outside. So, in *Did He Steal It?* (1869), Trollope's unperformed adaptation of *The Last Chronicle of Barset*, Grace Crawley's appeal to Mr Goshawk, as she touches his sleeve and wins his sympathy, is merely one sentimental moment, whereas the same incident in the novel depends for its effect on extended exploration of Archdeacon Grantly's troubled thoughts before that melting mood. Time and space were better organized in *Shilly-Shally* (1872), Charles *Reade's adaptation of *Ralph the Heir*, but the play ran for less than a month, and that unsolicited collaboration offended Trollope deeply. In the early 20th century, the dominance of realism and an antipathy for Victoriana kept his novels out of the theatre, with one or two exceptions. Curiously, in 1926, a Colonel Harding published his dramatized version of *Nina Balatka* without knowing the name of its 'anonymous' author (Sadleir 269). In 1927, *The Warden* was adapted for the Lyceum Stage Society by Michael *Sadleir and Gerard Hopkins: fifty years later, Terence Rattigan thought of creating another version for John Gielgud but was too ill to pursue it. When, in the 1960s, the stage again became an open, flexible space and the Victorians were back in vogue, Trollope's novels had already been revitalized as radio drama.

That phenomenon began in April 1938 with 'The Two Trollopes', a talk by V. C. Clinton-Baddeley, followed by twelve weekly readings, mainly from *Barchester Towers*, called 'Mrs Proudie and her Times'. Then the Second World War gave rise to serialized versions of entire novels. H. Oldfield Box has described the tranquillity they offered in troubled times and how he decided to dramatize *The Warden*. First broadcast in November 1942, this was soon followed by *Barchester Towers* (10 episodes, 1943), *Framley Parsonage* (12 parts, 1944), and *Doctor Thorne* (13 parts, 1945). As V. S. Pritchett wryly remarked, Trollope had 'become one of the great air raid shelters . . . and Barsetshire . . . one of the great Never-Never Lands of our time' (*New Statesman*, 8 June 1946). But this was more than escapist nostalgia. In a broadcast assessment (1945) of Trollope's drawing power, a dramatization in which the novelist appears to a drowsy young soldier during a railway journey, Elizabeth Bowen maintained that Trollope's characters were antidotes to hopelessness: 'It's essential for us, these days, to believe in people, and in their power to live.' In fact, Trollope's 'cheerful, confident people' had an appeal which extended far beyond the circumstances of war. Once the BBC completed the six Barsetshire novels, there were adaptations of books like *Phineas Finn* (1953) and *Orley Farm* (1967), and no decade has since gone by without a reworking of the Barset cycle (e.g. *SHA* 1997). As a genre, radio establishes extraordinary intimacy between characters and listeners (in the ordinary surroundings of home) and can move instantly from crowds to close-ups to internal thoughts. A listener participates in the creation of people and places just as a reader travels from one community to another in response to the author's words, and weekly instalments extend that relationship across time in the manner of any long novel. These adaptations concentrate on Trollope's dialogue and its nuance, and, in interior monologue, re-create the ambiguities and ironies that the narrator's commentary conveys on the written page. They have proved an ideal way to reproduce the novels' extensive range and delicate shading.

The novels have had varied fortunes on television. In the 1950s, as reception extended throughout Britain, BBC drama aimed at middle-class audiences who formerly listened in the evening to radio. So *The Warden* (1955) kept faith with the text and was cast with exceptional sensitivity to Trollope's characterizations. In those days before colour, star personalities, and videotaped exteriors, the narrative unfolded without distractions, and close-ups added to that intimacy. By the 1970s, the BBC had tapped an international market for dramatized classics, expensively produced in many episodes. Simon Raven, author of the *Alms for Oblivion* novels, was commissioned to write all 26 episodes of *The Pallisers* (1973–4) and so give the serial a unified structure. The result was less than happy. Though carefully advertised as 'based on the novels', Raven's adaptation horrified those who knew the originals, particularly in the way Glencora remained alive until the penultimate episode, Phineas Finn returned home to make an honest woman of his Irish love, and Silverbridge played cricket. Understandably, various subplots disappeared but, more insidiously, dialogue was broadened and social misdemeanour modernized to underline main points and leave room for picturesque landscapes and upholstered costumes: female rebellion was presented with democratic energy. An uneasy compromise between 'good television' and accurate Trollope, this production was too museum-like for general viewers (though informed of social themes by an 84-page *Radio Times* 'Special') and too cavalier for purists. A second foray into prestige Trollope combined *The Warden* and *Barchester Towers* in the seven-part *Barchester Chronicles* (1980). By emphasizing Archdeacon Grantly's comic bluster from the outset, Alan Plater's script achieved tonal unity, and the entire sequence centred on the story of Harding and his daughters. The dialogue was essentially Trollope's; the acting, though occasionally overemphatic, captured the characters' zestful ambitions and, in moments of silence or physical animation, created the emotive subtext which only visual media convey. This production proved that television, too, can portray Trollope's ordinary people in enthralling ways. Yet, as the film of *Malachi's Cove* (1973) revealed, there is much uncharted territory for adventurous exploration: *The Eustace Diamonds*, adapted for television by Rose Tremayne (1998), continues that journey.   AWJ

Bowen, E., 'Anthony Trollope: A New Judgment', first published in pamphlet form by OUP as a postwar Christmas gift for American clients (1945).
Box, H. Oldfield, 'Trollope on the Radio', *NCF* (March 1946), 23–5.

'Adventures of Fred Pickering, The', first published in *Argosy* (September 1866), as 'The Misfortunes of Fred Pickering' (reprinted in *LS*). Fred, 25 years old, married to Mary Pickering, has had some success writing for the papers in Manchester. Defying his father, he gives up his position in a lawyer's office and comes to London to make his fortune as a man of letters. After a year Fred and his wife and child are starving. He receives friendly advice from a Trollope-like author, Mr Burnaby, and goes back to Manchester and the attorney's office, resolving to return to authorship one day.   JS

agnosticism, atheism. For a devout believer like Trollope, these were alien concepts. When the *Fortnightly Review* was founded (1865), he wanted to exclude from the pages of this expressly liberal periodical any material that called into question the basis of the Christian faith; and when he interviewed the intellectual John *Morley for the editorship, he challenged his agnosticism outright.

In *Orley Farm* Trollope mounts a ferocious attack on the atheistic hedonism of the commercial traveller Mr Moulder and his friends, 'pigs out of the sty of Epicurus' (XXIV), as he calls them, for whom Christmas is merely a festival of consumption. Refusal to worship also transgresses the code of the gentleman and, as in the case of Daniel Thwaite, the revolutionary journeyman tailor in *Lady Anna*, is traditionally associated with political radicalism.

Atheism provides a particular problem for the Christian in *The Vicar of Bullhampton*. The vicar Frank Fenwick's talk of repentance and forgiveness is a language foreign to the atheist Jacob Brattle, the miller and tyrannical father of the 'fallen' Carry, who thinks only of his family's social disgrace. And there is the additional dilemma of dealing with Jacob Brattle's spiritual position in the presence of his pious wife.   GH

Ahalala, straggling, haphazard tent town in New South Wales, probably modelled on Currajong, where John Caldigate and Dick Shand strike gold. The 'streets' are bewildering tracks which wind around the holes and dirt heaps of claims. *JC*   SRB

Ahaseragh, village in Co. Galway, where Tom Daly keeps his kennels until they are burned by Landleaguers in an act of political violence. *L*
                    MRS

Ainsworth, William Harrison (1805–82), leading 19th-century historical novelist after Scott, noted for romances of dashing adventure such as *Jack Sheppard* (1839) and *The Tower of London* (1840). Founder of *Ainsworth's Magazine* (1842–54). In his Commonplace Book Trollope linked Sheppard and Byron's Corsair as characters which had excited admiration and emulation. Trollope's drawing power for *Cornhill Magazine* prompted George Smith's comment that if Ainsworth lured Trollope to write a story for *Bentley's Miscellany* it could be fatal to *Cornhill*.   RCT

al Ackbar, Mahmoud, Arab dignitary who mistakes lowly George Walker for his more emi-

nent namesake Sir George Walker. 'Walker' *TAC2*
GRH

Alasco the Wise, tutor to Euphemia, who tells
her that 'Love will still be lord of all'. 'Euphemia'
GRH

Albury, Lady. Wife of Sir Harry Albury and
mother of young children, 'a handsome, fashionable woman, always excellently dressed' (XXII),
she befriends Ayala Dormer and strongly advocates the cause of Colonel Jonathan Stubbs's love.
Her first name is either Rosaline (XXVII, XLV,
XLVII) or Rosalind (XXXIX). *AA*   WK

Albury, Sir Harry, husband of Lady Albury,
half-brother of Captain Benjamin Batsby, and
second cousin of Colonel Jonathan Stubbs. He
presides genially over Stalham, his 'handsome
country seat in the County of Rufford', and is
'Master of the Rufford and Ufford Pack' (XXII).
AA   WK

Aldersgate Street, site of the butcher's shop
owned by William Briskett, suitor of Maryanne
Brown. *SBJR*   RCT

Alf, Ferdinand, editor of the severely critical
Evening Pulpit newspaper, whose facts 'if not
true, were well invented'. He is immune to Lady
Carbury's pleas to be 'puffed' for her vapid writing. Clever, sly, and sardonic, Alf's primary characteristic is his aptitude for sarcastic abuse while
distancing himself from personal libel. He en-
hances his social prestige and interest by running
for Parliament in Westminster as the Liberal candidate against Augustus Melmotte. *WWLN*
SRB

Alford, Henry (1810–71), scholar, cleric; Dean
of Canterbury (1857–71); first editor of the *Contemporary Review* (1866–70). When Trollope's
Clergymen of the Church of England appeared
(1866) it received from Alford 'the most ill-
natured review that was ever written upon any
work of mine' (*Auto* XI). Alford found the work
frivolous and ill informed, especially about curates' incomes, and must have squirmed at Trollope's comment that a dean had little to do and a
good deal to get. See 'Mr Anthony Trollope and
the English Clergy', *Contemporary Review* (June
1866), 240–62.   RCT

'Alice Dugdale', first published in *Good Cheer*,
December 1878 (reprinted in *WFF*); a marriage-
dilemma short story. Sweet-natured Alice Dugdale lives in the village of Beetham in the south
of England, and is a main support of her doctor
father and ineffectual stepmother. The village
parson, who is very fond of Alice, as is everyone
in Beetham, has a successful son, Major John
Rossiter, who has returned from India with great

prospects. John is torn between marrying the
high-born, handsome, but cold-hearted Georgiana Wanless and humble Alice. He eventually
settles on Miss Dugdale.   JS

All the Year Round. In 1859, Charles Dickens
and William Henry Wills began this weekly, two-
penny magazine, to the later numbers of which
Trollope contributed novels. It succeeded *Household Words*, which Dickens had begun in 1850.
Bradbury & Evans had published *Household
Words* under the joint proprietorship of William
Bradbury, Frederick Mullett Evans, John Forster,
and Wills, with Wills serving as Dickens's assistant. After Dickens quarrelled with Bradbury &
Evans, he and Wills left to publish this new
magazine, which would be distributed outside
London by Chapman & Hall. Dickens, who
owned three-quarters, was editor, and Wills, who
owned one-quarter, was sub-editor.

Household Words had been an inexpensive,
high-quality periodical. Dickens's new venture
duplicated the former publication in size, at 24
pages, and format. Dickens then purchased
Household Words at auction in May, and, after the
fifth number of *All the Year Round*, added to its
title 'with which is incorporated *Household
Words*'. Like its predecessor, *All the Year Round*
continued to popularize periodical literature in
response to the gradual spread of education. The
increasing number of penny and halfpenny
magazines appearing between 1800 and 1850
demonstrated that the reading public of the
lower classes was growing. Dickens wanted to
offer a cheap, weekly journal of general literature
for the improvement of the social condition.

This was Dickens's third assignment as editor.
In 1836, when publishers Richard Bentley and his
brother Samuel proposed to begin a monthly
magazine, they asked Dickens to be editor. He
had already made a name for himself as a reporter beginning at age 19, as contributor of
short sketches by 'Boz' to various periodicals,
and as a novelist with the publication of the *Posthumous Papers of the Pickwick Club*. Dickens was
the major contributor to *Bentley's Miscellany*, and
both he and the magazine increased in fame and
popularity. Dickens's financial arrangements
with Bentley were unsatisfactory to him, so in
1839 he left the position of editor.

The first number of *All the Year Round* appeared on 30 April 1859 and contained the first
instalment of Dickens's *A Tale of Two Cities*. Articles were unsigned, but Dickens's letters reveal
that many of the contributors were the same as
in *Household Words*: Wilkie Collins, Edmund
Yates, Charles Collins, Bulwer-Lytton, Elizabeth
Gaskell, and Charles Lever.

After Dickens's death in June 1870, Charles Dickens junior carried on the publication until its close in 1895, when it was incorporated with a new *Household Words*, a reincarnation of the magazine that *All the Year Round* had absorbed when it began. Trollope never contributed to the magazine when Dickens was running it, but Tom Trollope, his wife Theodosia, and his second wife Frances Eleanor Ternan did. While Dickens's son was editing the magazine, Trollope published *Is He Popenjoy?*, *The Duke's Children*, and *Mr Scarborough's Family*, which was running when Trollope died. JWM

Allewinde, Mr, great barrister from Dublin employed by the Crown in prosecuting Thady Macdermot. A master in the legal arts of manipulation, intimidation, and coercion, Allewinde openly boasts of his ability to lead witnesses to perjure themselves. His questions during the examination of Pat Brady incriminate Thady in a premeditated plot to murder Myles Ussher. *MB* MRS

Allingham, William (1824–89), Irish civil servant (customs) and poet, whose first volume, *Poems*, appeared in 1850. After moving to England (1863) he made many friendships in literary circles, particularly with Tennyson. Crossing to the Isle of Wight in October 1864, he shared a coach to Freshwater with Trollope, who told him that he had visited every parish in Ireland (*I & R* 36 n.) and showered him with questions about the houses and landscape, but showed no interest in Tennyson. As editor of *Fraser's Magazine* (1874–9) he published Henry Trollope's article on Molière in June 1877. RCT

Allington, small village and parish just across the western border of Barsetshire, consisting of Squire Dale's estates, the church and vicarage, the Red Lion, the post office, and a handful of cottages and houses. *SHA* NCS

Alston, a pretty town near Noningsby where the second Orley Farm trial occurs. Despite Alston's proximity to London, the attorneys connected with the trial lodge in the town, giving Alston a great buzz of excitement. *OF* MT

Altifiorla, Miss Francesca, least-loved but most-seen friend of Cecilia Holt. She professes both a hatred of marriage and an exalted sense of her own Italian lineage, being descended from the Fiascos and the Disgrazias. She slyly inveigles Sir Francis Geraldine into proposing marriage, but incurs the Baronet's wrath by broadcasting the news to all of Exeter, whereupon he jilts her. Finally, she again takes up the cause of men's wrongs to women and plans a lecture tour of America. *KD* NCS

Altringham, Earl of, affable, worldly, and wealthy friend of George Hotspur, to whom he will not lend money and with whom he will not gamble. He advises George to end his affair with Mrs Morton in order to marry his cousin Emily Hotspur for the Hotspur property. *SHH* MG

Altringham, Lady, wife of the Earl. Believing property and title should remain together, and liking George Hotspur although she knows he is a rake and a gambler, his clever confidante aids him in the pursuit of his cousin Emily Hotspur. Like the Earl, however, she lends Hotspur advice but no cash. *SHH* MG

Amaillou, small village destroyed by General Westerman, from which he later retreats. *LV* GRH

Amberley, Viscountess Lady Katherine Louisa (née **Stanley**) (1844–74), outspoken fourth daughter of Lord Stanley of Alderley, whose feminist activism led Queen Victoria to say she deserved whipping. Her lecture 'The Claims of Women' at Stroud, 25 May 1870, provoked press controversy. Of *Rachel Ray* she said it bored her to death: 'a mere description of the feelings of a girl entering the world—I think one knows of them without reading of them' (Glendinning 334). Trollope dined with her and her husband, eldest son of Lord John Russell, several times. In April 1867, the hostess was irritated when Trollope's clamour at table drowned the more interesting conversation of Thomas *Huxley. RCT

Amedroz, Bernard, father of Charles and Clara Amedroz and proprietor of Belton Castle. He is a fretful man 'whose life had been very useless', but he 'looked as though he were one of God's nobler creatures' (I). His death leaves Clara homeless and nearly destitute. *BE* WK

Amedroz, Charles, dissipated son of Bernard Amedroz and brother of Clara Amedroz. Charles commits suicide at the age of 27, making Will Belton, a distant cousin, the heir to Belton Castle. Bernard has sold his life insurances to pay Charles's debts, depriving Clara of her inheritance. *BE* WK

Amedroz, Clara, daughter of Bernard Amedroz and sister of Charles Amedroz. Clara is 'a handsome young woman' of 25, 'tall, well-made, active, and full of health' (IV). She is also serious-minded and obstinate, risking homelessness and destitution for the sake of her own fixed ideas. The most wrong-headed of these is that she loves her fiancé, the spineless Captain Frederic Aylmer, rather than her ardently devoted cousin Will Belton. *BE* WK

'American Affairs' (letter). The defeated Confederate states may be readmitted to the United States after their proposed constitutions are approved. Equal rights for blacks are an unworkable requirement; racial war may result. The motivation is admirable but laws are impractical. *Pall Mall Gazette* (11 July 1868), 10–11.   AKL

American characters. North America fascinated and disturbed Trollope. He recognized that the United States provided a life and hope for many that the Old World could not provide, but his sensibilities were offended by the dynamism and rawness of the growing country. Like many English travellers, he was more comfortable in the eastern cities, especially Boston, than on the frontier or in the rude western cities like San Francisco. Trollope visited the United States five times, wrote a travel book, *North America*, about his second trip, and created some 37 American characters in his fiction.

Trollope's ambivalence about the United States, expressed in *North America* and other writing, is apparent in the Americans in his novels. They range from the delightful Isabel Boncassen in *The Duke's Children*, 'this American girl, [who] was to be the mother and grandmother of future Dukes of Omnium,—the ancestress, it was to be hoped, of all future Dukes of Omnium!' (LXXII), to the duplicitous and violent Lefroy brothers from Louisiana in *Dr Wortle's School*, and perhaps to Augustus Melmotte, the swindler on a grand scale in *The Way We Live Now*, of whom 'the general opinion seemed to be that his father had been a noted coiner in New York,—an Irishman of the name of Melmody' (XCVIII).

Trollope did not follow his mother's example in *The Refugee in America* (1832) and *Jonathan Jefferson Whitlaw* (1836) in placing any of his novels principally in the United States. Although part of *Dr Wortle's School* does take place in America, in general his American characters are seen in Britain, usually in England but, in *The Landleaguers*, in Ireland as well. Three of his short stories, however, are placed entirely in the United States. 'The Courtship of Susan Bell', the story of a heroine whose love for Aaron Dunn is opposed by her narrow-minded religious family, is a precursor to Trollope's English novel on the same theme, *Rachel Ray*. 'Miss Ophelia Gledd', his belle of Boston, must decide between two suitors, one American and one English. She rejects her countryman Hannibal Hoskins, and chooses the Englishman despite a fear that she will not be accepted by her suitor's family, a theme explored more fully in *The Duke's Children*. 'The Two Generals', with the Reckenthorpe brothers on opposing sides in the American Civil War, is not expanded upon in any of the novels but perhaps owes something to Thackeray's *The Virginians* (1857–9), where two brothers are in opposing armies during the American Revolution. Thus, American characters in his fiction are tied to English stories and issues.

In fact, Trollope sometimes used American characters to discuss issues that were too controversial to put into the mouths of English, or British, characters. So, for example, despite the fact that the 'Woman Question' was deeply implicated in political debates of the day in Britain, and despite the fact that Trollope knew several English as well as American feminists, his fictional feminists are not English. In *Is He Popenjoy?*, besides the German Baroness Banmann, there is the American Olivia Q. Fleabody, and in *He Knew He Was Right* Wallachia Petrie, 'the Republican Browning'. American poets are suspect. Ezekiel Sevenkings (*DC*), who shares a Christian name with the dignified and cultured Boncassen, is an uncouth man from the far west and the implication is that his verses are as well. In another politically charged arena we find that Gerald O'Mahony, father of Rachel—the heroine of *The Landleaguers*—an MP from Co. Cavan and Home Rule advocate, is not Irish but Irish-American.

Kate *Field undoubtedly influenced Trollope's American characters. Her opinions are caricatured in those of the feminists mentioned above and Rachel O'Mahony has a singing career like Kate Field. However, in keeping with Trollope's views on the proper role of women, both Fleabody and O'Mahony are 'rewarded' with husbands—Kate never married. Isabel Boncassen's quick wit and lively manner also owe much to Kate Field.

Not all attractive young American women fare well in Trollope. Isabel Boncassen (*DC*) and Caroline Spalding, who marries Charles Glascock (*HKWR*), are fortunate in their choice of partners, but the magnificent Lucinda Roanoake (*ED*), compared to both Juno and Minerva, is undone by her apparent success in the marriage market when she is captured by the vicious Sir Griffin Tewett. Lucinda (who shares her surname with Sir Walter Ralegh's colony in Virginia which, founded in 1587 and site of the birth of the first English baby in North America, had mysteriously disappeared by 1590) is herself lost as she renounces marriage on her wedding day and goes mad.

Elias Gotobed (*AS*) is enlisted to highlight the ways of the English as well as to skewer the manners of Americans. He is stereotyped as endlessly inquisitive, overly assured in his opinions, and obsessively concerned with 'institutions', even using the term to refer to fox-hunting (VII). At the same time Trollope uses Gotobed's American bluntness, which sometimes amounts to rudeness, to comment on English weaknesses and failings. Gotobed's diatribe against church patronage at Mr Mainwaring's table is both rude (the rector has bought his living) and reflects Trollope's own opinion (XLII).

In addition to American characters, there are characters who are exiled, or flee, to America, who in effect *become* Americans. These are inevitably scoundrels. Good English characters may go to America for a time but return to England. Paul Montague, who is entangled in the railroad scheme in *The Way We Live Now*, has lived in San Francisco but has returned home to England before the novel opens. However, at the end of that novel, Mme Melmotte, Marie Melmotte, and Mr Croll, Melmotte's confidential agent, all emigrate to America in the company of Mrs Hurtle and Hamilton Fisker who are returning to their homeland. Similarly George Vavasor in *Can You Forgive Her?* flees to America after, amid sundry other crimes, attempting to murder John Grey. And at least one unpleasant British character, Sir Louis Philippe Scatcherd in *Doctor Thorne*, is given American characteristics: his beard was 'cut in a manner to make him look like an American. His voice also had a Yankee twang' (XXX).   MG

American Civil War. The American Civil War caused intense concern in Britain. Economic, cultural, and ethnic ties between the two nations were never closer than in the mid-19th century. The USA was Britain's chief supplier of wheat, and above all cotton; Britain was the United States' chief source of capital. British audiences flocked to minstrel shows and Barnum's exhibits; Americans to hear Dickens and Thackeray. American popular culture fascinated the British, while the Americans were hypersensitive to British critics like Mrs Trollope and her son. For better or for worse the United States was seen as a crystal ball in which Britain's democratic future might be read.

Both the North and the South hoped for British support. The South was disappointed by Britain's neutrality; the North was angered. Polite society favoured the agrarian, 'gentlemanly' Southerners, while liberal intellectuals like Trollope and Goldwin Smith, and radical politicians like John *Bright, generally supported the dynamic, progressive North. Although anti-slave sentiment was profound in Britain, it was by no means evident that the war was about slavery, even after Lincoln's Emancipation Proclamation of 1863. It was the intense savagery of the war

that most struck many observers and is noted in Trollope's 'The Two Generals', a story about two brothers caught up in the conflict on opposite sides.

Britain had much at stake in the war, both domestic and imperial. The Northern blockade of Southern cotton triggered the Lancashire cotton famine, causing intense hardship. In Trollope's 'The Widow's Mite', a young bride forgoes a wedding gown and contributes its cost to the relief of unemployed mill workers. Britain's loyal colony Canada was generally pro-Southern but indefensible in the event of a determined Northern invasion. It was a hostage, and British fears that the Americans might provoke a war with Britain as a means of unifying public opinion were not groundless. When Trollope visited North America between August 1861 and May 1862, the war was going badly for the North. Anglo-American diplomatic relations hit a dangerous low during his stay, when a Northern naval vessel seized two Confederate diplomats from a British ship on the high seas. Fortunately the situation was carefully defused by both Palmerston and Lincoln, but relations remained tense. There was considerable feeling in Britain that it should intervene, perhaps as mediator in what many saw as a pointless bloodbath, but Palmerston resisted, realizing that it would only draw Britain into the conflict, and further antagonize the stronger North. As late as the summer of 1864, Northern victory was still not assured and many British observers shared Trollope's view that even such a victory could not prevent ultimate secession. The great lesson England had drawn from the American Revolution, that no Anglo-Saxon people could be held in a union against their will, seemed applicable to the South as well. Even Trollope underestimated the intensity of Northern resolve not just to defend but to enforce the Union. The other factor underestimated—not just in Britain but the United States also—was President Lincoln, whose greatness Trollope, like many others, finally acknowledged in obituaries. Lincoln was assassinated while watching that quintessential Anglo-American theatrical production *Our American Cousin*.   CK

Bourne, Kenneth, *Britain and the Balance of Power in North America, 1815–1908* (1967).

Jones, Howard, *Union in Peril: The Crises over British Intervention in the Civil War* (1992).

'American Conflict, The' (letter). The British get an incorrect sense of the Civil War from journalists sympathetic to the South. The North is in fact winning, and rightly so. The South seceded—i.e. rebelled—when the North won control of the government and Lincoln was elected. Had the North yielded to the imbecile guns of Charleston, all US prestige in the world would have been lost. The curse of slavery must be destroyed as a pestilence. *Pall Mall Gazette* (16 March 1865), 4. AKL

'American Conflict, The' (letter). When the Civil War ends, the winners may seek further war, obvious choices being Canada and Mexico; the former is more likely and would involve England. Hostility to England is strong among Northerners. However, most Americans and surely Lincoln would oppose further bloodshed. The free expression of opinion here should not be curtailed by fear. *Pall Mall Gazette* (6 April 1865), 3–4. AKL

'American Literary Piracy' (public letter to J. R. *Lowell). The lack of international copyright law and enforcement is a problem of justice as much as of money. Lippincott paid the author a fee for US publication rights to *North America*; he was cheated by Harper, who simply copied the British text and got it to market first. Our common language makes copyright law urgent. If US authors pressure Congress, a law will pass. Unscrupulous printers penalize American and British authors and publishers. *Athenaeum* (6 September 1862), 306–7. AKL

American literature. Despite his claim that he could 'seldom read with pleasure for above an hour and a half at a time, or more than three hours a day' (*Auto* IX), Trollope was a great reader. As a young man he kept a record of and notes on his reading and at one point planned a history of world literature.

However, his later comments on foreign authors are remarkably few. On American literature his longest remarks come near the end of the second volume of *North America* (1862) and his only essay devoted to an American author is his long appreciation of 'The Genius of Nathaniel Hawthorne' in *North American Review* (1879).

As regards *Hawthorne, Trollope was writing about a novelist whose fictional worlds were far from his own. He quoted the letter in which Hawthorne professed admiration for his own novels, and returned the compliment, admiring Hawthorne's mixture of 'austerity and romance', his 'ghastly spirit of drollery', and the 'peculiar mood of mind' required of the reader: 'a delight in looking round corners, and in seeing how places and things may be approached by other than the direct and obvious route'. He also noted, as a description with no intent of 'dispraise', that 'never surely was a powerful, active,

continually effective mind less round, more lopsided, than that of Nathaniel Hawthorne'.

While Trollope gave Hawthorne due credit for his individuality as an artist, he also placed him within an American tradition, separate from the English: 'The creations of American literature generally are no doubt more given to the speculative,—less given to the realistic—, than are those of English literature'. He claimed that even the 'broad humor' of Bret Harte, Artemus Ward, and Mark Twain contained an 'undercurrent of melancholy, in which pathos and satire are intermingled'. He included Cooper and Irving in this tradition and wrote that 'melancholy and pathos, without the humor, are the springs on which all Longfellow's lines are set moving'. This interesting view of American literature is not discussed. Trollope did not speculate on why there should be a difference between the two literatures that earlier, with a different purpose in view, he claimed to be one literature.

In the first volume of *North America* Trollope wrote of the 'gratuitous circulating library open to all Boston, rich or poor, young or old' with both scepticism and admiration. He found it difficult to believe that 'a great many of the books were not lost, stolen, and destroyed', but was pleased that his 'own productions were in enormous demand' and disingenuously wondered 'Why should not the great Mr *Mudie . . . open a library in London on the same system?' (1, XVI). Later in the same volume he said that he never 'examined the rooms of an American without finding books or magazines in them', and pointed out that, in contrast to the situation in England, he was not talking merely about the middle and upper classes: 'A porter or a farmer's servant in the States is not proud of reading and writing. It is to him a matter of course' (1, XIX).

The level of literacy achieved in the United States was often remarked upon by travellers from the Old World, from colonial times well into the 19th century. Trollope used this as one of his two central premises in the chapter 'Literature' (2, XV). He claimed 'that the literary character of a people will depend much more upon what it reads than upon what it writes', and that 'it is impossible to speak of the subject of literature in America without thinking of the readers rather than of the writers' (2, XV). His second premise was that the 'literature of the one country is the literature of the other'. That is, American literature is a branch of English literature. An American, he said, may divorce 'himself from England in politics and perhaps in affections; but he cannot separate himself in mental culture' (2, XV). Despite his professed admiration for Irving,

Prescott, and Longfellow, and his rhetorical 'What Englishman has devoted a room to books, and devoted no portion of that room to the productions of America?', 'Literature' is about the market for literature rather than about the works themselves, and it is clearly written by an Englishman with an English focus.

Authors are mentioned almost in passing, as examples of the point concerning the market that Trollope wishes to make: lack of a copyright treaty hurts both American and English authors. Since English is the common language the United States and England *need* a treaty more than countries who do not share a common language. Since English authors are more popular than American ones (he claimed) and can be pirated, lack of copyright drives down the market for American works in their own country. Since the American market is so large, English authors are deprived of a large portion of the just rewards for their work, and even though the English market is smaller, American authors do sell there and would profit from copyright protection. Trollope's remarks, unlike those of Dickens on the same subject in his *American Notes*, did not ignite a firestorm. The topic was no longer new and Trollope, although popular with the reading public, was not the object of adoration that Dickens was. The shameful state of copyright was not corrected for another thirty years.   MG

'American Question, The' (letter). Everyone must take sides on the US Civil War. America is a descendant of England, and thus of interest. Moral right is with the Northern side. The tendency to admire the South's chivalry must yield to the North's claim of justice. *Pall Mall Gazette* (7 February 1865), 3.   AKL

'American Reconstruction' (article). Understanding present conditions in the USA is important. Establishing equal rights for blacks and whites is ill conceived; whites will not accept black authority. Although slavery is immoral, and well abolished, equality of the races is a fatuous concept; implementation will invite enormous political corruption. *Saint Pauls* (September 1868), 662–75.   AKL

American Senator, The (*see opposite*)

ancestry of Trollope family. With a name so vulnerable to schoolboy ribaldry, Anthony and his brother Tom let it be known at Harrow that their family derived from Tallyhosier who came to England with William the Conqueror. During one hunt in the New Forest, he killed three wolves and so earned the name 'troisloup' which, over the centuries, became 'Trollope'. A clerical cousin, Edward, recalling that legend in his *The*

Family of Trollope (1875), chose a more earthy etymology: Trolls-hope, or Elf-dale. However, by that time, the name had created its own legend in America where, after Fanny Trollope's *Domestic Manners of the Americans* (1832), 'to trollope' (apart from its usual connotation) meant to hawk vulgarly (and publicly) into a spittoon (James Pope Hennessy, *Anthony Trollope* (1971), 47).

Historically, the senior branch of the family traced its origins to John Trowlope, of 14th-century County Durham, whose descendants were ruined by the Civil War. A younger branch was ennobled in 1642 when Charles I gave a baronetcy to Sir Thomas, who established his family at Casewick Hall in Uffington, Lincolnshire. Sir John (d. 1820), the 6th Baronet, was Anthony's father's first cousin. A second Sir John (1800–74) served for over twenty years as MP for South Lincolnshire. A fierce advocate of the Corn Laws and former President of the Poor Laws Board, he was created Baron Kesteven in 1868. Both titles were held concurrently until the 3rd Baron was killed in the First World War. The baronetcy then passed to a cousin, Sir William Henry Trollope, and, years later, to Anthony's Australian grandsons: Sir Frederic, 14th Baronet (1875–1957), and Sir Gordon, 15th Baronet (1885–1958). The title is at present held by the latter's grandson Sir Anthony, of Oakville, New South Wales. See Family Trees, p. 607.   AWJ

'Ancient Classics for English Readers' (review). For those unwilling or unable to read the classics in Greek, Collins's English version of Homer's *Iliad* and *Odyssey* will be useful. Descriptions of monsters and the sense of the times are particularly well done. *Saint Pauls*, March 1870, 664–8.   AKL

Anderson, Hugh, second secretary at the Brussels Legation, 'a fair-haired, good-looking young man, with that thorough look of self-satisfaction and conceit which attachés are much more wont to exhibit than to deserve' (XIV). *MSF*   MT

Angers, capital of Anjou, initially taken by the Vendeans, then surrendered. Barrère, Westerman, and Santerre meet there to plan their campaign. *LV*   GRH

Annesley, Harry, son of the rector of Buston and heir to his uncle Peter Prosper. 'He is a young man with more than a fair allowance of a young man's folly—it may also be said of a young man's weakness', but 'with nothing of falseness or dishonesty' (III). Harry is a decent

(*cont. on page 13*)

TROLLOPE began this novel in Australia (1875), where, as visiting dignitary, his public remarks could give offence, as could letters he sent home to the *Liverpool Mercury*. Trollope understood those delicacies. His mother's book on *The Domestic Manners of the Americans* (1832) was still contentious when he published his own views on *North America*. More particularly, his *Australia and New Zealand*, reflecting a previous journey to the Antipodes, had caused ill feeling. That uneasy context surrounds Elias Gotobed, the Senator from Mickewa, whose pronouncements on Britain's irrational institutions raise everybody's hackles. And Trollope's personal investment in that comic figure explains why, when his publisher complained, he was 'sure nobody can give a name to a novel but the author' (*Letters* 2, 673). For although the book's concluding chapter allows it 'might perhaps have been better called "The Chronicle of a Winter at Dillsborough"', the Senator is absolutely central to this condition-of-England novel.

Structurally, the Senator's arrival (VIII) drives readers below the novel's initial geniality to view country matters critically, and that estrangement leads in turn to the gentry's moral vacuity. At first, nothing seems more ordinarily English than Dillsborough, its one distinction being the way High Street changes into Bullock's Hill on top of which lies Ufford, 'a large county, with pottery, and ribbons, and watches . . . whereas Rufford is small and thoroughly agricultural' (I). This 'divided' society colours Trollope's intricate opening which maps the social and financial townscape and local family histories. Those past events have distanced the Mortons of Bragton Park from Cousin Reginald at Hoppet Hall, and the town takes sides. Similarly, the second Mrs Masters, an ironmonger's daughter, dislikes the gentry whereas her husband clings to old loyalties, though he is not the Mortons' lawyer as his ancestors were. On a public level, opinion divides (particularly amongst the Saturday Club at the Bush Inn) about Farmer Goarly's scandalous determination to sue Lord Rufford for crop damage. Throughout this prelude, Trollope moves from wide panoramas to intimate close-up at the Club or at the Dill footbridge where Mary Masters has to negotiate a tension between Reginald Morton and Larry Twentyman, who likes to be thought a gentleman. Thus dull Dillsborough's rhythms are governed by money and rank, a truth which impresses Senator Gotobed when he arrives at Bragton with his host, John Morton of Washington's British Embassy. The rhythms of the Rufford and Ufford Hunt turn peculiar under the Senator's rational gaze and, when the unusual happens and a fox is poisoned, he sees the suspect Goarly as a defiant individualist. Such republicanism, while intrinsically comic, does question British society and so prepares us for Trollope's acidic picture of the aristocracy. Arabella Trefoil and Lady Augustus arrive in a flurry of maids and luggage. Again Trollope depicts a busy surface before going behind closed doors where the ladies unburden themselves. Arabella's awful mother has never seen 'such a barrack' while she herself loathes the marriage game: 'I can't stand this any longer, and I won't. Talk of work,—men's work! What man ever has to work as I do?' (XIII). Whereupon Arabella tries to net Lord Rufford, risking all without abandoning John Morton, and sides are taken. Rufford's sister and her intimate friend Miss Penge (heir to a mining fortune) determine to save him from Arabella's charms.

The Senator also controls the novel's tonal unity. Contrasting the heartache of Mary's romance with the desperation of Arabella's, Trollope separates the two. Yet to underline their differing moralities, he develops each story in similar ways. As Mary is troubled by her stepmother over Larry Twentyman's suit, Arabella scorns Lady Augustus's counsel. Both are offered invitations to higher spheres (Cheltenham and Mistletoe) and both face a two-month delay before decisive action (Mary refuses Larry; Arabella ensnares Rufford). Ultimately, Arabella receives an expensive ring that acknowledges Rufford's admiration of the way she returned the money her mother bargained for (LXXVI); Mary accepts Larry's 'little ruby ring', moved by that token of past love (LXXIX). Those lives, while separate, do (for a reader) collide morally. At one point (XXXV) a dejected Larry Twentyman offers his farm to John Morton, himself at odds with Arabella. Seeing Larry's anguish, Morton perceives 'an honesty . . . [a] real love,—and though that love was not at present happy it was of a nature to inspire perfect respect. But in his own case he was sure of nothing.' Similarly, when Arabella learns of Morton's legacy, she momentarily regrets her treachery: she knew 'she belonged to a heartless world;—but she knew also that there was a world of women who were not heartless' (LXXV). Mary, though only a provincial attorney's daughter, is one of those women, and when Reginald Morton, heir to Bragton Park, makes her his wife, he loves her as she is: 'But suppose I had taken such a one as that young woman who was here with my poor cousin. Oh, heavens!' (LXXI). Only the Senator moves in both those worlds, bridging one plot's comedy of manners and the other's social satire. The most striking example of that unifying function occurs at 'Mr Mainwaring's Little Dinner' (XLII), where the rector has 'been driven to invite his curate' and sacrifices his best claret for hospitality's sake. When Mr Gotobed fails to appreciate that '57 Mouton, Mr Mainwaring can 'only groan and moan and look up at the ceiling'. This comedy slides into satire once the Senator directs the conversation to church patronage, and the injustice of 'one man getting £100 a year for working like a horse in a big town, and another £1000 for living an idle life in a luxurious country house'. The politics of that are embarrassing, yet the Senator, in quest of truth, soldiers on. The dinner party collapses but ends again in comedy as the rector doubts whether he 'ever met such a brute as that American Senator'.

Trollope thought of that scene when he described the Senator as 'not himself half so absurd as the things which he criticizes . . . With the parson my idea was not to hold an individual up to scorn but to ridicule the modes of patronage' (*Letters* 2, 701–2). Yet Gotobed is often foolish in his attitude to Trollope's beloved fox-hunting or in his estimation of Goarly's honesty, though there are moments when ludicrous self-satisfaction gives way to self-doubt. We last hear of him in the Senate, 'thundering' against his own nation: 'Don Quixote was not more just . . . nor perhaps more apt to wage war against the windmills' (LXXX). However, that was not the end of the Senator for Trollope. When *The American Senator* was serialized in *Temple Bar* (May 1876–July 1877), the publisher insisted on explaining that the book *was* about England. Once Chapman & Hall's three-volume edition appeared (June 1877), reviewers also worried about the Senator's prominence. The *Saturday Review* wished he 'had been left out'. *The Times* thought him 'too commonplace, too much of an American gentleman', while the *Athenaeum* suggested, 'his lecture on British institutions . . . is as near to being a bore as anything Mr Trollope could write' (Smalley 428–32). Understandably, readers who respected convention were irritated by that lecture's disruption of traditional joys and punishments at novel's end, but that ignores the book's consistent blend of comic satire.

Trollope himself expected reviewers to find Arabella 'unwomanly, unnatural, turgid,—the creation of a morbid imagination' (*Letters* 2, 710), but only the *Examiner* quailed at the 'rancour' of his portraiture. Trollope did mean 'to express the depth of [his] scorn for women who [hunt] down husbands' (*Letters* 2, 702) but his sensitivity to the toll of such a life gives Arabella a magnificent complexity. On the surface, she is all artifice. She has no loyalties except to 'her duty to marry well', yet her 'work' grows harder as she ages and as failures multiply and become more public. However, she is moved by the way John Morton stands by his word despite her shabby behaviour. So she attends his sickbed and bravely confesses her treachery. But her mother's willingness to accept Rufford's hefty bribe enrages her—'I would sooner be in a workhouse' (LXII)—and she courageously determines to outface him (LXVII). When she strides past obstructing servants and relatives, even Rufford admits 'it was almost a pity that he had not married her'. She was '. . . more beautiful, he thought, than ever.' She is just as terrifying when Trollope shows her 'haggard, lumpy, and almost hideous in her bewildered grief' (XLIX). Eventually he allows her what consolation he can. Mounser Green, appreciating her modest legacy and value as a duke's niece, stage-manages a society wedding at Mistletoe and takes his knowing consort to Patagonia where, as ambassador's wife, 'she need never again seem to be gay in order that men might be attracted' (LXXVI).

Apart from such subtleties of structure, tone, and character, the novel has elements which reflect a personal stock-taking: on his Atlantic crossing homewards, Trollope began *An Autobiography*. Hunting scenes become metaphors of Arabella's battle for Lord Rufford: 'You're a sort of five-barred gate' (XXXVII). That symbolism is especially effective in Captain Caneback's attempt to master his mount Jemima: rushing a fence, he is kicked senseless in the ensuing mêlée. Caneback's frenzy mirrors Arabella's, while the hollowness of his death—he 'had been dear to no one' (XXIII)—prefigures John Morton's (under his grandmother's unloving eyes) and Rufford's loveless union with Miss Penge. Along with the comedy of the Senator's reaction to the fictional Rufford and Ufford United, Trollope pays affectionate tribute to actual hunts like the Cottesmore, financed by his cousin Sir John. Other personal touches include an attempt to retrieve a letter from a postmaster, who hesitates then dutifully retains it, and the obsessive whist that preoccupies Arabella's idiotic father. Misunderstood in its time, *The American Senator* dramatizes England's reassuring solidity and the materialism and moral aphasia which threatened it. The manuscript is in the Robert H. Taylor Collection, Princeton University.   AWJ

young man, with no profession and no fixed income, who loves and finally marries Florence Mountjoy, despite her mother's wishes and his uncle's threat of disinheritance. *MSF*   MT

Annesley, Mary, eldest daughter of Revd Annesley and sister of Harry. She marries the young Buntingford brewer Mr Thoroughbung. *MSF*
                                                        MT

Annesley, Mr, rector of Buston, father of Harry Annesley and 'an idle, good-looking, self-indulgent man,—a man who read a little and

understood what he read, and thought a little and understood what he thought; but who took no trouble about anything' (XXII). He despises his foolish brother-in-law Mr Prosper. *MSF*
                                                        MT

Annesley, Mrs, Harry Annesley's mother. 'A dear, good, motherly woman, all whose geese were certainly counted to be swans,' Mrs Annesley 'was an excellent mother of a family, and a good clergyman's wife, being in both respects more painstaking and assiduous than her husband' (XXII). *MSF*   MT

annuals and keepsakes

annuals and keepsakes were popular varieties of Victorian coffee-table books. Customarily they were sumptuously bound in silk or velvet for drawing room display, and the illustrations by valued artists such as Turner and Martin—whose keepsake illustrations were influential on Charlotte Brontë—were often more highly regarded by middle-class purchasers than was their literary content. The publisher Ackermann introduced these books to the English publishing trade from Germany in 1822, and by mid-century works like *The Keepsake* and *Friendship* commanded sales of up to 30,000 copies.

Trollope contributed to such annuals and occasional books one or two otherwise uncollected short stories: 'Christmas Day at Kirkby Cottage' appeared in *Macmillan's Magazine*, 1870; *Good Cheer* for 1882 carried 'The Two Heroines of Plumplington'; in the same year the *Life* Christmas annual published 'Not if I Know It'. First publication of two short stories which eventually became part of *Lotta Schmidt and Other Stories* was in table books: The *Victoria Regia* carried 'The Journey to Panama' in 1861 and *A Welcome* (1863) first published 'Miss Ophelia Gledd'. TB
Glaister, G. A., *Glaister's Glossary of the Book* (2nd edn., 1979).

anthologies.

Since the power of Trollope's narration comes from the way he lures a reader step by step into an escalating plot, balancing the incidents of one strand of action against those of another and guiding that journey by means of authorial comment, the novels rarely lend themselves to excerpted quotation. So much depends on the width of each canvas and on repetitions, particularly the heart-searchings of apparently ordinary lovers; his world convinces because of the time each reader spends there. Yet, in the mid-1940s, post-war paper shortages made it difficult for readers, attracted by serialized versions on radio, to acquire even the more popular novels, so *The Trollope Reader* (1947), selected and edited by Esther Cloudman Dunn and Marion C. Dodd, and Lance Tingay's *The Bedside Barsetshire* (1949), fulfilled a genuine need. Those anthologies were superseded by OUP's expanding series of reprinted novels, but the effectiveness of *The Trollope Reader* was acknowledged (as late as 1993) by Graham Handley, who modelled his *Trollope the Traveller* on that earlier collection. His excerpts underlined the impact of foreign cultures on Trollope's psyche, as observer and commentator, by introducing modern readers to accounts of the West Indies, North America, Australia and New Zealand, and the conflicting societies of South Africa which so intrigued the novelist's contemporaries. Another

approach to Trollope's own words, particularly the authorial colloquy that controls each novel, appears in *Trollope-to-Reader: A Topical Guide to Digressions* (1983), in which Mary L. Daniels excerpts Trollope's personal intrusions under various subject headings, from 'Abuse' to 'Zeal, religious': multiple entries about a specific subject are arranged chronologically to convey the development of Trollope's thoughts on that subject. See also Richard Mullen, *Sayings of Anthony Trollope* (1992).

Anthologies like these depend on an editor's individual preferences. R. C. Terry's *Trollope: Interviews and Recollections* (1987) offers a comprehensive account of Trollope-the-man from letters, diaries, and published tributes of relatives, friends, and literary critics. The inclusiveness of those reminiscences allows one to construct a personal mind-portrait of a thunderously energetic individual whose good-hearted sensibility belied his blustering John Bull exterior. Equally representative is Donald Smalley's *Anthony Trollope: The Critical Heritage* (1969), a compendium of critical response to each novel by contemporary reviewers. That evidence counterbalances Trollope's own recollection (in *Auto*) of the way his books were received by writers who, 'especially from the 1860s onward, often convey surprisingly graphic insights into how Trollope's characters and their dilemmas struck their contemporaries' (26). Both these collections were treasure troves of source material for Trollope's recent biographers.

A third kind of anthology aimed at university students and interests surrounding the centenary of Trollope's death. In *Anthony Trollope* (1980), Tony Bareham edited a sequence of original essays to convey an up-to-date assessment of the novelist's place among his Victorian contemporaries. By the end of his life, critics had generally agreed that Trollope 'lacked any religious message, was deficient as a social prophet, wrote without a sense of poetical concentration, and [had no] critical self-awareness'. The essays, which range from the Irish novels and Barsetshire to Trollope's liberalism, show the limitations of that verdict. N. John Hall's *The Trollope Critics* (1981) presented a selection of previously published articles that extended from Henry James's obituary tribute of 1883 to Juliet McMaster's exploration of Trollope's authorial persona (1978). Their chronological arrangement allowed readers to appreciate the increasingly sophisticated response of Trollope's more perceptive critics and to assess the novelist's gradual acceptance within academic circles. A third collection, John Halperin's *Trollope Centenary Essays* (1982), confirmed that acceptance. Introducing his nine contributors, Halperin remarked that whereas Trollope had, since the 1940s, achieved 'indisputably major status' amongst general readers, now, in years leading up to the centenary, 'in terms of scholarly output alone, only Hardy among the Victorian novelists has kept pace with Trollope' (p. xi). A special issue of *Nineteenth-Century Fiction* (December 1982), ed. N. John Hall and Donald D. Stone, also marked the anniversary with an anthology of original essays.   AWJ

Anticant, Dr Pessimist, popular Scots reformer and author of diatribes on the follies of mankind, Trollope's caricature of Thomas Carlyle. 'No man ever resolved more bravely than he to accept as good nothing that was evil; to banish from him as evil nothing that was good' (XV). His pamphlet *Modern Chivalry* contrasts the goodness of the 15th-century John Hiram with contemporary greedy clergymen. *W*   NCS

Antwerp. Sights of this Belgian city include spire, paintings, and General Chassé's uniform. 'Chassé' *TAC1*   GRH

Apjohn, Nicholas. Intense study of Cousin Henry's behaviour leads him to guess the exact whereabouts of Indefer Jones's final will. Delighted by this detective work, he gladly assumes the costs of the abandoned libel suit against the *Carmarthen Herald*. In gratitude, the future heir to Llanfeare is christened 'Apjohn' as part of his 'grandiloquent name', and so (presumably) becomes the solicitor's godson. *CH*   AWJ

appearance, personality, character. Trollope's appearance was striking. In height about five feet ten inches tall, he was burly, overweight in fact, his face largely covered with reddish, wiry beard, his eyes bluish grey, and his gaze through small gold-rimmed spectacles intense. From an early age he had been awkward and ungainly. He was burdened by this, but traded on it when authority and success came his way. His loud, booming, but not unpleasant voice, and hearty boisterous laugh, were somewhat defensive ways of covering social unease. This had disadvantages. Many eyewitness accounts veer between being won over by his bluff heartiness and abundant good nature and being repelled by his shouts and mannerisms. He was given to extravagant gesturing, sometimes swishing his ebony cane through the air. Even those who knew him well sometimes quailed before the gale force of his company. What began as cover became the natural way of the man. His deportment was upright, his clothing immaculately clean, but carelessly worn and always rumpled. The outdoor life for the Post Office, travelling, hunting, made him fit and gave him a ruddy countenance. He

looked, as one observer put it, as if he had 'spent all his life in the country, growing turnips and preserving game' (George Smalley, *McClure's Magazine*, January 1903). A 'civilized and modernized Squire Western', declared Julian *Hawthorne, who left a perceptive description of him in *Confessions and Criticisms* (1887). G. A. *Sala noted that in company Trollope could get carried away with nervous excitement. At the first *Cornhill* dinner, he was pushy and opinionated, 'contradicting everybody; afterwards saying kind things to everybody, and occasionally going to sleep' then coming to, 'alert and pugnacious', on the prowl. Yet Trollope 'had nothing of the bear but his skin', Sala concluded. Plenty of evidence supports the view that Trollope acted the roaring boy, having found that it went down well in Ireland and made him popular among his rumbustious hosts. By the time of his fame in England he was a John Bull, playing up the role to some degree. George Smith's daughters, on the watch from upstairs as guests approached their dining room, delightedly observed Trollope look in a mirror, 'ruffle his hair and plunge into the room with a huge roar of greeting' (Sadleir 330). The John Bull image was characterized by several who noticed him stand with back to the fire, hands clasped behind him and feet firmly planted, 'a thorough Englishman in a thoroughly English attitude'. The ideal beefeater, Leslie Stephen called him. That aggressive posture was well drawn in pen and ink by R. Birch from a photograph by Sarony of New York (p. 598). (For this and other descriptions of Trollope see *I & R passim*.) But he had a quick temper too, inherited from his father. When, in the early days at the Post Office, Colonel Maberly virtually accused him of taking a letter containing banknotes from his desk and banged the table to make his point, Trollope banged back, shooting a bottle of ink over his superior's face and shirt-front (*Auto* III). Any unfairness of this kind made him see red. But Trollope was also impatient, always in a hurry; he bullied because he wanted quick answers and results from his colleagues in the postal service. Yates recounted gleefully a disagreement with one of the postal surveyors after which Trollope spluttered, 'I differ from you entirely! What was it you said?' If he liked winning an argument, he was also angered by cant and humbug, incivility, snobbery, and rudeness. One witness driving to a reception observed from her carriage a coatless Trollope squaring up to a local tradesman. Blessed with a strong constitution, Trollope toughened himself by riding and walking during his Post Office career and had the ability to take naps at will. All this enabled him to sustain a life of 'incessant toil', as Donald *Macleod put it. Edward *Bradley ('Cuthbert Bede'), weekending with him at a country house in January 1868, described his itinerary fully and with sheer amazement, never doubting that he was 'good for sixteen hours a day' (*I & R* 83, 108–9). Physical strength, combining with willpower, enabled Trollope to survive, and avoid serious health problems until late in life, when his extreme short-sightedness, and the family deafness, grew more aggravated. Writer's cramp, hernia, and gout added to his burdens, then angina and asthma. Such physical limitations made him depressed and moody. Yet the recollections of his immediate family and friends in the last few years stress the old appetite for work if not the old pleasures of the table, a prevailing optimism about life, deep compassion for others, a stubborn refusal to surrender to idleness or despair, a determination to die in harness. To read one of his earliest pieces of writing, the Commonplace Book sporadically kept 1835–40, with jottings about self-discipline, duty, order, and industry, is to see how early the basis of Trollope's character was formed. In the last phase of his life such principles remained firm, as he drove himself to research the novel which returned him to Ireland, revisiting the sources of his dedication to public service, his inspiration as a writer, his happiness with Rose and their sons. His last poignant letters to her bear witness to that strength of character. RCT

Appledom, Mr, one of Violet Effingham's many suitors. Mr Appledom is an unexceptionable middle-aged gentleman and upstanding Conservative member of Parliament, but perhaps too much of a dandy to suit Miss Effingham. *PF*
JMR

Arabin, Mrs Eleanor. See BOLD, ELEANOR (née HARDING).

Arabin, Revd Francis, fellow of Lazarus College, Oxford, and disciple of Dr Gwynne. A high churchman who almost follows Newman to Roman Catholicism but is dissuaded by Josiah Crawley; Professor of Poetry (although with little evidence of this talent) and polemical contributor to the *Jupiter*; an eloquent, energetic, conscientious 40-year-old clergyman, he receives the living of St Ewold's from Archdeacon Grantly to oppose the Slope–Proudie faction. A lifelong bachelor who knows or cares little about women, he falls under Signora Neroni's spell before finally engaging himself to Eleanor Bold. At the end of *Barchester Towers* his foes have been vanquished, though not through his efforts, and he becomes Dean of Barchester. In *The Last Chron-*

icle of Barset he supports his friend Josiah Crawley. *DT, FP, SHA* NCS

Arabin, Susan (Posy), 5-year-old daughter of Francis and Eleanor Arabin. With her own way of looking at the world, she becomes the great favourite of her dying grandfather Septimus Harding, as they play 'cat's cradle'. *LCB* NCS

Aram, Solomon, Jewish lawyer working for Lady Mason's defence. 'He was not a dirty old Jew with a hooked nose and an imperfect pronunciation of English consonants', rather 'a good-looking man about forty, perhaps rather over-dressed, but bearing about him no other sign of vulgarity' (LIII). *OF* MT

Arbuthnot, Isabella Staveley, elder daughter of Judge Staveley of Noningsby and mother of three. Mrs Arbuthnot is the first to caution her sister Madeline Staveley not to become romantically linked to Felix Graham. *OF* MT

Archer, Maurice. He offends Isabel Lownd by disparaging Christmas but falls in love with her, later proposes, and is finally accepted. 'Kirkby'
GRH

Ardkill Cottage. Half a mile (1 km) beyond the cart-track which ends at mean cottages and Liscannor's burial-ground, this ominously named dwelling suits Mrs O'Hara's brooding melancholy, as she strides through the winds and salt-spray of the Moher cliffs. But its sterile loneliness numbs her daughter. *EE* AWJ

aristocracy. Trollope's representations of aristocracy and people drawn from (as the Victorians would have it) the 'Upper Ten Thousand', taken together, form a complex response to the ever-shifting social and class boundaries of the 19th century. One detects a conservative longing for the mythical stability provided by a secure class system presided over by a governing aristocracy: 'The main duty of all aristocrats, and we may say their only duty, is to govern; and the highest duty of any aristocrat is to govern the state' (*NZ* II). This nostalgic strain is perhaps most evident in the 'Chronicles of Barsetshire', in which the county is presided over by a network of Whig and Tory grandees; in a famously anachronistic passage from the opening chapter of *Doctor Thorne*, Trollope's narrator writes— during the commercial boom of the 1850s—of a 'feudal' England still dominated by the land-owning families, and barely touched by the great social upheavals of the Reform Bill and the Industrial Revolution: 'England is not yet a commercial country in the sense in which that epithet is used for her; and let us still hope that she will not soon become so. She might surely as well be called feudal England, or chivalrous England. If in western civilized Europe there does exist a nation among whom there are high signors, and with whom the owners of the land are the true aristocracy, the aristocracy that is trusted as being best and fittest to rule, that nation is the English' (*DT* I). Accordingly, Barset is dominated by a cluster of aristocratic families such as the Luftons, the De Courcys, and the old Duke of Omnium. Trollope's most overwhelming endorsement of the aristocrat's right and duty to govern is, of course, his increasingly sympathetic account, over the six political novels, of the career of Plantagenet Palliser; not only is Palliser an aristocrat, he is—more importantly—'a noble gentleman, such a one as justifies to the nation the seeming anomaly of an hereditary peerage and of primogeniture' (*Auto* X). Nevertheless, despite such incipient conservatism, Trollope was always alive to the satirical possibilities in recording the aristocracy's discomfort in accommodating a rapidly changing society. Thus *Doctor Thorne* is in part a sustained satirical treatment of the aristocratic De Courcys, whose snobbery and opportunism is contrasted with the no-nonsense decency of Thorne himself; similarly, *The Way We Live Now* is savage in its portrayal of an increasingly desperate and impoverished aristocracy trying to buy its way into the reputedly vast wealth of the vulgar and ruffianly Augustus Melmotte. See also Senator Gotobed's lecture, near the conclusion of *The American Senator*, which is largely an attack on the unjust social privileges enjoyed by the aristocracy (LXXVII, LXXVIII). There is a correlated implicit privileging of middle-class virtues in Trollope's various presentations of that stock Victorian character-type, the vicious and dissolute—and sometimes downright villainous—aristocrat: Undy Scott (*TC*); the Marquis of Brotherton (*IHP*); the old Duke of Omnium (*DT, FP, SHA, PF, ED, PR*); all can be located, in varying degrees, within the novelistic and theatrical 19th-century tradition that sought to juxtapose the immorality and irresponsibility of the aristocratic class alongside a virtuous and meritocratic middle class. Generally speaking, however, Trollope resists such moral simplicities, and his satirical portraits of the aristocracy are balanced by a number of studies sympathetic to the accommodations the aristocracy in the latter half of the century need to make in order to preserve their ranks. Plantagenet Palliser's eventual acceptance of Lord Silverbridge's love for the American Isabel Boncassen (*DC*) is perhaps the most sustained of such studies; it is prefigured by the story of Hon. Charles Glascock's courtship of Caroline Spalding (*HKWR*), in which any satire

is directed not against the aristocracy—Glascock is presented as an exceptionally honourable man—but at the expedient abandonment of republican sentiments by Caroline's brash Senator father.   HO

Arkwright, Fanny. Having persuaded her husband to take the dangerous route 'home' from Costa Rica, she drowns in the Serapiqui river. 'Returning' *WFF*   GRH

Arkwright, Harry, young English planter en route to England from Costa Rica who sees his wife drown. Rather than continue, he returns with his baby and his brother-in-law to San Jose. 'Returning' *WFF*   GRH

Armstrong, Joseph, Protestant clergyman at Headford, near Morony Castle, Ireland, whose rampant anti-Catholic bigotry makes it impossible for him to offer 'aid, or counsel, or pleasant friendship' (XIII) to Philip Jones, an English landowner troubled by his young son's conversion to Catholicism. *L*   MRS

Armstrong, Revd Mr Joseph, impoverished but kindly rector at Ballindine, who, despite 'his nine poor children, his poor wife, his poor home, [and] his poor two hundred a-year', becomes 'love's ambassador' (XXVI), helping to reunite Lord Ballindine and Fanny Wyndham. His success is further crowned by his role in ousting Barry Lynch from Ireland. *KOK*   MRS

Armstrong, Toby, a 'squireen of three or four hundred a-year' (XIX) entrapped by Jonas Brown and his sons into an engagement with Julia, the daughter of the house, though he negotiates a bond for £2,000 before making her 'the mistress of Castle Armstrong' (XIX). *MB*   MRS

Arnold, Matthew (1822–1904), civil servant (Inspector of Schools 1851–86); distinguished poet and critic, whose essay 'The Function of Criticism at the Present Time' (1864) influenced Trollope and his fellow founders of the *Fortnightly Review* (1865), to which the poet contributed nine essays in the decade from 1877.   RCT

art and artists. Trollope was all his life an avid museum goer and art lover. (He recalled fondly his mother taking him when he was only 9 to the newly opened National Gallery at 100 Pall Mall.) Trollope wrote three fairly elaborate statements on art: the final chapter of *The New Zealander*, 1856, published 1972; 'The National Gallery', *St James's Magazine*, (September 1861); and 'The Art Tourist', *Pall Mall Gazette* (August 1865). All three reveal a tireless student of art, a man with recognizable Victorian preferences, such as that for works that 'tell a story', and an observer who mixed perceptive with highly questionable judgements, such as praising the excellence of Hogarth while equating A. W. Callcott with Reynolds.

In his fiction, Trollope's chief depictions of artists include the idle, scatterbrained, but likeable Bertie Stanhope of *Barchester Towers*—'[he] took lodgings and a workshop, at Carrara, and there spoiled much marble, and made some few pretty images' (X); the successful portrait painter Conway Dalrymple of *The Last Chronicle of Barset*—'There was . . . ever some story told in Dalrymple's pictures over and above the story of the portraiture' (XXIV); and a promising sculptor, Isadore Hamel (himself the son of a successful though dissolute sculptor), of *Ayala's Angel*, who marries Lucy Dormer, secondary heroine of the novel, who, with her sister Ayala, has been left penniless on the death of their artist father.

NJH

Ashley, Evelyn (1836–1907), biographer of Lord Palmerston. Ashley's work was a major source for Trollope when he wrote his own study of the statesman. Trollope was on the platform with Ashley at the conference on the Eastern Question in December 1876. RCT

Askerton, Colonel, retired army officer, living contentedly with his wife Mary at Belton Cottage, Belton. He is 'a slight built, wiry man, about fifty, with iron-grey hair and beard,—who seemed to have no trouble in life, and to desire but few pleasures' (V). *BE* WK

Askerton, Mrs Mary (née Vigo), wife of Colonel Askerton and close friend of Clara Amedroz. Long ago, in India, she fled from her first husband, the drunken Captain Berdmore, and was Colonel Askerton's mistress until Berdmore died. The revelation of this episode severely tests Clara's loyalty and courage. *BE* WK

'As to the Need of Caesars' (letter). Louis Napoleon's biography of Caesar is a self-justifying praise of despots. The book is un-researched, un-thoughtful, and ill written. Some Americans might approve this work; most English readers will ridicule it. *Pall Mall Gazette* (23 March 1865), 3. AKL

Athenaeum. Founded 2 January 1828 by James Silk Buckingham, this weekly, sixpenny, sixteen-page publication reviewed some of Trollope's novels. A Wednesday paper, it incorporated the *Literary Chronicle and Weekly Review*, a Saturday paper, which had begun in 1819. The earlier publication was almost entirely composed of book reviews or materials related to books and authors, as are some journals and literary supplements today. The popularity of reviews of current literature resulted from the high price of novels. Just when the public's appetite for novels was increasing, and the number of readers was expanding, the average reader was unable to afford the three-volume library edition, the form established between 1826 and 1830 as the norm. Since 1820, the standard three-volume novel had cost half a guinea (10*s.* 6*d.*) per volume for a total cost of 1½ guineas or 31*s.* 6*d.* per novel. Average readers could buy the 6*s.* reprint, available after the novel had been out for a few years, but new works were beyond their means. Not surprisingly, the *Athenaeum* stated in its first number that it was founded on the assumption that 'no Englishman in the middle class of life *buys* a book'.

In 1828, a number of other weeklies began, including the *Verulam*, which focused on non-literary topics. By May, it merged with the *Athenaeum*. Among the chief contributors during the first two years were Frederick Denison Maurice, theologian, and John Sterling, poet and essayist. At the end of its second year, Charles Wentworth Dilke, friend of Keats, acquired the paper. A contributor to numerous periodicals, Dilke took a stand against the general practice of inserting paid 'puffs', or promotional pieces for the book trade, reduced the price to fourpence, and changed the publication day from Wednesday to Saturday. Maurice and Sterling were his co-editors until December 1828, with Henry Stebbing continuing as assistant editor, as he had been since the founding of the paper. In its early days, the *Athenaeum* exceeded the circulation of similar publications.

In the 1840s, the paper took on the appearance of the ultra-conservative journals, despite its own more liberal stance, containing fine print and pages of small advertisements at the beginning and end, in a format that would continue until the 1890s. During the 1840s notable contributors were Thomas Carlyle, James Hogg, Thomas Hood, Leigh Hunt, Charles Lamb, Walter Savage Landor, followed later by Robert Browning, J. C. Jeaffreson, Andrew Lang, Theodore Watts-Dunton, and Walter Pater. In 1862 the price was reduced to threepence.

Over the years, Trollope had some association with the *Athenaeum*. In 1847, a reviewer of his first novel, *The Macdermots of Ballycloran*, advised Trollope to change his name to avoid having his work confused with his mother's and to develop his fine sense of humour. It later contained a positive review of *Barchester Towers*. By 1877, when the *Athenaeum* reviewed *The American Senator*, Trollope's growth in stature as a novelist was acknowledged: Trollope's readers, the reviewer said, included everybody. In 1862, Trollope wrote a letter to the *Athenaeum* about the harm being done to English novelists by American copyright laws. Five years later, in October 1867, when *Saint Pauls Magazine* began, the *Athenaeum* contained a full-page advertisement for it.

The *Athenaeum* increased in size over time. By 1905 it included about 6 pages of advertisements, mainly for books, followed by 20 pages of articles, reviews, and literary information, and ending with 4 pages of notices, for a total of 30 pages. From January 1916 to March 1919, it became a 28-page monthly with larger print and more attractive appearance, including a feature by A. L. Huxley. It resumed its former look and weekly publication in April 1919. Its list of contributions continued to be impressive, including a weekly story by Katherine Mansfield and fiction by Max Beerbohm and Virginia Woolf; poetry by Thomas Hardy, Edwin Arlington Robinson, Edith Sitwell, T. S. Eliot, and Wilfred Owen; and articles by George Saintsbury and J. Middleton Murry. In the 1920s, it changed from being a literary journal to a journal of literature, science, and art under the editorship of H. J. Massingham and Murry. In February 1921, the *Athenaeum* merged with the *Nation*, another weekly journal, begun in 1907, forming the *Nation and the Athenaeum*.   JWM

Graham, Walter, *English Literary Periodicals* (1930).

Aughacashel, inhospitable mountain above Loch Allen, Co. Leitrim, where Thady Macdermot hides after murdering Myles Ussher. Roadless, barren, and rocky, largely inaccessible to the 'the common blessings or restraints of civilization' (XXII), it affords some small freedoms from the trappings of England's colonial rule for a derelict population of Irish peasants such as Andy McEvoy who scratch out an existence as illegal squatters, making poteen and growing 'poor crops of potatoes' (XXII). *MB*   MRS

Augsburg, scene of Linda Tressel's rude awakening when Valcarm, her dream-lover, is arrested at the railway station. Discovering that the Black Bear, where he would have lodged her, is 'a house of a very bad sort' (XI), she finds refuge at the home of her friends the Bogens. *LT*   AWJ

Auld Reekie, Marchioness of, Alice Vavasor's greatest, but most distant, maternal relative. The Marchioness condescends to send disapproving messages to Alice when she has broken off her engagement with John Grey and condescends again to send her forgiveness when Alice decides that she will accept Mr Grey after all. *CYFH, WWLN*   JMR

Auld Reekie, Marquis of Lady Glencora M'Cluskie's uncle and guardian, father of Lord Nidderdale, and distant cousin of Alice Vavasor. The Marquis is beset with difficulties in managing the separate matrimonial prospects of his rebellious charge Lady Glencora and of his indifferent son. *SHA, CYFH, WWLN*   JMR

Austen, Jane (1775–1817). Trollope was an early admirer of Austen, who was not well known to Victorian novel-readers until the publication in 1870 of the *Memoir* by her nephew J. E. Austen Leigh. In his review of *Emma* in 1815, Scott had hailed a new development in fiction, but very little was written about her between her death and the publication of the biography. Until 1882 there was only one complete edition of her works, the five-volume set published by Richard Bentley in 1833, which Trollope owned.

In November 1869 Trollope, as editor of *Saint Pauls*, asked for a review copy of the *Memoir*, also published by Bentley, calling Austen 'my chief favourite among novelists'. The review, by Juliet Pollock, appeared in March 1870.

By the time he left school Trollope had decided that *Pride and Prejudice* was his favourite novel, and so it remained until Thackeray published *Henry Esmond* in 1852. All three wrote with careful attention to their prose style, and with attention to the weaknesses and vanities of men and women moving through society. Though Trollope said that Thackeray was his master, it can be argued that he owed more to Austen than to Thackeray. Certainly *The Warden* and *Barchester Towers*, his first successes, contain the same sort of sly humour, pellucid language, and moral instruction for which he praised Austen, and like her novels his aim is to show the details of everyday life.

Trollope tried to give his readers 'characters like themselves—or to which they might liken themselves' (*Auto* VIII). It was Austen who made the novel of common life, with its emphasis on the domestic scene and its descriptions of relations between men and women as they move through society, amusing and respectable and even inspiring; Austen who diverted the novel from panorama to human nature, from plot to character, focusing on people's weaknesses and vanities.

In *An Autobiography* and in his lecture 'On English Prose Fiction as a Rational Amusement' Trollope praises Austen and Maria Edgeworth for their truth to life and their moral lessons. 'The faults of some are the anvils on which the virtues of others are hammered till they are bright as steel', he said of Austen in the lecture. He recognized her as a great novelist who did what she did perfectly. Like her, he sought to describe human nature by depicting as fully as possible a corner of life that he knew well. On the end-papers of his copy of *Emma* he noted that though the male characters are weak, it would be remembered 'as a portrait of female life among ladies in an English village 50 years ago'. He was also taken with the portrait of clerical life in the novel.

Trollope's lecture noted that Austen's appeal lay in the clarity and validity of her presentation. 'She wrote of the times in which she lived, of the class of people with which she associated, and in the language which was usual to her'. This is, of course, precisely what Trollope did half a century later in a society that had traded in a fairly peaceful agrarian and feudal model for an aggressively democratic and industrial one.

There were even fewer heroes and heroines in Trollope's time than there were in Austen's, but it was not to heroic adventures but truth to life that each looked for substance. Indeed, both were staunchly anti-romantic and anti-sentimental. Both poked fun at their heroines' tendencies to succumb to the poetic or sublime. Young ladies who spent too much time daydreaming about being swept off by knights in shining armour were firmly brought down to earth. Like Austen, Trollope put his heroines through a learning process that novel-readers (mainly women) were expected to follow vicariously.

Trollope believed that the novelist must preach, but indirectly. He admired the way in which Austen did this, not by saying outright that a character who behaved dishonourably would have to suffer but by ensuring that she would be dishonoured in the estimation of all readers by her vices.

Both novelists did much of their preaching through comic irony. They delighted in drawing attention to ludicrous social behaviour, sometimes by exaggeration, sometimes by understatement, and at other times by simple, faithful delineation. Both excelled at conveying character through short, tart descriptions.

Though Trollope's world was urban and pressured and political and Austen's rural and slow-moving, both were peopled with clergymen, doctors, gentlemen, lovers—elevated characters made memorable by their vulgarity. We see what the leisured classes did, what they wore, what they said, where they went, how they regarded one another and were regarded by others. Major themes of both novelists concerned the mobility of property, money, and rank through marriage.

Both novelists felt that it was necessary to argue for the respectability of the novel. The narrator of *Northanger Abbey* insists, despite the vogue even among novelists for running down novel-reading, on our knowing that Catherine and Isabella read novels. Over the protestations of a young lady that she has been caught reading 'only a novel', the narrator insists: 'It is . . . only some work in which the greatest powers of the mind are displayed, in which the most thorough knowledge of human nature, the happiest delineation of its varieties, the liveliest effusions of wit and humour, are conveyed to the world in the best-chosen language' (V). Similarly, Trollope bemoaned the tendency for readers to indulge themselves guiltily, 'not without some inward conviction that the taste is vain if not vicious' (*Auto* XII), when all the while they were being instructed as well as entertained.   JK

Booth, Bradford, *Anthony Trollope: Aspects of his Life and Art* (1958).

—— 'Trollope on the Novel', in *Essays Critical and Historical Dedicated to Lily B. Campbell* (1950).

—— 'Trollope on *Emma*: An Unpublished Note', *NCF* (March 1949), 245–7.

Austin, Alfred (1835–1913), barrister turned writer after inheriting a fortune; editor of *National Review* (1887–93). From 1871 to 1908 he published twenty volumes of undistinguished verse, and became Poet Laureate (1896), in which capacity he assisted in securing a Civil List pension for widowed Rose Trollope. His *Autobiography* (1911) described Trollope as 'a delightful companion' but in no sense an intellectual, 'and as unhelpful and impatient an arguer as I ever met' (1, 166). Despite Austin's right-wing politics Trollope took to him and encouraged his versifying, offering detailed criticism of *The Seasons: A Satire* (1861) and other poems. It was to Austin that Trollope expressed his passion for work in May 1871: 'My only doubt as to finding a heaven for myself at last, arises from the fear that the disembodied and beatified spirits will not want novels' (*Letters* 2, 548). In January 1875, Austin asked him to propose his brother for the Garrick. Trollope replied that few acquirements were needed: 'I suppose the members can, most of them, read; but there are many who shew no signs of so much erudition' (*Letters* 2, 643).

RCT

'Australasia, England in' (letter series). Sydney Harbour is the loveliest on earth. New South Wales is the oldest Australian colony, from which the others separated. Problems exist between the colonies as to import and border duties. The original New South Wales squatters have become the aristocracy. There are still many problems in this young country—election security, economic capital, transportation of goods. Many jobs are available; this area is promising for English settlers. London *Telegraph* (23 December 1871, 13 February, 13 March 1872).   AKL

Australia and New Zealand. Trollope visited Australia and New Zealand twice in the 1870s. His first trip was to write *Australia and New Zealand*, and visit his son Fred, a sheep farmer in New South Wales. The second was to spend time with Fred; he also wrote twenty letters to the *Liverpool Mercury* (*The Tireless Traveller*, ed. B. Booth, 1941).

The Australian continent had been touched upon by European ships going to and from the Spice Islands since the 17th century, but was really introduced to the European world, as was New Zealand, by Captain James Cook in 1770. Cook took formal possession of the east coast of Australia, and the British government eventually established a penal colony there. The convict fleet arrived at Sydney, New South Wales, in 1788, transporting the first of some 160,000 convicts to the continent. From New South Wales new colonies were created, Van Diemen's Land (later Tasmania) first, then Victoria and Queensland. South Australia was settled in the 1830s as a result of the theories of Edward Gibbon Wakefield, the advocate of systematic colonization. Western Australia, first settled in 1829 as a convict-free colony, eventually for economic reasons was forced to accept transportation, and was the last to surrender it in 1867.

The free settlers who came soon established a commercial agriculture which flourished when it became apparent that fine wool could be sent to Europe cheaply enough to make a profit. On the plains of the interior, the 'squatters', who owned little of their pastoral lands, but depended on licensed sheep runs on government lands, partially by using convict labour, created a prosperity that attracted many new settlers. Free settlers demanded representative, and then responsible, government, and the various colonies gained these at the same time as they rejected further convict transportation. Gold strikes, beginning in 1851, greatly expanded the population and economic bases of several colonies.

Trollope's description of these southern colonies was meticulous, usually correct, and often critical, though he admired the achievements of the colonists. The maintenance of separate colonies often pursuing hostile fiscal and transportation policies he saw as folly, and he advocated rationalization and co-operation.

The Maori population of New Zealand was more capable of resisting intrusion than the Australian Aborigines, and European penetration was much slower. The islands were finally annexed in 1840, with the Maoris ceding sovereignty of primarily North Island by the Treaty of Waitangi. As land-hungry settlers increased in number, clashes in the mid-1840s led to the Maori Wars, 1860–72, and the loss of more Maori lands. Trollope predicted, as he had of the Australian Aborigines, that the Maoris would die out, a process he considered unjust, since the natives did have prior rights, but necessary in the face of advancing modern civilization.

Harry Heathcote of Gangoil and part of *John Caldigate* have Australian settings. His short story 'Catherine Carmichael' is set in New Zealand. See also AUSTRALIA AND NEW ZEALAND.   LK

Blainey, G., *A Land Half Won* (1980).
Sinclair, K., (ed.), *Oxford Illustrated History of New Zealand* (1990).

Australia and New Zealand is the travel book resulting from Trollope's trip to the Antipodes in 1871–2. He spent a full year in Australia (27 July 1871–29 July 1872) and two months in New Zealand (3 August–3 October 1872). The principal reason for both this visit, on which his wife accompanied him, and the later one which he made on his own in 1875 (4 May–28 August) was personal rather than literary. His younger son Frederic James Anthony had settled in Australia in 1865 and by 1871 had established himself, with his father's help, as a squatter (sheep farmer) in the central west of New South Wales. Frederic and his station are described in the chapter 'Station Life in the Bush' (*Australia*, ed. P. D. Edwards and R. B. Joyce (1967), XX). He was the model for the eponymous hero of *Harry Heathcote of Gangoil*, one of the two novels in which Trollope made direct use of his Australian experiences (the other being *John Caldigate*).

Besides staying in the capital cities of all the colonies, where he was entertained by political leaders and, usually, the colonial governor, Trollope travelled to all of the larger country towns, inspected most of the better-known gold mines (and even went down some of them), and was entertained at many large sheep stations as well as spending some time at his son's relatively small one, Mortray. At one station he rashly mentioned the prevalence of cockroaches and was told that he must have brought them with him. He hunted kangaroos at Mortray and on the Darling Downs in Queensland, attended a duck-shoot at Gippsland in Victoria, and found himself alone in the bush after being spilled from his mount while hunting what he was sure was a bagged hare on rough ground near Melbourne. Travelling in the backblocks, by buggy or on horseback, he often lost his way. He frequently sought out or ran into friends, including schoolfriends, or relatives of friends. Among the latter, not mentioned in *Australia and New Zealand*, was Dickens's son Alfred. Trollope and his wife would also, presumably, have seen Ellen Heseltine Davitt, his wife's eldest sister, who had emigrated to Australia, and whom Trollope called on in Ballarat in 1875, during his second visit.

In *Australia and New Zealand* Trollope looks at most aspects of life in the colonies with his customary shrewdness, fairness, and cosmopolitan broad-mindedness. He is much impressed by signs of that gradual 'diminution' of social inequalities, and improvement of the lot of the less fortunate, which is the core of the political doctrine of 'advanced conservative liberalism' propounded a few years later in *An Autobiography* (XVI). The colonial working man does not tug his forelock and housemaids bear their 'badge of servitude' lightly; the crowds at race tracks and other places of resort are orderly and the miners generally law-abiding and civil; no one who will work goes hungry (a rather roseate view). Trollope recognizes a common policeman who briefly acted as his guide in Victoria as essentially a 'gentleman' and rejoices when the cook he and his wife brought with them from England marries above her station. Notwithstanding that his own son was a squatter battling grimly for survival, he is convinced that the future of the colonies lies with small farmers, 'free-selectors', not with pastoralists grazing their flocks on vast tracts of leasehold land. 'I love a squatter,' he proclaims. 'But on principle I take the part of the free-selector' (*Australia*, X). Even as the house guest of one of New South Wales's leading squatter-politicians, he did not hesitate to state his views publicly when he became involved in an election campaign in the nearest town. The opinions he expresses on some of the other burning political issues of the day are equally liberal and progressive. He strongly supports the nascent federation movement, chiefly on free-trade grounds, just as he had done in Canada ten years earlier; and while he naturally emphasizes the value of the colonies to Britain as a repository for its surplus population and capital, he shares Gladstone's view that British policy must be guided solely by what will best contribute to the 'happiness' of the colonists themselves, and that this will almost certainly include independence from the mother country in the quite near future. He has no sympathy with Froude's vision of 'the indefinite and magnificent expansion of the English [*sic*] Empire', or with the Disraelian notion of the colonies as jewels in Britain's crown. Britain should be ready to part with them 'with a proud feeling that we are sending a son out into the world able to take his place among men' (*Australia* XXIII).

His 'advanced liberal conservatism' (*Auto* XVI) is not always so strongly in evidence, however. He is disappointed that the colonists have chosen to encumber themselves with voting by secret ballot as they take their first steps towards self-government (*Australia* XV, XLVIII), and his moral imagination fails him almost completely where the future of the dispossessed indigenous population is concerned. The Aborigines, he asserts, are 'ineradicably savage' and can never be Europeanized or Christianized; they are lower even than the negroes of whom he had written so slightingly in *The West Indies and the Spanish Main* (*Australia* IV, VIII). Even the Maoris, though certainly better fighters than the Aborigines and apparently more amenable to civilizing influences, still labour under the 'incubus of barbarous superstition', such as the 'tapu'. Efforts to be 'just and also generous' to them inevitably fail because 'our justice is not their justice', and because 'justice on our part is tantamount to weakness in their eyes'. The colonists may be 'humane', just as they would be to a horse, but the Maoris, like the Aborigines, are already 'melting away' and will inevitably 'go' (*Australia* XXIV, XXV).

Privately, Trollope confessed to finding colonial society wearisome after a while, and some reviewers of his book in Australia professed to find evidence of condescension on his part. The Melbourne *Argus*, for example, accused him of entertaining 'a very disparaging opinion of the things and persons' he encountered in the colonies and entering upon his task 'with the air of a man who believes that he is conferring a favour' upon them. But even after this caustic and seemingly gratuitous outburst the critic went on to praise the book in terms very similar to those employed by most other reviewers, both in the colonies and in the mother country: 'the book shows both acuteness of observation, industry in the collection, and method in the arrangement of facts. . . . In fact, he [Trollope] may be regarded as an unpaid and unbiased admiration agent, who is mainly anxious to depict these dependencies of the British Crown in their true colours, and who has succeeded as well in his self-appointed task as any man could be expected to do' (quoted *Australia*, editors' introd.).

Although Trollope travelled thousands of miles, almost entirely by coach or buggy, on horseback, or by coastal steamer, and suffered the usual extremes of heat and cold in Australia, and the rigours of winter in New Zealand, he yet found time to write all but 8 of the 51 chapters dealing with Australia by the time he reached New Zealand, and nearly all of the 12 New Zealand chapters by the time he reached San Francisco on his way home. Between October 1871 and October 1872, he also wrote 10 letters signed

'Antipodean' for the London *Daily Telegraph*, where they were printed between 23 December 1871 and 28 December 1872. (His second, shorter visit to Australia in 1875 produced a further 20 letters to the *Liverpool Mercury*—syndicated to eleven or more other provincial papers—but half of these were devoted to countries he passed through on his way out to and back from Australasia.)

Australia and New Zealand was first published in two hefty volumes by Chapman & Hall in 1873. A second two-volume edition appeared later in the same year, with minor corrections, and a third in 1876, the latter bringing together the four parts which had been issued separately in 1874–5, under the titles *New South Wales and Queensland*, *South Australia and Western Australia*, *Victoria and Tasmania*, and *New Zealand*. In Australia, the book was serialized in the weekly *Australasian*, from 22 February 1873 to 20 June 1874, and an authorized Australian edition in six parts (*Queensland*, *New South Wales*, *Victoria*, *Tasmania and Western Australia*, *South Australia and Australian Institutions*, and *New Zealand*), subsequently bound into a single volume, was published by George Robertson of Melbourne in 1873. Chapman & Hall, in which Trollope had recently bought his elder son a partnership, paid £1,250 for the book under an agreement signed on 12 January 1871, and Trollope received £50 more from other sources. The manuscript of *Australia and New Zealand* is in the National Library of Australia, Canberra; it lacks the first seven chapters devoted to New South Wales (1, XI–XVII).   PE

Trollope, Anthony, *Australia*, ed. P. D. Edwards and R. B. Joyce (1967).
—— *The Tireless Traveller: Twenty Letters to the Liverpool Mercury by Anthony Trollope, 1875*, ed. Bradford Booth (1941).

Autobiography, An. Trollope began writing an account of his life between 20 and 30 October 1875, on the transatlantic steamer *Bothnia*. One of his fellow passengers was Henry James, who assumed he was at work on a novel and who, in his great essay on Trollope in 1883, remembered Trollope's daily 'communion with the muse' on an overcrowded table in bad weather as a 'magnificent example of plain persistence' (H. James, *Partial Portraits* (1888), 99). At the time Trollope was on his way home from his second round-the-world trip to visit his son Frederic in New South Wales. He had completed his novel *The American Senator* on 24 September, two days before reaching San Francisco, and delayed commencing a new novel (*DC*) until after he completed *An Autobiography*. He resumed work on it on 2 January 1876 and finished it on 11

April. Rather than rely solely on his own memory, he had his wife compile a year-by-year list of the important events in their lives since their marriage. On 30 April he wrote a letter to his son Harry, bequeathing the book to him and instructing him how to edit it after his death: Harry was given discretion to delete passages or even to refrain from publishing the book at all, but not to add anything on his own account apart from a preface or introductory chapter. Both letter and manuscript were then locked away for two years before Harry was shown the manuscript and told of the letter. In the autumn of 1878 Trollope made some minor revisions, chiefly to bring the record of his publications up to date. He also cancelled three passages, probably at this time but possibly earlier; these are printed in an appendix to the Oxford Illustrated Trollope and subsequent World's Classics editions of *An Autobiography*, edited by Frederick Page. A few other passages were deleted by Harry before the book was published in two volumes in 1883, the year after Trollope's death. In conformity with his father's advice, Harry contributed a brief preface. A frontispiece photograph of Trollope by Elliott & Fry was the only illustration. The publisher was Blackwood, who paid Harry £1,000 for the book; Trollope had hoped that Chapman & Hall would publish it and that it would bring £1,800. Publication took place on 15 October 1883. All but 80 of the 4,000 copies printed had been sold by 26 March 1884. The printer worked not from Trollope's manuscript, but from a copy made by Harry, who appears to have often misread his father's handwriting. Frederick Page's edition was the first to go back to Trollope's manuscript.

An Autobiography comprises twenty chapters. The first five deal with Trollope's education, including his relations with his parents, his years as a clerk in the General Post Office, his work as a postal surveyor in Ireland, where he married, won promotion, and wrote his first three novels, and finally the conception and writing of *The Warden* which brought him his first glimmerings of literary success. The remaining fifteen chapters chronicle the development of his two careers as popular novelist and senior civil servant, his overseas travels, and his social and to a lesser extent domestic life back in England. Three chapters, interrupting the chronological narrative, give his opinions on 'Novels and the Art of Writing Them', 'English Novelists of the Present Day', and 'Criticism'. Another, 'Beverley', is largely devoted to his unsuccessful attempt to win a seat in Parliament. Apart from these four, all the chapters focus on and take their titles from his latest novels and other books, or his-

A page from the manuscript of *An Autobiography*, in the British Museum, which shows the difficulty Trollope's handwriting presents to the scholar. The passage details how by the time he wrote *Framley Parsonage* he was ready to make 'a map of the dear county' (VIII). The scribbled-over section relates to a row between Thackeray and Edmund Yates in which Trollope became embroiled.

work for new journals such as the *Cornhill Magazine*, the *Pall Mall Gazette*, and *Saint Pauls*. A table in the final chapter sets out his total receipts for each of the 45 books he had published by 1879: altogether they came to £69,939 17*s*. 5*d*.

What spurred Trollope to write his autobiography when he did must have been largely the consciousness that he had reached a watershed in his life: he had turned 60; he was still at, or barely past, the peak of his popularity and commercial success as a novelist; and although he had no reason to feel that his literary powers and mental energies were waning, his body, as he admits in the penultimate chapter, was demanding that he give up his most cherished physical pursuit, hunting. Some of his private letters suggest that his disgust at the recent publication of Dickens's 'hard words' about his parents in John Forster's *Life* of Dickens (1872–4) may have provided strong additional motivation. Writing to a friend just after he had begun his own 'Memoir', Trollope complained that both Dickens and Thackeray had exhibited a 'self-consciousness and irritated craving for applause' which they ought to have concealed however strongly they felt it, and which he himself had always been able to 'tread out' (*Letters* 2, 557, 671). In his treatment of his own early sufferings, and his later successes and disappointments, he presumably hoped to show how a successful author could review his career without such manifestations of vanity and lingering self-pity, and without false heroics.

The outcome fully justified his self-confidence. Although there is evidence that he may have exaggerated the miseries and humiliations he endured as a day-boy at Harrow, his dismal performance both there and at Winchester, and the orphan-like desolateness of some of his school vacations, it is not so much the pathos or injustice of his youthful sufferings that Trollope emphasizes as the emotional resources which enabled him to bear them: the sullen toughness, the thick defensive shell, and the never-failing refuge afforded by his imagination. And while he does not extenuate his father's egregious weaknesses and follies, or even his mother's limitations as a novelist—and, at least by implication, as a mother—he never questions their love for their children and concern for their welfare. His anger against three 'curled darlings' at Harrow who silently allowed him to be punished for crimes that they had committed still burns as fiercely as it did 50 years earlier, but it is a manly and righteous anger, similar to that which once brought him victory in an epic fight against a schoolfellow who goaded him too far (*Auto* I)—one of the rites of initiation for all oppressed schoolboys in Victorian novels. He is similarly frank and unashamed in acknowledging how almost childishly, almost 'womanishly' dependent on the goodwill and approbation of his friends the ostracism he suffered at school had left him throughout his adult life. The applause he most craves is not that of reviewers but that of his social peers, the huntsmen, whist-playing clubmen, and professional colleagues whose company he enjoys in his leisure hours, and many of whom were once among the curled darlings of schools like Harrow and Winchester. He makes no secret of the delight and pride he takes in the material rewards his slow rise to a senior position in the Post Office, and more especially to fame as a novelist, have won him. They have secured his position in the social class which tried to reject him in his schooldays. They have vindicated him. But it is not primarily a triumph over his boyhood persecutors or over adverse circumstances that he celebrates in *An Autobiography*. Nor is it a triumph of genius or inspiration. It is a much more modest, an essentially bourgeois triumph of character: of sheer persistence and hard work.

Trollope states in his opening sentence that he calls the book an 'autobiography' only for want of a better name. His intention is to speak not of the little details of his private life but of the failures and successes of his literary career and of literature as a means of livelihood. He correctly foresees, however, that he will not be able to avoid saying something of himself, recurring to 'the passages of his own life'; and although all but a handful of his twenty chapters purport to have literary topics as their primary focus, readers have always found his disclosures about himself more interesting than his criticisms of his own and other writers' work. Both his publisher William Blackwood and his close friend W. Lucas Collins, who reviewed the book in *Blackwood's Magazine* (November 1883, 577–96), regretted that he had not revealed more of himself, but most of the reviewers were surprised by much of what he did reveal, especially about his miserable schooldays, and commended his 'frankness', his 'unreserve'. One such was Alexander Innes Shand, in *The Times* (12 October 1883, 10), who found 'more of the sensational' in the book than in any of Trollope's novels, and who, along with other reviewers, favourably compared Trollope's manly treatment of his boyhood woes with Forster's treatment of Dickens's. In this regard the conclusion reached by the *Contemporary Review* (November 1883, 787) epitomized the general feeling: 'A happy, healthy nature, manifestly, in spite of a singularly depressing boyhood and a strangely unpromising young manhood.'

Trollope's frankness was seen also in his revelations about his mechanical methods of work: never waiting on 'inspiration', but grinding out 250 words every quarter of an hour in the chill early morning when at home; and keeping up a similar pace, regardless of distractions, in railway carriages or on board ship. True, he lays equal stress on the joy he obtains from constantly 'living with' his characters at other times, and most reviewers conceded that his creative processes had served him well, though the *Saturday Review* and Henry James were not alone in wondering whether he might have written better if he had written less. However, Michael Sadleir's contention that Trollope's copiousness, and his disclosures about his methods of work in *An Autobiography*, gravely damaged his reputation for at least a generation or two after his death is not really borne out by the evidence. In Trollope's own comments on his novels he never concedes that undue haste may be to blame for the shortcomings he identifies. Most often, his likes and dislikes among his own novels— as among those of his predecessors and contemporaries—appear to be matters of whim or prejudice rather than resting on any consistent literary criteria. The pertinacity, open-mindedness, and imaginative insight that he brought to his analysis of his characters within the novels hardly carry over at all to his analysis of the finished products, and even allowing that his apparent obtuseness about his own art may have been at least in part merely an affectation of innocence, designed to protect his creative imagination from intrusive scrutiny, *An Autobiography* amply validates Henry James's pronouncement that if Trollope was 'a knowing psychologist' and 'in any degree a man of genius'—as James maintained that he was—he was so by 'instinct' or 'grace', not by 'study' (James, *Partial Portraits*, 105).

Trollope fully adheres to his initial promise that his autobiography will 'set down naught in malice' and give neither himself nor others honour which he does not believe they have fairly earned. The three passages he cancelled in his manuscript all contain derogatory comments on other people which he may have feared would sound querulous. One included an attack on a former colleague in the Post Office, Edmund Yates, as a 'literary gutter-scraper' for making public a story Trollope had unwisely told him about the conversation at a *Cornhill* dinner; it may have been deleted after a partial reconciliation between Trollope and Yates effected early in 1878 by T. H. S. Escott, Trollope's first biographer, who was a close associate of Yates. Of the other passages, one accused Carlyle of 'silly and

arrogant' denigration of the novelists of the day and the other implied that Smith, Elder, the publishers, had not paid Trollope fairly for recent sales of *The Last Chronicle of Barset*. There was nothing Trollope needed to retract, or emend, in his treatment of the two great disappointments of his later life, the thwarting of his long-cherished ambition to become a member of Parliament and the failure of his application for the position of Under-Secretary in the Post Office. His chapter on the indignities he suffered as Liberal candidate for Beverley in 1868, and his resounding defeat, speaks almost as feelingly of his bewildered disillusionment at the time as does his fictionalized account of the experience in *Ralph the Heir*; but his lingering moral outrage is controlled, even more surely, by his wry consciousness of the absurdity of the situation and his own inadequacy, and his wounded pride is salved by the recollection that his successful opponents were subsequently unseated and the corrupt voters of Beverley disenfranchised: his signal failure to achieve what he considered 'an Englishman's highest ambition' had enabled him to perform a patriotic duty. The passage in which he expounds the creed of 'advanced conservative liberalism' that he would have tried to implement as member for Beverley—very similar to Plantagenet Palliser's creed as enunciated in *The Prime Minister* (LXVIII)—is one of the most thoughtful and heartfelt in *An Autobiography*. In the Post Office Trollope also feels that he was able to serve his country well in spite of disappointments; although his struggles with obstructive colleagues ended in defeat, just as his campaign for Beverley did, the stories he tells of them in *An Autobiography* are animated much more by recollections of the joy of battle, the 'delicious feuds' he engaged in—never doubting that he was 'right'—than by any lingering bitterness against his enemies. His chapter 'On English Novelists of the Present Day', though characteristically prejudiced and opinionated, and often far from gentle even in its judgements of the work of close friends (such as Thackeray, George Eliot, and Wilkie Collins), is free of personal animus and professional jealousy.

In the age of psychoanalysis, particularly after the Second World War, *An Autobiography* became a treasure trove for critics in search of biographical explanations for the symptoms of manic depression, Oedipal complexes, and other deep-seated neuroses which they detected in Trollope's novels. But most other critics, both before and since, have tended to endorse the original reviewers' reading of it as essentially the picture of a 'happy, healthy nature', even if a less untroubled and uncomplicated one than Trollope consciously sought to project. Refractions of his father (and to some extent of his own secret self) have been found, plausibly, in unhappy characters in his novels such as Josiah Crawley (*FP* and *LCB*) and Sir Thomas Underwood (*RH*), and of his mother in, among others, the exhilarating, mischievous, perhaps heartless Lady Glencora Palliser. *An Autobiography* explicitly reveals the autobiographical basis of other elements in the novels: notably Johnny Eames's youthful follies (in *SHA* and *LCB*), and the embarrassingly public harassment of Charley Tudor (in *TC*) and of Phineas Finn by moneylenders demanding 'punctuality'.

The frankness for which *An Autobiography* was widely praised does not extend to Trollope's marriage—which in a period famous for philoprogenitiveness produced only two children. It was, he said, 'like the marriage of other people, and of no special interest to any one except my wife and me' (IV). This reticence only makes it the more surprising that he did feel impelled to speak of his warm, though no doubt unconsummated, affection for another woman, the American actress and lecturer Kate Field, and to do so in terms that even the most innocent Victorian could hardly have failed to find almost erotic. ('She is a ray of light to me, from which I can always strike a spark by thinking of her' (XVII).) Trollope identified her as American, but his son discreetly deleted the reference to her nationality.

Just before the end of his 'so-called autobiography' Trollope reiterates that it has not been intended to give a record of his 'inner life'. No man, he believes, ever did so truly; Rousseau probably attempted to, but 'who doubts that Rousseau has confessed in much the thoughts and convictions rather than the facts of his life?' In the eloquent peroration that follows Trollope disarmingly insists that he himself has no worthwhile sins to confess anyway, and specifically no sexual sins. 'If the rustle of a woman's petticoat has ever stirred my blood; if a cup of wine has been a joy to me; if I have thought tobacco at midnight in pleasant company to be one of the elements of an earthly Paradise; if now and again I have somewhat recklessly fluttered a £5 note over a card-table;—of what matter is that to any reader? I have betrayed no woman. Wine has brought me to no sorrow. It has been the companionship of smoking that I have loved, rather than the habit. I have never desired to win money, and I have lost none. To enjoy the excitement of pleasure, but to be free from its vices and ill effects,—to have the sweet, and leave the bitter untasted—that has been my study. The preachers tell us that this is impossible. It seems to me that hitherto I have succeeded fairly well. I will not say that I have never scorched a finger,—but I carry no ugly wounds.'

When Trollope wrote this he had already lived longer than either Dickens or Thackeray and obviously felt he had reached an age when he could look back on his life with philosophical calm and moral balance, could see it steadily and see it whole like one of the ancients—his beloved Cicero, perhaps, or the Virgil whom he quotes in his farewell to the reader: 'Now I stretch out my hand, and from the further shore I bid adieu to all who have cared to read any among the many words that I have written.' The manuscript is in the British Library. PE

Hall, N. John, 'Seeing Trollope's *An Autobiography* through the Press', *Princeton University Library Chronicle* (winter 1986), 189–223.
James, Henry, 'Anthony Trollope', in *Partial Portraits* (1888).
Trollope, Anthony, *An Autobiography*, 2 vols. (1883); World's Classics edn., ed. Michael Sadleir and Frederick Page, with introd. and notes by P. D. Edwards (1992).

Awdry, Walter, school usher, then clergyman; died in poverty. A close friend of Trollope's adolescence, with John Merivale he made up the 'Tramp Society' walking through Hertfordshire and Buckinghamshire; he was described by Trollope as 'unfortunate in all things . . . He was most perverse; bashful to very fear of the rustle of a lady's dress; unable to restrain himself in anything, but yet with a conscience that was always stinging him; a loving friend, though very quarrelsome; and, perhaps of all men I have known, the most humorous' (*Auto* III). The lengthy tribute signifies some of the pangs of Trollope's own early manhood. RCT

Ayala's Angel (*see next page*)

Aylmer, Sir Anthony, husband of Lady Aylmer, father of Belinda and Frederic Aylmer, and squire of Aylmer Park. A gouty, elderly man, he is completely dominated by his wife and their staff of 'fat, and lazy, and stupid' servants (XVII). He subsists in mildly discontented idleness. *BE*

WK

Aylmer, Belinda, daughter of Sir Anthony and Lady Aylmer and sister of Frederic Aylmer. Over 40 and unmarried, she lives with her parents at Aylmer Park. She is 'as ignorant, meek, and stupid a poor woman as you shall find anywhere in Europe' (XVII). *BE* WK

Aylmer, Captain Frederic Folliott, younger son of Sir Anthony and Lady Aylmer and member of Parliament for Perivale, an indecisive, self-serving young man, wholly under the thumb of
(*cont. on page 30*)

TROLLOPE's '80th tale', as he emphatically called it (*Letters* 2,792), is a complex, light-hearted novel in which nothing goes permanently wrong and almost everyone enjoys a happy ending. *Ayala's Angel* begins, like a fairy tale, with the orphaning of two sisters, Lucy and Ayala Dormer. Their father Egbert Dormer, a rather desultory artist, has died shortly after the death of his wife Adelaide; the sisters, aged 21 and 19 respectively, must leave their 'most perfect bijou of a little house at South Kensington', where they have been raised amid witty conversations, blue china, and the other trappings of the artistic life (I).

Two very different sets of aunts and uncles are ready to take the sisters in. Adelaide's brother Reginald Dosett and his wife Margaret inhabit a 'genteel house at Notting Hill' (I), where they barely keep up appearances on Reginald's £900 a year as an Admiralty clerk (II). Meanwhile, Adelaide's sister Lady Emmeline Tringle—'with a house at the top of Queen's Gate, rented at £1,500 a year, with a palatial moor in Scotland, with a seat in Sussex, and as many carriages and horses as would suit an archduchess' (I)—has no such mundane worries. Her husband Sir Thomas Tringle is a partner in Travers & Treason, a 'great firm in Lombard Street' (I), and is widely known as 'the man of millions' (LVI). His incalculable wealth provides every material luxury for his wife and their three children Tom, Augusta, and Gertrude, as well as for whichever Dormer orphan the Tringles choose to adopt.

The contrast between Notting Hill and Queen's Gate, between the Dosetts' genteel poverty and the Tringles' nouveau riche splendour, forms a pervasive theme in *Ayala's Angel*. All of the novel's young lovers—there are nearly a dozen of them—must face some version of a choice between a poor life and a rich one. The choice is not merely financial: Augusta Tringle, who marries the Hon. Septimus Traffick, MP, in chapter XII, brings a dowry of £120,000 with her, more than enough to found a comfortable life, yet Septimus is so niggardly that the couple spend most of the novel billeted on the Tringles. Sir Thomas's increasingly unsubtle efforts to get rid of them make a running joke until chapter LVIII, when he finally succeeds in shaming his nearly impenetrable son-in-law.

Meanwhile, Lucy remains true to the sculptor Isadore Hamel, despite the sensible opposition of both her aunts and uncles. Hamel's monumental sculptures, such as his 'allegorical figure of Italia United', exist only in plaster of Paris, because no one will commission them in marble (XXXIII). The couple's financial prospects are dim indeed, but Lucy—in a fashion reminiscent of Emily Hotspur in *Sir Harry Hotspur of Humblethwaite*, Lucy Morris in *The Eustace Diamonds*, and several other Trollopian heroines—sticks to her lover simply because she loves him, whatever their elders may say or the future might hold. In the end Sir Thomas, very much the fairy godfather, pays for Lucy's trousseau and a lavish wedding. Isadore resolves to junk his unsaleable allegories and take up a more commercial style. Lucy and Isadore will enjoy the best of both worlds, romance grounded in reality.

The other two Tringle children, Gertrude and Tom, choose romance instead of reality, and though neither comes absolutely to grief, both suffer the bursting of their romantic bubbles. At first, Gertrude fancies herself in love with the dilettantish painter Frank Houston. But Frank—as he bluntly informs his loving cousin Imogene Docimer—is courting Gertrude only for the £120,000 she will presumably bring him, as Augusta has brought to Septimus Traffick. Disabused of this dream by Sir Thomas,

Frank drops Gertrude and returns to Imogene as a rather unconvincingly 'altered man' (XLII). With the aid of Frank's aunt and fairy godmother Rosina Houston, this couple, too, can look forward to a fusion of the romantic and the real.

Spurned by Frank, Gertrude sets her sights on the somewhat simple-minded Captain Benjamin Batsby. She persuades him to elope with her to Ostend, in search of a non-existent Anglican clergyman supposed to specialize in wedding runaways. Packed home in disgrace by Sir Thomas, Gertrude and the Captain eventually marry (in a double ceremony with Lucy and Isadore), though without the £120,000, since Batsby has a comfortable income of his own. Gertrude resigns herself to a well-padded, dull future: 'It was not interesting, as Gertrude felt; but she had not expected him to be interesting' (LXII). From the start, her romantic notions have been incompatible with any conceivable reality. She and Batsby are 'two fools', as Sir Thomas calls them (XLVIII); they deserve each other.

Tom Tringle, too, is something of a fool, though a highly sympathetic one. He falls in love at first sight with Ayala Dormer and spends the rest of the novel forlornly pursuing her. Ayala regards him as she would a Newfoundland dog that 'jumps all over you just when he has come out of a horsepond' (VI); she cannot bear the sight of him and repels all his advances. In despair, Tom takes to drink and rowdy behaviour in the wee hours; the only cure seems to be a round-the-world tour lasting at least a year. On the eve of sailing, he is still uttering romantic claptrap—'If the ship could be dashed against a rock I should prefer it!'—but in the end the narrator predicts for him 'a comfortable wife and a large family' (LXI). Unlike Gertrude, Tom will get over his romantic delusions.

These subsidiary love stories form an elaborate counterpoint to the story of 'our pet heroine', Ayala (LXIV). She receives no fewer than three marriage proposals—from Tom, Captain Batsby, and Colonel Jonathan Stubbs—but turns them all down, because no flesh-and-blood man can match the charms of her imaginary 'Angel of Light'. This vaguely conceived figure, who Ayala believes will come from heaven to claim her, seems at first to epitomize the romantic foolishness that misleads several other characters. Tom and the Captain are no prizes as men, perhaps, but they have money, and Ayala has none; prudence (expressed in the voices of her elders) dictates that she should accept one or the other of them. As for the Colonel, he possesses good financial prospects, a distinguished military career and the admiration of all who know him. But he also has 'ruby red' hair, an 'enormous' mouth, and, above all, that dreadfully unangelic name (XVI).

The reader might expect that Ayala has been set up to learn a hard lesson in the incompatibility of reality with romance. But something unexpected and delightful happens. Stubbs, it develops, has a streak of romance in him: he does not 'mind a little Byron now and then, so there is no nonsense', and his cottage at Drumcaller in Scotland fills the mind 'with a conviction of realized poetry' (XVIII). Instead of forgetting her Angel and embracing a real, ugly man, Ayala gradually learns that the Colonel and the Angel have been the same all along. When Stubbs proposes marriage a second time, she accepts him joyously, and in the novel's last line, 'to her own intense satisfaction, Ayala was handed over to her ANGEL OF LIGHT' (LXIV).

Trollope wrote *Ayala's Angel* between 25 April and 24 September 1878, a span that also included a month-long sailing trip to Iceland aboard the *Mastiff*. In late July, he joined his wife Rose at Felsenegg in the Black Forest, where he worked furiously on the novel, writing 3,000 words a day for 22 consecutive days (Hall 444). Though Trollope tried to place it with at least three other publishers, it was not published until June 1881, in three volumes, by Chapman & Hall. Its only serialization was in the American newspaper the *Cincinnati Commercial*, where it ran weekly between 6 November 1880 and 23 July 1881. Most reviews were brief and rather grudgingly polite, and *Ayala's Angel* has never counted among Trollope's favourites with the reading public.

Several modern critics—including R. C. Terry (*Anthony Trollope: The Artist in Hiding*, 1977), Walter Kendrick (*The Novel-Machine*, 1980), and Christopher Herbert (*Trollope and Comic Pleasure*, 1987)—have, however, sought to win for the novel the attention it deserves. From the man who had lately written such bitter satires as *The Way We Live Now* (1875), *The Prime Minister* (1876), and *Is He Popenjoy?* (1878), *Ayala's Angel* comes as a surprise; it is a thoroughly contemporary yet also light-hearted novel, in which even a multimillionaire can have a soft heart, and in which every difficulty 'solved itself, as do other difficulties' (*AA*, XVI). What it lacks in bite it makes up for in sheer comedy, and in its sunny assurance that even the most far-fetched dreams can, with luck, come true. The manuscript is held at Yale University. WK

his appalling mother. He promises his aunt Mrs Winterfield, on her deathbed, that he will propose marriage to Clara Amedroz. When Clara accepts with eagerness, Frederic supposes her love must be 'cheap' (X). In the end, he marries Lady Emily Tagmaggert. *BE* WK

Aylmer, Lady, wife of Sir Anthony Aylmer, mother of Belinda and Frederic Aylmer, and sister of Mrs Winterfield. A domineering, self-important, deliberately disagreeable woman, she displays 'a certain mixture of cunning, and power, and hardness in the slight smile that would gather round her mouth' (XXV). She browbeats her husband and son and tries the same tactic with Clara Amedroz, Frederic's fiancée. But Clara, revolted, defies her. *BE* WK

Aylmer Park, estate in Yorkshire, home of the Aylmer family, comprising three or four hundred acres (120–60 ha) and a pretentious house, with a wasteful staff of lazy servants: 'as the reader will at once perceive, Aylmer Park was kept up in the proper English style' (XVII). *BE* WK

Babington House, Suffolk country home of the Babingtons where hunting, sports, and games predominate. Young John Caldigate is made to feel welcome as a youth after his mother's death and his father's coolness make his own home less inviting. Aunt Polly forces John into an engagement with Julia Babington in the linen closet here. *JC* SRB

Babington, Humphrey, genial, good-hearted country squire and uncle of John Caldigate, considered stupid by John's father. The hospitality of his family and their sporting life make the young John feel at home when he quarrels with his father; later, the squire defends John against family animosity during the bigamy trial. *JC* SRB

Babington, John, son and heir of Humphrey Babington, who remains on good terms with John Caldigate despite the hatred of his mother and sister for his friend. *JC* SRB

Babington, Julia, cherry-cheeked country girl, intended by her mother to marry John Caldigate. When he deserts her, she feels scorned and speaks ill of him. She marries the Revd Augustus Smirkie who, with her, is piously grateful that she has been delivered from Caldigate's charge of bigamy. *JC* SRB

Babington, Maryanne (Aunt Polly), John Caldigate's loving aunt who tries to force a marriage between him and her daughter Julia. When John sneaks out of the engagement by running away to Australia, she and Julia hold a long-standing grudge against him, relieved only after Julia becomes Mrs Smirkie and John is vindicated after his trial for bigamy. *JC* SRB

Baden-Baden, famed German spa where Countess De Courcy flees her abusive husband, taking along her daughters Lady Margaretta and Lady Alexandrina Crosbie who has tired of her husband. *SHA* NCS

Bagehot, Walter (1826–77), editor of *The Economist* (1860–77), authority on banking and finance, better known as essayist in a wide sphere. A lucid and engaging stylist; from 1855 as editor of the *National Review* he strongly influenced political thinking and developments in social science. The first part of Bagehot's *English Constitution* ran in *Fortnightly Review*, May 1865, the periodical Trollope helped found. RCT

Baggett, Mrs, domestic in the employ of the Whittlestaff family for most of her life. Née Dorothy Tedcaster, she marries Sergeant Baggett but lives apart from him as the housekeeper at Croker's Hall. Devoted and deferential to her bachelor employer, Mr Whittlestaff, she also assumes the familiarity of an equal. *OML* RC

Baggett, Sergeant Timothy, ex-military man whose most distinctive features are a wooden leg and a red nose. An unemployed and unemployable alcoholic living in Portsmouth, he periodically visits his wife, housekeeper at Croker's Hall, to beg for money and demand her return. *OML* RC

Bagwax, Samuel, delightful postal clerk whose detective work with postage marks and stamps proves conclusively that John Caldigate's conviction for bigamy was wrong. He heroically sacrifices an official trip to Australia in order to release Caldigate from prison, and then is rewarded with the same trip for his honourable behaviour. *JC* SRB

Bailey, Catherine, former fiancée of Mr Whittlestaff. She jilts him for an Old Bailey barrister named Mr Compas. A 'fair-haired girl' of joyous good spirits, she 'blossomed out into the anxious mother of ten fair-haired children' (II). *OML* RC

Baillie, Joanna (1762–1851), Scottish dramatist and poet, issued four volumes of *Plays on the Passions* (1798–1836). Her most successful play, *The Family Legend*, was produced at Drury Lane in 1810 with a prologue by Sir Walter Scott. In his Commonplace Book, Trollope projected a critical account of the 'Excellencies and defects of the modern English' drama as displayed in selected works of five contemporary dramatists. Joanna Baillie's *Henriquez*, published in the three-volume collection *Dramas* (1836), was included, along with plays by Fanny Kemble, Sheridan

Knowles, Henry Taylor, and Sergeant Talfourd. RCT

Baker, Miss Mary, niece of Mr George Bertram, and Caroline Waddington's companion, one of Littlebath's unremarkable 'dear lad[ies]' courted by Sir Lionel for her comfortable income. *B*   MRS

Balatka, Josef. Once the partner of his Zamenoy brother-in-law, then in business with the Trendellsohns, he lives in penniless seclusion with his devoted daughter. Ever meek and indolent, he cannot forbid her to love Anton, though he fears for her Christian soul. His death leaves Nina vulnerable. *NB*   AWJ

Balatka, Nina. Passionately in love with Anton Trendellsohn, she bravely withstands her shrewish aunt's threats, her cousin's marriage proposal, the servants' outspoken criticism. Even St Nicholas and the Virgin cannot deflect her. Obedient to Anton's every word and touch, she patiently awaits the day he will claim her, while refusing her aunt's grudging charity and her lover's offers to lighten her poverty. When Anton is tricked into believing she has betrayed him, Nina becomes a wounded 'tigress' determined to end her misery and make him regret that distrust by plunging from the Charles Bridge. Anton learns to value her above the riches he gives up by marrying her. *NB*   AWJ

Baldock, Lady, respectable widowed aunt and dragon-like guardian of Violet Effingham. Though Lady Baldock conscientiously wishes to protect Miss Effingham's morals and substantial fortune, the dowager's vigilance is an awesome burden, full of scolding and distrust; and Miss Effingham often proposes wild schemes in an attempt to overthrow the caution of her aunt. *PF*   JMR

Baldock, Lord George (Gustavus), cousin of Violet Effingham and son of the dowager Lady Baldock of Baddingham and Berkeley Square. He enjoys teasing the ladies of his family, his mother particularly, but is otherwise a pleasant, well-behaved young man. *PF*   JMR

Baldoni, Marchesa, mother of Nina Baldoni and aunt of Colonel Jonathan Stubbs. An Englishwoman married to a usually absent Italian nobleman, she 'looked like a Marchesa;—or perhaps, even, like a Marchioness' (XV). Her first name is either Beatrice (XX) or Julia (LII). *AA*   WK

Baldoni, Nina, daughter of the Marchesa Baldoni, cousin of Colonel Jonathan Stubbs, and close friend of Ayala Dormer, whom she meets at Rome. Nina idolizes her cousin and speaks strongly in his favour to the stubborn Ayala. Nina marries Lord George Bideford, whom she also idolizes. *AA*   WK

Ball, John, bald, stout, past 40, a widower with nine children, sadly worn down with money cares. The son of Sir John and Lady Ball, he does not share his parents' haughtiness or irascibility. He courts Margaret Mackenzie first for her money, then for love; despite his rather dull and neglectful ways, she accepts him for the romance and poetry he brings to her life. *MM*   SRB

Ball, Sir John, the sarcastic, cross old Baronet who effects a reconciliation between the Ball and Mackenzie families in their long-standing dispute over inheritance by inviting his niece Margaret Mackenzie (whom he calls 'that old maid') to his home at the Cedars, where she meets and eventually marries his son John. *MM*   SRB

Ball, Jonathan. Eccentric and quarrelsome, he left money to his sister's children (the Mackenzies) rather than his brother's (the Balls). His legacy does great harm as he bequeathed money which was not legally his to give, creating much hostility between the families until lawyers discover the error 25 years later. *MM*   SRB

Ball, Lady, imperious wife of Sir John who meddles in her son John's relationship with Margaret Mackenzie. Often cold and unpleasant in her dignity, she cuts Margaret, who is a guest in her home. Trollope calls her a 'terribly stupid old woman' for interfering and valuing prestige over compassion. *MM*   SRB

Ballinamore. North-east of Mohill in Co. Leitrim, headquarters of Captain Greenough, sub-inspector of police, it also boasts a Bridewell, a jail for those guilty of minor offences. Paddy Byrne, Joe Smith, and Pat Reynolds, convicted of making illicitly distilled whiskey, are incarcerated in Ballinamore Bridewell. *MB*   MRS

Ballinaslow Asylum, madhouse where Barry Lynch threatens to have his sister Anty committed. *KOK*   MRS

Ballindine, Lord Francis (Frank O'Kelly), a rarity among Trollope's romantic heroes: a lover who is never seen wooing. Spendthrift owner of Kelly's Court who, though openhearted, banks on 'some happy matrimonial speculation' (II) to see him through his debts, instead he falls in love with minor heiress Fanny Wyndham. Separated from her when he fails to reform his wastrel ways, he repents, and through Revd Armstrong is reunited with her. *KOK*
MRS

Ballintubber, Irish estate adjacent to Morony, purchased by Philip Jones, an Englishman. *L*
MRS

Ballycloran, grand but dilapidated residence of the Macdermots, whose ruination paints 'a picture of misery, of useless expenditure, unfinished pretense, and premature decay' (I). It forms the setting for a struggle for cultural ascendancy between old blood (the Macdermots) and new money (Joe Flannelly and Hyacinth Keegan). *MB*
MRS

Ballyglass, town in Co. Mayo over ten miles from Castle Conor where Archibald Green stays. 'O'Conors' *TAC1*
GRH

Ballyglunin, small railway town, near where Florian Jones is murdered en route to Galway. *L*
MRS

Ballymoy, village in Galway close to Lough Corrib. 'Giles' *LS*
GRH

Ballytowngal, seat of Sir Nicholas Bodkin in Co. Galway, whose fox coverts are disturbed by local tenants under direction of the Landleaguers. *L*
MRS

Balsam, Mr. This mild-mannered barrister, as his name suggests, can be relied upon by Henry Jones's representatives to soothe him through his libel suit before confronting Mr Cheekey. *CH*
AWJ

Balzac, Honoré de (1799–1850), French novelist who conceived the grand design for the 90 novels and short stories that comprised his chronicle, *La Comédie humaine*, written between 1827 and 1847. Satisfaction among Trollope's readers at rediscovering familiar characters in subsequent novels was expressed at the Royal Literary Fund dinner on 15 May 1867 by Earl Stanhope, who called the strategy an 'invention, attended with the most successful results, of which, as far as I know, the original merit belongs to M. de Balzac'. Responding to the toast to literature, Trollope said he was happy to drink long life to Balzac: 'I am told that he was the man who invented that style of fiction in which I have attempted to work' (Hall 302). Other critics alluded to the affinity between them. The *Saturday Review* (December 1882) likened Trollope to Balzac for a similarly 'mechanical' mode of composition. In *Partial Portraits* (1888) Henry James commented that Louis Trevelyan in *He Knew He Was Right* at his desolate villa on a hilltop near Siena was 'a picture worthy of Balzac' (130). But James cited the historical realism of Balzac as a narrative ideal which Trollope violated each time he gestured towards the codes and conventions of novel-writing.
RCT

Bampfield, George Frederick Lewis (1827–1900). A zealous advocate of Roman Catholicism, he edited *St Andrew's Magazine* and wrote many pamphlets and essays. Original for Trollope's Catholic priest Father Barham, befriended by Roger Carbury in *The Way We Live Now*: 'a thoroughly conscientious man, . . . and a perfect gentleman, so poor that he had not bread to eat' (*Letters* 2, 645). The Trollopes opened their home to him 'in full friendship', but he so berated their religion, 'though I would not on any account have hinted a slur upon his', that 'He made himself absolutely unbearable'. Trollope loathed abuses of hospitality.
RCT

B&B, the Berkshire and Buckinghamshire Hunt which Ralph Newton (the heir) joins whenever possible, stabling his hunters Brag, Banker, Buff, and Brewer at the Moonbeam pub. *RH*
RCT

Bangles, Peter, partner of Burton & Bangles, wine-merchants and moneylenders, of Hook Court, London. He witnesses the death of Dobbs Broughton and later marries the predatory Madalina Demolines in the church of Peter the Martyr. *LCB*
NCS

banks and currency. English banking was transformed during the Victorian period from a mosaic of small local banks to a highly centralized branch system dominated by a few big London banks. The private country banks, of which there were hundreds earlier in the century and only a few survivors by its end, were dear to novelists like Trollope because of their rootedness in the local community. They were wholly owned and run by small partnerships, often family-based, comprising men of local consequence whose wealth, power, and reputation were tied directly and publicly to their unlimited personal liability as bankers. Nicholas Bolton, the Cambridge banker in *John Caldigate*, and Bartholomew Burgess of the Exeter bank Cropper & Burgess in *He Knew He Was Right*, exemplify this kind of banker. Joint stock banks, proliferating after the Bank of England's joint stock monopoly ended in 1827, increasingly drove out these private banks by their ability to mobilize a much larger shareholder capital base and tap into more deposits through branch banking.

Fraud and mismanagement were serious problems: government regulation was virtually non-existent, and effective accounting and auditing procedures were slow to take hold. John *Sadleir, one of several sources for Melmotte in *The Way We Live Now*, who embezzled huge sums before committing suicide, and Trollope's father-in-law Edward *Heseltine, who left the country to avoid enquiries into his lending practices, stood at the two ends of this spectrum. Banks were both vulnerable, and major contributors, to the boom–bust cycles of a *laissez-faire* economy punctuated by regular financial crises in 1836, 1839, 1846, 1857, 1866, 1875, 1882, and 1890. These caused runs on banks triggered by lack of customer confidence, or the domino effect of loans suddenly being called in. Successive panics shook out the smaller and weaker banks through failure or amalgamation.

The Bank of England was both a profit-driven commercial bank and the holder of a monopoly over government banking, but not over the issue of money. Its gold-backed paper money tended to be in short supply, and the resulting demand for currency was met by other banks issuing their own paper money freely, some too freely, as panics would reveal. Bills of exchange also circulated widely as currency equivalents. After the 1844 Bank Act, the Bank of England increasingly accepted the role of central banker and lender of last resort in times of crisis. It also began to exercise greater control over currency supply by actively discouraging other banks from note issue. The fast rising use of cheques, which were as good as cash and could even circulate uncashed as virtual currency, effectively increased the money supply. The stability of the monetary and banking system was further increased by the introduction of limited liability in banking, which freed shareholders from liability for losses and made banks much safer investments for cautious people like Trollope, who banked with, and became a shareholder of, the Union Bank of London.

Joint stock banks would become important alternatives to government bonds—the well-known 3 per cents in which Mary Bold's inheritance is invested in *The Warden*—for those seeking a secure income from their capital. Riskier, but potentially more profitable, was the swelling international bond market dominated from the City of London by specialized merchant bankers like Barings and Rothschild. Trollope knew Baron *Rothschild and hunted over his Buckinghamshire estate in 1873.

The everyday transactions of life, however, were conducted largely in a coinage which was defiantly antiquated, despite Plantagenet Palliser's lonely crusade to decimalize it in *The Eustace Diamonds* (LXXX). The basic penny was subdivided into half- and quarter- (farthing) pence coins, and multiplied in two-, three-, four- (groat), and sixpence coins. The shilling was twelve pence and multiplied in two- (florin), two-and-a-half- (half-crown), four- (double florin), five- (crown), ten- (half-sovereign), and twenty- (gold sovereign) shilling coins. Twenty

shillings made a pound and twenty-one shillings a guinea, which was no longer coined but was preserved as the unit of snobbery—fashionable tradespeople and professionals would commonly bill in guineas.   CK

Mathias, Peter, *The First Industrial Nation* (1969).

Banks, Mrs G. Linnaeus (née **Varley**) (1821–97), daughter of a Manchester chemist, publishing poems in the *Manchester Guardian* at 16. She gained fame as 'the Lancashire novelist' from several well-researched novels of working-class life, notably *The Manchester Man* (1876), about the 1819 'Peterloo Massacre'. Overcome by ill health, she was assisted by the Royal Literary Fund (to a total of £365 by 1882). In 1878 Trollope wrote: 'your rewards in literary life had fallen short of your desserts' (*Letters* 2, 802). She was awarded a Civil List pension in 1891.   RCT

Banmann, Baroness. An overweight and ugly German feminist, the Baroness sues Julia Mildmay in a factional dispute and is accused of swindling. Her appearance, her name, her foreign origin, and crooked dealings demonstrate the level of satire as does the refrain of her speech: 'De manifest infairiority of de tyrant saix—' (XVII). *IHP*   MG

Barchester, the cathedral city and county town of Barsetshire, lying in the county's eastern division, provides the setting of *The Warden* and *Barchester Towers*, is the important administrative centre dominating life in *Doctor Thorne*, *Framley Parsonage*, and *The Last Chronicle of Barset*, which largely take place in the county, and appears in *The Small House at Allington* and 'The Two Heroines of Plumplington', which do not. The narrator of *The Warden* invites us to suppose that it is 'a quiet town in the West of England, more remarkable for the beauty of its cathedral and the antiquity of its monuments, than for any commercial prosperity; that the west end of Barchester is the cathedral close, and that the aristocracy of Barchester are the bishop, dean, and canons, with their respective wives and daughters' (I). The city occupies an almost symbolic position on its own branch line off the main railway line from Paddington, so that it is at once connected to the modern world, and in a backwater. Practically every cathedral city in south and west England has at some time been supposed to be the original, and the opening of *The Warden* suggests that it may be any of 'Wells or Salisbury, Exeter, Hereford, or Gloucester'. Exeter and Worcester are popular candidates with some commentators on the grounds that Anthony and Rose lived in each for some time during the years 1851–3, while another obvious candidate is Winchester (not strictly West Country), where Trollope was at school for three years, and where there was a scandal connected with the Hospital of St Cross, to which *The Warden* frequently alludes, not to mention a parish church above a gateway (St Swithin-upon-Kingsgate) much like Septimus Harding's church of St Cuthbert's. On the other hand *An Autobiography* recounts that Trollope conceived Barchester when in Salisbury in 1852, and Barchester has a library not unlike Salisbury's Jewel Library. Shortly before his death Trollope told E. A. *Freeman, later Regius Professor of Modern History at Oxford 1884–92, that 'Barset was Somerset, but Barchester was Winchester, not Wells', despite the prominence of towers in Wells, and the presence there (unknown to Trollope) of 'a foundation for woolcombers' (*I & R* 224–5).

The history of Barchester Cathedral is not given. It is ancient as a building, but in terms of its organization it is not wholly an institution of the Old Foundation (that is, dating from before the Reformation). As precentor, Harding has the duty of supervising the cathedral's music, but the precentorship does not appear to carry the administrative responsibility which usually went with the office in cathedrals of the Old Foundation, in which the precentor was one of the four principal dignitaries, and usually second-in-command to the dean.

A number of institutions and parts of Barchester enjoy a prominent place in the novels. The Dragon of Wantly is the inn inherited in turn by John Bold and his widow, who later becomes Mrs Arabin, and unwisely passes on to Josiah Crawley as a gift a cheque made out to her for the rent on the inn (*LCB*), while the George and Dragon is most prominent in *Doctor Thorne*, when it is Mr Moffat's election headquarters. Hiram's Hospital, founded in 1434 by the will of John Hiram, a wool-stapler, 'for the support of twelve superannuated wool-carders, all of whom should have been born and bred and spent their days in Barchester', stands off the London Road by the bridge over the Little River (*W* I), and 'outside the town just beyond Hiram's Hospital' lie Pakenham Villas, a group of houses built by John Bold, senior (*W* II). In the High Street, we know of four of the shops belonging successively to John Bold, senior, John Bold, and his widow. Septimus Harding lodges above the chemist's shop while incumbent of St Cuthbert's. There is also a milliner's shop kept by the wife of a cathedral chorister, which Mr Moffat and then Frank visit when electioneering (*DT* XV, XVI). St Cuthbert's, 'a singular little Gothic building' above a gateway to the Close, is the church of 'the smallest possible parish, containing a part of the Cathedral Close and a few old houses adjoining', of which Septimus Harding is made rector when he resigns from Hiram's Hospital (*W* XXI). (See Maps, p. 615.)   DS

Barchester Towers (*see next page*)

Barham, Father John, ascetic Catholic priest whose attempts to convert everyone around him overstep good manners, much to the annoyance of his host, the courteous Roger Carbury, and the amusement of the mild Anglican Bishop. He is thrown out by Augustus Melmotte after his attempt to convert the worldly financier. See also BAMPFIELD, GEORGE FREDERICK LEWIS. *WWLN*
                                                                         SRB

Barker, Lady Mary Anne (1831–1911), born in Jamaica, daughter of the Colonial Secretary. She became a writer on domestic subjects and travel, notably *Station Life in New Zealand* (1873) and *A Year's Housekeeping in South Africa* (1880). After her first husband Sir George Barker died, she married Sir Frederick Napier Broome, who farmed sheep in New Zealand and became Colonial Secretary of Natal in 1877. Trollope was acquainted with both Broome and Lady Barker. Napier Broome had reviewed *He Knew He Was Right*, *The Eustace Diamonds*, and *Australia and New Zealand* for *The Times*. Lady Barker voted *The Way We Live Now* 'one of Mr Trollope's very best stories' (Super 327). Her review, in *The Times* (August 1875), was a notable exception to the execrations heaped on that novel in most journals. In *South Africa* Trollope referred to 'my old friend Napier Broome', and in June 1877 wrote to Lady Barker on behalf of a Mrs Christie, requesting patronage for that lady's son who was intending to visit Natal (*Letters* 2, 727).   RCT

Barkly, Sir Henry (1815–98), MP for Leominster (1845–8); colonial Governor for British Guiana, where he had estates; subsequently Governor of Jamaica, Victoria, Mauritius, and Cape Colony (1870–7). Barkly provided Trollope with letters of introduction for his South Africa visit. Concern over what Trollope might report about the religious and political controversies centring on Colenso, the Bishop of Natal, led to an informal exchange between governmental offices. Barkly wrote to the Prime Minister at Cape Town: 'Of course [Trollope] will write a dissertation on South Africa, which may or may not be more impartial than the productions of other literary men, but as it is better that he should have the opportunity of getting correct information if he chooses, I shall recommend him to your good offices' (*Letters* 2, 727 n.).
                                                                         RCT

THE second Barset novel opens four or five years after *The Warden* with the death of Bishop Grantly and the disappointment of his son the Archdeacon, who expects to succeed him, but whose hopes are dashed by a change from a Tory to a Whig government. The story centres on the struggle of the high-church party in the diocese, led by Archdeacon Grantly, against the new broad-church bishop Thomas Proudie, his domineering low-church Sabbatarian wife, and his low-church chaplain Obadiah Slope. The Archdeacon is aghast at Mrs Proudie's interference in the affairs of the diocese, and Mr Slope opens hostilities by preaching a calculatedly insulting sermon in the cathedral. Having been praised by the press for his upright behaviour (recounted in *The Warden*) in resigning the wardenship of Hiram's Hospital, Mr Harding is widely expected to be reinstated, while Mrs Proudie favours the appointment of Mr Quiverful, vicar of Puddingdale, whose need to support his fourteen children will ensure his obedience to her Sabbatarian demands which are repugnant to Harding. Mr Slope plays one off against the other, first goading Mr Harding into turning the post down, and then, on the discovery that Mr Harding's widowed daughter Eleanor Bold has an income of £1,200 per annum, deciding to ingratiate himself by backing her father. He therefore sides with the Bishop in the power struggle within the palace, attempting to induce the Bishop to act independently of his wife, and reappoint Mr Harding. In one of the acts of minor heroism in the novel, Mrs Quiverful makes her way to Barchester to put her case to Mrs Proudie. Meanwhile Barchester society has been enlivened by the arrival from north Italy of Dr Vesey Stanhope, who has lived in comfort on Lake Como for years, while drawing several large clerical incomes as a non-residentiary prebendary and absentee pluralist. Apart from the practical and worldly-wise eldest child Charlotte, the Stanhopes are all utterly selfish. The son Bertie is charming but totally irresponsible, the younger daughter Madeline, who styles herself 'Signora Vesey Neroni' and claims that her child is 'the last of the Neros', is a bewitchingly beautiful cripple who only appears in public draped on a sofa, while their mother cares for nothing but her clothes, and their father only for his dinner, his wine, and his collection of butterflies. This family's first public appearance is at Mrs Proudie's reception, where Bertie causes havoc, and Madeline begins the process of entrapping Mr Slope and scandalizing Mrs Proudie.

The Archdeacon persuades an Oxford Tractarian, Mr Arabin, to accept the living of St Ewold's, and do battle against the Bishop's party. Since Eleanor has found Mr Slope less objectionable as a clergyman than has her brother-in-law the Archdeacon, the latter and his party come to suppose that she is intending to marry the obnoxious chaplain, while the Stanhopes plot to marry her to Bertie. These complications are elaborated over the first two and a half volumes of the novel, and the virtuoso resolution of them commences at a '*fête-champêtre*' to which Miss Thorne of Ullathorne invites her brother's tenants, her neighbours, and the entire gentry and nobility of the county, including a number of characters destined to play major roles in later novels. The 'fête' itself is a comic masterpiece, as a myriad social tensions and rivalries are played out at all levels. The elderly Dean of Barchester, who has been on his deathbed for some time, dies off stage, while Mr Slope, having drunk too much, proposes to Eleanor, and has his ears boxed for his pains. Eleanor is then half-heartedly pursued by Bertie, who, although irresponsible, behaves more like a gentleman than Slope can ever do. Slope starts mustering support in London for his appointment to the vacant deanship, while Mr Quiverful is formally offered the wardenship. All this time the reader has known that Mr Arabin has been confusedly and incoherently aware of loving Eleanor, and that she has secretly reciprocated his feelings. The Signora draws him on the subject, and then in an unaccustomed fit of altruism informs Eleanor. Slope is unmercifully taunted when he declares his passion for the Signora, and his downfall and departure from Barchester are assured. Eleanor and Mr Arabin finally declare their love for each other. Mr Harding is offered the deanship, refuses it, and successfully proposes that Mr Arabin should be appointed in his stead. Stability returns to Barchester as Slope is expelled, the new Dean and the new Warden are installed, and the Bishop contentedly resolves to obey his wife in the future.

Barchester Towers expands the fictional world whose foundations were first laid down in *The Warden*, adding further parishes and clergy to the diocese, and extending the social range of the characters outside the Church, with the first extended treatment of the gentry in the persons of Mr Thorne of Ullathorne and his extraordinarily old-fashioned sister, and the first glimpse of the aristocracy in Lady De Courcy. Social competition is rife between the classes—the aristocracy and the older gentry, the traditional tenant farmers and their social-climbing neighbours, the church dignitaries and the lesser clerics—and Trollope derives some of his best comedy from the social strategies employed in these struggles. The novel also introduces fashionable conversational topics of the day, such as the rival hypotheses concerning 'the plurality of worlds', or the likelihood of intelligent life on other heavenly bodies. Despite this significant increase in social and intellectual range and analysis, the fiction claims to want the reader to believe that the world is of less importance than moral character and unquestioning religious faith, for the last chapter concludes with a description of Septimus Harding's virtues, so that, like *The Warden*, *Barchester Towers* does not end in a worldly victory for one of the warring factions, but for the near saintliness of this unassuming and reluctant protagonist: 'The Author now leaves him in the hands of his readers; not as a hero, not as a man to be admired and talked of, not as a man who should be toasted at public dinners and spoken of with conventional absurdity as a perfect divine, but as a good man without guile, believing humbly in the religion which he has striven to teach, and guided by the precepts which he has striven to learn' (LIII). To many readers, however, the impression left by the things of the world is more memorable, and the subjects which Trollope has set up for subsequent exploitation are resolutely temporal. Yet *Barchester Towers* is, with *The Bertrams*, the nearest Trollope came to systematic analysis of religious questions. Fiction about churchmen was not unusual at the time, and George Eliot's *Scenes of Clerical Life* appeared in the same year, while many another novelist, including Anthony's sister Cecilia Tilley, dealt more directly with theological issues, and (unlike Trollope and Eliot) wrote novels advocating one doctrinal position and utterly dismissive of all others.

Trollope probably began *Barchester Towers* in January 1855, and on 17 February wrote to William *Longman to ask whether this sequel to *The Warden*, of which one-third was written, would be welcome. When Longman reported that sales of *The Warden* were disappointing, Trollope interrupted the writing of *Barchester Towers* to work on *The New Zealander* for over a year, before resuming *Barchester Towers* on 12 May, and finally completing it on 9 November 1856. He reports, 'In the writing of *Barchester Towers* I took great delight. The Bishop and Mrs Proudie were very real to me, as were also the troubles of the Archdeacon and the loves of Mr Slope' (*Auto* VI).

Longman's reader Joseph Cauvin, reporting on 8 December 1856, is less enthusiastic than he had been about *The Warden*: 'the execution is so unequal, that while there are parts of it that I would be disposed to place on a level with the best morsels by contemporary novelists, there are others—and unfortunately these preponderate—the vulgarity and exaggeration of which, if they do not unfit them for publication, are at least likely to be repulsive to the reader.' There is 'hardly a "lady" or "gentleman" ' among the characters, and Madeline Stanhope 'is a great blot on the work' (*Letters* 1, 45–6).

Longman agreed to publish *Barchester Towers* if Trollope removed some supposed indecencies and shortened the novel from three to two volumes. Trollope recounts his response in *An Autobiography*: 'In my reply I went through the criticisms, rejecting one and accepting another, almost alternately, but declaring at last that no consideration should induce me to put out a third of my work. I am at a loss to know how such a task could be performed. I could burn the MS, no doubt, and write another book on the same story; but how two words out of every six are to be withdrawn from a written novel I cannot conceive. I believe such tasks have been attempted,—perhaps performed; but I refused to make even the attempt' (VI). Over the next month or more various changes were made to the manuscript, and at proof stage in March 1857 still more linguistic purification was called for, as a justly celebrated letter from Trollope to Longman reveals: 'At page 93 by all means put out "foul breathing" and page 97 alter "fat stomach" to "deep chest," if the printing will now allow it' (*Letters* 1, 51–4).

A few years later he declared, 'I shall never forget a terrible & killing correspondence which I had with W. Longman because I would make a clergyman kiss a lady whom he proposed to marry—He, the clergyman I mean; not he W Longman. But in that instance William Longman's church principles were perhaps at stake' (*Letters* 1, 116–17). Relations between author and publisher were unhappy on the question of payment too. When Trollope finally agreed to half-profits (a share of the publisher's net receipts, in circumstances where the publisher's accounts could not be inspected) with an advance against them of £100, he still objected to the general principle of granting an indefinite copyright to a publisher, acknowledging in the present instance that, as a novelist who was only in the process of establishing a reputation with the public, he had no power to insist further on this point.

Barchester Towers finally appeared in three volumes in May 1857 at a price of £1 11s. 6d., and, contrary to Trollope's wishes, the title-page identified him as 'Author of *The Warden*'. A letter of 21 August 1857 expresses his disquiet at receiving no positive news about sales from the publisher: 'From this I suppose I may imagine that you do not consider the sale satisfactory' (*Letters* 1, 57–8). Either Longman marketed this novel badly or he was not completely open with Trollope about his receipts, because as late as the end of 1867, when *The Last Chronicle of Barset* had rounded off the Barsetshire series and the reputation of the earlier books had been carried to new heights by the vastly successful later ones, Trollope was still reporting that he had not received any profits from *The Warden* or *Barchester Towers* for some time (*Letters* 1, 405). A one-volume edition followed the first edition in 1858, and the title was included in 'Tauchnitz's British Authors' the following year, with a New York edition in 1860. Thereafter a moderate number of editions followed in the 19th century, but in the 20th the novel clearly became a standard work, with over 50 distinct editions, including abridgements and simplified versions, which testify to its use in schools and English-language teaching.

Trollope's assessment of the success of the novel with the public in his lifetime is borne out by the evidence, although it is not clear whether Longman marketed the book as energetically as he might have done, and the author characteristically did not look forward to the great posthumous reputation this work would maintain: 'The work succeeded just as *The Warden* had succeeded. It achieved no great reputation, but it was one of the novels which novel readers were called upon to read. Perhaps I may be assuming more to myself than I have a right to do in saying, now, that *Barchester Towers* has become one of those novels which do not die quite at once,— which live and are read for perhaps a quarter of a century; but if that be so, its life has been so far prolonged by the vitality of some of its younger brothers. *Barchester Towers* would hardly be so well known as it is, had there been no *Framley Parsonage* and no *Last Chronicle of Barset*' (*Auto* VI).

The reviewers did not immediately develop a consensus on the terms in which they were to understand this new novelist. The *Spectator* (16 May 1857, 525–6) found *Barchester Towers* too diffuse for satire, and consisting of characters that are 'rather abstractions of qualities than actual persons' (Smalley 42), while in an anonymous review in the *Athenaeum* (30 May 1857, 689–90) H. St John praised its 'dramatic' construction, and the fact that an 'infusion of romance gives a lightness and brightness to the ecclesiastical picture' (Smalley 45). The *Saturday Review* (30 May 1857, 503–4) praised Trollope for handling 'theological disputes without bitterness, injustice, or profanity', and conceded that 'though his pudding may have the fault of being all plums, yet we cannot deny it is excellent eating'. 'He possesses an especial talent for drawing . . . the second-class of good people—characters not noble, superior, or perfect . . . but still good and honest, with a fundamental basis of sincerity, kindliness, and religious principle, yet with a considerable proneness to temptation, and a strong consciousness that they live, and like to live, in a struggling, party-giving, comfort-seeking world.' The clerical characters, the critic said, 'are thoroughly human, and retain the mixed nature of ordinary men . . . The author is not a party writer . . . He sees and paints the follies of either extreme' (Smalley 47–8). *The Times* too, in an anonymous review by E. S. Dallas (13 August 1857, 5), praised the novel's freshness and vitality, and the 'curious and interesting' side of social life it revealed (Smalley 52). The young George Meredith reviewed the novel in the *Westminster Review* (October 1857, 594–6), noticing the arrival on the literary scene of 'a caustic and vigorous writer, who can draw men and women, and tell a story that men and women can read', and who has 'without resorting to politics, or setting out as a social reformer, given us a novel that men can enjoy', in which the satire is 'cleverly interwoven with the story'. Yet 'Mr Trollope seems wanting in certain of the higher elements that make a great novelist. He does not exhibit much sway over the emotional part of our nature' (Smalley 53–4).

While the original reviewers worked to establish the terms in which to understand this relatively new novelist, many later critics have failed to notice that this novel is rather different from Trollope's fiction of the following decade, when the species of 'truth-to-life' exemplified in *Framley Parsonage*, *Orley Farm*, and *The Last Chronicle of Barset* became one of the dominant literary forms of the day. A belief in progress inherited from the Victorians has led them to believe that divergences from the later

Trollopian norm represent shortcomings which are soon to be purged, so that although the reputation of *Barchester Towers* was undoubtedly enhanced by the later Barchester chronicles, there has been a loss from reading this novel retrospectively through its successors. If the apparently recognizable rendering of contemporary life which many have seen in a novel like *Framley Parsonage* is taken as the norm, *Barchester Towers* may appear to fall short in those very features which are its distinctive strengths, such as dramatic form, self-aware narrative, satire, near-epigrammatic wit, and a distinctly 'non-realistic' treatment of history. Because of the relative formlessness of *Framley Parsonage*, it has been easy to assume that *Barchester Towers* too is casually planned, and some critics have followed William Longman in failing to recognize the care with which the novel is shaped to fit three volumes. On this mistaken premiss they have considered the ending to be clumsy, rather than a tour de force of comic resolution in a well-planned dramatic structure. Direct addresses to the reader on the progress of the story, so disliked by Henry James, are not blots but part of the narrative play to which we are alerted by a number of references to Sterne's *Tristram Shandy*. The treatment of church affairs, too, is 'unrealistic', as Barchester has survived unchanged from the days of Trollope's youth, and all the reforming activities of the past two decades appear at once in the midst of clerics as implausibly old-fashioned in their way as Miss Thorne is in hers. The satire has a mythic base, as it presents an impossible clash which collapses twenty years of church history into one brief drama. Then again, in few places in his works except *The Eustace Diamonds* is Trollope sharper or more economical than in chapter II, when describing Mr Slope's attempt to revive a past relationship with Olivia Proudie, now that her father can afford to provide for her: 'Olivia Proudie, however, was a girl of spirit: she had the blood of two peers in her veins, and, better still, she had another lover on her books; so Mr Slope sighed in vain, and the pair soon found it convenient to establish a mutual bond of inveterate hatred' (IV). And nowhere does he surpass the cogency of Archdeacon Grantly's apology for struggling for worldly wealth: 'If honest men did not squabble for money, in this wicked world of ours, the dishonest men would get it all; and I do not see that the cause of virtue would be much improved' (XIV). It is a few years later that Trollope comes near to creating the very realistic fiction which Hawthorne describes, and which is usually taken to be quintessentially 'Trollopian'. The manuscript is not extant.   DS

Barney (b. 1798), Trollope's groom. Identification of Trollope's long-serving groom has been complicated by differing surnames. The 1861 census of Trollope's household at Waltham Cross listed five servants, including Bernard Smith, groom, 63, born Ireland (*Letters* 1, 215). In 'What I Was Told', however, Muriel Rose Trollope, Trollope's granddaughter, gave the surname Fitz-Patrick, while James Pope Hennessy gave it as MacIntyre (*Letters* 1, 307 n.). Barney had been with Trollope since his days at Banagher. Scattered details suggest he became an integral part of the household. He told a story of Frances Trollope's charity to an old pauper breaking stones in the road, embroidering the tale till the original sixpence she had given him grew into half a crown bestowed daily for a month. 'Though he could neither read nor write', recalled Muriel Trollope, 'he was never a penny out in his accounts.' Not only did he christen the elder Mrs Trollope 'the mammy' but was also responsible, according to Muriel Trollope, for putting Harry and Fred on horseback before they could walk. In 1865, when Trollope's niece Beatrice received ten guineas, Trollope wrote to her, 'We must have a great consultation between you, and aunt Rose, and papa, and Barney, and all the other wise people, as to what you had better buy' (*Letters* 1,

306). Trollope paid Barney £5 a year extra for waking him every morning so he could be at his writing table at 5.30 a.m. 'During all those years at Waltham Cross he never was once late with the coffee which it was his duty to bring me. I do not know that I ought not to feel that I owe more to him than to any one else for the success I have had. By beginning at that hour I could complete my literary work before I dressed for breakfast' (*Auto* XV). In 1882 Trollope wrote to Henry Trollope: 'Barney has turned up again as fresh as paint. We wrote to the Protestant parson, and he says he saw him walking about Banagher every day,—only just a little the worse for wear' (*Letters* 2, 941). After more than thirty years with the Trollopes, Barney probably returned to Ireland. His successor was a groom-cum-manservant called Ringwood. RCT

Barnum, Phineas T. (1810–91), American circus proprietor; toured Europe (1844–5) with 'Tom Thumb'; author of *The Humbugs of the World* (1865). Trollope, who enjoyed joke names, gave Bishop Proudie's official signature as 'Thomas Barnum', explaining it derived from 'Baronum Castrum . . . [Barchester's] Roman name' (*LCB* XI). He leaves readers to connect that with the American showman. AWJ

Barrère, Bertrand (based on historical figure), one of the Commissioners of the Republic charged with exacting retribution on the Vendeans after their successes at Saint-Florent and Saumur: he quarrels with Westerman. *LV* GRH

Barry, Mr, partner in Mr Grey's law firm. After Mr Scarborough's death, he assumes legal responsibilities for the Scarborough affair. Barry is 'courteous and respectful' (XXXIII), but unsuccessful in wooing Mr Grey's daughter Dolly. *MSF* MT

Barsetshire is the setting of much of the action of *The Warden, Barchester Towers, Doctor Thorne, Framley Parsonage, The Last Chronicle of Barset*, and 'Two Heroines of Plumplington', and of considerable significance in *The Small House at Allington* and in the Palliser novels, particularly *The Prime Minister*. It is also mentioned in *The Claverings*. The county has two divisions. *The Warden* and *Barchester Towers* take place in East Barsetshire, while *Doctor Thorne* and *Framley Parsonage* introduce the reader for the first time to the western division, which is largely the preserve of landowners who are at odds with those characters in whose fates readers are asked to take the closest interest, being dominated by the Whig aristocracy (the De Courcys and Duke of Omnium) and the corrupting influence of Sowerby. The east, on the other hand, contains the staunch Tory Lady Lufton, and the great Tory squires Gresham and Thorne, as well as the nouveau riche Scatcherd, whose wealth is absorbed by the squirearchy through the marriage of Frank Gresham and Mary Thorne. It is only in the last two Palliser novels, when Plantagenet Palliser has inherited Gatherum Castle, that readers' sympathies are enlisted for a landowner in the western division. East Barsetshire contains Barchester, Barchester Junction, Boxhall Hill, Framley, Greshamsbury, Hogglestock and Hoggle End, Plumstead Episcopi, Puddingdale, and Silverbridge. West Barsetshire contains Courcy, Uffley, Chaldicotes, and Gatherum Castle, while Guestwick and Allington, two centres of *The Small House at Allington*, lie in a county bordering on West Barsetshire. There are four parliamentary constituencies in Barsetshire. East Barsetshire, which regularly returns a Conservative member, was represented at one time by John Gresham (Frank's grandfather) and Francis Gresham, senior, successively, and later by Mr Western in *Phineas Finn* and by Mr Daubeny from *Phineas Redux* onwards. In *Doctor Thorne* Sir Roger Scatcherd represents the city of Barchester, but is unseated after a petition by Gustavus Moffat. Silverbridge (which is a pocket borough of the Duke of Omnium's) is represented by Plantagenet Palliser in *The Small House at Allington* and by John Grey in *Can You Forgive Her?* and *The Prime Minister*. The seat is won by Arthur Fletcher in *The Prime Minister* in the contest from which Ferdinand Lopez is forced to retire, after wrongly claiming to have the Duke's support. In *The Duke's Children* the Duke, a Liberal, announces that he will no longer intervene in elections in the borough, and his son Lord Silverbridge is returned as a Conservative, while West Barsetshire, once represented by Nathaniel Sowerby in *Framley Parsonage*, is won by the Duke's protégé Arthur Fletcher.

The action of the relevant novels is almost always set shortly before the time when Trollope was writing, but with church institutions initially untouched by 20 years of reform, and some of the squirearchy, like the Thornes of Ullathorne, deriving as much from Washington Irving or even from Addison and Steele as from Trollope's own time, the fictional world is deliberately old-fashioned, to make sharper the impact of topicality on a comfortable version of traditional English ways. The way of life of landowners and clergy and other professionals is well documented, with some glimpses of lower-middle-class characters, and negligible presentation of working-class life. This country world is placed in symbolic contrast to London, the location of business and politics, and many of the stories of

Barsetshire concern the intrusion of this latter world into the life of the county. Hence derives an engaging mixture of security and manageable stress, which later readers have often allowed to decay into pure nostalgia. The name of the fictitious county and the places and people in it have been used connotatively in Trollope's day and ever since, by novelists, politicians, and journalists, to symbolize a representative, traditional southern county: Englishness, with a strong church atmosphere (see CHURCH OF ENGLAND). For example, as early as 1862 the *Spectator* dubbed the *Church and State Review* the 'Plumstead Episcopi Review', expecting its readers to know Archdeacon Grantly's views on the established Church; Angela *Thirkell is just one writer to have named characters, places, and stories after Trollopian prototypes, while William Golding ironically set his anti-idyllic novel *The Pyramid* in Barsetshire to emphasize its departure from traditional standards of morality and community. Most notable among attempts to continue the lives of the Barsetshire characters is *Barchester Pilgrimage* by Ronald *Knox (1935).

Trollope looked with an understandable pride and affection on what with justification he called 'the new shire which I had added to the English counties. I had it all in my mind,—its roads and railroads, its towns and parishes, its members of Parliament, and the different hunts which rode over it. I knew all the great lords and their castles, the squires and their parks, the rectors and their churches. . . . Throughout these stories there has been no name given to a fictitious site, which does not represent to me a spot of which I know all the accessories, as though I had lived and wandered there' (*Auto* VIII). While writing *Framley Parsonage* he drew a map of 'the dear county', which must have acted more as a stimulus to his memory than as a reference document, for when found among his papers, it was seen to be inaccurate, and a map produced by Ronald Knox has generally been judged to be more useful (see *London Mercury* February 1922), or his *Barchester Pilgrimage*, or Sadleir 153–4). There has been as much discussion of a possible 'original' for Barsetshire as there has for Barchester itself, and, as in the case of that city, it is obvious that Trollope drew on material he picked up all over the West Country in the course of his exhaustive travels on behalf of the Post Office. E. A. Freeman recounts that 'the week before his seizure . . . [Trollope] allowed Barset to be Somerset, though certainly Gatherum Castle has been brought to us from some other land' (*I & R* 225). For his part Michael Sadleir was convinced that the description of the church at Plumstead Episcopi and the name of the village itself derived

from Huish Episcopi in Somerset (155). See Maps, p. 615. DS

Barsetshire series. Six novels comprise the 'Chronicles of Barsetshire'. They are: *The Warden* (1855), *Barchester Towers* (1857), *Doctor Thorne* (1858), *Framley Parsonage* (1861), *The Small House at Allington* (1864), and *The Last Chronicle of Barset* (1867). A collected edition was published by Chapman & Hall in 1878 with an introduction by the author. He had formed 'so complete a picture of the cathedral town and county', wrote Trollope, and 'become by a long-continued mental dwelling in it, so intimate with sundry of its inhabitants, that to go back to it and write about it again and again have been one of the delights of my life'. For many readers, even in Trollope's day, the magic of the series lay in its meticulous creation of comings and goings in that county added to the English shires. Today the series exerts the same fascination through its characters and vividly delineated landscape, and newcomers to Trollope's world are well advised to begin with the Barsetshire novels, which remain the most popular and most reprinted of his books. Trollope writes about relations among families and friends, where loves are lost and gained, where self-interest clashes with other human obligations, and where principles of moral conduct are forever being put to the test. Such themes are manifest in stories of power struggles within the cathedral close and surrounding parishes among the spiritual leaders of the community, the conservative clergy and old-fashioned gentry, battling with evangelical zealots, reformers, and new wealth. Such clashes point to wider implications about the Church itself, then facing great tensions, and of society itself under pressure, in transition, and having to come to terms with inevitable change and the reforms of the 1850s and early 1860s during which the narratives unfold. The Chronicles produce some of Trollope's best-loved characters: Septimus Harding, Archdeacon Grantly, Bishop and Mrs Proudie, and Josiah Crawley. RCT

Bartley, George (?1782–1858), manager of Covent Garden Theatre and one-time comic actor to whom Trollope sent his play *The Noble Jilt* in June 1851. Bartley in retirement was asked his frank opinion and gave it: 'I found the serious parts deficient in interest, and the comic ones overlaid with repetitions. There is not one character serious or comic to challenge the sympathies of the audience' (*Letters* 1, 26). Trollope felt the blow but held his tongue, pronouncing many years later that some of the scenes were 'the brightest and best work I ever did' (*Auto* V). The play's materials were used for *Can You Forgive Her?* (1865). RCT

Basle, city in Switzerland, centre of the linen trade and home of Adrian Urmand. Michel Voss, not understanding the rules of the post office, travels to Basle in a futile attempt to retrieve a letter mailed to Urmand (*The Golden Lion of Granpère*). Also, one of the sites visited by Alice, Kate, and George Vavasor in *Can You Forgive Her?* MG

Baslehurst, town in Devon where the Tappitt & Bungall Brewery is located, and where Rachel Ray and Luke Rowan eventually settle. Baslehurst, in Devon's cider country, is loosely based on Kingsbridge in the South Hams region, where Trollope had spent some time in 1851. *RR* MT

Bates, Old, trusted Superintendent at Gangoil, well versed in lambing and foot-rot. Once a prosperous squatter, he had 'lost his all in bad times' (I). Reduced to living in a small cottage on a small salary, he serves as a fearful reminder to his employer of the precariousness of colonial life. *HHG* MRS

Bath. The association of Littlebath in *The Bertrams* (1859) and *Miss Mackenzie* (1865) with the spa town, made by W. G. and J. T. Gerould, *A Guide to Trollope* (1948), is now thought incorrect. A more likely source for Littlebath is Cheltenham. Archdeacon *Denison of Bath is alluded to in *Barchester Towers* (LIII). MRS

Batsby, Captain Benjamin. Half-brother of Sir Harry Albury, he is 'good-natured, simple, and rich', though generally regarded as a 'nuisance' (XXXIX). He proposes marriage to Ayala Dormer, who rejects him. He then elopes to Ostend with Gertrude Tringle, whom in the end he marries. *AA* WK

Battle, Mr, hired by Henry Lovelace and Lord George Germain to verify the legitimacy, or otherwise, of Lord Popenjoy. Known to the Dean through the Tallowaxes, the sharp but honest lawyer with chambers at Lincoln's Inn recommends dropping the enquiry when he can learn nothing definite in Italy. *IHP* MG

Battleax, Captain, commander of the *John Bright*, an English gunboat sent to Britannula to regain British sovereignty. He is courteous, respectful, and careful as to dress, using civilized manners to cover his determined purpose to depose and take away President Neverbend, although he is prepared to use violence if necessary. *FixP* SRB

Bauche, Adolphe. Craven youngest son of Mère Bauche who renounces his childhood

sweetheart Marie Calvert, even encouraging (under threat of losing his allowance) her marriage to Theodore Campan. 'Bauche' *TAC1* GRH

Bauche, La Mère. Green-spectacled owner of the Hôtel Bauche, who forces Marie Calvert to marry old Theodore Campan instead of her son. 'Bauche' *TAC1* GRH

Bawwah, Fritz, taciturn, cigar-smoking leather-cutter at Neefit's breeches-maker's shop in Conduit Street, rumoured to be paid £600 for his skills. Also referred to as 'the Herr', his name is probably an English corruption of 'Bauer'. *RH* ALS

Baylis, Thomas Henry (1817–1908), called to the bar (1856); judge of the Court, of Passage, Liverpool (1876–1903); author of *The Rights, Duties and Relations of Domestic Servants, and their Masters and Mistresses* (1857). He attended Harrow (1825–34). Trollope called for him on the way to school and they sat together in the sixth form (Super 13). Baylis recounted witnessing Trollope's 'great fight' (*Auto* I), saying it lasted for almost an hour. But he also thought Trollope exaggerated his sufferings at Harrow. Because of his size and strength, claimed Baylis, Trollope was persecuted 'less than other home-boarders who went young to school' (Hall 37). RCT

Bayne, Peter (1830–96), Scottish journalist and author; edited the *Glasgow Commonwealth* and the *Weekly Review* (1862–5), organ of the English Presbyterian Church. He was also a regular leader-writer for *Christian World*. He published essays on biographical and historical topics in several periodicals. While editor of *Saint Pauls Magazine*, Trollope sought out Bayne, whose 'Lord Palmerston' appeared in August 1868. In his own biography of the statesman, Trollope quoted some half-dozen pages from that article, returning the favour by recommending 'Shakespeare and George Eliot' to Blackwood when Bayne was having difficulty finding publishers for his work (Super 426). This article subsequently appeared in *Blackwood's* (April 1883). RCT

'Bazaars for Charity' (article). Of all fundraisers, bazaars are the worst. Men go seeking pleasant conversations, expecting to donate moderately. Women become unfeminine, aggressive, accosting men as 'pigeons' to buy outrageously overpriced penwipers and matchboxes. Competition in charity's name is disgusting. *Pall Mall Gazette* (21 April 1866), 12. AKL

Beamingham Hall, the Norfolk property, four miles (6 km) from Swaffham, purchased by Ralph Newton. 'Not grand enough for a squire's mansion, and too large for a farmer's homestead' (XLIX). *RH*   ALS

Beaumont, Francis (1584–1616), and **John Fletcher** (1579–1625). Part of Ben Jonson's circle, Beaumont, credited as sole author of *The Knight of the Burning Pestle* (*c*.1607), began collaborating on plays with fellow dramatist John Fletcher *c*.1606. Their association produced some fifteen plays notable for complex plots and surprising revelations, including *Philaster* (*c*.1609) and *The Maid's Tragedy* (*c*.1611). In 1850, Trollope began systematically reading their plays. By 1853, he had read 35. Trollope's aesthetic criteria, for both fiction and drama, demanded natural characters and situations, and propriety in content and expression. He criticized Fletcher's *The Island Princess* (1621) for an 'infinite absurdity in the manipulation, certain persons being infamous murderers in one scene, and magnanimous & noble in the next'. *The Coxcomb* (1612) he found in parts 'so offensive as to make the reader wonder that it should not have offended even the taste of the age of James I. It is not only that the fool should by stratagem have got his friend to lie with his wife, but that the wife, with whom the reader is intended to sympathize, should have debased herself by yielding' (Hall 416–17).   RCT

Beckard, Phineas, Baptist minister who respects Aaron Dunn, but pontificates about his courtship, as accepted lover of Hetta Bell. 'Bell' *TAC1*   GRH

Beeswax, Sir Timothy. His name indicates Trollope's and the Duke of Omnium's view of this Conservative politician. An able, courageous, intelligent man, he views Parliament as a means to personal greatness, not as a means of protecting or improving the well-being of the nation. He becomes leader of the House of Commons under Drummond's government. In *The Prime Minister* he serves as Solicitor-General under Daubney and quits the post during Omnium's coalition government. *DC*   MG

Beetham, parish in the south of England, 'half-village, half-town', where Dr Dugdale has his practice. 'Dugdale' *WFF*   GRH

Behn, Aphra (1640–89), dramatist and novelist, the first Englishwoman to have made a living by her pen. Behn wrote comedies such as *The Rover* (1677) and *The City Heiress* (1682), a satiric comedy on London life. Her most famous fiction is *Oroonoko: or the Royal Slave* (1688). Trollope's extensive survey of English prose and drama included the works of Behn, which he considered 'detestable trash' (*Auto* XII).   RCT

Beilby, Mr. The senior and much richer partner of Beilby and Burton, Civil Engineers, Beilby has constructed the world's widest single-arch bridge. He has a property worth two or three hundred thousand pounds, a seat in Parliament, and manages the London business of the firm from palatial riverside offices in the Adelphi. *C*   PJT

Belgium. Antwerp in 1834 was the setting for 'Relics of General Chassé', in which Trollope may have recalled his own experiences there in that year. Sir Magnus Mountjoy in *Mr Scarborough's Family* was English minister at Brussels, where English residents found educating children cheaper than at home and where Trollope himself went in 1834 to do some classics teaching. Blankenberg, about twelve miles (19 km) from Bruges, was the scene of Phineas Finn's duel with Lord Chiltern (XXXVIII). Bruges was also the setting for Trollope's play *The Noble Jilt*. His parents escaped creditors by fleeing to Bruges in 1834. The family took rooms at the Château d'Hondt just outside the city.   RCT

Bell, Hetta, the self-satisfied, interfering elder sister who objected to Aaron Dunn marrying Susan. Hetta marries Phineas Beckard. 'Bell' *TAC1*   GRH

Bell, Mrs Henrietta, mother of Hetta and Susan, apprehensive about Aaron Dunn, but finally supportive of Susan's love for him. 'Bell' *TAC1*   GRH

Bell, Robert (1800–67), journalist; biographer of Canning; edited several volumes of English poetry; unsuccessful playwright. Bell recruited Trollope to the Royal Literary Fund and proposed him for the Garrick Club in May 1861. Trollope invited him to become assistant editor of *Saint Pauls*, but ill health prevented him, and he died soon afterwards. Trollope paid tribute at the Literary Fund dinner (May 1867) and in *Pall Mall Gazette* (April 1867). When Bell's widow needed money from sale of his library Trollope bought it himself. Dickens congratulated him: 'I knew she could have no stauncher or truer friend' (*Letters* 1, 379). Trollope recalled ten years after Bell's death that his literary talents never had their due, that he had known no man better read in English literature, and that he was a good companion. 'He liked to hear the chimes go at midnight, and he loved to have ginger hot in his mouth' (*Auto* VIII). See 'MR ROBERT BELL'.
                                              RCT

'Bell, Robert'. See 'MR ROBERT BELL'.

Bell, Susan, 19-year-old younger daughter who reciprocates Aaron Dunn's love shyly and goes into a decline until his letter, and then his return, seal their love. 'Bell' *TAC1*   GRH

Bellfield, Captain Gustavus, debt-ridden dandy who competes with Mr Cheesacre for the hand and fortune of Arabella Greenow. Although his charms are questionable, Captain Bellfield ultimately wins Mrs Greenow both because she finds him manageable and because she believes he has a poetic nature. *CYFH*   JMR

Belton Estate, The (*see next page*)

Belton, Mary, unmarried elder sister of Will Belton, with whom she lives at Plaistow Hall. A 'poor sickly creature with a twisted spine and a hump back' (III), she has a sharp mind and a generous heart: 'all those who knew her loved her as they knew her' (XIII). *BE*   WK

Belton, Will, brother of Mary Belton and squire of Plaistow Hall. A distant cousin of the Amedroz family, he becomes heir of the Belton estate on the death of Charles Amedroz. A tall, broad, 'decidedly handsome' young man (III), he is also rough-hewn, impetuous, and thoroughly honest (perhaps a bit like Trollope himself). Will indefatigably woos Clara Amedroz until she recognizes that she has loved him all along. *BE*
WK

Bender, Carl, known as 'The German', a trusted old hand at Gangoil, and the only person able to tell Harry Heathcote he is too much the governor without raising his master's ire. As boundary rider, he helps patrol the homestead, and when the bushfire comes, works heroically to overcome it. *HHG*   MRS

Benjamin, Mr, jeweller, moneylender, pawn-broker, and dealer in stolen goods. Instrumental to Lizzie Greystock's schemes for marriage, Mr Benjamin permits her to borrow back jewels she has pawned to help her lure the wealthy Florian Eustace into marriage. Benjamin allows Lizzie to defer payment until she has become Lady Eustace, but when he later collects the debt, Benjamin helps to disillusion Sir Florian about his wife's character, thus contributing to the unhappiness of the Eustace marriage. Perhaps more significantly, Benjamin is the principal behind the complex plot to steal the valuable diamond necklace in the widowed Lizzie's possession, for which crime he is ultimately tried and convicted. *ED*   JMR

Bent, Fanny (d. 1860), spinster cousin of Frances Trollope. When the Trollopes fled from Harrow to Bruges in 1834, Fanny took care of Henry, Anthony's elder brother. Trollope portrayed her as Jemima Stanbury, in *He Knew He*

Was Right, to whom all changes were 'hateful and unnecessary'. (VIII).   RCT

Bentley, George (1825–95), son of Richard Bentley, and successor in the publishing house. He edited *Temple Bar* after 1867, which serialized *The American Senator*, October 1874–May 1875. Unhappy with the title, he was admonished by Trollope, who insisted on an author's prerogative in choosing a title for his novel (*Letters* 2, 673). At a meeting of authors and publishers in John Murray's house in February 1870, Bentley noted his impressions of the guests in his diary. Trollope was 'large-headed, bushy eyebrowed—heavy bearded, full faced, quick, fiery-eyed, but generous & warm' (Super 281).   RCT

Bentley, Richard (1794–1871), founder of the successful publishing house whose impressive authors' list included Ainsworth, Dickens, and Collins. Bentley published ten of Frances Trollope's works. She encouraged her son to handle some of her business with Bentley, and he took an opportunity in May 1835 of asking for the chance to get 'lucubrations of my own in any of the numerous periodical magazines &c which come out in such monthly swarms' (*Letters* 1, 1). Bentley declined *The Kellys and the O'Kellys* but accepted *The Three Clerks*.   RCT

Bergen, Anastasia, strong, calm, quiet, 'a woman that a man might well love', she defends herself courageously when violently attacked by a convict escaped from the penal settlement in Bermuda. She survives to marry her lover. 'Trow' *TAC2*   GRH

Bergen, Mr, cedarwood tradesman on Crump Island, Bermuda, who leaves his daughter Anastasia alone in the cottage three nights a week. 'Trow' *TAC2*   GRH

Bermuda, site of a penal settlement and isolated Crump Island where the Bergens live. 'Trow' *TAC2*   GRH

Berrier, Pierre, the ostler in Saint-Laurent whose resistance to conscription sparks the conflict between republicans and Poitou's royalists. *LV*   GRH

Berryhill, village on the Castle Richmond estate, where Herbert Fitzgerald builds an experimental mill for grinding corn for famine victims. *CR*   MRS

Bertram, George (the elder). A millionaire banker, he provides for his nephew George Bertram, his niece Miss Baker, and his unacknowledged granddaughter Caroline Waddington. Though fond of them all, his feelings and actions remain dominated by fiscal considerations: 'The
(*cont. on page 48*)

THE suicide of Charles Amedroz, before the novel begins, has left his 25-year-old sister Clara in a desperate situation. On the death of her 67-year-old father Bernard Amedroz, the family property will descend to a distant cousin, Will Belton, depriving Clara of her lifelong home at Belton Castle, Somerset. Mr Amedroz has sold his life insurances to pay his wastrel son's debts; Clara will therefore inherit no money either.

She has expected a small inheritance, enough to sustain her in modest gentility, from her 'aunt' (actually no blood relation) Mrs Winterfield. But two days before the news of Charles's death arrives, the old lady informs Clara that she has decided to keep all her property within her own family, the Folliotts. The house at Perivale and Mrs Winterfield's £1,200 a year will go to her sister's son Captain Frederic Folliott Aylmer. By the end of chapter I, Clara faces certain destitution, unless she marries well.

She has two prospects. Will, as soon as he learns of his impending good fortune, hurries to Belton from his home at Plaistow Hall, Norfolk, in order to inspect his future property and to assure Clara that he has no intention of evicting her. He falls in love with her on the spot, but not before she has persuaded him to treat her strictly as a sister. Nevertheless, in characteristically headstrong fashion, he proposes marriage, only to be told, 'Be my brother always' (V).

Clara has been thoroughly charmed by Will, and it is clear to the reader from chapter III that he is the right man for her. She, however, thinks she cannot love him, because 'her heart belonged to Captain Aylmer' (VI). Frederic has shown no reciprocal affection and, indeed, feels none. He is a cautious, wavering, expediently hypocritical man, who seems capable of no strong feeling. Nevertheless, Mrs Winterfield, on her deathbed, persuades him to promise that he will 'take a brother's care of Clara Amedroz' (IX).

Both Frederic and Clara understand this to mean that he will propose marriage—which he does, half-heartedly. Her enthusiastic response nearly knocks him over, and he immediately thinks of a certain Lady Emily, who 'might have suited' better than the overeager Clara (IX). Clara notes Frederic's hesitation and the cold formality of his occasional kisses, but at first her doubts concern neither her own love nor his, only the prudence of her behaviour.

The bulk of the novel, from chapter IX until nearly the end, centres on this favourite Trollopian dilemma: a woman placed between two men, one of whom loves her while the other does not, though she believes herself in love with the latter. Clara can be seen as a variant on Lily Dale, whose career in *The Small House at Allington* (1862–3) and *The Last Chronicle of Barset* (1866–7) frames *The Belton Estate* (1864–5). But Lily remains true to her mistaken love for Adolphus Crosbie, repeatedly rejecting the devoted Johnny Eames. Clara is more sensible, or perhaps luckier. In the end, she recognizes not only Will's excellence and Frederic's worthlessness but also that she has actually loved the better man all along.

Similar situations occur in other Trollope novels, including *Can You Forgive Her?* and *The Prime Minister*. But nowhere else is a woman's obstinacy explored with greater concentration. There are no sub-plots in *The Belton Estate*, and few subsidiary characters. The closest approach to a sub-plot concerns the shady past of Mrs Askerton, who lives with her husband Colonel Askerton in Belton Cottage, which for two years has been rented to them by Bernard Amedroz. Yet Mrs Askerton's story never detaches itself from Clara's, and it proves decisive in Clara's eventual enlightenment.

Unsavoury rumours have circulated in Belton since the Askertons' arrival, and though Mrs Askerton insists that her maiden name was Oliphant, Will Belton seems to remember encountering her nine or ten years before as 'fast-going' Miss Vigo, who married Mr Berdmore (III). It is, however, Frederic Aylmer who unearths the truth, to which Mrs Askerton admits when Clara confronts her. She was indeed Mrs Berdmore, but she fled from her brute of a husband into the arms of Colonel Askerton, with whom she lived as his mistress for three years, until Berdmore died and the Askertons legitimized their union.

Clara remains loyal to her friend, but Clara's prospective mother-in-law, the tyrannical Lady Aylmer, learns of the Askerton scandal (and Clara's loyalty) from her abject son. On a visit to Aylmer Park, the family estate in Yorkshire, where Clara goes as Frederic's fiancée, Lady Aylmer informs her flatly that Frederic will not marry her if she maintains an association with Mrs Askerton. Clara's response is emphatic: 'I shall let Captain Aylmer know that our engagement must be at an end, unless he will promise that I shall never in future be subjected to the unwarrantable insolence of his mother' (XXVI). Of course no such promise is forthcoming.

Yet even this fails to disabuse Clara of the idea that she loves Frederic Aylmer, not Will Belton. Finally, the combination of Will's persistence, Frederic's spinelessness, and some wise words from Mary Belton, Will's disabled sister, induces Clara to accept Will. Frederic, appropriately, marries the fortyish, penniless Lady Emily Tagmaggert, and the novel closes with a scene of domestic tranquillity in the bedroom of Will and Clara Belton, née Amedroz.

Clara ends up with everything—a devoted husband, a baby son, and the Belton estate—yet for most of the novel she seems determined to throw everything away. She refuses Frederic's offer of a small allowance from his Winterfield inheritance, and when Mr Amedroz dies and Will inherits Belton Castle, she refuses to stay on there despite his insistence. Trollope specialized in obstinate characters, but he never went further in that line than Clara Amedroz, who seems at times to verge on masochism or lunacy.

Clara is a distinctly 'serious' woman, as the narrator remarks several times, no longer in her first youth (she is 25 when the novel begins). She endures the deaths of her brother, father, and Mrs Winterfield, events that do nothing to lighten her spirits. Yet Clara's perverse preference for cold Frederic Aylmer over the vibrant, manifestly superior Will Belton stretches credibility almost to the breaking point, as the narrator seems to admit: 'I fear the reader by this time may have begun to think that her love should never have been given to such a man. To this accusation I will make no plea at present, but I will ask the complainant whether such men are not always loved' (XI). Changing the subject, however, does not answer the question.

With its obsessive heroine, gloomy atmosphere, and tight focus on a small cast of characters, *The Belton Estate* is on the whole a rather dreary book. This may account for its lukewarm initial reception and subsequent neglect.

Trollope wrote *The Belton Estate* between 30 January and 4 September 1865. It was published in instalments in the first sixteen issues of the *Fortnightly Review* (of which Trollope was one of the founders), from 15 May 1865 to 1 January 1866, and in three volumes by Chapman & Hall in December 1865. Trollope was nearing the peak of his popularity at the time, and most reviewers were polite, if unenthusiastic. A notable exception was 22-year-old Henry James, writing in the American magazine the *Nation* (2, 21–2), who demolished the novel, declaring it 'a *stupid* book. . . . It is without a single idea. It is utterly incompetent to the primary function of a book, of whatever nature, namely—to suggest thought.'

In a New Year's Eve 1865 letter, Trollope himself called *The Belton Estate* 'a good book' (*Letters* 1, 324), but ten years later, when he wrote *An Autobiography*, he had moderated his opinion: 'It is readable, and contains scenes which are true to life; but it has no peculiar merits, and will add nothing to my reputation as a novelist' (*Auto* X). Later critics have tended to agree. Only Michael Sadleir has rated the novel among Trollope's best, praising it for 'its smoothness, its subtlety and its faultless adjustment of character and circumstance'. But Sadleir issued a cogent warning: 'The theme is commonplace; the incidents unsensational; the treatment unassuming and serene. Perhaps, to those who demand of fiction what Trollope does not pretend to give, it may be an aimless irritation' (391).

Alone among more recent commentators, Christopher Herbert finds great 'psychological immediacy' in *The Belton Estate* (*Trollope and Comic Pleasure* (1987), 67), along with such hitherto unsuspected features as 'the enactment of a pagan rite of fertility' in Clara's final acceptance of Will (66). Most critics rank the novel among Trollope's lesser achievements. The manuscript is in the Huntington Library.   WK

---

iron of his wealth had entered into his very soul' (XXIV). Hence, while the Exchange has many 'good things' to say of this modern Croesus, at his deathbed 'he was not a good man' (XLIV). *B*   MRS

Bertram, George (the younger). A Trinity man poised for success with a double-first from Oxford, he stumbles amid delays and miscommunications into a lacklustre career and a broken engagement before settling into a 'quiet . . . but not unhappy' life with Caroline, Lady Harcourt, eight tortuous years after their betrothal. Though honest, loving, and well-meaning, he is also 'a stiff-necked stubborn mule' (XXIV), and this proud, uncompromising nature not only prevents him from courting his uncle's fortune, but also makes him unforgiving—'almost savage' (XX)—towards Caroline, so that his progress is marred with frustration and regret. *B*   MRS

Bertram, Sir Lionel, insolvent but dashing father of George Bertram, whose 'appearance was the best thing about him' (VIII). An erstwhile soldier-cum-diplomat who failed to provide for his child, he lives by sponging off his wealthy brother, his barely solvent son, and ladies of his acquaintance. He retires to Littlebath, where he dallies with Miss Todd and Miss Baker, plotting to marry whichever spinster will provide the surest income, only to be refused by both. *B*   MRS

Bertrams, The (*see next page*)

Bianconi, Charles (1786–1875), Italian immigrant entrepreneur who developed a coaching system in Ireland, which made a fortune. His 'Bians', four-wheeled cars drawn by three or four horses, carried mail and passengers. By 1843 he commanded a fleet of 100. Bianconi was elected mayor of Clonmel (1844). Trollope was quick to realize how the Bians would help his reorganization of postal services and used them plentifully. In his 'History of the Post Office in Ireland', he noted that Bianconi had probably done more than anyone to benefit the sister kingdom (*I & R* 31). Trollope's son Henry was ghost-writer of Bianconi's biography.   RCT

Bible. The King James Bible was part of the everyday cultural currency for reasonably well-educated Victorians, and many biblical allusions and quotations in Trollope's writings reflect this: his fictional characters are forever hiding their lights under a bushel (Matthew 5: 15), heaping coals of fire on one another's heads (Proverbs 25: 22), and tempering the guile of the serpent with the gentleness of the dove (Matthew 10: 16), while proclaiming that all is vanity and vexation of spirit (Ecclesiastes 1: 14, 2: 11, 17), and that sufficient unto the day is the evil thereof (Matthew 6: 34). The inexactness of many of these

(*cont. on page 51*)

TROLLOPE's eighth novel has a dual importance in his development, since it encompasses novel, travelogue, and episodes which are each effectively a story, a kind of fiction he was to develop from this period onwards. Early in 1858, Trollope went to Suez on a postal mission to evaluate the efficiency of mail shipments through Egypt to India and vice versa. Having drafted a treaty with Egypt (23 February) he had leisure for exploring the Holy Land, with Malta, Spain, and Gibraltar as main attractions on the way home. The immediate effect of the journey is felt in the novel: chapter VI, 'Jerusalem', establishes the symbolic biblical setting which activates the plot, the Mount of Olives having a central focus, since there George Bertram decides against a career in the Church. On this trip his feelings for Caroline Waddington emerge, and he meets his father Sir Lionel, unhappily discovering the desiccated and self-serving nature of this reluctant parent. Miss Todd's picnic and its aftermath (IX and X) are satirical of tourist 'doing' (they connect with later stories about the area) and prefigure the Littlebath sub-plot involving Miss Todd, Sir Lionel, and Miss Baker (and attendant curates), a comedy with pathetic overtones. Much later, in chapter XXXVIII, George and his cousin Arthur Wilkinson—the rather dull and oppressed subsidiary hero—visit Cairo, and again the location promotes an important plot development. Afterwards Arthur, who has been prevented by economic circumstances and his dominating mother from proposing to Ada Gauntlet, under George's influence declares himself. 'The Two Widows' (XXXIX), describing the shipboard romance of George on the way home, is effectively a story in itself, rather similar in tone to the short stories which Trollope's travelling experiences inspired.

The Bertrams traces the fortunes of George and to a lesser extent of Arthur from Oxford onwards. George gets a double-first, and after opting for the law becomes disillusioned and dilatory, turns to authorship, and in *The Romance of Scripture* attacks the supernatural elements of Christianity and other controversial matters, as a result of which he loses his fellowship. Since he is by now engaged to Caroline Waddington, and she will not marry him until they have sufficient money, their relationship deteriorates. George is largely in London, Caroline in Littlebath, and she confides her frustrations to George's friend Henry (later Sir Henry) Harcourt, who already loves and covets her. George and Caroline break off their engagement, and Caroline later marries Harcourt, in loveless and abject reaction.

Trollope employs contrast throughout the plot in tellingly weighted situations. George is a man of integrity, intelligence, sensitivity, trying to find fulfilment in life, rejecting the materialism of the age on the one hand and its religiosity on the other. His father Sir Lionel is self-seeking, importunate, a financial and amorous opportunist seen alongside his brother, George's namesake uncle, who is interested in money and the status money confers. This Bertram later reveals that Caroline Waddington is his daughter by a secret marriage, a Bertram too, and perhaps subject to his frailties. She is contrasted in turn with Adela Gauntlet, whose unaffected love and rejection of the importance of money in marriage complements the integrity and sincerity of George. Arthur Wilkinson is contrasted with George and George with Harcourt. Just as George in part depends on his uncle—who had contributed to his education—so Arthur becomes dependent on his mother after his father's death. He takes over his father's living when it is offered by Lord Stapledean, a degenerate, selfish, and aristocratic patron living at Bowes in the north, but Stapledean insists on his stipend being virtually allocated to his mother and sisters. Arthur's mother is insensitive to her son's needs, despising Adela, preventing the marriage until herself humiliated by Stapledean.

Gradually Caroline and George begin to meet again as Caroline's antipathy to her husband intensifies. Sir Henry Harcourt, Solicitor-General, becomes Sir Henry Harcourt, discarded politician, as the government falls. Mercenary and extravagant, he lives beyond his means and eventually commits suicide. Ultimately George and Caroline are married, but it is a muted coming-together, for 'The man's blood was upon her head' (XLVII). There is a bleakness at the end, as if love after debilitating experience is more punishment than reward, for George returns to 'the dusky purlieus of Chancery Lane' and the marriage is 'childless'.

Set in the 1840s, the general thrust of the novel is against materialism, competition, and pushing for advancement, with the historical ethos of the 1840s an important authentication of the action. Thus George's book resonates with Marian Evans's (later George Eliot) translation of Strauss's *Life of Jesus* (1846), and the loss of his fellowship is comparable to Froude's after publication of *The Nemesis of Faith* (1849). References to politicians and racehorses of the time and the emergence and ramifications of the Oxford Movement, for example, are direct historical allusions. But Trollope also continues his swingeing attack on competitive examinations (see *The Three Clerks* (1858) VI) following the Northcote–Trevelyan Report of 1854, and mentions the contemporary swindler Colonel Waugh (who absconded to Spain in 1857). Thus *The Bertrams* has the dual currency of the 1840s on the one hand and the 1850s on the other. Much of the novel is sombre, but a delightful sub-plot which parodies the main action of financial and marital acquisitiveness is set in Littlebath, where Sir Lionel opportunistically lines up first Miss Todd and then Miss Baker as wife-elect, and fails to secure either. Nor does he manage to siphon off any of his brother George's wealth. The latter, living quietly at Hadley, worships money, a theme sustained throughout the novel; the Littlebath gatherings, the card-party socializing, are a muted equivalent of higher stakes played for in public life. The selfishness of these men in office is complemented by an astute study of the position of women, trapped as spinsters and, in the case of Caroline Harcourt, as wives.

Such thematic constants give the novel structural and psychological cohesion, the realism of character supplemented by an intimacy of authorial tone from the beginning which ironically encapsulates the narrative itself—'This is undoubtedly the age of humanity—as far, at least, as England is concerned' (I). But although Miss Todd is vivacious and humorous, Miss Baker is pathetic and dependent, ending up at Hadley with the elder George Bertram. Humanity is in abeyance, and the rapier of Trollope's satirical and ironic cut and thrust is in evidence throughout. George's search for identity and fulfilment, his being at odds with his age and its requirements, carry the moral weight of the narrative and provide a sympathetic and searching examination of an individual and his responses to the moral, social, financial, and spiritual influences of his time. George is good without being cloying, helping Adela and Arthur, re-creating the broken Caroline, embracing selfless action in a selfish world. The particularities of place are integral, from George's crisis of decision at the Mount of Olives, through the touristy manœuvring, the sights, sites, sounds, smells of the early chapters, to the reclusive deadness of Hadley and the distant coldness of Bowes, the little world of Hurst Staple and the conventional world of Littlebath curates and card-parties. Despite the comedy, the notes struck are serious ones.

The Bertrams was written ('under very vagrant circumstances', *Auto* VII) 1 April 1858–17 January 1859, begun the day after Trollope finished *Doctor Thorne* in Egypt, and completed when he was in the West Indies on another postal mission. During the writing Trollope encountered problems in the postal service in Glasgow, to the stress of which he attributed the poor quality of the love scenes (*Auto* VII). Published in March 1859, it was well received, particularly in the *Examiner*, the *Spectator*, the *Saturday Review*, the *Athenaeum*, and the *Illustrated London News*. The manuscript is not extant.   GRH

Edwards, P. D., *Anthony Trollope: His Art and Scope* (1977).
Kincaid, James R., *The Novels of Anthony Trollope* (1977).
Polhemus, Robert M., *The Changing World of Anthony Trollope* (1968).

allusions, as John W. Clark has argued, indicates that Trollope's familiarity with the Authorized Version, like that of so many Victorians, is due to repeated hearings in church rather than to intensive scriptural study (John W. Clark, *The Language and Style of Anthony Trollope* (1975), 165). Moreover, this inexactness probably reveals the extent to which Trollope merely takes such scriptural allusions for granted as being semi-proverbial commonplace expressions. However, some allusions appear with such regularity in Trollope's novels that we might tentatively list them as being characteristically 'Trollopian'. These include: 'The lines are fallen unto me in pleasant places' (Psalm 16: 6, in *DT* VII; *FixP* II; *HKWR* XXXVI; *LCB* VIII, XLI, LXXVII; *OML* IX; *PF* LXXIII; *RH* XIV; *SHH* III); 'out of the abundance of the heart the mouth speaketh', normally rendered by Trollope as 'out of the full heart the mouth speaks' (Matthew 12: 34, in *KD* VIII; *LCB* XXIII; *RH* XXVI; *DWS* 'Conclusion', XI; *MSF* V; *BE* XIII); and 'whosoever shall not receive you, nor hear your words, when ye depart out of that house or city, shake off the dust of your feet' (Matthew 10: 14, in *MM* XXX; *VB* XXXIII; *BT* LI; *HKWR* XLII; *LA* XXI; *MF* XXXIII; *MSF* XVIII; *FP* XXV). No discussion of biblical allusion in Trollope's fiction should omit mention of Mr Quiverful, the impoverished clergyman featured briefly in *The Warden*, and much more prominently in *Barchester Towers*, whose name playfully indicates both his profession and his huge family: 'Lo, children are an heritage of the Lord: and the fruit of the womb is his reward. | As arrows are in the hand of the mighty man, so are children of the youth. Happy is the man that hath his quiver full of them' (Psalm 127: 3–5). As well as making specific textual allusions, Trollope also presumes his readers' familiarity with well-known biblical stories. See, for example, references to: Joseph and Potiphar's wife (*LCB* LI; *IHP* XXXII); Jeph-

thah's sacrifice of his daughter (*SHH* XXIII; *W* XI); Ahab and the vineyard of Naboth (*FP* II; *BE* XIII); Dives and Lazarus (*LA* XXII; *SHA* XXXII); and—from the Apocrypha—Judith and Holofernes (*SHA* XXIX; *LCB* XXIV). The biblical story to feature most prominently in the *plot* of any of Trollope's novels is the unsuccessful attempt by Conway Dalrymple to paint Jael's murder of Sisera (*LCB* XXIV ff.); although, in an interesting article, Sherman Hawkins has argued that Mr Harding and his twelve bedesmen are allegorical representations of Christ and the apostles. One should draw a distinction between Trollope's narrators' *alluding* to the Bible, and Trollope's characters' *quoting* from it: when his fictional characters quote Scripture they are almost invariably meant to be seen by the reader in a pejorative light, either as rigid dogmatists or smooth-talking hypocrites: it is no accident that such characters tend to be evangelical Christians, for whom Trollope had well-known disdain, and whose perpetual quoting from the Bible reflects the evangelical stress on scriptural authority. Mrs Proudie and Mr Slope (*BT*) are perhaps the best-known examples, but see also: Lady Macleod (*CYFH?*); Mr Emilius (*ED*); Mrs Bolton (*JC*); Mme Staubach (*LT*); Jeremiah Maguire (*MM*); and Mr Prong (*RR*).   HO

Clark, John W., *The Language and Style of Anthony Trollope* (1975).
Hawkins, Sherman, 'Mr Harding's Church Music', *English Literary History*, 29 (1962), 202–23.

bibliographies. Often considered mere catalogues of titles, bibliographies have played an important role in establishing Trollope's critical reputation since T. H. S. Escott appended a complete list of first editions to his *Anthony Trollope: His Work, Associates and Literary Originals* (1913). That bibliography, compiled by Margaret Lavington, documented the range of the novels and (with notes gleaned from *An Autobiography* and additional information from Trollope's son Henry) outlined each work's publication history. There were also brief accounts of Trollope's journalism, unpublished or 'projected' works, and a sketchy list of 'Articles of Biographical Interest'. During the next decade, Michael Sadleir took those explorations to more sophisticated heights in his *Excursions in Victorian Bibliography* (1922), where Trollope was one of his major exemplars, and *Trollope: A Bibliography* (1928). As a publisher himself, and an avid collector of Victorian first editions, Sadleir saw how Trollope's long career exemplified the whole business of writing, producing, and distributing books in the mid-Victorian period. In describing the precise details of lettering, binding, endpapers, inserted adverts, he not only showed other collectors what to look for but laid out the complexities of the author–publisher relationship. That prolonged work also impelled him to biography. *Trollope: A Commentary* (1927) presented the writer as a supreme man of business (matching the surface picture of *An Autobiography*) and, in the light of Sadleir's wide knowledge of 19th-century society, as representative *par excellence* of mid-Victorian energies and values. Those influential studies brought Trollope to a wider public, and to the attention of Mary Leslie Irwin, whose *Anthony Trollope: A Bibliography* (1926) moved beyond the novels to document short stories, journalism, public lectures, and to glance at the market for first editions: a copy of *Ralph the Heir* sold for $650 in 1919, sank to $190 in 1920, then rose to $450 in 1924. She also provided the whereabouts of portraits, photographs, caricatures, and the foundations of a checklist of contemporary reviews.

It was that latter topic which would eventually lead to the further sophistication of Trollopian studies. In 1966 a research team under Walter E. Houghton published the first volume of *The Wellesley Index to Victorian Periodicals* (the fifth and final volume, an epitome and index, appeared in 1989). Their aim was to catalogue the contents of every major Victorian journal and, crucially, to assign authorship, from various types of evidence, to articles that, under editorial conventions, had usually been published anonymously. Concurrently, David Skilton applied the same detective work to the contemporary reviewers of Trollope's fiction; by consulting editorial files, records, and archives, he was able to identify the authors of many such reviews. So *Anthony Trollope and his Contemporaries* (1972), while not a bibliography *per se*, showed that bibliographic research could lead to a dynamic reappraisal of an author's work. By examining a collection of reviews by individual critics (particularly Hutton of the *Spectator*), Skilton constructed a picture of

their moral and literary expectations in a time of increasing materialism, and then showed how Trollope wrote deliberately within and against those conventions. In that context, Trollope appeared a more self-conscious artist than the value-for-money journeyman he himself presented, and Skilton's reading of *An Autobiography* was tougher and more ironic than had been previously understood. Trollope's 'vision of society shows human ties of love and respect in danger, . . . in the midst of a crowded world, the individual is in the last analysis alone . . . Trollope recognizes this as a central contradiction in modern existence' (148). That darker view could also be traced in *The Reputation of Trollope: An Annotated Bibliography, 1925–1975*, by John Charles Olmsted and Jeffrey Egan Welch (1978), where academic sneers at novels that were 'quiet enough to please the most complacent Victorian' increasingly give way to a perception that Trollope's pleasing surface 'is a bitter farce and the life behind it is the desolate reality' (p. xxii). That survey was updated by Donald D. Stone, 'Trollope Studies 1976–1981', *Dickens Studies Annual*, 2 (1983), and by Nancy Aycock Metz, 'Trollope Studies 1982–1986', *Dickens Studies Annual*, 21 (1992). Other bibliographies have extended the 19th-century picture. Judith Knelman documented 'Trollope's Journalism', *Library*, 5 (1983). Anne K. Lyons's *Anthony Trollope: An Annotated Bibliography of Periodical Works* (1985) presented a chronological account of articles by and about Trollope 1847–1900. Those entries were enhanced by L. O. Tingay, *The Trollope Collector* (1985), revised as *Anthony Trollope: A Collector's Catalogue 1847–1990* (Trollope Society, 1992), and continue to be updated for the Modern Language Association and the *New Cambridge Bibliography of English Literature*, and *Annual Bibliography of English Language and Literature*. See also Donald Smalley in *Victorian Fiction: A Guide to Research*, ed. Lionel Stevenson (1966), and Ruth apRoberts in *Victorian Fiction: A Second Guide to Research*, ed. George H. Ford (1978).   AWJ

Biddy, kitchen-girl at Ballycloran, one of two barefoot domestic helps who provides company for Feemy Macdermot. *M*   MRS

Biddy, servant at Dunmore House who performs a pivotal action when she arranges her mistress's escape from the house. *KOK*   MRS

Bideawhile, Mr, Gresham family lawyer of the London firm of Slow & Bideawhile. He spends several hours talking to Frank Gresham about wine, Switzerland, and pumpkins rather than business. *DT*   NCS

Bideford, Lord George, fiancé of Nina Baldoni, to whom he will be married at Rome—'no doubt', says Lady Albury, 'by the Pope himself under the dome of St Peter's' (XLV). Nina asserts his 'absolute superiority . . . to any other man either alive or dead' (XLIX). *AA*   WK

Biffin, Major, military-looking gentleman on board the *Cagliari*, 'dry as a barber's block' (XL), who, having assiduously courted Mrs Cox all the way from India, is temporarily ousted by George Bertram. However, in consideration of his 'snug little income' (XL), he regains the widow's favour and before leaving the ship has been induced to make a proposal of marriage. *B*   MRS

Biggs, Martha, long-time friend of Mrs Furnival. Miss Biggs is a respectable woman who comes from the less than respectable Red Lion Square in London. 'She had not been a favourite of Mr Furnival, having neither wit nor grace to recommend her' (XXI), but she is a faithful friend to the often deserted Mrs Furnival. *OF*
MT

Biles, Miss, ally of Mrs Morony in an attempt to resist the sharp practice of Mr Jones when he refuses to sell a garment from the store display. *SBJR*   RCT

biographies of Trollope. While Trollope *mère* seems more interesting in life than fiction, her son Anthony packs away the more significant aspects of his personality in novelistic recesses. Thus where Fanny has courted biographers, Anthony Trollope has, until comparatively recently, dismayed and eluded them. T. H. S. Escott, author of *Anthony Trollope: His Work, Associates, and Literary Originals,* the first literary life, was only a half-willing recruit. A busy higher journalist who got to know Trollope quite well in the 1860s and 1870s, Escott waited until 1913 to record his impressions, probably too long. Errors of fact and memory creep in, and his book is under-edited. Nevertheless its tangles of forgotten professional grape-vines, and spunky if sometimes inconsequential anecdotes, have furnished indispensable materials for subsequent biographers. Escott emphasizes the official and even the officious side of the novelist, viewing him as thoroughly conservative in outlook, a lead followed by the next biographer, Michael Sadleir, in *Trollope: A Commentary* (1927), who felt Trollope's life and work 'embalmed' (13) the solidity and complacency of mid-Victorian England. Sadleir's book has been incalculably influential. It is written with flair and elegance, and is honourably zealous on Trollope's behalf in the face of a possibly exaggerated downturn in his reputation. On the debit side, Sadleir makes too much of Trollope's gaucheness and irascibility, and dismisses too many of his novels as drab and monotonous. *A Commentary* is light on archival material, and many of the sources consulted were not mined exhaustively, or else misunderstood, so much of its factual content has since been qualified or superseded.

Sadleir's remained the best biography for many decades. Despite remarkable industry (their meticulous listing of sources has been exploited by all subsequent workers in the field), the mother-and-son team of L. P. and R. P. Stebbins produced in *The Trollopes: The Chronicle of a Writing Family* (1945) a tetchy and intemperate study of family divisions. Their thesis, that Anthony's celebrated literary industry represented little more than an attempt to out-produce the mother who had spurned him, would scarcely merit consideration were it not pursued with such rigour and elaboration. As it is, the book retains dismaying curiosity value, its more wounding speculations about Anthony's jealousy long exploded. Bradford Booth's *Anthony Trollope* (1958) is circumspect enough, but a faint and uncomfortable read, the work of an author whose gift was less for biography than scholarship. Literary comment is uneven, the book lacks structure, and Trollope himself is viewed with a kind of blurred condescension. Altogether more swaggering in its judgements, and bright and brisk in tone, is James Pope Hennessy's *Anthony Trollope* (1971), though as little is offered beyond collation of familiar materials and mannered summaries of the novels, this may safely be ignored.

It is refreshing to turn from these offerings to C. P. Snow's vigorous and opinionated *Trollope: His Life and Art* (1975), much more than just a lively essay to suit the illustrations and coffee-table format. Snow writes with institutional authority about Trollope's conduct as a civil servant, and with psychological acumen of his mother's 'special kind of unfeelingness' (18) towards him. Speculations about the novelist's personality are as succulent as any that have yet appeared. Little original research lies behind the book, however, and the myths and misconceptions of previous biographers are sometimes perpetuated.

Despite Snow's efficient bridge-making, it was clear by the late 1970s there was a chasmal gap where the definitive biography ought to be, and no fewer than three American academics simultaneously and independently undertook to fill it. As their labours neared completion, they were joined by the professional biographer Victoria

Glendinning. Thus four serious and substantial lives of Trollope appeared in as many years, fatiguing even the best-intentioned reviewers, and provoking invidious questions as to pecking order. The emphasis in the first three, which may be considered as a group, is on events rather than personality. R. H. Super's *The Chronicler of Barsetshire* (1988) was first in the field. Growing out of a specialist monograph on Trollope's career in the Post Office (1981) and determined to redress the factual inaccuracies and abolish the unreliable sources used by previous biographers, Super's book sets a definitive standard of rigour and consistency, but purchases them at the cost of a certain austerity. N. John Hall, though equally scholarly, is a more companionable presence in *Trollope: A Biography* (1991). Hall has listened attentively to the wisdom of many Trollopians over a long period. His touch is light, decisive, but never opinionated. Building on the vertebral column of Hall's own impeccable *Letters of Anthony Trollope* (1983), the detailed movements of Trollope's daily living are picked up confidently, though random minutiae never obtrude. The emphasis of both Super and Hall is thus deftly to chronicle the chronicler: Richard Mullen's remit in *Anthony Trollope: A Victorian in his World* (1990) is to set him in his social and cultural context, and, of the 'professorial' biographies, this certainly possesses the most colour. Freighted with a satisfying thickness of reconstructed 19th-century life, and giving full weight to Trollope's subsidiary careers as journalist, aspirant politician, and indefatigable compiler of travel books, Mullen's register shifts between the informative and the racy. The result is an intriguing mix of the scholarly and popular biography. Victoria Glendinning's *Anthony Trollope* (1992), apparently written without knowledge that there were others labouring in the vineyard, is targeted at a general audience, but by no means to be disparaged on that account. The most readable effort since Sadleir and Snow, conversational in tone but never loquacious, it provides perhaps the most decisive vision of Trollope's personality so far, mainly by combing the pages of his fiction thoroughly and sensitively for indirect or inadvertent self-revelation. Much attention is paid to domestic context, especially to the contribution of Rose Trollope as companion, manager, and unsung literary adviser. Some 'intuition' comes into play here, as when Glendinning is 'sure' (316) Anthony and Rose had a scene over Kate Field, but there is no special pleading or wild guesswork. Glendinning's handling of her sources, though less detailed, is as rigorous as that of her rivals. PJT

Birdbott, Serjeant, skilful barrister brought in to add strength to the legal team led by Mr Chaffanbrass in defence of Phineas Finn in his trial for murder. *PR* RCT

Birmingham, large city in the West Midlands where the first congress of the National Association for the Promotion of Social Science is held. The lawyers in the novel descend on Birmingham to attend the legal reform sessions of the great congress. *OF* MT

Birmingham, Lord, absentee landlord of Mohill, where renters live in hideous squalor, dirt, and misery. Though well known for his charitable work, he has never visited his property, so remains unaware of the brutal social conditions that underpin his wealth. *MB* MRS

Bishopsgate Street. Partners in a haberdashery business set up at number 81, calling it 'Magenta House' and advertising it throughout London as '9 times 9 is 81'. *SBJR* RCT

Blackburn, Jemima (Mrs Hugh Blackburn). In 1878, six months after his return from South Africa, Trollope took a 2½-week expedition to Iceland with a party of 16 (and a crew of 34) in John Burns's yacht the *Mastiff*. A lively account of this voyage was given by one of the party, Mrs Jemima Blackburn, an artist from the West Highlands of Scotland, who specialized in drawing birds and animals. Her drawings often appeared in Norman Macleod's *Good Words*. During the expedition, she produced 56 illustrations. One sketch, entitled 'Siege of the Deck Cabin', showed the passengers attacking Trollope (unnamed) for commandeering the cabin as a smoking room. Jemima Blackburn regarded Trollope as 'a rough spoken good sort of fellow; one wondered how he came to write such good novels' (Glendinning 459–60). Lively political discussion ensued; he was the sole Liberal among Tories. Her account of the voyage, 'To Iceland', was published in *Good Words* (June–September 1879, 429–32, 480–6, 559–65, 622–8). Fourteen of her illustrations appeared in Trollope's *How the 'Mastiffs' Went to Iceland*. She recalled their chess games during the expedition, and Trollope saying one day 'that I was not like anyone else he had known—I wish it had occurred to me to ask how so!' (Glendinning 460). Jemima was one of very few friends to refer to him as 'Tony'. RCT

Blackfriars Bridge. Spurned by Maryanne Brown, Mr Robinson twice paces the bridge moodily to soothe his bleeding heart. *SBJR* RCT

Blackwood, John (1818–79), son of William Blackwood (1776–1834), founder of the publishing firm. Under his direction *Blackwood's Magazine* became a leading periodical. The Trollopes stayed frequently at Strathtyrum, the country house of the Blackwoods about a mile from St Andrews. On one visit in August 1868, Trollope clowned on the golf course and shocked the Revd A. K. H. *Boyd at dinner by his dishevelled appearance, swearing and insulting the memory of Sir Walter *Scott (*I & R* 94). Blackwood on the other hand recalled what fun they had and how they parted almost in tears after a farewell bathe at Lake Coruisk (*Chron* 80). Blackwood did not mince words when it came to business. He read and criticized Trollope's manuscripts frankly. Of *Linda Tressel* (1868) he said, 'I have read the whole story & I am very sorry to say that I fear you have made a blunder and so have I.' Trollope promptly offered to take the book back: 'your returning it to me will moult no feather between you & me' (*Letters* 1, 387, 389). Blackwood coaxed him into writing his book on Caesar, which brought them closer. RCT

Blackwood, Julia (née **Blandford**) (d. 1899), youngest daughter of Revd Joseph Blandford, wife of publisher John Blackwood, both close friends of the Trollopes. In January 1878 Trollope promised that when she was next in London he would try to improve her erratic play at whist (*Letters* 2, 75). RCT

Blackwood, William (1836–1912), nephew of John Blackwood. He acted for his uncle in negotiations over *Dr Wortle's School* as a serial for *Blackwood's Magazine* (May–December 1880). Trollope put him up for the Garrick Club in 1880. He continued his uncle's practice of commenting frankly on Trollope's work as in the case of *The Fixed Period* (1882). He also published *An Autobiography* (1883). RCT

Blackwood's Magazine. In 1817 Scottish publisher William Blackwood founded this monthly periodical as a Tory magazine to challenge the Whig *Edinburgh Review*. It carried original articles, poetry, fiction, including five novels by Trollope, and cost 2s. 6d. 'Maga', as Blackwood nicknamed it, was the successor of the *Edinburgh Monthly Magazine*, which he had founded earlier to counter the Whig monopoly of periodical literature in Edinburgh. After six numbers, Blackwood dismissed his editors, James Cleghorn and Thomas Pringle, changed the name to *Blackwood's Magazine*, and turned the magazine over to three young assistants, John Wilson, James Hogg, and John Gibson Lockhart, retaining the real editorial decisions himself. He was followed as editor by a long line of sons and Blackwood successors.

Articles were unsigned, but pseudonyms were freely used: Wilson (Christopher North), Hogg (The Ettrick Shepherd), and Thomas De Quincey (The Opium Eater). The magazine's satirical style and biting wit quickly gained readers. It was loaded with personal attacks, the most famous being 'On the Cockney School of Poetry', an attack on Leigh Hunt, by anonymous reviewer 'Z', actually Lockhart and Wilson. Later pieces ordered John Keats, who had studied medicine, to go back to the apothecary shop, and attacked Shelley and Hazlitt. Hunt and Hazlitt began a lawsuit for £2,000 in damages against the magazine which was settled privately for £100.

In 1822 Maga introduced the 'Noctes Ambrosianae', an ongoing feature discussing literature, philosophy, politics, and topics of the day. It was modelled on the then familiar idea of a club, a society of gentlemen, which had been so successful in Addison and Steele's Spectator Club. William Maginn, a witty Irishman and writer of parodies and humorous verses and later one of the founders of *Fraser's Magazine*, assisted Lockhart, Hogg, and Wilson in writing the 'Noctes', which became very popular. The magazine introduced foreign literature, particularly translations from German. Its politics supported a privileged, usually landowning class, rural rather than urban. *Blackwood's* strong Tory bias made it popular with military and colonial readers.

When Lockhart left to become editor of the *Quarterly Review* in 1825, the tone of the magazine became more restrained. The contents still included poetry, humorous pieces, fiction, and a defence of Scottish Tory life, but with a less savage tone. For years, *Blackwood's*, like many earlier magazines, ran a 'Chronicle' section, which included deaths, births, marriages, and stock prices. By 1827 that heading was gone, and such material appeared less frequently, totally disappearing in 1831, about the time that most new literary magazines were made up entirely of original articles, fiction, and poetry. In 1864 the *London Review and Weekly Journal of Politics, Literature, Art, and Society* listed *Blackwood's* as one of the outstanding miscellanies of the time. Contributors were eager to write for it, enjoying the anonymity, camaraderie, and prestige of being part of such a successful periodical.

In 1866, Trollope offered *Nina Balatka* to John Blackwood for publication and Blackwood sent a long critique of the manuscript stating his reservations about its profitability. The two settled on a price of £250, less than Trollope had earlier requested of Smith for its appearance in the *Cornhill*. It was published first in *Blackwood's*

The publisher John Blackwood, with whom Trollope developed a close friendship after *Nina Balatka* and *Linda Tressel* appeared anonymously in *Blackwood's Magazine*. The Trollopes often stayed with Blackwood at his home near St Andrews. Portrait by John Watson Gordon.

Magazine (July 1866–January 1867) and then in book form, both anonymously. Blackwood advised Trollope to make a number of changes in *The Fixed Period* to make it suitable for the periodical, including deleting words and phrases containing 'God' and 'Lord' so as not to offend readers. The magazine also reviewed a number of Trollope's works including *The Life of Cicero*, which it regarded as a pleasant book, even for those who could not share Trollope's enthusiasm for the topic. The *Blackwood's* reviewer did not like Trollope's *North America*, objecting to his use of fictional characters to discuss a complicated situation. A review by Margaret *Oliphant complained when Trollope killed Mrs Proudie in *The Last Chronicle of Barset*. Trollope published other novels in the magazine, Blackwood becoming one of his prime publishers along with George Smith and Chapman & Hall. Blackwood's imprint would eventually be on *An Autobiography*. By the end of the 19th century, *Blackwood's* was still a prosperous monthly of 160 pages of fiction and criticism.   JWM

Graham, Walter, *English Literary Periodicals* (1930).

Blagden, Isa (Isabella) (?1818–73). Well-known among the British expatriate community of artists and writers in Florence, daughter of an Englishman and an Indian woman, she lived with her dogs and independent women friends in rented villas at Bellosguardo (Glendinning 208). She was a close friend of Robert Browning, who found relief from caring for his ailing wife in her spirited company. From 1849 she was part of T. A. Trollope's circle and 'universally beloved' in Florence. Here she met Kate Field and tended Theodosia Trollope in her final illness. Blagden wrote poetry and novels, and both Browning and Trollope helped her career. Trollope persuaded George Smith to publish *Agnes Tremorne* (1860), although he commented, 'I do not suppose you will make a fortune by it;—nor, I suppose, will she' (*Letters* 1, 125). When her second novel, *The Cost of a Secret* (1863), appeared, Rose Trollope wrote to Kate Field, 'I hope it will have more common-sense than the former one—it can't well have less' (*I & R* 139).   RCT

Blake, Dr, physician at Mohill who attends Jonas Brown after he is shot in a duel. He also confirms Mrs McKeon's suspicion that Feemy Macdermot is bearing a child, and later ministers to her on her deathbed. *MB*   MRS

Blake, Montagu, university acquaintance of John Gordon, now a clergyman. His combination of silliness and self-satisfaction rivals that of Jane Austen's Mr Collins. Through no merit of his own, he rises to the comfortable position of

vicar of Little Alresford and secures the hand of a moderately wealthy and amiable woman, Kattie Forrester. *OML*   RC

Blake, Nicholas, a jockey at the Carrick races. *MB*   MRS

Blake, Thomas, friend of Philip Jones, who turns to him for advice when his young son becomes implicated in the activities of the Land-leaguers. As a Protestant, a landlord, and an Irishman, he successfully straddles the 'two nations' of colonial experience: English privilege and Irish identity. *L*   MRS

Blake, Walter (Dot), sharp gambler and sportsman who considers the turf not in the way of 'an expensive pleasure, but a very serious business' (X). An 'intimate friend' (III) of Lord Ballindine, he incites him to buy Brien Boru, an expensive racehorse, but when Lord Ballindine's engagement to Fanny Wyndham is thereby jeopardized, he sets aside his ruling passion—to make money—by relieving his friend, at no certain advantage to himself, of his horses. *KOK*   MRS

Bland, Florence Nightingale (1855–1908), orphaned daughter of Rose Trollope's sister Isabella and Joseph Bland. She came to live with the Trollopes at Waltham in 1863. Trollope's affection shows through bantering references to her in letters. She was, according to Cecilia Meetkerke, 'the tenderest and most devoted of daughters' (*I & R* 228). As Trollope increasingly succumbed to writer's cramp, she became his amanuensis. Large portions of manuscripts from *Cousin Henry* (begun October 1878) onward are in her hand. Trollope was none too easy to work for. It became a family joke that if she dared interrupt the flow he threw a tantrum. She catalogued the library after the move to Montagu Square (1873) and accompanied her uncle on two taxing trips to Ireland (1882). In June 1881 she was seriously ill. Trollope wrote to Millais, 'They put her under chloroform and did dreadful things to her. But they saved her life!' (*Letters* 2, 911). Something of Trollope's perception of young women in his fiction came from the proximity of Florence, whom he described as 'clever but not demonstrative' (*Letters* 2, 644). He left her £4,000 in his will, which she left with interest to Trollope's sons, Henry and Fred.   RCT

Bland, Isabella. See HESELTINE FAMILY.

Blankenberg, small fishing village near Bruges where Phineas Finn and his friend Lord Chiltern fight their infamous duel over Violet Effingham. The foreign location protects the combatants from England's anti-duelling laws and the secluded beach, thick with dunes, is a discreet location for the contest. *PF*　　　　　JMR

Blaze de Bury, Mme (née **Marie Pauline Rose Stuart**) (1813–94). Believed to be the illegitimate daughter of Lord Brougham, Mme Blaze de Bury was brought up by an army officer, William Stuart. She became hostess of a leading Paris salon, novelist, and contributor to the *Revue des deux mondes* and to *Blackwood's*. *Mildred Vernon: A Tale of Parisian Life in the Last Days of the Monarchy* was published in 1848 under the pseudonym Hamilton Murray. John Blackwood called her 'a sort of masculine female political *intrigante* (an awfully clever woman)' (*Letters* 1, 368–9). T. A. Trollope, who knew her in Paris in 1840, remembered her as a charming friend. In January 1867, Trollope wrote to Sir Charles *Taylor on her behalf. He felt her new novel would probably fail, as she had made no name for herself over the last decade, but he urged Taylor to have the manuscript read, and suggested he would read it himself. In the event, Trollope himself published her novel, *All for Greed*, in *Saint Pauls* from October 1867 to May 1868, alongside *Phineas Finn*. In February 1877, he wrote to George Smalley thanking him for a favour to Mme Blaze de Bury, but did not specify its nature (*Letters* 2, 708).　　　　　RCT

Blewitt, Octavian (1810–84), secretary of the Royal Literary Fund from 1839, during all the years Trollope was an active member. Trollope wrote approximately 70 letters, notes, and memos to Blewitt, mostly on business regarding the Fund, but occasionally offering instances of literary insight and humour. In February 1870, Blewitt submitted an article to Trollope, then editor of *Saint Pauls*, who promised to read it and pass it to other editors if he was unable to accommodate it before his tenure as editor ended (*Letters* 1, 501). Blewitt's 'Bricks and Mortar Charities' appeared in *Saint Pauls* in May 1870, and 'Suburban Houses' in March 1871. Blewitt was known for his handbooks for travellers to Italy published by John Murray.　　　　　RCT

Blomfield, Charles James (1786–1857), Bishop of London (1828–56); writer on classical subjects for the *Edinburgh Review* and *Quarterly Review*; moving spirit of ecclesiastical commission (1836), and vigorous advocate of expanding provision of churches, schools, and clergy in the rapidly growing population of London. He became embroiled in ritual controversy with the 'tractarian' clergy of his see. Trollope satirized him in *The Warden* as eldest son of Archdeacon Grantly.　　　　　RCT

Bluestone, Alice, younger of Serjeant and Mrs Bluestone's two daughters. She befriends Lady Anna but believes that her fiancé (Daniel Thwaite) cannot be a gentleman because he is a tailor. The 'young female Conservative' articulates the fundamental principle of distinct and hierarchical social classes: 'there was a gulf fixed. That is how it should be' (XXII). *LA*　　　RC

Bluestone, Mrs, supportive wife of Serjeant Bluestone and kindly mother of their children. She accepts her husband's client, Lady Anna, as a guest in her home as part of the effort to marry Anna to Frederic Lovel. Her good nature and patience are sorely tried by the protracted dispute among the Lovel family. *LA*　　　RC

Bluestone, Serjeant, aggressive lawyer employed by Countess Lovel and assisted by Mr Goffe. Although violent in court, he is reasonable and moderate outside it. He defends positions to Lady Anna that he does not personally hold because he believes that they are in the best interests of his client. *LA*　　　RC

Boanerges, Lord, smug and opinionated guest of the Duke of Omnium at Gatherum Castle, who teaches Miss Dunstable how to blow soap-bubbles on scientific principles (*FP* VIII). Appears also in *The Bertrams* and *Orley Farm* as President of an International Legal Congress (XVII). The name means 'sons of thunder'.

MRS

Bobbin, Mr, good-natured, indolent junior clerk in the Post Office, a fellow worker of George Roden's. *MF*　　　　　SRB

Bobsborough, home of the Greystock family and borough for which Frank Greystock sits as a Conservative member of Parliament. *ED*　　JMR

Bobtailed Fox, hunting inn in the Runnymede country where the members of the hunt meet to depose their MFH, Major Tifto. *DC*　　JMR

Bocage, wooded region of La Vendée ideal for the Vendeans' guerrilla tactics. *LV*　　　GRH

Bodichon, Barbara (1827–91), illegitimate daughter of radical MP Benjamin Leigh-Smith; painter and feminist, wrote *Women and Work* (1857) and *Reasons for the Emancipation of Women* (1866). Excluded from bourgeois society, she joined George Eliot's intimate circle, and was, along with Emily Davies, one of the 'Ladies of Langham Place'. Trollope first met her at Eliot's Sunday afternoon 'at homes'. She actively supported Caroline Norton's fight for a Married Women's Property Act (which became law in 1857) and was co-founder of the Women's Suffrage Committee in 1866. She also proposed the plan for, and endowed, Girton College, Cambridge, England's first degree-granting institution for women. RCT

Bodkin, Sir Boreas, probably based on Trollope's own superior in the Post Office, Lieutenant Colonel *Maberly. Referred to by his subordinates as Aeolus for his wrath and imperiousness, this Secretary in the Post Office nevertheless delays then decides against dismissing the errant clerk Samuel Crocker. *MF* SRB

Bodkin, Sir Nicholas, Irish Catholic owner of Ballytowngal. He is generally respected as a sportsman, but as a member of the Irish gentry his public standing shifts with the eddies of Ireland's political climate. *L* MRS

Bodkin, Peter, eldest son of Sir Nicholas Bodkin. His friendship with Black Daly not only successfully bridges ideological differences between Catholic and Protestant, but underlines how readily divisions based on religious prejudice can be overcome when common interests and values are fostered. *L* MRS

Boffin, Mr, thoroughly Conservative member of Parliament who works with Sir Orlando Drought to oppose the coalition ministry of the Duke of Omnium. *PM* JMR

Bogen, Max, Augsburg lawyer. Because he is 'well-to-do' and 'good-tempered' (II), Fanny Heisse chooses him from amongst her admirers. Their marriage works well since he adores his wife: 'so clever, and so wise' (XII). *LT* AWJ

Bokenham, William. Controller of the Circulation Department, Bokenham was in the thick of controversies concerning the Post Office in 1860 when *The Times* published a long article on its shortcomings. Bokenham recommended forming an internal committee, to examine charges that junior officers were overworked and underpaid, in which Trollope was a vociferous participant. Rowland *Hill regarded the committee as a cabal against him, largely orchestrated by John *Tilley, Trollope's brother-in-law. After 17 sessions and interviews with 116 witnesses the committee presented a 27-page report calling for higher wages for lower officers (Super 120–1). At a dinner on his retirement in February 1866, Trollope took the chair. His speech was described by *The Times* as 'admirable' (*Letters* 1, 326 n.). RCT

Bold, Eleanor (née **Harding**), widow of John Bold, younger daughter of Revd Septimus Harding, and sister-in-law of Archdeacon Grantly of Barchester. In *The Warden* aged 24, she marries the surgeon John Bold, whose well-intentioned reform has cost her father the wardenship of Hir-

am's Hospital. Left a widow at the beginning of *Barchester Towers*, with a baby and an income of £1,000, she becomes attractive prey for such impecunious men as Mr Slope and Bertie Stanhope. Not a dazzling beauty, she charms with sweetness and grace. An innocent involvement with Slope over Hiram's Hospital leads to suspicion and anger from the Grantlys and unspoken concern from her father. At the great fête of the Thornes, she endures first the unwelcome physical advances of Slope, which she repulses by boxing his ears, then the diffident but honest proposal of Bertie, while watching Arabin seemingly paying court to Signora Neroni. Encouraged by Miss Thorne and following Signora Neroni's unexpected advice, she accepts Arabin's proposal. As Mrs Arabin, she also appears in *Doctor Thorne*, *Framley Parsonage*, *The Small House at Allington*, and, more fully, in *The Last Chronicle of Barset*, where she has two young children and provides the final key to the overriding mystery. NCS

Bold, John, well-to-do Barchester surgeon and somewhat naive reformer. Aged 24, having practised for three years but taken few fees, he devotes himself to reforming state, church, corporation, medical, and general abuses in the world at large. His well-meaning attempt to eliminate perceived corruption at Hiram's Hospital angers Archdeacon Grantly and provokes London articles that upset the Warden, Septimus Harding, and spark his resignation. Bold loves Harding's daughter Eleanor, however, and tries to stop the suit to win her favour. He has died by the beginning of *Barchester Towers*. W NCS

Bold, Johnny, son of Eleanor and John Bold. Baby Johnny becomes the focus of several sessions of 'baby-worship' conducted by his mother and his aunt. In *The Last Chronicle of Barset* he is 'nearly a man'. *BT* NCS

Bold, Mary, sister of John Bold and confidante of Eleanor Bold. In *The Warden* she is just over 30, neither clever nor animated, but with a kindly disposition and a keen sense of right and wrong. After her brother's death, she joins Eleanor in baby-worship of her nephew and comforts her sister-in-law after embarrassments suffered in rejecting the unwanted proposals of Mr Slope and Bertie Stanhope. *BT, FP* NCS

Bollum, Richard, shady nephew of Timothy Crinkett, acting as go-between for Crinkett and John Caldigate. He suggests that Caldigate pay off previous gold-mining associates Crinkett and Euphemia Smith in order to prevent a bigamy scandal, thus exposing Caldigate to charges of bribery. *JC* SRB

Bolster, Bridget, one of the witnesses of Sir Joseph Mason's will who testifies at both trials. 'A poor slip of a girl' during the first trial, at the time of the second trial 'Bridget had risen in the world and was now head chambermaid at a large hotel in the west of England' (XXXII). *OF*   MT

Bolt, Sir Simon. Well known in sporting circles, he had been master of the Brotherton Hunt for fifteen years. *IHP*   MG

Boltby, John, lawyer to Sir Harry Hotspur who advises him that George Hotspur can be bought off and negotiates with the younger Hotspur's creditors. Boltby offends Sir Harry's familial and class pride by speaking forthrightly of George's character, but Sir Harry has to acknowledge that he has never known the lawyer to be mistaken. *SHH*   MG

Bolton, Daniel, pious son and banking partner of Nicholas Bolton. He and his wife side with Mary Bolton in her harsh judgement of John Caldigate, who marries Daniel's sister Hester. *JC*   SRB

Bolton, Hester (Mrs John Caldigate), innocent and lovely daughter of Nicholas and Mary who bring her up in a stern religious manner. John Caldigate falls in love with her at a glance and eventually marries her despite her mother's harsh disapproval. Hester deeply loves her husband, grateful that he has brought liveliness and joy into her life. When he is accused of bigamy she stoutly defends him, never wavering despite her family's strong, united opposition. She escapes incarceration in their house and is only reconciled to them after her mother unwillingly agrees to accept Caldigate as Hester's legitimate husband. *JC*   SRB

Bolton, Mrs Mary, fanatical and unforgiving woman who insists on dominating her daughter Hester and husband Nicholas. Her religious tenets override all comforts and her preaching only thinly disguises an obsession with personal power. She hates John Caldigate unreasonably, defaming him constantly to her daughter even after Hester has married him. She imprisons Hester in the house to protect her from charges of adultery when Caldigate is accused of bigamy. Her fanaticism is a fierce resistance to yielding to anyone; personal triumph is more important than maternal love or compassion. She begrudgingly accepts Caldigate only because of Hester's spirited refusal to bow to her mother's irrational demands. *JC*   SRB

Bolton, Nicholas (the elder), Cambridge banker who helps Daniel Caldigate buy the reversion of the estate from his son John, although it is later restored. His marriage causes him much suffering, cowed as he is by his sternly religious wife in her fierce opposition to the marriage of their beloved daughter Hester to John Caldigate. He finally stands up to his wife, thus making her bitter that she does not even have power over her weak old husband. *JC*   SRB

Bolton, Nicholas (the younger), eldest son and banking partner of Nicholas the elder. He and his wife are nearly as strict in religion as his parents. *JC*   SRB

Bolton, Robert, successful Cambridge attorney who, with his kind-hearted wife Margaret, encourages the marriage of his sister Hester to John Caldigate. Later, when Caldigate is accused of bigamy, Robert regrets not heeding his stepmother's harsh disapproval of the marriage. He turns against Caldigate to the point of encouraging Hester's imprisonment in her parents' home. Although reconciled later, he never understands why Caldigate would have voluntarily paid so much money to four reprobates out of a sense of honour. *JC*   SRB

Bolton, William, successful London barrister who encourages the family's incarceration of his sister Hester while her husband is convicted of bigamy. He is later instrumental in pacifying family animosity. *JC*   SRB

Bolton Abbey, ruined priory in Yorkshire dating from Norman times, an appropriately romantic setting for Earl Lovel to make love to Lady Anna and where she sprained her ankle jumping a gully (XV). Landseer's famous painting of the abbey was exhibited in 1834. *LA*   RCT

Boncassen, Ezekiel, father of Isabel Boncassen. An American scholar highly respected in American political circles, Mr Boncassen brings his wife and daughter with him for an extended trip to England so that he may take advantage of the resources of the British Museum. Discreet and intelligent, every inch the gentleman, Mr Boncassen becomes a favoured companion of the Duke of Omnium with whom he discusses politics and political theory. *DC*   JMR

Boncassen, Isabel, spirited American beauty who captures the heart of young Lord Silverbridge. Although Isabel is acknowledged as the crowning beauty of the London season, her freshness, intelligence, and sensitivity are what others find most winning. Courted by Lord Silverbridge, she refuses to engage herself to him unless he can obtain the permission of his father, thus showing a candour and self-respect, in sharp contrast to her rival, Lady Mabel Grex. *DC*   JMR

Boncassen, Mrs, mother of Isabel Boncassen, thoroughly good-natured and motherly, but perhaps not so well bred as her daughter. She is somewhat cowed by the high-born friends her daughter and husband make during the American family's extended visit to England. *DC*
JMR

Bonchamps, Charles, marquis de (based on historical figure), one of the royalist leaders of the Vendean rebellion, killed at Cholet. *LV*
GRH

Bonner, Mary, the orphaned niece of Sir Thomas Underwood, born and brought up in Jamaica, who returns to live with the Underwoods at Fulham. She is 'tall and somewhat large, with fair hair . . . dark eyes, and perfect eyebrows' (IV). She declines to marry Ralph, the heir, choosing his illegitimate cousin Ralph Newton instead. *RH*
ALS

Bonteen, Mr, immensely irritating political rival of Phineas Finn, for whose murder Phineas is tried. Though a hard-working Liberal member of Parliament, assisting Plantagenet Palliser with his decimal coinage bill, Bonteen is blessed with neither good manners nor intelligence. He treats Phineas Finn with great ill will, spreading rumours which cost Phineas political favour. *PF, ED, PR*
JMR

Bonteen, Mrs, ill-natured wife of Mr Bonteen, friend and protectress of the trouble-ridden Lizzie Eustace. Moving in fashionable parliamentary circles, Mrs Bonteen shares her husband's ill will towards Phineas Finn, to whom she is particularly unpleasant. When her husband is killed, Mrs Bonteen faithfully believes that Phineas is the murderer. *PR*
JMR

Boodle, Captain (Doodles), friend of Archie Clavering, who organizes the latter's pursuit of Lady Ongar. He lives off pickings from the billiard-table and by sniffing out stable-news, the turf supplying nearly all his conversational metaphors. His addiction to subterfuge later leads to embroilment with devious Sophie Gordeloup. *C, PR*
PJT

Booker, Alfred, editor of the *Literary Chronicle.* A 'hard-working' literary man 'with a large family of daughters', Alfred Booker, having abandoned his literary scruples, reviews, writes books, and details the social doings of fashionable parliamentary circles. Trollope may have based the character on real-life journalist Alexander *Shand. WWLN, PM*
JMR

Boolabong, dilapidated cattle run adjacent to Gangoil owned by the disreputable Brownbie family. *HHG*
MRS

Boothby, Mr, the kindly publisher who commissions an ineptly done index from Fred Pickering but sends him £10 none the less. 'Pickering' *LS*
GRH

Boreham, Augusta (Sister Veronica John), patient and understanding cousin of Violet Effingham and daughter of Miss Effingham's guardian, Lady Baldock. An apparently obedient young lady, Miss Boreham shocks her family by converting to Roman Catholicism and becoming a nun. *PF*
JMR

Boscobel (Bos), employee curtly dismissed by Harry Heathcote. He joins forces with the Brownbies to become yet another enemy of the intemperate young squatter. When fire threatens Gangoil, he not only hampers Heathcote's attempts to extinguish it, but prepares to assault his former master before being overcome by Jacko. *HHG*
MRS

Boston, Mass., the 'Athens of the States', where sleigh-riding is a favourite winter pastime. 'Gledd' *LS*
GRH

Bott, Mr, political ally of Plantagenet Palliser, whom both Glencora Palliser and Alice Vavasor find very disagreeable. Glencora complains that he is her 'duenna', perhaps with good reason, since Mr Bott suggests to Mrs Marsham that she inform Plantagenet when Glencora is seen waltzing 'wildly' with Burgo Fitzgerald at a party given by Lady Monk. *CYFH*
JMR

Boucher, Thomas, member of the Post Office Circulation Department, appointed to the internal committee set up in 1860 to examine allegations of exploitation and poor pay for junior officers. At a time when morale was low Boucher had to reassure John Tilley that members were not likely to go out on strike. Trollope was active in the committee's deliberations.
RCT

Bouncer, Mr, a 'literary gentleman' present at the Universe Club on the night of Phineas Finn's quarrel with Mr Bonteen. Mr Bouncer shows himself to be a reasonable and well-mannered man by his efforts to mitigate Phineas's justifiable wrath. *ED, PR*
JMR

Bowen, Sir George Ferguson (1821–99), first Governor of Queensland (1859), later Governor of New Zealand (1867), and then of Victoria (1872–9); pursued a policy of conciliation towards Maoris and settlers. He met Trollope several times in Australia and in Boston. In August 1878, Bowen was virtually relieved of his duties as Governor of Victoria for supporting the Premier, Graham Berry, against the upper house, the Legislative Council. Bowen had acted in the belief that, like the Queen in Britain, a governor should accept advice only from the majority leader in the lower house, in this case Berry. Trollope commented on the situation to G. W. Rusden (September 1878): 'I think that as Governor he [Bowen] has been right' (*Letters* 2, 792).   RCT

Bowes Lodge, Westmorland, seat of Lord Stapledean, who holds the living for Hurst Staple. A cold, cheerless mansion, green with damp, and surrounded by stunted trees, the comfortless state of Bowes Lodge reflects the mood of its owner, a discontented, unhappy misanthrope who believes 'in the justice and honesty of no one' (III). Dingy and derelict, his home offers no promise of hospitality: its door is hidden behind overgrown foliage, and the bell strains out 'a hoarse, rusty, jangling noise, as though angry at being disturbed' (XLIII). *B*   MRS

Bowick, village and parish where Dr Wortle settles after leaving his position at Eton. The Bowick School is built on several fields adjacent to the parsonage. *DWS*   RC

Boxhall Hill, part of Greshamsbury estate, halfway between Greshamsbury and Barchester, noted for its partridge and foxes. Squire Gresham sells the land to Sir Roger Scatcherd who builds a grand new house there. *DT*   NCS

Boyd, Revd Andrew Kennedy Hutchison (1825–99). Minister of Newton-on-Ayr, Scotland (1851), one of the best-known Presbyterian divines of his day; First Minister of St Andrews (1865); author of *The Recreations of a Country Parson* (three series, 1859, 1861, 1878); Moderator of the General Assembly (1890). A shrewd and humorous conversationalist, he was less stuffy than appears from his comments in *Twenty-Five Years at St Andrews* (1892), in which he described a dinner at John Blackwood's in August 1868. He found Trollope 'singularly unkempt . . . his clothes . . . wrinkled and ill-made'; he swore like a trooper, and made disparaging remarks about Walter Scott's novels being dull. 'It is sometimes very difficult to know what is a man's real and abiding opinion,' he concluded (*I & R* 94–5). Trollope was often a shock to the unprepared, especially when he sensed a disapproving eye.   RCT

Bozzle, Maryanne, supportive wife of the private detective. She opposes any effort to remove the child (Louey) from Mrs Trevelyan by force or cunning, but otherwise takes pride in her husband's work. She recommends that he gradually terminate his employment with Louis Trevelyan. *HKWR*   RC

Bozzle, Samuel, ex-policeman and private detective hired by Louis Trevelyan. Bozzle's pessim-

ism about human nature convinces him, wrongly, that Mrs Trevelyan is unfaithful to her husband. He plans and executes the kidnapping of Louey Trevelyan but is gradually persuaded that his employer has become unbalanced. Thus 'with a grain of humanity mixed with many grains of faithlessness' (LXXV), he betrays Louis to his wife's friends. *HKWR*   RC

Brackenbury, Sir Henry (1837–1914). After distinguished service in the Franco-German and Zulu wars (1879–80), he rose to the rank of major general and Director of Military Intelligence (1886–91). He contributed several articles on military topics to *Saint Pauls* including 'The Military Armaments of the Five Great Powers', and 'Parliament and Army Reform'. He also wrote *Some Memories of my Spare Time* (1909) in which he recalled Trollope's passion for cigars: 'One wall of [Trollope's] library where he worked was entirely hidden by small cupboards or bins, each with a separate glass door, and filled with cigars, stacked across each other "headers and stretchers" like timber, so as to allow free circulation of the air . . . There was a pointed stud stuck into the wood above the door of the bin in use, and the empty one filled from the chest. This had gone on for years' (*I & R* 89).   RCT

Bracy, Earl, tolerant father of Lord Carstairs. He relies upon Dr Wortle to prepare his son for Oxford and places no serious obstacle in the way of Carstairs's romance with Mary Wortle, despite both the difference in social status and the threat an early marriage poses to his son's university education. *DWS*   RC

Bradbury & Evans. Formerly printers, William Bradbury and Frederick Evans in 1844 began publishing Dickens, who then helped found and edited their periodical *Household Words* (1850–9). Their other journals included *Once a Week*, *Punch*, and the *Gentleman's Magazine*. Dubious dealings over publishing *The Vicar of Bullhampton*, conducted by E. S. Dallas on their behalf as editor of *Once a Week*, deeply offended Trollope.   RCT

Braddon, Mary Elizabeth (1835–1915). After leading an unconventional life as an actress, under the stage name 'Mary Seyton', and living with the publisher John Maxwell, Braddon produced her most popular and enduring work, *Lady Audley's Secret*, originally a serial for Maxwell's new periodical, later published as a three-decker (1862). Braddon wrote nine plays and over 80 novels, notable for dramatic ingenuity, as well as editing periodicals such as *Temple Bar* and *Belgravia*. Trollope disliked *sensation novels (*Auto* XII). He was acquainted with both Braddon and Maxwell in their capacity as editors.

RCT

Bradley, Revd Edward ('Cuthbert Bede') (1827–89), humourist and illustrator within the *Punch* circle, popular for tales of university life, *The Adventures of Mr Verdant Green, an Oxford Freshman* (1853) and its sequels. In 1868 he was guest at a country house (presumably near Stilton in Huntingdonshire) where Trollope was also staying. Bradley was amazed by Trollope's energy—'up at five in the morning to write, then hunting, dining, playing whist and smoking until the small hours'. When Trollope received some proofs for *Saint Pauls*, he requested Bradley's assistance in editing an article on the Irish Church. 'While I was [so] engrossed', wrote Bradley, 'he looked over the proofs and wrote several letters. I was much struck with the rapidity he showed in getting through this business, and also in keeping up a running conversation with those present, at the same time that he was reading proofs and writing letters.' Bradley also recorded Trollope's anguish over having to return manuscripts submitted by hopeful writers to the magazine with the words 'declined with thanks' (*I & R* 108–10).

RCT

Brady, Mary, sister of Pat Brady, and friend of Feemy Macdermot, whose marriage plans with Denis McGovery make Feemy anxious over her own unsettled status with Myles Ussher. Though desire for children propels her to marry McGovery, she remains childless at the end of the novel, tending instead to old Larry Macdermot. *MB*

MRS

Brady, Pat, manager of the Ballycloran estate who incriminates his young master, Thady Macdermot, in a plot to murder Myles Ussher. Though fond of Thady, his expedient, self-serving nature allows him to be manipulated by Hyacinth Keegan. At one time 'a leader to [the tenants] in their agrarian feelings and troubles' (III), by the end of the tale he is a thorough turncoat, spying for the revenue police until murdered by two Ribbonmen, one a former tenant of Ballycloran. *MB*

MRS

Bragg's End, sleepy and idyllic hamlet near Baslehurst where the Rays live. Bragg's End consists of 'a little green, and a little wooden bridge, over a little stream that trickled away into the Avon' in addition to 'half a dozen labourers' cottages, and a beer or cider shop' (I). The Rays live in a humble cottage across the green from Farmer Sturt and his wife. *RR*

MT

Bragton Hall, long-empty family home of the Morton family of Dillsborough. *AS*

MG

Bramber, Judge, a man highly reputed for his even-handed justice, but one who easily sways juries with his powerful summations of a case. He presides over John Caldigate's trial for bigamy. When the conviction is later subverted by new evidence, his painstaking investigation causes delay in the reversal of the verdict. *JC*

SRB

Brattle, Carry, the 'castaway' or fallen woman (about whom Trollope defended himself in one of his only two prefaces). Once her father's favourite, after she has been seduced she turns to prostitution. The vicar, Frank Fenwick, seeks to rehabilitate her. Sullen, suicidal, and fearful of her father's wrath, Carry returns to her parents' mill and is eventually accepted and forgiven. She stands as an emblem of Trollope's compassionate interest in the very real plight of outcast women. *VB*

SRB

Brattle, Fanny, the 'good' Brattle daughter, loved by all for her kind nature. A plain, useful woman, her destiny is to be a 'drudge'. She always believes the best of her sister Carry, a prostitute, and of her brother Sam, suspected of murder. Go-between for her erring siblings, she is also the mainstay of her aged parents. *VB*

SRB

Brattle, George, successful but grasping farmer who reluctantly puts up bail for his brother Sam but, out of fear of his wife, refuses to shelter his sister Carry, a prostitute. *VB* SRB

Brattle, Jacob, taciturn and hard-working mill owner, an old pagan whose unyielding stubbornness causes others to fear him. His deep, inarticulate feelings of shame, grief, and love for his wayward daughter Carry and son Sam cause the Brattle family much misery until he finally accepts both back into his household. *VB* SRB

Brattle, Maggie. Self-denying and patient wife of the tyrannical Jacob, she suffers much from his sternness in regard to their daughter Carry, a prostitute, and son Sam, suspected of murder. She is well loved by her husband and supportive daughter Fanny. *VB* SRB

Brattle, Sam, younger Brattle son who falls into bad company and is accused of murdering Farmer Trumbull. Aided by the vicar, Frank Fenwick, of whom he has been a favourite, he is eventually acquitted. Generally thoughtless of the grief he brings on his family, he nevertheless works well, if sporadically, at his father Jacob's mill, and supports his 'castaway' sister Carry. *VB* SRB

Brattle's Mill, home of Jacob Brattle and his family. Both the mill and house are large, old-fashioned, picturesque, and dilapidated. They are renovated by the owner, Harry Gilmore, in an attempt to impress Mary Lowther. *VB*   SRB

Brawl, Baron, respected judge who dines at Lord and Lady Harcourt's Eaton Square home and talks incessantly, loudly, and arrogantly (XXXIII). *B*   MRS

Brayboro' Park, the Berkshire seat of Sir George Eardham. *RH*   ALS

Brehgert, Ezekiel, wealthy banker and associate of Augustus Melmotte. A decent and honest widower, but middle-aged, fat, and greasy, he proposes to Georgiana Longestaffe and tolerates her family's bitter prejudice against his Jewishness. He chooses not to expose Melmotte's forgery when the evidence is in his hands. *WWLN*   SRB

Brentford, Earl of, Liberal cabinet minister and early political supporter of Phineas Finn. The Earl is head of an old 'Whig' family, and upholds his family's long-standing Liberal political involvement. His daughter Lady Laura Kennedy is an influential figure in his life, once urging her father to back Phineas Finn in his candidacy at Loughton, the Earl's 'own' borough. When Lady Laura is later forced to separate herself from her unreasonable husband, the Earl goes to live with her in obscurity, but the termination of his distinguished political career drives him into his dotage. *PF, PR*   JMR

Bribery Commissions were part of the post-1867 Parliament's concerted attack on electoral corruption. Royal commissions were appointed to examine three constituencies deemed notably corrupt—Bridgwater, Norwich, and Beverley, the ancient Yorkshire borough contested by Trollope in the 1868 general election. Beverley's undisputed political boss, the commission found, was its Conservative MP Sir Henry Edwards, whose railway wagon company was the town's biggest employer. Despite Edwards's energetic attempts to thwart the commissioners, they found that over a third of the borough's 2,700-odd voters took bribes. Beverley was deemed incorrigible and disenfranchised.   CK

O'Leary, Cornelius, *The Elimination of Corrupt Practices in British Elections, 1868–1911* (1962).

Bright, John (1811–89), MP for Durham (1843); President of the Board of Trade in Gladstone's first ministry (1868–73); known for powerful oratory in support of democratic liberal causes; thought to have been the model for Mr Turnbull, the demagogic politician in *Phineas Finn*. Trollope denied copying his political characters from life except where issues were concerned. He coyly named a British gunboat the *John Bright*, equipped with the ultimate weapon, a 250-ton 'steam swiveller', in *The Fixed Period*. Trollope was highly critical of Bright's later policies over Ireland. For discussion of politics and identities see *Letters*, 1, 468; John Halperin, *Trollope and Politics* (1977); J. R. Dinwiddy, 'Who's Who in Trollope's Political Novels', *NCF* (June 1967), 31–46.   RCT

Brisket, William, the butcher who is George Robinson's rival for the affections of Maryanne Brown. He eventually marries Emily, a drover's daughter, when he discovers that Maryanne's dowry is not forthcoming, owing to the ruin of her father's business. *SBJR*   HO

Britannula, fictional semi-futuristic island near New Zealand which has gained independence from Britain. Despite peace and prosperity, its distinctive policy of a fixed period of life for all inhabitants, ending in compulsory euthanasia at the age of 68, draws in British military force and reversion to British rule. *FixP*   SRB

British imperialism. The 19th century was the great age of British imperialism. Not only did the empire expand territorially into many parts of the world, but pro-imperial sentiment continued to develop, reaching its height at the end of Queen Victoria's reign. Imperial writings, both fiction and non-fiction, extolled the benefits of the empire, which was seen both as duty and sacred trust.

The empire was as diverse as the reasons for its expansion, but there were two major categories of colonies. The settlement colonies of Canada, Australia, New Zealand, and South Africa attracted British and other European immigrants throughout the century. They created communities based on European models, though modified by new environments, and replicas of the British parliamentary system which allowed them to be increasingly self-governing. The settlers came seeking economic opportunity and a new lifestyle and status, and most enjoyed at least a modest success. The colonies in Asia, Africa, and the majority of South Pacific islands would never be areas of settlement, and attracted instead entrepreneurs, missionaries, adventurers, and administrators. Though some were occupied for strategic reasons, in the background were economic incentives of varying intensity. The 'scientific racism' of the 19th century, reinforced by Social Darwinism, provided justifications of 'Anglo-Saxon' rule over so many native peoples; Kipling's famous phrase 'The White Man's Burden' described attitudes of many British imperialists long before it was articulated at the end of the century.

Critics of British imperialism were never lacking, from the classical economists who saw no benefit or reason for imperial acquisitions, to free traders like John Bright and Richard Cobden, for whom empire was both immoral and bad economics. Prime Minister W. E. Gladstone, though his governments did carry out annexations, saw imperial expansion as immoral and fiscally irresponsible. Events like the Boer War at the end of the century launched political economist J. A. Hobson into a critique of imperialism that was very influential in the 20th century.

Apart from occasional references in the Palliser novels Trollope's mention of empire and imperialism came primarily in his travel writings, the best expositions in *Australia and New Zealand* and in *South Africa*. Trollope was not a jingoist; his main interest in the British Empire, apart from Ireland which he anyhow saw as an integral part of the British nation, was in the settlement colonies. These colonies were of obvious benefit to enterprising British men and women who, by working hard, would enjoy comfortable lives and an enhanced sense of self-respect. The colonies would develop into autonomous but friendly states closely associated with Britain. Colonies which were full of native populations and which would never be areas of immigration were irrelevant to Trollope, and tended to illustrate aspects of British character he found unattractive. He firmly opposed the desire of the Australian colonies and New Zealand to take control of New Guinea and the islands of the South Pacific.   LK

Porter, B., *The Lion's Share: A Short History of British Imperialism, 1850–1980* (1984).

British Sports and Pastimes, single volume edited by Trollope of articles contributed to *Saint Pauls Magazine* between October 1867 and August 1868. It was published by James Virtue in November 1868 with a preface specially written by Trollope. Its contents were: 'On Horse Racing', two parts (Francis Lawley), 'On Hunting', two parts (Trollope), 'On Shooting' (Lawley), 'On Fishing' (Dr Bertram), 'On Yachting' (Edward Pigott), 'On Rowing' (Leslie Stephen), 'On Alpine Climbing' (Stephen), 'On Cricket' (Charles Merewether). The book has not been reprinted.   RCT

Brittany, refuge of the Vendeans after their retreat across the Loire. *LV*   GRH

Brittlereed, Mr, cricketer in an important match between England and Britannula. His poor play serves to enhance the heroic winning of the game by his team-mate Jack Neverbend. *FixP*   SRB

Brock, Lord, Prime Minister who sends the Duke of St Bungay to offer Plantagenet Palliser his first cabinet position as Chancellor of the Exchequer. Brock bears some resemblance to Lord *Palmerston. *CYFH, FP, PF, PR, PM*   JMR

Brodrick, Isabel. Devoted to her uncle and the welfare of his tenants, she is too proud to influence the way he should bequeath his estate and refuses to marry her detested cousin to secure that inheritance. Imperious and self-knowing, she will not placate her father and stepmother when she returns penniless to their household. Her sense of humour and forthright honesty lead her through a maze of scruples to the altar, with her beloved William Owen, and to happy possession of Llanfeare. *CH*   AWJ

Brodrick, Mr, Hereford attorney whose second marriage lowered him socially. Burdened with a growing family, he struggles to understand his eldest daughter's refusal of money from her uncle's estate. Somewhat lackadaisically, he assists in discovering the lost will that reinstates her. *CH*   AWJ

Brodrick, Mrs. Favouring her own children, she encourages her stepdaughter's removal to Wales as Uncle Indefer's companion. Awed by the girl's social superiority during annual visits home, she urges Isabel (after she returns permanently) to accept Cousin Henry's annuity and marry William Owen rather than burden the family's finances. *CH*   AWJ

Brodrick, Sir William, surgeon who attends to John Scarborough during his illness. Scarborough fears the arrival of Brodrick, who 'when he came, would come with his knife' (XXI). Brodrick sends Dr Merton to look after Scarborough in his absence. *MSF*   MT

Bromar, Marie, niece by marriage of Michel Voss, love interest of his son George, and tutelary spirit of the Lion d'Or. Except in one important instance she is obedient to her uncle, whom she loves as a father and whose inn she runs. George is exiled for choosing her and she is thereupon induced to accept Adrian Urmand. She breaks the engagement when she realizes George has been true to her. Their constancy is rewarded. *GLG*   MG

Bromley, Revd Thomas, the parson of Utterden who christens John and Hester Caldigate's son. His steadfast belief in Caldigate's innocence of the bigamy charge endears him to the Caldigate family. He is quizzed by the Babington family and Revd Smirkie for his defence of Caldigate. *JC*   SRB

Bronson, Katherine Colman DeKay (1834–1901), American socialite and lion-hunter whose friends included Browning, Ruskin, and Henry James. Sailing from New York to Liverpool in October 1875, she played whist with Trollope most evenings and brought out his mildly flirtatious camaraderie. He penned a mock advertisement for her: 'Wanted. A delicate-chested clergyman' to accompany a party travelling to the Nile. Later he wrote to her enquiring after fellow passengers, especially 'interesting young ladies who liked autographs from old men, and more tender acknowledgments from those who were younger' (*I & R* 205). High jinks on board were welcome to Trollope after driving a pen all day in his cabin.　　　　　　　　　　RCT

Brontë, Charlotte (1816–55). While Trollope negotiated with the publisher T. C. Newby over *The Macdermots of Ballycloran* (1847), Charlotte Brontë was complaining about Newby's delay in bringing out her sisters' combined volume of *Wuthering Heights* and *Agnes Grey*. Trollope thought highly of Charlotte's work and commended the realism of character in *Jane Eyre* (1847), a novel which would be read 'when many whose names are now better known shall have been forgotten' (*Auto* XIII). Her sensationalism in that novel, as in the scene 'of the mad lady tearing the veil of the expectant bride' (*Auto* XII), he did not care for, but on the whole her work met his criteria of 'characters with whom we can sympathize' and 'human truth as to men and women' (*Auto* XII). He included *Jane Eyre, Shirley* (1849), and *Villette* (1853) in 'On English Novelists of the Present Day'. Trollope's own work was compared with Charlotte Brontë's in the *National Review* (January 1863): 'People like Charlotte Brontë speak out of the fulness of their heart, when they depict the sufferings of our existence, and they infect us with sympathy for vicissitudes, disappointments, or regrets, with which each of us has something in common. They go nearer the truth, and they teach us a worthier lesson than he [Trollope] whom a good-natured superficiality and a perilous influx of success prevent from looking into the gloomy caverns which surround him' (Smalley 174).　　RCT

Brook Park, seat of the Wanless family. 'Dugdale' *WFF*　　　　　　　　　　　　GRH

Brooks, Charles William Shirley (1816–74), parliamentary reporter for the *Morning Chronicle*; playwright and novelist; joined *Punch* (1851) which he edited (1870–4). He said of Trollope, in January 1873, that he roared more than ever on return from Australia. Trollope bellowed to him at the Garrick Club that the illustrator (Frank Holl) for *Phineas Redux*, unable to draw a horse, had embellished a fox-hunt scene with a champagne picnic party.　　　　　　　RCT

Brosnan, Father, curate in Tuam, 'hot with righteous indignation' (III) over English rule in Ireland. He counsels Florian Jones, for political rather than spiritual reasons, to keep his oath to remain silent about having witnessed the flooding of his father's field by Landleaguers. *L*
　　　　　　　　　　　　　　　　MRS

brothers and sisters of Trollope. See TROLLOPE, THOMAS ADOLPHUS. Henry (1811–34) attended Harrow and Winchester. In 1827 he accompanied his mother on her ill-advised American foray. His health suffered badly. On returning to England in 1830 he enrolled at Caius College, Cambridge, though there were insufficient funds to keep him there. He died of consumption in Bruges on 23 December 1834. Arthur William, born in 1812, entered Harrow in 1823, already probably dying of the consumption to which he succumbed the following year. The first of the two daughters to be named Emily died the same day she was born in 1813. After the birth of Anthony in 1815 came Cecilia, one year later. She, like Henry, endured the family's catastrophic American trip. Cecilia seems to have been much attached to her mother; many of Fanny's heroines are modelled on the cool, remote, well-mannered Cecilia. In 1839 she married John Tilley, a Post Office friend of Anthony. They had four children. In 1847 she became a Puseyite and the same year began to evince signs of the consumption which carried off so many of the Trollopes. She died in 1849. *Chollerton: A Tale of our Own Times, by a Lady* appeared in 1846. Stebbins calls Cecilia's pietistic high-church novel 'a painful little book' (L. P. and R. P. Stebbins, *The Trollopes* (1945), 120). A second daughter named Emily was born 1818 and died in 1836.　　TB

Stebbins, L. P., and Stebbins, R. P., *The Trollopes: The Chronicle of a Writing Family* (1945).

Brotherton, cathedral town, home of Dean Henry Lovelace and nearest city to Manor Cross, seat of the Marquis of Brotherton. *IHP*　MG

Brotherton, Bishop of. Initially described as ascetic, strict, of evangelical cast, uncompromising, and disliking Henry Lovelace, the Bishop later demonstrates his fairness and worldly wisdom towards the Dean whom he secretly likes. His manners are old-fashioned and he is said to be the most respected man in Brotherton. *IHP*
　　　　　　　　　　　　　　　　MG

Brotherton, Dowager Marchioness of, mother of Frederick Augustus, Marquis of Brotherton, of George, and of Alice, Amelia, Sarah, and Susanna Germain. Despite the ill-treatment she and her other children receive from him, the Dowager remains loyal to her eldest son even as her mind fails. *IHP*   MG

Brotherton, Frederick Augustus, Marquis of, an evil, degenerate man in the Byronic mode, with 'a very devil in his eye' (XLI). He returns from Italy after an absence of years with a wife and putative heir, Lord Popenjoy. The Marquis mistreats his mother, sisters, and brother and abuses all who cross him. The ill, perhaps mad, Marquis no longer enjoys anything but causing trouble—an activity at which he excels. *IHP*
                    MG

Brotherton, Marchioness, Marchesa Luigi, Italian wife of Frederick Augustus, Marquis of Brotherton, and mother of Lord Popenjoy. Legally wed by the time they arrive in England, the question remains whether they were so at the time of Popenjoy's birth. Speaking no English, she returns to Italy with her mystery intact. *IHP*
                    MG

Broughton, diocese in which Bowick is located. The Bishop recommends that Mrs Peacocke leave the rectory at Bowick and take lodgings in the town of Broughton. *DWS*   RC

Broughton, Dobbs, speculator and money-lender, partner of Augustus Musselboro and Mrs Van Siever. High-living, poorly educated, ill-mannered, and increasingly given to drink and jealousy, he hosts pretentiously lavish parties at his Bayswater mansion. Adolphus Crosbie tries to renew a note with Broughton shortly before the business collapses. *LCB*   NCS

Broughton, Captain John, Miss Le Smyrger's nephew, who falls in love with Patience Woolsworthy, proposes, has second thoughts, and is rejected by her because of his snobbery. 'Colne' *TAC2*   GRH

Broughton, Maria Clutterbuck, beautiful, 30-year-old wife of Dobbs Broughton and patroness of artist Conway Dalrymple. Bored, she flirts with Dalrymple while trying to encourage his marriage to Clara Van Siever. Devastated by her husband's failure, she eventually marries his former partner, Augustus Musselboro. *LCB*
                    NCS

Broughton, Rhoda (1840–1920), popular writer whose novels occupied what Trollope called the borderlands of vice tempting to the novelist (*Auto* XII); her success came from a series of romances in which independent heroines kicked over the traces. Following the success of *Cometh up as a Flower* (1867) and *Not Wisely, but*

Too Well (1867), she became another queen of the circulating libraries. Intelligent and witty, she attracted dons and writers to her homes in Oxford and Chelsea, notably Henry James, who became a close friend. A keen detector of the absurd and ironic, Broughton gradually lost her edge. Late in life she wryly commented: 'when she was young she was Zola, and now she's Zola she's Yonge' (R. C. Terry, *Victorian Popular Fiction* (1983), 131). In June 1868, Trollope wrote to Broughton from America praising *Not Wisely, but Too Well*. Although he thought her guilty of exaggeration, nevertheless 'I read . . . with intense interest. I wept over it, and formed my wishes on it, and came to the conclusion that there had come up another sister among us, of whose name we should be proud.' Of her critics, he remarked: 'I do not understand the critics who, when there is so much that is foul abroad, can settle down with claws and beaks on a tale which teaches a wholesome lesson without an impure picture or a faulty expression' (*Letters* 1, 434). The letter renewed her confidence. In October 1874 Trollope invited her to lunch, stating that George Eliot was out of town, but he would try to help Broughton to know her better (*Letters* 2, 632). In *The Sands of Time* (1923), Walter Sichel mentioned a gathering at which Trollope, Rhoda Broughton, Elizabeth Braddon, and Marie Corelli were present (*I & R* 142).   RCT

Broune, Nicholas, practical-minded editor of the *Morning Breakfast Table*. Most prominent in *The Way We Live Now*, Mr Broune assists Lady Carbury in her literary career, advises her on family matters, and eventually marries her. In *The Prime Minister*, Broune attends and reports on the Duchess of Omnium's fashionable parliamentary parties.   JMR

Browborough, Mr, long-time Conservative member of Parliament for Tankerville. A staunch supporter of pre-reform parliamentary tactics, Mr Browborough believes that, so long as he pays well, he ought to be permitted to sit in the House. Mr Browborough loses his seat to Phineas Finn when the Tankerville election results are challenged. *PR*   JMR

Brown, Charles, hypochondriac husband of Mary Brown whose sore throat causes her to search out a hotel mustard jar with farcical consequences. 'Thompson' *WFF*   GRH

Brown, Fred, heir and favourite son of magistrate Jonas Brown, and friend of Myles Ussher. Fred offers to help Ussher elope with Feemy Macdermot. A wastrel like his father, he is devoted to money and 'everything that he called pleasure' (XIX). *MB*   MRS

Brown, George, second son of magistrate Jonas Brown, and friend of Myles Ussher. Best known as a gentleman jockey, he occasionally wins races but, as a ruthless, hard-paced rider, has also 'killed more horses under him than any man in Ireland' (XVII). *MB*   MRS

Brown, Jonas, magistrate and owner of Brown Hall, who challenges Councillor Webb to a duel over Thady Macdermot's murder of Myles Ussher, only to be wounded in the rear. An unsympathetic man, he is hated by the poor for his insistence on opposing 'every scheme for their improvement and welfare' (XXV). *MB*   MRS

Brown, Jonathan, editor intrigued by letters from Josephine de Montmorenci. He visits her to find she is a cripple, and out of sympathy arranges to publish her novel. See also EDITOR. 'Josephine' *ET*   GRH

Brown, Julia, only daughter of Jonas Brown, brought up to hunt, ride hard, and drink with her brothers. However, once they come to regard her as a financial burden, she is quickly married off to Toby Armstrong, a gentleman of small rank and fortune. *MB*   MRS

Brown, Mary, perpetrator of the farcical error of applying a mustard plaster to Mr Jones believing him to be her ailing husband. She eventually confesses the truth to him and later to the family Christmas gathering. 'Thompson' *WFF*   GRH

Brown, Maryanne, mercenary daughter of Mr Brown who flirts with George Robinson and William Brisket, but is left unmarried at the end of the novel. 'And thus she fell to the ground between two stools, and, falling, perceived that there was nothing before her on which her eye could rest with satisfaction' (XXI). *SBJR*   HO

Brown, Mr, weak-willed senior partner of the firm that is brought to bankruptcy through the dishonesty and grandiose schemes of his junior partners. *SBJR*   HO

Brown, Septimus, well-connected and respected Deputy in the Home Office, to whom Daniel Caldigate appeals on his son's behalf. Brown calms Caldigate's indignation without actually helping him, but later writes the letter informing him of John Caldigate's pardon. *JC*   SRB

Brown, Sir Ferdinando, the Governor brought to Britannula to depose John Neverbend and return the island to British rule. His smooth but empty speech to the citizens assumes a 'tone of domineering ascendancy', but he wins their support, much to Neverbend's disgust. *FixP*   SRB

Brownbie family, squatter family of 'four or five' dissolute sons (VI) headed by Old Brownbie, a former convict who has been unable to shake 'the thralldom of his degradation' (VI). Occasionally stealing sheep from their neighbour Harry Heathcote, whom they regard as 'a proud, stuck-up, unsocial young cub' (VI), the Brownbies plot to fire the Gangoil property, but their efforts are thwarted. *HHG*   MRS

Browne, Hablot Knight ('Phiz') (1815–82), brilliant illustrator of Dickens's novels, engaged for *Can You Forgive Her?*. Trollope was so troubled by the way the drawings were turning out that, after ten monthly numbers had appeared, he begged Millais to take over, offering to make up the fee (some five times as much per drawing). Millais was too busy. Trollope wrote to George Smith that Browne would 'take no pains to ascertain the thing to be illustrated' (*Letters* 1, 282). In one preliminary sketch he decorated Burgo Fitzgerald with a beard. Trollope had him replaced by a Miss Taylor of St Leonards. (See *Letters* 1, 267–8 and N. John Hall, *Trollope and his Illustrators*, 1980.)   RCT

Browne, Thomas A. ('Rolf Boldrewood') (1826–1915), police magistrate at Dubbo, near Gulgong, New South Wales, who welcomed Trollope at a luncheon in Gulgong (October 1871). Trollope somewhat rashly referred to the over-speechifying that went on in Australia, and Browne got his own back by calling a visitor from Britain Anthony Towers, an 'old Turk', in his novel *The Miner's Right*, serialized in 1880. Trollope's son Fred met Browne in 1881 and reported that he had quoted 'It's dogged as does it' (*LCB*) as a motive for continuing writing (P. D. Edwards, *Anthony Trollope's Son in Australia* (1982), 21–2).   RCT

Browning, Elizabeth Barrett (1806–61), invalid poet who married Robert Browning (1846) and lived her remaining years in Florence. The Brownings became friends of Tom Trollope and admirers of Trollope's books. 'Robert & I both consider him first-rate as a novelist,' she said, '*Framley Parsonage* is perfect it seems to me . . . I like both brothers very much. Anthony has an extraordinary beard to be grown in England, but is very English in spite of it, & simple, naif, direct, frank—everything one likes in a man' (*I & R* 135–6).   RCT

Browning, Robert (1812–89), leading narrative poet whose *The Ring and the Book* (1868–89) Trollope read aloud to his family in the winter of 1880. They met frequently at literary functions and clubbed at the Athenaeum and the Garrick. They dined at the Garrick two days before Trol-

Hablot Browne was best known as Dickens's illustrator, and Trollope was troubled from the start when he was commissioned for *Can You Forgive Her?*. Browne's style certainly strikes an odd note. 'Captain Bellfield proposes a Toast' (IX), for example, seems more appropriate to a scene from *David Copperfield*.

lope's stroke and Browning was one of the mourners at his funeral. Though they were good friends Trollope did confess to his son Harry that he found Browning's poetry stodgy (*Letters* 2, 941). RCT

Brownlow, Edith, sensible, sweet, and like a daughter to Sir Gregory Marrable, who wishes her to marry his son Gregory or his nephew Walter. Willing to oblige her friends, she nevertheless sees her dream dissipate when Gregory dies and Walter tells her of his love for Mary Lowther. *VB* SRB

Brownlow, Mrs, widowed sister-in-law of Sir Gregory Marrable, with whom she shares a tacit agreement that first his son, then his nephew Walter, should marry her daughter Edith. When consulted, she wisely and graciously suggests that Edith should speak for herself and Walter should marry his beloved Mary Lowther. *VB* SRB

Brownriggs, a 400-acre (160 ha) farm on the Newton Priory estate, worth some £12,000, and let to Mr Walker. It is not sold by Gregory Newton, though he considers the idea. *RH* ALS

Brumby, Lieutenant, half-pay, scruffy, drinking invalid, totally cowed by his wife. 'Brumby' *ET* GRH

Brumby, Mrs, aggressive woman who pesters the editor to publish her worthless essay on 'Costume', even threatening a lawsuit. 'Brumby' *ET* GRH

Bryce, Viscount James (1838–1922), jurist, historian, and Liberal cabinet member who wrote Trollope's obituary for the *Nation*, 36, January 1883. In *Studies in Contemporary Biography* (1903) he described the novelist as 'a bluff, genial, hearty, vigorous man, typically English in his face, his ideas, his tastes'. These were the qualities which made Trollope unsurpassed as observer of the contemporary scene (*I & R* 168–9). RCT

Buchanan, Robert Williams (1841–1901), minor poet, novelist, and playwright, notorious for attacking the Pre-Raphaelites in 'The Fleshly School of Poetry' (*Contemporary Review*, October 1871). His periodical *Light*, which lasted a few months, published Trollope's story 'The Lady of Launay' (April–May 1878). RCT

Buckinghamshire, divided from Berkshire by the river Thames but united to it in the name of the Berkshire and Buckinghamshire Hunt (the B & B). *RH* ALS

Budcombe, the parish of Revd Alexander Morrison. 'Launay' *WFF* GRH

Buffle, Sir Raffle, pompous, blustering, imposing Chief Commissioner of the Income Tax Office, whom Johnny Eames serves as private secretary. Known as 'Huffle Snuffle' to his inferiors, he is a liar whom no one believes and a bully whom no one fears. Trollope denied that he was based on an actual person, despite rumours to the contrary (*Auto* X). *SHA, LCB* NCS

Buggins, Mrs, old servant, then landlady, of Margaret Mackenzie, whose house in Arundel Street serves as a refuge for the beleaguered heroine after she loses her fortune. She gives Margaret down-to-earth advice in order to increase Margaret's chance of becoming a baronet's lady. *MM* SRB

Bullbean, Mr, never appears in the novel but is in a position to destroy George Hotspur. He was present when Hotspur fleeced the gullible Mr Walker at cards and is reported to be willing to testify against Hotspur in court. *SHH* MG

Bullhampton, parish and small town in Wiltshire, quiet, conservative, religious, and agricultural. Most of the land belongs to the Marquis of Trowbridge and Squire Henry Gilmore. *VB* SRB

Bulwer, Rosina (née **Wheeler**) (1802–82), estranged wife of Sir Edward Bulwer-Lytton. Her marital experiences provided raw material for novels. After the very public breakdown of the marriage in 1836, Lady Bulwer was befriended by Frances Trollope in Paris in 1839, where the two attended social functions at the British Embassy. In 1840, T. A. Trollope assisted Lady Bulwer in settling with Henry Colburn, the publisher, for her novel *The Budget of the Bubble Family* (1840), dedicated to Mrs Trollope (Glendinning 107). Around this time, Frances Trollope also wrote to Lady Bulwer about Trollope's near-fatal illness (*Letters* 1, 9). Contact was maintained with Lady Bulwer by Tom and Mrs Trollope when in 1843 they decided to make their home in Florence, staying with her in the Palazzo Passerini until they found their own accommodation. Trollope's Commonplace Book records that he read and commented on Lady Bulwer's novels. RCT

Bulwer-Lytton, Edward George Lytton (1803–73), highly successful author of *Pelham* (1828) and other novels of fashionable life, crime, and historical subjects, as well as plays. In his Commonplace Book of 1835, Trollope noted how 'wrong he is in his ideas on life & human nature'. His notes become a personal lament for his own frustrated desire to be a writer, 'I become weary of the labor, & do nothing; I am not contented with mediocrity—want the perseverance to accomplish superiority, & therefore fall into utter inferiority' (*Letters* 2, 1021). Bulwer-Lytton praised Trollope warmly for the conception and execution of *Miss Mackenzie* and other books (*Letters* 1, 319). At the dinner, chaired by Lord Lytton, honouring Dickens in November 1867, Trollope included the author of *Eugene Aram* (1832) among five great artists of fiction. But Trollope entertained a tepid view of Bulwer-Lytton's achievements (*Auto* XIII).　　　RCT

Bunce, Jacob, radical husband of Phineas Finn's lodging-house keeper. Bunce, a serious-minded law-stationer, holds strongly democratic views. His wife berates him for paying dues to a trade union and Phineas tries to talk him into more moderate political opinions, to no avail. *PF, PR*　　　JMR

Bunce, Jane, Phineas Finn's motherly lodging-house keeper. She is a caring and compassionate woman, though (in contrast to her radical husband) given to admiring those 'above' her a little too much. She is attentive to Phineas, proud to have a member of Parliament in her lodgings, and speaks strongly in Phineas's defence at his trial. *PF, PR*　　　JMR

Bunce, John, chief bedesman of Hiram's Hospital. A burly, handsome man over 80 in *The Warden*, over 90 in *Barchester Towers*, Bunce acts as 'sub-Warden' and friend of Mr Harding. Arguing against innovation and seeing the hospital as a wonderful home, he tries to dissuade his fellows from demanding changes that will surely worsen their condition. Blind and stooped in *The Last Chronicle of Barset*, he attends Mr Harding's funeral but dies within a fortnight. *W*　　NCS

Bunce, Mrs, housekeeper at Scroope Manor. Servants who behave submissively and attend Anglican services retain their places 'for ever'. *EE*　　　AWJ

Bundlesham, fine country house and estate of the Primero family in Suffolk. Its relative modernity 'savoured of trade' to the neighbouring squire, Roger Carbury. *WWLN*　　　SRB

Bunfit, Mr, one of the detectives who investigates the supposed theft of Lizzie Eustace's diamond necklace. *ED*　　　JMR

Bungall, Mrs, widow of partner in Bungall & Tappitt Brewery in Baslehurst, inherits a one-third interest in the brewery. She, in turn, leaves her interest to her great-nephew Luke Rowan, who has grand plans for changing the nature of the business. *RR*　　　MT

Buntingford, town in Hertfordshire where Mr Thoroughbung's brewery is located. *MSF*　　MT

Burgess, Bartholomew (Barty), second of four brothers and partner in the banking firm of Cropper & Burgess. Embittered when the family's money is left to Jemima Stanbury, Barty grows into an 'ill-tempered old man' whom 'no one liked' (XXXV). He and Miss Stanbury remain lifelong enemies, although their enmity is partially mitigated by the marriage of his nephew (Brooke) and her niece (Dorothy). *HKWR*　　RC

Burgess, Brooke (the elder), eldest of four sons of a banker in Exeter. He is engaged to Miss Stanbury, but both the lovers and their families quarrel. He never marries Jemima but leaves all his money to her, thereby deepening the rift between the two families. *HKWR*　　　RC

Burgess, Brooke (the younger), son of the fourth Burgess brother Harry, eldest in a large family, and clerk in the Ecclesiastical Record Office in London. Unlike his uncles, he is both good-natured and indifferent to Miss Stanbury's money. He becomes her heir, marries her niece (Dorothy Stanbury), and through her agency is brought into the firm of Cropper & Burgess in Exeter. *HKWR*　　　RC

Burke, Edmund (1729–97), parliamentary advocate of political freedoms; powerful orator and essayist. In September 1883 Trollope annotated a copy of Burke's *A Philosophical Inquiry into the Sublime and the Beautiful* (1757), noting that while one might indulge the romance of grief 'NO ONE CAN LIKE GRIEF'. His annotations were the most impressive surviving work of his early years (Super 16).　　　RCT

Burke's and Debrett's peerages first appeared in 1826 and 1806 respectively. Trollope owned a Burke, probably to cross-check on aristocratic names he invented. The complex web in his novels echoes real-life Victorian society. Lady Rowley consults Debrett to ascertain Charles Glascock's age in *He Knew He Was Right*; Burke is cited in *John Caldigate* as proof of the Smirke family pedigree.　　　TB

Burnaby, steward at Scroope Manor. His proficiency allows the 12th Earl to feel masterful but makes his heir feel purposeless. *EE*　　AWJ

Burnaby, Mr, compassionate author who, despite the poor job Fred Pickering makes of the index, pays him. 'Pickering' *LS*　　GRH

Burnand, Sir Francis Cowley (1836–1917). A founder of the Cambridge ADC, Burnand produced over 100 farces, burlesques, and adaptations of French comedies. His best-known play was *Black-Eyed Susan* (1866); an operetta, *Cox and Box* (1867), with music by Sullivan, also enjoyed great success. He was editor of *Punch* from

1880 to 1906. Word-play and punning came easily, and he parodied contemporaries well. On becoming editor he produced a serial from May to October 1880 called 'The Beadle—or, The Latest Chronicle of Small Beerjester', which he attributed to Anthony Dollop. Being parodied in this way proved Trollope's celebrity, but also reflected new tastes. In *Records and Reminiscences Personal and General* (1904), Burnand recalled meeting Trollope at the Athenaeum Club, 'bearded and rough in manner . . . a rough variation of the Tom *Taylor type' (*I & R* 154–5).   RCT

Burney, Frances (Mme d'Arblay) (1752–1840). Novelist, diarist, member of the Blue Stocking Circle, and friend of Dr Johnson, author of the highly successful *Evelina: or the History of a Young Lady's Entrance into the World* (1778), written in the form of letters. Other works included *Cecilia* (1782), *Camilla* (1796), and *The Wanderer* (1814), which, while savagely treated by critics, earned Burney a handsome sum of money. After marriage to a French refugee, General Alexandre d'Arblay, she spent ten years in France. In *The New Zealander*, Trollope noted appreciatively the pictures of society drawn by Pepys, Jane Austen, and Fanny Burney (Super 78).   RCT

Burney, Revd Charles (d. 1907), vicar of Halstead, Essex (1850–64), who persuaded Trollope to lecture. Trollope addressed the Halstead Literary and Mechanics' Institution in February 1864, on the American Civil War.   RCT

Burns, John (1829–1901), later Lord Inverclyde, chairman of the Cunard Steamship Company (founded by his father), the original aim of which was to carry mail (Glendinning 373). Burns owned the yacht *Mastiff* on which Trollope visited Iceland, a two-and-a-half-week expedition. At Burns's request, Trollope wrote (and Burns privately published) *How the 'Mastiffs' Went to Iceland* (1878). Burns and Trollope had been friends since the 1860s, when Trollope was one of a group, which included Norman Macleod, 'The Gaiter Club', which was dedicated to walking tours in Scotland, and held an annual dinner at which members told stories and reported on their activities. Trollope passed social evenings with Burns whenever he was in Glasgow (Super 384).   RCT

Burns, Robert (1759–96). The self-educated son of a poor Scottish farmer, he published *Poems, Chiefly in the Scottish Dialect* in 1786, and subsequently became the toast of Edinburgh. His main literary task from 1787 till his death was to contribute to and edit two compendia of songs, *A Select Collection of Original Scottish Airs* and *The Scots Musical Museum*. In *Barchester Towers* Trollope has the Signora Vesey Neroni rout Mr Slope with Burns's lines 'It's gude to be off with the auld luve | Before ye be on wi' the new'. The quotation is also used in *Doctor Thorne* (VI), *The Eustace Diamonds* (XXXV), *The Way We Live Now* (LXXII), and *Ayala's Angel* (LIX). In *The New Zealander* Trollope listed Burns among eighteen 'giants' of English literature.   RCT

Burrows, Anne, wife of 'Jack the Grinder', who refuses to divulge her husband's whereabouts when questioned by Constable Toffy. Sickly and weak, she lives with her mother-in-law at Pycroft Common. *VB*   SRB

Burrows, John ('Jack the Grinder'), notorious jailbird who is guilty of theft and the murder of Farmer Trumbull. He escapes with his accomplice, Larry Acorn, to San Francisco until returned by the police to stand trial and be hanged. Sam Brattle is briefly and harmfully associated with him. *VB*   SRB

Burrows, Mrs, canny but unscrupulous old woman, mother of Jack the Grinder, who is wanted for murder. She shifts suspicion onto Sam Brattle and briefly houses the outcast Carry Brattle. A clever witness at her son's trial, she is nevertheless unable to save him from the gallows. *VB*   SRB

Burton, Cecilia, wife of Theodore Burton, who wins Harry Clavering back for Florence Burton with a mixture of patience, flattery, and mild flirtation across the beds of her 'bairns'. She has three children, Cissy (7), Sophie (4), and the infant Theodore Burton junior. Harry Clavering is struck with her tall, slight, prepossessing figure. *C*   PJT

Burton, Florence, one of Trollope's 'little brown girls'. At first thought plain by the novel's hero, Harry Clavering, she endears herself by steadiness, constancy, and a trick of adjusting her expectations to his vacillating behaviour. Like all the Burtons, she is practical and resilient, and has little emotional energy to expend on the 'weaknesses of grief' (XXXII). *C*   PJT

Burton, Mr, junior partner of Beilby & Burton, Civil Engineers, who manages the firm's Stratton office and instructs Harry Clavering. His sons are civil engineers, and his daughters have all married into the same profession. Mr Burton also practises land surveying, valuing, and architecture. *C*   PJT

Burton, Mrs. Mother of a large family, she marries three of her daughters to civil engineers before *The Claverings* opens, and places the fourth, Florence, with her husband's pupil Harry

Clavering. A good manager, though somewhat vulgar in manner and speech, she turns tigress when Harry threatens to jilt Florence. *C*   PJT

Burton, Theodore. Eldest of Mr Burton's surviving sons, and his father's heir apparent in the family firm, he takes Harry Clavering somewhat proprietorially under his wing. Shares with his wife Cecilia a robust charm and, like his creator, philosophizes about the value of hard work. A considerable moral presence in the novel. *C*
PJT

business entrepreneurs. The Industrial Revolution brought unparalleled change to Western society. When once man's inventiveness for machines had been harnessed to the application of steam power, these forces exerted an ever-increasing demand for coal and for iron, which in turn fuelled the development of more engineering. Within a generation, urban rather than rural life became the norm. When Trollope was born the economy for most people revolved round a landowning squirearchy and aristocracy; by the middle of the 19th century, the economic landscape had changed dramatically. Many landowners had become immensely wealthy with the exploitation of natural resources on their property; wherever coal had been found and mined new towns grew; retail trade expanded exponentially; and with the demand for improved communication and transport, most importantly, came the railway, the great generator of engineering feats and a great consumer of iron and coal.

The financing of the industrial age promoted a massive growth in banking fields, and generated a new breed of financier to meet the new challenges. Sir Thomas Tringle in *Ayala's Angel* rose from humble origins to become senior partner in Travers & Treason, and 'was supposed to manipulate all the millions with which the great firm in Lombard Street was concerned' (I). Tringle, however, belonged in spirit with the banking types from earlier novels, generally shown approvingly despite the example of Trollope's crooked banker father-in-law Edward Heseltine. In *Framley Parsonage*, Mr Forrest, the Barchester bank manager, tries to help Mark Robarts over his financial difficulties (XLII). In *He Knew He Was Right* old Barty Burgess makes over his share of the banking firm of Cropper & Burgess of Exeter to his nephew Brooke Burgess (LXXXVIII). Similar continuity is observed in *John Caldigate* as Nicholas Bolton sees two of his sons follow him into banking. While celebrating such continuities, Trollope's imagination was gripped by the new forces in trade and commerce, although he makes a discrete judgement between men with the vision and skill to design and build, and

the men whose 'fortune was to be made, not by the construction of the railway but by the floating of the railway shares' (*WWLN* X). The railways are a dual symbol of social progress and degeneration in public life. The Industrial Revolution offered the possibility of immense wealth to men whose station in life was otherwise humble. Such a man was Sir Roger Scatcherd (*DT*), a stonemason by trade, who made his fortune by knowing how much stone and how many stonemasons were needed to build a railway line. Such were his entrepreneurial skills, he became internationally renowned, and was knighted for his achievements in building a railway in half the usual time. While he enjoyed the power his money gave him, his modest and humble wife was never comfortable out of her class, and his son, denied the necessity of earning his bread, was corrupted by a life of moneyed indolence and dissipation; his father, in drinking himself to death, died knowing that his son was soon destined for a similar end. Scatcherd's life and mores are explored against tales of financial embarrassment in the upper classes, and Trollope enjoys the ironic demonstration that both money, and the lack of it, can cause equal amounts of grief.

With the construction of the railways, possibilities of new professions opened for ambitious and well-born young men. Such was Harry Clavering's aspiration in *The Claverings*. His heroes are Locke, Stephenson, and Brassey—railway engineers and contractors—and he apprenticed himself to a firm where the leading partner has designed and built the longest single-span bridge in the world (II). Harry's ambition is ultimately greater than his moral fibre, and he is fortunate in the end that life provides him with an income he does not have to earn. Of greater significance in the new order of things is Theodore Burton, head of his father's business, one day destined to be as rich as Beilby, his father's partner. Burton is the man so bourgeois that he dusts his boots with his handkerchief, and wears cotton gloves, but who goes off in the morning to decide which bit of London will be knocked down next to make way for the railway, and who is called to Russia to advise on a railway from Moscow to Astrakhan. With the Burton family, Trollope suggests that the world now belongs to these new men, that our lives will be determined by the people who build railways, and can show the world how to build railways. The old world order gave wealth to the few. The advancement of the railways, led by a new middle class, becomes a paradigm for a world where hard work, knowledge, and vision thrust aside the structures of the old city to make way for the new.

Trollope deplored the lack of honesty in the times he lived in. 'Do we recognize the dishonesty of our tradesmen, with their advertisements, their pretend credit, their adulterations, and fake cheapness?', he asks in *The New Zealander* (XIII). When this work (written in 1855–6) failed to find a publisher, he reworked the themes in subsequent novels, beginning with *The Struggles of Brown, Jones, and Robinson*. This novel, begun in 1857, though not completed till 1861, satirizes the antics of tradesmen disguising the paucity of their stock with the puffery of advertising. *Doctor Thorne* (written in 1859–60) pokes fun at the origins of Miss Dunstable's enormous wealth, the profits from the sham Ointment of Lebanon. *Orley Farm* (written in 1860) has a sub-plot cast of commercial travellers, among whom is Kantwise with his line in folding metal furniture, 'all gilt in Louey Catorse' (VI). As Mrs Dockwrath wrathfully exclaims: 'They're got up for cheatery;—that's what they're got up for' (XLII). It is significant that while the supporters of the old order, their manners, and their values, represented by the Cleeve, stay put, the schemers, lawyers, and wheeler-dealers traverse the country by train, criss-crossing from London to Leeds to Birmingham, all now accessible in less than a day.

The Three Clerks, from the same period, similarly attacks dishonesty in public life. The clever, ambitious, but morally weak Alaric Tudor is led into corrupt share dealing by the unscrupulous member of Parliament Undecimus Scott. Scott uses privileged information to buy mining shares cheaply as they are just about to rise, and sells them as they reach their peak. He uses his political credibility to suck Alaric into his deals, and then blackmails him into betraying his position as a trustee of a young woman's fortune to use the capital for fraudulent speculation. It is Alaric who is prosecuted for his crimes, but while Scott escapes the arm of the law he is boycotted by members of his club, and expelled from the House of Commons. The book ends with Alaric manfully struggling back to some standing of dignity, while Scott is relegated to the life of a losing gambler in the seedier resorts of the Continent—Trollope's moral commentary and epitaph on his career.

Ferdinand Lopez in *The Prime Minister* is a similar opportunistic adventurer, who wishes to make large amounts of money from very little effort. He represents a new breed of entrepreneurs, men who seem very rich, and who appear to have sprung from nowhere. His lack of provenance reflects the prejudices of Trollope's age; he may not be a gentleman by birth, he may be foreign, he looks Jewish—and these prejudices

inform the assumptions that are made about the way he earns his money. In exploring Lopez's career and prospects, Trollope introduces the underworld of small-time stock market jobbers like Hartlepod, promoter of the mining company in Guatemala which Lopez hoped to represent. At a lower level of sordid commercial enterprise comes Sexty Parker with whom Lopez is also involved. Together they intend to promote 'Bios', a health tonic. Lady Eustace is invited to invest, and cautiously inquires, 'How are you to get people to drink it?' Lopez replies: 'By telling them they ought to drink it. Advertise it. It has become a certainty now that if you will only advertise sufficiently you may make a fortune by selling anything' (LIV). Parker's precarious living is destroyed by gambling on shares at great odds. Like Undecimus Scott, Lopez is seen as no better than a gambler, and his dubious origins allow Trollope to construct a persona where everything bad can be attributed to him. After his marriage to Emily Wharton, the heiress, he is shown to be a cash-hungry manipulator, concerned only with outward show. He pays extra for a main aisle seat in church, while Emily has to economize on the laundry; he is a man of vulgar taste and shallow feeling, who threatens his wife with violence, who cheats and deceives till his only escape is self-destruction under the wheels of a train.

But Lopez and Scott are small fry compared to Melmotte. *The Way We Live Now* was written in anger, to expose a dishonesty in public life and public finance which attacked the fabric of society. As Trollope says in *An Autobiography*, 'a certain class of dishonesty, dishonesty magnificent in its proportions, and climbing into high places, has become so rampant and so splendid that there seems reason for fearing that men and women will be taught to feel that dishonesty, if it can become splendid will cease to be abominable' (XX). Again Trollope chooses the Railway as his metaphor, his symbol of progress, modernity—and corruption. He drew on contemporary real-life swindlers who had achieved notoriety: John Sadleir, a banker and member of Parliament, a swindler, forger, and fraudulent dealer in railway shares, killed himself with prussic acid; Charles LeFevre, who was said to have escaped abroad with £1 million duped the public on a massive scale with worthless shares in a South American railway company. In *The Way We Live Now*, Roger Carbury, who belongs to an ancient squirearchy, sees his way of life and standards spurned by men of the machine age. His niceness about modest behaviour and probity is measured against the new riches of the families around him, who have bought their estates with fortunes made in trade. He is surrounded by people who flaunt the trappings of their wealth, who gamble and cheat at cards, bringing the same degenerate codes to their public lives as members of Melmotte's spurious board of directors. The Longestaffes, Grendalls, and Nidderdales are prepared to compromise all integrity to support the appearance of their moneyed lifestyle (VI and LV).

Melmotte is arrogant and vulgar, without scruple or principle, believing that if he operates on a large enough scale, on a high enough plane, he will be above society's constraints. Mrs Hurtle says, 'Such a man rises above honesty as a general rises above humanity when he sacrifices an army to conquer a nation' (XXVI). This New World sophistry embodies the attack of the book. Melmotte reaches both his zenith and his nadir when he entertains the Emperor of China. In a parody of the operating of the City, Trollope describes the trading in dinner tickets for the occasion; they rise as the rumours of the guest list circulate, fall back just prior to the event, and are worthless by 10 p.m. that evening. There is a neat irony in Melmotte's downfall starting from his meeting with 'the brother of the sun' (LIV), as, Icarus-like, the wax wings of one who aspires so high must inevitably melt, leaving him to crash down to his destruction.

This reflects a consistent voice in the novels, one which laments the passing of tradition and old world values. 'We have earls dealing in butter, and marquises taking their peaches to market,' says Maule, senior (*PR* XXX). However, Trollope himself enjoyed the comforts of progress, and the pleasures that his self-made wealth afforded him, and in his professional life he was one of those who helped make the world smaller, as he pursued his Post Office business round the globe.

MM

Buston Hall, Peter Prosper's property in Hertfordshire which is left to Harry Annesley. *MSF*
MT

Butler, Revd Dr George (1774–1853), headmaster of Harrow School 1805–29, which included the period of Trollope's first attendance when he was not yet 8 years old. Trollope recorded that he was disliked by him. 'I remember well, when I was still the junior boy in the school, Dr Butler, the headmaster, stopping me in the street, and asking me, with all the clouds of Jove upon his brow and the thunder in his voice, whether it was possible that Harrow School was disgraced by so disreputably dirty a little boy as I! . . . I do not doubt that I was dirty;—but I think that he was cruel. He must have known me as he was wont to see me, for he was in the habit of

flogging me constantly. Perhaps he did not recognize me by my face' (*Auto* I). RCT

Butt, Isaac (d. 1879), Irish advocate noted for his eloquence and skill in cross-examination; a founder of *Dublin University Magazine* (1834); later champion of Home Rule. For Trollope he was the prototype of many fictional aggressive barristers like Chaffanbrass. Called to give evidence in a case of post office theft at Kerry Assizes (July 1849), Trollope showed himself a match for Butt in court. Recalling that in *The Macdermots of Ballycloran* Trollope had portrayed a barrister named Allewind, Butt asked him if it had been his intention to show the world his ideal cross-examiner. 'Yes,' retorted Trollope, 'I dreamed of you.' An eyewitness, Justin McCarthy, noted in his *Reminiscences* (2 vols., 1899) that the lawyer 'could not puzzle Trollope, or bewilder him, or even cause him to lose his temper; nor did Trollope ever fail to give an effective and even droll answer to every effective and droll question' (*I & R* 39, 40–4). RCT

Butterwell, Mr, pleasant, middle-aged public servant who uses his tact to achieve a comfortable position with no enemies and some friends. He becomes a member of the Board of Commissioners of the General Committee Office, with Adolphus Crosbie replacing him as secretary. In *The Last Chronicle of Barset*, despite being snubbed, he eventually lends Crosbie £500. *SHA*
NCS

Buxton, Charles (1823–71), Liberal politician and something of a political mentor for Trollope, who reviewed his *The *Ideas of the Day on Policy* (1866) for the *Fortnightly Review* (January 1866). Trollope claimed that Buxton was instrumental in his decision to go in for politics in 1867 (*Auto* XVI) and steered him towards contesting Beverley, Yorkshire, in 1868. RCT

Byrne, Paddy, charged with making poteen, illicit whiskey, in the vicinity of Mohill, and, unable to pay his fine, sentenced to an indefinite period in Ballinamore jail. *MB* MRS

Byron, George Gordon, 6th Baron (1788–1824), best known for *Don Juan* (1819–24), which at first scandalized readers. In his Commonplace Book Trollope denounced the immorality of characters like his Corsair. Late in life he read Byron in the family circle (January 1877). His mother had idolized the poet and feuded with the Revd *Cunningham after he refused Byron's request to place a memorial tablet to his illegitimate daughter by Claire Clairmont in Harrow church. Frances Trollope's poem about the whole matter, *Salmagundi*, was published by N.

John Hall in 1975. In fiction Trollope mocked Byronic excesses in *The Eustace Diamonds*, where Lizzie Eustace dreams of a Corsair who would sweep her off her feet. Her candidate for the role, Lord George Carruthers, 'might have abused her to the top of his bent', but behaved like a coward and turncoat, 'no longer a Corsair but a brute' (LXIV).

RCT

Cairo, a favourite tourist destination, 'delightfully mysterious' city from which the group sets out to see the Pyramids. Also in *The Bertrams*, and where George Walker is sent for his sore throat. 'Pyramids', 'Walker' *TAC1, 2*   GRH

Caldigate, Daniel. Country squire at Folking, he is the undemonstrative but loving father of John, who buys his son's right of inheritance when they quarrel over John's debts. The two are reconciled when John proves his steadiness and maturity. Old Caldigate becomes an affectionate father to his daughter-in-law Hester and a great support to her during John's bigamy trial. *JC*
SRB

Caldigate, Daniel John, infant son of John and Hester who becomes temporarily 'nameless' while his legitimacy is questioned during his father's trial for bigamy. *JC*   SRB

Caldigate, George, nephew of Daniel, briefly considered as heir after John sold his right of inheritance. *JC*   SRB

Caldigate, John, eponymous hero, reckless and impulsive when young but maturing to become a settled country squire at Folking, Cambridgeshire. He quarrels with his father over gambling debts, sells his inheritance, and travels to Australia where he makes his fortune in gold. Flirtatious and naive, he is taken in by the dubious Euphemia Smith, with whom he lives for some years. Returning to England, he marries Hester Bolton despite resistance from her stern mother. His happy marriage is jeopardized when Euphemia Smith and former mining partner Timothy Crinkett charge him with bigamy. Largely because of Caldigate's misguided attempt at restitution, he is convicted and briefly imprisoned, but later pardoned. *JC*   SRB

Callander, Mrs. A fellow passenger on board the ship which takes John Caldigate to Australia, she warns him about Euphemia Smith. Caldigate later regrets that he did not listen to her. *JC*
SRB

Calvert, Marie. Inwardly loyal to her lover Adolphe Bauche, she marries the elderly Campan but commits suicide by leaping from rocks near the grotto where Adolphe forsook her. 'Bauche' *TAC1*   GRH

Cambridgeshire, setting for much of *John Caldigate* and the location of Folking, Utterden, Chesterton, and Puritan Grange. The land is flat, unattractive, and bisected by dikes. John Caldigate's trial is held here and his father expects the Cambridgeshire jury to be prejudiced, easily led, and rather stupid. *JC*   SRB

Cambridge University. Trollope's brother Henry gained a sizarship to Caius College (1830) but lasted there only a year because of the family's lack of money. Some fifteen of Trollope's fictional characters are Cambridge men, among them Frank Gresham (*DT*) and Gerald Palliser (*DC*). The most distinguished is Harry Clavering, a fellow of his college who played cricket for the Cambridge eleven and rowed in one of Trinity's boats (*C*). Charles Amedroz (*BE*) was sent down from Trinity. Dick Shand was obviously going wrong because he despised the University and left without a degree (*JC*). Cambridge's most despicable students were Obadiah Slope (*BT*), Louis Scatcherd, whose three terms failed to make him a gentleman (*DT*), and Augustus Scarborough, who was cordially disliked by everyone (*MSF*).   RCT

Cameron, Julia Margaret (née **Pattle**) (1815–79), born in Calcutta, married Charles Hay Cameron, jurist and member of the Supreme Council of India. With six children of her own and several adopted, she made her home a salon of art and letters. She took up photography when her daughter gave her camera equipment in 1863, and within a few months she was acclaimed for her portraits. She photographed Darwin, Tennyson, and Browning. In October 1864, she met the Trollopes while they were en route to Sir William *Pollock's house in the Isle of Wight, where the Camerons also lived. During the Trollopes' five-day stay on the island, Cameron secured a number of sessions, out of which emerged at least two photographs, 'one very familiar, hatless, and one relatively unknown, with a hat and with the same wrinkles in his jacket' (Super 176). Later the Trollopes and Cameron met socially at the Pollocks' London dinner parties (Glendinning 431).

RCT

Campan, Theodore ('le Capitaine'). Fifty-six, with a jet black wooden leg, he is persuaded by Mme Bauche to marry Marie Calvert, thus precipitating her suicide. 'Bauche' *TAC1*   GRH

Campbell, Dr John Logan (1817–1912), later Sir John, a prominent Auckland citizen who founded a successful mercantile business (*Letters* 2, 569). When the Trollopes visited Wellington in August 1872, they stayed at his home in central Auckland; Rose remained there while Trollope spent a fortnight visiting Maori settlements in the lake country. Trollope described bathing in the hot springs amidst welcoming Maori damsels (*ANZ* 2, XXIX). During the visit, Campbell supplied Trollope with a small writing room where he could work without interruption. Trollope spoke often of his disciplined habits, which Campbell remembered to the end of his life, but he did not talk about the travel book he was then writing. Campbell's unpublished memoirs commented on Trollope's strict routine, stating that he 'had no eyes for the beauties of nature' (*Letters* 2, 569 n.).

RCT

Camperdown, John, son and junior partner of Samuel Camperdown, the lawyer representing the Eustace estate in the dispute over Lizzie Eustace's infamous diamond necklace. John Camperdown later represents Lizzie in a suit against her bigamous husband Joseph Emilius. *ED*

JMR

Camperdown, Samuel Faithful lawyer representing the Eustace estate. Mr Camperdown sets in motion the dispute over the valuable diamond necklace held by Lizzie Eustace, insisting that the diamonds be returned to the estate for safe keeping. In his zeal, Mr Camperdown wishes to pursue the dispute almost against the wishes of the Eustace family. *ED*   JMR

Can You Forgive Her? (*see opposite*)

Canada. Trollope spent two short periods in Canada, in 1859 while returning from the West Indies, and about two and a half weeks in 1861, described in *North America*. He visited Quebec City, Montreal, Ottawa, Toronto, and Niagara Falls, and smaller communities along the St Lawrence river and Lake Ontario. The Falls impressed him immensely. Technically, the Canada of this time consisted only of the union of the two provinces of Upper and Lower Canada, and the rest of what is now Canada were separate colonies of British North America. These included New Brunswick, Nova Scotia, Prince Edward Island, and Newfoundland in the east, and Rupert's Land, the North-Western Territory, British Columbia, and Vancouver Island in the west.

Travellers, such as W. H. G. Kingston and Charles Dilke, who visited Canada in this period, like Trollope, contrasted, unfavourably, the quiet backwardness of the Canadian communities with the bustle and aggressive spirit of the American cities on their tours. Though many immigrants came to the Canadian provinces, a portion quickly continued on to the more economically promising American states. Partially for these reasons Canadian politicians were already beginning discussions which led to Canadian Confederation in 1867. Trollope supported Canada's independence from Britain. In *Phineas Finn* his hero at the Colonial Office is engaged in planning a railroad from Halifax to the Rockies (LIII).

LK

Brown, C. (ed.), *The Illustrated History of Canada* (1996).

Caneback, Major, officer in the Royal Horse Guards noted for dullness and horsemanship. He meets his match in the mare Jemima and dies slowly at Rufford Hall after a fall. Arabella Trefoil uses the accident to advance her intimacy with Lord Rufford, who pays the funeral expenses for the friendless man. *AS*   MG

Cann, Billy, one of the thieves involved in the theft of the Eustace diamonds. Billy Cann gives evidence against the principal culprits and is granted immunity for his own obscure role in the crime. *ED*   JMR

Cantor, Joseph (the younger), witness with his father to Indefer Jones's final will. His suspicious and accusing stares haunt Henry Jones, day and night. Letters, under his signature, form part of the *Carmarthen Herald*'s campaign against that interloper. *CH*   AWJ

Cantrip, Lady, long-time friend of the Palliser family who serves as a guardian for Lady Mary Palliser after the death of her mother, the Duchess of Omnium. Lady Cantrip's role as comforter is strained, however, by the interference of the Duke, who wishes her to act the part of duenna, protecting Lady Mary from an apparently disreputable marriage. Kindly and intelligent, Lady Cantrip realizes that it would be cruel and useless to separate Lady Mary from her beloved. She urges the Duke to reconsider his objections to his daughter's lover. *DC*   JMR

' **O** F *Can You Forgive Her?* I cannot speak with too great affection,' wrote Trollope in *An Autobiography*. 'The character of the girl is carried through with considerable strength, but is not attractive' (X). His confident tone is justified by the circumstances. Trollope's reputation was still growing, and at £3,525 his fee for this novel is among the highest he achieved. And with *Can You Forgive Her?* he launches on the second of his two great series: the Barset series with its concentration on church dignitaries and their domestic lives in and around a provincial town was still to reach its culmination in *The Last Chronicle of Barset*; in the new series the emphasis changes from Church to Parliament, and the setting moves largely from the provinces to London. The interaction of the professional life with the domestic, however, continues to be a major concern.

If Alice Vavasor, the main protagonist of *Can You Forgive Her?*, is 'not attractive', she was not meant to be, and her creator is satisfied. Josiah Crawley of *The Last Chronicle* is not attractive either, but he is nevertheless a great achievement in characterization. Alice is a girl with a problem, and she takes herself intensely seriously. For some readers, Lady Glencora Palliser, with her vivacity and her outspokenness, steals the show, and it is she who will figure largely in the subsequent novels as the Palliser series unfolds. The third lady of the triple plot is the cheerful widow Mrs Greenow, who, like the younger women, is faced with a choice of suitors.

Each of these women—maiden, wife, and widow—must choose between 'the worthy man and the wild man' (II). It is a familiar plot for Trollope, but this time he works out the pros and cons, the conflicting motives in reason and psychology, and the ironic parallels and contrasts, with more than his usual rich insight.

Alice Vavasor has a tendency to brood. She is motherless, her father neglects her, and she is much alone. While having strong moral principles, she is estranged from herself and out of touch with her real needs and desires. We hear of her that 'No woman had a clearer idea of feminine constancy than she had, and no woman had sinned against that idea more deeply' (LXXIV). If she is a jilt, as suggested by her changing engagements to two different men, her motives are noble, and she must be forgiven as a 'Noble Jilt'—the title of the play on the same theme that Trollope had written many years earlier.

The history of Alice's engagements is sufficiently complicated. Before the novel begins she was engaged to her cousin George Vavasor; but he behaved badly, and the engagement was broken off by mutual consent. At the opening of the novel she is engaged to John Grey. After a trip to Switzerland with George and Kate, his sister, Alice decides to end the engagement to Grey; and she re-engages herself to George. This engagement does not prosper either, and she finally breaks it and marries John Grey after all. Trollope follows her motives in each of these vacillations with fascinated attention.

Alice's 'worthy man', John Grey, is a Cambridge don and owner of a pleasant country estate; he is handsome, intelligent, well mannered, and well heeled. He has 'perfect command of himself at all seasons'—a degree of self-control that Alice finds rather daunting (XXXVI). He is steady in his love to her, even when she breaks their engagement, and persevering in winning her back. Her 'wild man', George Vavasor, has none of these advantages; but he makes the lack of them seem attractive. He has a scar on his face that becomes livid when he is moved; he is chronically short of money, but wants to take the expensive step of standing for Parliament as a radical; he is quick-tempered and violent; and he makes his second proposal to Alice not from an overmastering love but literally on the toss of a coin, because he is interested in her money and hates to lose her to Grey. He successfully presents himself to her as the 'brandy' in contrast to the 'milk diet' that Grey represents (V).

Alice's vacillations are agonizing to herself and the reader. Some critics have suggested that George is the powerfully sexual figure, and that her dilemma is the familiar one of passion against reason. But Trollope makes it very clear that George is physically repellent to her; his second proposal is made and accepted by letter, and when he is with her she will not return or even tolerate his caresses. But he is, as it were, politically attractive to her. Like several other women in the Palliser series, Alice longs for some action beyond the domestic sphere, but her world offers a paucity of opportunity. 'She was not so far advanced as to think that women should be lawyers and doctors, or to wish that she might have the privilege of the franchise for herself; but she had undoubtedly a hankering after some second-hand political manœuvring' (XI). In default of opportunities for first-hand political action, she must settle for second-hand; and George as radical candidate for a seat in Parliament is a cause she is ready to devote her money to. (She is more willing with her cash than her caresses.) The one great decision in life that women are allowed is the acceptance of a husband. To complicate, elaborate, and revise that decision is as close as Alice can get to political action, to doing something with her life (XI). That she is misguided in the choices she makes the novel proves at large. But her motives are explored, analysed, and respected.

Lady Glencora Palliser is already married to her worthy man, but is tempted to elope with the wild one. Before her marriage she had been in love with the strikingly handsome Burgo Fitzgerald, 'who had spent every shilling that anybody would give him, who was very fond of brandy, . . . who was said to be deep in every vice' (*SHA* LV); but since she was an heiress, young, and manipulable, her relatives detached her from him and made a marriage of convenience to the conscientious but colourless Plantagenet Palliser, heir to the Duke of Omnium. That part of her story was told late in *The Small House at Allington,* in which Palliser was first introduced as a character. Now Glencora is haunted by the sense of her loss, and the humiliation of having the most important choice of her life taken out of her hands. Her marriage is dreary, and her husband, who is a rising statesman and works late every night, is not good at making it absorbing. 'He was very dull. He rather prided himself on being dull, and on conquering in spite of his dullness. . . . If he was dull as a statesman he was more dull in private life' (XXIV). Such a husband is not likely to make his vivacious wife forget her handsome lost love, and when Burgo reappears in her life, and tries to persuade her to elope with him, she is deeply tempted.

The widow Mrs Greenow's two suitors serve as a parody of the more serious temptations of Alice and Lady Glencora. She is 40, and well off, and she values her independence. But she also admits, 'marriage is a comfortable thing'; and so she too is making a choice of suitors. Her worthy man is the burly farmer Mr Cheesacre, with his prosperous farm Oileymead; her wild man is 'Captain' Bellfield, who is chronically impecunious, and addicted to 'cigars and brandy-and-water' (brandy is a recurring trope for the wild men). She can see well enough that Cheesacre would be the prudent choice; but she also likes 'a little romance... —just a sniff, as I call it, of the rocks and valleys' (LXIV); and in spite of the brandy and cigars Bellfield has more of that whiff of romance than 'Cheesy'.

All three women have money; and the money seems to complicate their choices rather than to simplify them, for this is a society which makes it difficult for women to manage money, and removes that power altogether from the married woman. Alice cannot cash a bill without her father's agency, even though it is her money, for 'the City, by one of its mouths, asserted plainly that ladies' bills never meant business' (LX). These are all generous women, and their impulse is to lay their money out on those who need it rather than to accumulate more by marrying it. Each of them subsidizes her wild man at some point: it is her way of exerting a modicum of control. And, interestingly, the worthy men are all outraged, as by some lapse in chastity, at these financial transactions: they would rather pay off the wild men themselves. John Grey even arranges secretly that Alice's payments towards George's election expenses should come out of his pocket rather than hers. This can be seen as chivalry on the part of the worthy men; but it is also a means of winning power back into their own hands.

A little romance is to the taste of all three women, and their wild men, in being visible risks, offer it to them. There is some perversity in their leanings towards these dangerous suitors. Alice knows Grey is worthy and George is 'wild—very wild. And yet her thoughts were, I fear, on the whole more kindly towards her cousin than towards her lover' (II). Glencora 'knew Burgo Fitzgerald to be a scapegrace, and she loved him better on that account' (LXIX). For Mrs Greenow, 'strange to say, [Bellfield's] poverty and his scampishness and his lies almost recommended him to her' (XLVII). Each of them in her own way enjoys playing with fire. It seems that women relatively deprived of choice and action find some outlet for energy and passion in entertaining these temptations, as a soldier in a desk job hankers after action in battle.

However, Alice and Glencora are saved from their own perverse courage by their dull but devoted men. George realizes the latent violence always present in his character by shooting at Grey (and missing) and breaking his sister's arm, before heading for foreign parts, and Alice must submit to the mastery and forgiveness of John Grey, whose concession to her political ambition is to take to a seat in Parliament himself. Palliser nobly throws up his chance to be Chancellor of the Exchequer in order to take his wife on an extended holiday on the Continent, where she conceives a son and heir. Only Mrs Greenow, the widow who has a better chance of controlling her money, is allowed her sniff of the rocks and valleys: she marries her handsome scamp, and keeps him in order.

Notable minor characters include Kate Vavasor, who does all she can, and more than she should, to promote her brother George's marriage to Alice, while being herself so devoted to him that she cannot consider marriage. George's mistress Jane is treated with humane sympathy, though her role is a small one. In the cameo of Mr Pollock, the heavyweight literary man who wears out his hunters and bores his company with tales of novels written by candlelight, Trollope presents a wry self-portrait, like Hitchcock entering his own movies. The places too have their resonances, especially Matching Priory, the ruin near the comfortable country home of the Pallisers, where Glencora can indulge her romantic fantasies, and Basle in Switzerland, where the rushing Rhine makes Alice restless and rebellious.

A recurring theme, as Trollope unfolds his plot of women choosing, is a discontinuity between theory and reality, profession and performance, word and referent. George Vavasor, as we hear in a familiar Trollopian phrase, 'had taught himself some theories of a peculiar nature' (XXX), and he is not the only one. The three women who are persuading themselves to take an irrational step are reflections of a larger social tendency to create fictional constructs and to believe in them as reality. George as politician 'gets up' the subject of embanking the Thames as a project for his election as a member for Chelsea, but everyone knows this is a trumped-up issue that nobody really cares about. 'Of course it won't be done,' admits his agent serenely. 'But you can always promise it at the hustings, and can demand it in the House' (XLIV). This is the political dimension of Alice's merely verbal undertaking to marry a man she cannot bear to touch her: 'She had said that she would become George Vavasor's wife, but she wished that the saying so might be the end of it' (XXXIV). In the same way Glencora can convince herself that she would rather be 'a beggar' with Burgo than the rich wife of Palliser (XXVII); but when Burgo actually invites her to elope with him, 'words and things bore to her again their proper meaning', and she can recognize her constructed romance as merely a flight of fancy (L), and not a real programme for action. Trollope is exploring at the personal level the large social issues of propaganda and mass self-deception.

This first novel of the Palliser series provides opportunity for a brief lyrical intrusion by Trollope in his role as narrator. As George Vavasor takes up his hard-won seat for Chelsea, the narrator muses wistfully over the pillared entrance to the House of Commons: 'There are many portals forbidden to me, as there are many forbidden to all men; and forbidden fruit, they say, is sweet; but my lips have watered for no other fruit but that which grows so high' (XLV). By the time he had experienced his ill-starred election campaign for Beverley in 1868, Trollope himself may have been willing to concede that the forbidden fruit is much overrated. Even here he allows George Vavasor very little joy of his triumph. During his brief career as an MP he spends more of his time brooding on plans of personal revenge than on enterprises for the good of the nation. Trollope's ambivalence about grand schemes and romantic fantasies extends even to his political aspirations. It is surely not entirely accidental that a whist game among professional men should include 'Calder Jones the Member of Parliament, playing dummy' (XVI). The stirring and ennobling side of parliamentary politics is attached to Palliser, who serves his country by poring over blue books all night, and John Grey, who calmly accepts the pocket borough of Silverbridge virtually as a gift. But then these are the dull worthy men.

Social advancement, like political advancement, is treated with irony. Alice's father, the suave club man John Vavasor, who considers himself very ill used because he actually has to show up at this office occasionally in order to draw his salary of £800 a year, urges Alice to cultivate her relationship with the Pallisers: 'Everybody should endeavour to stand as well as he can in the world,' he urges Alice. 'If I had the choice of acquaintance between a sugar-baker and a peer, I should prefer the peer. . . . It's simply growing up, towards the light, as the trees do' (XXI). Thus he turns snobbery into a law of nature.

Trollope composed *Can You Forgive Her?*, as his working calendars show, between 16 August 1863 and 28 April 1864, and it ran in twenty serial numbers between January 1864 and August 1865. It was published in book form in two volumes by Chapman &

Hall in 1864. Hablot K. *Browne, better known as Dickens's frequent illustrator 'Phiz', illustrated the first volume, but he was past his prime, and Trollope chose a Miss E. Taylor to take over the illustration of the second. But the history of this novel's composition includes Trollope's failed attempt to become a playwright. His play *The Noble Jilt* is partly in blank verse, and it includes the first versions of the stories of Alice Vavasor and Mrs Greenow. (The names are all changed, except for that of Mrs Greenow's/Mme Brudo's maid Jeanette.) Trollope's friend the actor and stage manager George Bartley sternly rejected the play, adducing as his major objection that the character of Margaret, the noble jilt, 'meets but little sympathy' (*Auto* V). Although he claims to have accepted the judgement, Trollope was determined to find acceptance for this rejected product of his pen, and *Can You Forgive Her?* is partly the result of that determination. Bartley's judgement on the jilt as 'a most unbecoming character' probably accounts for his constant pleas, in the text as well as the title, that the reader should be ready to 'forgive' this erring heroine. The repeated pleas clearly irritated the young Henry James, who reviewed *Can You Forgive Her?* in the *Nation*: 'The question is, can we forgive Miss Vavasor? Of course we can, and forget her too, for that matter' (28 September 1865, 409–10). But Trollope was busy proving a point. In *The Eustace Diamonds* he again thrusts his rejected offspring into the limelight by sending his characters to see a production of *The Noble Jilt* ('from the hand of a very eminent author'), and allowing them to discuss it afterwards (*ED* LII).

The character of Lady Glencora Palliser, however, is original to *Can You Forgive Her?*, and it is she, Trollope says, who most endears the book to him. She, after all, became the dominating heroine of the new series, as the socially dull but psychologically interesting Plantagenet Palliser is its hero. 'I look upon this string of characters', wrote Trollope in reflective mood, '. . . as the best work of my life' (*Auto* X). The manuscript is in the Beinecke Library at Yale University.   JM

Levine, George, 'Can You Forgive Him? Trollope's *Can You Forgive Her?* and the Myth of Realism', *Victorian Studies* (September 1974), 5–30.
Morse, Deborah, *Women in Trollope's Palliser Novels* (1987).

Cantrip, Lord, long-time Liberal political colleague of the young Duke of Omnium. Serving primarily as Secretary of the Colonial Office, Lord Cantrip is notable for his good sense, his attachment to his work, and his loyalty. He is strong in defence of Phineas Finn when Phineas stands accused of murder. *PF, PR, DC*   JMR

Carbottle, Mr, Liberal parliamentary candidate who opposes Frank Tregear in the contest for Polpenno. He hopes to win by spreading about shillings from his heavy purse, but Tregear's agent prevents his generosity. *DC*   JMR

Carbuncle, Jane, aunt of Lucinda Roanoke and companion of Lizzie Eustace. Jane Carbuncle is a remarkably handsome woman, living in apparently genteel circumstances. An appropriate friend for Lizzie, Mrs Carbuncle's veneer of respectability conceals a somewhat less-than-genteel core. Constantly squabbling over money and marriage with her niece Lucinda, and living without her husband, there is a suggestion that Mrs Carbuncle may be involved in a romantic liaison with Lord George De Bruce Carruthers. *ED*   JMR

Carbury, Sir Felix, handsome, scapegrace son of Lady Carbury, unredeemed by a single act or word. Selfish and heartless, he has sufficient audacity to maintain an idle lifestyle, but gambling, drinking, and arrogance exhaust all friendships. Encouraged by his doting mother, he makes a listless attempt to pursue Marie Melmotte. He signs a despicable agreement with Augustus Melmotte to abandon Marie in return for promised wealth, but betrays both father and daughter, failing to elope with her after she has arranged the details. His dalliance with Ruby Ruggles results in a beating from her country lover, and this humiliation, added to his impecuniosity, finally forces him to slink off to Prussia. *WWLN*   SRB

Carbury, Henrietta (Hetta), meek daughter of Lady Carbury, who unjustly favours her son Felix despite Hetta's docile obedience. Passionately loved by her kind and gentlemanly cousin Roger, she nevertheless rejects his comfortable offer of marriage in favour of the younger and more adventurous Paul Montague. Sheltered, dutiful, and passive, she shows spirit and tenacity in this one act of resistance to her mother's wishes. *WWLN*   SRB

Carbury, Lady Matilda, false, well-meaning, ambitious woman who works hard to make her own way as an author. Her disturbing devotion to a worthless son, Felix, and emotional neglect of a deserving daughter, Hetta, are explained as resulting from her own sorrowful past as an abused and maligned wife. She indulges Felix's vices to the point of ruin, allowing herself and Hetta to be impoverished, yet makes Hetta feel that she is a burden for refusing to marry her cousin, whom she does not love. Lady Carbury's diplomacy, literary evenings, and carefully deployed wiles eventually win her the love of the editor Nicholas Broune, whose friendship improves her character. *WWLN*   SRB

Carbury, Roger, country squire of Carbury Manor in Suffolk. Trollope's ideal conservative gentleman, he espouses old-fashioned values, even living in a house surrounded by a moat. Respectable, honest, and confident, his role is largely that of rescuer, protector, and faithful friend to his family and tenants. He despises the way society lives now, running after the fame and money of the low-born swindler Melmotte. His deep love for his cousin Hetta proves his courage and nobility when he graciously concedes her preference for his own friend Paul Montague and resigns himself to bachelorhood. *WWLN*   SRB

Carbury Hall, small, unencumbered country estate of Roger Carbury, in Suffolk. The manor, an old Tudor building, is surrounded by a moat and is 'picturesque rather than comfortable'. The squire is very proud of its tradition and thoroughly established look. *WWLN*   SRB

card-playing. Domestic gatherings since the 18th century relied on card games for pleasant social intercourse. Trollope's fondness for cards developed in Ireland. Whist became a passion. Once elected to the Garrick he delighted 'to play a rubber in the little room upstairs of an afternoon . . . I think that without cards I should now be much at a loss' (*Auto* IX). Games were mostly played for shilling points. With fellow players at the Athenaeum Abraham Hayward, W. E. Forster,

and Sir George Jessel, Trollope was sketched by T. Walter Wilson. On one occasion Trollope joked to John Blackwood that he would give Mrs Blackwood lessons to improve her play. He wrote an article on the game, 'Whist at our Club', for *Blackwood's* (May 1877). Card-playing crops up in several novels. In *Sir Harry Hotspur of Humblethwaite* George Hotspur fleeces Mr Walker of £300 (XII). Cards are the downfall of Mountjoy Scarborough in *Mr Scarborough's Family*. In *The Duke's Children* Earl Grex has few pleasures left but cards and racing (IX), while his son Lord Percival lives from winnings at cards, taking £3,400 off Lord Gerald Silverbridge (LX). In narrowly religious circles, cards were frowned upon. Mrs Proudie was dismayed to hear of whist played in former days at the palace (*LCB* XLVII). Trollope was firmly in the opposite camp; 'if now and again I have somewhat recklessly fluttered a £5 note over a card-table;—of what matter is that to any reader?' (*Auto* XX).   RCT

Carlyle, Thomas (1795–1881), social prophet famed for his analyses of economic, political, and cultural questions of his age in such works as *Sartor Resartus* (1833–4) and *Past and Present* (1843). Trollope and Carlyle were not in sympathy. Trollope could never stomach his attacks on novelists, and Carlyle dubbed him 'Fat Trollope'. In 1851 Trollope declared *Latter Day Pamphlets* (1850) 'a grain of sense smothered in a sack of trash' (*Letters* 1, 29), and parodied him as Dr Pessimist Anticant in *The Warden*. Although he frequently countered the Sage's view of a downwardly spiralling society, Trollope manufactured some Carlylean thunder of his own in *The New Zealander*. But his review of Ruskin's *Sesame and Lilies* in *Fortnightly* (July 1865) caused Carlyle to explode to his wife, 'A distylish little pug, that Trollope; irredeemably imbedded in commonplace, and grown fat upon it, and prosperous to an unwholesome degree' (quoted *I & R* 128). This was four years after a meeting brought about by G. H. Lewes, when they got on well together, Carlyle having enjoyed Trollope's book on the West Indies. In March 1864 Trollope exclaimed of Carlyle, 'Oh, heavens;—what a mixture of wisdom & folly flows from him!' (*Letters* 1, 258).

RCT

'Carlylism, An Essay on' (article). The current idea that the world is progressively worsening is arguably inaccurate. People in general are not sloppier and/or less honest than in former times. As the population increases, the numbers of both the good and the less good will increase. In rebuttal to the argument that the increasing popularity of novel-reading illustrates generally lower standards of behaviour, the fact is that good literature illustrates the truth of one's duty to live virtuously. *Saint Pauls* (December 1869), 292–305. AKL

Carmarthen. Familiar with this country town through his postal duties, Trollope makes it a hive of gossip (on market-days) and speculation (at the Bush Inn) as to Henry Jones's right to his uncle's estate, and whether he will defend himself from public libel at the next assizes. *CH* AWJ

Carmichael, Catherine (Kate) (née **Baird**). Left destitute, Catherine Baird is obliged to marry the abusive Peter Carmichael. When she inherits his farm and money, she seeks out his cousin John, whom she has always loved. 'Carmichael' GRH

Carmichael, John, kind, hard-working lover of Catherine Baird, who eventually becomes her second husband. 'Carmichael' GRH

Carmichael, Peter, miserly, abusive sheep farmer who marries Catherine Baird, and is accidentally drowned. 'Carmichael' GRH

Carnlough, home of Mr Thomas Blake in Co. Galway where the murdered boy Florian Jones is carried. *L* MRS

Carrara, Italian commune famous for its marble where Bertie Stanhope has a workshop and can live cheaply. *BT* NCS

Carrick on Shannon, county town of Co. Leitrim, which holds the assize where Thady Macdermot is tried and executed for the murder of Myles Ussher. *MB* MRS

Carrick races, lively sporting event where Myles Ussher regales Fred Brown with his plan to run away with Feemy Macdermot. *MB* MRS

Carroll, Mrs, domineering wife of Captain Patrick Carroll and sister of Mr Grey. She and her scapegrace husband take a genteel house on the Fulham Road near her brother, who has to support her and her family. *MSF* MT

Carroll, Pat, Philip Jones's tenant. Carroll is a Landleaguer who refuses to pay rent, sabotages his landlord's property, and intimidates his son Florian, only to be released by the Crown when Florian, the main witness against him, is murdered by Carroll's friend Terry Lax, a known political assassin. *L* MRS

Carroll, Captain Patrick, brother-in-law to Mr Grey. 'An improvident, worthless, drunken Irishman' (XVI) who is 'vicious beyond cure' (XXXIV), Mr Carroll has to be financially supported by Mr Grey, who cares deeply for his sister. *MSF* MT

Carroll, Terry, murdered brother of Landleaguer Pat Carroll. He is killed in a crowded courtroom in Dublin, where he was to give evidence convicting his brother of flooding 80 acres (32 ha) of productive land at Morony Castle in return for a pardon and free passage to America. *L* MRS

Carroll family, six daughters of Captain Patrick Carroll, Amelia, Brenda, Georgina, Minna, Potsey, and Sophie. The eldest daughter, Amelia, 'entertained an idea that she was more of a personage in the world's eye than her cousin—that she went to more parties, which certainly was true if she went to any—that she wore finer clothes, which was also true, and that she had a lover' (XVIII). Sophie is 'a forward, flirting, tricky girl of seventeen, who had just left the school at which Uncle John had paid for her education' (XVIII). Georgina 'was sixteen and possessed of terrible vitality' (XVIII). *MSF* MT

Carruthers, Lord George De Bruce, dashing Byronic friend of Lizzie Eustace and Jane Carbuncle. Lord George is granted his title when his elder brother unexpectedly inherits the estate of Killiecrankie. A powerful, healthy man, scornful of aristocracy in general and given to hunting and to hanging about pretty women, Lord George has no visible means of support and is sometimes supposed to be a financial speculator. His rough but knowing manner and his unconventional lifestyle appeal to Lizzie, who thinks of him as her 'Corsair' and seeks unsuccessfully to lure him into marriage. *ED, PR* JMR

Carstairs, Lord, eldest son of Earl Bracy and student of Dr Wortle's at Bowick. His good nature and forthright character make him a favourite of all at school. Expelled from Eton, he returns to Bowick, where he befriends Mr Peacocke and falls in love with Mary Wortle. *DWS* RC

Carter, Mr, Protestant vicar visiting Ireland to oversee the administration of famine relief funds. *CR* MRS

cartoons and parodies. A writer's appearance in lampoons and satirical sketches is one measure of popularity. In Trollope's case publicity of this kind was widespread in the 1870s. His hirsute appearance and blustering manner was a gift to the cartoonists. The best-known cartoon was by Sir Leslie Ward, whose signature as 'Spy' accompanied drawings of many Victorian celebrities in *Vanity Fair*. Trollope's turn came in the issue of April 1873. James Pope Hennessy said he came out like 'an affronted Santa Claus who has just lost his reindeer' (*Anthony Trollope* (1971), 325). One cartoon by 'Sem' depicted him holding a

Trollope was often the subject of cartoons at the height of his fame in the late 1860s and early 1870s. Here 'Sem' had his subject clasping a huge quill pen. Trollope's hairy countenance and ferocious glare made him an easy target for caricature.

huge quill (*I & R* ills.). Another well-known illustration was by Frederick Waddy for *Once a Week* (1 June 1872), showing the novelist seated on a pile of his books with a puppet clergyman in his hand. Less well known is the cartoon showing him astride a train engine rushing through Australia, which appeared in the Melbourne *Punch* in August 1871. The caption reads 'The Good St Anthony', with a strapline 'The way that very fast writer, Mr Trollope, collected the information that enabled him to brand our girls as Gonerils and Regans.' A similar gibe in the South Africa *Observer* appeared on 13 September 1877. The drawing shows Trollope in a colourful magician's costume lifting a conical funnel (like a dunce's cap) marked 'A few months interval' from a pile of papers labelled 'rapid survey', 'hearsay', 'club gossip', and 'native tradition'. The caption reads 'A novel trick' and ' "There is no deception. I place the cover over these materials. On its removal you will find them transformed into my second colonial success." ' The cartoon is reproduced in *South Africa*, ed. J. H. Davidson (Cape Town, 1973). Trollope featured in *Punch* (11 March 1871; 20 June and 28 August 1874). He was also the subject of Linley *Sambourne's 'Fancy Portraits' No. 17, *Punch* (5 February 1881), with the legend 'O Rare for Anthony!' Parodies were also plentiful in the 1870s. Cecil Hay depicted Trollope as Mr Grizzly, 'pleasantest of romance writers, and gruffest and roughest of conversationalists' (*The Club and Dining Room*, 2 vols. (1870), 1, 236). Henry *O'Neill, an old friend, produced a dialogue dedicated to Trollope, *Satirical Dialogues* (1870), featuring vigorous exchanges between Painter and Writer on late nights, laziness, and the comparative merits of Art and Letters (*Chron* 170–8). These are friendly tributes. Parodies, like cartoons, can also signify a celebrity has been around a bit too long. The most famous *Punch* parody was by Francis *Burnand, 'The Beadle—or, The Latest Chronicle of Small-Beerjester by Anthony Dollop' and ran from 8 May to 16 October 1880 in nineteen instalments, 'Fishy Fin', 'The Prying Minister', 'He Knew He Could Write', and 'Can't You Forget Her?' Cartoons by Linley Sambourne accompanied several instalments. Swinburne amused his friends with obscene names for Trollope's Barchester clerics (*The Swinburne Letters*, ed. Cecil Lang (1959), 2, 87, 108, 141).   RCT

Cartwright, Mr, Englishman who regularly stays with Frau Frohmann and gives her practical financial advice. 'Frohmann' *WFF*   GRH

Casalunga, hilltop house seven miles (11 km) outside Siena to which Louis Trevelyan retreats with his son. It is an isolated, unattractive spot,

whose residents 'thought more of the produce of their land than of picturesque or attractive appearance' (LXXVIII). See p. 537. *HKWR*   RC

Cashel, Lady, mother of Lady Selina Grey and Lord Kilcullen, a nondescript figure who passes a listless existence. She 'slept the greatest portion of her time, and knitted through the rest' (XIV). When her niece Fanny Wyndham attempts to solicit some confidential advice concerning her future, so overwhelmed is she by the task that she promptly turns the matter over to her husband Lord Cashel. *KOK*   MRS

Cashel, Lord, pompous, voluble father of the dissolute Lord Kilcullen, and guardian of Fanny Wyndham, who persuades his ward to break off her engagement with Lord Ballindine because of his gambling. Well respected on account of his 'external dignity of appearance' (XI) and solemn demeanour, he walks the high moral ground, yet finds it convenient to propose a match between his unprincipled, debt-ridden son and his newly enriched ward. *KOK*   MRS

Casseway, Miss, elderly companion and would-be guardian of Lady Mabel Grex. Miss Casseway struggles valiantly to provide Lady Mabel with motherly guidance and support but is often thwarted in her attempts by the combined conditions of her own dependency and Lady Mabel's experience. *DC*   JMR

Cassidy, Mr, agent for Lord Birmingham, Mohill's absentee landlord. Though he lives in a large, comfortable house, Mohill's rack-rented tenants do not resent him, for they realize he is only an agent, and that within his limited power he is 'as good to the poor as he can be' (IX). MB   MRS

Castle Corry, the seat of Lord and Lady Altringham in Scotland visited by George Hotspur. *SHH*   MG

Castle Morony, Irish property purchased by Philip Jones, an Englishman, which becomes the setting for hostility against landlordism by local Landleaguers who refuse to pay rent, flood 80 acres (32 ha) of meadowland, and finally boycott the property. *L*   MRS

Castlemorris, seat of the Earl of Tulla in Co. Clare, Ireland. *PF*   JMR

Castle Reekie, family home of the Marquis and Marchioness of Auld Reekie. *CYFH*   JMR

Castle Richmond, idealized Irish estate on the river Blackwater, near Kanturk, Co. Cork, property of an English lord, Sir Thomas Fitzgerald. Prosperous and well stocked, it forms the setting for a drama of dispossession: the spectre posed by English fears over political agitation for tenant ownership of Irish land. *CR* MRS

Castle Richmond (*see opposite*)

Castlewell, Lord, confirmed roué who, despite his reputation for taking attractive young singers as mistresses, proposes to Rachel O'Mahony in good faith, only to be rejected by her. *L* MRS

Cathelineau, Mme Françoise, mother of the Vendeans' charismatic leader, bitter at his involvement in the rebellion and death, but somewhat placated by Agatha Larochejaquelin's declared love for him. *LV* GRH

Cathelineau, Jacques (based on historical figure), the Saint-Florent postillion. Much loved by the populace, he is elected as leader by the mix of aristocrats and others despite his humble origins. He is wounded at Nantes, and taken to the hospital at Saint-Laurent. On his deathbed he declares his love for Agatha Larochejaquelin. *LV* GRH

'Catherine Carmichael: or, Three Years Running', first published in the *Masonic Magazine*, December 1878, a rugged tale of New Zealand emigrant life. Catherine Baird is left alone in the world when her gold-digger father drinks himself to death. She is taken to wife by a sheep farmer, Peter Carmichael, an old man who treats her as his chattel. Although she is a good wife, Catherine secretly loves Peter's young cousin John Carmichael. When Peter is drowned, everything is left to John, nothing to the wife. After some awkwardness, John proposes and she becomes Catherine Carmichael for the second time. JS

Cauldkail Castle, country residence of Lord Gaberlunzie, surrounded by bleak mountains of Aberdeenshire and heartily disliked by his family. *TC* RCT

Cauvin, Joseph (d. 1875). Reader for William Longman, he reported favourably on *The Warden*, then called *The Precentor*. Of *The New Zealander* he wrote in April 1855 that it was a feeble imitation of Carlyle. He found *Barchester Towers* marred by vulgarity and thought Signora Vesey Neroni 'a great blot on the work'. He called for rigorous cutting. Mortified, Trollope agreed to attend to the vulgarities, but objected to reducing the manuscript by one-third (*Letters* 1, 45–7). RCT

Cavendish, Lord Frederick Charles (1836–82). Economic depression in *Ireland led to strong pressure for independence. Charles Stewart *Parnell became President of the Irish Land League (1879). The League advocated withholding rents, strike action, ostracism, while its extremists maimed cattle, flooded land, and even murdered. In 1881, Parnell was jailed in Dublin and the Land League outlawed. A few days after his release, in May 1882, the new Chief Secretary for Ireland, Lord Frederick Cavendish, and the Permanent Under-Secretary, T. H. Burke, were murdered in Phoenix Park, Dublin, eleven days before Trollope arrived with Florence *Bland to collect background material for *The Landleaguers*. Trollope included an account of the murder in his novel, commenting: 'I do not know why the deaths of two such men as were then murdered should touch the heart with a deeper sorrow than is felt for the fate of others whose lot is lower in life . . . But so it is with human nature' (XXXIX). RCT

Caversham, country estate of the Longestaffe family in Suffolk. Oppressive and ostentatious, the large mansion lends credibility to the family's extravagance. Social propriety is stretched when the Longestaffes actually invite the dubious Melmottes to this country home, rather than merely entertaining them in London. *WWLN* SRB

Cawston, parish in Devon about two miles (3 km) from Baslehurst. Cawston is located between Bragg's End, the hamlet where the Rays live, and the larger town of Baslehurst. *RR* MT

Cedars, the, the imposing but dreary and unkempt estate of impoverished Sir John Ball at Twickenham. *MM* SRB

Cervantes, Miguel (1547–1616), Spanish author of *Don Quixote* translated into English in 1612. Trollope's Commonplace Book, kept between 1835 and 1840, referred to Italian and Spanish writers of the past, including Cervantes. Responding to a toast by Earl Russell at the Royal Literary Fund's anniversary dinner in 1864, Trollope remarked that 'If any man has trod upon the heel of Cervantes it is Thackeray' (Super 174). In *An Autobiography* he wrote: 'I know no character in fiction, unless it be Don Quixote, with whom the reader becomes so intimately acquainted as with Colonel Newcombe' (XIII). What was faulty in Cervantes (as in Fielding) was episodes that distracted the reader disagreeably (XII). Trollope often relies on the standard allusion to tilting at windmills, as in the case of Senator Gotobed's strictures on English institutions (*AS* LXXX). RCT

Cetywayo (or **Cetshwayo**) (1826–84), de facto ruler of Zululand after 1857, was formally installed as king by Sir Theophilus Shepstone in 1873. In 1878 British troops invaded his territory, (*cont. on page 91*)

TROLLOPE's third Irish novel was begun in 1859, at the point when Trollope was at last coming into his own. It may be no coincidence that it is a story about inheritance and one that turns on a son's escaping from the blight that has over-shadowed his parents' lives.

Sir Thomas Fitzgerald, who owns an estate north of Cork, is a kindly but vulnerable man. For years he has been blackmailed by a father and son called Mollett, who threaten that it is in their power to disclose information that will bring ruin on the whole family. When the story opens Sir Thomas has reached a state of nervous col-lapse and it is his weakness, rather than his exercise of authority, that dominates the household.

The secret which has been used to terrorize Sir Thomas concerns his wife Lady Fitzgerald and it centres on the question of marriage. Her first husband may not have been dead when she married Sir Thomas, and in consequence Herbert and his sisters may not be legitimate, and Herbert unable to inherit as heir. But the sense of outraged delicacy exhibited by Sir Thomas in regard to his wife, his distress at having her even spoken of by a man like Mollett, strike a distinctly hysterical note. They seem to refer to an anxiety that cannot be named, unlike the risk of losing the estate, an anxiety about sexual intimacy itself, which is a quite different sort of secret.

The action of the novel ostensibly centres on the mystery of identity and inherit-ance: the Molletts are pursued to London and the secrets of their own past are un-veiled, but not before Sir Thomas has died and Herbert has been obliged to consider himself illegitimate. This disaster also meant that he risked losing the girl he loved, Lady Clara Desmond, the daughter of the widowed Countess of Desmond, who lives close by. The lonely impoverished Countess, who is still a beautiful woman, is herself in love with another of her daughter's suitors, Owen Fitzgerald, master of the local hunt, the man who would inherit both Castle Richmond and the title in Herbert's place. Once the threat to Herbert's legitimacy is removed by successful detective work on the part of his lawyers, he is free to marry Clara, but there is no question of the Countess marrying Owen, who goes off to Africa to shoot game.

These rather melodramatic issues of private experience are presented in tandem with a disaster of national proportions. The novel is set in the period of the Irish famine, the greatest peacetime catastrophe in Europe since the Black Death, and the action takes place around Mallow, the town where Trollope himself lived from 1849, towards the close of the famine years.

It is hard to disentangle the personal from the political in this novel. On the surface it presents a conventional fiction, where blackmailing villains and bigamous marriages threaten to shame the older generation and to prevent a set of young heroes and heroines from getting married, as if that was all they had to do to be happy. Yet that story is counterpointed by the business of famine relief, with which even the younger generation get involved when they set up a soup kitchen, and by images of desolation, to be found not only in the human figures of the starving and humiliated Irish but written into the landscape itself.

Towards the end of the novel, Herbert, the young heir, takes refuge from the wea-ther in a cabin, to find himself in the presence of a dying mother sitting by the corpse of her elder child, Kitty (XXXIII). That image has come to stand for *Castle Richmond* as a whole, for it is one incident that readers cannot forget. At the time Herbert is still not sure of his future, so his personal distress is linked by association with the suffering of the mother in the cabin, just as the main plot had linked his uncertain future with sorrows in his own mother's past. Both linkages suggest, as does the seamed and exhausted landscape Herbert views in the course of the same journey, that there are questions to be asked about the history that has brought this universal dereliction into being. What past has ground the virtue out of the fields and brought the landlord's son and his tenants to sit side by side in their despair?

The authorial voice Trollope adopts in this novel is one that firmly supports the British government in its handling of the famine. In the newspapers too he had published essays defending the policy of his government. In the final chapter of *Castle Richmond* he did not balk at describing the famine as a divine visitation which had in the end done good. Nevertheless, a different voice can be heard in the novel too, one that cannot so easily make terms with the fact that England took over Ireland by force and has kept it for many centuries as a possession.

When it gives the ancient names of Desmond and Fitzgerald to the landowning families in *Castle Richmond*, this voice carries an echo from that history and brings it into the account of present experience framed by the novel. The last serious armed opposition to English rule in Ireland had been offered by Gerald Fitzgerald, the last Earl of Desmond, a rebel who fought against Queen Elizabeth I and was driven off the lands that had been owned by his family in Kerry and killed in a cabin in the Kerry mountains in 1583. When Trollope writes a novel that asks whether the English heir really has got the right to inherit the Fitzgerald estate outside Mallow, he is voicing a question that is implicit in the history of Ireland's colonization at the hands of the English.

No novel of Trollope's was written in more charged circumstances, for when he began *Castle Richmond*, on 4 August 1859, he already knew that after nearly 20 years in Ireland, the place where he had been able to make good at last, he was about to leave and take up residence in England again. He had signed the lease on Waltham House in Essex a few days earlier. He was about to put his mature identity as a successful man to the test. This made him almost excessively alert to every opportunity. When he had completed the first volume of *Castle Richmond*, on 1 September, he interrupted himself to write short stories that he hoped to publish first in *Harper's New Monthly Magazine* in America, before bringing them out in a collection at home. Then, at the beginning of November, came the opportunity to write a serial novel for the new *Cornhill Magazine*, half of which had to be ready for the printers by Christmas. Before the New Year he was back at work on *Castle Richmond* and had finished it by 31 March, getting back the next day to *Framley Parsonage*, the sort of 'English' novel that George Smith, his publisher, knew was what readers really wanted.

Castle Richmond did not get much critical attention, though the *Saturday Review* observed that the most engaged writing in it concerned the famine. Within a few months *Mudie's were selling it off at nine shillings.

On the back of the working diary for this novel, Trollope drew up a plan dividing each volume into fifteen chapters: chapter XV 'Diplomacy' was intended to close the first volume and chapter XXX 'Pallida Mors', dealing with the death of Sir Thomas, was meant to have closed the second. Though he apparently intended to devote three chapters in the last volume to a fox-hunting sequence, in the event he could only spin the material out for two, leaving his last volume rather short; he preferred to shift the volume endings, rather than leave an impression of a scanty third volume.

On 2 August 1859 Chapman & Hall gave £600 for three years' copyright and a half-share in perpetuity of the still unwritten *Castle Richmond*, payable on publication, which it was agreed should take place in May of the following year. The manuscript was to be in their hands by the end of March, a deadline that Trollope only missed by a few days. Sadleir noted two different versions of the first edition of *Castle Richmond* in a purple-grey cloth binding and suggested that leftover first edition sheets were also issued in a dark green cloth. On 13 July 1860 the novel came out in a single volume at five shillings and by 1866 it could be bought for half a crown in cloth or two shillings as a 'yellowback'. The manuscript of *Castle Richmond* has not survived. It is not part of a series.   MH

Kelleher, M., '*Castle Richmond*: Famine Narrative and Horrid Novel', *Irish University Review*, 25/2 (1995), 242–62.
Overton, B., *The Unofficial Trollope* (1982).
Terry, R. C., *Anthony Trollope: The Artist in Hiding* (1977).

suffering a massacre at Isandhlwana. Trollope had foreseen much of that tragedy during his African tour and published an article, 'Kafir Land', in the *Fortnightly*, 1 February 1878. In March 1879, debate on Sir Charles Dilke's House of Commons motion censuring the conduct of Sir Bartle Frere in his war against Cetywayo, and that of the government in not recalling him, came to an end. Barely anyone, even on the Conservative side, spoke up for Frere, most people believing the war a blunder largely due to his provocation. In April 1879, Trollope wrote to Alexander Ireland: 'We are here all elated by the effect of the last . . . debate' (*Letters* 2, 821). To G. W. *Rusden he praised Frere as an individual, but denounced British action in Natal: 'we have already slaughtered 10000 of them, and rejoice in having done so. To me it seems like civilization gone mad!' (*Letters* 2, 826). In his one-volume abridgement of *South Africa* (1879), Trollope added a chapter, 'Zululand', in which he attacked Frere's policies. Lecturing in Nottingham in October 1879, Trollope was warmly applauded for condemning virtual genocide by Britain. In January 1880, Frere sent Trollope 105 pages of criticism on his interpretation of events in *South Africa*.   RCT

Chadwick, John, worthy steward to the Bishop of Barchester who farms property attached to Hiram's Hospital. Descended from a respected family, he holds a high position in Barchester society and is regarded by London lawyers as representing the temporalities of the diocese. With his wife and three daughters, he attends Mrs Proudie's reception and Miss Thorne's fête in *Barchester Towers*. W, FP   NCS

Chaffanbrass, Mr, barrister who first appears in *The Three Clerks* defending Alaric Tudor. His great skill is in browbeating witnesses in court. 'To apply the thumbscrew, the boot, and the rack to the victim before him was the work of Mr Chaffanbrass's life' (XL). He also defends Lady Mason in *Orley Farm* and Phineas Finn in *Phineas Redux*.   MT

Chaldicotes, Nathaniel Sowerby's country estate in West Barsetshire. The mansion, a large stone building of the time of Charles II, eventually becomes the home of Dr and Mrs Thomas Thorne. *FP, LCB*   NCS

Chamberlaine, Henry Fitzackerly, prebendary of Salisbury Cathedral and a wealthy, handsome bachelor who is popular with his congregation. He is self-indulgent, fussy, and careful of his comforts and happiness. Upon the matter of the controversial chapel built in his nephew Harry Gilmore's neighbourhood, he is eloquent but slightly overbearing. *VB*   SRB

Chambers Brothers, Robert (1802–71) and **William** (1800–83), founders of the publishing house of W. & R. Chambers, Edinburgh, in 1832. In the same year Robert established *Chambers's Edinburgh Journal*. He wrote widely on Scottish history, biography, and literature and was anonymous author of the bitterly attacked *Vestiges of Creation* (1844). William Chambers produced a multitude of cheap educational works, including *Chambers's Encyclopaedia* in 1859. In August 1868 Trollope met Robert at a large party hosted by John *Blackwood.   RCT

Chambers's Edinburgh Journal. In February 1832, publishers William and Robert Chambers began this weekly, eight-page miscellany, published each Saturday, and sold for 1½d. It was a highly successful Scottish literary and 'useful knowledge' miscellany, with a circulation of over 55,000, containing essays on a wide variety of literary, historical, and scientific subjects. Poetry, fiction, and biography made up the literary portion. Early numbers contained material reprinted from other sources, and the contributors were not of the first rank. Later numbers contained original material. After 1854, it continued as *Chambers's Journal of Popular Literature, Science and Art.* Its success in Edinburgh led to the establishment of a similar popular weekly, *Chambers's London Journal.* JWM

Chapeau, Jacques. Servant to Henri Larochejaquelin, he recruits for the Vendean cause, courts Annot Stein, displays constant resourcefulness, and finally, having married Annot, becomes a barber in Paris. *LV* GRH

Chapman, Edward (1804–80), bookseller and, with William Hall, co-founder of the publishing house Chapman & Hall (1830) of Piccadilly, which launched Dickens's career with *Pickwick Papers* (1836) and was his main publisher thereafter. When Trollope marched into Chapman hoping to sell him *The Three Clerks*, the publisher thought the experience was like facing a highway robber on Hampstead Heath (*Auto* VI), and held a poker in his hand during the interview. RCT

Chapman, Frederic (1823–95). Replacing his cousin Edward in managing the publishing house Chapman & Hall (1864), he suggested Trollope should help launch the *Fortnightly Review.* In their long relationship, the house published 22 of Trollope's novels, 4 travel books, 2 short story collections, 3 books of sketches, and 1 biography. In 1869 Trollope paid £10,000 to buy his son Henry a third-share in the company, noting wryly that the name should have been Chapman & Trollope (*Letters* 2, 86). Henry's partnership lasted under four years. Trollope grew increasingly dissatisfied with the firm's losses. He became a director of the limited company (1880) but found the work intolerable (*Letters* 2, 867). Alluding to this time, W. Lucas Collins said the company's affairs 'worried and disgusted him' (*I & R* 163). Chapman, gazetted for bankruptcy, had to resign from the Garrick Club, but Trollope stood by him. Chapman was among mourners at his funeral. RCT

Chapman, Robert William (1881–1960), critic and editor, best known for his works on Jane Austen and Dr Johnson. His studies of Trollope from the 1920s concentrated on correcting texts of many novels. RCT

'Characters and Criticisms by James Hannay' (review). This book is a collection of previously published essays, most quite admirable. The work shows the author's scholarship, skill, and industry; but there is too much party loyalty to be truly fair. Hannay overpraises Lord Eglinton (a Tory) and is ill-tempered toward the Russells because he disagreed with them. *Fortnightly Review* (1 September 1865), 255–6. AKL

charity and philanthropy, though often derided by novelists, were central to the Victorian welfare system. The middle classes were its chief pillars, generosity being a religious duty, an advertisement of prosperity, and an avenue of social advancement, as well as insurance against social upheaval. Charity being regarded as a particularly feminine vocation, fund-raising, bazaars, and home visiting provided socially sanctioned activities outside the home for women. The proliferation of charities raised concern that the poor would be 'demoralized' by excessive or too accessible relief. The Charity Organization Society was founded as a watchdog in 1869 and its volunteer investigators were forerunners of modern social workers. Charity bazaars were not to Trollope's taste. He depicts one scornfully in the chapter 'The Negro Soldiers' Orphan Bazaar' in *Miss Mackenzie* (XXVII). CK

Owen, David, *English Philanthropy 1660–1960* (1964).

'Charles Dickens' (article). The death of Dickens seems as sudden as did that of his friend Thackeray; he spoke last week at the Royal Academy, and spoke well. His arrangements with publishers should he not finish *Edwin Drood* illustrate both his fear and his integrity. Details of his life and critiques of his work are not necessary here, as they are available elsewhere. His immense popularity during his lifetime is a tribute to his understanding of art and human nature. His characters are as famous and familiar as Shakespeare's. Every household knows Mr Micawber, Mr Pecksniff and Sam Weller, Mrs Gamp, and Inspector Bucket. Dickens has occasionally been criticized for his word choice or exaggeration—but the greatness of his art overwhelms all such 'rules' of writing. He avoided politics; he believed social improvement moves upward from individuals, not down from government. He had no honorary titles, nor would have accepted any. His greatness was in himself and the regard in which he was held by readers everywhere. His loss will become only more evi-

Frederic Chapman. Long association with the publishers Chapman & Hall resulted in publication of 32 books by Trollope, beginning with *Doctor Thorne* in 1858. Trollope became a director in 1880. Frederic, cousin of the founder, joined with Trollope and others in establishing the *Fortnightly Review* in 1865.

dent with time. *Saint Pauls* (17 July 1870), 370–5.
AKL

'Charles Reade and *Shilly-Shally'* (letters).
1. My friend the author Charles Reade has announced he is producing a play, *Shilly-Shally*, adapted from my novel *Ralph the Heir*. While he means to share the credit, I was not consulted, have not consented, and do object on the grounds of fairness. *Pall Mall Gazette* (16 July 1872), 5.
2. Mr Reade has objected to your review of his play (listed jointly as mine) as 'indelicate'. This play was not authorized nor authored at all by me; it was adapted from a novel of mine without request or consent. *Daily Telegraph* (6 August 1872), 3. Both reprinted *Letters* 2, 562–3.   AKL

Chase of Chaldicotes, once an ancient forest near the Chaldicotes estate of Nathaniel Sowerby; the Crown has sold the timber and land. The purchase becomes a bone of contention between the Duke of Omnium and Martha Dunstable, finally won by the lady. *FP*   NCS

'Chateau of Prince Polignac, The', first serialized in Cassell's *Illustrated Family Paper*, 20 and 27 October 1860 (reprinted in *TAC1*). An English widow, Mrs ('Fanny') Thompson, has retired with her two daughters to live in the French town of Le Puy, where she is wooed by a local merchant, M. Lacordaire. He takes her and her younger daughter Mimmy on an excursion to the ruined castle at Polignac and proposes. Mrs Thompson has snobbish doubts about accepting him when she discovers that he is a tailor. But eventually she sees the wisdom of becoming Mme Lacordaire. Trollope returned to the theme in *Lady Anna* (1874).   JS

Châtillon-sur-Sèvre, small town used as headquarters by the Vendean leaders after Durbellière was retaken. *LV*   GRH

Chatto & Windus (1855–   ). Under Andrew Chatto the house published cheap editions of Trollope's novels at 3*s*. 6*d*. and in yellowbacks at 2*s*. In 1876 he bought the magazine *Belgravia* from John Maxwell. He was among the enterprising publishers who helped end the three-volume novel system. He brought out cheap editions of *The American Senator* at 6*s*. in one volume (1877) and *Marion Fay* at 2*s*. (1884). He also published *Kept in the Dark*, in two volumes, at 12*s*. (1882); *Mr Scarborough's Family*, in three volumes (1883); *The Landleaguers*, in three volumes (1883).   RCT

Chaucer, Geoffrey (*c*.1343–1400), creator of *The Canterbury Tales* (first printed by Caxton in 1477), which Trollope was accustomed to reading

aloud to his family. He made a record of the selections from October 1876 to April 1882. His list for January 1877 includes 'Canterbury Tales, Knights Tale, Squires Tale, Merchaunts Tale, &c' (*Letters* 2, 1033). He frequently used the patient Griselda motif, notably in *Miss Mackenzie* (for which it served as working title), *The Last Chronicle of Barset* (XXXIII), *He Knew He Was Right* (XI), *The Eustace Diamonds* (XXII), *The Duke's Children* (XXV).   RCT

Cheekey, John ('Supercilious Jack'). His reputation as a cross-examiner at the Old Bailey terrifies Henry Jones as he awaits their encounter in Carmarthen's assize court. *CH*   AWJ

Cheesacre, Samuel, one of two rivals competing for the hand and fortune of Arabella Greenow. Mr Cheesacre is certainly the less romantic of the two suitors but tries to make up for his indifferent charms by constantly reminding Mrs Greenow of his comfortable financial position, even condescending to show her the rich piles of manure in his farmyard. *CYFH*   JMR

Cheltenham, sleepy town wherein Lady Macleod keeps her modest home. The apartments are a little cramped and a little too close to the stables, but still respectable. Its best rooms are given up to Alice Vavasor when she makes her annual visit. *CYFH*   JMR

Cheshire. Revd Granger's parish of Plumstock is in Cheshire, close to Liverpool and the Cotton Famine. 'Widow' *LS*   GRH

Chesney, Sir George Tomkyns (d. 1895), military officer (promoted general in 1892), who served mainly in India. Trollope's setting for *The Fixed Period* may have been influenced by Chesney's 'The Battle of Dorking, or Reminiscences of a Volunteer'. Published in *Blackwoods Magazine* (May 1871) shortly before Samuel Butler's *Erewhon* (1872), Chesney's imaginary German invasion of England made a case for national defence volunteers. Trollope referred to this story in *The Life of Cicero*: 'In truth, the great doings of the world do not much affect individual life. We should play our whist at our clubs though the battle of Dorking were being fought' (1, X). Another reference occurs in his life of Palmerston (XIII, quoted Super 414).   RCT

Chesnut, Mrs Mary Boykin (1823–86). Wife of James Chesnut, Jr., Senator for Alabama and aide to Jefferson Davies, Mrs Chesnut kept a journal during the Civil War. Trollope was a favourite. After devouring an instalment of *Framley Parsonage* in February 1861, she wrote, 'How much I owe of the pleasures of my life to these much reviled writers of fiction.' Towards the end of 1863 she caught up on the last part when a friend smuggled a copy of *Cornhill Magazine* through a naval blockade; 'He knew how much I was interested in Trollope's story' (quoted Mullen 372). RCT

Chesterton, village near Cambridge and location of Puritan Grange, home of the Bolton family. *JC* SRB

'Child Care' (article). In reference to the article ('Babyland') proposing a wide-scale baby-care programme, the cost estimates cited seem too low, and the recommended level of care not possible on a large scale. *Saint Pauls* (November 1869), 214. AKL

Chiltern, Violet, Lady (née **Effingham**). The attractive, sprightly, intelligent, independent young woman is an heiress, an orphan, and an expert, fearless horsewoman. A childhood friend of Oswald Standish, she is urged by his sister and her friend Laura to marry him. She sees no reason why it is her duty to marry a man to save him. She claims to distrust Lord Chiltern but actually distrusts her own wild streak. She attracts many suitors including Chiltern's friend Phineas Finn and the dull Lord Fawn. Conversations between Violet and Laura about marriage's dangers for women are some of Trollope's most probing. Violet's reservations are serious but never cynical. To the delight of Chiltern and his family, and the horror of her aunt and erstwhile guardian Lady Baldock, Violet finally accepts Chiltern. In *Phineas Redux* she has accomplished the difficult task of having domesticated her husband without taming him. *PF, ED, AS* MG

Chowton Farm. Purchased by his grandfather from the Mortons, the 320 acres (130 ha) are farmed by Lawrence Twentyman. The prosperity of Chowton makes Twentyman an appealing suitor to her parents, if not to Mary Masters herself. *AS* MG

Christmas. Despite complaining of the 'humbug implied by the nature of the order' (*Auto* XX), Trollope wrote eight Christmas stories for the magazine market, and a ninth, *Harry Heathcote of Gangoil*, dealing with 'Christmas at the antipodes'. The festivities at Noningsby in *Orley Farm* (XIX) reflect those he organized at Waltham Cross in the early 1860s. PJT

'Christmas at Thompson Hall', first published in the *Graphic*, December 1876 (reprinted in *WFF*). The Browns have retired to Pau in France. They are invited to a Christmas in Mrs Brown's family home, Thompson Hall at Stratford-le-Bow. Mr Brown is petulant. In a Paris hotel he complains bitterly of a sore throat.

His wife resourcefully raids the dining room at one o'clock in the morning to fetch mustard for a plaster. On her return she mistakes rooms and puts the plaster on a sleeping stranger. Embarrassment ensues, and is multiplied when Mrs Brown's victim, Mr Barnaby Jones, reappears at the Thompson Hall Christmas party. JS

'Christmas Day at Kirkby Cottage', first published in Routledge's *Christmas Annual*, 1870. A Christmas story, set in the household of the Revd John Lownd, at Kirkby Cliffe in Yorkshire. Maurice Archer is set to propose to the daughter of the house, Isabel ('Bell') Lownd. But a rift develops between the lovers when he brusquely observes that 'After all, Christmas is a bore' and ignores the niceties involved in a proper Victorian courtship. A quarrel develops and it seems the match will not take place. Finally all is made well and Maurice is warned against ever again being rude about Christmas Day. JS

Church of England. The established Church permeated every aspect of 19th-century life, and membership was a mark of social respectability. Apart from Roman Catholics, Nonconformists, and Jews, and one or two agnostics and atheists, Trollope's characters regard themselves as members of the Church. He was himself steeped in the life of the Church of England. Both grandfathers had been clergymen, and his parents were practising Christians. His own faith is apparent in his essays in the *Pall Mall Gazette*, later published as *Clergymen of the Church of England*, and, unusually for his fiction, in *The Bertrams*. He also came to know intimately the structure of the Church, and the lives and roles of the various clergy, during his time reorganizing rural letter deliveries in south-west England.

The 1840s and 1850s were times of religious upheaval, but although Trollope sympathized with the need for reform within the Church, his basic instincts were conservative. A moderate high churchman, he respected the sacraments and the liturgy, preferring the formality and beauty of high-church worship to the sermons and emotionalism of the Low Church. He felt that, unlike the Low Church, and in particular the evangelicals, the High Church was marked by tolerance, reserve, and courtesy. *Clergymen of the Church of England* reveals Trollope's admiration for the Tractarian Movement in Oxford, especially its spiritual integrity, and this is also apparent in *Barchester Towers* and *Doctor Thorne*. Those who fear this leaning towards Rome, such as Miss Thorne, who still laments Catholic emancipation, are portrayed as reactionary Tories. But Trollope is critical of its excessive emphasis on the aesthetic and the liturgical, to which the sisters of the Marquis of Brotherton are so devoted in *Is He Popenjoy?* He also considered absurd the fashion for clerical celibacy. Francis Arabin in *Barchester Towers* is worryingly ascetic until he settles comfortably into married life in the deanery, and similarly in *Doctor Thorne* Caleb Oriel is persuaded to abandon this bizarre principle for marriage with Beatrice Gresham.

Trollope's Church was also that of the landed gentry, and there were close ties between them and the wealthier clergy. Dr Grantly in *Barchester Towers* and Henry Clavering in *The Claverings* both have dual roles as clergymen and members of the squirearchy. Successful clergymen such as Mr Arabin are the sons of country gentlemen, while the exotic prebendary Dr Vesey Stanhope in *Barchester Towers* is related to the peerage. Such clergymen may also gain their livings through family ties, as does Gregory Newton in *Ralph the Heir*, and Squire Prosper's brother-in-law in *Mr Scarborough's Family*. In Trollope's view, this need have no bearing on their performance as clergymen, and Gregory Newton is an example of a good parish priest.

But such connections do emphasize the gulf between wealthy and well-connected clergymen, and their younger, socially inferior curates; men such as the zealous Mr Saul in *The Claverings*, who effectively does all the work in the parish for a mere £70 a year, while the vicar, Henry Clavering, whose duties he carries out, has an annual income of about £800. Similarly, Dr Vesey Stanhope, who holds more than one living, spends long periods of time in Italy, while his parish work is undertaken by hired curates. Trollope disapproves of such cynical absentee clergymen. And he is also critical of the poverty of curates, partly because it encouraged recruitment from among the lower classes, as he points out in *Clergymen of the Church of England*. It opened the door to men such as Mr Thumble in *The Last Chronicle of Barset*, who is only too eager to take advantage of Mr Crawley's predicament and usurp his parish at Hogglestock.

While supporting the political establishment of the Church, Trollope exploits it for comic effect. In *Barchester Towers*, the high churchman Dr Grantly, who is dependent on the exercise of Tory patronage to enable him to follow his father as bishop, finds instead that the coincidence of his father's death with the installation of a Liberal government not only thwarts his ambition, but imposes on the intensely conservative diocese a low churchman, Dr Proudie. The ensuing battle mirrors those taking place in many dioceses during the period. The potential for human drama is also there within the structure of the Church.

The inherent contradiction between a bishop's authority and his circumscribed power over his clergymen, whose possession of their livings gave them a large measure of autonomy, is developed in *Dr Wortle's School*, where a source of comedy is the extensive correspondence between the stiff-necked clergyman Jeffrey Wortle and his peace-loving Bishop over Wortle's liberal treatment of the bigamous Peacockes.

For the purposes of fiction, Trollope views the Church as a human and political organization, riven by ambitions and rivalries. It is also an arena for conflict between the fanatical and the worldly. He makes one such conflict the centre of a delicate moral issue in *The Warden*, when a liberal reformer, the young doctor John Bold, challenges tradition in the form of his prospective father-in-law's wardenship of Hiram's Hospital, and rouses the forces of worldly opposition led by Archdeacon Grantly.

Trollope's requirements for a clergyman of the Church of England are social as well as spiritual. It is not enough to be a good man, such as the evangelical Revd Samuel Prong in *Rachel Ray*, without also being a gentleman. Trollope is ambivalent about men of humble origin, such as Dean Lovelace in *Is He Popenjoy?*, who has advanced himself through his own endeavour, and a wealthy marriage. His shame about his background in trade betrays itself in his assertiveness, but his innate gentlemanly instinct emerges when he stands up for his dignity. Trollope's most admirable clergyman is Frank Fenwick, in *The Vicar of Bullhampton*, a thorough gentleman, who performs his duties wholeheartedly, and exemplifies Christian love and courage in defending one of his parishioners, the 'fallen' woman Carry Brattle. GH

Baker, Joseph E., *The Novel and the Oxford Movement* (1932, repr. 1965).

'Cicero as a Man of Letters' (article). Cicero's power of expression is outstanding, both in oratory and in writing; the sound is charming to the ear, as the sense is to the mind. Those unfamiliar with his work should read it. *Fortnightly Review* (September 1877), 495–515. AKL

'Cicero as a Politician' (article). This Roman politician who lived in an age of unsurpassed corruption was 'especially clean-handed', driven by patriotism, courage, and honesty. His energetic and intelligent devotion to the public good arouses enthusiastic admiration centuries later. *Fortnightly Review* (April 1877), 495–515. AKL

'Civil Service, The' (article). The proposal in 'Papers Relating to the Reorganization of the Civil Service' is well intended but flawed. It suggests patronage is the cause of all problems, and

The General Post Office, St Martin's le Grand, in 1850. Trollope became a junior clerk in 1834 at a salary of £90 a year and was constantly in hot water with his superiors. Transferring to Ireland in 1841 he became a diligent civil servant for 33 years.

proposes that all jobs should be assigned after competitive examinations. Other inducements— better salaries, pensions—are omitted. The plan will not encourage good people to apply or to stay. *Dublin University Magazine* (October 1855), 409–26.   AKL

'Civil Service, The' (article). The tenth annual report of the Civil Service Commission reminds all that the board is not fairly supervised. Since reorganization some evils (patronage) have been abolished; others remain. Some suggestions are: the possibility of promotion to top positions, the extension of the vote to revenue-related jobs. *Fortnightly Review* (16 October 1865), 613–26.
                                               AKL

Civil Service, Trollope and the. Trollope's professional life, as an official of the Post Office, began in November 1834, when the future novelist was 'a hobbledehoy of nineteen' who described himself some months before as a 'desolate hanger on' to his family in Bruges who had no 'idea of a career, a profession or a trade' (*Auto* II). His clerkship at the Post Office also released him from the prospect of a career in the Austrian cavalry. This 'hobbledehoy' was to be transformed by residence in London and by a salary of £90 a year which should have enabled him 'to keep up [his] character as a gentleman, and be happy'. His nomination to a clerkship in the General Post Office in St Martin's-le-Grand was thanks to a connection of his mother's, Mrs Clayton Freeling, the wife of the Secretary of the Stamp Office, who had prevailed upon her father-in-law Sir Francis *Freeling, the Secretary of the Post Office 1797–1836. The appointment was in Sir Francis's gift, there being as yet no competitive entry to the civil service. Trollope was examined by another son of Sir Francis, Henry, the Assistant Secretary, by being asked to copy some lines from *The Times* (which he blotted) and questioned about his arithmetic proficiency, to which he replied: 'I know a little of it.' Having been warned that he would be re-examined on the following day, he found that no further hurdles were placed before him. Trollope was to be consistent in his opposition to the idea of competitive examinations for entry into the civil service when reforms were introduced in the 1850s, firmly believing in the gentlemanly validity of the system of patronage by which he had been recruited ('There are places in life which can hardly be well filled except by "gentlemen",' *Auto* III). In October 1855 he was to publish an article in the *Dublin University Review* strongly criticizing the civil service reforms proposed by Sir Charles *Trevelyan and Sir Stafford *Northcote.

Trollope's years as a junior clerk in the Secretary's Office of the General Post Office were, by his own account, years of drudgery in which he 'very soon achieved a character for irregularity' (he had a watch that was always ten minutes late). When Freeling was succeeded by Lieutenant Colonel William Leader *Maberly in 1836 Trollope found himself working under a Secretary who 'certainly was not my friend'. He also commenced what were to prove his lifelong 'quarrels with the authorities'. During this period he was treated, he said, as though he were unfit for any useful work and felt that he was always about to be dismissed despite his 'striving to show how good a public servant I could become, if only a chance were given me'. When the seven years were completed, however, his annual salary had risen from £90 to £140 (as a senior clerk) and then to £180, though Trollope frequently found it hard to manage on this income. Much of the drudgery, tribulation, debt, and diversion of this time are described in *The Three Clerks* and *Marion Fay* (see GOVERNMENT OFFICIALS AS CHARACTERS). In July 1841 Trollope successfully applied to Maberly for one of the newly created posts of clerks to the postal surveyors (there were seven surveyors for England, two for Scotland, and three for Ireland). Clerks travelled over the districts assigned to the surveyors, reporting regularly on the accounts and local deficiencies in the postal arrangements under their supervision. Despite the general conviction amongst clerks at St Martin's-le-Grand that 'nothing could be worse than the berth of a Surveyor's clerk in Ireland', Trollope was appointed to replace the clerk for the Central District of Ireland, one George L. Turner, who had proved 'absurdly incapable' in his post (Trollope had been lucky to be the first to read the report of this incompetence when it arrived in London). Maberly, he believed, was glad to be rid of him.

Trollope left for Ireland in September 1841, with an annual salary of only £100, augmented by travelling expenses (15s. a day when away from home, and 6d. for every mile travelled). By his own estimation his new annual income levelled out at £313 4s. 2d. (*Letters* 1, 10–11 n. 6). On 19 September he established himself at Banagher, King's County (now Co. Offaly), working under the surveyor James Drought. From here he travelled widely on official business through the province of Connacht. His journeys, which were gradually to extend into all four provinces, were to give him an intimate knowledge of Ireland. On 27 August 1844 he was transferred to Clonmel, Co. Tipperary, to work under the surveyor of the Southern District, James Kendrick. Here he proved assiduous in attention to his duties, exposing lax service and corrupt and corruptible local postmasters. In 1848 a fourth surveyor was appointed for Ireland, and Kendrick was moved to Mallow, Co. Cork. Trollope moved with him and remained there until August 1851 when, thanks to his reputation for the successful reorganization of rural deliveries, he was appointed to a temporary post in the South-West division of England in order to supervise the extension of rural postal services. (This was an especial concern of the new Secretary to the Postmaster General, the reforming Rowland *Hill, appointed in 1846 much to Maberly's chagrin.) Trollope's future career in the Post Office was also to be enhanced by the promotion of his brother-in-law John *Tilley to the post of Assistant Secretary. From his base in Exeter, Trollope was to visit Devon, Cornwall, Somerset, and Dorset, as well as the Channel Islands and those other southern and western counties which formed the basis of his fictional Barsetshire. Trollope spent two happy years on this special assignment. It was during his visit to St Helier in Jersey in November 1851 that he put forward the case for roadside letter boxes, 'pillar boxes', already in use in neighbouring France (*Letters* 1, 28–9). Trollope's suggestion was taken up by the Postmaster General, the first being erected in St Helier in November 1852, spreading to Guernsey in February 1853 and to the English mainland in the following September (the first being at Carlisle). At Trollope's bidding pillar boxes were subsequently installed at Gloucester and in the spring of 1855 at Ballymena and Belfast in Ireland. Thereafter their use spread throughout the United Kingdom. They were probably Trollope's most enduring and memorable innovation during his professional career (though he was more proud of his extension of the rural postal service). (See POSTAL MUSEUM, NATIONAL.)

In the autumn of 1852, Trollope's application for the post of Superintendent of Mail Coaches, which would have given him a London base, was rejected by the Postmaster General on Maberly's advice. In July 1853 he was recalled to Ireland as acting surveyor to the Northern District, and in October 1854 was formally appointed to the post on a salary of c.£650 (though he determined to base himself in Dublin rather than in the north). In January 1858 he was commissioned to go to Egypt by the 'great men at the General Post Office' in order to arrange a postal treaty which would facilitate the movement of mails to and from India and afterwards to inspect postal operations at Malta and Gibraltar. On returning from Egypt in June he was sent to Scotland for two months in order to reorganize the Glasgow Post Office. Here he 'walked all over the city with the letter-carriers, going up to the top flats of the houses . . . It was midsummer, and wearier work I never performed' (*Auto* VII). The organizational skills he had manifested in Egypt were to lead to a further complex mission to 'cleanse the Augean stables' of the West Indian Post Office in November 1858. Here he was to recommend new routes for the mail service and to reorganize the postal responsibilities divided between the London Post Office and the colonial authorities. He was also to negotiate treaties with the Spanish government over rates charged in Cuba and Puerto Rico. His work on both overseas missions was highly praised in the Postmaster General's Annual Report to Parliament. In the summer of 1859 Trollope finally left Ireland for the surveyorship of the Eastern District of England (though his appointment did not become official until January 1860). He based himself at Waltham Cross, within easy reach of the East Anglian counties, Huntingdonshire, and the eastern parts of Hertfordshire and Bedfordshire, for which he had responsibility. He was also in command of a salary of £700 plus expenses of 20s. per day when away from home and £30 a year rental if he used his home as his headquarters. In April 1860 Trollope testified before a parliamentary committee against the suitability of civil service examinations for junior entrants to the Post Office, and in the same month he was appointed to serve on a committee of inquiry, established by the Postmaster General, Lord Elgin, after *The Times* had criticized the pay and working conditions of letter-carriers, sorters, and messengers. Although Rowland Hill suspended the original committee (which he suspected of intrigue directed at him), Trollope was reappointed to a reconstituted committee in May. He was not, however, happy with the committee's deliberations on the questions of promotion, and was insistent about the undesirability of competitive entrance examinations for the 'minor establishment' despite Hill's advocacy of both. He managed further to antagonize Hill early in 1861 by organizing a series of lectures by literary men for Post Office employees and, in his own lecture, criticizing interference with the independence of civil servants by 'some big wig', complaining specifically about Hill's notion of promotion by merit—a system that, he believed, enabled a senior officer 'to put unfairly forward his special friends'. Trollope also published his lecture in the *Cornhill Magazine*. Hill was subsequently to oppose Trollope's application for a seven-month leave of absence in America, though in this he was overruled by the Postmaster General, Lord *Stanley. When Hill retired in March 1864, however, Trollope was to write him a conciliatory and flattering letter proclaiming him 'one of the essential benefactors, not only of your own country, but of all the civilized world' (*Letters* 1, 255–6).

With Hill gone, there was a further application for promotion within the Post Office, to an assistant secretaryship ('had I obtained this, I should have given up my hunting, have given up much of my literary work,—at any rate would have edited no magazine,—and would have returned to the habit of my youth in going daily to the General Post Office,' *Auto* XV). It was not to be. Perhaps as compensation, Trollope was to be offered a postal mission to the East in 1865, and in 1866 the position of Metropolitan Surveyor, but he declined both offers. He did, however, produce a report in 1866 on the feasibility of converting eight of the ten London postal districts into 'post-towns' each with its own postmaster, which, on implementation, required him to act as a temporary supervisor of a new district with his headquarters in Vere Street. On his appointment as editor of *Saint Pauls* in October 1867, with a salary of £750, Trollope finally resolved to give up his Post Office career, though this entailed forfeiting a pension of £500 which would have been his had he completed another eight years' service. In his letter accepting Trollope's resignation (printed by the novelist in *An Autobiography*), Tilley described him as one 'of the most outstanding servants of the Post Office', one who 'notwithstanding the many calls on [his] time' had never permitted other 'avocations to interfere with [his] Post Office work'. On his last day as a civil servant, 31 October 1867, Trollope was given a farewell dinner at the Albion Tavern by some hundred colleagues. He was reported in the *Spectator* as expressing 'melancholy at bidding adieu' to his old career (*Letters* 1, 396 n. 4). In February 1868, however, he was commissioned by the Postmaster General to negotiate a postal convention with the United States. His mission, though generally successful, did not finally induce the US Post Office 'to agree to such favourable terms as [the GPO] hoped to obtain' (*Letters* 1, 440 n. 5). ALS
Super, R. H., *Trollope in the Post Office* (1981).

'Civil Service as a Profession, The' (lecture).

Speaking as one civil servant to others, we will be frank. Such a career might not be one's first choice, but is selected as secure, and promoted by anxious parents. Certainly this was true for this speaker's generation whose parents had not the means to educate them to the law or the Church. However, one discovers that civil servants may have as noble, independent, and free lives as those in other professions. There are certain limitations, in exchange for financial security; one may be comfortable, but will not make a fortune. No occupation has a higher percentage of honest, noble men doing great things for others than does the civil service. Some self-styled reformers consider public money wasted on their salaries, and focus on various corruptions; these people know little or nothing about the reality. Actually very few temptations are available in civil service jobs. There is no motivation to 'water down' the product, nor to exaggerate the virtues of a thing, such as exists for merchants. There is no need to beg or grovel for favour or payment, as in other countries; salaries are reasonably liberal. Public work is of more benefit to more people than many other professions; civil servants can take pride in the value of their efforts. Society does seem to be improving with time, and governments also; Samuel Pepys's memoirs illustrate how difficult it was to be an honest public servant in times past. Civil servants now qualify for their jobs instead of receiving them as favours; the misuse of authority has been constrained if not totally removed. Promotion is still not completely fair, and this matter needs attention. The chief unfairness of public service, however, is the withholding of the vote from anyone who is in any way concerned with the collection of revenue. This rule takes from public servants the most basic right of citizenship. If all engaged in the civil service will work, this rule can be abolished. *Four Lectures*, 3–26. AKL

'Civil Service Commissioners' (letter).

The commissioners are now legally answerable only to the monarch. Their unquestionable power in personnel decisions can only be evil in the long run, though the present incumbents are of high integrity. *Pall Mall Gazette* (27 July 1865), 3–4.
AKL

'Civil War in America, The: An Address at the Last Meeting of the Manchester Union and Emancipation Society by Goldwyn Smith' (review).

The address has the language and rhetoric of a speech rather than an essay in the presentation of the belief that the North will win. The opinions are reasonable but not argued. *Fortnightly Review* (1 June 1866), 251–4. AKL

Clady, village in the barony of Desmond, where, hampered by lack of resources, the Countess of Desmond and Lady Clara attempt to establish a soup kitchen. It also provides the setting for Herbert Fitzgerald's harrowing encounter with a starving Irish family, an event that puts his own losses—of land and name—in a broader context of human deprivation. *CR* MRS

Clandidlem, Lady, Lady De Courcy's friend. Fat and heavy, she encourages the Countess's speculations about an affair between Plantagenet Palliser and Lady Dumbello. *SHA*   NCS

'Clarissa' (review). This is Richardson's novel as abridged by E. S. Dallas. The original work is prolix, incredible, and full of rogues—and worse. Shortening something that is terrible only makes it shorter, not better. *Saint Pauls* (November 1868), 163–72.   AKL

Clarke, Marcus Andrew Hislop (1846–81). Only child of a Chancery lawyer, he emigrated to Australia in 1863 and became theatre critic for the *Melbourne Argus*, playwright, and novelist. Commenting in *Australia and New Zealand* on the literature of the colonies, Trollope singled out Clarke's writings: 'I cannot . . . allude to the literature of the colony at large without mentioning the name of Mr Marcus Clarke, of Melbourne, whose Australian tales are not only familiarly known by all colonists, but are almost as familiar to English readers' (*Australia* (1967), 463). After receiving an advance copy of Clarke's classic convict tale *For the Term of his Natural Life*, Trollope wrote in November 1873 to compliment him, but he declined to review the novel on grounds that the role of critic did not sit well with his 'business as an author' (*Letters* 2, 603).   RCT

Clarke, Mary (Mme Mary Mohl) (1793–1883), bohemian hostess and friend of Mme Récamier in Paris, to whose salon she introduced Frances Trollope after she and her son Tom took apartments at 6 rue de Provence in 1835. Into this heady world Trollope briefly plunged in 1840, when he took Tom's place as his mother's escort. With Mrs Trollope, he attended Mary Clarke's salons and met members of her social set. Trollope encountered Mme Mohl again in the 1860s through the Ladies of Langham Place, amongst whom she was a vocal member on women's issues.   RCT

Clarkson, Mr, vulgar and impertinent moneylender who extends credit to Laurence Fitzgibbon for a bill signed by Phineas Finn. In an attempt to collect his money, Clarkson makes Phineas's life miserable, haunting his lodgings and attempting to embarrass him in the lobby of the House. *PF*   JMR

classical literature. Trollope's love of the Latin classics allegedly came to him in later life, the novelist having been, according to *An Autobiography*, an incorrigible dunce at school—even though he grudgingly concedes that the knowledge of Latin, 'acquired since I left school', was 'no doubt aided by that groundwork of the language which will in the process of years make its way, even through the skin' (*Auto* I). Wherever, and by what means, Trollope acquired his knowledge and love of the Latin authors, there can be no doubt of their importance to his writings. Not only did he write *The Commentaries of Caesar* for Blackwood's series 'Ancient Classics for English Readers', he also spent some four years reading and rereading, annotating and commenting upon, the works of Cicero, which bore fruit as two substantial essays, 'Cicero as Politician' (*Fortnightly Review*, NS 21, 495–515), and 'Cicero as Man of Letters' (*Fortnightly Review*, NS 22, 401–22), and, ultimately, a two-volume *Life of Cicero*. Indeed, as N. John Hall has written, '[o]n no book had Trollope ever worked with such assiduity and at such length' (Hall 471). Moreover, Trollope's familiarity with the classics is abundantly evident in his fiction, which teems with classical allusions, quotations, and translations buried in the main body of the narrative. Horace is overwhelmingly the main source of these, with references chiefly from his Odes and Epistles. A recurrent tag is 'the equal mind' (*Odes* 2. 3). Trollope was also fond of quoting from Virgil, Ovid, Juvenal, and Terence. John W. Clark, in his examination of Trollope's use of classical literature, claims there are 81 instances of quotations and translated quotations in Trollope's novels, 'just about all there are, I am sure' (*The Language and Style of Anthony Trollope* (1975), 178), but this is a gross underestimation: we can account for nearly 10 per cent of Clark's total merely by examining the frequency of just one of Trollope's regular allusions, from Terence's *Andria* (ll. 96–8), 'omnes omnia bona dicere et laudare fortunas meas, | qui gnatum haberem tali ingenio praeditum' ('All people said all good things, and praised my good fortune in having a son blessed with such a character'), which occurs at least eight times in his fiction (*B* I, XVI; *ED* XXXV; *FP* I; *HKWR* I; *PF* LVIII; *PM* XXXIX; *SHH* I). It should be noted, however, that, for the non-classicist hardly any of Trollope's Latin quotations impede the meaning of his novels; similarly, his buried translations can go unnoticed (hence Clark's underestimation) without any perceptible loss of understanding. Rather, the point of such quotations and translations is to reinforce the notion of a community of like-minded readers; in other words, Trollope is writing as a clubbable, middle-class, classically (and public-school-) educated male, and the readership his fiction takes for granted is of similar background, culture, and sex. As David Skilton has written, Trollope's deployment of classical tags 'does not stand in the way of the novel[s], as a pedantic obstacle would, but is a gesture of class recognition—a sign that the narrator is, like the novelist, "One of us" . . . . Having established their social credentials, the reader and narrator can now proceed on a friendly basis' ('Schoolboy Latin and the Mid-Victorian Novelist: A Study in Reader Competence', *Browning Institute Studies*, 16 (1988), 49). The one Trollope novel that features love of classical literature—and the solace it apparently provides in one's declining years—is *An Old Man's Love*, in which William Whittlestaff (the 'old man' of the title) habitually turns to the classics for comfort in times of emotional stress: 'he took to his classics for consolation . . . They did him good,—in the same way that the making of many shoes would have done him good had he been a shoemaker . . . Gradually he returned to a gentle cheerfulness of life' (*OML* II). Not only does this passage imply the presumed emotional power of classical literature; it also reveals (through likening knowledge of the classics to a *trade*) how far classical pursuits were deemed suitable as an 'occupation' for the well-to-do, gentlemanly middle and upper classes.   HO

Clark, John W., *The Language and Style of Anthony Trollope* (1975).

Skilton, David, 'Schoolboy Latin and the Mid-Victorian Novelist: A Study in Reader Competence', *Browning Institute Studies*, 16 (1988), 39–55.

Tracy, Robert, '*Lana Medicata Fuco*: Trollope's Classicism', in John Halperin (ed.), *Trollope: Centenary Essays* (1982).

class structure. Trollope's belief in the desirability of a gradual evening-out of class differences (see *Auto* XVI) means that, although a great many of his novels deal with such class differences (and the ensuing conflicts), relatively few are examinations of their underlying *causes*. There are, nevertheless, three notable—if only partial—exceptions: *The American Senator*, *Lady Anna*, and *Marion Fay*. *The American Senator* sets out to be the story of the eponymous Elias Gotobed's observations, over one winter, of the social and class system as it operates in the fictional town of Dillsborough, but descends at times into a squabble about the etiquette of fox-hunting. More importantly, the book's potential for analysis or satire is undermined by the presentation of Gotobed himself as being wilfully ignorant of English customs and institutions. Having said as much, the strand of the novel which deals with Arabella Trefoil's determined pursuit of Lord Rufford contains some finely nuanced observations on the social stratagems needed to overcome the etiquette arising from class distinctions. The class divide is confronted more directly in *Lady Anna* and *Marion Fay*, which both centre on the dilemma arising from an aristocrat's love for a commoner. Both novels have some sharp things to say about the arbitrariness of class divisions. Even so, the happy outcome of Lady Anna's love for the tailor Daniel Thwaite is wildly improbable, and indicates how far the analysis of class is subsumed in novelistic conventions. By contrast, the twin plots of *Marion Fay* both ultimately back away from the thorny social issues they seek to address: the humble Marion's love for Lord Hampstead is left unresolved through her tragic death; while Lady Frances Trafford's love for the Post Office clerk George Roden is only sanctioned by her family and friends when Roden is suddenly—and wholly implausibly—elevated to an Italian dukedom. Both plot resolutions thus preserve, in spite of the novel's many satirical gibes against class, the notion of the aristocracy as an exclusive social grouping. See also ARISTOCRACY; LANDED GENTRY, OLD; MIDDLE CLASS, NEW; WORKING CLASS.   HO

Clavering, Captain Archibald. Less intimidating than his brother Sir Hugh Clavering, and more inclined to work at his social obligations, his lifestyle is equally selfish, mainly revolving around gambling. He pays half-hearted court to Lady Ongar, in the hope of becoming master of Ongar Park, and dies with his brother on a fishing trip to Norway. C   PJT

Clavering, Fanny. Younger daughter of the Revd Henry Clavering, she is a pretty, gay-spirited girl, tireless in the practicalities of church and school affairs, until Mr Saul, her father's grimly energetic curate, surprises a spirit of unworldliness in her, and she falls in love. Like her father and brother she is capable of haughtiness, but proving more stubborn of purpose than either, she gradually wears down their opposition to the curate's suit. She occasionally operates as Harry's lively confidante. C   PJT

Clavering, Harry, self-absorbed and vacillating hero of *The Claverings*, haughty in manner and inclined to think himself marked out for special destiny. After a distinguished career at Cambridge and as a schoolmaster he goes to learn civil engineering at Beilby & Burton. For much of the novel he is not only unsure of his commitment to this unlikely profession, but also whether to renew his old suit to the fascinating Lady Ongar, or consummate his new one with the more prosaic Florence Burton. C   PJT

Clavering, Henry. The rector of Clavering and father of the hero, Harry Clavering, he considers himself one of the 'inner clerical familiarity' of 'country gentleman' clergymen (XXXIII). Though not without worldly wisdom, Mr Clavering has lapsed into quietly sybaritic habits, and is only energetic when blocking Mr Saul's suit to his daughter Fanny. C   PJT

Clavering, Mrs Henry. Wife of Revd Henry Clavering, she has largely abandoned attempts to stir her husband into activity. Her hackles rise, attractively on the whole, whenever she is in the presence of her insolent nephew-in-law Sir Hugh. She is both sensitive and resourceful during her visits to Clavering at the death of little Hughy, the heir. *C*   PJT

Clavering, Lady Hermione (née **Brabazon**), sister of Julia Brabazon, and melancholy wife of Sir Hugh Clavering of Clavering Park. Though she is afraid of the sound of his voice, and thinks that she hates him, Trollope insists that her love for her husband remains alive, and that no amount of ill usage on Sir Hugh's part is likely to destroy it. *C*   PJT

Clavering, Sir Hugh. Utterly careless of the opinions of others, the head of the Clavering family puts his hand down firmly during his marriage to Hermione Brabazon, and manages his estate, which he thinks 'dull', and his house, which he thinks 'gloomy', in an irascible and tight-fisted manner. Though greatly distressed by the death of his son and heir Hughy, he is remorseless in denying himself the love of his wife and the 'twaddling' consolations of religion. He dies in a boating accident off Heligoland. *C*
                    PJT

Clavering, Hughy, only son and heir of Sir Hugh Clavering and Lady Hermione Clavering. A 'poor, rickety, unalluring bairn' (XI), he soon dies, Trollope writing with some pathos of his 'little' body in its 'little cot' (XX). The main function of his death is to loose the last link that binds his parents. *C*   PJT

Clavering, Mary, elder daughter of Revd Henry Clavering, whose wedding to a neighbouring clergyman, Revd Edward Fielding of Humbleton, forms a focal point for the early action of the novel. Like all Claverings, she thinks much of social rank, and often merely echoes her husband's conventional opinions. *C*   PJT

Clavering Park, a 'large, square, sombre-looking stone mansion', the country seat of Sir Hugh Clavering. He resides there for six weeks of the year, during the partridge-shooting season, but compels his wife to remain there purgatorially. The neglected gardens form the setting for the memorable opening scene when Julia Brabazon jilts Harry Clavering. *C*   PJT

Claverings, The (see next page)

Clayton, Captain Yorke, handsome Irish policeman charged with directing forces against Landleaguers in Galway, Mayo, and Roscommon. He courts Edith Jones, the supposedly unattractive, but spirited, daughter of landowner Philip Jones, rather than her beautiful younger sister

Ada. He is presented heroically as an idealist who 'live[s] upon his hatred of a Landleaguer' (XV). Hence, while his zealous pursuit of Terry Lax, the suspected murderer of Florian Jones, earns him the enmity of Irish agitators, it inspires the murdered boy's two sisters to see him as the epitome of masculine virtues. *L*   MRS

Cleeve, Sir Peregrine Orme's estate, near Hamworth. In tune with Sir Peregrine's old-fashioned values, the Cleeve is a house built during the reigns of Elizabeth and Charles II. 'Everything was old, venerable, and picturesque' but 'it was for the beauty and wildness of its grounds that The Cleeve was remarkable' (III). *OF*   MT

clergymen as characters. Trollope is famous for clerical characters in his novels—it is one of his most notable originalities. There are some precedents in English fiction he would have been well aware of: Fielding's Parson Adams in *Joseph Andrews* is a kind of ancestor of Mr Harding; in *The Vicar of Wakefield*, Goldsmith, the son of a parson, creates a beautifully well-developed parson-hero. There is also Yorick, created *by* a parson, Laurence Sterne, as his alter ego in *Tristram Shandy*, who becomes his real ego in *A Sentimental Journey*, lively, witty, and 'sensible'. Trollope admired John Galt and would have found in *Annals of the Parish* (1821) a mine of affectionate clerical humour. But it is Trollope's special achievement to have made a whole clerical society in the Barsetshire novels.

Trollope said in *An Autobiography* (V) that he had no particular knowledge of clergymen or any cathedral town, but this is not quite true. His family had many clerical friends and relations, and he knew Winchester from attending school there. But his interest is not so much in the clergy as such as in their relationships to a changing society in the Age of Reform, their social relationships in the ecclesiastical hierarchy, and how they adjust their priestly vocations to financial, familial, and moral human exigencies. The cathedral town offers a little world where these relationships are played out. As Trollope says in *Framley Parsonage*, he has aimed to portray clergymen 'as they bear on our social life rather than to describe the mode and working of their professional careers' (XLII and see *LCB* LXXXIV).

His sympathies are perfectly clear: the old 'high and dry' Anglicans are much more to his taste than the new 'low' churchmen, or the Dissenters. His mother Frances *Trollope had written a virulently anti-evangelical novel, *The Vicar of Wrexhill*, the title character of which is an outright evangelical villain. It is not Trollope's way to work in such black and white. Of the

(*cont. on page 106*)

As its title suggests, *The Claverings* is as much concerned with a family and its attitudes as it is to follow the story of an individual hero and heroine. (Trollope started by calling the work 'Harry Clavering' but changed his mind, as his working papers indicate, though the moment when that happened is not clear.) The novel opens at the point where Harry Clavering, the son of the rectory, is rejected by the beautiful Julia Brabazon, who chooses to marry the debauched Lord Ongar rather than risk a life of poverty with Harry, who has no inheritance.

Harry's father, the rector of Clavering, is kindly but his laziness has stopped him from doing anything with his life. His uncle Sir Hugh, who lives at Clavering Park and has a house in town, is more powerful but he is harsh and repellent in his cruelty to his wife Hermione, particularly at the time when their young son dies. Sir Hugh's brother Archie is a wastrel who lives in town: it is no wonder that Harry has difficulty in knowing how to make a place for himself in the world as a man.

Deciding to train as an engineer, Harry leaves behind the surroundings that his class and upbringing have made familiar when he takes lodgings in Stratton, the manufacturing town where he is learning his new profession. He becomes involved with the demure little Florence Burton, the daughter of old Mr Burton who owns the engineering business, and before long they are engaged. At this point, Lady Ongar, now a widow of substantial fortune, returns to England, eager to renew her relationship with Harry.

His shamefaced enjoyment of the emotional intimacy that is offered him by Lady Ongar, and his failure to explain that he has asked another woman to marry him make for uncomfortable reading. Only when she is confronted by Florence's sister-in-law Cecilia does Lady Ongar learn that Harry is not free. Her marriage has left Lady Ongar wealthy but also vulnerable and neglected: since her husband put it about that she was unfaithful to him she is shunned by her own class and left the prey of fortune hunters who inhabit a seedy London subworld, like Sophie Gordeloup and Count Pateroff, the brother and sister who attempt to blackmail her. Even Archie Clavering, the ne'er-do-well brother of Sir Hugh, schemes to marry her.

The part that Cecilia Burton, the happy wife and mother, plays in this novel is powerful and ambiguous, for there is something suffocating about her moral certainties. She has more charm than her old mother-in-law Mrs Burton, whose intrusive questioning of Harry can be put down to lack of breeding, and she is more gracious in her ways than her husband Theodore, the engineer with his feet on the ground, but her presence is nevertheless felt as a threat. It was a marked innovation for Trollope to present a hero of good family who thought of becoming an engineer, but the use that he makes of the conjunction between the Claverings and the Burtons goes beyond simple observation of social change. Shifting class, to move among the Burtons, does not save Harry from being faced with disturbing behaviour in women.

Harry is brought back to Florence by the combined operations of his mother and his future sister-in-law, and saved from having to earn his living as an engineer by the shipwreck in which his unpleasant uncles are drowned. (His working papers show that Trollope hesitated for days before permitting himself this sensational solution.) Harry ends the novel with his father as the new baronet and himself as heir to the estate. A sub-plot, tracing the courtship of his sister Fanny, a young woman dedicated to church affairs, by her father's unprepossessing and penniless curate Mr Saul is also resolved by this injection of cash.

The novel's disillusioned inspection of this family from the landed gentry anticipates some of the bleak questions that Trollope would ask about those with authority and power in *The Way We Live Now*. But readers and reviewers had difficulty in taking *The Claverings* in: they seemed confused at not finding the mellow tone they expected from Trollope in accounts of the occupants of the rectory and the big house. As for Lady Ongar, with her beauty and her mercenary past, were they to pity her or to deplore her behaviour? they wondered uncertainly. There were signs that they warmed to her despite themselves. Some reviewers admitted they found her attractive. It puzzled readers, too, as the *London Review* indicated, when they registered that Trollope seemed to be showing absolute contempt for his hero and heroine.

The uneasy tone of this novel marks a refusal on the part of the author to offer readers characters with whom they could make comfortable identifications; if the weak rector and the mean squire invite criticism, so too do the good women, including the dull heroine who keeps the young man up to scratch.

The novel's scepticism extends even to its representation of Christianity. Julia Ongar, lonely and desperate in her fine house, is solemnly compared to Judas, a tricky move that risks several awkward questions, and Harry is shown on his knees praying to be kept true to Florence Burton, even as the writer is showing that Harry is too wrapped up in himself to treat either Florence or Julia with ordinary decency. It seems hard to believe that even the most pious reader could view Harry's devotions without irony; just as that reader must be unsettled by the novel's closing reference to the notion of Christian Providence, when it is suggested that 'Providence was making a great mistake when she expected him [Harry] to earn his bread' (XLVIII).

The Claverings was composed in 1864, only four years after Trollope returned from Ireland and from the time when *Framley Parsonage* was written, but it reads like a disillusioned rewriting of that 'thoroughly English' story.

Although this was the year when he joined both the committee of the *Royal Literary Fund and the *Athenaeum, Trollope had spent the spring and summer of 1864 in turmoil, disappointed when he did not get the job of Assistant Secretary to the Post Office and then passionately involved in a dispute over pay for himself and the other surveyors. Both disturbances set him at loggerheads with his brother-in-law John *Tilley, himself newly promoted to Secretary to the Post Office. These were steps in the process that would end, three years later, in his resignation. *The Claverings* seems to be written out of a loss of faith and a questioning of justice, changes that can be connected with Trollope's confusion on finding himself unfairly treated, as he thought, in a system in which he had come to feel secure.

The agreement between George Smith and Trollope for publication of *The Claverings*, dated November 1863, was unusual in being drawn up almost a year before Trollope began work. The novel was written in sixteen parts of 48 manuscript pages each, between 24 August and 31 December 1864. Publication was delayed and it did not begin coming out in the *Cornhill Magazine* till February 1866. It ran without interruption to May 1867.

Each of the sixteen serial instalments of the novel was accompanied by one full-page illustration and one vignette illustration of rather poor quality by M. Ellen Edwards;

the later volume publication included the full-page illustrations but not the vignettes.

When the type was reset for book publication the last page of the second instalment, which falls at the end of chapter VI, was overlooked by mistake and was lost from later issues of the novel; the missing material is supplied in the notes to the World's Classics 1986 edition.

In April 1867 Smith, Elder published *The Claverings* in two volumes. A two-volume edition from Tauchnitz came out in the same year and an American edition, in one volume, though dated 1866 is said by Sadleir (*Biblio* 85) to have been probably an 1867 issue. *The Claverings* forms part of no series. The manuscript is in the Robert H. Taylor Collection, Princeton.   MH

Edwards, P. D., *Anthony Trollope: His Art and Scope* (1977).
Hamer, M., *Writing by Numbers: Trollope's Serial Fiction* (1987).
Terry, R. C., *Anthony Trollope: The Artist in Hiding* (1977).

new-style low-church characters, Mr Slope is certainly almost all black, but we are eventually called on to feel pity for Bishop Proudie and even for his bully of a wife. On the other side, Mr Harding, the best of men, is party to a social injustice, old Bishop Grantly is ineffective, Archdeacon Grantly puts much value on worldly things, and is the last man to turn the other cheek, Mr Quiverful is too distressed financially to take any moral high ground, Mark Robarts yields to worldly temptations, and Josiah Crawley's fine spirituality is combined with an overbearing pride.

Trollope's breadth and charity are particularly evident in his vivid portrayals of Roman Catholic priests. His very first clergyman is Father John McGrath in the tragic *Macdermots of Ballycloran*. Realistically and lovingly drawn, he is virtually the hero of the book. The other Irish novels all have noteworthy priests. *Castle Richmond* portrays the narrow intolerance of the Irish Protestant clergy for their Catholic confrères, with whom, in the exigencies of the famine, they are obliged to co-operate. Here the Catholics come out ahead. In the short story 'Father Giles of Ballymoy' (*LS*), the English Protestant narrator declares the father 'one of the honestest fellows and best Christians' he ever knew, and a fast friend for twenty years. But English converts to Rome, or 'perverts', are not looked on favourably. Mr Arabin, exposed to the Tractarians at Oxford, had narrowly escaped 'going over to Rome'. And the Oxford-trained Roman Catholic priest whom Roger Carbury befriends in *The Way We Live Now*, while saintly in his devotion, becomes unbearable for his proselytizing. He is contrasted with the Anglican Bishop Yeld, who seems insouciant as to dogma, but exemplifies his religion

in his life, and is thoroughly effective and beloved in the community.

Few clergymen appear in the Palliser novels, for there the testing hierarchical institution is Parliament rather than the Church. But in the rest of his novels, a wide range of clergy appears from time to time. One of his most delightful and well-developed high churchmen is Frank Fenwick of *The Vicar of Bullhampton*. The test case of the novel is that of the 'fallen woman' Carry Brattle, and Puddleham, the Methodist minister, refuses to have anything to do with her. Trollope allows Fenwick to express a piece of doctrine in reproof of the Methodist, who says it is 'a very bad case'. Frank replies: 'And isn't my case very bad, and yours? Are we not in a bad way unless we believe and repent?' (XVII). Josiah Crawley is also allowed to express doctrine (*LCB* LXVIII). There are various objectionable low churchmen: Mr Prong in *Rachel Ray* is no gentleman and even drops his Hs; Mr Stumfold and Mr Maguire in *Miss Mackenzie* are thoroughly venal; Mr O'Callaghan in *The Bertrams* is very susceptible to tea and muffins. In *The Claverings*, however, Trollope refuses us the generalization and makes the charming high-church rector Harry Clavering into a 'hunting parson' who is lazy, and his zealous evangelical curate Mr Saul his moral superior, whom we get to like more and more. So does the heroine Fanny, whom he finally wins. And there is a thoroughly evil high churchman, Mr Greenwood, in *Marion Fay*. In *Dr Wortle's School* two excellent clergymen are first-rate schoolteachers, Mr Peacocke and Dr Wortle himself, as many clergymen were. There were occasional Jewish converts to Anglicanism, one such being Mr Emilius, a popular preacher and a thoroughly bad egg, a suitable mate for

Trollope avoided the more sensational elements of story-telling, but in this illustration for *The Claverings* he allowed his artist, M. E. Edwards, a dramatic encounter on the cliffs of the Isle of Wight with Count Pateroff's 'Lady Ongar, are you not rather near the edge?' (XXV). Edwards supplied sixteen full-page illustrations and sixteen vignettes for the serial in *Cornhill*.

Clergymen of the Church of England

Lizzie in *The Eustace Diamonds*. And in *Is He Popenjoy?* a very minor character, a Jewish convert, Mr Groschut, is presented chiefly to be discriminated against by the worldly Dean Lovelace.

In 1865–6, Trollope wrote for the *Pall Mall Gazette* a series of ten vignettes or 'characters', later published as *Clergymen of the Church of England* (1866). These essays present somewhat generalized types and cast light on them, and on the history of the Church. Trollope's understanding and accuracy are vouched for by Owen Chadwick in *The Victorian Church* (1966–70). He refers to Trollope from time to time for actualities. There is only one impossibility in *Barchester Towers*, he says (1, 473)—the appointment by Palmerston of the Tractarian Arabin to the deanship. The soundness and charity of Trollope's fictional clergymen satisfied no less a person than Cardinal Newman, a faithful reader of Trollope from 1858 onward.   R apR

> apRoberts, Ruth, introduction to *Clergymen of the Church of England* (reprint 1974).
> Chadwick, Owen, *The Victorian Church*, 2 vols. (1966–70).

'Clergymen of the Church of England'
(ten-article series).

1. The Archbishop's role is to be mysterious and lofty; appointed by the Prime Minister, he must seem to be in control, answer all mail vaguely, be good-humoured, patient, and diligent.

2. The Bishop, no longer lord or baron, must perform some work, but has livings to award (often for sons-in-law). This post is one of the last remaining sinecures.

3. The Dean, no longer required to oversee all the workings of the cathedral, now looks to its maintenance and the tourists. He usually likes literature, is studious but not fanatical, and deals well with ladies' groups.

4. The Archdeacon has more work and less pay than the dean; he must be well informed about the rectors and vicars, and alert to any possibility of scandal among them; once appointed to this post, he must not expect advancement. He is, ideally, a recognizable gentleman.

5. The Parson (sometimes rector or vicar) is the most virtuous and admirable of the clergy. He is a gentleman, educated at Oxford/Cambridge, and the social equal of squires; he is comfortable alike with rustics and royals. He believes earnestly that everyone should be in the Church of England, but is not a zealot; he lives comfortably but not ostentatiously.

6. The Incumbent has a less attractive post; he has a district, not a church proper; he must rent a house. His income depends on collections (inspired by his sermons). Social work does him no good; public speaking does. Most of this class trudge through life on a bare subsistence. This situation needs to change.

7. The College Fellow Who Has Taken Orders is another category in need of refining. Fellows are required to be celibate. Formerly, when fellows were monks, and lifelong celibates, it was reasonable to ordain them without further preparation. Ordination is now usually a preface to clerical life outside the university. Not every fellow is necessarily fit for or suited to a clergyman's life. Fellows should be thoughtfully prepared for the sacrament and for the responsibilities to follow.

8. The Curate in a Populous Parish is the most shamefully treated of clergy, exploited by bishops and other clergy. Although clerical stipends are rising, they are not yet fair. The curate no longer enjoys the social position, invitations, etc., which formerly compensated for his low salary; he is often nearly destitute.

9. The Irish Beneficed Clergyman usually has an unhappy life, isolated in a Roman Catholic environment where his efforts are often futile and his parish small. Efforts must be made to change this situation.

10. The Clergyman Who Subscribes for Colenso, often known as 'broad-church' or 'free-thinker', is not an admirable man. He is usually an urban clergyman, and often glib as well; this sort of man should not be supported; he is an infidel at best. *Pall Mall Gazette* (20 November 1865–25 January 1866).   AKL

Clifford, Lady Anne, widowed mother of two boys in *Dr Wortle's School*. She is 'a sweet, confiding, affectionate, but not very wise woman' (4. XII). Cowed by Mrs Stantiloup, she withdraws her sons from the school but later regrets the decision. *DWS*   RC

Clisson, Chateau of, home of the de Lescures, burned after the fall of Amaillou, the family narrowly escaping. *LV*   GRH

Clock House, residence in Nuncombe Putney rented by Hugh Stanbury and Louis Trevelyan, in order to provide a better home for the former's mother and sisters, and a respectable refuge for the latter's estranged wife and son. *HKWR*   RC

Close, Revd Francis (1797–1882), evangelical rector of Cheltenham (1826), Dean of Carlisle (1856–81). He published sermons and pamphlets between 1825–77 on ritualism, national education, and the evils of drink, tobacco, and racecourses. During his incumbency at Cheltenham he was involved with founding several churches and schools, including Cheltenham College. In *The American Senator* (I), Trollope refers to Lawrence Twentyman's three years at Cheltenham. To his friend Mary Holmes, Trollope confided that Twentyman's 'somewhat illiterate language' derived from a 'long-ago entertained dislike of Dean Close & Cheltenham School. *But that is quite for yourself* (*Letters* 2, 702). RCT

Cloudesdale, butler at Humblethwaite. He acts as a chorus to testify that Sir Harry Hotspur is greatly altered by the death of his son, and to indicate that the servants know of George Hotspur's bad reputation. *SHH* MG

clubs in the novels. Trollope's London settings inevitably involve a club or clubs. Although he mentions actual clubs—Brooks's, for example—most are given fictitious names, sometimes indeed facetious ones. A few are not named at all. The Acrobats (*HKWR*) is in Pall Mall: it is of some distinction and members spend much time playing whist. Louis Trevelyan, Colonel Osborne, and Sir Marmaduke Rowley are members. The Active Service Club (*PM*) is 'a new military club' where the parasitic Major Pountney and his friend Captain Gunner are to be found. The Alpine Club, in which Trollope took some interest, is mentioned in *Can You Forgive Her?* The Beargarden (recalling the Savage Club founded in 1857) is infamously prominent in *The Way We Live Now*, less so in *The Duke's Children*. In the former it accommodates the dissolute group of noblemen of whom Sir Felix Carbury is the most despicable (other members before its demise being Lord Grasslough, Dolly Longestaffe, and Lord Nidderdale). Scenes in the Beargarden run the length of the novel and mirror the wider corruption of society. Lord Silverbridge and the horse-nobbling Major Tifto are members. In *The Claverings* the Beaufort is a male haven, and Harry Clavering invites Count Pateroff to dine there. He spends most of his leisure in idleness at the club: in *The Duke's Children* Lord Grex plays whist there often, as Trollope himself did. Gambling is part of its *raison d'être*, and a high fee is payable by elected members. Brooks's (founded 1764, and after 1829 in Pall Mall) numbered Charles James Fox, Wilberforce, and Sheridan among its earlier members. It is casually mentioned elsewhere but is of focal importance in *Phineas Finn* and *Phineas Redux*. Phineas envies Mr Kennedy's membership since Brooks's is the cynosure of political news, gossip, and speculation, a cut above other clubs; he later becomes a member through the offices of Laurence Fitzgibbon. The Carlton, founded by the Duke of Wellington in 1832 and home of conservatism, has wide currency in the novels: Lord George Ger-

main uses it as unpolitical refuge (*IHP*), it is thought desirable that Lord Hampstead should be a member (*MF*), in *Lady Anna* Lord Lovel writes to his aunt from the Carlton Club, and in *The Way We Live Now* Melmotte stays there, his financial weight more than compensating for his vague political doctrine, while his family occupy the Longestaffes' town house in Bruton Street. Undy Scott is a member of the Downing Club (*TC*) and through him the upwardly mobile Alaric Tudor is elected to it. Both are expelled, Alaric on his conviction and Undy after his exposure at the hands of the merciless Chaffanbrass. Abel Wharton's club is one named, fittingly enough, after a strict Lord Chancellor, Lord Eldon (*PM*), while Jack De Baron (*IHP*) lodges close to the Guards' Club, which was then at 70 Pall Mall, its membership restricted to troops of the Royal Household. Lord Lufton and Mr Sowerby are members of the Jockey Club (*FP*), which was becoming increasingly influential in the racing world, although in this case it may merely suggest where the young men incurred their debts. Harry Annesley has his scuffle with Captain Scarborough coming 'down a passage by the side of the Junior United Services Club into Charles Street' (*MSF*), this junior branch dating from the amalgamation of army and navy needs in 1816. Tom Tringle is a leading light in the Mountaineers, a club which seems to have much in common with the Beargarden, and his friend Samuel Faddle is also a member in *Ayala's Angel*. Richard Roby belongs to the Nimrod Club (*PM*), Lord Hautboy, as befits the eldest son of Lord Persiflage, belongs to the Pandemonium (*MF*), Melmotte is anxious to get into Lord Alfred Grendall's club, the Peripatetics (probably a joke reference to the Travellers' Club), and equally ironically Ferdinand Lopez and Everett Wharton are members of the Progress (*PM*). In *The Claverings* those opportunistic and feckless men about town Archie Clavering and Captain Boodle belong to the Rag (an abbreviation for the United Services Club in Pall Mall?), while Phineas Finn gives his time to the Reform before his elevation to Brooks's (*PF*). Sir Thomas Underwood (*RH*) goes to the University Club (founded 1826) at the corner of Suffolk Street, Pall Mall. Pall Mall is also where the Oxford and Cambridge Club has its premises, completed at number 71 in 1838. This is where John Gordon stays in *An Old Man's Love*. In *Phineas Redux* the forthcoming big debate on the Church fills certain clubs with anxious clerics—'the Oxford and Cambridge, the Old University, and the Athenaeum,—were black with them'. Sebright's figures prominently in *The Small House at Allington*: Crosbie had been sponsored for membership

by his friend Fowler Pratt, who acts as buffer between him and the old Squire, Christopher Dale, when the latter arrives at the club to call Crosbie out after his shameful treatment of Lily. Bernard Dale is also a member. In *Phineas Finn* Phineas expresses a wish to belong to the Shakespeare, to which his associate Laurence Fitzgibbon already belongs; at the Shakespeare you could smoke wherever you liked and everybody was on Christian name terms. Among others, Lord Chiltern belongs to the Travellers' Club, founded 1819, which adjoins the Athenaeum in Pall Mall. Its members were required to have travelled 500 miles from London out of the British Isles 'in a direct line'. Chiltern observes to Phineas that he doubts 'whether the porter would let me go in' (*PF*), and Sophie Gordeloup tells Harry Clavering that her brother Count Pateroff is a member, though in fact he only has his mail delivered there (*C*). The Universe, almost certainly based on the Cosmopolitan Club, is especially important in *Phineas Redux*: its fictional luminaries include Mr Bonteen, Laurence Fitzgibbon, Phineas Finn, Barrington Erle, and, most important of all, the lifelong radical Mr Monk, who attracts the susceptible Phineas as a disciple.
GRH

Clyde, Mrs Charles (née **Mary Milton**) (1776–1880), widowed sister of Trollope's mother, one of several Devon relatives who contributed to Trollope's gallery of opinionated aunts and single women, with or without means.   RCT

Cobbold's Ashes, famed fox-hunting land halfway between Chaldicotes and Framley in Barsetshire, where Revd Mark Robarts becomes famous as a hunting parson. *FP*   NCS

Cockchaffington, Devon village. Colonel Osborne uses a visit to the vicar of Cockchaffington, an old schoolfriend, as the pretext for calling upon Emily Trevelyan at Clock House. *HKWR*
RC

Cogan, informer working for Myles Ussher, whose undercover work results in the seizure of illicit whiskey and the prosecution of three local men. After Ussher's murder, his cabin is burned down, indicating that his identity as a spy has been discovered. *MB*   MRS

Cohenlupe, Samuel, Augustus Melmotte's right-hand man in the City. Despite his Jewishness and broken English, he is the MP for Staines. When Melmotte's financial empire begins to crumble, Cohenlupe absconds with much of the funds, thus fuelling the panic and hastening Melmotte's downfall. *WWLN*   SRB

Colburn, Henry (d. 1855), founder of Colburn & Co. (1808–53), notoriously piratical publishers specializing in 'silverfork fiction' and pushing the market for three-volume novels for circulating libraries. Frances Trollope's main publisher, he also issued Trollope's *The Kellys and the O'Kellys* (1848) and *La Vendée*. After poor sales of the former (140 of a print run of 375), he told Trollope it was evident readers did not like Irish novels and that it was impossible to encourage him to continue writing (*Auto* IV). Yet Colburn did take *La Vendée*, though it fared little better. Trollope got £20 as an advance and no further payment.
RCT

Colenso, Frances Ellen ('Atherton Wilde') (1849–87). Daughter of Bishop Colenso, she wrote under the pseudonym Atherton Wilde. Trollope read for Chapman & Hall her book *My Chief and I; or, Six Months in Natal after the Langalibalele Outbreak* (1879). Trollope noted: 'The book is clever and will probably sell, but it is shamelessly personal.' He was also concerned over possible libel action. '[W]ere I the author's father and living in the Colony I should be most unwilling that such a book should be published' (*Letters* 2, 838). In a subsequent letter (September 1879), Trollope discarded the possibility of libel, but clarified his concern: 'My feeling has been as to what would be said and thought and felt in the Colony' (*Letters* 2, 843).   RCT

Colenso, Bishop John William (1814–83). Child of a poor Cornish family, he entered the Church and was eventually appointed Bishop of Natal in 1853, where he was called 'Sobantu' ('Father of the people') by the Zulus, whose status he defended. In 1875 he spoke out against official tyranny towards natives, and denounced the Zulu War in 1879. From 1861 Bishop Colenso came into increasing conflict with the Church. He attacked the sacramental system, and in 'Critical Examination of the Pentateuch' (1862–79) concluded that those books were pious forgeries. He was excommunicated in 1863 but was confirmed in possession of the see by the law courts in 1866. The Bishop's supporters, who included Darwin, sought contributions on his behalf. Trollope subscribed. In the *Pall Mall Gazette* (November 1865–January 1866) he published 'The Clergyman Who Subscribes for Colenso' in which a cleric stands against biblical literalism. When Trollope was planning to visit South Africa in 1877, the Colenso family prepared to receive him for an overnight visit. Frank Colenso noted that his father was 'a great admirer of Trollope . . . The *Barchester Towers* series gives him immense enjoyment' (*I & R* 214). Though the family were 'almost afraid lest he should fall completely into the hands of the officials and be hoodwinked', they believed he would prove too keen an observer. 'It will be a great triumph if we can supply him with really trustworthy facts about Zululand' (*I & R* 214). In the event, Trollope was reticent about his sympathies, and in *South Africa* recorded that hearing the Bishop preach would not upset innocent faith. Colenso's wife Frances subsequently wrote to Mrs Katherine Lyell (July 1878): 'If you see Trollope's book on South Africa, please to remember that he "looks through a pair of government spectacles", this is my Harry's [Harriet, their eldest child] expression. She took great pains to clear his vision, and to show him things as they are, but in vain' (*I & R* 214). RCT

Colligan, Dr, unprepossessing doctor, 'excessively dirty in his person and practice' (XXIII), who, on attending Anty Lynch, is horrified to be offered 50 acres (20 ha) of land by her brother Barry in return for ensuring Anty's death. Revealing this to Lord Ballindine, he becomes a factor in hounding Barry out of Ireland. *KOK*
MRS

Collins, Charles Allston (1828–73), son of the painter William Collins, brother of the novelist Wilkie Collins, and later husband of Dickens's daughter Kate. A member of the Pre-Raphaelite Brotherhood, he abandoned painting for literature, and published essays and novels, notably *The Bar Sinister* (1864). A friend of Thackeray and Millais, he formed part of the circle Trollope liked to entertain at home. Writing to Millais in June 1863, Trollope asked him to 'settle a day with the Thackerays and the [Charles] Collinses' to come to Waltham Cross for 'the consumption of all our cream and strawberries' (*Letters* 1, 220).
RCT

Collins, Revd William Lucas (1817–87), rector of Lowick, Northamptonshire (1873–87); editor of Blackwood's 'Ancient Classics for English Readers', for which Trollope wrote *The Commentaries of Caesar* (1870). Collins was impressed that he had read 'with an amount of industry really wonderful, when we remember how very limited were his leisure hours, almost the whole of the Latin authors'. They became close friends. Good hunting was available in the county, so Trollope visited Lowick several times, in April 1879 spending a month there. 'That I, who have belittled so many clergymen, should ever come to live in a parsonage,' he wrote. 'Shall I be required to preach, as belonging to the Rectory?' (*I & R* 162, 165). Collins reviewed *An Autobiography* for *Blackwood's* (November 1883). RCT

Collins, William Wilkie (1824–89), master of the suspense novel and, in *The Moonstone* (1868), creator of the full-blown British detective novel. Despite belonging to the Dickens set he became a friend of Trollope's, through whom he met the American actress and writer Kate Field (June 1873). Trollope's estimate of his work showed respect, but he found Collins all plot, and the machinery sometimes too evident; for Trollope character was a novel's primary motivator (*Auto* XIII). Dissimilar in temperament as well as fictional approaches, Collins found Trollope's boisterousness hard to take. 'To me he was an incarnate gale of wind. He blew off my hat; he turned my umbrella inside out. Joking apart, as good and staunch a friend as ever lived' (*I & R* 127). RCT

Colmar, a town on the Alsace side of the col de Schlucht. On the rail line to Basle, it is the site of Mme Faragon's Hôtel de la Poste. *GLG* MG

Cologne, home to the Grüners, who welcome their niece when she arrives, sick and exhausted, after a three-day journey by train and Rhine boat. She dies in that city four months later. *LT*
AWJ

Colza, Miss. Middle-aged, talkative friend of Mrs Tom Mackenzie, she dresses girlishly. Despite her outgoing and confident manner, she is behind on her rent. She invites Margaret Mackenzie's dislike and resentment with her indefatigable cross-questioning on behalf of Margaret's desperate suitor Mr Maguire, whom Miss Colza eventually marries. *MM* SRB

comedy in Trollope's work. One could easily illustrate a textbook on comedy using nothing but the novels of Anthony Trollope, so widely does he range over various forms and techniques. Many of these—comedy of humours, sentimental comedy—he touches on only lightly, however; and others, namely satire, he came to regard as more or less mistaken ventures. There was not much he did not try, from the boisterous and Dickensian *The Three Clerks* to the absurdist humour of *The Fixed Period*, but he soon settled down to the delicate and subtle effects achievable within the form and tradition of the comedy of manners.

He did, first, have to disabuse himself of the notion that he was born to be a satirist. He wrote, back to back, *The Warden* and *The New Zealander*, both exercises in the Swiftian mode, or so he thought. In *The New Zealander* he achieved a much more consistent satire but in *The Warden* an infinitely more interesting work, partly because he was a very poor satirist and a quite wonderful novelist. In *The Warden*, Trollope seems to have set out to take sides with the reformers attacking the evil, but soon found he was, as he said, attacking those who did the attacking, causing him, he acknowledges, to fall between two stools. Actually, the novel is fascinating for its shift away from a 'position' toward a wry look at both sides. Trollope seems to have found, in writing *The Warden*, the balanced comedy, far more poised and ambiguous, that ruined the satiric directness but that gave us so much in the books to follow.

Trollope's characteristic comedy is, like all comedy, suspicious of extremes and, in that sense, deflationary. But Trollope is usually more interested in defending obvious comic targets than blasting them, just as he loves to rub a little dust onto his most stainless creations. His comedy manifests a distrust of systems and systematic thought so strong that he might be suspected of being anarchic, were he not himself suspicious of anarchists. Trollope's moral comedy is, as Ruth apRoberts convincingly shows, highly flexible in its morality, trusting more to the complex demands of particular personalities and situations than to rigid codes.

This comic dexterity and the resistance to systematic and formal patterning takes its most radical form in Trollope's resistance to 'plots', his robust and joyous battle against the tyranny of coherent action. Using a million tricks and arguments, Trollope slices at the very plot he is writing, suggesting to us always that plots are wooden and linear things, false to life and to the comic agility necessary to deal with a world that runs its course never with the predictability of conventional plots.

Trollope could sometimes pretend that plots were simply beyond him, but that is chicanery. The truth is that he held passionately to the belief that plot is 'the most insignificant part of the tale' (*Auto* VII). Plots suggest that life is linear, coherent, and causal, tied together logically, and thus understandable in terms of ordered patterns. Plots further tell us that 'men and women when they are written about are supposed to have fixed resolutions', which, in fact, they seldom do and generally live by only if they are fools or monomaniacs (*CR* XVI).

Trollope further found plots pointing too resolutely toward completed actions, fulfilments, a drive quite contrary to comic openness. Thus he very often ends a romantic comedy with jokes about endings, about marriages, or about the artificiality of the whole thing. In short, plots or external actions are too gross to account for the really important aspects of life: the tiny daily acts of kindness and sensitivity (or the reverse) that

make up the moral life. These are the issues that translate into 'the minute ramifications of tale-telling' ('A *Walk in a Wood', Good Words* (September 1879), 595–600) Trollope says he thought about in place of plot. It is the precision and exactitude of his focus that makes possible the subtlety and power of his art, qualities that derive from his most important comic source, the comedy of manners tradition.

His attachment to this tradition is, however, as deceptive as it is central. While he accepts many of the values and assumptions dear to comedy of manners, he does not accept fully the comedy of manners form. The morality and grounds for behaviour are traditional, but there is a sense that the world at large no longer gives support to these assumptions and that they are, therefore, detached, sometimes even absurd. They seem no longer to provide the source for community; and the establishment of community, after all, is the basis of comedy. Unlike the novels of Jane Austen, a Trollope novel cannot merely test and confirm these communal values. In each novel they must be redefined, remade, and reinstituted. Trollope works, then, in the comedy of manners tradition without the comforts of the tradition. There is a complex of values, positions, and beliefs there ready-made, but where is that sort of life now manifest? Who will accept these values to the point of being guided by them? Who, even, will understand? All the old confidence is gone, and with it the patterned symmetry.

But the values themselves are there as they always were, making central the standards of enlightened and sophisticated civilization. The stability provided by these standards allows (or should allow) for understanding, for the expression of warmth and kindness through wit. The central discovery of the comedy of manners is perhaps that the confidence permitting indirection also allows for far more radiance than simple, blunt openness. Trollope writes to his brother, for instance, on hearing that they expect a child: 'The pleasures of paternity have been considerably abridged, since the good old Roman privilege of slaying their offspring at pleasure, has been taken from fathers. But the delights of flagellation, though less keen, are more enduring. One can kill but once; but one may flog daily' (*Letters* 1, 31–2). Often the civilized standards are supported by attacks on the naivety of alternative modes, particularly on modes of simplicity like the romance or pastoral: 'Robinson Crusoe could hardly have been particular about his bed' (*HMWI* II). This cool, urbane tone suggests the judicious insouciance of the undeluded, the sense that one's own being and one's civilization are so firmly rooted and secure that they can do very well without excitement. Excessive zeal is seen as immature, potentially dangerous, since it exhibits a distrust of the basic security and thus threatens it: 'I am no Puritan myself, and fancy that had I lived in the days of the Puritans, I should have been anti-Puritan to the full extent of my capabilities' (NA 1, III).

One naturally strives, therefore, for command and understanding of the self, not for radical transformations. Thus the great importance of the motif of education, though the novels manage to accept the belief in education without swallowing the rationalist premises that often accompany it. Trollope consistently stressed the superiority of age to youth, claiming that youth had no advantage whatever for real work. Youth had acquired so little in life of what was worth acquiring that, he often said, the young probably had no justification in speaking or writing at all, apart from a fear that maturity might never come to them. The means for reaching this maturity were, for Trollope, much more simple than they were to rationalists. In place of deliberate, careful training, Trollope put his trust in time and experience. The absolute opposite of James Mill, Trollope would have regarded a child of 5 who knew Greek and Latin as a freak, probably less mature, in his sense, than one who had banged about, in a miscellaneous, unplanned way, in the nursery and in schools. Over and over, his novels define education in terms of the training of the imagination through a complex and gradual battle with experience, not as a development of the intellect through a planned immersion in recognized fields of knowledge. Arithmetic may, perhaps, be taught in this way but nothing important: 'The simple teaching of religion has never brought large numbers of Natives to live in European habits; but I have no doubt that European habits will bring about religion' (SA 2, IX). The subtle 'habits' of a civilization are equivalent to its spiritual life, and one must develop the sensitivity to recognize that.

Trollope's works are neither sentimental nor naive about civilization, nor are they cynical. His basic myth is one of wholeness, of home and family. Despite the defects of that civilization, he understands that the stability of the myth requires continuity and that those who would 'improve' the civilization are therefore those who do not understand it, who have never been educated to full citizenship. Idealists and Utopian reformers in Trollope are usually, like Mr Turnbull in the political novels, men with no private being, unfortunate outcasts from the very civilization they seek to transform. Like Dickens, Trollope often uses America as a symbol for the rubbish heap where all uncivilized rationalist reformers

are piled, the capital, Washington, being a purely ordered and theoretically rigid town and thus unfit for comfortable life. The theoretical man is, finally, dead, divorced from life.

But the theoretical man, more exactly the unconscious man, seems in most Trollope novels to be everywhere. As a result there is in Trollope a characteristic tone of lost-cause melancholy. The values are there, as always, clear and firm, but they seem not to take material form or to be anywhere in action. As a result we often get the sense that the narrator is defining values that have no currency, that he is using the world of the narrative to plead for another world. He does not sentimentalize the past, surely; his conservatism is rather a feeling for a greater wholeness than can be found in modern life, a life now so pressured and so protected by layers of insensitivity that the delicate, imaginative behaviour at the heart of the moral life of the comedy of manners is nearly lost. Men are so hidden from one another, have so lost touch with their instincts, that, in his bleakest moods, Trollope pleads for simple honesty, no more. Maybe we have little to say or do, he suggests; but at least we can be straight about that little.

One must finally accept things as they are in this comedy, accept them as being imperfect. Such an acceptance of a muted, untransformed world is a brave act in Trollope's novels. Though absolutely central to the comedy of manners tradition, the rejection of illusion is far more dangerous in Trollope than in, say, Jane *Austen. Without some protective illusion, one always faces the possibility of desolation. One gains a kind of liberation from rose-coloured glasses, but the view is not always worth much.

Aware as Trollope is of the price one pays for often bleak awareness, he protects us from pain by insisting always on a sharp distinction between men and the abstractions they seem to need, between men and what they do, between man as a social being and as a private person. The former might be guilty of all sorts of stupidity and cruelty, but the individual as he really is, is generally well-meaning, if seldom innocent. We get ourselves in messes, 'teaching ourselves to think', as Trollope loves to put it, all manner of cruel and nonsensical things. At bottom, though, we are generally not bad sorts, not at all.

It is the privacy of decency Trollope is committed to protecting and, now and then, allowing us to gather in small groups to celebrate. His comedy is hedged round with cautions, never bursting forth for very long and often remaining underground, a set of possibilities seldom realized. It is this sense of what is never quite there that lends to the best of Trollope's novels their characteristic and distinctive comic power. It is often a melancholy comedy, made all the more moving by the passion with which Trollope believes in it and the fear he has that it is gone.

JRK

comedy of manners. Trollope inherits from Ben Jonson, from Restoration comedy, and from 18th-century novelists like Fielding the mannerism of giving minor characters 'humorous' names—Fillgrave for the doctor in *The Warden*, Dry & Stickatit, the lawyers in *The Bertrams*. Modern commentators find this mannerism clumsy and disconcerting. TB

Comfort, Charles, rector of Cawston and father of Mrs Butler Cornbury. As his surname suggests, Revd Comfort is complacent, and there is a 'discrepancy between his doctrine and his conduct' (I). This hypocrisy leads Mrs Ray to forbid Rachel from seeing Luke Rowan. *RR*
MT

Commentaries of Caesar, The. Trollope's friend John *Blackwood the publisher had initiated in 1869 a series of 'Ancient Classics for English Readers', edited by William Lucas *Collins, a clergyman and teacher. Trollope expressed admiration for the first volumes, the *Iliad* and the *Odyssey*, both done by Collins himself, and when it was proposed that Trollope contribute to the series, he volunteered to do *The Commentaries of Caesar*. He had made himself thoroughly familiar with the original and with the criticism—in Latin, in English, and in French. Trollope fell to the work in January 1870, completed it in April, and in June the book was published. He wrote to Blackwood that though the work was 'tough', he had 'enjoyed it amazingly. . . . It has been a change to the spinning of novels, and has enabled me to surround myself for three months with books & almost to think myself a scholar' (*Letters* 1, 510).

He starts with a sound and useful introduction aiming to make the book available to those with no Latin. He explains that *Commentaria* means *Memoirs*, and he communicates a sort of historical thrill, a sense of the unique and inestimable value of these records written right in the centres of action by the great historical figure himself. He celebrates the prodigious powers of the man, whose varied accomplishments seem tremendous even in an age when prime ministers write novels and translate Homer. He proceeds with a summary-plus-commentary of the seven books of the *Gallic Wars* and the three books of the *Civil War*, in a space about one-third of the bulk of the original. He is often more lively and informal than Caesar himself: Caesar proceeds by

forced marches 'as fast as he could lay leg to ground' (*quam magnis itineribus*), or the Britons are lurking about 'as thick as blackberries'. He supplies enough history to make the narrative intelligible, adds occasional illustrative anecdotes, gives helpful touches such as identifying Brutus at his first appearance as indeed that same Brutus we all know from Shakespeare, and gives the modern French and English place names so we can understand the geography. Finally he adds a conclusion summarizing the rest of Caesar's life: the sensational sojourn and 'dalliance' in Egypt, the political triumph in Rome as dictator, and the events of Shakespeare's play.

Throughout, he is, as the narrator of the Pallisers might be expected to be, deeply interested in character, motive, and manœuvring, and urgently concerned with the morals of public life. The historian Mommsen, he notes, and Napoleon III, both consider Caesar to be quite the ideal leader. It is generally thought today that Mommsen's picture of Caesar is in good part propaganda for emperors; and Napoleon III, as Trollope understood, adored in Caesar what impressed him in his uncle Napoleon I. Trollope applies another standard of judgement: he insists on the brutality of this man who preferred to be known for his clemency. Repeatedly, as Trollope records, he ordered 'with a wave of his hand' the complete and bloody annihilation of whole villages and tribes. In his later and more important classical work, his two-volume study of Cicero, Trollope explains his devotion to Cicero as by far the better man than Caesar: Cicero exhibits honesty, political purity, charity, and *humanitas*. However much Caesar is to be admired for his generalship, his political acumen, his efficient literary style, we are not allowed to forget his inhumanity, his cruelty. Trollope refuses to lend himself to any strong-man hero-worship.

The book received little scholarly acclaim, but it was a success for the publisher and was reprinted several times. The most recent reprint is of 1981 by Arno Press, with an introduction by Ruth apRoberts. R apR

Commonplace Book. Between 1835 and 1840 Trollope recorded his views on classics of world literature, notably by Italian and Spanish writers including Boccaccio, Petrarch, Cervantes, and Dante. His major sources of information on these writers were Simonde de Sismondi's *Historical View of the Literature of the South of Europe* (2nd edn., 1846) and A. W. Schlegel's *Dramatic Art and Literature* (2nd edn., 1840). Of greater interest are entries on English writers such as Bulwer, Pope, and Dr Johnson. In his lengthy commentary on Pope's *Essay on Man* Trollope upbraided himself for his idleness and slovenly thinking: 'I have lost in a measure the power of thinking and reflecting.' Under a heading 'Order—Method' he inscribed self-disciplinary rules which were to govern his life. 'I am myself in all the pursuits (God help them) & practices of my life most disorderly & unmethodical.' He listed areas in which order was vital: 'In Religion—in our studies—in accounts—in diet—and in cleanliness.' Trollope made a particular point of the need for order in careful monetary accounting. The young man entering life, he advised, 'wd. make no bad bargain in dividing half his last shilling to buying a red book with blue perpendicular lines—Those blue lines so hated by the young gentry of small fortunes, would fill themselves with figures on the right sheet, were they properly attended to in every monetary transaction.' The future Post Office surveyor would maintain meticulous records of his expenditures on official business. An early interest in drama is apparent in the attention given to contemporary playwrights, such as his favourite dramatist Henry *Taylor. The Commonplace Book forms appendix A to *Letters* (2, 1021–8) (see also entries under individual names). The manuscript is in the Beinecke Library at Yale. RCT

Como, Lake, resort lake in northern Italy where the absentee Barchester prebendary Dr Vesey Stanhope and his family have lived for twelve years. After a brief but eventful sojourn in Barchester they return to their hospitable villa, well known to élite English travellers. *BT, W,* 'Money' *TAC2* NCS

Cong, small village near Castle Morony, on the outskirts of which Mr Robert Morris is murdered, and Captain Yorke Clayton wounded. *L* MRS

Connor, Pat, one-eyed jockey from Strokestown who rides in the Carrick races. *MB* MRS

Conolin, Father, one of Frau Frohmann's two advisers who counsels her to lessen luxuries at the Peacock Inn. 'Frohmann' *WFF* GRH

Conservative and Liberal administrations

succeeded each other regularly after the passing of the 1832 Reform Act. The two parties became more alike as each realized that middle-class opinion would be increasingly important in determining election results. Sir Robert *Peel led the conservative Tories from their left wing, while the liberal Whigs were led from the right by aristocrats like Lords Grey and Melbourne. Peel's 1846 repeal of the Corn Laws (protective tariffs on grain) split the Tory Party between its

brains, Peel's talented ministers such as William *Gladstone who followed him faithfully, and the bulk of its largely rural backbenchers goaded by Benjamin *Disraeli, who were enraged by Peel's treachery to English agriculture. Sir John *Trollope MP, Trollope's cousin, was among the latter. Trollope, a lifelong liberal, disapproved of Peel's unprincipled abandonment of protection, but he liked the unscrupulous Disraeli even less. This split, which returned the Whigs to power under Lord John Russell, further blurred party differences as the Peelites became talented free agents wooed by Whigs and Tories alike, while the Tories, now led by Lord Derby and Disraeli, struggled to free themselves from the increasingly discredited policy of protection. The Peelites' eventual decision to join the Whig Party was central to its transformation into the Liberal Party in the 1860s. This was the context of Lord *Palmerston's dominance between 1850 and 1865. A former Tory, he appealed skilfully to middle-of-the-road sentiment in Parliament and the electorate.

Against this background, Trollope's description of himself as 'an advanced but still a conservative liberal' (*Auto* XVI) is not so strange. His Palliser novels deal particularly with the crucial period following Palmerston's death in 1865, when a change of political generation occurred in both parties. The Liberals and Conservatives, soon to be led respectively by Gladstone, the former Tory, and Disraeli, a former radical, jockeyed to gain advantage over parliamentary reform and a favourable image with the ever-expanding electorate which now included a significant working-class presence. The similarities between Conservatives and Liberals were favourable to political stability—not for nothing has the mid-Victorian period been called the Age of Equipoise. They could also be regarded as unhealthy evidence of political opportunism, with each party ready to 'steal the clothes' of the other for partisan advantage.

Trollope tended towards this view, though he regarded Disraeli (to whom Daubeny in *Phineas Finn* owes much) as the worst offender. Yet Trollope's attempts to identify the essential difference between Liberals and Conservatives—as expressed in *An Autobiography* (XVI) and through Lady Glencora Palliser (*PF* XIV)—would probably have met widespread assent. He believed that the difference was over inequality: the Conservative would maintain inequality as divinely ordained, though to be softened by paternalism; the Liberal would strive always to diminish inequality, though its complete elimination might be impossible. CK

Parry, Jonathan, *The Rise and Fall of Liberal Government in Victorian England* (1993).

Stewart, Robert M., *The Foundation of the Conservative Party, 1830–1867* (1978).

Contemporary Review. In 1866, Alexander Strahan launched a half-crown monthly review of signed articles to bridge the gulf between secular and sacred reading. Like the secular and liberal *Fortnightly Review*, which had invited contributors of varying opinions, the *Contemporary* welcomed discussion, but intended to attract contributors and readers who held to the Articles of the Christian Faith. Strahan employed Henry *Alford, Dean of Canterbury, as editor. Alford attacked Trollope's series 'Clergymen of the Church of England', which had appeared in the *Pall Mall Gazette*, as amateurish and almost entirely ignorant of clergymen. Trollope described it as the most ill-natured review he had ever received. Early numbers were heavily weighted toward theological topics. Strahan then tried to broaden the appeal of the magazine by including such contributors as Poet Laureate Alfred Tennyson, William Gladstone, Matthew Arnold, John Ruskin, and T. H. Huxley. JWM

Srebrnik, Patricia Thomas, *Alexander Strahan, Victorian Publisher* (1986).

'Convocation' (article). This periodic meeting of clerics to argue over proposed ecclesiastical changes is farcical. Parliament alone is empowered to alter laws. Convocations should be abolished, as participation is beneath the dignity of deans and bishops. *Pall Mall Gazette* (20 February 1865), 2. AKL

Cook, Thomas (1808–92). As secretary of the South Midland Temperance Association, he organized the first advertised train excursion in England from Leicester to Loughborough and back (1841). This induced him to organize excursions at home and abroad. He published tourist handbooks and from 1846 issued the *Excursionist*, a monthly travel magazine. In *The Eustace Diamonds* Trollope recommended holidays in Scotland, for 'Switzerland and the Tyrol, and even Italy, are all redolent of Mr Cook' (XXXII). In *The Prime Minister*, however, the attitude to Cook's tours was more positive, the narrator commenting that the travelling world 'divided itself into Cookites and Hookites,—those who escaped trouble under the auspices of Mr Cook, and those who boldly combated the extortions of foreign innkeepers and the anti-Anglican tendencies of foreign railway officials "on their own hooks"' (LXVII). Trollope was one of the latter. RCT

Cooper, James Fenimore (1789–1851), American author of five 'Leather-Stocking Tales', the best known being *The Last of the Mohicans* (1826). While living in Europe (1826–33), Cooper occasionally circulated through the same salons as Mrs Trollope. When she was ill in Cincinnati, she read her way through all of Cooper's novels, which she called 'raw-headed and bloody bones adventures' (Glendinning 36). At the Harrow Weald farmhouse, Trollope found consolation in the first two volumes of Cooper's *The Prairie* (1827), which, though it was incomplete, he read many times. In America (1861), Trollope bought an edition of Fenimore Cooper's novels (32 volumes) and shipped it home. RCT

Copyright, Royal Commission on. The first English Copyright Act was the statute of 1709 which gave authors, or the printers, booksellers, or publishers to whom they had sold the right, fourteen years' exclusive right. In 1814 a new Act of Parliament extended copyright to 28 years, or, if writers had lived beyond this period, it gave them lifetime's property of their work. In 1837 Serjeant Talfourd began a campaign to increase the length of copyright, a campaign that succeeded in 1842, partly thanks to two celebrated parliamentary speeches by Macaulay. The 1842 Act extended copyright to a period of 42 years from the date of publication, or to the lifetime of an author plus 7 years, whichever proved longer. Acts of 1838 and 1844 permitted foreign authors to benefit from British protection, provided they were nationals of countries extending reciprocal copyright to British writers. As Dickens had obstreperously protested during his American visit in 1842, the United States was conspicuous for its failure to agree to these reciprocal arrangements. As Trollope himself was to put it in *An Autobiography*, the want of an agreement with America was 'the one great impediment to pecuniary success which still stands in the way of English successful authors' (XVII).

Trollope's experience with *North America* in 1862 ensured that he had a personal stake in the issue. (See COPYRIGHTS, HALF-PROFITS, ROYALTIES; 'REJOINDER TO MR HARPER'.) Four years later the aggrieved Trollope wrote a paper (published as *'On the Best Means of Extending and Securing an International Law of Copyright') for a meeting of the National Association for the Promotion of Social Science. He was subsequently commissioned by the Foreign Office to reopen the issue of international copyright with Washington, during his official visit to the United States in 1868 to negotiate a new postal treaty. Nothing came of his efforts. In 1876, however, he was asked to serve on the Royal Commission on Copyright (1876–7). He proved to be one of the commission's most active members, despite his absence in South Africa in the spring of 1877. On his return, however, renewed pressure on his fellow commissioners occasioned Lord John Manners's comment that Trollope was irritating everyone by insisting on covering material that had been discussed in his absence. After the Commission reported, no change was made to English law, nor was one forthcoming in Trollope's lifetime. The issue of American copyright was not to be resolved until 1909.   ALS

copyrights, half-profits, royalties were key terms in assigning the profits of literary labour between writer and publisher, though the royalty system, where the writer receives a fixed sum for every copy sold, was not used by Trollope since it did not become established in Britain till late in the 19th century. Under the amended Copyright Act of 1842, writers were granted a statutory copyright in their own writings for 42 years from the date of publication or for 7 years after their death, whichever was longer.

Nearly all Trollope's earliest works, *The Macdermots of Ballycloran*, *The Kellys and the O'Kellys*, *The Warden*, and *Barchester Towers*, were sold to publishers on the terms that were known as the half-profits system. Under this the author assigned the copyright in his work to them for a limited period and agreed to accept as payment one-half of all receipts from sales, after various deductions such as manufacturing costs, advertising, and incidentals.

It was an arrangement which lent itself to false claims about costs on the part of the publisher. There were other disadvantages: publishers did not often risk printing many copies or go out of their way to promote novels published on these terms. Only 400 copies of *The Macdermots* and 375 of *The Kellys* were printed: even if a demand for these novels had arisen, buyers would not have been able to get their hands on them.

From 1858 onwards, Trollope's contracts with publishers were couched in terms of the sale of copyright, including a reference to foreign rights. In some cases the agreement would specify that the sale was for a limited period of three years, or a limited print run after which a half-share would revert to the author. By the time of his second serial, *Orley Farm*, it was agreed that a half-share should revert to Trollope after 10,000 copies had been manufactured. Variations on this agreement, by which the copyright reverted to Trollope entirely or in part some time after the work, or an agreed number of copies, had been published, were used in most subsequent contracts. In the case of *North America*, Chapman & Hall reserved an option to buy a half-share of the copyright after two years at a fixed price.

Smith, Elder would have been inclined to make an outright purchase of all rights when buying his work, but Trollope appears to have resisted this for some years, in order to retain ownership of his copyrights. Astute reissue of novels in cheaper formats and editions could make sure that they were continuing to bring in money long past their first appearance in print, as Dickens had demonstrated, and at that stage Trollope did not mean to let the reissue of his novels pass out of his own control. When it came to *The Small House at Allington*, he would let Smith, Elder have only the serial rights, with foreign and American rights while the serial was coming out and a licence to bring out book editions which must be taken up within eighteen months. He retained all foreign rights in his next major novel, *Can You Forgive Her?* Nevertheless, he allowed Smith to buy the entire copyright of *The Claverings*, within the first twelve months of its serialization, when he saw that it was not proving popular with readers.

Trollope was his own agent and his own manager, set on getting the best return for his work as a writer: if he allowed Virtue to buy the absolute copyright in *Phineas Finn* for £3,200, and accepted the same terms when they were offered a few months later for *He Knew He Was Right*, he may have felt that it was unwise to pass up such substantial immediate gains. Later he claimed that he had tired of dealing with the multiple negotiations necessary to sell off rights separately. It was a decisive moment in his career as a writer, for at this point he was giving up his Post Office work and moving into writing novels which made fewer concessions to popular appeal.

After 1867 Trollope did sell off copyrights, though the unit price came down even in the case of *The Way We Live Now*, which made only £3,000. By 1878, Chapman & Hall could buy the entire book-copyright of *The Duke's Children* for £1,000, while the price offered for book-copyright of *The Landleaguers*, the last novel he would write, was only £600. Trollope refused to make a matter of financial gain out of the copyright of *The Commentaries of Caesar* when he gave it as a birthday present to John Blackwood.

Baron *Tauchnitz of Leipzig paid the publishers directly for the rights when he brought out editions of more than 40 of Trollope's books in English under his own imprint for the European market. The three issued by his rivals, Asher of Berlin, *The Eustace Diamonds*, *Miss Mackenzie*, and *Phineas Redux*, were also authorized editions. In the States, however, most of Trollope's books made their first appearance in pirated editions issued by Harper, though Lippincott, who brought out *The Vicar of Bullhampton*, *North America*, and *The Belton Estate*, did pay for the American rights.

In the case of *North America*, however, in June 1862 Harper rushed out a pirated version at 60 cents before Lippincott's more expensive authorized one was ready. Trollope was provoked into writing a letter (reprinted in the *Athenaeum*) to James Russell *Lowell on the subject of international copyright quoting this experience: 'between no other nations can a copyright law be of the importance that it is between you and us, because no other two great reading people speak the same language. . . . I think you will admit that the difficulty is on your side of the water, and that such a law would be sanctioned here without doubt or dissent (*Letters* 1, 196, 197–8). He became associated with the campaign for international copyright, so that in 1868 he was commissioned by the Foreign Office to act in negotiations over international copyright during a visit he was making to Washington. Trollope was appointed to a Royal Commission on International Copyright in 1876. MH

Nowell-Smith, S., *International Copyright Law and the Publisher in the Reign of Queen Victoria* (1968).
Sadleir, M., *Trollope: A Bibliography* (1928).
Sutherland, J., *Victorian Novelists and Publishers* (1976).

Corcoran, Barney, delivers turf to Ardkill Cottage and so enlivens the O'Haras' solitude. *EE*
AWJ

Cornboro, small northern town in which Mary Gresley's father had been a medical practitioner. 'Gresley' *ET* GRH

Cornbury, Butler, eldest son of the squire nearest to Baslehurst and son-in-law of the Revd Charles Comfort. Persuaded by his ambitious wife, Butler Cornbury bids to represent Baslehurst in Parliament as a Tory. He wins by one vote after a lively campaign during which Mrs Butler Cornbury canvasses for support at Mrs Tappitt's ball (VII, VIII) *RR* MT

Cornbury, Patty (née **Comfort**), daughter of Revd Charles Comfort, wife of Butler Cornbury, and formidable member of local squirearchy near Baslehurst. Mrs Butler Cornbury campaigns fiercely for the election of her husband to Parliament and engages in a memorable verbal duel with Mr and Mrs Tappitt. She takes Rachel Ray under her wing at the Tappitts' ball and continues to support the union of Rachel with Luke Rowan. *RR* MT

Cornbury, Walter, cousin of Mrs Butler Cornbury. Walter flirts and dances with Rachel Ray at the Tappitts' ball, but Luke outwits him and takes Rachel in to supper himself. *RR* MT

Cornhill Magazine. Trollope frequently contributed to this monthly shilling magazine begun in January 1860. With Thackeray's name on the title-page as editor, anticipation for the new monthly ran high, advertisers predicting it would include the best-known writers of the day. Published by Smith, Elder, and Co., its first number was enormously successful, selling over 100,000 copies. In 128 pages, it offered five educational essays of the type that had been the speciality of the more costly quarterlies, the first instalments of *Lovel the Widower* and the 'Roundabout Papers' by Thackeray, *Framley Parsonage* with two full-page illustrations by John Everett Millais, all for one shilling. Contributions were unsigned. Thackeray wrote in the first number that this magazine would entertain while presenting information of the least disconcerting kind.

The *Cornhill* quickly became the most popular of the monthly magazines for educated readers, setting the style and appearance for later shilling magazines. Its attractive pages were not divided into columns, each article began on a new page, and each number contained an illustration and often poetry. It included no politics. A later editor, Leslie Stephen, Thackeray's son-in-law, complained that he could not make much of a magazine which excluded the two topics that interested reasonable men—politics and religion. Articles were informative, but not scholarly, seeking to entertain while instructing. Reviews said that the *Cornhill* had discovered a large, previously overlooked audience of readers of literature of a high class.

George Smith was trading on the popularity of serialized novels by giving his readers two first-class novelists along with the contents of a general review. Novels at mid-century were sometimes issued serially in monthly paper-bound parts costing one shilling. Smith offered his readers a monthly part of a novel along with a great deal more of literary interest, all for the price of the novel. *Macmillan's Magazine*, the first shilling magazine, begun in November 1859, had followed this general plan, but it had no particular speciality in fiction, whereas the *Cornhill* emphasized fiction by including such leading novelists as Trollope, Charles Lever, George Eliot, Elizabeth Gaskell, Wilkie Collins, Charles Reade, Thomas Hardy, and Henry James. Contributors of articles and poetry included Leslie Stephen, Harriet Beecher Stowe, W. S. Gilbert, Alfred Tennyson, Robert Louis Stevenson, G. H. Lewes,

Matthew Arnold, and Edmund Gosse. After publishing works in the *Cornhill*, Smith then published them in book form, thus acquiring a very good stable of writers. Smith assured the success of the magazine by paying first-rate contributors well and exercising excellent taste and business sense. Thackeray was editor in name only, Smith doing the real work. In the early numbers, circulation remained around 80,000, *Framley Parsonage* contributing to that success. Even Thackeray admitted that Trollope was more popular with readers than he was.

By 1862, when Thackeray's health was declining, Smith chaired an editing committee consisting of George Henry Lewes, later editor of the *Fortnightly Review*, of which Trollope was one of the proprietors; Frederick *Greenwood, journalist and later founder of the *Pall Mall Gazette* and *St James's Gazette*; and Dutton Cook.

Trollope's inclusion in the first number had come about quite by chance. He was writing a series of short stories, to be collected in two volumes after magazine publication as *Tales of All Countries*, and had offered them to *Harper's New Monthly Magazine*. *Harper's* had only wanted one story every other month. In October 1859, Trollope saw the advertisement for the new shilling magazine. He wrote to Thackeray offering his stories to appear in alternate months with *Harper's*. Smith, who made all editorial decisions, agreed to take the stories at the same price *Harper's* was paying, pointing out that his pages were half the size, but then said he preferred a full-length novel. Trollope offered *Castle Richmond*, which he had already begun. Smith did not want an Irish story, but agreed to publish it separately. Trollope had never published a novel in serial form, and was reluctant to begin with publication of an unfinished novel, but agreed to do so, realizing the importance of appearing in a new magazine edited by Thackeray. Trollope had just begun writing *Framley Parsonage* on his trip from Dublin to see Smith and continued it with some urgency. The success of the *Cornhill* helped Trollope's career greatly. After *Framley Parsonage* appeared in monthly parts, almost all Trollope's subsequent novels appeared first in magazines or in monthly parts. In the early years of the *Cornhill*, he contributed more than anyone else: for more than four years, scarcely a number appeared without one of his novels, including *The Struggles of Brown, Jones, and Robinson*, *The Small House at Allington*, and *The Claverings*; or an article, such as 'The Civil Service as a Profession'; or a review of his work. When Trollope became editor of a shilling magazine in 1867, *Saint Pauls Magazine*, he clearly had the *Cornhill* in mind.

Smith held monthly dinners for *Cornhill* contributors where Trollope met literary men who became his friends: John Everett Millais who illustrated *Framley Parsonage*, *The Small House at Allington*, and *Phineas Finn*; Charles *Taylor; G. H. *Lewes; Robert *Bell whom he would ask to be sub-editor of *Saint Pauls* and who contributed to the *Fortnightly*; and W. H. *Russell of *The Times*, among others. In 1865, Smith established an evening newspaper, the *Pall Mall Gazette*, taking the name from the fictional paper in Thackeray's *Pendennis*. Many *Cornhill* contributors wrote for this new publication, including Trollope, who became virtually 'a permanent member' of staff (*Auto* XI) between 1865 and 1868.

By 1868 the *Cornhill*'s circulation held at 26,000. It had inspired a number of imitators, including *St James's Magazine*, the *Belgravia*, and *Temple Bar*. By 1883, novelist James *Payn edited the *Cornhill*, which was then a sixpenny magazine with fewer essays and more light fiction. In 1896 it returned to being a shilling magazine and continued until 1975.   JWM

Cornwall, south-westernmost county of England, county seat Truro. Cornwall occupies the tip of a peninsula jutting into the Atlantic, between the Celtic Sea and the English Channel. It is a popular tourist area. Mudbury Docimer's country house, Tregothnan Hall, is located here (*AA*). See also POLWENNING (*DC*) and 'MALACHI'S COVE'.   WK

Cornwall, Gustavus C., Secretary of the Dublin Post Office (1850–85) to whom, in April 1857, Trollope wrote a report on house-to-house postal delivery. Trollope was by now a full surveyor and not involved in deliveries in rural areas, but his opinion was highly valued. His letter is a fair indication of the thoroughness and attention to detail he gave to his job (*Letters* 1, 54–7). Trollope visited his former colleague during his trip to Ireland with Florence Bland in 1882.   RCT

Cosby Lodge, country home of Major Henry Grantly, which he intends to close if his father Archdeacon Grantly carries out his threat of disinheritance. *LCB*   NCS

Costa Rica, Central American republic noted for its coffee plantations and Serapiqui river in which Mrs Arkwright drowns. 'Returning Home' *TAC2*   GRH

country houses and estates. Trollope's country houses and estates are primary indicators of the characters and class of his fictional families, and through them we become aware of a finely ordered social structure. The British country house was part of a rural economic system stretching back to Tudor times, with its roots in feudal tradition. The principle of primogeniture ensured that estates were handed down intact through the generations, though this often flew in the face of rational judgement; Roger Carbury (*WWLN*) and Sir Harry Hotspur (*SHH*) both face this dilemma. Owning land gave power and influence but carried with it many duties to be discharged in the local community, a precept clearly grasped by Lady Sarah Germain, but notably absent in the Marquis, her brother (*IHP*). Retainers felt an equal bond between place and moral order. The gardener Hopkins (*SHA*) is one example. He speaks loudly against the disruption of natural order threatened by the Dales leaving the small house (LIII). Andy Gowran, steward of the Portray estate (*ED*), is fiercely defensive of the property, telling Lady Eustace defiantly, 'There's timber and a warld o' things aboot the place as wants protection on behalf o' the heir' (XXVI). Thus a mutuality of respect between owner and estate was a principle of cohesion in the old social structure.

The Industrial Revolution disrupted this order and permanently changed the social significance of the country house. By selling the coal mined on their lands the older landed families helped create a new super-rich 'aristocracy', while success in trade and speculation funded the purchase of large houses for the nouveaux riches. This disruption of the old order undermined the position of Roger Carbury (*WWLN*), who was poorer than his neighbours but would not subscribe to the sordid commercial values of the age, unlike Adolphus Longestaffe, squire of Caversham, who coveted a place on Melmotte's railway board. Longestaffe's feckless son 'Dolly' has far more principle when he says, 'A fellow oughtn't to let his family property go to pieces' (XXVIII).

Trollope's satiric attack on self-made men like Melmotte is regularly made through descriptions of their houses. Robert Kennedy's mansion, built by his father, is made of stone, but it was 'cut only yesterday' (*PF* XIV). Timber is another significant indicator. 'The new trees show the new man. A new man can buy a forest, but he can't get park trees' (*PF* XIV). Earl De Guest (*SHA*) knows every tree on his land, though we know little of his house. Detail of Monkhams (*HKWR*) is also scanty, but George Glascock praises its ancient oaks in his wooing of Nora Rowley, and Mary Lovelace is said to have found the old elms of Manor Cross (*IHP*) very tempting. Studying the houses in *Orley Farm* is instructive for the distinction Trollope makes as to character and place. In this sphere he comes closest to Jane Austen.

Gardens are another telling feature. At Clavering Park (*C*), they are dry, dusty, and neglected, at some distance from the house, a metaphor for Sir Hugh Clavering's disposition. Courcy Castle's grounds, like their lord, are not very inviting, and Harry Gilmour symbolically betrays his office when he abandons his gardens half built (*VB*). In contrast, Lady Lufton's gardens were trim and neat (*FP*); at Nethercoats, the gardens are the greatest glory (*CYFH*).

The houses Trollope prefers have a domestic compactness to them. The Horns is 'a beautiful little place in Surrey' (*SHA* XLIII). Ongar Park, the prize of Julia Brabazon's dower, is described as perfect for an ordinarily wealthy family (*C*), while Nethercoats is said to be a model of comfort (*CYFH*). Trollope contrasts these sharply with Gatherum Castle, that monument to conspicuous consumption, built on so vast a scale that on completion, the Duke of Omnium could find nowhere in it comfortable to live, and went back to the smaller house his grandfather had built (*DT* XIX).

A great surge of interest in chivalric codes and medievalism occurred in the 19th century. St George's Hall, Windsor, was rebuilt in the medieval style in the 1820s and Queen Victoria commissioned portraits of Albert in medieval battle dress. Disraeli's fiction indulged the feudalist nostalgia. Trollope's contribution was Elizabethan tradition, represented by the Thornes' *fête-champêtre* with jousting and archery (*BT* XXXV). Some of Trollope's houses, like Ullathorne (*BT*), had never abandoned the trappings of their Tudor ancestors, but most people bought collections of armour for their halls. Trollope acidly remarks that the Duke of Omnium fills the hall at Gatherum with marble busts from Italy, and armour from Wardour Street—the centre of the antique auction trade (*FP* VIII).

Trollope's time was the heyday of the country house party, when hostesses vied to get the most prestigious guest list. Lady De Courcy scores a coup when she secures Plantagenet Palliser *and* Lady Dumbello for the same week (*SHA*). In the management of their guests, hostesses wield a power and influence that parodies the duties of the squirearchy of old. Mrs Montacute Jones pursues her matchmaking to fruition at Killancodlem (*IHP*); Ayala is cornered into accepting Jonathan Stubbs by Lady Albury at Stalham (*AA*). Lady Glencora goes to elaborate lengths to entertain guests useful to her husband's administration at Gatherum (*PM*). Adolphus Crosbie is perceived to be the perfect house guest because he is so pliable (*SHA*). Scottish country seats come into their own in the autumn for the shooting. Not surprisingly, fox-hunting is the most regular and popular entertainment supplied by Trollope's hosts. The debate about a landowner's duty to promote foxes is pursued with gusto. In an episode of mock-heroic irony, Plantagenet Palliser is persuaded he should spend up to £2,000 a year preserving foxes for his neighbour's sport (*PR* LXXV).

Trollope's houses are commonly dated by monarch. Courcy Castle is William III (1689–1702); Carbury Manor is Charles II (1660–85), but commonly thought to be Tudor; the Cleeve (*OF*) is Charles II extensions on an Elizabethan original. Trollope has little affection for the modern; Gatherum is a vulgar monstrosity, both in size and appearance. Built of white stone, with two long wings, and a huge portico with ionic columns, with great broad steps, it is probably an Italianate version of Blenheim. It cost a quarter of a million (*CYFH* XVIII), and was 'very cold, very handsome, and very dull' (LXXX).

Trollope makes no secret that he most admires the soft golden stone of the Tudor houses, their mullions mellowed with lichen. Ullathorne's 'beautiful rich tawny yellow colour, the effect of that stonecrop of minute growth that has taken three centuries to produce' (*BT* XXII), Allington's asymmetrical gables and windows (*SHA*), Greshambury's purest Tudor architecture (*DT*); these are Trollope's quintessential English country houses. The reader can visit Trollope's ideal country house: Montacute House, Somerset, was his model for Ullathorne.   MM

McMaster, Juliet, 'Trollope's Country Estates', in John Halperin (ed.), *Trollope Centenary Essays* (1982).

Courcy Castle, the De Courcy family home in West Barsetshire. A huge brick pile built in the days of William III, it has a castle gate, two stumpy towers, and grounds neither inviting nor extensive. Squire Gresham and his son find it dull. *DT, SHA, LCB*   NCS

courtship. In *An Autobiography*, Trollope refers to novel-writing as 'the fabrication of love-stories' (XIX). The remark is ironically self-deprecating, but it contains a good deal of truth. All Trollope's novels tell at least one love story; some tell several; and in his opinion, 'a novel can hardly be made interesting or successful without love'. Nor is this interest trivial. 'A vast proportion of the teaching of the day' is done by novels, and their main lessons are directed at young people. Young men 'unconsciously learn what are, or should be, or may be, the charms of love', a rather ill-defined course of instruction. But young women gain far more specific, even practical knowledge from novels: 'It is from them that

girls learn what is expected of them, and what they are to expect when lovers come' (*Auto* XII).

Probably few young women have ever learned from Trollope how to conduct a courtship, but his emphasis in *An Autobiography* indicates that, for him, love expresses itself in courting, and courting is chiefly a young woman's concern. Trollope's fiction presents many highly nuanced studies of married couples, most notably that of Plantagenet and Lady Glencora Palliser, which spans five novels, from *Can You Forgive Her?* to *The Prime Minister.* He can be painfully acute on the miseries that attend unhappy marriages, like those of Louis and Emily Trevelyan in *He Knew He Was Right*, Robert and Lady Laura Kennedy in *Phineas Finn* and *Phineas Redux*, and Cecilia and George Western in *Kept in the Dark.* But Trollope's married couples, especially those of long standing, are most often placid and settled; the great drama of their own lives is over, the great question answered.

That question—Whom shall I marry?—possesses crucial importance for young men as well as for young women. Trollope's novels offer several portraits of devoted young men who cannot win the young women of their choice, ranging from Johnny Eames in *The Small House at Allington* and *The Last Chronicle of Barset* to Larry Twentyman in *The American Senator* to the ridiculous but endearing Tom Tringle in *Ayala's Angel.* Sometimes, the man falls in love at first sight and pursues the woman until she surrenders, as Will Belton does in *The Belton Estate.* Many of Trollope's young men, however, drift aimlessly from one woman to another, as Frank Greystock does in *The Eustace Diamonds*; when a young man's first love is thwarted, he can usually find happiness with a second, as both Larry Twentyman and Tom Tringle do. Important as the choice of a wife is to Trollope's young men, they have professional or political concerns to distract them. But for most of Trollope's young women, 'Whom shall I marry?' is the only burning question, and courtship is the main event of their lives.

Trollopian courtship is a paradoxical business. In keeping with Victorian stereotypes, the man moves while the woman waits for him; he is active, she is passive. But that passivity is only apparent. In most cases, Trollope's women have decided whom they love far in advance of any proposal or even of their chosen man's awareness; when the chosen man speaks, it is the woman's victory, not his. Clara Amedroz's response to Captain Frederic Aylmer's half-hearted proposal is typical: 'Her first feeling was one of triumph,—as it must be in such a position to any woman who has already acknowledged to herself that she loves the man who then asks her to be his wife' (*BE* X). It is the triumph of self-willed submission: 'Hitherto she had been independent,—she had specially been careful to show to him her resolve to be independent of him. Now she would put aside all that, and let him know that she recognized in him her lord and master as well as husband' (*BE* XI).

Once the right men propose and are accepted, Trollope's women feel no qualms about expressing the love that they have kept to themselves until that moment. Clara responds so warmly that she terrifies the rather timid Captain Aylmer. Lucy Morris 'threw from her, at once, as vain and wicked and false, all idea of coying her love' (*ED* XV). Lily Dale agrees: 'She had seen girls who were half ashamed of their love; but she would never be ashamed of hers or of him. She had given herself to him; and now all the world might know it, if all the world cared for such knowledge' (*SHA* IX). Such frankness is refreshing, perhaps, as well as typically Trollopian. But there is a catch in it.

As the cases of Clara, Lucy, and Lily illustrate, Trollopian courtship is an almost wholly internal process that takes place within a young woman's mind; it may or may not find corroboration in the external world. Clara gives her love to Captain Aylmer in the absence of any encouragement or sign of reciprocation from him. Lucy has made the same secret gift to Frank Greystock; she is even willing to spend the rest of her life alone, if Frank should never wake up to the fact: 'She had given away her heart, and yet she would do without a lover' (*ED* III). When Lily is jilted by Augustus Crosbie, she learns that the gift of her love was misplaced, that he is, in fact, a cad and not at all the man she fell in love with.

In the end, Clara realizes that she never loved Captain Aylmer in the first place, that she has 'given her whole heart' instead to Will Belton, whom she marries (*BE* XXX). Lucy remains true to Frank throughout his repeated dalliances with Lizzie Eustace, and in the end Lucy is rewarded with his love. Lily never gives up her devotion to a non-existent man, despite the pleadings of Johnny Eames, who sincerely loves her. The narrator of *The Last Chronicle* dismisses her with the relieved assurance, 'in the last word I shall ever write respecting her, that she will live and die as Lily Dale' (LXXVII). A similar, even more extreme case is that of Emily Hotspur, who gives her love to her cousin George, only to be confronted with irrefutable evidence that he is 'a brute, unredeemed by any one manly gift; idle, self-indulgent, false, and without a principle' (*SHH* XXII). She cannot marry him, and she will not marry anyone else. But mere spinsterhood does not suffice for Emily. Having lost the imaginary man she loves, she devotes herself to good works among the poor, takes to reading 'dreary' books, and finally fades away, although the doctors can find 'nothing radically amiss with Miss Hotspur' (*SHH* XXIV).

The outcome of Trollopian courtship is variable: the man may prove worthy of the woman's love, he may vacillate a long time before reciprocating it, or he may turn out to be wholly other than what she imagined. In any case, it hardly matters what the man is or does; the woman, the apparently passive partner, makes the decisive move. Trollope often describes this act as a gift, and it is almost always an irrevocable one: 'My love was a thing to give', says Emily Hotspur, 'but when given I cannot take it back' (*SHH* VIII). If a woman has gone so far as to declare her love, the die is cast: 'When a girl has once brought herself to tell a man that she loves him', says Lady Frances Trafford, 'according to my idea she cannot give him up' (*MF* XII). Lady Mary Palliser concurs: 'She had told the man that she loved him, and after that there could be no retreat' (*DC* V). Such love persists despite all discouragement. Having declared her love to Ferdinand Lopez, Emily Wharton remains devoted to him even after his exposure as a blackguard and his suicide in front of a train; she eventually agrees to marry Arthur Fletcher, but only because it is her 'duty' (*PM* LXXIX).

Trollope, of course, does not ignore the manifold considerations of property and rank that courtship entails; nor does he neglect the rituals that attend it. But a man's wealth or lack of it seldom makes any significant difference in a woman's heart, and Trollope's young women are just as likely to refuse sincerely devoted suitors as they are to give their hearts to men who have hardly noticed them. The forms of courtship are irrelevant to women's love, which for them is a wholly internal matter until they declare it. The irrelevance of forms is most fully illustrated in *Ayala's Angel*, which offers every variety of male courting behaviour from Tom Tringle's dogged devotion to Frank Houston's cynicism to Benjamin Batsby's witlessness. In all cases, however, it is the women who choose, and they do so without regard for grace, money, or even the men's desire.

The most prominent young woman in *Ayala's Angel* is 'romantic, dreamy, poetic, childish' Ayala Dormer (VII), who starts out already in love with a non-existent, indeed impossible man, her 'Angel of Light'. This vague figure possesses a few unlikely characteristics, such as 'wings tinged with azure'; for the most part, however, he is 'confined altogether to the abstract', a mere 'conception of poetic perfection' (VI). The Angel exists in Ayala's mind and nowhere else; he seems to share some traits with Shelley, Byron, and possibly Tennyson's Arthur, but mainly he represents the fulfilment of Ayala's own yearning, which at first is as vague as he is. Yet the Angel has the power to make her reject marriage proposals from Tom Tringle, Captain Batsby, and Colonel Jonathan Stubbs, and thereby to put her future in jeopardy.

Gradually, however, Ayala comes to recognize that Stubbs *is* the Angel and has been all along. He starts as the Angel's opposite: 'Nothing could be more unlike an Angel of Light than Colonel Stubbs' (XVI); then she concedes that the Angel might have bristly red hair, as Stubbs does (XXVI). Later, she admits that there is 'something of the Angel about him' (XLV), then 'no more than a few of the real attributes of an Angel of Light' (XLIX), and finally 'all those attributes which should by right belong to an Angel of Light' (LII). The identity is complete and, more importantly, always has been: 'No!—her heart had never been predisposed to any one else. It was of him she had always dreamed even long before she had seen him' (LII).

In practical terms, of course, Stubbs is an ideal suitor. He has a brilliant military record, a comfortable income, and the boundless admiration of all who know him. But these material considerations mean nothing to Ayala. Nor does the Colonel's first marriage proposal. The second time he proposes, Ayala has already brought her imaginary Angel into accord with this real one, or perhaps the other way round. Then, and only then, can she accept him. This convergence of the imagined and the real, the internal and the external, in a woman's mind is the essence of Trollopian courtship. The rest is window dressing.

Trollope usually leaves the prudential aspects of courtship to his older, long-married characters, who offer his young people many pages of wise advice on the appropriateness of prospective husbands or wives. The young people themselves often spend many pages worrying about whether parental permission will be granted, or where the money will come from. Such matters sometimes postpone love matches, but they never decide them, although the matches may turn out to be disastrous for other reasons. Trollope, in fact, heaps pity and disdain on those of his younger characters—such as the wretched Lucinda Roanoke in *The Eustace Diamonds* and Arabella Trefoil in *The American Senator*—to whom rank and wealth are the primary considerations in seeking a mate. For all Trollope's meticulous attention to the minutiae of social and financial arrangements, his view of courtship is, at bottom, a thoroughly romantic one.   WK

'Courtship of Susan Bell, The', first printed in *Harper's New Monthly Magazine*, August 1860 (reprinted in *TAC1*); a trial run for the novel *Rachel Ray* (1863). Mrs Henrietta Bell is left a widow in Saratoga Springs, New York State, with two daughters. The younger, Susan, falls in love with a railway engineer, Aaron Dunn, who is lodging with the Bells. The evangelical elder Miss Bell and her mother disapprove of Aaron, thinking him a wolf. He leaves and, when he does not write, is assumed to have abandoned Susan. But he returns to claim her. Her family are reconciled to him.   JS

courts of justice. 'For the more speedy, universal, and impartial administration of justice between subject and subject', says Blackstone, 'the law hath appointed a prodigious number of courts.' Since the time covered by Trollope's novels, most of these courts have been consolidated. Those mostly concerned in his novels are magistrates' courts, assize and circuit courts, the Central Criminal Court (or Old Bailey), the Queen's Bench, and the Court of Chancery. Among other functions, a magistrates' court, composed of at least two lay justices, decides whether there is evidence sufficient to commit for trial or indictment, as in the charge of theft against Revd Crawley in chapter VIII of *The Last Chronicle of Barset*. In *Orley Farm*, though Trollope erred in many details, Lady Mason appears before a local magistrates' court which hears the grounds for prosecution, then before a grand jury which brings a 'true bill' against her, and then has a full trial before an assize court. Judges of assize from the superior courts, accompanied by barristers assigned to specific circuits, were sent regularly to each county to try actions and criminal cases. In London, the Queen's Bench was the supreme court of common law, taking cognizance of both civil and criminal causes. In *Lady Anna*, it figures in the case of 'Lovel versus Murray and Another', to decide who should inherit the old Earl's personal property, the Solicitor-General, Sir William Patterson, acting for the Earl. The most sensational trials, of course, occur in the Central Criminal Court, known as the Old Bailey. Sir Henry Hawkins (Baron Brampton), says in his *Reminiscences* (1904) that the Old Bailey was 'a den of infamy in those days [around 1843] not conceivable now. . . . Its associations were enough to strike a chill of horror into you' (38). The public regarded it as a place of entertainment, booing, catcalling, and applauding, and the sheriff's officers charged admittance (two shillings in 1848). It sat from 9 to

9, breaking for sybaritic dinners at 3 and 5 p.m. Barristers at the Old Bailey, savage in cross-examination and publicly notorious, had low professional status. Trollope, for whom cross-examination was his bugbear, epitomizes the Old Bailey barrister in the brash, untidy, and bullying lawyer Chaffanbrass, who defends Alaric Tudor, charged with embezzlement in *The Three Clerks*, Lady Mason, charged with perjury in *Orley Farm*, and Phineas Finn, charged with murder in *Phineas Redux*. The Court of Chancery, complementary to the courts of common law, was intended to do justice in cases where remedies at common law were inadequate, the Lord Chancellor, the highest law officer in the kingdom, being, as Blackstone says, the 'keeper of the king's conscience'. It had jurisdiction over such cases as those concerning trusts, the disposition and administration of property, frauds, wardship, and mistakes in deeds. The malicious waste to his estate that Mr Scarborough contemplates in order to spite his greedy son Augustus in *Mr Scarborough's Family* would be grounds for a Chancery case. RDM

Cousin Henry (*see opposite*)

Cowcross Street, home of Mr Jones, partner in a firm of haberdashers. *SBJR* HO

Cowley, Abraham (1618–67), royalist poet and essayist who published *Poems* (1656) and other works. In his Commonplace Book, Trollope, having read Johnson's 'Life of Cowley', commented: 'A poet who is more learned than enthusiastic & more witty than sublime or pathetic, is not to my taste. I shall therefore probably not take up much time in reading Cowley—or his fellows—' (*Letters* 2, 1023). RCT

Cowper, William (1731–1800). Rector of Olney, Buckinghamshire, he wrote *Olney Hymns* (1779) and *The Task* (1785), a poem on country life which brought him fame. Trollope listed Cowper among eighteen 'giants' of English literature. *The Task* was among works he read aloud to his family during January 1879 (*Letters* 2, 1034). RCT

Cox, Mrs Annie, young, attractive widow travelling with Mrs Price from Suez to Southampton on the *Cagliari*, who believes that 'when poverty comes in at the door, love flies out at the window' (XL). Her flirtation with George Bertram ends with her returning to her former beau, Major Biffin, when she learns that Bertram is not to inherit his uncle's wealth. *B* MRS

Cox, Lieutenant, friend of Ralph, the heir, in London and a fellow hunter with the B&B (Berkshire and Buckinghamshire Hunt). 'An open, good-humoured, shrewd youth . . . intelligent

enough to know that life at the rate of £1,200 a year, with £400 to spend, must come to an end' (XXVII). *RH* ALS

Crabstick, Patience, Lizzie Eustace's impertinent maid who crowns her career of unpredictable service by assisting the thieves who make off with her mistress's valuable diamond necklace. She eventually gives evidence about the crime, having been induced to do so by an offer of marriage from one of the detectives investigating the case. *ED* JMR

Crabtree Canonicorum, small Barchester parish which provides its rector, Dr Vesey Stanhope, an annual income of £400. *W* NCS

Crabtree Parva, small living near Barchester, worth £80 annually, belonging to Septimus Harding and served by his curate Mr Smith. *W* NCS

Crabwitz, Mr, senior clerk at Mr Furnival's chambers. Crabwitz had been working for Mr Furnival since the attorney's poorer days, and he 'considered that no inconsiderable portion of the barrister's success had been attributable to his own energy and genius' (XII). *OF* MT

Cradell, Joseph, intimate friend and co-worker of Johnny Eames, with whom he lives at Mrs Roper's boarding house. He flirts outrageously with Mrs Lupex, incurring the wrath of her husband, but eventually marries Amelia Roper and takes over her mother's establishment. In *The Last Chronicle of Barset* he has six children and money troubles. *SHA* NCS

Cranbourn House, Martha Dunstable's London mansion, known familiarly as Ointment Hall. Built by an eccentric millionaire in a rural style, it is the site of a triumphant evening party attended by the chief social and political figures, even Tom Towers and the Duke of Omnium. *FP* NCS

Crasweller, Eva, pretty, talented daughter of Gabriel, the first man set to be euthanized in Britannula. Her love for her father and for the son of President Neverbend sets in motion the rebellion against the Fixed Period law of predetermined death. Her emotional appeal makes Neverbend at least reconsider the effect of his cherished law. *FixP* SRB

Crasweller, Gabriel, citizen of Britannula whose time is the first to come up for compulsory euthanasia at age 68. His close friendship with President Neverbend and his own former enthusiasm for the law are taxed severely when his good health, prosperity, and love of life cause him to repudiate the death mandate. He stoically

(*cont. on page 127*)

ROLLOPE's thirty-eighth novel reflects a time of personal indecision. He had long worried how to provide for his niece Florence *Bland without injustice to his sons. By 29 October 1878, three days after commencing the novel, he made up his mind and, at his solicitor's, signed a will in which Florence would inherit £4,000. This was exactly the legacy the squire of Llanfeare awarded his niece Isabel Brodrick, as 'a charge on the estate' (I). Isabella was the name of Florence's dead mother. Those parallels cannot have escaped Florence as she wrote silently to her uncle's dictation of incidents focused on Indefer Jones's library. For when the Trollopes moved to Montagu Square it was she who organized their books, 'ticketing each one [and] . . . fixing the little blue-paper bookplate of her uncle's crest' (Sadleir 316). In her autographed copy of the published novel, Trollope pencilled a dedication (Mullen 612–13) from author to writer (the manuscript was almost entirely in her hand), and from uncle to niece.

Yet Trollope presented Uncle Indefer's anxieties comically, as is apparent from Isabel's bantering response. That comedy is underscored when Indefer insists his estate 'ought to go to a Jones', and his niece cannot help laughing at not being born 'a Jones' (I). Wales has notoriously few surnames, mostly formed by adding 's' or 'ap' to Christian names. Jones, derived from John, is amongst the commonest. Indeed, another Jones rents Llanfeare Grange (just as three Griffiths live on the estate). So, after all the fuss about primogeniture, the novel ends with a forward look to the christening of Isabel's son whose 'grandiloquent name' (William Apjohn Owen Indefer Jones) will distinguish him from any mere Jones.

Aside from that joke, Wales makes little impact. Trollope had lodged in Carmarthen during his postal survey of South Wales (1851), and knew how gossip coloured market-days and quarterly assizes. The town's long-established Ivy Bush becomes the Bush Inn, where flies can be hired to and from Llanfeare; the current Bradshaw supplied train-times from Hereford. Carmarthen may also have reminded him of Jeremy Taylor's *Sermons* in which Indefer leaves his last will: that fourth volume was written nearby at Golden Grove (Robert Tracy, *Trollope's Later Novels* (1978), 258). But Trollope has no feel for the rhythms of Anglo-Welsh, and his place names are impressionistic. Llancolly (XIX) sounds genuine, but is linguistically impossible; Llanfeare (Llanfair/Llan Mair/St Mary's) suggests Cousin Henry's fearful paralysis. Similarly the non-Welsh Indefer points to the way uncle, niece, and nephew defer their decision-making due to moral scruples. The rocks below Llanfeare dramatize Henry's suicidal misery but, in other respects, the landscape and its people are generalized.

However, that estranged viewpoint (as in the European tales) leads Trollope to concentrate on a socially isolated personality. His intricate account of Cousin Henry's psychology has remarkable power. It also makes subtle demands on our sympathies.

We first hear of Henry during the conversation between uncle and niece which (unusually for Trollope) starts off the novel in the middle of things. Indefer's conscience persuades him that his land ought to remain in the male line; Isabel's tells her she could never marry a man she 'loathes', and thus inherit jointly. The narrative then shifts to Indefer's lifelong concern for the family property and, in doing so, uncovers the chequered past of Isabel's despised cousin. Sole child of Indefer's disgraced brother, Henry was educated at his uncle's expense but, on visits to Llanfeare, was 'found to be a sly boy, given to lying' and is disliked by all. Sent down from Oxford 'for some offense not altogether trivial', he appeared to mend his ways by securing a job in a London office and living within his means. Although Indefer can now bury the past, Isabel cannot: 'Why can't he look any one in the face?' Yet, however unmanly, Henry is understandably mortified when his uncle tells him frankly that he invited him out of duty, that his affections are all Isabel's, that his will could again be changed (II).

Trollope's detached stance emphasizes Henry's calculated attempts to curry favour while revealing his mounting embarrassment when every move offends. So, even at his most cringing, Henry remains sympathetic, and that ambivalence prepares us to share his feelings when, on the evening of his uncle's funeral, he opens the book which he knows to contain the will that disinherits him. Stung by the 'injustice' he has encountered, he excuses himself with the thought that, had he been vengeful, he could have destroyed that document. The house is searched thoroughly; Henry neither helps nor hinders. Isabel surrenders her keys and leaves for her parents' home in Hereford (VIII).

At this juncture Trollope interrupted his daily regimen to prepare a lecture he would give in Manchester. While there, he arranged for the novel's serialization in the *Manchester Weekly Times* and the *North British Weekly Mail*. On his return to London, he completed the last sixteen chapters in as many days. That concentrated analysis of a haunted psyche unfolds with a logic that derives from the clarity and empathy of Trollope's imagination.

Henry sits for days in the library, mesmerized by a small stain on the spine of the 'fatal volume' and its exact position on the shelf. He longs to burn the will and swallow its ashes, but the thought of destroying it with his own hands terrifies him. If only he could parcel the book, weight it, drop it out to sea. But it would surely resurface, or someone might notice its absence from the library. These fears shape a dream in which he prepares to drown the book when a swimmer appears beside the boat, staring up at him with the face of Joseph Cantor who witnessed that missing will. He wishes someone would find it or that he could give Llanfeare away and end his misery. Ironically those thoughts are like his disapproving uncle's: the old man often wished an entail might save him from deciding between duty (to primogeniture) and love (for his niece-companion).

Henry's mind is also tortured by outside forces. His tenants notice his pallor and reclusiveness. The *Carmarthen Herald* questions the lost will and ensures the parish reads those insinuations. Pressured to answer in the courts, he tremblingly anticipates the arrival of John Cheekey, whose sardonic manner has reduced witnesses at the Old Bailey to helplessness. He knows he too must crumble unless he destroys that will: then guilty terror would make him lie convincingly. Yet he defers that crime, hoping, as long as he remains technically innocent, to sleep without visions of eternal perdition. At the last moment, when his lawyer and Isabel's father invade the library and move towards that book, he tries to seize it—driven finally to a decision.

Details like these graphically demonstrate the hell Henry has endured, so Trollope lets him resume his London clerkship with name intact (outside Carmarthenshire) and £4,000 from Isabel's largesse. Weak and contemptible, he was 'neither brave enough nor bad enough' (XXIV) to destroy Indefer's testament. Yet, in his own craven way, he is just as ruled by conscience as are his uncle and cousin.

Isabel's portrait, though not as engrossingly detailed, is also out of the ordinary. Imperiously certain of her position in the county and fiercely against her cousin, she might seem icy. Trollope softens her with early touches of humour, a loving understanding of her uncle's conservatism, a deep concern for every tenant. He also makes her vulnerable in that, though she is admired socially, she feels she is not the sort of woman men find attractive. In her scrupulous attempts at objectivity in financial or romantic matters, she has also 'something of the pride of a martyr' (IV). Strategically, Trollope shows her in Hereford, where her cool intellect would have succumbed to William Owen's ardent wooing had not a telegram summoned her to Indefer's deathbed. That episode establishes her as someone who, unwilling to seem grasping or to jump to unproved conclusions, could never wrangle over an inheritance. Even though her uncle's dying words suggest he favoured her, she keeps them to herself and soldiers on until, like some exiled queen, she is restored at last.

The novel is also distinguished by a gallery of lawyers who range from bland to bullying. Nicholas Apjohn, the Joneses' solicitor, is particularly useful in maintaining Trollope's double view of Henry. Wanting justice for Isabel, Apjohn traps Henry into a lawsuit; yet, pitying his client, he hopes that suit might exonerate him. Once convinced of Henry's lies, he remembers Indefer's habits and, after close study of the nephew, deduces the will's hiding place. However, his exuberant detective work goes more by instinct than design (Trollope had no taste for the constructed 'dovetailing' of that genre: *Auto* XIII); indeed, as he pounces on the will, Apjohn perceives that, had Henry 'been sharp enough', he could have said the lawyer had brought it with him (XXII). Though happily triumphant, he understands how Henry found no joy in deception. Such enlightening sympathy informs this unusual novel.

After serialization in six weekly parts of four chapters (8 March–24 May 1879), the book was published in two volumes by Chapman & Hall in October. *Cousin Henry* sold well, though reviewers felt that only Trollope could make its lost-will theme newly interesting. The manuscript is held at Yale University.   AWJ

succumbs, in order to keep his word, but is rescued by sympathetic citizens and British military interference. *FixP*   SRB

Crawley, Bob, young son of Revd Josiah Crawley of Hogglestock, with a taste for the forbidden pleasures of gingerbread and sugar-plums. The godson of Dean Arabin, he is attending Marlboro' School in *The Last Chronicle of Barset. FP*
                    NCS

Crawley, Grace, eldest living child of Revd Josiah Crawley of Hogglestock and distant cousin of Johnny Eames. Her intelligence, generosity, and love shine through her thinness and shabby clothes and endear her to all, especially the widower Major Henry Grantly. Educated in Greek, Italian, and philosophy by her father, the 19-year-old teaches at the Silverbridge school of the Misses Prettyman, and later becomes Lily Dale's friend. She refuses Grantly's offer of marriage while her father faces charges of theft; later, she charms Archdeacon Grantly by her manner and her refusal to bring disgrace into her lover's fam-

ily. Introduced as a girl in *Framley Parsonage. LCB*   NCS

Crawley, Jane, youngest child of Revd Josiah Crawley of Hogglestock. She divides her time between her mother's workbench and reading Greek to her distraught father. *LCB*   NCS

Crawley, Josiah. The Revd Josiah Crawley appears in *Framley Parsonage* as perpetual curate of the populous but unattractive parish of Hogglestock, but has first been mentioned in *Barchester Towers* as 'the poor curate of a small Cornish parish' who crucially influences Francis Arabin when the latter is tempted to convert to Roman Catholicism, explaining 'that the highest laws for the governance of a Christian's duty must act from within and not from without; that no man can become a serviceable servant solely by obedience to written edicts; and that the safety which he was about to seek within the gates of Rome was no other than the selfish freedom from personal danger which the bad soldier attempts to gain who counterfeits illness on the eve of battle'

(*BT* XX). Like the saintly and lovable Mr Harding, Crawley becomes one of the moral touchstones of the 'Barchester Chronicles'. His stipend at Hogglestock is a mere £130 per annum, on which he cannot uphold the appearance of gentility demanded by his profession, and in *Framley Parsonage* his family is the object of charitable attentions from Fanny and Lucy Robarts, who have to smuggle gifts into the house to Mrs Crawley without her husband's knowledge (*FP* XXII). He is prominent in *The Last Chronicle of Barset*, in which he is accused of stealing a cheque made out to Mrs Arabin by her tenant at The Dragon of Wantly. The advice of one of his parishioners during his tribulations, 'It's dogged as does it', has become proverbial (*LCB* LXI). When his name is finally cleared, he is fully integrated into the social system by an emotional exchange with the Archdeacon, when the latter asserts that, despite their difference in wealth, they meet on 'the . . . perfect level' since both are 'gentlemen' (*LCB* LXXXIII). Crawley is a devout and conscientious clergyman, and a man of difficult temperament, who torments himself with thoughts of his unworthiness, yet easily bears a grudge, and indeed has plenty to be aggrieved at. He 'understood fighting', is clear-minded on the subject of his legal rights, and wishes all official dealings to be utterly proper. Refusing to speak to Mrs Proudie on church affairs, he memorably silences her with 'Peace, woman', an utterance as startling then for social as it now is for gender reasons (*LCB* XVIII). He is a pedant but the best scholar in Barsetshire, and teaches Greek and Latin to his daughter Grace, who eventually marries the Archdeacon's son Major Grantly, while her father is finally made vicar of St Ewold's. In *An Autobiography* Trollope writes, 'I claim to have portrayed the mind of the unfortunate man with great accuracy and great delicacy. The pride, the humility, the manliness, the weakness, the conscientious rectitude and bitter prejudices of Mr Crawley were, I feel, true to nature and well described' (*Auto* XV). These personal qualities have caused many commentators to draw parallels with Trollope's equally difficult father. Crawley reappears in *Did He Steal It?*, Trollope's dramatized version of the plot concerning the cheque.　　　　　　　　　　　　　　DS

Crawley, Mary, long-suffering, well-educated wife of Revd Josiah Crawley of Hogglestock. Thin and haggard, she endures the pride and poverty of her strict husband without giving in to despair. Contracting typhus, she is nursed by Lucy Robarts, who forces the Crawleys to accept their friends' assistance. In *The Last Chronicle of Barset*

she supports her husband against criminal charges. *FP*　　　　　　　　　　　　　　NCS

Creagh, Columb, assistant to Father McCarthy, whose religious intolerance is matched only by that of his spiritual 'enemy' Father Townsend. *CR*
　　　　　　　　　　　　　　　　　　MRS

Creamclotted Hall, Squire Crowdy's Devon home, noted for pigs and milk, presided over by Blanche Crowdy. *FP*　　　　　　　　　NCS

Creech, Father, priest from Milltown Malbay, 'not half such a good fellow' as Liscannor's Father Marty. *EE*　　　　　　　　　　AWJ

Creswell, George H., Post Office surveyor for Western District of England, and Trollope's superior during his assignment in the south-west. In November 1851, Trollope suggested to him: 'I believe that a plan has obtained in France of fitting up letter boxes in posts fixed at the road side, and it may perhaps be thought adviseable [*sic*] to try the operation of this system in St Helier's . . . I think that the public may safely be invited to use such boxes for depositing letters' (*Letters* 1, 28).　　　　　　　　　　RCT

Crewe Junction, borough represented by Mr Green Walker under the patronage of his uncle Lord Hartletop. *FP*　　　　　　　　　NCS

cricket. Trollope, who lived into the age of test matches, introduces a strange one into *The Fixed Period* (V). Batsmen face a steam bowling-machine, probably based on a prototype at the Great Exhibition, and a fundamental rule of the game is broken when a run is scored off a skied ball before the catch is completed. Facetious names are given to his cricketers in this novel, Sir Kensington Oval and Sir Lords Longstop. In *Rachel Ray*, Mrs Prime has little regard for two local curates since 'they go to cricket-matches, and among young women with bows and arrows' (V). The objection from evangelicals was that cricket involved Sunday fixtures.　　PJT

Crinkett, Timothy (Tom), John Caldigate's partner at the Polyeuka gold mine in Australia. Canny, experienced, and initially prosperous, he buys out Caldigate's share in the mine just before its wealth runs out. He conspires with Euphemia Smith to frame Caldigate on a bigamy charge in order to force the latter to pay for the mining losses. *JC*　　　　　　　　　　　　SRB

Crippel, Herr, middle-aged musician, proficient on the zither, who, despite his shyness, succeeds in winning Lotta Schmidt. 'Schmidt' *LS*
　　　　　　　　　　　　　　　　　　GRH

Criterion, country home of Sir Francis Geraldine near Ascot. *KD*　　　　　　　　NCS

critical opinions of Trollope: 1882–1920. A day after Trollope's death, *The Times* spoke for the multitude of readers who felt they had 'lost a friend'. He would not rank, it added, with the major novelists of the century—'Scott, Balzac, Dickens, George Sand, George Eliot, Charlotte Brontë, Thackeray, Turguenieff'—but would stand alongside Austen 'at the head of the second order' (7 December 1882, 9). This provoked the *Saturday Review*, normally not Trollope's defender, to attack *The Times* critic and to claim for Trollope a 'genius' comparable to that of Balzac or Hugo (9 December 1882, 755–6). The most important memorial tributes came from R. H. *Hutton, in two essays, and from Henry *James, in a splendid 'partial portrait'. In his first piece Hutton repeated his long-standing conviction that Trollope had been reluctant 'to pierce much deeper than the social surface of life'; but he concluded that Trollope's 'name will live in our literature, and though it will certainly not represent the higher regions of imaginative life, it will picture the society of our day with a fidelity with which society has never been pictured before in history of the world' (*Spectator* (1882), 1573–4). A week later Hutton mourned the loss of stability which he perceived in the early 19th century. Austen and Trollope were both observers, but her world is quiet, while his is 'possessed with the sense of the aggressiveness of the outer world, of the hurry which threatens the tranquillity even of such still pools in the rapid currents of life as Hiram's Hospital' (*Spectator* (16 December 1882), 1609–11).

James's essay, first published in *Century Magazine* (July 1883), is one of his greatest critical performances. In it he balances criticism of Trollope's artistic weaknesses—his 'suicidal satisfaction in reminding the reader that the story he was telling was only, after all, a make-believe'—with generous praise for Trollope's truthfulness. As a realist, Trollope was on a par with, and in his moral soundness he was in advance of, the French school. And Trollope was capable of the highest flights, in *He Knew He Was Right*, for example. Trollope may have written not for posterity but 'for the day, the moment', James concludes; 'but these are just the writers whom posterity is apt to put into its pocket. . . . Trollope will remain one of the most trustworthy, though not one of the most eloquent, of the writers who have helped the heart of man to know itself' (H. James, *Partial Portraits* (1888), 116, 123, 129, 132–3).

Between the time of his death and the turn of the century, Trollope's critical fortune was at its lowest. Posthumous publication of *An Autobiography* provoked James Payn's comment in the *Cornhill* (July 1884) that Trollope did 'his literary reputation as much harm by the revelation of his method of work as by his material views of its result. He took almost a savage pleasure in demolishing the theory of "inspiration", which has caused the world to deny his "genius" ' (*Some Literary Recollections* (1884), 222). By 1895 Trollope seemed to have 'no place at all in Victorian literature', lamented Frederic Harrison in *Studies in Early Victorian Literature* (1895). 'It is the fashion with the present generation to assert that he is never anything but commonplace; but this is the judgement of a perverted taste.' Harrison predicted that posterity would salvage 'ten or twelve of Trollope's best' novels (N. John Hall, *The Trollope Critics* (1981), 21, 24–5). In the same year, a younger critic predicted a well-deserved 'comparative oblivion' for Trollope. 'His career is . . . something of a warning', George Saintsbury avowed, 'a proof that powers of observation are not enough if a writer lacks genius' (*Corrected Impressions: Essays on Victorian Writers* (1895), 172, 177). Two years later Herbert Paul declared, 'Trollope's books are dead' (*Nineteenth Century* (May 1897), 783).

In 1901 Leslie Stephen suggested that Trollope was not dead but in a state of 'suspended vitality'. To enjoy Trollope, Stephen remarks, 'we must cease to bother ourselves about art', and not look for deep thoughts or for 'romantic' subjects. What Trollope offers is a genial, peaceful world oblivious to the 'intellectual, political, and social revolution' that was in the air (*National Review*, 38 (1901), 68, 78, 84). Higher assessment of Trollope's powers came from William Dean Howells. In *Heroines of Fiction* (1901) Howells praised Trollope's female portraits. Two years earlier, in an unpublished essay, he confided that Trollope was 'the most artistic, that is to say the most truthful English novelist' (Hall, *Trollope Critics*, xviii). A more modest, and often cited, opinion was uttered by Lewis Melville in *Victorian Novelists* (1906). Trollope's fate has been 'the worst . . . that can befall a writer: he has not been abused; he has been ignored; and he is not disappearing: he has disappeared.' But Melville predicted that Trollope would recover from this 'temporary eclipse'. Moreover, 'the fact that he was for many years prior to his death the most popular of English writers of fiction is a tribute alike to his powers and to the public which had the discernment to recognize them' (168–9, 182, 187).

But the tide was already turning in Trollope's favour. Around 1912, W. P. Ker, lecturing at University College, London, called Trollope a realist by no means inferior to Balzac and one who ranks with Austen in his ability to give 'a sense of the movement of life'. 'Trollope's work is comedy', Ker exulted, 'the comic epic in prose' (Hall, *Trollope Critics*, 33, 29, 31). Meanwhile, the first biography of Trollope appeared in 1913, T. H. S. Escott's *Anthony Trollope: His Work, Associates and Literary Originals*, which drew on personal recollections. And in 1920 Saintsbury retracted his 1895 opinion. In a long essay, 'Trollope Revisited', he praised the novelist's ability to create real people (*Essays and Studies by Members of the English Association*, 41–66). DDS

critical opinions of Trollope: 1921–50. For the next three decades Trollope's reputation was on the rise, abetted indirectly by two world wars, and encouraged directly by Michael Sadleir, and Bradford A. Booth. In *Trollope: A Commentary* (1927) Sadleir wrote a serviceable biography, containing a vivid portrait of a man at once outwardly assured and inwardly uncertain (339–40). The book also attempted to account for the contradictions and division within Trollope's novels, works that 'are almost without exception novels of a conflict between individual decencies and social disingenuities' (153). 'Trollope deserves graver consideration than as a mere escapist author' (365), Sadleir cautioned. What distinguishes him from other major novelists is his 'almost pugnacious acceptance of reality' (368): Trollope did not rebel against his times; he was of 'all men the most tolerant of others' failings' (132); he was, in short, 'the supreme novelist of acquiescence' (367). Sadleir's apologetic tone may seem unwarranted nowadays, and his rating of the novels may strike rigorous critics as unseemly. But, to his credit, Sadleir created a rounded image of the author, and pointed to the variety and depth of Trollope's work, especially the later novels.

To an influential American academic and philosopher, there was no more need to apologize for Trollope. In *The Demon of the Absolute* (1928), Paul Elmer More admired both the ethical quality of Trollope's fiction and its aesthetic strength. He even defended the authorial interjections that had horrified Hutton and James. Trollope thereby 'converts his readers into accomplices with him in executing the law of poetic justice' (Hall, *Trollope Critics*, 54). For the time being, however, the academic world underestimated Trollope. In *Early Victorian Novelists* (1934), David Cecil chose to recycle Victorian clichés about Trollope's skills as observer, his refusal to go beneath the surface, his deficiencies as an artist. Ernest A. Baker, in *The History of the English Novel*, included Trollope with the Victorian romantics (vol. 8, 1936), as if to underscore his inferiority to Brontë and company. And F. R. Leavis

in 1948 refused to admit the 'ruck' of authors like Trollope to his 'great tradition'.

Novelists, however, were generally more charitable. In 'On Re-reading the English Novelists' (1927), Arnold Bennett had grudging praise for Trollope as a realist and a non-sentimentalist. 'His pictures of Victorian manners are far more exact and various and complete than those of either Thackeray or Dickens. There was no nonsense about him' (Samuel Hynes (ed.), *The Author's Craft and Other Critical Writings of Arnold Bennett* (1968), 262). Virginia Woolf was louder in her praise than Bennett or her father Leslie Stephen. In 1928 she referred to *The Small House at Allington* and *Pride and Prejudice* as 'those two perfect novels' (*Collected Essays*, 1 (1966), 231); and a year later, in 'Phases of Fiction', she included Trollope among the 'truthtellers' in fiction, alongside Defoe, Swift, and Maupassant. 'We believe in Barsetshire as we believe in the reality of our own weekly bills,' Woolf said and she compared Trollope to a shrewd 'family doctor or solicitor, too well acquainted with human foibles to judge them other than tolerantly' (*Collected Essays*, 2 (1966), 62–3). In *Anthony Trollope* for the 'English Men of Letters' series (1928), Hugh Walpole found 'rest and refreshment' (199) in the novels. He cited the post-war atmosphere as a reason for the escapist pleasure found in Barsetshire; but he also praised later novels, like *The Way We Live Now*, as proof of Trollope's being, unknowingly, 'in touch' with modernist trends (174). For Hilaire Belloc, in 1932 (in the *London Mercury*, 27, 150–7), Trollope's novels conjured up a blissful Victorian world, long gone. And for Elizabeth Bowen, in *Anthony Trollope: A New Judgement* (1946), they constituted a *dream* of ordinary life—one that had been shared by their author no less than by his wartime readers. V. S. Pritchett, also writing in 1946, was less impressed. 'Since 1918', he wrote, Trollope 'has become one of the great air raid shelters. He presides over the eternal Munich of the heart and Barsetshire has become one of the great Never-Never Lands of our time. It has been the normal country to which we all aspire' (*New Statesman* (8 June 1946), 415).

America in the mid-1940s also turned to Trollope. The distinguished Yale professor Chauncey Brewster Tinker, in the *Yale Review* (March 1947), praised 'Trollope's inexhaustible abundance' and even his authorial asides. 'Not even Henry Fielding associates with his readers on more agreeable terms' (Hall, *Trollope Critics*, 67, 72). A year earlier Harvard professor Harry Levin, noting a Victorian revival in the post-war air, referred to Trollope's 'substantial fantasies', which enable us to 'relive the warmth and comfort of the mid-

Victorians' (*Refractions* (1968), 318). Meanwhile, in 1945, Lucy Poate Stebbins and Richard Poate Stebbins published a readable, if overcoloured, family biography, *The Trollopes: The Chronicle of a Writing Family*. The main event that year for Trollope scholarship, however, was the publication in California of the first issue of the *Trollopian*. This journal, founded and edited by Bradford A. Booth, would change its title over the next 50 years—first to *Nineteenth-Century Fiction*, then to *Nineteenth-Century Literature*—but for much of that time it provided a forum for an increasing number of Trollope scholars, surveying everything from influences on his work to the structure of his novels, and calling attention to many overlooked gems in his fiction.   DDS

critical opinions of Trollope: 1951–80. In the 1950s a more complex image of Trollope began to circulate from British and continental critics. Starting from the Sadleiran premiss that Trollope was, 'more than any other English novelist of his time, completely at one with his age', Walter Allen, in *The English Novel* (1954), lauded the capaciousness and solidity of Trollope's created world and his 'ability to see a character wholly in the round'. Allen noted that 'Trollope has never received anything like adequate recognition for his sober appraisals of the psychologically abnormal and the part they play in society' (199, 206). Asa Briggs, in *Victorian People* (1954), called attention to the faithful 'impression of . . . everyday life in the middle Victorian years' in Trollope's novels (101). But A. O. J. Cockshut, in *Anthony Trollope: A Critical Study* (1955), and Mario Praz, in *The Hero in Eclipse in Victorian Fiction* (1956), discerned a darker, more passionate Trollope lurking beneath the (in Praz's term) 'Biedermeier' exteriors. Cockshut contended that 'Trollope is a gloomier, more introspective, more satirical, and more profound writer than he is usually credited with being' (9); and to justify his argument he turned to the later novels. Praz, for his part, found at least two Trollopes: one a benign, even-tempered photographer, who championed the values of 'Old England' and who opposed progress (290, 292); the other a subtle analyst of society, who anticipated Proust, who presented scenes of passionate behaviour with 'a vehemence and a truth that we meet with in no other Victorian except Emily Brontë' (314, 309, 298).

Among noteworthy essays in the 1950s, Joseph E. Baker's brief but suggestive 'Trollope's Third Dimension' (1955) stood out for its demonstration of how the novelist establishes an 'emotional background' to his work (232). Frank O'Connor, in *The Mirror in the Roadway* (1956), referred to

Trollope's psychological range, his 'power of exploring characters fully, of so understanding their interior perspective that by a simple change of lighting he can suddenly reveal them to us in a different way' (Hall *Trollope Critics*, 88). Jerome Thale, in 1960, usefully considered 'The Problem of Structure in Trollope'; while Hugh Sykes Davies, in the same year, analysed the moral cadences in 'Trollope and his Style'. In 1959 Elizabeth Bowen, in the Riverside edition of *Doctor Thorne*, discussed Trollope's 'inadvertent' artistry. 'Had he been a painter', she said, 'he would have been an inland Boudin' (p. xxv). Other studies of individual works included Wayne Shumaker's pioneering examination of *An Autobiography* (*English Autobiography*, 1954) and John Hagan's sensitive analysis of 'The Duke's Children: Trollope's Psychological Masterpiece' (*NCF* (June 1958), 1–21). Arguably the two most important essays of the 1950s appeared side by side in *From Jane Austen to Joseph Conrad* (1958). Arthur Mizener, in 'Anthony Trollope: The Palliser Novels', had nothing but praise for the novelist's psychological insight into human imperfection. But in the second piece, 'Trollope's *Orley Farm*: Artistry Manqué', the American dean of Trollope studies, Bradford A. Booth, judged Trollope by Jamesian standards and found him incapable of writing a 'perfect work of art' (159). Booth's *Anthony Trollope: Aspects of his Life and Art* (1958) elaborated on his view that Trollope achieved no more than 'journeyman' status (228).

The 1960s began with Gerald Warner Brace, in 'The World of Anthony Trollope' (*Texas Quarterly* (autumn 1961), 180–9), paying tribute to Trollope's 'fertility of invention' and to his humane, Chaucerian view of life. As for the un-Jamesian quality of Trollope's literary practice, Brace retorted, 'The *Autobiography* contains the most reliable advice to writers that I know of' (repr. Hall, *Trollope Critics*, 100, 106). In *English Criticism of the Novel, 1865–1900* (1965), Kenneth Graham examined Victorian ideas about fiction, including attitudes expressed toward and by Trollope on matters such as realism and didacticism, in an effort to show that James does not provide the only critical model. Meanwhile, influential new views of Trollope appeared. Gordon Ray celebrated 'Trollope at Full Length', arguing that it is in the long 'contrapuntal' novels, with multiple plots and space for character development, that Trollope displays his full powers (*Huntington Library Quarterly* (August 1968), 313–40).

A starker view of Trollope was provided, also in 1968, by J. Hillis Miller in *The Form of Victorian Fiction*. Expanding on his earlier view, in *The Disappearance of God* (1963), that Trollope creates 'a purely human world of intersubjective relations' (13), Miller applied his thesis to *Ayala's Angel*. Three years later James Gindin, in *Harvest of a Quiet Eye: The Novel of Compassion* (1971), repeated the view that for Trollope the self exists only in terms of interaction with other selves, not with something beyond. In another critical study of 1968 that aimed at reversing conventional wisdom, Robert M. Polhemus, in *The Changing World of Anthony Trollope*, demonstrated how wrong Leslie Stephen and others had been when they described the novelist as oblivious to change. 'Trollope made change', social and individual transformation, Polhemus argued, 'his predominant subject matter' (2–3).

The transformation of Trollope's critical fortunes was chronicled by Donald Smalley in the *Critical Heritage* volume devoted to his contemporary reception (1969); and in Smalley's entry in *Victorian Fiction: A Guide to Research* (1966), edited by Lionel Stevenson. Ruth apRoberts surveyed Trollope criticism from the mid-1960s to the mid-1970s in *Victorian Fiction: A Second Guide to Research*, ed. George H. Ford (1978); and Donald D. Stone covered 'Trollope Studies 1976–1981' in volume 11 of the *Dickens Studies Annual* (1983). Meanwhile, critics in the 1960s and 1970s proceeded to rethink Trollope titles and to examine under-appreciated books. Works in the first category included M. A. Goldberg on 'Trollope's *The Warden*: A Commentary on the "Age of Equipoise"' (*NCF* (March 1963), 381–90); James R. Kincaid on '*Barchester Towers* and the Nature of Conservative Comedy' (*Journal of English Literary History* (December 1970), 595–612); U. C. Knoepflmacher on the fictive nature of *Barchester Towers* in *Laughter and Despair: Readings in Ten Novels of the Victorian Era* (1970); Murray Krieger on the Swiftian quality of that novel in *The Classic Vision* (1971); and Hugh L. Hennedy on the thematic coherence of the Barsetshire novels in *Unity in Barsetshire* (1971). In the second category are the contrasting studies of a neglected title by Robert M. Polhemus ('*Cousin Henry*: Trollope's Notes from Underground', *NCF* (March 1966), 385–9) and Ruth apRoberts ('*Cousin Henry*: Trollope's Note from Antiquity', *NCF* (June 1969), 93–8); the complementary pieces on *The American Senator* by Edgar F. Harden ('The Alien Voice: Trollope's Western Senator', *Texas Studies in Literature and Language*, summer 1966, 219–34) and Ruth apRoberts ('Trollope's One World', *South Atlantic Quarterly* (summer 1969), 219–34); plus essays on the Irish novels by, among others, R. C. Terry ('Three Lost Chapters of Trollope's First Novel', *NCF* (June 1972), 71–80) and E. W. Wittig ('Trollope's Irish Fiction', *Éire-Ireland* (autumn 1974), 115–18).

David Skilton analysed Trollope's lone exercise in science fiction, '*The Fixed Period*: Anthony Trollope's Novel of 1980' (*Studies in the Literary Imagination* (Fall 1973), 39–50); and Donald D. Stone considered 'Trollope as a Short-Story Writer' (*NCF* (June 1974), 26–47). Mention should also be made of remarkable studies of *The Duke's Children* by George Butte, 'Ambivalence and Affirmation in *The Duke's Children*', *Studies in English Literature* (autumn 1977), 709–27, and Lowry Pei, '*The Duke's Children*: Reflection and Reconciliation', *Modern Language Quarterly* (September 1978), 284–302. Meanwhile, two full-length masterpieces received increasing critical attention. *He Knew He Was Right* was explored by Ruth apRoberts ('Emily and Nora and Priscilla and Dorothy and Jemima and Carry', in Richard Levine (ed.), *The Victorian Experience: The Novelists*, 1976), and *The Way We Live Now* attracted a legion of admirers, including Robert Lee Wolff in 'The Way Things Were: The Hundredth Anniversary of a Classic: Anthony Trollope's *The Way We Live Now*', *Harvard Magazine* (March 1975).

The 1970s was a boom period: nearly twenty book-length studies and collections, plus scores of articles, appeared between 1971 and 1980, with scarcely a word of apology. Ruth apRoberts, in her groundbreaking study *Trollope: Artist and Moralist* (1971), observed that Trollope needs 'a new and more workable theory' to do him justice (11). This she found, with the help of Cicero (the subject of one of Trollope's books), in Trollope's casuistry or 'situation ethics' (52, 54). His novels are the opposite of escapist. Reading them, we participate in the moral dilemmas at hand. The new level of sophisticated Trollope criticism continued with David Skilton's *Anthony Trollope and his Contemporaries* (1972), not only a useful account of Trollope's reputation and methodology, but also a newer-existential reading of the novels ('in the midst of a crowded world, the individual is in the last analysis alone' (148)). Skilton was suggestive on Trollope's 'realism', as were Richard Harter Fogle, in 'Illusion, Point of View and Modern Novel Criticism' (in John Halperin (ed.), *The Theory of the Novel: New Essays*, 1974), and George Levine, 'Can You Forgive Him? Trollope's *Can You Forgive Her?* and the Myth of Realism' (*Victorian Studies* (September 1974), 5–30). In *Trollope: His Life and Art* (1975) C. P. Snow held up the novelist's almost Tolstoyan 'percipience' as his great gift. Other fruitful pieces included Christopher Herbert on 'Trollope and the Fixity of Self' (*PMLA* (March 1978), 228–39), W. J. Overton on 'Self and Society in Trollope' (*Journal of English Literary History* (summer 1978), 285–302), and R. H. Super on the differences between Trollope and Thackeray in

'Trollope's *Vanity Fair*' (*Journal of Narrative Technique* (winter 1979), 12–20).

Publication of *The New Zealander*, in 1972, edited by N. John Hall, introduced an unknown Trollope to the 1970s. Ruth apRoberts studied the link between 'Carlyle and Trollope' in John Clubbe (ed.), *Carlyle and his Contemporaries* (1976). And James R. Kincaid, in several essays and in *The Novels of Anthony Trollope* (1977), brilliantly extended our sense of Trollope's diversity and intricacy. In his 1976 essay 'Bring Back the Trollopian' (*NCF* (June 1976), 1–14), Kincaid called for a new critical methodology to deal with so seemingly contradictory a writer. Many of the newer critical approaches to Trollope seem to have proceeded, knowingly or unknowingly, from that essay: e.g. the view that Trollope's novels are self-conscious fictions (see Walter Kendrick's *The Novel-Machine: The Theory and Fiction of Anthony Trollope*, 1980), awareness of his use of 'mixed forms', exploration of Trollope's reasons for drawing on Jacobean drama, examination of the tension between fixity of identity and a myth of transformation of self and society in his work. Kincaid's book similarly overflowed with paradoxical ideas about and approaches to Trollope. 'He reminds us over and over that what we are engaged with in reading this novel is art, not life', Kincaid avowed, 'and that art, unlike life, is an affair of convention, tradition, pure artifice' (38).

Other extended interpretations of the 1970s included R. C. Terry's *Anthony Trollope: The Artist in Hiding* (1977), which found in the principle of compromise a theme that continues throughout his work; John Halperin's study of real-life material in *Trollope and Politics: A Study of the Pallisers and Others* (1977); Juliet McMaster's examination of unifying principles in *Trollope's Palliser Novels: Theme and Pattern* (1978); and Arthur Pollard's view of the author's essential conservatism in *Anthony Trollope* (1978). A more complicated writer emerged in P. D. Edwards's *Anthony Trollope: His Art and Scope* (1978). Edwards noted 'two streams running through Trollope's work. One is the stream of common life, . . . the other the more "sensational" stream of "great and glowing incidents" ' (6). In *Trollope's Later Novels* (1978), Robert Tracy determined to save Trollope from the old-fashioned view that his novels lack art and coherence. Tracy demonstrated that Trollope's later novels, with their multiple plot structures, reveal indebtedness to Elizabethan and Jacobean dramatists: 'They constitute a non-Jamesian attempt to achieve the Jamesian end of unity' (39). Peter K. Garrett, in *The Victorian Multiplot Novel* (1980), draws on Mikhail Bakhtin's views on novelistic polyphony

to arrive at a similar conclusion. Still, Trollope remained for Tracy essentially the same author admired by James for his 'appreciation of the usual'. 'Trollope's acceptance of the world as he found it', remarked Tracy, 'and his dislike of romantic heroics, can easily become an impediment to taking him seriously as an artist. The modern reader is accustomed to regarding the artist as an outsider, a rebel. We have almost lost the ability to deal with writers who accept social and artistic conventions and create their art out of that acceptance' (95). This is well said, even if it has been said before. (Tracy's reading of Trollope's anti-romanticism might be read alongside Donald D. Stone's study of Trollope's suppressed romanticism in *The Romantic Impulse in Victorian Fiction* (1980).)

Geoffrey Harvey, in *The Art of Anthony Trollope* (1980), offered a more radical Trollope than most of the above. 'His belief in the supreme value of the individual and his right to self-determination', Harvey declared, 'demands a moral relativism which makes allowances for the special case and for the intense pressures of a rapidly changing social environment. His fiction therefore encompasses contradiction as the finest realism should, and it is this refusal to reduce his vision of the world, this determination to preserve its multifaceted quality, that gives to Trollope's novels their unique authenticity' (16). Perhaps the most succinct account of Trollope's paradoxical nature was offered by Robin Gilmour, in 'A Lesser Thackeray? Trollope and the Victorian Novel': the novels present simultaneously 'an intimate awareness of and respect for social and moral norms, and a fascination with characters who transgress those norms' (Tony Bareham (ed.), *Anthony Trollope* (1980), 201).

DDS

Hall, N. John, *The Trollope Critics* (1981).
Skilton, David, *Anthony Trollope and his Contemporaries* (1972).
Smalley, Donald (ed.), *Trollope: The Critical Heritage* (1969).

critical opinions of Trollope: contemporary. 'He never soars very high, nor digs very deep, but he hardly ever disappoints.' Trollope's contemporary critics, such as the friendly reviewer for *The Times* (25 December 1863), rarely advanced beyond the level of niggling praise and benign incomprehension. Trollope himself had few illusions on the subject of criticism. 'Critical ability,' he observed, 'for the price we pay, is not attainable. It is a faculty not peculiar to Englishmen, and when displayed is very frequently not appreciated.' At best, he might receive 'an equal measure of praise and censure' from an experienced reviewer such as R. H. Hutton (Trollope's favourite critic): but he was just as likely to find his work assigned to 'a young man making his first literary attempts, with tastes and judgement still unfixed' (*Auto* XIV), like the ambitious and inexperienced Henry James.

The most gratifying opinions almost invariably came from other writers: from George Eliot, for example, who praised 'the skill with which [in *Rachel Ray* he had] organized thoroughly natural everyday incidents into a strictly related, well-proportioned whole', demonstrating an artistic subtlety 'which can hardly be appreciated except by those who have striven after the same result with conscious failure' (*The Letters of George Eliot*, ed. Gordon S. Haight (1955), 4, 110). A demanding George Meredith, who found Trollope 'wanting in certain of the higher elements', described the author of *Barchester Towers* as 'a caustic and vigorous writer, who can draw men and women, and tell a story that men and women can read' (*Westminster Review* (October 1857), 594–6). Even more gratifying was the comment of 'a brother novelist very much greater than myself', Nathaniel Hawthorne: Trollope's novels perfectly suited his 'taste,—solid and substantial, . . . and just as real as if some giant had hewn a great lump out of the earth and put it under a glass case, with all its inhabitants going about their daily business, and not suspecting that they were being made a show of' (*Auto* VIII). Best of all Trollope liked the compliment received near the end of his life from Cardinal Newman: 'It is when I hear that such men as yourself have been gratified that I feel that I have not worked altogether in vain' (*Letters*, 2, 993).

Professional reviewers were another matter. Beginning with the notices for his first novel, *The Macdermots of Ballycloran*, critics made it clear that while they liked the lifelike quality of his characters, they wished he had chosen to write something else, in this case, something less painful. The reviewer of *The Kellys and the O'Kellys* for the *New Monthly Magazine* deplored Trollope's use of Irish subjects; the *Examiner* reviewer of *La Vendée* suggested that his talent was not in the field of historical romance. But even when Trollope wrote *The Warden* and found that 'it had not failed as the others had failed' (*Auto* V), he remained underestimated. A writer for the *Leader* criticized Trollope's authorial intrusions. 'The "illusion of the scene" ', he charged, 'is invariably perilled, or lost altogether', when the author becomes an active participant. 'This is a fault in Art' (17 February 1855, 164–5). *Barchester Towers* (1857), was also criticized on this account. In a generally favourable overview of 'Mr Trollope's Novels', a writer for the *National Review* (perhaps its co-editor, Hutton) reproved Trol-

lope's habit of 'frequently and somewhat offensively coming forward as author to remind us that we are reading fiction' (October 1858, 416–35). The success of the Barsetshire novels annoyed the writers for the *Saturday Review*, one of whom criticized *Barchester Towers* for being, 'if anything, too clever, . . . a series of brilliant but disjointed sketches' (30 May 1857, 503–4). As for *Doctor Thorne*, it gave signs that whatever Trollope might have gained in 'mechanical skill', he was 'losing what constituted the value and the promise of his style' (12 June 1858, 618–19). And when a fourth Barsetshire novel, *Framley Parsonage*, attained enormous popular success, the *Saturday Review* critic snidely remarked, 'If the present fashion continues, and the heroes of one novel reappear so constantly in the next, readers will begin to hope that funerals, and not marriages, may in future be made the *finale* in which all romances terminate' (4 May 1861, 451–2).

Despite the sporadically negative opinion of the *Saturday Review*, Trollope's novels from the late 1850s to the late 1860s were widely popular and widely reviewed. (David Skilton has counted twenty-four reviews from the *Spectator* alone, and a similar number from the *Saturday Review*, between 1857 and 1869.) When *The Last Chronicle of Barset* appeared, presumably to the *Saturday* critic's relief, the *Spectator* reviewer mourned, 'Life has lost one of its principal alleviations' (13 July 1867, 778–80). A commentator for the *Examiner* called the Barsetshire novels 'the best set of "sequels" in our literature' (20 July 1867, 452–3). As far as *Mudie was concerned, Trollope must be 'the greatest of living men', E. S. *Dallas wryly observed in *The Times*; but his popularity, he added, was distinctly 'of the circulating library sort' (23 May 1859, 12). 'More than a million people habitually read Mr Trollope', the *National Review* declared in 1863, 'and they do so because the personages in his stories correspond to something in themselves' (January 1863, 27–40). Critics were reluctant, however, to praise something that appeared so easy to do—his very prolificacy seemed proof of that—and that seemed based on 'commonplace' life. Such a practice, the *National Reviewer* continued, was 'low art', the result of someone taking photographs, but ignoring the inner depths explored by Charlotte Brontë and George Eliot.

Earlier in the century, Walter Scott had marvelled at Jane Austen's ability to draw interesting narratives from the 'paths of common life'. Trollope's reviewers would make a similar point. 'He sees a section of English life', the *Saturday Review* declared, 'and paints it with unerring truth, tact, and liveliness. . . . He can do, in fact, what Miss Austen did, only that he does it in the modern style, with far more detail and far more analysis of character' (14 May 1864, 595–6). However, reviewers were appalled by what they saw as the imaginative infertility of such a writer.

By the mid-1860s, however, it was discovered that Trollope did not resemble Charlotte Brontë. His novels might be 'the picture of English life which, for a brief space at least, will be accepted as the true one by those who wish to see English life represented in fiction'. But, the *Saturday Review* continued, while his 'novels are true, . . . they are not more true'. They lack excitement; they lack poetry. 'We wish fiction would do something for us besides giving us these accurate likenesses of the common run of those whom we see or know' (24 October 1863, 554–5). For years to come, Trollope would be reproached for not being Brontë—she whom George Henry Lewes had advised to become more like Austen. Reviewing *Orley Farm* (1862), the *National Review* took the occasion to praise those, like Brontë, who 'infect us with sympathy for vicissitudes, disappointments, or regrets, with which each of us has something in common. They go nearer the truth, and they teach us a worthier lesson than he whom a good-natured superficiality and a perilous influx of success prevent from looking into the gloomy caverns which surround him' (January 1863, 27–40).

Trollope's greatest sin was his popularity. The *Westminster Review*, dismissing *Framley Parsonage*, found it unconscionable that 'so trivial and purposeless' a work should be so widely read (July 1861, 282–4). Yet even when Trollope broke new ground, added tragic passions and psychological depth to his narratives, critical response remained largely non-comprehending. He had already demonstrated, in *The Macdermots* and *The Bertrams*, that he could handle a tragic theme. But with the creation of Lady Mason in *Orley Farm*, Lady Glencora in *Can You Forgive Her?*, Josiah Crawley in *The Last Chronicle of Barset*, and Louis Trevelyan in *He Knew He Was Right*, Trollope challenged critical opinion of his psychological powers head on. The reviewer of *Orley Farm* for the *Spectator* (probably Hutton) was not impressed. Compared to Brontë, Trollope remained an author relying on observation rather than drawing from within, and his characters consequently lacked an 'inward' dimension (11 October 1862, 1136–8). Dallas, in *The Times* (26 December 1862, 5), however, noted 'a tragic force, or something like it [in *Orley Farm*], which is rare in Mr Trollope's writings'. Another admirer of Trollope, Margaret *Oliphant, praised the 'perfect art' that had gone into the 'profound and . . . tragic' portrait of Mr Crawley (*Blackwood's Magazine* (September 1867), 277–8). But

while the *Spectator* was willing to concede that Trollope, in *He Knew He Was Right*, had chosen 'a more than usually painful subject' and that, for the first volume at least, he displayed 'a power of conception he has rarely equalled', much of the rest of the novel seemed coarse and padded (12 June 1869, 702–8). With the Barsetshire series finished, a writer for the *British Quarterly Review* (October 1867, 557–60) suggested that it was now time for Trollope to 'devote his high and varied powers to some themes quite worthy of him'. But in the first post-Barsetshire novel, *Phineas Finn*, Trollope's turn to politics and high society did not impress the *Spectator*: 'What we do think Mr Trollope sometimes fails in', wrote the reviewer, 'is in perceiving that there is, for most men at least, a depth of private character which barely gets to the surface of society at all, and which Mr Trollope rarely ever indicates' (20 March 1869, 356–7).

In 1865 a 22-year-old American wrote his first review of Trollope, confessing to a 'partiality' for the author 'of which [he felt] somewhat ashamed'. (He was not the last Trollope admirer to make the apology.) Despite his inexperience, Henry James had no hesitation in advancing his opinions—or those he had adopted from the *Spectator*—with regard to Trollope's deficiencies. Beginning with *Miss Mackenzie*, he recognized Trollope's right to select an anti-romantic theme, but he deplored the author's selection of 'ordinary mortals' and commonplace incidents. He is an 'admirable observer', but 'why does he not observe great things as well as little ones?', James asks. 'Why should we stoop to gather nettles when there are roses blooming under our hands?' (*Nation* (13 July 1865), 51–2). Two months later the *Nation* assigned James *Can You Forgive Her?* for review. Just as the *Spectator* had felt cheated of a 'darker ending' for Lady Glencora (2 September 1865, 978–9), so too James wished that Trollope had led 'the story to a catastrophe. . . . We are for ever wishing that he would go a little further, a little deeper' (28 September 1865, 409–10). When, four months later, Trollope produced a third prosaic novel, James accused him of writing 'for children; a work prepared for minds unable to think. . . . "The Belton Estate" is a stupid book' (*Nation* (4 January 1866), 21–2). Two years later, however, James showed his renewed partiality for Trollope in a favourable review of *Linda Tressel* (1868), which, like its predecessor *Nina Balatka* (1867), had appeared anonymously. By now James realized that Trollope was capable of writing a story with 'truly tragic interest and dignity'. He compared Trollope's achievement with Scott's more obviously romantic *The Bride of Lammermoor*, and found

critical opinions of Trollope

Trollope excelling in 'the sublime of prose' (*Nation*, 18 June 1868, 494–5).

The conventional wisdom dispensed by the reviewers of the 1870s was that Trollope's talents were in decline. There was also a falling off in his popularity, arrested temporarily by the success of *The Eustace Diamonds*. Having been typecast as the novelist of commonplace life, Trollope explored increasingly dark or difficult subjects. 'This is a sort of thing the reading public will never stand,' protested the *Saturday Review* with respect to *Lady Anna* (9 May 1874, 598–9). Outrage was expressed at Trollope's 'indiscriminate onslaught' against society in *The Way We Live Now* (*Saturday Review* (17 July 1875), 88–9). Meredith White Townsend was appalled by 'the oppressive vulgarity of the characters' and the 'sewage-farm' atmosphere (*Spectator* (26 June 1875), 825–6). *The Times*, for its part, applauded *The Way We Live Now* for being 'only too faithful a portraiture of the manners and customs of the English at the latter part of this 19th century' (24 August 1875, 4), and *The Times* was unique, again, in its praise of *The Prime Minister*. As far as the *Spectator* was concerned, the fifth Palliser novel contained only 'vulgarity' and indicated 'that Mr Trollope's power itself had declined' (22 July 1876, 922–3). And the *Saturday Review*, having detected 'a decadence in Mr Trollope's powers' in *The Prime Minister* (14 October, 481–2), gloated over his collapse in *Is He Popenjoy?*: 'We regard the present caricature of a corrupt state of society as an instance of the ill effects of over-writing, and of its deadening influence on the finer perceptions' (1 June 1878, 695–6). When praise was bestowed, it was on an unworthy title: the *Spectator* saluted *An Eye for an Eye* as a welcome exception to Trollope's recent excursions among 'sands and marshes and all kinds of muddy fencountries' (15 February 1879, 210–11). And there was praise of sorts for a Victorian relic—one who could not be judged as 'an artist according to the modern school of high art' (*Athenaeum* (29 May 1880), 694). 'He is . . . the last of the realists', noted one reviewer of *The Duke's Children*. 'No one ever, we fancy, read a novel of his without wishing that he might soon write another' (*Nation* (19 August 1880), 138–9).

DDS

critical opinions of Trollope: since 1980. A significant increase in the critical attention given to Trollope's work during the last fifteen years suggests that his writing, always popular, is now enjoying a critical renaissance; the extraordinary array of monographs, essays, and dissertations on Trollope produced since 1980 testify to both the enduring stature of Trollope's writings, and an increasing interest in Trollope studies. Certainly, Trollope's popular audience, always large, has expanded enormously; and critical attention, once limited to a small group of scholars, has also grown to include a much broader spectrum of the academic community, representing more diverse interests and approaches. The Barsetshire and Palliser novels, long considered Trollope's finest, remain popular both with critics and with general audiences, but some of Trollope's hitherto neglected writings—notably *An Autobiography*, *He Knew He Was Right*, and *The Way We Live Now*—have begun to compete with traditional favourites for a place in the Trollope canon. Similarly, traditional literary approaches to Trollope's work have begun to give way to more politically and theoretically inspired readings, though in the arena of postmodern criticism, interest in Trollope lags behind that in other major Victorian novelists. However, as more critics each year give attention to Trollope's complex ironic voice and the gap between his apparently staid middle-class aspect and his subtle subversive echoes, it seems likely that Trollope scholarship will assume a more theoretical bent.

The recent surge of interest in Trollope is evident from an abundance of new editions. While formerly it was sometimes difficult to find anything but the most popular of his novels, affordable editions of Trollope's works, including the short stories and travel writings, now abound. In the last ten years, a number of publishers (including, Arno, Dover, the Folio Society, Garland, Oxford, and Penguin) have undertaken to publish volumes that were previously almost unobtainable; Trollope's entire opus is now in print and the commercial success of new paperback editions is strong indication of a growing readership.

The last fifteen years have also seen the publication of four major biographies of Trollope including R. H. Super's *The Chronicler of Barsetshire* (1988), Richard Mullen's *Anthony Trollope: A Victorian in his World* (1990), N. John Hall's *Trollope: A Biography* (1991), and Victoria Glendinning's *Anthony Trollope* (1993). Other biographical works include R. C. Terry's *A Trollope Chronology* (1989) and *Trollope: Interviews and Recollections* (1987), the latter offering a series of first-hand accounts of Trollope's life and character. Also invaluable is Hall's two-volume edition of Trollope's *Letters* (1983). In addition to biographies and the *Letters*, a number of other reference texts have also appeared (see ANTHOLOGIES; BIBLIOGRAPHIES; GUIDEBOOKS).

These texts, however, represent only a small fraction of the work which has appeared during the last fifteen years. Critical interest in Trollope has soared since 1980 as evidenced by some 200 books and articles and 50 English-language dissertations on Trollope since that time. Though consistently strong, critical interest seems to have peaked in 1982, the centenary of Trollope's death, with the publication of approximately 30 books and articles. The years immediately surrounding 1982 were similarly prolific and are notable for publication of several collections of essays: John Halperin's *Trollope Centenary Essays* (1982), N. John Hall's *The Trollope Critics* (1981), and a special issue of *Nineteenth Century Fiction* (December 1982), edited by N. John Hall and Donald D. Stone, offer interesting and challenging new essays.

Though contemporary criticism has begun to offer more complex and appreciative readings, some criticism is still influenced by earlier, less favourable assessments of Trollope's work. Although Trollope is held in higher repute now, perhaps, than at any time since his death, many critics still begin their articles with apologias, explaining that Trollope's work is valuable *despite* the frequency with which it has been maligned. One eloquent defence, found in L. J. Swingle's *Romanticism and Anthony Trollope* (1990), argues that many critics naively regard Trollope as 'a quaintly rotund, garrulous, . . . Good Old Boy' (2). Indeed, Louise Weinberg ('Is it Alright to Read Trollope?', *American Scholar*, 62/3 (1993), 447–51) dedicates an entire article to an appreciation of Trollope's writing, defending the author in what she perceives as an anti-Trollopian climate.

In light of Trollope's growing stature, such defensive statements may seem unnecessary, a holdover from an earlier time. But in fact, rising interest in Trollope has given life to an old debate; Trollope's reputation has again become fertile ground for scholarly discussion. Fuelling the necessity for Trollopian apologias are articles like Fred Kaplan's in the *Times Literary Supplement* (11–17 November 1988), which asks that perpetual question: 'How Good is Trollope?' Sharing the view of many earlier scholars, Kaplan concludes that the virtue of Trollope's writing lies more in quantity than quality, a conclusion which inspired a volley of responses defending Trollope's literary merits. While such disagreements may indicate that Trollope's status within the Western canon is not perfectly secure, these debates also bespeak a lively interest. Vigorous conflict over Trollope's merits is a certain sign of his increasing stature.

Although some of Trollope's lesser-known writings are beginning to gain popularity, and though recent criticism incorporates some new theoretical approaches, much attention still focuses on the Barsetshire novels (especially *The Warden* and *Barchester Towers*) and relies on more traditional critical approaches.

Studies of influence, for example, continue to flourish, and include examinations of literary influences between Trollope and . . . Austen, Dickens, Eliot, Barbara Pym, and especially Henry James, no fewer than six articles on Trollope and James having appeared between 1982 and 1995. Other critics, notably Elizabeth R. Epperly, have examined the influence of Jacobean drama on Trollope's work (see DRAMA, ELIZABETHAN AND JACOBEAN). But influence studies have ranged far afield; one critic makes an intriguing comparison between Trollope's work and *The Tale of Genji* (Edward Seidensticker, 'Trollope and Murasaki', *NCF* (December 1982), 464–71).

With such a large opus to consider, Trollope students may be grateful for the publication of notes and other short articles offering 'readings' of various novels, characters, and symbolic elements in Trollope's work, though these offerings are scanty and sometimes unremarkable. The most valuable critical resource for an individual working on a particular novel, story, or character is likely to be the introduction found in the new Oxford World's Classics paperback editions.

Many critics also continue to express interest in Trollope's political and social attitudes, some insisting that the author's apparent conservatism belies a strongly 'cosmopolitan' spirit (Ann Marie Ross, 'Ploughshares into Swords', *Nineteenth-Century Literature* (June 1990), 59–72) or arguing that Trollope's attitudes about Ireland were progressive for their time (Tony Bareham, 'First and Last', *Durham University Journal*, NS 47 (1986), 311–17). Indeed, a number of scholars, John G. Hynes particularly, are giving greater attention to Trollope's Irish connection; and Trollope's Irish writings, *The Macdermots of Ballycloran* especially, are beginning to win greater appreciation. John Halperin ('Trollope's Conservatism', *South Atlantic Quarterly* (1983), 56–78), however, offers a critique of these more liberal interpretations, insisting that Trollope remains staunchly conservative.

One of the reasons, of course, that Trollope has traditionally lent himself to political readings is because of his own interest in politics, an interest which is now generating more serious reflection. The reputation of the Palliser novels (also known as the political or parliamentary novels), always highly regarded, continues to rise, and they may now be said to hold the place of honour in the Trollope canon, taking precedence even over the Barsetshire novels. This mounting interest in Trollope's political and social aspects has led scholars to pursue some interesting avenues. A number of critics, for instance, have written about Trollope and the law (Richard C. Burke, 'Accommodation and Transcendence', *Dickens Studies Annual* (1986), 291–307; Coral Lansbury, *The Reasonable Man: Trollope's Legal Fiction*, 1981); most useful, perhaps, among these works is R. D. McMaster's *Trollope and the Law* (1986), a detailed study of legal practices and intricacies pertaining to Trollope and his writings. Recent studies of Trollope in relation to society and culture range from essays on fox-hunting to essays on Trollope's moral code, his idea of 'the gentleman' (Shirley Robin Letwin, *The Gentleman in Trollope: Individuality and Moral Conduct*, 1982), and his alleged anti-Semitism.

In addition to the Palliser novels, Trollope's *An Autobiography* has also gained significantly in reputation. Part of the growing interest in the autobiography has no doubt been brought about by the recent profusion of Trollope biographies, but the trend marks an interesting departure from more traditional critical approaches. A number of articles, for instance, take a postmodern stance, entering into discussions of Trollope's 'Strategies of Self-Production' (Sarah Gilead, *Modern Language Quarterly* 47 (1986), 272–90), or examining the elusive boundary between 'reality' and 'fiction' (Sally Brown, ' "This So-Called Autobiography" ', *British Library Journal*, 8 (1982), 168–73; J. R. Kincaid, 'Trollope's Fictional Autobiography', *NCF* (December 1982), 340–9; J. Hillis Miller, 'Trollope's Thackeray', *NCF* (December 1982), 350–7; R. Tracy, 'Stranger than Truth', *Dickens Studies Annual*, 15 (1986), 275–89. In a similar vein, Andrew Wright's *Anthony Trollope: Dream and Art* (1983) considers the connection between Trollope's unhappy boyhood daydreaming and the development of his later narrative technique. In fact, recent studies have often suggested that there is a similarity in the narrative strategies employed by Trollope in *An Autobiography*, in his biographies, and in his fictions.

Recent writings about *An Autobiography* often take a structuralist or post-structuralist approach and, in fact, the use of structuralism, poststructuralism, and narrative theory to discuss Trollope's work has become increasingly prevalent, these approaches invited perhaps by *An Autobiography*'s detailed discussions of Trollope's extraordinary writing habits and methods. Perhaps as a result of these discussions, there has also been an increase in articles on publishing-related issues.

Among those exploring the influence of Trollope's writing habits on his narrative technique is Mary Hamer (*Writing by Numbers: Trollope's Serial Fiction*, 1987), who argues that the rigours of writing for serial publication had 'a paradoxically liberating' effect on Trollope 'from which he made rich imaginative gains' (p. ix). Other recent work discussing Trollope and narrative includes Christopher Herbert's noteworthy *Trollope and Comic Pleasure* (1987), which argues that Trollope's narrative voice is that of 'the wily comic dissembler' and that his texts are 'honeycombed with fissures, irregularities, [and] signs of disequilibrium' (4–9); Paul Lyons ('Morality of Irony and Unreliable Narrative', *South Atlantic Review* (January 1989), 49–54), offers another discussion of Trollope's 'unreliable' narrative voice, suggesting that the writer's 'surface jocularity and frequent light-handed digressions or intrusions underscore [his] serious thematic intentions and mask a pervasively manipulative, complicated, and ironic technique' (41).

The most notable trend in Trollope criticism is the array of books and articles which approach Trollope's writings from a feminist standpoint, or which discuss Trollope's importance from the perspective of gender and sexuality. Although Trollope has often been regarded as having a conservative attitude towards the role of women, many critics are now exploring the possibilities inherent in the author's narrative equivocations, and are intrigued by the openings created by his narrator's even-handedness, an important issue in Jane Nardin's *Trollope and Victorian Moral Philosophy* (1996). Nicola Thompson's 'Something Both More and Less than Manliness' (*Victorian Literature and Culture*, 1994) also discusses Trollope's fairness to his characters, proposing that the author's tendency to paint his characters in shades of grey, and the narrative gaps that are inherent in his writing, give him a kind of 'feminine' voice, an attribute which, she writes, has contributed in great measure to his uneven literary reputation.

Most prominent among the new gender-influenced criticism has been *Corrupt Relations: Dickens, Thackeray, Collins, and the Victorian Sexual System* (Richard Barickman, Susan MacDonald, Myra Stark, 1982), which proposes that the writings of the male authors in question are perhaps more subversive than those of their female counterparts. Publication of *Corrupt Relations* has helped to give rise to a mass of work defending Trollope's feminism. Among these works is Deborah Denenholz Morse's *Women in Trollope's Palliser Novels* (1987), which argues that Trollope's perception of women's roles, though 'limited', 'was much more elastic than that of most of his contemporaries' (6).

Also important in the new gender-oriented criticism has been the rising reputation of *He*

Knew He Was Right, generally thought to be Trollope's most explicitly feminist text. Christopher Herbert believes that this novel is a deliberate critique of 'the coerciveness of social institutions [and] the anomalies built into the code of Victorian marriage in particular' ('*He Knew He Was Right*, Mrs. Lynn Linton, and the Duplicities of Victorian Marriage', *Texas Studies in Language and Literature* (fall 1983), 448–69); in *He Knew She Was Right: The Independent Woman in the Novels of Anthony Trollope* (1989), Jane Nardin explores Trollope's transformation from a young conservative into a mature writer with more liberal, feminist views.

Recent trends in Trollope criticism employing narrative theory and feminist interpretations which propose subtextual readings of and 'gaps' in Trollope's apparently middle-class identity have suggested new possibilities for reading Trollope. Some theorists have begun to offer more playful readings of Trollope's works: Priscilla L. Walton's *Patriarchal Desire and Victorian Discourse* (1995) approaches Trollope from a Lacanian perspective; D. A. Miller's *The Novel and the Police* (1988) offers a Foucauldian reading of *Barchester Towers*; Barry M. Maid ('Trollope, Idealists, Reality, and Play', *Victorians Institute Journal*, 12 (1984), 9–21) interprets *The Warden* using Huizinga's game theory.

While postmodern interpretations of Trollope's work remain in the minority, and though the quality of these readings has sometimes been unremarkable, it seems likely that growing attention to the instabilities inherent in his narratives will invite further critical explorations of this kind.   JMR

Crocker, Samuel, irrepressible, obnoxious postal clerk who offends nearly everyone, especially the aristocrats with whom he boasts of being on intimate terms. His shoddy work habits result in near dismissal when it is discovered that he has destroyed official papers. *MF*   SRB

Crocket, Mrs, innkeeper of the Stag and Antlers in Nuncombe Putney. She befriends Mrs Stanbury and her daughters. It is said of her that 'no old woman in the public line was ever more generous, more peppery, or more kind' (XIV). *HKWR*   RC

Crofts, Dr James, Silverbridge physician for seven years. A slight, spare individual with bright dark eyes and dark hair, the 30-year-old surgeon attends Mrs Dale, her two daughters, and Lord De Guest. Shy, soft-spoken, and self-deprecating, he finally manages to propose to Isabella Dale. In *The Last Chronicle of Barset* they have two small children. *SHA*   NCS

Croker's Hall, country seat of Mr Whittlestaff in Hampshire. A mile (0.5 km) from Alresford, the hall is a comfortable but modest establishment. *OML*   RC

Croll, Herr, German clerk for Augustus Melmotte. Paid to overlook Melmotte's lack of scruples, Croll assents to the brutal beating of Marie and the forgery of her signature by her father, but refuses to sign as witness to the forgery. Later, he quietly returns the incriminating papers to Melmotte. He ends by marrying Melmotte's widow and moving to New York. *WWLN*   SRB

Crook, Sir William, old college acquaintance of Harry Annesley's, who offers Harry a position in America as his private secretary just at the moment that Peter Prosper is about to disinherit his nephew. *MSF*   MT

croquet. Originating in France, the game became very popular in the 1860s. Women took to it enthusiastically and by 1874 could compete in a national championship at Wimbledon. Waltham House, Trollope's home in Hertfordshire, had a large, well-kept lawn, where croquet could be played. In *The Small House at Allington* the glory of the Small House consisted of its lawn; Lily Dale vowed there was no point in playing croquet at the Great House which was all tufts (II). Lucy Morris knew every rule of the game (*ED* III). Croquet afforded opportunities for flirtation, which persuaded Jack De Baron to join Lady Mary Germain in friendly competition with the mallet (*IHP* LV).   RCT

Crosbie, Adolphus, ambitious secretary to the Board of the General Committee Office. Tall and good-looking, he talks well and seems destined to prosper. He proposes to Lily Dale, but then becomes engaged to Lady Alexandrina De Courcy. After jilting Lily, his life and career go downhill, despite his new connections. Thrashed by Johnny Eames, he loses most of his friends. In *The Last Chronicle of Barset*, after his wife's death, he fails to reconcile with Lily and falls deeper into financial trouble. *SHA*   NCS

Crosbie, Lady Alexandrina (née **De Courcy**), daughter of Earl De Courcy, and the beauty of the family. Encouraged by her mother the Countess, she engages herself to Adolphus Crosbie even when knowing he is engaged to Lily Dale. Their marriage, however, is not happy, and she leaves him to live with her mother in Baden-Baden, where she has died by *The Last Chronicle of Barset*. *SHA, DT, BT*   NCS

Cross Hall, dower house of the Dowager Marchioness of Brotherton located outside the gates of Manor Cross. *IHP*   MG

Crosstrees, Lieutenant, gallant young officer of the gunboat *John Bright*, entirely devoted to his profession and respected by all for his courage and military obedience. Despite disagreeing with John Neverbend's 'Fixed Period' philosophy of enforced euthanasia, he befriends the lonely, deposed President of Britannula while 'escorting' him into exile in England. *FixP*   SRB

Crowdy, Blanche (née **Robarts**), second and most beautiful of the three daughters of Dr Robarts of Exeter. Fanny Mansell's bridesmaid, she was expected to be noticed by Lord Lufton but marries instead Squire Crowdy of Creamclotted Hall in Devon, where she masters the mysteries of pigs, milk, cider, and green cheese. *FP*   NCS

Crowdy, Squire, husband of Blanche Robarts and squire of Creamclotted Hall in Devon. They take in Jane Robarts after her father's death. *FP*   NCS

Crowe, Thaddeus, intelligent and peculiarly successful lawyer who, once assured of Fred Neville's riches, arranges to pension off the disreputable Captain O'Hara. *EE*   AWJ

Crumb, John, simple-minded, well-off miller, usually dusty with flour, who is magnificently in love with Ruby Ruggles. He overcomes her love for Felix Carbury through his dumb obstinacy, great heart, and good-natured beating of Sir Felix, and is also aided in his pursuit by his more articulate friends. *WWLN*   SRB

Crummie-Toddy, Reginald Dobbes's Scottish hunting lodge, visited by Lord Silverbridge, Frank Tregear, and others. *DC*   JMR

Crump, Jonas, timber-merchant in Gloucester and brother of Mrs French. Although the Frenches look down upon the Crumps, Mrs French appeals to him for help after Camilla French is jilted in favour of her older sister Arabella. He removes his shrewish younger niece from Heavitree until a sororal truce can be established. *HKWR*   RC

Cruse, Mr, Mr Pott's travelling companion in Jerusalem, a clergyman of an unhappy frame of mind who finds that 'from Dan to Beersheba everything in truth was barren' (IX), but is nevertheless popular with the ladies. *B*   MRS

Cudlip, Mrs Pender (**Annie Hall** née **Thomas**) (1838–1918), Clergyman's wife and prolific writer of romantic novels. In 1867, Trollope rejected a story she had submitted to *Saint Pauls* for lack of space, but commented, 'I know your novels . . . and shall be very glad to use anything of yours if it would suit us' (*Letters* 1, 410–11). In 1868 he accepted her story 'For a Year', on condition that she changed the ending from a young girl's suicide to death from the effects of her trials. Mrs Cudlip revised the story as Trollope suggested, and the story appeared in June 1868 (*Letters* 1, 418). Chapman & Hall's reader, George Meredith, remarked of one of her stories: 'She has studied Trollope with advantage and throws in her hunting-bits very cleverly. It is written for the market and will suit the market' (Super 250).   RCT

Cullen, Father, illiterate, down-at-heel curate in the parish of Drumsna, and 'a violent politician' (V) who expresses vehement anti-English, anti-Protestant views. He takes Denis McGovery's incrimination of Thady in the plots of local Ribbonmen at face value, but is set to rights by Father John, and later urges his congregation not to attend Thady's execution. *MB*   MRS

Cumberland, with Westmorland, now Cumbria, a scenic region that includes the Lake District. Lovel Grange in *Lady Anna* is located there, as is the home of the Braeside Harriers in *Marion Fay* and the estate of Sir Harry Hotspur. *SHH*   RC

Cumberley Green, a hamlet in the parish of Clavering, three miles (5 km) distant from the church. Samuel Small undertakes the clerical work there. *C*   PJT

Cumming, Maurice, owner of the failed sugar plantation in Jamaica, beset by difficulties. He is pushed by his Aunt Sarah to propose successfully to her niece Marian Leslie, whom he loves anyway. 'Jack' *TAC1*   GRH

Cunningham, Revd John William (1780–1861), from 1811 for 50 years vicar of St Mary's, Harrow-on-the-Hill. A strongly evangelical churchman, dubbed 'Velvet' Cunningham after his book *The Velvet Cushion* (1814), he was loathed by the Trollopes for opposing Byron's wish to have a memorial tablet to his illegitimate daughter Allegra in his parish. Frances Trollope wrote the poem *Salmagundi* about the incident. *Salmagundi, Byron, Allegra, and the Trollope Family*, with foreword by N. John Hall, appeared in 1975. Mrs Trollope also satirized Cunningham in *The Vicar of Wrexhill* (1837), though she denied that connection.   RCT

'Curates' Incomes' (letter). This paper's recent report from an elderly curate confirms my statements on unreasonably low salaries for curates. Even twice the average cannot support a family. The country can afford better, and should. *Pall Mall Gazette*, 24 June 1866, 3–4.   AKL

Curlydown, Jemima, forward daughter of a postal clerk whose colleague Samuel Bagwax becomes engaged to her. She discourages her lover's dream of a trip to Sydney when it appears to supersede his interest in her. *JC*   SRB

Curlydown, Mr, one of two postal clerks who testify at John Caldigate's bigamy trial. He is jealous of his younger colleague Samuel Bagwax's success in discovering new evidence, but overcomes his envy and encourages his daughter's engagement to Bagwax. *JC*   SRB

Curragh, horse-racing track, close by Grey Abbey, frequented by Lord Ballindine. *KOK*
                                                        MRS

Currie, Sir Donald (1825–1909), founder of the Castle Steamship Co., MP for Perthshire (1880–5) and West Perthshire (1886–1900); art collector and patron. In 1872 he established a new shipping route between England and Cape Town. In June 1877, Trollope attended the Royal Colonial Institute where Currie lectured on 'Thoughts upon the Present and Future of South Africa, and Cen-

tral and Eastern Africa'. Trollope told the audience that, as he was about to sail for South Africa (on board one of Currie's ships), he would prefer to wait till his return nine months later when he would be better qualified to speak on the subject. The day after this meeting, he wrote to Currie asking for a copy of his lecture.   RCT

Curry Hall, country house in Gloucestershire owned by Mr Montacute Jones. Mrs Montacute Jones finds it dull but spends three months a year there. *IHP*   MG

Custins, Lord and Lady Cantrip's Dorset home, close to the sea. The Duke of Omnium's daughter, Lady Mary, is here introduced both to Lord Popplecourt and to Isabel Boncassen. *DC*   JMR

Cuttwater, Captain Bartholomew (Uncle Bat), pensioned navy officer and Mrs Woodward's uncle who comes to live at Surbiton Cottage. Although 'given to profane oaths' with 'a too strongly pronounced partiality for alcoholic drink' (IV), Captain Cuttwater is a gentleman 'with a soft heart' who assists Alaric Tudor financially. *TC*   MT

D

Daguilar, Maria, beautiful daughter of Mr Pomfret's Spanish partner, with a 'quiet sustained decision of character', much superior to John Pomfret, whom she none the less loves and marries. 'Bull' *TAC1* GRH

Daily Telegraph, a Liberal paper founded in 1855, the first London daily to sell for one penny. *The Times*, in contrast, cost sevenpence, while the Tory *Standard* and the Liberal *Daily News* sold for fivepence. By 1877, the *Telegraph* claimed a daily circulation of nearly 250,000, the highest in the world. The most significant of Trollope's interactions with the *Daily Telegraph* took place between 1869 and 1872. In a leading article on 31 March 1869, the *Telegraph* charged that several characters in *Phineas Finn* were 'thinly disguised' portraits of a number of living politicians, including Disraeli, Gladstone, Lord Russell, Lord Derby, and the radical politician John Bright. Trollope denied this in a letter published the next day: 'I intended neither portrait or caricature, and most assuredly I have produced neither' (*Letters* 1, 468). Privately, however, Trollope admitted that it was his practice to use well-known politicians as 'models' for his characters. In the same year, Trollope found himself in opposition to the *Telegraph* regarding a subject even closer to his heart: fox-hunting. This controversy commenced when the historian E. A. *Freeman attacked fox-hunting in an article in the *Fortnightly Review* of October 1869. Trollope, who was so closely connected to the *Fortnightly* that he regarded the publication of this article 'almost as a rising of a child against the father' (*Auto* X), re-

plied to Freeman in the December issue. John *Morley, editor of the *Fortnightly,* allowed Freeman a final rejoinder, but dissuaded Trollope from continuing the debate. None the less, Freeman contributed two lengthy letters to the *Daily Telegraph,* which endorsed his position. The *Telegraph* also published several other letters opposed to fox-hunting, including one from John *Ruskin. Despite these differences with Trollope, the *Telegraph* agreed in 1871 to publish a series of travel letters, to be written by Trollope from Australia, and signed 'Antipodean'. The series, which *The Times* had declined, began in the *Telegraph* on 23 December 1871 and concluded on 28 December 1872. Meanwhile, on 1 April 1872, a play entitled *Shilly-Shally* began a one-month run at the Gaiety Theatre. Although the play was announced as having been co-authored by Trollope and by the novelist Charles *Reade, it was in fact a dramatization of *Ralph the Heir* prepared entirely by Reade. When several critics, including Clement Shorter in the *Daily Telegraph,* attacked the play as coarse and indelicate, Reade wrote to the paper to announce that he was suing some of the critics for slander. (Reade eventually won his suit against the drama critic of the *Morning Advertiser* and was awarded £200 in damages.) Trollope, however, was not even aware that Reade had adapted his novel for the stage until 20 May 1872, when a letter from Reade, dated 7 March, caught up with Trollope in Melbourne. As Reade remarked, he had no legal obligation to consult Trollope before adapting the novel; indeed, Reade believed he was behaving generously by naming Trollope as his co-author and offering to share the profits. Trollope disagreed, and wrote to the *Pall Mall Gazette* to dissociate himself from the play. Trollope became even more angry when he learned of the negative reviews and saw Reade's letter to the *Daily Telegraph.* On 1 June, Trollope addressed his own letter to the *Telegraph,* in which he again disclaimed any responsibility for *Shilly-Shally.* Published on 6 August, it was his last contribution to the newspaper. The *Morning Breakfast Table* in *The Way We Live Now* was probably the *Telegraph,* which was gaining circulation steadily in the 1870s. PTS

Dale, Captain Bernard, son of Colonel Orlando and Lady Fanny Dale and heir presumptive of his uncle, Squire Dale of Allington. A small, slight man with moustaches and a confident air, he has succeeded with the corps of Engineers, though not with his cousin Isabella Dale, who rejects his proposal. In *The Last Chronicle of Barset* the 30-year-old lover marries Martha Thorne's niece Emily Dunstable. *SHA* NCS

Dale, Christopher, bachelor squire of Allington. A plain, dry, man with short grizzled hair, he is constant and sincere, but crusty and authoritarian. His generosity in allowing his sister-in-law Mary Dale to live with her two daughters on the Allington estate is tempered by his attempts to influence their choices of husbands. *SHA, LCB*
NCS

Dale, Isabella (Bell), elder daughter of the widow Mary Dale, with whom she lives in the Small House at Allington. Taller and prettier than her sister Lily, with the same fair hair, and soft and tender blue eyes, Bell refuses her cousin Captain Bernard Dale's proposal despite his love and her uncle's wishes. Clear-spoken, sympathetic, and honest, she eventually marries Dr James Crofts. Mentioned briefly, with two children, in *The Last Chronicle of Barset. SHA*   NCS

Dale, Lilian (Lily), younger daughter of the widowed Mary Dale of Allington. Shorter than her sister Bell, though with the same fair hair and complexion, she exhibits dignity, modesty, playfulness, and no fear of men. She falls deeply in love with Adolphus Crosbie, who jilts her in a matter of weeks for Lady Alexandrina De Courcy. Stoically, Lily devotes herself to her mother, rejecting the many proposals of her old friend Johnny Eames. In *The Last Chronicle of Barset* she befriends Grace Crawley and journeys to London where she encounters both Crosbie and Eames but becomes even more confirmed in her spinsterhood. *SHA*   NCS

Dale, Mary, mother of Isabella and Lily Dale and widow of Squire Christopher Dale's younger brother. Proud but poor, she lives in the Small House at Allington through the squire's generosity. Sympathetic to her daughter's troubles, she remains coldly civil to the squire's interventions. Basically kind-hearted, she takes in Grace Crawley. *SHA, LCB*   NCS

Dale, Colonel Orlando, brother of Squire Dale of Allington and father of Captain Bernard Dale. He and his wife Lady Fanny live in Torquay, an effete, listless couple with little interest in the world. Taller, thinner, and seemingly older than his brother, he has a dull dinner with Johnny Eames and Lord De Guest in London. *SHA*
NCS

Dallas, Eneas Sweetland (1828–79), critic. A Garrick Club colleague of Trollope, he boosted Trollope's reputation with an article in *The Times* (23 May 1859) about his fiction from *The Warden* (1855) to *The Bertrams* (1859) in which he declared that the novelist was the star of Mudie's Library. Trollope was not as appreciative when he reviewed Dallas's shortened version of Richardson's *Clarissa* (1748–9) in *Saint Pauls* (November 1868). As editor of *Once a Week* Dallas was involved with juggling arrangements for publishing *The Vicar of Bullhampton* (1870) to allow precedence to Victor *Hugo's *L'Homme qui rit*. It fell to Dallas to persuade Trollope first to accept a delay and, worse, to have his novel come out in an inferior journal, the *Gentleman's Magazine*. Trollope showed his contempt for the business in *An Autobiography* (XVII). He also criticized Dallas severely (without naming him) for accepting from Dickens a handsomely bound manuscript after reviewing *Our Mutual Friend* (1865). For Trollope it was a golden rule 'that there should be no intercourse at all between an author and his critic' (*Auto* XIV).   RCT

d'Almavivas, Marquis, good-natured Spanish nobleman who overlooks John Pomfret's rudeness in mistaking him for a 'torero'. 'Bull' *TAC1*
GRH

Dalrymple, Conway, artist friend of Johnny Eames. A bit of a dandy, he paints society women in classical and biblical settings, achieving some fame with Maria Broughton as *The Three Graces*. His painting of Clara Van Siever as Jael leads to a flirtation with Mrs Broughton, a conflict with Clara's mother, and a proposal to Clara herself. *LCB*   NCS

Daly, J., young untried lawyer who is employed by Barry Lynch to pressure his sister Anty to forfeit her inheritance. Though repelled at the prospect, he feels economically compelled to take on the case, but does so with an eye to protecting his client's sister. *KOK*   MRS

Daly, Kate, younger sister of Mrs Heathcote, attracted to Giles Medlicot, a neighbour in dispute with Harry Heathcote. She functions as a bridge between the antagonists after they are reconciled, cementing their friendship when she accepts Medlicot's proposal of marriage. *HHG*
MRS

Daly, Tom (Black Daly), master of the Galway Hounds, whose sense of identity and self-worth is threatened when Landleaguers marshal the Irish tenantry throughout Co. Galway to disrupt the gentry's favourite sport, fox-hunting. *L*
MRS

Daly's Bridge, residence of hunt master Tom Daly, a small property inherited from his father. *L*   MRS

Damer, Fanny, pretty daughter of the Damers. She is successfully courted by the American Jefferson Ingram on the trip up the Nile. 'Pyramids' *TAC1*   GRH

Damer, Mr, English tourist, insular and condescending towards the American whose betrothal to his daughter he greets with utter astonishment and then acceptance, having been occupied with the vexations of travel including Sabrina Dawkins. 'Pyramids' *TAC1*   GRH

Damer, Mrs, a most unwilling and somewhat comic tourist. 'Pyramids' *TAC1*   GRH

Dana, Richard Henry (1815–82), American writer and lawyer, admitted to the bar in the year he published his classic *Two Years before the Mast* (1840). Trollope consulted him about the US constitution and judiciary for his *North America*. Dana's first impressions of Trollope were unfavourable; a diary note of a breakfast meeting in January 1862 pronounced Trollope 'intolerable, no manners, but means well & would do a good deal to serve you, but says the most offensive things—not a gentleman' (*I & R* 75). They eventually became friends. When Rose and Trollope spent two weeks in Paris in April 1874, they met Dana and his wife on friendly terms. Later Trollope told Dana's son that his father was one of the most entertaining raconteurs he had ever met, and spoke of his wit and wide information (quoted Super 330). Trollope supported Dana's nomination for US ambassador to Britain, writing to him in March 1876 that it was fortunate the President had 'recourse to a man whom all would esteem, and of whom his country may be proud in all relations' (*Letters* 2, 682). The appointment was not ratified.   RCT

dancing. All his life Trollope enjoyed dancing. As a youth, with his brother Tom he walked fourteen miles (22 km) to Vauxhall to see the fireworks, danced for several hours, and walked home again to Harrow 'without having touched bite or sup' (T. A. Trollope, *What I Remember* (1887), 1, 240). Later in life he teased a friend of Florence *Bland, 'In your letter you have taken the very last way to get a middle aged man like me to come to your ball. You only offer to put me in a corner to play cards! If you had promised to dance three round dances with me, I should have come at once' (*Letters* 2, 605). Dancing is often deployed in the novels to further flirtations, dalliance, and mutual engagements of feeling. Maryanne Brown flirts with two suitors at a dance emporium called the Hall of Harmony (*SBJR*). In *Can You Forgive Her?* Burgo Fitzgerald and Lady Glencora Palliser whirl around the dance floor at Lady Monk's party 'till they were stopped by want of breath' (L). Clearly, illicit romance is in the air. The waltz has overtones of sexual excitement here as in *Rachel Ray*, where the heroine, having waltzed with Luke Rowan,

asks herself, 'was it very wicked? She had her doubts' (VIII). Married ladies are advised to stand up for the quadrille: 'When a woman has five children', says Mrs Butler Cornbury in *Rachel Ray*, 'I don't think she ought to do more than that' (VII). But Lady George Germain in *Is He Popenjoy?* shocks her husband by displaying herself with Jack De Baron in the latest dance craze, the Kappa-Kappa (XXXVIII).   RCT

Darvell, John Caldigate's gardener before whom Timothy Crinkett first denounces Caldigate as a thief and a bigamist. *JC*   SRB

Darwin, Charles (1809–82). Intended by his father for his own profession of medicine, but showing no talent either for that or for the Church, Darwin embarked in 1831 as a naturalist on board the *Beagle* bound for South America. By 1844 Darwin had developed his theory of evolution by natural selection. However, it was not until 1859 that he produced *On the Origin of Species by Means of Natural Selection*, followed by *The Descent of Man* (1871). In 1868, Trollope turned down an article on Darwin's theories for *Saint Pauls* because 'I am afraid of the subject of Darwin. I am myself so ignorant on it, that I should fear to be in the position of editing a paper on the subject' (*Letters* 1, 447). Trollope was none the less open to new ideas about human origins. Like Darwin he was also drawn to *Colenso's challenges to biblical literalism. He sent his sons Harry and Fred to Bradfield School in 1860, where the headmaster, the Revd Stephen Poyntz Denning, included such controversial topics (Glendinning 261).   RCT

Daubeny, Mr, one of the great prime ministers who serve as head of Tory governments in Trollope's Palliser series. A one-time member for East Barsetshire, Mr Daubeny is a confirmed Conservative, but he is still friendly with the Duke of Omnium, recommending the Duke as Prime Minister when his own administration fails. Mr Daubeny is perhaps modelled after Disraeli, a possibility suggested both by his being called 'a political Cagliostro' and by a similarity of nicknames ('Dizzy' and 'Dubby'). *PF, PR, PM*   JMR

Davies, Sarah Emily (1830–1921), feminist educator and one of a group known as the Ladies of Langham Place among whom Trollope warily moved, sympathizing with their crusade for greater career opportunities for women, but in fiction making capital out of militant feminism. Davies, later a co-founder of Girton College, produced *The Higher Education of Women* (1866) in which she scathingly cited Trollope as saying that 'we like our women to be timid' (*Letters* 2,

996 n.). Trollope used the title of her book for a lecture he gave several times offering an unsympathetic view of the feminist cause. RCT

Davis, Julia. As flirtatious as her friend Marian Leslie, she calls Maurice Cumming 'the knight of the rueful countenance'. 'Jack' *TAC1* GRH

Davis, Mr, moneylender to whom John Caldigate becomes heavily indebted through horse racing while at Cambridge University. *JC* SRB

Davis, Mrs, landlady of the Cat and Whistle. Mrs Davis's pub is frequented by London's clerks and navvies, 'young men who, like Charley Tudor and his comrades, liked their ease and self-indulgence' (XX). She tries to force Charley to marry her barmaid Norah Geraghty. *TC* MT

Dawkins, Sabrina, An unsympathetic portrayal of a young single woman who attaches herself where she can in order to see the sights. Rejected, she is spiteful. 'Pyramids' *TAC1* GRH

'Day and the Hour, The, by Capt. W. A. Baker' (review). Baker, a mathematician for the Royal Bombay Engineers, insanely devised these prophecies, based on arithmetical applications to the Book of Revelation. Examples: Victoria will abdicate in favour of a Prince Regent; Christ will descend over Mount Olivet at sunset on 20 September 1878; Napoleon III will be named Pope and prove himself the Antichrist. *Fortnightly Review* (15 September 1865), 379–80. AKL

Deans Staple, beautiful property adjacent to the parish of Hurst Staple in Hampshire, owned by Lord Stapledean, who chooses, however, to make his seat in the bleak district of Bowes, Westmorland. *B* MRS

De Baron, Jack. Cousin and intimate of Adelaide Houghton, this attractive Guards officer is a disturber of marital peace. Lady George Germain, suspected of loving him, recalls him to his better nature. Jack eludes the marital pursuit of Guss Mildmay, until a mischievous legacy from the Marquis of Brotherton forces him to redeem his promise to marry her should he obtain a sufficient income. *IHP* MG

De Baron, Mr, father of Adelaide Houghton, proprietor of Rudham Park, and the only friend of the Marquis of Brotherton, whom he receives at his house. *IHP* MG

De Courcy, Lady Alexandrina. See CROSBIE, LADY ALEXANDRINA.

De Courcy, Lady Amelia, one of Earl De Courcy's four daughters. Convinced of her family's superior blood, she persuades Augusta Gresham to reject the lawyer Mortimer Gazebee, then

at the age of 33 marries him herself. In *The Small House at Allington* she assists her sister Alexandrina to marry Adolphus Crosbie. *DT, BT* NCS

De Courcy, Earl, Whig nobleman of West Barsetshire, a 'Court Whig' who delights in visiting Windsor and Balmoral, and in receiving royal favours. He encourages the political aspirations of Gustavus Moffat in an election against the radical Sir Roger Scatcherd. In *The Small House at Allington*, gout-ridden, irascible, and miserly, he returns to Courcy Castle to live, and with his abuse drives his wife away, thus hastening the disintegration of the family. *DT* NCS

De Courcy, George, second son of Earl De Courcy who proposes by letter to the heiress Martha Dunstable but eventually marries Maria, the daughter of a coal-merchant with £30,000. After his marriage he becomes parsimonious, quarrels with his father, and is turned out of the house. *DT, BT, SHA* NCS

De Courcy, John, troublesome, malicious third son of Earl De Courcy. Addicted to cigars and an extravagant bachelor life, he affects an intimacy with Adolphus Crosbie until his future brother-in-law throws him out. *SHA, BT, DT, LCB* NCS

De Courcy, Lady Margaretta, unmarried daughter of Earl De Courcy. Proud and disdainful, she acts under the self-imposed duty of being a De Courcy. Her mother the Countess takes her (her favourite daughter) with her to live in Baden-Baden. *SHA, BT, DT* NCS

De Courcy, Maria, George De Courcy's wife, condescended to and known as 'Mrs George' by the great family she has married into. Daughter of a coal-merchant, she is neither beautiful, clever, ugly, nor unbearably stupid, though she does have £30,000, and her pregnancy could provide a De Courcy heir in the event Lord Porlock fails to marry. *SHA* NCS

De Courcy, Countess Rosina, wife of Earl De Courcy of Barsetshire and sister-in-law of Lady Arabella Gresham. A cold, calculating woman, she considers herself the pinnacle of Barsetshire society. She attempts to find a suitably wealthy wife for her nephew Frank Gresham in *Doctor Thorne* and arranges the marriage of her daughter Alexandrina to the already-engaged Adolphus Crosbie. When her abusive husband returns to Courcy Castle, the Countess leaves him to live in Baden-Baden with her favourite daughter Margaretta and her married daughter Lady Alexandrina. *SHA, BT, LCB* NCS

De Courcy, Lady Rosina, energetic, unmarried, and healthy daughter of Earl De Courcy who tyrannizes servants and acquaintances with her religious fervour. *SHA, BT, DT*   NCS

Deepbell, Lady, a purveyor of news, especially when Major Rossiter's projected union with Georgiana Wanless is 'off'. 'Dugdale' *WFF*
GRH

Defoe, Daniel (1660–1731), journalist and novelist, whose *The Life and Strange and Surprizing Adventures of Robinson Crusoe, of York, Mariner* (1719) Trollope considered the first 'really popular' novel. In his list of major figures of English literature, Defoe and Johnson are the only two prose writers included. Planning his 'History of World Literature', Trollope intended to begin with *Robinson Crusoe*.   RCT

De Guest, Lady Julia, spinster sister of Earl De Guest and mistress of Guestwick Manor. Thought tedious, dull, and virtuous, she attempts to make Adolphus Crosbie recognize his responsibility to Lily Dale and then becomes Johnny Eames's fierce partisan and confidante in his pursuit of Lily, a project she continues in *The Last Chronicle of Barset*. *SHA*   NCS

De Guest, Earl Theodore, unmarried nobleman of Guestwick Manor who breeds cattle and enjoys the country; brother of Lady Fanny Dale and Lady Julia De Guest. A short, stumpy man with red cheeks, round face, and old clothes, he has gradually rebuilt the family fortunes. He befriends Johnny Eames, supporting with money and advice the young man's efforts to win Lily Dale. By *The Last Chronicle of Barset* he has died and left Eames a few thousand pounds. *SHA*
NCS

Delabordeau, M., French tourist with canal interests who resists the blandishments of Miss Dawkins. 'Pyramids' *TAC1*   GRH

de la Contrie, François Charette (based on historical figure), Henri de Larochejaquelin's friend and fellow leader when the royalists were defeated at Nantes. *LV*   GRH

Delane, John (1817–79), called to the bar in 1847 but passionately drawn to journalism, he became editor of *The Times* at 23, holding that post for 36 years (1841–77). During his tenure he saw thirteen governments rise and fall. He ensured that reporting of the Crimean War exposed official blunders and the troops' sufferings. At mid-century, *The Times* was facetiously named 'The Thunderer'; Trollope parodied the paper as the *Jupiter* in *The Warden* (1855). It was widely believed that Tom Towers, leading writer of the *Jupiter*, was modelled on Delane, but Trollope denied it: 'at that time, living away in Ireland, I had not even heard the name of any gentleman

connected with *The Times* newspaper, and could not have intended to represent any individual by Tom Towers' (*Auto* V). In 1875, on publication of *The Way We Live Now*, an editorial in *The Times* wholeheartedly endorsed the book's viewpoint. Apparently written by John Delane and Tom Mozley, it did not mention the novel, but made oblique reference to the 'commercial profligacy' Trollope claimed had inspired the novel.   RCT

de Larochejaquelin, Agatha. The 'Rose of Poitou' is beautiful, intelligent, sensitive, and active in the Vendean cause. Henri's sister is close to her cousin Marie de Lescure, desired by Adolphe Denot, whom she dislikes and rejects, and adored by the postillion-leader Cathelineau, whose love she accepts as he lies dying in the Saint Laurent hospital. She confesses her feelings to Cathelineau's mother, and after the Vendeans' defeat she escapes to Spain with Marie and Mme de Lescure. *LV*   GRH

de Larochejaquelin, Henri (based on historical figure). Only 20, Henri is one of the main activists in the Vendean rebellion, supporting Cathelineau as leader, true to his friend Denot, loyal to Charles de Lescure, his cousin (whose sister he marries), brave in action. His home, Durbellière in Poitou, is central to the action. He leads the Vendean forces in the final phases of the revolt until his death. *LV*   GRH

de Larochejaquelin, Marquis. The old Marquis is crippled, and tenacious of clinging on to Durbellière through his children Henri and Agatha. He reveals his dignity when the chateau is overrun and, despite his disabilities, agrees to join the flight into Brittany. *LV*   GRH

de Lescure, Charles (based on historical figure). At 27 Charles is an enlightened and humanitarian leader of the Vendeans, an idealist at first sympathetic to the Revolution but opposed to its excesses. He is tolerant of Denot's cowardice. Mortally wounded at Cholet, he insists on accompanying the army and dies in Brittany. He represents the man whose public conscience overcomes his love of domesticity and privacy. *LV*   GRH

de Lescure, Marie. Dark, vivacious, and good-humoured sister of Charles, an intimate friend of Agatha de Larochejaquelin, whose brother Henri she loves and marries. She works for the Vendean cause and, after the defeat and the death of her husband, flees to Spain, but later returns to Poitou during Napoleon's reign. *LV*   GRH

de Lescure, Victorine (based on historical figure), wife of Charles, constantly concerned on his account, appreciative of Marie's support, warmly friendly to her. Sustained by her religion, she later marries Henri's younger brother Louis de Larochejaquelin after Charles dies from his wounds. *LV*   GRH

Demijohn, Clara, pert, nosy young woman who watches the doings of her neighbours in Paradise Row and gossips about them, going so far as to write an anonymous letter to Lord Hampstead's stepmother about his engagement to Marion Fay. Clara dallies with two young men, eventually marrying Tribbledale for his larger income. *MF*   SRB

Demijohn, Jemima, old gossip with a penchant for brandy and water who lives in Paradise Row with her niece Clara. She is reputed to have money hidden away, but she declares that a £100 wedding, a clock, and a harmonium are ample dowry for Clara. *MF*   SRB

Demolines, Lady, elderly widow of Sir Confucius Demolines and mother of the predatory Madalina. Rarely seen except when necessary to express outrage and spring a marriage trap on one of her daughter's visitors. *LCB*   NCS

Demolines, Madalina, predatory daughter of Lady Demolines. A remarkable if not beautiful woman, with large dark eyes and tangled dark hair, she delights in being mysterious, sending anonymous letters, and attempting to trap a husband, first setting her sights on Johnny Eames before settling for Peter Bangles. *LCB*   NCS

de Montmorenci, Josephine, alias of Maryanne Puffle, whose saucy letters and novel intrigue Jonathan Brown. She is crippled and too 'metaphysical in her writing', but he arranges to publish her novel, which is quite a success. 'Josephine' *ET*   GRH

Denison, George Anthony (1805–96), combative high churchman, created Archdeacon of Taunton (1851). He became embroiled in doctrinal controversy with the Bishop of Bath and Wells and was prosecuted in the ecclesiastical courts, but was vindicated (1857). In *Barchester Towers* Eleanor Arabin sent, anonymously, 'a handsome subscription towards certain very heavy ecclesiastical legal expenses which have lately been incurred in Bath' (LIII). Such wranglings in the higher echelons of church power doubtless whetted public appetite for Trollope's fictional cathedral clashes.   RCT

Denot, Adolphe, Henri de Larochejaquelin's close friend. An orphan with property. Ambitious, jealous of Cathelineau, his cowardice is witnessed by de Lescure. Rejected by Agatha de Larochejaquelin, he defects to the republicans, enters Durbellière seeking to take Agatha by

force, is captured, reprieved through Henri, disguises himself, and becomes a royalist. As the 'Mad Captain' of the Breton rebels, he leads the resistance and is mortally wounded. *LV*   GRH

Derby, Edward George Geoffrey Smith Stanley, 14th Earl of (1799–1869), leader of the moderate reformers, able administrator, and tactician who introduced the Reform Bill for Ireland in 1832. During his third administration (1866–8) he collaborated with Disraeli in the Reform Bill of 1867. He was devoted to classical scholarship and sport, especially horse breeding and racing. He became Chancellor of Oxford University (1852), and published miscellaneous works, including a version of the *Iliad* (1864). On the death, in 1867, of Robert Bell, prospective sub-editor of *Saint Pauls*, Trollope drew up a petition to Lord Derby, asking for a government pension for Bell's widow. Following publication of *Phineas Finn* readers could not resist identifying its fictional politicians with real-life counterparts. Lord Derby was seen in Lord De Terrier, who in *Phineas Redux* hands party leadership to Daubeny (Disraeli). Although Trollope strenuously denied that Turnbull was a portrait of John Bright, he did not specifically deny other identifications; in a letter to Mary Holmes, however, he maintained that in general his political characters were 'pure creations' (*Letters* 2, 693). Nevertheless, living politicians appear in a number of novels, and Lord Derby is mentioned in passing in *He Knew He Was Right* (1869).   RCT

Derby, Edward Henry Stanley, 15th Earl (1826–93), Conservative statesman, Foreign Secretary (1861–8, 1874–8), President of the Royal Literary Fund (1875–93), chairman of the Copyright Commission (1876–7) for which as member Trollope missed only one of 48 hearings. An incident concerning Derby's handling of who should chair the Literary Fund dinner (May 1876) almost caused Trollope's resignation. Derby had blocked a move to invite the son of the French Emperor, and Trollope, a stickler for protocol and principle, was enraged. Diplomacy ensured that Trollope stayed on the committee. Derby's phrase 'leap in the dark' in his final speech on the Reform Bill was used by Trollope to describe young people embarking on marriage.   RCT

descendants and relatives of Trollope. '[R]emember, dear Tom, that in a family like ours, *everything* gained by one is felt personally and individually by all.' Thus Frances Trollope encouraged her 'praefect' son to protect his younger brother at Winchester. But, as Anthony would remember bitterly, Tom regarded his prefectship as licence for daily whippings at school,

Tom was 'of all my foes, the worst'. Such misery was one more instance of the friendless adolescence described in *An Autobiography*, yet his mother's assumptions reflected those of any Victorian family with social pretensions who depended on relatives (and a network of mutual friends) to further their interests in good times and shield them in bad. Behind the Trollopes when they settled, as newlyweds, in Keppel Street were their Lincolnshire relatives—a present of silver forks from Casewick Hall; an obligatory footman (in family livery) in Bloomsbury—and the Meetkerke inheritance. After that, great expectation crumbled and tuberculosis struck; sickly Arthur was hurried to Grandfather Milton; Cousin Fanny Bent took Henry, who was too ill to join the exodus to Bruges; and while he and Emily fought death, their elder sister Cecilia found safety with Uncle Henry Milton in Fulham. Trollope saw himself as the forgotten youngest son (his mother's American adventure separated them for more than three years after he turned 12), yet Tom remembered him as mother's 'Benjamin' and his education in England and Belgium depended on their friends, the ubiquitous Drurys; his Post Office appointment also came through the family's network. However, during that unhappy apprenticeship, Trollope seems to have deliberately cut himself off from those connections because he felt unworthy of their notice as an aimless drifter and lowly clerk, though his mother did everything she could for him after her return, as a widow, to England.

However that may be, once Trollope discovered his identity in Ireland, and married Rose, the family became an important part of his life. Immediately after his wedding, he took his bride to his sister's house in Penrith (Cecilia had married Anthony's Post Office colleague John Tilley), where she was introduced to Frances Trollope and Tom; that relationship prospered. The couple's elder son Henry Merivale was named after Anthony's dead brother and an old schoolfriend, John Merivale, who stood as godparent; the other two were Grandmother Trollope and Uncle Tom. John Tilley and Rose's sister Isabella joined James Kendrick, Trollope's Post Office chief, as godparents of Frederic James. As Trollope's career flourished, he maintained connection with his mother's family in the west of England: Fanny Bent at Exeter would become the model for Jemima Stanbury of *He Knew He Was Right*. There were regular visits to Casewick Hall, where Sir John was master of the Cottesmore Hunt and, as MP for the county, a useful ally: the family's crest headed Anthony's personal stationery. Cecilia, second wife of the heir to the Meet-

kerke estates, became a good friend: Trollope helped prepare her poetry for publication. When their sister Cecilia Tilley succumbed to tuberculosis, Rose and Anthony took temporary care of her daughter Edith, and remained close to John Tilley, despite disagreements at the Post Office. Years later, Trollope stood godfather to Tilley's second son and was with that family when he suffered his fatal stroke. After Rose's sister died, her 8-year-old daughter Florence Bland joined the Trollope household (1863) and would later be her uncle's amanuensis and, on his death, her aunt's companion. A third niece, Beatrice, Tom's adored and only child, was sent to boarding school in England after her father's remarriage (a union Rose and Anthony had fostered) and was cared for at Waltham during the holidays. It was Trollope who supervised the negotiations (and proprieties) of her engagement to Charles Stuart-Wortley, grandson of Lord Wharncliffe. A year after the marriage, Bice was dead, having borne a daughter. Charles would be a pallbearer at Anthony's funeral and a constant source of aid to the widowed Rose in family matters. Among those concerns were her Australian grandsons. Before Trollope's death, arrangements had been made for Frank, Fred's 10-year-old son, to come to school in England. But his accent and dilatoriness made life difficult there: at 17, he joined the navy and jumped ship when he got to Australia. He became a bank clerk and later fought in the Boer War. A younger brother, Frederic, was also a bank officer and eventually inherited the Trollope baronetcy. That title passed to yet another brother, Gordon (born after Trollope's death), and through him to his son and grandson, the present Sir Anthony. Shortly after Trollope died, his elder son proposed to Ada Strickland, one of Florence Bland's close friends. Their daughter Muriel wrote a brief memoir, 'What I Was Told', before her death in 1953. Neither she nor her brother Thomas Anthony (1893–1931) married.

AWJ

Edwards, P. D., *Anthony Trollope's Son in Australia* (1982).

Trollope, Muriel, 'What I Was Told', *NCF* (March 1948), 223–35.

Desmond, Clara, Dowager Countess of,

impoverished widow and mother of Lady Clara, who falls in love with her daughter's suitor Owen Fitzgerald. Having married a 'wrinkled earl with gloating eyes' (XLIII) at an early age for his rank, she later discovers that commodifying the heart's affections bears bitter fruit: hopeless passion for a younger man, alienation from her daughter, and living interment in the lonely precincts of Desmond Court. Though rivalry for her daughter's suitor made her seem 'almost revolting' to Trollope (*Auto* IX), her predicament is sympathetically presented. *CR*　　　　　　　　MRS

Desmond, Lady Clara, impressionable heroine who accepts her second suitor, the wealthy Herbert Fitzgerald, before fully renouncing her first, the portionless Owen Fitzgerald. Though somewhat insipid—Trollope himself felt she lacked character (*Auto* IX)—she eventually defies her mother's prudence to assert a personal sense of loyalty to the apparently disinherited Herbert. Indeed, the passion of her first love is all the better quelled by the prospect of mortification at the hands of her second: 'Clara's love for Herbert had never been passionate, till passion had been created by his misfortune' (XXX). *CR*　　MRS

Desmond, Patrick, Earl of, heir of Desmond Court, an Eton schoolboy who develops a 'strong boyish love' (XXXVI) for Owen Fitzgerald. At first, under his mother's influence, he sees his hero's betrothal to his sister Clara as imprudent, but overcome by his crush he not only promises to press his friend's suit, but later travels with him overseas. *CR*　　　　　　　　MRS

Desmond Court, near Kanturk, Co. Cork, vast but dilapidated residence of Lady Clara and her impoverished mother, the Countess of Desmond. An extravagant mansion built by the late Earl, its cement 'thickened with human blood' (I), it becomes a solitary prisonhouse for the Countess, where she remains immured after the marriage of her daughter. *CR*　　　　　　　MRS

De Terrier, Lord, Tory leader, modelled on Lord Derby, who becomes Prime Minister in a short-lived government. He attends Martha Dunstable's London gala just before dissolution. *FP, PF*　　　　　　　　　　NCS

Devon, county in the south-west of England. The primary locations for *Rachel Ray*—the town of Baslehurst, the village of Cawston, and the hamlet of Bragg's End—are all located in the South Hams region of Devon. Trollope knew the county well, having visited as a child and then later when working as a surveyor for the Post Office. The lushness of the Devon countryside is particularly appropriate for the pastoral values which collide with commercial values in the novel. The county also provides settings for *He Knew He Was Right*, *Framley Parsonage*, and *Kept in the Dark*. In the short story 'The Parson's Daughter of Oxney Colne', Revd Woolsworthy is 'the antiquarian of Dartmoor', and Devon 'the prettiest scenery in all England'.　　　MT

Dibdin, Thomas Frognall (1776–1841), nephew of Charles Dibdin, songwriter and play-wright; rector of St Mary's, Bryanston Square, from 1824, who wrote 'Bibliomania' (1809) and other works. A close friend of Henry Drury, he rhapsodized about Harrow in *Reminiscences of a Literary Life* (1836). Dibdin officiated when Trollope's sister Cecilia and John Tilley were married at St Mary's in 1839.　　　　　　RCT

Dicey, Edward James Stephen (1832–1911), editor of the *Observer* (1870–1911). He succeeded Robert Bell as assistant editor of *Saint Pauls* (1867). As member of the Royal Literary Fund committee Dicey mediated a squabble (May 1876) by which Trollope's resignation was averted. He was among mourners at Trollope's funeral.　　　　　　　　　RCT

Dickens, Alfred Tennyson D'Orsay (1845–1912). Most independent of Dickens's sons, he emigrated to Australia and took up sheep farming. He initially settled in New South Wales, became a friend of Fred Trollope, and met Trollope and Rose when they visited their son in 1871–2. In 1872, when Alfred moved to Melbourne, Fred wrote of having 'one neighbour less with whome [*sic*] you can exchange an idea' (Glendinning 410).　　　　　RCT

Dickens, Charles (1812–70). Trollope's response both to Dickens the novelist and to Dickens the man was at best ambiguous, at worst antipathetic. The two men were acquainted, both professionally and personally, but scarcely intimate. In 1869 Trollope noted that it was not often that he heard from Dickens 'but such things do occur, now & then' (*Letters* 1, 476). In November 1867 he had acted as a steward and spoken at a dinner given in Dickens's honour at the Freemasons' Hall. Although he described Dickens as 'a great chieftain in literature', he made little other reference to him in his speech and he had earlier commented on the organizers of the dinner: 'I am not specially in that set, but having been asked I did not like to refuse' (*Letters* 1, 394 n., 397). Dickens was far closer to Thomas Adolphus Trollope (a relationship made all the more distinctive by Thomas's marriage in 1866 to Frances Ternan, sister of Dickens's mistress Ellen Ternan). It was to Thomas Adolphus that Dickens commented that Anthony was 'the heartiest and best of fellows' (*Letters* 1, 423 n.) and later described his ambition to stand for Parliament as 'inscrutable', but with the proviso that 'the honester the man . . . the better for the rest of us' (*Letters* 1, 452 n.). In April 1868, as Dickens was just about to leave New York harbour on his homeward voyage, Trollope, who had himself just arrived in America, made a point of shaking hands 'most heartily' with him on shipboard (*Letters* 1, 423 n.).

Trollope was far less generous privately and in print. Dickens is famously caricatured in *The Warden* (XV) as 'Mr Popular Sentiment', a serial novelist 'of all reformers . . . the most powerful'. The first number of Mr Sentiment's novel the *Almshouse* is 'a direct attack on the whole system' which goes a long way 'to put down Rochester, and Barchester, and Dulwich, and St Cross, and all such hotbeds of peculation'. Trollope's narrator goes on to comment, letting the fictional veil slip: 'Mr Sentiment's great attraction is in his second-rate characters. If his heroes and heroines walk upon stilts . . . their attendant satellites are as natural as though one met them in the street . . . yes, live, and will live till the names of their calling shall be forgotten in their own, and Buckett and Mrs Gamp will be the only words left to us to signify a detective police officer or a monthly nurse.' The tenor of these comments may well be related to what we can suppose would have been Trollope's defence of the civil service against Dickens's peccant Circumlocution Office in the rejected, and now lost, article on *Little Dorrit* submitted to the *Athenaeum* in 1856 (*Letters* 1, 43). His obituary of Dickens (*Saint Pauls* (17 July 1870), 370–5) lays great stress on the justice of the novelist's popularity, but subtly declines to answer the criticism that Dickens's novels are deficient in both 'art in the choice of words' and 'nature in the creation of character' ('they have justified themselves by making themselves into a language which is itself popular; and his characters, if unnatural, have made a second nature by their own force'). Trollope praises Dickens's acting skills ('as an actor he would have been top of his profession'), but then admits that he had never actually seen him act, let alone read. At the Royal Academy dinner in April 1871, Trollope replied to the President, Sir Francis Grant's, allusion to the deceased Dickens by expressing the narrow and somewhat Podsnapian sentiment: 'He has gone to his grave with the conviction that by no word he wrote did he ever damage a youthful mind, by no word he wrote did he ever harm a human heart.' When the first volume of Forster's *Life of Charles Dickens* appeared in 1872, he wrote to George Eliot complaining that: 'Dickens was no hero; he was a powerful, clever, humorous, and, in many respects, wise man;—very ignorant, and thick-skinned, who had taught himself to be his own God' (*Letters* 2, 557). He was also singularly offended by Dickens's fictional representation of his father '& the hard words he intended to have published of his own mother'. Trollope's sense that Dickens was both vulgar and self-pitying

was to remain constant. In 1875 a reading of Macready's *Reminiscences* stimulated the sentiment that it was 'disgusting to see the self-consciousness and irritated craving for applause which such men as Macready & Dickens have exhibited' (*Letters* 2, 671). It is in *An Autobiography*, however, that Trollope's ambiguity emerges most vividly. Again, and with a tinge of professional jealousy, he dwells on Dickens's popularity and his sales: 'The primary object of a novelist is to please; and this man's novels have been found more pleasant than those of any other writer.' Again he stresses the purity of Dickens's mind and the morality of his art ('His teaching has ever been good'), but he places him in third rank amongst contemporary novelists, after Thackeray and George Eliot, believing Dickens's 'drollery . . . very much below the humour of Thackeray', his pathos 'stagey and melodramatic'. Dickens's style, he believed, was 'jerky, ungrammatical, and created . . . in defiance of rules' and he advised that 'no young novelist should ever dare to imitate the style of Dickens. If such a one wants a model for his language, let him take Thackeray' (XIII).

During the so-called 'Garrick Club affair', which pitted Dickens against Thackeray during the winter of 1859–60, Trollope, still relatively innocent when it came to the factions of 'literary London', naturally took Thackeray's side. He nevertheless unwittingly exacerbated the personal tensions by talking about recent *Cornhill* dinners to Edmund Yates (a protégé of Dickens and the subject of the dispute). Yates subsequently wrote up this gossip for the *New York Times* of 26 May 1860, an article partly reproduced in the *Saturday Review*, and Trollope was obliged to apologize to George Smith, the proprietor of the *Cornhill* (*Letters* 1, 111 n.).   ALS

Boll, E., 'The Infusions of Dickens in Trollope', *NCF* (September 1946), 11–24.

Dickens, Charles, *The Letters of Charles Dickens*, ed. Walter Dexter (Nonesuch Edition), 3 vols. (1938), vol. 3.

Roos, David A., 'Dickens at the Royal Academy of Arts: A New Speech and Two Eulogies', *Dickensian* (May 1977), 100–7.

Dickens, Charles, Jun. (1837–96), after his father's death (1870) proprietor of *All the Year Round*, which published *Is He Popenjoy?* (October 1877–July 1878); *The Duke's Children* (October 1879–July 1880), to which Dickens requested, and got, substantial cuts; *Mr Scarborough's Family* (October 1879–July 1880). Henry Trollope prepared *Dickens's Dictionary of Paris, 1882: An Unconventional Handbook* (1882) for Dickens's travel guide series.   RCT

Dictionary of National Biography. Trollope died the year the *DNB*, founded by George Smith, was begun. It collected biographies of noteworthy inhabitants of Britain and the colonies who had died before 1900. The entry on Trollope, by Richard Garnett, is three and a half pages, as compared with, for example, three for G. H. Lewes and five and a half for George Eliot. Garnett's biography draws heavily on *An Autobiography*, overemphasizing Trollope's routine and discipline. Though he insists that the writing is mechanical and Trollope 'never creates—only depicts', Garnett correctly predicts that his faithfulness to detail in the depictions of 19th-century life will enhance Trollope's reputation in the 20th. JK

Did He Steal It? Asked for a play (by John Hollingshead), Trollope extracted the Crawleys from *The Last Chronicle of Barset* and shaped their misfortunes into three acts. The first two largely reproduce dialogue from equivalent chapters in the novel, though not in the same order and with minor elisions, yet the result travesties the original. Nevertheless, its adaptation required some ingenuity.

Given the sensitivities of stage censorship, which would certainly not have countenanced a clergyman suspected of theft, Crawley becomes master of a municipal school, where his only daughter Grace assists him. These changes also conform to *The Last Chronicle*'s conclusive farewell to Barset. Though the schoolmaster now lives in Silverbridge and his troublesome cheque still bears Lord Lufton's signature, the play makes no reference to Barset or its politics.

Crawley's persecutor is Mrs Goshawk, whose husband, a magistrate and school-trustee, summons him to an interview which reproduces the famous defeat of Mrs Proudie (*LCB* XVIII). Having killed off that redoubtable prototype, Trollope could not bring himself to resurrect her name for a character who, by Act III, behaves like a fishwife. He does, however, retain Thumble (as replacement schoolmaster, single and young enough to propose to Grace), Mick Stringer and the waiter (at the Dragon of Wantly), and Toogood (a splendidly comic 'turn' who devolves into a functionary of the plot). Dan Morris and Giles Hoggett amalgamate into Dan Hoggett, whose son Giles is Crawley's pupil. Henry Grantly transmutes into Charles Oakley, Mrs Goshawk's son by a previous marriage.

The play was rejected for reasons Trollope claimed to 'forget' (*Auto* XV). One might speculate that the manager was disappointed by the play's jejune rendering of the original, but that is unlikely. Had he wanted a staged version of a novel, he could, under the liberties of Victorian copyright, have employed some hack to supply it. On its own terms, the play fails as domestic drama: its emotional climaxes create no forward-moving line of suspense; its characters make preposterous entrances and exits into and from scenes ill suited to the action.

For example, Act II begins in Hoggett's cottage. After a sequence between Crawley and the brickmaker, Captain Oakley enters to ask for Grace's hand. That unlikelihood is partially explained by his being directed there by Mrs Crawley, but the comments of Mrs Hoggett, from her sickbed behind a screen, are socially inappropriate and would not have pleased audiences who liked their proposal scenes straightforwardly emotive. In scene ii, Oakley's confrontation with his parents ends with mother's stormy exit and father's invitation to 'come along . . . to my room'. Moments later, both Goshawks return to interview Crawley. This clumsy stage management continues to a final episode between Grace and Oakley in which she behaves more frankly than theatre conventions allowed.

Fundamentally, the story of the cheque is undramatic, depending on narrative explanations rather than staged actions. That Trollope chose it seems all the stranger when one recalls his unease about that story's credibility in the novel *The Last Chronicle* (*Auto* XV). In the play, Mrs Lofty's appearance early in Act III to explain all, 'like a Queen's messenger', trivializes the plot and robs the final scene of all suspense. The script was privately printed by James Virtue, 1869. AWJ

Didon, Élise, Marie Melmotte's maid. Her services are essential in abetting Marie to elope with Felix Carbury but, when they are apprehended at the train station in Liverpool, she abandons Marie and escapes to New York. *WWLN* SRB

Die, Neversaye, the 'great and enduring Chancery barrister' (XII) whose success is based on discretion and expediency. Although a staunch Tory, he advises his young friend Harcourt, a political aspirant, not to trust to party philosophies, but to align himself with the winning side. *B, CR, DT* MRS

Dillsborough, scene of much of the action in *The American Senator*, which Trollope notes could have been called 'The Chronicle of a Winter at Dillsborough' (LXXX), a town of 3,000 with little to recommend it. *AS* MG

'Disabilities', located in London in Marylebone Road, formally named the 'Rights of Women Institute. Established for the Relief of the

Disraeli, Benjamin

Disabilities of Females.' The 'Disabilities', a parody of the women's rights movement of the day, dissolves in an internecine dispute. *IHP*   MG

Disraeli, Benjamin (1804–81) charismatic leader of the Conservatives, Prime Minister (1868, 1874–80); Earl of Beaconsfield (1876); novelist. Trollope's political bête noire, he became Daubeny ('Dubby') in the Palliser novels, most prominent in *Phineas Redux*, as a Cagliostro, a conjurer, and a powerbroker without principle. Disraeli's pro-Turkish position over the Bulgarian Atrocities (1876) caused Trollope to label him 'the meanest cuss we have ever had in this country' (*Letters* 2, 699–700). Meeting Trollope at Lord Stanhope's, he congratulated him for showing the same deft touch with an adventuress in *The Eustace Diamonds* he had already demonstrated with his clergymen (T. H. S. Escott, *Anthony Trollope* (1913), 280). Trollope remained implacable. He judged Disraeli's novels unjustly as 'the wit of hairdressers . . . and the enterprize of mountebanks . . . a smell of hair-oil, an aspect of buhl, a remembrance of tailors . . . paste diamonds' (*Auto* XIII).   RCT

Dixon, William Hepworth (1821–79), biographer and historian, authority on Bacon; editor of the *Athenaeum* (1853–69). Trollope offered him an article on the third number of *Little Dorrit* (including the 'Circumlocution Office', chapter X). It was rejected and has not survived. Trollope's long paper on international copyright appeared in the *Athenaeum* (September 1862). At the banquet in Liverpool (April 1873) to mark the end of Dickens's farewell readings, Trollope joined Dixon in responding to the toast of 'Modern Literature'.   RCT

Dobbes, Reginald, fanatical sportsman who leads a shooting party at Crummie-Toddie including Lord Silverbridge, Silverbridge's brother Gerald, and Frank Tregear. Austere in his eating and drinking, Dobbes despises all life's pleasures outside sport. He is furious when Silverbridge temporarily absents himself from the shoot at Crummie-Toddie. *DC*   JMR

Dobbs, Montgomerie, special friend of Adolphus Crosbie, member of Sebright's Club, and owner of a Scottish home. He serves as groomsman at Crosbie's wedding, suggesting that not all the world had deserted him. *SHA*   NCS

Dobson, Henry Austin (1840–1921), biographer of Hogarth (1879), Goldsmith (1888), and others, writer of light verse, one of the younger poets Trollope encouraged. His poems frequently appeared in *Saint Pauls* and were commented on in letters. 'No contributor who has worked with me has given me more pleasure than yourself' (*Letters* 1, 498). Dobson dedicated his *Vignettes in Rhyme* (1873) to Trollope.   RCT

Docimer, Imogene, sister of Mudbury Docimer and cousin of Frank Houston, whom she loves despite his cynical courtship of Gertrude Tringle. Imogene is 'a young lady of marvellous beauty' (XIV); she is also nearly penniless, as is Frank. But love triumphs over calculation, and they are married. *AA*   WK

Docimer, Mary, wife of Mudbury Docimer and sister-in-law of Imogene Docimer. Mary sides with her husband in opposing Frank Houston's continuing attachment to Imogene, even when he is supposedly engaged to Gertrude Tringle. But in the end, husband and wife resign themselves to the lovers' union. *AA*   WK

Docimer, Mudbury, husband of Mary Docimer, brother of Imogene Docimer, and owner of Tregothnan Hall, Cornwall. As head of the Docimer family, Mudbury strenuously objects to Frank Houston's calling on Imogene, to the extent of refusing him dinner (LX). But Mudbury's efforts are to no avail. *AA*   WK

Dockwrath, Miriam, daughter of Jonathan Usbech and wife of Samuel Dockwrath. Miriam inherits £2,000 from the codicil to Sir Joseph Mason's will. Bullied by her vengeful lawyer-husband, Mrs Dockwrath informs Lady Mason that he has found new and important evidence in 'The Great Orley Farm Case'. *OF*   MT

Dockwrath, Samuel, husband of Miriam Dockwrath, a tenant of Orley Farm for many years, and lawyer who discovers evidence leading to the second trial. 'A young attorney with a questionable character' (I) at the time of the first trial, Dockwrath is a mean-spirited, envious, and vengeful bully at the time of the second trial. *OF*   MT

Doctor, the, generous scholar who hands a lifetime's work to Julius Mackenzie for indexing, and behaves magnanimously after its destruction. 'Dog' *ET*   GRH

doctors as characters. In Trollope's fiction, doctors have a social rather than a medical role. There is a feud between Dr Thorne and the grandly dignified Dr Fillgrave, who appears throughout the Barsetshire novels and who knows how to preserve the mystery of his profession: 'the amount of secret medical knowledge of which he could give assurance by the pressure of those lips was truly wonderful' (*DT* XII). Short, rotund, with built-up shoes, he is a caricature. In *Doctor Thorne* he visits Sir Roger Scatcherd during his fatal illness, and he attends the death of old Mr Harding in *The Last Chronicle of Barset*; but his words of comfort are insincere and trite.

The really eminent doctors practise in London, but make occasional expensive visits in the provinces, as does the famous Sir Omicron Pie, whose reputation is based more on his title than on his professional expertise. However, the great and the good of both Barsetshire and London cannot die without Sir Omicron Pie, who attends Bishop Grantly and Dean Trefoil in *Barchester Towers*, and later the august Duke of Omnium in *Phineas Redux*. His charges are high: £20 for a visit to old Mr Bertram's deathbed in *The Bertrams*. Of course distinguished surgeons, such as Sir William Brodrick in *Mr Scarborough's Family*, could command huge fees. He charges £300 to perform a major operation on the courageous Mr Scarborough in his own home in Staffordshire, enabling him to extend his life long enough to cheat the entail on his estate.

Trollope particularly respected those unpretentious, caring practitioners, such as the exemplary physician Dr Crofts, who appears in *The Small House at Allington*; or John Bold, the young surgeon in *The Warden*. Bold's profession is almost incidental to the plot, but his use of his inheritance to practise on his own account among the poor of Barchester endorses his moral worth as a suitor for Mr Harding's daughter Eleanor.

The doctor who is of major importance as a character is Dr Thorne, 'my hero' as Trollope calls him. Although he is connected to the landed gentry, professionally he is a reformer; and in the novel that bears his name, his controversial practice of making up his own prescriptions, and sending out bills to his patients, gains him notoriety, and gives rise to debate in the medical press. He also charges a reduced rate of 7s 6d. for home visits, rather than the traditional one guinea; and visits his patients on horseback instead of in a grand carriage. The conservative medical profession, which relies for its mystique on the doctor's status as a gentleman, and on the charging of substantial fees, is scandalized. Thorne's more illustrious rivals, Dr Fillgrave and Dr Rerechild, also resent his superior expertise. Trollope places this admirable man in a moral dilemma at the centre of a conflict of loyalties, in the resolution of which he shows himself to be also a social and moral healer. GH

Doctor Thorne (*see next page*)

Dr Wortle's School (*see page 158*)

Dolan, Corney, tenant of Thady Macdermot, associate of Ribbonman Joe Reynolds, and Daniel Kennedy's partner in distilling poteen, or illicit whiskey. He accompanies Thady in his flight from Ballycloran after the murder of Myles Ussher, and later joins Reynolds in the assault on Hyacinth Keegan. *MB* MRS

Dolan, Widow, Irish tenant living near Ballyglunin who reveals that Terry Lax, the suspected assassin, had taken refuge in her cottage after the shooting of Florian Jones. *L* MRS

Doncaster, town where the St Leger is run. Lord Silverbridge's horse Prime Minister is deliberately lamed before the great race. *DC* JMR

Donellan, Captain, hunting guest at Hap House whose breakfast is interrupted by the unexpected arrival of Aby Mollett and Mr Prendergast. *CR* MRS

Donne, Arthur, fiancé of Mary Gresley who dies of consumption. 'Gresley' *ET* GRH

Dormer, Ayala, younger daughter of Egbert and Adelaide (Dosett) Dormer and sister of Lucy Dormer. Orphaned at 19, and penniless, Ayala nevertheless receives marriage proposals from three men: hopeless Tom Tringle, ridiculous Captain Benjamin Batsby, and ugly but eventually adorable Colonel Jonathan Stubbs. Her 'long dark black locks' are known as 'the loveliest locks in London' (I); she sings beautifully, speaks French like a native, and can paint. But Ayala's most attractive quality (and most serious disadvantage) is her romantic nature. She expects an ideal hero to come for her—and, in the end, he does. *AA* WK

Dormer, Egbert, deceased father of Ayala and Lucy Dormer, an artist who inhabited 'the most perfect bijou of a little house at South Kensington' (I). Although Dormer surrounded himself with all the suspect trappings of aestheticism, there was 'a sweet savour about his name' (I). *AA* WK

Dormer, Lucy, elder sister of Ayala Dormer. Lucy is 'fairer than Ayala, somewhat taller, and much more quiet in her demeanour' (I). Also unlike Ayala, Lucy is devoted to a flesh-and-blood lover, the impecunious and impractical sculptor Isadore Hamel, to whom she remains true throughout. *AA* WK

Dorset, location of Custins, Lord and Lady Cantrip's country residence. Scroope Manor in *An Eye for an Eye* is also in Dorset. *DC* JMR

Dosett, Margaret, wife of Reginald Dosett, sister-in-law of Lady Emmeline Tringle and aunt (*cont. on page 161*)

FOR his seventh novel, the third to be set in Barsetshire, Trollope took the unusual step of asking his brother Thomas Adolphus for the plot. The resulting work, *Doctor Thorne*, attained a success that astonished its author. Looking back at this 'most popular' of his books, Trollope used the occasion, in *An Autobiography*, to decry novels whose interest lies more in their plot than in their characters (V, VII). But if *Doctor Thorne* is unusually well plotted—perhaps overplotted—it also contains some of Trollope's most memorable characters, beginning with the good doctor himself, and it transports us to East Barsetshire, an idyllic rural world threatened by change. The principal squire of the region, Francis Newbold Gresham, is the owner of Greshamsbury, an estate that has fallen on hard times, largely as a result of the aristocratic ambitions of Lady Arabella Gresham, née De Courcy, a member of the great Whig family that lives in West Barsetshire.

After a flashback to the time of the First Reform Bill (1832), a period covering the squire's marriage, his failure to sustain his Tory principles, and his increasing financial embarrassments, Trollope begins the novel proper in 1854 with a splendid set piece: the coming of age party for the heir to Greshamsbury, young Frank Gresham. Among the guests are members of the De Courcy family, some of whom, like the Countess and the Hon. John, we first met in *Barchester Towers*. The Countess is anxious that Frank do his 'one great duty', in the eyes of the De Courcys: he 'must marry money' (V). This is an especially pressing obligation as Greshamsbury is now heavily mortgaged. A portion of the property, Boxhall Hill, has already been sold to the wealthy contractor Sir Roger Scatcherd, who is also the squire's creditor to the amount of nearly £100,000. Frank, however, is in love with the doctor's niece Mary Thorne, a woman with no money and of mysterious parentage. When Frank declares himself to Mary, she is driven to ask her uncle a long unasked question: where does she rank in society?

What Mary does not know, and what the doctor does not have the heart to tell her, is that she is the illegitimate child of his dissolute brother Henry Thorne, who seduced the sister of the future baronet in the days when the latter was a local stonemason given to excessive drinking. The enraged Scatcherd killed Henry, and while he was in prison his sister Mary gave birth. She was offered the chance to marry and emigrate from Barchester, but on the condition that she give up the child. Thomas Thorne adopted his brother's daughter as his ward, but only the doctor's close friend Squire Gresham knew of the circumstances. (Scatcherd assumed the child to be dead.) Because of the doctor's friendship with the squire, and his attendance on Lady Arabella and her children, Dr Thorne, along with his niece, has gained a footing at Greshamsbury. But the Gresham–Thorne relationship is now threatened because of Frank's feelings for Mary.

Each of the novel's three main characters is faced with a dilemma: Frank is torn between love for Mary and the duty to marry money to save Greshamsbury; Mary is torn between her own feelings for Frank and her deep-seated pride which scorns the idea of sullying the Gresham blood and impoverishing her lover; and the doctor is torn between his own veneration for 'good blood' and the 'democratic' instincts which have led him to a doctor's calling (II, III). Dr Thorne wants his niece to be happy, and he expects to be treated on an equal basis with the Greshams. (As second cousin to the Thornes of Ullathorne, he feels toward his own blood that there was none 'better . . .

to be had in England' (II). But he deeply respects the existing order of things, and what Trollope says of his niece could be applied to the doctor too: each 'came forth armed to do battle against the world's prejudices, those prejudices she herself still loved so well' (VIII).

Barely a fifth of the way into the novel, however, Trollope indicates to the reader how the plot will be happily resolved. Sir Roger Scatcherd, dying of alcoholism, tells his friend Dr Thorne that he has made a will leaving his fortune—in the event that his alcoholic son Louis should die before the age of 25—to his sister's eldest child. The doctor is obliged to tell the Baronet of his niece's existence, but he refuses to allow him to see her or to let Mary know, for the moment, of her other uncle's existence. 'Her life is not like your life', he explains, 'and her ways are not as your ways' (XIII). From this point in the novel until the end, the reader enjoys an uneasy confidence with the narrator: waiting, in effect, for the Baronet to die (which occurs at the novel's halfway point) and then waiting for Louis's death, all for the sake of a happy ending. The doctor's dilemma is that he must attend conscientiously to two self-destructive patients, whose lives lie in the way of his niece's happiness and of the salvation of Greshamsbury. ' "I will never hanker after a dead man's shoes, neither for myself nor for another," he had said to himself a hundred times; and as often did he accuse himself of doing so. One path, however, was plainly open before him. He would keep his peace as to the will; and would use such efforts as he might use for a son of his own loins to preserve the life [of Louis] that was so valueless. His wishes, his hopes, his thoughts, he could not control; but his conduct was at his own disposal' (XXXVII).

Frank Gresham, following his mother's and aunt's wishes, goes to Courcy Castle in a half-hearted effort to woo the Ointment of Lebanon heiress, Miss Dunstable. Among the visitors at the castle are Bishop and Mrs Proudie, who set an 'example of . . . conjugal affection' (XV). Frank arrives at his relations' home while an election is in progress between the Courcy (Whig) candidate, Mr Moffat, and the radical candidate Scatcherd. Frank canvasses on behalf of Moffat, who is engaged to his sister Augusta. Trollope deftly compares the race for Barchester with the contest for Miss Dunstable's hand. Moffat, the enterprising son of a tailor, joins in the fruitless pursuit of the heiress. (When he subsequently breaks off the engagement to Augusta, he is horsewhipped by Frank.) He also loses the Barchester election, although the election results are subsequently repealed on grounds of voting irregularities. Frank, during his stay at Courcy Castle, has an opportunity to dine with the Duke of Omnium himself, but he is disgusted by the Duke's bad manners. He does, however, become friendly with Miss Dunstable, who makes him promise to be faithful to Mary.

Lady Arabella, horrified to learn of her son's attachment, does everything she can to thwart the union. She closes the doors of Greshamsbury to Mary, and she quarrels with Dr Thorne. Her efforts to prevent a misalliance are curiously paralleled by the doctor's refusal to countenance an engagement between his niece and the smitten baronet Sir Louis Scatcherd: 'Had Sir Louis been a Hottentot, or an Esquimaux, the proposal could not have astonished him more. The two persons were so totally of a different class, that the idea of the one falling in love with the other had never occurred to him' (XXVIII). Mary admits her love for Frank, and she even stands up to Lady Arabella: 'I will not listen to your calculations as to how much or how little each of us may have to give to the other' (XLII). But with Sir Louis's death—occurring a mere chapter after Mary's defiance of Lady Arabella, followed by her letter to Frank releasing him from the engagement—all ends happily for the lovers. After a three-year wait, Frank's fidelity is rewarded; and he turns out to have been true to Mary and to his duty. The novel ends in 1857 (a year before the book's publication) with another set piece: Frank's marriage to Mary, attended by various De Courcys and by the Duke of Omnium himself. 'And thus Frank married money, and became a great man' (XLVII).

This all makes for a 'good plot', but Trollope is aggrieved by the thought that this 'most insignificant part of a tale' is what the public likes best (*Auto* VII). Hence, in *Doctor Thorne* he makes use of the hand-me-down plot to tease the reader's expectations about plot and to raise moral issues affecting his characters' and our worldly values. After all, as the doctor reflects, 'Frank, though he might find [Mary] rich, was bound to take her while she was poor' (XL). One reviewer of *Doctor Thorne* took the occasion to criticize novelists whose 'heroes make desperate efforts to marry beggary and infamy; but when they try to do so, the desert blossoms as the rose' (*Saturday Review*, 12 June 1858). But Trollope himself calls repeated attention to the artificiality of his plot. Mary, baffled by Dr Thorne's air of knowing a deep secret, complains, 'Uncle, I think you're going to take to writing mysterious romances, like Mrs Radcliffe's' (XLVI). In *Barchester Towers* Trollope promoted the 'doctrine . . . that the author and the reader should move along together in full confidence with each other'—without resorting to the secrecy employed by Mrs Radcliffe (XV). By eschewing the suspense element—since early in the book the reader knows the novel's outcome—Trollope is able to focus on the human element of his tale and to consider moral ambiguities faced by reader and characters alike. For, despite Trollope's attitude toward *Doctor Thorne*, it is the characters and not the plot that make this one of his masterpieces.

Pre-eminent among them is Dr Thorne himself, whose moral delicacy and combination of contradictory qualities mirror those of his creator. Skilled in his professional calling, proud of his heritage, Thorne is (like Trollope) both a self-made man and a traditionalist. As such, he naturally mediates between the various inhabitants of Barsetshire. He can stand up to rival doctors, as well as to the mighty Greshams, De Courcys, and Scatcherds, but he is also at home in 'the society of children' (III). He is friend to the squire as well as to Sir Roger, sharing personal attributes with both. (The latter's addiction to spirits is paralleled by the doctor's addiction to heaping pots of tea.) As a high Conservative with 'subversive professional democratic tendencies' (III), he serves to reconcile two of the novelist's major themes: a respect for tradition and a respect for needful change. If the doctor is Trollope's 'hero', Mary is 'our heroine' (II). Simultaneously independent-minded and deferential, she has traits in common with both her uncles: her 'spirit of democracy' maintains that a person be respected for 'absolute, intrinsic, acknowledged, individual merit', while her 'spirit of aristocracy' upholds the claims of the establishment (VI). Henry James, in his famous 'partial portrait' of the author, lists Mary first among Trollope's 'affectionate' gallery of heroines (*Partial Portraits* (1888), 128). Her standing up to Lady Arabella (XXIX) is worthy of Elizabeth Bennet's defiance of Lady Catherine de Bourgh. (*Pride and Prejudice* was one of Trollope's favourite novels.) Her tender moments with her uncle, her lover, and her friend Beatrice Gresham are described by Trollope with wonderful delicacy.

Toward the reader's 'favourite young man' (I), Frank Gresham, Trollope displays a mixture of humour and kindliness. He traces Frank's growth from the boyish lover of

21 to the manly suitor of 24, willing to brave the world's prejudices with regard to 'blood' and to take an extraordinary (if unnecessary) vow to 'do something for his living!' (XXXIX). Elizabeth Bowen has observed of two other major characters that Trollope should 'have leased them out to other novelists, better equipped to handle them—Lady Arabella to Balzac, Scatcherd to Dostoievsky' (introd. to *DT* (Riverside edn., 1959), p. xxii). But that is to overlook the many ways in which Trollope humanizes these two potentially stereotypical figures. Despite her overbearing nature, Lady Arabella is also a worried mother and a patient fearful of cancer. And Scatcherd is not allowed to become merely a warning against drunkenness. He too is a worried parent, as well as a sympathetic prankster and avenger. (His reaction to his sister's dishonour foreshadows Frank's treatment of his sister's former suitor.) Especially noteworthy among the minor characters is the strong-willed Miss Dunstable, who amusingly fights off her presumed admirers and who urges the hero not to 'sell one jot of liberty for mountains of gold' (XX). Trollope concludes the novel with the wild rumour 'that Dr Thorne, jealous of Mary's money, was going to marry her' (XLVII). Yet in *Framley Parsonage* this improbable scenario becomes fact.

Written during Trollope's most Carlylean phase, *Doctor Thorne* begins with a defence of England's 'old symbols', its rural values. 'England', he maintains, 'is not yet a commercial country in the sense in which that epithet is used for her; and let us still hope that she will not soon become so. She might surely as well be called feudal England, or chivalrous England' (I). But in his handling of the theme of inter-class marriage, Trollope takes a more liberal position, anticipating such novels as *Lady Anna* and *The Duke's Children*. The 'democratic nuptials' between blood and money which end the novel (XLVII) suggest, as is so often true in Trollope, that individual cases outweigh general precepts. Oddly, for a Barsetshire novel, religion figures very little in the book. When the Revd Caleb Oriel says of his bride-to-be Beatrice Gresham that 'she's so sincerely religious', her brother looks 'solemn as became him' (XLV). On the other hand, this is the first Trollope novel in which English politics figure. Plantagenet Palliser's forebear, the Duke of Omnium, makes his first appearance here, albeit in an unpleasant light. Although in his depiction of the Moffat–Scatcherd election Trollope presents human nature at its weakest, he also asserts, 'To be or not to be a member of the British parliament is a question of very considerable moment in a man's mind' (XVII). Neither Scatcherd's discomfiture nor Moffat's humiliation dissuaded Trollope from making his own unsuccessful bid for a seat in Parliament ten years after the publication of *Doctor Thorne*.

Stylistically, the novel also looks backward and forward. Chapter XXXVIII, 'De Courcy Precepts and De Courcy Practice', shows Trollope at home in the epistolary mode of 18th-century fiction. The letters between Augusta Gresham and Lady Amelia De Courcy, the former pleading in vain for her cousin's permission to marry a commoner, are Trollope at his most Austenish, mingling satire with ruefulness. Once again the implied theme is that individuals need not be sacrificed to traditional strictures. One also detects traces of Trollope's mentor Thackeray, in the satire directed at the aristocracy and in the occasional epigrams. Regarding Lady Arabella's refusal to nurse her progeny, Trollope writes, 'Nature gives them bosoms for show, but not for use' (II). Trollope's good-natured irony is evident throughout the book, although it was not always evident to contemporaries, who interpreted literally, for example, his apology for having begun 'a novel with two long dull chapters full of description' (II). The

Saturday Review critic was disturbed by this bit of ironic self-deprecation. (The chapters establish the context of the Gresham–Thorne story with economy and wit.) And, like James after him, he deplored Trollope's narratorial asides as disturbances of the 'reasonably perfect illusion as to the reality of the events which he relates' (see also James 116–17). Nowadays, Trollope's habit of exposing his novelistic machinery might be seen as a sign of literary postmodernism. In his asides to the reader, implicating us in the novel's moral issues, Trollope anticipates the ideas of reader-response theorists. Trollope's contemporaneity is particularly well displayed in his dialogue. C. P. Snow observes that, in comparison to Dickens, Trollope sounds 'entirely natural' and up-to-date (*Trollope* (1975), 156). He cites *Doctor Thorne* in proof of this.

Doctor Thorne was published in three volumes by Chapman & Hall in June 1858. It was begun 20 October 1857, and completed 31 March 1858, a substantial portion being written while Trollope was undertaking a postal mission to Egypt. Contemporary reviewers were highly favourable, welcoming Trollope (in the words of the *Leader*) 'among the illustrious living writers of fiction whom we are able to count off upon our fingers'. Trollope was praised for his 'healthy and sturdy' realism, and for his 'real insight into human character and into the complexities of human motives' (Smalley 69). His characters, in the words of the *Athenaeum* reviewer, 'are real creatures of human nature, flesh and blood, vigorously and broadly drawn' (Smalley 71). Michael Sadleir praised the 'sensational perfection' of *Doctor Thorne*. In terms of composition and characterization, it constitutes 'the proud apex of the pyramid of Trollope fiction' (Sadleir 375, 401). According to N. John Hall, the novel was 'reprinted during Trollope's lifetime more often than any other of his novels', 34 reissues altogether (Hall 165); and by the mid-20th century it had proved one of the half-dozen most popular of his novels. Only one notable voice has ever denied the novel's greatness: Trollope himself. The manuscript is not extant.   DDS

Bowen, Elizabeth, introd. to *Doctor Thorne* (Riverside edn., 1959).
James, Henry, *Partial Portraits* (1888).
Snow, C. P., *Trollope: His Life and Art* (1975)

Dr Wortle's School

THIS short novel, which deals with attitudes towards irregular sexual relationships, is unique in Trollope's fiction for its subversive moral view. Two main narrative concerns are interwoven: the status of marriage, which had come under intense scrutiny during the late Victorian period; and the nature of moral judgement. Trollope was no doubt preoccupied with the strain and unhappiness caused to his friends George Henry *Lewes and George *Eliot, who lived together for many years, by Lewes's inability to obtain a divorce from his wife; for he had recently written Lewes's obituary.

A recurrent theme in Victorian fiction was bigamy, which Trollope treats in several novels, particularly *Castle Richmond* and *John Caldigate*. In *Dr Wortle's School* it is the catalyst for a tale that challenges social conventions. His publisher, William Blackwood, was anxious until he saw how this dangerous theme was to be handled. Trollope's changing of his working title, 'Mr and Mrs Peacocke', to *Dr Wortle's School* indicates a shift of interest from the bigamous relationship to the moral psychology of Dr Wortle. Indeed, it has often been observed that there are striking similarities between Wortle's personality and Trollope's own—he is stubborn, generous, proud, choleric, and loyal. Jeffrey Wortle may be seen to some extent as a self-portrait; and this late novel as something of a personal statement about contemporary sexual morality and essential human values.

Aspects of Trollope's story involving the gun-carrying American ruffian smack of melodrama, but at its core is an abstract moral problem which the plot serves to make concrete. Dr Wortle, the rector of Bowick, who runs a preparatory school that sends pupils to Eton, engages as his assistant the Revd Henry Peacocke, formerly an Oxford scholar, who had been Vice-President at a classical college in St Louis, Missouri (now Washington University). He brings with him his American wife, and they serve the school excellently as teacher and matron. However, their social reclusiveness attracts the spiteful gossip of Dr Wortle's long-standing antagonist the Hon. Mrs Stantiloup, and the secret that Ella's brutal first husband is still alive is revealed with the arrival of her brother-in-law, the degenerate blackmailer 'Colonel' Robert Lefroy. Dr Wortle accepts Peacocke's explanation of their unfortunate situation, and shelters Mrs Peacocke, while her husband, pursuing a hint from Lefroy, leaves with him for San Francisco to verify his brother's death.

The serious social consequences of Dr Wortle's moral stance—the Bishop interferes, the school is threatened with ruin, and a London newspaper picks up the salacious story—are resolved by Peacocke's triumphant return from America. The romantic complication involving Dr Wortle's daughter Mary, who at this inopportune juncture falls in love with one of the school's former pupils, Lord Carstairs, serves to expose her parents' difference of moral perception.

Trollope is keenly interested in the 'situational ethics' of the Peacockes' unique relationship. The judgement of the social world, which is an absolutist reflex, is represented by the kindly Mrs Wortle's unthinking allegiance to its rigid codes. It is voiced more publicly in the Bishop's entirely reasonable anxiety about the conduct of a clergyman in his diocese. But while the Church, the law, and social convention regard the Peacockes as living in sin, the Peacockes themselves, having married for love and in good faith, do not. Trollope's achievement lies in the extraordinarily subtle treatment of the translation of Dr Wortle's principles into action. His interview with Mr Peacocke is a meeting of gentlemen, and he responds with quixotic tenderness to the individual human dilemma, judging Peacocke according to his motives, and admitting that he would probably have acted in the same chivalric fashion. He understands that in unique moral situations normal rules do not serve. Of course, Wortle's problem is that of reconciling his private moral view with his social obligations—for he recognizes the claims of his parish and his school—and squaring it also with his legitimate self-interest.

Dr Wortle's moral response is what fascinates Trollope. It is muddled by his obligation to Peacocke, who saved one of his pupils from drowning; by his susceptibility to the beauty and dignity of Ella Peacocke; and also by his inability to brook antagonism not only from his Bishop, but from society at large. The Hon. Mrs Stantiloup's correspondence with Lady Grogram aims at persuading parents to withdraw their pupils, and the London press, in the shape of *Everybody's Business* (Edmund *Yates's *World*), takes up the story for its sensational value. Trollope's treatment of the vicious

Mrs Stantiloup, and the letters that fly between Dr Wortle and the Bishop, are reminiscent of the Barsetshire series, but in this novel the moral issue is serious and intractable.

Trollope's employment of a moral yardstick serves to complicate the reader's judgement. A benevolent tyrant at home and in his school, Wortle's fundamental principle is to act according to his own will, and so he has triumphed over meddling bishops before; but there is one man, a humble clergyman, to whom he will force himself to listen, the uncomfortably candid Mr Puddicombe. Just as Wortle's personal warmth is tempered by social circumspection, so the hard logic of Puddicombe's moral censure is qualified by his emotional approval of Wortle's human feelings. A further agent of sympathy is the moral endeavour of the submissive Mrs Wortle to place herself by an act of imagination in the position of Mrs Peacocke.

In this novel Trollope argues for moral relativism. He acknowledges the importance of law, custom, and the need for openness in social relationships, but these may be flawed by ignorance and prejudice, just as individual morality may be muddied by stubbornness and pride. And indeed, the introduction of the post-Civil War American South, where Peacocke met Ella, and the lawless West which he visits in pursuit of Lefroy's grave, encourages a broader perspective of social custom, from which English provincial middle-class morality seems extremely insular. However, in the end it is Dr Wortle's moral posture, the assertion of the importance of an individual rather than a collective morality, which the novel endorses. It is very much a novel of its period, anticipating the challenges to the wisdom of social conventions as they affect personal relationships.

As a matter of narrative principle, Trollope eschews mystery: it is part of his open relationship with the reader. It is also an aspect of the novel's moral rhetoric. His revelation of the Peacockes' secret very early in the story signals that his interest lies in the effects of this bombshell on the communities of the school, the Church, and county society. But more importantly, it frees the reader from the leading-strings of plot to focus on what is central: the moral problem, and the response to it of Dr Wortle.

Associated themes are Trollope's assault on the Church as the voice of the moral society; on the way its judgement is prejudiced by the social tittle-tattle of the clerical wives and the local squirearchy, and blinkered by convention. It is presented as a very human and flawed institution, too blunt an instrument to deal with complex moral questions.

Unusually bold is Trollope's raising of the issue of the Victorian double standard in sexual morality. Mrs Wortle is aware of the different ways in which men's and women's sexual irregularities are judged by society. Although overborne by her husband's will, she expresses, not entirely ungenerously, society's feelings about a woman whose sexual situation is simply unthinkable, intensified by her immediate anxiety about its effects on her daughter's marriage prospects. In view of the professional, social, and personal forces arrayed against him, Dr Wortle's spirited defence of the bigamous 'wife', which opposes their collective, covert support of the double standard, is all the more remarkable.

Dr Wortle's School was written in unusual circumstances, when the Trollopes were staying at Lowick Rectory in Thrapston, Northamptonshire, which they had been loaned by a friend, the Revd William Lucas *Collins, for a holiday. Kept indoors by heavy snow showers, Trollope wrote this novel between 8 April and 29 April 1879. The name of the rectory was changed to Bowick, but he used local features such as Collins's school for young men, and the lawn tennis court, on which Mary Wortle and Lord Carstairs play in the novel; and in addition he drew on events in his own experience, ranging from witnessing the saving of a boy from drowning, and the name of a dog, to his visits to America, including St Louis and San Francisco.

The novel was serialized in eight parts in *Blackwood's Magazine* from May to December 1880, and published in two volumes by Chapman & Hall in January 1881. Critical reviews were kind. The manuscript is in the Yale University Library.　　GH

Cockshut, A. O. J., *Anthony Trollope* (1955).
Kincaid, James R., *The Novels of Anthony Trollope* (1977).
Maxwell, J. C., 'Cockshut on "Dr Wortle's School"', *NCF* (September 1958–9), 153–9.

of Lucy and Ayala Dormer. Though Mrs Dosett discourages her nieces' romantic dreams, she is not immune to romance: 'there was a tender corner in her heart which was still green' (X). *AA*
　　　　　　　　　　　　　　　　　　WK

Dosett, Reginald, husband of Margaret Dosett, brother of Lady Emmeline Tringle, and uncle of Lucy and Ayala Dormer. Fifty years old and childless, a clerk in the Admiralty, Dosett manages to maintain gentility, and a house at Notting Hill, on a salary of £900 a year. The taking in of Lucy (then Ayala, then Lucy again) compels still stricter economies, but he will not ask his rich brother-in-law for help. *AA*　　　　　WK

Dove, Thomas, brilliant legal mind who writes an opinion at the behest of the Eustace estate lawyer, Mr Camperdown, as to the possible heirloom status of the Eustace diamonds. The legal opinion offered by 'Turtle' Dove was actually written by Trollope's friend Charles *Merewether. *ED*　　　　　　　　　　JMR

Doyle, Sir Francis Hastings Charles (1810–88). Poet, and inferior successor to Matthew Arnold as Professor of Poetry at Oxford, Doyle published several volumes of verse, the best known being *The Return of the Guards and Other Poems* (1866); his *Reminiscences and Opinions* appeared in 1886. When Robert *Bell died in 1867, Doyle followed Trollope in presenting a toast in his honour at that year's Royal Literary Fund dinner.　　　　　　　　　　RCT

drama, Elizabethan and Jacobean. Trollope chose to root *An Autobiography* in an 'unhappy' childhood and a self-castigating account of his seven-year wilderness as postal clerk until, despairing and maligned, he arrived in Banagher, where his energies immediately became focused and appreciated. Yet that novelistic epiphany,

while emotionally accurate, scarcely indicates the early stirrings of his antiquarian interest in drama (English literature was not then studied academically). Behind the dejection of his childhood, one sees him in his father's 'old deserted' chambers in Lincoln's Inn 'reading [immersed in] Shakespeare out of a bi-columned edition, which is still among my books' (I). Then, as a feckless clerk, his ambition to write, and be like the rest of his family, led to grandiose dreams of a 'History of Literature' (*Letters* 2, 1029–30) and a reading list which included Schlegel's *Dramatic Literature*, which he notated in his Commonplace Book (*Letters* 2, 1021–8). Trollope glides over that: 'For history, biography, or essay writing I had not sufficient erudition' (III); but those studies were eventually realized and became so important that he ends *An Autobiography* by acknowledging his 'greatest pleasure in our old English dramatists', hoping, in his remaining years, to complete 'written criticisms on every play' in his extensive collection (XX).

In 1850, when creating his own first play, he acquired a 1647 folio of Beaumont and Fletcher (now owned by the Shakespeare Institute at Stratford-on-Avon) and, in the next three years, read 35 of their works (as he noted in that volume). After settling at Waltham Cross, he built up a library of early drama and, with accustomed thoroughness, entered comments and dates-of-reading into those books. Most of that collection is now in the Folger Library, and, as Elizabeth Epperly's transcription of those notes makes clear, Trollope's studies began in earnest once he resigned from the Post Office (September 1867); after he left the editorship of *Saint Pauls* (1870), they became a passionate hobby which lasted till September 1882 (just before his fatal paralysis). On the long voyage to Australia, he spent two months rereading Shakespeare

(January–July 1871) and resumed his researches as soon as he had returned from his travels and rehoused his library in Montagu Square (June 1873). Even at Christmas, he snatched a few spare hours and then wrote a substantial comment that ends in 'self-irony' (E. Epperly, *Anthony Trollope's Notes on the Old Drama* (1988), 14): *Cynthia's Revels* 'will have no future readers, unless it be some . . . determined idler like myself'. On Boxing Day, he was engrossed in *Volpone*.

His guidelines through those texts (over 270 in all) were a deep knowledge of Shakespeare, a novelist's appreciation of plot-structure and character-development, a Victorian's feeling of poetic sentiment and manliness. Though no bardolator, he could not find those aesthetic qualities in any other dramatist, though he was prepared to allow, as with Shakespeare's less satisfactory work, that a play can be 'better for the stage than the closet' (*The Taming of the Shrew*). Having read an extraordinary amount of Beaumont and Fletcher, he could state authoritatively that the latter was 'infinitely superior . . . and would rank next to Shakespeare, had he not too often . . . done his work in such hot haste'. Overall, he appreciated 'the healthiness of the fun' in Tudor plays, which 'In the days of Elizabeth . . . still existed;—but in James I time men going to the theatre expected to be excited by seeing men in women's clothes act parts [and speak words] which no women could undertake.' A comment on Marston's *Dutch Courtesan* typifies that overview: 'full of obscenity, ill arranged, crowded with all possible faults that can disgrace a play;—but nevertheless there is in it a certain wit.' As he grew confident as a critic, he became more impatient with the carelessness of clergymen who had (in their own spare time) compiled those editions, sprinkling their margins with 'oh!' and other exclamations and confuting their comments: 'never was such far-fetched nonsense.' His critique of *The Queen of Arragon*, by the unknown Habington, epitomizes his independence and consistent viewpoint: 'almost faultless in plot, sentiment & language . . . yet no one has read it . . . His play has crept in here [Robert Dodsley's *Old English Plays*, 1825], without a word of praise, by accident.'

Those passions had their effect on Trollope's novels. Each is studded with Shakespearian phrases that create a texture of educated converse between narrator and reader; the sprightly dialogue of the Slope–Eleanor–Arabin romance (*Barchester Towers*) echoes the mood of Shakespeare's comedies; his comment on Brutus—'the ill adaptation of the man's honesty to political exigencies'—foreshadows Palliser's circumstance in *The Prime Minister*. Most importantly, the early drama showed Trollope ways to construct multiple plots whose interrelation places the dilemmas of leading characters within a complex social network (R. Tracy, *Trollope's Later Novels* (1978), 44–7). So the simple plot/sub-plot of Trollope's first play (*The Noble Jilt*) grows into the triple structure of *Can You Forgive Her?* The multiplying schemes of *Mr Scarborough's Family* reflect the elaborate intrigue of trickster plays like *Volpone* (B. A. Booth, *Anthony Trollope* (1958), 130–1), though this novel's debt to George Wilkins's 'Scarborow' family (Tracy 307) is unlikely, since Trollope had not then read *The Inforced Marriage*. At the end of his life, this Jacobean patterning enabled him to assimilate political events which were unfolding randomly in Ireland as he wrote. The fictive sub-plot of *The Land-leaguers*, in which Rachel O'Mahony fights to control a dreamlike world of gossip and treachery that surrounds her, acts as a metaphor for actualities which Trollope himself fought to control and shape.

He may also have intended to use his knowledge of early drama more directly, in an eventual monograph, just as he encouraged his son Henry to publish essays on French playwrights from the time of Louis XIV. Trollope's expertise earned the respect of G. H. *Lewes and Icelandic friends (who presented him with *Macbeth* in their language). Yet, with his usual bluff objectivity, he refused to contribute to Charles Flower's Memorial Theatre at Stratford-on-Avon: 'If there be any one who does not want more memorials than have been already given, it is Shakespeare!' (*Letters* 2, 770). AWJ

Epperly, Elizabeth, *Anthony Trollope's Notes on the Old Drama* (1988).

Tracy, Robert, *Trollope's Later Novels* (1978).

Dresden, a 'clean, cheerful' German city, where Laura Kennedy and her father Lord Brentford take refuge from the importunate demands of Laura's estranged husband. Dresden also serves as George Western's retreat when he breaks with his wife in *Kept in the Dark*. PR JMR

Dribble, Revd Abraham, low-church suitor of Mary Tomkins (recalling Mr Slope) who abandons her, woos her afresh without success, becomes Bishop of Rochester, and marries well. 'Never'. RCT

Drought, James, one of Ireland's three Post Office surveyors, when Trollope applied for the post of surveyor's clerk. Working under Drought in the Central District, after seven unhappy and unproductive years in London as a junior clerk, was later judged by Trollope as the commencement of his fortune and happiness. RCT

Drought, Sir Orlando, 'Consistent old Tory' who becomes one of the chief troublemakers within the Duke of Omnium's coalition ministry. Though he serves the Duke's ministry as First Lord of the Admiralty, Sir Orlando's pride and ambition stand in the way of his contentment. Excluded from the Duchess of Omnium's lavish parties, he is continually dissatisfied with the Duke and his government, eventually resigning in an effort to divide the coalition. *PR, PM, WWLN*   JMR

Drumbarrow, parish in the vicinity of Castle Richmond, where bigotry makes for a religious war between the vicar and the priest, until they are forced to work together for the famine relief committee. *CR*   MRS

Drumcaller, Colonel Jonathan Stubbs's uncomfortable, 'beautifully romantic' (XVIII) cottage on Loch Ness. *AA*   WK

Drumleesh, near Mohill, Co. Leitrim, an area renowned for the illicit distilling of whiskey and for Ribbonism. *MB*   MRS

Drummond, Lord, the Minister of State for Foreign Affairs who arranges for Elias Gotobed to attend the opening of Parliament and chairs Gotobed's unfortunate lecture. He serves in the Duke of Omnium's coalition government in *The Prime Minister*, appears in *Phineas Redux*, and figures as Conservative Prime Minister in *The Duke's Children*. *AS*   MG

Drumsna, a 'quiet little village' (I) in the neighbourhood of Ballycloran, where Father John is parish priest. *MB*   MRS

Drury, Anna Harriet [Henrietta?], granddaughter of Mark Drury, second master at Harrow when Trollope was a pupil, and minor novelist whom Trollope often helped in dealings with publishers. He negotiated with *Good Words* over *The Brothers* (1865), *The Three Half-Crowns* (1866), and others, but apart from one short piece, 'The Story of a London Fog', which appeared in November 1867, none of her works was accepted.   RCT

Drury, Revd Henry ('Old Harry') (1778–1841), assistant master of Harrow School for over 40 years; tutor and friend of Byron. He recommended Trollope's transfer to Sunbury where another Drury (Arthur) taught. Trollope learned little from the move but made a firm friend in John Merivale. Henry Drury conducted the funeral service for Allegra, Byron's illegitimate daughter.   RCT

Drury, Revd Joseph, head of Harrow School (1785–1805) whose family members influenced the school's development in the period of the Trollopes' residence in Harrow.   RCT

Drury, Revd Mark, second master at Harrow when Trollope was a pupil. Extreme obesity, which affected most of the family, prevented him climbing the hill to school, so pupils had to come to his house. The Drurys were hopeless in money matters. In 1826 Mark fled from creditors, and the following year Henry Drury went bankrupt.   RCT

Drury family, friends of Trollope's parents, housemasters and tutors at Harrow. Mark Drury, brother of Joseph Drury, headmaster of Harrow School until 1805, became Tom Trollope's first tutor in 1818. The Drurys were unsuccessful in money matters. In 1826 Mark and his son William fled from creditors to the Continent, allegedly leaving behind debts to tradesmen of some £40,000. When Mrs Trollope visited Belgium in 1833 with Hervieu and Henry, she rediscovered friends 'long valued and long lost', while writing *Belgium and West Germany* (1833). These were the Drurys—Mark, William, and William's wife. In 1834, Trollope became a classical usher (instructor) at William's school in Brussels.   RCT

Dryden, John (1631–1700), poet, dramatist, critic, and translator of Juvenal and Virgil. Trollope included Dryden in his list of eighteen 'giants' of English literature, and referred to the poet as 'certainly a great master of English' (*Letters* 2, 632). He was fond of the line 'None but the brave deserves the fair' from 'Alexander's Feast', 1. iv, which he used in *The Duke's Children* (IV) and *Sir Harry Hotspur of Humblethwaite* (XIX).   RCT

Dublin, scene of the State Trials of Repealer John O'Connell, where Martin Kelly visits his brother, an attorney's clerk who attends the court proceedings, and where he meets with his landlord Lord Ballindine, to arrange a deed of settlement on Anty Lynch. Before pursuing his parliamentary career, Phineas Finn attends Trinity College in Dublin. *KOK, PF*   MRS

Dublin Review. In 1836, Nicholas Wiseman, rector of the English College at Rome, began this Catholic review in imitation of the popular Whig *Edinburgh Review* and Tory *Quarterly Review*. Wiseman wanted to reconcile the tensions between old and newly converted Catholics, followers of John Henry Newman who had left the Church of England. In its early years, the *Review* was the central voice of Catholicism in England.

The *Review* praised *Phineas Finn*, saying Trollope truly understood the Irish spirit and calling him the leading novelist of the day. Another review said no Irishman could have written *The Macdermots of Ballycloran* with such candour and impartiality. JWM

Dublin University Magazine. In January 1833, Isaac *Butt, a Dublin barrister, began Ireland's first successful magazine, a monthly with strong Tory bias aiming to unite Irish and British interests through the education of the Irish people. Modelled after *Blackwood's Magazine* and *Fraser's Magazine*, its 110 pages included unsigned articles on politics, Dublin University politics, academic reform, fiction, and poetry.

Trollope's lengthy review of Charles *Merivale's *History of the Romans under the Empire* appeared in it, and an article disagreeing with the civil service report which had called for reform. Works by Trollope were reviewed in its pages. JWM

Du Boung, Mr, local brewer of Silverbridge who enters the parliamentary contest with Ferdinand Lopez and Arthur Fletcher, thus splitting the vote and allowing Fletcher to win the seat. Cautiously supportive of the Duke of Omnium's coalition ministry, Du Boung represents Silverbridge's Liberal interests despite his Conservative allegiance. *PM* JMR

Dugdale, Alice. Dumpy but attractive, she devotes herself to her stepmother's children. Unconscious of status, practical, cheerful, and selfless, she hides her love for Major Rossiter until his proposal. 'Dugdale' *WFF* GRH

Dugdale, Dr, a kindly, liberal man, not good at household matters, proud of Alice, his daughter by his first wife. 'Dugdale' *WFF* GRH

Dugdale, Mrs, stepmother of Alice, 'overworn and idle' (IV), beset by her large family of seven children. 'Dugdale' *WFF* GRH

Duke's Children, The (*see opposite*)

Dumbello, Lady Griselda. See HARTLETOP, GRISELDA, MARCHIONESS OF.

Dumbello, Lord Gustavus, heir of the Marquis of Hartletop, later MP for West Barsetshire. An eligible bachelor noted for lack of conversation and devotion to eating, he eventually marries Griselda Grantly. In *The Small House at Allington* his jealousy of Plantagenet Palliser is overcome by his wife's assertion of innocence. *FP, LCB* NCS

Dunckley, Henry (1823–96), editor of the *Manchester Examiner and Times* (1855–89), commentator on public issues under the pseudonym 'Verax'. Given the chance of meeting him in November 1878, Trollope responded: 'Mr Dunkley

[*sic*] . . . is quite a prophet after my own heart. A member of the late Govt assured me the other day that if I wished to be considered a Liberal I was bound to know his article in the XIX Century by heart' ('The Progress of Personal Rule', *Nineteenth Century* (November 1878) 785–808; *Letters* 2, 801). RCT

Dunmore, market town in Co. Galway, where the Widow Kelly keeps the Dunmore Inn and grocery store, and location of Dunmore House, the Lynches' residence. *KOK* MRS

Dunmore House, residence of Simeon Lynch that divides Barry Lynch and his sister Anastasia when inherited equally by both. Originally filched from the O'Kelly estate, it reverts to the family when a distant relative, Martin Kelly, marries Anastasia. *KOK* MRS

Dunn, Aaron, the direct, open engineer who draws a picture for Susan Bell which is rejected because of over-strict propriety. He impulsively burns it. This forms an obstacle to their love, which they finally overcome. 'Bell' *TAC1* GRH

Dunn, Onesiphorus (Siph), stout Irish gentleman friend of Martha Thorne. He serves as a safe, well-liked intimate of almost everyone in London, living easily with neither income nor fortune. He escorts Lily Dale in London. *LCB* NCS

Dunripple Park, seat of Sir Gregory Marrable on the border of Warwickshire and Worcestershire, and good hunting country. Sir Gregory makes his nephew Walter welcome here and leaves the estate to him upon the death of his son Gregory. *VB* SRB

Dunstable, Emily, niece (or cousin) of Martha Thorne. An heiress worth £20,000, good-humoured, and kind, she becomes an intimate friend of Lily Dale after her engagement to Captain Bernard Dale. *LCB* NCS

Dunstable, Martha. See THORNE, MRS MARTHA.

Duplay, Eleanor. 'Robespierre's Love' is a beautiful woman of about 25, whose attempt to persuade Robespierre to moderate his vengeance against the Vendeans makes him suspect her loyalty to himself and the Republic. *LV* GRH

Durbellière, Chateau of, the de Larochejaquelin estate, close to Saint-Florent, scene of much of the action, eventually abandoned to the republicans. *LV* GRH

Trollope's thirty-ninth novel (1880) is the final volume of the Palliser series, having been preceded by *Can You Forgive Her?* (1865), *Phineas Finn* (1869), *The Eustace Diamonds* (1873), *Phineas Redux* (1874), and *The Prime Minister* (1876). For many readers, these six books form the most remarkable sequence of novels in the language. It is true that individual novels from the Barsetshire series have attained greater fame. In Trollope's time *Doctor Thorne* sold more copies in book form (it was not serialized) than any other of his novels. *Framley Parsonage* was given the most favourable reception of any of his works. Since his death *Barchester Towers* has become the quintessential Trollope novel, surely his most popular, and *The Last Chronicle of Barset* probably deserves the place Trollope himself gave it as the best novel he ever wrote. And yet Trollope also said he looked upon the 'string of characters' comprising the old Duke of Omnium, Plantagenet Palliser (the young Duke), and his wife Lady Glencora 'as the best work of my life' (*Auto* X).

Ideally the reader should come to *The Duke's Children* after having read the five other novels, some 1,300,000 words. Still, *The Duke's Children* is a self-contained work which can be read nicely on its own terms. The person approaching this novel un-initiated will read a work slightly different from that read by someone acquainted with the earlier novels, but this is really not a problem. The first-time reader (provided he or she has a Trollopian sensibility) will be enchanted, and unaware of missing any-thing. Moreover, Trollope's huge and varied world is so absorbing that it can be entered pleasurably at just about any place, even at the wrong end, so to speak. Later, having gone back to the other books, one will discover that rereading *The Duke's Children* (and Trollope readers are almost always rereaders) is a remarkably fresh experience. The novel certainly will not suffer from the reader's knowing how it will turn out.

The six-book saga that ended with *The Duke's Children* actually began one novel previous to the Palliser series. For Plantagenet Palliser and Lady Glencora make their first appearances, rather unpromisingly, in *The Small House of Allington*, the fifth of the Barsetshire novels. Here an unprepossessing Palliser is about 25, unmarried, and rich, a man with prospects of enormous wealth as heir to the Duke of Omnium. A rising politician, dedicated and hard-working, he is indifferent to hunting or shooting, or any amusement; a great reader of serious books, he is a 'thin-minded, plodding, respectable man, willing to devote all his youth to work, in order that in old age he might be allowed to sit among the Councillors of the Land' (*SHA* XXIII). Palliser becomes involved in what seems—from what we later learn of him—an unlikely flirtation with a married woman, Lady Dumbello, daughter of one of the leading figures of the Barsetshire series, Archdeacon Grantly. But one word from Mrs Grantly sends Lady Dumbello hurrying back to her husband, and Palliser ends up in the unwilling arms of Lady Glencora M'Cluskie. This wealthy young woman, who in this novel occupies scarcely two pages and speaks not a word in her own voice, is in love with a scapegrace adventurer named Burgo Fitzgerald. But pressures from her family and Palliser's prevail. Palliser had 'danced with her twice, and had spoken his mind', had done his duty, and the two marry. From this inauspicious beginning grew the Palliser novels, which Trollope would embark upon half a year later with *Can You Forgive Her?* He would lavish more attention on this frequently unhappy couple than on any other of the hundreds of characters he created. He explained in *An Auto-biography* that he used these two favourite fictional creations time after time to express his political, social, and moral convictions. Palliser and Glencora, he wrote, 'have been as real to me as free trade was to Mr Cobden, or the dominion of a party to Mr Disraeli; and as I have not been able to speak from the benches of the House of Commons, or to thunder from platforms, or to be efficacious as a lecturer, they have served as safety-valves by which to deliver my soul' (X). Trollope modestly said that if he were to be among the English novelists read in the 20th century this 'permanence of success will probably rest on the characters of Plantagenet Palliser, Lady Glencora, and the Revd Mr Crawley [of *The Last Chronicle*]'.

Palliser and Glencora, as we come to know them in *Can You Forgive Her?*, are an ill-matched pair. He is a solemn, formal, cold, austere man, altogether devoted to the work of his life, politics. Proud but shy, intelligent but plodding, he never manages to fathom his wife, so completely his opposite. Glencora is outgoing, warm, spirited, witty, irrepressible. Whereas he is proper, conventional, she is rebellious, irreverent. She is his equal in intelligence, but quicker. Trollope engages more sympathy on her behalf, and he treats with sensitivity both her continuing love for the handsome, impoverished Fitzgerald and the way she is brought to the brink of leaving her husband for Fitzgerald. After she has been reconciled to marriage and to Palliser, she retains the mischievousness that is her most charming quality: as for example, when pregnant at last with the heir apparent to the greatest dukedom in the land, she tells the old Duke of Omnium that she hopes the baby is a girl. Although the Pallisers find a *modus vivendi*, in this and in subsequent novels Trollope never blinks the harsh facts of her story. 'The romance of her life is gone' with Burgo, and the tale of her difficult marriage to Palliser will form a large part of the six-novel series that begins with *Can You Forgive Her?* In them is a colossal exception to the time-honoured comic tradition Trollope so often followed, that of ending stories with wedding bells and happy prospects. The story of Glencora and Palliser begins with their marriage, one of the least 'romantic' marriages in English fiction.

On taking up *The Duke's Children*, the reader familiar with the earlier Palliser books learns to his or her dismay (and in the very first sentence) that Glencora, Duchess of Omnium, has died. *How*, one asks, can this novel come up to the others if the more attractive, amusing, and sympathetic of its central pair is gone? So much of the previous novels had hinged on the interaction of these two, their differences, clashes, their strange abiding regard and love for each other. It is almost as if Trollope dared himself, with an impulsiveness worthy of Glencora herself, to take the risk. One recalls how he had impetuously killed off Mrs Proudie in the final Barsetshire book (although she had already played a major role in that novel).

But, of course, Trollope succeeds. He manages to write a Palliser novel without Glencora Palliser. For one thing, her spirit pervades the book. One could even say that in this book she ultimately triumphs. Her daughter Mary is in some respects like her. Though lacking her mother's verve, effusiveness, wit, and irreverence, she has some of Glencora's independent-mindedness; her stubbornness, unlike her mother's, is gentle but, if anything, more determined. And Lady Mary, in love with someone that her family, especially her father, feels is unworthy of her, is positioned somewhat as was Glencora with Burgo Fitzgerald (although Frank Tregear is a much more suitable young man than Burgo). Certainly the Duke sees a parallel, sees in fact more similarities than the case warrants. Another reason for the novel's success as a Palliser novel may stem, ironically enough, directly from Lady Glencora's absence. With her removed from the scene, Trollope could concentrate more squarely on her husband. Palliser is less fun than Glencora, but he is also more complicated, more enigmatic, and, in his own peculiar way, more fascinating.

Additionally, *The Duke's Children* succeeds in spite of Glencora's absence because Trollope moves confidently forward with an array of engaging new characters, the coming generation. These include the three Palliser children, Lord Silverbridge, Lord Gerald, and Lady Mary, plus Mary's suitor Frank Tregear, Lady Mabel Grex, and the American Isabel Boncassen. Through these youthful characters Trollope develops a number of his favourite motifs, including the age-old one of young lovers overcoming parental objections, in this case objections centring around differences in wealth, class, and nationality. Another related and abiding Trollope interest, the clash between father and son, gets its fullest, subtlest, and gentlest treatment in this novel. All of these issues are neatly fitted to the novel's overarching theme, the Duke's gradual bending, as he mellows, becomes more human, more accepting of what would have been Glencora's reading of people and events.

One can see some correlation to Trollope's own life here. He did not get along with his father, a failed barrister, an angry, strange, irascible, disappointed man (in a literal sense, of all Trollope's characters the Revd Mr Crawley, driven to near madness by money worries, most resembles his own father). And Anthony's mother was a high-spirited, happy, congenial, witty, unconventional woman, from whom a good deal of Glencora's irreverence and rebellious spirit may have derived. It is probably significant that Trollope wrote *The Duke's Children* immediately after finishing *An Autobiography*, the work in which he had put on paper the revelations about his unhappy childhood and youth, including the long passages about his father's total inability to get along with his children. Sadly, the reconciliation possible in the novel was never within reach in Trollope's own life. But in *The Duke's Children* (except in the case of Lord Grex who hates his son 'worse than any one else in the world', XX), reconciliation eventually prevails. This tale of the Duke's trials and sorrows at the hands of his three children, and the sorrows he inflicts on them, is moving, at times even sad. Both sons are rusticated from University; both incur gambling debts; the elder, Lord Silverbridge, decides to become a Tory, and wants to marry an American, Isabel Boncassen. Moreover, the Duke's beloved daughter Lady Mary wants to marry a penniless Tory commoner. The novel chronicles Palliser's slow coming to terms of understanding and regard for his two sons and his acceptance (or partial acceptance) of his daughter's choice of the man who will be his son-in-law. Plantagenet Palliser mellows, but reluctantly and painfully.

Curiously, much of the Duke's character resembles Trollope's own. Although the polar opposite of the brash, blustering Trollope, Palliser exhibits an (apparent) intractability and an almost abnormal sensitivity very much like his creator's. The Duke also shares with Trollope a seemingly preternatural devotion to work: in this novel, the Duke, considerably older, his early ambition for decimal coinage unrealized, his tenure as Prime Minister having been unsatisfactory, and feeling rather useless, 'knew that if anything could once again make him contented it would be work' (LXVIII), and at the close he becomes President of the Council of the new Liberal cabinet. Moreover, in connection with the Duke's troubles with his children, the narrator remarks that had he been required to give in only with reference to the lovely Isabel Boncassen, he could have done so easily: 'There are men, who do not seem at first sight very susceptible to feminine attractions, who nevertheless are dominated by the grace of flounces, who succumb to petticoats unconsciously, and who are half in love with every woman merely for her womanhood. So it was with the Duke' (LXXIV). (The words echo those from a closing passage in Trollope's *Autobiography*: 'If the rustle of a woman's petticoat has ever stirred my blood . . . of what matter is that to any reader?' (XX).) And the woman whom the Duke finds relatively easy to accept as daughter-in-law is an American, beautiful, witty, clever, lively. Isabel Boncassen is in many respects drawn from Kate Field, the young American woman to whom Trollope had a long-standing romantic attachment. Like Kate in the 1870s, Isabel is a huge success in London; she is a good conversationalist, can talk politics with great liveliness, and has unmarried men such as Barrington Erle, Mr Warburton, and Mr Monk enraptured. Like so many of Trollope's young women she is considerably cleverer and more quick-witted than the men who woo her. Henry James said that Trollope was 'evidently always more or less in love' with all his heroines, but this must have been especially the case with Isabel Boncassen.

Another young woman, Lady Mabel Grex, is even more prominent in the novel than the American. Through Mabel Grex, made wretched by her frustrated love for both Tregear and Silverbridge, Trollope develops with sympathy and insight the burdens imposed upon women by society. She tells Tregear, 'because you are not a woman . . . you do not understand how women are trammelled. . . . Only think how a girl such as I am is placed; or indeed any girl. You, if you see a woman that you fancy, can pursue her, can win her and triumph, or lose her and gnaw your heart;—at any rate you can do something. You can tell her that you love her; can tell her so again and again even though she should scorn you. . . . What can a girl do?' (X). She understands that 'as an unmarried girl she was a burden', something her disagreeable old father Lord Grex keeps reminding her ('I don't see why the deuce you don't get married', XX). But when a girl like herself 'works hard' at getting a husband, 'everybody feels that they are sinning against their sex'. That she is particular about whom she would marry adds greatly to her problem: she is too bright, too quick for most young men, and they sense it. (Silverbridge worries that 'Lady Mabel as his wife would be his superior, and in some degree his master', XIX.) She says, 'With nineteen men out of twenty, the idea of marrying them would convey the idea of hating them' (XL). Most young men, in her view (and Trollope's), hardly know what they are doing in marrying; they 'seldom mean'; rather, 'they drift into matrimony' (XXXI). In her frustrated passion, Lady Mabel is one of Trollope's saddest and most powerful figures, the equal of Lady Laura Kennedy from the Phineas books.

Lady Mabel's fate aside, the novel will come to a quietly happy conclusion. We know hundreds of pages ahead of time that the Duke will relent. A comic spirit, but a muted comic spirit, presides over this tale of the Duke's slow, grudging acceptance of his children's choices. The 'family dinner' in chapter LXXIV, where the Duke, his three children, Isabel and her parents, and Tregear have a kind of ritual of reconciliation in which the Duke fails in spite of himself at being less than solemn and 'funereal' towards Tregear, must rank among the great scenes in all of Trollope. Palliser may be mellowing, but he remains the difficult man he always was.

The Duke's Children, which Trollope wrote between 2 May and 29 October 1876, first appeared serially in *All the Year Round* in weekly instalments from 4 October 1879 to 14 July 1880 (Trollope, ordinarily so opposed to any kind of revising or cutting, had reduced the manuscript by about one-quarter, to accommodate the nine months' run of short weekly instalments in the magazine). Chapman & Hall published the work in three volumes in May 1880.

The novel enjoyed an excellent press. Trollope's reputation with the critics had gradually declined with *Lady Anna*, continuing through *The Way We Live Now*, *The Prime Minister*, *The American Senator*, and *Is He Popenjoy?* Then *John Caldigate* had mixed but on balance good reviews, and a short novel, *Cousin Henry* (published the same year), did even better. But *The Duke's Children* seemed completely to restore Trollope's reputation with the critics. The *Westminster Review* wrote: 'Those who fancied that Mr Trollope had been falling off will be delighted to read "The Duke's Children", and to meet again their old friend the Duke of Omnium, the only duke whom all of us know. Mr Trollope is upon old ground, and describes it with all the ease of his best days. The death of the Duchess so early in the tale will be a great shock to many worthy people, but even duchesses must die that novels may be written' (Smalley 474). The *Saturday Review* praised Trollope's presentation of the domestic trials of 'our old friend, now Duke of Omnium' (Smalley 468). Both the *Athenaeum* and the *Illustrated London News* found Trollope's representation of society true to life. The *Spectator* wrote, 'No novelist of whom we have any knowledge seems to possess so sane a comprehension of the mode of life and thought of the British aristocracy as Mr Trollope.' It lauded Isabel Boncassen, saying that 'Her character, speech, and manners are so carefully and justly presented by Mr Trollope, that few even of his most critical American readers would, we fancy, be inclined to raise objections to the portrait.' This reviewer pronounced the novel 'thoroughly readable and one of the most edifying that Mr Trollope has yet produced' (Smalley 470–1). And in New York, the *Nation* called *The Duke's Children* 'one of Mr Trollope's most successful novels' (Smalley 473). Today, despite continuing widespread disagreement about which novels represent Trollope at his best, many readers rank *The Duke's Children* very high among his 47 novels. The manuscript is in the Beinecke Library at Yale University.   NJH

Durham, county in which Tankerville borough is situated and where the Hotspur Scarrowby estate is located. *PR, SHH*   MG

Durton Lodge, Berkshire country home, little more than a cottage, of George and Cecilia Western. *KD*   NCS

E

Eames, John, energetic, impetuous son of Mrs Eames, widow of Squire Christopher Dale's most intimate friend. Eternally rebuffed by Lily Dale, Johnny becomes a clerk in the Income Tax Office, and spends the period of his hobbledehoydom rising in wealth and career, becoming Lord De Guest's friend and Sir Raffle Buffle's private secretary. He also thrashes Adolphus Crosbie for jilting Lily and flirts with Amelia Roper. In *The Last Chronicle of Barset,* having inherited money from Lord De Guest, he continues his luckless pursuit of Lily while amusing himself with Madalina Demolines and travelling to Europe to find Mrs Arabin, key to the Josiah Crawley affair. *SHA*
NCS

Eames, Mrs, widow befriended by Squire Dale and doting mother of John Eames and his sister Mary. *SHA*   RCT

Eardham, Augusta (Gus), the second daughter of Sir George Eardham of Brayboro' Park, 'Certainly a fine girl . . . [but who] . . . would have no money' (LII). Thanks to the calculating manœuvres of her mother she marries Ralph, the heir, and becomes mistress of Newton Priory. *RH*
ALS

Eardham, Sir George, a Berkshire baronet, the owner of Brayboro' Park and of a mansion in Cavendish Square. He is the father of Marmaduke and of three dowerless daughters, the second of whom, Augusta, marries Ralph, the heir. 'A stout, plethoric gentleman, with a short temper and many troubles' (LV). *RH*   ALS

Eardham, Lady, wife of Sir George, characterized by Ralph Newton (the heir) as 'an inter-fering old fool' and 'the old harridan' (LV). Arranges the marriage of Ralph and her daughter Augusta (Gus). *RH*   ALS

Earlybird, Earl of, obscure Earl whom the Duke of Omnium, as Prime Minister, makes a Knight of the Garter, much to the disgust of parliamentary society. Though Lord Earlybird is an acknowledged philanthropist, it is agreed that the honour of a Garter is thrown away upon him. *PM*   JMR

'Eastern Question, On the' (speech at the 'St James's Hall Conference'). England should consider present Turkey as a wayward relative, already given extra chances. Its barbaric behaviour precludes more extra chances. Our agreements were with the previous ruler. If the Turk is to live in Europe, he must adopt the customs and behaviour of civilized men. *The Times* (9 December 1876), 7–8.   AKL

Easyman, Dr, personal physician to Martha (Dunstable) Thorne. *FP, DT*   NCS

Échanbroignes, home of the Stein family and refuge for Mme and Marie de Lescure after Clisson is destroyed. *LV*   GRH

Edgeworth, Maria (1767–1849), Irish novelist renowned for *Castle Rackrent* (1800), the first regional novel in English. Fanny Milton gave her future husband Thomas Trollope a copy of Edgeworth's *The Modern Griselda* (1805), which deals with the nature of marriage. The following morning, Thomas wrote from his chambers that he could not put it down. Anthony Trollope was well read in Irish fiction and admired Edgeworth's, although in *Is He Popenjoy?* her novels were sickening to his heroine Mary Lovelace (XLV). He paid tribute in his first novel, *The Macdermots of Ballycloran,* having the Dublin coach pass through Edgeworthstown, the guard referring to the residence 'of the authoress of whom Ireland may well be so proud' (appendix, World's Classics edn., 642). The *John Bull* (May 1847) review of *The Macdermots* noted: 'events are made to bring out all the peculiar features of Irish life among the peasantry, with a fidelity of description and knowledge of character equal to anything in the writings of Miss Edgeworth' (Smalley 549).   RCT

Edinburgh Review. Begun by Sydney Smith, Francis Jeffrey, Francis Horner, and Henry Brougham in 1802, it became one of the great, widely imitated quarterlies and an influential Whig organ. In long articles, contributors introduced the practice of writing an essay under the pretext of writing a review, presenting the reviewer's ideas on the subject rather than reactions to the book being reviewed. It appealed to a conservative, aristocratic audience and increasingly emphasized politics. The *Edinburgh's* impressive group of contributors included Brougham, Smith, Walter Scott, William Wilberforce, Thomas Arnold, Thomas Carlyle, and William Hazlitt. In 1883, it reviewed Trollope's *An Autobiography* favourably.   JWM

editions. See MANUSCRIPTS AND EDITIONS.

Editor (sometimes anonymous, sometimes Jonathan Brown), narrator of six stories in *An Editor's Tales*, elderly, wise, kindly, sometimes gullible, beset by conflicting loyalties to his readers and the often indigent writers, and clearly the alias of Trollope himself.   RCT

editor, Trollope as. Many Victorian publishers, for example Blackwood and Macmillan, established their own periodicals. Frequently these were edited by the publishers themselves, but Dickens's expert conduct of *Household Words* and *All the Year Round* established the alternative model, of the prominent novelist/editor who showcased his own fiction while drawing upon his literary contacts to enlist other contributors of note. In *An Autobiography*, Trollope observed that few magazines were 'lucrative', although they did serve their publishers by 'bringing grist to the mill' (XV). This was certainly true of the *Cornhill Magazine*, which was launched in 1860 under the nominal editorship of Thackeray, although most of the day-to-day work was done by the publisher, George Smith of Smith, Elder. Smith spared no expense in the purchase of novels for serialization, which he then published in volume form. Trollope was flattered to be invited by Thackeray to supply a novel for the inaugural issues of the *Cornhill*; he was also gratified to be paid £1,000 by Smith for the copyright of *Framley Parsonage*. Trollope's novel certainly worth the money Smith paid: its immense popularity had much to do with the immediate success of the *Cornhill*, a success which in turn encouraged many other publishers to suppose that a magazine could earn them profit as well as prestige. By 1864, Smith purchased three more novels by Trollope, to be serialized in the *Cornhill* and then published by Smith, Elder in volume form.

Trollope was an obvious candidate to become editor of any magazine modelled upon the *Cornhill*, and as early as 1861 he was invited to become editor of *Temple Bar*. He was assured that, beyond providing a novel for serialization, he would not be expected to do the actual work of editing. Trollope replied that he would not undertake a 'mock editorship'. He was more re-

ceptive when approached by Frederic *Chapman, of the firm of Chapman & Hall, which from 1858 to 1865 published every novel by Trollope not purchased by Smith for the *Cornhill*. Trollope and Chapman discussed in detail the possibility of starting a 'New Weekly—Conducted by Anthony Trollope', but the project was for some reason abandoned. A year later, Trollope and Chapman were two of a group of investors that formed a small company to launch the inappropriately named *Fortnightly Review*, edited by G. H. *Lewes. Trollope was chairman of the board of directors, and it was also his responsibility to provide a novel—*The Belton Estate*—to begin serialization in the first issue, dated 15 May 1865. As well, Trollope acted as substitute editor of the *Fortnightly* when Lewes was obliged to be away, and again for a few weeks after Lewes's resignation in November 1866.

The *Fortnightly* was printed by James *Virtue, who operated a publishing firm in conjunction with his far larger printing works. In 1866, Virtue, having decided either to purchase or establish a monthly magazine, invited Trollope to assume the editorship. In *An Autobiography*, Trollope claimed that he 'strongly advised' Virtue 'to abandon the project, pointing out to him that a large expenditure would be necessary to carry on the magazine in accordance with my views' (XV). Virtue, however, insisted on proceeding with plans for a new periodical to be called *Saint Pauls Magazine*. He agreed that all arrangements with contributors were to be made by Trollope, and that Trollope was to be solely responsible for the content of the magazine. Trollope proposed to include a political article every month. Virtue was more concerned that the first issue commence serialization of a novel by Trollope: in addition to Trollope's salary as editor, he agreed to pay £3,200 for *Phineas Finn*, which appeared in *Saint Pauls* from 17 November 1866 to 15 May 1867, and was then published in two volumes under Virtue's imprint.

Trollope committed much time, thought, and effort to editing *Saint Pauls*. In an editorial preface to the first issue, he explained that the magazine would be distinctive in achieving a balance between fiction and non-fiction; the editorial also committed *Saint Pauls* to support for the Liberal Party. Trollope's own contributions reflect these goals: the emphasis on political matters is evident in *Phineas Finn*. In addition to the serialized fiction that was, as Virtue recognized, essential to any successful magazine, Trollope also wrote, for *Saint Pauls*, twenty-one non-fiction articles, many on political topics. He contributed as well a series of six short stories, eventually collected under the title *An Editor's*

Tales, in which he drew upon his own experiences to describe the trials of an editor. In 'The Panjandrum', for example, a group of young men and one woman decide to establish the perfect magazine, but are unable, as a result of their constant disagreements, to put their plans into practice. Other stories describe the difficulties of the editor in dealing with contributors—the talented and the untalented, the charming and the 'hateful'. In more than one story the editor refers to his susceptibility to attractive young women. In 'The Spotted Dog', he tries in vain to induce a drunken scholar to make one last effort at literary work. There are references also to the burden of reading piles of worthless manuscripts; in *An Autobiography*, Trollope recalled how difficult it was to tell a friend his work was 'trash' (XV).

Trollope described his conduct of *Saint Pauls* in *An Autobiography* (XV). He 'omitted nothing which I thought might tend to success'. He believed that in his list of contributors he 'succeeded in obtaining the services of an apparently excellent literary corps'. He recalled also that 'I read all manuscripts sent to me, and endeavoured to judge impartially'. Contemporary observers confirm these remarks, while casting doubt upon Trollope's judgement. R. H. *Hutton, editor of the *Spectator*, believed that Trollope's editing was 'conventional. He did not really know how to use contributors, how to make the most of them.' John *Morley, editor of the *Fortnightly*, believed Trollope took infinite pains, but thought his practice of reading every manuscript submitted 'a waste of time absolute and unredeemed' (quoted Super 273).

Although Virtue, according to Trollope, was willing to invest a large amount of capital in *Saint Pauls*, he was soon disappointed by its lacklustre success, which fell far short of his expectations in terms of circulation. Virtue's business interests were entangled with those of the publisher Alexander Strahan, who published and conducted a variety of periodicals, ranging from the serious and scholarly *Contemporary Review* to the lightweight *Argosy*; several of Trollope's stories had appeared in another of Strahan's periodicals, *Good Words*. In May 1869, Virtue transferred the management of *Saint Pauls* to Strahan, who decided that the ailing magazine could no longer afford Trollope's services. The last issue edited by Trollope was that of July 1870. In *An Autobiography*, Trollope graciously asserted 'that publishers themselves have been the best editors of magazines, when they have been able to give time and intelligence to the work' (XV). In fact, *Saint Pauls* was even less successful after Trollope's departure. PTS

Srebrnik, Patricia Thomas, *Alexander Strahan, Victorian Publisher* (1986).

editors and journalists. See DELANE, JOHN; RUSSELL, SIR WILLIAM HOWARD.

Editor's Tales, An, one volume, Strahan, 1870. A volume of collected short stories written and published while Trollope was editor of *Saint Pauls Magazine*, November 1869–May 1870. The stories are unified through the editor-narrator persona, although his name (when it is given) varies. JS

education in Trollope's England was largely unregulated. A wide variety of schools corresponded to the gradations of social class and religious sectarianism. Although education was fee-based and voluntary, a large majority of children received at least some education to the age of 10. The cheap schools of the poor were often little more than child-minding services, yet England's literacy rate—80.6 per cent for males and 73.2 per cent for females in 1871—exceeded most other countries'. There were two extensive school systems for the lower classes, the Anglican-supported National Society and the Nonconformist-supported British and Foreign Society. Both combined private funding with some government funding to provide primary education at low cost by employing the monitorial system in which younger students were largely taught by older ones. Sunday schools, which provided more than just religious instruction, also contributed significantly to lower-class education. At the bottom of the scale, charity-supported Ragged Schools attempted to reach children living in extreme poverty.

The government only very cautiously increased its involvement in education due to religious rivalries and suspicions of its intentions. It did, however, provide encouragement, as in the Factory Act of 1833, which required that children working in factories receive a certain amount of education. It also provided grants to schools that met certain standards, enforced by government inspection, and it supported teacher training. The potent examples of France and Germany, Britain's rivals, suggested to many that the British state had to become more directly involved in national education. The result was the Education Act of 1870 brought in by W. E. *Forster (a whist-playing crony of Trollope), which provided for non-sectarian state schools governed by locally elected school boards to fill the gaps. Legislation enforcing free, compulsory education followed shortly thereafter. Trollope advocated national elementary education in his Beverley campaign in 1868.

For the middle classes a wide variety of schools existed, many of them proprietorial, especially the junior or preparatory schools for children up to about age 13. They were a popular resource for clergymen such as Trollope's Dr Wortle, whose school prepared boys for Eton. Schools varied widely in quality and expense, the two not always corresponding. Social status and religious domination were very important, exclusivity being heavily emphasized. Basic divisions were Anglican versus Nonconformist and commercial versus classical. Trollope was concerned almost entirely with the gentlemanly classical sector, having himself received one-half of a gentleman's education almost free of charge at two of England's best and most exclusive public schools—Winchester and Harrow ('public' meaning endowed and governed by trustees rather than privately owned). Etonians and Harrovians—about a dozen from each—and a few Wykehamists (including Francis Arabin in *Barchester Towers*) are the only characters identified by their school in Trollope's novels (see ETON COLLEGE; HARROW SCHOOL; WINCHESTER COLLEGE).

The fortunes of public schools took off in Trollope's time. Previously of such doubtful moral and intellectual reputation that many well-to-do parents preferred to have their children tutored at home, they underwent reform inspired by Thomas Arnold's well-publicized transformation of Rugby into a hothouse for new model gentlemen. So great was the demand that many new public schools sprang into existence with instant traditions. Significantly their curricula changed very little. Latin and Greek continued to predominate because they were needed to win the university scholarships for which the schools' star students competed.

Although there were four ancient Scottish universities and two colleges of the newly established University of London, Oxford and Cambridge were the gentlemanly institutions. They were largely Anglican seminaries and finishing schools for the upper classes, controlled through their constituent colleges by clerical fellows. In the 1850s and 1860s, however, a strong reform movement opened the universities to non-Anglicans, raised the standards of teaching, and broadened the curriculum to include subjects such as modern history, and eventually the natural sciences. Characteristic of both universities was their conviction that the intellectual gymnastics of mastering the classics prepared their graduates for leadership in any sphere of activity. Another distinctive feature of Oxford and Cambridge was their remarkable faith in competitive exams as the infallible measure of intellectual ability. Their beauty, in the eyes of such enthusiasts as Mr Job-

bles, the Cambridge don satirized in *The Three Clerks*, was their quantifiability and impartiality: the best man *always* won. During the 1850s and 1860s the universities were trying to assert a claim upon the best jobs in the expanding civil service for their graduates. This rankled with Trollope, whose resentment is perhaps reflected in the number of university men in his novels who fail to measure up (see CAMBRIDGE UNIVERSITY; OXFORD UNIVERSITY).

Women's education lagged behind men's in all sectors because investing in the education of male children seemed to offer the greatest economic return. Free and compulsory primary education would have the greatest impact on working-class girls: by the end of the century female literacy equalled male. Education for middle-class girls was more likely to be conducted at home, but their schooling benefited from a growing concern about the 'surplus women problem'—the realization that large numbers of women never married and had to support themselves. In the 1870s women's colleges were founded at Oxford and Cambridge, but neither university would confer degrees on women.

Though scientific and technical education was neglected by elite schools and universities it was available through a network of institutions such as provincial colleges, the Royal School of Mines, and several schools sponsored by the rich guilds of London. These were also part of the lively adult education sector that included numerous literary institutes, athenaeums, and mechanics' institutes, which attracted self-improving artisans and the middle class to evening lectures on a wide range of topics. Mindful perhaps of his own uncompleted education, Trollope was a frequent lecturer to such audiences. In his final years he actively supported the local school at Harting, Sussex. CK

Adamson, J. W., *English Education 1789–1902* (1930).

Rothblatt, Sheldon, *The Revolution of the Dons: Cambridge and Society in Victorian England* (1968).

Edwards, Amelia Ann Blanford (1831–92). A precociously talented novelist (her first story was published when she was 12), she was praised for lively women characters. Fascinated by the Middle East, she helped found the Egypt Exploration Fund (1882) and provided in her will for a chair of Egyptology at University College, London. Trollope became acquainted with her through their mutual friend Frances *Elliot in 1868. In December 1869, he commented at length on her novel *Debenham's Vow* (1870). Excusing his delay in responding, he explained that there were 'two ways of acknowledging books,—the instantaneously courteous way which does not involve reading, and the slower mode which comes after perusal' (*Letters* 1, 489). Trollope offered positive criticism: 'The man's character is admirably kept up, and is, as you no doubt intended, the pearl of the book. The singularity of the story to me is that so good a novel should hang so entirely on one character. Had I been writing it, I should have endeavoured to divide, and should probably have frittered away, the interest between him and Claudia.' He also praised her setting, 'All the American scenes are excellent and full of life', and provided pointers towards improving the story: 'To my seeming the fault of the story,—for there always is a fault,—is in the want of sympathy with Debenham in jilting Juliet—I think you should have made the girl accede to the arrangement by some mutual terms with him. He not only throws her over, but does so without noticing her.' RCT

Edwards, Sir Henry, Tory member for Beverley, Yorkshire, for ten years and incumbent when Trollope challenged the seat in 1868. Edwards's position was impregnable since he was a major employer as chairman of a firm making railway trucks and farm machinery. He also supported local charities. Trollope noted that he kept his seat 'with a fixity of tenure next door to permanence' (*Auto* XVI). Not in the least disturbed by Trollope's candidacy, Edwards came out top of the four contestants. In one of his campaign speeches he played the religious card, declaring that Gladstone was a Roman Catholic. After the borough was disenfranchised he was put on trial and acquitted. RCT

Edwards, Mary Ellen (1839–1908), illustrator much in demand for periodicals such as *Argosy, Cassell's Magazine,* and *Good Words.* She did her best work for Trollope's *The Claverings* and M. E. Braddon's *Birds of Prey* (1868). Trollope offered subjects for the vignette at the opening of his novel, and for the full-page illustration of the first instalment: 'I would suggest that the subject for the illustration should be the entrance into the little parish church of Clavering of Lord Ongar with Julia Brabazon as his bride. | Page 24. "A puir feckless thing, tottering along like" | That should be the legend to the picture' (*Letters* 1, 321). Edwards did sixteen illustrations in all. Trollope's suggestions for the first number (*Cornhill,* February 1866) were followed. For the book edition the full-page illustration was chosen as frontispiece, but the vignettes were omitted throughout. Hall placed Edwards among the better illustrators of Trollope's novels, though not in Millais's class (*Trollope and his Illustrators*, 1980). RCT

Effingham, Violet. See CHILTERN, VIOLET, LADY.

Egham, location of the Bobtailed Fox, a hunting inn frequented by members of the Runnymede Hunt. *DC* JMR

Eiderdown, small Barsetshire parish joined with Stogpingum, under the cure of the absentee Dr Vesey Stanhope. *BT* NCS

'Election of M. Prevost-Paradol, The' (letter). Prevost-Paradol's winning the election to the French Academy over Jules Janin is a happy event. The Emperor's choice has been defeated; the French reject the 'necessity of Caesars' approach. A revolutionary journalist's success is encouraging. *Pall Mall Gazette* (12 April 1865), 3–4. AKL

election scenes in Trollope's novels. Elections to Parliament are dramatized in ten of Trollope's novels, from *The Three Clerks* to *The Duke's Children.* These election episodes are some of Trollope's most vividly presented scenes, and develop his fundamental political themes about community and class. Trollope's elections function in a variety of ways, from broad comedy to a darker drama, and from organic connection to their host narrative to the merely tangential.

Trollope's most-often discussed election episode is Sir Thomas Underwood's campaign at Percycross in *Ralph the Heir.* Trollope wrote this novel soon after his own frustrating experience as a losing candidate for Parliament at Beverley in 1868. The election story in *Ralph the Heir* bears many similarities to Trollope's experience, and marks a change towards pessimism in Trollope's election accounts. Of course, people's motives in Trollope for supporting a candidate had rarely been political conviction: Trollope's narrator in *Rachel Ray* observes about Mr Tappitt's voting record, 'He was no doubt a liberal as was also [the candidate] Mr Hart; but in small towns politics become split, and a man is not always bound to vote for a liberal candidate because he is a liberal himself' (XVII); in fact Tappitt's vote is determined by very local matters (and Hart's Jewish identity). But in *Ralph the Heir* motivations become more narrowly venal, focused on money, drink, and mean self-interest. The comedy is more bitter, as a local Tory, Mr Pile, complains that Underwood's refusal to bribe makes him sick. And although the borough is a town, not a city, its voters are becoming more working class and more anonymous, a trend that the ballot, which Trollope distrusted anyway, would only exacerbate.

Everything that Trollope disliked about Beverley shows up at Percycross: the supporters who care not what the out-of-town candidate thinks, the indifference on all sides to important political questions, the endless speeches, the voters whose interest seems limited to how much money or beer they can wheedle from each candidate, and the endless rain. Rain will recur regularly in Trollope's later election chapters, notably at Polpenno in *The Duke's Children*, though by now with a more light-hearted humour. Percycross, like Beverley also, will finally be disenfranchised for its corruption.

However, it is worth noting that fiction and life were not identical. Trollope the Liberal was at the bottom of the poll at Beverley, but Sir Thomas the Tory wins his seat at Percycross, only to lose it when the borough is disenfranchised for a corruption he could not control, and fought against. Like Trollope, Sir Thomas felt humiliated by his political experience, but his humiliation is also physical, when his arm is broken in the turmoil that breaks out after a speech he gives. Trollope's experience is refracted and distanced by art (see also POLITICAL ISSUES IN TROLLOPE'S FICTION; POLITICIANS AS CHARACTERS; POLITICS, TROLLOPE AND). The election chapters in *Ralph the Heir* are also tangential to the central narrative. Trollope will not be able to connect his new grasp of political process to the deeper structure of his stories until he writes *The Way We Live Now* and *The Prime Minister*.

Melmotte's campaign for Parliament to represent Westminster, the heart of Victorian empire, in *The Way We Live Now* is Trollope's only London election. Melmotte, the dishonest financier, is successful in part because working-class voters had 'that occult sympathy which is felt for crime, when the crime committed is injurious to the upper classes' (LXIV). But Trollope's view of latter-day democracy is not always quite so pessimistic. In *The Duke's Children* Tregear the Conservative, not a rich man, is elected because bribery is forestalled, though Trollope admits that 'ten shillings a head would have sent three hundred true Liberals to the ballot-boxes!' (LVI). Throughout Trollope, elections are mostly a game, practised equally without scruple by both national parties. The odd result is none the less that some men of integrity are elected, like Phineas and Arthur Fletcher and Frank Tregear.

Trollope's election scenes by novel and chapter include: *The Three Clerks* (VIII, XXIV, XXIX), *Doctor Thorne* (XVII, XXII), *Rachel Ray* (XVII, XXIV), *Can You Forgive Her?* (XLIV), *Phineas Finn* (XXVII, XXXII), *Ralph the Heir* (XXIX, XXXIX, XLIV), *Phineas Redux* (IV, LXXI), *The Way We Live Now* (LXIII–IV), *The Prime Minister* (XXIX, XXXIV), and *The Duke's Children* (XIV, LV) (see W. G. and J. T. Gerould, *A Guide to Trollope* (1948), 77).   GB

Cockshut, A. O. J., *Anthony Trollope* (1955).
Gerould, W. G., and Gerould, J. T., *A Guide to Trollope* (1948).
Halperin, John, *Trollope and Politics* (1977).

Eliot, George (1819–80). Trollope came to know Eliot through her common-law relationship with G. H. *Lewes, whom he met in January 1860 at a *Cornhill* dinner. She noted in her journal that on 20 November of that year he dined with them 'and made us like him very much'. She appears to have been particularly fond of him on account of his regard for Lewes.

In *An Autobiography*, Trollope identifies the couple as dear friends. He obviously enjoyed the companionship of both. But he was broad-minded about the relationship only to a point. Though he was entertained at their home many times it was without Rose, and when Lewes was invited to Trollope's home he was not accompanied by Eliot. A man who had a wife still living was not welcome to appear in society with her replacement.

Both Eliot (in the voice of the narrator of *The Mill on the Floss*) and Trollope (in *DWS*, *EE*, and *HKWR*) commented in their fiction on women's tendency to ostracize other women who were guilty of unorthodox sexual behaviour. Her biographers have remarked that Eliot was careful not to solicit attention from those she suspected were too narrow-minded to accept her position. Trollope appears to have attempted to protect her: he wrote to Rhoda Broughton in 1874 that she was 'somewhat difficult to know', meaning that she shied away from ordinary social intercourse (*Letters* 2, 632). To Kate Field, who on Eliot's death asked him for background on her relationship with Lewes for an article that she was writing for the New York *Tribune*, Trollope wrote that she had 'lived down evil tongues' and her 'private life should be left in privacy,—as may be said of all who have achieved fame by literary merits' (*Letters* 2, 892).

In 1860, after Thackeray turned down his short story 'Mrs General Talboys' on grounds of indecency, Trollope reminded him that not only was Thackeray's own Becky Sharp a courtesan, but *Adam Bede*, published the previous year, was about a fallen woman. Like Eliot, Trollope did not flinch at describing irregular sexual relations, though certainly neither author promoted them.

Eliot's first fiction, 'Amos Barton', published in *Scenes of Clerical Life*, was begun in 1856, a year after *The Warden* was published. Both describe the clergy in England at about the same

George Eliot, drawn by Frederick Burton in 1865. Deep friendship with Trollope began in 1860 through her companion G. H. Lewes. She praised Trollope's books as 'pleasant public gardens', while he placed her second to his beloved Thackeray among contemporary novelists.

time, though her approach is to examine the motivation of her characters while his is to describe their behaviour. She later said that her stories always grew out of her psychological perception of the characters. He admired her work but found the emphasis on psychology too deep.

Though Trollope's novels were much more directed by plot, they appealed to Eliot: 'Anthony Trollope is admirable in the presentation of even, average life and character, and he is so thoroughly wholesome-minded that one delights in seeing his books lie about to be read,' she wrote to a friend in 1862. Prone to depression, she admired his ambition and industriousness, even suggesting that had it not been for his example she might not have made *Middlemarch* so panoramic. After he sent her *Rachel Ray* she praised him for his organization of everyday incidents into 'a well-proportioned whole, natty & complete as a nut on its stem' (*Letters* 1, 238). She was also impressed with his ability to convey moral lessons while entertaining his readers. A free thinker, she said in a letter to Clifford Allbutt in 1868 that her own purpose was to 'help my readers in getting a clearer conception and a more active admiration of those vital elements which bind men together and give a higher worthiness to their existence'. She told Trollope she found his books 'like pleasant public gardens, where people go for amusement, & whether they think of it or not, get health as well' (*Letters* 1, 238). In her letters and journals she mentions having read a number of Trollope novels and sometimes recommends them to others. His regard for her writing was tempered by his belief in the importance of accessibility in novels. He appears to have respected her ability and achievement, admiring especially her moral purpose, while at the same time shrinking from the task of wading through the psychological analysis that entwines and impedes her plots. 'She is sometimes heavy,' he wrote in a letter in 1874, '—sometimes abstruse, sometimes almost dull,—but always like an egg, full of meat' (*Letters* 2, 627). In *An Autobiography* he acknowledges that she was the greatest English novelist alive at the time he was writing, but confesses that though he admires the characterization in *Adam Bede*, *The Mill on the Floss*, *Silas Marner*, and *Romola* he has found the more complicated *Felix Holt*, *Middlemarch*, and *Daniel Deronda* difficult to read. In a curiously restrained letter of congratulation, written in 1862 after he had read the first number of *Romola*, Trollope suggested that perhaps she was trying too hard. 'Do not fire too much over the heads of your readers,' he advised (*Letters* 1, 187). Far from taking offence, she recorded in her journal: 'This morning I had a de-

lightful, generous letter from Mr Anthony Trollope.'

Around the same time as Trollope met Eliot, he met Kate Field, a strong feminist, and developed an interest in the movement for women's rights in both England and the United States. Through Eliot he met Barbara *Bodichon and other Ladies of Langham Place. Though he sometimes ridicules the idea of equality for women in his novels, there are also portraits of highly individual, intelligent women like Lady Laura Standish (Kennedy) and Marie Goesler (Mme Max) who do not quite fit the feminine stereotype.   JK

Ashton, Rosemary, *George Eliot: A Life* (1996).
Haight, Gordon S., *Selections from George Eliot's Letters* (1985).

Eliot, William Greenleaf (1811–87), American Unitarian minister, author of *Discourses on the Doctrines of Christianity* (1855) and other theological works, founder of Washington University, Illinois. He met Trollope during his stay at St Louis in January 1862 and had a conversation about Kate Field, which Trollope reported to her later: ' "Let her marry a husband," said he [Eliot]. "It is the best career for a woman." I agreed with him—and therefore bid you in his name as well as my own to go & marry a husband' (*Letters* 1, 175). Trollope drew on his visit to Washington College and his acquaintance with Eliot for the character of Mr Peacocke in *Dr Wortle's School*. Eliot's *In my Anecdotage* (1925) recalled dining in the company of Trollope, John Millais, Arthur Sullivan, and Lord James of Hereford. In the course of that evening, Eliot witnessed Trollope in one of his blustery moods: 'young man rather nervously remarked to Trollope, who had all this time been munching his dinner in silence: "They tell me, Mr Trollope, that before sitting down to write one of your— may I say?—delightful novels, you always make a prefatory sketch!" "Never did such a thing in my life sir, and never shall!" bawled the angry Anthony' (*I & R* 148).   RCT

Eliot, Frances (née **Dickinson**) (1820–98), prolific writer on European social history. Although a divorcee she played in Dickens's *The Frozen Deep* before Queen Victoria in July 1857, went through a form of marriage to a doctor whose identity is unknown, and married in 1863 the Very Revd Gilbert Elliot, Dean of Bristol, twenty years her senior. Wilkie Collins dedicated *Poor Miss Finch* (1872) to her and Dickens tried to mediate between the Elliots when their marriage broke down. She contributed to the first two issues of *Saint Pauls*: 'Madame Tallien: A

Biographical Sketch' (January 1868) and 'Madame de Sévigné' (June 1868). Trollope did not feel warmly towards her. In 1877 Frances Eleanor Trollope wrote to Bice, Trollope's niece, that 'Mrs Dean of Bristol Elliot "declares she has *not* quarrelled with your Uncle. This will be a severe blow to poor Anthony should he ever hear of it" ' (*Letters* 1, 374 n.). RCT

Elliot, Revd Gilbert (1800–91). Rector of Trinity Church, Marylebone, Elliot moved to Bristol, where he became dean. A remarkably handsome man and eloquent preacher, he married Frances Dickinson in 1863 when he was 63. By 1866 the marriage was in ruins, though Dickens tried to mediate between them. In November 1867, the Dean was a steward at the dinner for Charles Dickens at the Freemasons' Hall on the eve of his departure for a reading tour in the USA. RCT

Elliotson, Dr John (1791–1868), Professor of Medicine at London University (1831–8); first physician in England to use the stethoscope; negotiated the founding of University College Hospital. He published numerous papers on physiology and mesmeric treatment of pain. In 1838, he was compelled to resign his practice for unauthorized interest in mesmerism after the *Lancet* denounced the Okey sisters, whom Dr Elliotson employed as subjects of public experiments. Thackeray dedicated *Pendennis* (1850) to him; he was also a friend of Dickens who was deeply interested in mesmerism. Mrs Trollope called him in when Trollope was struck down by a mysterious illness in 1840. At this time, Elliotson was still employing the Okey sisters, who seemed able to predict the deaths of hospital patients whenever they 'saw Jack' nearby. T. A. Trollope recalled in *What I Remember* (1887) that the Okey girls 'were very frequently in the lodgings occupied by my brother at the time, during the period of his greatest danger, and used constantly to say that they "saw Jack by his side, but only up to his knee" and therefore they thought he would recover—as he did!' (*Letters* 1, 9). Trollope later wrote sceptically on mesmerism in *The New Zealander*, dwelling on its potential for fakery. See *Letters* 2, 682, 786. RCT

Elliott & Fry. One of the best-known firms of commercial photographers in London, Joseph John Elliott and Clarence Edmund Fry began their partnership in 1863. According to one observer in 1865, the main feature of their studios at 55 Baker Street was 'an elongated canopy stretched over the cameras, 12 feet long, so that the photographer looked at the sitter through a tunnel'. During the 1860s, press and commercial photography created a market for celebrities and the *carte de visite* became one means of satisfying autograph seekers. Famous people were besieged for these miniature portraits, which usually measured two inches by three inches. Photographers charged their customers about one guinea for twelve or eighteen *cartes*. Fry was good at making his sitters relax during the ten minutes, or sometimes five, he required them to stay still. Trollope sat for Elliott & Fry in February 1867 with satisfactory results. RCT

Emerson, Ralph Waldo (1803–82), American philosopher, poet, founder of the Transcendental Club promoting ideas on philosophy, theology, and literature. *Essays* (1841) and *Essays: Second Series* (1844) earned him the status of prophet. During their stay in Boston in 1861, the Trollopes dined at the Fields' with Emerson, Hawthorne, Russell Lowell, and Wendell Holmes. Lowell commented: 'Emerson and I, who sat between them [Trollope and Holmes] "crouched down out of range" ' (*I & R* 78) of their heated exchanges. Trollope attended Emerson's lecture on 'American Nationality' at Tremont Temple. He had feared the lecture might be too transcendental, but there was nothing 'mystic' in it, and Trollope 'especially relished Emerson's caveat about the American eagle becoming the American peacock' (Hall 232). After hearing Edward Everett lecture on 'The Causes and Conduct of the Civil War', he remarked that Everett 'was neither bold nor honest, as Emerson had been' (quoted Super 139). In *North America* Trollope included Emerson as one of the leading lights of Boston, the 'western Athens'. In his tribute to G. H. *Lewes, however, he claimed to know 'nothing of philosophy or science and admitted that he simply could not comprehend one book by Emerson' (Mullen 569). RCT

emigration took over sixteen million people from the United Kingdom between 1815 and 1914. Considerably over half went to the United States, most of the rest to Australia and Canada about equally, and the remainder elsewhere, particularly South Africa. A disproportionate number were Irish, some six million (with at least a million more Irish emigrating to England and Scotland), and Scots, nearly two million (excluding migration to England). Some of this was 'crisis' emigration, notably that triggered by the Irish famine of the late 1840s, and most of the Irish, Scots, and Welsh emigrated from rural poverty. Irish emigration apart, it was rarely a flight from destitution, since emigration cost money and under 10 per cent of emigrants received assistance. Earlier in the century, Malthusian fears of overpopulation had bred numerous schemes for 'shovelling out paupers' to Australia and Canada, but these colonies were understandably wary of such projects. As they gained greater autonomy they became increasingly concerned with attracting emigrants of quality.

British emigration rose along with Britain's prosperity throughout the 19th century, though it surged in periods of recession. Happily the cycles in the American economy tended to move counter to those in Britain. Most English emigrants came from towns and though most were general labourers, skilled miners, artisans, and increasingly white-collar workers formed a significant portion. An important factor in rising emigration was falling transportation costs. New steamships from the 1860s cut fares by 40 per cent and passage time by up to 75 per cent. Reduced risk and improved communications made emigration less of a leap in the dark, making it increasingly attractive to single young men and even women (though the latter were always significantly fewer). Since people of British ethnicity were dominant in most settlement colonies apart from Latin America, UK emigrants had a cultural and linguistic advantage over their European counterparts. Nor was emigration irrevocable. As many as half of English emigrants 1850–1914 returned to England, not necessarily out of disappointment, though the rates of return were lower for Irish, Welsh, and Scots. Never before or since were there such conditions of unrestricted population mobility within the English-speaking world. Without passports, visas, or quotas, *laissez-faire* ruled. On gaining autonomy, Australia and Canada both worked to attract immigrants. The USA did not need to. Generally British emigration was the result of informed decision rather than a desperate response to extreme circumstance.

In addition to dramatic 'pushes' to emigration, like the Irish famine, there were occasional dramatic 'pulls', such as the gold rushes to Australia, South Africa, and the Yukon which stirred many middle-class men in search of adventure. Gentlemen or would-be gentlemen in search of status, authority, cheap acres, or a new identity were a small but visible segment of those attracted particularly to Australia and Canada. Such were Trollope's speciality. His son Frederic's emigration to Australia gave him excellent sources which he put to use in *Harry Heathcote of Gangoil*. Emigration to Australia (for Alaric Tudor in *The Three Clerks*) or America (George Vavasor in *Can You Forgive Her?*) was also a convenient way for Trollope to dispose of awkward characters without killing them. CK

Baines, Dudley, *Migration in a Mature Economy: Emigration and Internal Migration in England and Wales 1861–1900* (1985).

Erickson, Charlotte, *Invisible Immigrants: The Adaptation of English and Scottish Immigrants in Nineteenth Century America* (1972).

Emilius (Mealyus), Joseph, Hungarian Jew turned fashionable London preacher, who bigamously marries Lizzie Eustace and murders her would-be protector Mr Bonteen. Despite 'a slight defect in his left eye' and his 'hooky nose', Joseph Emilius has dark good looks and a 'sweet, oily tone' that women find attractive. His propensity for lies and false drama make him the perfect match for Lizzie. *ED, PR* JMR

Emly, William Monsell, Baron (1812–94), Liberal MP for Limerick, 1847–74; raised to the peerage (1874). He had been at Winchester with Anthony and Tom Trollope, and was Postmaster General, 1871–3. Trollope stayed with Baron Emly in Ireland during his research for *The Landleaguers* in 1882. Noting how badly Trollope suffered from asthma, Emly mentioned it to his friend Cardinal *Newman, who sent Trollope specifics for a remedy. Trollope thanked Emly (October 1882) but doubted its efficacy. 'Great spasmodic want of breath is the evil which affects me, and which at night sometimes becomes very hard to bear' (*Letters* 2, 993). RCT

'England and America' (letter). While the government is officially neutral on the American Civil War, English newspapers should research, publicize, and persuade readers of the truth of issues. The North's stances on abolition and unity will triumph; the South is gallant but wrong. *Pall Mall Gazette* (27 February 1865), 3. AKL

'England and the United States' (letter). Mr Conway says in the *Fortnightly Review* that England owes the USA for the *Alabama*; he must know England cannot bear humiliation, and will refuse to pay for dockworkers' treachery. The situation is a very unlikely *casus belli*, despite Conway. *Pall Mall Gazette* (8 January 1866), 2–3. AKL

'English Aspect of the War, The' (article). England should honour its pledge to protect Belgium, despite understandable reluctance to join the Franco-Prussian War. It will probably not come to fighting, but England must not deny its promise, and devalue its word throughout the world. *Saint Pauls* (September 1870), 562–71. AKL

'English View of the President's Impeachment, An' (letter). The visitor to the United States who witnessed the narrow vote to acquit

Johnson believes that tension is inherent in the US system between the two houses, and between Congress and the President. The widespread belief is expressed that bribery and corruption have affected this outcome; the writer does not himself think so. *Pall Mall Gazette* (15 June 1868), 10.

AKL

Ennis, assize town of Co. Clare. Its cavalry barracks house a detachment of the 20th Hussars to which Fred Neville is assigned. Mrs O'Hara pushes past the guard to those rough quarters, demanding to know when Fred will marry her daughter. *EE*

AWJ

Ennistimon, nearest town to Liscannor Bay. Fred Neville lodges at the inn there on the night before his death. Kate O'Hara is taken there to recover from that trauma and later gives birth to a stillborn child. *EE*

AWJ

Erle, Barrington, important behind-the-scenes political figure on the Liberal side, appearing most prominently in *Phineas Finn*, *Phineas Redux*, and *The Prime Minister*. A middle-aged youth, cousin to Lady Laura Standish, Erle is a devoted follower of William Mildmay, 'the great Whig Minister of the day', and is a party politician to the core, absolutely scorning independence in politics. Erle introduces Phineas into Liberal political circles and assists in launching his parliamentary career.

JMR

Escott, Thomas Hay Sweet (1850–1924), author and editor of *Fortnightly Review* (1882–6) and Trollope's first biographer. He benefited from interviews with the novelist resulting in his article 'A Novelist of the Day' in *Time* (August 1879, 626–32) and 'The Works of Anthony Trollope', *Quarterly Review* (January 1909, 210–30). This led to a full-length study, *Anthony Trollope: His Work, Associates and Originals* (1913), which, though inaccurate in details, gives useful data on contemporaries and a vigorous close-up of the man himself. In *England: Its People, Polity, and Pursuits* (1879) Escott saw the novels as unrivalled pen-and-ink photographs of 19th-century life.

RCT

essay, contemporary. Trollope was a serious social reformer who took an active interest in the debate as to whether extension of the franchise, which by the 1860s seemed inevitable, would assist or impede the progress of civilization. Though, with Matthew Arnold, he was aware that the energy to govern productively existed potentially in the middle class, he saw and wrote about instability in Europe, dissension in Ireland, and civil war in America as the result of power taken too quickly.

His designation of himself in *An Autobiography* as an advanced conservative liberal meant that, though he regarded democracy as a force for the good of mankind, he did not think that progress should be headlong. He was a moderate, believing, as he said metaphorically many times in his fiction, that the speeding carriage of liberalism needed the political brake of conservatism so that traditions could be slowly modified rather than thrown out wholesale and replaced.

Though he found the idea of extended individual freedom inviting, he thought *Mill's prescriptions for liberty and the emancipation of women went too far. At the other extreme, he found *Carlyle's dire warnings of an inevitable plunge into anarchy tiresome. His parody of Carlyle as Dr Pessimist Anticant in *The Warden* is well known. 'An Essay on Carlylism' credits Carlyle with having 'founded a school of thinkers . . . vehement in their forebodings of a coming day of wrath'. He twitted Mill in *He Knew He Was Right*, begun the year Mill moved, in the Reform Bill debate, to replace the word 'man' with 'person' and thus extend the franchise to women. In the novel an American minister remarks to an Englishman that Mill is 'a great man' for advocating equality between the sexes. Trollope's mouthpiece replies: 'Can he arrange that the men shall have half the babies?' (LV)

The more restrained liberalism of G. H. *Lewes Trollope could accept. Lewes earned Trollope's respect for his staying power as a philosopher and essayist who earned his living by writing for periodicals. On his death, remarking that 'there was no form of literary expression in which he did not delight and instruct', Trollope marvelled at how much of England's best thought was handed out cheaply to the public in the nation's magazines and newspapers. Intellectuals and conservatives tended to dismiss Trollope as vulgar and insensitive. After he ran down *Ruskin in a review in 1865 of *Sesame and Lilies* for preaching like Carlyle and for denouncing the popular taste in reading, Carlyle, commending the book to his wife, observed that Trollope was 'irredeemably imbedded in commonplace, and grown fat upon it' (*I & R* 128).

Though Arnold disparaged 'philistinism' there is no evidence that Trollope thought himself included in this label. Indeed, he appears to have been influenced by Arnold's essay 'The Function of Criticism at the Present Time', first published in 1864, shaping the *Fortnightly Review* as a kind of Arnoldian 'organ for a free play of the mind' and later, in *An Autobiography*, arguing for the elevation of literary criticism from hack-work to art.

It can be inferred from Trollope's own influence as an editor that, despite his distaste for Carlyle, he believed the strongest essay was one that could translate into social action. Though he read all current essays and recognized the need for more serious and direct analysis of contemporary issues than was possible in fiction, he was not nearly as convincing an essayist as he was as a novelist. His fiction sparkles; his serious essays are for the most part dull.

His most successful essays were not political commentary on events and ideas of the day, but timeless, extemporaneous descriptions of, for example, fox-hunting, or the clergy, or types of tradesmen. Trollope was much more successful at describing than at prescribing. However, he felt a strong responsibility to do more than amuse. The essay form appealed to him because it allowed him a pulpit.

He was well aware, as he reminded Kate Field in a letter about one of her stories, that the moral message of fiction had to be much more subtle than that of the essay. 'If you are writing an essay', he told her, 'you have to convey of course your own ideas and convictions, to another mind. You will of course desire to do so in fiction also. . . . We are very jealous of preachers. We admit them at certain hours & places for certain reasons' (*Letters* 1, 430–1).   JK

Trollope, Anthony, review of *Sesame and Lilies*, *Fortnightly Review* (15 July 1865), 633–5.
—— 'An Essay on Carlylism', *Saint Pauls Magazine* (December 1869), 292–305.
—— 'George Henry Lewes', *Fortnightly Review* (January 1879), 15–24.

Essex, favourite hunting county for Trollope but scarce in fictional locations. George Bertram, senior, lives at Hadley about a mile from Barnet (*B*). The Shands live at Pollington (*JC*).   MRS

Eton College. Founded in 1440–1, its pupils provided the elite of English law and politics. In the 1860s the education and administration of the nine leading public schools came under fire, largely as a consequence of an article in *Cornhill* (May 1860). A commission of inquiry was set up in July 1861. Trollope weighed in with 'Public Schools', *Fortnightly* (October 1865). In 1876 Mrs Oliphant tried to get Trollope as a speaker at Eton. He was not enthusiastic 'about the hardest audience in England to please' (*Letters* 2, 683). Trollope chose not to send his sons to the ancient foundations, enrolling them in the progressive St Andrews College, Bradfield, near Reading. Twelve Etonians appear in his fiction, an odd assortment, including Lord Ballindine and Barry Kelly (*KOK*), Patrick Desmond (*CR*), Lord George Germain (*IHP*), Frank Tregear, Lord Popple-court, and Lord Silverbridge (*DC*), Mountjoy and Augustus Scarborough (*MSF*), Louis Scatcherd (*DT*), Bertie Stanhope (*BT*), and Tom Tringle (*AA*).   RCT

Euphemia asserts her independence of love but, seeing Lord Mountfidget fall by a poisoned arrow, gets an antidote and effects a cure. 'Euphemia'   GRH

Europe, eastern. In the 19th century, eastern Europe, particularly the Balkans, became one of the most volatile regions of Europe, giving birth to a number of crises ultimately culminating in the Sarajevo assassination of July 1914, which helped precipitate the First World War. The background to the particular crisis that involved Trollope, the 'Bulgarian Atrocities' agitation of 1876, goes back to the 14th century, when the Ottoman Turks erupted from central Asia, swept across Anatolia, and invaded the Balkans. In the ensuing centuries, the Turks captured Constantinople, extinguished the Byzantine Empire, expanded south into the Arab lands, and continued their progress into central Europe, until twice beaten back from the walls of Vienna. For several centuries the Turks controlled the areas in which the modern states of Romania, Bulgaria, Greece, Albania, and the states created by the collapse of Yugoslavia are located. During this period, while the Christian populations enjoyed relative freedom of religion, there were forcible conversions to Islam, which meant that in many regions an ethnically similar Slavic population was now divided by religion. Though Muslims and Christians usually coexisted, there were enough bloody persecutions and revolts that fierce hatreds developed and remained in the collective memories.

Continuing resentment over Turkish domination helped fuel growing nationalism in the 19th century, and Greece, aided by the French and English, gained independence in 1829, while Moldavia, Wallachia, and Serbia became autonomous. These successes encouraged restlessness in the other Balkan provinces, and also stimulated Russian interests. The tsars, eager for access to the Mediterranean, hoped to convince the rest of Europe to partition the ailing Ottoman state, and planned to use Russian co-religionist status and the Pan-Slavic ethnic relationship to the Balkan peoples to expand Russia's influence throughout the region (ironically, though the Russians thereby promoted Balkan nationalisms, these nationalisms could become as strongly anti-Russian as anti-Turk).

In 1876 a revolt in a Bulgarian region led to Turkish use of local Muslim irregulars, the bashi-bazouks, to suppress the Christians, with the result that the conflict now had something of the nature of a civil war, and atrocities were committed by both sides. Approximately 4,000 Christians were killed, and a larger number of Muslims, but reports reaching western Europe greatly exaggerated the death toll—it was reported that as many as 100,000 Christians were massacred, with fearsome atrocities, including impalement.

Liberal leader W. E. *Gladstone, now semi-retired from politics, was stirred by the reports, and stormed back into the political limelight in a great moral crusade against the 'anti-human' Turk. His pamphlet *Bulgarian Horrors and the Question of the East* sold hundreds of thousands of copies, and stimulated fervent public protest against the foreign policy of Conservative Prime Minister *Disraeli. This policy was the propping up of the Turks as a barrier to Russian expansion into the eastern Mediterranean, which would put Russia in position to threaten British routes to India. Trollope read the pamphlet aloud to his family in October 1876. On 8 December, in London, Trollope spoke at a protest meeting at which Gladstone was the main speaker. Trollope enthusiastically lambasted the Turks, who were everything bad in comparison to the Christian English; his fervour was so great that he carried on considerably past his time limit.

Meanwhile, in 1877, open war broke out between the Russians and the Turks; the Turks were heavily defeated and forced to agree to a treaty that would have created a 'Big Bulgaria', autonomous, but a Russian satellite. At this point traditional policies reasserted themselves, and Russophobia proved to be as fervent as the previous anti-Turkish sentiment. The Disraeli government sent fleet units to the Dardanelles, and troops from India to Cyprus. At least a portion of the British public clamoured for war, exhibiting an outburst of 'jingoism', an emotion named from an anti-Russian music-hall song popular at this moment. In the end, at the Congress of Berlin in 1878, Russia was forced to retreat from some of its gains. A part of Bulgaria remained nominally under Turkish sovereignty, but most Balkan states were now independent, and effectively the Turks were eliminated from Europe, except for Istanbul and the area which controlled the European side of the passage between the Black Sea and the Mediterranean. The British stayed in Cyprus. In the whole Bulgarian controversy in Britain there is no evidence to suggest that either side understood what was really happening in the Balkans.   LK

Saab, A. P., *Reluctant Icon: Gladstone, Bulgaria, and the Working Classes, 1856–1878* (1991).

Europe, western. Because Britain became a well-publicized imperial state from the 17th century on, it is easy to think of the British as world citizens by the 19th century, rather than as Europeans. But Britain was and still continues to be a European state, with strong historical, cultural, and economic links to the Continent, which also had the virtue of being on the doorstep. Though British exports to the empire, the United States, and the rest of the world were to expand impressively, especially after the Industrial Revolution vastly improved Britain's trade capacity, in Trollope's lifetime almost a third of British goods flowed to European countries, about the same amount as to the colonies. The Foreign Office maintained consuls in the major cities of western Europe, who, among their other duties, provided economic and commercial information.

Apart from trading connections, which were often centuries old, there were also political similarities that were greater than with most other parts of the world. Except for Switzerland and France (which fluctuated—monarchy 1815–48, republic 1848–52, empire 1852–70, and once more republic) most European states were monarchies of familiar types, and had easily recognizable aristocracies of birth and wealth. Historically, most of Britain's significant wars had been against European states, primarily France, and had been fought with the aid of European allies, primarily the Germanic states. Europeans shared similar tastes in music, art, architecture, and, increasingly, technology. Though Englishmen travelling through Europe could be put off by differences in languages and local customs, they would usually be more comfortable than in more exotic locales.

Europe was accessible to the British traveller without the preliminary of a time-consuming ocean voyage, and so travels in western Europe were extensive. In the 18th century wealthy families had often sent their young men on a grand tour, to extend their knowledge and complete their educations. They learned a smattering of the languages and the art and literature of the countries where they spent some time. On a more limited scale, this was to continue in the 19th century. Trollope's travellers, for example, were often determined to expose themselves to European culture, both ancient and modern, and in doing this they emulated about 150,000 travellers a year from the upper and middle classes of Britain.

In the 19th century a new travel link opened up with western Europe. Thomas *Cook, who started out running excursions to English seaside resorts, and then expanded to Scotland, took a group of tourists to the Paris Exhibition of 1855.

Quickly, tours to France became a regular feature of Cook's service, and he soon included Switzerland and Italy. Though upper-class travellers looked down on these tourists, thousands of men and especially women of modest means became better acquainted with European neighbours and their ways. A proudly independent traveller, Trollope joked in *The Eustace Diamonds*, 'Switzerland and the Tyrol, and even Italy, are all redolent of Mr Cook' (XXXII).

Many of the British did more than just travel in Europe. For a long time English workmen, especially those involved in railway construction, could find jobs in Europe, which they accepted for a variety of reasons—better pay, or simply employment where none was available at home. They were often joined by those of their 'betters' whose finances were distressed at home, who found that their incomes went further, as did for a time Trollope's parents, in countries like Belgium. Trollope's brother Tom settled permanently in Italy, as later did his mother, attracted by climate and culture as well as the more comfortable lifestyles available on their incomes; there were a great many European cities with English communities where the inhabitants remained abroad for the same reasons.

Britain was fortunate that, until the emergence of united Germany in 1871, there was a roughly equal power balance in Europe, which meant that British foreign secretaries could be influential in continental politics even though they did not have massive conscript armies behind them. Though wars frequently occurred in western Europe, such as the conflicts in the revolutions of 1848, and the wars for Italian and German unification, Britain remained largely neutral. The British treated the French with considerable caution because of historical rivalries, but the Germans evoked feelings of friendship and often admiration because of their solid, hard-working qualities.

Trollope, the European traveller, became an expert on railway food, missed connections, obnoxious travellers, quantities of luggage, and lost tickets. He and Rose were ardent holiday-makers in Europe and shared a fondness for Felsenegg, Switzerland. They enjoyed mountain scenery (see HOLIDAYS ABROAD; 'TRAVELLING SKETCHES').

Trollope wrote travel books but not travel novels. Consequently, though many of his characters, especially of his political novels, did travel in Europe, Trollope did not go in for a great deal of physical description, except for the Italian scenes of *He Knew He Was Right*. Some of his novels were set in western European countries, and the protagonists were Europeans rather than British. Here more local colour emerged. *Nina Balatka* was set in Prague, the leading city of Bohemia in the Austro-Hungarian state, and *Linda Tressel* took place in Nuremberg, Germany. The setting for *The Golden Lion of Granpère* was in the French province of Lorraine. *La Vendée* was set in the west of France during the French Revolution.

Several of Trollope's short stories also had European settings. 'Why Frau Frohmann Raised her Prices' occurred in the Tyrol, and 'La Mère Bauche' in the Pyrenees. 'John Bull on the Guadalquivir' took a young Englishman to Spain; another Englishman encountered adventures in Italy in 'The Man Who Kept his Money in a Box'. 'The Last Austrian Who Left Venice' also took place in Italy, as did 'Mrs General Talboys'. 'Lotta Schmidt' was set in Vienna, and 'The House of Heine Brothers in Munich' in Germany. Two other stories involved English visitors to Europe: 'Relics of General Chassé: A Tale of Antwerp' in Belgium, and 'The Chateau of Prince Polignac' in France.   LK

Stearns, P. N., *Life and Society in the West: The Modern Centuries* (1988).

European literature. Trollope's interest in European literature does not seem to have been especially extensive, and apart from the odd reference to *Don Quixote* (1605–15), *Gil Blas* (1715–35), and Molière's comedies, allusions to European literature are practically non-existent. One notable exception, in *The Warden*, is the revelation of Archdeacon Grantly's secret fondness for Rabelais (*W* VIII), a disclosure that does much to augment the Archdeacon's characterization; the French writer's twin satires *Pantagruel* (1532) and *Gargantua* (1534) both mock (among other things) the church hierarchy for its unshakeable belief in its own authority. This fact alone makes them a deeply ironic choice of reading matter for the Archdeacon; their numerous scatological references merely compound the point. Trollope's reputation as one of the great 19th-century practitioners of the realist novel, and, especially, his habit of reintroducing characters into subsequent novels, facilitates comparison with Honoré de *Balzac's massive series of interlocking novels, the *Comédie humaine*, and there is much fruitful research to be done by enterprising students of comparative literature. Trollope, however, does not seem to have been particularly familiar with Balzac's works; he admitted as much at the annual Literary Fund dinner, May 1867, when, responding to a toast, he declared that '*I am told* that he [Balzac] was the man who invented that style of fiction in which I have attempted to work' (my emphasis; see Hall 302–3). In fact, the only European novelist about whom Trollope has anything substantial to say is Victor *Hugo; in *An Autobiography,* he criticizes the Frenchman's dilatory attitude to meeting publishers' deadlines which had affected publication of *The Vicar of Bullhampton* (see also DALLAS, ENEAS SWEETLAND). Trollope castigated Hugo's novels as 'pretentious and untrue to nature. To this perhaps was added some feeling of indignation that I should be asked to give way to a Frenchman. . . . From week to week and month to month he had put off the fulfilments of his duty. And because of these *laches* on his part,—on the part of this sententious French Radical,—I was to be thrown over!' (*Auto* XVIII).

HO

Eustace, Sir Florian, wealthy but ailing dupe who marries Lizzie Greystock, convinced of her purity and innocence. Though he lives only a year following their marriage, Sir Florian's eyes are opened to Lizzie's true character before his death. *ED*　　　　　　　　　　　　　　JMR

Eustace, John, easygoing brother of the late Sir Florian. He maintains cordial family relations with his brother's widow Lizzie Eustace, although he knows his sister-in-law is a liar and even though he realizes it may cost the Eustace estate £10,000 to replace the diamond necklace which she has taken for her own. It is a tribute to his family devotion that John graciously accepts the widowed Lizzie's invitation to stay at Portray Castle with other guests of dubious respectability. *ED*　　　　　　　　　　　　　　JMR

Eustace, Lady Lizzie (née **Greystock**), the brilliantly dishonest young widow of Florian Eustace who attempts to defraud her late husband's estate of £10,000 worth of diamonds. Strongly reminiscent of Thackeray's Becky Sharp, Lizzie Eustace is magnificently beautiful but artful and scheming, marrying Sir Florian from wholly mercenary motives. Lizzie's appeal lies partially in her devoted love of pretence: she pretends to read and enjoy reams of Romantic poetry she has barely skimmed; she imagines that she is in love alternately with Lord Fawn, Frank Greystock, and Lord George De Bruce Carruthers. With her flair and determination, Lizzie makes some headway in society, temporarily winning the interest of figures like Lady Glencora Palliser. But despite her cleverness and beauty, Lizzie is both too audacious and too ignorant to convince the world that she is pure-minded. Obsessed with keeping the valuable diamond necklace which belongs to the Eustace estate, often living beyond her means, and choosing indifferently respectable companions in her widowhood, Lizzie ultimately loses her standing as a woman

of fashion as people realize what the reader observes from the start—that she is false to the core. After a disreputable remarriage, Lizzie is forced to mix with a less genteel set. *ED, DC*

JMR

Eustace Diamonds, The (*see opposite*)

evangelicalism. The evangelical wing of the Church of England was at its most powerful in the 1850s, and then began to decline as the Oxford Movement gained influence. It came under attack for its lack of a coherent basis of faith, absence of clear doctrine of the Church, little sense of community, and sloppy emotionalism. In Trollope's novels it is noted for ostentatious piety, conviction of sin, zealous attitude to private morality, suspicion of pleasure, dislike of church tradition, and detestation of Roman Catholicism.

Trollope's intense dislike for evangelicalism stemmed from his antagonism to J. W. *Cunningham, the vicar of Harrow, whom his mother lampooned in her novel *The Vicar of Wrexhill* (1837), and on whom Trollope based Mr Slope, the Bishop's hypocritical chaplain in *Barchester Towers.* An ambitious man, he is attacked for his hatred of the Puseyites, his Sabbatarianism, and for having been a sizar (a poor scholar) at Cambridge. Such unbalanced assaults on evangelical clergymen principally caricature the young and ambitious; both Mr Emilius in *The Eustace Diamonds* and Mr Maguire in *Miss Mackenzie* have a symbolic squint. Although, like Mr Groschut, the Bishop's odious chaplain in *Is He Popenjoy?*, who fulminates against Dean Lovelace's fox-hunting and smoking, they disapprove of innocent pleasures, hypocritically, like the gluttonous curate Mr O'Callaghan in *The Bertrams,* they succumb readily to temptation.

Evangelicalism belonged to the world of the lower middle class, and Trollope persisted in his perverse view that evangelical clergy were not gentlemen. In *Rachel Ray,* Trollope emphasizes not Samuel Prong's sincere practice of Christian principles, but his dropped 'Hs', and his theological training at Islington. A rare exception is Mr Saul, the 'enthusiastic' curate in *The Claverings*: a gentleman, but regarded nevertheless as an interloper in the Clavering social circle.

Outright religious fanaticism belongs to the women. The best known is Mrs Proudie, the Bishop's wife in *Barchester Towers* and *The Last Chronicle of Barset,* whose desire to control and deny is seen in her obsession with Sabbatarianism. In *Rachel Ray* there is Rachel's morose sister Dorothea Prime, whose oppressive religion fuels her opposition to Luke Rowan's courtship. But

(cont. on page 190)

(cont. on page 190)

As many critics have noted, *The Eustace Diamonds* employs some of the strategies used in Wilkie Collins's classic detective story *The Moonstone*, which was published in 1868. Its main plot concerns Lizzie Greystock, a well-born adventuress, who lures the consumptive Sir Florian Eustace into marriage. His death leaves Lizzie in possession of an ample jointure and a priceless diamond necklace, which she claims he had given her. Sir Florian's solicitor, who cannot prove that she is lying, retorts that the Baronet had no legal right to dispose of this family heirloom. When Lord Fawn, the timid, scrupulous man to whom Lizzie has engaged herself, learns that his fiancée has seized property that may not be her own, his desire to marry her evaporates. But because the legality of Lizzie's claim is still in dispute, Fawn fears that public opinion would not support him were he to break the engagement, which therefore continues.

While defending her claim by lies and evasions, Lizzie keeps the diamonds with her in a strongbox. Eventually, the box is stolen, but the thieves miss the necklace, which Lizzie has hidden under her pillow. On oath, Lizzie states that the necklace was in the stolen box. Soon, the thieves arrange a second robbery, and this time they do get the jewels. Lizzie again lies on oath, simply to avoid admitting her previous perjury. When the truth comes out, Lizzie is offered immunity from prosecution in exchange for her help in convicting the thieves. She is saved from punishment, but her reputation is in tatters. Lord Fawn escapes from his engagement, and Lizzie weds the clerical conman Joseph Emilius, a converted Jew.

The novel's sub-plots concern the marriage prospects of two young women who are very different from Lizzie—and from one another. Lizzie's childhood friend Lucy Morris, a penniless governess, becomes engaged to Lizzie's cousin, the impecunious barrister Frank Greystock. Though Frank adores the honest, unselfish Lucy, he is tempted by Lizzie's wealth, and considers jilting Lucy to marry her. After Lizzie's lies are exposed, Frank returns to his true love. Lizzie's acquaintance Lucinda Roanoke agrees under extreme financial and social pressure to marry a man she despises. But Lucinda's hatred for her fiancé is so intense that the prospect of marrying him drives her to madness.

Though *The Eustace Diamonds* is technically the third novel of the Palliser series, the Pallisers themselves play only a minor role. Plantagenet's obsession with decimal coinage precludes his taking much interest in the Eustace scandal. But Glencora, seeing Lizzie as a fellow rebel, decides to champion her. When Lizzie's perjuries are exposed, however, Glencora realizes that she is beyond redemption.

On its initial appearance, *The Eustace Diamonds* received much attention in the press. Most of the reviews were highly positive. In *An Autobiography*, Trollope remarked that the novel did 'much to repair the injury which I felt had come to my reputation in the novel-market by the works of the last few years' (XIX). He believed that the unusual characterization of Lizzie Eustace, and not Lucy Morris's love story, accounted for the book's success.

An examination of contemporary reviews confirms Trollope's judgement on this point. Even the *Spectator*, which found Lizzie a 'very unattractive' heroine, was fascinated by her combination of 'cowardice and sly mendacity . . . without the vestige of a sense of right and wrong, without a vestige of passion' (Smalley 372). And *The Times*, in an otherwise enthusiastic review, found the novel's romantic sub-plot unsatisfying and clichéd, remarking that 'there is too strong a family likeness between our old favourite, Lucy [Robarts], in *Framley Parsonage,* and a certain very charming Lucy in these pages' (Smalley 374).

Contemporary reviewers judged Lizzie an original and striking character in spite of her obvious resemblance to Thackeray's Becky Sharp, a resemblance which Trollope also noted in *An Autobiography.* In calling Lizzie 'but a second Becky', Trollope asserted an identity where contemporary reviewers saw only a similarity—and on this point, the reviewers were certainly right (XIX). Like Becky, Lizzie is a greedy adventuress whose conduct has more in common with that of her supposedly respectable neighbours than readers might initially realize. But there the resemblance ends. Becky is a self-conscious hypocrite, who knows the difference between truth and falsehood, and who lies only in pursuit of clearly defined goals. But by the time Lizzie reaches adulthood, she has told so many lies that she can scarcely discriminate between the invented and the real. Her falsehoods often have a strangely purposeless quality. She lies about the first robbery, for example, although she has nothing clear to gain by doing so—and much to lose.

One reason why Lizzie has puzzled many readers is that her manœuvres are so frequently pointless. It is hard to guess what might be motivating a woman who generally seems to have her eye on the main chance, yet whose conduct is often impulsive and self-destructive. A second reason why Lizzie is puzzling concerns the relationship between her crass materialism and her apparently sincere longing for a life filled with poetry and romance. Is the longing for romance one of those many lies that Lizzie is unable to distinguish from truth, a veneer of self-deceived idealism covering the reality of greed? Or do her deceptions testify to a sincere dissatisfaction with her emotionally and morally impoverished existence, a dissatisfaction, in short, with the world she inhabits?

For if Lizzie's character poses the first significant interpretative problem in *The Eustace Diamonds,* that problem cannot be separated from a second problem, concerning her relationship to the social world that the novel depicts. Is Lizzie the recognizable product of a hypocritical society, whose secret vices her behaviour both illuminates and punishes? Or is she an innately evil woman whose behaviour transgresses society's laudable moral norms and who is therefore a fit subject for condemnation, punishment, and ostracism? Who, in other words, is the object of moral judgement in *The Eustace Diamonds,* Lizzie or society? The answers that Trollope's recent critics have offered to this question range from James Kincaid's remark that Lizzie 'is a judgement on the world' that produced her (*The Novels of Anthony Trollope* (1977), 209) to Stephen Wall's emphatic assertion that Trollope does not see Lizzie's misbehaviour 'as symptomatic of some pervasive social malaise' (*Trollope and Character* (1988), 264).

Whether or not they see Lizzie as its symptom, readers have generally agreed that a pervasive malaise, if not something worse, characterizes the world of *The Eustace Diamonds.* Thus the *Spectator*'s 1872 review lamented that, in the amoral society the novel depicts, 'the few good characters are so insignificant that you almost resent the author's expectation that you shall sorrow in their sorrows and rejoice in their joys' (Smalley 373). It would be fair to say that almost all of Trollope's modern critics reach similar conclusions. Bill Overton argues that the novel shows dishonesty to be 'epidemic in fashionable life' (*The Unofficial Trollope* (1982), 165), Juliet McMaster concludes that it exposes a world 'in irrational pursuit of artifice, rumour, and other people's property' (*Trollope's Palliser Novels* (1978), 102), while Robert Polhemus says rather quaintly that 'the society of *The Eustace Diamonds* turns rotten with public-relations mentality' (*The Changing World of Anthony Trollope* (1968), 172). Stephen Wall is a notable exception to the critical consensus in his belief that this world is not exceptionally corrupt.

The Eustace Diamonds portrays an upper-class milieu where everyone pays lip service to the old English virtues of honesty, loyalty, and responsibility, but few practise them. From Lord Fawn to Frank Greystock, from Lucinda Roanoke to Frank's respectable mother, the characters are engaged in a more or less passionate search for wealth, one not noticeably restrained by moral considerations. James Kincaid notes that in this novel 'everywhere we look we see the same fluidity, the same impotence of the old values, the same crass thought and language triumphant' (Kincaid 203) We see hypocrisy as well, because the narrator so frequently calls our attention to it. 'The one offence which a gentleman is supposed never to commit is that of speaking an untruth,' he remarks. 'The offence may be one committed oftener than any other by gentlemen . . . nevertheless, it is regarded by the usages of society as being the one thing which a gentleman never does' (XXIX).

In this world, the few virtuous characters who remain, like Lucy's kind and responsible employer Lady Fawn, seem confused and ineffectual, especially in comparison to their counterparts in Trollope's earlier novels. When her daughter tells her 'that under the new order of things promises from gentlemen were not to be looked upon as binding', Lady Fawn finds herself unable to 'disbelieve it all, and throw herself back upon her faith in virtue, constancy, and honesty' (LX). 'Laws, mamma, how antediluvian you are!' this daughter exclaims, when Lady Fawn opines timidly that an ambitious man like Frank Greystock might really want to marry for love (LX).

What relationships have readers discerned between Lizzie's vices and those of the admittedly corrupt society that produced her? According to Kincaid, both Lizzie's dishonesty and her romantic longings result from her need to escape an impoverished, materialistic world, 'to improve it, to make it more alive and more exciting' (Kincaid 205). But because the cultural milieu which has produced Lizzie does not offer her models of real transcendence, a pathetic parody of romance is the best thing she can construct out of the materials at hand.

According to another line of argument, however, Lizzie's dishonesty is best understood not as an attempt to escape a corrupt society, but as an attempt to fight it with its own weapons. *The Eustace Diamonds* suggests that ignorance has played a large role in making Lizzie what she is. She knows almost nothing about law and not much more about custom. Though Lizzie twice commits perjury, she hardly knows what perjury is. Hearing this word applied to her own conduct alarmed Lizzie only because it 'sounded like forgery and burglary', the narrator comments wryly (LII). But Lizzie's ignorance is no different from that of many Victorian ladies, who received a systematically superficial education designed to ensure that they would never be as well informed as their husbands. And this ignorance places Lizzie at a disadvantage in dealing with the greedy and manipulative men who surround her.

The Eustace family lawyer is not above using his legal expertise to bamboozle her. When she meets him with deception, Lizzie believes that she is merely shortening the odds against her—and she has a point. If she tells the truth, Lizzie fears, those who understand the world better than she does, but who are no less self-interested, may use her admissions against her. She feels safe only when she is keeping something back. But her ignorance is so dire that she is never sure what, exactly, she needs to conceal, and this may explain why her deceptions are often purposeless. She starts to lie automatically, even when there is no reason to do so, for 'to lie readily and cleverly, . . . according to the lessons which she had learned, [is] a necessity in woman' (LXXIX).

Lizzie's romantic role-playing can also be seen as an initially effective strategy run amok. In a society which commodifies women, girls must profess to be guided by only the purest, most romantic motives as they seek advancement and security in marriage. Having played this part for several years, Lizzie comes to believe that she is really capable 'of surrendering herself and all her possessions to a great passion' (V). In fact, however, the romantic role that circumstances thrust upon her was in such extreme tension with the young Lizzie's true motives that playing it finally destroyed any authentic sense of self she might initially have possessed. And so 'the guiding motive of her conduct [becomes] the desire to make things seem to be other than they were. To be always acting a part rather than living her own life was to her everything' (XIX).

The sub-plot concerning Lucinda Roanoke's misadventures offers support to those who read the novel in this manner. Like Lizzie, Lucinda is pressured to perpetrate the deceptions most likely to ensnare a rich husband. But Lucinda naturally loves the truth so much that she is simply unable to play the role the situation demands. Nor is she able to lie about her feelings to the repulsive man who proves willing to take her without such role-playing. When Lucinda's sanity snaps under the strain of these conflicting pressures, we see what would have happened to Lizzie if she had been less morally and emotionally malleable. But although this sub-plot poses no problem for readers who see Lizzie as a social product, the Lucy Morris sub-plot certainly does create difficulties. For if Lucy and a few characters, like Lady Fawn and Frank's sister Ellinor, who share her values, embody traditional English virtues in an acceptable form, then the society the novel depicts *does* offer a moral standard in terms of which Lizzie can be judged wanting, an alternative which she could have known about and should have chosen.

Juliet McMaster and Stephen Wall believe that Lucy's sub-plot does indeed affirm a set of traditional moral standards by which Lizzie can be condemned. McMaster argues that Lucy and Lizzie are allegorical characters representing truth and falsehood, like Una and Duessa in *The Faerie Queene*. The novel portrays their struggle for the soul of Frank Greystock, who plays the role of a feckless Redcrosse Knight, a struggle in which Lucy ultimately and rightly triumphs. Wall also sees Frank's final allegiance as the acid test of moral value in the novel. Even though Trollope finds Lizzie a fascinating character, Wall claims, 'there is bound to be a limit to the official sympathy she can expect, as the fact that in the end she is consigned to Emilius rather than Frank shows' (Wall 272).

But by making Frank's allegiance both the touchstone of value and the reward of virtue, this approach privileges form over content in a highly questionable manner. The heroines of romantic comedy are often rewarded for exemplifying approved moral values by marriage with a deserving hero. But if the hero is not particularly deserving, it becomes much more difficult to view his allegiance as either the reward or the proof of the heroine's virtue. And many critics of *The Eustace Diamonds* have indeed found Frank to be a deeply compromised character, whose eleventh-hour reformation is by no means sufficient to reassure the reader that he deserves Lucy or will make her happy. Thus Kincaid argues that Frank 'does more than touch pitch lightly; he wallows in it' (Kincaid 203).

On such a reading, this sub-plot is not the straightforward romantic comedy, ending in the vindication of Lucy's moral commitments, that McMaster and Wall take it to be. Rather it is an ironic parody of true comedy that ends in moral compromise, when Lucy ensures her own social salvation by accepting a man who has proved himself unworthy of her love. If she is to marry Frank, Lucy must convince herself, against decisive evidence to the contrary, that 'there was no sin to be forgiven. Everything was, and had been, just as it ought to be' (LXXVII). Were Lucy to acknowledge how badly Frank has behaved, she could hardly promise him obedience at the altar with a happy heart or a clear conscience. To avoid this alternative, Lucy begins to deceive herself—and so takes a moral giant step in Lizzie's direction. If Lucy's integrity has proved susceptible to the same pressures that buffeted Lizzie and Lucinda, how can she be said to embody a standard by which their conduct can be judged? And if she does not embody such a standard, where in the novel can it be found?

Readers of *The Eustace Diamonds*, from its earliest reviewers to its most recent critics, who have found the romantic sub-plot clichéd or generally unsatisfactory may be reacting exactly as Trollope wished them to react. When he wrote this novel, Trollope was at the height of his powers, so one need not immediately attribute the uneasy sensations that Lucy's story has evoked to a failure of his art. One can at least entertain an alternative explanation: the novel's romantic sub-plot may confirm the moral pessimism of its central story.

Trollope conceived *The Eustace Diamonds* in December 1869, when he began writing a four-volume novel with that title. He offered the projected work to John Blackwood for serialization in *Blackwood's Edinburgh Magazine*, beginning in the spring of 1871, but Blackwood declined to make an arrangement so far in advance. Trollope then sold the novel to Chapman & Hall for £2,500. In January 1870, Trollope stopped work on *The Eustace Diamonds* in order to write his *Commentaries of Caesar*, a foray into classical scholarship that excited him more than the prospect of producing another work of fiction. He returned to the novel three months later and completed it in August. Chapman & Hall arranged for *The Eustace Diamonds* to begin serialization in the *Fortnightly Review* (which at this time appeared only once a month) in July 1871. Trollope was then touring Australia and New Zealand. The novel continued its run during most of his nineteen-month absence and was published in book form in late 1872. The manuscript is in the Robert H. Taylor Collection, Princeton University.   JN

Kincaid, James, *The Novels of Anthony Trollope* (1977).
McMaster, Juliet, *Trollope's Palliser Novels* (1978).
Wall, Stephen, *Trollope and Character* (1988).

an extreme and frightening portrait of puritanism seeking to repress normal instincts is Mrs Bolton, the heroine's tyrannical mother in *John Caldigate.*

In *Rachel Ray*, the evangelicals are cold, prudish, obsessed with money, and converse through biblical quotations. And Rachel spiritedly objects to the 'Dorcas Meetings', because the women who attend them are vulgar. But it is in the claustrophobic Littlebath of *Miss Mackenzie* that Trollope best reveals the intimate workings of provincial evangelical society—the tea parties and church bazaars, the backbiting, the manipulation of women by clergymen, and the unhealthy cult of personality among the flock of 'Stumfoldian ladies'. Here the excessive individualism of evangelicalism, which gives rise to rivalry between the clergy, also results in a comic loss of reserve, when Mr Stumfold slanders his curate.　　　　　　　　　　　　　　GH

Cunningham, Valentine, *Everywhere Spoken Against* (1975).

Evans, Gregory, editor of the *Carmarthen Herald.* He campaigns to force Henry Jones to defend himself publicly against the paper's libellous suggestions that he interfered with his uncle's will. *CH*　　　　　　　　　　　　　AWJ

Everett, Edward (1794–1865), Professor of Greek Literature at Harvard (1815–20), Governor of Massachusetts (1836–40), minister to the Court of St James (1841–5). Everett was sought out by Frances Trollope during her American sojourn, and became a family friend. In Boston (November 1861) Trollope attended a lecture by Everett on 'The Causes and Conduct of the Civil War'. He disliked the lecture for its anti-Southern fervour and uncomplimentary references to England. In *North America* he elaborated: 'I did not like what he said, or the seeming spirit in which it was framed. But I am bound to admit that his power of oratory is very wonderful' (*NA* 1, 349).　　　　　　　　　　　　　RCT

Ewing, Captain, dancing partner for most of the evening with flirtatious Marian Leslie, complicating her relationship with Maurice Cumming. 'Jack' *TAC1*　　　　　　　　GRH

Exeter. Jemima Stanbury lives here in the Close, near the cathedral. Trollope's attachment to Exeter and the West Country shows in many locations in *He Knew He Was Right*. In *Framley Parsonage* Dr Robarts practises in the city, which also provides locales in *Kept in the Dark*.　　RC

Eye for an Eye, An (see below)

Eyre, Governor Edward John (1815–1901). He emigrated to Australia in 1832 where he worked as sheep farmer and overlander. Appointed resident magistrate (1836), his humanitarianism won him the title 'Protector of the Aborigine'. In 1854 he was sent to the West Indies and became Governor of Jamaica in 1862. His administration initially engendered difficulties with the white planters and the Assembly, but in 1865 his harsh suppression of a native uprising through imposition of martial law, floggings, and executions caused uproar in England and forced his recall. A government inquiry was launched, and the public debate that ensued, known as the Governor Eyre Controversy, centred around use of martial law to control colonial populations. It focused middle- and upper-class anxieties about maintaining the empire and fears over working-class agitation for suffrage. Eyre's supporters, including Dickens, Carlyle, and Ruskin, feared similar domestic agitations and formed the Eyre Defence and Aid Fund. J. S. Mill's Jamaica Committee sought to prosecute Eyre for murder (1866). The effort to indict Eyre failed. Trollope's attitude to the Eyre Controversy was never explicit, but he was probably in Mill's camp, since his friend Charles *Buxton had helped organize the Jamaica Committee.　　　　　　RCT

Eye for an Eye, An

TROLLOPE wrote this short novel in less than a month (13 September–10 October 1870) before commencing *Phineas Redux.* In June he had returned to Ireland, after many years' absence, and may have recalled the time he and his wife lived at Milltown Malbay, Co. Clare (February–June 1845), in the course of his postal duties (Super 283). Some miles north of that town stand the Cliffs of Moher: the ideal setting for a romance which, in certain respects, reworks the earlier story of Phineas Finn who relinquished political power and a brilliant marriage in order to keep faith with his Irish fiancée Mary Flood Jones. Fred Neville also returns to his Irish love, but with fatal results.

This tale of innocence betrayed unfolds with the simplicity of folk ballad or (depending on one's viewpoint) the creakings of Victorian melodrama. Fred is handsome, sociable, and, as nephew and heir to Lord Scroope, generously funded. But he is not yet ready for the responsibilities of his position, preferring to remain with the 20th Hussars in Ireland for a year's 'adventure'. Posted to Ennis, he is relieved to find a man of means can still grace Limerick's balls and coverts or even those of Galway. In Clare he appears in nautical kit to shoot seals and seagulls. Meeting the O'Hara ladies on the cliffs, he behaves charmingly to both until continued proximity to the beautiful Kate leads to that flower which, once plucked, loses its attractions. Then letters arrive from the dissolute Captain O'Hara, and Fred thinks the ladies have deceived him: it might now be possible to break his troth. Detecting that change in him, Mrs O'Hara bursts into Fred's rooms at Ennis, demanding satisfaction: the same sort of embarrassment happened (less pregnantly) to Charley Tudor (*TC*), Johnny Eames (*LCB*), and, as he would later confess (*Auto*), young Trollope. Fred hurries to England when his uncle dies. The new Earl could have stayed there, but his conscience forbids that. He returns to offer Kate everything except legal wedlock. Maddened by this, Mrs O'Hara sends him over the cliff-edge: an eye for an eye.

Read for its story (a short 'foreword' in a private asylum encourages this how-did-things-happen approach), the novel seems trite: Kate is an innocent cipher and Fred, for the most part, a naive dreamer. Mrs O'Hara emits melodramatic ferocity with her hard eyes and flaring nostrils, the dagger she draws on her sottish husband, her threats to destroy Fred if he betrays her daughter. But the scene on the cliffs is strangely muted: Fred is so used to those heights that he feels no danger, and Mrs O'Hara's intentions are harmless until the last brief moments. Unlike Trollope's other short novels, which explore the dynamics of lonely, troubled minds, this tale lacks intensity. Its interests lie beyond plot or character in the book's thematic patterning.

The novel was originally designed for serialization in six segments of four chapters each. Trollope balances those units against each other to illustrate the way Fred gravitates, with increasing urgency, between social and moral principles until he topples to his death. For example, the first segment concentrates almost exclusively on Scroope Manor. Welcomed as his uncle's heir, Fred finds things gloomy and old-fashioned. The Earl is sedentary; his Countess selflessly devout; like their mansion, which backs onto the village street in long lines of Tudor brick, they seem to have turned from the world (Robert Tracy, *Trollope's Later Novels* (1978), 137). But Trollope takes us beyond that dullness to the old Earl's daily conference with his steward, groom, and butler, his occasional talks with the parson 'so that he might know the wants of the people', moments of silent tenderness with his wife: 'Few men perhaps did less—but what he did do was good; and of self-indulgence there was surely none' (1. II). By the end of these chapters, when news of Fred's first adventures in Ireland has filtered back to Scroope, the Earl's warning that his carefree nephew is 'bound by every duty to God and man' to marry suitably carries weight and substance (1. IV).

The second sequence, in Co. Clare, reverses things. Moher's gloomy isolation deepens Mrs O'Hara's melancholy and locks Kate in a lifeless prison. But the screaming gulls and whirling spray enrapture Fred; Quin Castle's ladies cannot vie with the O'Haras' wild beauty; dinner at Father Marty's cottage seems adventure indeed. We perceive the callowness behind such 'freedom'. But Fred, when cautioned by the priest to respect Kate's virtue, cannot imagine hurting her. She will be his bride once his uncle dies.

A third sequence brings Fred's social and moral obligations into collision. Scroope's dullness is increased by the Earl's illness, brought on by rumours from Ireland: the heir has nothing to shoot or hunt; days end early. Yet Lady Scroope's appeals to duty have an effect which Trollope symbolizes in an episode where Fred stares abstractedly at his ancestors' fusty portraits: manly duty and feminine grace. Gradually Fred considers a morganatic union, is irritated by Kate's 'French hand-writing', and ashamed to show her letter to Sophie Mellerby, a duke's granddaughter. Touring the estate, he resents the steward's lecture but does begin to care and, impressed by his uncle's minute concern for the land and its tenants, 'understood . . . Kate O'Hara ought not to be made Countess of Scroope' (1. XII).

Yet despite these resonant patterns, Fred remains a *Boy's Own* romancer who thinks difficulties are every adventurer's lot. Those difficulties are far more interesting, particularly as they concern Victorian proprieties: the marriage market, sexual double standards, a gentleman's responsibility.

Sophie Mellerby understands her role. Knowing Fred's status, she will fall in love if his character accords with his wealth, good looks, and affability. Fred feels put upon, despite the tact of those behind the scenes, but, when his younger brother Jack proposes, Sophie is too well schooled to accept a misalliance. Kate O'Hara is also a lady, though she has neither fortune nor ancestry, and her Catholicism is anathema to the Protestant Scroopes. Mrs O'Hara would defend her like a tiger against wolves, but, as Father Marty advises, nothing ventured nothing gained. The risks Kate runs are greater, but so are the rewards. Her breeding places her above Ennistimon's swains, but her protector, Father Marty, 'entertained no prejudice against a good looking Protestant youth when a fortunate marriage was in question' (1. VII). Quin Castle and Scroope Manor would see that as the design of 'an unscrupulous intriguing ruffian', but Trollope implies that Kate and Sophie are essentially similar, though on different levels of sophistication.

Lady Scroope and Mrs O'Hara share a fierce morality, though on different sides of the sexual balance. The Countess is prepared to lower her standards for young men but, should they go too far, she has no compassion for women: 'Lady Scroope had the name of being a very charitable woman . . . But she would have no more mercy on such a one as Miss O'Hara, than a farmer's labourer would have on a rat!' (1. IX). Moral scruples give way to social principles as she entreats Fred to dishonour his pledge rather than sully the earldom of Scroope. Mrs O'Hara also bends to men, knowing that the world would otherwise offer her daughter nothing 'but hopes of eternity' (1. V). Yet despite her complicity in Kate's seduction, she too puts family honour above the ten commandments and exacts a justice that no 'Court in the world [would] have given' (2. XI). 'Raging with a maddened pride', she ends her days in an asylum, whereas the Countess shuts herself away in guilt-ridden solitude, knowing in her conscience she was wrong.

But it is Fred's ultimate awakening to his responsibilities as a gentleman that leads him to the cliff-edge. He tries to balance his promise to the Earl against his pledge to the O'Haras by suggesting that his brother should live at Scroope (and marry Sophie) while he roams the world with Kate (as Mrs Neville). But Jack sees the folly of that and, with his own sense of gentlemanly honour, urges him to marry Kate legally. Fred tries again with Father Marty, hoping the worldly priest may perform some sort of counterfeit marriage. But Marty is no romantic either and commands him to keep his word to Kate. Fred is no blackguard. Through his uncle's exemplar, he has come to understand the family's motto, *sans reproche*, and so returns to Ireland to answer the reproaches of Father Marty and Mrs O'Hara. He will offer Kate everything except the title that would shame him and bring her misery. 'What an ass had he made himself . . . in quest of adventures! . . . he could see no way out of the ruin he had brought upon himself' (2. XI). In his own eyes he is a gentleman; in Mrs O'Hara's he is a monster.

The manuscript remained in Trollope's strongbox until 1878, when it was serialized by the *Whitehall Review* in 24 weekly parts (24 August–1 February 1879), thus obscuring the novel's ethical schema. It was published in two volumes by Chapman & Hall, January 1879. Reviews were few and unenthusiastic. Only the *Spectator* found it praiseworthy. The manuscript is held at Princeton University.   AWJ

F

Faddle, Samuel, fatuous young friend of Tom Tringle and fellow member of the Mountaineers Club. Faddle's foolish behaviour leads his father to banish him to Aberdeen: 'Our friend Tom saw nothing more of his faithful friend till years had rolled over both their heads' (XXXVI). *AA*   WK

Fairlawn, Mr, master of the hounds of the Hitchin Hunt, who intrudes upon Mr Harkaway's coverts during the Cumberlow Green Hunt, an act of territorial violation which pits the members of each hunt against the other. *MSF*   MT

Fairstairs, Charlotte (Charlie), young woman a little too long in the marriage market. Though neither young, attractive, nor having a particularly mild temper, Miss Fairstairs benefits mightily from the tuition of Arabella Greenow, and ultimately manages to persuade the wealthy Mr Cheesacre to marry her. *CYFH*   JMR

Faithfull, Emily (1836–95), advocate of women's issues, particularly employment; lecturer and founder of the Victoria Press (1860). Her base of operations was Langham Place, which housed the Society for Promoting the Employment of Women, its activists being 'the Ladies of Langham Place'. Trollope associated with them sympathetically, but never budged from his stand on the best women's right being a husband. Emily Faithfull founded a printing company staffed by women. Trollope dubbed her 'that female Caxton of the Age' (*Letters* 1, 220). He contributed without charge 'A Journey to Panama' to her *Victoria Regia* (1861) and 'Miss Ophelia

Gledd' to another of her publications, *A Welcome* (1863).   RCT

Fane, Lady Rose Sophia Mary (1834–1921), second daughter of the 11th Earl of Westmorland, keenly interested in the arts. In 1866 she married the artist Henry Weigall, a member of the Athenaeum Club, to which Trollope also belonged. As guest of Lord Houghton at Fryston in January 1866, she met the Trollopes, and wrote of them to her mother with cordial disdain: 'I wish I had never seen Mr Trollope, I think he is detestable—vulgar and noisy & domineering—a mixture of Dickens vulgarity & Mr Burtons self-sufficiency—as unlike his books as possible' (*Letters* 1, 321). Of Rose Trollope she observed: 'a quiet sort of woman & wd. be well enough only she has perfectly white hair which is coiffé en cheveux [bareheaded]—in the most fashionable way with (last night) a little rose stuck in it wh: looks most absurd.' *Letters* 1, 321 n.   RCT

Faragon, Mme. A fierce, suspicious old woman with a romantic soul, she is a distant cousin of Michel Voss and proprietor of the Hôtel de la Poste in Colmar. *GLG*   MG

Farmer, nursemaid to the Trollope family. One of Trollope's earliest memories was of himself aged 3 being helped by her to his 'minced mutton mixed with potatoes and gravy' (Mullen 16). Farmer made clothes and repaired shoes for the children, and when Trollope and Tom were at Winchester sent cake as an occasional treat. Her grimness and austerity produced a ditty: 'Old Farmer is an Anabaptist! | When she is gone, she will not be missed!' (quoted Mullen 17). However, she remained a loyal retainer for many years.   RCT

farmers as characters. One aspect of the perennial appeal of Trollope's novels is his concern with land, both as an enduring source of traditional values, and as a potent symbol of continuity. It is reflected in his interest in farmers and farming. His fiction shows that agriculture was still very much the basis of English life. The tenant farmer in *Rachel Ray*, Farmer Sturt, with his dialect and simple wisdom, and his wife with her utilitarian parlour, although marginal figures, contribute a detailed realism to the portrayal of a significant provincial community. In *The Last Chronicle of Barset*, Mary Crawley feels able to call on Farmer Mangle to spare her husband a long walk between Hogglestock and Barchester.

In his novels Trollope drew on his own experience of living close to the land as a boy, when he saw at first hand his father's disastrous venture in farming 160 acres (65 ha) of land leased at Harrow, an enterprise he combined with his work as a Chancery barrister. (Their farmhouse, called Julian Hill, was the original for 'Orley Farm' in the novel of that name.)

Trollope admires those gentlemen farmers who take an interest in their land such as Larry Twentyman in *The American Senator*, although, in the same novel, farmer Dan Goarly is suspected of poisoning foxes. Will Belton in *The Belton Estate* pursues his career in spite of doubts raised about his gentlemanly status. Above such anxieties are Earl De Guest in *The Small House at Allington*, Lord Grassangrains in *Is He Popenjoy?*, and in *Barchester Towers* Archdeacon Grantly, who is both clergyman and landowner, and whose concern with the latest development in fertilizers is shared by the experimental farmer Lucius Mason in *Orley Farm*.

Farmers also provide comedy. There is the social climbing of the aptly named Lookalofts in *Barchester Towers*, who call their house Rosebank, and are contrasted with the unpretentious tenant-farming Greenacres. In *Can You Forgive Her?* there is the comic portrait of one of Widow Greenow's suitors, the dull gentleman farmer Cheesacre. GH

Farrar, Sir George Herbert (1859–1915), director of the East Rand Proprietory Mines and member of the Transvaal Legislative Council; served in the South African War (1899–1900); was made baronet in 1911. Trollope met him in 1877, while preparing to visit the Kimberley diamond mines. Farrar was an adventurous 18-year-old, the kind of youth who appealed to Trollope: 'a gentleman of about a third of my own age, who had been sent out by an agricultural machinery company to sell to farmers.' Together they bought a cart and four horses and made the exhausting journey to Kimberley, camping out on the veld. Trollope wrote to Henry: 'Heat here— 96—shade, 160—sun; supposed heat in Infernal Regions—94—shade(?), 156—full brimstone' (*Letters* 2, 743). Six miles (10 km) out of Kimberley they lost a portmanteau and retraced their steps in search of it without success. It contained Trollope's manuscript for his travel book *South Africa*. Next day it was recovered. RCT

Farrar, Thomas Henry (1819–99). Beginning in politics at the Board of Trade (1850), Farrar became Permanent Secretary until 1886; he was created baronet (1893) for public service. He wrote copiously on finance and trade issues, notably *Free Trade versus Fair Trade* (1882) and *Studies in Currency* (1898). Trollope knew him through the Athenaeum. They crossed swords, however, when Farrar, testifying at the Copyright Commission, said he would be 'sorry' to hear that men like Scott or Dickens wrote for money.

This raised a Trollopian storm as he rounded on the witness: 'Do you not think an author is in exactly the same category as any other workman, who has it upon his conscience to use his life for doing good work for the world around him and who cannot do that good work unless he is paid for it' (quoted Mullen 599). RCT

fashion. The dress of Victorian woman was restrictive, and even when adapted for work, hampered activity: her long skirts could weigh between fifteen and twenty pounds (7–9 kg). Crinolines came into fashion in the late 1850s, and continued to be an indicator of taste and style until 1866 or 1867.

Trollope accurately places a woman in her class and in her type by describing her dress. His description of Lily Dale's muslin party dress, goffered by her mother, which billows out like a bud bursting into flower as she gives Crosbie a deep curtsy, is observant, knowledgeable, and a significant metaphor (*SHA* IX). Marion Fay (*MF*), loved almost on the strength of her simple brown dress, is typical of many of his brown merino-clad heroines. The whiteness of their collars and cuffs is a telling barometer of approval. His satiric attack often focuses on grubbiness of dress: Sophie Gordeloup's morning wrapper (*TC* XXIV), Feemy's visible underwear and dirty hair curlers (*MB* VIII), and Lizzie Eustace's dress soiled from her train journey—such smuts would not have stuck to Lucy Morris (*ED* LXXVI).

Trollope detested all extremes of fashion, particularly crinolines and false hair. When *Millais drew a picture of Lucy Robarts in an elaborately flounced crinoline for the first edition of *Framley Parsonage*, Trollope wrote to his publisher that the picture was simply ludicrous—a burlesque. One of his chief signifiers of virgin-heroine is that her hair is simply dressed, and all her own. Dorothy Stanbury gets extra approval for her ringlets 'that won't be hurt by a little cold water' (*HKWR* VIII).

Trollope's burlesques on extremes of fashion reach their apogee with attacks on Arabella and Camilla French (*HKWR*), with their bare shoulders, lace that is none too clean, and, above all, their hair. It was fashionable to slick back one's own hair with pomade and fasten onto it a false front, with a chignon bulking up the back hair. Arabella's chignon grows by the day, and develops a personality of its own; in a passage of high comedy, Mr Gibson imagines being married to it. MM

'Father Giles of Ballymoy', first published in *Argosy*, May 1866 (reprinted in *LS*). Archibald Green (who also appears in the 'The O'Conors of

Castle Connor' and 'Miss Ophelia Gledd') finds himself in an Irish village on business for a week. He puts up at Kirwan's, the local hotel, and wakes up to find a strange man in his room, evidently intending to get into bed with him. A scuffle ensues and the intruder, who turns out to be the wholly respectable local priest, Father Giles, is thrown downstairs. Everything is cleared up and the two men become fast friends in subsequent years. JS

Fawkes, Lionel Grimston (1849–1931), subaltern in the Royal Artillery and amateur artist. His drawings for *The Way We Live Now* (1875) have been described as 'the very nadir in illustrations' for Trollope's novels (N. John Hall, *Trollope and his Illustrators* (1980), 482). Trollope had introduced him to Chapman. After the fourth instalment Trollope may have realized his error, but would not admit it. RCT

Fawn, Viscount Frederick, practically useless fixture of the Liberal government. Divided between pride and fear, spoiled by his mother and sisters, the easily daunted Lord Fawn seeks unsuccessfully to fortify his family's failing fortunes through matrimony, first pursuing Violet Effingham, then Mme Goesler (*PF*), before entering into a tumultuous engagement with Lizzie Eustace (*ED*). Ultimately, Lord Fawn falls into marriage with a 'pretty, mincing' flirtatious woman many years his junior. Perhaps most memorable for his role in the trial of Phineas Finn, Lord Fawn offers evidence against Phineas during the investigation of Mr Bonteen's death, but he is forced to retreat from society after being crushed by the vigorous cross-examination of Mr Chaffanbrass. *PR, PM, DC* JMR

Fawn, Lady, dowager of the Fawn family, doting mother of Frederick and his eight sisters, and affectionate mistress to her governess Lucy Morris. Full of matronly advice and good humour, though reluctant to interfere, Lady Fawn is especially anxious to save Lucy Morris and Lord Fawn from unwise marriages. *ED* JMR

Fawn Court, the well-appointed but economical suburban residence of Lord Fawn and his mother and sisters. Here Lucy Morris resides as governess for the younger Fawn girls and here she meets with her lover Frank Greystock. *ED*
JMR

Fay, Marion, graceful and earnest eponymous heroine whose romance revolves around her steadfast mutual love with Lord Hampstead. Despite his passionate entreaties and 'womanly' devotion, she continually refuses to marry him, fearing that her middle-class Quaker background and manners would detract from his high rank;

awareness of her impending death by consumption confirms her refusal. A strong sense of duty to her father and to her lover's right to happiness, combined with her untimely death, make her one of Trollope's few tragic heroines. *MF*
SRB

Fay, Zachary, stern, serious Quaker clerk whose only love in life is his daughter Marion. He accepts Lord Hampstead's suit for Marion's hand but protects Marion's privacy and nurses his own grief when she is dying of consumption, as did her mother and siblings. *MF* SRB

Fenwick, Frank, imprudent, friendly, well-meaning vicar of Bullhampton, popular and zealous in his parishioners' interests. His combative nature makes him fight midnight intruders in his garden, take on the offensive Marquis of Trowbridge, and strive for justice for his young friend Sam Brattle and for reformation of the fallen Carry Brattle. He is gracious to his rival Mr Puddleham, the Dissenting minister, despite the building of an ugly Methodist chapel beside the vicarage. He and his wife unsuccessfully urge an unfortunate match between his good friend Harry Gilmore and Mary Lowther. *VB* SRB

Fenwick, Janet, the engaging, cheerful wife of the vicar of Bullhampton. She loves and admires her husband enormously and works tirelessly to encourage a match between his close friend Harry Gilmore and her friend Mary Lowther, but she finally admits it is a failure. She is particularly offended by the ugly Methodist chapel built upon her doorstep, and strongly defends her husband's right to resist it. *VB* SRB

Fiasco, Major, discontented member of the Board of Commissioners of the General Committee Office. Brooding over injuries and slights, Major Fiasco now merely fills a chair, signs his name, and contends with the chairman, Mr Optimist, believing all men to be sly, dishonest rogues. *SHA* NCS

Field, Mary Katherine Keemle (Kate) (1838–1896), American feminist, actress, and journalist; daughter of actor-playwright Joseph M. Field. She sought out celebrities in England and Europe, such as Dickens, Landor, and the Brownings. Friendship with the Trollopes began with Thomas Adolphus at the Villino Trollope in Florence, where she first met Anthony and liked his 'almost boyish enthusiasm'. In the autumn of 1860 she wrote to her aunt, 'Anthony Trollope is a very delightful companion. I see a great deal of him.' He sent her a copy of *Arabian Nights*, and henceforth ensued the lifelong attachment to the woman who, outside his own family, became his closest friend (*Auto* XVII). The precise nature of-

Kate Field, a crayon drawing by Vanderweyde, London (1878). An attractive and vivacious American, who became an actress and journalist, she undoubtedly influenced Trollope's heroines, especially American girls. In *An Autobiography* Trollope wrote of her as 'out of my own family, my most chosen friend … a ray of light to me, from which I can always strike a spark by thinking of her' (XVII).

this relationship has aroused much speculation. It proceeded on his part in terms of coyly avuncular flirtatiousness, not without erotic overtones. He ended one letter (July 1868) 'with a kiss that shall be semi-paternal—one third brotherly, and as regards the small remainder, as loving as you please' (*Letters* 1, 438), which seems a masterly exercise in the sanctioned pattern of Victorian flirtations. Her responses are tantalizingly brief, like her diary note in May 1868: 'Met Anthony Trollope. Same as ever.' She was extremely vital, personable, and physically attractive, and being photographed with him in sultry New York (mid-July 1868) does suggest an intimacy which might have troubled Rose had she not been broad-minded. If she felt pangs of jealousy she accepted the situation gracefully, although the only surviving letter to Rose suggests a crisis of some kind in December 1862. Kate was ambitious in her career as lecturer and advocate of women's issues, both of which gave Trollope opportunities for playful scolding. He criticized her frankly, mostly because she dabbled. 'I fear you are idle,' he admonished in January 1862 (*Letters* 1, 168). For the reader of Trollope's novels what matters is how this friendship influenced his portrayal of young heroines (particularly Americans) and the vicissitudes of long-standing marriages.   RCT

Field, Nora. Her principles demand a real sacrifice after she receives a legacy of £100, and she insists on merino instead of white silk for her wedding to save £15 for victims of the Cotton Famine. 'Widow' *LS*   GRH

Fielding, Edward. Bridegroom of Harry Clavering's sister Mary, he holds the family living of Humbleton, a parish near Clavering. Though he has more social grace than his father-in-law's curate Mr Saul, he is not morally as considerable. He preaches a dexterous sermon on the virtues of those contemptible brothers Sir Hugh and Archibald Clavering. *C*   PJT

Fielding, Henry (1707–54), author of *Tom Jones* (1749) and other robust picaresque novels whose work Trollope preferred to that of his contemporary Samuel Richardson. In the lecture 'On English Prose Fiction' Trollope noted that Dickens's characters had not the likeness to human nature that Fielding's had. When the collected 'Chronicles of Barsetshire' were published (March 1878), Trollope pointed out that neither Fielding nor Dickens had ventured on the series form.   RCT

Fields, James Thomas (1817–1881), partner in Ticknor & Fields, publishers, of Boston; editor of *Atlantic Monthly* (1861–70). He first met Trollope at a *Cornhill* dinner and took to him immedi-

ately. Visiting Waltham House in May 1860, he passed on Hawthorne's praise of his novels, which Trollope quoted in *An Autobiography* (VIII). Trollope met Hawthorne at Fields's home in September 1861, and (Fields reported) liked him at first sight (*I & R* 77). The Fields connection put Trollope in touch with American men of letters.   RCT

Fildes, Sir Samuel Luke (1844–1927). Fildes began his career illustrating for *Cornhill Magazine*, *Once a Week*, and the *Graphic*, and provided illustrations for Dickens's *The Mystery of Edwin Drood* (1870) and Mark Twain's *Roughing It* (1872). He became famous for documentary subjects, of which 'The Doctor' (1891) is the best known. Early biographers mistakenly identified Fildes as the illustrator of *The Way We Live Now* (1875), although those drawings were actually by Lionel Grimston Fawkes.   RCT

Fillgrave, Dr, Barchester physician who quarrels with Dr Thomas Thorne in the papers and in the treatment of Sir Roger Scatcherd. Pompous and probably ineffective, he nevertheless is called to oversee the deaths of many prominent Barchester citizens, including Dean Trefoil and Septimus Harding. *DT, BT, FP, LCB*   NCS

Finn, Dr Malachi, Irish Roman Catholic physician, father of Phineas. A practical man, Dr Finn urges Phineas to forgo his parliamentary aspirations for a law career, but despite the doctor's moderate means, he generously offers to support his son's political vocation. *PF*   JMR

Finn, Phineas, young Liberal politician, the principal subject of two of the Palliser novels. Phineas Finn is the son of an Irish doctor from Killaloe, in Co. Clare. He overcomes prejudice against his Irish Catholic background and the disadvantages of youth and poverty to achieve great success in English politics. Initially elected to represent Irish Loughshane, Phineas later serves as Liberal member of Parliament for the English boroughs of Loughton and Tankerville. Always popular, Phineas wins the friendship of such luminaries as Joshua Monk and the young Duke of Omnium. His social and political success may be attributed largely to abiding honesty, hard work, and natural intelligence, but his charm, easy manner, and good looks are also important assets. These characteristics, too, make him a favourite with women, including Lady Laura Kennedy, Mme Goesler, and the Duchess of Omnium. Somewhat fickle in his youth, Phineas is beset by romantic difficulties, political upheaval, debt, even a murder trial. Despite adversity, however, Phineas always seems to land on his feet, explaining perhaps why he is typically regarded as Fortune's child. In the later Palliser novels, Phineas, devoted husband of the former Marie Goesler, appears as a regular parliamentary fixture. *PF, PR, PM, DC*   JMR

Finn, Mrs Phineas. See GOESLER, MARIE.

Finney, Mr, Barchester attorney who induces John Bold to reform Hiram's Hospital. He dreams of financial and political advancement when the *Jupiter* takes up the cause. He attends Mrs Proudie's reception in *Barchester Towers* and the Duke of Omnium's dinner in *Doctor Thorne,* where he also acts for Sir Louis Scatcherd. *W*
                                          NCS

Finucane, Mr. His 'various rings' and Ennistimon 'demesne' fail to impress Fred Neville, who circumvents his desire, at Father Marty's dinner party, to go adventuring. *EE*   AWJ

Fisker, Hamilton K., dapper American entrepreneur. He makes Augustus Melmotte head of a questionable American railway scheme, thus involving enormous English financial speculation. Untroubled by scruples, he supplies confidence and dash to the enterprise. When it crashes, he marries Marie Melmotte and takes her back to San Francisco with him. *WWLN*   SRB

Fitzallen, Albert, young druggist who marries Mary Snow: 'a pale-faced, light-haired youth, with an incipient moustache, with his hair parted in equal divisions over his forehead, with elaborate shirt-cuffs elaborately turned back, and with a white apron tied round him so that he might pursue his vocation without injury to his nether garments' (LVII). One kiss under a lamp-post seals his love for Mary. *OF*   MT

Fitzapplejohn, Anastasia, abandoned love of John Thomas. 'Never'   RCT

Fitzgerald, Burgo, stunningly handsome and wildly impetuous young man who seeks first to elope with Lady Glencora M'Cluskie and then to run off with her after she has become Lady Glencora Palliser. Although Lady Glencora loves Fitzgerald deeply, she is frightened out of marrying him because he is considered 'dangerous' and immoral. Sweet-tempered and kind, whatever Fitzgerald does, he does with absolute vigour and without the least care for the future. Thus he waltzes with Lady Glencora Palliser at a party given by his aunt Lady Monk, regardless of the shocked faces of those looking on. Thus he hunts, constantly risking his neck. And thus he seeks to gamble away his last coin when the Pallisers happen upon him abroad. Trollope suggests that perhaps Fitzgerald's beauty has led him astray, as people seem always to be more impressed with the man's 'brightly blue' eyes and

'godlike' form than with his character. *CYFH*
                                          JMR

Fitzgerald, Edward (1809–83), Poet, translator of *The Rubáiyát of Omar Khayyám* (1859). He paid a young man to read Trollope's novels aloud, expressing forthright opinions on them. In March 1860 he found that his enjoyment of novels returned whenever Trollope's arrived. *Framley Parsonage* was almost as fascinating as the *Tichborne case, and he thought *The Prime Minister* his only dull novel. Usually Fitzgerald wanted to argue with his reader (who never replied) about what was said and done by Trollope's characters. Changing once to *The Mill on the Floss,* he could not endure it and exclaimed, 'Oh for some more brave Trollope' (*I & R* 129–33). See *Letters of Edward Fitzgerald* (2 vols., 1980). Trollope consulted him when writing his short biography of Thackeray.   RCT

Fitzgerald, Emmeline and **Mary,** sisters of Herbert Fitzgerald, who loyally urge their disinherited brother to pursue his suit with Lady Clara Desmond. *CR*   MRS

Fitzgerald, Herbert, wrongly disinherited English heir of Castle Richmond, Ireland. Productive in helping to relieve the Irish famine, loyal to his family despite being deemed 'nobody's son', and steadfast to Lady Clara despite her former attachment to Owen Fitzgerald, he is more acted upon than acting, making for a quiescent though stalwart hero. *CR*   MRS

Fitzgerald, Letty, unmarried elderly sister of Sir Thomas, who, though living in Ireland, a predominantly Catholic country, harbours extreme anti-Catholic feelings. She is unsentimental, strong, and proud of family rank, but when faced with the shame of her family's apparent illegitimacy, she demonstrates that love is stronger than pride when she determines to leave Castle Richmond with Lady Fitzgerald, loyally declaring that 'Whither she goes, I will go, and where she lodges, I will lodge; her people shall be my people, and her God my God' (XXXII). *CR*
                                          MRS

Fitzgerald, Lady Mary (née **Wainright**). Victim of a bigamous marriage in early youth, but later married to Sir Thomas Fitzgerald, her indeterminate marital status provides the motor of a disinheritance plot of tragic dimensions. Presented as an ideal of gentle womanhood, she nevertheless displays greater courage than her husband. While he escapes grief and ruin through an early death, she, who 'was made of more enduring material' (XXVII), lives to see her family rights reinstated. *CR*   MRS

Fitzgerald, Owen. Strong, bold, and handsome, a compound of all the manly virtues except a large inheritance, he is first accepted then rejected by Lady Clara, adored by her mother the Countess, and hero-worshipped by her brother the Earl. Though generally accounted a roué, he not only proves unswervingly loyal to Lady Clara, but refuses to accept the title to the Fitzgerald estate. *CR*   MRS

Fitzgerald, Percy Hetherington (1829–1925), journalist, biographer, minor novelist, close friend of Dickens, and founder of the Boz Club. Trollope put him up successfully for the Garrick (January 1876) and sealed his friendship. In some embarrassment Fitzgerald reviewed *Reade's Shilly-Shally*, adapted from *Ralph the Heir*, for the *Observer*.   RCT

Fitzgerald, Sir Thomas, respected Baronet blackmailed by his wife's first husband, whose reappearance threatens the legitimacy of his marriage, his children, and his son's right of inheritance. Devoted to his family, Sir Thomas nevertheless lacks the courage to rise above the burden of their dispossession: the 'hot iron had entered his soul, and shrivelled up the very muscles of his mind's strength' (XXII). Crushed by his family's loss of name and estate, he dies before evidence arrives to ensure their triumphant reinstatement. *CR*   MRS

Fitzgibbon, Aspasia, elderly spinster sister of Laurence Fitzgibbon, the only Fitzgibbon with any fortune. Slightly eccentric and with an acerbic sense of humour, Miss Fitzgibbon has a warm-hearted affection for her brother, manifested by her relieving Phineas Finn of one of Laurence's debts. *PF*   JMR

Fitzgibbon, Laurence, Liberal member of Parliament and political friend of Phineas Finn. Though an eloquent speaker, Fitzgibbon is without political convictions, and is willing to say whatever is most convenient to his party; he cares little for parliamentary honours except in so far as they keep him out of debtor's prison. Fitzgibbon stands as Phineas's second in the duel with Lord Chiltern. *PF, ED, PR, PM*   JMR

Fitzpatrick, Barney. See BARNEY.

Fixed Period, The (*see opposite*)

Flannelly, Joe, builder of the Macdermots' 'fine, showy house' (II) and holder of the mortgage, who offers his daughter Sally in marriage to Larry Macdermot. When she is rejected because of her lowly origins, he and, later, his son-in-law Hyacinth Keegan become intent on the Macdermots' ruin. *MB*   MRS

Fleabody, Olivia Q., American feminist who wrests control of the *'Disabilities'* from Baroness Banmann. Unlike her rival she is good-looking, at least without her glasses, and is rewarded with marriage to a New York shopkeeper and children. Perhaps a composite of American feminists Elizabeth Peabody, Dr Elizabeth Blackwell, and Kate Field. *IHP*   MG

Fletcher, Arthur, faithful suitor of Emily Wharton. Though Emily initially refuses Arthur Fletcher's proposals in part, perhaps, because her family approves the marriage, she also seems unimpressed by her suitor's boyishness. When he finally wins Emily's hand, Arthur has matured immensely from his parliamentary experience and from his suffering over Emily's troubled marriage with Ferdinand Lopez. *PM*   JMR

Fletcher, John, Arthur Fletcher's elder brother, head of the family, and owner of Longbarns. Both loyal and loving, he is a man of sound judgement, asking straightforward questions about Lopez's finances and advising his brother well when Arthur is disappointed in love. *PM*
                                                     JMR

Fletcher, Mr, Silverbridge butcher and creditor of Revd Josiah Crawley. He complains to Bishop Proudie and threatens to publish Crawley's debts, then receives a cheque from the clergyman that may have been stolen, which precipitates criminal charges. *LCB*   NCS

Fletcher, Mrs, mother of Arthur and John Fletcher. Mrs Fletcher is a respectable old woman but is bitterly angry at Emily Wharton's marriage to Ferdinand Lopez. Though she initially wants Emily to marry Arthur, Mrs Fletcher later suggests that her son ought not to marry the widowed Emily. *PM*   JMR

Flick, Mr, attorney for the young Earl, Frederic Lovel. 'In his way, an honest man' (V), he works diligently for his client, but turns a blind eye to evidence that might support the other side. *LA*
                                                     RC

'Flood, Field, and Forest by Mr Rooper' (review). Unlike many previous books on field sports, this one is well written and interesting. A great deal of helpful information is given without slang or jargon. *Fortnightly Review* (June 1869), 748–50.   AKL

Florence, northern Italian city, briefly the capital, and centre of foreign diplomatic activity. Charles Glascock courts and marries the niece of the American ambassador here in *He Knew He Was Right*. Florence was well loved by the Trollopes. 'Villino Trollope', home of Thomas (*cont. on page 203*)

Fixed Period, The

ONE of Trollope's most unusual novels, *The Fixed Period* blends a futuristic setting and technology with an exploration of euthanasia and cremation. The story is set in 1978–9 in the fictional island of Britannula, a thriving antipodean 'empire', which has peacefully gained independence from Great Britain. The inhabitants are the 'élite' of New Zealand, who settled the island some 30 years ago, bringing stock and plants to establish a prosperous agricultural society. Trollope includes a system of decimal coinage (Plantagenet Palliser's pet scheme in the Palliser novels) in Britannula. Ruled by the popular President Neverbend, Britannula especially prides itself on its legislative autonomy. Its most distinctive law, besides the removal of capital punishment, is that of the 'Fixed Period', a policy which determines that every citizen will undergo compulsory euthanasia at the age of 68, a year after being 'deposited' in Necropolis, a college which prepares its residents for a peaceful and honourable death. (The veins of the individual will 'be opened' while the person is tranquillized with morphine and a warm bath.) Ambiguity pervades the presentation of these concepts, from Orwellian euphemisms to Neverbend's statement, 'When I say educated I mean prejudiced' (IV).

Neverbend's first-person narration renders the telling ironic as he remains unaware of his own weakness: he does not understand the importance of emotions and the strong will to live which characterize human nature. He employs rational, utilitarian arguments in defence of the policy: people are commodities and are spoken of in terms of currency; they are 'deposited'; statistics are quoted to prove that 'by the use of machinery the college could almost be made self-supporting'; the savings will effect progressive infrastructure in railways, bridges, and transportation. The excellence of the fixed period lies more in financial savings to the country than in the general lessening of misery for feeble, useless citizens.

The fatal flaw of the system, strangely unforeseen despite years of public debate, surfaces when the first 'victim', Gabriel Crasweller, happens to be hale, prosperous, useful, loved, and, not surprisingly, quite unwilling to relinquish his life voluntarily. Crasweller's beautiful and talented daughter Eva has never shared her father's former support for the law (neither does the only other woman in the novel, Neverbend's wife Sarah) and her appeal to the emotions of the Britannulans is heightened when her first suitor, Abraham Grundle, appears to advocate the fixed period merely to hasten his appropriation of Crasweller's prosperous farm. Neverbend's son Jack also firmly resists the policy, more so when he and Eva fall in love and he champions his lover's cause while rebelling publicly and eloquently against his father's cherished project. Thus, the love story and the family dynamics provide a framework for debate about the fixed period.

Neverbend, whose name clearly indicates his total inflexibility, is caught by surprise at every objection. He does not have any strong allies once the day of Crasweller's 'deposition' arrives; in fact, a mob surrounds what Neverbend had hoped would be his triumphal escort of Crasweller to Necropolis. Further complications arise with the arrival of the British gunboat the *John Bright* at this very moment, pointing its 250-ton steam-swiveller gun at the capital city of Gladstonopolis, ready to level it if Neverbend does not instantly abdicate power so that the fixed period law can be annulled. Trollope has some fun here, speaking of the British Minister of Benevolence, whose envoys, says Crasweller to Neverbend, 'have come here in their horror, and have used their strength to prevent the barbarity of your benevolence' (XI).

Because of the first-person narration, the reader is never sure of Trollope's own voice in the novel's troubling premiss. His handling of Neverbend lacks that sureness of touch necessary for plausibility. Neverbend confesses himself an 'enthusiast' and we are privy to his long musings, but his agonies of doubt centre, not on misgivings as to the policy, but on being ahead of his time and fighting the sentimental prejudices of others. He likens himself to Galileo and Columbus, lonely men who steadfastly achieved their goals in the face of ridicule and opposition. Neverbend's relations with his wife and son evince a man out of touch with his own emotions: he suppresses his paternal affection, and, when exiled, leaves his affectionate, spirited wife without apparent regret, even using 'that tone of sarcastic triumph' (XI) which reveals a conviction that his wife and son 'had always successfully conspired against' him (IV).

Trollope's attempt at science fiction is not a happy one. His futuristic technology includes steam bicycles which can travel six miles (10 km) in fourteen minutes, a gun which can level a city with one shot, 'hair' telephones, and a steam-bowler and paraphernalia for cricket. The underlying assumption of futurity rests in the prescient notion of agreeable euthanasia and cremation, the latter being one of Trollope's own interests. He was a member of the Cremation Society of England. (*Letters* 1, 409 n.) (See also THOMPSON, SIR HENRY.) Most notably, however, the novel fails in innovative perspectives by being so thoroughly Victorian in its values of class and status consciousness, financial parameters of success, the role of women, the rules of courtship and marriage, and the continuing sovereignty of Britain. Thus, Trollope seems to place the daring concept of euthanasia for the aged in a fantastic setting in order to offset immediate public disapproval, rather than to try his hand at science fiction.

Reactions to *The Fixed Period* have always been mixed at best. Contemporary critics called it 'essentially ghastly', a *jeu d'esprit*, a grim joke, a clever flight of fancy, a Swiftian satire (Smalley 487–92). More recent critics find it 'unfortunate' (R. C. Terry, *Anthony Trollope* (1977), 144), 'outside his ken' (Hall 112), and 'surprising' (Glendinning 491). The comfortable style of the Palliser and Barsetshire novels is much less evident in *The Fixed Period*, thus upsetting preconceptions and increasing the reader's uneasiness. W. L. *Collins's oft-quoted line, that Trollope exclaimed, 'It's all true—I *mean* every word of it' (Hall 487), brings us no closer to the author's intention: did he *mean* the premiss, the ironic rendering, or the satire on obstinacy and closed minds? The modern reader may well find the novel appealing for these complex ironies and ambiguity.

Trollope wrote *The Fixed Period* near the end of his life, a year before the very age (67) when Britannulans would be 'deposited' in Necropolis. Feeling his own increasing decrepitude and fearing forced idleness (*Letters* 2, 691), he began the novel the day after completing *Kept in the Dark* and worked on it from 17 December 1880 to 28 February 1881. It first appeared anonymously in serialized form in *Blackwood's* between October 1881 and March 1882, and then was published as two volumes in March 1882. Upon Blackwood's apprehension of objections by the public—'they may bring down upon us a religious storm'—Trollope agreed to 'put out all the profanities' (*Letters* 2, 923). However, he did restore most of the cuts for the two-volume edition, as indicated in R. H. Super's edition of the novel (1990, University of Michigan), showing the variants between the manuscript, serial, and two-volume edition. After offering Trollope £200 for the book, Blackwood agreed to pay £100 when serialization began, another £100 at completion, and a further £250 for publication in book form. Blackwood told Trollope, 'the story is thoroughly fresh and the novelty of the situation and the strangeness of the circumstances should make it very attractive and bring you fresh honours' (*Letters* 2, 908 n.). Regarding the length of the novel, Trollope wrote, 'it is very hard to make a story not too short and not too long. I am far from saying that I have hit the medium correctly. But I fear it cannot be altered now' (*Letters* 2, 944). Blackwood lost money on the novel, which sold only 877 copies. The manuscript is held at the University of Michigan.   SRB

Adolphus, was a centre of expatriate English cultural life, and Anthony frequently visited. *HKWR*
                                                                                    RC

Folking, estate near Cambridge, home of Daniel Caldigate for which his son John sells, then buys back, the inheritance rights. *JC*   SRB

food and drink. Trollope was a big, active man and therefore liked plenty to eat, hearty breakfasts taken late in the morning and a dinner with a roast of beef or good mutton, despite unhappy memories of mutton dinners at school. In March 1882, Trollope invited himself for lunch with the children of his brother-in-law John Tilley, declaring that he needed only a crust and some cheese. They led him into a back room where they had set out 'the tail end of a stale loaf, some mouldy bits of cheese, and a jug of water'. He looked at the table with loathing, and was then informed there was a real lunch in the dining room, at which he roared with delight (*Chron* 1882). In August 1882 he wrote home to Rose from Ireland that Charles Booth, the gin-maker, had given him 'the best dinner that I ever ate' (*Letters* 2, 980). In his last novel he had a diminutive heroine confess, 'I'm very fond of eating.' He knew he ate and drank too much, and dieted now and then. In 1864 he followed the regimen popularized by William Banting, author of *A Letter on Corpulence, Addressed to the Public* (1863). George Eliot found him thinner because of it and 'better for the self-denial' (*I & R* 138). But the weight came back always. Dressing formally for dinner was part of the ritual. In *Ayala's Angel* he wrote, 'The man who ceases to dress for dinner soon finds it to be a trouble to wash his hands' (XVII). Julian Hawthorne observed him as one of the few in evening dress at a function in 1879. While travelling abroad he had trouble keeping track of his formal wear and getting the laundry done. But Trollope also liked gatherings at home without ceremony, and even picnics at Waltham if planned properly. In the novels the offering or withholding of food is, as in Dickens, an index of

fellowship. This is well deployed in *Orley Farm*, where Moulder (gluttony), Mrs Mason (parsimony), and Judge Staveley (generosity) are shown in the context of food.   RCT

Fooks, Captain, in the same regiment as Lieutenant Cox. A loyal hunting friend of Ralph, the heir, in London and at the Moonbeam. *RH*
                                                                                    ALS

'Formosa' (review). Much criticism of Dion Boucicault's popular drama now playing in London is misguided. The weakness of the play is not the presentation of criminals and prostitutes; such people exist and are legitimate subjects. However, immoral people are not happy and successful. This work is untrue and thus inartistic, despite popularity. All who profit from this production deserve censure. *Saint Pauls* (October 1869), 75–80.   AKL

Forrest, Mr, Barchester bank manager who attempts to relieve Revd Mark Robarts's financial problems. *FP*   NCS

Forrest, Ralph, widower bound for California who befriends Emily Viner on the voyage, but she refuses his offer to accompany her back to England, despite the mutual attraction. 'Panama' *LS*   GRH

Forrest, Sergeant, police officer who investigates the fire at Harry Heathcote's sheep station. *HH*   MRS

Forrester, Kattie, clergyman's daughter and fiancée of Mr Blake. She good-humouredly tolerates his bad manners and insufferable self-complacency, but she also unerringly points out his mistakes—a tutelage to which he is impervious. *OML*   RC

Forster, Ada, orphan heiress with Northern sympathies who loves the Kentucky Southern 'General' Tom Reckenthorpe, is loved by his brother Frank, but stays loyal to Tom after he has lost a leg. 'Generals' *LS*   GRH

Forster, John (1812–76), literary adviser for Chapman & Hall (1837–60); editor of the *Examiner*, which ran Trollope's letters 'The Real State of Ireland' (August 1849–June 1850). Reviewing *The Warden* in the *Examiner* he disliked the satirical sketch of Dickens as 'Mr Popular Sentiment' but admired its invention and much of the writing (Smalley 30–1). Trollope was dismayed at Forster's *Life of Dickens* (1872) for displaying so much in public. 'Dickens was no hero,' he wrote. 'Forster tells of him things which should disgrace him,—as the picture he drew of his own father, & the hard words he intended to have published of his own mother' (*Letters* 2, 557). Dickens's vulgarity and vanity was the focus of Trollope's distaste, but personal dilemmas surrounding his own childhood were an unacknowledged part of that psychological antipathy. The catalogue of Trollope's library was inscribed to Forster, and is in the Victorian and Albert Museum.   RCT

Forster, William Edward (1818–86), Liberal statesman; chief architect of the elementary Education Act (1870); fellow member of the Athenaeum and Cosmopolitan and keen whist-player. A sketch shows him at the card table with Trollope, 'A Memorable Whist Party at the Athenaeum'. As Chief Secretary for Ireland (1880), he resigned from cabinet in protest at Gladstone's policies over *Parnell and Home Rule. His view accorded with Trollope's.   RCT

Fortescue, Chichester Parkinson (1823–98), later Lord Carlingford; Irish-born MP for Louth (1847–74), Under-Secretary for the Colonies (1857–8), and Chief Secretary for Ireland (1865–6, 1868–70), both offices Trollope conferred on Phineas Finn. Some critics have suggested that Finn was based on Fortescue (see John Halperin, *Trollope and Politics* (1977), 83). Other candidates have included Colonel King-Harman, Joe Parkinson, and James Pope Hennessy. Trollope doubtless agreed with his mother that novelists pulped their acquaintances before serving them, so that it was impossible to see the pig in the sausage (R. C. Terry, *Anthony Trollope* (1977), 16).   RCT

Fortnightly Review. In December 1864, Trollope and a group of prominent literary figures and intellectuals, including Frederic Chapman, publisher; Henry Danby Seymour, Liberal member for Poole; Charles Waring, successor to Seymour; James Cotter Morison, writer and biographer; Charles Rea, Trollope's Post Office colleague; James Sprent *Virtue, Morison's brother-in-law, printer for the *Fortnightly*, and future publisher of *Saint Pauls Magazine*; and Lord Houghton, established an innovative journal based on the *Revue des deux mondes*, the successful Paris periodical. They were influenced by Matthew *Arnold, Professor of Poetry at Oxford, whose lecture 'The Function of Criticism at the Present Time' had appeared in Walter *Bagehot's new *National Review* in 1864. Arnold had said that the bane of criticism at the time in England was that its vehicles served men and parties. In contrast, the *Revue des deux mondes* had as its main function to understand and utter the best that is known and thought; it was a medium for free play of the mind. Arnold's remarks focused the attention of the group as they met to set up their new publication. Each of the founders contributed £1,250; Trollope was elected chairman of the board and chose the name for the magazine. Chapman & Hall were the publishers.

This 130-page, fortnightly journal, selling for two shillings, was to be open to all opinions, with signed articles, an unusual practice for the time, later adopted by the *Contemporary Review* and the *Nineteenth Century*. Trollope was against including a serialized novel because it would distract from the serious purpose of the journal; others disagreed, and Trollope's *The Belton Estate* appeared in the first number. Trollope persuaded his friend George *Lewes, editor of the *Leader* and a frequent contributor to the *Westminster Review*, to be the first editor.

The first number appeared on 15 May 1865; the preface said the magazine would further the cause of progress 'by providing illumination from many minds, with every contributor expressing his own point of view. It contained an unprecedented mixture of reviews, stories, serious articles, poems, critical discussions, and notices of new books. Contributors included George Eliot, Robert Buchanan, Thomas Henry Huxley, Lewes, and Walter Bagehot. The *Fortnightly* succeeded in becoming the most intellectual of the reviews and magazines of its day, coming close to Arnold's ideal.

In 1866, Lewes resigned due to ill health. It was also in August 1866 that the *Fortnightly* became a monthly, for financial reasons, although it retained the name. John *Morley, a friend of Cotter Morison's, took over from Lewes. (Trollope had been considered for the position, having filled in during June and July while Lewes was abroad.) Morley, editor for the next fifteen years, increased the circulation, attracted good contributors, and improved this already well-respected periodical. In 1882, Morley resigned, to be succeeded by T. H. S. *Escott, who favoured attracting more Conservative contributors. Escott became ill in 1885 and resigned in 1886. Frank Harris, the next editor, doubled the circulation in his first year, and began paying contributors very well, sometimes from his own pocket, thereby attracting high-quality literature and criticism. After eight years, he was followed by W. L. Courtney, who edited the *Fortnightly* for 34 years until his death in 1928. Under his editorship unsigned articles appeared. The journal continued until 1954 when it was absorbed by the *Contemporary Review*.

Trollope was a frequent contributor. He wrote articles on anonymous literature, the Irish Church, the civil service, public schools, travel, and book reviews. Reviewing the ballad 'The Rose of Cheriton' by Mrs Mary Sewell, mother of Anna Sewell (author of the best-selling novel *Black Beauty*, 1877), Trollope criticized it for being so one-sided that it preached for its own sake. Although Trollope's interest in the *Fortnightly* fell off as he became more and more involved with *Saint Pauls Magazine*, he still made the occasional contribution: *The Eustace Diamonds* (July 1871–February 1873), *Lady Anna* (April 1873–April 1874). In 1877 appeared *'Cicero as a Politician' and *'Cicero as a Man of Letters'. In 1878, he contributed *'Kafir Land'. When Lewes died in 1878, Trollope wrote a moving tribute to him. Later that year an account of his trip to Iceland on the ship *Mastiff* appeared.

Trollope became embroiled in a public argument about fox-hunting, a topic dear to him, in the *Fortnightly*. In 1869, an article by Edward *Freeman condemned the cruelty and immorality of fox-hunting. Trollope had not written for the *Fortnightly* for two and a half years, but he felt compelled to respond, pointing out the skill and courage involved in the sport and arguing that the end justified the means, and that a minimum of suffering for the fox produced a maximum of recreation for the many. Freeman responded, but Morley, then editor, prevented Trollope from continuing the debate. Other publications took up the topic, including the *Saturday Review* and the *Daily Telegraph*. Years later when Trollope met Freeman, he was surprised to find that he thoroughly enjoyed talking with him, in spite of their strong difference of opinion.   JWM

Foster, replacement officer brought in to Drumsna after the murder of Myles Ussher, who is so far intimidated by death-threats, a stoning, and arson that he informs the head office in Dublin that the area cannot be secured against violent political unrest. *MB*   MRS

Fothergill, Mr, West Barsetshire magistrate who manages the Duke of Omnium's estates. Good-natured and popular, fond of eating and drinking, he is tenacious in the Duke's interests: helping elect Lord Dumbello to Parliament, hosting the Duke's dinner for Barsetshire gentry in

Doctor Thorne, and conveying the Duke's displeasure over Plantagenet Palliser's supposed flirtation in *The Small House at Allington. FP, LCB, PR*   NCS

Four Lectures. Several important lectures by Trollope were edited by Morris L. Parrish and published by Constable & Co. in a limited edition of 150 copies (1938), reprinted in 1969. It contains 'The Civil Service as a Profession' (1861), 'The Present Condition of the Northern States of the American Union' (1862–3), 'Higher Education of Women' (1868), 'On English Prose Fiction as a Rational Amusement' (1870). The manuscript is in the Parrish Collection at Princeton.
                                    RCT

'Fourth Commandment, The' (article). Dr Norman *Macleod's recent sermon denying the necessity of spending all of Sunday in church or in tedious non-activity is defensible and reasonable. Rules for sabbath observance must be understood in terms of their long history. Hard labour is forbidden, but not all non-religious activity. *Fortnightly Review* (15 January 1866), 529–38.   AKL

Framley Court, Lady Lufton's Barsetshire home, a pleasant country place of two storeys, devoid of architectural pretensions. Warm and comfortable, noted for its gardens, it later becomes chief home of Lord Lufton and his wife. *FP*   NCS

Framley Cross, junction of two Barsetshire roads in Framley parish which constitutes the entire village: the Lufton Arms where the hounds would occasionally meet, and a post office kept by a shoemaker. *FP*   NCS

Framley Mill, located between Barchester and Hogglestock, near the Barchester Road. Farmer Mangle drives Josiah Crawley there in Mrs Crawley's scheme to save her husband a long walk. *LCB*   NCS

Framley Parsonage (see page 207)

France. Despite his mother's love of Parisian society, Trollope nursed a traditional English antipathy to French institutions and customs. His European destinations focused on Italy, Switzerland, and south Germany, although France's cathedral cities like Chartres appealed, as did mountainous regions like the Pyrenees. His historical novel *La Vendée* was located in the Loire region. 'The Chateau of Prince Polignac' takes place in Le Puy, and 'La Mère Bauche' at Vernet-les-Bains. Paris is where snow and hail are colder than in England ('Thompson'). Wine was about the only French commodity to receive Trollope's wholehearted approval.   RCT

Lord Lufton and Lucy Robarts, drawn by J. E. Millais, one of many fine illustrations for *Framley Parsonage*, which consolidated Trollope's position as a novelist of the day. Collaboration with the celebrated artist got off to a bad start when Trollope was so enraged by a drawing of his heroine, all bustle and flounces (XVI), that he doubted Millais should continue. The drawing here, though, is charming, the subjects neatly framed by parsonage gate and doves.

Framley Parsonage

THE fourth of the Barchester novels marks a turn in Trollope's career. In 1860, Smith, Elder had announced a new monthly magazine, the *Cornhill*, to be edited by Thackeray, whom Trollope considered the best of living novelists. Trollope offered some short contributions, and the publisher's answer was positive. There was also a heart-warming letter from his admired Thackeray, and the gratifying invitation to contribute a novel to be serialized. Trollope offered *Castle Richmond*, the Irish novel he was working on, but there was a clear preference for 'an English tale . . . with a clerical flavour' (*Auto* VIII). He obliged, possibly with some relief at being able to return to Barchester and material he had proved his mastery on. At this point he had moved his family home to England from Ireland, and was taking up an important new position in the Post Office with an increase in salary. And the payment for *Framley Parsonage* was to be £1,000, almost double what he had received for any previous novel. He set to work with a will. As he says in *An Autobiography*, 'By placing *Framley Parsonage* near Barchester, I was able to fall back on my old friends Mrs Proudie and the Archdeacon. . . . There was a little fox-hunting and a little tuft-hunting, some Christian virtue and some Christian cant. There was no heroism and no villainy. There was much Church, but more love-making. And it was downright honest love. . . . Each of them longed for the other and they were not ashamed to say so' (*Auto* VIII). It would seem from this that Trollope knows very well just what he is doing. And the writing has become less tentative and more steadily confident. When he learned it was to be illustrated by Millais, his cup was full, and he might now feel himself to be a comfortably established novelist.

Framley Parsonage was his first novel to be serialized. This brought out his customary professional punctiliousness: he deplored the practice of serializing a novel before it was completely written. Dickens, Thackeray, and Mrs Gaskell, he later noted, all died leaving a novel unfinished. Twenty-six more of his novels were to be serialized, but only for *Framley Parsonage* did he break this principle. An instalment consisted of three chapters, and at the end of each, he would sharpen the focus, leaving the reader with some memorable insight, usually in dialogue; this in turn invited more interest in what was to follow in the next instalment. Serialization also seems to have led to more careful artistry in arrangement of alternating plots. Unquestionably it brought Trollope a vastly increased audience, and he later said that *Framley Parsonage* was the most favourably received of all his novels.

It is concerned with the delicate gradations of interplay between the clerical vocation and worldly life, and between true love and social hierarchy. Framley is in the thoroughly Tory eastern division of Barsetshire, and the dowager Lady Lufton of Framley Court is the local power. She takes a keen interest in clerical matters, and the living at Framley is in her gift. Her son Lord Lufton had formed a close friendship with Mark Robarts, first at Harrow, then at Oxford. Mark, a country doctor's son, was destined for the Church, and Lady Lufton had sensed in him a high-church tendency, as well as an amiable disposition. In due course the Revd Mark Robarts was made vicar at Framley. Lady Lufton had arranged for him to meet young Fanny Mansell, and Mark and Fanny had obligingly fallen in love and married. There is much social intercourse and genuine affection between the great house and the parsonage. At the beginning of the novel, though, there is an incident showing that Mark will accede to his patroness's will in some minor points, in order, he says to Fanny, to hold out against her in others.

Young Lord Lufton, to his mother's chagrin, has shown some Whiggish sympathies, and frequently joins in hunts away from his home part of the country. He has fallen in with the Whig Nathaniel Sowerby, MP for East Barsetshire, who is supported by the powerful old Whig reprobate the Duke of Omnium, whom Lady Lufton regards as something like Lucifer himself. Sowerby is of an old landed family with the country seat of Chaldicotes, but he has wasted his patrimony and is now in the hands of the moneylenders. Sowerby's sister has married Harold Smith, a dedicated Whig MP, very much the professional politician and something of a bore. Mrs Harold Smith, very worldly and witty, is a friend of Mrs Proudie, wife of the low-church Bishop of Barchester, and when the Harold Smiths are at Chaldicotes the Proudies are liable to be there. Sowerby has inveigled Lord Lufton into some financial entanglements, but he trusts to solve all his financial troubles through his sister's help, by marriage with the wealthy heiress Miss Dunstable. Such is what Lady Lufton calls the 'Chaldicotes set', and she deplores her son's connection there.

The Revd Mark Robarts accepts an invitation for ten days at Chaldicotes, rather flattered by connection with the great. Ostensibly his visit is proper: he will meet his Bishop and various MPs; Harold Smith is to give a lecture in Barchester on the need for English investment to civilize the Australasian archipelago, and Mark is to preach a sermon on the need for missionaries there. While at Chaldicotes, he is led to accept an invitation to the Duke of Omnium's Gatherum Castle. And so Mark writes to Fanny, to make arrangements to cover his parochial duties, and also to 'make it as smooth at Framley Court as possible'.

The Chaldicotes set amuse themselves very well. Mrs Harold Smith and Miss Dunstable love to bring out Mrs Proudie, on her notorious historic troubles with Mr Slope (see *BT*), and they make deliciously cruel fun of Harold Smith's pompous lecture. The lecture itself is punctuated by an outburst from Mrs Proudie proclaiming that sabbath observance is what the Australasians need above all. Poor Smith finishes lamely. Miss Dunstable, whom we know to be good at heart as well as witty (see *DT*), proffers friendship to Mark. And when we hear that she and her retinue are departing to visit a certain country doctor, we surmise that the Dunstable–Sowerby liaison will not take place. And when Sowerby presses Mark to put his name to a bill for £500, we surmise disaster. Trollope's characteristic mastery is evident in all this: Sowerby, for instance, is something close to a villain, and yet on the one hand Trollope is able to make us see the man's wily charms, enough to persuade even so perceptive a person as Mark, and on the other to exact from us a degree of sympathy for the misery of his shabby morality.

Concurrently there is the love story of Mark's sister Lucy and Lord Lufton. The father of Mark and Lucy has recently died, and Lucy has come to make her home at the parsonage. She is much loved and valued by Mark, Fanny, and their children, and as she emerges from mourning is invited into the Framley Court–parsonage social nexus. Young Lord Lufton in his kindly way attempts to bring her out of her shyness. It turns out there is plenty to bring out: a fine intelligence and style and humour. She is small and brown and lacking in regular beauty, but her grey-green eyes have a striking fire. From her charming conversational sallies, the reader can see why Lord

Lufton falls in love with her. Lady Lufton, however, has other plans. She and Arch-deacon Grantly's wife have agreed that Lord Lufton will marry Griselda Grantly. Griselda's background is satisfactorily Tory and anti-Proudieite, and although her lineage is not aristocratic, it is quite adequate when one considers she has some money, and she is very beautiful. She has been introduced to society in London and has been much admired, especially drawing the attention of the son of the Dowager Marchioness of Hartletop, Lord Dumbello. Lady Lufton has invited the Grantlys to a dinner party, and Griselda is to stay on over Christmas. Lord Lufton is not averse to Griselda's beauty, her statuesque carriage, and elegant clothes. The trouble is that Griselda's conversation is a little slow. In fact, she is about as diverting as a block of ice. She is occasionally moved by the compelling subject of clothes, but even her supportive mother finds her at last emotionally lacking, when she fails to win Lord Lufton, and eventually accepts Lord Dumbello.

The story takes us to London, where anybody who is anybody has a house for 'the season'. Mrs Proudie aims to get the most mileage for the least expenditure by enter-taining everybody at a conversazione: for two hours people stand up while cake and tea are passed about. Griselda Grantly encounters Lord Dumbello there, and the courtship inches along with brief remarks about the weather. The Whigs are in now, and Mr Harold Smith is appointed Lord Petty Bag, and Mrs Harold Smith spends most of his salary to give a party—not a 'pure-minded *conversazione* like Mrs Proudie, but a downright wicked worldly dance' with fiddles, ices, and champagne (XX). Lord Lufton persuades his mother to attend with Griselda, who is her house guest, and she agrees, thinking to further the match. Lord Lufton dances with Griselda, and this further inflames Lord Dumbello's passion for her. But for Lord Lufton, the encounter with Griselda only makes Lucy more desirable.

The next great social occasion is Miss Dunstable's party. While Mrs Harold Smith has been trying to engineer the Dunstable–Sowerby alliance, Dr Thorne's niece Mary Gresham (née Thorne) is working toward another alliance—Dunstable–Thorne. She manages to persuade Dr Thorne to come up to London for Miss Dunstable's party, although such great social occasions are not much to his taste (but Miss Dunstable herself is). Their mutual understanding progresses. Absolutely everybody is there, even the old Duke, and now Lady Lufton encounters the prince of darkness himself. In her exaggerated curtsy to him she manages to convey a sense of irony, and is considered to have come off the victor. Even the powerful Tom Towers of the *Jupiter* is present. He starts a rumour that Parliament may be due for dissolution, and this rumour in fact *causes* it in a few days. The Whigs are out, and Harold Smith's brief glory is over, but not before, with a word from Sowerby and a word from the Duke's man Fothergill, he has arranged for Mark Robarts to be given a remunerative prebendal stall in Bar-chester. It is in fact a way of buying Mark, and unfortunately he accepts.

Lady Lufton is quite willing to patronize Lucy, but cannot conceive of her as a wife for her son. Her family background is good enough for a parish parson, but not for the Lady of the Manor. It is hard for her to say just what the deficiencies are, but Lucy has no wealth, is not very tall, and is not stunningly beautiful. In sum, she is 'un-distinguished'. And Lady Lufton takes it on herself to tell Fanny to warn Lucy against the attachment. But Lord Lufton has condescended to stay at home, to hunt with the local hunt, and to court Lucy. When he declares his love, she rejects him: she will not be considered inferior and a drawback to him. Her pride is a sense of self-worth. In time, she makes it clear that indeed she loves him but will accept him only if his mother asks her.

Dean Arabin had arranged for his old friend and fellow scholar Josiah Crawley to become perpetual curate at Hogglestock, near Framley. It *is* a living, but a very poor one for a man with a family. Crawley is one of the most remarkable of all Trollope's characters: psychotic and depressive, we would call him, full of self-pity, bitterly resentful of receiving charity from his peers, endlessly self-dramatizing in his despair. At the same time, he is punctilious in his pastoral duties. He is so known for his learning and piety that Lady Lufton persuades him to counsel Mark against his worldly associates, and indeed this has some effect. But the poor man's troubles accumulate when his overworked wife is stricken with typhus. Josiah Crawley is a difficult man to help, but the Robartses conspire to take care of the children, while Lucy volunteers to go and nurse Mrs Crawley. Lucy, with all her tact and courage, is able to mollify the prickly husband, and heroically cares for the sick woman and the household. Meanwhile, Mark at last rebels against Sowerby's machinations and resigns the prebendal stall, to face the consequence—which is bankruptcy: the bailiffs are at the door. But through the good offices of Lord Lufton, Lady Lufton is persuaded to the financial rescue of Mark, just as she had previously rescued her son from Sowerby, treating the whole matter good-humouredly as similar foibles of young men. And she realizes Lucy's moral and intellectual worth, and begs her forgiveness.

The last chapter is entitled 'How They Were All Married, Had Two Children, and Lived Happily Ever After'. The 'two children' leads one to think the Victorians knew something of birth control (except for Mr Quiverful). Trollope himself had only two children. At any rate, Griselda Grantly is married to Lord Dumbello, after the Archdeacon retrieves him from an attempted escape to France. Mary Gresham is able to soften up both parties so that Miss Dunstable is happily married to Dr Thorne. She has purchased Sowerby's Chaldicotes to save it from the Duke's greedy hands, and eventually it becomes home to the Thornes. And of course Lucy and Lord Lufton are married, and Lady Lufton gladly makes way for the new mistress of Framley Court.

Framley Parsonage is full of enjoyable allusions to the previous Barchester novels, and in all these we appreciate the passage of time and concomitant development of characters and situations. What is more remarkable, is the anticipation of so many elements of the Palliser novels yet to come. Here appear the old Duke of Omnium and Gatherum Castle, his man of business Mr Fothergill, the Marchioness of Hartletop, Lord Boanerges, the Prime Ministers Lord Brock and Lord De Terrier, a person called Sidonia who anticipates Daubeny, Trollope's portrait of *Disraeli. There are scenes of London social life, and of the working of Parliament, presented here in mock-heroic style (compare 'The Warden's Tea-Party', W VI), which Trollope was to give up in favour of a dramatic ironic realism. The interesting question is: how much did Trollope envisage of the later political novels when he was writing *Framley Parsonage*? At any rate, we see him here in the midst of his far-ranging interwoven alternative world. As he wrote *Framley Parsonage*, he made a map of 'the dear county' (*Auto* X) which he had invented and added to the English shires (see Maps, p. 615).

There is a pretty general consensus that *Framley Parsonage* is vintage Trollope. Mrs *Gaskell at the time of its serialization wished it would go on for ever. Elizabeth Barrett Browning pronounced it 'superb' (Smalley 140). Lucy Robarts was, for Henry James, one of those women of Trollope who have something of the 'fragrance' of

Shakespeare's women (Smalley 543). True that Sadleir gave it only one star in his three-star-maximum classification, but everyone ever since has complained about that. Bradford Booth said, 'If it is not his best book, it is the most characteristic, the most Trollopian of all his stories' (*Anthony Trollope* (1958), 48). Mary Hamer sees it as variations on the theme of pride, and admires the way the variations are manipulated in the multiple plots. Trollope's women have recently led to some good feminist readings, and Jane Nardin sees in Lucy Robarts and Lady Lufton two powerful women, engaged in a struggle, Lady Lufton exercising her power in the community, and Lucy in her fierce self-determination (*He Knew She Was Right* (1989), 77 ff.) Perhaps the wisest analysis of the book is Andrew Wright's: he sees the centre of it as a comparison of the very fortunate Mark Robarts with the very unfortunate Josiah Crawley, and no doubt, as Wright says, Trollope is bitter against the economic inequities in the Church. Nevertheless, Wright points out that it is not an ideological work, and much closer to Jane Austen than to Dickens or Thackeray. And in all the facets of its rich comedy, it is marked by the Trollopian quality of 'a sense of forgiveness'. He leads us to see how these things happen, and how we might have done the same as Lucy, or Lady Lufton, or Mark Robarts—or even Josiah Crawley (*Anthony Trollope* (1983), 60). Wright's term, the 'sense of forgiveness', can be understood to apply to a great deal of Trollope's work.

Framley Parsonage was composed 1859–60, sold to Smith, Elder for £1,000, published in sixteen parts in the *Cornhill*, January 1860 to April 1861, illustrated by Millais, and published in three volumes in 1861. The incomplete manuscript (XIX–LVIII) is in the Vaughan Library, Harrow School.   R apR

Hamer, Mary, *Writing by Numbers: Trollope's Serial Fiction* (1987).
Nardin, Jane, *He Knew She Was Right* (1989).
Wright, Andrew, *Anthony Trollope: Dream and Art* (1983).

Fraser, Francis Arthur (fl. 1867–83), landscape and genre painter, exhibited at the Royal Academy four times (1873–8). He did most of the illustrations for *Good Words* in 1869, and illustrated *The Last Chronicle of Barset*. The plate showing Mr Crawley being admonished by Giles Hoggett with the words 'It's dogged as does it' makes its impact. This illustration for the second volume has been thought superior to G. H. Thomas's for the frontispiece of volume 2 of the original issue. 'The driving rain, the mud, and the wet sheen reflecting the human figures all contribute to create an environmental gloom that adumbrates Crawley's state of mind' (N. John Hall, *Trollope and his Illustrators* (1980), 143). Fraser also illustrated *Ralph the Heir*.   RCT

Freeborn, Dr, 70-year-old rector, source of wisdom in the parish, who successfully promotes the marriages of the two heroines. 'Plumplington'
                                                                      GRH

Freeling, Mrs Clayton, friend of Trollope's mother from her Bristol days. She prevailed upon Sir Francis, her father-in-law, who, as Secretary of the Post Office, had the appointment in his gift, to find Trollope a place. She also tried to help Trollope socially, inviting him to various gatherings during his London clerkship, but Trollope usually refused. When he was near dismissal it was Mrs Freeling 'who with tears in her eyes, besought me to think of my mother' (*Auto* III).   RCT

Freeling, Sir Francis (1764–1836), for many years Secretary of the Post Office; created baronet 1828. Like Trollope's mother, he came from Bristol, where a memorial tablet in St Mary Redcliffe praises his 38 years of public service. When Trollope applied to enter the Post Office in 1834, the Secretary was solicited by his daughter-in-law Mrs Clayton Freeling to offer Trollope a place. On 4 November this appointment was routinely approved. 'Mr. Trollope has been well educated and will be subject to the usual probation as to competency,' commented Sir Francis (R. H. Super, *Trollope in the Post Office* (1981), 1). Trollope spoke kindly of him: Sir Francis died '—still in harness,—a little more than twelve months after I joined the office. And yet the old man showed me signs of almost affectionate kindness, writing to me with his own hand more than once from his death-bed' (*Auto* III). RCT

Freeling, Henry and **Clayton,** sons of Sir Francis Freeling, Secretary of the Post Office; Henry, the elder son, was Assistant Secretary, Clayton in the Stamp Office. Clayton took Trollope to be examined at the Post Office. For a test Henry asked Trollope to copy some lines from *The Times*, which Trollope did badly, making many blots and false spellings, jeopardizing his prospects: ' "That won't do, you know," said Henry Freeling to his brother Clayton. Clayton, who was my friend, urged that I was nervous, and asked that I might be allowed to do a bit of writing at home and bring it as a sample on the next day' (*Auto* III). Clayton urged Trollope not to be discouraged and that evening, 'under the surveillance of my elder brother' he made 'a beautiful transcript of four or five pages of Gibbon'. Trollope returned next day with his sample, at which point 'I was seated at a desk without any further reference to my competency. No one condescended even to look at my beautiful penmanship.' RCT

Freeman, Edward Augustus (1823–92), historian, best known for his *History of the Norman Conquest* (1867–79); regular contributor to the *Saturday Review* (1855–78); Regius Professor of Modern History at Oxford (1884–92). He threw down the gauntlet with 'The Morality of Field Sports', *Fortnightly Review*, October 1869, provoking Trollope's defence of his favourite sport two months later. He returned to the topic in *An Autobiography* (X). Meeting in Rome in March 1880 they discussed Cicero, and Freeman discerned Trollope's deep knowledge of Roman history. At Freeman's home near Wells, Somerset, they wrangled amiably in autumn 1882 about the location of Barchester. It had to be Wells, said Freeman. Trollope insisted it was Winchester, although Barset was Somerset. They had one more meeting the day before Trollope's stroke. 'He talked as well and as heartily as usual' (*I & R* 225–6). RCT

French, Arabella, elder sister whose marital expectations are upset when Mr Gibson becomes engaged to her younger sister (Camilla) but fulfilled when she lures him back. The sisters are like two pigs 'at the same trough, each striving to take the delicacies of the banquet from the other, and yet enjoying always the warmth of the same dunghill in amicable contiguity' (XLIV). *HKWR* RC

French, Camilla, younger sister whose effort to win Mr Gibson takes a number of turns. Her vain, selfish, and shrewish nature leads to her being jilted and to Mr Gibson's retreating to the cold comfort of his first object of desire, her elder sister Arabella. *HKWR* RC

French, Mrs, widow of an army captain. She tolerates Mr Gibson's vacillation between her daughters Arabella and Camilla—and even his brief defection to Dorothy Stanbury—on the condition that he marry one of her children. She finally sacrifices the younger's feelings to the elder's interests, sanctioning the engagement of Arabella and Gibson. *HKWR* RC

Frere, Sir Henry Bartle (1815–84). He entered the Bombay civil service in 1834, the first non-Bengal civilian to be appointed to the Viceroy's council (1859). In 1872 he was sent to Zanzibar to negotiate suppression of the slave trade; in 1877 appointed Governor of the Cape, the first High Commissioner of South Africa. His governorship was plagued by controversy. In 1879 he made demands on Cetywayo, King of the Zulus, which resulted in the war of 1879. He was censured by the government and recalled (1880). In a letter to G. W. *Rusden (April 1879) Trollope professed respect for Frere, whom he had met in South Africa, but condemned his actions: 'Frere . . . is a man who thinks that it is England's duty to carry English civilization and English Christianity among all Savages. . . . he has waged war against these unfortunates,—who have lived along side of us in Natal for 25 years without ever having raised a hand against us! The consequence is that we have already slaughtered 10000 of them, and rejoice in having done so. To me it seems like civilization gone mad!' (*Letters* 2, 826). In an abridged edition of *South Africa* (1879), Trollope included a chapter on 'Zululand' in response to current events, and completed arrangements for two lectures on the Zulus, one in Nottingham and one in Birmingham. In his chapter in South Africa, he declared: 'I have no fears myself that Natal will be overrun by hostile Zulus;—but much fear that Zululand should be overrun by hostile Britons' (Hall 434); the crowds who heard his lecture in Nottingham, which took much the same line as his chapter on 'Zululand', 'applauded him vigorously in his condemnation of the English colonial policy of extermination' (Super 401). Frere sent Trollope a 105-page criticism of his 'Zululand', but Trollope remained unmoved. RCT

Frew, Frederic. American suitor of Nora Field, who good-humouredly argues with her uncle Mr Granger on North and South in the Civil War

and British/American differences. 'Widow' *LS*
GRH

Friswell, James Hain (1825–78). A miscellaneous writer, dubbed 'Frizzle' in literary circles,
his *Modern Men of Letters Honestly Criticised*
(1870) drew a libel suit from G. A. *Sala and a
fine of £500. As a friend of Edmund *Yates, he
portrayed Trollope unsympathetically, suggesting
his work was inferior to both his mother's and
elder brother's. Trollope, he declared, was 'a man
one would hardly choose to confide in' (*I & R*
121). RCT

Friswell, Laura Hain (later **Myall**) (d. 1908),
author of children's books and a memoir of her
father J. H. Friswell. Meeting Trollope at the
Dickens banquet in November 1867, she was impressed by the 'nice old gentleman' (then 52)
who told her that authors never forgot those who
admired their works (*I & R* 98). Trollope's old
world courtesy and skittishness were directed towards many young ladies. RCT

Frith, William Powell (1819–1909), celebrated
genre painter known for crowded canvases like
Derby Day (1858). His painting *The Private View
of the Royal Academy* (1881) had Trollope at one
end earnestly taking notes, and Oscar Wilde in
aesthetic pose at the other. Frith joined Trollope
and others (May 1874) in raising funds for the
widow of Shirley Brooks, the noted *Punch* editor.
Frith and Trollope were together at a prize-giving
for students of City and Spitalfields School of Art
(November 1876). Frith noted in *My Autobiography and Reminiscences*, 'Trollope made a good
speech, and I made a bad one' (1888, 3, 387). Like
many others, Frith was bemused by Trollope:
'The books, full of gentleness, grace and refinement; the writer of them, bluff, loud, stormy and
contentious' (quoted *I & R* 142). RCT

Frohmann, Amalia (Malchen) daughter of
Frau Frohmann who supports her lover Fritz
Schlessen in his advocacy of raising prices at her
hotel, while fretting over the 'mitgift' (dowry) so
that she can marry. 'Frohmann' *WFF* GRH

Frohmann, Frau, staunchly conservative,
warm-hearted innkeeper who resists raising

prices, and tries to buy provisions at lower prices,
angering local suppliers. She finally increases
prices selectively, thus winning back those who
had left her. 'Frohmann' *WFF* GRH

Frohmann, Peter, innkeeper's son initially
against the price increase, but who comes to appreciate its necessity. 'Frohmann' *WFF* GRH

Froude, James Anthony (1818–94), historian;
edited *Fraser's Magazine* (1860–74); author of
History of England, 12 vols. (1875), and biographer
of Carlyle (1882). His travels to South Africa
(1874–5) made for mutual interests, but he and
Trollope were never close, although both served
on the Royal Literary Fund committee. Trollope
heavily annotated his copy of Froude's *Caesar*
(1878) with critical notes. Froude commented in
the 1870s of Trollope's travels that he had 'banged
about the world' more than most (T. H. S. Escott, *Anthony Trollope* 133). RCT

Fuller, Mrs, tenant of River's Cottage, Willesden, where Trevelyan goes after abducting his
son. *HKWR* RCT

Furnival, Kitty, wife of the barrister and MP
Thomas Furnival. Sacrificially devoted to her
husband during the long, lean years of his early
legal career, Mrs Furnival finds herself more or
less abandoned in middle age. She is jealous of
Lady Mason and eventually leaves home to reside
near her friend Martha Biggs. *OF* MT

Furnival, Sophia, daughter of Kitty and
Thomas Furnival. Sophia is 'a clever, attractive
girl, handsome, well-read, able to hold her own
with the old as well as with the young, capable of
hiding her vanity if she had any', but 'she was
not altogether charming' (X). She is fleetingly
engaged to Lucius Mason. *OF* MT

Furnival, Thomas, London barrister and MP
for Essex Marshes who defends Lady Mason. A
dedicated lawyer whose success comes late in life,
Mr Furnival neglects his duties to his wife. In
middle age, he 'was obtaining for himself among
other successes the character of a Lothario' (X).
Mrs Furnival suspects his devoted attentions to
Lady Mason. *OF* MT

G

Gager, Mr, gifted young detective who investigates the theft of the Eustace diamonds. He marries Lizzie Eustace's maid Patience Crabstick, in part to secure her testimony at the trial of Mr Benjamin. *ED*   JMR

Galway, assize town in Co. Galway, where the trial of Landleaguer Pat Carroll is to take place, and where Captain Yorke Clayton has his constabulary headquarters. *L*   MRS

Gangoil, a 120,000-acre (50,000-ha) sheep ranch surrounded by thick forest, west of the Mary river in Queensland, which, rented from the Crown by Harry Heathcote, forms the parched setting for class animosities that explode in conflagration. *HHG*   MRS

gardening. Having missed the rootedness of childhood Trollope set great store by normal domestic routines, especially the rituals of garden care. Rose was integral to this domestic pattern. During a visit to the United States in November 1861 he reported to Kate Field that Rose had gone home because 'She has a house, and children & cows & horses and dogs & pigs—and all the stern necessities of an English home' (*Letters* 1, 161). This was Waltham House, which he always preferred to Montagu Square, since it had a large productive garden. 'Out of my little patches', he wrote, 'I have enough for all domestic purposes.' He then proudly listed 21 vegetables (*NA* 1, XI). The asparagus bed and strawberries were favourites. The lawn was kept in good shape. George Smith once saw Trollope dashing around with a roller with typical energy. At the end of his life he wrote wistfully to Rose from Ireland, 'How is the

garden [North End, Harting, their last home], and the cocks & hens, & especially the asparagus bed?' (*Letters* 2, 966).   RCT

Garnett family. After the death of John Garnett (1750–1820) his widow and three daughters, Julia, Harriet, and Fanny, moved amongst the intellectual circles in Paris, where Frances Trollope became their friend. Julia married a Dr Pertz, royal librarian and archivist in Hanover. Mrs Trollope told her (November 1831) of Anthony's winning a prize at Harrow. Her dearest wish, she said, was to see her sons in situations 'where their talents and good conduct might enable them to gain their bread' (quoted Super 442). To Harriet she lamented (December 1828) her husband's ungovernable temper and its dire effects on the children (quoted Mullen 46).   RCT

Garrow, Elizabeth (Bessy), independent-minded only daughter whose 'reverence for martyrdom' causes her to reject Godfrey Holmes initially. After his Christmas visit she comes round to accept him. 'Mistletoe' *TAC2*   GRH

Garrow, Theodosia (1825–65), poet and essayist; married Thomas Adolphus Trollope (1848). They settled in the Brownings' circle in Florence. Later there were rumours (said to have emanated from Robert Browning) about the paternity of the daughter Beatrice (Bice). After Theo's death Bice stayed with her uncle at Waltham Cross. For a while Frances Ternan (sister of Dickens's mistress) gave her singing lessons.   RCT

Garrow family, headed by Major Garrow, a retired officer of Engineers, of modest means, and his warm-hearted wife. Concerned and careful parents, they are anxious about their daughter Bessy's matrimonial qualms, while her younger brothers Frank and Tom provide pranks, vitality, and laughter during Christmas. 'Mistletoe' *TAC2*   GRH

Gaskell, Elizabeth Cleghorn (1810–65), author of socially realistic novels such as *Mary Barton* (1848), *North and South* (1855), and domestic subjects. She admired Trollope's work, but they never met. She wrote to George Smith, 'I wish Mr Trollope would go on writing *Framley Parsonage* for ever. I don't see any reason why it should ever come to an end, and everyone I know is always dreading the last number' (*The Letters of Mrs Gaskell*, ed. J. A. V. Chapple and Arthur Pollard (1966), 602).   RCT

Gatherum Castle, palatial castle near Silverbridge constructed by the old Duke of Omnium as his formal ducal seat. Despite its splendour, the castle is shunned both by the old Duke and by the young Duke and his family except during the Christmas season and other periods of forced occupancy. Frequently mentioned in all the Palliser novels and in *Framley Parsonage* and *Doctor Thorne*. JMR

Gauntlet, Adela, dutiful daughter of the vicar of West Putford, 'a pure, true, and honest girl' (XLVII), who loves Arthur Wilkinson. Though he informs her that he cannot afford to marry, she feels she could 'live on potato-parings could he have been contented to live with her on potatoes' (IV). Disdaining fear of poverty, she resolves to wait for him, her fidelity rewarded when Arthur finally plucks up courage to risk love on a small income. *B* MRS

Gauntlet, Miss Penelope, one-time instructor of her motherless niece Adela Gauntlet, and one of the ladies of Littlebath, where she is subsequently joined by the recently orphaned Adela. *B* MRS

Gay, Susan Elizabeth, daughter of William Gay, Post Office surveyor for the Manchester district; author of a children's book, a study of Annie Besant, and other works. Campaigning for women's rights, she wrote *Woman and a Future Life* (1876). Of Trollope in *Old Falmouth* (1903) she recalled: 'No more repose was left in the house when he awoke in the morning. Doors slammed, footsteps resounded, and a general whirlwind arose, as he came or returned from his bath, or walked out in the garden, and from that time until nightfall, he was as busy as a man could be. He had a scorn of everything in the way of pretention—even of justice to time-honoured institutions—and slurred over his family history, and belittled "the service" right royally. "Post Office" (he always omitted the "General" or departmental style and title)—he would write with a little "p" and a little "o", as though it were a village sub-office, retailing stamps with tobacco and onions. Such was his nature which, as I recollect it, was full of fiery and energetic bluntness . . . Yet as regards imagination, he was unusually gifted, as shown by his best works of fiction, and he would describe a woman's feelings and ideas in regard to a lover better than a woman herself' (*I & R* 61–2). RCT

Gay, William (1812–68) Post Office surveyor for the Manchester District. When important alterations regarding mails were to be considered, the surveyors would convene to arrange connections through each postal district, calculations often too complex to be carried out by correspondence. Hence Trollope was an occasional house guest at William Gay's, where official business

was 'enlivened by good dinners, and an agreeable social time' (*I & R* 61). RCT

Gaynor, Bob, Tony McKeon's friend from Roscommon, 'one of the best gentlemen riders in the country' (XVII), who wins the Carrick race riding McKeon's horse Playful. *MB* MRS

Gazebee, Mortimer, London lawyer who takes over the financial affairs of Squire Francis Gresham. Elegant, fashionable, bald with remarkable whiskers, the 38-year-old lawyer with £1,500 a year and a nice place in Surrey proposes to Augusta Gresham, but is turned down on the advice of Lady Amelia De Courcy, whom he later marries. In *The Small House at Allington* and *The Last Chronicle of Barset* he has become the De Courcys' financial manager who exacerbates Adolphus Crosbie's money problems. *DT* NCS

Genet, Chapel of, refuge for Father Jerome after Cholet and for Mme de Lescure and Marie fleeing from Clisson. *LV* GRH

'Genius of Nathaniel Hawthorne, The' (article). Hawthorne knows and clearly illustrates the truths beneath unlikely characters and incidents. *The Scarlet Letter* is his best work, and the one most read in England; it reveals 'black deeps of the human heart'. Hawthorne, an American, is bound to be more speculative than the British. Other recommended books are *The House of the Seven Gables* and *Mosses from an Old Manse*. *North American Review* (September 1879), 203–22. AKL

genre painting. Trollope had a special liking for Flemish and Dutch genre painters: Teniers, Dou, Steen, Ostade, Mieris. Visiting Amsterdam in 1862, Trollope so marvelled over a Dou painting of a young woman handing a basket out of a window that he confessed to leaving the Jan Six House 'coveting my neighbour's goods' ('My Tour in Holland', *Cornhill Magazine*, November 1862, 616–22). NJH

'Gentle Euphemia, The', first published in the *Fortnightly Review*, May 1866, subtitled 'Love Shall Still be Lord of All'. The tale comprises eight chapters, each with a poetic epigraph from Keats, Tennyson, Scott, etc. The Gentle Euphemia lives in a castle with her father, Lord Grandnostrel, and the wise Alasco, who tells her, 'love will be lord of all'. Euphemia is beloved by Lord Mountfidget, but when his beeves are lost, the young man is repulsed by Lord Grandnostrel and wounded by a poisoned arrow. Euphemia follows him, disguised as a page, and saves his life, proving that love is indeed lord of all. JS

George, witness to Augustus Horne's discomfiture in Antwerp, sees his friend's trousers cut up as relics by women tourists, and turns the tables on the scissor-wielding ladies. 'Chassé' *TAC1*

GRH

'George Henry Lewes' (obituary). George Henry Lewes's life and career were advanced by his excellence, not overwhelmed by any of several major disappointments. He began as a journalist, critic, and novelist, and taught himself to be a mathematician, physicist, chemist, and philosopher. He agreed to be the first editor of this journal despite frail health; he advanced scholarship and honesty in journals. His thoughtful analysis of Dickens's work is perhaps the best yet written. His popularization of science and philosophy was outstanding. A great friend and matchless storyteller, his drollery and wisdom are sorely missed already. *Fortnightly Review* (January 1879), 15–24.

AKL

'George Walker at Suez', first published in *Public Opinion*, 28 December 1861 (reprinted in *TAC2*). George Walker goes to Egypt for his health and is persuaded by a friend to accompany him to the port of Suez, where George finds himself obliged to spend five wretched days alone waiting for his onward passage. Mysteriously, a local dignitary, Mahmoud al Ackbar, treats him with elaborate generosity, even arranging a luxurious expedition to the nearby Wells of Moses. It emerges that he has mistaken the humble Englishman for his namesake Sir George Walker, the new Lieutenant-Governor of Pegu. George is cruelly snubbed. JS

Geraghty, Mr, good-humoured but incompetent junior clerk and co-worker with George Roden in the Post Office. *MF* SRB

Geraghty, Norah, barmaid at the Cat and Whistle who loves Charley Tudor. Norah 'was a fine girl' and 'could make an excellent pudding, and was willing enough to exercise her industry and art in doing so' (XX). Unsuitable as a match for middle-class Charley, she finally marries the widower Mr Peppermint. *TC* MT

Geraldine, Sir Francis, ill-tempered, egotistical, mean-spirited Baronet who adores the bachelor life of gaming and drinking and who wishes to marry only to keep his estates from going to his detested cousin. The 40-year-old Sir Francis avenges himself on Cecilia Holt, who had jilted him, by implying that he had renounced her; he later informs her husband George Western of the previous engagement. He nearly becomes entrapped in marriage by Francesca Altifiorla, but jilts her instead. *KD* NCS

Geraldine, Captain Walter, wealthy young cousin and heir of Sir Francis Geraldine. He mar-

ries Mary Tremenhere after she jilts George Western. *KD* NCS

Germain, Lady Alice (later **Holdenough**). The only Germain sister to marry, she remains removed from the family quarrel with the Marquis of Brotherton and meets him socially at Rudham Park. Lady Sarah stays at her house in Brotherton while acting as peacemaker between Lord and Lady George. *IHP* MG

Germain, Lady Amelia. Less severe than the other unmarried Germain sisters, she is less annoying to her sister-in-law Lady George Germain. *IHP* MG

Germain, Lady George (née **Mary Lovelace**). To please her loving and ambitious father Henry Lovelace, the low-born but carefully raised and wealthy Mary marries the well-born but poor Lord George. A bright, lively young woman who likes to enjoy herself, she suffers from the snubs of her husband's rather grim family. When her high-spirited but innocent behaviour leads to a brief rift with her husband, she demands the respect due to a married woman from her in-laws as well as from her husband. Her place in the hierarchies of family and society is assured when she becomes marchioness and bears the new Lord Popenjoy. *IHP* MG

Germain, Lord George. A poor, younger son refused by Adelaide De Baron, he marries Mary Lovelace. An extremely handsome man, he is obstinate, weak, and overwhelmed by family pride. He resents his dependence upon his wife's fortune and he resents his father-in-law Henry Lovelace, who drives him to enquire into the legitimacy of Lord Popenjoy. His embarrassingly public jealousy of Jack De Baron causes a rift with Lady George. The deaths of his brother and nephew make him the new marquis, a position he fills with the requisite responsibility and dignity. *IHP* MG

Germain, Lady Sarah. Oldest of the Germain sisters, she is the only one unafraid of her brothers. She advises Lord George and relishes the notion of a battle with the Marquis of Brotherton. Severe, good, and proud of her family, she at first thinks Lady George is frivolous, but later becomes her advocate and friend. *IHP* MG

Germain, Lady Susanna. As severe as but less wise than her sister Lady Sarah, she is sent to London to keep an eye on Lady George who deliberately and easily annoys her. *IHP* MG

Giblet, Lord, young man about town ensnared in Mrs Montacute Jones's matchmaking schemes. He marries Olivia Green, settles into happy domesticity, and, much to the disgust of his father, becomes a pillar of the Entomological Society. *IHP*   MG

Gibson, Thomas, rector of St Peter's-cum-Pupkin and minor canon at Exeter Cathedral—'a sort of tame-cat parson' (XLIX). At Miss Stanbury's suggestion, he proposes to but is rejected by Dorothy Stanbury. Passive and weak, with the unjustified reputation of a Lothario, he vacillates between the French sisters, ultimately but unhappily settling upon Arabella. *HKWR*   RC

Giles, Father, elderly parish priest of Tuam who, having preached to his flock on the virtues of political obedience and the importance of valuing 'the good things of this world' (III) for 40 years, finds himself troubled in old age by the agitational fervour of his young curate Father Brosnan. *L*   MRS

Giles, Father, good-humoured Irish priest expecting to share a bedroom with Archibald Green, but is flung down the stairs. He is bruised but forgiving. 'Giles' *LS*   GRH

Gilliflower, Gabriel, unassuming curate who performs Arthur Wilkinson's pastoral duties while the latter convalesces in Egypt. *B*   MRS

Gilmore, Harry. Squire of Bullhampton and a relaxed country gentleman, 'he is to be our hero'. A good friend of the vicar and his wife, he falls deeply in love with their friend Mary Lowther. She rejects his suit but, after her engagement to Walter Marrable is broken off, she accepts Gilmore from a sense of duty. Her cold, passive acceptance wounds him deeply, and when she finally rejects him again, he goes abroad, heartbroken, for several years. *VB*   SRB

Gissing, George (1857–1903), late 19th-century chronicler of the working class and master of social realism, noted for *New Grub Street* (1891). *The Private Papers of Henry Ryecroft* (1903), a fictitious author's journal, contains amusing comment on Trollope, 'an admirable writer of the pedestrian school'. Gissing was undeterred by Trollope's *An Autobiography*, 'so cynically sprung upon a yet innocent public' who preferred ignorance of 'the processes of "literary" manufacture and the ups and downs of the "literary" market' (213). As to whether it contributed to Trollope's decline in popularity, he wrote, 'It would be a satisfaction to think that "the great big stupid [public]" was really, somewhere in its secret economy, offended by that revelation of mechanical methods which made *An Autobiography* either a disgusting or an amusing book to those who read it more intelligently' (213). Henry Ryecroft thought 'the notable merits of Trollope's work are unaffected by one's knowledge of how

that work was produced' (212) and he admired the writer for being a hard-nosed businessman: 'A big, blusterous, genial brute of a Trollope could very fairly hold his own, and exact at all events an acceptable share in the profits of his work' (214).   RCT

Gladstone, William Ewart (1809–98), Liberal statesman, twice Prime Minister in Trollope's lifetime (1868–74, 1880–5). Trollope disagreed strongly with Gladstone's policy over Ireland. His last unfinished novel, *The Landleaguers*, contains a denunciation of Gladstone's Land Acts in the chapter 'The State of Ireland' (XLI). Politics of the Second Reform Bill form a background to *Phineas Finn* in which the Liberal Prime Minister, Mr Gresham (Gladstone), is opposed by an opportunistic leader of the Conservative Party, Mr Daubeny (Disraeli). In *Phineas Redux* the political events behind the story concern Irish church disestablishment. As usual with his fiction, current policies rather than a living politician's character direct Trollope's presentations. In 1875 he strongly supported Gladstone over the Bulgarian/Turkish dispute. He read Gladstone's pamphlet *The Bulgarian Horrors and the Question of the East*, and spoke at a rally condemning Disraeli's pro-Turkish stance. In *The Fixed Period* Trollope gave the name 'Gladstonopolis' to the capital of 'Britannula'. Feeling himself snubbed at the Royal Academy banquet (May 1880), he wrote to ask if he had offended the great man. 'My sympathies are with you in all things; and as I want nothing from the Prime Minister, I can dare to endeavour to put you right if there be a mistake' (*Letters* 2, 864–5). Such forthrightness stemming from sensitivity as to others' opinions is typical. Gladstone tried to reassure him. It was during a Gladstone administration that Trollope was considered for a peerage.   RCT

'Gladstone's Irish Land Bill' (article). To the great relief of many, Gladstone's proposal for land reform in Ireland does outlaw fixity of tenure (granting to tenants an absolute right to use of the land for a stated number of years). Gladstone's oratorical persuasiveness is almost dangerously effective; even on close examination, however, this bill seems fair to tenants and landholders. The proposal for arbitration of disputes seems bound to help only the lawyers. *Saint Pauls* (March 1870), 620–30.   AKL

Gladstonopolis, capital city of Britannula and hence the centre of a notable cricket match between England and Britannula, but more especially of the country's notorious policy of compulsory euthanasia. Independence from Britain is lost when the ship the *John Bright* trains its huge gun on the city, forcing President Neverbend to give up his power. *FixP*   SRB

Glascock, Charles, eldest son of Lord Peterborough, who assumes the title upon his father's death. Twice rejected by Nora Rowley, he marries Caroline Spalding, niece of an American diplomat. He is a thorough gentleman, an unimposing but decent man, and an unpretentious aristocrat. He is instrumental in arranging the return of Louey Trevelyan to his mother and provides a home for Nora until she can be married to Hugh Stanbury. *HKWR*   RC

Gledd, Ophelia, Boston beauty of independent views, acutely sensitive to the cultural differences between her American and her English lover, who eventually opts for the latter, 'Gledd' *LS*
          GRH

Glenbogie, Sir Thomas Tringle's Scottish country house, twenty miles (32 km) from Inverness. *AA*   WK

Glenn, William Wilkins (1824–76). Born into a wealthy Baltimore family, Glenn became part owner of Baltimore's *Daily Exchange*, a newspaper opposing Lincoln's government, for which he was briefly imprisoned. For the Confederacy Glenn smuggled visitors into the South. During his American tour of 1861–2 Trollope had hoped to cross into the blockaded South, but although acquainted with Glenn he did not try the 'underground' route. However, he made several visits to Baltimore, which enabled him to hear the views of Confederate sympathizers. Glenn kept a diary (published in 1976 as *Between North and South . . . The Narrative of William Wilkins Glenn, 1861–9*), in which he noted that Trollope was 'exceeding Republican [i.e. pro-Lincoln] and believed in the great history of Democratic institutions' (quoted Mullen 407). In a letter (March 1864), Trollope described him as 'a distinguished rebel from Maryland and a particular friend' (1, 256). Glenn paid several visits to Waltham. In November 1863, Trollope offered to take him 'to see so thoroughly British an institution as a fox hunt' (*Letters* 1, 241) and invited him to spend Christmas with his family. Trollope also put him up for the Garrick. Glenn revealed one reason Trollope spent so much time in his garden, for 'even Anthony Trollope in his snug little house only smoked in an outhouse, beyond the kitchen' (Glenn 103). Glenn did not like hunting, although he acknowledged that it allowed Trollope to release his competitive spirit.   RC

Glomax, Captain, itinerant master of the Ufford and Rufford United Hunt. Dissatisfied with the funding and the kennel arrangements, he quits at the end of the season. He rides with the hunt in *Ayala's Angel* and also surfaces in *The Duke's Children. AS*   MG

Gloucestershire, county in western England where Curry Hall, country home of Mr Montacute Jones, is located. Mary Masters travels to Gloucestershire to visit Lady Ushant at her home in Cheltenham in *The American Senator*. Mary Lowther lives at Loring in the county (*VB*). *IHP*
          MG

Goarly, Dan, shifty, shiftless farmer suspected of poisoning foxes. Elias Gotobed becomes involved in Goarly's claim against Lord Rufford for damages done by pheasants. After giving evidence against Scrobby in the fox-poisoning trial, he offers to sell his land to Lawrence Twentyman rather than have it go to Lord Rufford. *AS*   MG

Godby, Augustus, Secretary of the Post Office in Ireland to whom Colonel Maberly sent advance warning in 1841 that his new clerk, Anthony Trollope, was unreliable. Godby assured the newcomer he would be judged on his merits.
          RCT

Godley, John Robert (1814–61), attended Harrow (1828–32). In 1847 Godley published five letters in the *Spectator* describing the condition of the poor in Ireland. Horrified by the famine, he advocated emigration and became a zealous Colonial Reformer. He played a key role in founding the Canterbury Association for settlement of Canterbury, New Zealand. Trollope devoted a chapter to Godley in *Australia and New Zealand*. He remembered him 'as a boy at school thoroughly respected by all his schoolfellows' (*ANZ* 11, 356). Of Godley's letters, he wrote: 'no volume of correspondence ever fell into my hands which left upon my mind a higher impression of the purity, piety, philanthropy, truth, and highminded thoughtfulness of the writer.' He regarded Godley's endeavours as nobly philanthropic and based on 'the best of everything English'.   RCT

Goesler, Marie (Mme Max). Clever, beautiful, fashionable, and wealthy, she wins the friendship of Lady Glencora Palliser and the love of both the Duke of Omnium and Phineas Finn. Though Mme Goesler lives in fashionable Park Lane, where she entertains with great elegance, her obscure background somewhat clouds her social success. 'The World' believes, at least, that she is a foreigner, and suspects that she may be Jewish. Her former marriage, which has left her a wealthy widow, is also a subject of distrust. Mme Goesler fiercely guards her reputation, cultivating only the best society and behaving with the utmost discretion and gentility. Her beauty and intelligence charm the old Duke of Omnium to such an extent that he proposes to marry her in his old age. But with characteristic caution, Mme Goesler refuses the coronet, thus winning Lady Glencora's lifelong friendship. As the Duke is charmed by Mme Max, so is she charmed by Phineas, to whom she offers her hand and her fortune, though it is several years before he can accept her offer and make them both happy. *PF, PR, PM, DC, ED*   JMR

Goffe & Goffe, solicitors acting for Countess Lovel in her attempt to assert her right to the Lovel title and estate. *LA*   RCT

Golden Lion of Granpère, The (*see next page*)

Goldfinder, the ship which takes John Caldigate and Dick Shand to Australia, on a voyage which shows shipboard life and social classes as well as Caldigate's meeting and romance with Euphemia Smith. *JC*   SRB

Goldsmith, Oliver (1729–74), Irish journalist, dramatist, novelist, poet; part of Johnson's circle, best known for *The Deserted Village* (1770) and his comedy *She Stoops to Conquer* (1773). Goldsmith was among Trollope's favourite dramatists and he read several of his poems to the family (December 1878). In *The American Senator* Trollope used Elias Gotobed, a visiting Republican, to ask damning questions about society in much the same way as Goldsmith's Chinese 'Citizen of the World' (Super 348).   RCT

Golightly, Clementina, daughter of Mrs Valentine Scott, and an heiress. Clementina is a 'doosed fine gal' (XVII) whose only passion is for the latest polka. Her £20,000 fortune proves too tempting for her trustee Alaric, who speculates with her money. She marries the Frenchman Victoire Jacquêtanàpe, and dances happily ever after. *TC*   MT

Gondin, M. le Curé ('Goudin' prior to chapter XIII, 'Gondin' thereafter). As Granpère's Catholic priest and confessor to Mme Voss, he is enlisted in the effort to convince Marie Bromar it is her duty to marry Adrian Urmand. *GLG*   MG

Good Words. In 1860, the same year the highly successful monthly shilling magazine the *Cornhill* was begun, Alexander *Strahan, a Scottish publisher of religious books, began *Good Words*, selling it for sixpence, half the price of *Cornhill*, but just out of reach of many working-class readers. Strahan, who already published the *Sunday Magazine*, introduced this new household magazine to bridge the gap between improving and entertaining literature. As a popular religious periodical, its success was unparalleled.

Appealing to the lower middle class, it was edited by Dr Norman *Macleod, a liberal minister in the Church of Scotland like his father before him. Both were leading figures in the religious life of Scotland, and both had been appointed chaplains to Queen Victoria. *Good Words*' readership was made up principally of evangelicals, Scottish Presbyterians, and English Nonconformists.

The first number, containing 64 pages, displayed a quotation from George Herbert on the title-page, 'Good Words are Worth Much and Cost Little', and included no fiction or illustrations. Articles, averaging less than two pages, were unsigned. Macleod promised that he would be assisted by writers from various denominations, in an effort to attract readers from varying sectors of evangelical Christianity. The first number sold 30,000 copies, outselling the *Cornhill* in Scotland.

Strahan seemed to use the *Cornhill* as his model. Like George *Smith, proprietor of the *Cornhill*, Strahan did more of the editorial work than his editor. By the second number, *Good Words* included illustrations of the Scriptures and a serialized story, as well as the names of contributors (perhaps in an effort to demonstrate their diverse religious backgrounds). Dinah Mulock (Mrs Craik), author of the best-selling novel *John Halifax Gentleman* (1856), and Sarah Tytler, a *Cornhill* writer, began contributing. Articles on subjects of general interest, including science, began to appear. Illustrations later became a special feature, including some by Millais. Contributions to early numbers came mainly from ministers of the Church of Scotland, as well as Free Churchmen, Scottish Baptists, Scottish Congregationalists, Wesleyans, and evangelical Anglicans. Contributors appealing to English readers appeared too, including A. P. *Stanley, who became Dean of Westminster in 1864, and social reformers and religious liberals like Charles *Kingsley. The *London Bookseller* said it was the best and cheapest of the religious monthlies. Its circulation reached 70,000 by 1862. *Cornhill*'s circulation at that time was between 80,000 and 85,000.

Strahan looked to the *Cornhill* for more writers, including John *Hollingshead, who also contributed to Dickens's *All the Year Round*. In a letter asking him to provide scenes describing London working-class life, which Hollingshead was already writing for *Cornhill* and *All the Year Round*, Strahan stressed the difference between *Good Words* and those publications, saying that in his magazine everything had to have a purpose. To interest and amuse the reader was not

(*cont. on page 221*)

THE story is set in Alsace-Lorraine, which Trollope and his wife visited in 1867. Since the Franco-Prussian War (1870–1) occurred between writing and publication, however, Trollope had to recognize the annexation of the area (hitherto all in France) by Germany (I), though elsewhere (VII, for example) he failed to do the requisite tidying up. It does not affect the impact of the story, which is single-stranded in plot, concisely structured, and precisely told. Michel Voss, proprietor of the Lion d'Or in Granpère, has a son George by his first marriage. By his second, he provides for his wife's niece Marie Bromar, to whom he becomes devoted. Michel obdurately sets his face against George marrying Marie, and George, having declared his love to Marie and found it reciprocated, leaves to work in a hotel in Colmar, nominally run by a relative, Mme Faragon, though George bears the main responsibilities. Michel arranges for a wealthy linen-merchant from Basle, Adrian Urmand, to court Marie, but she resists his advances. George returns to Granpère on rumours of Marie's marriage, but he and Marie fail to communicate their real feelings for each other and, after he leaves, she is once again pressured by Michel to accept Urmand. George again returns, but this time the lovers acknowledge their passion. Michel is still adamantly opposed, but he has already recognized that if Marie marries Urmand he will lose her. She is, moreover, a model of dedication and efficiency; popular with everyone, she effectively runs the hotel. Gradually, Michel sees where his best interests lie, and he contrives a picnic at which all three lovers appear with the leading residents: amity is established, since Urmand does not lose face because he is seen to be an intimate of the family, and George and Marie are reconciled with his father. The much-ado-about-nothing structure of the story does not diminish its charm. The touch is light and relaxed, the style pleasantly descriptive of the setting. Within the easy-flowing, controlled, simple narrative is a strong psychological focus on Michel and his obsession, complicated and enlivened by Trollope's depiction of the workings of gossip in the small community; of the obstinacy which George has inherited from his father; of the resistance, loyalty, and courage of Marie; and of the vapid but not unsympathetic Urmand. Mme Voss exercises her own ameliorating influence on her husband, while the latter's reduction of Marie to his fixed wish is counterbalanced by his warmth and a developing capacity to accept what he has irrationally opposed. The plot, neat and economical, incorporates Trollope's postal expertise: Marie's letter of rejection to Urmand, a copy of which she shows to Michel after she has posted it, sends him successfully in pursuit of it to Basle, where he persuades Urmand to return with him despite its contents. And the all's-well-that-ends-well motif is fittingly climaxed by the picnic, the reconciliatory occasion redolent of happiness, pathos, and humour in equal proportion.

Originally intended to be published anonymously, its seven-week writing time close to that of *Nina Balatka* and *Linda Tressel*, *The Golden Lion* is slight but assured, Trollope's travel once more feeding his fiction. The urbane, sometimes arch manner provides a smooth gloss, but the narrative tension is maintained through the dexterous combination of outward normality—the daily ritual of hotel life—and the inward conflicts and sufferings of the protagonists. Part of the impact derives from the sense of separateness from the familiar world, a cut-off claustrophobia, a paradoxical inversion of space. The journeys from Colmar to Granpère and the anti-climactic returns encapsulate the love crises of George and Marie, but although the ending is never in doubt reader-identification with this small and unsophisticated world is never in doubt either. *The Golden Lion* was written 1 September–22 October 1867, and serialized in *Good Words* January–August 1872. It included 24 drawings by F. A. Fraser. Book publication was in May 1872. The manuscript is not extant.   GRH

Smalley, Donald (ed.), *Anthony Trollope: The Critical Heritage* (1969).
Trollope, Anthony, *The Golden Lion of Granpère*, (ed. David Skilton 1993).

enough, and while he did not expect Hollingshead to turn into a parson, he did need a week-day preacher.

Strahan attracted Gladstone as a contributor, as well as Tennyson, Poet Laureate. *Good Words'* reputation was such that by 1868 Henry *Kingsley asked his publisher if he could write something for the magazine because it would give him greater prestige, since all the best writers were appearing in it.

Macleod, a friend of Trollope's and fellow member of the Garrick Club, wrote to him in 1862 to describe *Good Words* and to ask for a novel. Trollope met Strahan and agreed to submit *Rachel Ray*, to begin serialization in 1863. Before the novel appeared, Trollope's story 'A Widow's Mite' appeared in the Christmas number, with an announcement that a novel by Trollope would be forthcoming, illustrated by Millais.

In April, a number of ministers of the Free Church of Scotland passed a resolution condemning *Good Words* because it undermined the sabbath by encouraging readers to read amusing tales or papers by writers such as Trollope on worldly matters on the Lord's Day. Macleod then asked Strahan if he could take a stronger role in evaluating material for the publication. As a result, when he read *Rachel Ray* for the first time, in galley form, Macleod decided it was unfit for *Good Words* because Trollope presented dancing until 4 a.m. as enjoyable and meetings of the Dorcas Society as dull. Worse still, Trollope ridiculed Prong, a clergyman with evangelical tendencies. Trollope took the rejection with good humour, advising Millais that *Good Words* had determined he was too wicked to be included. He remained friends with Macleod until the editor's death in 1872. Donald Macleod, his brother, then became editor.

Trollope continued to make contributions over the years, including the short story 'Why Frau Frohmann Raised her Prices'; and the novels *The Golden Lion of Granpère* (January–August 1872) and *Kept in the Dark* (May–December 1882), which Macleod edited to make it acceptable, changing 'damnable' to 'pernicious', 'damning' to 'condemning', and 'd—— my relatives' to 'never mind my relatives'. A novelette, 'The Two Heroines of Plumplington', the final story set in Barset, which Trollope wrote during the last months of his life, was published in the Christmas issue after his death.   JWM

Goose and Gridiron, The, Fleet Street club frequented by Mr Robinson, in which political issues are debated according to House of Commons procedures. The name recalls a Goose and Glee Club formed by John Merivale and Trollope in London. *SBJR*   RCT

Gordeloup, Sophie, a Franco-Polish woman of 50, of dry, hard, bright appearance, carelessly intimate in both dress and confidence. Much more obviously an exotic than her brother Count Pateroff, her English is colourful rather than correct, and what she says shrewd but rarely trustworthy. She is Lady Ongar's limpet-like companion for much of the novel, and though decidedly tough, she shows hints of past misery, as when she sheds a tear for the loss of her child. *C*   PJT

Gordon, Revd Henry Doddridge, vicar of Harting where Trollope had his last home; author of *The History of Harting* (1877) and *Among the Birds of Harting* (1886). On Trollope's death, he wrote an obituary for *Publisher's Circular* (December 1882). 'He was the life of our school manager meetings, and a generous patron of the education of the poor. He sympathized with the farmers in their troubles, and was always a promoter of the union of the classes . . . He rarely, even when his health was failing, missed Sunday morning service, always punctual to the minute—an alert and reverent and audible worshipper, and a steady communicant' (*I & R* 236–7). Gordon also left a written memorial of Trollope in the *Guardian* (December 1882), describing how his gardener had caught a man stealing apples: 'Trollope rushed from his library and found the man seated under a tree munching a purloined apple. "Who allowed you to take some of my apples?" Trollope roared. "I had nothing but bread and it's better with an apple", was the pert reply. Trollope rushed back into the kitchen, and returned with ham and cheese, commanding: "Eat and be better" ' (quoted Mullen 636–7).   RCT

Gordon, John, son of a Norwich banker. His father's financial ruin forces him to leave Oxford and prevents his marriage to Mary Lawrie. He leaves for the South African diamond fields, makes a fortune, and returns three years later to propose to Mary. Upon learning that she has just accepted Mr Whittlestaff's proposal, he is prepared to return to South Africa but is quickly— and gratefully—betrothed to Mary when Mr Whittlestaff releases her from the engagement. *OML*   RC

Gorse Hall, cottage and hunting lodge in Northamptonshire belonging to Lord Hampstead. It is at one of the hunts here that Hampstead is rumoured to have died in a fall with his horse, giving rise to concern and speculation. *MF*
                                                SRB

Gortnaclough, village near Castle Richmond where the famine relief committee meets every fortnight, and where the Fitzgeralds establish a soup kitchen. *CR*   MRS

Goschen, George Joachim, 1st Viscount Goschen (1831–1907), brilliant businessman, a director of the Bank of England at 27, known as the 'Fortunate Youth'. He became Chancellor of the Duchy of Lancaster (1866), devoting himself to Liberal policies. Trollope persuaded him to contribute articles to the first two numbers of *Saint Pauls*: 'The Leap in the Dark' (October 1867) and 'The New Electors' (November 1867). Goschen hosted a dinner in 1878 for the Crown Princess of Prussia (Queen Victoria's eldest child) to which Trollope was invited.   RCT

Gotobed, Elias. The American Senator of the title, used by Trollope as the proverbial man from Mars to comment on English mores, is an intelligent, politically concerned man who does not understand why he offends almost everyone he talks to. His lecture on 'The Irrationality of Englishmen', given to help them correct their faults, provokes a near-riot and he feels hardly used. He reappears in *The Duke's Children* as the American minister in London. *AS*   MG

Gould, Catherine, daughter of Colonel and Mrs Grant, close friends of the Trollopes at Harrow, and wife of John Nutcombe Gould (?1806–78), rector of Stokeinteignhead, Devon (1847–78). As a child she and her sisters helped the Trollopes rescue portable property from Julian Hill when they decamped. 'I still own a few books that were thus purloined' (*Auto* II). To Catherine's enquiry about successful authorship, Trollope said it required what few outsiders appreciated, 'considerable training, and much hard-grinding industry—My belief of book writing is much the same as my belief as to shoemaking' (*Letters* 1, 100). The analogy was often repeated.   RCT

government in Trollope's England was cheap and honest, if not particularly efficient. 'Old Corruption', the system of sinecure, patronage, and graft which characterized most *ancien régime* governments, was largely defeated by about 1840. It was a residue of the old suspicion of civil service corruptibility that, as a Post Office official, Trollope was disqualified from voting in parliamentary elections. Civil servants were appointed by merit, paid an adequate stipend rather than charging fees, and insulated from direct political interference by a hierarchy of permanent nonpolitical officials. Civil servants were relatively few in number—around 21,000 in 1832, increasing by 1881 to 51,000 (excluding the armed forces), an indicator of broadening government activity. Cheap and honest government was one of the chief benefits of the creed of financial orthodoxy, its trinity being Free Trade, Balanced Budgets, and the Gold Standard. Consecrated to upholding these doctrines was the Treasury, the central department which controlled and audited all government expenditure.

Government expenditure as a proportion of net national income was roughly constant at 10 per cent, while the national debt actually declined significantly over the 19th century due mainly to the absence of major wars. Debt servicing fell from 54 per cent of government expenditure in 1830 to 34 per cent by 1880. However, maintaining the armed forces remained the main item of government expenditure, absorbing about a third of the budget. By contrast education expenditure was 0.2 per cent in 1830; by 1880 it was 4 per cent. Law and order rose from 0.7 per cent to 8 per cent. Paying for this was, of course, the taxpayer. Britain was a lightly and, comparatively speaking, fairly taxed country. Free trade meant that revenue from customs and excise duties fell drastically (though tobacco and alcohol taxes remained indispensable). They were replaced in 1842 by a flat tax of 3 per cent on incomes over £150 p.a. This tax fluctuated from year to year according to government needs, doubling to 6 per cent during the Crimean War, and the great but unrealized ambition of Gladstone, high priest of government economy, was its abolition. It fell briefly to under 1 per cent in 1874. Estate taxes were minimal until 1894. Such things were so well known to Trollope's characters, and readers, that he did not have to mention them.

As for efficiency, some parts of government were worse than others, the War Office being notably bad, as the Crimean War demonstrated. Institutional inertia could be immense, and blind devotion to tradition obstructed adaptation to new circumstances and needs. Yet, with the help of an outstanding civil servant, great things could often be achieved, as Sir Edwin Chadwick and Sir John Simon showed in public health administration, and Sir Rowland *Hill at the Post Office. Fortunately, Trollope worked in one of the most efficient government departments, as one of its most efficient members, though he clashed with Hill. Contrary to common belief, *laissez-faire* was not an unchallenged dogma of Victorian government: the Post Office took over the telegraph system and Gladstone advocated nationalization of the railways. One of the ways in which government was most active was in regulation and inspection of industries and services, where it was able to exert influence, without having to spend much money, by enforcing higher standards in education, housing, transportation, sanitation, and the like, especially on local governments.

CK

Roseveare, Henry, *The Treasury: The Evolution of a British Institution* (1969).
Smellie, K. B., *A Hundred Years of English Government* (1936).

government officials as characters. In the original version of *The New Zealander* a whole chapter was dedicated to Trollope's view of the present and future state of his own profession, the civil service. The fact that this chapter did not survive his revision of the rejected manuscript may suggest that much of the material was reused in the extraneous chapter XII ('The Civil Service') of *The Three Clerks* in 1857 (though this chapter was in turn cut from the one-volume edition of the novel of 1859). It is also possible that further material was used in Trollope's rejected, and now lost, review of the third number of Dickens's *Little Dorrit* (February 1856), the number in which Dickens had introduced his deeply unflattering picture of the Circumlocution Office. Further material may well have also surfaced in an article ('The Civil Service') published anonymously in the *Dublin University Magazine* in October 1855. The fact that other deleted passages from the manuscript of *The New Zealander* were worked into the chapter of *The Three Clerks* entitled 'The Parliamentary Committee' (now XXXII) also suggests the intimate linkage between that particular novel and Trol-

lope's determination to defend his profession against ill-informed or prejudiced opinion.

Although Trollope was never to be uncritical of the civil service, and of both senior and junior government officials in his fiction, he was clearly offended by such overstated caricature figures as Dickens's gentlemanly Tite Barnacles ('a very high, and a very large family . . . dispersed all over the public offices, and [holding] all sorts of public places') (*Little Dorrit*, X). Unlike Miss Marrable in *The Vicar of Bullhampton* (IX) he was also clear in his mind that the civil service was a proper profession for gentlemen and, as he reiterated in *An Autobiography*, that gentlemen were constitutionally proper to 'berths' in the civil service. In *The Three Clerks* the 'Office of the Board of the Commissioners for Regulating Weights and Measures' is 'a well-conducted public office' with 'a very excellent secretary, and two very worthy assistant secretaries'. The Office has proved such a paragon of order and efficiency that the 'exoteric crowd of the Civil Service, that is, the great body of clerks attached to other offices, regard their brethren of the Weights as prigs and pedants' (I). To junior clerkships in the Weights and Measures are nominated the public-school- and university-educated Henry Norman ('the second son of a gentleman . . . in the north of England') and Alaric Tudor (who somehow contrives to 'pass the scrutinizing instinct and deep powers of examination possessed by the chief clerk'). Alaric's cousin Charley, the third and youngest clerk in the story, is the son of a Shropshire clergyman who 'could never have passed muster at the Weights and Measures' and is tied to a dull job in the Internal Navigation Office. The character of the scrutinizing chief clerk at the Weights and Measures, Mr (later Sir Gregory) Hardlines, who is enthusiastic about the 'much loathed scheme' of civil service examinations, was, the novelist admitted, based on that of Sir Charles Trevelyan. The 'excellent' Sir Warwick Westend, 'full of the best intentions', one of the examining board of the civil service in the same novel, is, Trollope said, a 'feebly facetious name' for Trevelyan's associate and fellow reformer Sir Stafford Northcliffe.

Trollope was to return to his own youthful experience and to dealing prominently with civil service clerkships in *Marion Fay*. George Roden may be a modest, gentlemanly clerk in the Post Office, but he will finally succeed to the Italian dukedom of Crinola. Roden shares his office with four other clerks: the senior, Mr Jerningham ('a quiet civil, dull, old man'), the 'pleasant and good-natured enough' juniors, Bobbin and Geraghty, and the 'ill-mannered' Samuel Crocker, who proves particularly objectionable to his superior Sir Boreas Bodkin ('Aeolus'), the Secretary of the Office (whom Trollope modelled on his own antipathetic superior at the Post Office, Lieutenant Colonel *Maberly).

Apart from the generous Lucy Graham, the 'Telegraph Girl' in the short story of that name, and her invalid room-mate Sophy Wilson, the most prominent government officials in Trollope's other novels are John Robarts, a clerk in the Petty Bag Office and private secretary to the Lord Petty Bag ('a place of considerable trust, if not hitherto of large emolument') (*FP* X); the worthy John Eames, a clerk in the Income Tax Office at Somerset House; the ambitious Adolphus Crosbie, a clerk in the General Committee Office; Eames's colleague and fellow boarder at Mrs Roper's, Joseph Cradell; Mr Butterwell, 'who had never set the Thames on fire, and had never attempted to do so' (*SHA* XXVIII) but who has a seat on the Board of Commissioners; Sir Raffle Buffle, the 'great bully' who is head of the Income Tax Office, and Major Fiasco, a member of the General Committee who had been sent to the General Committee Office 'because he was not wanted anywhere else' (*SHA* XXVIII); Reginald Dosett, the generous uncle of Ayala and Lucy Dormer, and a clerk at the Admiralty on a salary of £900 p.a. (*AA*); and the barrister John Vavasor in *Can You Forgive Her?* who had once been appointed an assistant commissioner in 'some office which had to do with insolvents, which was abolished three years after his appointment' (I), but who still receives an income for attending three times a week for three hours (during term time) and simply signing his name. In *Miss Mackenzie*, Miss Mackenzie's Scottish father 'became a clerk in Somerset House at the age of sixteen, and was a clerk in Somerset House when he died at the age of sixty' (I). Her brother Walter, 'a poor sickly creature', now also deceased, followed his father's profession. In *John Caldigate*, he was still the spokesman for industrious public servants. Samuel Bagwax, a Post Office clerk, uncovers crucial evidence of a forged postmark on an envelope to clear the hero's name.   ALS

Gowran, Andy, Scottish steward of Lizzie Eustace's Portray estate. Gowran distrusts and despises his mistress, whom he suspects of all manner of evil, reporting against her that she has been improperly involved with her cousin Frank Greystock. Despite his bellicosity, Gowran is an eminently capable and trustworthy bailiff. *ED*
                                                              JMR

Graham, Felix, junior defence lawyer for Lady Mason. Felix is 'by no means a handsome man' but he is 'full of enthusiasm, indomitable, as far

as pluck would make him so, in contests of all kinds, and when he talked on subjects which were near his heart there was a radiance about him which certainly might win the love of the pretty girl with the sharp tongue and the hatful of money' (XVIII). One of Trollope's idealistic young men, Felix tries to educate Mary Snow into the perfect wife, but fails in the endeavour and eventually marries Madeline Staveley. *OF*
                                                              MT

Graham, Lucy, independent, selfless working girl who helps Sophy Wilson to the point of going hungry. She finds happiness with the engineer Abraham Hall. 'Telegraph' *WFF*   GRH

Graham, Mr, concerned and perceptive family lawyer of George Western. He interviews the deserted Cecilia Western, sympathizes with her situation, recognizes her beauty and will, and attempts to convince his employer of the severity of the punishment inflicted on her. *KD*   NCS

Grandnostrel, Count. He orders his archers to attack Mountfidget when he arrives without cattle at the castle. 'Euphemia'   GRH

grandparents of Trollope. Both of Anthony's grandfathers were rural clergymen. Although he would later disclaim any intimate knowledge of country rectories and cathedral closes, his family background, with its connections by marriage or friendship to the landed gentry, the law, the military, and (let it be whispered) hints of trade, exactly reflects the social texture of the Barsetshire novels.

As the youngest son of Sir Thomas Trollope, 4th Baronet, of Casewick Hall, Lincolnshire, Anthony's paternal grandfather could not share that estate, which was entailed upon his senior brother. Accordingly, he took holy orders, after an education at Wakefield School and Pembroke College, Cambridge, and acquired the rectorships of Cottered and Broadfield in Hertfordshire, along with the honorary title of 'Chaplain to the Duchess of Somerset'. He was also a qualified barrister (Mullen 3) but remained a country vicar for the next 40 years, earning 'the Esteem of all good men', according to his memorial tablet, for 'Christian harmony and benevolence' (Glendinning 9). Such ancestry and affluence also earned him the hand of Penelope Meetkerke, daughter of the neighbouring squire of Rushden. Her family had lived in Hertfordshire since Adolphus Meetkerke, Dutch ambassador to the court of Elizabeth I, had married the heiress of Julians, Penelope Stone. Since those times, the Meetkerkes had also acquired Rushden manor and, because Mrs Trollope's brother Adolphus had no children, that double inheritance was an inviting prospect. Together, the Revd Anthony and Mrs Trollope produced three daughters and a son. One daughter married a Sussex landowner; another married a cousin, the Revd Henry Trollope; the youngest also married a clergyman. The Trollopes' only son, with an eye to his landed future, followed Uncle Adolphus to Winchester and New College, Oxford, and then sat for the bar. When the Revd Anthony died in 1806, his heir had sufficient means to buy a London house and settle £6,000 on his bride-to-be Frances Milton (Mullen 7).

Her father had become a gentleman by education and ordination. The son of a Bristol tradesman, who was perhaps an apothecary or distiller, perhaps a saddler, William Milton had also been to Winchester and Oxford and, through those connections, received a benefice near Bristol, where Fanny was born, and, somewhat later, at Heckfield in Hampshire. He rose still further from his commercial beginnings when he married Mary Gresley, the daughter of wealthy landowners. The respectful thrill of that splendid relationship would later be detonated by Trollope when he used his grandmother's name for the title of one of his short stories, about a nobody whose prettiness persuades an ageing editor to further her writing career. He used it again, more pointedly, for a rejected suitor, Lord Alfred Gresley, in *Sir Harry Hotspur of Humblethwaite*. The actual Mary Gresley died relatively young. William Milton survived to marry Sarah Partington, who did not endear herself to her stepchildren, and to be remembered by Trollope's brother Tom as 'an excellent parish priest after the fashion of his day': 'He was a charming old man, markedly gentlemanlike and suave in his manner; . . . clever unquestionably in a queer, crotchety sort of way. . . . But he would have had no more idea of attempting anything of the nature of active parochial work or reform . . . than he would have had of scheming to pay the national debt' (*What I Remember* (1887), 1, 13). Long before his eccentric old age, he had devised ways to improve and enlarge the port of Bristol. His plans for a floating harbour were rejected, with suitable thanks, by the city fathers, but at Hexfield he continued to ponder ways of improving society. Hating the sound of knives on dinnerware, he invented a plate with a central disc of silver on which to cut one's meat. His coach-house was crammed with prototypes of a stage-coach which could not be overturned, and shares in the prospective revenues from that remarkable 'patent cart' formed part of his daughter's settlement when she married Thomas Anthony Trollope.

That union of gentility, money, and inventiveness ought to have turned out well. But, alas, Thomas Anthony's brusqueness belied the motto beneath his family-crest, *audio sed taceo* ('I hear, but am silent'), and offended Uncle Meetkerke, as did Fanny's raffish friends. On the death of his wife, Adolphus remarried and produced an heir for the Meetkerke estates. But the Trollopes' dashed hopes, which led to financial disaster, also resulted in Anthony's fascination with the complexities of family bloodlines, marriage settlements, and legacies. AWJ

Granger family. Revd Robert Granger is dedicated to alleviating the misery of those suffering in the Cotton Famine through collecting donations, and the family, including his wife and two sons, Charles and Bob, and Nora Field, discuss the problem constantly, without being able to agree on a remedy. *LS* RCT

Granpère, village in the Vosges mountains on the Lorraine side of the col de Schucht noted for its linen. Prosperous without great gradations of wealth and poverty, the Protestant and Catholic inhabitants mix together easily. The Lion d'Or is a centre of the village. *GLG* MG

Grant, Albert (1830–99), son of W. Gottheimer; assumed the name of Grant; company promoter for schemes such as the notorious Emma silver mine (1871) for which investors got back one shilling on £1 shares; MP for Kidderminster (1865–8, re-elected 1874). Grant built a mansion next to Kensington Palace; he also purchased Leicester Square, which he converted to a public garden and handed over to the metropolitan board of works (1874). He was made Baron Grant by the King of Italy (1868). Obvious parallels exist between Grant and Augustus Melmotte in *The Way We Live Now*, as Escott suggested (*Anthony Trollope* (1913), 297). RCT

Grant, Lady Bertha, widowed sister of George Western. Kind-hearted, perceptive, and knowing his stubborn and suspicious character, she sympathizes with his estranged wife Cecilia, and selflessly travels from her Scottish home to Dresden to bring him back to England and responsibility. *KD* NCS

Grant, Colonel James (d. 1852) and **Mrs Penelope** (1795–1861). The Grants were neighbours of the Trollopes at Julian Hill. The children of both families played together and started a family magazine, 'The Magpie'. After bailiffs had repossessed Julian Hill, 'the whole family bivouacked under the Colonel's hospitable roof, cared for and comforted by that dearest of all women, his wife' (*Auto* II). RCT

Grant family, neighbours of the Trollopes in Harrow who took part in smuggling portable property from Julian Hill to beat the bailiffs in 1834. Colonel James Grant took in some furniture, while his daughters Anna, May, and Kate helped rescue china, glass, books, and silverware through a gap in the hedge. The family are possibly figured in the Dales of *The Small House at Allington* (1864).   RCT

Grantly, Bishop, kindly Bishop of Barchester, father of Archdeacon Grantly, and lifelong friend of Septimus Harding, with whom he attempts to temper his son's angry and ambitious actions. Over 70 and idle, the Bishop rules his diocese with benevolent ease. His peaceful death at the beginning of *Barchester Towers* sets in motion the struggle for power in the diocese. He is remembered as a symbol of virtue in *The Last Chronicle of Barset*. W   NCS

Grantly, Charles James, eldest son of Archdeacon Grantly of Barchester, who uses him as a threat to disinherit his second son, Henry. An exacting and decorous London clergyman, he marries the Lady Anne, and may become a bishop, perhaps an archbishop. A child in *The Warden*. The character was intended as a satire on Charles James *Blomfield. LCB   NCS

Grantly, Edith, 3-year-old motherless daughter of Major Henry Grantly. According to her grandfather Septimus Harding, she resembles her aunt, Eleanor Arabin. *LCB*   NCS

Grantly, Florinda, eldest daughter of Archdeacon Grantly, named after the wife of the Archbishop of York. Aged 16 in *Barchester Towers* (and the younger daughter) she acts as bridesmaid at Eleanor Bold's wedding. She has died by *The Small House at Allington*. W   NCS

Grantly, Griselda. See HARTLETOP, GRISELDA, MARCHIONESS OF.

Grantly, Major Henry, second son of Archdeacon Grantly of Barchester. Having won a Victoria Cross in India, he returns to Barsetshire, a widower under 30 with a young daughter, Edith, and falls in love with the talented Grace Crawley, an attachment that causes his father to threaten cutting off his portion. Enraged, Major Grantly threatens to sell off Cosby Lodge and move to Pau. His boyhood is described in *The Warden* and *Barchester Towers*. LCB   NCS

Grantly, Samuel ('Soapy'), third son of Archdeacon Grantly of Barchester. Soft, gentle, courteous, and affable, he defends himself against his more active brothers with vocal wit. He returns from university for his aunt Eleanor Bold's wedding in *Barchester Towers*, but is never

heard of again. The character satirized Samuel *Wilberforce. W   NCS

Grantly, Susan (née **Harding**), eldest daughter of Septimus Harding and wife of Archdeacon Grantly. She values power but knows her place, nevertheless managing to express her opinions and exercise 'beneficent sway' over her difficult husband. Though often suspicious of her younger sister Eleanor's actions, she does her best to support her. She strives to find a good husband for her beautiful daughter Griselda, attempting to arrange an alliance with Lord Lufton in *Doctor Thorne* but achieving greater success with Lord Dumbello. She has a trying time defending her son Henry's choice of bride against her husband in *The Last Chronicle of Barset*. Appears often in all the Barsetshire novels. *BT*   NCS

Grantly, Dr Theophilus. Dr Grantly, Archdeacon, and rector of Plumstead Episcopi, son of Bishop Grantly (who dies at the opening of *BT*), married to Susan, elder daughter of Septimus Harding, is a principal character in *The Warden*, *Barchester Towers*, and *The Last Chronicle of Barset*, and appears frequently in *Doctor Thorne* and *Framley Parsonage*. He is the champion of the high-church party in Barchester against evangelicalism and Liberal reforms. A wealthy man, and proud of his position, he is equally proud in *Framley Parsonage* of marrying his daughter Griselda to Lord Dumbello, heir to the marquisate of Hartletop, despite Dumbello's dubious reputation and the scandal attaching to his mother as an intimate friend of the old Duke of Omnium. He has a keen eye to the temporalities of the Church, and scant understanding of the scrupulosities of conscience of Septimus Harding, whom he bullies persistently but unsuccessfully over the wardenship. He is described as 'an ecclesiastical statue': 'the broad chest, amply covered with fine cloth, told how well to do was his estate; one hand ensconced within his pocket, evinced the practical hold which our mother church keeps on her temporal possessions; and the other, loose for action, was ready to fight if need be for her defence' (*W* V). His forcible style of expression is typified by his habitual exclamation, 'Good heavens!', which has become part of his wife's repertoire too. Although formidable by day, he has to submit to 'curtain lectures' from his wife by night. When his father lies dying, he is conscious that he has been almost promised the bishopric by the present administration, but that a change of government is about to take place, which threatens to take this plum from him, and at his father's bedside he 'dared to ask himself whether he really longed for his father's death. . . . The proud, wishful, worldly man . . . prayed that his sins might be forgiven him' (*BT* I). His favourite son, Henry, serves in the army in India, reaching the rank of major, and winning the Victoria Cross. In *The Last Chronicle of Barset* he falls in love with Grace Crawley, and wins his father over to the match, inducing the latter to recognize the social equality of Grace's father as a cleric and a gentleman. Trollope took pride in this character: 'My archdeacon, who has been said to be life-like, and for whom I confess that I have all a parent's fond affection, was, I think, the simple result of an effort of my moral consciousness. . . . [A]s far as I can remember, I had not then even spoken to an archdeacon' (*Auto* V). Some commentators have made a case for linking the Archdeacon's combativeness to Trollope's own character, but efforts to equate their views on religion have been misguided.   DS

Graphic, The. Founded by William L. Thomas in 1869, this weekly magazine quickly rivalled the *Illustrated London News*, and became renowned for its illustrations. Arthur *Locker (editor 1870–91) serialized *Phineas Redux* (19 July 1873–January 1874); he ran *Harry Heathcote of Gangoil* as a Christmas story (1873) and published *Marion Fay* (3 December 1881–3 June 1882). 'Christmas at Thompson Hall' also appeared in the magazine.   RCT

Grascour, M., member of the Belgian Foreign Office who loves Florence Mountjoy. A good-looking and well-educated young man, Grascour 'was a man of singularly good temper, and there was running, through all that he did, somewhat of a chivalric spirit which came from study rather than nature' (XLVI). *MSF*   MT

Grasslough, Lord, dissolute member of the Beargarden Club. He gambles regularly with Sir Felix Carbury, Lord Nidderdale, and Miles Grendall. *WWLN, DC*   JMR

Gray, Mr, old college friend whom John Caldigate asks to act as witness that he is not resorting to bribery when he compensates Timothy Crinkett and Euphemia Smith for their mining losses. *JC*   SRB

Graybody, Mr, decrepit curator of the 'College' of Necropolis in Britannula wherein citizens were to be prepared for compulsory euthanasia. *FixP*   SRB

Green, Mrs Adolphus, wife of the curate at Groby Park. In payment for several years of singing lessons to the Mason daughters, Mrs Mason gives the poor curate's wife a broken 'set of metallic "Louey Catorse furniture," containing three tables, eight chairs, &c., &c.' (XXIII), which Mrs Mason purchased at a bargain price from Mr Kantwise. *OF*   MT

Green, Archibald, narrator of three stories, based on Trollope himself. Staying at Castle Conor, he finds himself without dancing pumps. He browbeats the servant Larry into loaning him his shoes in return for his hunting boots ('O'Conors' *TAC1*). In Ballymoy, Green awakes to see a man in his room, and throws him down the stairs, only to find it is the parish priest ('Giles' *LS*). Privy to Ophelia Gledd's dilemma over her American and English suitors, he recognizes her superior qualities, but, acknowledging English prejudices, invites the reader to consider whether or not she is a lady ('Gledd' *LS*).   GRH

Green, Bessy, Cecilia Holt's 'humble' friend and confidante. Married to the minor canon and a bit of a gossip, she represents, in her advice to her friend, the conventional wifely attitudes of submission and humility, which Cecilia, by the end, largely comes to embrace. *KD*   NCS

Green, Captain, co-conspirator of Major Tifto who takes part in the plot to lame Lord Silverbridge's horse before the St Leger. *DC*   JMR

Green, Joseph, solicitor and legal adviser to the Amedroz and Belton families, with chambers in Stone Buildings, Lincoln's Inn. He is 'a man not yet forty years of age, with still much of the salt of youth about him' (XIV). *BE*   WK

Green, Miss, first-class passenger whose social freedom is resented by Euphemia Smith on board the ship to Australia. *JC*   SRB

Green, Mounser, clerk in the Foreign Office who becomes minister to Patagonia and marries Arabella Trefoil. Handsome, six feet tall, popular, playful, and appearing idle, Green is a dedicated civil servant who works hard, knows several languages, and entered the service prior to competitive examinations. *AS*   MG

Green, Olivia. One of the performers of the daring Kappa-Kappa, she marries, with the aid of Mrs Montacute Jones, Lord Giblet. *IHP*   MG

Green, Mrs Patmore. This first cousin of the late Marquis of Brotherton, and mother of Olivia, hosts a dinner where the feelings of the extended family towards Lord and Lady George and the current Marquis of Brotherton are revealed. *IHP*   MG

Greenacre, Harry, eldest son of Farmer Greenacre of Barchester and favourite of Miss Thorne, who thinks him an excellent English yeoman. To encourage his fellows, he rides at Miss Thorne's quintain during the Ullathorne fête, but is unhorsed and thought dreadfully injured. *BT*   NCS

Greene family. Wealthy Mr Greene, amiable but nervous, is on his marriage journey with his new wife, who is close in age to her stepdaughter Sophonisba (Sophy). All are extremely indiscreet about their box and its valuable contents, the saga of its loss and rediscovery setting them at odds with Robinson, the narrator. 'Money' *TAC2*
GRH

Greenmantle, Emily, Less spirited than her friend Polly Peppercorn, and more frightened of her father, her stratagem of not eating is nevertheless as successful as Polly's in persuading her father to let her marry Philip Hughes. 'Plumplington'   GRH

Greenmantle, Mr. A banker intent on his daughter's marrying well—perhaps Harry Gresham—he proposes taking her abroad, but abandons the idea, allowing her to marry Philip Hughes. 'Plumplington'   GRH

Greenough, Captain, sub-inspector of police from Ballinamore, and friend of Myles Ussher, whom he joins at the Carrick races. *MB*   MRS

Greenow, Arabella, dubiously honest widowed aunt of Alice and Kate Vavasor who, though supposedly inconsolable after the death of her much older husband, nevertheless carries on an extended courtship both with Mr Cheesacre and with Captain Bellfield. Taking Kate Vavasor under her wing, Mrs Greenow attempts to school her niece into marrying a rich husband, but desists when Kate comes into a small inheritance. Aunt Greenow's charms have a decidedly Thackerayan flavour. *CYFH*   JMR

Greenwood, Frederick (1830–1909), impressively talented publisher's reader and editor; completed versions of Thackeray's *Denis Duval* (1864) and Mrs Gaskell's *Wives and Daughters* (1866); edited *Cornhill* (1864–8) and *Pall Mall Gazette* (1865–80). Greenwood remembered Trollope as 'he who with the aspect of a wild boar, and with not infrequent resemblance to the manners of the same' strode into the editorial offices with his copy (*I & R* p. xviii).   RCT

Greenwood, Thomas, unctuous, sly chaplain/secretary who has lived luxuriously off the Kingsbury family for 30 years. Idle, hateful, and utterly selfish, he sides with the Marchioness against her husband over the rights of the Marquis's eldest children, even to plotting the murder of Lord Hampstead. When he tries to blackmail the Marchioness, he is dismissed. *MF*   SRB

Gregory, Miss, sympathetic relative of the rector who looks after Bessy Pryor when she is banished by Mrs Miles. 'Launay' *WFF*   GRH

Gregory, Sir William (1817–92), MP for Dublin (1842–7) and Galway (1857–71); Governor of Ceylon (1871–7). He attended Harrow when Trollope was a pupil, and later recalled (with some help from *An Autobiography*) how derided and avoided he had been; 'the most slovenly and dirty boy I ever met' (*I & R* 24). When Trollope came to Ireland as a Post Office clerk he was a guest of the Gregorys at Coole Park, Galway, where he met the gentry and Irish writers. En route for the second time to Australia (1875), Trollope stayed with Gregory but did not relish the Governor's lifestyle: 'A Governor has a great deal of luxury but very little comfort. He can admit no equals, and lives in a sort of petty bastard vice royalty which would kill me' (*Letters* 2, 659).   RCT

Grendall, Lord Alfred, idle, impoverished lord who becomes Augustus Melmotte's private secretary and yes-man. He sells his aristocratic integrity for the empty but moneyed position of director on Melmotte's board, but resents Melmotte's familiarity and hates his own servitude. *WWLN*   SRB

Grendall, Miles, aristocratic lackey of Augustus Melmotte, like his father Lord Alfred. He serves as Melmotte's secretary, screening visitors. Also a gambler and cheat at his club, the Beargarden, and hopelessly in debt, his only good point is his dislike for Felix Carbury. *WWLN*
SRB

Gresham, Lady Arabella (née **De Courcy**), wife of Squire Gresham of Greshamsbury, sister of Earl De Courcy, and devoted mother of six children. Condescending, tyrannical, insecure, and bolstered by the De Courcy belief in heredity, she quarrels with Dr Thorne and ostracizes his niece Mary in hopes that her son Frank will save the family estate by marrying money. *DT, FP*
NCS

Gresham, Augusta, eldest daughter of Squire Gresham of Greshamsbury. Considering herself strong-minded and useful rather than rich, witty, or beautiful, she plays her trump-card of heredity in the marriage game, though without success. *DT, LCB*   NCS

Gresham, Beatrice, second daughter of Squire Gresham of Greshamsbury and friend of Mary Thorne. Imprudent and unlike the De Courcys, she nevertheless shares their veneration for bloodlines and feels she cannot further Mary's love for her brother. She marries a wealthy clergyman, Caleb Oriel. *DT*   NCS

Gresham, Francis (Frank) (the younger), handsome son of Squire Gresham of Greshamsbury whose family duty is 'to marry money' in order to save the estate. Boyish enthusiasm leads him to propose to his penniless childhood friend Mary Thorne, earning the displeasure of his family and his aunt Countess De Courcy. Encouraged to court the heiress Martha Dunstable, he instead becomes confirmed in his first love. He also whips Augustus Moffat who had jilted his sister. Appears in *Framley Parsonage* as an upcoming MP candidate. *DT, LCB*   NCS

Gresham, Francis Newbold (the elder), squire of Greshamsbury who, as a young man, was MP for East Barsetshire, though lukewarm, indifferent, and prone to associate with political enemies. His large fortune and estate dwindles from the cost of three unsuccessful elections, and by the time of his son's majority much of the estate has been sold or mortgaged to Sir Roger Scatcherd. *DT*   NCS

Gresham, Harry, the son of the superior Greshams, seen by Mr Greenmantle as an appropriate husband for his daughter Emily. 'Plumplington'   GRH

Gresham, Mr, one of the great Liberal prime ministers of the Palliser series. Although conscientious, Mr Gresham is also worldly, having a business-like attitude that makes him a particularly effective Prime Minister. Mr Gresham may be modelled after Gladstone. *PF, ED, PR, PM*
                              JMR

Greshamsbury, East Barsetshire village, fifteen miles (24 km) from Barchester and consisting of one long, straggling street, where Dr Thorne lives and practises. *DT*   NCS

Greshamsbury Park, heavily mortgaged home of Squire Gresham of Greshamsbury. Its mansion, said to be among the country's finest specimens of Tudor architecture, stands just outside the Park proper which consists of an expanse of abrupt hills and oak groves, along with some celebrated gardens. *DT*   NCS

Gresley, Lord Alfred, younger son of an old friend of Sir Harry Hotspur and member of Parliament. Among his qualifications as a suitor for the hand of Emily Hotspur is his willingness to assume the name Hotspur. Emily finds him and other approved men to be 'walkingsticks'. *SHH*
                              MG

Gresley, Mary. In November 1869, Trollope received a commonplace book inscribed 'Mary Gresley | 1740–' from Elizabeth Bent, wife of Trollope's second cousin Major John Bent. William Milton (b. 1743 in Bristol), Trollope's grandfather, had married Mary Gresley (June 1774), distantly related to the Gresleys of Derbyshire and Leicestershire, who were holders of an old baronetcy. The couple had four children, Mary, Cecilia, Frances (the mother of Trollope), and Henry. Mary Gresley died shortly after the birth of Henry. Trollope used his grandmother's name in the short story 'Mary Gresley', published in *Saint Pauls* (November 1869).   RCT

Gresley, Mary, physician's daughter determined to be a writer. The poor curate to whom she is engaged never approves, however, and when he dies she burns her manuscript, eventually marrying a missionary. 'Gresley' *ET*   GRH

Grex, Earl, violent spendthrift father of Lady Mabel Grex. The Earl's pedigree is among the finest in England but his gentility may certainly be questioned. Selfish and abusive, the Earl uses Lady Mabel's fortune to pay his never-ending gambling debts, then continually swears at her because she is slow to marry. *DC*   JMR

Grex, Lady Mabel, daughter of an ancient noble family who almost becomes Lord Silverbridge's wife. Lady Mabel is tormented by her father and brother, hardened gamblers who have ruined her fortune and who speak to her without courtesy or respect. Due both to this mistreatment and to an early affection for the penniless Frank Tregear, Lady Mabel acquires an air of wisdom which does not appeal to her young suitors. Lord Silverbridge loses interest when she is unable to requite his love with the freshness and innocence he expects. *DC*   JMR

Grex, Lord Percival, brother of Lady Mabel Grex. Like his father, Lord Percival is a hardened gambler who loses more than he wins. He is no friend to his sister, whose fortune he helps to ruin, nor to his father, who owes him money from a discontinued entail. *DC*   JMR

Grey, Dorothy (Dolly), spinster daughter of John Grey, 'motherless, brotherless, and sisterless' but absolutely devoted to her father, 'the only man for whom she had ever felt the slightest regard' (XVI). She despises her cousins, the eldest Carroll daughters, and refuses a match with Mr Barry. *MSF*   MT

Grey, John, London attorney for John Scarborough and father of Dolly Grey. An honest and old-fashioned lawyer, he has complete faith in the letter of the law. He supports his sister, her dissolute husband, and their six daughters, in the call of duty. His retirement after the end of the

Scarborough affair signals a passing of generations and values. *MSF*   MT

Grey, John, thoroughly upright and gentlemanly lover of Alice Vavasor whom she first accepts, then jilts, before finally marrying him. It is his stalwart character which first makes Alice suspect that she would be unhappy living with him in the quiet solitude of his country home. Though remaining almost 'a shade too good', as Alice's father puts it, Grey takes on added dimension and appeal when he enters upon a successful parliamentary career. *CYFH*   JMR

Grey, Lady Selina, haughty, unmarried daughter of Lord Cashel, dutiful and 'always useful' (XXVIII), but rendered inhuman by her exaggerated devotion to rank. She 'tried hard to love her neighbours, in which she might have succeeded but for the immeasurable height from which she looked down on them' (XII). *KOK*   MRS

Grey Abbey, Lord Cashel's estate in Co. Kildare, which, like the family residence, is devoid of historical or picturesque appeal. *KOK*   MRS

Greystock, Ellinor, eldest sister of Frank Greystock who serves for a brief and comfortless period as Lady Eustace's companion at Portray Castle. Though 'good-humoured' and 'kindly', Ellinor cannot bring herself to real friendship with Lizzie Eustace. *ED*   JMR

Greystock, Frank, young Conservative member of Parliament for Bobsborough, and fiancé of Lucy Morris. Though he is intelligent and conscientious, Frank Greystock's parliamentary success relies largely on the flexibility of his political opinions. Perhaps equally flexible in the romantic arena, Frank toys with the idea of marrying his wealthy, beautiful, but dishonest cousin Lizzie Eustace, but he ultimately follows his heart, and is true to his existing engagement with the plainer but more worthy Lucy Morris. *ED*   JMR

Greystock, Lizzie. See EUSTACE, LADY LIZZIE.

Greystock, Mr, Dean of Bobsborough, Frank Greystock's father. Dean Greystock is 'a fine old Tory of the ancient school' from a family which has no money of its own, but which inevitably prospers from church patronage. The Dean's pleasures are simple: family, Church, and complacent Conservative politics. *ED*   JMR

Greystock, Mrs, Frank Greystock's overprotective mother. Mrs Greystock wants the best for her children, but is perhaps a little too ambitious for their sake. She tries to prevent Frank's marriage to Lucy Morris, but her disapproval is ultimately overcome by her son's devotion to his beloved. *ED*   JMR

Griffenbottom, Mr, Conservative member of Parliament for Percycross; stands again with Sir Thomas Underwood as his running mate. 'A heavy, hale man, over sixty, somewhat inclined to be corpulent, with a red face and a look of assured impudence about him . . . he could boast neither birth, nor talent, nor wit' (XXV). *RH*   ALS

Griffith, John (sometimes **Griffiths**), good-natured tenant of Coed farm at Llanfeare to whom Henry Jones almost reveals his uncle's missing will. But Henry's suspicious behaviour finally alienates him, too. *CH*   AWJ

Griffith, Mrs (sometimes **Griffiths**), Indefer Jones's housekeeper whose good heart eventually responds to his defeated nephew Henry. As with John Griffith(s), Trollope inconsistently adds an 's'. They are not married to each other. The housekeeper's title merely indicates her domestic status; the farmer's wife is introduced briefly at Coed. *CH*   AWJ

Griffiths, Lady Cashel's servant and confidante, notable for providing her mistress with a ready supply of small talk. *KOK*   MRS

Griggs, Adolphus, bachelor son of a Baslehurst wine-merchant. Unlike the romantic hero Luke Rowan, Adolphus is the bachelor nobody wishes to dance with at the Tappitts' ball. The 'singular arrangement of Mr Griggs's jewellery' (VII) contrasts with Luke's confident manliness. Young Griggs incorrectly tells the Tappitts that Luke has left town without paying his bills. *RR*   MT

Grimes, Jacob, politically inclined publican of the Handsome Man tavern who is paid to back George Vavasor in his first bid for a seat in Parliament. *CYFH*   JMR

Grimes, John, landlord of the Spotted Dog. He is sympathetic to Julius Mackenzie but eventually angered by his and Mrs Mackenzie's drunkenness. 'Dog' *ET*   GRH

Grimes, Polly, pretty, sympathetic landlord's wife who is supportive to Julius Mackenzie and accommodates him at the pub. 'Dog' *ET*   GRH

Groby Park, Joseph Mason's estate, seven miles (11 km) from Leeds. Supposedly the only property left to Joseph Mason in his father's will, Groby Park is spacious but 'flat and uninteresting' with a house 'Greek in its style of architecture—at least so the owner says' (VII). *OF*   MT

Grogram, Miss, the 'rednosed harpy', instigator of the destruction of Augustus Horne's trousers. 'Chassé' *TAC1*   GRH

Grogram, Mr, Squire Vavasor's attorney who executes the squire's last will and reads it in the presence of John and George Vavasor. Though sorely provoked by George Vavasor's violent accusations against him, Mr Grogram behaves consistently as a gentleman. *CYFH*   JMR

Grogram, Sir Gregory, Liberal member of Parliament for Clovelly, Lord Chancellor under Mr Gresham. As Attorney-General, Sir Gregory is a resolute upholder of the law, but the cases he tries are not much to his taste. In addition to prosecuting Phineas Finn for the murder of Mr Bonteen, Sir Gregory is required to try Mr Browborough for bribery at the Tankerville election. Sometimes confused with Mr Gogram, an attorney in *Can You Forgive Her? PR, PM*   JMR

Groschut, Joseph. An evangelical converted Jew, the assistant to the Bishop of Brotherton uses his influence over the *Brotherton Church* journal to attack Henry Lovelace. This unpleasant, unpopular, and humourless man is rewarded with an unpleasant, unpopular, and poor parish, and a wife, when he is discovered to have trifled with the affections of a bookseller's daughter. *IHP*   MG

Growler, Mrs, Mrs Heathcote's elderly maidservant, 'as good as the bank', but apt to feel low-spirited. When the homestead is threatened with fire, Mrs Growler urges her mistress to leave, but her advice is overridden. *HHG*   MRS

Grundle, Abraham, first suitor of Eva Crasweller until she learns that he is more interested in her father's prosperous farm. Young Grundle becomes an increasingly articulate and disagreeable advocate of the 'Fixed Period' policy of compulsory euthanasia because Eva's father would be the first to die, thus enriching her. *FixP*   SRB

Grüner, Frau, wife of Madame Staubach's estranged half-brother, a Cologne lawyer. As a Catholic, she bristles at her Calvinist sister-in-law's fanatic treatment of their niece: 'she will have been murdered by your prayers' (XVII). Her loving, fair-haired children visit Linda's sickbed daily, until their cousin's death. *LT*   AWJ

Guadalquivir, Spanish river down which John Pomfret journeys to Seville. 'Bull' *TAC1*   GRH

Guestwick, market town neighbouring on Allington, just over the western border of Barsetshire, where Johnny Eames and his mother live and Dr Crofts practises. Lily Dale and her mother contemplate moving there. *SHA*   NCS

Guestwick Manor, home of Earl De Guest and his spinster sister Lady Julia. *SHA*   NCS

guidebooks. Because Trollope wrote so extensively and since several of his characters appear, however fleetingly, in more than one novel, a guide to those crowded and overlapping canvases can prove useful. When, for instance, the Duchess of Omnium overhears the Duchess of Mayfair chiding her niece for refusing afternoon church and afterwards says, 'That makes me feel so awfully wicked' (*AS* XXXVIII), reference to the turbulent story of 'Palliser, Lady Glencora' adds ironic dimension to that brief episode. Until recently, Winifred and James Gerould's *A Guide to Trollope* (1948) has been the standard Bradshaw to such interconnections. With remarkable economy, they describe the role played by every significant character and usually follow that summary with a crisp quotation from Trollope himself. Entries are arranged alphabetically as are the plot synopses of each novel, along with publication details and notes, if any, from *An Autobiography*. They also include maps of Barset and country estates as well as a conversion-table which enables readers to translate the chapter numbers of their own editions into those of the compilers. A number of thematic headings, such as *doctors, lawyers, hunting, courtroom scenes,* create a view of Trollope's particular interests. As might be expected, there are errors of fact and transcription (Trollope himself made mistakes as his early-morning pages flowed from him). John Griffith is not the husband of Indefer Jones's housekeeper (*CH*); Captain Carroll has six daughters, not four (*MSF*); Usbech not 'Usbeck' (*OF*); Brodrick not 'Broderick' (*CH*); and so on. Nevertheless, the Geroulds offer a truly effective passport to the novels and short stories. Michael Hardwick's *Osprey Guide to Anthony Trollope* (1974) is less comprehensive and more subjective. That book provides a biography and then recounts the plot of each novel in order of publication, except for the Palliser series which is retold in narrative sequence. Aimed at readers whose interest in Trollope has been heightened by televised adaptations, the book is coloured by its editor's somewhat grudging tone (for an audience 'hungry for good story-telling and fed up with obliquity and obscurity, [Trollope] has much to offer') which, in turn, dictates the way he determines a book's relative importance so that his verdict on *La Vendée*, 'this insignificant novel', is likely to discourage a reader's own exploration. A dictionary of major characters rounds out this guide; those entries, for reasons of space, are again governed by Hardwick's editorial selectivity.

The Penguin Companion to Trollope (1996) by Richard Mullen (with James Munson) is designed for readers who feel cut off from Trollope's mid-Victorian assumptions. So, along with essays on each of the works and descriptions of major characters, entries focus on moral and socio-economic themes and details which 19th-century readers took for granted. As Mullen's introduction indicates, a character's manœuvres for a place on the hearth-rug often reveal Trollope's appreciation of life's comedy: 'Until the invention of central heating any position near the fireplace was historically one of pre-eminence' (438). This lively compendium is as much a guide to Trollope's world as it is to the details of each novel. R. C. Terry's *A Trollope Chronology* (1989) provides a different type of route-map. Here, in readily accessible format, is a chronicle of events in Trollope's life as a writer: a sort of skeleton biography. Naturally the documentation of his early years is somewhat sparse, but as month-by-month entries accumulate (from his and other notable letters, account books, and *An Autobiography*) one can see, at a glance, the circumstances which surrounded the creation of a particular novel: how, for instance, Senator Gotobed's observations were impelled by Trollope's own outsider's viewpoint while writing *The American Senator* during his second visit to Australia. Looking up that novel in Mullen's *Companion*, one also learns that 'lengthy trips abroad . . . led the liberal side of Trollope's mind to question aspects of English society' (10). AWJ

Gunliffe, Barty, farmer's son who invades the Trenglos seaweed-gathering cove, is nearly drowned, but is saved by Mally, who becomes his wife. 'Malachi' *LS*   GRH

Gunliffe, Farmer, Barty's father, who believes Mally Trenglos responsible for his son's injuries,

but soon recognizes she has saved his life. 'Malachi' *LS*   GRH

Gunliffe, Mrs. Willing to condemn Mally Trenglos for her son's accident, she accepts her as a daughter when she learns the truth. 'Malachi' *LS*   GRH

Gushing, Miss, friend and relative of Mrs Umbleby of Greshamsbury, a 'pretty young thing', who seeks to marry Revd Caleb Oriel by imitating his high-church practices. When he becomes engaged to Beatrice Gresham, Miss Gushing becomes an Independent Methodist and marries a preacher, Mr Rantaway. *DT*   NCS

Guthrie, Thomas Anstey ('F. Anstey') (1856–1934), comic novelist and *Punch* contributor. After the runaway success of *Vice Versa, or a Lesson to Fathers* (1882) he produced a succession of fantasy novels, notably *The Brass Bottle* (1900). On 2 November 1882, when Trollope dined at John *Tilley's, Edith Tilley read aloud to her father and uncle from *Vice Versa*, the story of a father and son who change identities by magic, so that the father, trapped in a schoolboy's body, suffers the miseries of school life. Doubtless this aspect of the story struck a chord, and Trollope laughed uproariously. Sadleir linked the episode to the fatal stroke. A note in Tilley's hand to a letter of Trollope's more prosaically records that the novelist was taken ill at ten o'clock 'just as he was leaving' (Glendinning 498). Anstey's *A Long Retrospect* (1936) includes recollections of Trollope.   RCT

Gwynne, Dr, Master of Lazarus College, Oxford, and friend of Archdeacon Grantly. Extremely religious and thoroughly practical, Dr Gwynne sends his protégé Mr Arabin to Barchester, attends Miss Thorne's fête, and arranges final appointments for the vacant deanship. Married with a large family, he serves as an occasionally gout-stricken *deus ex machina*. *BT*   NCS

habits, interests, opinions of Trollope. See CARD-PLAYING; DANCING; FOOD AND DRINK; GARDENING; HOLIDAYS ABROAD; HOUSE PARTIES; HUNTING; LIBRARY; LONDON: CLUBS; MUSIC-MAKING; SEA-BATHING; SMOKING; WINE.

Hadley, village in Essex, near London, where Mr George Bertram lives quietly, comfortably, and without ostentation. His home becomes the refuge of Lady Harcourt when she leaves her husband, and when Mr Bertram dies, it is left to his niece, Miss Baker. *B*   MRS

Haggard, Sir Henry Rider (1856–1925), in 1875 secretary to the Governor of Natal, then with the Special Commissioner of the Transvaal in 1877, experiences which provided material for such novels as *King Solomon's Mines* (1886). Visiting South Africa in 1877, Trollope stayed at Pretoria overnight at Government House as guest of Sir Theophilus Shepstone. Rider Haggard was an aide. 'My first introduction to him [Trollope] was amusing,' wrote Haggard in *The Days of my Life: An Autobiography* (1926). Entering the darkened room 'where I was then sleeping I began to search for matches, and was surprised to hear a gruff voice, proceeding from the bed, asking who the deuce I was. I gave my name and asked who the deuce the speaker might be. "Anthony Trollope," replied the gruff voice, "Anthony Trollope".' He thought Trollope was 'a man who concealed a kind heart under a somewhat rough manner, such as does not add to the comfort of colonial travelling' (*I & R* 214).   RCT

Hale, Edward Everett (1822–1909), clergyman, short story writer; chaplain of US Senate (1903–9). In the 1860s, according to his son, Hale would read Trollope's novels aloud on summer evenings. He published *The Way We Live Now* in his periodical *Old and New* from January 1874 until it merged with *Scribner's Magazine* in June 1875.   RCT

Hale, Susan (1833–1910), American watercolourist, writer, brother of Edward Everett Hale; part of the circle Trollope met during his visit to America in 1875. Susan Hale edited *Sheets for the Cradle*, a short-lived Boston publication, to which Trollope contributed 'Never, Never,— Never, Never: A Condensed Novel, in Three Volumes, after the Manner of Bret Harte'. It appeared on 6, 8, and 10 December 1875. Each 'volume' consisted of three chapters of about 25 lines each.   RCT

Hall, Abraham, courteous, concerned engineer and widower, kind to Sophie Wilson and Lucy Graham, to whom he declares his love with dignity and sensitivity. 'Telegraph' *WFF*   GRH

Hall, Mrs Anna Maria (1800–81), author of two plays, nine novels, and several plays; editor of *St James's Magazine* (1862–3). She collaborated with her husband, author and editor Samuel Carter Hall, and helped found Brompton Consumption Hospital and other benevolent institutions. In 1861 Mrs Hall approached Trollope to join *St James's*, but Trollope refused. His lecture 'The National Gallery' appeared in the magazine in September 1861. Trollope declined to sign a testimonial commemorating the Halls' golden wedding anniversary, thus indicating that he was among those, like Dickens, who thought S. C. Hall a humbug.   RCT

Hall, Mr, squire of Little Alresford with four unmarried daughters. Frugal rather than cruel, he refuses to assist John Gordon's father during the financial crisis that ruined the family. Now 70, he 'never had a headache in his life' (XIII)—a sign not only of good health but also of modest and quiet living. *OML*   RC

Hallam, Jack, young writer and member of the group founding a magazine. He worked hard and became a millionaire. 'Panjandrum' *ET*   GRH

Hallam Hall, George Wade's large rambling house outside London. 'Not If'   GRH

Hamel, Isadore, handsome, impractical sculptor, 26 years old, raised at Rome by his disreputable father, whose profession (though not his morals) Isadore has followed. Despite his dim financial prospects, he remains true to Lucy

Dormer, resolving to give up his grandiose artistic notions once they are married. *AA*   WK

Hamilton, Mr Baron, judge at the Carrick-on-Shannon assizes who passes sentence of death on Thady Macdermot after the jury finds him guilty of murder. *MB*   MRS

Hamley, Edward Bruce (1824–93), career soldier and minor novelist; regular contributor to *Blackwood's*, for which he wrote a strongly critical review of Trollope's *North America* as simplistic and carelessly written. Hamley urged him to stick to novels: 'We like his plots better than his travels' (quoted Mullen 417). Trollope came to like him; and his treatment after the British expedition under Sir Garnet Wolseley to quell a rebellion in Egypt (1882) seemed to him quite unfair: Wolseley had scarcely mentioned Hamley's role in the campaign (*Letters* 2, 975, 984–5).   RCT

Hampshire. The estate of Ralph Newton in *Ralph the Heir* is 'where that county is joined to Berkshire: and perhaps in England there is no prettier district, no country in which moorland and woodland and pasture are more daintily thrown together to please the eye' (XI). It is also the location of Mr Whittlestaffe's house in *An Old Man's Love*. Both the Wilkinsons and the Marquis of Stapledean in *The Bertrams* live in the county.   MRS

Hampstead, Lord (John Trafford), affable eldest son of the Marquis of Kingsbury. His radical politics dismay his father and stepmother (who particularly hates him for superseding her own son's right as heir), especially when he wishes to marry the humble Marion Fay. His luxurious life of hunting and yachting belies his democratic principles, but his passionate, hopeless love for Marion proves his sincerity. Her refusal to marry him and her early death leave him heartbroken. *MF*   SRB

Hampton, old-fashioned little village outside London where the Woodward family lives. *TC*   MT

Hampton Privets, home of the squire of Bullhampton, Harry Gilmore, the lavish refurbishing of which he calls off when Mary Lowther breaks her engagement to him. *VB*   SRB

Hamworth, town nearest to Orley Farm, about 25 miles (40 km) from London. *OF*   MT

Handcock, Harry, early suitor of Margaret Mackenzie, easily extinguished by her brother's disapproval. Now bald and stout, with little aptitude for romance, he again proposes, coldly and unsuccessfully, by letter after the death of Margaret's brother leaves her rich. *MM*   SRB

Handicap Lodge, Dot Blake's home near the Curragh races, frequented by Lord Ballindine. *KOK*   MRS

Handy, Abel, former Barchester stonemason pensioned to Hiram's Hospital by Septimus Harding. He leads the rebellion of dissatisfied pensioners, hoping to gain £100 a year rather than their daily 18*d*. Of sour and ill-omened appearance, he finally apologizes to Mr Harding and survives to greet the new Warden in *Barchester Towers*. *W*   NCS

Haphazard, Sir Abraham, Attorney-General, consulted for definitive legal opinions. A tall, thin, self-sufficient, witty, and friendless man, he believes in success and power. His opinion on John Hiram's will favours the Grantly faction, but when visited by Septimus Harding he becomes disconcerted by the Warden's moral views. In *Doctor Thorne* he advises Thomas Thorne on Sir Roger Scatcherd's will. *W*   NCS

Hap House, residence of Owen Fitzgerald, close to Castle Richmond. Endowed with 'a comfortable little slice of land', and surrounded by 'pleasant grounds and pleasant gardens' (I), it is regarded as an asset by mothers of unmarried daughters, except by the Countess of Desmond, who sees it as unworthy of her daughter's rank. Lacking a feminine presence, it soon acquires ill repute as the scene of riotous living. *CR*   MRS

Harcourt, Lady Caroline (née **Waddington**), headstrong 'donna primissima' (VI) engaged to George Bertram, whose proud and intransigent nature belies Trollope's claim that *The Bertrams* 'was relieved by no special character' (*Auto* VII). Caroline's strength of will is massive: she is a Juno in spirit, as well as beauty and bearing. She refuses to bend to Bertram's will, just as later she refuses to brook the prospect of returning to Sir Henry Harcourt, indicating her preference for the noble Roman exit—suicide—over submission to a hated marriage. *B*   MRS

Harcourt, Sir Henry, ambitious young lawyer and career-politician, associated rhetorically with the imagery of gaming, who marries Caroline Waddington, mistakenly believing her to be an heiress whose money and beauty will 'adorn his drawing-room' (XXVIII). Though gallant in his social triumphs, he is, however, a coward under misfortune. Deserted by his wife, sinking in popularity, and mired in debt, he shoots himself in his extravagant Eaton Square home. *B*   MRS

Harcourt, Sir William George Venables Vernon (1827–1904), Professor of International Law at Cambridge; Liberal MP for Oxford; asked by Trollope to act as steward at Royal Literary Fund dinners. A particular attraction of the Cosmopolitan Club for Trollope was that Liberal politicians there, such as Vernon Harcourt, 'used to whisper the secrets of Parliament with free tongues' (*Auto* IX). Doubtless materials gleaned there helped flesh out the political novels.   RCT

Harding, Eleanor. See BOLD, ELEANOR.

Harding, Robert Palmer (1821–90), founder of the Imperial British East Africa Co.; accountant for, and a director of, Chapman & Hall (along with Trollope) when it became a limited company in 1880. Ever scrupulous in business, Trollope wrote to Harding about accounts for *The Duke's Children*, for which rights had been negotiated for £1,000 in 1878: 'The company loses £120 by the venture. I cannot allow that. It is the first account I have ever seen of one of my own books . . . I will repay the Company the amount lost, viz £120, if you think that fair' (*Letters* 2, 880).   RCT

Harding, Septimus, warden of Hiram's Hospital and incumbent of Crabtree Parva, subsequently rector of St Cuthbert's and rector of St Ewold's, father of Susan, wife of Archdeacon Grantly, and of Eleanor, wife first of John Bold and then of Francis Arabin. In *The Last Chronicle of Barset* (LXXXVIII) Trollope forgets that he has not recounted Harding's appointment to St Ewold's in any previous novel. Mr Harding is in some sense the most important character in the 'Chronicles of Barsetshire', which start with him as principal character of *The Warden*, and end with his death and burial in *The Last Chronicle* (LXXXI), after which a few fictional ends are tied up but no further developments occur, apart from the rapprochement between Archdeacon Grantly and Josiah Crawley, which ensures stability in the fictional society. Harding is one of the few purely good characters in English fiction, 'without guile, believing humbly in the religion which he has striven to teach, and guided by the precepts which he has striven to learn' (*BT* LIII). His resignation of the wardenship of Hiram's Hospital and its stipend, which seems like cowardice to the worldly Archdeacon, is the action which defines his character, for his motive is that he cannot be sure, however conscientiously he has done his duty and however innocent he was in the matter of his appointment, that his position is as blameless in other people's eyes as his conscience requires it to be. The praise which the *Jupiter* eventually accords him does not gratify him, and moreover is, exceptionally in Trollope, presented quite unironically. Declining the deanship singles him out as the one truly just man in Barchester, and he alone of Trollope's characters is presented as having no mixed motives when recommending a family connection (Francis Arabin) to an important post, the deanship of Barchester (*BT* XLIX). Similarly we are told unequivocally that Scandal had lied when it connected his appointment to the wardenship with his daughter's marriage to the Bishop's son, the Archdeacon. In the later Chronicles, when he has little action to carry, he is used as a moral touchstone: his disdain for society, for example, provides a standard against which to judge Adolphus Crosbie's unworthy ambition. The two men meet briefly in *The Small House at Allington*, and Crosbie is surprised to learn that the saintly old man is Lady Dumbello's grandfather. Millais's illustration of them together (*SHA* XVI) has been much admired (see p. 499). The character of Septimus Harding is in marked contrast to the unbelievable and often unattractive portraits of Christian virtue found in religious novels of the period. One of his pleasing features is his unwillingness to launch personal attacks on those who have injured or insulted him, and typical of the accuracy and mildness of his adverse judgements is the remark to Eleanor following Obadiah Slope's sermon: 'Christian ministers are never called on by God's word to insult the convictions, or even the prejudices of their brethren' (*BT* VIII).
DS

Hardlines, Sir Gregory, head of the Weights and Measures Office and later Chief Commissioner of the Board of Civil Service Examination. Based on the civil servant Sir Charles *Trevelyan, powerful Sir Gregory introduces a rigorous but ultimately foolish examination system for the appointment of clerks. *TC*   MT

Hardman, Sir William (1828–90), from 1865 until his death Chairman of Surrey Quarter Sessions for which he was knighted in 1885; editor of the *Morning Post*, 1872–90. Meredith portrayed him as Blackburn Tuckham in *Beauchamp's Career* (1876). Harding met Trollope at the Alpine Club and recalled 'a good fellow, modelled on Silenus, with a large black beard. . . . Silenus made a funny speech, assuring the Club that he was most desirous of becoming a member, but the qualification was the difficulty, and both time and flesh were against him. He added that not very long since, in the city of Washington, a member of the US Government asked him if it were true that a club of Englishmen existed who held their meetings on the summits of the Alps. "In my anxiety," he said, "to support the credit of my country, I may have transgressed the strict limits of veracity, but I told him what he had heard was quite true. (Great cheers.)" ' (*I & R* 155). Harding also commented on Trollope's

North America. Trollope's dismay at seeing pickles fed to babies 'stands out most prominently in my recollections of the two fat volumes, filled up by a background of gigantic hotels, towns with vast untenanted and tenanted blocks of buildings . . . hot stoves, disagreeable be-crinolined women, hard-featured unpleasant men, railway cars without distinction of class, and a large amount of immature twaddle about the American Constitution and the War' (*I & R* 156).   RCT

Hardwick, Charles Philip, 4th Earl of (1799–1873), MP for Reigate (1831–2), and for Cambridge (1832–4). In 1852, with a seat in cabinet, he was appointed Postmaster General. That year, Trollope, hoping for promotion, applied for the post of Superintendent of Mail Coaches. Sir John Trollope, MP for Lincoln, wrote on his behalf. Trollope himself cited '18 years in the service' and 'confidently' directed him to Colonel *Maberly for reference 'as to my fitness for the situation' (*Letters* 1, 32). In the end, Trollope was passed over. Appointment of Superintendent of Mail Coaches was in fact in Maberly's gift, and Trollope was no favourite of his. The failure was probably a blessing in disguise. The Mail Coach Office was abolished during an administrative reorganization, while the time Trollope spent in western England in his old position was two of the happiest years of his life.   RCT

Hardy, Mr, counsel for the young Earl Frederic Lovel. 'He hated compromise and desired justice,—and was a great rather than a successful lawyer' (V). *LA*   RC

Hardy, Thomas (1840–1928), creator of the Wessex novels. Hardy was in the audience at the conference on the Eastern Question, St James's Hall, December 1876, when Trollope would not stop speaking even when the Duke of *Westminster, as chairman, tugged at his coat-tails. On another occasion, Hardy noted that 'in conversation [he] just went on, indifferent to attention and to other people' (*I & R* 220). Hardy consulted him about getting copyrights back and returns from cheap editions and serialization. By this time (1877) Trollope was convinced that the most advantageous arrangement for an author was to sell everything out to the publisher and have no further bargaining. He had no doubt that the royalty system was best (*Letters* 2, 715).   RCT

Harford, Dr, rector of Baslehurst for over 40 years before the arrival of his arch foe, the low-church evangelical Mr Prong. Once a Liberal, now at times a violent Tory, Dr Harford is ultimately inflexible, and 'now in his old age, he was

discontented and disgusted by the changes which had come upon him' (XVIII). *RR*   MT

Harkaway, Mr, master of the hounds of the Cumberlow Green Hunt, 'a sincere, honest, taciturn, and withal, affectionate man' (XXVIII) whose life is his hounds. He becomes angry with Mr Fairlawn for poaching on his hunting territory. *MSF*   MT

Harper, Fletcher (1806–77), one of four brothers of Harper & Brothers, New York, who published *Harper's New Monthly Magazine.* The magazine ran two of Trollope's stories, 'The Courtship of Susan Bell' (August 1860) and 'Relics of General Chassé' (February 1860). It also purchased, but did not publish, 'La Mère Bauche'. In September 1859, Trollope wrote to Fletcher offering 'Tales of all Countries'. 'Each would refer to some different nation or people; and in each case to some country which I have visited. They would run to from 24 to 28 pages in number, & would average in length 10 of your monthly magazine pages' (*Letters* 1, 86). Trollope also wanted to clarify the situation regarding copyright: 'Of course it would be understood that I should have the power of republication in England as soon [as] a series of 12 (say) has appeared in your magazine.' Only one other story appeared in Harper's, 'The O'Conors of Castle Conor, County Mayo' (May 1860). Trollope was paid £20 for each story—or £2 a page for ten pages (*Letters* 1, 89)—but in the absence of international copyright laws, payments and book-rights were acrimonious issues: Harper 'had been reprinting his books, sometimes paying some little sum to the English publisher. In 1859 he had declined to buy early sheets for *The West Indies,* but then published the book anyway' (Hall 230). In 1862 Trollope called on Harper in New York 'and explained to him, with what courtesy I could use, that I did not quite like his mode of republishing my books. He was civil enough to assure me that the transaction had been gratifying to him' (*Letters* 1, 195). However, Harper promised Trollope that if he reached agreement with another American publisher for his new book, *North America,* he would not reprint it; but although Trollope came to an arrangement with the Philadelphia publisher J. B. Lippincott, Harper broke his word, and Harper Brothers brought out a cheap pirated copy that made Lippincott 'positive losers in the enterprise' (quoted Mullen 415), while Trollope received nothing. Harper's action prompted a letter from Trollope to James Russell Lowell in Boston, condemning 'literary piracy' (*Letters* 1, 193–8). However, the letter produced no concrete results, and Harper 'continued to publish Trollope's books—thirty-one titles by the end of Trollope's life, for most of which he paid nothing' (Super 146). RCT

Harper's New Monthly Magazine. In June 1850, New York publishers Harper Brothers, who often published cheap reprints of English fiction, began a monthly magazine selling at $3 per year. Their goal was to sell the wealth of English fiction in periodical form while also advertising their publications. *Harper's* reprinted materials from British periodicals, among them *Household Words*, *Bentley's Miscellany*, and the *Dublin University Magazine*. In its first number, the publisher stated that they would 'transfer' to their pages, as quickly as possible, all the tales of Dickens, Lever, and others and make them available to the public. At that time, American copyright laws offered no protection to foreign authors. Many English novels were quickly published in America after their first appearance in England. Trollope was among those fighting for stricter copyright laws.

In 1859 Trollope offered his first attempts at short stories, later published collectively as *Tales of All Countries*, to *Harper's* for publication, one each month, but *Harper's* decided to run them every other month. The magazine published *Orley Farm* without Trollope's authorization. Harper Brothers published numerous other works of Trollope's including *The Three Clerks*, *The Bertrams*, *Castle Richmond*, *Doctor Thorne*, *Framley Parsonage*, *The West Indies*, and *The Struggles of Brown, Jones, and Robinson*. *Harper's Magazine* reviewed Trollope's *North America* and praised it, saying only one other foreigner, de Tocqueville, had produced a better book about America. JWM

'Harriet Parr's *Life and Death of Jeanne d'Arc'* (review). This account has both essentials for good biography: it is informative and pleasant to read. The only flaw is the obviously partisan stance. *Fortnightly Review* (15 October 1866), 632–6. AKL

Harrington Hall, home of Lord and Lady Chiltern and centre of the Brake Hunt, managed by Lord Chiltern. The house is cheerful and homy but is pervaded throughout with the flavour and concerns of the hunt. Phineas Finn is a frequent visitor. *PR, DC* JMR

Harrison, Frederic (1831–1923), philosopher and prolific writer on historical and literary topics. His *Studies in Early Victorian Literature* (1895) praised Trollope's frankness, honesty, and modesty about his talents and accomplishments. This was exemplified by what Harrison observed during dinner at George Eliot's. Trollope told the usual tale of sitting down every morning for three hours at 5.30 with watch on desk and producing 250 words every quarter of an hour. George Eliot quivered with horror; she could write only when she felt in the right mood and often sat at her table without writing a line. Trollope countered immediately that with imaginative work like hers it was only to be expected, 'but with my mechanical stuff it's a sheer matter of industry. It's not the head that does it—it's the cobbler's wax on the seat and the sticking to my chair!' (*I & R* 189). This self-deprecation was apparent in the company of intellectuals. When Trollope came to write his memorial essay on G. H. *Lewes for the *Fortnightly Review* (February 1879) he enlisted Harrison's help for the section dealing with philosophy. RCT

Harrow School, scene of Trollope's juvenile misery, began taking pupils in 1611. When Trollope started there in 1823 there were about 200 pupils. As a home-boarder (day-boy) Trollope was scorned by the sons of wealthier parents resident in the school houses. The home-boarders 'were often sadly bullied and pursued with stones on their way home', said one contemporary (*I & R* 27). Trollope studied under two headmasters, Dr George Butler, whose term lasted from 1805 to 1829, and Dr Charles Longley (who became Archbishop of Canterbury in 1862), between 1829 and 1836. Discipline was harsh in all public schools. Education proceeded mainly in the classics with groups meeting in one cold room, the clergymen tutors listening to the recitation of chunks of translations. The brighter, more vocal, more secure types fared best. Trollope was not among them, although he did win a prize for an English essay. In his fiction Charles Amedroz is expelled from Harrow (*BE*). More distinguished Harrovians include Frank Gresham (*DT*); Lord Lufton and Mark Robarts (*FP*); Harry Gilmore (*VB*); Peregrine Orme (*OF*); Hugh Stanbury (*HKWR*); John Caldigate (*JC*); Lord Hampstead (*MF*); two sons of Revd Charles Lovel (*LA*). Trollope recounts his schooldays in *An Autobiography* (*I*). RCT

Harry Heathcote of Gangoil (see next page)

Hart, Abraham, one of George Hotspur's major creditors, an ugly stereotype of the Jewish moneylender complete with dialect spelling of his speech. He threatens to expose George's 'card-sharping' and forgery of a cheque, but instead negotiates with Mr Boltby in order to recoup his money. *SHH* MG

Hart, Mr, candidate in the parliamentary election at Baslehurst, and opponent of Mr Butler Cornbury. Hart is a Jewish clothier from London,

(*cont. on page 239*)

TROLLOPE's thirty-first novel is his shortest, and the only one in the form of a Christmas story. It is also the only Trollope novel, apart from *The Fixed Period*, set entirely in the New World.

Trollope admitted that its hero was modelled on his younger son Frederic James Anthony, who was a sheep farmer in New South Wales. He and his wife had stayed with Frederic for extended periods during their year-long visit to Australia in 1871–2, and *Harry Heathcote* was inspired by the most vexed political issue in the Australian and New Zealand colonies at the time: the contest between 'squatters' like Frederic, who grazed their sheep on large tracts of mainly leasehold Crown land, and 'free-selectors', who could purchase segments of the squatters' runs cheaply and turn them into dairy or crop farms. To lessen the likelihood that any of his hero's enemies would be identified with Frederic's, Trollope located Gangoil in the Mary River district of Queensland, 1,000 miles (1,600 km) away from Mortray, Frederic's sheep station in central-western New South Wales. Although he remembered the Mary River district's summer humidity and its mosquitoes, most of the local colour for his novel is drawn from Mortray and its environs as described in the chapter 'Station Life in the Bush' in *Australia and New Zealand* (1, XX). Strict realism in matters of geography would hardly have seemed necessary in a Christmas tale with so outlandish a setting. As always, however, Trollope succeeds in making his characters believable enough for the purposes of the story, and the descriptions of bush scenery and customs in *Harry Heathcote* ring at least as true as those in most other colonial novels of the period— Henry Kingsley's *Geoffrey Hamlyn* (1859), for example.

Harry Heathcote tells of the struggles of a young squatter beset by human enemies in a harsh and dangerous climate. He aggravates his problems by an 'imperiousness' clearly out of place in the egalitarian world of the bush. Although his property is much larger and accommodates many more sheep than Frederic Trollope's, Harry Heathcote's economic survival is likewise under constant threat from drought, from bush-fires (some of them the work of arsonists), from neighbours who 'duff' (steal) his sheep, from disgruntled employees, from passing swagmen who sponge on him and often rob him (the 'nomad tribe of the bush', Trollope called them in *ANZ*), but most of all, or so Harry believes, from free-selectors. In reality, his most dangerous enemies prove to be a neighbouring family of squatters. Shiftless, hard-drinking ex-convicts who duff his sheep, they collude with a station hand he has recently dismissed in setting fire to some of his paddocks. Giles Medlicot, a free-selector who has created a thriving sugar farm on what was formerly part of Harry's choice riverfront land, helps him fight the fires, and they are reconciled. In traditional Christmas-story fashion the reconciliation is sealed on Christmas Day when they and their families dine together, and Medlicot proposes to Harry's sister-in-law Kate Daly, and is accepted.

While in Australia, Trollope had made a point of siding with the free-selectors against the squatters as a matter of political principle, notwithstanding his loyalty to his son and his enjoyment of many other squatters' hospitality. He knew that squatters would have to accept free-selectors, and often make way for them. Equally, however, he knew that acceptance would not be made as easy for the vast majority of squatters, including his son, as it is for Harry Heathcote, whose free-selector, altogether atypically, is a social equal, a 'gentleman' fresh from England, at bottom a natural ally in spite of their conflicting economic interests. Trollope was indulging in a little wishful thinking on his son's behalf.

Harry Heathcote was written between 1 and 29 June 1873, six months after Trollope's return to England from Australasia. It was serialized in the Melbourne *Age* (15 November 1873–3 January 1874) before appearing as the Christmas number of the *Graphic* (25 December 1873). The *Graphic*, which had bought the entire copyright from Trollope for £450, sold the book-rights to Sampson Low, who published the novel in one volume in October 1874, at the standard price of 10s. 6d.; an illustrated edition, selling for 5s., followed shortly afterwards. Harper & Brothers had published the book in America earlier in 1874. The manuscript is in the Beinecke Library, Yale University.

PE

Edwards, P. D. (ed.), *Anthony Trollope's Son in Australia: The Life and Letters of F. J. A. Trollope* (1982).
Trollope, Anthony, *Australia*, ed. P. D. Edwards and R. B. Joyce (1967).

and much is made by the Cornbury camp of the need to keep a Jew out of Parliament. Hart is expected to win by two votes, but in the end Butler Cornbury beats him by a single vote. *RR*
MT

Hart, Samuel, Jewish moneylender to whom Mountjoy Scarborough is indebted. Hart 'was small, and oily, and black-haired, and beaky-nosed, with a perpetual smile on his face, unless when on special occasions he would be moved to the expression of deep anger' (XI). *MSF*   MT

Harte, Bret (1836–1902), poet, storyteller, famed for *The Luck of Roaring Camp and Other Sketches* (1870); part of the Boston literary circle that welcomed Trollope during his American visits. He dined with Trollope at his London clubs and attended a Royal Literary Fund dinner where he responded to the toast 'Literature'. Trollope's parody, 'Never, Never—Never, Never' was inspired, he said, by the American. 'As Bret Harte says I have no sense of humour, and won't laugh at me, I must try to laugh at myself, and make fun of the heroine I have loved best [Lily Dale]' (*Letters* 2, 664).   RCT

Hartington, Spencer Compton Cavendish, Marquis of, later 8th Duke of Devonshire (1833–1908), Postmaster General (1868–71); Secretary of State for India (1880–2). Early biographers of Trollope, Escott and Sadleir, saw him as a model for Lord *Chiltern.   RCT

Hartlebury, seat of the Marquis of Hartletop in Shropshire. *FP, SHA, LCB*   NCS

Hartlepod, Mr, self-important secretary of the San Juan Mining Company which proposes to send Ferdinand Lopez to Guatemala. Though he fills an important role in the company, Mr Hartlepod's 'greasy face' and his exaggerated talk of anticipated profits inspire anything but confidence. *PM*   JMR

Hartletop, Griselda, Marchioness of (née **Grantly**), daughter of Archdeacon Grantly and wife of Gustavus, Lord Dumbello, Marquis of Hartletop. Reputed to be one of the most beautiful women in Barsetshire, she is launched into the marriage market with high expectations. Her mother and Lady Lufton try to arrange her marriage with Lord Lufton, but instead she chooses the silent, stolid, and much richer Lord Dumbello. Her perfect beauty, cool manner, and impressive silences make her the central attraction of London society. Described often as a statue, she becomes a Carlylean symbol of beauty without depth, style without understanding. Her few comments to the equally silent Plantagenet Palliser spark a flurry of rumours concerning a possible adulterous affair, but she deflects the jealousy of her husband with a typically cool explanation that gains her a gorgeous necklace. *SHA, W, BT, FP, CYFH, PF, LCB, MM*   NCS

Hartletop, Marquis of. See DUMBELLO, LORD GUSTAVUS.

Hasell, Elizabeth Julia (1830–79), miscellaneous writer who published on Calderón and Tasso; contributed to *Blackwood's* and *Quarterly Review* from 1858. Unable to use Hasell's piece on Robert Browning, Blackwood recommended it to Trollope for *Saint Pauls*: 'you will not find any where a more elaborate or better written piece of Criticism than this.' Although Trollope replied, 'I have matter to last me up to the end of my reign'

(*Letters* 2, 501), the article did appear as 'Browning's Poems.—*The Ring and the Book*' in December 1870 and January 1871. RCT

Hatfield, Duke of, British Minister for the Crown Colonies and 'Secretary of Benevolence', by whose order the 'Fixed Period' policy of Britannula is overruled in the form of a gunboat and the 'civilized' removal of President Neverbend. He appoints Sir Ferdinando Brown as new governor. *FixP* SRB

Hautboy, Lord, eldest son of Lord Persiflage, beautiful but profligate, and thus a source of pride to his mother and of concern to his father. *MF* SRB

Hautboy Castle, prettily situated in Westmorland, the home of Lord Persiflage, to which he and his wife invite Lord Hampstead and Lady Frances while the two are in social disgrace. *MF* SRB

Hauteville, Lady Amaldina, beautiful, self-assured daughter of Lord Persiflage. She cheerfully plans marriage to the dull, older Lord Llwddythlw because his wealth and respectable reputation suit her ambition. Self-centred in a good-natured way, she is among the first to accept socially Lady Frances Trafford's lowly fiancé George Roden. Her own wedding is magnificent. *MF* SRB

Hawthorne, Julian (1846–1934), author of sensation novels and biographer of his father Nathaniel Hawthorne. He first met Trollope during winter 1879, in London, possibly at Chapman & Hall's offices, and left a striking portrait in *Confessions and Criticisms* (1887). Trollope stood out from the company, 'a broad-shouldered, sturdy man, of middle height, with a ruddy countenance and snow-white tempestuous beard and hair'. Hawthorne sensed a finer sensitivity beyond 'the modernized Squire Western, nourished with beef and ale' (a key phrase of his own father's estimate) and noted a complexity about his nature together with a self-doubt and insecurity, which manifested itself in a concern about what others thought of him. Hawthorne concluded 'he was something of a paradox' (*I & R* 143–5). Hawthorne warmly reviewed *Cousin Henry* in the *Spectator* (October 1879): 'His touch is eminently civilizing; everything, from the episodes to the sentences, moves without hitch or creak; we never have to read a paragraph twice, and we are never sorry to have read it once' (Smalley 461). RCT

Hawthorne, Nathaniel (1804–64), American short story writer and novelist of Puritan New England, best known for *The Scarlet Letter* (1850);

served in Boston Custom House (1839–41); American consul at Liverpool (1853–7). His comment on Trollope's novels in a letter to James T. *Fields was devotedly copied into *An Autobiography*. 'Have you ever read the novels of Anthony Trollope? They precisely suit my taste; solid and substantial, written on the strength of beef and through the inspiration of ale, and just as real as if some giant had hewn a great lump out of the earth and put it under a glass case, with all its inhabitants going about their daily business and not suspecting that they were made a show of. And these books are just as English as a beefsteak' (VIII). Coming from a writer whose allegorical fantasy and symbolism were so different from his own style, this delighted Trollope, who longed to meet him. Fields brought them together in September 1861, and reported back to Hawthorne: 'Trollope fell in love with you at first sight . . . He swears you are the handsomest Yankee that ever walked this planet' (*Chron* 43). Trollope wrote 'The Genius of Nathaniel Hawthorne' for *North American Review* (September 1879). RCT

Hayward, Abraham (1801–84), barrister, prolific essayist. His review of the *Greville Memoirs* in *Quarterly Review* (January 1875) was not hard enough, Trollope thought, on 'a most blackguard production', one that made him feel 'that all gentlemanlike faith is dying out in the land' (*Letters* 2, 659). At this time *The Way We Live Now* was causing a stir for its bleak assessment of contemporary mores. Hayward was one of the players portrayed with Trollope in the picture *A Memorable Whist Party at the Athenaeum*. RCT

Headford, small village by Morony Castle, where Florian Jones is intimidated by the Man in the Mask and sworn to secrecy by the Landleaguers. *L* MRS

health and medical practice. The health of the English population improved notably during Trollope's lifetime, as evidenced by the declining death rate, from about 25 per 1,000 in 1815 to around 20 per 1,000 in 1880. The decline was most marked in the years up to 1840, and again from 1870 onwards. The reasons for this decline are the subject of debate, though it is widely accepted that improvement in medical treatment of disease was not among them. The majority of people saw doctors rarely if at all in the course of their lives, due to their expense, and reasonable doubts as to their benefit. Trollope's numerous fictional portraits of doctors generally confirm this attitude: they are not a particularly impressive lot and little is said in favour of their professional skills (see DOCTORS AS CHARACTERS).

Nor do doctors seem to have been able to do much for Trollope in real life, except perhaps the unorthodox Dr John Elliotson, whose hypnotic ministrations may have helped him recover from a mysterious but severe asthmatic crisis as a young man. Trollope suffered from extreme near-sightedness, increasing deafness, asthma attacks, and a hernia—all beyond medical intervention. He tried to reduce his considerable weight by 'banting', one of the earliest popular dietary regimes, promoted not by a doctor but a London undertaker named William Banting. He rode zealously to hounds, bathed naked in the sea, and, a heavy smoker from earliest manhood, eventually cut back on his considerable cigar consumption. He drove himself hard, and died in the aftermath of a stroke, having apparently worn his body out. Contemporary medical practice could do nothing for him, yet he did manage to live somewhat beyond the average life expectancy for his generation—and perhaps just beyond what he felt appropriate for the population generally, if the practice of euthanasia by age 68 proposed in *The Fixed Period* is any indication.

Women had already begun to outlive men—a distinctive characteristic of modern societies—by an average of over three years in 1880 and rising. Eliminating all childbirth-related deaths would have further lengthened female life expectancy by only about 0.6 years, yet Trollope's favourite niece Beatrice died of puerperal fever, a childbirth hazard for which medical practice had no effective treatment. Nor did it have any power over tuberculosis ('consumption'), which was on the increase in Britain until the 1870s and was the leading cause of death throughout the century. Three of Trollope's siblings would die of it, a brother and two sisters, as did Marion Fay. It was a peculiarity of tuberculosis that it killed significantly more females than males, due probably to lower female resistance resulting from poorer diet, and to women's care-giving role, tuberculosis not being recognized as an infectious disease until about 1870.

The other major causes of death were more explosively infectious, often reaching epidemic proportions. Respiratory diseases such as scarlet fever, measles, and whooping cough, and the newly arrived diphtheria, spread through contact and were particularly deadly to children. Waterborne diseases such as typhoid and cholera, another new arrival, were more likely to affect adults. Collectively, infectious diseases caused about a third of all deaths in all ages. Hospitals generally excluded victims of infectious diseases to safeguard other patients. Doctors were reluctant to study infectious diseases, both because of personal risk and their demeaning habit of af-

flicting mainly the poor. In any case medicine had no effective preventive or cure to offer. One exception was smallpox, for which vaccination was compulsory from 1853, though extensively resisted by sceptics and civil libertarians. Mental disease, which figures prominently in several of Trollope's novels, notably *Phineas Redux* and *He Knew He Was Right*, attracted considerable medical attention. A surprisingly large amount of public expenditure was devoted to building insane asylums, which were generally humanely managed.

Although Victorian medical practice was little advanced in terms of treatment, it made much greater progress in diagnosis and prevention. Knowledge of physiology expanded through laboratory research on cadavers, and vivisection of animals. Crucial developments occurred in bacteriology, such as John Snow's discovery of the waterborne nature of cholera, which lent the weight of science to government-sponsored public health reforms. These began to address the bad sanitation and overcrowding that bred infectious disease. One area of dramatically visible medical progress was in surgery from about the 1870s, where the spread of Lister's practice of antisepsis combined with that of anaesthesia made possible operations hitherto impossible—such as appendectomies. Such developments gave a much needed boost to medicine's popular prestige. The profession also took important steps to improve medical education and to enforce qualifications. Traditional hierarchical rivalries between physicians, surgeons, and apothecaries were negotiated, and the Medical Act of 1858 united the profession and helped to promote the interests of the growing number of well-trained and almost, but not quite, exclusively male general practitioners.   CK

Peterson, M. Jeanne, *The Medical Profession in Mid-Victorian London* (1978).

Smith, F. B., *The People's Health, 1830–1910* (1979).

Heathcote, Harry, magistrate and proud owner of Gangoil, an Australian sheep farm, squatter-hero of a Christmas story set amid the scorching heat of Queensland. Based on the character and the tribulations of Trollope's son Frederic, Heathcote emigrates to Australia with a small fortune after having been orphaned as a youth. He counts himself master of 120,000 acres (50,000 ha), but his often intemperate air alienates those around him. His fear of the hot summer, coupled with distrust of all but his own people, results in paranoia, leading him to suspect his closest neighbour, Giles Medlicot, of arson. He is not only proven wrong when Medlicot helps him to extinguish a raging fire, but comes to see that those with whom he has disagreements need not be counted enemies, but can indeed be friends. *HHG*   MRS

Heathcote, Mrs Mary. Daughter of a bankrupt squatter from Sydney, and mother of Harry Heathcote's two infant sons, she idolizes her husband, and aspires to 'agree with [him] in everything', but feels occasionally oppressed by the doggedness of his opinions, especially those concerning her sister's prospective suitor, Medlicot. But she remains loyal to Heathcote, and is rewarded when the rift between the two men is healed and Medlicot proposes to her sister. *HHG*   MRS

Heavitree, home of the Frenches in Exeter and location of Revd Gibson's courtship of Arabella and Camilla. *HKWR*   RC

Heavybed House, Devon estate neighbouring on Creamclotted Hall, whose squire needs a wife, perhaps the orphaned Jane Robarts. *FP*   NCS

Heine, Isa, dutiful eldest child of Ernest Heine, who asks her formidable uncle to advance promotion of Herbert Onslow so that she and Herbert can marry sooner. 'Heine' *TAC2*   GRH

Heine, Mme. Twenty years younger than her husband, she sympathetically supports the marriage hopes of Isa and Herbert Onslow. 'Heine' *TAC2*   GRH

Heine, Uncle (Hatto). Senior partner in the bank whose word is law, he succumbs to the pleas of his niece Isa to advance Herbert Onslow's promotion so that they can get married. 'Heine' *TAC2*   GRH

Heisse, Fanny, Linda Tressel's ex-schoolfriend and neighbour whom she has been taught to view as worldly. After a carefree adolescence, she happily settles down with a husband who has solid prospects and will allow her to continue dancing. The way she handles Linda's arrival in Augsburg shows a splendid maturity. *LT*   AWJ

Heisse, Jacob, Nuremberg upholsterer who regards his children's flirtations with easygoing humour. In neighbourly concern, he joins those who persuade Steinmarc to press on with marriage. But when his daughter worries over Linda's 'mad' response, he scurries back to comfy neutrality. *LT*   AWJ

He Knew He Was Right (*see page 244*)

Helps, Sir Arthur (1813–75), miscellaneous writer and civil servant; Clerk of the Privy Council (1860–75); close adviser to Queen Victoria, whose writings he prepared for the press. He is best known for *Friends in Council*, four series of

pious discourses (1847–59), and *Realmah* (1868), a political fable. Receiving a copy, Trollope framed a diplomatic answer. 'I was surprised when I heard that you had descended into our arena, feeling that you had fought your battles on a nobler battlefield' (*Letters* 1, 459).   RCT

Hendon Hall, Lord Hampstead's residence in suburban London where he shelters his sister Lady Frances after their stepmother has made Frances's life miserable. *MF*   SRB

Henniker, Mother, dirty, disreputable old landlady of the hotel in Nobble, New South Wales, where John Caldigate briefly stays. *JC*   SRB

Henniker's Hotel, rough, extremely dirty shanty where John Caldigate boards when he first arrives in New South Wales. *JC*   SRB

'Henry O'Neill: Obituary'. A Royal Academy Associate Fellow, he died 13 March. Once widely acclaimed for *The Rivers of Babylon*, *Eastward Ho*, and *Home Again*, his best painting was *The Wreck of the Royal Charter*. Also a violinist and writer, 'and it may be doubted whether he best loved his palette or his fiddle'. He was buried simply at Kensal Green. *The Times* (15 March 1880), 6.   AKL

'Henry Taylor's Poems' (review). It is a good thing to praise living authors; too often we wait until their decease. Tennyson and Browning are fortunately still able to enjoy critics' applause. Taylor's works are also well worth having. Especially recommended is the early 'Van Artevelde'; like the best poetry, it is thoughtful but not obscure or difficult. There is some regrettably inflated diction, such as 'the gibbous moon' and 'the vegetable dead', but the poems as a whole are admirable. *Fortnightly Review* (29 May 1865), 129–46.   AKL

'Henry Wadsworth Longfellow' (article). One hesitates to write about a living man, but there is nothing hurtful to say. Longfellow as a person is uncommonly pleasant; as a poet, he shows rare purity. He never offends, never amazes. His work is marked by soft melancholy. Note the beauty of image and thought throughout *Evangeline*, *Hiawatha*, and *Miles Standish*. The stories overcome the sing-song metre problem. *North American Review* (April 1881), 383–406. See also LONGFELLOW, HENRY WADSWORTH.   AKL

Herbert, Henry Howard Molyneux, 4th Earl of Carnarvon (1831–90). Entering official life as Under-Secretary for the Colonies (1859), Carnarvon pressed for the federation of Canada (*cont. on page 249*)

Vignettes embellishing the serial publication of several novels are often as striking as full-page illustrations. Marcus Stone's for *He Knew He Was Right*, shown here, were particularly effective. Millais did nineteen splendid vignettes for *The Small House at Allington*, and sixteen by Mary Ellen Edwards for *The Claverings* are also highly atmospheric.

Oᴺ a visit to the Mandarin Islands, Louis Trevelyan falls in love with and marries Emily, eldest daughter of the Governor, Sir Marmaduke Rowley. They return to England, bringing with them Nora, the second of Sir Marmaduke's numerous daughters. Handsome, affluent, socially superior, Trevelyan sits in Parliament and is an esteemed member of society. Emily is attractive, strong, clever. But as Trollope comments ominously, both of them are people who too much like their own way—people who in a crisis will stubbornly know they are right.

Colonel Frederick Osborne knew Emily when she was a child. He now ingratiates himself by arranging, under seal of secrecy from Trevelyan, for her father to be called home to testify before a Commons committee. Osborne is vain, self-opinionated. Though innocent of sexual intent, his letters and visits to Emily persist, until old Lady Milborough, a family friend, feels obliged to warn Trevelyan that his wife is being compromised by Osborne's attentions. This casual social intercourse provides the core of an increasingly irrational and intransigent jealousy on Trevelyan's part, countered by Emily's obstinate and equally unyielding refusal to break off the relationship, and fuelled by Osborne's cantankerous persistence.

Trevelyan commands Emily to end the connection; she, incensed by what she perceives as an affront to her integrity as wife and as woman, refuses, or offers compliance on such bitter terms that it widens rather than heals the rift. Trollope skilfully manipulates the accumulating trivia which slowly form an impenetrable wall between husband and wife.

Trevelyan sends Emily into exile at Nuncombe Putney, near Exeter. Even here Osborne engineers the opportunity to visit her. His activities are now subject to the scrutiny of Bozzle, a private detective whom Trevelyan has degradingly employed to spy on his wife. These actions naturally further the rift between the couple.

After Osborne's visit to Emily at Nuncombe Putney she is forced to return to London to live purgatorially at her uncle's East End rectory. Trevelyan arranges the abduction of their child Louey and hides with him at a dismal cottage in Willesden. Throughout this section of the novel, Trollope develops the gradual but inevitable decline of Trevelyan's mental stability. Both author and characters debate his sanity as he becomes increasingly morbid, distraught, and unbalanced.

Alienated from his friends, and abandoned even by his evil genius, the predatory Bozzle, Trevelyan decamps to Italy with young Louey and settles at Casalunga, a desolate farmstead outside Siena, where he holds the child with him in terrible isolation; Trollope's use of the barren landscape to depict the declining mental and physical state of his protagonist is particularly skilful and unusual. Efforts by friends to mediate are unavailing until Emily visits her now dying but still intransigent husband, and persuades him to give up the child and to leave Italy. The price she pays is to yield her own pride and integrity, finally agreeing to repeat a form of words which virtually acknowledge a guilt she never in fact incurred. This most moving and most unjustly wrung 'confession' persuades Trevelyan to return to England, where he dies, still deeply disturbed and, to the last, convinced he was right.

This uncharacteristically grim main plot is leavened and interwoven with some poignant social comedy. 'Sub-plot' is an inadequate description of the supporting material in *He Knew He Was Right* for the themes of the main story are closely echoed in the rest of the novel. Three households and three separate love affairs—all destined for a happy ending—counterbalance the tragedy of the main story. In Exeter lives Miss Jemima Stanbury, a wealthy spinster utterly fixed in her ways and full of gloriously comic prejudices. She had been jilted as a young woman by Brooke Burgess, a local businessman, who, dying repentant, had left her all his money. Deep friction between the elder Stanburys and Burgesses is the inevitable consequence. Her sister-in-law Mrs Stanbury lives outside Exeter in the village of Nuncombe Putney, with her two daughters Priscilla and Dorothy. Her son Hugh, formerly Miss Stanbury's protégé, has deeply offended his aunt by giving up the law and taking to penny-a-line journalism. After Hugh offends, she takes under her wing and brings to live with her the younger of Hugh's sisters, Dorothy. There is an ancillary comic sub-plot in which Dorothy is wooed by an Austen-esque cleric, Mr Gibson. Rejected by Dorothy the unfortunate Gibson is contracted to Camilla French, a local husband-hunter. Brought to realize how horrid she really is, he ludicrously shifts his affections to her elder sister Arabella. A sharpness of satirical tone informs this grotesque wooing, leavening the straightforward sweetness of the other love-plots.

Hugh Stanbury falls in love with Nora Rowley and eventually wins her, despite the prior attentions of the Hon. Charles Glascock, heir to Lord Peterborough. Miss Stanbury attempts to boycott Hugh's plans. Her efforts are, of course, finally unavailing, and she is brought to forgive him. Dorothy Stanbury attracts the admiration of young Brooke Burgess, son of Miss Stanbury's arch enemy Barty. Again Miss Stanbury's ancient prejudices and grudges threaten the relationship. Young Brooke is simply too breezy, too affable, and too determined for Aunt Jemima. Her objections to Dorothy's marriage are swept aside and she is reconciled to the Burgess clan.

The last of the emotional entanglements involves Caroline Spalding, a young American whom Mr Glascock meets in Italy, where he has gone to visit his dying father. Trollope complicates this relationship by showing Caroline's hesitations about marrying an English nobleman, and leavens it with a brilliant but acid satire on rampant American feminism in the person of Caroline's poetess friend, 'the Republican Browning', Wallachia Petrie. Social scruples are overcome by Charles Glascock's own quiet confidence and the novel latterly gives us a picture of Caroline settling to be a model Lady Peterborough. Each of these subsidiary relationships is bound quite closely to the main Trevelyan plot. Emily Trevelyan is exiled to the Stanbury family at Nuncombe Putney through Hugh Stanbury's friendship with Louis Trevelyan at Oxford. Dorothy's residence in Exeter with Miss Jemima and her attachment to young Brooke link Stanbury and Burgess material, whilst Hugh's determined wooing of Nora Rowley also links the characters in the various subsidiary stories. The Glascock/Trevelyan thread is strengthened by the future Lord Peterborough having once thought himself in love with Nora Rowley. This association involves him in mediation between Trevelyan and his wife in Italy.

Thus, around his deeply tragic and moving main story Trollope is able to arrange a series of alternative and happier love-interests which all have close links with his principal tale.

The major themes of *He Knew He Was Right* are obsession, mastery, self-will, individuality, and the problems of accepting social change. These are presented in binary opposition to balance, sharing, self-abnegation, corporate responsibility and conservative stasis. Thus the novel is unusually full and unusually assertive. Normally a Trollope novel is 'about' the brilliantly observed vicissitudes (often romantic) of ordinary people fulfilling their very ordinary business; the youngsters falling in love, the elders scheming and manipulating their social relationships. But Trollope takes new turnings in *He Knew He Was Right*. The wooing and wedding in the main plot are completed before the story opens, and is described in an ominously satirical tone. From the outset things go awry, and then from bad to worse. The Trevelyan marriage ends in the husband's derangement and death and the wife's withdrawal into virtual purdah. Very few of Trollope's love-plots are as inexorably grim as this, nor accorded such meticulous psychological investigation.

Many of the characters in *He Knew He Was Right* are obsessive. Obsession destroys Louis Trevelyan, exacerbated by his wife's equally obsessive pride. Jemima Stanbury is stubborn, self-centred, and reactionary. Her world has been ordered to conform to her own whims, and she resorts to emotional blackmail when thwarted. She is obsessive about her money, about her unhappy romantic past, about her social status, and about controlling the lives of everybody with whom she has contact, even down to dictating the clothes they wear. It is a miracle that this crusty old woman yet manages to emerge as a comic and sympathetic character. Trollope achieves this by breaking down most of her silly prejudices through the agency of the love she learns to give to other people. Dorothy, Hugh, and Brooke all resist her urge to dominate, and she yields as she realizes she wants to love them more than she wants to control them. Many of her obsessions are so cranky, and are dealt with in such a slyly subversive and comic manner, that we come to relish Miss Stanbury despite all her faults. Her monomania about Camilla French's new-fangled chignon is deliciously funny, and her conversation always manifests a pungent ability to observe and capture her friends' absurdities. But it has taken most of her 60 years for the new and more charitable Jemima to emerge from the carapace of stubborn self-regard.

Frederick Osborne evinces a malign obsessiveness. He does not love Emily, does not intend marriage or even courtship, but to satisfy his inordinate vanity he is prepared to persist in his attentions and to watch the Trevelyan marriage disintegrate. Self-will smothers in him any charitable or compassionate instinct.

Bozzle is also obsessive. Almost admirable, his dogged loyalty to his employment at first sight looks like virtue, but is actually fired by the ex-policeman's prurient desire to pursue his victim regardless of good taste or compassion. Trollope finds a remarkable stylistic device to underline this trait: whenever Bozzle's name occurs on the page, it is repeated, time and time again, until the very typography becomes obsessive. On one page the name Bozzle recurs sixteen times. His conversation, which Trollope captures with uncanny skill, is characterized by vulgarity and dullness.

The more congenial characters reveal a capacity to temper self-will with self-abnegation. Hugh Stanbury categorically refuses to comply with his aunt's objections to his career as a journalist. For a time he is content to swing out of her orbit, to deny the old woman the love she fostered in him as a youth. But the good offices of a larger love save this relationship after he becomes betrothed to Nora.

Priscilla Stanbury is one of the book's most interesting and original obsessives. Her self-assessment is painful and honest: ' "I stand alone, and can take care of myself . . . I defy the evil tongues of all the world to hurt me. My personal cares are limited to an old gown and bread and cheese. I like a pair of gloves to go to church with, but that is only the remnant of a prejudice. . . ." "And you are contented?" "Well, no.

. . . I am not fit to marry. I am often cross, and I like my own way, and I have a distaste for men." ' (XVI).

Trollope presents us with a moving and unusual portrait of a woman self-willed yet self-aware. She alone perceives the essential pettiness of the Trevelyans' quarrel and declares that it comprises 'twopenny-halfpenny pride'. 'We all live on self-esteem,' she asserts. 'Everyone thinks himself the centre and pivot of the world, and wants praise because it enables him to think well of himself.' This is a keynote of the novel. Few women of marriageable age speak with this self-lacerating but self-comprehending intelligence in Victorian fiction. Priscilla holds to her ideas as compulsively as Trevelyan or Osborne, but they are informed by ruthless appraisal of herself and her true place in the world.

As the book's title makes clear, knowing one is right is always obsessional. Nora's advice to Emily to 'be right and give way' sounds simple. But stubbornness defies common sense. Desire for mastery interferes with charitable compassion. The success of the Hon. Charles Glascock stems from his gentlemanly pliancy; he possesses no desire for mastery. He is extraordinarily unheroic, but extraordinarily skilful in making social accommodations—to the point where he becomes the first British peer in either fact or fiction to marry an American.

Self-abnegation counterpoises obsession in the novel. Hugh struggles manfully to judge the rightness of his pursuit of Nora. Should a young man with no adequate income pursue a girl no matter how much he loves her? Chapter XXV is particularly articulate on this theme. Caroline Spalding summons the altruism to ask herself if it is fair for an American girl to saddle an English lord with a transatlantic connection, regardless of their mutual affection. Dorothy is sensitive about causing her aunt distress in choosing Brooke Burgess for her mate, and old Miss Stanbury learns to abandon her fortress of prejudice in forgiveness and readjustment on many social levels. Prudence opposing love is a theme familiar enough to readers of Trollope. In the supporting plots the message is, as always, that love should conquer all. Hugh and Nora finally dare to adventure their love, with or without the wherewithal for domestic comfort. But if the theme is familiar, the intensity and the elaboration with which it is played is unusual.

He Knew He Was Right is curiously and disturbingly haunted by prescient glimpses of a changing and threatening world. The characters mostly leave the stage to enjoy an assured and comfortable personal future, yet they all seem aware of times coming soon when these comfortable lives will need readjustment: times when women will have the vote, will smoke in public, will adopt Wallachia Petrie's strident transatlantic feminism as their social manner. Chapter XL offers a sharp-edged analysis of the emancipated self-assurance of American females: 'they fear nothing . . . and talk with as much freedom as though they were men.' In allowing Caroline Spalding to marry the future Lord Peterborough, Trollope pre-dates the first actual wedding of an American woman to a British aristocrat by something like five or six years. Chapter XCV contains a remarkable conversation in which Nora pretends to deprecate the seriousness with which women should take their wedding vows, and old Lady Milborough presages a time to come when the vowing of these oaths really will be for young women no more than a necessary social strategy to buy their independence. Throughout the novel issues of female rights and female responsibility create an uneasy undercurrent to the usual affable surface of Trollopian male-dominated love-making.

The density and range of the thematic discussions in *He Knew He Was Right* make it one of Trollope's most responsible and thoughtful novels, though its length and its intensity make it unlikely ever to be one of his most popular.

Trollope commenced *He Knew He Was Right* in November 1867, and finished it in America in the spring of 1868. It first appeared, published by Virtue in 32 weekly sixpenny numbers, from 17 October 1868 to 22 May 1869. Starting in November 1869, it then appeared in monthly bound parts. In 1869 the novel appeared in two volumes, published by Strahan. Illustrations were by Marcus Stone.

The novel, the first he wrote after resigning from the Post Office, is one of Trollope's longest. It was also, along with *Phineas Finn*, the most highly paid of all his works. He received £3,200 for it from Virtue, a sum the publisher never recouped.

Trollope was disappointed with the story. None of his other novels fell so far short of his intentions. He confessed in *An Autobiography* that he had failed to create an intended sympathy for Trevelyan. He thought that the material involving Miss Stanbury was lively and entertaining, but that this could not redeem the failure of the main story.

Reviewers were not generally enthusiastic. Whilst aspects of the book were singled out—Bozzle and Jemima Stanbury in particular—few critics felt the novel's parts cohered satisfactorily. *Academy* took the line that Trollope had created a disproportionately strong moral ferment out of unwarrantably slim and innocuous material. This 'wild affliction' is, of course, exactly what modern critics have praised in the book. The *Spectator* was forthright in attributing equal blame to Emily: 'There is real genius in the conception of breaking a husband's heart and ruining his mind on so meagre a basis of fact as this . . . on the absurd foundation of an old gentleman's foppish vanity, a young lady's bitter wilfulness, and a self-occupied husband's angry, suspicious, and brooding sense of indignity' (Smalley 324). Not all the reviewers were so percipient. *The Times* thought Trollope in this mood a mere sensation novelist, whose prosaic mind managed to make his story unsensational, and the *British Quarterly Review* was indignant that Trollope should bring such uncompromising reality into a work of fiction.

The characterization of Bozzle elicited general praise. *The Times* was delighted to see the hitherto romanticized figure of the private detective reduced to 'an ordinary vulgar rogue'.

Edward *Fitzgerald found the opening of the book excellent, but thought it drifted off into longueurs, a judgement frequently repeated. Henry *James was moved by Trollope's success in evoking the atmosphere which surrounds Trevelyan in his mad isolation at Casalunga, likening Trollope in this mood to Balzac. Other discussion topics carrying into 20th-century criticism centre upon the degree and definition of Trevelyan's 'madness', and the novel's sombre and often caustic tone. The manuscript is in the Pierpont Morgan Library, New York.   TB

Gatrell, S. J., 'Jealousy, Mastery, Love and Madness . . .', in T. Bareham (ed.), *Anthony Trollope* (1980).
Overton, Bill, *The Unofficial Trollope* (1982).
Wall, S., *Trollope: Living with Character* (1988).

and of South Africa. Colonial Secretary in Disraeli's second administration, he supported Irish disestablishment, and was later responsible for abolishing slavery on the Gold Coast (1874). He resigned in January 1878 because he opposed sending the fleet to the Dardanelles in the Russo-Turkish War, fearing another Crimean War as well as breaching neutrality. After *South Africa* appeared in 1878, the Trollopes were regularly invited to Highclere, the Carnarvon country house in Berkshire.   RCT

Herbert, Sidney (1810–61), 1st Baron Herbert of Lea, 1860; Colonial Secretary under Palmerston, 1855; Secretary for War, 1859. In *Memoirs of an Ex-Minister* (1884), Lord Malmesbury recalled Herbert's anecdote about the origin of the name of Trollope, based on what he had heard as a contemporary of Anthony at Harrow. Claiming that the origins of the family were from Norman times cost Trollope many a beating from other pupils. This was corroborated by another Harrovian, Sir G. F. Duckett, in *Anecdotal Reminiscences of an Octo-nonogenarian* (1895). See also ANCESTRY OF TROLLOPE FAMILY.   RCT

Hereford, named, with no local detail, as home to the Brodricks and William Owen. *CH*   AWJ

Herefordshire. Both Wharton Hall and Longbarns are situated in this county in *The Prime Minister*, as well as Maurice Maule's country estate in *Phineas Redux*.   JMR

heroes and heroines of Trollope. The 19th-century sense of true history as the record of unheroic deeds performed by the decidedly unheroic is strong in Trollope. He accepted as fully as Jane Austen and Thackeray the belief that events of great moral consequence occur at Box Hill, not at Waterloo. Trollope not only does not believe in but detests notions of perfection—perfect character or perfect beauty. He sees in the world just as few noble heroes as did Thackeray. Unlike Thackeray, however, Trollope can view the absence of exalted heroism with great flexibility. He can sometimes leave behind the laments for vanished heroism or the sarcastic attacks on the smallness of modern men and substitute small celebrations of a displaced form of quiet, undemonstrative heroism, or, if not heroism exactly, inner strength and, more important than strength, imaginative flexibility and charity.

Trollope's biases are those of most novelists in the realistic tradition, though he pushes harder than almost anyone at the flim-flam generally associated with what he caustically refers to as 'true heroism'. We find, instead, a host of central figures who, admirable as they usually come to seem, are erring and uncertain, or, when certain, often wrong. More important, the results they produce, the plots they direct, are never of the size or consequence that would qualify as heroic. They get by, living the best they know how by their lights, retricking their beams when necessary, and never, ever, knowingly telling a lie. This instinctive aversion to a lie, however difficult that may be to put into practice, is the cornerstone of Trollope's definition of a 'gentleman', and the gentleman is the closest he gets to romantic notions of heroism.

With heroines, the matter is somewhat different and even less orthodox. For many of Trollope's heroines, life offers no choices at all beyond the narrow challenge of making the best marriage they can. Failure means absolute emptiness, but so may success. Success in any case may mean a loss of freedom or selfhood, a very limited victory indeed. Trollope raises explicitly for his heroines the central question, 'What is a woman to do with her life?' and refuses to give any easy answers. Sometimes it appears that there are no answers, which means that his heroines are without a plot, without any means for exercising power.

Trollope often traces with great insight the common paths women follow through courtship, where their attempt to preserve their independent being leads them finally to feeling isolated, perverse, and consequently guilty. This course results so often in a desire for punishment that a devastating masochistic psychology becomes characteristic. Men who sense this in the novels often do then punish the women and grant them the submission they are forced into desiring: the desire for freedom becomes by its very strength the neurotic desire to submit. Alice Vavasor is Trollope's fullest treatment of this twisted psychological progress, but many of his marriages are haunted by the notion that a heroine can exist as a real being only in sacrifice.

Even women who have been successful in marriage and withstood the temptations to masochism often find that they have triumphantly made their way into nothing at all. The most moving image of this state in Trollope is that of Lady Glencora, whose whole life as heiress, wife, and Duchess of Omnium may be seen as a fight to escape being nothing. And she, the strongest and wittiest of women, fails. As many recent feminist critics have observed, Trollope's heroines are portrayed with an unmatched sensitivity to the enormous difficulties in that culture of translating personal merit and power into any sort of meaningful action.

A different sort of unheroic failure from that which awaits Glencora traps Trollope characters who, deliberately or not, elevate themselves above their community or in some way find themselves isolated, even isolated by their virtue. Some of the most fascinating heroes and heroines are those who stick to their guns, who remain steadfast, even unto perversity. Turning the psychological screw on these isolates, Trollope shows how their very stubbornness makes them very nearly unfit for civilized life, exalted as that stubbornness may, from some points of view, undoubtedly be.

But these cross-grained, single-minded heroines and heroes are among Trollope's most fascinating explorations of both the demands and the limits of the sophisticated, not to say corrupt, world he is portraying. They tend to become disgusted with the compromises demanded by the world and to define for themselves a standard of integrity, honour, devotion correspondingly rigid and, often, as self-serving and self-defeating as it is lofty. Many of these characters cause themselves (and others) great pains by way of their steady principles, and many come not simply to exalt in that pain but to enjoy it.

Lily Dale in *The Small House at Allington* is a good example. Treated to a severe but not uncommon flightiness in her lover, she has decided, somehow, that she will herself be loyal, loyal long after any reason for that loyalty has disappeared. She simply decides that her identity involves sticking absolutely to her man, and stick she does, even when she has nothing but the false ideal before her. At first she declares, 'I believe, in my heart, that he still loves me' (XXX), but her firmness is not shaken by clear evidence that he does not. Evidence does not matter to her; she is what she is: 'I have made up my mind about it clearly and with an absolute certainty' (XLII). Lily lives in the midst of a pastoral world eager to be born, and she has at hand as a would-be lover one of Trollope's favourite anti-hero types, the hobbledehoy Johnny Eames. But a combination of sentimental idealism, masochism, and pride keeps her almost stupidly true.

Just as firm is the Revd Josiah Crawley, though he is certainly not stupid. It gives him, however, delicious pleasure to reflect on the ways in which his sufferings are more exquisite than those of St Simeon Stylites (*LCB* XLI) and to imagine what a 'grand thing' it would be 'if the judges would condemn him to be imprisoned for life' (LXII). He revolves the tragic formulas in his head: 'Great power reduced to impotence, great glory to misery, by the hand of Fate,—Necessity, as the Greeks called her' (LXII), and he runs stubbornly and contentedly into a perverse absolutism much like Lily's, isolating himself from a loving community and, even in his obstinacy, somehow towering over it. He wants justice and right to

prevail, and he says, 'in the adjustment of so momentous a matter there should be a consideration of right and wrong, and no consideration of aught beside' (LXVIII). As always with these characters, the matter is not so very 'momentous', and right and wrong are never so clearly to be determined as such a textbook code would demand.

Giles Hoggett's famous advice to Crawley— 'It's dogged as does it'—is therefore by no means the moral of the tale but a poison to Crawley's system, causing an unnatural growth in his determination to be King Lear. He cannot finally resist the role and incorporates tragic elevation into his everyday language, which is so oratorical, so directly transplanted from the Old Testament, that his wife wonders sometimes if he is, without knowing it, acting: 'she could not quite believe that her husband's humility was true humility' (XXXII). Certainly he has become a bully of humility, daring anyone to abuse him more than he can abuse himself, and greeting every other human being with what amounts to a sanctimonious snarl. Tragic heroism really cannot operate very well in Trollope's urbane and relativistic fictional world, but it is very interesting to watch it try.

The heroism we do receive is usually muted, with the hero finding himself moderately successful at best, misunderstood, and often a little sore. Trollope's favourite hero, the Duke of Omnium, is never at home in his world and is able to accomplish very little that one could point to. He does not understand his wife or children and is imperfectly understood in return; his stint as Prime Minister is certainly not glorious; he often finds the world sliding away from him; he feels very much alone. Still, he is a perfect gentleman and acts always with an integrity that can be glowing in its generous ferocity. He never in his life does anything unfair, unjust, or unkind; now and then he acts with a sweetness of heart that startles him as much as those who know him. Never able to bring much of his character into action or even into his own full awareness, he none the less is as heroic as Trollope's hard, unsentimental realism will allow.

It is a displaced heroism, certainly, but still close to an identifiable heroic tradition. More common in Trollope is the radical displacement of the centre of the novel away from the romantic leads—the young lady and her lover—and onto an older male. Trollope engages romantic comedy often only to play with it, mock it lightly, show us that his (and our) interest is elsewhere. Notice, for instance, how often he ends a novel by mocking marriages and by displaying his own hand in bringing them about. He thus makes them seem arbitrary, artificial, insignificant, as here, for instance, at the close of *Ayala's Angel*: 'If marriage be the proper ending for a novel,—the only ending, as this writer takes it to be, which is not discordant,—surely no tale was ever so properly ended, or with so full a concord, as this one. Infinite trouble has been taken not only in arranging these marriages but in joining like to like,—so that, if not happiness, at any rate sympathetic unhappiness, might be produced' (LXIV).

Trollope often adds this sort of self-reflexive play to explicit ridicule of his technical romantic leads, forcing us to look elsewhere for the hero. A wonderful example is in *Barchester Towers*, where the romantic centre is occupied by the silly Eleanor Bold, whose mindless devotion to her dead husband (whom the narrator says he disliked) is likened to the action of deadly parasites, and by an ageing adolescent, the Revd Francis Arabin. By a variety of means, Trollope clears out a centre in this novel for one of his most compelling and unorthodox heroes, Mr Harding.

While Mr Harding's virtues are defined largely by negation, he does display a strength of resistance, the true power of the pacifist, surrounded by idiots bent on warring. He demonstrates those beatitudes which the narrator cites repeatedly as vital: 'Blessed are the meek, for they shall inherit the earth—Blessed are the merciful, for they shall obtain mercy' (IV). Mr Harding has no goals for himself, no long-term plans, no strategy. He simply wants to do good and cause no trouble; he wants not to trouble his neighbours, nor upset long-established ways of living. He withdraws from conflict and gains thereby a great clarity and an important capacity for self-doubt. Like a woman, we are told, he has 'a nice appreciation of the feelings of others' (LII). A tolerant man, he has, all the same, absolutely sure moral instincts, dislikes all the right people (Slope, Mrs Proudie), and wins by not fighting. Trollope's narrator announces that, generally speaking, the wrong man always wins in a fight, since the very weakness of his cause forces him always to be honing his tools, whereas the man in the right, easy and confident, always loses (XXXVII). Hence, one does not fight.

Heroic action, then, amounts to quiet withdrawal, not the only shape for Trollope's unusual figurings of the heroic, but one of the most unconventional. One does not, however, go to Trollope to look for the conventional anyhow, certainly not when it comes to heroes and heroines. JRK

Herriot, Arthur, penniless lawyer fond of grouse shooting, who accompanies his friend Frank Greystock to Portray Castle to stay with Lizzie Eustace. *ED* RCT

Hertfordshire, one of the shires north of London and chief setting for *Mr Scarborough's Family*. While not one of the beautiful counties of rural England, Hertfordshire still has pleasures such as fox-hunting to recommend it. The Cumberlow Green Hunt, where Mr Thoroughbung is triumphant, 'was a popular meet in that county, where meets have not much to make them popular except the good-humour of those who form the hunt' (XXVIII). *MSF* MT

Hervieu, Auguste (?1794–1858), French artist and close friend of Fanny Trollope who stayed with the family in Harrow, tutoring the children in drawing, for which Anthony's talents were minimal. His romantic portrait of Trollope in youth is in the National Portrait Gallery. Hervieu accompanied Fanny on her mad journey to found a community in Tennessee (1827). He designed the bazaar in Cincinnati known as 'Trollope's Folly', in which Fanny sold gimcrack goods imported from England. He helped out when funds ran low by sketching the locals, and later illustrated several of Fanny's novels. Scurrilous newspaper stories in the American press capitalized on Hervieu's relations with Fanny. Traces of her cheerful bohemian *compagnon* may be seen in some of Trollope's artists and European characters, such as Conway Dalrymple (*LCB*) and Édouard Pateroff (*C*). RCT

Heseltine family. A daughter, Rose, became Trollope's wife in 1844 (see TROLLOPE, ROSE). Little is known about Martha Heseltine (d. 1841), Rose's mother, or her origins: she appears to have borne the same name as her husband even before she married him in Hull. Edward J. Heseltine (?1783–1855) was born in Hull, one of eight children, the son of a merchant clerk. He became a bank clerk himself.

Two daughters of the marriage, Eliza Ann (b. 1813) and Mary Jane (b. 1815), were born in Hull and baptized there in the Anglican faith although the two younger children born after the family moved to Rotherham, Rose (1820–1917) and her sister Isabella (1823–63), were baptized in the Hollis Unitarian Chapel there, which suggests a parental conversion.

From 1828 Heseltine was manager of the bank situated on Rotherham High Street, which from 1836 on became known as the Rotherham office of the Joint Sheffield and Rotherham Stock Bank, though the directors of the new joint stock company allowed him a continuing latitude in the conduct of its business which they came to regret.

Heseltine's job brought in a salary probably of about £300 a year and free quarters for his family, who lived above the premises in the High St., where they had two live-in servants. He later became a director of the Sheffield and Rotherham Railway and was a respected local figure, known for his collection of armour.

Martha, his first wife, died in 1841 as a result of injuries she sustained in an accident on the North Midland Railway: he was a widower of 60 when his daughter Rose got engaged. Just a year after the death of his first wife, Heseltine married a woman half his age. Charlotte Platts (b. 1813), the daughter of John Platts, a well-known Unitarian minister, bore him two sons, Ned and Frank, at about the same time that her step-daughter Rose Trollope was giving birth to her own children.

At the time when Rose became engaged, Eliza Ann had already left home, having married an Irishman, Samuel Anderton, but the next sister, Mary Jane, was still living with her husband and child over the bank. Isabella would marry Joseph Bland, who was also a bank employee.

The Heseltines' connection with the bank, however, turned out to be painful in several respects: though the accommodation was free, the house, like others in the street, stank from the standing ordure in the inadequate drains, making the children ill and encouraging servants to leave quickly. The cellars might have as much as four feet (1 m) of water in them, needing to be pumped six or seven times a day. Heseltine gave evidence to this effect in the course of an inquiry into the town drains: in the report he was given the title of 'Esquire', which may be an indication of the gentlemanly status of his work.

When Heseltine retired in 1852 at the age of 72, the new manager found that he had been embezzling the funds. He had been doing it since 1836 and at least £4,000 was missing. (It has been suggested that he was transferring money to the railway of which he was a director (Glendinning 223–6).) His son-in-law Joseph Bland was head clerk at the bank and would have been involved in making the audit which exposed the shortfall, so Heseltine may have had some prior warning of the investigations which followed. He escaped them by moving about from Torquay to Plymouth and then on to Bristol and Gainsborough and by getting Charlotte to answer the bank's letters and fend off their demand that he should attend for interview by claiming that he was ill. Eventually he fled to the Continent, where he died at Le Havre in September 1855.

It seems impossible that Rose and her husband should not have known of this disgrace, but no reference to it can be found in their letters. It

may help to explain the fact that when Rose drew up a memo of the events of their married life for Trollope, who was thinking of writing his autobiography in 1875, she recorded many visits to members of the Trollope clan but made no mention of the Heseltine family, with the exception of her sister Isabella, and of her sister's daughter Florence Nightingale *Bland (1855–1908). Rose appears to have remained close to Isabella, who acted as godmother to the Trollopes' second son Fred in 1847. Trollope and his wife took in Isabella's 8-year-old daughter Florence and brought her up as their own when both her parents died in 1863, leaving their four children orphaned.

MH

Glendinning, Victoria, *Anthony Trollope* (1992).
Mullen, Richard, *Anthony Trollope: A Victorian in his World* (1990).

Heytesbury, county seat for Bullhampton in Wiltshire and location of trial for Farmer Trumbull's murder. *VB*   SRB

Higgins, Matthew ('Jacob Omnium') (1810–68), journalist who wrote under the name 'Jacob Omnium' (lit. 'Jack of all Trades'), taken from the title of his first published article. He was active on behalf of sufferers in the Irish famine (1847) and contributed to the Peelite *Morning Chronicle*, *The Times*, the *Pall Mall Gazette*, and *Cornhill Magazine* (under Thackeray). Many of these articles were re-edited in 1875 as *Essays on Social Subjects*. Trollope first met Higgins at *Cornhill*'s inaugural dinner, in January 1860, and soon numbered him among his 'most intimate associates' (*Auto* VIII). In November 1860 Trollope congratulated George Smith on an article by Higgins exposing abuses at Eton which contributed to public debate and the Clarendon Commission (July 1861), inquiring the nine most distinguished public schools. Publication of the report in 1864 led to Trollope's article 'Public Schools' in the *Fortnightly* (October 1865) about his experiences at Winchester and Harrow.

RCT

'Higher Education of Women, The' (lecture). Women's exclusion from universities is unjust and unreasonable. Women can, however, exercise their minds and pursue independently such subjects as geography, history, art, music, foreign languages. Perhaps ironically, this novelist advises restraint in novel-reading. Women's education should differ in scope and nature from men's education, as their roles in society differ; the American co-education system will prove socially damaging by encouraging competition between, rather than within, the sexes. *Four Lectures*, 67–88.   AKL

Hill, Frederic (1803–96), brother of Rowland Hill; Assistant Secretary of the Post Office, 1851–75. Trollope reported on negotiations with Nubar Bey, the Egyptian diplomat, about passage of mail through Egypt and projected changes in the routes of West Indian packets. Regarding the two brothers, he declared: 'I never came across anyone who so little understood the ways of men [as Rowland Hill],—unless it was his brother Frederic. To the two brothers the servants of the Post Office . . . were so many machines who could be counted on for their exact work without deviation, as wheels may be counted on, which are kept going always at the same pace and always by the same power' (*Auto* VIII).   RCT

Hill, Octavia (1838–1912), influential housing reformer, sister-in-law of G. H. *Lewes. In January 1869 Lewes sent Trollope her essay for *Saint Pauls*, possibly 'Organized Work among the Poor; Suggestions Founded on Four Years' Management of a London Court', which proposed regular inspection of poor people's houses by lady rent collectors. Trollope declined the article: 'It is not that I do not respect her and her cause, or that she does not plead for it well; but that she is Utopian, and at the same time not so clear in the theory of her Utopia, as to make it probable that any thing should come of good from a suggestion so made' (*Letters* 1, 459). He added: 'Education is the only cure,—not Utopian inspection—such a good man or woman may make in his own family or own Court. You cannot inspect people into Godliness, cleanliness, and good grub. I do think you may educate them to it, and we are doing so,—only education wont go as quick as population. Then comes in Malthus & all the rest of it' (460). Hill's piece appeared in *Macmillan's* (July 1869), later reprinted in *Homes of the London Poor* (1875).   RCT

Hill, Rowland (1795–1879), originator of the penny post; Secretary of the Post Office (1854–64) and Trollope's heartily loathed chief; knighted in 1860. Although impressed by Trollope's abilities and the results he achieved in reorganizing rural postal deliveries, Hill was thin-skinned and paranoid with colleagues, especially with Trollope's brother-in-law John *Tilley, who was, as Assistant Secretary, in close proximity. Suspecting a cabal, he suspended one committee (1860) on working conditions. He also took offence at Trollope's publishing a version of his lecture 'The Civil Service as a Profession' in *Cornhill* (February 1861) and was uncooperative when Trollope asked for seven months' leave to go to America (1861). In September 1862 he confided to his diary that Trollope was suspected of neglecting his official duties for his writing, and that he doubted

his honesty or sincerity—both assumptions wide of the mark. His daughter Eleanor Smythe noted an awkward two-hour meeting at their home with Trollope in full cry, perched on a flimsy chair that looked as if it might collapse at any moment (*I & R* 54). Trollope looked back in high glee at his 'delicious feuds' with Hill (*Auto* XV), insisting, 'I had thought very much more about the Post Office than I had of my literary work, and had given to it a more unflagging attention.'   RCT

Hippesley, Dean, Dean of Exeter Cathedral, father of Cecilia Western's friend Maude, and brother-in-law of Sir Francis Geraldine of whom he greatly disapproves. *KD*   NCS

Hiram's Hospital, Barchester almshouse established in 1434 by John Hiram for the support of twelve elderly working men. The revenue has increased manyfold in 400 years, offering its Warden a picturesque house and an annual income of £800, whereas the pensioners receive only 18*d.* daily. It becomes a *cause célèbre* when John Bold seeks its reform and the London *Jupiter* uses it to attack mercenary clergy. W, BT, SHA, LCB.   NCS

historical fiction. Sir Walter Scott popularized the English historical novel and many 19th-century novelists emulated him with stories set in previous periods which mixed real and fictitious characters. *La Vendée*, Trollope's only historical fiction, has never received the critical acclaim it deserves.   TB

'History of English Prose Fiction'. At some time in the 1850s Trollope contemplated this ambitious project, acknowledging in *An Autobiography* that the task 'came to have a terrible aspect to me', as he realized 'it would be necessary to read an infinity of novels' with extensive commentary on each (XII). He planned to begin with *Robinson Crusoe* and continue with Defoe's successors, except for living authors. With typical thoroughness he began his studies with earlier authors than Defoe, spending time on Sidney's *Arcadia* and Aphra Behn's stories, before his spirit flagged; 'I still think that the book is one well worthy to be written.' Michael Sadleir copied two pages from the manuscript, reproduced in his *Commentary* (appendix III), which indicate Trollope's purpose to vindicate his profession and show the educative value of fiction. It was to become the theme of several lectures he gave up and down the country in the 1870s and at *Royal Literary Fund dinners. Although poetry 'takes the highest place in literature', the novelist's purpose is the same 'and his lessons all tend to the same end'—the teaching of 'true honour, true love, true worship and true humanity'. The rest of Trollope's brief introduction refutes Carlyle's attacks on novel-writing and extols the example set by Walter Scott. The fragment is in the Bodleian. RCT

'History of the Post Office in Ireland', Trollope's lively anecdotal report over seven pages which traced the development of postal services in the country since the 18th century. Trollope was instructed to make this report for the Postmaster General and it was submitted to Parliament (House of Commons, *Sessional Papers*, 1857, 4, 354–60). His expertise in this area had already been acknowledged in July 1855, when he testified on postal arrangements in Ireland before a select committee of the House of Commons (*Parliamentary Papers*, 1854–5, 11, 431–532). In nearly four days he argued the case for the efficiency of mail links by Bianconi's cars over the railway for which an amount of lobbying had been going on. His statement drew a commendation from the Postmaster General. RCT

'History of World Literature'. In early adulthood, probably in 1840 or 1841, Trollope proposed an ambitious plan, to create single-handedly a vast reference work. It was to be divided into nineteen chronological divisions and twelve subject areas. The undertaking may have been influenced by Trollope's knowledge of his father's attempt to compile an *Encyclopaedia Ecclesiastica*, of which the first and only volume was published (1834). With his father's example in mind, he confidently hoped to publish one volume at a time. In his outline for the project, Trollope theorized that the book would be structured by periods of years, time divisions being irregular according to how much literature any given period yielded. Another principle governing the shape would be by subject, of which twelve were listed comprising Poetry, Practical Philosophy, History, Ethical Philosophy, Theology, Political Economy, Works on Literature, Romance, Biography, Fine Arts, Periodical Literature, and Miscellaneous. The manuscript is among Trollope family papers in the University of Illinois. The document was reproduced as appendix B in the *Letters*. RCT

Hittaway, Clara, interfering oldest sister of Lord Fawn. Mrs Hittaway is a sensible, worldly woman married to an important man of business. To protect the respectability of the Fawn family, she does her utmost to break off the engagement between Lizzie Eustace and Lord Fawn. *ED* JMR

Hittaway, Orlando, busy, self-important husband of Clara Hittaway and chairman of the Board of Civil Appeals. Though he is concerned primarily with his life 'among official men', Mr Hittaway supports his wife in her effort to separate his brother-in-law Lord Fawn from Lizzie Eustace. *ED* JMR

Hodgson, Christopher, Post Office surveyor for the Northern District, one of nine (along with Trollope) who negotiated in 1864 with John Tilley for increased salaries. In a letter to Hodgson he confided, on leaving the service in 1867: 'It is not so much that the office is no long[er] worth my while, as you say, as that other things have grown upon [me] so fast that I feel myself beginning to neglect the office and I am sure you will acknowledge that when that is the case it had better be given up' (*Letters* 1, 396). RCT

Hoff, Herr, Innsbruck butcher who angrily tells Frau Frohmann to buy meat elsewhere when she asks for lower prices, but makes up his quarrel, advising her to 'swim with the stream'. *'Froh-mann' WFF* GRH

Hoggett, Giles, elderly brickmaker of Hoggle End whose philosophy of endurance, 'It's dogged as does it', profoundly influences the meditations of the troubled Revd Josiah Crawley. *LCB* NCS

Hoggle End, small colony of impoverished, rough brickmakers two miles (3 km) from Hogglestock Parsonage. Revd Josiah Crawley spends much of his time in this part of his parish where he is respected for his hard work and hard life. *LCB* NCS

Hogglestock, small, poor parish in northeastern Barsetshire. Bleak and ugly, with few trees and large fields of turnips and wheat, it has none of the beauties of English cultivation. The only gentleman's house—ugly, straight, and small—is inhabited by Revd Josiah Crawley. *FP, LCB* NCS

Holdenough, Mr, widowed canon, on good terms with the Dean of Brotherton, who marries Lady Alice Germain. They remain aloof from the quarrels of her family. *IHP* MG

holidays abroad. The grand tour, once exclusively limited to the sons of the privileged, spread widely among the newly wealthy, and filtered down to the middle class with the growth of rail travel and excursions organized by cruise lines and business entrepreneurs. The Trollopes took annual holidays abroad and became experts at handling luggage and itineraries. Trollope, of course, wrote solidly during vacations, although continental tours were necessary escapes from the ferociously ordered pattern of English routines and engagements. In July–August 1867, for example, they toured Reims, Nancy, the Vosges (which Trollope loathed), the Engadine, St Moritz. They crossed the St Bernard Pass and the Simplon, and went down the Rhône Valley to Geneva. Such journeys fed into the fiction. Immediately after this trip Trollope launched into *The Golden Lion of Granpère*. Trollope became an expert on all the perils of travel by land and sea, including delays, lost luggage and tickets, and poor food. He noted in *He Knew He Was Right*, 'the real disgrace of England is the railway sandwich,—that whited sepulchre, fair enough outside, but so meagre, poor, and spiritless within' (XXXVII). Experiences on the Luxembourg route (1874), when his tickets were lost, caused him to write to *The Times* twice. His most favoured destinations were Hollental in the Black Forest and Felsenegg near Zug, Switzerland (first visited in 1874). Here were ideal 'hunting grounds' for thought ('A Walk in a Wood', *Good Words*, September 1879). From Felsenegg he wrote to George Eliot in August 1878, 'Here we are on the top of a mountain where I write for four hours a day, walk for four hours, eat for two, and sleep out the balance satisfactorily' (*Letters* 2, 785). Eager traveller though he was, Trollope was always glad to return to England, sentiments he expressed in the story 'Returning Home'. After Trollope's death Rose kept up the holiday ritual. See also TRANSPORTATION AND TRAVEL; 'TRAVELLING SKETCHES'. RCT

Holl, Francis Montague (1845–88), genre painter famed for scenes of working-class life. His most famous picture, *Newgate—Committed for Trial*, was exhibited at the Royal Academy in 1878. He illustrated regularly for the *Graphic*, in which his 26 illustrations for *Phineas Redux* appeared, July 1873 to January 1874. Holl's Phineas 'seems to have lost all his dash and verve' and the artist 'overstated the changes that suffering has wrought upon Lady Laura' (N. John Hall, *Trollope and his Illustrators* (1980), 144–5). RCT

Hollingshead, John (1827–1904), journalist and theatre manager; contributor to *Household Words* and *Cornhill*; succeeded Edmund *Yates as drama critic of the *Daily News*. He opened the Gaiety Theatre specializing in burlesques (1868) and ran it for eighteen years. Asked by Hollingshead for a play, Trollope offered his comedy *Did He Steal It?* (1869), based on the cheque mystery of *The Last Chronicle of Barset*. It was rejected. This must have made the later *Shilly-Shally* episode all the more galling, since Charles *Reade's unauthorized stage adaptation under that title of *Ralph the Heir* ran for 28 performances at the Gaiety. Trollope assured Hollingshead in March 1873 he felt no bitterness towards him: the fault was all Reade's. RCT

Hollycombe, Jack. A malt salesman working for Peppercorn, he aspires to Polly and by persistence wins her. 'Plumplington' GRH

Holmes, Godfrey, Bessy Garrow's suitor. The young banker has a difficult time persuading her to accept him but eventually wins her. 'Mistletoe' *TAC2* GRH

Holmes, Isabella, blunt sister of Godfrey. She tries to influence Bessy Garrow towards accepting Godfrey. 'Mistletoe' *TAC2* GRH

Holmes, Mary (?1815–1878), governess to Thackeray's daughters. She found consolation in Roman Catholic faith, music, literature, and cultivating friendships with eminent figures like Newman. After *Thackeray's death (1863) she latched on to Trollope and became, next to Kate Field, one of his most assiduous female correspondents. He greeted her literary efforts patiently but firmly, and tried to further her musical aspirations (*Letters* 1, 473), unavailingly. He confided about his own writing, in one letter informing her that he had used Disraeli and Gladstone as characters for their policies not their persons (*Letters* 2, 692–3). In another lengthy letter he tactfully explained how a publisher's reader went about the business (her novel had been rejected by Chapman & Hall) and described his own miseries as editor (*Letters* 2, 636). He frequently commented to her on his own work and that of others. RCT

Holmes, Oliver Wendell (1809–94), Professor of Anatomy and Physiology at Harvard (1847–94); leading contributor to *Atlantic Monthly*; author of *The Autocrat of the Breakfast-Table* (1858). In literary Boston of the 1860s, Trollope could hardly wait to cross swords with the Autocrat who was noted for his lively conversation. The opportunity came in September 1861, when James Lowell observed their combat: 'It was very funny. Trollope wouldn't give him any chance.' Visiting England, Holmes called on the Trollopes in 1865 and 1874. RCT

Holt, Cecilia. See WESTERN, CECILIA.

Holt, Mrs, widowed mother of Cecilia Western. A woman of comfortable means, she supports, largely in silence, her daughter's actions, and resents those of George Western. *KD* NCS

Holt, Ralph, loyal tenant farmer on John Caldigate's estate, delighted that Caldigate resumes the estate after first selling his inheritance. He strongly supports the Caldigate family during the bigamy trial. *JC* SRB

homes of Trollope. 16 Keppel Street, Russell Square, the house Thomas Anthony owned and

Demands of business and social engagements in the 1870s obliged Trollope to find a
home in central London. He chose 39 Montagu Square, and moved in during April 1873,
modifying the interior for his huge library. Eventually London fogs and declining health
caused him to move to his last home in the Sussex countryside in July 1880.

where he began married life with Frances Milton in 1809. Fanny's brother Henry Milton lived at No. 27. The Trollopes' first five children were born here, including Anthony on 24 April 1815. A footman clad in the Trollope livery proclaimed the family's status as gentry. The house no longer exists. In *Orley Farm* Mrs Furnival pines for by-gone days at Keppel Street. When Anthony was 3 his father leased some 160 acres (65 ha) around Illots Farm, Harrow, from Lord Northwick and built a large house called Julians, moving the family there in 1818. It was, said Trollope, 'the grave of all my father's hopes, ambition, and prosperity' (*Auto* I). Forced to move into the farmhouse, which he promptly enlarged, Thomas renamed it Julian Hill. It became the model for *Orley Farm.*

In 1827 another farm was leased at Harrow Weald, 'a wretched tumble-down farmhouse . . . in danger falling into the neighbouring horse-pond'. Here Anthony solaced his lonely hours flirting with the bailiff's daughter (*Auto* I). The success of Fanny's *Domestic Manners of the Americans* (1832) enabled the family to return to Julian Hill. Thomas Anthony's financial position grew worse. By October 1833, he was being threatened by Lord Northwick with legal action. In March 1834, he fled to Ostend, where the family soon followed. Anthony hung around in Bruges for about six months, thence to Brussels to become a classical usher (*Auto* II), before his great opportunity arrived to work for the General Post Office in London.

After a short stay with his brother in Little Marlborough Street, Trollope moved into 22 Northumberland Street (now Luxborough Street), grimly situated by Marylebone Work-house, 'a most dreary abode' (*Auto* III). In *Phineas Redux* (1874) he has the fugitive Emilius take lodgings there. His deliverance from a round of debts, poor food, and mild dissipation, relieved by visits to his mother, now in Hadley, came with transfer to Ireland. Trollope went to Banagher, staying in the hotel by the river Shannon. Post Office business kept him on the move in the west of Ireland. At Drumsna, Co. Leitrim, for several weeks, he discovered the ruined house which sparked the idea for his first novel, *The Macdermots of Ballycloran.*

Marriage to Rose Heseltine (June 1844)—'the commencement of my better life'—(*Auto* IV) led to their first real home, in Clonmel, Co. Tipperary, where his two sons, Henry Merivale (1846–1926) and Frederic James Anthony (1847–1910), were born. Happily married, and a family man, his homes now took on special significance in his life and fiction. He was to write in *The Bertrams* 'To neither man nor woman

does the world fairly begin till seated together in their first mutual home they bethink themselves that the excitement of their honeymoon is over' (XXX).

Between 1855 and 1859 the family lived at 5 Seaview Terrace, Donnybrook, a roomy, three-storey red-brick house near Dublin.

Transfer to England and special responsibilities in Wales and Scotland involved moves to a variety of lodgings, but in 1859 Trollope leased Waltham House, Waltham Cross, Hertfordshire, about twelve miles (19 km) from London, in many ways Trollope's favourite home. It was an elegant 18th-century house with two wings, one ideal for official business, the other serving as stables for his hunters. Iron gates and gravel driveway led to the front steps. Inside were spacious rooms, a fine staircase, and the library Trollope prized. The property had a walled garden, lawns, and summerhouse. Trollope now lived the role of English squire, with a household staff of five servants, including his Irish groom *Barney. Numerous accounts testify to the Trollopes' hospitality and congenial way of life here, and the novelist always spoke fondly of the place 'where we grew our own cabbages and strawberries, made our own butter, and killed our own pigs. I occupied it for twelve years, and they were years to me of great prosperity' (*Auto* IX). Among many visitors, Anne *Thackeray noted in her journal in 1865 that it was 'a sweet old prim chill house', while Sir Frederick and Lady Juliet *Pollock called it 'an old-fashioned red-brick house . . . with a good staircase and some large rooms . . . and standing in equally old-fashioned grounds'. The garden had 'a square pond at one end of it and a smooth grass lawn at the other'. Here on summer evenings, W. Lucas *Collins recalled, guests assembled after dinner for wines and fruit and good stories (*I & R* 88–91, 161).

Returning from Australia Trollope leased a four-storey house, 39 Montagu Square, north of Marble Arch, taking possession in early April 1873. They stayed seven years, until city bustle began to take its toll. A National Trust plaque marks the building.

The Trollopes' last home was North End, South Harting, in Sussex, where they moved in July 1880. The house was notable for its Italianate tower and was set in about 70 acres (28 ha), which Trollope rented out, keeping one meadow. The property had an apple orchard and large conservatory, stabling, sheds for pigs and cows, other outbuildings, and two enclosed yards. T. H. S. Escott considered the house among the best and prettiest buildings in the district, and it was said that Alfred Austin found in North End inspiration for his book *The Garden That I Love*

(1894), although text and illustrations show no direct connection. Rose had her garden once more, and Trollope busied himself with his wine racks and library. The Trollopes still entertained, rode through the countryside, regularly attended church, and got to know the locals. But with failing health, and restless, Trollope complained of the damp, and feeling cut off from his London haunts. When possible he booked in at his favourite Garlant's Hotel, Pall Mall, not far from the Haymarket Theatre, 'a certain quiet clerical hotel at the top of Suffolk Street, much patronized by bishops and deans of the better sort' (*LCB* LXX). It was at Garlant's that on 3 November 1882 he had a furious row with the leader of a German street band playing under his window, precipitating the stroke which killed him.   RCT

'Honesty in Statesmanship' (letter). The discovery of villainous fraud in the life of the late duc de Morny seems not sufficiently publicized. Wealth, rank, and success in fraud should not soften the judgement of guilt; a large tombstone and family connections are no credit to such a person. *Pall Mall Gazette* (16 March 1865), 3–4.
AKL

Honybun, Mr, lawyer friend of Sir John Joram, whose invitation to a shooting holiday in Suffolk sorely tempts Joram as he works long hours on the Caldigate case. *JC*   SRB

Honyman, Mr, Baslehurst lawyer who suggests that his client, Mr Tappitt, the brewer, settle his dispute with Luke Rowan out of court. Tappitt refuses his lawyer's sound advice and takes up with the disreputable legal team of Sharpit & Longfite. *RR*   MT

Hopkins, Mr, venerable head gardener of the Great House at Allington who cultivates Lily and Bell Dale as well as the flowers and grounds of the estate. He knows his master's true worth and his own, and he vociferates masterfully against Adolphus Crosbie's actions. *SHA*   NCS

Hopkins, Mrs, housekeeper at Bragton Hall. Although she works for John Morton, her friendship and loyalty belong to Reginald Morton. *AS*
MG

Hoppett Hall, a substantial house with three acres (1 ha) in Dillsborough owned by Reginald Morton. *AS*   MG

Horace (65–8 BC), Roman soldier and poet, best known for his 'Epodes' on a variety of political and satirical themes, his 'Odes'; three books of 'Epistles', of which one is the literary essay 'Ars Poetica'; and two books of satires. Although Trollope claimed that little attempt had been made at Harrow to teach him the classics, he told T. H. S.

Escott that during 1840 he found to his delight he could read Cicero and Horace in the original. Sceptical views on satire's capacity to reform mankind were articulated in May 1870 to Alfred Austin. Doubting Juvenal's efficacy in suppressing vice he praised Horace as 'goodnatured,— almost I may say a trifler,—in his satyres' (*Letters* 1, 516). Preparing for his *Fortnightly* articles on Cicero in 1877, Trollope reread works by Horace, and others. To the end of his life he frequently quoted Horace. In 1876 his valediction to hunting was underlined by poignant Horatian allusion. In *An Old Man's Love*, Mr Whittlestaff likes walking among the beech trees reading Horace: 'Many a morsel of wisdom he had here made his own' (XVI).   RCT

Horne, Revd Augustus, dandified clergyman. Intrigued by the size of General Chassé's 'what's the names' (trousers), he tries them on, has his own discarded trousers cut up in mistake for them, and suffers comical embarrassments. 'Chassé' *TAC2*   GRH

Horns, the, luxurious Richmond residence of the Pallisers. With beautiful gardens fronting the Thames and within easy reach of London, the Horns is often used for fashionable parties during the London season. The property was a gift to Lady Glencora from the old Duke of Omnium upon her marriage. *SHA, CYFH, PM, DC*   JMR

Horsball, Mr, obliging manager of the Moonbeam, the inn at Barnfield where members of the Berkshire and Buckinghamshire Hunt (the 'B&B') stable their horses. Known in the sporting world as 'a man who never did ask for money' (VIII). *RH*   ALS

Horton, Mary. Wife of Wilfred, she does much to reconcile her husband to her brother George Wade. 'Not if'   GRH

Horton, Wilfred. Annoyed by his brother-in-law's refusal to sign a paper, he threatens to leave Hallam Hall until reminded by his wife and the sermon of peace and forgiveness. 'Not if'
GRH

Hoskins, Hannibal, persistent and likeable American suitor of Ophelia Gledd who confides in Green. 'Gledd' *LS*   GRH

Hôtel de la Poste, Mme Faragon's inn in Colmar where George Voss works after leaving the Lion d'Or. *GLG*   MG

Hotspur, Lady Elizabeth. A good woman twenty years younger than her husband Sir Harry Hotspur, she is no match either for her daughter Emily or for George Hotspur, whom, like many of the women in the novel, she likes. Her attempts to convey her husband's warnings to her daughter fail due to her timidity and awe of Emily. *SHH*   MG

Hotspur, Emily, daughter of Lady Elizabeth and Sir Harry Hotspur. Knowing that she cannot inherit the Hotspur title, and believing with her father that title and property should remain together, Emily is willingly attracted to her charming cousin George Hotspur. By the time her father is convinced George is not fit to be her husband, it is too late—she has given him her heart. Emily believes the Victorian mythos that no matter what the errors of a man the love of a good and pure woman can save the reprobate and that for a woman to love more than once is to sully her purity. Thus, when George proves unworthy, she dies. *SHH*   MG

Hotspur, George, heir to the title of the Hotspurs, although not the estate, and second cousin to Emily Hotspur. Allowed into polite society, he is none the less 'a very black sheep indeed'. He appeals to both men and women, but is untrustworthy and cannot resist immediate gratification in order to gain Emily and, thus, the estates to go with his title. He is deeply in debt, drinks, has a mistress, and, perhaps most damning, cheats at cards. *SHH*   MG

Hotspur, Sir Harry. Torn between his duty to his daughter Emily and to society, he fails both. He firmly believes that keeping title and estate together is necessary for the maintenance of England as a great nation, but George Hotspur, heir to the title, is corrupt. Sir Harry's vacillation over the depth of George's iniquity allows the rogue to gain Emily's promise of marriage. After Emily's death, Sir Harry wills the estates to his wife's nephew. *SHH*   MG

Houghton, Adelaide (née **De Baron**). Recognized as a kindred spirit by the Marquis of Brotherton, the amoral woman tries to cause trouble between her former flame Lord George Germain and Lady George for the excitement it brings her and for the pleasure of destroying any happiness they enjoy. Judging by herself she assumes all manifestations of love and virtue are hypocritical. After her machinations are discovered, she unashamedly attempts to cultivate Lady George, who rebuffs her. *IHP*   MG

Houghton, Hetta. A good-natured, rich spinster who enjoys life. The sister of Jeffrey Houghton, she conducts a flirtation with the Dean of Brotherton when he visits his daughter in London. *IHP*   MG

Houghton, Jeffrey, gambler and friend of Mr De Baron, married by Adelaide De Baron for the comfort and position his wealth provides her. Although he (ineffectually) forbids her to hunt, he is in general a complaisant husband. *IHP*   MG

household management. Advice on household management was a popular topic in magazines of the period, and Trollope's close accounts of his characters' domestic circumstances mirror this. The average income of the fast-growing middle class was between £150 and £300 a year, and on this a household would probably be able to afford one maid to help do everything. The Crawleys, with £130 a year, have 'a red-armed little girl' (*FP* XLVI). To keep a carriage required an income of at least £600 a year. Mark Robarts has a pony carriage, a saddle horse, and a second horse for his gig—and lives right up to his income of £900 a year (*FP* IX).

Trollope focuses on the seemingly endless purse of the Pallisers and the immensely rich, and mocks those families, like the Longestaffes (*WWLN*), brought to financial embarrassment by their aspiration to powdered footmen. He has more respect for Lady Fawn, budgeting carefully to keep within her income of £3,000 a year, while maintaining a household with thirteen staff (*ED*). Trollope himself, as a married man, budgeted cautiously and carefully; he never risked repeating his childhood experiences with the bailiffs once he had extricated himself from the scrapes of his 'hobbledehoyhood'. His budget for 1859, on an income of £1,580, demonstrates the cost of a comfortable life (Glendinning 256). In 1863, with his income more than doubled, financial prudence still prevailed (Mullen 425).

While Trollope married on £400 a year, his single men regularly agonize about the visible economies necessary to marry on £600–£800. This is often the comic theme of a sub-plot. Jack De Baron foolishly relies on his poor financial prospects to protect him from matrimonial commitment to Augusta Mildmay (*IHP*). Gerald Maule and Adelaide Palliser contemplate a budget of stringent economy with masochistic enthusiasm (*PR*); and poverty, cabbages, and cradles run like a refrain through Frank Houston and Imogene Docimer's on-and-off romance (*AA*). Crosbie's prevarications over the sacrifice of his bachelor pleasures if he marries Lily, and the irony of his ultimate impoverishment, are a primary theme in *The Small House at Allington*.

The problem was one of aspiration and class. Adolphus Crosbie (*SHA*) wants a wife who is leisured, not occupied with chores and the care of children. Johnny Eames knows this cannot be done on a clerk's salary of £90 p.a.; his friend Cradell accepts the necessity of taking in boarders to make ends meet. Alexandrina's determination to match Crosbie's aspirations means they sacrifice clean shirts and beef steaks for a carriage, while Crosbie borrows money to buy fashionable furniture, and ties up his income with life insurance.

The Trollope heroine is much more practical, and often remarks that if he will have the potatoes, she will have the peelings. The Stanbury women (*HKWR*) maintain respectability on less than £70 a year by doing all their own housework. Mrs Ray (*RR*) has £120, one little maid, and darns the carpet. Miss Marrable (*VB*) and Mary Lowther manage to keep two maids, dress smartly, and entertain friends to sherry and cake six times a year on £350, by living where rents are low.   MM

Banks, J. A., *Prosperity and Parenthood* (1954).
Beeton, Isabella, *The Book of Household Management* (1861).

House of Commons. The House of Commons numbered about 650 members in Trollope's day: 490 for England and Wales, 103 for Ireland, and 53 for Scotland. About 400 seats were for boroughs, most of them small pre-industrial towns in agricultural areas. Urban and industrial Britain was still significantly under-represented. The other 250 seats were for counties. MPs in the 1865 House included 82 baronets or their elder sons, 37 peers or their elder sons, and 106 younger or grandsons of titled aristocracy. Over 100 more MPs were very closely related to the aristocracy—making a total of over half the membership of the House—and many more yet came from landed families. Under 150 MPs were businessmen, but there were 100 barristers, 227 educated at public schools, 246 Oxbridge graduates, and 550 Anglicans. In short, the House of Commons was very socially homogeneous, and hardly 'common'.

Such was 'the finest club in London' to which the inveterate clubman Trollope aspired to belong. He spoke from the heart when he declared in *Can You Forgive Her?*, 'It is the highest and most legitimate pride in an Englishman to have the letters M.P. written after his name' (XLIV). The legal qualifications were few: one had to be male and over 21; there was no property qualification, and one might be a Jew (after 1858) but not an atheist until 1888. Since MPs were unpaid some independent means were essential, though membership could bring financial opportunities: 179 MPs were railway directors, 79 bank directors and 60 insurance company directors. 'City' interests were well represented.

Most MPs owed their election to their own personal standing, money, and effort, rather than to party labels or patronage, though party identity was increasingly important, and party discipline. Most were not ambitious of office and under half took any active part in proceedings. The politically active and ambitious often sat for boroughs which were cheaper and easier to contest at the mandatory by-election on appointment to office. Even after 1867 nearly 50 boroughs were under the effective control of an aristocratic patron. Such seats still provided nurseries for young men of promise: a long apprenticeship was deemed necessary to learn the procedural intricacies and special code of the House—to acquire its tone and win its confidence. To be able to address it in the easy non-oratorical style was important when speeches could be decisive in determining a vote. Trollope was doubtful of his abilities in this respect (*Auto* XVI).

*Dickens, who was dumbfounded to hear that Trollope was standing for Parliament, may have derided it as a 'talking shop' but that was indeed its role. Private members' bills and petitions occupied considerable time, while public legislation was less frequent, though increasing in volume especially after 1867. Its procedure was still remarkably free from rules, though the increasing legislative demands on government led to increasing ministerial control over the timetable. Systematic obstruction, particularly by the Irish Home Rule party in the 1870s and 1880s, necessitated stricter rules to prevent abuse of procedural freedoms.

The power of the House of Commons rested above all on two chief pillars: its absolute control of financial legislation over which the House of Lords had no veto, and its power to vote non-confidence in a government, which necessitated that government's resignation.   CK

Le May, G. H. L., *The Victorian Constitution: Conventions, Usages and Contingencies* (1979).

'House of Heine Brothers, in Munich, The',

first published in *Public Opinion*, 16 and 23 November 1861 (reprinted in *TAC2*). The Heine banking house in Munich is run by two brothers, the elder a confirmed and crusty bachelor, the younger a married man with a pretty but stolid daughter, Isa. She and a young English clerk in the firm, Herbert Onslow, fall in love. Although distantly related to the Heines, Herbert is poor. At first the brothers decree that the lovers must wait at least four years. Isa finally goes to her old Uncle Hatto and wins him over. Herbert will be made a partner.   JS

House of Lords. The House of Lords consisted of the English peerage, which increased from about 420 to 540 members between 1832 and

1886, 16 representative Scottish and 28 representative Irish peers, and 30 (later 26) Anglican bishops. Its political complexion was predominantly, and increasingly, Tory throughout the century. It suffered from low attendance; only about 15 per cent bothered to take their seats each year. Proxy voting was permitted until 1867 and a quorum was three members. None the less it had to approve all House of Commons legislation, holding power of veto over all but money bills. Though it rarely initiated legislation it frequently altered Commons bills substantially, especially on Irish matters where it claimed special expertise due to the extensive Irish landholdings of many peers. It was also the country's final court of legal appeal.

A very agreeable club, it lacked the electrical atmosphere of the Commons. One member likened addressing it to 'speaking to the dead in a torchlit crypt'. It usually met for less than an hour each day while in session to conduct its undemanding business. This was convenient for government ministers having other claims on their time. Indeed most of the prime ministers and cabinet ministers during Trollope's lifetime sat there. Most of them, however, had previously sat in the House of Commons. Several of them, like the Duke of Omnium, regretted 'the golden inanity of the coronet which in the very prime of life had expelled him from the House of Commons' (*PM* XLII).

Having challenged the Commons in 1832 over the First Reform Act and then backed down under the threat of dilution by the mass creation of compliant peers (the Crown's right), the House of Lords enjoyed generally smooth relations with them during the ensuing fifty years. Many questioned its value, however, and even more expected its eventual demise with the advent of democracy. Trollope discusses the shortcomings of the House of Lords, particularly the unsuccessful attempt to introduce life peerages, in *The New Zealander*. In 1881 the historian Lord Acton, a political confidant of Gladstone, discussed the possibility of making Trollope a peer to shore up the dwindling Liberal ranks in the Lords: he noted, however, that 'Trollope is condemned as noisy'. CK

Le May, G. H. L., *The Victorian Constitution: Conventions, Usages and Contingencies* (1979).

house parties. Trollope loved entertaining both at Waltham House and Montagu Square. Guests at Waltham such as Revd W. Lucas Collins, Annie Thackeray, Sir Henry Brackenbury, and the Pollocks left impressions of a thoroughly considerate and generous host (see *I & R* 87–8, 89–91, 161). He was a frequent and conspicuous guest at others' country houses too. With friends like John Blackwood and his hunting cronies he became opinionated and excitable. One such visit recalled by Mrs Gerald Porter showed how much Trollope enjoyed teasing Blackwood with 'daring assaults upon the most cherished articles of the Blackwood faith', golf, the monarchy, the Conservatives, and especially Disraeli. ' "You *know*, Blackwood, you think exactly about Dizzy as I do; you *know* you would be very glad to hear he had been had up for shoplifting" Tableau! all holding up their hands, and Mr Trollope delighted with the sensation he had produced' (*I & R* 95). Mrs M. Evangeline Bradhurst remembered how cheerfully he dressed for a hunt, talking to garments as he searched for them (*I & R* 116). Indoors, feasts, musical events, and card games provided entertainment. Trollope enjoyed solo voices and often spoke warmly of his niece Bice's singing. Among many scenes of family parties in the fiction are the Christmas at Noningsby scenes in *Orley Farm* (XXII). Garden parties for tenantry and local people on feast days are best represented by Miss Thorne's *fête-champêtre* and the Ullathorne sports in *Barchester Towers* (XXXV–XXVII). On a grander scale vast entertainments are given by landowners such as the Duke of Omnium, asserting their wealth and influence. In *Phineas Finn* Lady Glencora Palliser entertains royalty at the Horns at Richmond, given her as a wedding present by the old Duke (LXIII), planning the event precisely and selecting 'the five hundred . . . who were to be blessed . . . The grounds were opened at four. There was to be an early dinner out in tents at five; and after dinner men and women were to walk about, or dance, or make love—or hay, as suited them.' On still grander scale she spends thousands of pounds entertaining at Gatherum Castle trying to boost her husband's popularity in *The Prime Minister* (XVIII). RCT

Houston, Frank, a painter and 'a young man of family, with a taste for art, very good-looking, but not specially well off in regard to income' (VII). In love—as 'far as his nature could love' (XXXVIII)—with his cousin Imogene Docimer, Frank cynically courts Gertrude Tringle, counting on her presumable dowry of £120,000. When this scheme fails, he returns to faithful Imogene, supposedly 'an altered man' (XLII). *AA* WK

Houston, Rosina, aunt of Frank Houston, 'a neat, clean, nice-looking old lady' inhabiting a small house in 'Green Street, Hyde Park' (LX). She comes to the rescue of Frank and Imogene Docimer by offering to let them live there with her once they are married. *AA* WK

Howard, Henry (1826–1905), Governor of Rhode Island (1873–4) who wrote to Trollope in 1881, asking if he would bring back the Proudies, Mr Crawley, Glencora, etc.—in some future work. Trollope thanked him but said he was too old to do so. 'I am nearly seventy years of age, and cannot hope to do what you propose in reference to bringing back our old friends' (*Letters* 2, 920). The 'new characters', he wrote, 'are much less troublesome than the old ones; and can be done without the infinite labour of reading back again and again my old works'.   RCT

Howells, William Dean (1837–1920), American man of letters; consul in Venice (1861–5); assistant editor of the *Atlantic Monthly* (1866), and thereafter editor-in-chief. In 1865 he met Trollope at Waltham, but the visit was inauspicious. Mildred Dean Howells, in *Life in Letters of William Dean Howells* (1928), recounted that Trollope scarcely spoke to him. However, Howells confessed that, during his Venetian years, 'I was not yet sufficiently instructed to appreciate Trollope, and I did not read him at all' (quoted Super 196), which might explain the coolness. Howells, like Hawthorne, associated Trollope with bovine imagery: 'Trollope with his immense quiet, ruminant reality, ox-like cropping the field of English life and converting its succulent juices into the nourishing beef of his fiction' (*I & R* 81). His anonymous review of (Trollope's) *Thackeray* in the *Atlantic Monthly*, August 1879, was savage. In *Criticism and Fiction* (1891) he criticized narrative confidences and asides to the reader, but insisted, 'Trollope's books have been a vast pleasure to me through their simple truthfulness' (quoted Super 196).   RCT

How the 'Mastiffs' Went to Iceland. This brief, light, playful, and affectionate narrative of a three weeks' trip admirably complements Trollope's more measured treatment of Iceland in his article in the *Fortnightly Review* of 1 August 1878. A group of 16 friends plus a crew of 32 left Castle Wemyss, seat of their host/organizer John Burns, on 22 June, on board the *Mastiff*, a yacht of 870 tons, 220 horse power, according to the fact-loving narrator. There is a touch of schoolboy humour in the usurpation of the ladies' snuggery for a smoking room on board, a general party atmosphere in these 'private pages' (I) before the arrival at St Kilda, uttermost Hebridean island, '45 miles from humanity' (II), where there is one church and eighteen cottages. The land is poor, there is some trading in birds' eggs and woollen stockings, but the islanders' diet of porridge, bread, stew, and fulmar typifies the low standard of living, and rheumatism and scrofula are common. This sombre survey is succeeded by a three-hour visit to Thorshavn (25 June), capital of the chief Faeroe island, Stromo. The tone lightens with the 24 hours of daylight. Trollope finds it a delightful place despite its 'ancient and fish-like smell' (III), and approves the English-speaking postmaster who looked like Gladstone. Next they sail along the south/south-west shores of Iceland, noting huge glaciers 30–40 miles (50–60 km) long, and are received at Reykjavik where they meet the Bishop's daughter Thora. She makes a vivacious addition to the group, and Trollope indulges in an innocently avuncular flirtation. The Icelanders are healthy, comely, strong, sell leather, export oil, fish, import timber, sugar, tea. Still the fishy smell prevails, but Trollope acquires a copy of *Macbeth* in Icelandic (IV)! There is a ceremonial dinner on board the *Mastiff*, with the ladies prettily dressed: white hat, light veil, 'jaunty jacket', brightly coloured skirt; and next day a church service comprising a 2½-hour sermon, impressive but incomprehensible (V). The party rides to visit the geysers, the sixteen-stone (100-kg) Trollope recording their pony pace of seven miles (11 km) an hour. He admires the beauty of the river Bruara, notes the ladies' enjoyment of spirited riding (VI), and then describes the great geyser, 'a pool of boiling water about 50 yards in circumference', with a funnel 8 feet (2.5 m) broad descending as far as the eye can see. They bivouac and dine among the springs, the sights 'curious' but not beautiful (VII). The return to Thingvalla, Trollope's favourite spot, takes two days and nights, and on the way they sleep in a church. There is much boisterous fun and laughter, particularly involving the ladies, and later the party is photographed on its ponies. Elated by their experiences, they are melancholy at parting. The illustrations in the text, rightly praised by Trollope, are by Jemima *Blackburn, who wrote her own account of the excursion, 'To Iceland', published in *Good Words* in 1879. Trollope's charming account was privately printed by Virtue & Co. in 1878. It was not for sale: John Burns paid the costs, and each traveller had a copy.   GRH

Hudson, George (1800–71), known as the 'Railway King'. Anathematized in Carlyle's *Latter Day Pamphlets* (1850), he made his fortune as a draper, founded a banking company, and became mayor of York (1837 and 1846); he was owner of several railway companies, before queries about his business practices caused early retirement to the Continent in 1854. By 1846 the Sheffield and Rotherham Railway was under Hudson's control and Rose Trollope's father Edward Heseltine was a director. 'Mr Heseltine was one of the thousands who swindled in a small way in the shadow

John Burns, head of the Cunard Steamship Company, invited Trollope and friends on a brief journey to Iceland. Jemima Blackburn sketched incidents on the voyage and Trollope produced a light-hearted account in *How the 'Mastiffs' Went to Iceland*, privately printed in 1878.

of George Hudson—millionaire, master-swindler and entrepreneur of genius' (Glendinning 225). Hudson has been considered a source for Melmotte in *The Way We Live Now*. RCT

Hudson, George, resident magistrate at Mossel Bay, most eastern harbour in Cape Colony. Trollope's expedition with him is described in *South Africa* (1, VII). RCT

Hughes, Philip, bank cashier in love with Emily Greenmantle. He refuses to be put down by her father's snobbery, winning her with the help of Dr Freeborn. 'Plumplington' GRH

Hughes, Thomas (1822–96), trained for the legal profession and QC (1869); MP for Lambeth from 1865; best known for *Tom Brown's Schooldays* (1857). Trollope enlisted him among speakers in a lecture series for Post Office employees (1860). At a dinner for Joaquin Miller hosted by Trollope in July 1873, another guest, Mark Twain, noted that Hughes and Trollope gave all their attention to the Hon. Frederick Leveson-Gower. Hughes was later involved with Trollope in the Free Libraries Association. RCT

Hugo, Victor (1802–85), French novelist, poet, dramatist, best known for *Notre-Dame de Paris* (1831) and *Les Misérables* (1862). In 1852 he was expelled from France for opposing the coup of Napoleon III. He returned in 1870 and was elected to the Senate in 1876. In 1869, Trollope was offended by Bradbury & Evans proposing to transfer publication of *The Vicar of Bullhampton* from *Once a Week* to the less prestigious *Gentleman's Magazine* to make way for Hugo's *L'Homme qui rit*, which had come in late. E. S. Dallas asked Trollope to accept the arrangement. Trollope refused, and his novel was issued in eleven monthly parts between July 1869 and May 1870. That smart was not forgotten. A very critical commentary on *L'Homme qui rit* entitled 'M. Victor Hugo's England', by Juliet Pollock, a close friend, appeared in *Saint Pauls* (July 1869). Seven years later Trollope recalled his 'indignation that I should be asked to give way to a Frenchman' (*Auto* XVIII) and a procrastinator. 'With all the pages that I have written', he thundered, 'I have never been a day late.' Moreover, Hugo's later novels were 'pretentious and untrue to nature'. RCT

Humblethwaite Hall. Primary residence of Sir Harry, Lady Elizabeth, and Emily Hotspur, the property has been in the family for nearly four centuries. Built and rebuilt over the years, it combines a variety of styles, creating a beautiful manor in a beautiful Cumberland setting. *SHH* MG

Hundlewick Hall, Maurice Archer's home a few miles from Kirkby Cliffe, Yorkshire. 'Kirkby' GRH

Hunter, Captain Clayton's bodyguard whose surveillance proves ineffectual against the sniper's bullet. *L* MRS

hunting, Trollope and. Trollope began to hunt in Ireland in 1841. It was one of his greatest passions for almost 40 years, and many of his novels make references to the fox-hunt or contain full-blown scenes. 'Nothing has ever been allowed to stand in the way of hunting,—neither the writing of books, nor the work of the Post Office, nor other pleasures' (*Auto* IV). Trollope rode hard and courageously. Weight and poor eyesight did not deter him from going at full speed, and he would ride at a gate while it was being opened. Spills and injuries he had in plenty: a sprained foot in December 1873, a nearly fatal throw in January 1875 (*Letters* 2, 644). His favourite hunting areas were around Hertfordshire and Buckinghamshire, but he would send his horses up north to the Pytchley and Fitzwilliam hunts. He defended the sport against E. A. *Freeman's attacks in the *Fortnightly* (October 1869), and championed it in *Hunting Sketches* (1865). His letters abound with notes on meets, train timetables, stopovers, lending togs to guests, 'supplying sherry and sandwiches and small-talk' (*Letters* 1, 142). In fair weather and foul, usually foul, it remained his sublime recreation. As he said in December 1862, 'I have become a slave to hunting' (*Letters* 1, 206). At Waltham his house had stabling and was within easy reach of several meets. Hunting cheered him up. A friend with whom he stayed observed that he would talk loudly in his dressing room as he searched for his kit. 'Now, Mr Top Boot, where is your twin? Can't go hunting alone, you know' (*I & R* 116). Only when he saw an end to the sport would he ride home in melancholy state. Moving to Montagu Square after returning from Australia (1875) meant parting with his horses; the winter of 1876 was his last season, then he stopped entirely in March 1878. 'Alas—alas—my hunting is over,' he wrote to John Blackwood. 'I have given away my breeches, boots—and horses' (*Letters* 2, 759). Trollope's last riding was a regular outing with Florence Bland in Hyde Park's Rotten Row. In *Ralph the Heir* (1871) two of the horses are given the names Banker and Buff after Trollope's own horses. RCT

hunting and horse racing in novels. Trollope confessed in the *Autobiography* that hunting had been 'dragged . . . into many novels . . . I have always felt myself deprived of a legitimate joy when the nature of the tale has not allowed me a hunting chapter' (IV). Hunting scenes in the fiction, of which there are at least seventeen, are more than the author's indulgence; they often forward plot and provide fertile ground for blossoming romance. Trollope's passion for the sport started in Ireland, and his first two novels have horse-riding scenes. In *The Macdermots of Ballycloran* tensions surrounding Thady's downfall are relieved by an exuberant description of Carrick races (XIX). In *The Kellys and the O'Kellys* with his first fox-hunting scene Trollope discourses at length on cross-country riding strategies and skills (XXII). In *Orley Farm* Trollope devotes two chapters to the Hamworth Hunt and introduces the two Misses Tristram, both skilled and fearless riders, but the hunt significantly furthers the story by indicating Madeline Staveley's love for Felix Graham after his accident, described in 'Another Fall' (XXX). The hunting metaphor is well used in 'Aaron Trow', when the pursuit of the violent criminal is compared with that of a fox, 'the agonizing struggles of the poor beast whose last refuge is being torn from over his head. The Rufford and Ufford Hunt Club features prominently in *The American Senator*, where conflicts within the community arise from Senator Gotobed's support for a farmer suspected of poisoning foxes, and Major Caneback dies from a fall (XXII–III). In this novel Trollope jokes against himself as John Runce, 'too heavy and short-winded;—too fond of his beer and port wine; but . . . a hunting man all over' (XXII). A more direct self-portrait occurs in *Can You Forgive Her?*, where he is Pollock the 'heavyweight sporting literary gentleman'. On seeing him at the Edgehill Hunt a rider observes: 'I'll bet half a crown that he's come down from London this morning, that he was up all night last night, and that he tells us so three times before the hounds go out of the paddock' (XVI). When ladies ride there are opportunities for flirtation and conquest. This is why Jeffrey Houghton in *Is He Popenjoy?* dislikes his wife's fondness for riding to hounds. Arabella Trefoil grieves loudly for Caneback in order to gain Lord Rufford's intimacy (*AS* XXIII). In a later scene she sits at the window on the night prior to the hunt at Mistletoe, Lincolnshire, imploring the gods that there will be no frost, so that the going will be good (XXXIX). It is a poignant moment. Trollope had his share of accidents; thus in several novels characters are badly injured or killed. Besides Caneback, Squire Gregory Newton in *Ralph the Heir* conveniently breaks his spine and dies from a fall, after the best run of his life in Barford Wood (XXXI), complicating the main issue of the novel as to which Ralph comes into the estate. Typic-

ally, Trollope allows himself a long passage about the techniques of riding and drawing the fox in different terrains. In this novel, as in *Marion Fay*, he uses the names of two horses he owned. Another notable horse name is Lord Chiltern's Bonebreaker in *Phineas Finn*, but it is with another mount that he breaks his collar-bone and three ribs (XXIV). Both horse races and hunting are incorporated into *The Duke's Children*. Turf and bones, the downfall of several Trollope characters, are a cause of great misgiving to the Duke over his son Lord Silverbridge, who has formed a partnership with Major Tifto in Prime Minister, a likely winner of the St Leger. After a dispute Tifto lames the horse, leaving Silverbridge with debts of £70,000. Fox-hunting, on the other hand, is celebrated, despite the Duke's long history of neglecting the coverts. As the huntsmen dine they contemplate the morrow and 'good sport . . . . the delight of having a friend in a ditch, or the glory of a stiff-built rail were fitting subjects for a lighter hour' (LXII). Lord Chiltern can even forgive the Duke's poor preservation of the foxes in Trumpeton Wood about which he was once very angry (*PR* XIV). The hunting scenes in the Brake country are done with great spirit. Silverbridge is shown in much kindlier light (LXII–III) and Frank Tregear breaks a few bones after a fall, thereby becoming even more desirable in Lady Mary Palliser's eyes (LXIII–IV). The hunting party in *The Eustace Diamonds* is far less distinguished, comprising only 'a lord or two, a dozen lairds, two dozen farmers', and sundry men of business (XXXVI), but among them Lady Eustace looks splendid, and enjoys learning the finer points of the sport as she rides through Craigattan Course flanked by Lord George Carruthers and Frank Greystock: 'what could the heart of woman desire more?' (XXXVIII). Hunting scenes also include the Dunhallow Hunt in *Castle Richmond* and the Braeside Harriers in *Marion Fay*. A fox-hunt in Co. Mayo opens the short story 'The O'Conors of Castle Connor'. After a lifetime celebrating the sport, Trollope tried to include a hunt in his last unfinished novel *The Landleaguers*; ironically, the Galway Hounds and the riders find their meeting blocked by demonstrators, and the hunt has to be abandoned.   RCT

'Hunting Sketches' (eight-article series).
1. The Man Who Hunts and Doesn't Like It. This fellow feels compelled to hunt and tries to enjoy it. Chiefly he enjoys the off-season, talking hunting and dealing with his tailor and bootmaker. He rides badly, falls, gets bruised, has a miserable time, and never really is part of the hunt.

2. The Man Who Hunts and Does Like It. Envied by the above, this man has problems also; he pays £500 a year for perhaps one really good day. Must get up early, endure bad weather, often misses the close, and goes home frustrated.

3. The Lady Who Rides to Hounds. Hunting women always enjoy the sport; they have taken lessons and are consequently very capable. Their presence improves the language and manners of male hunters. Some ladies demand help in everything and are nuisances; most, however, are a pleasure to watch and talk with.

4. The Hunting Farmer. His good nature and generosity as to the use of his land are essential to hunts. Thoughtful riders avoid barley fields and new-sown meadows; wheatfields will hold their own. The farmer usually wears a heavy black coat, brown breeches, and top boots either white or mahogany; he is usually taciturn but very knowledgeable about land. The good master will consult with him. The farmer enjoys hunting but not inordinately; he rides one sensible horse, not a fancy stable-full.

5. The Man Who Hunts and Never Jumps. Hunters must be prepared to jump always or not at all; injuries happen to those in between. The non-jumper is quite acceptable; usually not a flashy dresser, and very sensitive to sound, scent, wind, and land. He keeps up with the chase by this knowledge. He never gets lost, and is a helpful guide for those who do. He does not boast, nor suffer those who do. He does miss some of the excitement of the chase.

6. The Hunting Parson. The general public, especially old ladies and bishops, feel most recreations, including hunting, are vaguely 'wicked' and inappropriate for clergy. This (unsound) judgement affects the clergyman who enjoys hunting; he is usually a very good sportsman and an interesting conversationalist, but still aware he suffers disapproval.

7. The Master of Hounds. The master as usually described is not anyone's first choice. Ideally, he should be a wealthy English country gentleman, a resident of the area. Although hunts are 'subscribed', he pays much more than is collected. He needs £500 for each day of week there is hunting; he usually has three subscriptions per week and one (free) for neighbours. He has great authority, and should deserve it. It is a great deal of work, a demanding and happy occupation.

8. How to Ride to Hounds. Novices should watch the experienced. Let the dogs go first; stay with the crowd so the fox has an avenue to run from cover. Spare the horse's energy and the rider's, to be fresh for the final run. Learn to listen and watch; experience is the best instructor. Impatience is the worst fault. To succeed

in following the chase for up to seven miles (11 km) without stopping or falling is an achievement, and a source of intense pleasure. *Pall Mall Gazette* (9 February–20 March 1865); reprinted 1981. See also 'IN THE HUNTING FIELD'.   AKL

Hurst & Blackett (1852–1926), publishing house established by Daniel Hurst (?1802–70) and Henry Blackett (1826–71), who took over Henry Colburn's. When Macmillan sold them the rights to *Sir Harry Hotspur of Humblethwaite* the firm set about printing the novel in two volumes. Always a stickler for fair dealings with the public, Trollope objected, and the book was issued in one volume, Macmillan having picked up the extra printing costs. The firm also published *Ralph the Heir*.   RCT

Hurst Staple, quiet country parish in Hampshire in the gift of Lord Stapledean, held by Revd Arthur Wilkinson and, following his death, by his son Arthur. Arthur junior in turn becomes the new vicar of Hurst Staple, where he eventually settles with Adela Gauntlet. *B*   MRS

Hurtle, Winifred, beautiful, feisty American who pursues Paul Montague to England. Her self-assertiveness, as well as her violent history of duelling with her husband and shooting another man, makes Paul apprehensive, so despite her rages, pleas, and aggressive demands for justice, he leaves her for the gentle, English Hetta Carbury. She proves her good nature in a gracious interview with Hetta as well as in kindness to her adoring landlady Mrs Pipkin. *WWLN*   SRB

Hutton, Richard Holt (1826–97), wide-ranging critic on theological, social, and literary topics; edited with Walter *Bagehot the *National Review* (1855–64); joint editor of *Spectator* from 1861 until his death. Trollope's career was helped by his review 'Mr Trollope's Novels' in *National Review*, October 1858. Hutton was among the first to recognize the identity of the anonymous author of *Nina Balatka*. In *An Autobiography* Trollope mistakenly thought Hutton had written a harsh review of *The Prime Minister*, but noted that he was a fine critic, 'inclined to be more than fair to me' (XX). One of Hutton's most striking critical observations concerned Trollope's command of 'the moral "hooks and eyes" of life' (Smalley 198). Trollope reviewed Hutton's *Studies in Parliament* in *Fortnightly Review* (April 1866), a work which influenced his political fiction. Hutton's review of *An Autobiography* in *Spectator* (October 1883) paid tribute to his liberal outlook.   RCT

'Hutton's *Studies in Parliament.* By R. H. Hutton: Critical Notice' (review). Publishing under his name seventeen previously anonymous sketches from the *Pall Mall Gazette* is a brave act. The descriptions are fair and need no apology. Personal traits are legitimate considerations in evaluating public figures; unless journalists deal with them, the public remains uninformed. Here Lords Russell, Palmerston, and Cranbourne, Earl Grey, and Messrs Bright and Forster are particularly well described, including tones of voice, types of arguments, faults, and virtues. *Fortnightly Review* (1 April 1866), 510–12.   AKL

Huxley, Thomas Henry (1825–95), scientist and seminal thinker on natural history; President of the Royal Society (1883–85). Author of many works rousing widespread debate, such as *Man's Place in Nature* (1863) and *Science and Morals* (1873). His essay 'The Physical Basis of Life' ran in *Fortnightly* (February 1869). At Lady Amberley's (April 1867) Trollope disappointed the hostess by drowning out 'Huxley's pleasant quiet voice which was certainly better worth hearing' (*I & R* 148–9).   RCT

Hyde Park riots. The Hyde Park riots of July 1866 occurred when crowds gathered to protest the government's ban on a Reform League rally pressed down the park's railings and surged peacefully in. They occupied Hyde Park for several days until George Odger, the league's leader, negotiated their departure in return for a police withdrawal. This moral victory for the reformers was confirmed in May 1867, when the government banned another meeting and the league called its bluff, proceeding to meet peacefully in the park while troops stood by. Subsequent legislation in 1872 guaranteed the right of public meeting in Hyde Park won by these 'riots'. The violence in *Phineas Finn*, which Trollope began writing in November 1866, reflects the turbulence in central London at this time.   CK

Richter, Donald C., *Riotous Victorians* (1981).

'Iceland' (article). A recent expedition to Iceland on a friend's boat was interesting and surprising. The Icelanders are remarkably sophisticated considering their geographic isolation. Drunkenness is not a problem. The people are hard pressed when supply ships are delayed by ice. A trip to 'the geysers' was truly fascinating. The public officials were interesting and hospitable. *Fortnightly Review* (August 1878), 175–90.   AKL

'*Ideas of the Day on Policy, The,* by Charles Buxton: Critical Notice' (review). This book purposes to summarize the state of British public opinion on current matters of state politics. It is a curious work, of possible interest to politicians out of touch with general opinion. *Fortnightly Review* (15 January 1866), 650–2.   AKL

illustrators and illustrating. Fifteen of Trollope's 47 novels were illustrated in their original magazine-serial or part-publication: more than 300 full-page illustrations and 100 quarter-page vignettes, most of which were included in the first book editions. Any discussion of these illustrations must focus on the former Pre-Raphaelite John Everett *Millais, who illustrated four Trollope novels and supplied frontispieces for two others (*RR* and *KD*), 87 full-page drawings and 19 elaborate vignettes in all. Other illustrators did one book apiece.

Millais's illustrations for Trollope began in 1860 with *Framley Parsonage*, the work which inaugurated Trollope's career as a serial novelist and enormously enhanced his reputation. The story appeared in the newly launched *Cornhill*

Magazine, published by George Smith and edited by Thackeray. No record survives of Trollope's reaction to Millais's first illustration to *Framley Parsonage*, but when he saw in proof the second illustration, that of Lucy Robarts in a crinoline dress weeping on her bed, Trollope wrote angrily to Smith that the drawing was 'simply ludicrous', and that some people would think it intentionally so. Smith calmed his author, as did the next illustration: 'The Crawley family is very good,' Trollope wrote to Smith, '& I will now consent to forget the flounced dress.' Millais supplied only six drawings for *Framley Parsonage*, but the collaboration had begun, of which Trollope later wrote: 'I do not think that more conscientious work was ever done by man. . . . In every figure he drew it was his object to promote the views of the writer whose work he had undertaken to illustrate, and he never spared himself any pains in studying that work, so as to enable himself to do so. I have carried on some of those characters from book to book, and have had my own early ideas impressed indelibly on my memory by the excellence of his delineations' (*Letters* 1, 104, 111; *Auto* VIII). Millais was the quintessential 1860s-style illustrator: representational, naturalistic, realistic, the very opposite of the stylized, exaggerated style of earlier illustrators like Cruikshank and Browne. Millais's style accorded nicely with that of Trollope, who was frequently accused by reviewers of a 'photographic realism' and was even called a 'Pre-Raphaelite in prose'.

Millais's most ambitious work for Trollope came with *Orley Farm* (40 plates). Trollope, now a very close friend of the artist, was ecstatic over them: he went so far as to have the narrator say in a late chapter that the reader's idea of Lady Mason's sorrow 'will have come to him from the skill of the artist, and not from the words of the writer', and he even suggests that the reader turn back hundreds of pages and look again at the illustration (LXIII). Trollope wrote, 'I have never known a set of illustrations as carefully true, as are these, to the conception of the writer of the book illustrated. I say that as a writer. As a lover of Art I will add that I know no book graced with more exquisite pictures' (MS, Taylor Collection, Princeton). In *An Autobiography* Trollope called Millais's illustrations for *Orley Farm* 'the best I have seen in any novel in any language' (IX). This claim was a bit of a stretch, but these illustrations probably rank as the most accomplished to any novel during the 1860s, the 'golden decade' of English black and white wood engraving.

Millais again did the illustrations for *The Small House at Allington* (18 plates, 19 vignettes); but, because of his commitment to lucrative oil paint-

gForgeription

ings, he declined to illustrate *The Last Chronicle of Barset*. However, when in 1867 Trollope launched his own magazine, *Saint Pauls*, which was to serialize *Phineas Finn*, he pleaded special circumstances and Millais obliged (20 plates).

The first illustrations to Trollope other than by Millais were by Hablot Knight *Browne, formerly Dickens's illustrator. Trollope was disgusted with Browne's work for *Can You Forgive Her?*: it seemed to him that Dickensian, i.e. 'inhuman' and 'unnatural', characters had wandered onto his pages. He begged Millais to take over, and even offered to make up himself the difference in price (Browne was getting about £5 a drawing, Millais five times as much). But Millais refused, and halfway through the novel, Trollope had Browne dismissed, and replaced him with a Miss Taylor of St Leonards, an amateur of very little talent. But she was a Millais-style '1860s' illustrator, and this was what Trollope wanted.

George Housman *Thomas's drawings for *The Last Chronicle* drew mixed appraisals from Trollope: Thomas's Grace Crawley 'has fat cheeks & is not Grace Crawley'; Mr Crawley before the magistrates 'is very good. So is the bishop. Mrs Proudie is not quite my Mrs Proudie' (*Letters* 1, 355). Two other '1860s' artists illustrated Trollope novels: Mary Ellen *Edwards, *The Claverings*, and Marcus *Stone (the man with whom Dickens had displaced Browne), *He Knew He Was Right*. It is not known what Trollope thought of these two illustrators, but he soon ceased to take any active interest in the illustrations that accompanied his later novels, as supplied by post-1860s artists: Henry *Woods, *The Vicar of Bullhampton*; F. A. *Fraser, *Ralph the Heir*; Francis Montague *Holl, *Phineas Redux*; William Small, *Marion Fay*. All these illustrators worked in the so-called 'Graphic School' manner, a style marked by prettiness and sentimentality, with 'wash' substituting for 'line'. (Ruskin termed the new style 'Blottesque'.) The very nadir in illustrations to Trollope was reached in the 40 drawings to *The Way We Live Now* by an amateur named Lionel Grimston *Fawkes. The stiff, awkward figures, contorted limbs, paw-like hands, and frighteningly ugly children positively deface the text. While the book was appearing in shilling parts, a friend complained to Trollope about the illustrations. He replied, 'What you say of illustrations is all true,—not strong enough in expression of disgust. But what can a writer do? I desire, of course, to put my books into as many hands as possible, and I take the best mode of doing so' (*Letters* 2, 613). There was to be but one bright reminder of the past days when in 1882 he

persuaded the always busy Millais to provide one illustration for *Kept in the Dark*. NJH

Incharrow, home of old Sir Walter Mackenzie in Scotland. *MM* SRB

India and Ceylon. Trollope considered writing a book on India in 1860, but the project fell through, and he never visited 'the brightest jewel in the English crown'. His visit to Ceylon en route to Australia in 1875 was described in a series of letters to the *Liverpool Mercury* (*The Tireless Traveller*, ed. B. Booth 1941). His portrayal of Britishers from India in *The Bertrams* was not flattering.

British rule in the subcontinent of India in 1860 was close to its maximum extent, and had recently survived a massive challenge in the Indian Mutiny of 1857–8. The Indian civil service ruled a large portion directly, in provinces of various sizes, and British residents monitored the Indian princes, tied to the Crown by treaties. The actual British presence was small, apart from the military, but it controlled a paternalistic administration which, by the end of the century, was facing a nascent nationalist movement. The British public at home saw India as a place of adventure and exotic glamour, increasingly celebrated in literature by writers such as Rudyard Kipling.

Much of Ceylon fell under Portuguese control in the 16th century; the Dutch replaced the Portuguese in the mid-17th century, and the British expelled the Dutch in 1796, and gradually conquered the whole island. British planters established a flourishing coffee culture, which Trollope extolled, but the plants were hit by a leaf disease in 1880, and tea replaced coffee. The plantation economy brought a large Tamil population from south India because the native Sinhalese were not greatly interested; the background was thus created for violent civil disturbances between these peoples in the late 20th century. In Trollope's time, Ceylon was famous for elephant hunting, but Trollope was unsuccessful in arranging an expedition, even though his host was the Governor, Sir William Gregory, a friend from his Irish days. LK
Wolpert, S., *A New History of India* (1997).

Ingram, Jefferson, good-natured American tourist who puts up with the opinionated and condescending Mr Damer and eventually proposes successfully to his daughter. 'Pyramids' *TAC1* GRH

Innsbruck, closest town to the pretty Brunnenthal valley in the Tyrol, where Frau Frohmann keeps the Peacock Hotel. 'Frohmann' *WFF* GRH

269

Inns of Court. The four Inns of Court in London, where barristers are trained, examined, and called to the bar, are Lincoln's Inn, the Inner Temple, the Middle Temple, and Gray's Inn. Each belongs to a separate society. Members of the Inns of Court are benchers (Masters of the Bench, with sole power to call students to the bar), barristers, and students. (Until the late 19th century, there were also Inns of Chancery, occupied by solicitors, and a Serjeants' Inn.) As in Trollope's novels, many barristers have their chambers, solicitors their offices, and students their rooms, in or near the Inns of Court. Trollope's father, a Chancery lawyer, kept dingy, almost suicidal chambers at Lincoln's Inn (*Auto* I). Sir Thomas Underwood, former Solicitor-General, actually lives in his chambers in Chancery Lane (*RH* I). Mr Harding, in *The Warden*, consults the Attorney-General, Sir Abraham Haphazard, at his chambers in Lincoln's Inn. The profoundly respectable Slow & Bideawhile, solicitors who appear in several of the novels, have their professionally dreary offices in Lincoln's Inn Fields. Phineas Finn is called to the bar after studying for three years at the Middle Temple. From the Middle Ages on, the Inns of Court (where singing, dancing, and playing musical instruments were originally included) were looked on as good preparation for a life of affairs. Phineas, too, is assured that though he might fail to succeed in court or in chambers, he would doubtless have given to him some of those numerous appointments for which none but clever young barristers are supposed to be fitting candidates (*PF* I). Charles Lamb, who was born there, wrote a nostalgic essay on 'The Old Benchers of the Inner Temple' in *Essays of Elia* (1823), and Thackeray's Pendennis and George Warrington have rooms in the Temple in *Pendennis* (1849).

RDM

'In the Hunting Field' (article). Few people understood the sport, supposing it to consist of jumping over five-barred gates. For Trollope it meant recreation and exercise. Hunting was a gracious social occasion with due courtesies at the meeting place before the whip led the way followed by the Master deeply aware of his responsibilities 'for the amusement of a hundred and fifty gentlemen . . . who have turned out of bed at seven o'clock on a winter morning'. Farmer Rudge represented the slow and steady kind of hunting to which Trollope pledged his allegiance. 'Fifty years of close study in any art will teach an attentive man many secrets.' The rest of the article, however, celebrates in literary vignette another kind of hunting—fast and dangerous—with 'a happiness and joy quite its own', clearly where Trollope's real pleasure resides. 'Let a man at any rate find out what he can do, what he is fit for,' Trollope concludes, 'and then let him set to work accordingly.' The essay was to have been the first of a four-part series called 'Half-Hours in the Fresh Air'. *Good Words* (February 1879), 98–105.

RCT

'Introduction to *Saint Pauls Magazine*' (article). The editor welcomes readers of the first issue. This genre is sometimes unfairly labelled as trivial; in fact it is a supplement to great literature. This journal will combine entertainment, instruction, politics, and poetry, but not criticism. Both well-known and amateur authors will be published. *Saint Pauls* (October 1867), 1–7.

AKL

Ireland was the place of Trollope's rebirth, the country in which he found the means to reinvent himself at the age of 26. It was the special form taken by the class system there that allowed him to make this move: as a Protestant Englishman in Ireland he was automatically a member of the Ascendancy or ruling class with no risk of sinking out of it by becoming an Irishman. This class system, like the system of land tenure with which it was bound up, was produced by a history of colonial exploitation on the part of England. As an artist, Trollope repaid his debt to Ireland and its people by engaging in his fiction with the question of Ireland and of Irish distress. The answers that he could accept in his capacity as a civil servant were not always enough to satisfy his imaginative response to the ruin that confronted him in Ireland, England's oldest colony.

It was a literal ruin, seen by chance in Co. Leitrim, that prompted Trollope to start his first novel, *The Macdermots of Ballycloran*. The abandoned house was the sign of the failure and departure of a landlord. Such sights became so common in Ireland after the famine that the Encumbered Estates Act of 1849 was passed to allow Irish landlords or their creditors to sell off estates that had previously been bound up by legal entanglements. Philip Jones, in *The Landleaguers*, bought his estate under the provisions of that Act.

But accurate historical reportage was too simple to deal with the complex questions that were raised by contemplating the Irish scene. The degraded landscape viewed by Herbert Fitzgerald towards the close of *Castle Richmond* bore witness to a history of abuse that Trollope did find ways of addressing, even while he continued to justify British policy towards Ireland. When Herbert stares over fields divided and subdivided and let out to the poorest tenants at an absurdly high price per acre, the reader is offered an image of the degradation of Ireland and its people at the hands of the English colonizers. The original form of the cultivated landscape has been obliterated, just as Irish ways and Irish culture have been systematically made of no account under British occupation.

The problems of landlords and tenants are the recurring theme in Trollope's Irish novels. There was a historical basis for such difficulties, although Trollope tacitly went along with the popular racism that attributed Irish problems to the extravagance and weakness of Irish people and their absurd hankering after a romanticized past. (See *MB* II.) The displacement of the Irish began in the 12th century, when incursions from England began. Ownership of Irish land was systematically removed from the native inhabitants: the estates of the last Irish leaders to offer armed resistance to English rule were confiscated in 1583 and subsequently settled by 12,000 Protestant English. Loyalty to the Church of Rome and to the unreformed Catholic faith became associated with national identity and with decreasing social power. At the same time grounds for mutual suspicion between Protestant and Catholic, of the kind that Trollope's stories repeatedly record (see *L* IX), were installed.

At the start of the 18th century the Test Acts forbade Catholics to hold land, to bear arms, or to receive education. Wealth, power, and social influence were reserved almost exclusively to Protestants, and to those of English ancestry. This also meant that the terms on which tenants held their land were a crucial factor in the economic well-being of the community. Relations between landlord and tenant bore traces of the feudal, which, taken with the widespread hostility against middlemen, the landlords' agents, helped to paralyse initiative on both sides, prevented modern agricultural development, and kept Ireland poor. The rise in population increased the numbers dependent on the land and reduced farming to a subsistence level by the 1840s. Landlords could not make their estates pay under these conditions: Lady Desmond in *Castle Richmond* cannot afford to keep a carriage.

Guerrilla resistance to English rule was an Irish tradition. The old crape mask spied by Florian Jones in *The Landleaguers* might have seen service in many campaigns designed to protect tenants and to resist paying tithes to the Protestant Church of Ireland from the 18th century onwards. But in 1799 the Act of Union between Britain and Ireland was passed, when the members of the Irish Parliament, bribed by the offer of seats in the House of Lords—the grandfather of Francis O'Kelly in *The Kellys and the O'Kellys* got one—voted to dissolve itself, agreeing that legislation for Ireland should henceforward be made in Westminster. That move generated a formal political opposition in the Repeal Association, dedicated to repeal of the Act of Union and founded in 1842.

The famine of 1845–7 drained away energy from the cause of Repeal, which had been attracting vast crowds to its meetings. Two million people died and millions more emigrated. Scholars continue to debate how a disaster of such magnitude was allowed to occur: though Trollope was stalwart in his defence of government policy and of the relief programme, both in *Castle Richmond* and the series of *Letters he wrote to the *Examiner*, recent historians have questioned the blend of doctrinaire economics and providential determinism that characterized the government response.

Tenants kept up the struggle against landlords in Ireland in the decades that followed, with the short-term aim of improving their own current income. In the agricultural distress of the late 1870s the Land League was founded, to reclaim Irish land for Irish tenants. Sensing that the whole social framework by which he had oriented himself was unravelling, and horrified at the violence which attended it, Trollope set out to write *The Landleaguers*.   MH

Cairns, D., and Richards, S., *Writing Ireland* (1988).

Mokyr, J., *Why Ireland Starved* (1983).

Solow, B., *The Land Question and the Irish Economy 1870–1903* (1971).

Ireland, Alexander (1810–94), Scottish journalist, publisher of the *Manchester Examiner and Times* (1846–86) and *Manchester Weekly Times*. When Trollope lectured at the Manchester Athenaeum (November 1878), he met Ireland and offered *Cousin Henry* for serial publication. Ireland was given three titles: 'you may choose out of the following three names—Cousin Henry. Getting at a Secret. Uncle Indefer's Will. The second is exactly apposite. My wife says that it sounds claptrap' (*Letters* 2, 805). Trollope's correspondence with Ireland shows his assiduous attention to ethical business dealings. After receiving proofs, February 1879, he asked Ireland to delete the words 'An original novel'. 'It would seem to imply a special claim to originality as made by the author himself. It is an original novel, but it is not for me to say so. What you want to imply is that it is not a republication. Could you not put "Now first published"? You will at any rate see that "Original" will not do' (*Letters* 2, 818). In April, he wrote expressing concern over maintaining the integrity of his layout for the novel. 'May I ask you to ask your printers to let me have my own way about my own paragraphs. They have an idea as to the arrangement of dialogue opposed to my idea. I will not contest the question with them as [to] which is right. But I am exasperated. It is my duty to write as I think best, and theirs to print as I write.' He added a tactful critique of Ireland's printers: 'They read my bad writing, and no doubt often correct my bad spelling. But they should not alter my forms of expression, because they do not, and cannot, know my purpose' (*Letters* 2, 820–1).　　RCT

'Irish Church, The' (article). The Irish Church will certainly be disestablished. Many pamphlets have circulated lately, proposing tax disbursement schemes. The money now collected from the Irish must be distributed equitably, and Roman Catholics must get their proportional share. *Fortnightly Review* (15 August 1865), 82–90.　　AKL

'Irish Church Bill in the Lords, The' (article). Members of the House of Lords are not inefficient and dilatory; the recently passed Irish church bill is better for the scrutiny, debate, and alterations than the original version. *Saint Pauls* (August 1869), 540–55.　　AKL

'Irish Church Debate, The' (article). The disestablishment of the Irish Church is both inevitable and imminent; Disraeli's delays have been an unnecessary and unhelpful difficulty. Gladstone is sure to succeed him as prime minister, partly because of this issue. *Saint Pauls* (May 1868), 147–60.　　AKL

Isbister, William (?1838–1916), partner in Strahan & Co. (1859–72) publishing house, which became W. Isbister & Co., then Daldy, Isbister & Co. He published *Why Frau Frohmann Raised her Prices* (1882), *Lord Palmerston* (1882), and *Kept in the Dark* (1882).　　RCT

Ischel, Austrian resort visited by the Duke of Omnium and his daughter Lady Mary. *DC*
　　JMR

Is He Popenjoy? (see below)

Italy. The northern lake region around Lake *Como and Lake Maggiore is the tourist destination where Robinson meets the Greene family. 'Money' *TAC2*　　RCT

Is He Popenjoy?

TROLLOPE's most artfully duplicitous novel leads us into one trap after another, snatching from us, again and again, the bait that had lured us there. From the first page of *Is He Popenjoy?*, with its entirely deceptive chattiness, we are misled, as the amiable and garrulous narrator slowly disappears and we are left in the clutches of a plot that never seems to go where we thought or hoped it would. Domestic comedy yields to a darker world of sexual intrigue, which declines to one darker still, a bitter battle over property, which becomes a reckless assault on legitimacy and male prerogatives. The happy ending, such as it is, comes to us courtesy of two deaths and some very uncivilized howling. This is not the amiable Trollope of legend.

But it is a Trollope one might suppose would accord with modern tastes, which are expected to run to such ironic cynicism. That the novel has been neglected is due partly to its absurd and repellent title but also to a rhetoric of chicanery too strong even for us. Certainly contemporary reviewers did not like it, insisting unanimously that it was Trollope at his worst. The *Spectator* even called it 'unwholesome' and Charles Dickens Junior, serializing it in *All the Year Round*, took it upon himself to bowdlerize it. We would not use the same terms or methods to deny this novel's power; we simply avoid it, which is a pity.

Trollope starts us off by boldly marrying his hero and heroine—why wait until the end to do that?—and assuring us that we are inside what looks like a domestic comedy, complete with a country setting, clerical characters, and all the trappings of Barsetshire. The only problem, we suppose, is to convince 'gaunt' and 'sombre' Lord George Germain to let his young bride Mary have some fun: a house in London, some parties, some dancing. Mary's worldly father, the Dean of Brotherton, sets out to convince his stolid son-in-law that London gaiety is the answer to all life's problems, and we are likely, at first, to agree. London seems to offer nothing more threatening than balls and roaring feminists, the latter and their Institute ('The Female Disabilities') providing an easy caricature of women's wrongs, as if they had any.

But they do. Just as we are about to settle into a broad comedy of manners, Trollope forces on us new enemies and new problems, really a new novel. It is not, we discover, simply a question of overcoming puritanical repression, of relaxing into the happy ways of the world; for the ways of the world are not at all happy. Lord George quickly becomes enmeshed with an old flame, Adelaide De Baron, now Houghton, who knows those ways and who has nothing better to do than try to manipulate them for her pleasure. At first, her raciness and vulgarity seem sprightly, even to Mary, but she is both thoroughly bored and very dangerous. Life has offered her nothing but a clear intelligence that has brought her no profit, so she tries to find whatever amusement she can in playing with the naive Lord George, forcing from him finally a declaration of love.

Meanwhile, back in the country, things have gone from placid to putrid. Lord George's older brother, the Marquis, returns from Italy with an Italian bride and, what is worse, a sickly little boy that he claims is his heir, the true Lord Popenjoy. Now this Marquis is a truly vicious man, perhaps the most brutal in all of Trollope, and he proceeds at once to eject his own mother and sisters from their house and to treat everyone about him with a rudeness they cannot counter. He demonstrates, that is, the impotence of those caught within the assumptions of civility in the face of those who scorn those assumptions.

And, to make matters worse, the domestic plot deteriorates quickly. Discovering a love letter from the terrible Mrs Houghton in her husband's coat, Mary is shaken but quick to forgive. Lord George, relieved and vowing to dis-ensnare himself from the temptress, also finds that his misstep has caused him to lose his position of unquestioned moral superiority in the marriage. As a result, he twists his own guilt and pain into a scrupulousness as regards his wife's conduct that becomes almost a positive wish that she do wrong. It is not long before he can find what he imagines is, in fact, such a deep offence to his name and honour: a dance she dances with Mrs Houghton's brother. This entirely harmless dance, the notorious and ridiculous Kappa-Kappa, becomes somehow the centre of the novel, and it is, of course, no centre at all, merely a psychological chimera that causes great and prolonged pain.

Through all of this the Dean is bustling about like some displaced God of the Festivity, with a vigorous and manly disregard for forms and a hearty taste for pleasures, pleasures of the table and of the field. It is very easy for readers to approve of the Dean—at first; he is merely 'some schoolboy out on a holiday' (XIX). But selfish children cause great harm when they act as heedlessly and, ultimately, selfishly as does the Dean. In an exceptionally artful reversal, Trollope turns the Dean inside out, showing the callousness that underlies his heartiness, the defensive snobbery that makes him seem so open. He forces his daughter roughly into the very world that is so dangerous to her, all in the name of 'fun', and he launches an enquiry into the legitimacy of the Marquis's poor little child that proceeds with so little taste that even Lord George, who stands to gain most, is sickened.

By this point, roughly two-thirds of the way through the novel, the readers have been stranded, left with no favoured perspective that will be safe. Only the women, or some of them, have been left untainted. The feminists, it would seem, have a case after all, as there is not a lot to choose among the men, among this weak Lord George, the rapacious Dean, and the malignant Marquis, as they battle over money and land, battle over the body of a helpless and ailing child. Trollope disrupts any easy position: even the Marquis, who had seemed a reliable villain, is given very strong arguments, even while he is made more repugnant personally. When he complains that his enemies, the Dean and his brother, are spurred on mostly by 'pigheaded English blindness' that makes them detest everything not English (XXX) he is backed by a great deal of evidence Trollope supplies: both the Dean and Lord George are ignorant and bigoted and are fuelled by their unrepentant insularity. The Marquis, after his little boy's death, is reflective, even wry, in wondering what it all mattered anyhow and whether he would have fought so hard had his enemies not gone about their own fight 'in such a dirty way' (LIII).

The dirty fight seems to be all there is, and we are left in the end with no clean spot for ourselves. Is it Popenjoy? turns out to be the wrong question: the boy dies and so does the Marquis, leaving Lord George and the Dean winner of the field. Mary even has a baby, the new and undoubted Lord Popenjoy, and Lord George assumes his brother's title. Minor characters are disposed of, not very warmly, and all should be happy. But what kind of happiness can we wring from 'pagan exaltation' (LXI) over the death of a dissolute Marquis and a baby who never had a chance? We have come a long way from the comic victories in Barsetshire. Now all triumphs seem dusty.

Is He Popenjoy? was begun 12 October 1874 and finished 3 May of the next year. Halfway through the writing, Trollope had departed for Ceylon and then for Australia, writing the last half of the novel on his voyages and actually finishing it while at sea. He kept it in his desk drawer until serializing it in *All the Year Round* from 13 October 1877 to 13 July 1878. Chapman & Hall published it in book form in April 1878. The manuscript is not extant. JRK

Tracy, Robert, *Trollope's Later Novels* (1978).

Jack, Sarah. Aunt to Maurice Cumming and Marian Leslie, she helps to bring about their marriage by her force of character, determination, and generosity. 'Jack' *TAC1* GRH

Jacko, nomadic character of unspecified origins, possibly Aboriginal, attached to Gangoil as a tracker. Aged 16, he is marked by 'that wild look which falls upon those who wander about the Australian plains' (I), but is implicitly trusted by Heathcote. A minor character, Jacko nevertheless performs a pivotal role in shaping Harry's judgements and actions. Moreover, when a fire threatens Gangoil, Heathcote's trust is rewarded by Jacko labouring intensely to extinguish it. *HHG* MRS

Jacobi, Ruth. Oppressed by her grandfather's gloomy house and her uncle's scoldings, she longs for gaiety with a young husband before settling into domesticity. Orphaned and lonely, she is befriended by Nina Balatka, whom she finds romantically exotic, and by Rebecca Loth, whose brother Samuel would (according to her guardians) be a suitable match. It is she who brings the two women together. *NB* AWJ

Jacquêtanàpe, Victoire. He marries Clementina Golightly for her fortune. Victoire is a 'well-made, shining, jaunty little Frenchman' who 'was one of those butterfly beings who seem to have been created that they may flutter about from flower to flower' (XXV). *TC* MT

Jamaica, magnificent scenery amidst which the Leslies live under the Blue Mountain peak, but 'in its decadence' with the labour problems, caused by emancipation, for plantations like Maurice Cumming's Mount Pleasant. 'Jack' *TAC1* GRH

James, George Payne Rainsford (1799–1860), consul-general at Venice (1856–60); historical novelist, best known for *Richelieu* (1829). His production-line methods yielded three novels annually for some twenty years; he was parodied by Thackeray in *Punch* (1847). In his Commonplace Book, Trollope noted of James's *Corse de Leon, or the Brigand*: 'I trust this will be [the] last of the modern adventurous class of novels I shall be tempted to read—for nothing gives me so great an idea of wasting my time—no not even idleness and castle building—It appears to me, that no talent—no industry—no energy was put to this work—that it consists of an improbable string of adventures very badly put forth in bad writing, and without any single charm, but that to me very poor

one—the desire to know what becomes of the people' (*Letters* 2, 1023). RCT

James, Henry (1843–1916), American novelist who settled in England (1875), master of subtly organized novels like *Portrait of a Lady* (1881) and *The Golden Bowl* (1904). Prior to his own success James wrote four reviews of Trollope's fiction in the New York *Nation*. The first, on *Miss Mackenzie* (1865), patronized Trollope for describing the obvious. 'Life is vulgar, but we know not how vulgar it is till we see it set down in his pages' (July 1865). *Can You Forgive Her?* prompted a facetious parody of its title (*Nation*, September 1865). James was then 21. Some fourteen years later with four novels behind him he was praised by one English reviewer but 'compared with Mr Trollope almost a tyro'. James found *The Belton Estate* (1866) 'as flat as a Dutch landscape . . . Mr Trollope is a good observer; but he is literally nothing else' (January 1866). By the time *Nina Balatka* and *Linda Tressel* appeared anonymously, James had no trouble identifying the author. James's attitude was changing, however. 'These short novels are rich with their own intrinsic merits . . . they contain more of the real substance of common life and more natural energy of conception than any of the clever novels now begotten on our much-tried English speech' (June 1868). When both were on board the SS *Bothnia* in the autumn of 1875, James found Trollope 'the dullest Briton of them all' with 'a gross and repulsive face and manner' (*Henry James: Letters*, ed. Leon Edel, 1 (1974), 486). Later he judged him 'a very good, genial, ordinary fellow—much better than he seemed on the steamer' (James, *Letters*, 2 (1975), 94). He marvelled at Trollope's capacity to write in his stateroom in rough weather and play cards all evening. At the Cosmopolitan Club in 1877 he found Trollope much the same, amidst 'a little knot of Parliamentary swells, "all gobble and glare" as he was described by someone' (James 2, 101). Meeting Anthony's niece Beatrice in June 1875, he wondered, 'How could such a flower have blossomed on that coarse-grained Trollope stem?' (James, 2, 246). Old misgivings returned when *An Autobiography* appeared; condemned for 'its density, blockishness and soddenness. Not a voice has been lifted to say so. But I must do it sometime and somewhere' (James, *Letters*, 3 (1980), 14). Fortunately, he had also had his say four months earlier in the *Century Magazine* (July 1883), later published in *Partial Portraits* (1888), one of the most perceptive contemporary estimates of Trollope's fiction.   RCT

James, Sir Henry (1828–1911), lawyer and statesman; Attorney-General under Gladstone (1873 and 1880); Lord James of Hereford (1895); a close friend of Trollope, and an occasional steward at Royal Literary Fund dinners, where they eagerly disputed. At a dinner party, hosted by Henry O'Neill, 'There was a great scene between Trollope and James. Trollope raging and roaring with immense vehemence against the system of cross examination as practised and James defending it with charming calmness and good-nature' (*Letters* 2, 950). In 1874 when Thomas *Hughes was seeking nomination as a Liberal candidate for Parliament Trollope put his case to James 'with vehement debate until one-thirty the following morning' (*I & R* 220). When Trollope moved to South Harting, James was among friends invited to provide the parish with cultural entertainment.   RCT

Jay, Mr. Ironmonger of Warminster and brother-in-law of Sam Brattle, he refuses to put up bail for the young man accused of murder, and is unkind to Carry Brattle, the outcast. *IMP*   RCT

Jenner, Sir William (1815–98), physician to University College Hospital (1849); physician extraordinary to Queen Victoria (1861); established the distinct identities of typhus and typhoid fevers. When Trollope suffered his stroke in November 1882, he was attended by William Murrell, the heart specialist, Sir William Jenner, who had been called in as consultant, and Sir Richard Quain, his regular London physician. In the following weeks, Murrell and Jenner issued thirteen bulletins in *The Times* on his condition.

Initially these were optimistic, but after ten days the reports ceased for two weeks. When they resumed, Murrell and Jenner announced that their patient had lost strength. A few days later, they declared his condition critical; the following day, 6 December 1882, Trollope died.   RCT

Jerningham, Mr, quiet, civil, dull old supervisor who tries to keep the peace among his subordinates in the Post Office where George Roden works. *MF*   SRB

Jerome, Father, the Balatkas' confessor. Aunt Sophie expects to enlist his authority and the Church's anathema against Nina's Jewish lover, but Jerome is too honest to deny Bohemia's laws permit mixed marriages or that God's forgiveness is all-embracing. *NB*   AWJ

Jerome, Father, curé of St Laud's who, though banned from his church, preaches expressively to his congregation, fights in the Vendean cause and is badly wounded, and plays a major part in their discussions. *LV*   GRH

Jerrold, William Blanchard (1826–84), journalist, playwright, novelist, biographer; son of Douglas Jerrold; edited *Lloyd's Weekly* from 1857; published *Life of Napoleon III* (1874–82), also lives of Douglas Jerrold and Cruikshank. He was secretary of the National Book Union (1861), a scheme for making books available to the working classes. In April 1861 he asked Trollope's help. Trollope replied: 'I shall be most happy to assist the Book Union in any way, and shall be proud to see my name on the list of patrons. My name I fear will do you but little good. If I can serve you in any other way I shall be very glad' (*Letters* 1, 146). Jerrold also joined the English delegation to the Paris International Literary Congress debating copyright, republication, and translation (June 1878), issues close to Trollope's heart. Again, Trollope offered assistance.   RCT

Jessel, Sir George (1824–83), Master of the Rolls (1873–83); Vice-Chancellor of London University (1881–3); Liberal MP for Dover (1868–73); one of the great English equity judges. Jessel collaborated with Trollope in the Royal Literary Fund and played whist with him at the Athenaeum Club. Amidst the rabid anti-Semitism aired by several characters in *The Way We Live Now*, depiction of the Jewish merchant Brehgert may owe something to Trollope's affection for Jessel. As Lady Pomona rails against Jews, 'An accursed race; . . . expelled from Paradise . . . Scattered about all over the world, so that nobody knows who anybody is', Trollope has Georgiana Longestaffe retort, 'One of the greatest judges in the land is a Jew' (LXXVIII). Jessel became Master of the Rolls about two months before Trollope wrote that chapter. RCT

'John Bull on the Guadalquivir', first serialized in Cassell's *Illustrated Family Paper*, 17 and 24 November 1860 (reprinted in *TAC1*). John Pomfret, son to one of the partners of Pomfret and Daguilar, is sent to Spain with a view to his marrying Maria Daguilar, the daughter of the other partner. In Cadiz, John is met by a friend, Thomas Johnson. They take a boat for Seville, along the Guadalquivir. On board they scoff at the exotic dress of a Spaniard. When they arrive at the Daguilars' house a mortified John discovers that the Spaniard was the Marquis d'Almavivas. Despite this display of crassness, John and Maria marry. JS

John Caldigate (*see next page*)

Johnson, Samuel (1709–84), the great lexicographer, poet, and essayist, whose *Dictionary of the English Language* appeared in 1755 after nine years of labour. His final work was *Lives of the English Poets* (1779–81), which Trollope threw out of the window 'because he spoke sneeringly of *Lycidas*' (*Auto* III). In his Commonplace Book, he commented on Johnson's 'Life of Cowley': 'The unmeaning pomposity of his style is . . . the same in this as in all his works. I think his opinions on those whom he terms metaphysical poets—that is most of the poets of the 17th Century . . . are true—though Metaphysical is not the proper word by which their tortuous ingenuity should be ascribed' (*Letters* 2, 1023). Despite finding fault with Johnson's style, Trollope placed him among eighteen masters of English literature. RCT

Johnson, Thomas, friend of John Pomfret who misjudges the appearance and status of the Marquis D'Almavivas. 'Bull' *TAC1* GRH

Johnson of Manchester, name of cotton goods manufacturer made up by Mr Robinson to cover his firm's failure to supply goods promised to customers. *SBJR* RCT

Johnstone, Captain (sometimes **Johnson**), Fred Neville's superior officer at Ennis. Barely older but equally devoted to Irish sport, he fails to check Fred's ardour for Kate O'Hara. *EE* AWJ

Jones, faithful servant and companion of Lady Fitzgerald who stoutly defies Mr Prendergast's best efforts to make her positively identify Matthew Mollett. *CR* MRS

Jones, Ada, eldest daughter of Philip Jones, 'tall, fair-haired, and very lovely' (I). Seen by others, especially by her less attractive sister Edith, primarily in terms of her physical beauty, she is not only predominantly viewed as a love-object, but is led to regard herself as such. However, when rejected by the handsome Captain Clayton, she refuses to play the role of lovelorn lady, and works instead to help Clayton win her sister. *L* MRS

Jones, Charles Burnaby. The victim of Mrs Brown's mustard plaster meant for her husband, he suffers pain and indignity, but at Thompson Hall is reconciled to her. 'Thompson' GRH

Jones, Edith, younger daughter of Philip Jones, who, feeling herself inferior to her sister Ada, in terms of feminine beauty, maps a future full of marital happiness for Ada, but not for herself. Despite her own attraction to Captain Clayton, she constructs a fanciful match between him and her sister, with unhappy consequences for all when it becomes clear that she, not Ada, is the Captain's real object of desire. *L* MRS

Jones, Florian (Flory), 10-year-old murder victim, son of Philip Jones, an English Protestant landowner living in Ireland. A beautiful child, both 'clever and sharp' (I), Florian turns Catholic, colludes with the Landleaguers, and lies to his father, only to be murdered by Terry Lax, a political assassin, after he is persuaded by his family to give evidence against Pat Carroll, a known Landleaguer. *L* MRS

Jones, Frank, eldest son of Philip Jones, an English landowner in Ireland, who falls in love with Rachel O'Mahony, an Irish-American opera singer on the London stage. Far outmatched in both character and ability by his fearless, unconventional fiancée, 'his feelings as a man' are wounded by Rachel's air of independence (XVII) and their engagement is broken when, penniless himself, he cannot bring himself to live on 'the earnings of a singer' (XXXIII). When she loses her voice, and their engagement is renewed, he regards it as a happy sign that she 'had knocked under to him' (XLVI). *L* MRS

Jones, Henry. Nobody at Llanfeare likes this 'unmanly' insurance clerk. Justified by that antipathy, he takes the volume of sermons in which his uncle left a will that disinherits him back to its library shelf. But fear of worldly and eternal punishment and of what he might say under cross-examination makes his inheritance a misery. His guilty behaviour eventually leads to the will's discovery, and he returns to London with relief, thanks to the generous contempt of the new heiress and her lawyer. *CH* AWJ

PERHAPS the most 'sensational' of Trollope's novels, *John Caldigate* was partly inspired by Trollope's travels in Australia in 1871–2, and by the celebrated Tichborne case (1871–4) in which a butcher from Wagga Wagga in New South Wales unsuccessfully laid claim to the name, property, and title (a baronetcy) of Sir Roger Tichborne (see TICHBORNE CASE). While he was writing it, Trollope initially called the novel *John Caldigate's Wife* and later *Mrs John Caldigate*, titles which would better have drawn attention to the central interest of the plot: the grave doubt cast on the legality of John Caldigate's marriage after Euphemia Smith, a woman who claims he had married her in Australia, returns to England, and he is jailed for bigamy. Her story is both more easily believable and harder to disprove than that of the claimant in the Tichborne case, with whom she privately compares herself. She had certainly been Caldigate's common-law wife for a time on the goldfields of New South Wales, and her claim that there had been a legal marriage ceremony is corroborated by a fellow conspirator, Timothy Crinkett, who had been Caldigate's partner in a highly successful gold mine, Polyeuka. Their chief aim is to blackmail Caldigate into paying them £20,000, ostensibly as compensation for the money they lost on the mine after Caldigate sold his share to Crinkett and the gold was found to be worked out. Caldigate at first rejects their demand, but then decides to accede to it as a matter of honour. It is a rash, almost perverse decision, of a kind Trollopian heroes are prone to. At his trial for bigamy it is naturally seen as having been an inducement to Smith to change her story, almost tantamount to a confession of guilt on Caldigate's part. But the most damning evidence against him appears to be an envelope addressed to Smith as 'Mrs Caldigate', in his handwriting. He maintains that he addressed the envelope when they were living together on the goldfields and he had conditionally promised to marry her; it was intended simply as a form of endearment and reassurance. She points to the postage stamp and Sydney postmark on the envelope as evidence that he had in fact publicly addressed and acknowledged her as his wife. He is predictably found guilty and imprisoned, only to be pardoned, after some months, when a clever and assiduous postal worker, improbably named Bagwax, demonstrates that the postage stamp had not even been issued at the time when the letter was supposed to have been sent, and that the Sydney postmark had almost certainly been obtained by fraud and stamped on the envelope at a later date than the one it bore. (Trollope holds Bagwax up as an example of the skill and dedication of Post Office employees.) Smith is sentenced to three years' imprisonment for perjury, having previously resolved that rather than lose her ill-gotten gains she would endure 'fourteen years . . . like the Claimant'.

John Caldigate was Trollope's first thoroughgoing 'bigamy novel', belonging to the distinctive sub-genre of the sensation novel which had been inaugurated in the early 1860s by Mrs Henry *Wood's *East Lynne* (1861) and Mary Elizabeth *Braddon's *Lady Audley's Secret* (1862). The scenes in which Caldigate's disreputable past, and especially the story of his quasi-marriage in Australia, begins to catch up with him are in the best traditions of the sub-genre. Trollope, however, without detracting from the underlying menace, narrates them with a calmness and an amused moral irony all his own. When Caldigate first sees Crinkett in England, the man who will so dreadfully shatter his peace is sleeping on a bench in St John's Gardens, Cambridge, a sardonic commentary on Caldigate's complacent assurance that his past misdeeds have been put to rest; and the appearance, soon after, of Crinkett and one of his henchmen at the christening of Caldigate's first child, filling the tiny village church and arousing an irrational fear in Caldigate's mind that they may stop the ceremony, epitomizes the shock, the seeming absurdity, of this convergence of the opposite poles, the very antipodes, of his moral experience: his buried past on the goldfields of Australia and his present as a fledgeling English squire. Bored, in debt, and virtually estranged from his father, he had left England in search of 'more conventional freedom than one can find among the folk at home'. He had expected to exchange the 'washy fen' of his father's estate in Cambridgeshire for a 'wild and beautiful world', a spot among the gold-bearing mountains of New South Wales that would be 'most lovely' and 'in all respects romantic' (I). The other romance of his life, he had hoped, would be Hester Bolton, the girl he left behind him, whom he marries after he returns to England to 'topdress the English acres with a little Australian gold' (XXIII). Euphemia Smith symbolizes his confusion of true romance with false, a confusion that persisted even after he sold his goldmine, the 'imperious mistress' he was 'wedded' to—as he cynically characterizes it—and began what he called new 'mining operations' at a 'second Ahalala', the heart of Hester Bolton (XIV).

Ahalala, the site of the Polyeuka mine, had signally failed to live up to Caldigate's romantic dreams of a mountain paradise. Its real-life model was a settlement called Currajong that Trollope considered 'the most hopelessly disappointing place' he visited in Australia. It was at Currajong that the germ of the idea for *John Caldigate* was clearly sown in his memory, when he met a softly nurtured, well-educated, handsome young gentleman whom he had known as a boy in England, sitting in front of his tent and 'eating a nauseous lump of beef out of a greasy frying-pan with his pocket-knife' (*Australia* XIX). Ahalala is 23 miles (37 km) away from Nobble, the first goldfield on which Caldigate tried his luck. Nobble was based on Grenfell, the nearest town to Trollope's son Frederic's sheep station Mortray. It had struck Caldigate as the 'foulest place' he had ever seen; its streets, deep in mud and slush when he arrived, ironically recall the muddy fields of Cambridgeshire which his romantic eyes had found so dreary.

Only four chapters of the novel are set in Australia, but the vividness and authenticity of the goldfield scenes, unmatched in any other English novel of the period, are crucial to the daring plea for moral tolerance, even moral relativism, that is the implicit message of the novel. At the time of Caldigate's trial there is a widespread feeling that 'anything done in the wilds of Australia ought not to "count" here at home in England', and while Trollope knew better than to try to represent the Australian bush as lawless like the Wild West, the novel does appear to endorse this feeling, at least with regard to the 'conventional freedom' of which Caldigate had availed himself in his relationship with Euphemia Smith. It does not even reproach him, or have him reproach himself, for lying about the relationship both to his future wife and to her brother; and when he does eventually tell Hester the truth, after their marriage, she quickly forgives him. Notwithstanding that in Scotland, as John Blackwood pointed out to Trollope, Caldigate would have been regarded as legally married to Smith, he never accepts full blame for his plight but insists that 'any man might be made the victim of a conspiracy' in the way he has been (XXXVII). Blackwood, after at first sympathizing with Trollope's 'involuntary Don Giovanni', thinking him 'a fellow not better or worse than the rest of us', was increasingly repelled by his failure to show any sign of contrition (*Letters* 2, 749–50). Instead of having him repent, Trollope deflects attention away from his intransigence in order to concentrate on that of the enemies who are loudest in their condemnation of him: his wife's family, especially her mother. The Boltons of Puritan Grange are among the most extreme of all the numerous low-church fanatics in Trollope's novels. At one stage they virtually lock Hester up in order to prevent Caldigate from seeing her. If their self-righteous sexual puritanism is the only alternative to the pragmatism of Caldigate's less harsh judges, most readers even in Trollope's own day would have known where they stood.

Trollope began writing *John Caldigate* on 3 February 1877 and finished it on 21 July 1877. There were interruptions between 22 February and 12 March, when he was at work on *The Life of Cicero*, and between 14 and 21 April, when he was ill. The last three parts were written at sea, on his way to South Africa. Under agreements dated 26 and 27 June 1877, Chapman & Hall paid £1,200 for exclusive book-rights and Blackwood's £600 for serial-rights. The novel was serialized in *Blackwood's Magazine* from April 1878 to June 1879, and published in three volumes in June 1879. It was more warmly received than most of Trollope's recent novels, although some reviewers complained, with good reason, that the concluding chapters were unnecessarily eked out. The manuscript is in the Arents Collection, New York Public Library.   PE

Trollope, Anthony, *Australia*, ed. P. D. Edwards and R. B. Joyce (1967).

Jones, Indefer, squire of Llanfeare whose conscience bids him leave the estate in the male line rather than to his beloved niece. Despite his scrupulosity, he reverses that decision in his final days, without informing his lawyer, and so, through the best of intentions, brings confusion upon the entire parish. *CH*   AWJ

Jones, Mary Flood (later **Finn**), first of Phineas Finn's numerous love interests, ultimately his wife. Irresistibly attractive, Mary is hopelessly in love with Phineas long before he decides to propose to her. Though she attempts reserve, Mary's affection is obvious to her beloved. As Mrs Finn, Mary dies during her first pregnancy. *PF*   JMR

Jones, Mr, lawyer who defends Sam Brattle at his trial for the murder of Farmer Trumbull. *IMP*   RCT

Jones, Mr, son-in-law and junior partner of Mr Brown, who robs the firm. After the partners' bankruptcy, he opens a small hairdresser's shop in Gray's Inn Lane. *SBJR*   HO

Jones, Mr, traveller across Palestine in the company of John Smith (Julia Weston, disguised as a man). Her uncle meets them and accuses Jones of eloping with his niece. 'Palestine' *TAC2*   GRH

Jones, Mrs (Sarah Jane), scheming elder daughter of Mr Brown and wife of his partner in a haberdashery business who 'played the part of Goneril' (II) in family matters. *SBJR*   RCT

Jones, Mrs Montacute, wife of a wealthy industrialist, notable for her excellent hospitality. Mrs Montacute Jones's life is dedicated to giving garden parties in Roehampton and shooting parties at her Scottish residence, Killancodlem. Under the auspices of her hospitality in London and Scotland, Lord Silverbridge meets and proposes to Isabel Boncassen. She is an ally of Lady George Germain in *Is He Popenjoy? DC*   JMR

Jones, Philip, English Protestant owner of Morony Castle in Ireland who, though fair and equitable with his Irish tenants, finds himself 'wretched in heart' (XL) on being caught up in the fractious history of Ireland's colonial politics. Not only are his lands sabotaged and his family boycotted, but his favourite son, 10-year-old Florian, lends allegiance to the Irish cause, and is subsequently murdered by Terry Lax, a political assassin. *L*   MRS

Jones, Septimus. A friend of Augustus Scarborough, he occupies chambers on the same floor in London. He 'had always been submissive to Augustus; and, now that Augustus was a rich man, and could afford to buy horses, was likely to be more submissive than ever' (VII). *MSF*   MT

Jonson, Ben (1572/3–1637), playwright, contemporary of Shakespeare, famed for his humours comedies, notably *Volpone, or the Fox* (1607) and *The Alchemist* (1610). Trollope, who studied the old drama, faulted Jonson's plays for their characterization of women. Jonson, he declared, 'hardly even tries to make a woman charming. They are all whores or fools—generally both' (quoted Hall, 417). He also felt that while writers such as Shakespeare could successfully rely on the writings of others to frame their own imaginative works, Jonson failed to achieve Shakespeare's delicacy of touch in this matter. *Cynthia's Revels* (1600) he regarded as 'altogether inept', claiming 'The work will have no future readers, unless it be some additional Editors or determined idler like myself' (quoted Hall 417–18). *Mr Scarborough's Family* 'may have drawn on *Volpone* (re-read by Trollope in August 1882) for the deviousness with which the old man played upon the greed of his presumed heirs' (Super 353). RCT

Joram, Sir John. The light-hearted Jacky Joram, barrister in the Percycross election case in *Ralph the Heir*, becomes the dignified lawyer who defends John Caldigate unsuccessfully in a bigamy trial, but works successfully to secure his pardon. JC SRB

'Josephine de Montmorenci', first published in *Saint Pauls*, December 1869 (reprinted in *ET*). The editor of the *Olympus Magazine*, Mr Jonathan Brown, receives the manuscript of a novel, 'Not so Black as he's Painted', from an authoress who calls herself Josephine de Montmorenci and who accompanies her submission with a stream of importunate letters. When he visits Miss de Montmorenci, he discovers he has been hoaxed. She is a wizened invalid, called Maryanne ('Polly') Puffle. Although the novel is bad, the sympathetic Mr Brown is induced to accept 'Not so Black as he's Painted' for publication. Perversely, it is 'quite a success'. JS

journalist, Trollope as. Trollope's career in journalism did not really develop until the 1860s, in the wake of his success as a novelist. He became an important figure in the expanding world of magazines because he could supply so much of their staple, serial fiction.

In 1849–50, while he was in Ireland, the *Examiner* ran a series of seven articles by Trollope on Ireland during the famine, and in the 1850s he had two book reviews and an article on the civil service in the *Dublin University Magazine*. In 1859, his last year in Ireland, he offered some short stories to a periodical that was to begin publishing in January 1860. This was the *Cornhill*

Magazine. Thackeray, the editor, promptly invited him to write articles as well as fiction for the new magazine. 'Whatever a man knows about life and its doings, that let us hear about' (*Auto* VIII). Though he was turning out novels faster than ever and still working at the Post Office, he decided to take the opportunity to diversify.

In the early 1860s Trollope wrote several articles for the *Cornhill*, *St. James's Magazine*, and the *Athenaeum*, not all of them signed. He increased his journalistic output substantially in 1865, when the *Fortnightly Review*, which he helped found and whose board he chaired, began publication. For the *Fortnightly*, an independent and eclectic review, Trollope wrote five full-scale articles and fourteen book reviews in a little more than two years. All these, in line with magazine policy, were signed. Thus his constant appearance in the *Fortnightly* identified him as an established man of letters of the calibre of Walter Bagehot, G. H. Lewes, and Frederic Harrison. His articles were mainly about literature, the Church, education, and the civil service.

In 1865 Trollope also became a newspaperman. For a year and a half he was a regular columnist for the *Pall Mall Gazette*. This was a new intellectual evening paper with a bent for social reform. He remarks in *An Autobiography* that he found that he was not suited to newspaper work; he particularly disliked being given assignments and having his copy edited. To add insult to injury, the amount of money he made in his newspaper career was small in comparison with the amount of time it took.

As was the custom in newspapers, his *Pall Mall* articles were unsigned, but they have been identified from his record of earnings (Trollope Papers III, Bodleian Library, University of Oxford). Besides whimsical sketches on hunting, travelling, and the clergy (all reprinted in book form) he wrote substantial articles on the United States, France, English political corruption, reform at home and abroad, the advancement of women, and the Church. His opinions on the events and ramifications of the American Civil War, English politics, and the implications for England of current foreign affairs mark him as a serious recorder and interpreter of history. In addition, they amplify situations and characterizations in his novels. Many of the articles explain points of view to be found in the fiction: the strong interest in Americans, for example, and the move from church to government politics. One of his lighter pieces, a description of a charity bazaar, was imported into *Miss Mackenzie*. The list goes only from February 1865 to July 1866, but he took up the connection with the *Pall Mall* again in

1868 in order to write a series of post-war dispatches from the United States. The wide scope of his reading and travels reflected in these articles shows an active intelligence stimulated by his access to publication in an important daily newspaper. Trollope provided the *Pall Mall* with so much copy that he had to resort to the stratagem of appearing variously in the characters of Anthony Trollope, the foreign correspondent; 'An Englishman', the prolific letter-writer; an anonymous reporter and author of leading articles; and a bemused observer of human nature.

Through George *Smith, proprietor of the *Cornhill* and then the *Pall Mall*, Trollope moved among influential writers, politicians, diplomats, and scholars, including Thackeray, Matthew Arnold, and William E. Forster, who would later become a member of Gladstone's cabinet. 'I have met at a Pall Mall dinner', he says in *An Autobiography*, 'a crowd of guests who would have filled the House of Commons more respectably than I have seen it filled even on important occasions' (XI).

In 1867, year of the Second Reform Act, he became editor of another new magazine, *Saint Pauls*, a position he held until 1870. He promised his readers an education in politics. The magazine's writers included Leslie Stephen, Edward Dicey, G. J. Goschen, Tom Trollope, Charles Lever, Austin Henry Layard, Lewes, Charles Merewether, Sir Charles Trevelyan, and Margaret Oliphant. As well as fiction, the editor wrote articles on domestic, American, and Anglo-Irish politics and classical and contemporary literature.

In 1869, in addition to editing and writing for his own magazine, he wrote a review and an article for the *Fortnightly*. From the autumn of 1870, when his twentieth (and last) *Saint Pauls* article appeared, his appearances in newspapers and magazines were mostly in the form of travel articles on Australia, New Zealand, the United States, and South Africa. Between 1877 and 1881 he wrote for the *Fortnightly*, *Blackwood's*, *Nineteenth Century*, *Good Words*, and the *North American Review* eleven articles in all. In 1880 he wrote a dozen light articles for the *Pall Mall*.

Trollope's newspaper and magazine articles are a mirror of his time. Journalism was the means through which every facet of the complex mid-Victorian period was recorded and debated. Writing as the growth of democracy was transforming Europe and America, he examined closely such issues as faith in political progress and reform, doubts about the authority of the Church, England's position in the international community, and directions in contemporary literature. His journalism is also highly descriptive of human nature and society. JK

Knelman, Judith, 'Trollope's Journalism', *Library*, 2 (1983), 140–55.

Trollope, Anthony, *Miscellaneous Essays and Reviews* (1981).

—— *Writings for Saint Paul's Magazine* (1981).

journalists as characters. Despite his admiration of two high-profile newspapermen, John *Delane, editor of *The Times*, and the foreign correspondent W. H. *Russell, Trollope's fiction shows journalists as contemptible and manipulating Grub Street hacks. The relentlessly crusading reporter Tom Towers and the populist editor Quintus Slide shrewdly use their positions to control public figures. Even Mr Groschut wields enough influence through the *Brotherton Church* to cause trouble for the Dean of Brotherton in *Is He Popenjoy?* From church bulletins through Slide's *People's Banner* to Tom Towers's *Jupiter*, modelled on *The Times* (popularly known as 'The Thunderer'), Trollope's journalists abuse their power.

Tom Towers is described as a god dispensing thunderbolts from Mount Olympus. In *The Warden* he alleges in a leader that the Warden of Hiram's Hospital, Mr Harding, gets too much money and the old men who live there too little. Towers, a trained barrister who does not hesitate to make judgements, demands reform and succeeds in embarrassing Mr Harding into resigning. In *Barchester Towers* the sly and grasping Mr Slope seeks and receives Towers's endorsement in his campaign to be dean. In *Framley Parsonage* Towers again interferes in the promotion of a clergyman, protesting the gift of a prebendal stall to Mark Robarts through political patronage. Though Towers's victories are usually short-lived, they show how arbitrary and opportunistic the press can be.

Towers can be perceived as misguided but well-meaning; the same cannot be said of Slide, an unscrupulous, low-class scandalmonger whose vocation is to expose corruption in the establishment even if he has to invent it. Slide appears in *Phineas Finn* and *Phineas Redux* as the nemesis of Phineas, running against him for Parliament and then attempting to discredit him socially as well as politically. In *The Prime Minister* Slide attacks the Duke of Omnium and his coalition government in retaliation for a social snub.

Trollope disparages the integrity of Nicholas Broune, Alfred Booker, and Ferdinand Alf, three editors with whom the hack novelist Lady Carbury curries favour in *The Way We Live Now*. John Sutherland links Broune's paper the *Morning Breakfast Table* with the *Daily Telegraph*, and Booker's *Literary Chronicle* with the *Saturday Review*. Alf's *Evening Pulpit* reflects the rise of evening papers at this period (*WWLN*, World's Classics (1982), 464–5). Not all Trollope's portraits of journalists focus on their egotism and sensation-seeking. With Hugh Stanbury in *He Knew He Was Right* he shows the power of the press in a better light. The impecunious Stanbury has chosen to work for a penny paper, the *Daily Record*, churning out political leaders, rather than pursue a career as a barrister. He tells his prospective father-in-law (*HKWR* LI) that journalism is not only as stable and respectable an institution as the law, but one that is as necessary to society.

In *Mr Scarborough's Family* we meet Quaverdale, a writer for the *Coming Hour*, who, having quarrelled with his father, has made his way in the world through discipline and industry. A similar figure is the hero of his short story 'The Adventures of Fred Pickering', who left a job as a law clerk in Manchester to work six nights a week for the *Morning Comet*, a penny daily, in London. Press tactics are shown in *John Caldigate* (XXXVII, XL, LV) and for a summary of Trollope's views see *The New Zealander* (III).   JK

'Journey to Panama, The', first published in the *Victoria Regia* (1861) (reprinted in *LS*). Ralph Forrest takes ship for California, driven by 'the accursed hunger for gold'. On board the *Serapiqui* he befriends a young woman, Emily Viner. She is going out to marry a man, twenty years her senior, whom she does not love. The young travellers fall in love. When she arrives in Panama she discovers that Mr Gorloch, her intended, has died. She is free but, on a noble impulse, she refuses Ralph's offer of marriage and returns to England. He goes on to the goldfields.   JS

Jowett, Benjamin (1817–93), Master of Balliol College, Oxford, from 1870; promoter of the Act to abolish religious tests for university degrees. One of Trollope's 'unholy trinity' involved in the report 'Organization of the Permanent Civil Service' (1853) advocating competitive examinations for new entrants. In *The Three Clerks* he joined Sir Charles Trevelyan and Sir Stafford Northcote as 'the three kings' 'destined to revivify, clarify, and render perfect the Civil Service'. Translated to Cambridge, Jowett was Mr Jobbles who 'had passed his life in putting posing questions, in detecting ignorance by viva voce scrutiny, and eliciting learning by printed papers' (XI).   RCT

Joyce family. In August 1882 fifteen men, four of them named Joyce, were arrested for the murder of the Joyce family at Maamtrasna, Co. Galway. Ten were brought to trial on 2 November and convicted; three were executed on 15 November. Trollope incorporated the murders into *The Landleaguers*, in which five members of a peasant family named Kelly are killed in their hovel (XLVII). In September 1882 Trollope mentioned the execution in Limerick of Francis Hynes for murdering a shepherd, adding, 'I trust that they will also hang . . . all the Joyces that are left' (*Letters* 2, 985). In his novel, Trollope implied that the murders were the work of the Irish Land League, although a local feud seems likely (Hall 504).   RCT

Judaism and the Jews. Trollope is warmly sympathetic to Judaism and the Jews. His friends included the Rothschild banking family, with whom he hunted, and in his introduction to *South Africa* he notes the traditional generosity of Jewish people. The European context of 19th-century Judaism is assumed in *Nina Balatka*, where Anton Trendellsohn's racial insecurity, and his love for the Catholic Nina, are treated subtly; and his leaving the ghetto with Nina represents in microcosm the response of Judaism to historical change.

English anti-Semitism is evident in the gibes about the parliamentary candidate in *Rachel Ray*; but it is more virulent in the areas of sex and class. Ferdinand Lopez, the alleged Portuguese Jew adventurer in *The Prime Minister*, provokes the hostility of the upper class when he marries Emily Wharton, as does the proposed union of Georgiana Longestaffe with the banker Ezekiel Brehgert in *The Way We Live Now*. However, as in the case of the great financier and suspected Jew Melmotte, anti-Semitism is often masked by self-interest.

Like other Victorian writers, Trollope utilizes the Jewish stereotype for fictional purposes in his treatment of the impresario in *The Landleaguers*, and in his more traditional presentation of the moneylenders, the rapacious Jabesh M'Ruen in *The Three Clerks*, or Samuel Hart, whom Mr Scarborough delights in duping in *Mr Scarborough's Family*.

Trollope's criticism of anti-Semitism in *The Way We Live Now*, in his revelation that Mr Brehgert is a complete gentleman and superior to the ancient Longestaffes, is matched by a double slap at racial and religious prejudice in *Phineas Redux*, in Phineas Finn's marriage to Mme Max Goesler, thought to be a Jewess, who snubs English society by refusing the Duke of Omnium for a middle-class Irish Catholic.   GH
Rosenberg, Edgar, *From Shylock to Svengali* (1961).

Juniper, Richard. A Newmarket horse trainer who loaned money to Mountjoy Scarborough, Juniper was 'a well-featured, tall man, but he looked the stable and he smelt of it' (XXXV).

Juvenal

Juniper is willing to marry Amelia Carroll, but only if he receives £500, which sum is not forthcoming. *MSF*   MT

Juvenal (*c*.55–*c*.140), Roman poet whose sixteen satires deployed rhetorical indignation against vices of his age; thought to have been banished to Egypt for lampooning a favourite of the Emperor Domitian. An avid reader of the classical authors, Trollope liked to sport with incidental meanings created by the crossover of sounds between Latin and English. Writing to John Merivale about a motto for their Goose and Glee Club (mentioned in *LCB* XLII), he puns on Juvenal's 'Cantabit vacuus coram latrone viator' ('The traveller with an empty purse will sing in the presence of a robber', *Satires* 10. 22). Nearly fifteen years later (May 1870) his more serious reading of Juvenal arose in the context of Austin's *The Seasons: A Satire* (1861). 'I doubt whether Juvenal ever aided at all in the suppression of vice' (*Letters* 1, 515).

RCT

'Kafir Land' (article). A recent trip to South Africa proved illuminating. This century's five Kafir wars have been costly in every way. European settlers' farms have been destroyed, and some killed (never women or children). The public needs to understand that the natives feel invaded, devoured by Europeans. Withdrawal now, however, would produce more inter-tribal wars. Civilization is good; the Kafirs begin to see British law is more safe, just, and pleasant than Kafir law. *Fortnightly Review* (1 February 1878), 191–206. AKL

Kanturk Hotel, low-class drinking establishment in the Irish city of Cork, owned by Mr O'Dwyer and tended by his daughter Fanny, which provides temporary headquarters for the Mollets while they blackmail Sir Thomas Fitzgerald. *CR* MRS

Kantwise, Mr, commercial traveller selling metallic furniture for the Patent Steel Furniture Company. 'He looked as though a skin rather too small for the purpose had been drawn over his head and face so that his forehead and cheeks and chin were bright and shiny', and his nose 'seemed to have been compressed almost into nothing by that skin-squeezing operation' (VI). He sells a broken set of furniture to stingy Mrs Mason. *OF* MT

Kate, servant girl at the Dunmore Inn who assists Mrs Kelly in running the establishment. *KOK* MRS

Katty, kitchen-girl at Ballycloran, one of two barefoot domestic helps who provides company for Feemy Macdermot. *MB* MRS

Keegan, Hyacinth, the 'oily attorney of Carrick' (II), whose foot is hacked off by three Ribbonmen in vengeance for his persecution of the Macdermots. Son-in-law of builder Joe Flannelly, and agent for absentee landlords, he is driven by ambition to become master of Ballycloran. Having turned Protestant to align himself with the English, the ruling powers in Ireland, he makes himself so hated and feared by the local Irish tenantry that he is finally driven out of Drumsna. *MB* MRS

Keegan, Sally, daughter of builder Joe Flannelly, who had offered her, together with the building of Ballycloran as dowry, to Larry Macdermot. Rejected by him on account of her lowly bloodline, she is subsequently married off to the attorney Hyacinth Keegan. Though she remains with him when he loses all and is forced to leave, their relationship is soured by battles over his attentions to other ladies. *MB* MRS

Kellogg, Clara Louise (Mme Strakosch) (1842–1916), celebrated opera singer who made her New York debut in *Rigoletto* in 1861 and first appeared in London in 1867. Meeting Trollope in Boston (1861) she found him 'filled with conceit', and wrote: 'Mr Trollope knew nothing of America, and did not seem to want to know anything. Certainly, English people when they are not thoroughbred can be very common! Trollope was full of himself and wrote only for what he could get out of it. I never, before or since, met a literary person who was so frankly "on the make". The discussion that afternoon was about the recompense of authors, and Trollope said that he had reduced his literary efforts to a working basis and wrote so many words to a page and so many pages to a chapter. He refrained from using the actual word "money"—the English shrink from the word "money"—but he managed to convey to his hearers the fact that a considerable consideration was the main incentive to his literary labour, and put the matter more specifically later, to my mother, by telling her that he always *chose the words that would fill up the pages quickest*' (*I & R* 80). RCT

Kelly, Jack, the 'family fool' (II) at Kelly's Court, a 'dirty, barefooted, unshorn, ragged ruffian' (II) who offers Captain Kelly, owner of property filched by Simeon Lynch, the pointed observation that 'I and the lord are both Sim's fools now' (II). *KOK* MRS

Kelly, Jane, youngest sister of Martin Kelly, who helps her mother and sister Meg run the

Dunmore Inn, where she befriends Anty Lynch, and tends to her during her illness. *KOK*   MRS

Kelly, John, older brother of Martin, an avowed Repealer, whose position as attorney's clerk in Dublin, where John O'Connell is being held, allows Trollope to frame his second Irish novel around an incident of Irish politics. *KOK*   MRS

Kelly, Larry, jockey from Roscommon, 'something under eight stone' (XVII), who rides at the Carrick races. *MB*   MRS

Kelly, Martin, avowed Repealer, youngest son of Mrs Kelly, and tenant of Lord Ballindine, who, while keeping a pragmatic eye on her fortune, falls in love with Anty Lynch. Like the novel's 'other hero' (X), Lord Ballindine, he is seen exercising little in the way of romance; instead, he is presented as son and brother, political observer, and shrewd tenant farmer. *KOK*   MRS

Kelly, Mrs Mary, industrious owner of the Dunmore Inn, and widowed mother of Martin, John, Mary, Jane, and Meg Kelly, a prudent but kindly woman who offers Anty Lynch safe refuge from her brother Barry. She 'could face the devil, if necessary, across her own counter' (VI), and virtually does when she faces down a blustering Barry Lynch. *KOK*   MRS

Kelly, Meg, sister of Martin Kelly, who helps her mother and sister Jane run the Dunmore Inn, where she befriends Anty Lynch, and furtively assists her courtship with her brother, Martin. *KOK*   MRS

Kellys and the O'Kellys, The (*see opposite*)

Kelly's Court, old, unkempt residence of the Kellys in Co. Roscommon, slowly 'humanize[d] . . . and civilized' by Captain Kelly, Lord Ballindine's father. *KOK*   MRS

Kemble, Frances Anne (1809–93), daughter of Drury Lane actors Charles and Theresa Kemble, herself a well-known actress, appearing with great success in Shakespearian roles. She began a series of Shakespeare readings (1848), and published several autobiographical works, poetry, and drama. In his Commonplace Book, Trollope included her *Francis the First: An Historical Drama* (1832) among five plays best representing contemporary drama.   RCT

Kennard, Edmund H. Captain Edmund Kennard, 'a young man of fortune in quest of a seat' (*Auto* XVI), was one of two Conservative candidates in the 1868 election at Beverley (N. Yorks), in which Trollope ran as a Liberal. When the polls closed, Sir Henry Edwards, Conservative incumbent, came in first, and Kennard second;

Trollope came last. When they arrived shouts of 'Bribery!' and 'We'll soon have you unseated' erupted, and rocks were thrown. Edwards and Kennard retreated 'only just in time to escape by a back street when the crowd rushed to meet them' (Hall 327).   RCT

Kenneby, John, one of two witnesses at the signing of Sir Joseph Mason's will, and a bookkeeper at Hubbles & Grease. Although not at all clever, Kenneby is a 'good, honest, painstaking fellow' (XXIV) who marries Mrs Smiley at his sister Mrs Moulder's bidding. *OF*   MT

Kennedy, Abraham, crippled brother of Daniel Kennedy, a man of keen intelligence responsible for making illicitly distilled whiskey. When Thady Macdermot is brought to the mountain retreat where he lives with his brother, he administers an oath of secrecy to Thady. *MB*   MRS

Kennedy, Daniel, Corney Dolan's partner in the illicit distilling of whiskey, whose cabin in the mountains of Aughacashel is used to conceal Thady Macdermot. A surly man whose 'desperate contempt of authority' is coupled with 'a cruelty of disposition' (XXII), he joins Joe Reynolds's brutal assault on Hyacinth Keegan. *MB*   MRS

Kennedy, Lady Laura (née **Standish**). Lady Laura Kennedy was thought by Trollope to be the best character in the two novels, *Phineas Finn* and *Phineas Redux*, in which she appears. She is the daughter of the Whig politician the Earl of Brentford and sister of Lord Chiltern, whose debts she uses her own fortune to pay; later, she is the wife of Robert Kennedy MP, philanthropist and millionaire. Laura instructs Phineas Finn, as a newcomer to Westminster, speaking without irony in the solemn terms used by men to describe their political business. But Laura does not seem to know how to live the life of a woman. When she does speak from the heart, to ask Phineas if he will make an effort to get to know her brother, she breaks down and weeps.

When Phineas proposes to her she has already made up her mind to accept Robert Kennedy, a disastrous decision, for Kennedy removes her from the social scene and subjects her to a dreary discipline of prayers and religious duties in the country. It takes the outrage of her subjection to the whims of a pedantic and tyrannical husband to rouse her to scepticism and irony. Even though she decides to leave Kennedy when he accuses her of inappropriate intimacy with Phineas, there can be no return for her to the life she enjoyed as a young woman: her father takes her away to a discreet exile in Europe. As for Phineas, (*cont. on page 290*)

TROLLOPE'S second novel, subtitled 'Landlords and Tenants', was published in 1848, a time of intense political ferment, with revolution in Europe, Chartist agitation in England, and struggles for national independence in Ireland. The politics of disaffection were reflected in such novels as Charlotte Brontë's *Jane Eyre* (1847) and Elizabeth Gaskell's *Mary Barton: A Tale of Manchester Life* (1848), 'agitational' novels designed to draw attention to the oppressions of women and of workers. Thus for Michael Sadleir *The Kellys and the O'Kellys* was, like *The Macdermots of Ballycloran*, too political in scope. Trollope's absorption in the Irish question, he complained, reduced the novel to little more than a pamphlet in fictional guise (139). Yet while the action of Trollope's novel is framed by the state trials in Dublin, 1844, of Daniel O'Connell and other prominent Repealers—and while its subtitle might anticipate a concern with Disraeli's infamous two Nations, the rich and the poor—*The Kellys* in fact offers a different kind of story, recalling robust Irish novelists like William Carleton rather than the reformist fiction of Brontë or Gaskell.

Principally about two courtships, and the important role of money in each, *The Kellys* pays tribute to the time-honoured, conservative wisdom that while it may be unconscionable to marry for money, it is impossible to marry happily without it. When Lord Ballindine, one of the novel's protagonists, protests 'that he was not going to marry Fanny Wyndham for her money', his mother promptly rejoins, 'but you know you could not marry her without the money' (XXXIX).

The Kellys traces the courtships of Martin Kelly (tenant) and Lord Ballindine, Frank O'Kelly (landlord), two handsome young men looking for wives and material advancement. Martin Kelly, youngest son of the industrious widow Kelly, a small innkeeper at Dunmore, Co. Galway, is a farmer, renting the lands of Toneroe from his distant relative Frank O'Kelly. Martin is engaged to Anastasia (Anty) Lynch, ten years older than himself, but with £400 a year of her own. After years of servitude living with her drunkard brother Barry Lynch and her father Simeon Lynch, Anty suffers from lack of self-esteem; but her generous and gentle nature endears her to the locals, as well as to Martin. However, when Sim Lynch, after having defrauded his absentee landlord, 'the O'Kelly', of a small estate (Dunmore House), quarrels with his son and leaves half his estate to her, Barry grows to hate his sister, especially when, in an unexpected show of independence, she employs Mr Moylan in his capacity as a legal agent to protect her interests. Enraged at the prospect of losing half his inheritance, Barry terrorizes his sister to prevent her marrying, threatening to put her in Ballinasloe madhouse and physically assaulting her. The servants, fearful for Anty's life, call on the Widow Kelly, who offers Anty safe keeping at the inn. Barry then resorts to Mr Daly, the attorney at Tuam, and the two concoct charges of conspiracy against the Kellys to intimidate them into returning Anty. Under these pressures, Anty falls dangerously ill. Using her deathbed privileges, she takes the opportunity to upbraid Barry; then, having voiced her recriminations, proceeds, significantly enough, to recover. Dismayed, Barry intimates to the physician, Dr Colligan, that he will be handsomely rewarded should Anty *not* recover from her illness.

Alongside these events, a parallel plot unfolds. Although determined to wed for money in order to finance his gambling and sport, Frank O'Kelly (Lord Ballindine) nevertheless falls in love with Fanny Wyndham. Her guardian, Lord Cashel of Grey Abbey, approves the match on condition that Frank give up his horses as proof he can live with Fanny on a modest income. Frank neglects to comply, but then, hearing the engagement has been broken off, visits Grey Abbey to make reparations, not knowing that the sudden death of Fanny's brother Captain Harry Wyndham has made her the sole heir of her father's estate, valued at £100,000. The sanctimonious Lord Cashel, misunderstanding Frank's motives in renewing his suit, dismisses him; but then speculates that his own son, the dissolute Lord Kilcullen, whose mounting debts threaten to bankrupt the Cashel estate, might well benefit from his ward's fortune. Lord Kilcullen proceeds, albeit reluctantly, to court Fanny, but instead she enlists Kilcullen's promise to help reunite her with her lover. With no prospect of winning Fanny's fortune, Lord Kilcullen, hounded by creditors, escapes abroad, but not before persuading his father to reconsider Frank's suit. Frank meanwhile enlists the help of the Revd Joseph Armstrong, who also appeals to Lord Cashel on Frank's behalf. A reconciliation ensues.

At this point in the novel, the two plots ostensibly merge as Dr Colligan, troubled by Barry's murderous proposals, decides to visit Grey Abbey to speak to Lord Ballindine, who is the local magistrate as well as a friend to the Kellys. Together, Dr Colligan, Frank, and the Revd Armstrong visit Barry, and, in return for waiving due process of law, insist that he write a letter not only agreeing to Anty's marriage and Martin's future management of the Kelly estate, but also promising to leave the country forever. Barry reluctantly consents, and finally settles at Boulogne. The novel concludes with a flurry of marriages and a glimpse of ensuing marital bliss, complete with well-stocked nurseries and prosperous estates.

In 1848 Trollope asked his mother, Frances Trollope, to offer *The Kellys* to her own publisher, Henry Colburn. It was accepted, but, like *The Macdermots*, on conditions Trollope considered unfavourable: no payment, except the promise of a half-share in profits from future sales. But Trollope agreed to the terms, and the novel came out as a three-decker in 1848. Like his first novel, it proved a financial loss, selling only 140 copies of 375 printed (*Auto* IX).

After Trollope's later successes with *The Warden* and *Barchester Towers*, Chapman & Hall agreed to reissue a second edition of the novel in one volume. This edition, printed in 1859, differed from the original three-decker only in its chapter breaks, with Trollope dividing chapters IV and VII of volume 1, chapter IX of volume 2, and chapter X of volume 3 into two chapters each.

Modern printings follow Chapman & Hall's second edition of 1859.

With publication of *The Kellys*, claimed Trollope, 'I made my first acquaintance with criticism' (*Auto* IV), after a friend solicited notice for the book from 'the gods of *The Times* newspaper'. Out of this significant first encounter came Trollope's vow that 'I would have no dealings with any critics on my own behalf', believing that to *request* critical notice was merely a prelude 'to crawling at the critic's feet'.

Trollope's own opinion was that *The Kellys* was inferior to *The Macdermots* in plot, but superior in the execution, a view with which most reviews concurred. The *Athenaeum* (July 1848) preferred the second novel to the first 'because though not more powerful, it is less painful' (Smalley 553). There was a general consensus that Trollope's tone had been leavened by the use of humour. *Douglas Jerrold's Weekly Newspaper* (July 1848) commented that '[a]ll readers who dislike to be wrought up to a pitch of strong sensation, and at the same time wish to be positively amused by a novel, will find the present work very much to their taste' (Smalley 554), while *Sharpe's London*

Magazine rather more drily noted that it was remarkably easy to read. There was also a general agreement that, as in *The Macdermots*, Trollope had produced a novel remarkably free 'from that outrageous exaggeration which is so common in sketches of Irish life and character' (Smalley 554). There were also complaints: *The Times*, the only review of *The Kellys* Trollope claimed to have read, deemed that, like mutton, the novel was 'substantial' but 'very *corse*' (Smalley 557).

The *Kellys* has not enjoyed the kind of critical reassessment accorded to *The Macdermots*: few articles have been devoted to it alone. It is, perhaps, most interesting as what Sadleir termed Trollope's 'prentice work'. Many of the qualities we associate with Trollope's mature writing are featured. *The Kellys* initiates Trollope's literary tendency to democratize his narrative focus: the singular concentration on a central protagonist that characterized *The Macdermots* moves to a narrative structure that disperses the reader's interest among several main characters in differing social milieux. The resulting structure in *The Kellys* is arguably less coherent than that of later works. But this fissure between plot-lines may also have been due to the demands of writing an 'Irish novel' which, unlike its English middle-class counterpart, emerges from a fragmented and historically unsettled context. Certainly the opening chapter, with its focus on the trial of prominent Irish Repealers for treason, underlines Ireland's state of national dis-union. From this point of view, without sustaining an overt concern with Irish politics, the novel may be said to thematize the 'condition of Ireland' indirectly through use of divided—and only tenuously united—plot-lines.

Characterization in *The Kellys* also anticipates directions in Trollope's later fiction. Frank O'Kelly, Lord Ballindine, undergoes a slow but carefully mapped transformation, not unlike Lord Silverbridge in Trollope's final Palliser novel, *The Duke's Children*, moving from recklessness to a heartfelt sense of responsibility. The feisty Mrs Kelly, an industrious widow struggling to do well for herself and her family, looks forward to hard-working female figures, such as Lady Carbury in *The Way We Live Now*, who straddle the gap between an ideology which confines women to the home, and economic necessity which brings them into the public domain. Similarly, though Anty Lynch and Fanny Wyndham are ostensibly constructed as feminine stereotypes, each displays moments of self-will and independence which not only prefigure such later characters as Lily Dale, but also highlight the debilitating conditions of women's subordination.

Barry Lynch is perhaps an experiment in genre that Trollope chose not to pursue. One of his few explicitly evil characters, compounded of Gothic touches of madness and sensationalist schemes to incarcerate his sister in a lunatic asylum, Barry is an alcoholic whose drinking fires his sense of injury to murderous rage. As in Anne Brontë's *The Tenant of Wildfell Hall* (1848), excessive consumption of alcohol is directly related to aggressive and destructive behaviour. Barry is the first of several of Trollope's male characters who inflict violence on a woman, anticipating representations of domestic violence in later novels. One of Trollope's accomplishments was to show how broader structures of power tended to construe women as weak and passive, subject to male will.

Readers taking up *The Kellys* after Trollope's tragically intense first novel will be entertained by its dialogue and ear for the vernacular. The charting of its twin love stories points to the course of much of his future storytelling. There is much to enjoy also in what was to become a regular theme, the clash of youth and age, conveyed here particularly in the relations of the Earl of Cashel and his son Lord Kilcullen. Like its predecessor the novel includes spirited horse riding, and the first of many fox-hunting scenes. The original manuscript is no longer extant.   MRS

he has already forgotten that he once loved Laura but she herself is now tormented by the intensity of her own response to him, a passion that she insists on imagining she can master. She returns to England in *Phineas Redux* after Robert Kennedy's death but despairs and withdraws into seclusion when Phineas marries Mme Max Goesler.   MH

Kennedy, Robert, Lady Laura Kennedy's austere, unbalanced husband. Though not born of an ancient family, he is enormously wealthy and has substantial land at his beautiful Scottish estate, Loughlinter. Given his fortune and his long-standing career as a Liberal member of Parliament, Mr Kennedy initially seems an ideal husband for the politically interested Lady Laura Standish, but his religious melancholy, his sternness, and his gloomy sense of responsibility combine to make him a tyrant to his young wife. A strict moralist, he attempts to discipline Lady Laura into his idea of appropriate Sunday behaviour: church twice a day, no novels, and no political discussion. At one time a gracious host, Mr Kennedy comes to desire a private, almost reclusive life for himself and his wife. When Lady Laura separates herself from him, Mr Kennedy's brooding tyranny escalates into madness and his body deteriorates at the same rapid pace as his mind. In *Phineas Redux*, his madness finally manifests itself when he shoots at Phineas Finn, whom he comes to believe is his wife's lover. Though violently angry with Lady Laura, Mr Kennedy maintains the generous settlements made upon her at their marriage, leaving her an immensely wealthy widow. *PF*   JMR

Kensal Green, site of first cemetery in London opened in 1832. Many famous people were buried here including Thackeray (1863), whose funeral Trollope attended. The cemetery is mentioned in *The Struggles of Brown, Jones, and Robinson*. Trollope was buried here on 9 December 1882 not far from Thackeray's grave.   HO

Kent, William Charles Mark (1823–1902), minor poet and journalist; editor of the *Sun* (1853–71). One of the Dickens circle, he helped organize the banquet at Freemasons' Hall, 2 November 1867, as a send-off for Dickens's American tour. Trollope was a slightly reluctant steward, saying to a correspondent, 'I am not specially in that set, but having been asked I did not like to refuse' (*Letters* 1, 397). In a speech he hailed Dickens as a great chieftain of literature. Kent reviewed *Sir Harry Hotspur of Humblethwaite* in the *Sun* (December 1870) and wrote an appreciative notice of Trollope's work in *Illustrated Review* (May 1871).   RCT

Kentucky, state in the front line of the Civil War, where the Reckenthorpes live in the capital, Frankfort. 'Generals' *LS*   GRH

Kept in the Dark (*see page 292*)

Kerrycullion, village near Castle Morony, the scene of a multiple political murder that decimates the Kelly family. *L*   MRS

Keswick, Cumberland town where Thomas Thwaite's tailor shop and Lovel Grange are located. *LA*   RC

Keswick Poet, the, one of the 'poets of the lakes, who had not as yet become altogether Tories' (IV). Friend of Thomas Thwaite, he leads a solitary and melancholy life. He counsels Daniel not to marry Lady Anna, comparing aristocrats to 'hothouse plants' and the tailor to 'a blade of corn out of the open field' (XXVI). *LA*   RC

Kilcullen, Lord Adolphus, dissipated son of Lord Cashel, a reckless gambler who, urged by his father, woos Fanny Wyndham for her wealth. Despite his reputation for heartless worldliness, she wins him over, and he helps reunite her with her lover Lord Ballindine, before creditors hound him out of the country. *KOK*   MRS

Killaloe, home of Phineas Finn, his parents, and his five sisters, in Co. Clare, Ireland. *PF*   JMR

Killancodlem, house of Mrs Montacute Jones in Scotland where she entertains lavishly and pursues her matchmaking ventures. Also in *The Duke's Children* where Lord Silverbridge proposes marriage to Isabel Boncassen. *IHP*   MG

Kimberley diamond mines, diamond fields in South Africa where John Gordon makes a fortune. *OML*   RC

Kinglake, Alexander William (1809–91), historian; author of *Invasion of the Crimea*, 8 vols. (1863–87), and the Oriental travel book *Eothen*
(*cont. on page 294*)

Agonies at the writing desk were frequent subjects for illustration. Here is one of the best examples, used as frontispiece for *Kept in the Dark* (1882). The artist was J. E. Millais, and the caption reads 'When the letter was completed, she found it to be one which she could not send' (V). Trollope's skilful deployment of letters illustrating character and event enrich the novels.

Tᴴɪꜱ late domestic study has a simple plot: girl jilts disreputable baronet, then marries more conventional man; husband discovers prior engagement and deserts her; they reconcile. Trollope focuses almost entirely on four main characters, with little attention to setting, action, or description.

Engaged to Sir Francis Geraldine, Cecilia Holt dismisses him for ignoring her. In Europe with her mother, she meets the 40-year-old George Western, recovering from being jilted. He tells Cecilia his story, but she never manages to tell hers either before or after their marriage. A friend, the marriage-hating Francesca Altifiorla, urges Cecilia to confess, but then the vengeful Sir Francis writes to Western, who, outraged and suspicious, leaves his wife and goes abroad. His widowed sister Lady Grant sympathizes with Cecilia, who has spurned Western's monetary support and returned to Exeter to live with her mother. Finally, Lady Grant brings her brother back from Dresden to reunite with Cecilia. In a comic sub-plot, Miss Altifiorla nearly traps Sir Francis into marriage through flattering and witty letters, though he manages to escape at the last minute.

Trollope seems mainly concerned with depicting the four main characters, who, though interesting, are not particularly sympathetic. The brooding George Western is perhaps the most intriguing: a shy, silent, almost middle-aged man of good but not large fortune, and a former MP who had found Parliament a waste of time, he has just been jilted by a beautiful, fortune-hunting girl when he finds, apparently for the first time, genuine happiness in the person of Cecilia. Impetuously he first believes Sir Francis's letter a lie, then accepts it as solemn truth even though aware of the writer's dubious character. Moreover, his wife's silences lead him to misread her character, as he invents a 'secret' between the two and even asserts that Cecilia had accepted his proposal when still engaged. Both his sister and his wife comment upon Western's stubborn unforgiving nature and his inflated moral sense; his enemy Sir Francis calls him, not without some justice, a prig.

Cecilia is perhaps more sympathetic, though one wonders about her taste in men. Her hesitancy in telling of her prior attachment seems generally reasonable, and she recognizes that she has been unjustly punished by desertion. With a pride typical of Trollope's heroines, she refuses Western's money and determines to elicit *his* apology rather than meekly to confess to wrongs greater than those she committed. While waiting for her husband to return, she dreams that their coming child will lead to a romantic reunion, though the actual reconciliation is far more prosaic, clearly illustrating Trollope's comment that 'the man is silent, not because he would not have the words spoken, but because he does not know the fitting words with which to speak. His dignity and his so-called manliness are always near to him, and are guarded, so that he should not melt into open ruth' (XVIII).

The two 'villains'—Jamesian villains though far less complex—remain fairly conventional, though fully revealed. A confirmed bachelor, interested mainly in horse racing, clubs, and male companions, Sir Francis wishes to marry only to preserve his considerable estates to his own line rather than have them pass to a detested cousin. Miss Altifiorla begins as a companion to Cecilia who warns against marriage, dabbles in the marriage market in pursuing Sir Francis, too loudly proclaims her engagement, and finally, having been jilted, decides to go to America to initiate a great movement to redress the wrongs of her sex.

Minor characters serve primarily as advisers and confidantes, although all the main characters are too stubborn and proud to take advice. Cecilia's three friends include Maude Hippesley, the Dean's daughter, who usually displays a common-sense approach to life; Mrs Green, a gossipy married lady, who reflects conventional attitudes toward marriage and wifely submission; and Miss Altifiorla, who speaks against marriage. Lady Grant and Mr Graham, Western's lawyer, both try, without much success, to convince the misguided husband of his unjust treatment. Even Sir Francis has his sycophants, including the impoverished Dick Ross, who finally leaves his benefactor over his attitudes toward women.

What may seem the obvious morals of the story—that marriage partners should not be kept in the dark about earlier attachments and that jilting can have serious social consequences—have little importance today; even one contemporary review called the tale 'much ado about nothing' (*British Quarterly Review*, January 1883; Smalley 501). These characters, indeed, make mountains out of molehills, though the extent of the mountains, in the form of Western's false allegations, is fascinating. More significant are Trollope's variations on the notion of duty. All the main characters speak of duty, generally personal rather than moral. For instance, Miss Altifiorla deems it dutiful for Cecilia to tell her husband her secret, but she then offers to tell it herself, more interested in her own role than in the truth. Likewise, Sir Francis says to Dick Ross, 'you have no idea of duty. . . . Now, if a man does me good, I return it,—which I deem to be a great duty, and if he does me evil, I generally return that sooner or later' (X).

George Western, disillusioned with love and politics, considers his actions as a duty to his own moral sense. His overriding sense of injustice that cannot be ignored or forgiven is, as his sister says, like 'a running sore; and, alas, it is not always an injustice, but a something that he has believed to be unjust' (XV). Even Cecilia has her personal motivation when she rails against the unfair treatment by her husband; yet her thoughts on the duty of husbands, later expressed in a letter to Western, ring the truest of any: 'As her husband had he a right so to dismiss her from his bosom? . . . As his wife she had a right to his care, to his presence, and to his tenderness. She had not married him simply to be maintained and housed. Nor was that the meaning of their marriage contract. Before God he had no right to send her away from him, and to bid her live and die alone. . . . But though he had no right he had the power' (XIII). At the end of the novel, however, she has 'softened' enough to accept her 'duty' as a wife and not to extract his forgiveness, thereby wounding his male pride.

Typically, too, Trollope creates a limited, interconnected world where society seems almost a fifth character. The interrelations of the main characters sometimes strain credibility but suggest this small world: Western has been jilted by a woman who marries a cousin of the Sir Francis Geraldine who had earlier wronged Western; Cecilia jilts Sir Francis, who takes up with Miss Altifiorla and then jilts her. Meanwhile 'the world of Exeter' reacts to all three engagements, 'everybody in Perth' knows that Lady Grant has gone to her brother in Dresden, and 'the aristocracy express[es] an opinion' about the supposed engagement of Sir Francis and Miss Altifiorla. Though neither of the Westerns seems concerned with the world's opinions—the deserted Cecilia returns to Exeter while George dismisses comments about what people will think of his actions—there are constant reminders that all society knows and judges one's actions.

The first notices of *Kept in the Dark* found the novel a typical and rather insignificant work. The *Athenaeum* called it 'an amusing "society" story, told in the well-known style of the author about whose health society is now genuinely anxious'; W. E. Henley in the *Academy* thought it 'interesting from the first line to the last'; the *Graphic* said it 'might be made the text of a criticism upon his style and process generally'; and the *Spectator* saw it as 'one of the least important of Mr Trollope's works [though] a very pleasant little book, altogether' (Smalley 497–500).

Comparatively little critical attention has been paid the short novel. Although A. O. J. Cockshut (*Anthony Trollope*, 1955) called it one of Trollope's misunderstood novels, James Pope Hennessy (*Anthony Trollope*, 1971) dismissed it as 'flimsy' and a 'potboiler'. Robert Tracy's *Trollope's Later Novels* (1978) treated it as a 'study of morbid reticence and self-delusion'.

Kept in the Dark, written from July to December 1880, was sold for £200 to *Good Words*, where it appeared in eight monthly parts from May to December 1882. Chatto & Windus published the book version, for which Trollope received £250, in two volumes, on 14 October, the last novel published during his lifetime. After a 'new edition' in 1891, it disappeared for nearly a century. A frontispiece by John Everett Millais, which had appeared in the serial, depicted Cecilia Holt in Rome composing a letter to Western. A manuscript of about two-thirds of the novel in the Hatcher Library of the University of Michigan shows some toning down of profanities requested by William Isbister of *Good Words*. NCS

(1844); fellow member of the Cosmopolitan Club. Kinglake would not involve himself with Trollope's Royal Literary Fund affairs, but agreed to donate (March 1878), 'mindful of the unnumbered hours of pleasure that I owe to your delightful books' (*Letters* 2, 767). RCT

Kingsbury, Clara, Marchioness of, aristocratic, cold wife of the Marquis. Affectionate only to her own three 'darling' sons, she fiercely resents her stepson Lord Hampstead, wishing him dead. Because of her idolatry of social prestige, she makes life miserable for the Marquis and his daughter Lady Frances when the latter falls in love with the clerk George Roden. MF   SRB

Kingsbury, Marquis of. Although once a radical himself, he deplores his son Lord Hampstead's even more democratic policies and his daughter Lady Frances's desire to marry a postal clerk. Now a valetudinarian, he quarrels with his wife Lady Clara; his petulance is exacerbated by Mr Greenwood, a former confidant who sides with Lady Clara against him. MF   SRB

Kingsley, Charles (1819–75), Christian Socialist; ordained (1842) and served at Eversley, Hampshire, the rest of his life; author of *Alton Locke* (1850) and the highly popular fantasy *The Water-Babies* (1863); stalwart campaigner for working poor. Trollope was a reluctant contributor to a memorial fund (February 1875) for restoration of his parish church and for a bust in Westminster Abbey. RCT

Kingsley, Henry (1830–76), author of sixteen novels and tales between 1863 and 1876; brother of Charles Kingsley; went to the Australian goldfields (1853–8) which provided materials for *Geoffrey Hamlyn* (1859) and *The Hillyars and the Burtons* (1865). *Ravenshoe* (1862) is his best-known novel. Kingsley was a beneficiary from the Royal Literary Fund while Trollope was associated with it. In May 1881 Trollope advised the daughter of Professor Charles Badham of the University of Sydney on novel-writing. Speaking from bitter experience he observed: 'historical novels do not at present pay.' Australia was still too narrow a sphere for a first novel, but 'if the Australian novel be good, men will read it,—as they did those of Henry Kingsley' (*Letters* 2, 908). In this letter Trollope shows his shrewd sense of the market and the beginner's task: 'the opinions of fathers and mothers and brothers *and sisters are worthless* . . . The cruel, hard-hearted, indifferent public must be the judge and you must fight your way before the judgment seat as best you may.' RCT

Kirkby Cliffe, Yorkshire home of the Lownd family. 'Kirkby'   GRH

Kirwan, Mrs, landlady of the inn, aggressive towards Archibald Green, though Father Giles's influence softens her attitude. 'Giles' *LS*   GRH

Knatchbull-Hugessen, Edward (1829–93), Liberal MP for Sandwich (1857); Lord of the Treasury (1859–60, 1860–6); Baron Brabourne (1880). One of those in the corridors of power with whom Trollope liked talking politics informally at the Cosmopolitan Club.   RCT

Knower, Mary (?1840–1931), daughter of Harriet, widow of Edmund Knower of Albany, New York. She met Trollope on board ship crossing the Atlantic to Liverpool (1859). Mary married Samuel Penniman, an oil-merchant (1866), and was herself widowed (1876). Trollope enjoyed a close friendship with her, as with several young women. When she was invited to Waltham (1860) he volunteered, 'I will be your humble slave, & come and fetch you at any time or point' (*Letters* 1, 98). She sent her picture, which adorned the bedroom wall. At her husband's death he recalled that first meeting: 'I can see her now, as she used to be then, just springing out of childhood—almost too young to be treated by one like myself otherwise than as a child' (*Letters* 2, 695).   RCT

Knowles, James Sheridan (1784–1862), prolific playwright and actor. His greatest success, a comedy, *The Hunchback*, played at Covent Garden in 1830. It was among the plays noted in Trollope's Commonplace Book.   RCT

Knox, Mr. The estate agent is the only one who hears regularly from the Marquis of Brotherton. Loyal to the family, rather than to the Marquis personally, he declares he will quit rather than enforce some of his employer's decrees. *IHP*
    MG

Knox, Father Ronald Arbuthnott (1888–1957), ordained Catholic priest, 1919; chaplain at Oxford (1926–39); writer of light verse, six detective stories, and Trollopian *jeu d'esprit Barchester Pilgrimage* (1935). His essay 'A Ramble in Barsetshire', with a map, drawing attention to *Framley Parsonage* as *locus classicus* of Barset geography, is in *Essays in Satire* (1928) (see Maps, p. 615). His tribute in *London Mercury* (February 1920) epitomizes the appeal Trollope held for the post-First World War generation: 'Trollope's rose-hued world, like a cloistral port . . . is all the better for keeping; Barchester, caught once for all by the artist's brush in a moment of mellow sunset, lives on, uncontaminated by change, in that attitude' (*I & R* 59).   RCT

Königsgraaf, beautiful German castle in the Alps on the river Elbe, belonging to the Marquis of Kingsbury. His daughter Lady Frances is brought here by the Marchioness to separate her from her inappropriate suitor George Roden, the postal clerk. *MF*   SRB

Königstein, fortress close to Lord Brentford's home in Dresden, the scene of Laura Kennedy's dramatic confession to Phineas Finn that she loves him. *PR*   JMR

Krapp, Suse, wild fruit gatherer and general supplier to Frau Frohmann, who reasons with her about prices. 'Frohmann' *WFF*   GRH

L

Lacordaire, M. de, middle-aged suitor of Fanny Thompson, attentive, courteous, soft. He proposes to her with trepidation because he is 'tailleur'. 'Polignac' *TAC1*　　　　　　GRH

'Ladies in the Hunting Field' (letter). The fears expressed by 'Paterfamilias' regarding ladies hunting are groundless. Good exercise, the excitement of a hard run, and occasional falling are the truths of hunting. Bloody accidents and improper behaviour are extremely rare. *Pall Mall Gazette* (28 February 1865), 3.　　　　AKL

Lady Anna (*see opposite*)

'Lady of Launay, The', first serialized in *Light*, 6 April 1878 to 11 May 1878 (reprinted in *WFF*). Bessy Pryor, a penniless orphan, has been brought up as a daughter of the household by Mrs Miles, mistress of Launay Park. Her foster-brother Philip Miles, the future heir to the Launay property, falls in love with Bessy. Mrs Miles, after trying to arrange a marriage between her ward and the Revd Alexander Morrison, 'banishes' Bessy to a friend's household in Normandy. Finally, the good-hearted old woman overcomes her snobbish objections and consents to the match. Bessy becomes Lady of Launay apparent.　　　　　　　　　　　　　JS

Lafayette, Marie-Joseph, marquis de (1757–1834), French statesman whose contributions to liberty in America and France earned him the title of 'hero of two worlds'. He served the American cause after the Declaration of Independence, urged moderation after the French Revolution, and supported freedom movements wherever they occurred. Mrs Trollope and her husband met this charismatic figure through Fanny Wright in 1823. Lafayette invited the Trollopes to his country estate, La Grange, where, as Mrs Trollope noted in her journal, they were royally entertained. Lafayette dined with them at their farewell dinner given by Wright in Paris in 1824. Of Lafayette, Mrs Trollope wrote: 'Never did I meet with a being so every way perfect' (Hall 21). When Mrs Trollope embarked on the disastrous scheme hatched by Fanny Wright for the Nashoba commune in Tennessee, Lafayette marvelled 'at the determination of a London lady to make herself a forest pioneer' (Mullen 49). However, with the publication of *Domestic Manners of the Americans* (1832), relations with the General deteriorated. Her son's one historical novel, *La Vendée*, included Lafayette. Trollope drew on his mother's manuscript (Trollope MS, University of Illinois).　　　　　　RCT

Lahinch, village at the southern end of Liscannor Bay where Fred Neville keeps the canoe in which he 'adventures' along the Clare coast. *EE*　　　　　　　　　　　　　　　　　　AWJ

'La Mère Bauche', first published in *Tales of All Countries: First Series*. Bauche, stern proprietor of a hotel in the French Pyrenees village of Vernet, is affronted when her favourite son Adolphe falls in love with a charity girl whom she has taken in, Marie Calvert. Adolphe is sent away and Mme Bauche arranges a 'suitable' marriage between Marie and Theodore Campan, known as 'le Capitaine'. Campan is ancient, unappealing, and has a wooden leg. Adolphe returns. It is clear he no longer loves her enough to defy his mother, and Marie throws herself from a cliff to her death.　　　　　　　　　JS

landed gentry, old. Trollope's treatment of the landed gentry, while often critical, tends to be sympathetic. His affectionately satirical portrait of the Thornes of Ullathorne, for instance, is warm towards the Thornes themselves, even though it pokes fun at their 'Anglo-Saxon attitudes' (*BT* XXII). However, one should be mindful of the distinction, in Trollope's earlier fiction at least, between Saxon and Norman ancestry. Trollope, as with many novelists writing in the wake of Sir Walter Scott, has more satirical fun at the expense of the old Norman families than he does with good Anglo-Saxon stock. Hence, in *Barchester Towers*, his satirical gibes at Lady De Courcy are more pointed than those at the Thornes; the De Courcy family is again mocked throughout *Doctor Thorne* and *The Small House at Allington*. Nevertheless, the Barset novels as a
(*cont. on page 298*)

TROLLOPE's thirtieth novel works intricately on tensions of social status, legality, and justice. In it an earl's granddaughter, courted by both a radical Lake District tailor with whom she has grown up and a handsome young aristocrat to whom she is greatly attracted, eventually marries the tailor. Trollope was quite pleased with himself over the outrage some readers felt at this turn of events: 'If I had not told my story well, there would have been no feeling in favour of the young lord. The horror which was expressed to me at the evil thing I had done, in giving the girl to the tailor, was the strongest testimony I could receive of the merits of the story' (*Auto* XIX). Legal validation of class plays a large part in *Lady Anna*, and zealous lawyers abound. But much as Trollope loves the accepted structures of British life, this time victory seems to go to the unconventional: an aristocratic lady marrying a tailor, and helped in her course by an opposing lawyer, Sir William Patterson, who, unlike most of Trollope's lawyers, seeks accommodation and the general good. However, both Lady Anna and Sir William are motivated by the Trollopian lodestar of truth: Lady Anna true to her early love, the tailor, and Sir William to an inner vision of justice—'some romantic idea of abstract right', as a hostile colleague puts it (XXXIII).

Married for six months, Earl Lovel, owner of a diminished estate near Keswick, tells his wife Josephine that their marriage is illegitimate, he being already married to a woman in Italy. Leaving the Countess, his wife, with their daughter Anna, he returns to Italy. To establish what is legitimate, the Countess prosecutes him for bigamy, but he is acquitted and the status of her marriage left in doubt. In their poverty, the Countess and Anna are supported for many years by Keswick's tailor, Thomas Thwaite. Anna grows up with and loves his son Daniel. The Earl returns with an Italian woman, Signorina Camilla Spondi, and soon dies, bequeathing his large personal property to her, his impoverished land going by entail to a distant heir, Frederick Lovel. Most of the novel deals with sorting out the legal intricacies of this complicated situation. (Among Trollope's papers in the Bodleian Library is a sheet of paper on which, in parallel columns, he asks questions about the legal niceties and receives answers from a legal consultant.) The Earl's will is contested. If it can be set aside because the Earl was mad, Frederick, now the Earl, may inherit everything. However, if the Countess can prove her marriage and thus the legitimacy of her daughter Anna, he will inherit only the land, the Countess a widow's portion, and Anna all the rest, a major fortune.

The Countess and Sir William dominate the novel. Another Trollopian study in obsession, the Countess, grimly determined to claim her status, would like to reject the tradesman Thwaites, who had supported her in her poverty. Incensed at the idea of Anna marrying Daniel and thus confounding the social hierarchy she has striven to maintain, the Countess even goes to the length of shooting him. It suits both Trollope's and Sir William's ideas of social rightness that the young Earl should have the wealth to support his estate. It seems appropriate to Sir William, acting for Lord Lovel, that Lady Anna should marry him, thus conveniently combining their property. And Anna herself finds Frederick attractive. The complicated drama of class and personal honour is indicated in Lady Anna's comment: 'I am ashamed to marry Mr Thwaite,— not for myself, but because I am Lord Lovel's cousin and mamma's daughter. And I should be ashamed to marry Lord Lovel . . . Because I should be false and ungrateful!' (XXII). However, in the end, when the Countess's marriage is accepted as legitimate and Lady Anna inherits her father's personal fortune, she gives half of it to Lord Lovel but marries Daniel.

Perhaps the most interesting character in the book is the Solicitor-General, Sir William Patterson. The other barristers—Mr Hardy for the Earl, Serjeant Bluestone for the Countess—are vehement and combative, Mr Hardy 'a gruff man' who 'hated compromise and desired justice', and Serjeant Bluestone 'a very violent man, taking up all his cases as though the very holding of a brief opposite to him was an insult to himself' (V). Sir William is suave, a public-school man, a believer in the social hierarchy, comfortably at home with 'the right sort'. Though he starts out with the bracing determination to 'make mince-meat of the Countess' and cross-examine her 'off her legs, right out of her claim, and almost into her grave' (III), and considers the notion of Lady Anna marrying a tailor as 'a grievous injury to the social world of his country' (XX), his sense of poetry, romance, and rightness leads him to champion accommodation and compromise, to the outrage of his colleagues and the general curiosity of the legal community. He ignores legal etiquette, holds irregular meetings with the opposing parties, and seems, awful thought, to be acting for the general good rather than simply for his own client. The bemused legal establishment speculates that he will ruin his career. Unusual among Trollope's barristers in following inner light and conviction, in the end he manages everyone and everything in the light of 'truth', and establishes harmony, which culminates in his benignly furthering the marriage of Daniel and Lady Anna.

Lady Anna plays subtly with social constructions, status, and conflicts of value and validation both in the legal and general social worlds. Though not much discussed, it deserves a place among Trollope's more interesting novels.

Written wholly on shipboard during Trollope's trip to Australia in 1871, *Lady Anna* was serialized in the *Fortnightly Review*, April 1873 to April 1874, and published in two volumes by Chapman & Hall, May 1874. The manuscript is in the Robert H. Taylor Collection, Princeton. RDM

Edwards, P. D., *Anthony Trollope: His Art and Scope* (1978).
McMaster, R. D., *Trollope and the Law* (1986).

whole display a fondness towards the old landed gentry, nowhere better exemplified than in the famous eulogy to feudalism in the opening chapter of *Doctor Thorne*: 'England is not yet a commercial country in the sense in which that epithet is used for her; and let us still hope that she will not soon become so. She might surely as well be called feudal England, or chivalrous England. If in western civilized Europe there does exist a nation among whom there are high signors, and with whom the owners of the land are the true aristocracy, the aristocracy that is trusted as being best and fittest to rule, that nation is the English' (I). This nostalgic, conservative narrative perspective ensures that even the villainous Nathaniel Sowerby of *Framley Parsonage* is treated sympathetically in the depiction of his frittering away Chaldicotes, the family property;

and often in Trollope's fiction, the challenges faced by old landed families in the face of the immense social upheaval of the mid-19th century are represented in financial terms, as the old squirearchy, like Sowerby and the Greshams of *Doctor Thorne*, find the sheer cost of maintaining the family property ruinously expensive. However, the difficulty of adjustment faced by the old families is also portrayed in generational terms, as the sons and daughters of the squirearchy pose, in various ways, problems of inheritance. The law of entail, for instance, in which the present owner is legally merely the custodian of the property for future generations, is the cause of a great deal of anxiety for Trollope's squirearchy: thus, in *Ralph the Heir*, Squire Newton is desperate to ensure that the property of Newton Priory will not fall into the hands of his dissolute nephew Ralph; therein also, in *Doctor Thorne*, lies the need for Frank Gresham to marry money in order to ensure continuance of the property, in the face of the threat from the arriviste Scatcherd family. Similar problems underpin the plots of *Cousin Henry* and *Mr Scarborough's Family*. Often, however, it is the different cultural expectations of the younger generation from the older that form the basis of narrative interest: this is true of the Longestaffes in *The Way We Live Now*, and also of Plantagenet Palliser and his children in *The Duke's Children*. In each case, the determination of the younger family members to marry whom they please does not necessarily threaten the property as such; what *is* threatened, however, is a way of life and the cultural values that sustain it. HO

Landleaguers, The (*see next page*)

Landon, Letitia Elizabeth (L.E.L.) (1802–38), famous poet and novelist, whose best novel was probably *Ethel Churchill* (1837). Her mysterious death by prussic acid two months after marrying George Maclean, Governor of Cape Coast, Ghana, made her notorious. Subsequent inquiries could not establish whether she died by accident, suicide, or murder. When the Trollope fortunes briefly improved after publication of *Domestic Manners of the Americans* (1832), Landon was one of his mother's 'dear friends among literary people' (*Auto* II). Trollope knew her work. Considering Kate Field's poetry he suggested how few succeeded: 'What is the reputation of Poe or Holmes, or [our] own L. E. L.? What good have they done?' (*Letters* 1, 171). RCT

Landor, Walter Savage (1775–1864), poet, essayist, and literary lion, who may have inspired Trollope to offer George Smith in 1865 'Imaginary Meditations' for *Pall Mall Gazette*. Smith accepted one, 'Napoleon on the Death of Morny', *Pall Mall Gazette* (March 1865). In 1860 in Rome Trollope called on the 85-year-old Landor with Tom. Landor also met Kate Field at this time and, like Trollope, was smitten by her, saying she was the most charming young lady he had ever seen. RCT

Landseer, Edwin Henry (1802–73), landscape painter and portraitist, best known for animal paintings, such as *The Monarch of the Glen*. Landseer formed part of Trollope's social milieu from the 1860s; he was present at the farewell banquet for Charles Dickens at the Freemasons' Hall (November 1867) prior to his reading tour in America, when Trollope toasted Dickens as 'a great chieftain' (*I & R* 100 n.). RCT

Langalibalele (1813–89), chief of the Hlubi tribe, a clan of about 10,000 people. In 1873 Langalibalele had refused to appear before British authorities in Natal, who then pursued him, with bloodshed on either side. Under house arrest near Cape Town, he requested that his 70 wives and numerous children be allowed to join him. Bishop Colenso supported him. Trollope devoted chapter XVIII to Langalibalele in *South Africa* (1878), agreeing that his disobedience had to be punished for opposing British law. Similarly, the 'troublesome old Pagan' was not to be allowed to go against marriage laws: 'it could hardly be that Exeter Hall and the philanthropists should desire to encourage polygamy by sending such a flock of wives after the favoured prisoner.' Visiting the captured chieftain at his farmhouse he found 'a stalwart man . . . in whose appearance one was able to recognize something of the Chieftain' (XVIII). RCT

Langford, Joseph Munt (1809–84), drama critic; head of Blackwood's London branch; Cosmopolitan and Garrick Club friend of Trollope's; 'Joe' in correspondence negotiating business concerning his books. Langford helped arrange the partnership of Trollope's son Henry with Chapman & Hall and was in the know over his involvement with a woman (1872) which resulted in Henry's hasty departure for Australia. RCT

language and style of Trollope. According to Henry James, 'with Trollope we were always safe' (*Partial Portraits* (1888), 100), so safe that 'to become involved with one of his love stories is very like sinking into a gentle slumber' (*Nation*, January 1886, 21). Trollope might have been amused at this sneer, recognizing in it the risk he was running in developing a language so perfectly transparent that it might indeed seem to the unwary simply to be nothing more than 'safe', a language so at home with itself as to be snoozing. This language appears not to be 'working' at all, a language we would take in through our pores, it would seem, without noticing the process or even noticing that it *was* language. It was language, somehow, without style, 'dribbled into the reader's intelligence . . . in such manner that he shall himself be insensible to the process' (*IHP* I). For hostile or inattentive readers, such art would seem artless in the worst sense: naive, complacent, hardly written at all.

It is a style brilliantly crafted to seem uncrafted: its characteristic tone is chummy, inviting ease. It appears to ask for so little that, like a very old and dear friend, we scarcely notice that it is around, even when it truly is asking for a very

(*cont. on page 301*)

TROLLOPE's last novel was a labour of love and sorrow which took him back to his beloved Ireland, now entering its most troubled phase since the potato famine (1845–7). In failing health he took two exhausting trips with his amanuensis Florence Bland, the first mid-May to mid-June 1882, the second mid-August to early September. The impetus was to write, he told Richard Bentley, on the condition of the country, which seemed lamentable (*Letters* 2, 957). Thus political themes were to shape a plot, which centres on the family of Philip Jones, an English Protestant landlord in Co. Galway, and his neighbouring landowners beset by a wave of violence and agitation led by the Irish nationalists and backed by Irish-American sympathizers in the cause of Home Rule. Jones has a 400-acre (160-ha) estate by Lough Corrib and when sluice gates are secretly opened, flooding part of his land, he faces ruin. His 10-year-old son Florian, a convert to Catholicism, witnessed the sabotage, but is afraid to tell what he knows. When, by the end of the first volume, Florian has named the saboteurs to the investigating authorities led by Captain Yorke Clayton his death is certain, and he is shot and killed (XXX).

A secondary romantic plot, which at first reading seems far removed from the political concerns of the novel, involves Rachel O'Mahony, an American opera singer, daughter of Gerald O'Mahony, who has come over from New York to support the fight against the English oppressors. Rachel falls in love with Frank Jones, eldest son of Philip Jones, but their romance is checked by the family's misfortunes. The ramifications of this sub-plot take the reader to London's theatreland where, in scenes quite risqué for Trollope, Rachel gets involved with a sleazy singer-impresario, Mahomet M. Moss, and a womanizing stage-door johnny, Lord Castlewell. Further love interests are introduced by Clayton's involvement with Jones's two daughters Ada and Edith. How the story was to have been developed is known from what Trollope's son Henry Merivale added to the uncompleted manuscript: Clayton would have married Edith Jones and Frank Jones would have married Rachel O'Mahony. One of the most vicious terrorists, Terry Lax, was to hang for the murder of young Florian.

Sixty chapters were intended, and Trollope completed 48 before his stroke on 3 November 1882. Trollope had approached Bentley for publication in *Temple Bar* for £400 (March 1882), but Bentley declined. The novel was serialized in *Life* (16 November 1882–4 October 1883). A £600 agreement for book publication with Chatto & Windus had to be renegotiated by Henry Trollope for the unfinished book at £480.

The book's reception was not enthusiastic, the *Spectator* calling it 'a long pamphlet, under the guise of fiction' (Smalley 518), a view that has persisted. Polemic is certainly prominent, one chapter, 'The State of Ireland' (XLI), being devoted to Irish politics. Trollope was disaffected with Gladstone's Irish policy, loathed the nationalist leader, Charles Stewart *Parnell, and, like most Englishmen, was enraged at the Phoenix Park murders of the Chief Secretary for Ireland, Lord Frederick Cavendish, and his deputy, Thomas Burke, a few weeks before he began the novel. In its favour some have praised the gathering sense of doom involving the boy Florian, and the spreading fears of terrorism among the community of mainly decent citizenry, as relevant today as in Trollope's time. The apparatus of terrorism is well conveyed. Fear keeps people silent. 'There must be some terrible understanding among them, some compact for evil, when twenty men are afraid to tell what one man has been seen to do' (IV). Trollope even manages to convey some supernatural impulse to the moral disease, from the very soil of Ireland he knew so well. 'All the want of evidence in this country', says Clayton, desperately trying to enforce the law, 'comes from belief in the marvellous' (XXXIX). Some critics have been inclined to dismiss the sexually daring section of the novel involving Rachel O'Mahony in London, although it contains some lively, spirited writing. Rachel speaks her mind with a freedom never given to earlier heroines. 'I am a singing girl; but I don't mean to be any man's mistress' (XXVIII). As Mary Hamer has noted, this is part of a world rapidly undergoing transformation, gender difference being one glaring example (introd. to World's Classics edition, 1993). Tony Bareham has argued that Trollope's concern with responsibility in private and public spheres unifies the seemingly dissimilar plots. This is no broken-backed novel as early critics argued. In fact the theatre plot was an inspiration. All the operatic excesses, such as Rachel brandishing her knife, counterpoint the Grand Guignol of Yorke Clayton's world of masked men and assassins. Trollope portrays a mad world where traditional values are turned upside down. With the Phoenix Park and Joyce murders happening even as he writes, Trollope is in the midst of a world gone mad, of alienating politics and domestic disorder. Sons will betray fathers and daughters will take on parental authority. In despair Trollope imposes order on events out of control by having Rachel lose her voice. The projected end restoring harmony and normal human ties was never completed.

Another aspect of the novel worth noting is the pleasure Trollope evinces from old haunts and memories, displayed in several in-jokes. At one point a 'little bill' is mentioned, which recalls his dealings with moneylenders in early days (VII). His old groom Barney is recalled in a character's name (XX). An angry old gentleman is glimpsed scolding a porter (VI), recalling Trollope's temper tantrums as a traveller. Rachel's admission that she is very fond of eating is much Trollope's own sentiment. Rachel brings back memories of lively Americans like the real-life Kate Field. The voice of his niece Bice is surely being remembered in Rachel as opera singer. Letters to Rose at this time show how deeply the return to Ireland affected him, both from reminders of mutual pleasures and poignant homesickness. 'How is the garden, and the cocks & hens, & especially the asparagus bed', he writes in June 1882 (*Letters* 2, 966). At one point Trollope seems to be talking directly to Rose. 'In all those ways of giving aid, which some women possess and some not at all,—but which, when possessed, go far to make the comfort of a house,—she was supreme' (XL). The incomplete novel was published by Chatto & Windus, 1883. The manuscript is in the Robert H. Taylor Collection at Princeton.   RCT

Bareham, Tony, 'First and Last: Some Notes towards a Reappraisal of Trollope's *The Macdermots of Ballycloran* and *The Landleaguers*', *Durham University Journal*, 47 (1986), 311–17.

great deal. This transparency is, of course, the goal of low-mimetic realism, a realism which rejects show and mere 'literary' convention in order to portray 'real life'. Hating the 'exaggerations' of Dickens, Mrs Stowe, and Rhoda Broughton, even of his own mother's fiction, Trollope, like most of his contemporaries, claimed he was writing life itself.

But such 'life', Trollope saw, did not offer itself easily to language, was, in fact, to be reproduced only by being artfully created. Trollope did not, in other words, mistake realism for 'the real' or imagine that a plain language would give us immediate access to something called 'life'. Realism, for him, was a convention very difficult to capture and employ, certainly not available by copying life or holding a mirror up to everyday speech: 'And yet in very truth the realistic must not be true—but just so far removed from truth as to suit the erroneous idea of truth which the reader may be supposed to entertain.' Realism is defined as 'that which shall seem to be real' (*T* IX), a *seeming*, of course, which only the most skilled writer can produce.

Such 'seeming-to-be-real' realism was to be obtained, Trollope argued, primarily through a careful use of language. One must not, as Scott so often did, 'leave on the mind of the most un-practised reader a sensation of made up words'. Instead, the writer must locate a language so carefully constructed around a reader's idea of reality that the language itself will seem to be-come transparent. The style will be so artfully developed as to disappear, creating the illusion of a direct participation with 'reality', not with 'made up words' but with a world unmediated by words.

This idea of clarity is inseparable, then, from ideas of rhetoric: when Bell, in *The Small House at Allington*, tells her mother, 'I like a book to be clear as running water, so that the whole mean-ing may be seen at once,' Mrs Dale answers, 'The quick seeing of meaning must depend a little on the reader, must it not?' (XLIV). It is remarkable, then, that Trollope's transparency can work so well with so many readers, given that the illusion of reality is so rhetorical, so dependent on the novelist's ability to form through language just the reader he wants and to make us into that reader.

When we think of how often artists like Dick-ens asked their language to do what it could not, it is astonishing how seldom Trollope's style fails to provide for him the transparency he wants. There are times in *La Vendée*—'female beauty and female worth will be made to suffer ten thousand deaths from the ruthless atrocities of republican foes' (XIV)—and in *Nina Balatka*—'She is to me my cup of water when I am hot and athirst' (VI)—when Trollope depends on style to give a certain foreign flavour, and the results are ludicrous enough. Trollope mastered a disap-pearing style and generally knew better than to ask it to appear and to work for him.

He achieves his effects largely through a uni-form and plain style, a liberal use of what David Aitken calls 'imprecise, multi-purpose words like "pretty"' that appear to make no special de-mands on us and claim no attention (' "A Kind of Felicity": Some Notes about Trollope's Style', *NCF* (March 1966), 337–53). The same may be said for his use of offhand non-specific cover-terms like 'thing', 'someone', 'they', and easy qualifiers like 'probably'. The style is so unmeta-phoric that the very rare bursts—'the air was as soft as a mother's kiss to her sleeping child' (*VB* II)—are startling. Even passages of analysis tend to mask their art by leading us, at their climax, to the styleless comfort of a proverbial saying about touching pitch and being defiled, the wind being tempered to the shorn lamb, and the like.

Very often the simple, unpretentious diction allows for and hides a syntax that is repetitious and thus obviously arranged, artificial: ' "Because you have been bad," say those who are not bad to those who are bad' (*VB* LII). The bald repetitions alert us to the simple-mindedness of what is to come. This deceptively plain language can be used to make the most intricate artistic man-œuvrings unobtrusive—psychological probing and analysis, for instance: 'And though, after a fashion, [Lizzie] knew herself to be false and bad, she was thoroughly convinced that she was ill-used by everybody about her' (*ED* XXI). The easygoing 'after a fashion' tells us, without seem-ing to, how Lizzie can hold contradictory notions in her mind; it indicates levels of consciousness with quiet delicacy.

In a similar way, the Duke's anger at his wife's vulgar transformation of Gatherum Castle is analysed: 'It angered him to think that there was so little of simplicity left in the world that a man could not entertain his friends without such a fuss as this. His mind applied itself frequently to the consideration of the money, not that he grudged the loss of it, but the spending of it in such a cause. And then perhaps there occurred to him an idea that all this should not have been done without a word of consent from himself' (*PM* XIX). As the Duke's thoughts proceed from the blandly general to the intensely personal, the sentences become more roundabout, circumlo-cutionary. The first motive stated is easy, flatter-ing, and directly available to his mind: 'It angered him.' The second is more difficult, brings up troubled associations (since some of the money was originally Glencora's): 'His mind applied itself frequently to the consideration' (as if the mind were doing it on its own). The last issue, the inner circle, is at the heart of his di-lemma and the secret power struggle he is en-gaged in with his wife: 'And then perhaps there occurred to him an idea.' The layers of the Duke's mind, from the outer shell of public mor-ality to the inner doubts of his own position, are exposed with great suggestiveness. And with fine indirectness: notice how much that 'perhaps' in the last sentence does for Trollope and for us. A writer more self-consciously 'psychological' would have required several sentences to accom-plish the work of that 'perhaps'.

Style is seen by Trollope, then, as a means for creating an illusion, particularly the illusion that there is no style. Language, he would have us believe, does not so much create as serve; in *The Duke's Children* style is spoken of as a mere 'vehicle' for the important wares (XXVI). The wares in this case are the details of the pure story: 'Now among us plain English,' Trollope said, 'a plain narrative, whether in verse or prose, is everything.' The idea is that style should clear the way for and not get in the way of the narrative, as if the narrative existed somehow before or outside language. This is hocus-pocus, of course, but Trollope pulls it out of the hat.

One notices, for instance, how unlike the typical materialist, *seen* world of conventional realism Trollope's worlds are. Typically, in realism, we are shown a crowded world that presses on us its reality by convincing us of the reality of the objects in it. Trollope's world, however, is much more aural than visual; a less cinematic art would be difficult to imagine.

Trollope does seem materialistic in the loose sense: he admires money. Really, though, he admires the getting of money, not the thing itself, admires ambition. His materialism, in other words, is really non-objective. With important objects like Gatherum Castle, the symbolism is made to work psychologically and not physically. The Castle is the cluster of associations it calls forth: fear, worship, awe, envy, hatred, discomfort. None of these being has any compelling reference to its physical being, nor does Trollope expect us to be able to draw a map of it, to see it. It exists as a matter of affect, rhetorically, created by a language which is non-mimetic, working through us and not the external world.

There is rarely much sense of setting—'I myself cannot describe places,' Trollope lamented—and even less of physical objects. People are there, of course, but they are defined by their talk. Talk becomes about the only objective correlative in Trollope. That is why the narrator, the best talker of all, is such an important character.

And it is this narrator, often disruptive and deliciously self-reflexive, who best illustrates the artistry of Trollope's disappearing style. Were the narrator less convincingly chummy, he would give the game away. As it is, his sharpest observations are so lightly couched that we do not notice the sting. Trollope's narrators employ a language so companionable and confidential that the subversive effects come on us unawares. Frank O'Connor observed that Trollope's narrator's 'favorite device is to lead his reader very gently up the garden path of his own conventions and prejudices and then to point out that the reader is wrong' ('Trollope the Realist', in *The Mirror in the Roadway: A Study of the Modern Novel*, 1956). We are, further, often nudged,

against our conscious knowledge and probably against our will, into accepting a most extraordinary value system.

Perhaps the clearest example is found in *Barchester Towers*, where the apparently friendly and chatty narrator is used with great subtlety, and we are induced to relax into heightened insight. The narrator works from the beginning to establish a surface rhetoric of intimacy and relaxation. 'Our doctrine', he says, 'is, that the author and the reader should move along together in full confidence with each other' (XV). The point of this comment and, to a large extent, of the novel itself is that we are all of us men, whether bishops, archdeacons, authors, or readers. This levelling language denies explicitly the author's special claim to knowledge and authority, and also appears to deny his fiction the prerogative to surprise, lecture, and edify. On the first level, the rhetoric works by direct flattery, giving the sense that we—the author and the reader—are undeluded, tolerant, realistic, and not bamboozled, as are the characters, by power of position. Such easy language gives us no choice but to accept its terms and we find ourselves relaxing our cautions and identifying with the novel's most important point: that the joy of life comes in renouncing power and its corollary notions of progress and in accepting the common, the kindly, and the established. Unlike most moral comedies, where the dominant mode is attack and where the reader is asked to sharpen his critical faculties, here we are asked not to be so eager to judge. The tactful comedy involving Mr Quiverful and the wardenship, for instance, makes just this point. Trollope establishes the entirely understandable impatience of Mrs Quiverful with her husband's apparent 'sentimental pride' and over-scrupulousness. At the same time, he shows the equally understandable judgement of 'the outer world' that Mr Quiverful was rapacious and dishonourable. The narrator concludes, 'It is astonishing how much difference the point of view makes in the aspect of all that we look at' (XXIV). This moderate, kindly prose asks for a matching moderation and kindness from us.

At the same time, this soothing language is promoting, beneath the surface, a startling set of values. For instance, the narrator early injects some facetious complaints about sermons: 'There is, perhaps, no greater hardship at present inflicted on mankind in civilized and free countries, than the necessity of listening to sermons. No one but a preaching clergyman has, in these realms, the power of compelling an audience to sit silent, and be tormented' (VI). He goes on through a rather long paragraph on this 'bore of the age', using direct language to effect the expansive, unbuttoned attitude in the reader that can recognize the experience as a common one and respond to that recognition with laughter.

The next paragraph begins in the same vein, and the reader is encouraged to lean back and companionably agree some more. But the tone and direction are quietly changed. The 'preaching clergyman' becomes 'the young parson', 'my too self-confident juvenile friend', 'my insufficient young lecturer', and the attack is shifted from the general target of boring preachers to the quite specific one of ignorant youth presuming to lecture age. Young clergymen are advised to 'read to me some portion of those time-honoured discourses which our great divines have elaborated in the full maturity of their powers'. Otherwise, 'it all means nothing'.

The shift in focus and in tone has been managed by a perfect control over the diction and an unfailing feel for a rhetoric of pleasantness. The true harshness and severity of the closing comment—'it all means nothing'—and of the pervasive attack on youth are masked by the jocund language and by a rhetoric which leads us ever so gently into the subject. The chummy platitudes disappear without our knowing it, and the reader is skidded into the narrator's position, recognizing without being fully aware of it a shared, really secret set of values altogether different from those common to the romantic comedy we thought we were reading. We find ourselves massaged into an odd oppositional role by this language, siding with age in the face of a romantic comedy celebrating the triumph of youth.

Later in the novel, the attacks on the young can be introduced without the elaborate preparations. When Mr Arabin is preparing to read himself in at St Ewold's, the narrator reflects with deceptively genial irony on the fact that it 'often surprises us that very young men can muster courage to preach for the first time to a strange congregation' (XXIII). He continues in mock wonder at how those 'who have never yet passed ten thoughtful days' 'are not stricken dumb by the new and awful solemnity of their position'. After a few paragraphs of this, the irony, again without our sensing it, has become much sharper: perhaps the process of ordination 'banishes the natural modesty of youth'.

A genial tone and a language that works to hide itself thus perform sophisticated and amazing work, burrowing into and beneath us to direct our sympathies and establish complex counter-movements in the novels. To imagine

that this is 'no style at all', as George Meredith remarked, or that, as James supposed, it is supremely 'safe' is to fall into the deep spell that devious style is casting. Trollope's language does a wonderful job of convincing us that it is 'natural' but it is, he would say, simply natural-seeming, just as his apparent simplicity is the result of a hard-won complexity. In so far as he can make his language disappear, and no one does it better, he has us trapped. But, come to think of it, it is not a bad trap to be in.   JRK

Aitken, David, ' "A Kind of Felicity": Some Notes about Trollope's Style', *NCF* (March 1966), 337–53.
apRoberts, Ruth, 'Anthony Trollope, or the Man with No Style at All', *Victorian Newsletter* (spring 1969), 10–13.
Herbert, Christopher, *Trollope and Comic Pleasure* (1986).

Larry, old retainer who suffers agonies carrying out his duties when obliged to wear Archibald Green's hunting boots. 'O'Conors' *TAC1*   GRH

'Last Austrian Who Left Venice, The', first published in *Good Words*, January 1867 (reprinted in *LS*). A story set in Venice at the crisis of the 1866 war of Italian independence. Hubert von Vincke is a captain in the occupying forces. He befriends a young Venetian, Carlo Pepé, and falls in love with his sister Nina. Nina, however, cannot marry 'an enemy of Italy'. Hubert is posted to Verona. After Austria's defeat, Nina goes to the other city and discovers Hubert wounded, in hospital. They are finally united. Hubert discovers he will be the last soldier to leave Venice, but is 'triumphant'.   JS

Last Chronicle of Barset, The (*see page 306*)

Launay, Philip, younger son of Mrs Miles. Despite her disapproval, he remains true to Bessy Pryor, and ultimately brings about the reconciliation and his mother's agreement to the marriage. 'Launay' *WFF*   GRH

Launay Park, large Somerset property of Mrs Miles. 'Launay' *WFF*   GRH

Laurence, Samuel (1812–84), eminent artist, whose portrait of Trollope is in the National Portrait Gallery. Commissioned by George Smith in 1864, the picture was a gift immensely touching for the novelist. He told Smith, 'When I look at the portrait I find myself to be a wonderfully solid old fellow' (*Letters* 1, 285). Smith also gave Trollope one of the chalk pictures Laurence made of Thackeray.   RCT

Laval, town in Brittany, scene of a late Vendean victory and headquarters of Denot, the Mad Captain. *LV*   GRH

La Vendée (*see page 311*)

Trollope's response to illustrations by G. H. Thomas for *The Last Chronicle of Barset* was lukewarm, possibly because he was disappointed at Millais turning down the assignment. Thomas did his best work here in showing the proud, shamed Mr Crawley making his way through his parishioners (LXIX). The caption reads 'They will come to hear a ruined man declare his own ruin'.

Last Chronicle of Barset, The

THE sixth and final book in the Barsetshire series is one of the longest of Trollope's novels—only *The Prime Minister* is longer. It is very rich, very various, and, in the views of many critics, his greatest novel. Trollope himself thought it his best work (*Auto* XV). It brings together strands from all five of the previous Barsetshire novels (*W, BT, DT, FP, SHA*). In the four years since completing *The Small House at Allington*, he had written no fewer than six non-Barsetshire novels, including the first of the Palliser series, *Can You Forgive Her?*, as well as considerable periodical work, all the while carrying on his work for the Post Office. Now he returns to Barsetshire, with affectionate nostalgia, and a sense of farewell which the title indicates. The gap in novel-time between *The Small House at Allington* and this is about four years, the same as the gap in the writing.

At its centre is Josiah Crawley, who had first appeared in *Barchester Towers* as the clerical colleague of Francis Arabin, whom he had saved from 'going over to Rome', by his wise spiritual counsel. Then he was elaborately developed in *Framley Parsonage*, as the poverty-stricken 'perpetual curate' of Hogglestock. Crawley's stiff and formal style, flavoured with the Authorized Version, contrasts wonderfully with the easy convivial colloquialism of Mark Robarts. But the Robartses and Luftons as well as the Arabins are his supporters in the high-church Tory anti-Proudie factions of the community.

The donnée of the book is that he is accused of having appropriated a cheque for £20, and in fact cannot remember where he had got it. Bowed down with debt, he is especially pained to receive charity from his peers like Arabin, his fellow in learning. Indeed, he is the better Hebraist of the two, as he reminds himself bitterly, and a great classical scholar. His joy is to recite the great Greek dramatists and to impart his learning to his daughters, and to feel his own suffering in terms of the tragic heroes. When he is accused of theft, he is taken before a magistrate's court in Barchester, and committed to appear at the next assizes some months off. He refuses to have any lawyer, and is set free on bail, the bailsmen being Mark Robarts and Henry Grantly. A good deal of the drama of the book lies in how the various members of the community react to the charge against Crawley.

Mrs Proudie, the Bishop's wife, offended by his poverty as well as his high-church stance, assumes he is guilty and expresses horror at the idea of the good souls of Hogglestock being ministered to by a thief. She bullies the Bishop into sending his man Thumble to take over the duties. Crawley refuses any exchange with Thumble, insisting in a letter to the Bishop that the inhibition is illegal. At times he is crippled by depression, but articulating his good cause energizes him with the joy of battle. Mrs Proudie sees that the Bishop summons him to Barchester, and he determines to walk the many miles there, as a sort of dramatization of his poverty, although his loving wife manages surreptitiously to have a local farmer pick him up part-way there. The interview with the Bishop is one of the great scenes of the book: the Bishop makes mild remonstrances, and Mrs Proudie interrupts repeatedly with stronger terms, and frets the Bishop dreadfully, while Crawley steadily and pointedly ignores everything she says. At one point Crawley himself is driven to smile at her badgering of the poor Bishop, and she sees the smile and is ever more furiously galled. But the high point is Crawley turning to her to say 'Peace, woman!' (XVII). The Bishop is crushed, and Crawley leaves more or less triumphant.

The townspeople are interested in the scandal of a criminal charge against a clergyman, and many believe him guilty, even the sympathetic lawyer for the prosecution, Mr Walker. In fact, Walker believes him mad, and suggests a plea of temporary insanity. Crawley himself, unable to remember where he got the cheque, believes he is mad at times. His supporters rally to discuss strategy, and lament the absence of Crawley's chief friends, the Arabins: Dean Arabin is on a protracted visit to the Holy Land, and Mrs Arabin is in Europe. Robarts goes to Crawley to try to persuade him to use a lawyer, but Crawley is adamant. But it turns out that Mrs Crawley has a lawyer cousin in London, Mr Toogood, willing to take an interest in the case, and Crawley is persuaded to travel to London to see him. Toogood is touched by this peculiar man who somehow 'revels in the sense of injustice done to him' (XII). In some of Crawley's darkest moments he contemplates suicide, or even the murder of his wife and children, for only that is lacking to his agony. Toogood comes to Barchester to investigate on Crawley's behalf, and calls on the aged Mr Harding to write to his daughter Mrs Arabin to cast light on the case. It is agreed that Mrs Crawley's cousin Johnny Eames will go on a mission to her in Italy.

Mrs Proudie has not abated her hostility. She goads the Bishop to call on Dr Tempest, the Rural Dean, to set up a commission to inquire into Crawley's conduct. The august Doctor Tempest answers the summons to the palace—and here is another great confrontation. Tempest waits for Mrs Proudie to leave, the Bishop tries to instruct him in his duties, and Mrs Proudie persists in contradicting the Bishop every time he opens his mouth. Tempest holds out for a private audience, and at his request the Bishop asks his wife to leave the room. She refuses. Tempest then refuses to speak, and leaves, undertaking to communicate in writing. It is all at long last too much for the Bishop, and he turns on her: 'You have disgraced me' (XLVII). He is a broken man, and finds himself wishing for her death. From here on, he refuses her in everything. For some days, Mrs Proudie tries to urge him into activity, and even takes it on herself to send Mr Thumble once more to Hogglestock to take over. But her reign is at an end; the Bishop castigates her for the action and says he will resign his high office. Mrs Proudie is at last humbled and locks herself in her room. Here Trollope, typically, invites us to sympathize with Mrs Proudie! She, it seems, had kept secret a heart condition, and now, in her anguish, it kills her. But she dies heroically, standing up, clinging with one hand to the bedpost. The stunned Bishop prays to be forgiven for being glad of her death.

The clerical commission meets and determines that they will make no decision till after the trial. Crawley takes some comfort in visiting his poor parishioners, and from one, a stolid brickmaker, borrows a motto: 'It's dogged as does it' (LXI). Doggedly, he decides on his own that he will resign the living, and so informs Dr Tempest in a visit, and Dean Arabin in a letter. Johnny Eames at last finds Mrs Arabin in Venice, and she informs him simply that she had given the cheque to Crawley, along with some other moneys in an envelope for him from the Dean. They speed home with this saving news and there is general rejoicing in the Crawley party. Toogood finds out that the cheque had in fact been stolen earlier, from Soames, Lord Lufton's agent, by a corrupt employee at the pub the Dragon of Wantly. The pub is among Mrs Arabin's real estate holdings and the cheque had found its way to her as part of the rent. Mrs Arabin, anxious to augment her husband's assistance to the Crawleys, had added it to the envelope, somewhat in error in treating it as cash. Mr Toogood rejoices in the happy outcome and delights to spread the news. He has been astounded and impressed by the peculiarities and the virtues of Crawley: 'Somebody ought to write a book about it' (LXXVII).

Mrs Arabin, Eleanor Harding that was, has arrived home to find her beloved father near death—a peaceful death. His deathbed is attended by his two daughters, his favourite Eleanor and Susan Grantly, his two sons-in-law Dean Arabin and Archdeacon Grantly, and his granddaughter Posy Arabin. The death of Mr Harding gives Trollope occasion to look back on the whole series through the focus of this most beloved character, one of the most believable saints in all literature. Harding, of course, had been warmly interested in Crawley's case and is much relieved at the outcome. Hesitantly he had proposed to the Archdeacon that Crawley might have the living of St Ewold's, which is in the Archdeacon's gift. And this is what eventually is arranged. Crawley is at last obliged to relinquish his suffering and live comfortably. At Harding's funeral, the Bishop makes his first appearance since his wife's death, a suggestion of recovery and peace to come.

The love story of Grace, the Crawleys' daughter, takes place in the shadow of her father's trouble. Grace has been outstandingly well educated by her father, in Latin and Greek as well as algebra and geometry, has been a student at the Misses Prettyman's school in Silverbridge, and has remained there as a valued teacher. Her intelligence and beauty have won her the love of Major Henry Grantly, son of the Archdeacon. Henry, after a distinguished military career in India, has been left a widower with a young daughter, Edith, living at Cosby Lodge near Plumstead. When the shadow of suspicion and gossip falls on her father, Grace insists on leaving the school and is persuaded to stay with the Dales at the Small House at Allington. When Henry's parents are informed of his interest in Grace, they are displeased by the connection with a poverty-stricken family under suspicion of theft; the Archdeacon is especially horrified, particularly when he thinks, as he often does, of how the family has been honoured by the marriage of their daughter Griselda to the Marquis of Hartletop. This is galling to Henry, who knows that the vapid Griselda cannot hold a candle to Grace Crawley. The parents seek the Marchioness's advice, which is simply to cut back Henry's income until he gives up. When Henry threatens to propose to Grace, the Archdeacon says that is what he will do (though Mrs Grantly knows he would not really do it). This steels Henry in his resolve, although in fact he has been hesitating because of the Crawleys' trouble. It would be doing 'the magnificent thing' (VII) to offer marriage when her father is under suspicion, and he wonders whether he will do it. In this mood, he encounters his sympathetic friend Mrs Thorne, and puts the problem to her. Her advice is characteristically unequivocal: Marry her, of course! It is typical of Trollope and his realistic psychology that Henry's 'heroism' is clinched by his annoyance with his father and by Mrs Thorne's exhortation. He goes to Allington and proposes to Grace. Lily Dale has urged her to accept, but Grace refuses on the grounds that the time of her father's tribulation is no time for lovemaking.

Henry has put Cosby Lodge up for sale, taking his father at his word, and plans to live cheaply in France with Grace and his daughter Edith. When his parents hear of Grace's refusal, they are given pause, and much regret the plan to sell Cosby Lodge. Young Lady Lufton, Lucy Robarts that was, is intimate with the Crawleys from old association (see *FP*), and the Luftons now persuade Grace to stay at Framley, with the

Robartses at the parsonage. The Grantlys have been good friends for years with the Framley people, and now the Archdeacon feels betrayed by their making Grace so available to Henry. He journeys to Framley, and is led to an encounter with Grace herself. Hostile at first, he is quickly won over into his true charitable self by Grace's high principles, and by her beauty. She vows she will never marry Henry so long as her father is suspected. The Archdeacon in turn vows that he will welcome her as a daughter when the cloud has passed away. But at last the plan to sell Cosby Lodge is given up, and when Crawley's innocence is established Henry comes to terms with his good fortune in marrying Grace and in reconciling with his father.

Concurrently, we follow the continuation of the story of the Lily Dale–Johnny Eames situation of *The Small House at Allington*. Lily had been heartlessly jilted by her fiancé Adolphus Crosbie so that he could marry into the aristocracy with the Lady Alexandrina De Courcy. The Lady Alexandrina has died, and Crosbie, now deeply regretful of losing Lily, resolves to try her again. He has become somewhat bald, somewhat fat, and financially disadvantaged by his dead wife's grasping family. He approaches Lily through a letter to her mother, and Lily directs her mother to rebuff him. Her cousin Bernard, once disappointed in love by her sister Bell, has become engaged to Emily Dunstable, the niece of Mrs Thorne. Bernard's father the squire persuades Lily to come to London to become acquainted with Emily, and Lily takes part in London social life. Two chance encounters with Crosbie confirm her in her rejection of him. She will never love anyone else, she says, but is in a way emotionally crippled by his betrayal.

Johnny Eames her faithful suitor is now private secretary to Sir Raffle Buffle, and as protégé of the Earl De Guest is well regarded in London. His old flame Amelia Roper is now married to Cradell, Johnny's old friend. Eames tends to plume himself on his faithfulness to Lily, and plans to try her again. He has moved somewhat upmarket in his social life and his friend the painter Conway Dalrymple introduces him to the Dobbs Broughton circle. There at a dinner party he encounters Crosbie whom he had once thrashed for jilting Lily—but now Crosbie no longer seems a threat. Johnny is in need of distraction and finds it among the Dobbs Broughtons. Broughton is a city financier, whose partners are the repulsive Mr Musselboro and the wealthy old woman Mrs Van Siever. Conway has painted Mrs Dobbs Broughton, who likes to flirt with him, as the three graces (all three!), and he fancies Mrs Van Siever's good-looking daughter Clara, and proposes to paint her. His sense of the rapaciousness of these women makes him first think of her as Judith with the head of Holofernes, but he declares rather for Jael in the act of driving a tent-peg through the head of Sisera. The painting proceeds *sub rosa* at the Dobbs Broughton house, and gives Mrs Dobbs Broughton a pleasant sense of surreptitious activity. Meantime Johnny amuses himself with another member of the group, Madalina Demolines, who enjoys dramatic flirtations, and twits him with his faithful love for 'L.D.' Johnny takes leave from his office to go on his mission to Mrs Arabin for the Crawley case. He takes pride in this heroic trip, and Lily is proud too of his generosity. While he is gone, Madalina makes mischief with an anonymous letter to Lily. Lily is under pressure from all directions to accept Johnny—from the De Guests, Squire Dale, Grace Crawley, Emily Dunstable, Mrs Arabin, but when he proposes again, she finds she cannot oblige her friends—the anonymous letter does not help—and she refuses him yet more definitively than ever, vowed to the motto inscribed in her book: O.M.—for Old Maid. Johnny's shabby

London friends finish shabbily: Dobbs Broughton, bankrupt and drunken, blows his brains out, Conway Dalrymple manages to marry the heiress Clara-Jael, Musselboro runs off with Mrs Dobbs Broughton. And Madalina, failing to entrap Johnny, in good time marries the wine-dealer Peter Bangles appropriately at the church of St Peter the Martyr.

It was for this novel that Frank O'Connor put Trollope in the big league, with Stendhal and Tolstoy (*The Mirror in the Roadway* (1957), 167). And it was in an analysis of this novel that Jerome Thale defended Trollope from the charge of being loose and rambling, arguing that the accumulation and grouping of events and characters gave him his special perspective, his 'wonderful disenchanted clarity of vision, his tolerance and accuracy . . . his complex and balanced vision of human life' ('The Problem of Structure in Trollope', *NCF* (September 1960), 147–57). Peter K. Garrett argues that Trollope's double perspective in this book puts in tension the opposing claims of society and the individual (*The Victorian Multiplot Novel: Studies in Dialogical Form* (1980), 191–203). The compelling character of Crawley has led some biographers to speculate that Trollope based him on his own father, 'a strange, stubborn, proud, learned, self-pitying impoverished man' (Hall 35). However that may be, he is one of the most striking characters in all Victorian fiction. Generally, we never hear Trollope's clergymen in their professional capacity as preachers; it is their social selves he is concerned with. But he allows Crawley to state a piece of doctrine. Talking to Robarts on the death of Mrs Proudie, on how the deaths of the great are more shocking than those of the humble, he says he will blame no one for this, for all men are faulty. 'It is in his perfection as a man that we recognize the divinity of Christ. It is in the imperfection of men that we recognize our necessity for a Christ' (LXVII). And both his spirituality and his pride are beautifully clear when he is talking to Arabin just back from the Holy Land. Arabin has just been saying that no one is quite sure of the exact location of Calvary. 'I fancy that I should know,—should know enough,' said Mr Crawley (LXXIX).

With this conclusion of the Barsetshire series, something new was established in English literature: the *roman fleuve*, made famous in France by Balzac's *La Comédie humaine*. Thackeray had made some connections between novels, but it is Trollope who really establishes the genre, to be later practised by such as Galsworthy and Anthony Powell. Trollope does not appear to have been influenced by Balzac and so we might be the more inclined to give him credit for his profound originality. In a landmark essay of 1968, Gordon Ray argued that Trollope is at his best in his longer novels ('Trollope at Full Length', *Huntingdon Library Quarterly* (August 1968), 313–40). We might extend the idea to imply that his two series, the Barsetshire novels and the Palliser novels, are the best of all. The cogent picture of a whole society reaches its greatest richness in this last.

The Dobbs Broughton sequences in the novel have not been much admired, and some critics have considered them a grave flaw. The tawdry circle in which Johnny Eames seeks distraction makes for rather unpleasant reading, and somehow the styles of tawdriness seem dated. But it can be argued that they serve a function in the book. Eames, so likeable, so good-hearted, so quick and bright, and generally so suitable a mate for Lily Dale, shows himself as less than fastidious, susceptible to the shallow games of Madalina Demolines. Moreover, the venality of the whole group, the self-dramatizing of the women especially, make a contrast with the Barsetshire crowd.

What if this novel were taken to be variations on the theme of self-making, from the despicably dishonest mode of Madalina, to the heroic near-tragic mode of Crawley, to the slight dereliction of Johnny in failing quite to act the hero?

But what is unquestionably effective is the two deaths concluding in elegiac mood this 'last' chronicle—Mrs Proudie's and Mr Harding's. There is a well-known account of Mrs Proudie's in *An Autobiography*: Trollope tells us he overheard two clergymen at the Athenaeum Club complaining about the reappearance of characters in his novels. They were especially tired of Mrs Proudie. Trollope revealed himself to them, and said he would go home and kill her before the week was out (*Auto* XV). A good story. But maybe at that point he was indeed just ready to do it. At any rate, the novel demands the death just where it is. Mrs Proudie's occupation's gone, and she *must* die. Mr Harding's death is simply sublime. Some readers have refused to let this be the *last* chronicle: modern updated Barset stories have been written by Ronald *Knox and Angela *Thirkell.

The Last Chronicle of Barset was composed 1866–7, sold to Smith, Elder for £3,000 half-copyright, came out in 32 separate weekly parts 1 December 1866 to 6 July 1867, and was published in two volumes in 1867, illustrated by G. M. Thomas. The manuscript is in the Beinecke Library at Yale. R apR

Ray, Gordon, 'Trollope at Full Length', *Huntington Library Quarterly* (August 1968), 313–40.
Thale, Jerome, 'The Problem of Structure in Trollope', *NCF* (September 1960), 147–57.
Wall, Stephen, 'Trollope, Balzac, and the Reappearing Character', *Essays in Criticism*, 25 (1975), 123–44.

La Vendée

HOPING to attract readers, after the failure of his two first Irish novels, Trollope devised 'An Historical Romance' about the royalist uprising in western France that occurred after the Revolution and Louis XVI's execution (January 1793). Actual and fictitious characters are enmeshed in his narrative. Trollope himself acknowledged two sources: the *Memoirs of the Marquise de la Rochejacquelein* (in Sir Walter Scott's anonymous translation, 1816) and Archibald Alison's *History of Europe* (1833–42). But he was also responding conservatively to the contemporary overthrow of Louis Philippe by republican activists in February 1848. For topographical detail he used his brother Tom's *A Summer in Brittany* (1840) and *A Summer in Western France* (1841)—both edited by his mother, Frances—which also included anecdotes from the Marchioness's *Memoirs* and introduced the spelling, 'Larochejaquelin'. Yet, as W. J. McCormack suggests, Trollope reworked those sources 'to establish himself as . . . distinct from other writers in the family' (p. xxx).

Trollope imagined Charles de Lescure and his young friend Henri de Larochejaquelin (both historical personages) as aristocratic leaders of the rebellion in La Vendée, a *département* created in 1790 from the Poitou region. Their initial success, due mainly to the charismatic postillion Jacques Cathelineau (historically a carter and pedlar), in expelling the republicans from Saumur led to the Directorate's vengeful destruction of the population and their dwellings. Those actual events support the 'Romance' between Henri and Lescure's sister Marie, and an idealized love between the peasant Cathelineau and Henri's sister Agatha. She is also desired by Henri's longtime friend Adolphe Denot, the most remarkable character in the novel. He moves from jealous vanity to madness and redemption with an intensity that anticipates Trollope's later and more convincing studies of obsession. Denot even has the trademark livid scar on the cheek like George Vavasor (*CYFH*). Cathelineau dies (XV), with Agatha at his bedside, and that releases Trollope from the consequences of love across the classes, an alliance which is grounded in the novel's account of the way landowners, peasants, and Catholic clergy support each other, particularly through the leadership of Father Jerome.

Trollope is far too dependent on his sources, describing events from an essayist's distance, but occasional chapters are spirited and exciting, beginning with the resistance at Saint-Florent (II), and the seizure of the factual (and symbolic) cannon 'Marie Jeanne', the capture of Saumur (IX–XI)—including the released prisoners' shaved and painted heads—and the Vendeans' subsequent defeat at Nantes and desperate retreat across the Loire (XXVIII). But too often this is costume drama or melodramatic fustian, as in Denot's defection to the republicans, the seizing of the chateau of Durbellière and rescue of its family and servants, the unconvincing meeting between Agatha and Cathelineau's mother, and the reappearance of Denot as 'Mad Captain' of the Breton royalists. In reshaping history, Trollope failed to inhabit his characters' minds. Structurally, however, the novel has its credits: the sub-plot of Jacques Chapeau and Annot Stein, a peasant equivalent of patrician romance, and—in Chapeau's uneasy relationship with Annot's father Michael—a racy humour, which neatly contrasts the idealistic and curdling sentiment of the nobler characters. In the third volume a description of the painted wood and stone figures in the garden at Durbellière symbolizes an idyllic past that is shortly to be smashed, and the entire novel exhibits a tolerance to Catholicism that typifies Trollope's later work, as do two seemingly gratuitous chapters which balance the pros and cons of Robespierre's godless rationalism (XXIII–XXIV).

Inflated and artificial dialogue, some tedious recapitulation of events, characters as wooden as the painted figures in the garden, no real sense of place—one of Trollope's later strengths—all muddy the novel, yet historical figures like Santerre and Westerman are tellingly individualized. Trollope wrote later, 'I read the book the other day, and am not ashamed of it' (*Auto* V). Despite that, the novel was generally ignored or denigrated until critics, like McCormack, sifted it for evidence of its author's stylistic and psychological liberation. It was written 1848–9 and published in three volumes, for which Trollope received £20. The manuscript is not extant.   GRH

Trollope, Anthony, *La Vendée*, ed. W. J. McCormack (1994).
Walpole, Hugh, *Anthony Trollope* (1928).

law and society. Law pervades Trollope's novels. Lawyers accordingly abound, from solicitors guarding family estates generation by generation, to learned Chancery barristers, to the flamboyant stars of the Old Bailey dealing with the extremes of theft, perjury, and murder. Many of his lawyers hold high office, or jockey for position as judges and Law Officers of the Crown. But it is not the mere machinery and personnel of law that interest him. The novels return again and again to the possession, management, and inheritance of property. For Trollope, property has a spiritual dimension. Fundamentally, he sees law as a spiritual armature for the English way of life, an acknowledgement and articulation of its accumulated practices, traditions, and eccentricities, a tissue of connections between place and person, present and past. He agrees with Edmund Burke (in *Reflections on the Revolution in France*, 1790) that 'We receive, we hold, we transmit our government and our privileges, in the same manner in which we enjoy and transmit our property and our lives.' For Burke, the perpetuation of that property 'tends the most to the perpetuation of society itself', and the particular contracts that ensure it are but clauses 'in the great primeval contract of eternal society'.

That may sound rather grand for the operation of Trollope's famously down-to-earth, practical world, but the novels, frequently turning on matters of primogeniture and entail, bear out Burke's emphasis on the transcendent and even irrational claims of possession. Will Belton in *The Belton Estate* reflects that 'There is much in the glory of ownership,—of the ownership of land and houses, . . . but there is much more in it when it contains the memories of old years, when the glory is the glory of race as well as the glory of power and property. . . . and now he was the Belton of the day, standing on his own ground,—the descendant and representative of the Beltons of old,—Belton of Belton without a flaw in his pedigree!' (XXXI). In *Ralph the Heir*, Trollope so arranges the plot that, even against justice and common sense, Providence seems to intervene in preserving the principles of entail. The proper heir, Ralph, is a feckless booby, indifferent to the estate. Sir Gregory Newton, who has a life interest, would like to buy up the reversion of the estate so that his illegitimate son, also named Ralph, may inherit it. The illegitimate Ralph takes a keen and humane interest in the estate and its tenants, and they appreciate him. Just as the deal is about to be concluded, Gregory breaks his neck hunting. Rather than lamenting, however, the tenants, the local gentry, even the admirable Ralph himself, agree that 'It was in proper conformity with English habits and English feelings that the real heir should reign' (XXXV). In *The American Senator*, the Senator is shouted down for lecturing on the irrationality of this system and retires reflecting 'that the want of reason among Britishers was so great, that no one ought to treat them as wholly responsible beings' (LXXVIII). Like Burke, Trollope sees English law and society slowly moulded not only by reason but by instinct and tradition, not lightly to be tampered with.

Ideally, as in Burke's semi-religious vision, all contracts would be part of a chain 'connecting the visible and invisible world', but Trollope tends to see his society in a state of disintegration. Entails invite generational conflict, as elders try to hold property together in perpetuity and youth tries to get its say in the present. The novels are full of such machination and accommodation, as in the extraordinary gyrations of *Mr Scarborough's Family*, where Mr Scarborough schemes to have one son, then the other, then the first again, inherit. The law has no divine tinge

for Scarborough as it has for his solicitor Mr Grey. In *The Way We Live Now*, we not only have nouveau riche financiers like Melmotte, aspiring to sanctify their stock market jobberies by buying themselves country estates and becoming part of the landed gentry, but upstart solicitors like Mr Squercum, taking the side of sons against fathers. In the same novel, Roger Carbury, exemplar of moral values, inhabits a manor symbolically surrounded by a moat, a figure of embattled probity in a dishonest age. (Here, even though there is no entail, Roger feels impelled to leave the estate to a second cousin he despises, feeling himself 'constrained, almost as by some divine law, to see that his land went by natural descent' (XIV).) Trollope is highly inventive not only in ways to imperil the right and mystical order of things but also in styles of behaviour that reveal inherent iniquity in the possessors of estates. To spite his son, Mr Scarborough contemplates cutting down the timber (Jane Austen and Thackeray would both recognize that sign of social delinquency). In *Lady Anna*, the incumbent not only indulges himself sexually with Italian ladies, he also has more regard for money than land, 'converting unentailed acres into increased wealth, but wealth of a kind much less acceptable to the general English aristocrat than that which comes direct from the land' (I). Un-English on both scores.

In Trollope's attitudes towards law, one can see the reflection of a major historical shift in the conception of what laws are. In the theory of 'natural law', stretching back to antiquity and Christianized in the Middle Ages, particular laws are seen as a faint reflection of the divine will and reason, a human attempt to discern and maintain the original order of the universe before the fall. Those lawyers in Trollope's work, like Mr Grey, 'Turtle' Dove, and Mr Camperdown, inspired by an idea of the law as majestic, aligned with fundamental truth and honesty and with principles of abstract justice, probably reflect this theory. On the other hand, 18th-century sceptical philosophy made a sweep of natural rights, self-evident truths, and immutable laws of morality. From the sceptical point of view, laws are merely expediential, enacted by parliaments for immediate practical ends, convenience, or preference. This is the theory of 'positive' law. The two theories are not always clearly distinguished: Blackstone wanders between both, and Jeremy Bentham flays him for it, mocking his notion of the Law of Nature and even his idea of positive law as having to do with 'right' and 'wrong' (see Bentham's posthumous *A Comment on the Commentaries and A Fragment on Government*, ed.

J. H. Burn and H. L. A. Hart, 1977). *Mr Scarborough's Family*, where Mr Grey is appalled by his client's irreverent juggling of legalities to suit his momentary whims, reads like an exploration of these two basic notions of law.

Trollope's Burkean, almost mystical, reverence for estates, entails, and primogeniture suggests a vestigial sympathy with the idea of natural law. But one aspect of the theory takes us further into a reason for Trollope's lifelong exasperation with criminal lawyers, barristers like his famous Mr Chaffanbrass. The enactment of laws in accord with the Law of Nature assumes an inbuilt moral faculty in human beings that recognizes right and wrong axiomatically. As the Americans say, 'We hold these truths to be self-evident.' Trollope was perennially annoyed with the adversarial system, because he thought that in most cases a right-minded person could intuitively recognize guilt or innocence, and that elaborate and systematic argument was unnecessary if not gross imposture. As early as *The Macdermots of Ballycloran* his barristers are called O'Blather and Allewinde, forerunners of Chaffanbrass. In Trollope's view, a barrister will do anything for his client, guilty or not, argue with partisan zeal, and badger to distraction witnesses only trying to tell the truth. In *Orley Farm* the witness Kenneby is made to feel himself unfit to live, and in *Phineas Redux*, under Chaffanbrass's cross-examination, Lord Fawn 'felt that he had been disgraced forever' (LXIII). Trollope never really understood or sympathized with the adversarial system of the criminal courts. Even in the late 1870s, J. M. *Langford, Blackwood's London manager, records a dinner scene where Trollope roars and rages at the eminent advocate Sir Henry *James about the iniquities of cross-examination. To Trollope, in this mood, there seems to be little problem in intuitively recognizing truth. Thomas Carlyle, the lapsed Calvinist with his oft-repeated evangelical argument that the great soul of the world is just and that all men have the inner light to recognize it, probably reinforced Trollope's belief in the presence and availability of moral intuition. 'The Universe', says Carlyle, 'is made by Law. . . . The fact of Gravitation known to all animals, is not surer than this inner Fact, which may be known to all men' (*Past and Present*, 3 (1843), p. xv). Though he later parodied Carlyle as Dr Pessimist Anticant in *The Warden*, in 1850 Trollope himself wrote a social survey called *The New Zealander* (unpublished until 1972) in which he adopted Carlyle's belligerent pontificating manner, and in which, in an argument stretched pretty far, bullying Mr Allewinde is a member of the bar, and the bar, through its many voices in Parliament and

the newspapers, casts its baleful influence over the whole world. One side of his personality was let loose in the experiment—Trollope was personally given to a good deal of bluster. However, as novelist, he was also a master of nuance, fine discrimination, rumination, and moral subtlety —and remarkable at sympathetically presenting characters who do not share his outlook. Even when he does his best to denigrate Mr Chaffanbrass, the bullying advocate wins our amused affection, and by the end of *Phineas Redux*, where he defends Phineas Finn indicted for murder, Chaffanbrass holds his own very impressively on the practice and consequences of his art. Similarly, in his last novel, Trollope's Mr Scarborough, who plays games with the truth, derides law, and sees honesty as affectation, earns both the reader's and Mr Grey's respect. The structure of a typical Trollopian novel often involves both characters and readers in finely shaded reconsideration upon reconsideration. In *The Reasonable Man: Trollope's Legal Fiction* (1981), Coral Lansbury (who derives Trollope's structures from the pattern of legal pleadings used as a model for writing Post Office reports) argues that this technique of reflection approximates that of the judicial process, with reader and narrator involved in a series of fine readjustments in order to arrive at a final judgement.

Trollope's lawyers are mirrors of society in many ways. In his elegiac mood Trollope suggests that solicitors are descending from the respectable honesty of former times into the sharp practice of the present day. Old Slow and Bideawhile (*OF, MM, WWLN*), old Round of Round & Crook (*OF*), old Mr Grey (*MSF*), are all, in their honesty and concern for traditional values, out of joint with the times, unhappy with the newer and sharper practices of their younger partners and colleagues. The barristers of the criminal courts, however, are for Trollope an evolutionary hold-over, savages surviving into a more civilized era: Chaffanbrass, for example, is 'one of an order of barristers by no means yet extinct' (*TC* XL). Historically, both views were wrong. Solicitors were better trained and disciplined over the course of the century, and Chaffanbrass, in fact, is a relatively new phenomenon, consequent to the Trials for Felony Act of 1836, which specified that a prisoner charged with a felony had the right to 'make full answer and defence thereto by counsel learned in the law'. Chaffanbrass is also a specialist in that, though English barristers can act for either prosecution or defence, he chooses the defence—no doubt the better to vent Trollope's vexation about defence of the 'obviously' guilty.

Despite Trollope's crusades, his treatment of the law has considerable philosophical depth. Along with some mistakes and perversities, he has an extensive awareness of legal subtleties and practices, and for his later novels he had several of the most eminent lawyers in the land among his friends to advise him. His lawyers, as well as covering a great range of personal types, are intimately expressive of the ideologies and niceties in his highly elaborated picture of English society.   RDM

Lansbury, Coral, *The Reasonable Man: Trollope's Legal Fiction* (1981).
McMaster, R. D., *Trollope and the Law* (1986).

Lawley, Francis Charles (1825–1901), journalist and sportswriter; elected for Beverley in 1852 as an advanced Liberal; served as private secretary to Gladstone to whom he was devoted. Political indiscretions drove him to the United States for nine years, in which he sent lively dispatches to *The Times* on the Civil War. He contributed four articles to *Saint Pauls*, two of them on horse racing, to which he was addicted, having lost a small fortune on the turf. The articles were: 'Conditions and Prospects of the Turf' (October 1867), 'Our Fortifications' (January 1868), 'On Shooting' (February 1868), 'About Horse-Racing' (April 1868). He was among friends who accompanied Trollope's hearse to Kensal Green Cemetery in December 1882.   RCT

lawn tennis. Immediately popular after Major Wingfield patented the unenclosed court in 1874, the first world championship was held at Wimbledon in 1877. Tennis aids flirtation in a number of Trollope's later novels. Nina Albury plays in *Ayala's Angel*; Isabel Boncassen is an adept in *The Duke's Children*, as is Lord Carstairs, in *Dr Wortle's School*, and Georgiana Wanless plays the game tirelessly to capture Major Rossiter in 'Alice Dugdale'.   PJT

Lawrie, Mary, daughter of Mr Whittlestaff's best friend, Captain Patrick Lawrie. Alone and penniless after the deaths of her father and stepmother, she resides at Croker's Hall. She accepts Mr Whittlestaff's marriage proposal out of gratitude rather than love but will not go back on her promise when her lover John Gordon unexpectedly returns. Willing to sacrifice herself to her promise, she is released from the engagement by Mr Whittlestaff and free to accept John Gordon's proposal. *OML*   RC

lawyers as characters. Trollope creates over a hundred lawyers. Some are caricatures as their names suggest: bullying barristers like Allewinde (*MB, NZ*), O'Laugher (*MB*), and Cheekey (*CH*), otherwise known as Supercilious Jack; or unscrupulous solicitors like Mowbray and Mopus (*ED*). Some are fully developed professional and character studies, like the solicitors Mr Camperdown (*ED*) and Mr Grey (*MSF*), or the barristers Sir William Patterson (*LA*) and Mr Chaffanbrass (*TC, OF, PR*). Many, though they make briefer appearances, are vividly memorable: Mr Dove, learned and inspired by the poetry of the law, who gives his opinion on whether or not the Eustace diamonds are heirlooms; Mr Quickenham, who devotes a vacation to finding a defect in the title to Puddleham's Dissenting chapel (*VB*); brisk Sir Abraham Haphazard, so amazed at the simplicity of the Warden, Mr Harding, 'that he hardly knew how to talk to him as to a rational being' (*W* XVII); formidable Sir John Joram, who defends John Caldigate charged with bigamy and assists in getting him pardoned (*JC*); cheerful Thomas Toogood, who finds the real culprit and clears his stiff-necked and grudging client Mr Crawley from suspicion of having stolen a cheque (*LCB*); or slovenly but energetic Squercum, despised by respectable solicitors but much in vogue among elder sons, like Dolly Longestaffe, in contention against their fathers (*WWLN*).

Among his barristers, Trollope's greatest achievement is in the evolution of Mr Chaffanbrass, denizen of the Old Bailey. Chaffanbrass characteristically acts for the defence. Appearing first in *The Three Clerks*, defending Alaric Tudor on a charge of embezzlement, he is dirty, slovenly, and baleful, wears his wig awry, brushes others' papers off their tables, and carries himself with aplomb: 'Mr Chaffanbrass was the cock of this dunghill, and well he knew how to make his crowing heard there' (XL). He is so sarcastic and aggressive in cross-examination that prosecutors and witnesses alike cringe. He is said to put his clients' interests above truth and not to care about their guilt; in short, to delight in 'dressing in the fair robe of innocence the foulest, filthiest wretch of his day' (*TC* XL). In all this, Trollope conceives him polemically as representative. Nevertheless, Trollope recognized he had created an outstanding character: 'I do not think', he says, 'that I have cause to be ashamed of him' (*Auto* VI). In *Orley Farm*, Chaffanbrass defends Lady Mason on a charge of perjury, this time associated with the somewhat disreputable solicitor Solomon Aram, on the one hand, and, to set them off, the righteous young barrister Felix Graham on the other. By Chaffanbrass's third appearance, defending Phineas Finn on a charge of murder, Trollope, however, has mellowed, has more understanding of the adversarial system, and shows Chaffanbrass in a more sympathetic light. He still demolishes Lord Fawn on the stand, improperly interviews a witness, and behaves with his usual courtroom brashness. But Trollope lets him make the point that truth absolute is not the counsel's business but the truth of the evidence, since there must always be some shadow of doubt. And Chaffanbrass, dismissing his skill at cross-examination as a trick of the trade, tellingly concludes, 'You forget it all the next hour. But when a man has been hung whom you have striven to save, you do remember that' (*PR* LX). Outside the court, however, Chaffanbrass is a lamb, pooh-poohed by his daughters, a philanthropist who contributes to hospitals for the poor. In the end, Trollope lets him consent to take a silk gown.

Mr Furnival in *Orley Farm* is a fine psychological study of a dignified, middle-aged barrister, eminent in his profession, who allows himself to be enchanted and manipulated by the pretty pathos of his client, Lady Mason. He is in his fifties, a Trollopian time of danger, and tempted to pursue strange goddesses.

More distinguished in the profession is Sir William Patterson, Solicitor-General, counsel for young Earl Lovel in *Lady Anna*. Patterson is a puzzle and a scandal to his colleagues, who watch with keen interest his eccentric behaviour, and calculate what the political effects of his actions will be. Unlike many of Trollope's barristers, he is humanely devoted to justice and looks at the issues in the interests of all concerned. He sees no reason why he and the opposing counsel should not sit together, with their briefs and evidence in common. He even has a sense of romance. Acting with suavity, benevolence, and reason, he is a kind of superintending deity in the plot. Everyone is interested in his unconventional performance and curious about the various possible consequences for his professional career.

Trollope sees solicitors like the massively respectable Slow & Bideawhile (*OF, DT, MM, FP, WWLN*) as having a semi-religious function in preserving the integrity of estates and thus of the whole social fabric of England.

Perhaps his most interesting solicitor is Mr Camperdown (*PR, ED*), deeply identified with the estate and the affairs of his clients, the Eustaces, to the point of protecting them not only against the avariciousness of Lizzie Eustace but against their own weakness and lack of determination. Trollope is good at obsession, and *The Eustace Diamonds* turns on two obsessions: Lizzie's to hold on to the Eustace diamonds, Camperdown's to retrieve them. The law for Mr Camperdown is poetic and majestic. Consulting the learned barrister Mr Dove for an opinion on heirlooms, he is inspired by 'Turtle' Dove's discourse on the chivalry of the law—though deeply disgusted by the opinion that the diamonds are not heirlooms. Camperdown's mixture of energy, scruple, hatred of Lizzie, and love of the law makes him a dynamic character and a major force in the novel's development. Lizzie's adamantine, pig-headed, determination to hold on to what is not hers is an irresistible spur to his professional lawyerly zeal.

The notion of the lawyer as 'Lar' of the estate reaches a peak in *The American Senator*, where the solicitor Gregory Masters, grieving and unmanned in youth by losing the management of the Bragton property, almost regains his youth at the news that his daughter will marry its present owner and 'His grandson, should she be fortunate enough to be the mother of a son, would be the squire himself!' (LXXI).   RDM

Lax, Terry, notorious assassin for the Landleaguers, who is believed to be responsible for the murders of Florian Jones and Terry Carroll, and the attempted murder of Captain Clayton. *L*
MRS

Layard, Sir Austen Henry (1817–94), archaeologist famed for his excavation of Nineveh (1845–6); Chief Commissioner of Works (1868–9); Under-Secretary for Foreign Affairs in Whig ministries of Palmerston and Russell (1852, 1861–6); British minister in Madrid (1869). Layard wrote for *Saint Pauls* 'England's Place in Europe' (December 1867), 'What is the Eastern Question?' (June 1868), and 'How to Settle the Eastern Question' (July 1868).   RCT

Leake, Mrs, a sharp-tongued lady of Rissbury, near Littlebath, whose acerbic comments make her unpopular among the ladies (XXIX). *B*
MRS

Leatherham, Sir Richard, Solicitor-General and leading counsel for the prosecution in Lady Mason's trial. He opens the second trial 'with wonderful perspicuity' (LXVIII), explaining the nature of the Orley Farm case past and present, without damning Lady Mason too severely. *OF*
MT

Lecky, William Edward Hartpole (1838–1903), MP for Dublin University (1895–1902); best known for *History of England in the Eighteenth Century* (1878–92). Trollope asked him to be a steward for the Royal Literary Fund dinner (1878).   RCT

lectures and speeches. From 1861 Trollope was increasingly seen on public platforms. He spoke regularly at the *Royal Literary Fund's annual dinners, and lectured on subjects of special expertise such as the civil service and literary affairs, America, politics, education, and South Africa. The man once described as 'all gobble and glare' in conversation was not a brilliant speaker like Dickens, although his lectures were carefully prepared. On a public platform nervousness got in the way and he grew over-excited before an audience. Speaking on the Bulgarian Atrocities at a conference on the Eastern Question in St James's Hall, Regent Street, London, on 8 December 1876, he was so carried away that the Duke of Westminster as chairman tugged at his coat-tails to make him sit down. Views varied as to his speaking abilities. He acquitted himself well at the banquet for Dickens in St George's Hall, Liverpool, on 10 April 1869, responding to the toast to modern literature, but the *Liverpool Daily Courier*, while praising the common sense, manliness, and quiet humour of his speech, noted that his voice was not agreeable. Four years later the *Liverpool Daily Post* pronounced after a speech on novel-reading that he was no orator. On the other hand when he spoke at St James's Hall in support of J. S. Mill's re-election to Parliament for Westminster in the autumn of 1868 'the clear, ringing accents of his short and forcible speech' were thought far superior to the candidate's scarcely audible voice (Super 252). According to Viscount Bryce he was direct and forceful, and would have had the ear of the House of Commons. In the series of stump speeches during his inglorious run for Parliament (1868) reports showed that he kept his head and got his points across despite the clamorous nature of such meetings. Lectures of a formal kind, rather than off-the-cuff, after-dinner affairs, suited him better. One of his earliest was an in-house affair, at the opening of the Post Office Library and Literary Association on 6 November 1859, in the Returned Letter Room at St Martin's-le-Grand. It was a project dear to his heart, and he spoke well, praising the donors of books and suggesting that the library's Reading Room 'should partake of the nature of a club' (appendix B, *Chron* 148–56). Trollope again addressed the association (4 January 1861) on 'The Civil Service as a Profession'.

Political addresses stemmed from his essay 'Politics as a Daily Study for the Common People', delivered on 18 February 1864 to Leeds Mechanics' Institution and Literary Society and fully reported in the *Leeds Mercury* next day. Another essay, 'The Present Condition of the Northern States of the American Union' (1862–3), was given as a lecture at Bury St Edmunds Athenaeum, 26 January 1864. He also spoke on the Civil War at the Literary and Mechanics' Institution, Halstead, Essex, on 25 February 1864. Another political and social subject opened up after his trip to South Africa. He spoke on 'The Trans-

vaal', 14 January 1878, at the Royal Geographical Society; on South Africa, 30 March 1878, at the Working Men's Club and Institute Union, London; on 'The Native Races of South Africa', 15 November 1878, at Manchester Athenaeum; on 'The Zulus and Zululand', 23 October 1879; and 'The Condition of the Zulu People', 28 October 1879, at Harborne and Edgbaston Institute, Birmingham.

The most polished of his talks on literary themes was 'On English Prose Fiction as a Rational Amusement' (1870), a copy of which he inscribed to Rose 'from her obedient slave | The Lecturer'. The talk was given at Hull (24 January 1870), Glasgow (27 January), Edinburgh (28 January), and in 1871 at Leeds Philosophical and Literary Society (17 January), Walsall Lecture Institute (19 January) and Stourbridge, Wiltshire (20 January). The lecture was also among his topics in Australia (1871–2), where his first engagement was at Rockhampton, Queensland, in September 1871. He had come, he said, as a ready listener to learn all he could about the country. In late October he spoke at the gold-mining town of Gulgong, New South Wales, expressing admiration for the miners' pride in their labour. 'Modern Fiction as a Rational Amusement' was delivered at Melbourne, December 1871, before an immense audience. At Hobart, Tasmania, he gave early in 1872 'Modern Fiction as a Recreation for Young People' to help raise funds for a new Church of England cathedral. These speeches on literary topics dealt with the moral efficacy of fiction, and its role in teaching the young, a theme first announced in his response to Charles Merivale's toast at the Royal Literary Fund dinner, 13 May 1863, when Trollope observed that novel-writers were the great instructors of the country: 'They teach ladies to be women, and they teach men to be gentlemen' (quoted Super 157). Trollope spoke on 'Modern Literature' at Liverpool (10 April 1869); 'Novel Reading and Popular Education' at the Liverpool Institute (13 November 1873); 'On the Art of Reading', Quebec Institute, London (2 March 1876), and Spitalfields School of Art (28 November 1876) An essay on 'Higher Education of Women' (1868) was given as a lecture in several places. Blank spaces in the text allowed Trollope to substitute the name of the town he was visiting. There were speeches for school and club functions and other public occasions. This aspect of Trollope's public life provides eloquent testimony to his extraordinary constitution and passion for work. See ROYAL LITERARY FUND.   RCT

Booth, Bradford, 'Trollope and the Royal Literary Fund', *NCF* (December 1952), 208–16.

Super, R. H., 'Trollope at the Royal Literary Fund', *NCF* (December 1982), 316–28).

Terry, R. C., *A Trollope Chronology* (1989), appendix A.

Leeds, large industrial city in Yorkshire, seven miles (11 km) from Joseph Mason's estate at Groby Park. Lees is the home of the Bull Inn, where Messrs Moulder, Kantwise, and the other commercial travellers meet for chops and chat in the Commercial Room. *OF*   MT

Lefroy, Ferdinand, elder son of a Confederate general, known like his brother as Colonel Lefroy. After the Civil War, he marries Ella Beaufort but soon abandons her. He reappears briefly after her remarriage only to disappear for a second time. He dies of alcoholism in destitute circumstances in San Francisco. *DWS*   RC

Lefroy, Robert, younger son of a Confederate general. Wanted for fraud in California, he travels to England, seeking to extort money from the Peacockes. In exchange for $1,000, he returns to the United States with Mr Peacocke in order to provide definite proof of his brother's death, thereby allowing the Peacockes to be legally (re)-married. *DWS*   RC

legal system and officials. The chief judicial officer of England, the Lord High Chancellor, highest civil subject of the land, Keeper of the Great Seal, a privy counsellor, presiding over the House of Lords and the Chancery Court, is appointed by the Crown upon nomination by the Prime Minister. He makes recommendations for the appointment of High Court judges. And he is, as Blackstone says, 'the general guardian of all infants, idiots and lunatics'. As speaker of the House of Lords, he sits upon the Woolsack. The Law Officers of the Crown are the Attorney-General (e.g. Sir Abraham Haphazard, *W*) and the Solicitor-General (e.g. Sir William Patterson, *LA*). They are MPs appointed from the party in power. The Attorney-General is head of the bar, and manages legal affairs and suits in which the Crown is interested. The Solicitor-General is his assistant and deputy. Before 1895, both were allowed to have private practices as well, thus Mr Harding's consultation with Sir Abraham, and Sir William's acting in an inheritance case. The Law Officers have a traditional right of judicial preferment. Sir William hopes to be at least a Chief Baron of the Court of Exchequer, if not appointed as a Lord Chief Justice of the Court of Queen's Bench or of the Court of Common Pleas, and eventually, perhaps, Lord Chancellor, depending on vacancies. The Courts of Queen's Bench and Common Pleas both had Lord Chief Justices before the Judicature Acts of 1873–5, but

the Lord Chief Justice of England presided over the Queen's Bench and was nominal head of all three courts. A puisne ('puny') judge, such as Judge Staveley of *Orley Farm*, is a superior-court judge inferior in rank to the Chief Justices (and the best that Patterson's critics think he can hope to become). The Judicature Acts consolidated the several superior courts into one Supreme Court of Judicature consisting of the High Court of Justice (with divisions of Queen's Bench, Common Pleas, Exchequer, Chancery, Probate, Divorce, and Admiralty), and the Court of Appeal. Inferior courts are local, district, or county courts, the lowest of which are those of justices of the peace. By an Act of 1842, serious offences such as murder, treason, forgery, bigamy, etc. were only triable by a superior court or assize court presided over by a superior court judge. London, of course, has its high criminal court, the Central Criminal Court or Old Bailey.

The legal profession in England is divided into barristers and solicitors (or attorneys), with separate functions, rights of court appearance, relationship with clients, and status. In the 19th century, barristers, trained and called to the bar at the Inns of Court, were superior in learning and status. Solicitors had a lower social and professional reputation throughout the 18th and early 19th centuries. Barristers are independent though they may share chambers; solicitors may have firms and partnerships (like Trollope's Slow & Bideawhile, Camperdown & Son, Grey & Barry, etc.). Barristers reside in London; solicitors are spread throughout the country. Solicitors consult with and are hired by the public directly; barristers, who do not deal directly with clients, are then sought out by the solicitors. (Lady Mason in *Orley Farm* frequently consults with the barrister Mr Furnival, but this lapse of etiquette is a sign that she has him charmed.) Solicitors advise their clients on business, deal with property, draft documents such as wills, trusts, and settlements, take evidence from witnesses, appear in inferior but not generally in superior courts, and tend to become identified with the interests of their clients. They range from the intensely respectable Slow & Bideawhile to the shady Mowbray & Mopus, 'sharks', says Mr Camperdown, 'that make one blush for one's profession' (*ED* XI).

Barristers also vary in prestige by rank and areas of specialization, the highest grade of counsel being Serjeants-at-Law (dissolved in 1877), who had their own Inn, and from whom were appointed the judges of the Queen's Bench and Common Pleas. Trollope has Serjeants Birdbott (*PR*), Bluestone (*LA*), and Burnaby (*RH*). Next came the rank of Queen's Counsel, conferred by

the Queen upon the Lord Chancellor's recommendation. Old Bailey lawyers such as unruly Mr Chaffanbrass, though champions in the public eye, were considered relatively weak in learning, besides trailing the criminal atmosphere. (Trollope does give him a QC's silk gown late in life (*PR* LIII).) Chancery lawyers, like Mr Low, were and are considered the cream of the profession.
RDM

Le Gros, M., agent for Covent Garden Opera House who offers Rachel Mahony a lucrative singing contract. *L* MRS

Leighton, Frederic (1830–96), made Baron Leighton of Stretton one day before he died; distinguished artist; President of the Royal Academy (1878). His interest in Florentine Renaissance subjects brought him a commission to illustrate *Romola* (1863). In June 1862 Trollope complimented Eliot on her descriptions: 'little bits of Florence down to a door nail' and of the eponymous heroine, 'a picture exceeded by none that I know of any girl in any novel' and 'nobly aided by your artist. I take it for granted that it is Leighton' (*Letters* 1, 186–7). Trollope's Post Office retirement party at the Albion Tavern on 31 October 1867, with 100 friends present, had entertainment from the Moray Minstrels, a glee club to which Trollope belonged. Leighton was also a member. In 1879, Trollope pressed Leighton to chair the next dinner of the Royal Literary Fund, but he declined. Nettled, Trollope noted: 'I am very much surprised by Leightons [*sic*] decision' (*Letters* 2, 850). RCT

Leipsic (Leipzig), **University of,** German university which Bertie Stanhope attends for two years, learning German and a taste for the fine arts. *BT* NCS

Lemon, Mark (1809–70), known among his friends as 'Uncle Mark'; wrote farces, melodramas, and operas; collaborated with Charles Dickens on *The Frozen Deep* (1854); contributed to *Household Words* and other periodicals; best known as one of the founders and first editor of *Punch* (1841–70). Lemon was a friend and fellow member of the Garrick Club. When he died he was heavily in debt, partly due to unsuccessful speculations. In June 1870 Trollope urged the Royal Literary Fund to assist his widow. She was given a grant of £100. RCT

Le Puy, picturesque small town in the Haute Loire where Mrs Thompson is staying, above which is the ruined chateau of Polignac. 'Polignac' *TAC1* GRH

Leslie, Marian, banker's daughter, flirtatious, surrounded by suitors. Marian eventually accepts Maurice Cumming's proposal and renounces dancing and flightiness to marry him. 'Jack' *TAC1* GRH

Le Smyrger, Penelope, wealthy spinster who welcomes the attachment between her friend Patience Woolsworthy and her nephew until he shows himself shallow and snobbish. 'Colne' *TAC2* GRH

'Letter from Anthony Trollope, A', description of Trollope's visit to California in 1875, published in a special edition of 500 copies in San Francisco (1946). See also Bradford Booth, 'Trollope in California', *Huntington Library Quarterly* (3 October 1939), 117–24. RCT

letters. Trollope's letters were first published in a selected edition by Bradford Booth in 1951, following their use by Michael Sadleir for his authorized biography. Booth reproduced many only as summarized by Sadleir, considering that they did not rate a full edition like Gordon Ray's four-volume edition of Thackeray's letters: 'The fame of Thackeray justifies an all-embracing inclusiveness. But with Anthony Trollope the case is altered' (*Letters*, ed. Booth, p. xxiv). The case was altered again by 1983, when Trollope's burgeoning critical reputation justified a complete two-volume edition by a major Trollopian of the succeeding generation, N. John Hall.

In conceding that a selected edition was appropriate, Booth had admitted, 'Too many of [the letters] are concerned with minor details of business' (p. xxiv). But the details of business can themselves be fascinating to readers increasingly interested in the publication and history of the book. Thanks to the archival habits of publishers, a large proportion of the surviving letters are about Trollope's professional dealings as an author: they are minute and particular about contractual arrangements and the intricate adjustments of serial publication—whether monthly or weekly or both at once, whether in a journal or in separate numbers, whether published immediately on delivery as he preferred or deferred to accommodate some more tardy author such as Victor Hugo. Fittingly, the very first letter in the collection is to his mother's publisher Richard Bentley, to whom the young Trollope is hopefully offering 'lucubrations of my own' (*Letters* 1, 1). The letters record long and varied relations with an astonishing number of publishers, for in his prime he produced enough to keep several busy at once. Letters and notes furnish the often intriguing inside story of his fiction. Some of his stories, to his own surprise and chagrin, proved too hot to handle. Queen Victoria's chaplain, Norman *Macleod, invited

Trollope in fulsome terms to contribute a story to his evangelical magazine *Good Words*, coaxing him, 'I think you could let out the *best* side of your soul in Good Words—better far than even in Cornhill' (1, 178). Trollope agreed, but rather tactlessly supplied *Rachel Ray*, in which he makes the evangelical characters almost as disagreeable as Mr Slope of *Barchester Towers*. Macleod was dismayed, and backed out of the agreement. '[*Good Words*] has thrown me over,' Trollope announced to Millais. 'They write me word that I am too wicked' (1, 220). Similarly, Thackeray and George Smith turned down 'Mrs General Talboys' for *Cornhill* because it included adultery. Trollope boldly took his story to the *London Review*, which published it but got into trouble for doing so. One outraged reader told the editor, 'You must make your election whether you will adapt your paper to the taste of men of intelligence & high moral feeling *or* to that of persons of morbid imagination *& a low tone of morals*' (1, 140–1). Such stories make more juicy reading for the modern reader than the rather tame 'Mrs General Talboys' itself.

His letters are characteristically short and to the point. And so it is worth quoting one whole, to convey the flavour of their style. Arthur *Locker, editor of the *Graphic*, had objected to Trollope's title *Harry Heathcote of Gangoil* for his story of Christmas on an Australian sheep station. Trollope replied (*Letters* 2, 600):

'My dear Mr Locker,

I have written a good many novels,—more I believe than any man alive,—and I have thought much of the names of them. I think the name I have given the tale for the Christmas number of The Graphic is a good name, and I do not wish to change it. The question of the name of a novel is one which must be left to the author. No one else can be in a condition to give a name to his story. I must trust you will not think me stiff-necked,—but there are matters in which a man must go by his own judgment.

Yours very faithfully,
Anthony Trollope

It is typical of him to regret appearing stiff-necked, but to insist that a line must be drawn somewhere, and this is where he draws *his* line. Many of his letters to publishers take similar stands on principle.

Hall's edition includes much of Trollope's official correspondence from files of the General Post Office. Even these letters make entertaining reading, especially as augmented by ample annotations, which maintain the narrative interest. 'I think that as an old, and I believe I may say meritorious, officer of the Crown', he writes in huffy officialese, during one of his Post Office rows, 'I have a right to ask the Postmaster General to reconsider' (1, 277).

His letters are expressive rather than revealing. They are full of 'crusty, quarrelsome, wrong-headed, prejudiced, obstinate, kind-hearted and thoroughly honest old Tony Trollope', as *Sala described him; but they are seldom deeply introspective. Thackeray's and Charlotte Brontë's letters record more of the 'blue devils' and secret anguish of their private lives, and Dickens's play on a wider keyboard of exhilaration and desperation. But Trollope likes to take his stand on principle and on common sense.

A letter to G. W. *Rusden, written at 61, is more than usually explicit about his views on that stage of his life. After writing *An Autobiography*, he says, he is 'ready to go. No man enjoys life more than I do, but no man dreads more than I do the time when my life may not be enjoyable.' He suggests that Christian humility is a virtue much overrated, while recognizing that, among his own kind, 'I must belittle myself. I must say that [my work] is naught. But if I speak of it to my God, I say, "Thou knowest that it is honest;—that I strove to do good . . ."' And I own that I feel it is impossible that the Lord should damn me, and how can I be humble before God when I tell him that I expect from him eternal bliss as the reward of my life here on earth' (2, 691). He expects even his Maker—in fact especially his Maker—to honour the terms of a contract.

To an enquiry about George *Eliot's irregular liaison with Lewes, Trollope responded evasively. He certainly did what he could to keep his own private life private, even in *An Autobiography*, and he would not have approved of his personal correspondence being published. Nevertheless, even here he has covered his tracks well, and his letters do not lay him embarrassingly bare. It is the ones to Kate *Field, the young American whom he called his 'ray of light', which show him most fully engaged in the intricacies of a complex relationship; but here too he is constantly on his guard. The strong erotic content of the relation coexisted with a genuine and successful determination on his part to be a faithful husband. His wife Rose knew all about Kate, and invited her to Christmas dinners; and moreover Trollope conscientiously mentions Rose in almost every letter to Kate (he seldom mentions her to anyone else). The tension in the situation is manifested in Trollope's compulsion to lecture Kate. Her poems are bad, her stories and lectures will not do, her favourite causes, whether women's rights or a Stratford Memorial Theatre, he pillories as misguided. And of course a recurring burden is that she must 'go & marry a husband'

(1, 175). Not surprisingly, this finally exasperated Kate. 'I don't in the least understand why you fly out against me as to matrimony,' he remonstrates naively (1, 509). In various postures intended to announce his sexual distance, he classes himself with 'old fogies' (1, 191), and mocks his ample physique: 'I have another horrible carbuncle on the small of my back—(If my back has a small)' (1, 173).

Aside from the professional dealings, Trollope's letters are short of comment that illuminates his own writing; for that we still need to go to *An Autobiography*. If he mentions his characters or his works, it is usually in passing. Still, there are revealing passages. Offering advice to Kate in her writing of fiction, he scolds her for choosing first-person narration. 'It is always dangerous to write from the point of "I." . . . In telling a tale it is, I think, always well to sink the personal pronoun. The old way, "Once upon a time," with slight modifications, is the best way of telling a story' (1, 429). While Dickens, Thackeray, the Brontës, Wilkie Collins, and James were elaborating their experiments in point of view, Trollope succeeded in telling his own 47 novels in 'the old way', and with that astonishing evenness of quality that has left his critics still undecided as to which are the best. But in his letters, fortunately, he has not entirely sunk the personal pronoun. They may not lay him bare, but they present a thoroughly personal, if cautious and respectably garbed, image of the man who was Trollope.   JM

Trollope, Anthony, *The Letters of Anthony Trollope*, ed. Bradford Allen Booth (1951).
—— *The Letters of Anthony Trollope*, ed. N. John Hall, 2 vols. (1983).

'Letters from South Africa'. Fifteen letters commissioned from Trollope by Nicholas Trübner for a total of £175 were published in the *Cape Times* (10 November 1877 to 4 March 1878) and various British newspapers. They formed the basis of his travel book *South Africa*.   RCT

'Letters to the *Examiner*' (series of seven letters).

1. 'Irish Distress': Recent well-intentioned letters in *The Times* from S.G.O. [Lord Sidney Godolphin Osborne] betray a lack of understanding of the state of Ireland. This writer's eight years of living and travelling there give a truer focus. The statistics cited by O. are doubtless true, but incomplete and misleading. The situation is in fact improving—disease is lessening, and the harvest this year was equal to any. The disorganization of work projects is due to time pressures; no alternatives are likely to be better. 25 August 1849.

2. 'Real State of Ireland, The': Progress in Ireland through the winter proves my August optimism was sound. Public complaints are loud but invalid. Land values rose fast, and artificially inflated the economy; some decline was inevitable, exacerbated by the potato blight. The blight early in 1846 was alleviated by Peel's relief shipments. The true disaster was in early 1847. The best possible efforts were made by the clergy and government. 30 March 1850.

3. 'Real State of Ireland. No II': Nearly £7 million was made available for Irish relief; there is much debate now about the wisdom and worth of that. Lord Russell faced an unprecedented situation; most funds were well spent. Some fraud was inevitable in attempt to feed three million people and restore the economy immediately. Massive evils were prevented. 6 April 1850.

4. 'Real State of Ireland': Earlier statements about Irish land value need explanation. Large landholdings were bought by people ignorant of good farming; the land was then sublet and overcropped. The immediate high revenues were bound to fail long-term. 11 May 1850.

5. 'Real Condition of Ireland. No. IV': Irish agriculturists now bewail their poverty. Earlier escalated values are now being corrected; this process is good for society, though the landowners disagree. The tenants cannot afford their former rents; land lies fallow; estates deteriorate. The encumbered Estates Bill was passed to sell land quickly and reactivate farming. These lands are a good long-term investment for knowledgeable hard workers. 1 June 1850.

6. 'How to Make Assassins': The recent article on the murder of Mr Mauleverer stated the facts of the crime correctly, but not the facts about Ireland. 'Pauper tenants' are entitled to food and shelter under law. Encumbered estates are being sold and rejuvenated. 8 June 1850.

7. 'Real Condition of Ireland, The, No. V': Irish politics are now at low ebb; the earlier activism has burned out, replaced by feelings of apathy and despair. A leader is needed for people longing to follow one. Representatives in Parliament are not assertive or vocal. New confidence is needed; all hope it will develop. 15 June 1850. Reprinted *Princeton University Library Chronicle* (winter 1965), 71–101.   AKL

Lever, Charles (1806–72), Irish comic novelist celebrated for robust tales like *Charles O'Malley* (1841); British consul at La Spezia (1867); died in Trieste. Trollope made his acquaintance in his early days in Ireland and later wrote of him fondly, 'His was a kindly friendly nature, prone to cakes and ale' (*Letters*, 2, 819). His tribute in *An Autobiography* was equally cordial: 'Surely

never did a sense of vitality come so constantly from a man's pen, nor from a man's voice, as from his' (XIII). Lever was less kindly towards Trollope, 'He is a good fellow, I believe, *au fond*, and has few jealousies and no rancours; and for a writer, is not that saying much?' (*I & R* 128). *Saint Pauls* published Lever's *Paul Gosslett's Confession in Love, Law and the Civil Service* (February 1868) and 'The Adventurer' (October 1868).
RCT

Leveson-Gower, Hon. Edward Frederick (1819–1907), brother of Lord Granville; incurable gossip and one of many MPs whose chief business in going to the House of Commons was to collect their mail. The *DNB* said of him: 'Gifted with agreeable manners, conversational tact, and a good memory, he excelled as a diner-out and giver of dinners' (R. C. Terry, *Anthony Trollope* (1977), 268 n.). Mark Twain in 1873 at dinner with Trollope, Thomas Hughes, Joaquin Miller, and Leveson-Gower described himself as an 'obliterated' guest, noting with sharp republican eyes that Trollope was 'but vaguely aware that any other person was present excepting him of the noble blood, Leveson-Gower'. RCT

Leveson-Gower, Sir George Granville (1858–1951). A nephew of Earl Granville, he was a pupil of Revd W. L. *Collins at Lowick Rectory and rode there with the Woodland Pytchley and Fitzwilliam hunts. Trollope would spend several weeks at the rectory, and the two often came home together. He recalled Trollope in a memoir, *Years of Content* (1940), as 'a big, bearded, red-faced, jovial man with a loud voice and hearty manner'. Leveson-Gower noted that he 'brought down a string of seven hunters, which excited my envy' (*I & R* 115). RCT

Levy, Mr, a 'little dark man with sharp eyes . . . [and] a beaked nose' (LX), who visits Alice Vavasor's house to show her how to fill out 'bills' in the amount of £2,000 for her cousin George Vavasor. *CYFH* JMR

Lewes, Charles Lee (1842–91), son of G. H. Lewes, whose desire to enter the civil service Trollope assisted, advising on the admissions process (1860). When Lewes came of age (1863) he passed the entrance examination with flying colours, and Trollope offered sage advice to his father that 'exertion will give a man a decent gentleman's income not late in life' and afford scope for other pursuits without sacrifice to public duties (*Letters* 1, 118). Lewes did not heed this advice and was soon on the carpet for laxness and carelessness (not unlike the young Trollope at the start of his career). Lewes changed his ways and rose to the rank of Principal Clerk. RCT

Lewes, George Henry (1817–78), literary critic, philosopher, partner of George Eliot, and close friend of Trollope; science writer for *Cornhill*; edited *Fortnightly Review* (1865–6) to which he contributed 'The Principles of Success in Literature' (June 1865). In 1861 Lewes gave a lecture, 'Life from the Simple Cell to Man', to postal employees. In the same year he introduced Trollope to Carlyle. They grew closer when Trollope tried to help Lewes's son to a Post Office job. Trollope was a regular guest at the Priory, their home in Regent's Park, taking their 'marriage' in his stride and once referring to 'Mr and Mrs Felix Holt . . . blooming like garden peonies' (*Letters* 1, 349). Trollope confided in him when his son Henry became involved with 'a woman of the town' (*Letters* 2, 575). Lewes contributed 'The Dangers and Delights of Tobacco' to *Saint Pauls* (November 1868). He dedicated his book *On Actors and Acting* (1875) to the novelist. Trollope's tribute after Lewes's death appeared in *Fortnightly Review* (January 1879). More personal than the note in *An Autobiography* (VIII), it confesses perplexity over Lewes's conversation on philosophy and ends, 'There was never a man so pleasant as with whom to sit and talk vague literary gossip over a cup of coffee and a cigar.' RCT

Lewis, Arthur James (1825–1901), wealthy partner in Lewis & Allenby, silk mercers; founded the Arts Club (1864) of which Trollope was briefly a member; married Kate Terry and entertained artists, actors, writers and prominent business people at Moray Lodge, Kensington, throughout the 1860s. Lewis organized the Moray Minstrels, among whom at different times were Dickens, Thackeray, Trollope, Millais, Dante Gabriel Rossetti, Landseer, and Holman Hunt. The minstrels entertained at Trollope's farewell party when he left the Post Office. RCT

library. W. H. *Pollock observed that Trollope was a well-read man in the truest sense. In youth he trained his mind by keeping a Commonplace Book of his reading. Late in life he read aloud to the family circle. He collected books wherever he went and in 1867 acquired a vast stock from the widow of his friend Robert Bell, which included works of the old English dramatists. These he studied and annotated devotedly. Over the years he amassed a library of which he was very proud. He owned some 5,000 volumes by the time he moved to Montagu Square in 1873, 'dearer to me even than the horses which are going, or than the wine in the cellar, which is very apt to go, and upon which I also pride myself' (*Auto* XX). James Virtue printed a new catalogue for him (1874), now in the Victoria and Albert Museum. The books were kept in a 'quaint and quiet book-

George Henry Lewes, formidable critic, essayist, and biographer, was one of Trollope's closest friends. At Trollope's urging he became first editor of the *Fortnightly Review* in 1865. Trollope helped find a job for his son in the Post Office. Rudolf Lehmann made this drawing in 1867.

room', 'more a workshop than a library', on the ground floor at the rear of the house, which overflowed upstairs in a recess at the end of the double drawing-room. Sometimes visitors were welcomed into the sanctum. The books had to be taken down and dusted twice a year with Florence Bland's help. The last move to Harting in 1880 caused much anxiety over arranging the books once more. 'You may imagine what a trouble the library has been,' he wrote to Henry Trollope in July 1880. All was 'in confusion so that sometimes I am almost hopeless' (*Letters* 2, 875). RCT

Lichfield, Thomas William Anson, 1st Earl of (1795–1854), Postmaster General during Trollope's early, troubled years with the service. Archives show that the Postmaster General was kept informed about the smallest administrative detail (Mullen 89). Just before Christmas 1838 the Assistant Secretary reported to Lichfield on Trollope's carelessness. Lichfield replied: 'Let Mr Trollope be suspended from pay for one week and let him be most seriously warned' (quoted Mullen 90). The warning had little effect. The following year Trollope was again in hot water, having returned late from weekend leave. His nemesis, the Secretary, Colonel Maberly, requested Trollope should make up the time by staying at his post an extra two hours a day. He added the nasty touch, that when a vacancy for higher rank arose he should be passed over. By good fortune Maberly saw his chance to get rid of his troublesome clerk when an opening arose in Ireland in July 1841. Lichfield approved the transfer. RCT

Life of Cicero, The. In Trollope's maturity he recouped a poor school record by becoming a distinguished Latinist. In 1876, *aetat* 61, he tells of having finished reading or rereading all of Cicero's works from beginning to end, and he envisaged this *Life* as the 'opus magnum for my old age' (*Letters* 2, 702, 842). It is to be remembered that Cicero's output was enormous: it occupies no less than 27 volumes of the Loeb Classical Library. Trollope's research was careful and exhaustive, and the work is thoroughly annotated. In the hundreds of notes, I have found no errors.

In the introduction he explains his motivation: he finds current a misreading of Cicero's character and, loving the man, determines to defend him. He finds that Caesar has been idealized by Macaulay, Mommsen, Merivale, and Froude, always at the expense of Cicero. Caesar is admired for political success—Cicero dismissed for failure. 'The one has been lauded because he was unscrupulous, and the other has incurred re-

proach because, at every turn in his life, scruples dominated him.' He traces Cicero's very *engagé* career—as student, lawyer, soldier, politician—and his private life as a family man and friend. The documentation is rich, especially perhaps in those intimate, witty, compendious *Letters to Atticus*. The novelist Trollope has a sense of Cicero's character as quite as vivid and many-sided and sympathetic as his own fictional characters, and a sense of Cicero's milieu as just as ambiguous and demanding as that of his own novels. Cicero found himself repeatedly at the centre of dilemmas where the moral decisions were difficult and sometimes exacted peculiar compromises. Here lies the great interest of Cicero for Trollope, and of Trollope's *Life of Cicero* for readers of Trollope's fiction, and even for general students of history and morals—the great moral questions of how to shape a course of action through an engaged public (and private) life wherein the decisions are not easy, wherein right and wrong are not immediately self-evident.

Trollope loves Cicero's wit that comes out of the ability to see the many sides of things. There was no moment, Trollope avers, when Cicero was not able to laugh. Trollope generally in his works takes a more or less Christian stance, orthodox but cool; significantly he notes that Cicero recommends an orthodox stance as a public example. But Trollope himself gives signs of a larger view. He proposes that the Eleusinian mysteries, which horrified the early Christian Fathers, have much to do, as Cicero felt, with something like a true and larger 'religion'.

Punch in 1881 published a caricature by Linley *Sambourne showing a very recognizable Trollope standing by a pile of books—his own novels—plus a stack of Latin dictionaries and cribs, all surmounted by a bust of Roman Cicero on which Trollope is placing the top hat of a 19th-century English gentleman. Critics of Trollope generally grant that the concept of 'gentleman' is a key to Trollope's novels, and this concept, under the terms *honestum* and *humanitas*, as contrasted with *utile* and *turpe*, Trollope demonstrates as the subject of Cicero's moral treatise *De officiis*, which had long been a central text of the public schools. In Edith Hamilton's opinion 'the gentleman, the English gentleman . . . was fostered by, the English schoolboy's strenuous drilling in Cicero' (*The Roman Way* (1957), 50). The fun of the *Punch* cartoon, then, goes along with a good deal of truth (see CARTOONS AND PARODIES).

The book is bright and readable, and far from the dry-as-dust school. In 1971 William A. West found in Trollope's Cicero illuminating parallels to Plantagenet Palliser. In the same year, Ruth apRoberts showed how the book relates to Trollope's moral and political interests, and how the title *The Way We Live Now* and the attitude in it echoes Cicero's wry comment to his friend Atticus: 'Sic vivitur!' (*Trollope: Artist and Moralist* (1971), 55–72). She argues also that at least one plot—that of *Cousin Henry*—is taken from Cicero's collection of cases, the *De officiis* (apRoberts 1969). Now, contemporary classicists' views are much in line with Trollope's view of Cicero, and a generation that has seen Hitler is not inclined to idealize Caesar. R. H. Super calls the book a 'genuine masterpiece' (368). N. John Hall insists on Trollope's informed sense of Cicero's historical context (Hall 472).

The Life of Cicero, written intermittently 1877–80, was published in two volumes in December 1880 by Chapman & Hall, on a modest royalty agreement. The manuscript is in the Parrish Collection, Princeton University Library.

R apR

Jones, Frank Pierce, 'Anthony Trollope and the Classics', *Classical Weekly* (15 May 1944), 227–31.
Tracy, Robert, '*Lana Medicata Fuco*: Trollope's Classicism', in John Halperin (ed.), *Trollope Centenary Essays* (1982).
West, William A., 'Trollope's Cicero', *Mosaic*, 4 (1971), 143–52.

Limerick, on the Dublin rail-line, garrisoned by the 20th Hussars. *EE*   AWJ

Lincoln, Abraham (1809–65), sixteenth president of the United States who preserved the Union during the Civil War and brought about emancipation of the slaves. On his North American tour Trollope visited Washington, where the 200,000 soldiers disturbed him. He attended the Congress and the Senate. Here Sumner's speech on the boarding of the British vessel *Trent* to remove two Confederate diplomats did not impress him. He wrote to Kate Field: 'I have seen most of the bigwigs here except the President, but have not as yet been to the White House' (*Letters* 1, 169). In *North America*, Trollope criticized the Lincoln government for suspending habeas corpus. While he wrote extensively on the constitutional office of the President, he made little comment on Lincoln, but clearly saw him as a pivotal figure in resolving the North/South divide. Lincoln was one subject of Trollope's intended series of 'Imaginary Meditations' (along the lines of Landor's *Imaginary Conversations*, 1824–9) suggested to George Smith in March 1865, but the idea was not taken up. However, when Lincoln's assassination followed shortly afterwards, Trollope wrote to the *Pall Mall Gazette* (May 1865) on the subject. His letter drew fierce criticism from the *Saturday Review* in an article 'Mistaken Estimates of Self', saying that he should stick to novel-writing not political commentary. *Pall Mall* immediately came to Trollope's defence, stating that the mere novelist had long predicted Northern victory, while the *Saturday Review*'s political pundits had been insisting that the South would never surrender.   RCT

Lincolnshire, county in eastern England bypassed by the Industrial Revolution and remaining mostly rural in the 19th century where Mistletoe, the country house of the Duke of Mayfair, is located. *AS*   MG

Linda Tressel (see next page)

Linlithgow, Lady Penelope (sometimes **Susanna**), fiercely honest dowager aunt of Lizzie Eustace. Lizzie, Lucy Morris, and Julia Macnulty each live with her for a time, but suffer much from the lady's uneven temper. Her dragon-like qualities, however, stem more from impatience than malice and her no-nonsense attitude is often refreshing. Due to a small slip, Trollope designates her both as Penelope and as Susanna. *ED*   JMR

Linton, Mrs Eliza Lynn (1822–98), novelist, essayist, reviewer; staffer on the *Morning Chronicle* (1848–51); achieved success with her novel *Joshua Davidson* (1872). In December 1867 she contributed 'Cumberland Photographs' to *Saint Pauls*. She wrote essays for the *Saturday Review*, collected as *The Girl of the Period* (1868). Although a dedicated anti-feminist, Linton was herself thoroughly emancipated. Separated from her husband, the engraver William James Linton, she enjoyed a vigorously independent career. In *He Knew He Was Right*, Trollope parodies some of Linton's views through the American feminist Wallachia Petrie (LXXXI). *The Vicar of Bullhampton* offers another Lintonism. The narrator states his belief that 'woman's one career' is marriage, yet 'Saturday Reviewers and others blame them for their lack of modesty' (XXXVII). Linton claimed that women had become immodest by going to any lengths to attract a man (R. C. Terry, *Anthony Trollope* (1977), 156). In *My Literary Life* (1899) Linton commented on Anthony's mother: 'just a vulgar, brisk and good-natured kind of well-bred hen wife, fond of a joke and not troubled with squeamishness' (*I & R* 4 n.).   RCT

Lion d'Or, inn owned by Michel Voss in the village of Granpère and home to Marie Bromar. *GLG*   MG

Lippincott, J. B., & Co., Philadelphia publishers with whom Trollope negotiated to supply
(*cont. on page 327*)

As an established author, Trollope wondered if success derived simply from his name or whether he could make a career anonymously. This short novel, 'by the author of *Nina Balatka*', was serialized, like its predecessor, in *Blackwood's* and then issued in two volumes (1868). Neither format sold well, and Trollope, with his usual integrity, did not press his publisher to continue the experiment. However, that relationship did lead to personal friendship and other publications.

Both anonymous novels evolved from European travel. Prague dominates *Nina Balatka* as a symbol of racial, religious, and social division. Since so many episodes occur at night or in gloomy interiors, the lovers move within a palpable atmosphere of distrust and secrecy. In *Linda Tressel*, Nuremberg is comparatively one-dimensional: tidily Lutheran and picturesque, islanded by city walls from Catholic Bavaria. That tourist's eye-view is established at the outset: 'They who have seen the [red] house will have remembered it, not only because of its bright colour and its sharp gables, but also because of the garden which runs between the house and the water's edge' (I). Later, with Murray's *Handbook for Travellers* at hand, Trollope describes the Ruden Platz across the river and the 'quaintness' of Herr Molk's mansion in the Egidien Platz.

This reliance on surface appearances controls the novel, which concerns an orphan brought up by her joyless aunt, Charlotte Stanbach, who is determined that Linda shall marry the elderly Peter Steinmarc. Madly in love with his cousin, a revolutionary, Ludovic Valcarm, she elopes, but after his arrest she returns home broken-hearted, and dies. Trollope maintains a distance from this story of religious mania so that we perceive the (increasingly dark) comedy of Aunt Charlotte's battle to save Linda's soul. That stance begins with the first paragraph's detached account of the way Linda's 'sorrows . . . arose from the too rigid virtue of her nearest and most loving friend'. Only in the four last chapters do we move below this comedy to feel that fanatic campaign's effect on Linda's mind and spirit, whereupon events turn 'lachrymose', as Trollope confessed (*Auto* XI).

External features also explain the novel's main characters. Linda's struggles are encapsulated in the way her eponymous 'tresses' break free from their confinement. Also 'the half-soft, half-wild expression of her face' signals an obedience to her aunt's moral tutelage and a spark of wilfulness that questions beliefs to which she genuinely subscribes.

Such inexperience would naturally see Valcarm as a dream-figure who invades the house by leaping from the river, breaching a window, or dropping from the rafters. Blackwood thought him 'a myth', but that romantic emblem is ironic. Linda looks under this image during their escape to Augsburg. In the icy train-carriage, believing herself a 'castaway' in the eyes of other passengers, she huddles up to her hero who is comfortably asleep. Awakened by the dejected 'queen of his heart', he talks incoherently about his (dubious) father and plans to lodge her at the (still more dubious) Black Bear. After the police hustle him from the train, Linda has no idea what to do with the incriminating papers he stuffed into a window-frame and is left, in all-too-real bewilderment, to the sophisticated mercies of her schoolfriend Fanny, who cleverly erects a respectable front over that disgraceful adventure.

Linda has no illusions about Peter Steinmarc who, as her dead father's assistant and possessor of the first-floor apartments, creaks around the house with middle-aged seediness. She loathes his shabby hat, his tobacco-ridden clothes, the enormous shoes that ease his bunions, the way he arranges strands of hair to disguise his baldness. When he assumes a spruce façade as town clerk and suitor, Linda scorns his pretensions. Yet there is another level, of greed and smug vindictiveness, which readers perceive long before his craven behaviour makes it apparent at the red house: a perception Aunt Charlotte quickly covers over, believing men are naturally less spiritual than women are. Trollope was in his fifties when he drew this portrait, yet he sustains it with comic objectivity while understanding the little details of day-to-day living that can seem so vile.

He is also sympathetic to Aunt Charlotte, despite a lifelong antipathy (learnt from his mother) towards religious extremism. Unlike Nina Balatka's pretentious aunt, a mean-spirited bully, Frau Staubach loves her niece and strives, with prayerful tears, to 'crush' worldly desire. This 'wicked old saint' (XII) truly believes that women need special guidance and elects Steinmarc (who appears respectable) to govern her niece's life and property. Linda trusts and loves her; Trollope delights in the ironies of her limited imagination. When Linda finally dies in her aunt's arms, Trollope pulls back from sentiment to suggest how Charlotte cloaks her sudden doubts in tattered remnants of faith.

Linda Tressel was serialized in eight monthly parts (October 1867–May 1868). Reviews of the two-volume edition were tepid; even the *Spectator*, which praised the novel, did not think its setting was used as dynamically as that of *Nina Balatka*. The manuscript is not extant. AWJ

early sheets of *North America* (1862) on the understanding that Harper, in the absence of international copyright laws, would by common courtesy not release a pirated copy of the book in advance. Lippincott was not offering generous terms—'no advance, and royalties of 12½% only after 2,000 copies were sold'—but the alternative for British writers in America was likely to be nothing at all (Glendinning 308). However, despite a verbal agreement not to do so, Harper rushed into print before Lippincott with a cheap 60-cent edition. The effect, Lippincott explained, was that 'we find ourselves *positive losers* in the enterprise. . . . Of course I shall be quite willing to have an account of this matter given to the public' (*Letters* 1, 189). Trollope did go public, writing a lengthy open letter to the *Athenaeum* (20 December 1862), detailing Harper's actions in the context of a broader discussion of the need for agreement over international copyright laws. Nevertheless, he confided to James T. *Fields that he considered Lippincott somewhat culpable in the matter: 'he allowed the grass to grow under his feet while he had the sheets, and while Harper who had no such advantage was hard at work' (*Letters* 1, 208). In the end, Lippincott had to do the best he could to recover his losses, and Trollope got nothing. In 1862, Trollope was again plagued by the absence of international copyright

laws, although this time the culprit was Chapman & Hall, his English publishers for *The Belton Estate* (1866), who contrary to their agreement with Trollope sold printed early copies of the novel to Lippincott before it was published in England. Trollope wrote indignantly to Chapman & Hall: 'I have expressly kept the foreign rights in my own hands . . . . it is not within your rights to sell unpublished matter of mine to any one' (*Letters* 1, 320). But Trollope's protest was disregarded, and Lippincott issued his first edition of the novel with an English imprint on the reverse side of the title-page and on the last page (*Letters* 1, 320 n.). RCT

Liscannor, adjacent village to the Cliffs of Moher, Co. Clare. In this desolate spot, Mrs O'Hara and her daughter find refuge after misfortunes in France. *EE* AWJ

'Literature'. Just prior to Dickens's departure for America the Royal Literary Fund honoured him at its banquet on 2 November 1867. Trollope was a steward and responded to the toast to 'Literature' citing Dickens as its 'great chieftain'. He took the opportunity to refute Carlyle's criticism of novels, pointing to the example of Thackeray, Charlotte Brontë, George Eliot, Bulwer-Lytton, and Dickens as promoters of morality, noble action, and self-denial. His speech was received with loud applause. See *Letters* 1, 394, 397.   RCT

'Literature of England, The'. As a steward (financial backer) at the Royal Literary Fund's annual dinner on 15 May 1861, Trollope responded to this toast.   RCT

Little, William, business manager and, with Laurence Oliphant, an owner of the *London Review and Weekly Journal*, which began publication in July 1860. Little asked Trollope for a story. Trollope declined but offered 'Tales of all Countries' at £50 per story. By December 1860 the magazine had purchased rights to eight stories, but published only three. 'The Banks of the Jordan' and 'Mrs General Talboys' appeared in January and February 1861, causing complaints of immorality. 'The Parson's Daughter of Oxney Colne' came out in March 1861. Little sold the remaining five stories to *Public Opinion*.   RCT

Little Alresford, parish of Revd Blake adjacent to Croker's Hall. Also place of residence of Squire Hall, whose estate is familiarly known as the Park. *OML*   RC

Littlebath, in Somerset, inhabited mostly by lodgers of three classes: the 'heavy fast' set, the 'lighter fast set', and 'the pious set' (XIII). Possibly based on Cheltenham, Littlebath is home to Miss Baker and Caroline Waddington, where they are visited by Bertram and Harcourt. It is also the residence of Miss Todd and Miss Penelope Gauntlet, and, following the death of her father, of Adela Gauntlet. *B*   MRS

Little Britain, location favoured by Mr Brown for a haberdashery shop from which he and his partners hope to make their fortune. *SBJR*   HO

Little Christchurch, pretty and thriving farm belonging to Gabriel Crasweller, near Gladstonopolis. *FixP*   SRB

Liverpool. Marie Melmotte is detected here in her failed attempt to elope with Felix Carbury. It is also the city where Paul Montague consults with Mr Ramsbottom regarding his involvement with Melmotte's empire. *WWLN*   SRB

'Liverpool Institute Address' (lecture). A novelist's invitation to speak here suggests respect for literary amusement. Properly pursued, mental amusement is very educational; novels are today's sermons. This institute is better as an educator than public schools, provides more practical learning, and is efficiently and economically managed. Reprinted *NCF* (March 1947), 1–9. See LECTURES AND SPEECHES.   AKL

Llanfeare, Indefer Jones's cliff-top estate, four miles (6 km) south of Carmarthen on the Kidwelly side of the Towy estuary. *CH*   AWJ

Llwddythlw, Marquis of, extremely wealthy eldest son of the Duke of Merioneth. His steadiness and dedication to parliamentary tasks are mocked, especially as he can barely schedule time to marry the good-natured Lady Amaldina, but he is respected despite his social stiffness. *MF*   SRB

Locker, Arthur (1828–93), writer of popular novels such as *Sweet Seventeen* (1866) and *The Village Surgeon* (1874); editor of the **Graphic* (1870–91) to which Trollope was asked to contribute. Trollope offered *Phineas Redux*, which ran from July 1873 to January 1874. Locker worried that the public would think 'Redux' was the hero's name; Trollope declared he 'had no objection to them doing so' (Super 308). Locker also objected to the title *Harry Heathcote of Gangoil*, which ran July 1873–January 1874. Trollope was firm: 'The question of the name of a novel is one which must be left to the author' (*Letters* 2, 600). Problems over length arose over *Marion Fay*. This was 'the only one of Trollope's books that shows confusion in publishing arrangements' (according to Sadleir, quoted *Letters* 2, 915). Locker complained that chapter lengths created complications. Trollope responded: 'The book is a regular 3 volume novel, *exactly* of the same length as my other 3 vol. novels . . . No writer ever made work come easier to the editor of a Periodical than do I' (*Letters* 2, 914). The novel finally ran to his satisfaction from December 1881 to June 1882, allowing book publication to take place, on schedule, two weeks before the end of the serial run, in mid-May.   RCT

Locker-Lampson, Frederick (1821–95), civil servant at Somerset House and the Admiralty; minor poet, best known for *London Lyrics* (1857) and *Lyra Elegantarium* (1867). One of the young poets Trollope took to and encouraged. They were fellow members of the Cosmopolitan Club and the Athenaeum. Locker-Lampson's 'A Nice Correspondent' appeared in *Saint Pauls Magazine* (June 1868). Trollope wanted him to be a treasurer of the Royal Literary Fund (1877), but he declined. As a token of their friendship Trollope gave him the manuscript of *The Small House at Allington*, morocco bound (March 1882). In *My Confidences* (1896) Locker-Lampson left his tribute. Like others he stressed the outwardly formidable Trollope, 'hirsute and taurine', with a voice that shook windows in their frames, but 'he may well have been the most generous man of letters, of mark, since Walter Scott . . . He indulged in no professional jealousies; . . . He only had much nobility of nature' (*I & R* 142–3).

RCT

Loire, northern boundary of La Vendée, a river barrier which affords the royalists an escape into Brittany. *LV*
RCT

London, Trollope's. Despite his much-travelled life and widely flung fiction, Trollope is essentially the celebrator of London. GRH

Gerould, W.G. and J.T., *A Guide to Trollope* (1948).
Glendinning, Victoria, *Anthony Trollope* (1993).
Mullen, Richard, *Anthony Trollope: A Victorian in his World* (1990).

London: assembly rooms. In the fiction two significant references occur, the first in *The American Senator* where Senator Gotobed gives his provocative lecture on 'The Irrationality of Englishmen' at St James's Hall. This was in Regent's Street, probably the best London hall of the period, with fine acoustics. It was there on 8 December 1876 at a conference on the Eastern Question that Trollope exuberantly condemned Disraeli's pro-Turkish stance. Popular concerts were held there until 1898. The second reference in the fiction is in *Is He Popenjoy?* in the famous sequence from 'The Rights of Women' Institute in the Marylebone Road, the location based on the actual Home for Crippled Girls. Lady *Amberley spoke at the Hanover Rooms on Women's Suffrage in 1870. Trollope was honoured at the Royal Literary Fund dinner at Freemasons' Hall, Great Queen Street, as early as 15 May 1861, and soon became heavily involved with the Fund's activities. Dickens's farewell dinner before his reading tour of America was held in the same place on 2 November 1867. Annual dinners of the *Royal Literary Fund often took place here. Trollope was a regular attender, speaking on several occasions and serving six times as steward. Willis's Rooms were another favoured venue for the Fund. Here on 8 May 1869, at the 54th Annual Festival of the Artists' General Benevolent Institution, Trollope joined Millais for the occasion. From *The New Zealander* onwards Exeter Hall (built 1831) in the Strand, the site of many lecture meetings, concerts, and evangelical addresses, is mentioned; Trollope himself squirmed at one of the interminable religious gatherings, a 'May Meeting' in 1865. In *The Eustace Diamonds* Lucinda Roanoke's reception, which has to be cancelled, is to be held in a banqueting hall in Albemarle Street. GRH

London: churches. The most commonly mentioned church in the fiction is St George's, Hanover Square. Lady Amaldina Beaudesert marries Lord Llwddythlw there in *Marion Fay*; in *Ayala's*

Angel the reference to 'St George's-Hanover-Square-ceremonies' is an indication of its fashionable status, then as now. Westminster Abbey and St Paul's Cathedral figure prominently as landmarks on the London skyline, the first memorably captured during Mr Harding's long day in the capital when he has to pay the statutory visitor's fee to enter (*W*), the second as a presence overlooking the small administrations of men in several novels. *The Warden* has a reference to the 'bell-smiting bludgeoners' of St Dunstan's, Fleet Street, one of the few churches to escape the Great Fire of London in 1666. In *Lady Anna* Daniel Thwaite wants the marriage banns read at Bloomsbury church (probably St George's, where Trollope was baptized), and Margaret Mackenzie buys a bun, goes past Bloomsbury church, and thence 'back to the Strand' (*MM*). In the same novel, Mr Maguire, an evangelical curate and Margaret's persistent suitor, eventually gets a chapel in Islington, where Mr Slope finds a post-prelate's existence in a church off the New Road in *Barchester Towers*. Osnaburgh church, attended by Maryanne Brown and her friend Miss Twizzle in *The Struggles of Brown, Jones and Robinson*, is also situated in Islington. The Goose and Gridiron in the same novel is in one of the lanes behind the church in Fleet Street (possibly St Dunstan's-in-the-East, above) while Robinson walks slowly 'down the passage to St Botolph's church' at the end of the novel. In *He knew He Was Right* the Trevelyans' wedding is celebrated at St Diddulph's-in-the-East. In *The Way We Live Now* Father Barham tries to persuade Melmotte to provide St Fabricius's church in the metropolis with the gift of an altar. In 1839 Cecilia Trollope married John Tilley at St Mary's, Bryanston Square, another fashionable church. Evidence of Trollope's own taste is seen in his admiration for the new polychrome brick church by Butterfield in Margaret Street. Despite his support for cremation, Trollope himself was buried in All Souls Cemetery, Kensal Green, which had been opened in 1832, and where Thackeray had been interred in 1863. GRH

London: clubs. For Trollope the measure of his social acceptance, status, and security was to belong to a club, and the move to Waltham Cross in 1859, with its ease of access to London, provided him with the opportunity. The early to mid-19th century is the period of clubland expansion, and within two years of his return he had been elected to the Cosmopolitan (April 1861). This club was at 45 Charles Street, Berkeley Square, where, according to *Escott, the meetings were held in a single room on Thursdays and Sundays during the session. Among the members of the 'Cosmo' during Trollope's membership were Tennyson and Monckton Milnes, and there was plenty of political discussion and gossip to fuel his imagination. The club just survived into the 20th century. A year later almost to the day he was elected to the Garrick, founded in 1831 at 35 King Street, Covent Garden, whose purpose was to bring together men interested in the theatre and to provide those of literary tastes with a meeting place for discussion and socializing. It is indelibly associated with Thackeray, who always mentioned it affectionately. In 1864 it moved to New King Street, renamed Garrick Street, to an imposing new building with a 96-foot (30-m) frontage. Also in 1862, Trollope became a member of the Athenaeum, founded in 1824 originally on the Pall Mall site which had once been the Carlton Club.

An Autobiography provides eloquent testimony to Trollope's pride in his membership of these clubs, particularly the Garrick, 'the first assemblage of men at which I felt myself to be popular' (IX). He enjoyed playing whist in the afternoons at the Garrick in its old premises in Covent Garden. After Thackeray's death in December 1863 Trollope was moved and gratified to fill his place on the committee. He was instrumental in forming the Arts Club in Hanover Square, but withdrew after a couple of years because he was never there. He was also a major instigator of the Civil Service Club at 86 St James Street, perhaps more from a sense of obligation than choice, and left for the same reason. He played whist for high points at the Turf Club, which had once been the Arlington in Arlington Street, spoke at dinners of the Alpine Club (his *Travelling Sketches* (1866) includes 'The Alpine Club Man'). He probably paid casual visits to the Arundel Club (Salisbury Street, Strand), the Fielding, and the Sterling, but his loyalties were reserved for his chosen clubs. Invited to join the Reform Club in June 1874, he replied that he already belonged to three clubs, 'which are two more than a man needs'. He became a life member of the Garrick in 1867, and his correspondence, whether of a personal or business nature or both, was frequently conducted from the Garrick or the Athenaeum. In August 1881 he was elected to the United Services Club in Pall Mall, and was amused and flattered to be called 'Sir Anthony' by one of the 'old generals'. In February 1882 he successfully canvassed friends to get his son Henry elected to the Athenaeum. One of Trollope's last public appearances was with Browning at a dinner at the Garrick on 1 November 1882. For Trollope the clubs were his second home, the whist, the dinners, the talk, the leisure for reading and writing providing him with a social milieu essential to his development

as a writer. The opening of the final chapter of his last fully completed work, *An Old Man's Love*, is written on Athenaeum Club notepaper. This small irony is perhaps complemented by the larger one of his failure to get into the most select male club of all, the House of Commons. See CLUBS IN NOVELS. GRH

London: hotels and inns. These are relevant in Trollope's life and fiction. During his stays in London Trollope frequently used Garlant's Hotel at 14 Suffolk Street, off Pall Mall. Early in October 1882 he was occupying the first and second floors prior to his stroke on 5 November. In *The Last Chronicle of Barset* Eleanor Arabin and John Eames stay at a quiet hotel in Suffolk Street which would appear to correspond to Garlant's, and Dean Lovelace stays there in *Is He Popenjoy?* Hotels, whether given fictional names or retaining their real ones, are indicators of the status or aspiring status of their guests. Thus Sir Marmaduke and Lady Rowley stay at Gregg's Hotel, Baker Street, in *He Knew He Was Right*: Rachel O'Mahony and her father have rooms in Brown's Hotel in *The Landleaguers*, as does Lord Lovel in *Lady Anna*, the actual hotel being small, discreet, and eminent. Mr Harding stays at the Chapter Hotel and Coffee House during his eventful visit to London in *The Warden*, and Mr Gotobed stays at Fenton's when he first comes to the capital (*AS*). Phineas lives at Fowler's Hotel after he returns to London following the death of his wife Mary (*PR*), and Frank Gresham uses the Gray's Inn Coffee House during his visits (*DT*). Clara Amedroz stays at the Great Western Railway Hotel (*BE*), as does Johnny Eames after leaving Burton Crescent (*SHA*). In *The Eustace Diamonds* Frank Greystock stays at the Grosvenor Hotel. Macpherson's Hotel in Judd Street is the site of Mr Kennedy's murderous attack on Phineas (*PR*), while the Boncassens stay at the Langham Hotel in *The Duke's Children*, as does Hamilton K. Fisker in *The Way We Live Now*. Arabella Trefoil writes to Lord Rufford from Murray's Hotel in Green Street (*AS*), Parker's Hotel is the scene of the abduction of his son by Louis Trevelyan (*HKWR*), and Pawkins Hotel in Jermyn Street cushions the London visits of Lord De Guest (*SHA*). Scumberg's Hotel is the location for the assault by Dean Lovelace on the vicious Marquis of Brotherton (*IHP*).

Pubs or inns are class indicators in the fiction. Thus Crocker has whisky at the celebrated Angel in Islington (*MF*), the Banks of Jordan pub (in Sweeting's Alley, just behind the Exchange) is where M'Ruen urges Charley to be prompt (*TC*), while the Blue Posts restaurant, located in Cork Street, is where Harry Clavering dines with

Count Pateroff (*C*). Bolivia's Eating House in Leicester Square is mentioned in *Ayala's Angel*, and Bozzle arranges the meeting between Lady Rowley and Trevelyan in the Bremen Coffee House in Poulter's Alley, which is in the City behind the Mansion House (*HKWR*). Coal Holes, Cider Cellars, and Shades are the lures for young men in *The Three Clerks*, the first being a public house in the Strand, the third in Upper Thames Street. The Handsome Man pub (located in the Brompton Road) houses that aspiring politician George Vavasor (*CYFH*), and at the other end of the social scale, in a pub just off the Strand, the Cat and Whistle, Charley Tudor only just evades the wiles of Nora Geraghty and her supportive employer Mrs Davis (*TC*). Ontario Moggs is the star political turn at the Cheshire Cheese (*RH*), Lord De Guest entertains Johnny Eames at Cox's in Jermyn Street (*SHA*), a favoured resort of Ralph Newton is Evans's Tavern in Covent Garden (*RH*), Mr Neefit's expressed preference is for a 'steak at the Prince's Feathers in Conduit Street' (*RH*), while from the Full Moon near St Diddulph's-in-the-East Bozzle keeps Emily Trevelyan under surveillance (*HKWR*). At the Goat and Compasses (a few hundred yards from the New Road) the Tozers, moneylenders, deal with unfortunate debtors like Lord Lufton and Mark Robarts (*FP*). The Goose and Gridiron (in one of the lanes behind the church in Fleet Street) is where the 'Geese' hold their spirited, ceremonial debates (*SBJR*), and Robinson and Poppins drink at the Mitre, which is in Fleet Street itself. In *The Prime Minister* Abel Wharton treats Arthur Fletcher to dinner at the Jolly Blackbird, which is near Portugal Street. Gager interrogates Billy Cann at a small public house at the corner of Meek Street and Pineapple Court, which is one minute from the top of Gray's Inn Lane (*ED*). In *Lady Anna* the Countess goes into the City to meet her daughter at the Saracen's Head, while the Spotted Dog in Liquorpond Street is where Julius Mackenzie struggles to survive by words alone ('Dog', *ET*). Trollope was himself a great diner out, and the farewell dinner to mark his retirement from the Post Office was held in the Albion Tavern close to St Martin's-le-Grand on 31 October 1867.   GRH

London: houses of friends and associates.
Robert Bell, Trollope's good friend, lived at 14 York Street, Portman Square. When he died in 1867, Trollope did much to raise money for his widow. The publisher Henry Colburn had a large house in Bryanston Square. Wilkie Collins lived at 90 Gloucester Place, Portman Square. At this period Lewes and George Eliot were at Holly Lodge, but they moved to Harewood Square in

1860. Then they moved to 16 Blandford Square and finally in August 1863 to the Priory, 21 North Bank, Regent's Park, where Trollope was a frequent guest at George Eliot's Sunday gatherings. John Morley, who succeeded Trollope as editor of the *Fortnightly*, was at 18 Old Burlington Street. Sir Frederick Pollock and his wife, close friends of the Trollopes, lived at 59 Montagu Square from 1858; Trollope and Rose frequently dined there. Charles Reade was at 2 Albert Terrace, Knightsbridge, during the course of the *Shilly-Shally* affair. In January 1860, the first *Cornhill* dinner was held at the home of George Smith, which was then at 11 Gloucester Square. Among others, Thackeray, Lewes, and Millais were present, thus giving Trollope his first real entrée into literary society. Smith moved to Oak Hill Lodge, Hampstead, in 1863. Much later, when Smith had a house in Waterloo Place, Trollope met Annie Thackeray there and they resolved differences arising from Trollope's monograph on her father. Only 21 months before his death Thackeray had moved to a Queen Anne Mansion at 2 Palace Green, Kensington. John Tilley and Cecilia lived at 6 Allen Place, Kensington, where she died on 4 April 1849. Trollope was at John Tilley's house in St George's Square on 5 November when he suffered a stroke. The Trollopes themselves moved in January 1873 to 39 Montagu Square, which is north of Oxford Street but only a few hundred yards away from his early lodgings. Samuel Warren, author of *Ten Thousand a Year* (1841), lived at 16 Manchester Square. Trollope's letters are full of a sense of place, from offices to houses to rooms where he worked and took his leisure.

GRH

London: landmarks.
St Paul's Cathedral was the tallest structure in London. Other significant buildings were Westminster Abbey, Somerset House in the Strand, St James's Palace in Pall Mall, the Tower of London, the Horse Guards in Parliament Street, the Mansion House, the Albany complex in Piccadilly. The Houses of Parliament were burned down in 1834 and rebuilt, the new House of Lords being occupied from 1847, the Commons from 1852. The British Museum was completed in 1837, the National Gallery was opened in Trafalgar Square in 1838, and Nelson's column was erected in 1843, the full opening of the square being celebrated in the following year. The Post Office headquarters at St Martin's-le-Grand was completed in 1829 and could accommodate 1,000 employees. The Great Exhibition opened in Hyde Park in 1851 with Paxton's Crystal Palace. Green spaces are another index to Trollope's London, and in the late 1870s his niece Florence Bland accompanied him on his

daily ride in Hyde Park. Regent's Park, and the new Zoological Gardens, where Miss Mackenzie takes her nieces, as well as St James's Park, the Green Park, Kensington Gardens, and the Temple Gardens—'Where can retirement be so complete as here?' (*W*)—are other notable green spots. The Vauxhall pleasure gardens gave way to the Cremorne gardens, King's Street, Chelsea, which had a pagoda and two theatres among other attractions, but became increasingly disreputable and were closed in 1877. London was expanding rapidly, and new areas—like that of Princess Royal Crescent, off Bayswater Road, the destination of Lady Alexandrina and Crosbie in *The Small House at Allington*—contrasted with old. In *Castle Richmond* Trollope described the new suburb in Spinney Lane—'Of such streets there are thousands now round London.' The opening of the railways was significant: 'they have turned the country into a city' (*TC*). King's Cross was opened in 1852, Paddington, where Johnny Eames gave Crosbie a black eye (*SHA*), in 1864. Trollope, at Waltham Cross from 1850, travelled in to Shoreditch, which gave way to Liverpool Street in 1875. Pimlico station was replaced by Victoria from 1860. Underground stations were appearing and from the 1870s onwards the novels refer to them: in *Ayala's Angel* there is the Temple station, completed 1870, and 'the underground cavern at the Gloucester Road station', opened 1868. The New London Bridge, opened 1831, and Hungerford Bridge (1845) were landmarks as well as movers of traffic. In the West End impressive club façades spread along St James's Street into Pall Mall. Large houses, like Lady Blessington's Gore House, hosted literary and political groups. At the other end of the scale were the slum areas of St Giles and Seven Dials, still in existence. Fortnum's was the main store for the purchase of groceries in Piccadilly. In *Lady Anna*, set in the 1830s, Anna goes to Swan & Edgar for clothes. Marshall & Snelgrove was founded in 1837. Hatchard's were the established booksellers and Mudie's, the circulating library so important to the contemporary novelist, moved in 1860 to larger premises on the corner of Museum Street and Oxford Street. In this period the Haymarket was a low-life resort, and Piccadilly Quadrant haunted by dropouts. Somerset House contained many government departments: in *Miss Mackenzie* Walter Mackenzie has a clerkship there. In *Ayala's Angel* Reginald Dosett works at the Admiralty, where the offices of the Internal Navigation are located in *The Three Clerks*. By the time he wrote *The Warden* Trollope could refer to the new Houses of Parliament as 'Barry's halls of eloquence' in tribute to Sir Charles Barry, who designed them. He also makes mention of Temple Bar, which defined the old boundary of the City, and was not removed until 1878. In *Marion Fay* and elsewhere there are references to the Monument built by Sir Christopher Wren to commemorate the Great Fire of London in 1666, to the Duke of York's column (about 120 feet high at the south end of Waterloo Place with a fine view over London), and to the whispering gallery of St Paul's, which is more than 90 feet (27 m) from the floor. Trollope's awareness of the great and small landmarks of change is seen, for example, in *Kept in the Dark*, where Sir Francis Geraldine sees Miss Altifiorla off at Waterloo. There is a neat contemporary reference (identified by John Sutherland) in *Is He Popenjoy?*, when Lady George goes with her husband to see a painting displayed by gaslight at the New British Institution which opened in Old Bond Street in November 1874. In the same novel there is a reference to the Albert Memorial in Kensington Gardens, finished in 1876, as well as a glance at the large houses in Kensington as one of Trollope's favourite locations, Capel Court, entrance to the Stock Exchange. In *The Landleaguers* Mr O'Mahony goes to the British Museum in Great Russell Street (begun 1823, Reading Room constructed 1832–7). In *The Vicar of Bullhampton* there is mention of the fact that the new law courts were not yet built (they were constructed 1874–82). The Old Bailey occupies a central position in *The Three Clerks* and *Orley Farm*, with two key trials described. Downing Street—frequently mentioned in the political novels—and Buckingham Palace are the contrasting centres of national decision and royal habitation. The imposing façades of the Albany contrast with the mention of Cheapside and of the Foundling Hospital (1739) near Grays Inn Lane. In *The Claverings* London University and King's College in the Strand are mentioned, while another contemporary reference is to the lions by Landseer in Trafalgar Square (*RH* XIII), placed there by Landseer in 1866 under Nelson's statue. The Lord Mayor's banquets were held at the Guildhall, as we know from *The Way We Live Now*, Millbank Prison was Alaric's destination in *The Three Clerks*, Mr Turnbull received the radical petition at Westminster Hall (*PF*). The wide reference overall indicates Trollope's factual, architectural, and social range in the London of his day.

GRH

London season. The London season, from the opening of the Royal Academy's summer exhibition in early May to the beginning of the shooting season on 12 August, was a highly ritualized succession of fashionable cultural and sporting events, parties, and balls which made residence

in London a social essential for its duration. Among young ladies of marriageable age it was the ideal husband-hunting opportunity. Lady Macleod in *Can You Forgive Her?* saves up in Cheltenham so she can spend a month in London for the season. The season provided Trollope with plot-lines and changes of scene. In *The Way We Live Now* Mr Longestaffe's decision to economize by closing his Bruton Street town house and returning to Caversham in mid-season forces his unmarried daughter Georgiana to compromise her social position by staying in London with the Melmottes. One of Trollope's best uses of the season occurs in *Is He Popenjoy?* Pining for excitement, Lady George Germain lets her hair down at Mrs Montacute Jones's ball in Grosvenor Place, joining in the latest dance craze, the 'Kappa-Kappa', almost ending on the floor but saved by Captain Jack De Baron's entwining arm, much to her husband's disgust (XXXVIII).   CK
> Davidoff, Leonore, *The Best Circles, Society Etiquette and the Season* (1973).

London: streets and squares. London place names resonate in Trollope's life as in his fiction, from his birth in Keppel Street on 24 April 1815, to his death at a nursing home in Welbeck Street on 6 December 1882. He soon made acquaintance with his father's rooms at 23 Old Square, Lincoln's Inn (where a pupil had committed suicide) and with other 'dark gloomy chambers in and about Chancery Lane' (*Auto* I). At the age of 19 he began work at St Martin's-le-Grand (November 1834). His brother Tom was already living in Little Marlborough Street, between Regent Street and Soho, and Anthony joined him there on his arrival. He later moved into Northumberland Street (now Luxborough Street) overlooking Marylebone Workhouse. In *An Autobiography*, he describes how he fell into the hands of a money-lender 'who lived in a little street near Mecklenburgh Square' (III), his original debt of £12 mushrooming to £200. After his father's death, his mother and sister Emily moved into Northumberland Street with him, and from 1838 to 1840 he lived with his mother, Tom, and Cecilia at 20 York Street, close to Baker Street (Emily had died in February 1836). In 1840 Mrs Trollope and Tom took lodgings at 3 Wyndham Street, New Road, and here Anthony was nursed through a debilitating illness by his mother in June and July. His posting to Ireland in 1841 meant that visits to London over the next eighteen years were infrequent, but after his move to Waltham Cross in 1859 he was constantly in town for professional, literary, and social reasons. When he and Rose returned from Australia at the end of 1872, they initially took lodgings at 3 Holles

Street, off Cavendish Square, but early in 1873 the Trollopes moved into a house at 39 Montagu Square, where they lived until early July 1880. Trollope was in London visiting John Tilley at his home in St George's Square on 5 November 1882 when he suffered a stroke.

Trollope may be celebrated for Barsetshire, but the heart of his work is the capital. He recognized the primacy of London in every way: culture, society, the accessibility of publishers, his dual status (as it evolved) of high-ranking Post Office official and literary man. *The New Zealander* (written before the end of May 1856), *An Autobiography* (written 1875–6), and his series of articles *London Tradesmen* (published 10 July–7 September 1880, ed. Sadleir (1927)) emphasize his lifelong intimacy with London. The first is full of contemporary references to government, the law, 'our Exeter Halls', the ongoing pollution of the Thames, the clubs, Tattersalls ('the celebrated London horse auction rooms', VII), bridges, landmarks, the new Houses of Parliament, society and the West End, art (the National and private galleries). *The New Zealander* is effectively Anthony Trollope, contemporary Londoner. Twenty years on in *An Autobiography* he recalls early London days, rolling off his tongue the names of publishers from T. C. Newby of Mortimer Street, Henry Colburn of Great Marlborough Street, to Longman's in Paternoster Row and Chapman & Hall in Piccadilly. He ranges through clubs and fame and friends and all the attachments of the London context. And scarcely five years after *An Autobiography*, at the age of 65, he undertook a mini Mayhew-type investigation (early hours no deterrent) of London tradesmen. The glancing commentary includes Marshall & Snelgrove's, Meekings, Whiteleys, advertisements for products from quack medicines to coal-merchants given space 'in the Underground Railway carriages', and a nostalgic recollection of the Smithfield butchers of his youth. He addresses the current problem of the congestion caused by street hawkers of food, especially in the environs of Covent Garden, Smithfield, and Billingsgate. Traffic from the latter begins to jam below the Monument, 'where Thames Street turns to the east at London Bridge, and covers all the lanes between Thames Street, Eastcheap, and Tower Street' (*London Tradesmen*, 59). Trollope's own range is from Hampstead to Camberwell, from the Bank to beyond Hammersmith. The zest here is a factual equivalent to the fictional recreation of London.

Streets and squares of the city, its circulatory system, add oxygen to the novels, provide an index to class and status, register seediness or upward mobility, indicate expansion, change, the lodgings of the socially disadvantaged, the homes of the aristocratic or rich, the chambers of lawyers or politicians—the solid context of fictional events. In Trollope's London there is a high premium on place, with fine distinctions between Mayfair, Belgravia, the West End, the City, law in Lincoln's Inn and law in the Temple, the fashionable old districts as well as the fashionable new.

The use of place is literary and social art, and here Trollope, like Dickens, is a master. In *Phineas Finn* and *Phineas Redux*, it authenticates sensational incident. In the first there is the attempted garrotting of Mr Kennedy: Phineas sees the men lurking to attack in Orchard Street and saves Kennedy in nearby Park Street. Phineas's suspicions lead him to go 'down North Audley Street to the corner of Grosvenor Square, and thence by Brook Street into Park Street' (XXX). Such particularity is typical, witness Lord Fawn's detailed evidence at Phineas's trial of a small area bounded by Curzon Street, Bolton Row, and Clarges Street—a passage separating the gardens of Devonshire and Lansdowne Houses (*PR* LXII). Houses of the rich and aristocratic are thick on their superior ground. Belgrave Square has the town house of Lord Grex (*DC*), Berkeley Square has the houses of Lady Baldock (*PF*), of the tyrannical Hugh Clavering (*C*), of the mischief-making Adelaide Houghton (*IHP*), and of the shallow Mrs Roby (*PM*). Brook Street is the residence of the Marchesa Baldoni, where Ayala first sees her angel (*AA*) and where the affluent Boncassens take a house (*DC*). Another cluster has town houses in Bruton Street: Lady Lufton (*FP*), Sir Harry Hotspur (*SHH*), the Proudies (*BT*), Mr Longestaffe (*WWLN*). Carlton Terrace is a fitting location for the town house of the Duke of Omnium. Cavendish Square is for a time home to the desiccated Marquis of Brotherton (*IHP*), and Cranbourn House ('Ointment Hall') is undoubtedly in the area (*DT*). The early discords of *He Knew He Was Right* occur in the Trevelyans' house in Curzon Street. Gloucester Place has another Proudie town house where the prelatess holds her conversazione (*FP*). Lady Monk's house, where Burgo Fitzgerald's plan to elope with Lady Glencora is just thwarted (*CYFH*), is in Grosvenor Square. Melmotte lives, appropriately, in Grosvenor Square (*WWLN*), which also witnesses Lady Laura's suffering after her marriage to Mr Kennedy (*PF*). Park Lane is the site of Mme Goesler's 'cottage', visited by the old Duke and Phineas, while Lord Brentford (*PF*), the Greshams (*DT*), and the execrable De Courcys (*SHA*) live in Portman Square. More modestly 75 Tavistock Square houses the Toogoods (*LCB*), and Warwick Square the Hittaways (*ED*). Mount Street is a favourite choice for lodgings, selected by the fickle Captain Aylmer (*BE*), by the pre-marital Crosbie (*SHA*), and by the scheming Lizzie Eustace and her downmarket equivalent Sophie Gordeloup (*ED*, *C*); it is also the site of Archdeacon Grantly's town house (*FP*). Harry Clavering visits Lady Ongar at her lodgings in Bolton Street (*C*), Rachel O'Mahony has rooms in Cecil Street (*L*), and even further down the social scale the seething Roper boarding house is in Burton Crescent, now Cartwright Gardens (*SHA*). Mrs Val Scott (née Golightly) lives in Ebury Street but exercises her power over Gertrude Tudor at 5 Albany Row, Westbourne Terrace (*TC*). Phineas Finn lodges with Mr and Mrs Bunce at Great Marlborough Street (*PF*, *PR*), Mr Emilius with the Meagers at Northumberland Street (*PR*), both places where Trollope himself lived. Mr and Mrs Furnival have graduated, not without regrets on her part, to a house in Harley Street (*OF*), while Lizzie and the like-minded Mrs Carbuncle operate from Hertford Street (*ED*). Lady Anna and the Countess Lovel live temporarily in Keppel Street, which 'cannot be called fashionable' (*LA* XX), Reginald Dosett has a house in Kingsbury Crescent (*AA*), and Theodore Burton in Onslow Crescent, where Harry Clavering constantly confides (*C*). The attractive Suffolk Street is where John Grey lodges and where he is attacked by George Vavasor (*CYFH*).

The exact placing of legal or company offices often provides a density of reference. Both Alaric Tudor and Phineas Finn find themselves at Bow Street (*TC* and *PR*), both are subsequently tried at the Old Bailey and Phineas is held in Newgate. Lincoln's Inn and the Temple provide a rich supporting legal cast: Cox and Cummins and the Attorney-General Sir Abraham Haphazard (*W*) are in the first, as are Neversaye Die (*BE*, *BT*, *CR*) and Abel Wharton (*PM*), both of whom are in the Stone Building. Mr Low (*PF*, *PR*) and Mr Furnival (*HKWR*) are, like Trollope's father, in Old Square. Tom Towers (*W*) also lives in the Temple, and Frank Greystock's chambers are there in *The Eustace Diamonds*. George Bertram's are in the Middle Temple (*B*), where Augustus Staveley is a member. The canny solicitor intent on exposing sharp practice, Mr Squercum, operates from Fetter Lane on behalf of his client Dolly Longestaffe, a location appropriately inferior to that of the family lawyers Slow & Bideawhile of Lincoln's Inn, whose presence is felt not only in *The Way We Live Now* but also in *Doctor Thorne*, *Framley Parsonage*, *Miss Mackenzie*, *He Knew He Was Right*, and *Orley Farm*. Abchurch Lane is the site of Melmotte's City 'cover' (*WWLN*); Beilby & Burton (*C*), the firm of engineers where Harry

Clavering attends (sometimes), are located in Adam Street, Adelphi. Magenta House, with its large advertisements, is found in Bishopsgate (*SBJR*), and Mr Neefit's more modest tailoring establishment is in Conduit Street (*RH*). Quintus Slide of the *People's Banner* has offices in Fetter Lane (*PF*), and in Great Broad Street Pogson & Littlebird, commission agents, employ Marion's father Zachary as their chief clerk (*MF*). The ill-fated Dobbs Broughton and his opportunistic partner (and marital successor) Mr Musselboro have an office in the City in Hook Court (*LCB*), while from a dingy court close to the Bank of England Sexty Parker does his financial wheeler-dealing (*PM*). Sir Thomas Tringle, powerful partner in the banking business of Travers & Treason, is naturally located in the financial amplitude of Lombard Street (*AA*). The *People's Banner* is published from Quartpot Alley, Fleet Street. Sir Thomas Underwood has offices in Southampton Buildings (*RH*), while Gumption & Gazebee, who attract superior clients, have a suitably superior location, their offices, available to Mr Fothergill acting on behalf of the Duke of Omnium (*FP*), being in South Audley Street. Rarely does Trollope invent a place name. His London references are informed with familiarity, particularity, and affection: the mesh of streets and squares is the register of fact embedded in the fiction.

GRH

London: theatres. In 1851 Trollope sent his play *The Noble Jilt* to George Bartley, the retired manager of the Covent Garden Theatre, who rejected it ('There is not one character serious or comic to challenge the sympathy of the audience', *Letters* 1, 26). It was later used as the basis of *Can You Forgive Her?*, but the author enjoys a private joke with his readers in *The Eustace Diamonds*, where Lizzie and Mrs Carbuncle go to the Haymarket Theatre to see ' "The Noble Jilt", from the hand of a very eminent author'. Trollope had a celebrated falling-out with Charles Reade, who adapted *Ralph the Heir* without the author's permission into *Shilly-Shally*, which ran at the Gaiety Theatre from 1 April 1872 for a month. In the spring of 1877 Kate Field appeared at the St James's Theatre in the comedy *Extremes Meet*, which she had translated from the French. Trollope's uncompleted *The Landleaguers*, because of Rachel O'Mahony's career as an opera singer, has a number of theatrical references, notably to Mahomet Moss's Embankment Theatre—a Trollopian invention—the Charing Cross Opera, perhaps a glance at the Charing Cross Theatre (in King Street off the Strand), closed down in 1882, Covent Garden, where Rachel O'Mahony is acclaimed, and the Queen's

Theatre in Long Acre, shut in 1879. Away from Covent Garden and theatreland, in a chapter called 'The City Road' (*WWLN*), there is the Music Hall of the Eagle Tavern and Grecian Theatre in Shepherdess Walk, notorious for its low life and the refrain 'in and out the eagle'.   GRH

'London Tradesmen' (eleven-article series).

1. The Tailor. Conversations with one's tailor show him knowledgeable on many topics. He tends to be slow and high-priced, as proof of quality. Paying customers must compensate for non-payers. He is usually an honest man, doing his best with the bodies he has to clothe.

2. The Chemist. The value of the chemist seems questionable unless he is unavailable. His knowledge is essential; if he errs, he is liable to fast and serious ruin. His allegedly inflated prices are not unreasonable in light of the required education, examinations, and practice.

3. The Butcher. People wonder that he thrives in a business of killing and dismembering animals. He sometimes sells inferior meat as good; after a complaint, he deals fairly for some weeks, then cheats again. The cost of meat includes the percentage demanded by cooks, a custom butchers could unite to stop. Some become wealthy, but many fail.

4. The Plumber. Everyone knows him to be dishonest; he does his work so it will need redoing. His aim is profit, his demeanour sullen. It is doubtful if any plumbers go to heaven, though perhaps as many as government officials.

5. The Horse Dealer. Traditionally of bad reputation, modern horse dealers must be scrupulous, or they will soon be out of business (unlike private owners selling occasionally). The buyer should clearly describe his preferences and his budget; he will get an honest deal, probably a bargain. He should deal directly; coachmen or grooms will demand a percentage (higher than the cook's).

6. The Publican. The publican must admit anyone; thus, drunkards, rowdies, and disreputable women may come. His heart hardens as his customers' weakness becomes his fortune. His political views are totally self-serving. Upon retirement (early if possible), he becomes again his better self.

7. The Fishmonger. Freshness of fish is essential to this business. Bad or stale fish is rare; that not sold by the afternoon is often sent back to Billingsgate or given away. The London fish industry needs another market; Billingsgate is not large enough; there is much confusion, traffic problems, and delays as a result.

8. The Greengrocer. This tradesman is handicapped by the crowds at Covent Garden Market.

Limited space causes mishandling, delays, and non-fresh vegetables on the table. The market is a crowded, noisy, unpleasant workplace. Two or three additional Covent Garden style markets are badly needed.

9. The Wine-Merchant. There are several levels of wine-merchants. One has imperturbable effrontery and is a great nuisance. The best is fully knowledgeable, has very good wine, and a modest humour; 'to dine with him is, according to our ideas, the acme of human bliss'. Others exist, whose judgement and selection are erratic or worse.

10. The Coal-Merchant. Newer dealers use expensive advertising, mailed in sealed envelopes to great numbers of households. These notices misrepresent the senders as colliery owners and experts; this nuisance must add considerably to the price of coal. Old reliable businesses are best.

11. The Haberdasher. The haberdasher's store has become a great mart, selling not only clothing but linens, furniture, even food and wine. The quality of the merchandise is sometimes doubtful. Men usually prefer to deal with shop-owners; women tend to enjoy the social aspects of large stores. Men clerks are slower to train than women, but stay longer; thus they are cheaper help in the long run. *Pall Mall Gazette* (10, 17, 24, 29 July; 5, 11, 18, 23, 26, 28 August; 7 September 1880). AKL

Longbarns, prosperous home and farm of John Fletcher, a Herefordshire squire, and his family. *PM* JMR

Longestaffe, Adolphus, overbearing, financially constrained squire of Caversham, who is constantly at odds with his son Dolly and his daughter Georgiana. Proud of his position, he nevertheless compromises the family name through his dealings with Augustus Melmotte. The dispute arising over the sale of Pickering, one of his houses, eventually brings about Melmotte's downfall. *WWLN* SRB

Longestaffe, Adolphus (Dolly), well-heeled but infinitely laconic young man who always follows the path of least resistance. Devoted chiefly to playing cards and smoking cigars, Dolly Longestaffe rouses himself occasionally to fight with his father about money. He shows some rare spirit also in objecting to his sister's residence with the Melmottes in *The Way We Live Now*, and in asking Isabel Boncassen to marry him in *The Duke's Children*. JMR

Longestaffe, Georgiana, haughty, sharp-tongued daughter of a country squire. Twenty-nine and desperate to be married, she lowers herself to accept a 'vulgar, upstart Jew', but her family's horror and lover's plain speaking prevent the marriage. Enraged by her family's cold indifference and the humiliation of her position as a dependent daughter, she eventually runs off with a curate. *WWLN* SRB

Longestaffe, Lady Pomona, high-living, proud wife of Adolphus, squire of Caversham. She bemoans the family's financial straits, largely brought on by her own extravagance, and cruelly rejects her daughter Georgiana for attempting an escape through marriage to Ezekiel Brehgert. *WWLN* SRB

Longestaffe, Sophia, spiteful elder daughter of Adolphus. Unable to catch a rich, smart husband in London, she accepts the dull George Whitstable, much to her sister Georgiana's contempt. However, her socially acceptable alliance is flaunted before the once scornful Georgiana, who falls into disgrace for engaging herself to a Jew. *WWLN* SRB

Longfellow, Henry Wadsworth (1807–82), American poet much loved in England. During 1868–9 he was given honorary degrees by Cambridge and Oxford and received by the Queen. He became the only American honoured by a bust in Poet's Corner, Westminster Abbey. Trollope met him in November 1860, and called him 'poet-laureat of the West' (*NA* 1, XVI). He asked Whitman's autograph for Rose and received a signed poem. Trollope sent him a copy of *North America* in May 1862. His article **'Henry Wadsworth Longfellow'* appeared in *North American Review* (April 1881). RCT

Longley, Charles Thomas (1794–1868), Doctor of Divinity (1829), headmaster of Harrow School (1829–36) during Trollope's time in the sixth form; Archbishop of Canterbury (1862–8). He was the one teacher Trollope recalled with any respect or affection. Lord Bessborough, a schoolmate, noted that in recalling his utter failure academically Trollope had forgotten that he received an English prize from Longley, who said to Bessborough hoping for his own prize, 'You did well, but, you see, Trollope writes better English than you do, at present' (quoted Hall 44). Trollope had his old headmaster in mind when he drew Bishop Yeld in *The Way We Live Now*, labelled in his notes for the novel 'Old Longley'. RCT

Longman, William (1813–77), partner in the publishing firm founded in 1724 by Thomas Longman. *The Warden*, accepted for publication October 1855, followed by *Barchester Towers* in 1857, launched Trollope's writing career. When Longman dickered over payment for *The Three Clerks* (1858), suggesting the firm's imprint mattered more, Trollope took it to Bentley, commenting in *An Autobiography*, 'I did think much of Messrs Longman's name, but I liked it best at the bottom of a cheque' (VI).   RCT

Longroyston, family seat of the Duke of St Bungay. *PR*   JMR

Longstop, Sir Lords, cricketer in the great match between England and Britannula. He represents English aristocracy and fine manners, which are ambiguously respected and mildly derided by the independent Britannulists who, significantly, win the cricket match. *FixP*   SRB

Longsword, Major, brought in by Jonas Brown to act as his second in a duel with Councillor Webb. He attempts to negotiate between the two men, being 'a great hand at an apology', but his 'mission of peace' is unsuccessful (XXVI). *MB*   MRS

Lookaloft, Mr, tenant farmer of Squire Thorne of Ullathorne. Having more sense or less courage than his wife, he chooses not to attend the Thornes' fête. *BT*   NCS

Lookaloft, Mrs, social-climbing wife of one of Squire Thorne's tenant farmers. At the Ullathorne fête, she pluckily manœuvres her overdressed daughters into the Ullathorne drawing room to hobnob with the country nobility, much to the dismay of neighbours relegated to the outlying park. *BT*   NCS

Lopez, Emily (née **Wharton**), Abel Wharton's imprudent daughter, wife of Ferdinand Lopez. Emily Wharton is replete with feminine virtues and demonstrates enormous grace and maturity as her husband's villainous character becomes apparent. But her strength may also be regarded as stubbornness, a serious flaw in her character. Emily's obstinacy is seen in her insistence on marrying Ferdinand Lopez despite the fact that she knows little of his character. Similarly, after Lopez's suicide, believing herself permanently shamed by her imprudent marriage, Emily initially refuses to marry Arthur Fletcher, a man she can truly love and trust. *PM*   JMR

Lopez, Ferdinand, unscrupulous financial adventurer of questionable extraction who wins the hand of Emily Wharton. Considered by most of the conservative Wharton family to be a 'foreign cad' and a 'greasy Jew adventurer out of the gutter', he is, in fact, a good-looking and well-educated young man with genteel manners. Unfortunately for his wife Emily, Lopez is also without honour or honesty; he leads his business partner into financial ruin, manipulates Emily to try to get at her father's fortune, and dallies shamelessly with Lizzie Eustace. But while Lopez

is without morals, he is not without feelings. Miserable in the life he has created for himself, he exits dramatically, throwing himself in the path of an oncoming express train. *PM*   JMR

'Lord Brougham and Mr Edmunds' (article). The Edmunds scandal is now widely known; the condition of his appointment as Patent Clerk for over 30 years required paying most of his salary to others. As Chancellor, Lord Brougham must have known the situation. A thorough investigation and publication is called for. *Pall Mall Gazette* (11 March 1865), 1–2.   AKL

'Lord Chancellor, The' (letter). The continuing abuses of patronage exercised by Lord Westbury are a disgrace to all English people. Only Westbury's resignation from the lord chancellorship can be acceptable following this latest misbehaviour. *Pall Mall Gazette* (28 June 1865), 4.

AKL

Lord Palmerston. Henry John Temple, 3rd Viscount Palmerston (1784–1865), was the subject of a memoir by Trollope begun in November 1881 and completed 1 February 1882. As Lord *Brock a potent presence or memory throughout the Palliser novels, Lord Palmerston was surely Trollope's greatest political hero. He seemingly had it all: tall, dark, handsome, and intelligent, he succeeded to his father's title (an Irish peerage which did not confer membership of the House of Lords) and extensive estates at age 18. He entered the House of Commons at age 22, and at 23, having modestly declined the office of Chancellor of the Exchequer and a cabinet seat, accepted that of Secretary at War. At Trollope's birth he had already served over six years as a government minister. When Trollope turned 50, Palmerston was still a minister—the Prime Minister.

Palmerston was not spoiled by early advantages. For twenty years he worked hard in the same demanding and unglamorous position, earning a reputation for reliability, toughness, and tact as administrative head of the army. He did not break into the political front ranks until the Tory government began to fragment after the departure of Lord Liverpool in 1827. Showing hitherto unnoticed political and oratorical skills Palmerston moved deftly leftwards and in 1830 exited his party to accept the office of Foreign Secretary in the newly formed Whig government of Lord Grey.

For 25 of the next 35 years, Palmerston shaped his country's foreign policy at the time of its greatest power and influence. He was alert and assertive in pursuing Britain's traditional policy of preventing the emergence of a dominant continental power, and became accustomed to conducting foreign policy largely unchecked. Queen Victoria and Prince Albert resented Palmerston's high-handedness, particularly in the aftermath of the 1848 revolutions, and managed to have him ousted as Foreign Secretary in 1851. Palmerston then demonstrated his political power by bringing down the government. It has been plausibly argued that had he remained Foreign Secretary the Crimean War might have been avoided. Certainly it was the unsatisfactory conduct of that war that made Palmerston the inevitable choice as Prime Minister in 1855. Apart from a short spell in opposition in 1858–9, he remained Prime Minister until his death.

Trollope wrote *Lord Palmerston* in the last year of his life, and though, as reviewers noted, it is scantily researched and contains several errors, it none the less offers within its brief compass a fairly convincing impression of Palmerston's character and career as it appeared to a well-informed and sympathetic onlooker. Trollope begins by defending him from the charge of having 'behaved badly to the Queen' (*Letters* 2, 935), but his simplification of complex foreign policy matters, particularly the famous Don Pacifico affair, so often seen as the quintessence of Palmerstonism, makes it rather cruder than it was. In calling Palmerston a bully Trollope applied a highly charged epithet to his fellow old Harrovian. None the less Palmerston had most of the attributes of a Trollopian hero, and Plantagenet Palliser was given several of his most notable qualities, particularly his stubbornness, though not his easy affability. Like Palliser, Palmerston was dogged and diligent, working long hours at a special stand-up desk which he could not fall asleep over. Ordinarily an indifferent speaker, perhaps calculatingly avoiding the 'rock of eloquence' with his frequent 'ahs' and 'ums', he could occasionally rise to brilliance, as in his legendary 'Civis Romanus Sum' speech of 1850. He was thick-skinned, optimistic, and upright in his political dealings—'manly', in short, to use a favourite Trollopian epithet. Crucial to Palmerston's indispensability was his liberal conservatism: a lapsed Tory, but never a true Whig, he was widely acceptable across the political spectrum, and had a sharp sense of the political tides. He was notably lukewarm towards parliamentary reform, essentially stonewalling it during his premiership. Despite his opportunism he had principles: he was an early supporter of Catholic emancipation and free trade and a passionate enemy of the slave trade, and, like Trollope, of the cowardly idea of the secret ballot. As Prime Minister he presided over the emergence of the Liberal Party and the further liberalization of the economy.

In his private life, Palmerston was a keen horseman who rode hard until the end of his life. He was a good landlord to his Irish tenants. He increased his wealth with some bold but ultimately profitable mining investments. He neither gambled nor drank heavily, but had a large appetite for food and women. A pattern Regency buck, Palmerston energetically and successfully pursued some of the greatest beauties of his time. One of them, Emily, Countess Cowper, the sister of Palmerston's great friend and ally Lord Melbourne, was his mistress for some 30 years and several of her children were almost certainly fathered by him. When her complaisant husband died she married Palmerston, and became an enormous asset to him as London's most effective political hostess. Lady Glencora Palliser owes something to her.

An astute manager of his political image, Palmerston won great popularity from the late 1840s onwards as the personification of John Bull, in which role *Punch* frequently portrayed him. Even his evergreen reputation as a ladies' man contributed to his popularity as when, at age 78, he was accused of adultery by the husband of a pretty Irishwoman: 'She may be O'Kane', said the wags, 'but is Palmerston Abel?' The manuscript is in the Taylor Collection, Princeton University. See also PALMERSTON, HENRY JOHN TEMPLE, 3RD VISCOUNT. CK

Bourne, Kenneth, *Palmerston: The Early Years 1784–1841* (1982).
Southgate, Donald, *The Most English Minister* (1966).

'Lord Westbury and Mr Edmunds' (letter). The recent treatment of the dishonest civil servant Edmunds by the Lord Chancellor is disgraceful. Allowing the resignation with a pension of a proven thief of public funds is an insult to all in the civil service and an outrage to decent citizens. *Pall Mall Gazette* (8 May 1865), 4. AKL

Loring, factory town in Gloucestershire, home of Pastor John Marrable, his relative Sarah Marrable, and her niece Mary Lowther. *VB* SRB

Lorraine, incorporated into Germany after the Franco-Prussian War (1870–1). It is the site of Granpère and the Lion d'Or. *GLG* MG

Loth, Rebecca, urges Nina to give up the man they both love, rather than ruin him in Jewish society. Their nervous rivalry changes to sisterly affection when the queenly Jewess aids Nina during her father's sickness and rescues her from death. *NB* AWJ

'Lotta Schmidt', first published in *Argosy*, July 1866 (reprinted in *LS*); a short story set in 1860s Vienna. A beautiful young Viennese girl, Lotta Schmidt, has two suitors. One is a handsome and dashing young man, Fritz Planken. The other suitor is a 45-year-old, physically unprepossessing musician, Herr Crippel. Crippel plays violin in a beer hall. After some internal wavering, Lotta finally chooses the older man, largely persuaded by the beauty of his playing on the zither, an instrument particularly associated with Vienna. The story ends with the couple intending to marry in a fortnight. JS

Lotta Schmidt and Other Stories, one volume, Strahan, 1867. Called by Trollope, in *An Autobiography, Tales of All Countries: Third Series*, this volume of short stories covers work mainly published in magazines between December 1862 and January 1867. As in its predecessors, the settings are largely foreign. JS

Lough Corrib, waterway used to irrigate part of Philip Jones's property until Landleaguers open the sluice gates, flooding 80 acres (32 ha) of meadow. *L* MRS

Loughlinter, immense Scottish estate of Mr Robert Kennedy. Until his marriage, Mr Kennedy is a popular host, and his property is a favourite country retreat for the Liberal élite. With the advent of the Kennedys' marital difficulties, however, the retreat becomes a cold, dark, isolated, and prison-like place. *PF* JMR

Loughshane, borough in Co. Galway, Ireland, represented in Parliament by Phineas Finn. *PF* JMR

Loughton, borough for which Phineas Finn is elected member of Parliament through the influence of Lord Brentford. *PF* JMR

Louisiana, Southern American state and site of the plantation owned by the Lefroys until the end of the Civil War. *DWS* RC

Lovel, Lady Anna (Murray), only child of Earl Lovel and Josephine Murray. She refuses to marry her cousin (Frederic Lovel) in order to secure her claim to the Lovel name and wealth. She remains loyal to Daniel Thwaite, the tailor who is her childhood friend and grown-up lover and to whom she is secretly engaged. Although swayed by the Earl's attentions and situation, her firm belief in the sanctity of her promise to Daniel leads to their marriage. *LA* RC

Lovel, Charles, Tory clergyman and uncle of the young Earl, Frederic Lovel, who is virulently opposed to the claims of the Murrays. He is 'passionate, loud, generous, affectionate, and indiscreet' (V). His militant and inflexible conservatism prompts the narrator to comment on 'the difficulty of drawing the line between political sagacity and political prejudice' (XLVIII). *LA* RC

Lovel, Earl, wealthy libertine who lives primarily abroad. He claims to have been already married when he marries Josephine Murray, but he is subsequently acquitted of bigamy. His deathbed will acknowledges Anna Murray as an illegitimate daughter but leaves his estate to his current companion, Signorina Camilla Spondi. The will is set aside on the grounds of insanity. *LA* RC

Lovel, Frederic, successor to Earl Lovel and youthful head of the family. An affable, honourable, but poor man, he courts Lady Anna in the hope of securing the Lovel wealth in addition to the title he indisputably holds. He loses Anna to Daniel Thwaite but accepts her offer to divide the Lovel estate between them. *LA* RC

Lovel, Jane, well-to-do wife of Revd Charles Lovel. She is quickly won over by Lady Anna, despite her husband's conviction that the Murrays are ill-bred impostors. *LA* RC

Lovel, Countess Josephine (née **Murray**), beautiful and ambitious daughter of Captain Murray, who marries Earl Lovel despite his disreputable character and her romantic indifference. Abandoned by him, the legality of her marriage contested, she spends nineteen years as 'a wretched, unacknowledged, poverty-stricken countess' (VIII) befriended only by the Thwaites. Although ultimately acknowledged and wealthy, she remains wretched because her daughter marries a tailor. She wishes that Anna were dead and goes so far as to attempt to murder Daniel Thwaite. *LA* RC

Lovel, Julia, unmarried and strong-minded aunt of the young Earl, Frederic Lovel. She carries a good deal of authority in the Lovel family. More tolerant than Charles Lovel but more stern than his wife, she combines suspicion of Lady Anna's claim with appreciation of her character. *LA* RC

Lovel, Minnie (Mary), daughter of Charles and Jane Lovel. Unlike her father, she immediately recognizes in Lady Anna one 'of such nature and breeding as made her fit to be a cousin' (XIII). She cannot understand Anna's rejecting her cousin (Frederic Lovel) in favour of a tailor (Daniel Thwaite). *LA* RC

Lovel Grange, home of the Lovel family, located in the mountains between Cumberland and Westmorland. *LA* RC

Lovelace, Henry. The Dean of Brotherton rose from humble beginnings by his own merits, but has been unable 'to get rid of the last porcine taint' (II). A loving father, he none the less encourages his daughter to marry Lord George Germain to gratify his rather pagan ambitions. When the Marquis of Brotherton insults her, the usually urbane Dean most unclerically tosses him into a fireplace. His energy and monetary power are often resented by his son-in-law. The driving force behind the inquiry into the legitimacy of Lord Popenjoy, the Dean's dreams are realized when he becomes grandfather of a future marquis. *IHP*　　　MG

Low, Georgiana, sympathetic and motherly wife of Mr Low. Protective of her husband's social standing, she is somewhat jealous of Phineas Finn's parliamentary honours, but her loyalty to her husband does not prevent her being a true friend to Phineas. *PF, PR*　　　JMR

Low, Mr, respectable middle-aged barrister who reads law with young Phineas Finn. Mr Low is initially displeased by Phineas's parliamentary ambitions, believing that a barrister should enter Parliament only after his law career is established. His displeasure is conquered, however, when he himself becomes Conservative member for North Broughton. *PF, PR*　　　JMR

Low, Sampson (1797–1886), bookseller-stationer turned publisher; inaugurated *Publisher's Circular* (1837) which became his sole property (1867); issued *English Catalogue* (1853–82). As Harper's agent in England he negotiated publication from early sheets of Trollope's *Life of Cicero* (1880). Trollope rapidly grew disillusioned with American publishers, labelling them 'dishonest beasts' (*Letters* 2, 913). Low acquired the rights of *Harry Heathcote of Gangoil* and published it in a single volume in October 1874. By 1878 Trollope was so aggrieved by Harper's piracy that he turned his dealings with Low over to Chapman. 'I hate the American doings so utterly', he wrote to William Blackwood in April 1878, 'that I wash my hands of them altogether' (*Letters* 2, 775).　　　RCT

Lowe, Robert, Viscount Sherbrook (1811–92), fellow Wykehamist (1825–9); first MP for London University (1868–80); Chancellor of the Exchequer (1868–73); Home Secretary (1873–4); created Viscount (1880). At Winchester, where scourging was commonplace in the 1820s, if screams were heard they were probably those of Anthony being beaten by his brother; 'if you heard particularly loud screams, they would be those of both the Trollopes being beaten by Bob Lowe' (Glendinning 24). Escott commented: 'Lowe was for many years the one politician in the front rank with whom Trollope had real intimacy' (quoted Super 8).　　　RCT

Lowell, James Russell (1819–91), American diplomat, poet, critic, and original editor of the *Atlantic Monthly* (1857–61). He met Trollope at a dinner in Boston (1861): 'a big, red-faced, rather underbred Englishman of the bald-with-spectacles type. A good roaring positive fellow who deafened me (sitting on his right) till I thought of Dante's Cerberus.' Lowell found that he 'rather liked' Trollope. In his hearing Trollope made his customary claim that he went to work on a novel 'just like a shoemaker on a shoe, only taking care to make honest stitches' (*I & R* 77). Trollope wrote at length to Lowell on the vexed issue of international copyright, a letter reprinted in the *Athenaeum* (September 1862). See COPYRIGHTS, HALF-PROFITS, ROYALTIES.　　　RCT

Lowestoffe (sometimes **Lowestoft**), seaside resort where Roger Carbury surprises his friend Paul Montague and Mrs Hurtle in their compromising stay there. Paul nearly loses his engagement to Hetta Carbury when she learns of it. *WWLN*　　　SRB

Lownd, Isabel. Loving Christmas, she responds angrily to Maurice Archer's depreciation of it, but their tiff does not last long, and she accepts his renewed proposal of marriage. 'Kirkby'　　　GRH

Lownd, Revd John. The rector approves of Maurice Archer as his daughter's suitor and believes that constancy and perseverance will win her. 'Kirkby'　　　GRH

Lownd, Mabel, bouncy younger sister of Isabel who wants her to marry Maurice Archer. 'Kirkby'　　　GRH

Lownd, Mrs. Anxious about her daughter's state of mind (and heart), she 'trembled for her girl' in respect of Maurice Archer. 'Kirkby'　　　GRH

Lowndes, William Selby (1807–86), master of the Whaddon Chase Hounds with whom Trollope hunted in the early 1870s after returning from Australia. For a few years he travelled from London three days a week to Essex or Leighton Buzzard, joining Lowndes or Baron Meyer *Rothschild. Trollope preferred riding with the Baron.　　　RCT

Lowther, Mary, beautiful, graceful, self-reliant friend of the vicar of Bullhampton and his wife. Urged by them and her Aunt Sarah Marrable to marry Harry Gilmore, a man she greatly respects but does not love, she makes herself miserable trying dutifully to please others. After much vacillation on the nature of marrying for love or for a good match, she eventually marries the man she loves, her cousin Walter Marrable. *VB*   SRB

Lowther Arms, the inn at Shap where Kate Vavasor meets her brother George. *CYFH*   JMR

Lufton, Lady. Widowed mother of Lord Lufton, she resides at Framley Court, Barsetshire. Though not worldly, she delights in arranging and ordering parish affairs. Having successfully married off her daughter Justinia, she arranges the marriage of Justinia's friend Fanny Mansell to her protégé Mark Robarts, the vicar. Devoted to her son, she attempts to arrange his marriage to Griselda Grantly and opposes his interest in Lucy Robarts, the minister's 'insignificant' sister. Strongly high-church, she has a memorable encounter with the Duke of Omnium, whom she considers the Devil incarnate, at Martha Dunstable's London soirée. *FP, LCB*   NCS

Lufton, Lord Ludovic, Baron Lufton of Lufton, Oxfordshire. A good-humoured, sweet-tempered, bright-looking bachelor of 26, he cheerfully puts up with his beloved mother's attempt to marry him to Griselda Grantly, while falling in love with Lucy Robarts. He introduces his friend Revd Mark Robarts to a set of fashionable companions where they both fall into debt. He finally helps Mark settle his debts. *FP, LCB*   NCS

Lufton Park, uninhabited, ramshackle, former family home of the Luftons in Oxfordshire. *FP*   NCS

Lupex, Maria, one of Johnny Eames's fellow boarders at Mrs Roper's house in Burton Crescent, London. When her improvident, drunken, and jealous husband is away, the clever, worldly woman maligns love and marriage while flirting unconscionably with Joseph Cradell. *SHA*   NCS

Lupex, Orson, husband of Maria Lupex for eight years, with whom he has lodgings at Mrs Roper's in Burton Crescent. An easy, listless, self-indulgent scenery-painter, he often displays drunken, jealous rages over his wife's behaviour. A failed artist, he cautions Johnny Eames about marrying. *SHA*   NCS

Lupton, Mr, discreet sporting gentleman, member of the Beargarden Club. Mr Lupton tries unsuccessfully to warn Lord Silverbridge against

making large bets before the running of the St Leger. He subsequently leads the movement to have the dishonest Major Tifto expelled from the Beargarden. *DC*   JMR

Luxa, Lotta. 'A sharp little woman' who hates Jews, Mme Zamenoy's servant and confidante predicts that Nina will inevitably be jilted. In such a situation, 'I would drown myself' (V). It is Lotta who thinks up a way to ensure Trendellsohn's defection, without considering how that might indeed send Nina to her death in the Moldau river. *NB*   AWJ

Lynch, Anastasia (Anty), unlikely heroine of Trollope's second novel, an Irish Catholic ten years older than her suitor Martin Kelly, who despite the bullying of her murderous brother Barry keeps her property and wins a husband. Though her self-esteem, talent, and beauty have been diminished by years of abuse in her father's household, once Anty inherits half his estate, she quickly rallies from habitual docility to fend for her rights against her brother, who aims to terrorize her into forfeiting her property. Eventually, the Kellys provide a safe home, but not before the heroine demonstrates her capacity to withstand intimidation. *KOK*   MRS

Lynch, Barry, heir of Simeon Lynch of Dunmore House, a murderous alcoholic, whose relentless objectification of others, especially his sister Anty, makes him one of Trollope's blackest villains. Perhaps an experiment in genre, appearing as he does in Trollope's 'prentice second novel, he combines Gothic touches of madness with sensationalist plots to appropriate his sister's inheritance involving physical assault, threats of incarceration, and murder. He serves as a cautionary figure, dramatizing the horrors of alcohol abuse, as well as the dangers of gender ideologies that encourage men to dominate women. *KOK*   MRS

Lynch, Simeon (Sim), father of Barry and Anastasia Lynch who filched his estate, Dunmore House, from the O'Kellys. When, in a fit of anger against Barry, he bequeaths half the estate to his daughter, he sows seeds of implacable rage in his son, whose attempts to appropriate her share of the inheritance drive the main plot of the novel. *KOK*   MRS

Lytton, Edward George Lytton Bulwer-.
See BULWER-LYTTON, EDWARD GEORGE LYTTON.

Maberly, Colonel William Leader (1798–1885), Secretary of the Post Office (1836–54). He was 'not my friend', Trollope recalled (*Auto* III). Maberly treated him 'as though I were unfit for any useful work'. Trollope was constantly admonished by Maberly, not without cause, and came close to losing his position. After seven unsatisfied years as a junior clerk in the Secretary's Office, an opportunity came for Trollope to volunteer for a post in Ireland. Maberly, he states, 'was glad to be so rid of me, and I went'. However, when Trollope later applied for the post of Superintendent of Mail Coaches (1852), he not only cited Maberly as a reference, but Maberly wrote a favourable letter to the Postmaster General, the Earl of Hardwicke, commending Trollope for his prompt and effective reorganization of rural posts (*Letters* 1, 32). The appointment as Superintendent went to another officer, W. T. Wedderburn, who outranked Trollope in seniority. Sir Boreas Bodkin ('Aeolus') in *Marion Fay* is probably based on Maberly.

RCT

Macaulay, Thomas Babington (1800–59), historian, critic, poet, and statesman; achieved celebrity through his essays in the *Edinburgh Review*. Ranked among the greatest stylists of the day by Trollope (*Auto* VI), who recommended that all writers take note of Macaulay's insistence on 'the all-important art of making meaning pellucid' (*Auto* XII). Macaulay's 'prophecy' in the *Edinburgh Review* in 1840 that a visitor from New Zealand in the future would sketch the ruins of St Paul's Cathedral inspired the title of Trollope's

The New Zealander, which in Carlylean terms warned of Britain's downward spiral through money-worship. To G. W. Rusden in 1878 he suggested that both Froude and Macaulay had made themselves masters of a certain historical purpose, and, though inexact, they had 'left a picture of their periods which the world of readers has acknowledged to be true' (*Letters* 2, 791).   RCT

M'Buffer, Mr, MP for Tillietudlem. M'Buffer accepts the stewardship of the Chiltern Hundreds (resigns from Parliament), 'having been a managing director of a bankrupt swindle, from which he had contrived to pillage some thirty or forty thousand pounds' (XXIV), leaving his parliamentary seat vacant for Undecimus Scott. *TC*

MT

McCann, Judy, Father McGrath's faithful servant. *TMB*   MRS

McCarthy, Father Bernard, parish priest of Drumbarrow, respected by the Catholic Irish peasantry, but demonized by the Protestant rector, Mr Townsend, his wife, and Aunt Letty. He abjures their prejudices, yet makes for an eager, even 'malicious antagonist' (X). He prides himself on his clean, starched apparel, in dramatic contrast to the grubby rector, but, according to the narrator, it cannot disguise inferior birth and education. *CR*   MRS

Macdermot, Euphemia (Feemy), Trollope's first fictional heroine, regarded by Hugh Walpole as showing 'a certain poetry and tragic inevitability' not found in later heroines (*Anthony Trollope* (1928), 27). Sister of Thady Macdermot, impoverished heir of Ballycloran, she is 'ardent and energetic' (II), but lack of education and companionship make her susceptible to Myles Ussher, a police officer in the pay of the English, who seduces her. When Ussher is killed by her brother, Feemy's evidence could vindicate him, but she dies of pre-natal complications before being called to the stand. *MB*   MRS

Macdermot, Lawrence (Larry), demoralized, alcoholic father of Thady and Feemy Macdermot, whose pride in his chieftain ancestry is the catalyst for Joe Flannelly's hatred and persecution of the impoverished family. Subject to a 'despairing apathy' (VI) that, coupled with drink, impairs his reason, he falls victim to his greatest tragedy: not eviction from the ancestral home, but loss of faith in the son who loves him. *MB*   MRS

Macdermot, Thaddeus (Thady), care-worn heir of Ballycloran, a heavily mortgaged estate in Co. Leitrim, whose unintentional killing of Myles Ussher, his sister Feemy's lover, results in execution by hanging. The death of Ussher, a police officer in the pay of the English, is construed by the courts as murder: a premeditated political act intended to strike against British authority. Thady is consequently seen as heinous criminal by the representatives of English justice, and as heroic martyr by the local Irish tenantry. Betrayed by his own naivety, trapped by codes of family honour, and cornered by colonial powers, Thady is one of Trollope's few protagonists denied successful agency, his plight dramatizing a lack of autonomy that in turn exemplifies the predicament of the colonial subject under foreign rule. *MB*   MRS

Macdermot, Captain Tom, police officer who assumes control after the assault on Father Giles and helps to restore peaceful relations. 'Giles' *LS*   GRH

Macdermots of Ballycloran, The (*see next page*)

Macdonald, George (1824–1905), Scottish author of *David Elginbrod* (1863) and *Robert Falconer* (1868), best known for children's stories such as *At the Back of the North Wind* (1871). In August 1868, Trollope requested a Christmas story for *Saint Pauls* of about twenty pages. 'Let it not be sensible;—but weird rather, and of a Christmas-ghostly flavour, if such be possible' (*Letters* 1, 442). Macdonald offered 'Uncle Cornelius: His Story', which appeared in January 1869. Trollope considered him 'a clever, honest, industrious, imaginative man, with a large intellect' (*Letters* 2, 716) but found him no great stylist. However, he acknowledged him among the writers without whose assistance *Saint Pauls* would not have succeeded (*Auto* XV).   RCT

Macdonnel, Major, steward at the Carrick races, and an aspirant Tory politician, who is brought in by Councillor Webb to act as his second in a duel with Jonas Brown. *M*   MRS

McEvoy, Andy, ancient Irishman who speaks no English and lives with his daughter Meg in extreme poverty in the mountains of Aughacashel where Thady Macdermot takes refuge after the murder of Myles Ussher. Tortured by 'the vulture in his stomach' (XXIII), he sits still and silent all day, a living emblem of the paralysis of Irish culture, until his terrible apathy drives Thady to return to Ballycloran to yield himself to the authorities. *MB*   MRS

McEvoy, Meg, dishevelled daughter of Andy McEvoy, who tends to Thady Macdermot when he takes refuge in her father's hovel at Aughacashel. *M*   MRS

M'Gabbery, Mr, one of the travelling party at Jerusalem bent on attending to Caroline Waddington till ousted by George Bertram. He suffers wet feet on her behalf when he attempts to rescue her from a fall into the pool of Siloam, a minor event but subsequently highlighted as 'an oasis in his otherwise somewhat barren life' (IX). *B*
                                        MRS

McGovery, Denis, blacksmith in the village of Drumsna, Co. Leitrim, who proposes to Mary Brady in consideration of her 'two small pigs and thrifle of change' (VIII). Their marriage party provides Trollope with the opportunity for a description of Irish merry-making, while allowing Thady Macdermot to be set up as a conspirator in the planning of Myles Ussher's murder. *MB*
                                        MRS

M'Gramm, Captain, Mrs Price's unofficial beau on board the *Cagliari*, who, as a married man, is quickly jettisoned in favour of the unmarried Arthur Wilkinson. *B*   MRS

McGrath, Father John, parish priest of Drumsna who acts as councillor, confessor, and comforter to Feemy and Thady Macdermot. A sympathetic portrait of a Catholic priest, he appears not only well born, well educated, well dressed, and well mannered, but also goodnatured, temperate, merciful, and generous. But when Thady turns to him for help, the priest cannot protect him from Ireland's turbulent history, and henceforth his role is to oversee the ruination of the Macdermot family. *MB*   MRS

McGrew, Peter, aged butler at Morony Castle, who despite receiving a death-threat remains loyal to his English master Philip Jones, subject of a general boycott. *L*   MRS

MacHugh, Mrs, widow of a former dean of Exeter Cathedral. She is Miss Stanbury's 'most intimate friend' (VII) and a fellow enthusiast of whist. *HKWR*   RC

Mackenzie, Clara, self-assured, wealthy wife of Walter Mackenzie who rescues Margaret Mackenzie from loneliness and neglect with an invitation to her home in Cavendish Square. She eases the strained relationship between Margaret and John Ball, sympathetically advising and supporting the two lovers, and eventually orchestrating a renewed engagement between them. *MM*
                                        SRB

Mackenzie, Julius, fine scholar, a sympathetic character, once a gentleman, who, after his drunken wife burns the Doctor's manuscript, for which he was making an index, cuts his throat. 'Dog' *ET*   GRH

TROLLOPE's first novel, largely ignored when it appeared in 1847, has become appreciated only in the last two decades. It is a 'condition of Ireland' novel, much in the vein of social problem novels of the 1840s, dealing with that afflicted nation just prior to its greatest trials in the potato famine (1845–9), a subject taken up in his third novel set in Ireland, *Castle Richmond*. Its genesis, described in *An Autobiography*, was a walk he took at Drumsna, Co. Leitrim, with his friend John Merivale, when they came across a ruined house. 'It was one of the most melancholy spots I ever visited' (IV). The moment is worked up as a prelude in which the narrator conjectures about that ruin. This segue into the narrative, resembling the device framing *Wuthering Heights* (published in the same year by the same publisher), speculates: 'The usual story, thought I, of Connaught gentlemen; an extravagant landlord, reckless tenants, debt, embarrassment, despair, and ruin' (I). It will be all these things, of course, but in terms the 'outsider' narrator will scarcely comprehend. Indeed, it is the guard of the Boyle coach who actually transmits to him the 'true' story of what the downfall of the house of Macdermot really signified. Rapidly the novel opens out in the way films so often do from a tracking shot which blurs into flashback to the 1830s. Thaddeus (Thady), *de facto* head of the Macdermot family, his sister Euphemia (Feemy), and their alcoholic father Lawrence (Larry), remnants of an Irish Catholic gentry, eke out a bare existence from rents scraped together by their destitute tenants. The Macdermots are in debt to Joe Flannelly, builder of their ostentatious but ramshackle mansion, and persecuted by an attorney, Hyacinth Keegan, who is married to Flannelly's daughter. Thady is reduced to harassing his tenants for rent to pay the mortgage on the estate; while Feemy, lacking education and company, escapes from her poverty by reading romantic novels. Into this situation comes Captain Myles Ussher, a police officer in the service of the English, an outsider from the northern county of Antrim, and a Protestant. Although illegitimate, and so without lineage, he is handsome and ambitious, and courts Feemy, who falls deeply in love; but he makes no formal declaration, and has no intention of making so poor a match. Ussher is hated by the locals for his determined prosecution of poteen (illicit whiskey) making, which solaces them and provides some small income. The disgruntled tenantry begin voicing rumours about Ussher's dishonourable intentions toward Feemy, which are conveyed to Thady via Pat Brady, Thady's manager and confidant. Thady grows to hate Ussher, while at the same time alienating his sister, whom he deeply cares for. Keegan brings Flannelly's offer to buy Ballycloran, but in a fit of drunken pride Larry drives him from the house. As Flannelly's heir, Keegan swears to gain possession of house and land.

Thady is urged, while drunk at the wedding of Mary Brady and Denis McGovery, to join a conspiracy by his more desperate tenants-cum-Ribbonmen (local groups struggling against English rule and unjust landlords) to 'rid the country' of Captain Ussher. When he comes to his senses, however, he refuses further involvement, a decision supported by Father John McGrath, the parish priest of Drumsna. Unable to dissuade Feemy from her attachment to Ussher, at least until a formal declaration, Father John arranges for her to stay with a respectable family, the McKeons, in the hope that the motherly Mrs McKeon may convince Feemy of her dangerous situation. A promotion involving transfer from Drumsna enables Ussher to bully Feemy into an elopement, promising that marriage will follow. During the elopement, Feemy faints, and as Ussher drags her to a coach, Thady spots them. Believing that Ussher is abducting

Feemy against her will, he clubs and kills him. After turning the body over to the authorities, Thady escapes into the mountains of Aughacashel with the aid of Joe Reynolds, one of the Ribbonmen. Because he is not present to give evidence, the coroner's inquest, having heard rumours of Thady's involvement in a plot to kill Ussher, finds that Thady should be tried for premeditated murder, rather than man-slaughter. After two nights as a fugitive, Thady returns to Father John, and together they go to the authorities, since the priest is convinced that once Thady gives his account, he will be vindicated. Feemy meanwhile falls ill and, although her evidence could clear Thady, has no recollection of the elopement, and declares she cannot forgive her brother for Ussher's death.

Thady spends six months in jail awaiting the assizes. Larry, incapable of grasping the situation, believes his son has betrayed him. Mrs McKeon suspects that Feemy may be pregnant, a diagnosis confirmed by the doctor. Only Father John and the hapless tenants remain committed to helping Thady. On the final day of the trial, Feemy, Thady's key witness, dies. Thady is found guilty of murder, and sentenced to hang. One week later the sentence is carried out with Father John at Thady's side. As part of the people's protest against British justice, shops remain closed, and Joe Reynolds and his men muster outside Carrick jail to block views of Thady's public hanging. 'As to the plot itself,' said Trollope, 'I do not know that I ever made one so good,—or, at any rate, one so susceptible of pathos' (*Auto* IV).

Even though he considered the novel had 'truth, freshness, and a certain tragic earnestness' (*Letters* 2, 613), Trollope was 'sure the book would fail, and it did fail most absolutely' (*Auto* IV), but while it was not a financial success, it was praised by several periodicals for narrative technique and natural characters. It possessed 'a fidelity of description and knowledge of character equal to anything in the writings of Maria Edgeworth', wrote *John Bull*. 'It is a story of intense interest, and is written by a bold and skilful hand', said *Howitt's Journal* (Smalley 549, 550). In Trollope's lifetime critics recalled its fidelity to Irish life, Irish characters, and Irish speech. The *Dublin Review* praised him in 1872 as a critical spectator who had no 'side' in the awful plight of Ireland. Indeed the *Spectator* critic (probably R. H. Hutton) in July 1879 went so far as to declare 'the Irish novels will be regarded as the high water mark of his ability' (52, 916). T. H. S. Escott, Trollope's first biographer, said it 'Formed the microcosm of an entire people' (*Anthony Trollope* (1913), 66). He rightly stressed its allegorical reach, which adds considerable breadth and power to the work. Such verdicts still warrant attention.

The Macdermots has an unusual publishing history. First published by the un-scrupulous T. C. Newby in 1847 in three volumes, it was promoted as the work of Trollope's mother Frances Trollope. But partly because Newby published only 400 copies, poorly advertised, and partly because, with the Great Famine at its height, the English public preferred to avoid contact with Ireland's troubles, the novel did not sell. In 1848, however, with the appearance of Trollope's second novel, *The Kellys and the O'Kellys*, Newby reissued it, this time crediting Trollope, but adding the misleading subtitle 'A Historical Romance', in hope of increasing its appeal. Little more is known of the novel's history until 1860, when Trollope regained copyright, and arranged with Chapman & Hall, his regular publishers from 1858, to reissue the novel. This edition was cut by three chapters, chapters II, III, and XII of volume 3 (see R. C. TERRY, 'Three Lost Chapters of Trollope's First Novel', *NCF* (June 1972), 71–80). In addition to new chapter headings, numerous minor stylistic changes were made, including the excision of a key sentence that made Feemy's death the result of abortive childbirth. The original also amplified the role of the kindly priest, McGrath. There is no concrete evidence that Trollope authorized any of these revisions—he does not, for example, refer to them in *An Autobiography*. Hence, Robert Tracy in his introduction to the World's Classics edition (1989) believes it is 'unthinkable that [Trollope] would let anyone else alter his text' (p. xxx), and Owen Dudley Edwards in the Folio Society edition (1991) remarks that 'quite probably [he] did not' initiate the revisions (p. xiii). Clearly, their status must remain problematical. Most editions of *The Macdermots* have traditionally reproduced the text of 1860, although the World's Classics edition includes the three omitted chapters in an appendix. The original 1847 text became available in 1981 with N. John Hall's Arno edition, followed by Owen Dudley Edwards's 1991 Folio Society edition. The manuscript is lost.

The Macdermots is a compelling story because it stems from a newcomer's fully awakened sensibility to new surroundings. Trollope arrived in Dublin in September 1841, as surveyor's clerk responsible for keeping track of complaints and defaulters in the postal system. This might have proved dangerous and certainly could have made him unpopular. Quite the reverse occurred. 'It was altogether a jolly life,' he noted (*Auto* IV). He got married, started a family, bought a hunter, and rode to hounds. Two years after his arrival he began his first novel and became miraculously transformed, noted his brother on a visit in 1842—a dedicated public servant. His love of the country and its people led to a series of letters to the *Examiner* (March–June 1850) and took him back to Ireland for his last book, *The Landleaguers*, unfinished at his death. 'It has been my fate to have so close an intimacy with Ireland', he wrote, 'that when I meet an Irishman abroad, I always recognize in him more of a kinsman than I do in an Englishman' (*NA* 2, XVI). Feeling distanced from the English establishment, and sensing affinity with the wildness and recklessness of the Irish, were part of that early recognition. Riding from village to village he listened well and caught the vernacular without strain. Cadence, rhythm, and linguistic feature are rendered with total actuality. ' "Deed then, Sir, and I do" said he, "and good reason have I to know; and well I knew those that lived in it, ruined, and black, and desolate as Ballycloran is now" ', says the Boyle coachman to the narrator (I). Trollope's love of Irish people helped him avoid the parodic tones of contemporary English observers and the stock 'Mick' ribaldry of Irish writers like Lover and Lever. Instead he tapped into authentic Celtic voices of passion and disequilibrium, responding to dark strains he found in writers like William Carleton and Gerald Griffin, whose *The Collegians* (1829) offered similar themes of flight and pursuit. He benefited also from Maria Edgeworth's regionalism, alluding to her respectfully in one of the chapters excised after the first edition. The rhythmic pattern of the novel is remarkably mature. Cumulatively the sense of Thady's tragic and representative fate at the heart of the story increases the reader's pity for the well-intentioned but helpless individual caught up in the muddle of Ireland's rural economy under English rule. Scenes of robust vitality like the McGovery wedding (XII, XIII), betting and horse racing (XVII–XIX), and a farcical duel (XXVI) throw into relief violent events, such as the severing of Keegan's leg, the wretchedness of Feemy's decline, Larry's dementia, and the agony of Thady's nights and days in Aughacashel (XXIII, XXIV). Here the writing has a strange phantasmagoric quality seldom found again in Trollope's fiction. The reader accustomed only to Barsetshire may be surprised by those Gothic touches. Trollope dares a great deal in this so-called 'prentice work, making a story of family downfall the paradigm of an oppressed country's misfortune. Thady's dark night of the soul in Aughacashel is climactic and central to personal and public themes (XXIII–XXIV). This is the place where Ussher had arrested Joe Reynolds's brother for poteen-making, reminding us of tyrant and subject people. Venturing further, where the inhabitants are a 'lawless, reckless set of people', Thady sees 'no road or sign of a road'. At the limits of endurance Thady stumbles into a cabin to meet life at its most animal level. After agonies of conscience and remorse Thady emerges from this limbo to face the law of the oppressors, triumphing over anarchy within and becoming a martyr for Ireland. The novel also includes Trollope's first equestrian scene and first courtroom drama. Another notable first is the device of a character arguing out internally the pros and cons of an action, as when Thady ponders his involvement with Keegan's enemies (XV). In maturity Trollope used such arguing of choices and an individual's emotional baggage with great subtlety.

The modern reputation of *The Macdermots* is as strange as its publishing history. Following Michael Sadleir's disparagement of Trollope's Irish tales it was neglected by publishers and critics alike. Since the 1960s, however, studies have recognized its merit not as a novel set in Ireland, but as a genuine exploration of the collision between colonizer and colonized. Ussher, the excise officer, is an Antrim man, but fills the role of English oppressor, feeding off the subject people through his job and deriding their nexus of community. Ussher's use of spies and informers Trollope despises as a state apparatus of control. Such incompatibilities between Irish character and English administration were clearly intended in the narrative framing of the novel (I), and it is significant that it should have been remarked by Escott, who knew Trollope well. By making the embodiment of power a vicious seducer of common goodness and innocence (Escott viewed Feemy as symbol of the people of Ireland, a manifestation of the iconic Cathleen), Trollope deepens the texture of subjected national identity. Thady's love for her is poignantly conveyed through Father John's comments to Mrs McKeon, who had given her temporary shelter after Ussher's death: 'if you could know how much more anxious he is on her account and his father's, than on his own' (XXVII). The parish priest plays a vital role throughout the novel as mediating presence of conscience, compassion, and higher morality measured against the iron secular law exercised by the judiciary through the trial scenes and hanging (XXVIII–XXXIII) which bring the story to an end. To return to the opening of the novel alerts the reader to the larger dimensions it intends to engage; Trollope's prose strains for the rhetorical gesture with a disquisition on Time and Ruin. If the novel shows the beginner's uncertainty over technique and is at times verbose and repetitive, it is unquestionably an auspicious beginning to Trollope's writing career. In his mature art he would refine those themes of integrated personal and public issues surrounding love, honour, duty, and moral responsibility, but these were announced in his first novel.   RCT

Johnston, Conor, 'Parsons, Priests and Politics: Anthony Trollope's Irish Clergy', *Éire-Ireland*, 25/1 (1990), 71–92.

Tracy, Robert, ' "The Unnatural Ruin": Trollope and Nineteenth-Century Irish Fiction', *NCF* (December 1982), 358–82.

Mackenzie, Margaret, unattractive, middle-aged eponymous heroine who leads a weary life nursing her father, then her brother for fifteen years. She is neglected by all until she gains her brother's fortune. When she enters 'the world' at Littlebath, her naive susceptibility and emotional insecurity are replaced by increasing self-assurance. Snubbed by her aunt, abused by her sister-in-law, and exploited by her suitors, she reflects the quiet courage and pride of an unmarried woman who gains respect and admiration through her enduring goodness and generosity. The quiet support of her cousin John Ball, which culminates in their marriage, teaches her that she is loved for her own sake. *MM*   SRB

Mackenzie, Sarah, Ungracious wife of Tom, she demands attention and money from his sister Margaret Mackenzie after Margaret inherits the family fortune. A nervous hostess, a penny-pinching landlady, and a self-pitying shrew, she never flags in venting her anger about her life on the mild, forbearing Margaret. *MM*   SRB

Mackenzie, Susanna, teenage niece, young-looking and sweet, whom Margaret Mackenzie undertakes to educate and care for, despite the mother Sarah's ingratitude and distrust. Susanna supplies affection and companionship to her lonely aunt and spiritedly defends Margaret to her mother. *MM*   SRB

Mackenzie, Thomas, Margaret's brother in the oilcloth business, who brings some disgrace to the family name through his trade and through financial mismanagement. He is ashamed of the liberty he and his partner Samuel Rubb take with his sister Margaret's generous loan. After his death, Margaret determines to help his widow and their seven children. *MM*
SRB

Mackenzie, Walter. Son of Sir Walter of Incharrow and husband of Clara, he becomes interested in his cousin Margaret following her notoriety from the scandalous journalism of Mr Maguire. He encourages his wife to befriend Margaret, who is eventually married from his prestigious home. *MM*   SRB

Mackenzie, Walter (the younger), invalid elder brother of Margaret, nursed by her for fifteen years. He had not distinguished himself in his earlier years as a clerk, but created considerable stir after his death by leaving the family fortune to his sister Margaret. *MM*   SRB

McKeon, Mrs, respectable neighbour of Feemy Macdermot, a 'kind, good, easy creature' who invites Feemy Macdermot to stay with her family in order to mitigate the circumstances of her other-

wise unchaperoned courtship with Myles Ussher. When Feemy proves pregnant, Mrs McKeon pleads with the priest on her behalf, and not only offers Feemy a home, but 'a mother's solicitude for her in her sorrows' (XXVII); Feemy dies holding Mrs McKeon's hand. *MB*   MRS

McKeon, Tony, contented family man and prosperous farmer who works hard but enjoys life's pleasures. When Thady Macdermot is charged with murder, he publicly supports him while defending Feemy's honour, and working with Father John McGrath to vindicate him. *MB*
MRS

Mackinnon, Conrad, American author who, after a passing flirtation with Arabella Talboys, is critical of her. 'Talboys' *TAC2*   GRH

Mackinnon, Mrs. Self-denying and tolerant of her husband's flirtations, she enjoys salon life in Rome. 'Talboys' *TAC2*   GRH

Mackintosh, Major, hard-working Scotland Yard official who investigates the theft of the Eustace diamonds. His kind manner finally induces Lizzie Eustace to admit that she perjured herself when giving evidence about the burglary at Carlisle. As head of the London Constabulary, he is also called to investigate the murder of Mr Bonteen in *Phineas Redux. ED*   JMR

Macleod, Revd Donald (1831–1916), chaplain to Queen Victoria (1857–72); brother of Norman Macleod and his successor as editor of *Good Words* after 1872, which published four stories of Trollope's, three articles, and the novel *Kept in the Dark.* Trollope's connection with the magazine exemplifies his scrupulous regard for deadlines, attention to contractual obligations, and business integrity. In October 1876, Macleod wrote to Trollope asking for a 'storiette'. Trollope submitted 'Why Frau Frohmann Raised her Prices', serialized February to May 1877. That year Trollope also wrote an article and another story, 'The Telegraph Girl', for the magazine. After *An Autobiography* appeared, Macleod wrote a reminiscence of Trollope in *Good Words,* 35 (1884), expressing surprise over his revelations of hardships in early life: 'For no trace of sorrow . . . could be detected in that bluff and cheery presence' (*I & R* 82). Trollope's powers of concentration and conscientious work habits made him 'a comfort for any editor . . . for there was never any anxiety as to "copy" being forthcoming at the appointed time'. As to revelations of his work methods, Macleod recognized some 'padding', but 'If he worked hard, he very properly expected to be paid for his work' (83).
RCT

Macleod, Lady, Alice Vavasor's closest maternal relative, much given to offering Alice unwanted advice. Trollope describes her as a 'good woman', but deplores her severe religious belief and near-worship of her great relatives. She is particularly loud in demanding that Alice honour her engagement to John Grey. *CYFH*   JMR

Macleod, Revd Dr Norman (1812–72), editor of *Good Words* from 1860 until his death. In April 1862 he approached Trollope for a contribution to his journal, which catered for varying sectors of the evangelical community of the Scottish Free and Anglican Church. In words which must have raised Trollope's eyebrows, he urged that here was the chance to 'let out the *best* side of your soul' (*I & R* 82). Trollope supplied 'The Widow's Mite' for the January 1863 issue. But when, under contract, he submitted *Rachel Ray*, Macleod, 'full of wailing and repentance' (*Auto* X), rejected it because of its uncomplimentary picture of professing Christians as full of 'weaknesses—shams—hypocrisies—gloom' (*Letters* 1, 223). Trollope claimed afterwards that *Rachel Ray* was not very wicked; 'the fault had been with the editor' (*Auto* X). Trollope continued publishing short stories in *Good Words*, which serialized *The Golden Lion of Granpère*. He supported Macleod's criticism of Scottish Sabbatarians in 'The Fourth Commandment' for *Fortnightly Review* (15 January 1866).   RCT

Macmanus, the Misses, two maiden ladies, appalled by the story of how the souvenir hunters in Antwerp came by the relics. 'Chassé' *TAC1*   GRH

Macmillan, Alexander (1818–96), Scottish co-founder (with his brother Daniel) of the publishing house of Macmillan & Co. who offended Trollope by publishing a single-volume novel in two-volume format. Macmillan purchased copyright of *Sir Harry Hotspur of Humblethwaite* for £750, his interest piqued by learning from the author that it was 'a common love story—but one that ends sadly' (*Letters* 1, 464). Serialized in *Macmillan's Magazine* (May–December 1870) it did not improve circulation, so Macmillan sold the book-rights, for a nine-month period, to Hurst & Blackett for £300. Their intended two-volume edition disgusted Trollope, who wrote to Macmillan: 'as one pound of tea wont make two by any variance in packing the article,—so neither will a one-volumed tale make two volumes . . . the quantity is too well and too nearly fixed to admit of such violent stretching' (*Letters* 1, 532–3). Although nearly half the book was already in type, Trollope had his way. Macmillan and Blackett came to an accommodation, Mac-

millan paying for part of the reprinting. The novel subsequently appeared in one volume. Macmillan remained a friend. His 'English Men of Letters' series published Trollope's *Thackeray*. Macmillan entertained Trollope to dinner the night before his fatal stroke.   RCT

Macmillan's Magazine. Appearing from 1859 to 1907, the first monthly, shilling magazine included one novel by Trollope. In 1859, a year in which 115 periodicals started in London, Alexander Macmillan began a new kind of magazine. In mid-century, novels were sometimes published in monthly, paperbound parts, costing one shilling per number. This monthly, 80-page magazine offered a part of a novel, poetry, reviews, and articles appealing to educated readers on politics, religion, and travel.

The magazine retained many characteristics of earlier monthly periodicals such as *Blackwood's Magazine* or *Fraser's*, which cost 2*s*. 6*d*.: pages were unattractively divided into double columns, one article following immediately on the other, without illustrations, but *Macmillan's* added the innovation of signed articles. *Macmillan's* too was political, but from a philosophical rather than a partisan point of view. Articles were more serious than they would be in later shilling magazines, including such topics as Darwin's theories. Because of its distinctive selection of topics and serious tone, readers might read it along with subsequent shilling magazines like the *Cornhill Magazine*, which would begin two months later, or *Saint Pauls* which Trollope would begin in 1867. *Macmillan's* success was immediate, its first number selling 10,000 copies in eighteen days, requiring a second printing. By 1864 a contemporary weekly publication wrote that *Macmillan's* was one of the outstanding miscellanies of the time.

One of its consistent features was the inclusion of a serialized novel. Novels frequently overlapped, a new one beginning during the final parts of the current novel. *Macmillan's* attracted writers of the highest quality. Thomas Hughes's *Tom Brown at Oxford* was the first novel in the magazine, overlapping with one by Henry Kingsley, whose better-known elder brother Charles wrote often for *Macmillan's*. Trollope's *Sir Harry Hotspur of Humblethwaite* was serialized May–December, 1870. In 1879, Trollope offered the magazine *Ayala's Angel*, but Alexander Macmillan declined, saying they were filled with fiction until 1881. Henry James's *The Portrait of a Lady* was scheduled to appear after a story by Mrs Oliphant concluded. Bret Harte and Thomas Hardy also contributed fiction.

Alexander Macmillan. He and his brother Daniel were well established publishers by 1850 with a list of many distinguished Victorian novelists. Trollope joined them with *Sir Harry Hotspur of Humblethwaite*, serialized in *Macmillan's Magazine* during 1870. Macmillan's also published Trollope's volume on Thackeray. Alexander Macmillan became a close friend, and was Trollope's guest on the evening before he suffered his fatal stroke in 1882.

Matthew Arnold began contributing in 1863 and continued until 1887, the year before his death. Poems appeared by Christina Rossetti, and by Tennyson, who was a contributor for 30 years, and whose poem 'Sea Dreams' was printed in the January 1860 number to compete with the appearance of the *Cornhill*, the new shilling magazine, edited by W. M. Thackeray. There were essays by Thomas Carlyle, Elizabeth Gaskell, W. M. Rossetti, Herbert Spencer, and Harriet Martineau. Alexander Macmillan turned to his fellow Scotsman David Masson to be the first editor (1859–68). George Grove, a musicologist who later edited *Grove's Dictionary of Music and Musicians*, followed 1868–83, then John Morley, 1883–5, who also edited the *Fortnightly Review*, with which Trollope was involved as a proprietor; and lastly Mowbray Morris, 1885–1907.　　JWM

MacNuffery, Dr, disagreeable doctor whose job is to maintain the well-being of the English cricket team in their match against Britannula. His strict rules of diet make him an object of ridicule. *FixP*　　SRB

Macnulty, Julia, long-suffering companion first of Lady Linlithgow, and then of Lizzie Eustace. Kind and even-tempered but too honest for her own good, Miss Macnulty is prey to the various humours of the wealthier ladies with whom she is obliged to live. Her calmness and steadiness contrast with both Lizzie Eustace's bursts of enthusiasm and Lady Linlithgow's fits of choler. *ED*, *PR*　　JMR

Macready, William Charles (1793–1873), distinguished actor and stage manager, whom Trollope described to G. H. Lewes as 'a man of supreme intelligence, but with no histrionic genius. He never moved me to tears' (*Letters* 2, 665). His assessment of Macready's memoirs published in 1875, which Trollope read alongside Forster's *Life of Charles Dickens* (1872–4), was less generous. 'These books', he wrote to G. W. Rusden (November 1875), 'do not make one pleased with humanity. It is disgusting to see the self-consciousness and irritated craving for applause which such men as Macready and Dickens have exhibited' (*Letters* 2, 671). Macready's religion was discussed in another letter. Responding to Rusden's claim that Macready was humble before God, Trollope rejoined: 'to my God I can be but true, and if I think myself to have done well I cannot but say so' (*Letters* 2, 691). Trollope doubted whether Macready's 'humility before God will atone for his want of manliness'.
　　RCT

M'Ruen, Jabesh, moneylender to whom Charley Tudor is indebted. The first of several nasty moneylenders in Trollope's fiction, M'Ruen is a 'sharp-clawed vulture' (XVIII) who preys on young men such as Charley and his fellow clerks by lending small amounts at extortionate interest rates. *TC*　　MT

Maggott, Mick, rough but well-meaning miner who works in partnership with John Caldigate and Dick Shand, teaching them how to mine for gold. Excessive drinking eventually causes his death. *JC*　　SRB

Magruder, Major, aged member of Parliament for Killiecrankie and long-time critic of British colonial policy. His Committee of Inquiry solicits testimony from Sir Marmaduke Rowley, and its six-week investigation into colonial government yields a blue book but no actual reforms. *HKWR*
　　RC

Magruin, Mr, moneylender who provides funds for Burgo Fitzgerald's proposed elopement with Lady Glencora Palliser. *CYFH*　　JMR

Maguire, Jeremiah, overweening evangelical curate who pursues Margaret Mackenzie for her money in order to establish himself in an independent church. His terrible squint repels Margaret who is otherwise attracted to him at first. However, he loses his advantage by pushing beyond social propriety, embarrassing Margaret before her aunt Lady Ball, and especially by exposing what he presumes is a conspiracy by John Ball against Margaret in journal articles entitled 'The Lion and the Lamb'. *MM*　　SRB

Mainwaring, Mr, rector at Dillsborough, fond of dining and of fine wine, whose curate attends to all church duties. Having used his wife's money to obtain his living, he is unintentionally insulted at his own table by Elias Gotobed who expounds on the evil of that practice. *AS*　　MG

Malachi, Father, Catholic priest who welcomes Florian Jones's conversion to Catholicism as 'a miracle' (XIII). *L*　　MRS

'Malachi's Cove', first published in *Good Words*, December 1864 (reprinted in *LS*); a regional tale. Old Malachi Trenglos has supported himself over the years by gathering seaweed from a cove on the Cornwall coast. Now that he is old, 'Glos' is helped by his granddaughter Mahala ('Mally'). Friction develops between Mally and a neighbouring young farmer, Barty Gunliffe, who also gathers weed from the cove which Mally (wrongly) regards as her family's private property. When Barty falls in the swirling water of the cove she intrepidly rescues him, and the young people realize they are in love.　　JS

Maltby, Baron, judge presiding at Lady Mason's trial. A friend of Judge Staveley's, the Baron stays at Noningsby during the trial, where he lets it be known that he disapproves of legal reform of the sort discussed at the Birmingham congress. *OF*   MT

'Man who kept his Money in a Box, The', first serialized in *Public Opinion*, 27 January and 1 February 1861 (reprinted in *TAC2*). The narrator, Robinson, recalls an encounter with an English family, the Greenes, in Bellaggio, by Lake Como. Mr Greene is accompanied by his wife and daughter Sophonisba, to whom Robinson is attracted. When the Greenes' box of valuables disappears, suspicion falls on Robinson. To add to his chagrin, he is obliged to pay the Greenes' bills. The misplaced box is finally found in Robinson's luggage. He and the Greenes part on bad terms.   JS

Manchester, northern industrial city where Fred Pickering is articled to an attorney, and to which he returns after failure in London. 'Pickering' *LS*   GRH

Mancrudy, Sir Peter, Exeter physician who attends Miss Stanbury during her nearly fatal illness (bronchitis). He takes over the case after Mr Martin, an apothecary and Miss Stanbury's regular doctor, has mistreated her condition. *HKWR*   RC

Mandarin Islands, fictional tropical British colony of which Sir Marmaduke Rowley is Governor, and where Louis Trevelyan meets and marries Emily Rowley. *HKWR*   RC

Manners, Lord John James Robert (1818–1906), 7th Duke of Rutland; Postmaster General (1874–80 and 1885–6); member of the Copyright Commission; from 1878 a treasurer of the Royal Literary Fund. The Copyright Commission (1776–8) was a passion for Trollope. After a 'cheery dinner' in February 1878 at the Trollopes', John Blackwood noted that Manners complained, '[Trollope] is like to drive them all mad at the weary Copyright Commission, going over all the ground that has been discussed in his absence [in South Africa]' (*Letters* 2, 759 n.). Manners also testified 'to the anxiety [Mr Trollope] constantly manifested that the relief administered by [the fund] should be efficacious and generous' (quoted Super 434).   RCT

Manning, Henry Edward (1808–92), attended Harrow School when Trollope was a pupil. As son of a director of the Bank of England and Tory MP he received a generous allowance. He entered the Church (1832), became a Roman Catholic (1851), and became Archbishop of Westminster (1865). In June 1879 he wrote warmly to Trollope that when readers recalled his many works they would 'bear witness to you the witness you bear to Thackeray' (*Letters* 2, 831).   RCT

Manor Cross, grim, dark house nine miles (14 km) from the city of Brotherton, the family residence of the Marquis of Brotherton. The old Marchioness, her daughters, and second son (Lord George Germain) live there until turned out by the Marquis. Lady George is brought to this house as a bride. *IHP*   MG

manuscripts and editions. Manuscripts that relate to Trollope and his family are housed in four major collections, of which the two most important are held at Princeton, the Morris L. Parrish and the Robert H. Taylor collections. *The New Zealander*, which was never published in Trollope's own lifetime, survives in manuscript form in the Taylor Collection, which also contains the six notebooks in which Trollope kept a record of his travel expenses. The Trollope Family Papers, which contain material relating to his mother, wife, sons, and brother, are held at the University of Illinois at Urbana-Champaign. In the United Kingdom the Bodleian Library's holdings include Trollope's working diaries for *Barchester Towers* and each of the novels that followed it, with the various contracts he made with publishers, also his letters to George Smith; there is also a collection of letters from his sister-in-law Frances Eleanor Trollope, which give an account of Trollope's later years.

Only the partial manuscript of *Framley Parsonage* (the final ten of its sixteen instalments in *Cornhill*), which was given by Trollope himself to Harrow School, is still in England. The rest of the surviving novel manuscripts are held in the United States, as follows: Cornell University: *Mr Scarborough's Family*; Henry E. Huntington Library and Art Gallery: *The Small House at Allington*, *The Belton Estate*; Houghton Library, Harvard: *The Vicar of Bullhampton*, *Ralph the Heir*; University of Michigan: *The Fixed Period*, *Kept in the Dark*; New York Public Library, Arents Collection: *John Caldigate*, *Nina Balatka*, *The Prime Minister*, *Rachel Ray*, and, in the Berg Collection, *Miss Mackenzie*; Pierpont Morgan Library: *He Knew He Was Right*; Carl H. Pforzheimer Library: *Orley Farm*; Princeton University: *An Eye for an Eye* and, in the Robert H. Taylor Collection, *The American Senator*, *The Claverings*, *The Eustace Diamonds*, *Lady Anna*, *The Landleaguers*, *Marion Fay*, and *An Old Man's Love*; Yale University: *Ayala's Angel*, *Can You Forgive Her?*, *Cousin Henry*, *Dr Wortle's School*, *The Duke's Children*, *Harry Heathcote of Gangoil*, *The*

Last Chronicle of Barset, Phineas Finn, Phineas Redux, and *Sir Harry Hotspur of Humblethwaite*.

Among other works, the manuscript of *Australia and New Zealand* is at the National Library of Australia, Canberra; *North America* is in a private collection; *An Autobiography* is in the British Library; *The Life of Cicero* is in the Robert H. Taylor Collection; *South Africa* is in the Huntington Library; and *The Noble Jilt* is at the University of Texas, Austin.

Seven manuscripts, *Cousin Henry, Dr Wortle's School, The Fixed Period, Kept in the Dark, Marion Fay, Mr Scarborough's Family*, and *An Old Man's Love*, are mostly written in the hand of Florence Bland, Trollope's niece, who worked as his amanuensis in his later years when he began to suffer from writer's cramp.

Trollope did not redraft his stories nor, like Thackeray, start amending them when he saw them in proof: with the exception of the manuscript of *The Duke's Children*, a late long novel which Trollope had to cut very heavily after it was written in order to get it published, there are usually signs only of minor emendations to his original draft.

From 1847, when Trollope began to publish fiction, until 1860, when his first serial novel, *Framley Parsonage*, appeared in the *Cornhill Magazine*, all his novels came out in three-volume form. *The Warden*, a short work, which came out in a single volume at 10s. 6d., was anomalous, both as regards Trollope's own work and contemporary publishing practice.

The three-volume novel sold at 31s. 6d., or half a guinea per volume, to the public, though Mudie's Circulating Library, where most readers obtained their copies, bought them at a lower price. It was the standard form in which new fiction appeared in Britain before Dickens made serialization an option in the 1840s, and did not finally go out of use until 1894. Three-volume publication was almost invariably followed up by a cheaper edition, usually at five shillings, in one volume or at most two. (From 1858 Baron Tauchnitz of Munich brought out Trollope's novels in English under his own imprint for the European market. Editions that appeared in America were pirated by Harper Brothers.)

Sadleir's *Bibliography* offers a detailed account of the publishing history of each of Trollope's books. After its first appearance, issuing so-called new editions was the publisher's way of exploiting the interest and value of a novel that might still invite more readers to buy if the price came down low enough. Over the fifteen years after its initial publication *The Small House at Allington* came out in editions priced from six shillings down to half a crown.

Many instances of speculative reissue resist classification but a few major series can be identified as follows: from 1859 Chapman & Hall reissued various works that Trollope had published earlier in their five-shilling series 'Standard Editions of Popular Authors': *The Bertrams, Doctor Thorne, The Macdermots of Ballycloran, Rachel Ray*, and *Tales of All Countries*. From 1866 the same publisher brought out a cheaper series of reissues, in their 'Select Library of Fiction': these were 'yellowback' or railway novels at two shillings per volume. The works of Trollope included in this series were *The Macdermots of Ballycloran, The Kellys and the O'Kellys, La Vendée, Barchester Towers, Doctor Thorne, The Bertrams, The West Indies, Castle Richmond, Rachel Ray, Tales of All Countries, Can You Forgive Her?, Miss Mackenzie, Orley Farm, The Belton Estate, Lotta Schmidt and Other Stories, Phineas Finn, He Knew He Was Right, The Vicar of Bullhampton, An Editor's Tales, Ralph the Heir, The Eustace Diamonds, Phineas Redux, Lady Anna, The Prime Minister, Is He Popenjoy?*, and *Cousin Henry*.

Between 1864 and 1871, following their serial- or part-publication, Smith, Elder brought out a number of Trollope's illustrated novels, *The Small House at Allington, The Last Chronicle of Barset*, and *The Claverings*, in their series 'Illustrated Editions of Popular Works'. Other collections included Tauchnitz's British authors, 1858–84 (45 titles); Library of Select Novels, New York, 1862–77 (12 titles); Franklin Square Library, New York, 1879–84 (16 titles); Seaside Library, New York, 1881–4 (46 titles); World's Classics, 1907–48 (38 titles); *Selected Works of Anthony Trollope*, New York, Arno, 1981 (36 titles).

No complete edition of Trollope's novels was issued in his lifetime, and it was not until a hundred years after his death that initiatives were taken to put one out and to keep it in print. The World's Classics series, the Folio Society, and the Trollope Society have made this attempt. The Penguin Trollope comprises reprints of all the novels, collected short stories, and *An Autobiography*. MH

Mullen, R., *Anthony Trollope : A Victorian in his World* (1990).

Sadleir, M., *Trollope: A Bibliography* (1928).

Manylodes, Mr, Cornish stockjobber connected to the Wheal Mary Jane tin mine. With his ally Undecimus Scott, Mr Manylodes bribes Alaric Tudor to write a favourable government report about the mine in order to increase the stock value. Manylodes is 'as vulgar a fellow as you ever met, and as shrewd' (IX). *TC*　MT

Marion Fay (*see next page*)

CONTEMPORARY reviews of *Marion Fay* (1882) were mixed, ranging from the *Athenaeum*'s judgement that the novel exhibits 'much of the brightness and light-ness of touch which characterize [Trollope's] early work' to the New York *Critic*'s scathing assertion that the book 'indulges in an excess of feeble sentiment' (Smalley 493, 495). A few months after these reviews appeared, Trollope was dead and *Marion Fay* sank into oblivion. During the 20th century, it has not received much critical attention.

The story concerns the love affairs of Lord Hampstead and Lady Frances Trafford, children of the Marquis of Kingsbury. In his youth the Marquis sat in Parliament as a Liberal. His first marriage, which produced Hampstead and Frances, represented a compromise between his democratic views and his social responsibilities as a heredi-tary aristocrat. His wife, though not noble, came from a prominent political family. But after her death, the Marquis, whose political 'convictions had been blunted by that sinking down among the great peers which was natural to his advanced years', chose a conservative noblewoman as his second wife (I).

Because Hampstead and Frances not only remain true to the liberal opinions their father originally held, but embrace an even more advanced brand of radicalism, trouble arises in the family. Frances engages herself to one of her brother's political friends, George Roden, a well-conducted clerk in the Post Office. Her father and stepmother are horrified, but she remains firm. Worse is to come. Hampstead falls in love with Roden's neighbour Marion Fay, whose Quaker father is a clerk in a modest commercial establishment. Hearing this news, Lady Kingsbury decides that Hamp-stead is a traitor to his class and begins to long for his death.

But Marion refuses Hampstead's offer. Though she loves him, she is rightly con-vinced that an early death from consumption will be her fate. Her death leaves Hamp-stead broken-hearted. As Marion declines, a long-standing secret concerning Roden's birth comes to light: he is the heir of the Duca di Crinola and is related to the most aristocratic families of Europe. Though Roden refuses to use his title, the mere fact that it is known to possess it smooths his path to marriage with Frances.

Two farcical sub-plots lighten the novel's mood. The first concerns Lord Llwddythlw, who is so busy that he cannot find the time to solemnize his marriage with the thoroughly suitable bride he has chosen. The second concerns Roden's incor-rigibly lazy fellow clerk Sam Crocker, who is constantly on the verge of losing his job—and is as constantly saved from this awful fate by his soft-hearted and indecisive superior.

Most of the critics who have recently discussed *Marion Fay* focus upon the social issues raised by the hero's and heroine's unorthodox romantic choices. And there has been virtual unanimity among them that Trollope succumbed to the conservative expectations of his readers by crafting an ending that did not permit either character to marry outside the aristocracy. Such critics view both Marion's death and Roden's ennoblement as serious defects, improbable attempts to sidestep the social problems which are the novel's most interesting feature.

In a typical appraisal, David Skilton writes that *Marion Fay* ends with an almost total capitulation to the standards of circulating library fiction. Marion's sentimental-ized decline gets Hampstead off the hook, while Frances's story sacrifices plausibility 'to the reader's desire to have his cake and eat it. Having identified with the young lovers in their adversity, the reader is . . . able to glory in the young man's superior rank after the *deus ex machina* has done its work' (*Anthony Trollope and his Contemporaries* (1972), 97). Marion's death is indeed improbably devoid of all medical unpleasantness, as Skilton notes, but his contention that Frances's marriage can be explained only as a failure of art is less convincing.

In arguing that Trollope adopted the deplorably low standards of contemporary popular fiction in ennobling Roden, Skilton and his critical allies ignore the fact that contemporary reactions to this episode were largely negative. The New York *Critic* found the old-fashioned device of transforming the young plebeian into a duke both tiresome and unnatural. The *Spectator*'s reviewer criticized Roden's story as improbable, while the *Saturday* cited it as an example of pernicious sentimentality. It is unconvincing to assert that Trollope was pressured into ending this plot as he does, when many contemporaries faulted its conclusion.

A second problem with the notion that Trollope took the easy way out of a real difficulty by ennobling Roden is to be found in the ironic circumstances surrounding the episode. London society is thrilled by the clerk's accession to a foreign title that brings him no wealth, but this exaggerated worship of rank in its emptiest form appears absurd to the reader. R. H. Super's discovery that Trollope substituted the comic title Duca di Crinola, or 'Duke of Horsehair', for the more dignified title Duke of Cremona, which he originally intended to confer on Roden, also suggests that the novel is mocking the conventions of sentimental fiction, rather than using them in a straightforward manner.

The shape of *Marion Fay*'s main plots may be explained upon premises unrelated to its readers' presumed conservatism. Super notes that 'the pious remark, "it is in God's hands"', occurs so frequently as to be almost thematic in the book, but the implications of the statement are not simplistic' (*Marion Fay*, ed. R. H. Super (1982), p. viii). Read in the light of this 'pious remark', *Marion Fay* becomes an extended, tragi-comic meditation on the limited efficacy of individual effort.

As political radicals, Hampstead, Frances, and Roden all hope to change the world. And the world is indeed moving in the direction of democracy, though not quite as fast as they wish. In spite of their political commitments and the generally favorable tenor of the times, however, the radical characters cannot break convention's grip on their own lives. The Kingsbury family finds it impossible to abide by their secret agreement to call Lord Hampstead by his first name rather than his title. Frances makes no progress in her endeavours to marry a commoner until chance ennobles him. Hampstead finds, to his own surprise, that he is disturbed by his sister's desire to marry beneath her. Roden fights to keep his name, but, like Hampstead, discovers he will eventually be forced to use his title.

But if the novel's radicals cannot bring about the changes they desire, its conservatives are equally powerless to secure social stasis. Though Lady Kingsbury believes a liberal marquis to be an oxymoronic abomination, she cannot prevent the spirit of a democratic era from throwing up radical noblemen in her own family. Nor is she able to prevent Hampstead from inheriting the marquisate, though at times she appears to be inciting her chaplain to murder him. Wiser conservatives, like the worldly Lord Persiflage, hope only to slow the pace of change. Thus Persiflage smooths Roden's entrance into the aristocracy by offering him something that the clerk values more than rank, namely money. Persiflage finds Roden a well-paid post in the Foreign

Office, initiating a chain of events that will eventually result in Roden's assuming his title.

When a radical clerk is enabled to marry a noblewoman solely because a chance discovery reveals him to be the penniless Duke of Horsehair, we are not in the realm of either realism or sentiment, but in that of the absurd. In the plot concerning Marion's death, however, Trollope's meditation on the limited efficacy of individual effort takes a tragic turn. No matter how passionately Hampstead loves Marion, he cannot save her life. Marion's death demonstrates that there are natural obstacles to fulfilment which have no comic dimension whatever.

Rounding out this pattern, the novel's farcical sub-plots treat situations where effort ought to succeed more easily than it does. Thus the habits of a lifetime cause Llwddythlw to imagine that an endless series of routine public engagements makes it impossible for him to fix his wedding date, though this is clearly not the case. When Crocker tears up a bundle of official papers, his superiors can and should dismiss him—only soft-hearted weakness prevents them from doing so. The comic paralysis revealed in these sub-plots throws Hampstead's tragic frustration into sharper relief.

Marion Fay was composed as follows. In December 1878, Trollope outlined the plot for a long novel, tentatively entitled *Lord Hampstead*. After writing four chapters, he laid the manuscript aside and embarked on *Thackeray* and *Dr Wortle's School*. In August 1879, Trollope returned to his unfinished book, now called *Marion Fay*, completing it in November. In March 1881, he sold the serialization rights to the *Graphic*, where *Marion Fay* appeared in 26 instalments, from 3 December 1881 to 3 June 1882. In May 1882, Chapman & Hall published a three-volume edition, followed by a one-volume 'cheap' edition from Chatto & Windus in 1884. A seven-inch by nine-inch illustration, by the Scottish-born artist William Small, accompanied each instalment of the serial. In one of the drawings, Small appears to have used Trollope himself as the model for the Marquis of Kingsbury. The illustrations were not republished in the first two book editions of the novel. The manuscript is in the Robert H. Taylor Collection at Princeton University. JN

Harvey, Geoffrey, introduction to *Marion Fay* (1992).
Skilton, David, *Anthony Trollope and his Contemporaries* (1972).
Super, R. H., preface to *Marion Fay* (1982).

Marlboro' School, preparatory school attended by Bob Crawley to ready him for Cambridge. *LCB* NCS

Marmaduke Lodge, Matilda Thoroughbung's home in Buntingford where Peter Prosper proposes. *MSF* MT

Marrable, Colonel, a 'wicked old colonel' who disgraces the family name with debt, dishonour, and quarrelling. His smooth manners and polished style enable him to live fashionably on borrowed money. He cheats his own son Walter of his fortune, creating lasting animosity between them. *VB* SRB

Marrable, Gregory, good-natured, retiring, learned son of Sir Gregory. His chronic invalidism makes him old before his time, and upon his early death his father makes Walter the heir to Dunripple Park and the baronetcy. *VB* SRB

Marrable, Sir Gregory, quiet, self-indulgent semi-invalid who, after the death of his son, makes his nephew Walter his heir. Honourable and charitable, he nevertheless meddles slightly in urging a marriage between Edith Brownlow and Walter, but is willing to be talked over to Walter's marriage to Mary Lowther. *VB* SRB

Marrable, John, kindly hearted and sincere rector whose rather low opinion of women and marriage drives him to discourage his nephew Walter's marriage to Mary Lowther. For this Walter considers him a crafty, selfish old bachelor, despite his hospitality to Walter. *VB*   SRB

Marrable, Sarah, dainty, independent old aunt of Mary Lowther, proud of being a lady. Bewildered by Mary's desire to marry the near penniless Walter Marrable, Sarah gives Mary solid advice cautioning the young woman against marrying without money, and unsuccessfully advises a more suitable and socially acceptable match with Harry Gilmore. *VB*   SRB

Marrable, Captain Walter, impetuous, self-centred, and handsome son of Colonel Marrable. Returning home from India, he learns that his father has robbed him of his fortune, and he nurses his injury bitterly. He falls in love with Mary Lowther but they break their engagement until he learns he will be heir to his uncle Sir Gregory's estate. His fickle affections are swayed by money and opportunity, but his headstrong, fierce character is ultimately rewarded with an estate, baronetcy, and the beautiful Mary. *VB*
SRB

marriage and divorce. Trollope's novel-writing career spanned the years of major changes to the laws concerning married women and access to divorce. While these laws, and the changes to them, are rarely primary themes, the legal backdrop constantly informs his plots, and there is a noticeable regular narrative voice which draws our attention to the rights, and wrongs, of women.

When Victoria came to the throne in 1837, a woman's legal position upon marriage was bleak. She ceased to have an independent existence. She was known legally as *feme covert*: her husband owned her property, owned her earnings, owned the children, owned the right to her company known as *consortium*. He was responsible for her actions, and responsible for her debts. His rights over her began as soon as she agreed to marry him. If she owned property before her marriage, having agreed to marry him she could not dispose of it before the marriage without his consent. This becomes an issue in *Lady Anna* where Lady Anna wishes to give Frederick Lovel half her inheritance. The lawyers point out that she can only do this with Daniel Thwaite, the tailor, that she can only do this with his permission. If her husband died intestate, a woman was entitled to a third of his property, or half if the marriage was childless. This is how Earl Lovel's property is divided up in *Lady Anna*. The rest of the estate, unless it was land, would pass to the state, regardless of a wife's needs or whether the estate had been hers in the first

place. In his will a husband could choose to leave his wife destitute, even totally depriving her of what had once been hers. It was her husband's inadequate provision for her and their child in his will that pushed Lady Mason to forge the codicil in *Orley Farm*.

The world at large constantly counselled care to a woman who had any property and was contemplating marriage. Her vulnerability urged the imperative of knowing a man's antecedents. This is why the people of Baslehurst (*RR*) caution Dorothea Prime against marriage to Mr Prong, because they fear he will run away with the money once he has married her. There were, however, ways to circumvent the financial stringencies of the law, in the establishment of settlements and trusts, and the rich always had access to good advice on such services. In *Barchester Towers* Mrs Arabin has kept control of the money left to her by her first husband, and Lady Glencora has all the spending of her enormous wealth, a significant issue in the refurbishment of Gatherum Castle in *The Prime Minister*. It was also easier in Victorian times to obscure one's antecedents, and a bigamous marriage was always a possibility. Bigamy is the focus in *Castle Richmond*, *John Caldigate*, *Mr Scarborough's Family*, *Dr Wortle's School*, and features in many others.

Legal custody of the children belonged to the husband. Unless declared insane, he could take them from his wife and arrange their care as he thought fit. Largely due to the lobbying of Caroline Norton, an abused wife who was denied access to her three small children, an Infant Custody Act passed in 1839 entitled a mother to apply for custody or contact with her children after separation: but not if she had been proved adulterous. This is a critical issue in *He Knew He Was Right*, a novel which (along with much else) starkly exposes implications of the infant custody laws for the Trevelyans' baby. If Bozzle can produce evidence of Emily's adultery, Louis Trevelyan will be able to deny her access to their child. As it is, he is perfectly within his rights when he snatches his son from his wife and takes him to Italy.

These inequalities did not begin to be remedied until the Matrimonial Causes and Divorce Act of 1859, which gave women competence to sue for divorce if they could prove adultery and a further offence, such as desertion, cruelty, bestiality, sodomy, or incest: men could sue for divorce on the grounds of adultery alone. This Act also gave women who separated from their husbands some financial protection for any future earnings or property that they might acquire. A slightly more comprehensive Married Women's

Property Act was passed in 1870, but not until the 1882 Act did a married woman have the same property rights as her unmarried sister.

The legal requirements of grounds for separation or divorce influence the remedies that are available to Emily Wharton in *The Prime Minister*. Although Lopez's behaviour makes him intolerable to live with, it falls short of any strict matrimonial offence, and Emily's father knows he treads a narrow line in his wish for Emily to remain with him, since Lopez could sue her for alienating his wife's affections in any action taken to restore his conjugal rights. While the telling of his tales exposes women's vulnerability in marriage, Trollope's tone is never crusading. His purpose is ever to entertain. Heiresses, even when modestly endowed, are regularly targeted by impoverished men on the make. Clergymen, particularly evangelicals, are frequently the butt of this joke. The Revds Jeremiah Maguire (*MM*) and Samuel Prong (*RR*) chase after Miss Mackenzie's and Mrs Prime's few hundreds, while the passions of Revds Slope and Emilius are fired by the greater size of Eleanor Bold's and Lizzie Eustace's fortunes.

But Trollope the novelist is in truth more interested in the dynamics of a relationship than in the legal mechanics. The effects of abuse on a generous heart, and the undermining of Emily Wharton's self-esteem, are more pertinent to the plot of *The Prime Minister* than the legal detail, and Sir Hugh Clavering's cruelty to the long-suffering Hermione in *The Claverings* is a fine study of emotional abuse. Thus, while changes to the law affect the shape of so many plots and sub-plots, acute examination of the relationships is Trollope's especial forte. His favourite themes are the problems that young people encounter en route to the altar when they fall in love, and he particularly notices their sexual attraction. Nearly all Trollope's betrothals are sealed with embraces of some passion. Arms go round waists, lips are pressed against lips, faces are covered in kisses. And while the man is often the initiator, a significant number of women show their pleasure in love-making. Of Mary Lowther in *The Vicar of Bullhampton* we read, 'Then she came back to him, and laid her head upon his shoulders, and lifted his hand till it came again around her waist' (XXIX). Lily Dale's arousal by Crosbie's caress is explicit: ' "When he held me in his arms"—and, as the thoughts ran through her brain, she remembered the very spot on which they had stood—"oh, my love!", she had said to him as she returned his kisses—"oh, my love, my love, my love!" ' (*SHA* LVII). It is implied by Rachel Ray's account of her honeymoon (*RR* XXX)

that their sexual compatibility lasted all their married life.

A significant group of novels begin with the nuptials, and examine what goes on within the marriage (*HKWR, KD, JC, IHP, DWS, PM*). In these novels Trollope exposes the minutiae of the intimate relationship between a man and woman. In *He Knew He Was Right* he takes us into the Trevelyans' bedroom to show us how it is their mutual inflexibility on very small points that ultimately leads to their rift on a major one. *Is He Popenjoy?* explores a marriage where problems of consummation allow sexual jealousy to fester till it nearly destroys the union. Rigid clinging to a posture threatens to separate George Western and Cecilia Holt permanently in *Kept in the Dark*. That marriage was ultimately saved by a wife's refusal to let go of her love for her husband, in spite of his jealousy and desertion. Taking a different angle, *John Caldigate* explores a wife's interpretation of her vows of obedience when her husband is accused of bigamy, and found guilty. Hester Caldigate feels that the jury's verdict makes no difference to the troth she plighted.

Obedience is a common issue in the marriages and marriage plans of his plots. Young women are regularly urged to obey their parents and relatives and marry the man they do not love, or abandon their plans to marry the man they love: Rachel Ray (*RR*), Mary Masters (*AS*), Ayala Dormer (*AA*), Bell Dale (*SHA*), Lucy Robarts (*FP*), Dorothy Stanbury (*HKWR*), Henrietta Carbury (*WWLN*)—the complete list is a very long one. Rachel Ray reflects ironically that if she behaved when married as she is being urged to behave and abandon her lover because the world thinks ill of him, she would be betraying the most hallowed of her marriage vows. Since most of Trollope's heroines are justified by the plot outcomes in their refusal to comply with their parents' demands, we might surmise a Trollope who prevaricated over the conventions of the obedient and submissive daughter.

Obedience within marriage is exposed in a similarly equivocal way. For while Nora Rowley (*HKWR*) declares, 'I don't mean to submit to him at all . . . I am going to marry for liberty' (XCV), his young women marry assuming they will owe obedience to their husbands. However, the reality of a contented relationship is regularly proved to depend on a different arrangement of dues. 'Equality is necessary for comfortable love,' says Trollope in *Is He Popenjoy?* (XXXII), or, rather more dramatically, 'There sometimes comes a terrible shipwreck, when the woman before marriage has filled herself full with ideas of submission, and then finds that the golden-headed god has got an iron body and feet of clay' (*BE* XI). Some of his marriages are clear examples of the joining of two equals, like Cecilia and Theodore Burton in *The Claverings*. But Trollope often notes that in many stable unions, the reality is that women are in control. It is clear that Lady Glencora is usually at the helm in the Palliser marriage, and Revd Clavering regularly abdicates control. Trollope tells us that the man's best days are when he is courting, before he has persuaded his love to marry him. After the betrothal he is so often like an ox dressed for sacrificial slaughter, a prize to be displayed. Beyond that, when a young couple settle down to married life, wives tend to have the last say. In *The Warden*, Susan Grantly says her piece, and rolls over for the night—and the Archdeacon knows that that is the end of it, for once he has taken his trousers off and put his nightshirt on, he is 'an ordinary man'.

Trollope's vein of high comedy often hits its peak when he describes the power women exercise within marriage. Mrs Proudie is his most famous portrayal of a woman wielding marital power, and Lady Aylmer in *The Belton Estate* plays a comic masterpiece in her cameo role. The Tappitt marriage in *Rachel Ray*, which has been comfortable for both partners for 30 years, offers some of the most fertile ground for humour. Trollope's gently satirical style, his timely use of bathos and understatement, his feel for the timing of a circumlocutory phrase, so that the slowing down to absorb what he really means heightens the joke, show him to be master of his comic script. Besting a tipsy husband, preferably with his trousers down, is the bedrock of farce, and in a scene of great humour and sharp observation, Mr Tappitt knows he will not get his clothes back until he accepts retirement to the villa in Torquay (XXVII).

Of his own marriage, Trollope, in *An Autobiography*, makes the single bald statement, 'My marriage was like the marriage of other people' (IV). It is diverting to wonder at the degree to which he drew on personal experience for his intuitive revelations of how marriages really worked. MM

Marsham, Mrs, friend of Plantagenet Palliser's late mother with whom he wishes his wife to be intimate. Unable to abide Mrs Marsham's prudish ways, Glencora rejects her husband's friend, insisting that the woman is simply a 'duenna'. Mrs Marsham is responsible for fetching Mr Palliser when Glencora 'misbehaves' at a party. *CYFH* JMR

Martha, confidential servant who has lived with Miss Stanbury for twenty years. She deals calmly and wisely with her mistress's idiosyncrasies and

imperious temper, remaining in her position after Brooke Burgess and Dorothy Stanbury marry and move into the Close with her aunt. *HKWR* RC

Martin, Sir James (1820–86), Premier of New South Wales (1863–5; 1866–8; 1870–2), later that colony's Chief Justice. In Sydney (1875) Trollope was fêted at a river trip and picnic during which Martin said, 'we have as much affection for his character as we have respect for his attainments' (quoted Super 344). RCT

Martin, Sir Samuel (1801–83), barrister and QC; Liberal MP for Pontefract (1847); Baron of the Exchequer (1850–74). Martin heard the bribery and corruption case after the Beverley election in which Trollope came bottom of the poll (9–11 March 1869); 109 witnesses were heard (Trollope did not testify); 104 persons were found guilty of corrupt election practices; and the election was declared void. A government commission, held over 38 days, examined over 700 witnesses, including Trollope. Trollope was exonerated, but Beverley was disenfranchised. RCT

Martin, Sir Theodore (1816–1909), poet, translator, essayist; author of the five-volume *Life of His Royal Highness the Prince Consort* (1875–80), which Trollope read for his book on Palmerston, challenging Martin's view of the statesman's conduct. Trollope made his disagreement with Martin explicit to his brother, claiming that 'the Queen and Prince Albert, and Baron Stockmar behaved badly to Lord Palmerston' (*Letters* 2, 935). But despite his contention, Trollope presented Martin with a copy of his book, inscribed 'with the Authors kind Regards' (quoted Super 427). RCT

Martineau, Harriet (1802–76), essayist, novelist, social reformer; author of *Illustrations of Political Economy* (1832–4). At a dinner party given by the Milmans of Pinner, friends of the Trollopes, she was scornful of Frances Trollope's book on America (Glendinning 73 n). Mrs Trollope's Cincinnati Bazaar she called 'the great deformity of the city' (quoted Hall 28 n.). RCT

Marty, Father, priest of Kilmacrenny who tries to balance duty as Kate O'Hara's protector against hope that she can make a fine marriage. Despite an earthy manner and fondness for whiskey, Marty is as honest as the day. When Fred Neville suggests some hole-and-corner ceremony, he finds the priest is no 'romantic'; instead, he brings down curses on the young lord's head, commanding him to make an honest woman of his wild Irish love. *EE* AWJ

Marygold, home of the Connop Greens often visited by Lady Augustus and Arabella Trefoil. *AS* MG

'Mary Gresley', first published in *Saint Pauls*, November 1869 (reprinted in *ET*). The editor receives a piece of fiction from a pretty young author who lives in the country with her widowed mother. Mary is engaged to a penniless curate, the Revd Arthur Donne. The editor perceives promise in Mary's manuscript, and works with her to render it publishable. But her fiancé sickens with tuberculosis and on his deathbed exacts a promise that she will give up fiction. Some years later Mary marries a missionary and goes to Africa. The editor kisses her for the first and only time. JS

Marylebone, Lord, young Marquis and leader of the English cricket team which plays against Britannula. Despite his host President Neverbend's aggressive Britannulan patriotism, he remains good-natured and diplomatic throughout his stay. *FixP* SRB

Mason, Diana, wife of Joseph Mason. Mrs Mason's primary characteristic is her stinginess: 'there are women, wives and mothers of families, who would give the bone-scrapings to their husbands and the bones to their servants, while they hide the ortolans for themselves; and would dress children in rags, while they cram chests, drawers, and boxes with silks and satins for their own back. Such a woman one can thoroughly despise, and even hate; and such a woman was Mrs Mason of Groby Park' (VII). *OF* MT

Mason, Joseph, son of Sir Joseph Mason by his first wife and heir to Groby Park. Having failed in the first trial to gain Orley Farm as part of his inheritance, Joseph Mason delights in Lady Mason's trial. He is a severe father and husband, however dutiful, 'but yet he was a bad man in that he could never forget and never forgive. His mind and heart were equally harsh and hard and inflexible' (VII)—a damning indictment in Trollope's world. *OF* MT

Mason, Lucius, only child of Sir Joseph and Lady Mason. Lady Mason forged the codicil to her husband's will in order to provide for Lucius. Having come of age, Lucius returns from Germany to take his place as head of Orley Farm. Lucius is a clever, handsome, and well-mannered young man who hopes to combine his interests in philology with agriculture: 'And thus he became an agriculturalist with special scientific views as to chemistry, and a philologist with the object of making that pursuit bear upon his studies with reference to the races of man' (II). He is

briefly engaged to Sophia Furnival, and dutifully stands by his mother. *OF* MT

Mason, Lady Mary, widow of Sir Joseph Mason and mother of Lucius, who is tried twice in the Great Orley Farm Case. Lady Mason forged Sir Joseph's will in order to ensure that Orley Farm would be left to their son Lucius, and her forgery is revealed by the conclusion of *Orley Farm*. 'Accused of matrimonial prospects' in her marriage to Sir Joseph and suspected of wishing to marry her friend and neighbour Sir Peregrine Orme, Lady Mason is a middle-aged woman, melancholy in her face rather than in her character, which was full of energy,—if energy may be quiet as well as assured and constant' (II). After the second trial, Lady Mason leaves England with Lucius. *OF* MT

Masters, Gregory, Dillsborough attorney who has come down in the world. An easygoing man, he is harried by his second wife who meddles in his business. He resists her pragmatic advice and thereby repairs the family fortunes by gaining the patronage of Lord Rufford and of the Mortons. *AS* MG

Masters, Kate (later **Twentyman**), half-sister of Mary Masters who loves to hunt, borrows Lawrence Twentyman's pony, and wants Mary to marry him. Although she is still too young at the end of *The American Senator*, her mother hopes Kate will wed the rejected Twentyman, as she has by the time she appears briefly in *Ayala's Angel*. *AS* MG

Masters, Mary, pretty, demure daughter of Gregory Masters from his first marriage. Having lived with Lady Ushant as a child, Mary is more genteel than the rest of her family, to the annoyance of her stepmother, who accuses her of snobbery when she refuses Lawrence Twentyman. Her reticence and refusal to demonstrate her love of Reginald Morton provide a contrast to Arabella Trefoil. Their respective marriages point a Trollopian moral lesson on female behaviour. *AS* MG

Masters, Mrs, the second wife of Gregory Masters. An unimaginative and domineering woman, she believes Mary has been spoiled by Lady Ushant and poetry and tries to force her into a marriage with Lawrence Twentyman for her own good. She interferes as ineffectually and wrongheadedly in her husband's business. *AS* MG

Matching Priory, beloved Yorkshire home of the Pallisers. Though the seat of the Duke of Omnium is Gatherum Castle at Silverbridge, the family prefers the more human scale of Matching. The comfortable house sits in the midst of the ruins of an old monastery through which Lady Glencora delights to walk, especially in moonlight. The property is supposed to have been a royal gift made to Sir Guy de Palisere, perhaps sometime in the 14th century. Sir Guy's lookout is a favourite spot both of the young Duke and of his children. *CYFH, PF, ED, PR, PM, DC* JMR

Matterson, Mr, clergyman who marries Amelia Carroll. John Scarborough settles £500 on Amelia for her marriage to Matterson, 'a very shy gentleman', 'not very young, nor very rich', with several children (LXII). *MSF* MT

Maule, Gerard, young gentleman nearly ruined by his vain and selfish father. As a youth, Gerard Maule seems indifferent to everything but hunting, in pursuit of which he often lives beyond his means. He is saved from near certain ruin by marrying Adelaide Palliser, who helps settle him and whose money allows him to live more respectably. Like his wife, Gerard Maule remains an avid hunter. *PR, DC* JMR

Maule, Maurice, ageing dandy who seeks to mend his fortunes by making a profitable marriage, preferably to Mme Max Goesler. Mr Maule lives a remarkably selfish life, taking pains to maintain his youthful appearance, and caring for nothing beyond his own comfort and entertainment. Though he does not live on the decaying family property, Maule Abbey, he refuses to allow his son and heir to live there, as he wishes to keep the place vacant in the event of his own remarriage. *PR* JMR

Maule Abbey, decaying manor of Maurice Maule, who refuses to allow his son Gerard to restore the place and live there with his bride. *PR* JMR

Maxwell, Marmaduke Francis Constable (1837–1908), became 11th Lord Herries of Terregles; Trollope's running mate in the 1868 Beverley election, which Trollope called 'the most wretched fortnight of my manhood' (*Auto* XVI). Maxwell received marginally more votes than Trollope (895 to 740), but both Liberal candidates lost to the Conservatives. The Liberal *Beverley Recorder* declared that Trollope and Maxwell were greeted with an ovation that made them seem like victors. RCT

Mayfair, Duchess of. The proper and pious Duchess distrusts Arabella Trefoil, her niece by marriage, but feels compelled to accept her assertion that Lord Rufford has proposed and attempts to aid her. She bars Arabella from her home after this fiasco, but relents, allowing her to marry Mounser Green from Mistletoe. *AS* MG

Mayfair, Duke of. Arabella Trefoil's uncle is a pattern aristocrat who entertains lavishly at Mistletoe and in London in their proper seasons. He gets along with his son Lord Mistletoe, his daughters are properly married, and he dutifully sits in the House of Lords where he never opens his mouth. *AS* MG

Meager, Mr, drunken and impecunious husband of Mrs Meager, a lodging-house keeper. His overcoat plays a central role in the trial of Phineas Finn: this coat, worn by Revd Emilius, is mistaken for one worn by Phineas, thus casting suspicion on him for the murder of Mr Bonteen. *PR* JMR

Meager, Mrs. Keeping lodgings opposite Marylebone Workhouse, the long-suffering Mrs Meager tries her best to make ends meet, but her efforts are often threatened by her drunken and impecunious husband who resides intermittently with his family. Mrs Meager helps Mme Max Goesler find evidence that clears Phineas Finn of Mr Bonteen's murder. *PR* JMR

Medlicot, Giles, a free-selector, whose purchase of Crown land offends Harry Heathcote. Harry feels the new Scottish immigrant, handsome and well dressed, is not only a fop but an interloper. Medlicot prepares to 'commence hostilities' (III), but sets differences aside when arson threatens his neighbour and, at risk to himself, rallies to his aid. He is rewarded by Heathcote's friendship, and an engagement to Kate Daly, Heathcote's sister-in-law. *HHG*

MRS

Medlicot, Mrs, aged mother of Giles Medlicot who stoically shares her son's isolated life on a sugar plantation in Queensland. *HHG* MRS

Medlicot's Mill, experimental sugar mill built by Giles Medlicot on disputed property adjacent to Gangoil. *HHG* MRS

Meetkerke, Adolphus (1753–1840), wealthy cousin of Thomas Anthony Trollope, whom, in the absence of any other successors, he declared heir to Julians, his estate in Hertfordshire. The Trollope family were welcome visitors; the children addressed Meetkerke familiarly as Uncle Adolphus. Anticipating his inheritance, Thomas Anthony built an impressive red brick house in 1817, also called Julians. But on the death of his wife, Meetkerke remarried and fathered six children, including a son and heir, Adolphus. The Trollopes' hopes of fortune were dashed. RCT

Meetkerke, Cecilia (?1823–1903), minor author; daughter of the Hon. Edward Gore; second wife of Adolphus Meetkerke (1819–79), Trollope's second cousin. She enjoyed modest success in periodicals and as a writer for children, publishing *The Guests of the Flowers; A Botanical Sketch for Children* in 1880 (*I & R* 227). Over the years, she received much advice from Trollope about writing. 'Never use italics', he once cautioned her. 'They are the struggles of imbecility' (*Letters* 2, 212). Meetkerke left two tributes to Trollope after his death: 'Anthony Trollope', *Blackwood's Magazine* (February 1883, 316–20) contains the fullest account of Trollope's decision to 'kill Mrs Proudie'; 'Last Reminiscences of Anthony Trollope', *Temple Bar* (January, 1884, 129–34), was wrongly attributed for many years to Alfred Austin (*I & R* 227). Both accounts emphasize Trollope's geniality (alongside his sometimes startling outbursts), his industrious work habits, and his great integrity. She regretted that *An Autobiography*, while an 'exact and faithful portrait of the man', did not convey 'how simple, how straightforward, how sincere he was, with what a tender heart, and what an open hand' (quoted *I & R* 230). RCT

Melbourne, port of entry for John Caldigate's gold-mining venture in New South Wales. *JC*
SRB

Mellerby, Sophie. Mellerbys have lived in Mellerby since King John's time; the Ancrums, on her mother's side, are amongst England's oldest, richest families. Sophie is 'every inch a lady' and is willing to marry Fred Neville should his character accord with his fortune and appearance. Nothing comes of this, but she is too well trained to consider his younger brother Jack. However, four years after Jack becomes Lord Scroope, Sophie becomes his Countess. *EE* AWJ

Melmotte, Augustus. Melmotte dominates London's financial and social worlds in *The Way We Live Now*, exemplifying a deterioration in moral probity and social discrimination. Possibly Irish or Jewish, he claims to be English, but has a slight foreign accent. His real name may be Melmody. He has lived in Hamburg, New York, and Paris, arriving in London after Napoleon III's fall (1870) ended the Second Empire as a speculator's paradise. Rumours claim that he 'made a railway across Russia . . . provisioned the Southern army in the American civil war . . . supplied Austria with arms, and . . . at one time bought up all the iron in England. He could make or mar any company by buying or selling stock, and could make money dear or cheap as he pleased.' Other rumours call him a swindler, forced to leave Paris, denied residence in Vienna (IV).

With offices in the City and a mansion in Grosvenor Square, Melmotte schemes to estab-lish himself in England. His public image swells as he lavishly entertains society and even royalty. Eager investors take shares in his enterprises, especially his projected South Central Pacific and Mexican Railway, to link Salt Lake City with Vera Cruz. He tries to buy a country estate and a titled husband for his daughter. As a representative 'merchant-citizen of London' he hosts a dinner for the Emperor of China, and is elected Conservative MP for Westminster. Dangerously, he comes 'almost to believe in himself' (LVI).

The dinner and election are Melmotte's triumphs, but rumours that he is insolvent and about to be arrested deter many guests from attending the dinner. As public confidence wanes, he struggles to survive. He forges Dolly Longestaffe's signature to obtain the deeds of a Longestaffe estate, then mortgages that estate. Threatened with exposure, he forges the signatures of his daughter and clerk, a ruse which fails. Trollope grants Melmotte 'a certain manliness' (LXXXI), as he realizes he is 'about to have a crushing fall' and decides that 'the world should say that he had fallen like a man' (LXXXII). He shows himself in the City, then in the House of Commons, where he literally falls on rising to speak. When he kills himself, Trollope suggests he has been 'driven as far beyond his powers of endurance as any other poor creature who ever . . . felt himself constrained to go' (LXXXVIII).

Trollope based Melmotte on several spectacular and speculative failures: Henry Fauntleroy, banker and suicide; John *Sadleir, railway speculator, forger, MP, and suicide; George *Hudson, railway speculator, Conservative MP, host to royalty; and perhaps on Dickens's Mr Merdle, speculator and suicide, in *Little Dorrit* (1855–6). He is also a study of the Napoleonic type and its incompatibility with social order. Trollope knew Napoleon III's biography of Julius Caesar, which claimed that great men are above the law, implicitly justifying illegalities committed by both Napoleons. The American Mrs Hurtle compares Melmotte to Napoleon, declaring, 'Such a man rises above honesty' (XXVI); Lady Carbury argues that 'One cannot measure such men by the ordinary rule' (XXX). But to Roger Carbury, the moral conscience of the novel, he is 'a miserable imposition, a hollow vulgar fraud from beginning to end' (LV). RT

Melmotte, Mme, generally despised wife of Augustus Melmotte. Fat, cowed, and dim-witted, she is also maligned for her Jewishness and obscure origins. Socially incapable of living up to the magnificence of her husband's income, she is also a poor stepmother to Marie, defending physical abuse and taking it herself. After Melmotte's suicide, she only cares for anonymity and financial security and marries Melmotte's secretary, Herr Croll. *WWLN* SRB

Melmotte, Marie, daughter of the wealthy swindler Augustus Melmotte. As the marketable daughter and only child of a prestigious, rich man, she suffers the ignominy of the 'Marie Melmotte plate', up for sale among impoverished, idle lords, knowing she is both courted and despised for her father's dubious wealth. Her father beats her and is astonished when she shows enough spirit and intelligence to refuse signing over a trust fund he had put in her name. Her passive, intimidated stepmother gives her no support or comfort. The man she chooses to love is the utterly worthless Felix Carbury but he cannot even bother to elope with her as planned. Undefeated, she turns the disillusionment of her struggles into a growing independence until she alone controls her life. After her father's suicide, she considers her options and calculates that marriage to the entrepreneur Hamilton Fisker and the freer society of San Francisco will suit her best. Marie stands as an emblem of victimhood to female roles and unprincipled social ambition in this most bleak of Trollope's novels, yet she rises above abasement through her own intelligence, perseverance, and courage. *WWLN* SRB

Meredith, George (1828–1909), novelist, poet and critic, best known for *Modern Love* (1862), a sonnet sequence portraying a broken marriage, and novels such as *The Ordeal of Richard Feverel* (1859), *The Egoist* (1879). In *Westminster Review* (October 1857), Meredith gave unstinting praise to *Barchester Towers*, admiring its plot, 'as simple as the siege of Troy' (Smalley 53). Trollope did not involve Meredith with the new *Fortnightly Review*, but expressed respect for Meredith as reader for Chapman & Hall, a role performed 1862–94. Trollope contacted him regarding Lady Pollock's *Little People, and Other Tales* (1874), 'not at all to influence your verdict . . . but that you might understand my anxiety and oblige me by sending the Mss back to me with your report as early as you conveniently do [*sic*]' (*Letters* 2, 583). When Mary Holmes complained in 1874 that she had been badly treated by Meredith, Trollope was quick to defend his judgement on the firm's behalf. (*Letters* 2, 636). RCT

Meredith, Sir George, husband of Justinia Lufton, daughter of Lady Lufton. *FP* NCS

Meredith, Lady Justinia, first child of Lady Lufton of Framley, married to Sir George Meredith for several years. Her friend Fanny Mansell has married the ambitious Revd Mark Robarts,

and Lady Meredith helps defend his worldly actions to her mother. *FP* NCS

Merewether, Charles (1823–84), barrister, MP for Northampton, and friend of Trollope, who gave a legal opinion on the issue of heirlooms and 'paraphernalia' in *The Eustace Diamonds* (*Letters* 2, 858). Trollope was careful to seek advice on legal matters in his fiction after having been taken to task over the matter of 'theft' in *The Last Chronicle of Barset*; 'those terrible meshes of the law', he lamented in *Phineas Finn* (XXIX). RCT

Merioneth, Duke of, father of the Marquis of Llwddythlw and one of the richest men in England. *MF* SRB

Merivale, Revd Charles (1808–93), chaplain to the House of Commons; Dean of Ely; historian, essayist, author of *History of the Romans under the Empire* (1850–64), reviewed by Trollope. He was also a contributor, with Trollope, to the *Pall Mall Gazette*. Trollope reviewed five volumes of the *History* for the *Dublin University Magazine*, 1851 and 1856. Those articles revived interest in the classics and subsequently led to his *The Commentaries of Caesar* (1870) and *Life of Cicero* (1880). Trollope was deeply wounded by Merivale's reference to his 'comic Caesar'. RCT

Merivale, Herman (1806–74), Eldest son of John Herman Merivale; political economist, best known for *Historical Studies* (1865); Under-Secretary for India (1859). Trollope invited him to write for the *Fortnightly Review*; he contributed six articles between 1865 and 1871. Trollope sponsored his son Herman Charles (1839–1906) for the Garrick Club in 1864. RCT

Merivale, John Lewis (1815–86), barrister; attended Harrow (1827–33); long-time registrar in the Court of Chancery; close friend of Trollope for 50 years from the age of 10. They formed the Tramp Society for hiking in the Home Counties. These walks with Merivale were 'the happiest hours of my then life' (*Auto* III). Merivale sponsored his application for a reader's ticket for the British Museum. Walking with Merivale in Co. Leitrim in 1843 Trollope came across the ruined house that inspired his first novel, *The Macdermots of Ballycloran* (*Auto* IV). Through Merivale Trollope met William Longman, who agreed to publish his first successful novel, *The Warden* (*Auto* V). He was godfather to Trollope's son Henry Merivale. RCT

Merivale family. John Herman Merivale (1779–1844), barrister-poet, and his wife Louisa, daughter of Revd Joseph Drury, former head of Harrow School (1785–1805), were friends and neighbours in Keppel Street, London, of Trollope's parents. The eldest son, Herman, recited Dante, much to Mrs Trollope's delight (*Chron* 3). The Merivales visited the Trollopes after their move to Julian Hill. Three of their sons, Herman, John, and Charles, attended Harrow. Of the three John, being closest in age, became Anthony's closest friend.   RCT

'Merivale's *History of the Romans'*, volumes 1 and 2 (review). This is possibly the finest history in English of the Roman Empire. This is a work much needed today. Merivale is less narrow and much easier to read than most university people; he has the simplicity of style missing in Macaulay and Grote. Roman culture's influence on modern languages, customs, and laws is immense. The only flaw here is excessive 'hero-worship' of Caesar and exaggeration of his political prowess at the expense of other elements of the period. *Dublin University Magazine* (May 1851), 611–24.   AKL

'Merivale's *History of the Romans'*, volumes 3–5 (review). In the years since volumes 1 and 2 were produced, the author has become even better at his task of explaining the ancients. There is no error of overemphasis on one figure here; Antony and Augustus are kept in proper perspective. The frequent use of 'pedantic Latinity', such as 'cremation' and 'Etruscan cult', is a minor flaw. Merivale's scholarship is not to be doubted. Octavius is seen as the most cruel person in history, without even a misguided religious motive for his persecutions. *Dublin University Magazine,* (July 1856), 30–46.   AKL

Merle Park, Sir Thomas Tringle's comfortable country house in Sussex, near Hastings. *AA*
                                                     WK

Merton, Dr, doctor at Tretton Park who cares for John Scarborough during the ongoing illnesses which lead to his death. Merton understands that Scarborough is thoroughly dishonest but completely loving and unselfish. *MSF*   MT

Mickewa, one of the western states of the United States, home of Senator Elias Gotobed. *AS*
                                                     MG

middle class, new. Trollope is highly ambivalent in his treatment of the new middle class. This is clearly demonstrated by the fates of two of his earliest arrivistes, Sir Roger Scatcherd (*DT*) and Miss Dunstable (*DT, FP, LCB*). Despite his sympathetic portrayal in the novel, Scatcherd, the former stonemason and railway magnate, is clearly shown to be unsuitable for the new life his vast fortune has brought about: alcoholic excess causes his early death (as it does with his son

Louis); and, significantly, his wealth is used ultimately to rescue the ailing Greshamsbury estate, and ensure the continued dominance of the old, squirearchical Gresham family. The equally vast fortune of Miss Dunstable, daughter of a patent-medicine peddler, however, is ultimately bestowed upon Dr Thorne, rather than various impecunious squires and aristocrats who seek to marry her, thus ensuring the consolidation of middle-class professionalism that the doctor represents. Both Scatcherd and Miss Dunstable are to some extent objects of satire: in both cases we are asked to smile at their nouveau riche vulgarity, as we are at the equally wealthy and equally vulgar Neefit, the breeches-maker, in *Ralph the Heir*. The tradesmen of *The Struggles of Brown, Jones, and Robinson* are equally marked out as objects of ridicule. Nevertheless, if Trollope could sneer at trade, he was fundamentally at one with a different sort of newly emerging middle-class existence: that of the *professional*. Indeed, the professional classes probably come off best in Trollope's fiction, and feature prominently in it (virtually the entire male cast of *Orley Farm* is composed of lawyers). Trollope's young heroes, for instance, tend to be drawn from the new occupations that were seeking respectability in the mid- to late 19th century. Thus, for instance, Hugh Stanbury and Brooke Burgess (*HKWR*) are, respectively, a journalist and a banker; Harry Clavering (*C*) is an engineer; Phineas Finn (*PF, PR, PM, DC*) is the son of a doctor, a struggling barrister, and, ultimately, one of the new breed of professional politicians; John Eames and Adolphus Crosbie (*SHA, LCB*) are civil servants, as are Harry Norman and Alaric and Charley Tudor, the three male protagonists of *The Three Clerks*. Common to nearly all these characters (and many more) is an anxiety concerning money; Trollope returns time and time again to the dramatic possibilities arising from a society not yet fully meritocratic, where young, well-educated men have to make their way in a world that respects their intelligence, but has not yet the social and financial structures in place to accommodate them properly. Indeed, the difficulty for respectable people to acquire hard cash is arguably Trollope's overwhelming concern in his fiction. If his male protagonists are struggling to make their way in the world, however, so too are his female protagonists, and Trollope is equally sympathetic to those women who are 'genteel' by birth and education, but isolated because of society's inability to accommodate them: such vulnerable characters include the governess Lucy Morris (*ED*), the orphaned Mary Lawrie and Mary Bonner (*OML* and *RH*, respectively), the Dormer sisters (*AA*), and Clara Amedroz (*BE*).

All these women are virtually helpless because of the socio-cultural formations which excluded so many middle-class women from the Victorian social sphere, and in each of the cases cited above, only marriage can save the woman in question from a lifetime of poverty. Trollope's identification with the problems of the newly emerging professional middle classes is obviously demonstrable in his endorsement of the Smilesian self-help ethic in *An Autobiography*, where the message to his readers is plain enough: work hard at your profession and, in the face of considerable adversity, you will reap the requisite pecuniary awards. HO

Middle East. The Middle East that was of concern to the British in the 19th century was largely ruled by the Ottoman Turks. Many areas of this financially troubled empire were semi-autonomous, left alone in return for an annual tribute. This was the case in Egypt, where the Khedives followed virtually independent policies. Britain's interests in the area grew in proportion to the progress of British trade and empire in India and China, and intensified when a fast route to India, via Egypt, was developed in the 1830s. The Suez Canal, the building of which Britain initially opposed, opened in 1869, and increased British strategic involvement. British foreign policy was designed to thwart or balance French interests in the eastern Mediterranean, and prop up the Turks sufficiently to keep the Russians out of Istanbul and the Dardanelles.

When Egyptian rulers plunged deeply into debt, European governments became involved in Egyptian politics on behalf of their bondholders; Egypt's financial situation deteriorated to the point that the British invaded in 1882, and set up a 'temporary' behind-the-scenes administration designed to restore the country's finances, and keep other nations out of this strategically vital area. At the same time, British diplomats attempted to curb Russian infringements on the Turkish state, on Persia, and on Afghanistan in order to deflect any possible threat to British India.

The Middle East was also of interest for several other reasons. Palestine contained Jerusalem, Bethlehem, and other places of sacred relevance to Christians (as well as to Muslims), and attracted a steady stream of pilgrims and sightseers anxious to explore areas familiar to them from biblical references. Archaeology was born in the 19th century, and many Middle Eastern sites were investigated and uncovered. The Arabs on the southern fringes of the Ottoman Empire, particularly the desert-based tribes, exerted a fascination for British travellers, and Richard Burton,

Gifford Palgrave, and Charles Doughty, among others, wrote of their adventures in the area. Burton travelled disguised as a Muslim doctor to the holy places of Mecca and Medina. Also, interest in the economic exploitation of the region grew as 20th century technology created the need for oil. All these factors led to Britain seeking and getting mandates over Palestine, Transjordan, and Iraq after the First World War.

Trollope travelled to the Middle East twice. In 1858, the Post Office sent him to Egypt to improve postal service, and he visited the Holy Land. In 1875, he travelled through the area by way of the Suez Canal en route to Australia; his letters from here are published in *The Tireless Traveller*. Several of Trollope's short stories are set in the region, as is a portion of *The Bertrams*. The stories are: 'An Unprotected Female at the Pyramids', 'A Ride across Palestine' (first published as 'The Banks of the Jordan'), and 'George Walker at Suez'. LK

Perry, G. E., *The Middle East* (2nd edn., 1992).
Tidrick, K., *Hearts Beguiling Araby: The English Romance with Arabia* (1989).

Middlesex, location of the Cedars, home of Sir John Ball. *MM* SRB

Middle Wash, immense dike in the Cambridgeshire fens, bisecting the Folking estate of Daniel Caldigate. *JC* SRB

Midlothian, Lady Margaret, Great but distant relative of Alice Vavasor who attempts to interfere in Alice's matrimonial arrangements. Alice regards this interference as impertinent both because of Lady Margaret's manifest lack of interest in Alice's earlier life and because of the lady's own 'unfortunate' marriage. *CYFH* JMR

Milborough, Dowager Countess of, friend of Louis Trevelyan's mother. Old-fashioned and a bit stodgy, she is nevertheless a 'good, motherly, discreet' woman (II). Initially Louis's ambassador to his wife, she ultimately recognizes that Emily is more sinned against than sinning. She subsequently befriends Nora Rowley, and it 'may be doubted whether any old lady since the world began ever did a more thoroughly Christian and friendly act' (XCIV). *HKWR* RC

Mildmay, Augusta (Guss). On the marriage market too long, she imprudently loves the impecunious Jack De Baron. In a most unladylike pursuit Guss forces him to promise marriage in the unlikely event of his acquiring suitable funds. She holds him to his word. *IHP* MG

Mildmay, Julia (Aunt Ju). The spinster aunt of Guss Mildmay is an active member of the 'Disabilities' to which she invites Lady George Germain. She is sued by Baroness Banmann over

an internal dispute in the organization. *IHP*
MG

Mildmay, William Great Whig Prime Minister who heads the government immediately after Phineas Finn's first election to Parliament. Though honest in his desire for reform and popular among other government Liberals, Mr Mildmay is resolute in his decision to exclude the ballot from his reform bill. *PF, PR, PM*   JMR

Miles, Mrs. Pride in the Launay family makes her try to thwart her son's love for Bessy Pryor, but she is defeated by love in the end. 'Launay' *WFF*   GRH

military characters. Army and navy affairs and types have little place in Trollope's novels, although over 80 characters bear some kind of service rank. Thackeray made Waterloo central to the theme and plot of *Vanity Fair* (1848), but Trollope had no such interest. The possibility of an army career loomed briefly when he was barely out of his teens: his mother sought a commission for him in an Austrian cavalry regiment, for which he was supposed to prepare by learning French and German in Brussels while serving as a school usher (*Auto* II). This was not as bizarre as it sounds, since military service was among the more attractive career options in the 19th century. Although commissions had to be bought, until 1871, and could cost as much as £1,200, the profession had status and glamour, especially for younger sons who were not going to inherit the family estate. The most valued commissions were in the Household Troops around the royal family, in the cavalry and in the various regiments of the Guards. Misconduct could lead to being cashiered which, apart from disgrace, meant that the commission could not be exchanged for cash. Captain Gustavus Bellfield (*CYFH*) has sold out of the army, because he cannot exist on his lieutenant's pay: 'The price of his commission had gone to pay his debts' (LXIV). The Crimean War (1854–6) raised the status of soldiering, and Trollope argued for a beefed-up standing army in *The New Zealander* (V). In fiction he presents few good soldiers in their professional roles. Colonel Stubbs (*AA*), with short back and sides and a thick red beard, 'each bristle almost a dagger' (XVI), is the youngest colonel in the British Army, and has been 'thrown a good deal about the world', possibly serving in India, before undertaking vague duties in Aldershot. Major Henry Grantly (*LCB*), son of the Archdeacon, has won the Victoria Cross in India but the circumstances are not specified (XVI). Bellfield (*CYFH*) has quasi-military employment drilling volunteers at Norwich, but his chief occupation is paying court to Widow Greenow by boasting of previous exploits 'on the plains of Zululand, when with fifty picked men I kept five hundred Caffres at bay for seven weeks; . . . [and] at the mouth of the Nitchyhomy River, when I made good the capture of a slaver by my own hand and my own sword!' (XX). Another serving soldier is Captain Walter Marrable (*VB*), conveniently on leave from India and thus able to court Mary Lowther. Gerald Robarts (*FP*) has been a captain in the Crimea; Colonel Askerton (*BE*) has served in India; Sir Lionel Bertram (*B*) has held a vague military post in the Middle East. Lord George De Bruce Carruthers (*ED*) is a colonel of Volunteers. Military action occurs only in 'The Two Generals', in which the two Reckenthorpe brothers are on opposite sides in the American Civil War, and in *La Vendée*, which deals with an uprising during the French Revolution. Many of Trollope's military characters appear in this book, notably General François-Joseph Westerman, who was based on a man who rose from the rank of private. Soldiers in the fiction, other than heroes like Grantly and Stubbs, are gamblers, toadies, and ne'er-do-wells, and have no connection with actual service. Colonel Frederic Osborne (*HKWR*) 'was fond of intimacies with married ladies' (*I*), and drove a wedge between the Trevelyans. Similarly, the young Guards officer Captain Jack De Baron (*IHP*) flirts with the wife of Lord George Germain and almost ruins their marriage. Major Moody and Captain Vignolles (*MSF*) are gamblers who fleece Mountjoy Scarborough at cards. Captain Valentine Scott (*TC*) tries to persuade Alaric Tudor to venture his ward's fortune in a stock market venture. Major Pountney (*PM*) offends the Duke of Omnium by asking outright for the Silverbridge seat in Parliament and is sent packing. Major Tifto (*DC*) nobbles a horse to ruin Lord Silverbridge who has a share in it. Captain Frederick Aylmer (*BE*) breaks off his engagement to Clara Amedroz, while Fred Neville (*EE*), a lieutenant in the cavalry, seduces Kate O'Hara; in the same novel, her father Captain O'Hara is a blackmailer. Captain Stubber (*SHH*) is a moneylender who has George Hotspur in his clutches. Hotspur, who holds a commission in a cavalry regiment, courts his cousin Emily, breaks her heart, and marries his long-term mistress. The navy is even less well represented in the fiction. Captain Bartholomew Cuttwater (*TC*) is a retired navy man much given to drink, swearing, and outspoken comments. Lieutenant Crosstrees (*FixP*) is second-in-command of the warship *John Bright*, of which Captain Battleax is commander. Captain Munday (*JC*) is skipper of the ship *Goldfinder* which takes John Caldigate to Australia.   GH

Mill, John Stuart (1806–73), philosopher, author of *On Liberty* (1859), *Utilitarianism* (1861), *The Subjection of Women* (1869), co-written with Harriet Taylor, and *Autobiography* (1873). Mill expressed a wish to meet Trollope, who was delighted: 'Stuart Mill is the only man in the whole world for the sake of seeing whom I would leave my own home on a Sunday,' he told a friend, but the meeting was scarcely a success. As usual in such encounters, Trollope came on strong. The contrast, 'was too violent between the modesty and courtesy of the host and the blustering fashions of Trollope . . . It was a relief to get the bull safely away from the china-shop' (*I & R* 192). Trollope publicly supported Mill's candidacy for Westminster, giving a 'short and forcible' speech on his behalf (Hall 278). Trollope was sceptical of Mill's advocacy of women's rights but alluded sympathetically to them in *Phineas Finn* through Violet Effingham's declaration that she might 'knock under to Mr Mill and go in for women's rights and look forward to stand for some female borough' (LI). He had mixed feelings about Mill's ideas on land being given to tenants in Ireland with compensation for owners and said so in *Saint Pauls* (March 1870).   RCT

Millais, Sir John Everett (1829–96), entered Royal Academy at 14; a founder of the Pre-Raphaelite Brotherhood (1848); in 1855 married Effie Gray, formerly Ruskin's wife; Trollope's favourite illustrator. The collaboration began unpromisingly when Trollope found fault with his depiction of Lucy Robarts in a billowing dress (*Framley Parsonage*), but thereafter Millais, a fellow Garrick member, became one of his closest friends. As Trollope lay dying, Millais wrote to William *Russell: 'is there one word necessary for me to say what I think of the man we have both lost? "Fill up the ranks and march on"—as Dickens said when he heard of Thackeray's death' (quoted *Chron* 140). Millais attended the funeral at Kensal Green, 9 December 1882.   RCT

Millepois, Mr, French chef employed by the Duchess of Omnium to provide fashionable dinners at Gatherum Castle during the early days of her husband's coalition ministry. *PM*   JMR

Miller, Cincinnatus Hiner ('Joaquin') (1839–1913), American poet known as 'the Oregon Byron', a celebrity in England after *Pacific Poems* (1870) and *Songs of the Sierras* (1871). Trollope invited Miller to a dinner at the Garrick Club which he was hosting for Mark Twain, who found Miller 'a disturber and degrader of the solemnities' (*I & R* 156). Trollope gave as good as

he got: 'He and Trollope talked all the time and both at the same time, Trollope pouring forth a smooth and limpid and sparkling stream of faultless English, and Joaquin discharging into it his muddy and tumultuous mountain torrent, and—Well, there was never anything just like it except the Whirlpool Rapids under Niagara Falls' (*I & R* 157). They met again at a hunting party, at which, on a challenge from Trollope, Joaquin later recalled, 'I threw my saddle on the grass and rode without so much as a blanket', leaving all the rest behind and being unhorsed in the process (*I & R* 159 n.).   RCT

Milnes, Richard Monckton (1809–85), later Baron Houghton; MP (1837); patron of many writers. His major literary work was *Life and Letters of Keats* (1848); he was an early champion of Swinburne and was well known for his generous hospitality at Fryston, Yorkshire, to which Trollope was invited. He notified Trollope of his election to the Cosmopolitan Club (1861) and served with him on the Royal Literary Fund. When Trollope was planning to tour the United States, Milnes provided him with letters of introduction. Like Trollope, he was a contributor to *Pall Mall Gazette*, and together with Trollope helped found—and fund—the *Fortnightly Review* (1865). In 1866, as a mark of esteem, Trollope presented Milnes with a first edition of *The Warden*, the last of 750 copies originally printed by Longman (*Letters* 1, 363). Speculation over what Disraeli had been paid for *Lothair* (1870) led Trollope to bet Milnes £10 that no publisher would offer £10,000 for a novel: 'no house could afford to give such a sum' (*Letters* 1, 520). He lost. Trollope was evidently not aware how high the upper end of the pay scale could go. Under complex profit-sharing agreements Dickens made more than £10,000 from several works. Longman gave that sum for Disraeli's *Endymion* (1880).   RCT

Milton, John (1608–74) There are more references and allusions to Milton in Trollope's fiction than to any other English writer except Shakespeare. Trollope's juvenile enthusiasm for the poet may have been fired by the coincidence that Milton was his mother's family name. In *An Autobiography* he tells us that the 'music of the Miltonic line' was familiar to him when he joined the Post Office at 19 (*Auto* III). His favourite poem at this time (and afterwards) was 'Lycidas' (1638), his favourite lines, according to Tom, those on fame as the 'last infirmity of noble mind' ('Lycidas' ll. 70–2). There is an anecdote of his offering a £5 note to each of his nieces if they could get the poem by heart, and all three of them did so (Alfred Austin, *Autobiography* (1911), 1, 211). After *Macbeth* and *Hamlet*, 'Lycidas' is the

John Everett Millais, photographed by Lewis Carroll, 1865. Publication of *Framley Parsonage* not only established Trollope's popularity, but began his association with Millais, who became his favourite illustrator. Trollope judged his illustrations for *Orley Farm* the best he had seen in any novel. Millais also illustrated *The Small House at Allington* and *Phineas Finn*. Millais contributed a total of 86 full-page plates for Trollope's fiction.

work Trollope alludes to most frequently, and the poem accounts for over three-quarters of his references to Milton. In addition to those on 'fame', the lines most frequently cited refer to sporting 'with Amaryllis in the shade' (ll. 68–9, *TC*, I; *FixP*, IV), and the day-star 'flaming in the forehead of the morning sky' (ll. 169–71, *C* (V), *WWLN* (LXX), *SHH* (XXIII)). The most imaginatively charged Miltonic allusion comes in *The Last Chronicle of Barset* (LXII), where the grimly self-dramatizing Josiah Crawley compares himself with Samson, 'Eyeless in Gaza, at the mill with slaves' (*Samson Agonistes* l. 41). Trollope alludes to *Paradise Lost* comparatively infrequently, though he read the poem aloud to his family in 1881 (*Letters* 2, 1034). Rose Trollope presented the novelist's bust of Milton to the Athenaeum Club after his death.   PJT

Miss Mackenzie (*see next page*)

'Miss Ophelia Gledd', first printed in *A Welcome* (1863) (reprinted in *LS*). Ophelia ('Pheely') Gledd is the 'belle of Boston'; beautiful, intelligent, and high-spirited. The English narrator, Archibald Green (a recurrent figure in Trollope's short stories), first encounters her resourcefully dealing with a sleigh accident. He observes Miss Gledd's dilemma about whether to accept the addresses of a sturdy young American, Hannibal H. Hoskins, or a rich upper-class Englishman, John Pryor. After much heart-searching, she eventually chooses the Englishman. Ophelia is thought to be based on Trollope's American friend Kate Field.   JS

'Miss Sarah Jack, of Spanish Town, Jamaica', first serialized in *Cassell's Illustrated Family Paper*, 3 and 10 November 1860 (reprinted in *TAC1*). Maurice Cumming is proprietor of the Mount Pleasant sugar plantation in Jamaica. Following the abolition of slavery in 1833, the business has fallen on hard times. At the instigation of his amiable busybody of a maiden aunt Miss Sarah Jack, Maurice is elected to the House of Assembly in Spanish Town. Here he falls in love with Miss Jack's niece Marian Leslie. They fall out when she dances with other partners at a ball. Finally, all is made well by Miss Jack.   JS

'Mr Anthony Trollope and Baron Tauchnitz' (letter). The author of this letter is not, nor has been, nor expects to be, engaged in a lawsuit with the Leipzig publisher Baron Tauchnitz, despite rumours to the contrary. *Pall Mall Gazette* (21 May 1869), 1743.   AKL

'Mr Anthony Trollope and the *Saturday Review*' (letter). Criticism of this novelist for writing on public issues is annoying (as examples, witness responses to observations on

Lincoln's assassination and on fourth-commandment observance). Surely all citizens, including newspaper editors, must (and should) have interests other than their jobs. *Pall Mall Gazette* (5 February 1866), 395.   AKL

'Mr Disraeli and the Dukes' (review). Mr Disraeli's new novel *Lothair* is vulgar, ill-written, and absurd; it commits every possible fault of a novel except indecency. Disraeli has cynically written this, sure of success because of his name. *Saint Pauls* (August 1870), 447–51.   AKL

'Mr Disraeli and the Mint' (article). The Prime Minister has appointed as Master of the Mint one of his secretaries, passing over a man with much better experience and reputation. Such actions damage not only the better man, but, in fact, the whole civil service. *Saint Pauls* (May 1869), 192–7.   AKL

'Mr Freeman on the Morality of Hunting' (article). Freeman's (1 October) criticism of fox-hunting as cruel and inhumane is inaccurate. Hunters do not take pleasure in the animal's pain; fox-hunting is not comparable to bear-baiting. Freeman does not define 'cruelty'; it could be applied to hunting animals with fur or shells, or even killing wasps. The foxes' pain is exaggerated and the value of recreation underrated. Mawkish sentimentality is as misguided as the alleged cruelty practised by fox-hunters. *Fortnightly Review* (1 December 1869), 616–25.   AKL

'Mr Robert Bell' (obituary). Mr Bell died yesterday. His contributions to periodical literature, as writer and editor, were significant. He also wrote a novel, a biography, and dramas. More accomplished than famed, he was much admired for his wit, kindness, affection, and integrity. *Pall Mall Gazette* (13 April 1867), 11.   AKL

Mr Scarborough's Family (*see page 371*)

Mistletoe, home of the Duke of Mayfair, an ugly, enormous, comfortable house set in dull surroundings, always full of fashionable guests hunting, shooting, and flirting. In an effort to borrow the glamour of her uncle Arabella Trefoil wages part of her campaign to marry Lord Rufford there. *AS*   MG

Mistletoe, Lord, eldest son of the Duke of Mayfair, as inexpressibly handsome as his father. He retains his childhood affection for his cousin Arabella Trefoil but tells her he cannot force Lord Rufford to marry her. He is a conscientious member of Parliament who hopes to 'become a useful Under Secretary' (*L*). *AS*   MG

ORIGINALLY titled 'The Modern Griselda', *Miss Mackenzie* was a deliberate attempt on Trollope's part to write a novel without love interest. He sets out instead to reframe the question of the choices that a woman has to make, taking for his heroine Margaret Mackenzie, a woman of 35. She could not fit the role of romantic heroine, even though she is almost as inexperienced as a young girl, since her life has been passed in caring first for her father, then for her invalid brother Walter.

On Walter's death, Margaret inherits an estate which brings her an income of £800 a year. She finds herself free to taste the pleasures of independence for the first time but at the price of having incurred the hostility of the rest of the Mackenzie family.

She moves to Littlebath and takes lodgings in the home of the sceptical Miss Sally Todd, who refuses to be frightened off her game of cards by the evangelical pieties of her neighbours. (Miss Todd, who also appears in *The Bertrams*, is often taken as a portrait of the activist Frances Power Cobbe.)

In spite of this bracing example, Margaret becomes involved with a pious set, where, once it is known that she has independent means, she begins to receive attentions from the Revd Jeremiah Maguire, a handsome gallant only disfigured by a severe squint. As the rather crude detail of that squint suggests, in this novel Trollope's satirical touch is not always assured. His impatience with self-deception makes him ruthless in the caricature of evangelical manners. In *Rachel Ray*, possibly because Trollope confines himself almost entirely to a world of evangelical manners, the comedy gives pleasure by highlighting the self-deception of the characters rather than by mocking their vulgarity.

The Revd Maguire is not the only man to pursue Margaret: she has two other suitors, Samuel Rubb, a man of 40, who is the partner in her brother Tom's business, and John Ball, an older cousin of her own, a widower with nine children. This cousin, who will be a baronet one day, has a domineering mother, Lady Ball, who would be pleased to make use of Margaret and her fortune. The widow of her brother Tom, who has her own children to provide for, has her eyes on Margaret's money too.

Margaret is fully conscious that she is the object of desire for many different people. Just being a focus for others seems to help her to admit to longings of her own. In an unmistakably sexual image, she pulls her clothing tighter at her breast and leans forward to kiss her own face in the glass, in a gesture that Charles Swann has argued came to be borrowed by Gwendolen Harleth in Eliot's *Daniel Deronda* (*Notes and Queries*, 43 (1996), 47–8). It was with reference to this novel that Trollope declared in *An Autobiography* that he felt it a pity that some independent women should find it hard to admit that they wanted to marry: he chose to emphasize the part played by active sexual desire in a mature woman's choice of marriage.

Margaret decides to use her money to help Tom's widow and children. But when she makes a visit to her lawyer, old Mr Bideawhile, to arrange this, she finds that there has been a mistake and that the money she thought she had inherited in fact belongs to John Ball.

Although she respects and trusts Ball as a friend, Margaret has already turned down his proposal of marriage when this news breaks. The Revd Maguire makes a show of attempting to defend her interests against her cousin, bringing the case a short-lived notoriety. Samuel Rubb does better: knowing that she is now penniless he repeats his offer of marriage. If Margaret can finally accept John Ball, confident that he is not after her money, the reader has also learned something about what satisfactions marriage might offer a mature woman: sexual fulfilment, along with friendship and respect and an active life organizing a busy household.

Though Sir Edward Bulwer-Lytton wrote to him out of the blue to say how much he admired the conception of Margaret Mackenzie's character, most reviewers did not think it was one of Trollope's best books. Some did applaud his boldness in choosing to experiment with an older heroine: the *London Review* observed that Trollope delighted in setting himself problems in order to overcome them, while others found his choice in the matter perverse. Henry James, at 22 a young reviewer for the *Nation*, complained that we did not know how vulgar life is until we saw it set down in Trollope's pages (see Smalley 228, 233–7).

This was the only novel of Trollope's after 1860 that was not written for serial publication but was intended to make its first appearance as a short novel in two volumes. *Miss Mackenzie* was commissioned by an agreement of 23 February 1864: Chapman & Hall agreed to pay £1,200 for the right to print 3,000 copies and for half the copyright thereafter. Trollope did not start work on it till 22 May and he finished it 18 August. It was a period of intense productivity: in July there was a stretch of fourteen days when he churned out eighteen pages of *Miss Mackenzie* every day. After finishing it he would fit writing *The Claverings*, a three-volume novel, into the remaining months of that year.

Miss Mackenzie was published in two volumes by Chapman & Hall in February 1865 and reissued in a single volume in 1866 with an illustrated title-page and frontispiece not previously published. There were no further editions until it was published in World's Classics in 1924. The manuscript is in the Berg Collection in the New York Public Library. It does not form part of any series.   MH

Cunningham, V., *Everywhere Spoken against* (1975).
Riffaterre, M., 'Trollope Metonymies', *NCF* (December 1982), 272–92.

Mr Scarborough's Family

TRIBULATION over the inheritance of estates is a staple of Trollope's novels. As in Burke, contracts are a bond not only between individuals but between generations, ultimately joining the temporal interests of mankind with the spiritual and God. In this context, one could see Trollope's lawyers as even more important to the network of interests, material and spiritual, that make up English life than his clergymen. In *Mr Scarborough's Family*, these issues come to the fore in a contest between the cunning of Mr Scarborough, who delights in playing ingeniously with the law to suit his changing interests, and the respectable decency of his solicitor Mr Grey, who regards the law with reverence. At its most abstract the contest is between the idea of law as an expediential construction of rules (whatever it suits Parliament to enact), and the older notion of natural law (as the human reflection of divine providence). To Scarborough, 'law was hardly less absurd . . . than religion' (XXI). To Mr Grey, laws are 'as Holy Writ' (LV). The novel, Trollope's forty-fifth, is intricate and neat in its plot, and the character of Mr Scarborough gives it an incisive, sardonic, acerbic edge, often touched with grim humour.

Mr Scarborough owns a sizeable estate enriched by a town and clay workings on its land. Afflicted by an incurable disease, he lies slowly dying. Like many of Trollope's characters (Lizzie Eustace, for example), Scarborough has a limpet-like attitude to property, and if, facing death, he cannot keep it, he is determined that it will be disposed as he wishes. He has two sons: Mountjoy, his heir, a captain in the Guards and a gambler, who has already gambled away his inheritance in post-obit debts; and Augustus, a calculating, thoroughly selfish lawyer, who thinks that 'The making of all right and wrong in this world depends on the law' (V). Mr Scarborough, however, 'had lived through his life with the one strong resolution of setting the law at defiance in reference to the distribution of his property; but chiefly because he had thought the law to be unjust' (VIII). According to the rules of primogeniture and entail, the elder son inherits. But Mr Scarborough, in his youth, had married his wife twice, Mountjoy being born between the two ceremonies. Disgusted by Mountjoy's profligacy, Mr Scarborough produces proof of his second marriage as though it were the first, to show that Mountjoy is therefore illegitimate and thus cannot inherit. Disgruntled, Mountjoy disappears for a while and is even thought murdered. The estate would now go to Scarborough's second son Augustus, but Augustus, epitome of callous greed, makes his eagerness for his father's death so evident that Scarborough changes his mind. He now produces proof of his first marriage, and so reinstates Mountjoy as heir. In the meantime, to avoid possible claims and harassment, Augustus has paid off Mountjoy's creditors, who, thinking Mountjoy penurious, are willing to settle for a fraction of his debts. Mr Grey, like Trollope's other respectable solicitors (Mr Camperdown, or Slow & Bideawhile) a faithful guardian of his client's interests, is nevertheless outraged by Scarborough's ingenious legal juggling, and in touching night-time conferences disburdens himself of his grievances to his daughter.

The novel's sub-plot, also a story of entail and disinheritance, provides the usual set of Trollopian young lovers. Harry Annesley is heir to his mother's brother Squire Prosper, who sends him to Charterhouse and Cambridge and gives him an annual allowance. Prosper loves to preside over family sermons and takes it ill when Harry airily absents himself: 'A tacit contract had been made on his behalf [attending sermons], and he had declined to accept his share of the contract' (XXV). Prosper finds further grounds for disapproval when Harry fights Mountjoy Scarborough over Florence Mountjoy, whom they both love. (For a while Harry is suspected of murdering Mountjoy.) Motivated by the desire to punish Harry by disinheriting him, Prosper, a 'sickly little man about fifty', looks about him for a wife with whom he can beget an heir and upon whom, as Harry's mother observes, he can 'settle a jointure . . . which would leave the property not worth having' (XXIII). He chooses Matilda Thoroughbung, a brewer's daughter 42 years old with £25,000, but also, as he finds to his chagrin, with strong views about women's rights, and scorn for the way in which legal arrangements are always made in favour of 'the fathers and the brothers, and the uncles and the lawyers'. As Prosper puts it succinctly, 'I hate woman's rights' (XXVI). He objects to her conditions but also fears a suit for breach of promise. She eventually mocks and releases him. Mortified but relieved, he is ready to accept Harry as his heir.

Both plots contemplate age and generational conflict. The fact that Scarborough is dying accentuates the zest with which he attempts to impose his will on society, the law, and his sons. Not only is he obsessively determined that his property will go wherever he himself decides, he seems to have anticipated the moves in his game of legal chess for many decades—as, for example, in his double marriage ceremonies: 'it had all been done in preparation for the plot in hand,—as had scores of other little tricks which have not cropped up to the surface in this narrative. Mr Scarborough's whole life had been passed in arranging tricks for the defeat of the law' (LV). Scarborough's machiavellian gusto is backed by an appropriately thorough knowledge of the laws of entail. Becoming disgusted with Augustus, he not only plans to leave Mountjoy all his personal property (including the library over which the rather slow-witted guardsman muses in melancholy fashion, estimating that three or four days' gambling at the club would see the end of it), he also contemplates leaving the real estate 'bare'—'Underscore that word', he says—by cutting down the timber, and defacing the front of the house with a huge conservatory (XXXVIII). He would like to scrape the paper off the walls, too. But when his secretary Merton questions his powers to destroy the timber and stay within the law, Scarborough replies that he would use the timber to mend the tenants' barns and gates; in short, making a nice distinction between legitimate and 'equitable' waste (that is, actionable in a court of equity). Grey will consent to the general stripping of moveables for Mountjoy's benefit, but restrains Scarborough's malice in regard to the timber (regard for timber, as usual in the English novel, being an almost sacred indicator of a moral responsibility in the management of estates). His solicitor's reproachful comments on Scarborough's legal trickery, so far from abashing him, are a source of great enjoyment. He is fundamentally possessive, and his possessiveness is psychologically part of his affection for those he likes: 'Mr Scarborough', says Trollope, 'was fond of people who belonged to him' (II). But he is also 'one who could hate to distraction, and on whom no bonds of blood would operate to mitigate his hatred' (LVIII). He characteristically expresses his feelings for people through the manipulation of property.

Trollope is remarkable at portraying with sympathy and conviction characters whose attitudes to life are very far from his own, and Mr Scarborough is interesting as a protagonist who defies most of the qualities that Trollope holds dear throughout his fiction. Truth is one of Trollope's watchwords: Scarborough delights in playing fast and loose with it, to Mr Grey's annoyance. Trollope values honesty: Scarborough 'had a most thorough contempt for the character of an honest man. He did not believe in honesty, but only in mock honesty. . . . The usual honesty of the world was with him all pretence' (XXI). Trollope, though alive to nuance, is a moralist: Scarborough reduces all vice and virtue to 'good nature' and 'ill nature'. Trollope believes in the sanctity of oaths: Scarborough makes light of words—'That one set of words should be deemed more wicked than another, as in regard to swearing, was to him a sign either of hypocrisy, of idolatry, or of feminine weakness of intellect.' For Trollope the principles of entail and primogeniture are guarantees of the English way of life (even here, though Mountjoy at the end will still gamble away the estate, the elder son inherits): Scarborough, true to his theory of words, considers law 'a perplexed entanglement of rules got together so that the few might live in comfort at the expense of the many' (XXI). Cynical though all this makes him sound, nevertheless, Trollope treats him sympathetically. He 'was kind to many people, having a generous and an open hand' (XXI). Dominating, caustic, and relentless, he is at the same time sensitive to other people's moral qualities, though he has to find contorted reasons for approving them. In so many ways the antithesis of Trollopian virtues, Scarborough is undoubtedly the most sympathetically rendered character in the book.

The novel's contest of moral viewpoints is primarily located in Scarborough's relationship with his solicitor Mr Grey, who has a deserved reputation for acuteness and honesty, and who tells himself that having been tricked once by Scarborough he cannot be tricked again. Of course he is tricked again. With his respect for the majesty of the law, Grey thinks Scarborough's behaviour outrageous. But in this ironic novel of qualification and reversal, that is not the final judgement. ' "He is the greatest rascal that I ever knew," he said again and again. . . . But yet he did not regard him as an honest man regards a rascal, and was angry with himself in consequence. He knew that there remained with him even some spark of love for Mr Scarborough, which to himself was inexplicable' (XXXIX). On Scarborough's part, we find a similar breakdown of moral definition. First, he tries to fit Mr Grey's apparent virtues into his own amoral universe: 'The usual honesty of the world was with him all pretence, or, if not, assumed for the sake of the character it would achieve. Mr Grey he knew to be honest; Mr Grey's word he knew to be true; but he fancied that Mr Grey had adopted this absurd mode of living with the view of cheating his neighbours by appearing to be better than others.' Nevertheless, though Scarborough is a good hater, 'Mr Grey, who constantly told him to his face that he was a rascal, he did not hate at all. Thinking Mr Grey to be in some respects idiotic, he respected him, and almost loved him. He thoroughly believed Mr Grey, thinking him to be an ass for telling so much truth unnecessarily' (XXI). Such mutual affection in spite of differences might seem to assure a happy outcome, but the ingenious gyrations of his client leave Mr Grey feeling old and superannuated, his confidence gone, and his suitability to his profession and to his times in doubt. Both are old men, but Scarborough has somehow stayed young, 'ever so much younger than I am', says Grey. He feels at odds with his own partner Mr Barry, who thinks Scarborough the best lawyer he ever knew.

Grey's disgruntlement expresses a cultural theme running through many a Trollopian novel and implicit in the title *The Way We Live Now*: that the degenerative modern age has become one of loose principles and sharp practice. ' "How am I to get on with such a man as Mr Barry" ', Grey asks. ' "I have been at my business long enough. Another system has grown up which does not suit me. . . . It may be that I am a fool, and that my idea of honesty is a mistake. . . . When I find that clever rascals are respectable, I think it is time that I should give up work altogether." ' And he does give up his work in disillusion, leaving the firm to Mr Barry, in whose condescending judgement 'poor old Grey was altogether off the hooks' (LXII). In modern terms, it is as though *Mr Scarborough's Family* were an allegorical conflict between the superego and the id, with the id winning (Mr Grey's daughter Dolly invites us to see an allegorical pattern in which Mr Grey is Reason, Dolly is Conscience, and Mr Barry is the Devil). Dr Merton, who attends Scarborough, concludes, ' "if you can imagine for yourself a state of things in which neither truth nor morality shall be thought essential, then old Mr Scarborough would be your hero" ' (LVIII). In this heavily qualified and finely nuanced novel, that is not the whole story; nevertheless, dying Scarborough remains the dominant figure of life-force, energy, enjoyment.

Mr Grey's trials of conscience are analysed in recurrent scenes of heart-searching with his daughter. Dolly is 32 years old, but the only man for whom she has ever felt any regard is her father. Their bedroom discussions of the day's events before retiring are 'the very salt of her life' (XVI). She declines an offer of marriage from Mr Barry, and in contemplating matrimony in general she assures herself that death would be preferable: 'there was but one man with whom she could live, and that man was her father' (XXXIII). Grey is of the opinion that, through their living so long together, Dolly has acquired his habits and thoughts, that they have stringent ideas about who is or is not a gentleman (Barry does not quite measure up), that they are both fastidious. Age and death hover in the background. Dolly reflects that her father is 66, that he cannot live much longer, and that she will be left alone, but she is nevertheless resolved. From one point of view, their relationship is touching. Their late-night communings are deeply gratifying to both. From another, Dolly's fastidiousness is another expression of Trollope's theme of the age being out of joint. Mr Barry, as we have seen, is an expression of the age to Grey, and Dolly takes a similar view—' "to know that your husband is not a gentleman!" ' (LII). But to what extent is their rigidity merely eccentric, another sign of disintegration? As Grey virtually renounces life in his feeling of being out of sympathy with his calling and his times, Dolly, in seeing her father as the only possible man that she could live with, makes a similar morbid choice. James R. Kincaid (in *The Novels of Anthony Trollope*, 1977) puts the matter bluntly: 'Trollope's most open excursion into twisted sexuality marks an appropriate symbol for a world that so distorts all the values which count' (256).

The sub-plot of *Mr Scarborough's Family* parodies its main plot—both deal with the disinheritance of wayward heirs, and they are further connected by Mr Grey's acting as solicitor for both Scarborough and Peter Prosper, and by Mountjoy Scarborough's and Harry Annesley's both courting Florence Mountjoy. The Peter Prosper plot, however, is comic, a contrast with the sardonic and disintegrating world of the Scarboroughs. Scarborough, though possessive, feels strongly about those around him: Prosper is thoroughly self-centred. Miffed about Harry's attitude to his sermons, he seeks marriage out of petulance. And once again, Trollope presents his action through a coalescence of psychology and legal niceties, this time the niceties of jointure. Prosper's prospective bride, Matilda Thoroughbung, is 42, just within child-bearing age. If she produces an heir, Harry Annesley is displaced. Here Trollope may be recalling his own father's tribulations when 'as a final crushing blow, an old uncle, whose heir he was to have been, married and had a family!' (*Auto* I). But producing an heir is no safe bet, and Prosper's pique is extreme, so he also plans a jointure, which is a settlement in lieu of dower, for Matilda. One way or the other Harry will be out in the cold. Matilda Thoroughbung, however, is no shy maiden. She believes in women's rights and has her own views about the legal exploitation of women by fathers and husbands and lawyers. In her conditions for a jointure, she even thinks of provision for a possible daughter! Having sought her to spite Harry, Prosper now longs to be rid of her because he cannot bear a woman with ideas—and particularly these ideas. Moreover, as Grey and Dolly hold to the manners of a vanished world, and consider Mr Barry not quite a gentleman, Prosper now sees a lack of dignity in Miss Thoroughbung herself. Another of the several old men in this book, Prosper is the typical comic bachelor, opinionated, self-absorbed, and finicky. His fussiness is comically expressed in the letter-writing on which he prides himself. Dearly longing to withdraw from their engagement, but timorous about breach of promise, he sets himself to writing an appropriate letter, but he 'was afraid that he might commit himself by an epithet. He dreaded even an adverb too much. He found that a full stop expressed his feelings too violently, and wrote the letter again, for the fifth time, because of the big initial which followed the full stop' (L). Full of suppressed mirth, Matilda confronts him on it, humiliates, and dismisses him. The pattern of comic romance, complete with the discomfiture of blocking elders, rises, and the book ends with the reinstatement of Harry and his marriage to Florence.

There is plenty of comedy in *Mr Scarborough's Family*, including such sardonic passages as that in which Scarborough wickedly contemplates stripping the estate, but the dominating impression, though illuminated by Scarborough's wit and basic unconventional decency, is of a world out of joint.

Mr Scarborough's Family was serialized in *All the Year Round* from May 1882 to June 1883, then published as three volumes in 1883. The manuscript, only partially in Trollope's hand, is in the library of Cornell University.   RDM

Kincaid, James R., *The Novels of Anthony Trollope* (1977).
McMaster, R. D., *Trollope and the Law* (1986).

'Mistletoe Bough, The', first published in the *Illustrated London News*, 21 December 1861 (reprinted in *TAC2*). A Christmas story, with household preparations for the annual festival in the background. The Garrows live in Thwaite Hall, in the Lake District. Various members of the family are coming home for the holiday. Also visiting is Godfrey Holmes, a young man who is in love with Elizabeth (Bessy) Garrow. There is a misunderstanding which almost leads to the engagement not taking place, but by the twelfth day of Christmas all is made well and marriage is again in prospect.   JS

'Mrs Brumby', first published in *Saint Pauls*, May 1870 (reprinted in *ET*). The 'editor' is persecuted by a Mrs Brumby who bombards him with wholly unpublishable pieces of writing. She ignores his rejections, and insists that he has undertaken to accept her work. She threatens the editor first with the wrath of her husband, a retired (and wholly unbelligerent) former lieutenant in the Duke of Sussex's regiment. Subsequently she recruits the assistance of dubious lawyers, Badger & Blister. Against his better judgement, the editor is bullied into making over £10 and writing a letter of apology to the pertinacious Mrs Brumby.   JS

'Mrs General Talboys'. Rejected by a prudish *Cornhill Magazine*, it was first published in the *London Review*, 2 February 1861 (reprinted in *TAC2*). Ida ('Mrs General') Talboys, a respectable English wife and matron, decides to spend the winter of 1859 in Rome. She likes to scandalize company with her libertarian views and encourages the dangerous attentions of an Irish artist, Wenceslaus O'Brien, a married man. On an expedition to the tomb of Cecilia Metella, he proposes that she run away with him to Naples. She

indignantly repulses him, and it is all her friends can do to induce her to remain in Rome.   JS

'Mrs Mary Sewell's *The Rose of Cheriton*' (review). This verse essay illustrating the dangers and sinfulness of drunkenness among the working class is unlikely to convert readers. Like most 'do-good' pamphlets, this is illogical, implausible, and inartistic. *Fortnightly Review* (February 1867), 252–5.   AKL

Mitford, Mary Russell (1787–1855), writer of historical dramas such as *Rienzi* (1828), *Charles I* (1834); best known for the rural sketches of *Our Village* (1843); met Trollope's mother in 1802 and became a lifelong friend. Mrs Trollope persuaded Macready to take *Rienzi* to America, while Miss Mitford, in turn, provided her friend with a letter of introduction to her publisher George Whittaker, who agreed to issue *Domestic Manners of the Americans*. In *The New Zealander* Trollope expressed appreciation of the society pictures drawn by Pepys, Fanny Burney, Jane Austen, and Mitford.   RCT

Mixet, Joe, baker of Bungay and good friend of John Crumb. With his 'rare eloquence', he serves as the inarticulate Crumb's mouthpiece in the latter's courtship of Ruby Ruggles, much to her disgust. His comic speech as best man at their wedding draws the admiration of all but Ruby. *WWLN*   SRB

'Modern Fiction as a Rational Amusement'. See LECTURES AND SPEECHES.

'Modern Fiction as a Recreation for Young People'. See LECTURES AND SPEECHES.

'Modern Literature' (speech). The guest of honour here [Dickens] is more fit to respond to this toast. Novelists work hard to please. If amusement comes without the sacrifice of manly nobility or feminine purity then authors do great and good work. Reprinted in *The Speeches of Charles Dickens*, ed. K. J. Fielding (1960), 389–93. See LECTURES AND SPEECHES. AKL

Moffat, Gustavus, mercenary young Barchester MP, a tailor's son. A dapper little man, he proposes to Augusta Gresham, demanding £10,000 dowry but settling for £6,000; however, he pursues Martha Dunstable, jilts Augusta, and is whipped in the London streets by her angry brother. *DT* NCS

Moggs, Mr, a London bootmaker of the firm of Booby & Moggs of Old Bond Street. He objects to his son Ontario's radical politics and looks upon his striking workmen 'with the eyes of Coriolanus glaring upon the disaffected populace of Rome' (XVI). *RH* ALS

Moggs, Ontario, son of Moggs the bootmaker and so christened by a Canadian godfather. In defiance of his father he holds 'horrible ideas about co-operative associations, the rights of labour, and the welfare of the masses' and regularly addresses political meetings of artisans at the Cheshire Cheese (VIII). Invited to stand for the radical interest in the Percycross election. Despite the failure of his political ambitions, he successfully woos and wins Polly Neefit. *RH* ALS

Moher, Cliffs of, dramatic outcrop, 600 feet (180 m) above the Atlantic, in Co. Clare. Fred Neville shoots seals and seagulls below Hag's Head and, from the edge of those cliffs, falls to his death at the hands of Mrs O'Hara. *EE* AWJ

Mohill, small Irish village populated with dingy hovels that is rumoured to be the headquarters of local Ribbonmen. *MB* MRS

Molk, Herr. As former burgomaster, Nuremberg's senior magistrate listens sympathetically to Linda's distress until he learns of her attachment to Valcarm, a political subversive. He urges her to marry Steinmarc and dangles possession of the red house before that nervous town clerk's ambition after Linda's disgraceful liaison with the rebel. *LT* AWJ

Mollett, Abraham (Aby), degenerate son of Matthew Mollett, who seconds his father's blackmailing of Sir Thomas. Despite mustachioed good looks, 'two rings, a gold chain, and half a dozen fine waistcoats', he alienates even his prospective bride, Fanny O'Dwyer, by his 'cruel and insolent' behaviour (XVII). *CR* MRS

Mollett, Mary (Swan), unmarried daughter of Matthew Mollett, who lives with her mother. Though decent-looking, she is prematurely worn by the perpetual sorrow of poverty, worry, and work. *CR* MRS

Mollett, Mary (Mrs Swan), long-suffering, estranged wife of Matthew Mollett, whose marriage certificate authenticates the legitimacy of the Fitzgerald family. Brow-beaten by years of poverty and neglect, she retains a sense of dignity, and though she pleads for mercy for the husband who deserted her, she also insists that he reveal the truth to Mr Prendergast. *CR* MRS

Mollett, Matthew, bigamist who illicitly marries Mary Wainright (Lady Fitzgerald), then later blackmails her husband, Sir Thomas Fitzgerald, becoming 'the Warwick who was to make and unmake the kings of Richmond Castle' (XLI). Though not vicious, he is likened to a leech that 'will not give over sucking . . . as long as there is a drop of blood left within the veins' (XX). *CR* MRS

Molloy, Michael, Irishman who pesters an editor with worthless manuscripts, obtains money by his charm, and turns out to be slightly mad. 'Bath' *ET* GRH

Molloy, Mrs, nurse and breadwinner who loves and cares for her somewhat deranged husband. 'Bath' *ET* GRH

Molteno, Sir John Charles (1838–1923). Prime Minister of Cape Colony (1872–8), he dismissed Sir Bartle *Frere over the conduct of the Frontier War (1877); he was one of several influential leaders Trollope interviewed in 1877 for his book on South Africa. RCT

Momont. Butler at Durbellière, devoted to the family and particularly to the Marquis, he conducts himself bravely when the chateau is taken, but is a little jealous of Chapeau's role in the Vendean cause. *LV* GRH

Momson, Lady Margaret, daughter of the Earl of Brigstock and first cousin of Mrs Stantiloup. She is instrumental in having her nephew (Augustus Momson) removed from Bowick School. Married for 30 years to a clergyman, she remains 'quite as much the Earl's daughter as the parson's wife' (4. XI). *DWS* RC

Momson, Mr, squire whose eldest son Augustus is a pupil at Bowick School. He resists but ultimately submits to efforts by Mrs Stantiloup and by his brother's wife (Lady Margaret Momson) to withdraw his child from the school. Dr Wortle implies that the squire's morals are not all that they should be. *DWS* RC

monarchy. Trollope's recorded comments on the institution of the monarchy in general, and of

Queen Victoria's reign in particular, are notable by their scarcity, although one might locate an implicit endorsement of the British constitutional status quo in his satirical portrayal of American republicanism in the characters of Jonas Spalding and Wallachia Petrie in *He Knew He Was Right*, and, to a lesser extent, of Senator Gotobed in *The American Senator*. More explicitly, Trollope's historical novel *La Vendée*, which tells of the royalist Vendeans' struggle against the French revolutionaries in the aftermath of 1792, is clearly on the side of the monarchists, and ends with a hope that the current French republic will also fail (Trollope was writing in the wake of the 1848 revolution): 'How long will it be before some second La Vendée shall successfully, but bloodlessly, struggle for another re-establishment of the monarchy? Surely before the expiration of half a century since the return of Louis, France will congratulate herself on another restoration' (XXXV). Revolutionary excesses were too strong for the stomach of the self-described 'advanced conservative liberal', who preferred a 'tendency to equality' rather than equality itself; for Trollope, the word was 'offensive and presents to the imagination of men ideas of communism, of ruin, and insane democracy' (*Auto* XVI). Hence it is no surprise to find that in his two non-fictional discussions of the monarchy—chapter IX of *The New Zealander*, 'The Crown', and his essay for *Saint Pauls Magazine* 'On Sovereignty'—he is adamant that preservation of the monarchy is absolutely necessary to Britain's well-being, but only because the British constitutional monarchy has in itself a 'tendency to equality': 'We recognize no divine right in any one to reign over us. We proclaim that the sovereign is the servant of the people, and not the people the servants of the sovereign' (*NZ* IX). In both pieces Trollope likens the British monarchy to the steeple of Salisbury Cathedral, on the grounds that, just as a steeple cannot support the cathedral, so too the monarch should not attempt to be the foundation of the society over which he or she governs. Rather, 'the spire was built that it might be seen from afar off, and recognized as the symbol in those parts of the religion of the country. So we think is it with such a sovereignty as that which we possess' (*Saint Pauls Magazine* 1, 76–91). The *Saint Pauls* essay (published in 1867) also contains an implied criticism of Victoria, who had withdrawn from public life following the death of Albert in 1861: 'A sovereign with us cannot be dreaded;—but he should be loved, and to be loved he should be seen.' Trollope was adding his voice to a substantial body of opinion, which gained increasing momentum as the decade progressed, that the Queen was abnegating her duties as sovereign. Such a criticism, of course, is one with Trollope's general belief in the responsibility of the Crown to its subjects, and contrasts strongly with his remarks about Prince Albert in the first chapter of *Lord Palmerston*: 'To have found genius and conscience and industry, with assured moral convictions and a tender loving heart, to fill such a place as that occupied by the Prince Consort, has been the good fortune of England' (I).   HO

Mondyon, Arthur. 'Le petit chevalier' is distinguished for his attachment to the De Larochejaquelin family, his assistance to Henri, and his defence of the family, particularly Agatha, when the chateau is taken by Santerre with Denot in attendance. *LV*   GRH

moneylenders as characters. Trollope's moneylenders have a symbiotic relationship with his young men who live beyond their means. Names differ, but most Trollope moneylenders are essentially the same character, based on a man who visited the young Trollope daily at the Post Office, urging him to ' "be punctual" ' (*Auto* III). He reappears, punctual injunction and all, as Jabesh M'Ruen (*TC* XVIII–XIX), Mr Magruin (*CYFH* XXX), and Clarkson (*PF* XXI). Other moneylenders include the Tozer brothers (*FP*), Abraham Hart and Captain Stubber (*SHH*), and Mr Davis (*JC*).

Moneylenders are depicted as persistent, chiding, flashy but dirty. Stereotypically Jewish in appearance, they speak with the adenoidal intonation then supposed to be used by Jews. Trollope may not share, but certainly reflects, his society's disdain for Jews, and accepts the convention that made Jew and moneylender interchangeable terms. Bertie Stanhope is in debt to Sidonia, 'a dirty little old man' (*BT*) named for Disraeli's aristocratic Jew in *Coningsby* (1844). Snubbed and despised by their clients, moneylenders are often cheated, even ruined. Augustus Musselboro (*LCB*) and Sexty Parker (*PM*) ally themselves with apparently respectable partners, although Parker is ruined by his partner Lopez. A whole posse of cheated moneylenders pursue Mountjoy Scarborough at his father's funeral, having been swindled by Mr Scarborough's legal tricks.   RT

moneylending enjoyed a golden age in Britain between the repeal of the old usury laws in 1854 and the Moneylending Act of 1901. It had always existed, but never so brazenly as in this period of virtually no legal restraints. Unlike bankers, who lend other people's money, moneylenders lend their own. Their loans were generally unsecured, the borrowers often poor risks, and the expenses for a small loan—most were under £50—as great as for a large one. Consequently interest rates were high: 60 per cent per year was standard. They were not all as ruthless, or as numerous in Victorian life, as in Trollope's fiction, but he specialized in the sort of people they thrived on, particularly young gentlemen, or would-be gentlemen. A feature of gentility was not paying cash: tradesmen were supposed to wait, and they charged more in this expectation. Sometimes they sold their unpaid bills to moneylenders: Trollope fell victim to this as a young man in London when a £12 tailor's bill 'grew monstrously' to over £200 (*Auto* III). Paradoxically, unlike tradesmen's debts, gambling losses were deemed debts of honour and were supposed to be paid immediately—another gentlemanly convention which profited moneylenders.

The harassing tactics of moneylenders like Jabez M'Ruen, who torments Charley Tudor in *The Three Clerks* with the refrain 'Only be punctual', were notorious, but they also resorted to legal trickery to ensure that the courts would enforce collection, which was much more effective than mere harassment. Various strategies were used to conceal the true rate of interest, and devious means were sometimes employed to get the borrower's family or friends to guarantee the loan. Phineas Finn and Mark Robarts both suffer the consequences of endorsing a friend's bill. The 'preliminary fee' fraud enabled some moneylenders who advertised widely to prosper without ever lending any money. They would charge applicants a fee to cover alleged credit investigations and then refuse to lend.

The spectrum of moneylending extended from pawnbrokers, important players in the economy of the poor who lent on the security of goods at a legally limited 25 per cent per year, through the smaller lenders of up to about £300—the group among whom fraud was most prevalent—to élite West End moneylenders. The prime example of these was Sam Lewis, who rose from poor Jewish street pedlar to lender of sums up to £325,000 to the highest aristocracy. Younger sons resentful of primogeniture might turn to the moneylender to embarrass their families, knowing they would be bailed out. Future heirs might borrow 'post-obit', the loan to be repaid when they inherited, a way of eluding parental restraint. The post-obit figures largely in *Mr Scarborough's Family*. Moneylenders offered ready money on the spot with no bankerly moralizing. Sam Lewis flourished on his reputation for being straightforward and trustworthy in his dealings. He was accused of abetting the destruction of the aristocracy, and certainly he helped some young rakes along the

road to ruin. But his entire fortune, a remarkable £2.5 million, eventually went to charities benefiting the poor, making him a significant redistributor of upper-class wealth before the advent of large estate duties.   CK

Black, Gerry, *Lender to the Lords, Giver to the Poor* (1992).

Mongrober, Lord, a do-nothing gentleman who knows a great deal about food and wine. He is a fixture at fashionable London dinners, but is unable to return the hospitality he is shown. As a guest at Mr Roby's table, Lord Mongrober is remarkable for his rudeness to his host. *PM*   JMR

Monk, Sir Cosmo, cold-hearted and close-fisted husband of Lady Monk. He deeply resents having to take responsibility—financial or moral—for his wife's errant nephew Burgo Fitzgerald. *CYFH*   JMR

Monk, Joshua, Liberal member of Parliament, frequent office holder, and ultimately Prime Minister. Though a great defender of Liberal causes, he is fiercely independent, sometimes upsetting the plans of his Liberal colleagues by opposing them. His early friendship with Phineas Finn helps shape Phineas's political career. *PF, PR, DC*   JMR

Monk, Lady, respectable but immoral aunt of Burgo Fitzgerald who encourages her nephew in his plan to persuade Lady Glencora Palliser to leave her husband and run away with him. Lady Monk helps both plan and finance the project, apparently with a view to gaining some part of Lady Glencora's vast wealth. She calls Burgo 'cowardly' when he shows some reluctance to pursue the scheme. *CYFH*   JMR

Monkhams, expansive estate with famous oaks in Worcestershire belonging to Lord Peterborough. *HKWR*   RC

Monkshade, country seat of Lord and Lady Monk, often visited by Burgo Fitzgerald. *CYFH*   JMR

Monkton Grange, an old farmhouse property, the site of a hunting meet near Noningsby, where 'sportsmen and ladies congregate by degrees' (XXVIII) and where Felix Graham gets injured. *OF*   MT

Monogram, Sir Damask Fashionable appurtenance for London dinners. In contrast to the snobbish social pretensions of his wife, Sir Damask is notable for the almost democratic nature of his civility. He is friendly, for instance, to the less-than-perfectly-genteel company at a dinner party given by Mrs Roby in *The Prime Minister*. *WWLN*   JMR

Monogram, Lady Julia (née **Triplex**), fashionable but snobbish lady who cements her social position by a strategic marriage. Cold and manipulative, Lady Monogram bullies her softhearted husband and behaves with only moderate civility to persons of questionable fashion. *WWLN, PM*   JMR

Monsell, William (1812–94), later Lord Emly (1874); Postmaster General (1871–3). He conveyed a saltpetre remedy for asthma offered by Cardinal *Newman to Trollope in October 1882, shortly before a stroke felled the novelist. Trollope replied gratefully but thought the treatment would not help. 'I am indeed obliged to sit upright so as to catch my breath or to remedy the disease by taking chloral' (*Letters* 2, 993). What Trollope thought, or hoped, was that asthma was part of a heart condition.   RCT

Montague, Paul, friend of Roger Carbury, although the relationship is strained when they both fall in love with Hetta Carbury. An earnest businessman, he becomes involved in the shady financial world of Augustus Melmotte, but eventually defies Melmotte and the disreputable operation of their shareholding business in the South Central Pacific and Mexican Railway. His affiliation with the infamous Beargarden Club further discredits him temporarily. He vacillates in his treatment of his former love, Winifred Hurtle, but finally manages to disengage himself from her in order to marry Hetta. *WWLN*   SRB

Montgomery, Alfred, reputedly illegitimate son of Marquis Wellesley, and therefore nephew of the 1st Duke of Wellington. Legendary man about town and gossip who, according to Escott, supplied Trollope with hints for Barchester characters and anecdotes on political events.   RCT

Montreuil, town where the Vendeans meet before their attack on Saumur. *LV*   GRH

Montrose, James Graham, Duke of (1799–1874), Postmaster General (1866–8); accepted Trollope's resignation. In October 1867 John Tilley forwarded Trollope's letter outlining terms in which the Duke might wish to express his appreciation of Trollope's long service. The Duke took his cue, and six days later Tilley presented the Duke's response. Clearly gratified by its contents, which mentioned his 'great abilities' and energetic performance of his duties, Trollope copied the letter verbatim into *An Autobiography*, using it as official 'evidence' that, despite extensive literary output, his work for the Post Office was never neglected (XV).   RCT

Moody, Major, professional gambler, 'a grey-headed old man of about sixty, who played his cards with great attention, and never spoke a word,—either then or at any other period of his life' (XLII). He is one of the gamblers who fleeces Mountjoy Scarborough at Captain Vignolles's table. *MSF*   MT

Mooney, Kit, baker from Claregalway 'turned Landleaguer' (XI) whose insolence to hunt master Black Daly illustrates the growing resistance to landlords among the Irish population. *L*
      MRS

Mooney, Teddy, father of Kit, a car-driver who joins the boycott against Philip Jones and other political undesirables, only to find himself in such reduced circumstances, 'suffering much himself from want of victuals', that he determines 'to serve the other side' (XXXIX), and writes to Captain Clayton informing him of the identity of Florian Jones's murderer. *L*   MRS

morality and fiction. Trollope never doubted that good fiction ought to teach good moral lessons. The best novels, Trollope wrote, make vice appear ugly to their readers. 'The novelist', he added, 'if he have a conscience, must preach his sermons with the same purpose as the clergyman, and must have his own system of ethics' (*Auto* XII). These remarks tell us something of Trollope's moral aims as a novelist, but nothing about the means by which he seeks to achieve them. How does he go about making his vicious characters seem unalluring to his readers? What, exactly, is the 'system of ethics' which his own novels advocate?

   Though a few remarks in the letters and autobiography suggest the contrary, in fact Trollope's fiction does not try to make vice repellent by showing that it is inevitably punished in this world or the next. Contemptible characters sometimes suffer well-deserved calamities, as a result of chance or as a direct consequence of their own actions. Thus Sir Hugh Clavering, in *The Claverings*, the quintessence of callous selfishness, is drowned in a yachting accident, while the financier Melmotte, in *The Way We Live Now*, commits suicide when his shady speculations fail. But for every character who experiences this sort of poetic justice, there are ten who get off almost as lightly as George Hotspur, the villain of *Sir Harry Hotspur of Humblethwaite*. This gambler, cheat, and womanizer, whose romantic deceptions kill an innocent girl, has gained a loving wife and a comfortable annuity by the time the tale closes. Further, many characters in Trollope's novels are defeated by situations where a morally acceptable course of action is difficult to identify or follow, rather than by their own vices. Thus her inability to satisfy the contradictory demands of feminine propriety and common honesty destroys Lady Mabel Grex, a well-intentioned, intelligent character in *The Duke's Children*.

But if Trollope refuses to make virtue alluring and vice ugly by an appeal to their consequences, he must do so by some other means. He must show that the 'ethical system' his novels advocate is attractive or authoritative for intrinsic reasons, since no reliable extrinsic sanctions enforce it. In general, readers and critics agree that Trollope's novels do indeed offer remarkably subtle, balanced, flexible, and convincing analyses of the moral issues they raise—that the ethical system upon which they are grounded is exceptionally persuasive. But there is less agreement about why this is so.

In *Trollope: Artist and Moralist* (1971), the first book-length study of Trollope as moralist and moral philosopher, Ruth apRoberts notes that several of Trollope's novels focus upon a particularly perplexing moral problem. She thinks that the ethical system his novels use to assess these problems closely resembles that described by the theologian Joseph Fletcher in *Situation Ethics: The New Morality* (1966). There Fletcher argues that all general, abstract laws of morality should give way to whatever seems most loving in a given situation. According to apRoberts, Trollope creates plots involving baffling moral dilemmas in order to show that 'any [moral] theory or precept can be invalidated, in *some* case', and that unfettered sympathy is therefore the most reliable guide to moral conduct (apRoberts 39). Several subsequent critics have agreed that the 'moral system driving [Trollope's] fiction is reducible to no rigid calculus, but always remains fluid and problematical' (Christopher Herbert, *Trollope and Comic Pleasure* (1987), 163).

Others disagree. These dissenters are not convinced that the application of a vague principle of human sympathy is sufficient to account for the nuanced moral analysis that distinguishes Trollope's fiction. As James Kincaid puts it, Trollope's morality is 'tied to situations, but only because situations test and make solid an ethical code that would otherwise remain abstract and superficial' (James Kincaid, *The Novels of Anthony Trollope* (1977), 15). Following this line of reasoning, we are once more thrown back upon the question: what, exactly, *is* the ethical code that undergirds Trollope's fiction?

Recently, two books have offered similar answers to this question. Shirley Letwin's *The Gentleman in Trollope* (1982) and Jane Nardin's *Trollope and Victorian Moral Philosophy* (1996)

both argue that Trollopian morality is grounded in a system of abstractions that are deployed with great casuistical sophistication. Letwin believes this system, which she calls the 'gentleman's morality', to be a peculiarly English creation. She compares its rules to 'the grammar of a language which has been spoken without being identified'. It is the purpose of her study to reconstruct this grammar from examples 'of the variety of [its] usage' offered by the conduct of Trollope's characters (Letwin 57). Letwin's reconstruction of the gentleman's morality includes many principles that are central to the Stoic-Judaeo-Christian moral tradition: 'The Golden Rule, "Treat others as you would have them treat you", is not a bad summary of the idea that controls a gentleman's relations with others', she says at one point (Letwin 68). But Letwin grants equal authority to many Victorian mores as constituents of the gentleman's morality.

Jane Nardin agrees with Letwin that Trollope believes morality to be a cultural practice, so deeply ingrained as to become an integral part of an individual's identity. For this reason, she argues, his novels might be expected to advocate an ethical system that was accepted in his own time—and indeed they do. But unlike Letwin, Nardin considers that Trollope draws a sharp distinction between the core of the Stoic-Judaeo-Christian moral tradition and the local mores of Victorian Britain. The central precepts of this long-lived tradition—do not lie, do not steal, respect the autonomy of your fellow men, do not do evil so that good may come of it, and so forth—are absolutely authoritative in Trollope's moral universe. And these precepts provide the means by which Trollope shows certain contemporary English customs to be morally unacceptable. Most of Trollope's readers—from his day to the present—think about moral issues in terms of the Stoic-Judaeo-Christian tradition, simply because it *is* the dominant tradition of Western ethics. Trollope's 'ethical system' owes its persuasiveness to the subtle way he uses the principles of this widely accepted and internally coherent tradition to analyse the dilemmas in which Victorian mores entangle his characters.   JN

apRoberts, Ruth, *Trollope: Artist and Moralist* (1971).

Letwin, Shirley, *The Gentleman in Trollope* (1982).

Nardin, Jane, *Trollope and Victorian Moral Philosophy* (1996).

Morecombe, Sir Marmaduke, minor political character useful for the utter predictability of his thoughts, words, and actions. Though rewarded with the title Lord Mount Thistle, he is actually no more than 'a serviceable stick who can be made to go in and out [of office] as occasion may require' (*PF*, LXVIII). *ED*   JMR

Moreton, Mr (sometimes **Morton**), agent for the young Duke of Omnium. Mr Mor(e)ton provides the Duke's sons with their allowances and looks after their other financial needs. The agent's compassion and good sense are invaluable both to the Duke and to his son when Lord Silverbridge loses more than £70,000 at the St Leger. *DC*   JMR

Morison, James Augustus Cotter (1832–88), biographer of Gibbon and Macaulay; contributor to the *Saturday Review*; one of the original proprietors of the *Fortnightly* (*Letters* 1, 271).   RCT

Morley, John (1838–1923), Liberal MP (1883–1908), later Viscount Morley of Blackburn (1908); prolific writer on historical, biographical, social topics; edited *Fortnightly Review* (1867–82); *Pall Mall Gazette* (1881–3); wrote *The Life of Gladstone* (1903). Morley was agnostic and rationalist and his appointment to the *Fortnightly* was not entirely to Trollope's liking. At the interview he thundered, 'Do you believe in the divinity of our blessed Lord and Saviour Jesus Christ?' (*I & R* 193–4). A row blew up at once when in January 1867 Morley wanted to sack his sub-editor, John Dennis. When Morley accepted E. A. Freeman's article against fox-hunting (October 1869) Trollope saw it as 'almost the rising of a child against its father' (*Auto* X). More trouble occurred over serial lengths of F. E. Trollope's novel *Anne Furness* (*Fortnightly*, July 1870–August 1871). In April 1876, Trollope told Cecilia Meetkerke that 'the learned and indefatigable editor . . . will weigh every word you write down to the last pronoun' (*Letters* 2, 684). Trollope was uncomfortable with men of Morley's high intellect, especially when their views seemed 'much advanced' (*Auto* X). Morley, with Mrs Humphry Ward, reviewed *An Autobiography* for *Macmillan's Magazine* (November 1883).   RCT

Morony, Mistress, aggressive customer of haberdashery shop who demands to buy a pelisse from a display rather than an identical item from stock. *SBJR*   RCT

Morris, Dan, poor Hoggle End brickmaker. He cashes the disputed cheque that leads to charges of theft against Revd Josiah Crawley and later offers to commit perjury to save his friend. *LCB*   NCS

Morris, Lucy, spirited young governess who becomes engaged to Frank Greystock against the advice of her well-meaning mistress Lady Fawn. Though Lucy is poor and has no family, her cheerfulness, self-confidence, and intelligence win the favour both of Frank Greystock and of the Fawn family. Unusually perceptive, Lucy sees Lizzie Eustace's falseness more clearly than most. *ED*   JMR

Morris, Matthew, worldly wise traveller who befriends Ralph Forrest and comments laconically on his shipboard romance with Emily Viner. 'Panama' *LS*   GRH

Morrison, Alexander, good-humoured young parson chosen by Mrs Miles as suitor for Bessy Pryor, who rejects him. 'Launay' *WFF*   GRH

Morton, Caleb, Presbyterian clergyman engaged to Anastasia Bergen, who hunts down her attacker and fights with him in the sea. 'Trow' *TAC2*   GRH

Morton, John, squire of Bragton and Secretary of the British Legation in Washington, known as the Paragon because he never makes mistakes; but he makes one in proposing to Arabella Trefoil. In coldness of temperament they are a fit match but she sets her sights higher. Even he is infuriated by Elias Gotobed's criticisms of England. He forgives Arabella on his deathbed, leaves her £5,000 and Bragton to his cousin Reginald Morton. *AS*   MG

Morton, Lucy, actress and mistress of George Hotspur, superior in all ways to her lover. In her advice to him she responds both to what he says he wants and to what she knows his true character to be. She marries George hoping to reform him but, of course, fails. *SHH*   MG

Morton, Mrs, cold, narrow, domineering grandmother of John Morton, who maintains a family quarrel long past its natural lifespan. She tries to force John Morton on his deathbed to leave Bragton away from the next-in-line, Reginald Morton, who she (falsely) insists is a bastard. *AS*   MG

Morton, Reginald. The owner of Hoppet Hall inherits Bragton when his cousin John Morton dies. Raised by Lady Ushant and hated by Mrs Morton, the saturnine and scholarly Reginald dreads being squire of Bragton but will fulfil the social contract with the aid of his wife, the former Mary Masters. *AS*   MG

Moses, Well of, in Asia near the Red Sea, the 'dirty pool' visited by George Walker. 'Walker' *TAC2*   GRH

Moss, Mahomet M., American-Jewish impresario responsible for launching Rachel O'Mahony on the London stage. Despite being subjected to her virulent anti-Semitism, he courts her to become his mistress, then his wife, only to have her stab him when his sexual harassment threatens to turn violent. *L*   MRS

Motley, John Lothrop (1814–77), Boston historian and diplomat; met Trollope in July 1867, and found him extremely likeable and friendly. They met also at the Cosmopolitan Club (the 'Universe Club' in *PR*) where members gathered late every Sunday and Wednesday and smoked bad cigars. He quoted Thackeray saying, 'Everybody is or is supposed to be a celebrity; nobody ever says anything worth hearing; and every one goes there with his white choker at midnight, to appear as if he had just been dining with the aristocracy' (quoted Super 219).   RCT

Moulder, Mary Anne, wife of Mr Moulder and sister of John Kenneby. 'The work of her life consisted in sewing buttons on to Moulder's shirts' (XXIV), but she was a happy woman, enjoying her hot kidney in the morning, roast fowl in the afternoon, and *Reynolds's Miscellany* in the evening. She arranges the marriage between Mrs Smiley and John Kenneby. *OF*   MT

Moulder, Mr, commercial traveller selling tea, coffee, and brandy for Hubbles & Grease of Houndsditch. Moulder is a short man whose 'body had been overcome by eating, but not as yet his spirit' (VI). He rules the roost at the Commercial Room, Bull Inn, Leeds, where he meets Mr Dockwrath en route to Groby Park. *OF* MT

Mountfidget, Lord, young man who goes to Grandnostrel to see Euphemia, whom he loves. Dying from a poisoned arrow, he is saved by the antidote she administers. 'Euphemia'   GRH

Mountjoy, Florence, niece of Sir Magnus and Lady Mountjoy and daughter of Sara Mountjoy. The heroine of the novel, Florence 'had no idea that she was better than anybody else; but it came to her naturally, as the result of what had gone before, to be unselfish, generous, trusting, and pure' (X). Florence's family all press her to marry Mountjoy Scarborough in order to become mistress of his large fortune, but Florence loves Harry Annesley, whom she eventually marries. *MSF*   MT

Mountjoy, Lady, formidable wife of Sir Magnus, and Florence Mountjoy's aunt. 'There were those who declared that Lady Mountjoy was of all women the most overbearing and impertinent' (X), and her particular wish is that Florence marry Mountjoy Scarborough. *MSF* MT

Mountjoy, Sir Magnus, British Minister plenipotentiary at Brussels. A lifetime diplomat, Sir Magnus was a popular host in Brussels, despite his overbearing, domineering wife. Together

with Lady Mountjoy and Mrs Mountjoy, Sir Magnus conspires to prevent Florence from marrying Harry Annesley, and they spread false stories about a fight between Harry and Mountjoy Scarborough. *MSF*   MT

Mountjoy, Sarah, Florence Mountjoy's mother, who wishes her daughter to marry the reckless gambler Mountjoy Scarborough. After Mountjoy's disinheritance, Mrs Mountjoy believes that Florence should 'be transferred with the remainder of the property' (X) to Mountjoy's brother, the new heir, Augustus Scarborough. *MSF*   MT

Mowbray & Mopus, unscrupulous London solicitors engaged to represent Italian interests in the Lovel case (*LA*). Also active on behalf of Lady Eustace in her bid to hold on to the family heirlooms (*ED*).   RCT

Moydrum, family home of Lord Claddagh, Laurence Fitzgibbon's father, in Co. Mayo, Ireland. *PF*   JMR

Moylan, Mr, unscrupulous agent employed by Anty Lynch to protect her interests until bribed by her brother to switch allegiances. *KOK*   MRS

Moytubber, gorse covert where local tenants assemble to disrupt that traditional sport of landowners, fox-hunting. *L*   MRS

Mudie, Charles Edward (1818–90), Scottish bookseller who founded Mudie's Lending Library in 1842 and changed the reading habits of the nation. By 1859 (a great year for Trollope) *The Times* would trumpet, 'To be unknown to Mudie is to be unknown to fame' (quoted *Chron* 39). Trollope, whose output and material dovetailed perfectly with Mudie's market, was now one of his stars. Julian Hawthorne quipped that Trollope 'was afraid of nobody except God and Mudie' (*I & R* 147). Trollope had his fun with the library. In *The Eustace Diamonds* Lady Linlithgow cancelled her subscription because every time she ordered *Adam Bede* they sent her *The Bandit Chief*. Lady Carbury in *The Way We Live Now* hopes to get her novel on Mudie's shelves. In *Ayala's Angel* Mudie volumes were 'as much a provision of nature as water, gas, and hot rolls for breakfast' (II). Other references occur in *The Bertrams* and *Orley Farm*.   RCT

Mudie's Library. In 1840 Charles Edward Mudie opened his premises at Upper King Street, and commenced his lending library two years later. For all his acumen and energy Mudie was lucky; he caught the rising tide of reader interest in the generation of novelists we now recognize as the great Victorians. By setting up in Bloomsbury, he also caught the trade associated with the

Mulready, Mrs

university, and found avid readership in the new bourgeoisie who occupied the surrounding area.

Although not the first or only lending library, Mudie's was by far the most successful. Victorian novels usually appeared in three volumes—'the three-decker' as it was known—and Mudie was largely responsible for this format, since it meant three subscribers could be reading the same book at the same time, thus boosting his membership. Mudie's own strait-laced morals were imposed upon the authors he bought for his library. Thus he exercised a powerful sway on the tone, the format, and the content of middle-class fiction. Trollope, like all his contemporaries, was dependent upon his publishers' sales to Mudie, and thus upon Mudie's implicit judgement of his works.

Mudie charged a guinea a year per ticket per volume, and within ten years had moved to expanded premises at 510 New Oxford Street. By 1860 his premises had extended from 509 to 511, with additional space in 20–1 Museum Street. From early days he claimed a subscribing membership of over 25,000, and when he moved yet again due to expansion in the early 1860s, he was ordering something like 180,000 volumes a year, at least half of them from publishers of fiction. Mudie's advance orders at a special rate were of vital importance to the novel trade. For instance, virtually half of all the novels the publisher Bentley sold by subscription in 1864 were sales to Mudie. Mudie alone took nearly one-third of the first edition, in three volumes, of Trollope's *Barchester Towers*, at his own specially negotiated discount price.

Later in the century he opened branches in Birmingham and Manchester. His distribution system, via the new railways, was not only nation-wide: tin boxes of loans from Mudie's Library found their way all over the world.

It was in Mudie's interest to preserve the high price of English novels, and the cumbersome three-volume format. At 31s. 6d. for a new three-decker, readers were better off with a number of borrowers' tickets from Mudie than buying for themselves. The extended demands of the three-decker did not always suit the integral structure of what the novelist planned. Much of the undoubted padding which characterizes many Victorian novels is Mudie-motivated. The generally bland moral tone of middle-class fiction is deferential to Mudie's influence on publishers; the mere threat of Mudie's disfavour was enough to motivate Longman's reader to make Trollope change the phrase 'fat stomach' to 'deep chest' in *Barchester Towers*. Mudie's influence on publishers, novelists, and readers lasted for much of the 19th century. *The Times* commented thus on

Trollope as Mudie's ideal author when reviewing *The Bertrams* (23 May 1859, p. 12): 'The wide world of authors and the wide world of readers alike regard . . . [Mudie] . . . with awe; nay, even the sacred race of publishers have been known to kiss the hem of his garments. . . . He is the mighty monarch of books that are good enough to be read, but not good enough or not cheap enough to be bought. . . . This majestic personage, whom authors worship and whom readers court, knows that at the present one writer in England is paramount above all others, and his name is Trollope. . . . He writes faster than we can read, and the more that the pensive public reads the more does it desire to read. [He] is, in fact, the most fertile, the most popular, the most successful author— that is to say, of the circulating library sort . . . and so long as Mr Anthony Trollope is the prince of the circulating library our readers may rest assured that it is a very useful, very pleasant, and very honourable institution' (Smalley 103).

Towards the end of the century more independent-minded authors and changes in the publishing trade weakened Mudie's autocratic grip, but the lending library survived into the 1930s.   TB

Sutherland, J. A., *Victorian Novelists and Publishers* (1976).

Mulready, Mrs, 'Strong, red-faced, indomitable-looking' widow who keeps a shebeen, an unlicensed drinking establishment, in a two-room hovel in Mohill frequented by 'the wicked, the desperate, and the drunken' (IX), including a band of local Ribbonmen. *MB*   MRS

Mulroney, Barney, Fred Neville's oarsman during his Co. Clare adventures. When romance turns sour, Fred hates the sight of him. *EE*
                                                                AWJ

Munday, Captain, captain of the *Goldfinder*, the ship on which John Caldigate meets Euphemia Smith. He later testifies to their presumed engagement against which he had warned Caldigate. *JC*   SRB

Munich. Heine Brothers have their banking business in the old Market Place. 'Heine' *TAC2*
                                                                GRH

Murray, Alec, young man who goes out with Sophy Wilson, intent merely on a good time. 'Telegraph' *WFF*   GRH

Murray, John (the elder) (1778–1843), celebrated publisher, best known for connection with Byron, for the *Quarterly Review*, and for travel guidebooks. He published the first volume of Thomas Anthony Trollope's *Ecclesiastical Encyclopedia* in 1834, but with nothing like the enthusiasm he had felt for Mrs Trollope's *Domestic Manners of the Americans*: 'It will sell like wildfire!', he exclaimed, 'the cleverest thing I ever read' (Hall 40). The book took off in 1832, puffed by a laudatory 40-page review in the *Quarterly*. In January 1835, Mrs Trollope asked Murray if Anthony could do some proof-reading, but nothing came of the request (*Letters* 1, 3 n.).   RCT

Murray, John (the younger) (1808–92), son and successor of Murray the publisher; producer of the Family Library and Cabinet Cyclopedia. In 1850 Trollope sent him a partial manuscript of a proposed guidebook on Ireland, but it lay unopened for nine months before being returned 'without a word' after Trollope's angry letter reminding Murray of his promise to deal with the manuscript 'within a fortnight' (*Auto* V). Had he been 'less dilatory', wrote Trollope, 'John Murray would have got a very good Irish Guide at a cheap rate'. Trollope never published with the house.   RCT

Murrell, Dr William (1853–1912), winner of French Academy of Medicine medal in 1880 for *Nitro-Glycerine as a Remedy for Angina Pectoris* (*Letters* 2, 938 n.). When Trollope fell ill he sought out the heart specialist, who declared he did not show symptoms of angina. 'I am disposed to believe him', wrote Trollope, adding with relief that he would henceforth keep on walking 'up all the hills in the country' (*Letters* 2, 939). According to Cecilia Meetkerke, Trollope's health seemed to improve under Murrell's care, but Trollope continued to tax himself, and in November 1883 suffered a stroke. Murrell and Sir William Jenner, Physician in Ordinary to the Queen, as consultant, issued thirteen bulletins in *The Times* during the month-long course of Trollope's final illness.   RCT

museums and exhibitions. As a boy Trollope gained some appreciation of drawing through his mother's friend Auguste Hervieu. Lodging in London after his appointment to the Post Office, he frequented galleries, especially the National Gallery, then in Pall Mall, and museums, acquiring an appreciation of art and architecture. The Royal Academy summer exhibition became a regular event in his calendar. Travelling abroad always included a city's art and architecture, a taste first developed in Florence and Rome when

visiting his brother Tom. In the Great Exhibition (1851) in Hyde Park, Rose Trollope exhibited an embroidered screen. Rather sombrely anticipating the great show in Sir Joseph Paxton's Crystal Palace, Trollope wrote to his mother in May 1850 that he intended to exhibit four novels '—all failures!—which I look on as a great proof of industry at any rate' (*Letters* 1, 22).   RCT

music-making. The 19th-century practice of music-making within the family and in groups was part of Trollope's leisure. He enjoyed solo voice and instrumental music. He was also fond of glee singing. In the late 1850s he and his friend John *Merivale organized the Goose and Glee Club in a London tavern, with its own rules and a Latin motto. The name crops up in *The Last Chronicle of Barset* (XLII). At his Post Office retirement party (31 October 1867), entertainment came from the Moray Minstrels, a group he had sung with. His favourite instrument, the violoncello, was accorded to the Revd Septimus Harding, whose playing gave such comfort to the bedesmen in *The Warden* (1855). In January 1873 he recalled as a young man hearing the great cellist Robert Lindley and being moved to tears (*Letters* 2, 577). Music was often heard in the Trollope circle. His niece Bice had a wonderfully pure soprano and was praised by Arthur *Sullivan, the composer, and Jacques Blumenthal, pianist to Queen Victoria.   RCT

Musselboro, Augustus, disreputable partner of Dobbs Broughton and Mrs Van Siever in their speculation and moneylending schemes. Goodhumoured and somewhat good-looking with lots of chains and elaborate whiskers, though with dirty hands, he attempts to take over the business, wants to marry Clara Van Siever, and finally ends up with his partner's widow. Conway Dalrymple wishes to paint him as Sisera to Clara's Jael. *LCB*   NCS

'My Tour in Holland' (article). This trip was made primarily to visit art museums (which were rather disappointing). The Dutch appear small, neat, merry, and not heavy drinkers; they have better bathing machines than the English. Holland seems a pleasant place to live. *Cornhill*, November 1862, 616–22.   AKL

N

Nantes, important city on the Loire, site of the battle which costs Cathelineau his life. *LV*

GRH

Napoleon I (1769–1821). Soldier, statesman, and self-proclaimed Emperor of France (1804), he was among the Trollope family's list of 'great men' of history (*Letters*, 1, 23). In 1865 Trollope proposed writing a series of 'Imaginary Meditations' for the *Pall Mall Gazette*, including 'Napoleon on the death of Morny'. RCT

Napoleon III (1808–73), French Emperor (1852) who lived in England after two unsuccessful attempts to overthrow the French monarchy (1836 and 1840); incited the Franco-Prussian War (1870); died in exile (1873). Trollope's article (signed 'An Englishman') in *Pall Mall Gazette*, 'As to the Need of Caesars', was a response to Napoleon III's *History of Julius Caesar*. Trollope was strongly critical of Napoleon's militarism in Italy in 1867 (*Letters* 1, 395) and characterized him as a man without wisdom or honour (Mullen 285). In *Lord Palmerston* (1882) he wrote that 'even the memory of the Emperor is distasteful' (quoted Super 426). Napoleon, who had supported extravagant commercial speculation, may have contributed to the creation of Melmotte in *The Way We Live Now*, a novel set in the year of the Emperor's death, 1873 (Hall 381). RCT

'Napoleon III's *History of Julius Caesar*' (review). The Emperor-author links Julius Caesar, Charlemagne, and Napoleon as men who dramatically advanced civilization, implicitly including himself in this line. The paragraph here quoted [in French] illustrates the foolish, invidi-ous comparisons of England with Rome. *Pall Mall Gazette* (7 February 1865), 2. AKL

'Nathaniel Hawthorne' (article). Hawthorne is one of those respected by a circle of peers but not truly famous; however, this is changing, chiefly in response to *The Scarlet Letter*. He has a 'thoroughly English style', with delicacy reminiscent of Longfellow. Read *Mosses from an Old Manse* first; it is 'breezy and wholesome'— especially 'P's Correspondence'. *The House of Seven Gables* is the most complete and pleasing of his tales. The only weakness is the excessive premonition of events. The attempt at biography in the *Life of General Pierce* is unfortunate; his tolerance of slavery is obvious. He is, withal, a man of genius. *Dublin University Magazine* (October 1855), 463–9. AKL

'National Gallery, The' (article). William Wilkins's controversial National Gallery (completed in 1838) was a better building than critics allowed. Admittedly its exterior was 'very poor', but Wilkins had done his best, being 'crippled' as to space, money, and materials ('he was called on to use columns from other places'). The Louvre is a grander building, but England cannot expect anything like that 'until, as a first step, we bless ourselves with a French government'. But as a place for *seeing* pictures, the National Gallery is superior. The building ought to open at eight, not ten, in the morning. *St James's Magazine*, (September 1861), 163–76. See ART AND ARTISTS; MUSEUMS AND EXHIBITIONS; PRE-RAPHAELITES.

NJH

Nearthewinde, Mr, celebrated parliamentary agent who assists Gustavus Moffat in the Barchester election, though more loyal to Lord De Courcy. A 'sharp fellow', he scrupulously defends the doctrine of purity of election while encouraging friendly publicans. His detection of an irregularity overturns the election. *DT* NCS

Necropolis, the 'college' and crematorium wherein Britannula's citizens were to be 'deposited' and prepared for one year for compulsory euthanasia at the age of 68. *FixP* SRB

Neefit, Maryanne (Polly), only daughter of Thomas Neefit. 'As pretty a girl as you shall wish to see . . . her laughing dark eyes were full of good-humour, and looked as though they could be filled also with feeling . . . somewhat given to frank coquetry, and certainly fond of young men' (V). Determined to resist her father's campaign to make a 'lady' of her, she refuses Ralph, the heir, and marries Ontario Moggs. Determinedly signs herself 'Mary Anne' after marriage. *RH*

ALS

Neefit, Mrs, wife of Thomas Neefit, mother of Polly, and mistress of Alexandrina Cottage, Hendon. A staunch supporter of Ontario Moggs's courtship of her daughter. *RH*   ALS

Neefit, Thomas, prosperous breeches-maker of Conduit Street 'whose manners to his customers contained a combination of dictatorial assurance and subservience' (V). Aspiring to gentility for his daughter Polly, he determines to marry her to Ralph Newton, the heir, putting pressure on him by advancing him money beyond his existing debts. When Polly chooses Ontario Moggs he grudgingly comments: 'She might a' done a deal better, but women is always restive' (LIII). *RH*
ALS

Neroni, Julia, spoiled 8-year-old daughter of Signora Neroni, presented by her mother as the 'last of the Neros'. Dressed outlandishly and extravagantly, she rejects Squire Thorne's overtures, though she likes the attentions of young gentlemen. *BT*   NCS

Neroni, Signora Madeline (neé **Stanhope**), crippled younger daughter of Dr Vesey Stanhope. Her beauty, especially her lovely basilisk-like eyes, and exotic dress mask a heartless soul. Courage, cunning, and a mischief-making wit are her chief attributes. Lounging on her sofa, she becomes the focus of male attention at public functions, much to the annoyance of Mrs Proudie and Countess De Courcy. She captivates nearly all the men in Barchester, including Mr Slope, Mr Arabin, and Squire Thorne. She dismisses the former with a satiric display of wit, but, remarkably, helps Mr Arabin win Eleanor Bold. Her perception, intelligence, and disdain for social niceties lend life and energy to the somewhat prosaic affairs of Barchester. *BT*
NCS

Neroni, Paulo, absent husband of Signora Neroni, a captain of the Pope's guard, of no birth and no property. His harsh temper is rumoured to have been the cause of his wife's crippling accident. *BT*   NCS

Nethercoats, John Grey's Cambridgeshire residence. Like Grey himself, the place is eminently comfortable and respectable, but it is also quiet and somewhat removed from society. The surrounding countryside, though 'well adapted for agricultural purposes', is deficient in 'rural beauty'. *CYFH*   JMR

'Never, Never—Never, Never', 'A condensed novel, in three volumes, after the manner of Bret Harte', parodies Lily Dale's constancy (*SHA*). It appeared in Susan Hale's *Sheets for the Cradle* (Boston, 6, 8, 10 December 1875), reprinted in

Collected Short Stories (1981). Mary Tomkins is beloved of John Thomas, a lazy Post Office clerk (recalling Johnny Eames), who begs for her hand, but she refuses him, recalling a kiss from the Revd Abraham Dribble, who had abandoned her. Dribble woos her afresh. To all entreaties Mary answers 'Never, never'. Dribble becomes Bishop of Rochester and John Postmaster General for inventing a farthing stamp. Both marry well. Mary embroiders a gown with the words 'Old Maid', which she vows to wear for ever. Thus Trollope had fun with Hawthorne's *The Scarlet Letter* (1850) as well as Bret Harte, who had said he had no sense of humour (*Letters* 2, 664).   RCT

Neverbend, Fidus, clerk in the Woods and Forests Office and co-commissioner with Alaric Tudor in reporting on the Wheal Mary Jane tin mine. Fidus is 'an absolute dragon of honesty' (VII) but overly confident and self-satisfied. *TC*
MT

Neverbend, Jack, boyish and enthusiastic son of the President of Britannula. A great cricketer and popular young man, he matures through his increasingly public opposition to the law of enforced euthanasia. This specific clash with his father gains impetus when Jack falls in love with Eva Crasweller, whose father will be the reluctant first victim of the law. The farewell between son and father when the latter is being exiled reconciles the two emotionally if not politically. *FixP*
SRB

Neverbend, John, President of Britannula and fanatical advocate of compulsory euthanasia for all citizens after a 'Fixed Period' of useful life. His narration of the story renders ambiguous the account of vacillation, rebellion, and ultimate betrayal of his interests by his own family, friends, and citizens. His actions betoken a respectable, courteous gentleman and popular leader, but his private reflections indicate prejudice, egocentrism, and obstinacy. Although secretly proud of his son and fond of his wife, he embraces exile as a necessary means of furthering his euthanasia gospel. *FixP*   SRB

Neverbend, Lactimel, unmarried sister of Fidus and Ugolina Neverbend. Already past her prime, Lactimel's charms 'consisted of a somewhat stumpy dumpy comeliness' (XXV). She and her sister Ugolina toady to the pretentious Mrs Valentine Scott and happily accept the cast-offs of Clementina Golightly. *TC*   MT

Neverbend, Sarah, irreverent wife of the President of Britannula, who is quick to berate her husband for fanatical loyalty to his policy of compulsory euthanasia. Her devotion to and support of their son Jack seems a 'conspiracy' in her husband's eyes. She is more interested in her husband's creature comforts than his politics, and often uses curtain lectures to impart common sense to him. *FixP* SRB

Neverbend, Ugolina, unmarried sister of Fidus and Lactimel Neverbend. When dancing, 'Ugolina was apt to be stiff and ungainly and to turn herself, or allow herself to be turned, as though she were made of wood' (XXV). She 'read poetry and professed to write it' (XXV) and is wholly without charm. *TC* MT

Nevill, Dr, kindly doctor who treats Trevelyan in his last illness. *HKWR* RCT

Neville, Fred. Offered Scroope Manor, ample funds, a London town house (if he marries suitably), Fred prefers a year's adventure before accepting responsibility as his uncle's heir. In Ireland he hunts seals and seagulls, then seduces Kate O'Hara. Once she succumbs, he realizes his mistake and sees, through the exemplar of his uncle's nobility, that she could never be Countess of Scroope. But he is too honourable (or sentimental) to abandon her and would give her anything (except his title). That is too little for Mrs O'Hara who furiously exacts the price of her daughter's honour. *EE* AWJ

Neville, Jack. Despite his raffish sobriquet and ugly features, he is as four-square as any christened John. Fred tries to delegate the responsibilities of the earldom to his younger brother, but Jack's ambitions have nothing to do with rank. He would endeavour, in any circumstance, 'to live as an honourable gentleman' (2. VI). When he becomes Lord Scroope, Jack supports the O'Haras and, as much through character as title, finally wins Sophie Mellerby. *EE* AWJ

Neville, Mrs Julia (neé **Smith**). Once a great beauty, rumoured to be 'fast' and 'loud', the elderly widow of Lord Scroope's brother idolizes her two sons and is timidly grateful to the Earl who is so good to them. *EE* AWJ

Newby, Thomas Cautley (1798?–1882), published Trollope's first novel, *The Macdermots of Ballycloran* (1847) at 'half-profits', an unfavourable arrangement for authors. (See PUBLISHERS AND PUBLISHING.) Newby claimed that, while the novel was cleverly written, Irish stories were unpopular. He agreed to print 400 copies; once half were sold, author and publisher would split profits. But Newby was a cheat. His sharp practice with the Brontës so riled Mrs Gaskell that she suggested he should be hanged. He first advertised the novel as by Trollope's mother, an already successful writer, and then he compromised sales by keeping back copies, which he then

reissued as a second edition the following year. Because Newby distributed so few copies of the book—Trollope thought that perhaps 50 copies had been sold—first editions of *The Macdermots* are very rare. Only three perfect copies are supposed to exist. RCT

'New Cabinet and What it Will Do for Us, The' (article). Liberals rejoice at the recent election results; fierce party battles like this are healthy. The long-needed disestablishment of the Irish Church was clearly mandated. Tax relief, budget cuts, and military administration are other pressing issues, demanding careful thought. *Saint Pauls* (February 1869), 538–51. AKL

Newman, John Henry (1801–90), vicar of St Mary's, Oxford, from 1828; converted to Roman Catholic faith (1845); made cardinal (1879). Trollope heard him preach in Oxford in the 1830s. Newman's novel *Loss and Gain* (1848) deals with the religious ferment of the time. Trollope sympathized with Newman's struggle and some of this is reflected in the history of Mr Arabin of *Barchester Towers* (XX). A long-time admirer of Trollope's novels, he once said that he woke up laughing out loud having read *Barchester Towers* before going to bed (*The Letters and Diaries of John Henry Newman*, ed C. S. Dessain (1968), 482). When he came to *The Bertrams* (1859) Newman was amazed at its tragic power until the third volume disappointed him. He enjoyed long novels and praised Trollope's multiple plots for adding variety to the narrative. When Trollope was in severe pain from what he described as asthma, Newman sent a saltpetre treatment, expressing his admiration for the novels. 'Many of them I read again and again' (*Letters* 2, 994). RCT

Newton, Gregory (the elder), the squire of Newton Priory who attempts to buy the reversion of the estate from Ralph Newton (the heir) so that he may leave it to his illegitimate son, also named Ralph, his child by a German lady. His plans are thwarted by his accidental death on the hunting field. *RH* ALS

Newton, Gregory (the younger), rector of the family living of Newton Peele in Hampshire, younger brother of Ralph, the heir. 'A tall slender man . . . he always went with his hands in his pockets, walking quick . . . He was a man with prejudices,—kindly gentlemanlike, amiable prejudices' (XIV). He finally marries Clarissa Underwood, whom he has long loved. *RH* ALS

Newton, Ralph, much-loved illegitimate son of Gregory Newton and a German lady. Prevented from inheriting the entailed Newton estate by his

birth and by his father's untimely death, he nevertheless uses his financial inheritance to purchase Beamingham Hall in Norfolk and marries Mary Bonner. 'He was tall . . . and broad across the chest, and strong and active . . . had been educated abroad . . . German and French were the same to him as his native tongue' (XI). *RH*
ALS

Newton, Ralph (the heir), the 'unsteady, extravagant and idle' heir to the Newton Priory estate. Formerly the ward of Sir Thomas Underwood. Much addicted to hunting with the B&B (Berkshire and Buckinghamshire Hunt), stabling his horses at the Moonbeam. Despite his initial declaration of love for Clarissa Underwood, his debts to Thomas Neefit, the breeches-maker, oblige him to pay suit to Neefit's daughter Polly. Released from this obligation by his inheritance of the estate, and rejected by Polly, he marries Augusta Eardham. *RH*
ALS

Newton Peele, also known as Peele Newton, the north Hampshire living of the Revd Gregory Newton. *RH*
ALS

Newton Priory, north Hampshire seat of the Newton family. 'The house was neither large nor remarkable for its architecture:—but was comfortable . . . it had been built in the ungainly days of Queen Anne, with additions in the equally ungainly time of George II . . . in a park of some two hundred acres' (XI). *RH*
ALS

New Zealand. See AUSTRALIA AND NEW ZEALAND.

New Zealand. Peter Carmichael's sheep station, Warriva, is in the Southern Canterbury province. See AUSTRALIA AND NEW ZEALAND. 'Carmichael'
GRH

New Zealander, The. A somewhat misleading title identifies Trollope's single work devoted to social, political, and cultural essays. It was written in 1855–6 and remained unpublished until N. John Hall edited the manuscript (in the Robert H. Taylor Collection at Princeton) which Clarendon Press published in 1972. Its title originated in a comment by Macaulay in 1840, reviewing a book on the longevity of the Roman Catholic Church, claiming that it would last to the time when a traveller from New Zealand should arrive in a London wasteland to sketch the ruins of St Paul's. An epigraph declares, 'It's gude to be honest and true', a line from Burns used to good effect in *Barchester Towers*. Being honest and true is Trollope's theme in *The New Zealander*, as he ranges through the nation's institutions and cultural features in a world of rapid social change and apparent moral decline. 'Is England in her

decadence?' The question is posed in his opening paragraph. The book is meant in a Carlylean way to make the reader pause and examine what exactly is meant by 'progress' and how social advance must be measured by quality of life. For Trollope, as for Carlyle, the dominant fear is that materialism and greed are eroding standards of honesty and fair dealing, particularly in business, but also in other spheres of human intercourse. Business ethics became the focus of *The Struggles of Brown, Jones, and Robinson, The Three Clerks*, and, most notably, *The Way We Live Now*.

Thirteen chapters, an introduction, and conclusion form the book's appraisal of a society Carlyle had already prophesied was going to the dogs. Writing at high speed and with topical allusions Trollope thought it a significant contribution to contemporary debate, and presented the manuscript confidently to William Longman requesting rapid consideration. Joseph Cauvin, Longman's reader, was baffled. Having responded warmly to *The Warden* he could hardly believe it came from the same hand. He advised against publication, calling it a feeble imitation of Carlyle's *Latter-Day Pamphlets* (1850). Trollope put the manuscript away, although he used some of the text in novels. A section on 'Trade' went, after changes, into *The Struggles of Brown, Jones, and Robinson*, and a whole chapter, 'The Civil Service' (missing from the manuscript), slightly amended, was included in *The Three Clerks*. Hall's introduction provides useful insights into other Trollopian concerns which feed into his later fiction.

Charges that *The New Zealander* followed poorly in Carlyle's tracks are valid. The speaking voice is Carlyle's down to the biblical cadences, finger-wagging, and sometimes laboured phrasing. In the chapter on the press, for example, there are apostrophes and rhetorical questions: 'The truth, sayst thou. Thou wilt write the truth! How is the truth known to thee in these matters? In these matters there is no truth. There is but opinion which for certain purposes is to be made public' (III). Criticism of irresponsible power wielded by the press is one major target, and Trollope refers specifically to *The Times*, defending free speech on principle but blaming the 'Leviathan' for abusing its power by one-sided reporting, and by pillorying anyone who dares challenge its view. 'The tomahawk of the dread Editor is brandished over his head' (III).

The plea for honesty underscoring his consideration of the fifth estate also dominates his treatment of politics (over several chapters). A chapter on the House of Commons (VII) catalogues a number of offences against truth, notably in debates where calculated ambiguities on the one side meet with the equivalent of badger-baiting on the other. Similar arguments concerning lawyers browbeating witnesses and engaging in gladiatorial combat with each other are raised in the chapter on law (IV), which deals with Trollope's primary legal conundrum of getting at the truth or getting a verdict. Trollope's discourse on the purity demanded of leaders will sound familiar to modern ears. 'This leads to hypocrisy, since "it is not given to mortal man to assume infallibility except at the expense of truth"' (VII). Cynicism lurking beneath moral outrage evident in debates, bribery and corruption in elections, the tactics of special committees, and the degree to which self-serving ambition and building a power base erode honesty, are further topics in Trollope's analysis of what ails Parliament.

In his chapter on the Church (VI) Trollope's focus is the hypocrisy of churchmen exhorting their flock to despise material goods, and—a familiar hobbyhorse—the advocacy of Sabbatarian severities quite beyond normal human resources and natural appetites. 'The desire of wealth is planted in every bosom. The love, nay the necessity of pleasure, is a part of our nature. Without it the life of man could not have been joyous and mirthful as our Creator has intended.' Other essays are devoted to 'The People and their Rulers', 'The Army and Navy', 'The Crown', and three topics treated with more hopeful conclusions, on Society, Literature, and Art. Here Trollope is more at ease and escapes the Carlylean stereotype. He makes much of the importance of national education and improving conditions for the poor. In 'Literature' (XI) he offers eighteen models of excellence among poets, an odd assortment with Henry Taylor between Southey and Tennyson, and no mention of Wordsworth or Coleridge. An energetic case for extending and preserving Britain's legacy of art and architecture ends the volume on a positive note. While it is apparent that Trollope's credentials as a serious social thinker in Carlyle's image are slight, the book's merit lies in the balancing of judgements about controversial issues, so intrinsically part of Trollope's ability to see both sides of a question and to maintain 'the equal mind' so evident in his later life as a novelist.   RCT

Nickem, Samuel. Gregory Masters's clever clerk obtains permission to spend his time ferreting out evidence against Scrobby and Goarly. His success leads him to abandon his employment, plunging his family into destitution despite Lord Rufford's aid. *AS*   MG

Nidderdale, Lord, well-connected Liberal member of Parliament and young man about town. Dominated by his ill-tempered father, the Marquis of Auld Reekie, Lord Nidderdale makes several feints for the hand and fortune of Marie Melmotte. Though he backs out of his engagement before Melmotte commits suicide, Lord Nidderdale's help and sympathy prove invaluable. He eventually marries Lord and Lady Cantrip's younger daughter. *DC*   JMR

Nightingale, Florence (1820–1910) 'the Lady of the Lamp', founder of the nursing profession, whose selfless work began during the Crimean War (1854–6). She was presented to Queen Victoria, and from 1857 advised on public health issues. Trollope was sceptical about career-oriented females. In *Orley Farm* (1862), when Madeline Staveley read a paper by Florence Nightingale the narrator states that her mother had no wish for her to 'take to the Florence Nightingale line of life . . . it was a young woman's duty to get married. For myself I am inclined to agree with her' (LVIII). Trollope grew more inclined to the self-sacrificing lives of nurses when he saw hospitals in the Kimberley diamond fields (*SA* 2, VIII). Trollope's niece, born in 1855, was Florence Nightingale *Bland.   RCT

Nina Balatka (see opposite)

Nobble, rough, ugly gold-digging town in New South Wales, probably modelled on Grenfell, and location of Henniker's Hotel where John Caldigate first stays. *JC*   SRB

Noble Jilt, The. Trollope's first attempt as playwright reflects his conservative response to events of 1848. Uprisings in Europe's principal capitals and Chartist demonstrations in London seemed uncomfortably reminiscent of the French Revolution. So, having produced two unread Irish novels, Trollope turned first to the Breton revolt of 1793 (*La Vendée*) and then wrote a play set in that same year in Bruges, hoping to make his name one way or the other. But history creates a flimsy backdrop to the heroine's idealism and her bourgeois aunt's panic. As political statement, the play 'might have been contrived by a scholarly yet unskilled adolescent' (James Pope Hennessy, *Anthony Trollope* (1971), 137).

All mid-Victorian drama could be dismissed as 'adolescent' but, in that context, the play sets out not unskilfully to imitate Bulwer-Lytton, epitome of contemporary high seriousness (see THEATRE, VICTORIAN). That explains Trollope's seemingly odd choice of blank verse for the main plot, where archaic poesy obscures the characters' motives. Trollope reproduces Bulwer's manner without achieving the clear-cut tensions that propel

(*cont. on page 392*)

Nina Balatka

RECALLING this novel's anonymous publication (1866), Trollope confessed to having felt that success, 'once earned', could accrue automatically: 'Aspirants coming up below me might do work as good as mine . . . and yet fail to have it appreciated' (*Auto* XI). He had always worried about producing too many books but, in the late 1860s, felt particularly restless about his established career. In the next three years he would put an end to Barset, resign from the Post Office when passed over as Under-Secretary, edit *Saint Pauls Magazine*, stand (unsuccessfully) for Parliament, and write a second play. He also distrusted the way authors and their critics fed off each other (*Auto* XIV) so was curious to see if his books could succeed without his imprimatur. The *Cornhill* balked at such experiment, but *Blackwood's*, with an eye to future contracts, agreed to serialize the novel. This provoked some interest, but not enough to sell a two-volume edition (later published as Trollope's in one volume, 1879). He tried again with *Linda Tressel* and, had he reduced his fees, might have continued to pursue a 'second reputation'. His last attempt (*The Golden Lion of Granpère*) appeared later under his own name in *Good Words* (1872).

To disguise *Nina Balatka*, Trollope adopted a romantic style and setting for the story of his heroine's battle with her rigidly Christian family, particularly her aunt, Sophie Zamenoy, to marry a Jew, Anton Trendellsohn. After many trials the couple marry and move to Frankfort.

This tale of 'a maiden of Prague' begins with folk-like simplicity, establishing a clash between feuding religions, and then takes on a biblical flavour—'it came to pass', 'as water to a thirsting man'—to evoke the story's Jewishness. Nevertheless, certain turns of phrase alerted the *Spectator*'s R. H. *Hutton to the novel's authorship. The way Trollope describes Prague is unusually graphic in its detail and symbolic impact. Its topography underscores divisions between Catholics (in the Kleinseite around St Nicholas's church), Jews (centred on their synagogue), and nouveaux riches (in New Town). Above those districts looms the Hradschin, cavernous residence of Austria's ex-emperor, Ferdinand, and his soldiers. Nina turns that into a candlelit fairy tale. In actuality, this severe bastion presides over the chiaroscuro and pretension that characterize the novel's distinct societies. Nina's life is so isolated that it comes as a shock when, driven by despair to the Charles Bridge, she joins worshippers beside the Virgin's statue, and is recognized, before crossing to the figure of St John Nepomucene behind which, in bitter cold and darkness, she contemplates suicide.

Death by water pervades the novel with Dickensian forcefulness. Trollope establishes that motif early on when Lotta Luxa, the Zamenoys' clever and prejudiced servant, remarks that she would drown herself rather than be jilted by a Jew. That thought haunts Nina, as Anton Trendellsohn becomes increasingly distrustful, until she cowers desperately beside the statue of Prague's drowned martyr which overlooks the Moldau river. But Nina and water are also subtly linked in Anton's imagination, since he responds to her liquid gentleness that 'refreshed and cooled him' (XI), as opposed to the queenly determination of Rebecca Loth who seems so fitted, socially and ethnically, to be his wife. In that contrast, Nina typifies the little woman who cleaves bravely to her man and obeys his every word. She seems less cloying when, angered by his suspicions, she becomes a 'tigress' and decides to make him ashamed by leaping to her death.

Having toured Bohemia the previous autumn, Trollope saw his characters from an outsider's viewpoint, in social isolation. Fascinated by Jewish otherness, he describes their women's festival dresses and, through the eyes of a stranger, Ziska Zamenoy, depicts a sabbath in Europe's oldest synagogue. But his own memories of rejection in adolescence move him beyond the stereotype of Jewish greed and hard-bargaining to the centre of Anton's lonely sensitivity (interestingly they share the same initials). On the one hand, Anton responds bitterly to Christian contempt by testing Nina's love for himself and her father. At a deeper level, his puzzled disappointments give him an individuality beyond creed or race.

That empathy is itself Trollopian; however, the novel's romantic atmospherics and detailed exoticism took him beyond the interconnections of rural English politics and explain his fond regard for that experiment. He thought the novel as good as *Phineas Finn* and 'much better' than *The Small House at Allington* or *The Eustace Diamonds* (*Auto* XVIII). Yet, although the Austro-Prussian War of 1867 added an immediacy, especially as regards laws that affected Jews in the Hapsburg Empire, this account of a Jewish leader's ambitions to lead his people to freedoms they enjoyed in Europe's more sophisticated capitals made little impact on the reading public. There was curiosity about its authorship when *Blackwood's* ran its seven monthly instalments (July 1866–January 1867), and reviews of the two-volume edition (February) were generally favourable. Yet, as Blackwood put it, 'the book is telling although not selling'. The manuscript is in the Arents Collection, New York Public Library.   AWJ

his model's dramatic structure. Instead, the play's conflicts are blurred by moral ambiguities which confuse one's sympathies.

Under the rhetoric lurk the pains of Margaret de Wynter who, though genuinely in love with Count Upsel, feels that adoration cannot reconcile her to tranquil domesticity. Eager for heroic action, she is persuaded to break her engagement and re-ally herself with Steinmark, leader of Flanders's patriots. Naively she offers herself as soul-mate, but pulls back when Steinmark refuses to bend his republican principles by submitting to a church marriage. Yet, in soliloquy, he admits that, had she loved him, he would have given way. A chastened Margaret begs Upsel's pardon. But to forgive instantly would be to forget his love and grief, so Upsel suggests (peculiarly) that forgiveness must take time. However, when Margaret confesses she always loved him, he immediately proclaims her 'my own, my love, my wife'.

Passion conquers all in the sub-plot, too. Margaret's ridiculous aunt, widow of an elderly ironmonger, encourages (with much protestation) the attentions of Van Hoppen, the burgomaster, and Belleroach, an adventurer who sees the widow and republicanism as ways to make his fortune. In a series of farcical episodes, Mme Brudo becomes entangled with this deceiver, whose youth and good looks outweigh the burgomaster's sincerity. Once married, though, she rules the roost. What that says about love (and idealism)—so bewailed in the main plot—is unclear.

Trollope sent the script to the actor-manager George Bartley, an old friend of his mother's, whose critique was 'altogether condemnatory'. Trollope bowed to professional wisdom but kept that letter, quoting parts in *An Autobiography* (V), years later, when he good-humouredly recalled that 'blow in the face' to his theatrical aspirations while accepting it 'as gospel'.

Yet he remained fond of the play, using its two plots for the Alice Vavasor/Mrs Greenow segments of *Can You Forgive Her?* where a novelist's detailed analyses give their behaviour substance and credibility. The play turns up again, with amusing irony, in *The Eustace Diamonds* as 'a new piece, . . . from the hand of a very eminent author' for which Mrs Carbuncle and party reserve box-seats at the Theatre Royal, Haymarket (LII). Unpublished until Michael Sadleir's edition, 1923. The manuscript is at the University of Texas, Austin.   AWJ

Nokes, William, an employee subject to instant and violent dismissal by Harry Heathcote, who subsequently fears arson at his hands. His abrupt dismissal rankles, and he plots with the Brownbies to bring down the high-handed squatter. After he is seen setting a fire adjacent to

Heathcote's property—a capital offence—he flees, living thereafter as a pariah. *HHG*   MRS

Nonconformism. Baptists, Methodists, Congregationalists, Presbyterians, Unitarians, and Quakers all stood outside the Anglican tradition, dissenting vigorously from the Church of England, and frequently calling for its disestablishment. Trollope would have encountered Nonconformism in its stronghold in the West Country when he was there on behalf of the Post Office, and he found their brick chapels aesthetically distasteful, as he makes clear in *The New Zealander*.

Nonconformism was alien to Trollope's liberal culture. It was exclusive and socially divisive, thriving on antagonism to other branches of the Christian faith. It stood for evangelical zeal, puritanical morality, and doctrinal fanaticism. Socially, it was the religion of the lower middle class; of the poorer sort of tradesmen and clerks. It was not the religion of gentlemen; and its ministers were not properly educated. This point is made in *Doctor Thorne*, when, having failed to secure the high-church Anglican clergyman Mr Oriel, Miss Gushing turns in desperation to the lower-class Revd Mr Rantaway, minister of the 'independent' Methodist chapel.

Essentially provincial, and peripheral to Trollope's social experience, the representatives of Nonconformism are encountered only occasionally; as for instance in *Ralph the Heir*, when the Conservative candidate for the parliamentary constituency of Percycross seeks the vote of the Wesleyan Methodist minister. But Trollope does offer a portrait of intolerant puritanism in Clara Amedroz's Aunt Winterfield, in *The Belton Estate*; and a similar figure, in the Prague of *Linda Tressel*, is Linda's tyrannical Calvinistic Anabaptist aunt Charlotte Staubach, who attempts to crush her spirit in a life-denying marriage with a much older man.

Trollope's most extensive treatment of Nonconformism occurs in *The Vicar of Bullhampton*, in which the qualities of the Primitive Methodist minister, Mr Puddleham, are examined in direct contrast to those of Frank Fenwick, the vicar. Trollope was aware of the severe doctrines of Primitive Methodism, which was established in rural parts, but he strives to be fair. Mr Puddleham, though ignorant and clearly not a gentleman, achieves some good among the poor. However, his condemnation of the 'fallen' woman Carry Brattle, whose cause the young vicar courageously takes up, voices an extreme puritanism. The ugly new chapel, built on land immediately opposite the vicar's church, symbolizes the aggressive posture of sectarian bigotry.

However, Trollope does acknowledge that perhaps for the uneducated rural poor the long sermons, the hymns, and fervent emotional atmosphere may minister to them more effectively than the formality and more elaborate language of the Anglican service.

Another example of Trollope's religious tolerance occurs in *Marion Fay*, in which he portrays a Quaker family. Zachary Fay works as a clerk in the City, and his family lives in lower-middle-class Paradise Row in Holloway. Much as Trollope disliked the Quakers for their exclusivity, their eschewal of ordinary ways, and their quaint speech, his portrayal of the Fays is imaginatively generous. Especially so is his treatment of Marion Fay: the integrity of her self-denying refusal of Lord Hampstead, and the serene courage of her illness and death.   GH

Noningsby, the Staveley family home near Alston. 'There could be no more comfortable country-house than Noningsby. . . . It was a new house from the cellar to the ceiling, and as a house was no doubt the better for being so. . . . The gardens were also new, and the grounds around them trim, and square, and orderly. Noningsby was a delightful house; no one with money and taste at command could have created for himself one more delightful; but then there are delights which cannot be created even by money and taste' (XXII). Noningsby can be contrasted with the Cleeve. *OF*   MT

Norfolk. Ralph Newton first rents then buys the 400-acre (160-ha) farm known as Beamingham Hall. 'It's as flat as a pancake . . . it is under the plough throughout, and famous for its turnips' (*RH* XLIX). He proposes to hunt there, though his neighbours are not sporting. Norfolk is also the location of Will Beeton's farm (*BE*) and of Mr Cheesacre's Oileymead Farm (*CYFH*).   ALS

Norman, Henry (Harry), cousin of the Woodwards, clerk at the Weights and Measures, and later squire of Normansgrove. A thoroughly honest young man and the most trustworthy of the three clerks, Harry is Mrs Woodward's favourite. He introduces Alaric and Charley Tudor to the Woodwards and continually helps both out of trouble. Having lost Gertrude Woodward to Alaric, Harry eventually marries Linda Woodward. *TC*   MT

Normandy. Bessy Pryor is banished from Launay to Avranches to stay at Mrs Gregory's. 'Launay' *WFF*   GRH

Normansgrove, seat of Henry Norman's family in the north of England. Harry Norman inherits Normansgrove after the death of his elder brother, enabling him to resign from the civil service and take up life as a country squire with his new bride, Linda Woodward. *TC*   MT

North America. Prior to requesting leave from the Post Office to make a trip to North America, Trollope negotiated terms for publication of a book on the subject with Chapman & Hall. Despite opposition from Rowland *Hill, the Secretary of the Post Office, Trollope got his way with the help of Lord *Stanley of Alderley, the Postmaster General. He sailed for America from Liverpool on 24 August 1861 and returned 25 March 1862. Within a month he had completed his manuscript and Chapman & Hall had the two volumes of *North America* on sale in London by 19 May 1862. Rose, his wife, accompanied him on the first part of the trip but sailed for home on 27 November 1861. He had 'visited all the States (excepting California) which had not then seceded' (*Auto* IX), as well as parts of Canada including Quebec, Ottawa, and Toronto. The bulk of his trip and his book are concerned with the United States. He noted 'in going from the States into Canada, an Englishman is struck by the feeling that he is going from a richer country into one that is poorer, and from a greater country into one that is less' (*NA* 1, IV).

Looking back in *An Autobiography*, Trollope wrote of the Americans he met while travelling during the Civil War that 'nothing struck me more than their persistence in the ordinary pursuits of life in spite of the war around them' (1, IX). *North America* reflects that—the Civil War is contained in the pages, and chapters, assigned to it such as 'An Apology for the War' and parts of 'From Boston to Washington' in the first volume and 'The Causes of War' and 'The Army of the North' in the second.

Trollope disliked war, the military, and mindless patriotism. He wrote to Kate Field 'that a man should die rather than be made a soldier against his will' (*Letters* 1, 192). However, although his comments on 'The Army of the North' (2, VII) are full of his usual facts and figures, including a discussion of the scandals concerning government contracts, he also found space to complain that the officers 'never enforced the cutting of hair. No single trait has been so decidedly disadvantageous to the appearance of the American army, as the long, uncombed, rough locks of hair' (2, VII). Elsewhere he noted that the 'American cavalry have always looked to me like brigands' (2, VI).

Trollope was proud of the fact that although his book was published when 'the hopes of those who loved the South were the most buoyant, and the fears of those who stood by the North were the strongest . . . it expresses an assured confidence—which never—wavered in a page or in a line—that the North would win' (*Auto* IX). While this is true, he did not believe that the Union would survive the war. He envisioned that to be 'a low and debased nation . . . will be the fate of the Gulf States' and the Northern ambition 'for an entire continent under one rule will not, I should say, be gratified' (*NA* 2, VIII).

More prescient perhaps were his remarks on the sheer agricultural, and therefore economic, power of the United States. He devotes a whole chapter to '*Ceres Americana*' in which he remarks that 'the price of wheat in Europe will soon depend, not upon the value of the wheat in the country which grows it, but on the power and cheapness of the modes which may exist for transporting it' (1, XI). In the case of England the 'Protectionists . . . will have grown sleek upon American flour before they have realized the fact that they are no longer fed from their own furrows' (1, IX).

More than most English visitors to the United States, and certainly more than most novelists, he was always aware of the economic aspect of almost any topic. The one place this economic acuity failed was in his assessment of 'The Rights of Women'. In his chapter on the topic he acknowledges that money and power are related, that many women need to work because they will never marry, that women are capable of paid work, but ends with an exhortation for young women to seek husbands. He could not overcome, despite his recognition of the plight of many women in horrible marriages and the large numbers of women who would never marry, his fixed idea that 'the best right a woman has is the right to a husband' (1, XVIII).

As he demonstrated in the Palliser novels and elsewhere in his fiction, Trollope was master of the daily life of politicians in England. As a political theorist he was perhaps less adept. The chapters he felt obliged to include on 'The Constitution of the United States', 'The Government', 'The Law Courts and Lawyers of the United States', and other comments on the political *system* of the United States in *North America* are the most unreadable of the book. Richard H. Dana, who was a lawyer as well the author of *Two Years before the Mast*, assisted Trollope with these more technical chapters but refused to have his aid acknowledged.

Unlike many visitors to the United States Trollope was not only relatively undisturbed by the lack of civility (or servility) of those in subordinate positions, he understood that it was an improvement upon such relations in England. For someone placed as he was, England was best, but someone lower in the hierarchy could only improve his or her situation in the United States. This is true not only economically but also psychologically and spiritually—even the poor in America 'walk like human beings made in God's form' (1, XVI). That the United States has provided an 'increasing population rights and privileges' that England had not, and perhaps could never have, was a sign of the strength of the country.

It was this ability to see both his side and that of the other that made Trollope's fear of offending his American friends with his book unfounded. *North America* was more popular in the United States than in England. A fiercer, or even a more personal book, might have made a greater impression, but in this Trollope was perhaps handicapped by his determination to write a book very different from his mother's *Domestic Manners of the Americans* which had so offended the Americans in 1832.

Trollope declared 'I am not going to write a guide-book' (*NA* 1, III), but much of the volumes is taken up with an evaluation of which landmarks are worth seeing, which are not, and the best months for visiting them. At the same time he had wished 'so to write my travels, as to introduce, on the sly, my political opinions' (*Letters* 1, 192). Travelogue, guidebook, and political commentary jostle each other awkwardly and Trollope was critical of the result: 'It contained much information, and with many inaccuracies, was a true book. But it was not well done. It is tedious and confused' (*Auto* IX). However, those items that some of his contemporaries, notably Sir William Hardman, found trivial, such as 'the gigantic hotels . . . hot stoves . . . railway cars without distinction of class' (*I & R* 156), are precisely the details that we today find fascinating.

As Trollope himself knew, his interest was not in theories but in individual men and women. In *North America* Trollope was handicapped by the reality of those he wrote about, by the fact they might read his words. The disjunction that contemporaries noted between the inner and outer man is played out in the disjunction between his non-fiction and fiction. He was hampered by the inability to let his daydreams order what he saw. We read *North America* because it was written by Anthony Trollope whose fictional people we feel we know, no matter that they are separated from us by over a century, and all that century has wrought, but we fret over its flatness and turn with relief to the rounded world of his imagination. The manuscript is in a private collection.

MG

Northamptonshire, hunting country including Willingford, frequented by Lord Chiltern and Phineas Finn, and location of Rufford Hall, home of Lord Rufford. *PF, PR, AS*   JMR

North Broughton, borough for which Mr Low sits as member of Parliament. *PR*   JMR

Northcote, Sir Stafford (1818–87), MP for North Devon (1866); governor of the Hudson's Bay Company (1869–74); Chancellor of the Exchequer (1874–80). In the 1850s under Sir Stafford and Sir Charles Trevelyan, assisted by Benjamin Jowett, the civil service, especially its recruiting system, began to be reorganized. Their report recommended competitive entry exams, an idea Trollope opposed anonymously in *Dublin University Magazine* (October 1855). Trollope, who had entered the civil service through patronage—and who certainly would not have passed any testing as proposed by the report— regarded it as totally unfair. Despite his opposition, a Civil Service Commission was established (1853–4) to implement and oversee examinations. Northcote figured in *The Three Clerks* as Sir Warwick Westend; Trevelyan was Sir Gregory Hardlines.   RCT

Northwick, John Rushout, 2nd Baron, leased Illots Farm on his estate at Harrow to Thomas Anthony Trollope in 1813. After Anthony's birth, the family left Keppel Street, London, and moved into the farmhouse, which they enlarged and named 'Julian Hill'. Increasing debts, rising by 1834 to some £500 in arrears in rent, led Northwick to order the Trollopes' assets seized. Some of the family goods were spirited away before the sheriff's men arrived and the family found temporary sanctuary with their friends and neighbours, the Grants, before decamping to Belgium.   RCT

Norton, Mrs Caroline Elizabeth (1808–77), novelist, poet, and social reformer noted for such poems as 'A Voice from the Factories' (1836). Victim of an abusive husband, the Hon. George Chapple Norton, her very public divorce (1836) made her advocate changes in the laws on child custody and married women's property. Such highly visible signs of victimized wives deprived of their children (Rosina Bulwer's similar domestic plight was familiar to the Trollopes) possibly coloured the Trevelyans' marriage break-up in *He Knew He Was Right*.   RCT

Norton & Flick, lawyers acting for Frederick Lovel in the suit over title and estate claimed by Lady Lovel. *LA*   RCT

Norwich, Norfolk town visited by Arabella Greenow and Kate Vavasor, perhaps because of its proximity to Widow Greenow's suitors. *CYFH*   JMR

'Notes on the Brazilian Question' (review). This is an attempted self-justification of W. D. Christie's conduct as minister in Brazil. He appears thin-skinned and imperious. Demands for payment for losses from ships prevailed, but are no doubt the major cause of the current bad relations with that country. *Pall Mall Gazette* (11 February 1865), 6–7.   AKL

'Not if I Know It', first published in *Life*, December 1882. Trollope's last completed piece of writing. The phrase in the title is used by George Wade when his brother-in-law Wilfred Horton asks him to sign a document. Wilfred and his wife Mary (George's sister) are making their annual Christmas visit to Hallam Hall where George, a bachelor, lives. After his outburst Mary goes to her brother and gently remonstrates with him. Perceiving that there is minimal financial risk, that it is Christmas, and that he has behaved churlishly, George relents and makes a graceful apology.   JS

Nott, Revd George Frederick (1767–1841), prebendary of Winchester Cathedral; translator and editor; family friend of Trollope's parents. Nott, visiting the family, and making the customary enquiry about behaviour, was told by Tom Trollope that if the children were not always good, it was because their nurse, Farmer, was an Anabaptist (Hall 14). Clerics of Nott's stamp, with a taste for Italian literature and the pleasures of life, probably influenced Trollope's depiction of clergymen like Dr Stanhope in *Barchester Towers*.   RCT

novel, contemporary British. Trollope, the most prolific of the Victorian novelists, saw himself as a critic as well as a practitioner of novel-writing. He was very conscious that in his own time novel-reading had become, as he put it in the title of a lecture in 1870, 'a rational amusement'—a pursuit that was not only popular but also respectable. The English had become a novel-reading people. Now that cheap fiction was readily available through serialization or circulating libraries, everyone who could read was reading and talking about it. He himself had benefited from this phenomenon, publishing fourteen novels in the 1860s alone.

None the less he felt that the English read novels as they ate pastry after dinner—not without some inward conviction that the taste was 'vain if not vicious'. In his lecture and in *An Autobiography* he protested that novel-writing as a profession was not held in high enough regard. He rejected out of hand Carlyle's charge that fiction consisted of lies, insisting that fiction, in its way, could be as true as fact.

Trollope had no illusions that the novel was as high a form of literature as poetry, whose impact derived from refinement of language and universality rather than from mere storytelling. It was the task of novelists to describe the manners of their own age so that readers could better understand their lives, and this mandate made prose fiction especially attractive to young people. Since novels were read far more than other forms of literature, their influence was considerable.

Trollope could not imagine a novel without a love story. He believed that young men and women of his time grew to understand what to expect in their own love affairs from having read over and over in novels of what went on in others' love affairs.

With popular attention focused on fiction, the novelist, in Trollope's view, had an obligation to provide moral instruction as well as entertainment—'to make virtue alluring and vice ugly'. For this reason he admired Thackeray and George Eliot above all the novelists of his age. Thackeray, he said, could view his characters from either the male or female perspective and modulate his satire from sly to broad. He had reservations about Dickens (parodied as Mr Popular Sentiment in *W*), whose characters he felt were memorable but exaggerated and whose style was idiosyncratic and jerky. None the less he placed him third. Charlotte *Brontë, if she could be judged only for the powerful characterization of Rochester and Jane in *Jane Eyre* and Paul in *Villette*, he would rank in this top group, and probably also Mrs *Gaskell, cited for the soundness of the moral guidance offered in her novels.

We can infer from *An Autobiography* that he would (reasonably enough) have placed himself in this top group as well. In the second rank were Bulwer-Lytton, whose intellect he admired but whose novels he found mannered, and Charles *Lever, whose writing, he said, was droll but lacked memorable characters. He thought Charles *Reade's novels, especially *The Cloister and the Hearth*, entertaining though probably ephemeral. He admired but did not enjoy the sensation novels of Wilkie Collins, who he felt depended too much on tight construction.

He includes in the list of the best-known English novelists in *An Autobiography* Anne *Thackeray, whose characterization he admired but whose style he found wanting, and Rhoda *Broughton, who he felt made her female characters more emancipated than was credible. He strongly disapproved of Disraeli's novels on account of their artificiality. Meredith is conspicuous by his absence. Hawthorne, who of course did not fit into discussions of English novelists, is praised at length in an article Trollope wrote for the *North American Review* (September 1879). Hawthorne was drawn to Trollope's novels for their realism, and Trollope, in turn, admired the 'weird, mysterious, thrilling charm' of Hawthorne's imaginative but highly implausible novels.

Henry Esmond was his favourite novel on account of the completeness of its historical plot and its truth to life. *Esmond, Jane Eyre*, and *Adam Bede*, he predicted, would have lasting popularity; *Pickwick Papers, Pelham*, and *Harry Lorrequer* would be forgotten.

A novel, said Trollope, had to be easy to read, its story thought out in advance and told in a lucid way. George Eliot's novels had no plot, he complained, whereas Wilkie Collins's were all plot. But plot was secondary to character. To create characters that would ring true or seem lifelike he thought the hardest and most important task of the novelist, and also the most rewarding. The most significant legacy from novelist to reader, he believed, was a portrait gallery of realistic characters.   JK

novel, 18th-century British Trollope seems to have had a thorough knowledge of 18th-century fiction, perhaps augmented by his reading for a projected 'History of English Prose Fiction', for which he began research in the early 1850s, but which he abandoned in the early 1870s (*Auto* XII). Trollope intended to begin his study with Defoe's *Robinson Crusoe* (1719), 'which is the earliest really popular novel which we have in our language' (*Auto* XII); and Defoe is the only novelist (with the partial exception of Oliver Goldsmith) to earn a place on Trollope's list of the eighteen giants of English literature in *The New Zealander* (XII). Elsewhere in the same work, however, he is dismissive of other 18th-century writers, arguing that in the fiction of the period, 'we are again at a loss for any trustworthy views of general society'. Accordingly, Trollope reckons Fielding 'but a caricaturist', states that Samuel Richardson 'clearly knew nothing of the world of which he was writing', and objects that Fanny Burney is 'too much like an artist in waxwork' (*NZ* X). Trollope also wrote a long review of E. S. Dallas's abridgement of *Clarissa* (1748), in which he finds the epistolary novel 'as impossible as it is cumbersome', and judges Dallas's attempt to revive interest in Richardson's novel to be fundamentally misconceived: 'The very admission that *Clarissa* is not read, is of itself proof to us that *Clarissa* is unreadable' (*Saint Pauls* (November 1868), 163–72). Trollope pastiches the epistolary novel himself in *Doctor Thorne*, in an episode in which Lady Amelia De Courcy counsels her

cousin Arabella Gresham to reject the lawyer Mortimer Gazebee, only to marry him herself. Trollope's narrator cheekily calls the epistolary method 'one which is very expressive when in good hands', even as he suspects he will 'break down and fall into commonplace narrative, even before the one chapter be completed' (*DT* XXXVIII); arguably, deployment of the epistolary method is meant to reflect formally the old-fashioned aristocratic precepts by which Lady Amelia seeks to govern her cousin, even as the reversal to 'commonplace narrative' reflects her fundamental hypocrisy in not practising what she so eloquently preaches. The most significant—if brief—use of an 18th-century novel in Trollope's fiction is unquestionably the deployment of Sterne's *Tristram Shandy* (1760–7) in *Barchester Towers*: Obadiah Slope's apparent descent from Sterne's Dr Slop (*BT* IV) alerts the reader to the *kind* of novel Trollope is writing; *Barchester Towers*, like *Tristram Shandy*, is a self-reflexive *jeu d'esprit* which constantly revels in its own status as a novel, and which draws its readers' attention relentlessly to the conventions of novel-writing itself. Just as Mr Slope is a lineal descendant of Dr Slop, we are to infer, so *Barchester Towers* is a novelistic descendant of *Tristram Shandy*. Sterne is also the source of Trollope's favourite allusion from 18th-century fiction: his frequent observation that 'God tempers the wind to the shorn lamb' derives from the rendering of a French proverb ('A brebis tondue Dieu mesure le vent') in the section 'Maria', in Sterne's *A Sentimental Journey* (1768). Trollope must have thought it appropriate for *La Vendée*, in which it crops up at least three times.   HO

novelist, Trollope as. See COMEDY IN TROLLOPE'S WORK; HEROES AND HEROINES OF TROLLOPE; LANGUAGE AND STYLE OF TROLLOPE; WORKING HABITS OF TROLLOPE.

'Novel-Reading: The Works of Charles Dickens; the Works of W. Makepeace Thackeray' (article). Novels are replacing sermons and codebooks for the young. Social and moral values are strongly influenced by reading. Thus, it is important to select carefully what the young read. Virtue should be shown as good, attractive; vice must be seen as base. Truth to life demands this distinction. Most of Defoe's works are unsatisfactory because they do not castigate evil. Satirists who 'linger lovingly' over the vice being criticized do little good. Gothic fiction contributes to an undesirably morbid imagination, but something of the sensational is natural to novels. If a novel is true, it cannot be too sensational; realism is essential to this genre and must not be compromised for other values. Of modern novels, Walter Scott's are exemplary: true, moral, and interesting. Dickens is less realistic, but always thoroughly moral and to be recommended. Thackeray's characters are perhaps more lifelike than Dickens's, but the lessons taught are the same. *Nineteenth Century* (January 1879), 24–43. AKL

Nubar Bey (1825–99), later Nubar Pasha; Armenian-born Egyptian diplomat; subsequently Premier of Egypt on three occasions. Trollope negotiated with him in 1858 for the conveyance of mail overland from Alexandria to Suez via the railway line then being built. Nubar Bey visited Trollope almost daily at his hotel, bringing 'servants, and pipes, and coffee' (*Auto* VII), and Trollope found him most courteous. The treaty was signed in July 1858, and Trollope was commended in the Postmaster General's Annual Report. When Escott met Nubar Bey in the 1880s,

he recalled that Trollope's brusque negotiating tactics owed less to the diplomat than to the author 'who might have meditated scolding his publisher if he did not come round to his terms' (T. H. S. Escott, *Anthony Trollope* (1913), 123–4). RCT

Nuncombe Putney, village twenty miles (32 km) east of Exeter where Mrs Stanbury and her daughters live. The surrounding country 'is perhaps as pretty as any in England' (XIV), especially Niddon Park, 'a beautiful wild slope of ground full of ancient, blighted, blasted, but still half-living oaks' (XXIV). *HKWR* RC

Nuremberg Two Protestant 'cathedrals' and red-brick, gabled houses, which meticulously preserve their medieval origins, create a placid enclave where traditional appearances matter and where ne'er-do-wells and girls who love them are frowned on by city magistrates. *LT* AWJ

obituaries of Trollope. From the time of Trollope's seizure on 3 November 1882 until his death on 6 December, *The Times* issued thirteen bulletins on his condition. When the end came tributes appeared in all the major newspapers and periodicals testifying to the immense public regard in which he was held. *The Times* itself, true to its perceived role as the paper of record, was muted in its estimate of his place in literature, although Mrs Humphry Ward, in an anonymous contribution commented, 'He has enriched our English fiction with characters destined to survive.' Richard Littledale in the *Academy* called him 'the most representative figure of contemporary literature and one who had achieved the rare distinction of having become an object of personal goodwill to uncounted readers'. 'No one', said Viscount Bryce, in the *Nation*, was 'so representative of English fiction both by his books and by his personality'. The *Edinburgh Review* called him 'capable, indefatigable, and conscientious', while the *Graphic* praised him for 'wholesome and innocent mental pleasure'. The *Athenaeum* thought he was at his best in 'kindly ridicule of the approved superficialities of life'. The *Saturday Review*, often hostile to his novels, praised his 'instinctive revelation of life which delighted the most fastidious critic'. From the *Spectator* came the assertion that 'probably no English writer of his day has amused Englishmen so much as Mr Trollope, or has given them that amusement from sources so completely free from either morbid weaknesses or mischievous and dangerous taints'. In the *Dublin Review* he was praised for giving 'more innocent amusement and entertainment than any other writer of this generation'. *Macmillan's Magazine* judged 'his worst work . . . better than a great many people's best', and *Blackwood's Magazine* summed up a majority opinion saying, 'he was in all things, in thought and deed, the high-minded English gentleman he delighted to portray'. (See R. C. Terry, *Anthony Trollope* (1977), 50–1, 269.) From abroad there were similar tributes, notably in *Harper's Weekly* and *Princeton Review*. Rome newspapers also ran notices. Among the best articles were those of R. H. Hutton (*Spectator*), Walter Herries Pollock (*Harper's New Monthly*), Cuthbert Bede (*Graphic*), the *Saturday Review*, and Revd H. D. Gordon (*Guardian*). A further spate of tributes, mingled with some shock, attended publication of *An Autobiography* one year later.   RCT

O'Brien, Charles, young Irish sculptor attracted to Arabella Talboys. He asks her to elope to Naples, having taken her daring statements at face value. 'Talboys' *TAC2*   GRH

O'Callaghan, Mr, evangelical clergyman at Littlebath who, though 'always hot in argument against the devil and his works', condescends to join the ladies' card games under the mellowing influence of tea and muffins. *B*   MRS

O'Connell, Daniel (1775–1847), Irish patriot known as the 'Liberator'; elected MP for Co. Clare (1828); founded the Repeal Association (1840); indicted and tried in Dublin (1844). His trial provided Trollope with the opening scene for his second novel *The Kellys and the O'Kellys*. The novel ends with a wedding in the summer of 1844, after the verdict of the packed jury had been reached (Super 49). Despite friendship with ardent supporters of O'Connell such as Charles *Bianconi, mayor of Clonmel, and William Smith O'Brien, MP for Co. Limerick, Trollope doubted the extent of Irish disaffection and believed O'Connell was its major *provocateur*.

RCT

O'Conor, Tom, fox-hunting father of five. Temporary host to Archibald Green, he enjoys the comedy of Larry's ineptitude at dinner. 'O'Conors' *TAC1*   GRH

O'Conor family. Large and lively Irish hunting family, with three teasing daughters, Fanny, Kate, and Eliza, all of whom are highly entertained by Archibald Green's trouble with his footwear. 'O'Conors' *TAC1*   GRH

'O'Conors of Castle Conor, County Mayo, The', first printed in *Harper's New Monthly Magazine*, May 1860 (reprinted in *TAC1*). Trollope notes, in *An Autobiography*, that the story is based on one of his own early experiences in Ireland. After a day's hunting, Archibald Green is invited to spend the night at Castle Conor. He finds himself without dancing pumps, having only his hunting boots, and borrows some comically inadequate footwear from the butler Larry. Much mirth ensues, especially among the young ladies of the household. All ends happily although Archibald does not, as expected, win the hand of pretty Fanny O'Conor. JS

O'Donnell, senior counsel for Pat Carroll who intends to build his defence on the defamation of Florian Jones's character. *L* MRS

O'Dwyer, Fanny, niece of Father Bernard, and barmaid at the Kanturk Hotel, briefly attracted by Aby Mollett. Said to belong to a class of women incapable of discerning 'what is good in tone and character' (VI), she nevertheless recognizes Aby's mean and callous ways, and rightly decides that 'her English lover was not a man to be loved' (XVII). *CR* MRS

O'Dwyer, Mick, brother of Mr O'Dwyer, the proprietor of a public house in Kanturk, and part-owner with his brother of the Cork–Kanturk car. *CR* MRS

O'Dwyer, Mr, owner of the shabby Kanturk Hotel, Co. Cork, and part-owner of the Cork–Kanturk passenger car. Solid and thick-set, he appears 'incapable of deep inquiry' (XIII), but is in fact a successful entrepreneur and loyal, well-informed tenant of Sir Thomas Fitzgerald who keeps a sharp eye on the suspicious Mollets. *CR* MRS

O'Hagan, Judge John (1822–90), judge of the High Court of Justice (1881–90) whom Trollope consulted in 1882 while researching *The Land-leaguers*. Ireland was at this time in the grip of the 'Land War', in which small farmers and distressed tenants were pitted against landowners in acts of boycott, arson, and murder. O'Hagan was in charge of the Land Commission Gladstone had initiated to settle the fair rents issue. Trollope was firmly against the Irish Land League, founded by Parnell in 1879, and maintained that the British government should clamp down on agitators. RCT

O'Hara, Captain. This ex-convict's sudden appearance at Liscannor opens Fred Neville's eyes to the unsuitability of his liaison with O'Hara's daughter Kate. Feeling he has been treated less than honestly, he nevertheless buys off the Captain on condition he returns permanently to France. Later, Fred's brother Jack Neville persuades the Captain to care for Kate by giving her a generous annuity. *EE* AWJ

O'Hara, Kate. Wearied by solitude, she gives herself completely to the god-like Fred Neville. Refusing to see her mother, after the latter's vengeance, she is spirited away to France thanks to Jack Neville's charitable concern. *EE* AWJ

O'Hara, Mrs. Enchanted by a cruel wastrel at 18, she finds uneasy peace in western Ireland. When Fred Neville refuses to make her daughter his legitimate wife, she thrusts him over the cliffs to his death. But her mind cracks, and she lives out her days in an asylum, continually harping on that act of biblical vengeance. *EE* AWJ

Oileymead, prosperous Norfolk farm of Mr Cheesacre. Oileymead is a thriving place, but the riches of genuine mahogany beds and ample piles of manure are perhaps too close to one another. *CYFH* JMR

O'Joscelyn, Revd, bigoted Protestant rector invited to dine with Lord and Lady Cashel. He 'spent his life . . . in denouncing the scarlet woman of Babylon and all her abominations; and he did so in season and out of season; in town and in country; in public and in private' (XXXVIII). *KOK* MRS

O'Kelly, Augusta (Guss) and **Sophia (Sophy),** sisters of Lord Ballindine who share fondness for dancing, musicianship, and attentions of young men. *KOK* MRS

O'Kelly, Hon. Mrs, 'prudent and self-denying' (XXI) matriarch, who, concerned for the well-being of her three children, espouses the wisdom that money is an essential ingredient of a happy marriage. *KOK* MRS

Okey sisters, subjects of Dr John Elliotson's public mesmerism experiments; called to Trollope's bedside in 1840 when he was stricken with a mysterious, near fatal illness. Elizabeth and Jane Okey were reputedly able to predict the deaths of hospital patients when they 'saw Jack'. In Trollope's case they 'saw Jack', but only up to his knee, and therefore prophesied recovery. Mrs Trollope became increasingly concerned for the welfare of the Okey girls and consulted her friend Mrs Grant about their future. A daughter of one of the Okeys became housemaid for some years at the Trollopes' Waltham Cross home. RCT

old age. Trollope's novels abound with characters whose old age is central to their peculiarities. The expected rewards of old age are respect, status, and comfort, and many characters such as the Revd Harding in *The Warden*, the old Duke of Omnium in the Palliser novels, and Monica Thorne in *Barchester Towers* represent this fulfilment. Of course old age has its distresses as well, as testified by the querulous Sir John Ball of *Miss Mackenzie* and the cowed, feeble Nicholas Bolton of *John Caldigate*, among others. Trollope's interest in elderly characters is evident in the attention he gives to them, especially as they are troubled by conscience, as is Revd Harding regarding his position as Warden, or William Whittlestaff, who releases the much younger Mary Lawrie from her engagement to him in *An Old Man's Love*. Trollope reveals his compassionate understanding for the losses and disruptions of old age in the last years of the Proudie marriage in *The Last Chronicle of Barset*, and the grief of Plantagenet Palliser upon his wife's death, depicted in *The Duke's Children*.

Trollope himself tended towards valetudinarianism, implying that old age began in the fifties in his life and in his fiction. Troubled as he was with angina and deafness, he expresses indignation over the frailties of old age to several friends: 'Why should there be decay?—why death?' (*Letters* 2, 599). When he was 60, he wrote, 'After a man has done making love there is no other thing on earth to make him happy but hard work' (*Letters* 2, 671). He dreaded physical inability and mental lethargy, and his novel *The Fixed Period*, written the year before he died, explores in detail the advantages of compulsory euthanasia at the age of 68 as a means of alleviating the afflictions of old age. SRB

Oldeschole, Mr, Secretary of the Internal Navigation Office where Charley Tudor works. Mr Oldeschole heads the least respectable branch of the civil service with the most dissipated and fast young civil servants. The useless Office is finally closed down by Sir Gregory Hardlines. *TC*   MT

Oldham, Richard Samuel (1823–1914), rector of St Mary's Episcopal Church, Glasgow; Dean of Glasgow (1877–8). He accompanied Trollope incognito on his tour of Glasgow's worst slums. In its obituary on Oldham, *The Times* (26 June 1914) noted that his tour with the author led Oldham to establish day and Sunday schools and mission chapels. In 1879 Oldham engaged Trollope in a scheme for persuading writers to produce short novels for the Society for Promoting Christian Knowledge. Trollope volunteered a contribution at £50 for an entire copyright, half his current rate. Meticulously he gave the SPCK an escape clause if the material was unsuitable 'because it is incumbent on the Society to put forth nothing but that of which it approves' (*Letters* 2, 849). The scheme did not materialize. RCT

Old Man's Love, An (*see next page*)

Oliphant, Laurence (1829–88), Scottish writer born in Cape Town; called to the colonial bar

(1849); MP for Stirling (1865–8); author of the popular novel *Piccadilly* (1870); like Trollope a member of the Cosmopolitan Club. A proprietor of the *London Review*, which published 'The Banks of the Jordan' and 'Mrs General Talboys', Oliphant broke the news that these stories had been badly received, but he firmly believed in their merit and morality (*Letters* 1, 140). Trollope noted, 'A wonderful letter' (*Letters* 1, 140–1). RCT

Oliphant, Mrs Margaret (1828–97), author of almost 100 novels, notably her seven-part series 'The Chronicles of Carlingford' (1863–76), whose clergy and village community reflect, at lower social level, Trollope's Barsetshire series. Her novel *The Three Brothers* (1870) ran in *Saint Pauls* (June 1869–September 1870). She was one of the few to recognize Trollope as the anonymous author of *Nina Balatka*. In her review of *The Last Chronicle of Barset* for *Blackwood's* (September 1867), she reproved Trollope for the 'murder' of Mrs Proudie, but thought the conception of Mr Crawley had tragic grandeur. Writing to Trollope in March 1869, she observed that 'hot discussions' went on at home over Louis Trevelyan's behaviour (*HKWR*). She also reviewed Trollope's *Commentaries of Caesar* for *Blackwood's* (November 1871), telling John Blackwood privately that it made her laugh. Editing *Blackwood's Foreign Classics* she took on Henry Trollope's *Corneille and Racine* (1881) with some misgivings about the editor's competence. It always puzzled Oliphant, desperately pouring out copy to support her demanding sons, how Trollope made so much money; 'it [his revealing what he earned from books] gave anything but an agreeable sensation, for his worst book was better paid than my best' (quoted R. C. Terry, *Victorian Popular Fiction 1860–80* (1983), 33). Her review of *An Autobiography* for *Good Words* (24, 1883) was generous and perceptive: 'no man ever took more pains to show the way in which the mind justified to itself a certain course of action' (quoted *I & R* 103). RCT

O'Mahony, Gerald, Irish-American political agitator, father of opera singer Rachel O'Mahony, who comes from America to lecture on England's exploitation of Ireland. Although Trollope condemns his firebrand rhetoric, he presents a sympathetic portrait of a man who marries the ideal of national sovereignty to the issue of personal autonomy. Thus, while insisting on Ireland's right to shape its own historical destiny, O'Mahony also affirms his daughter's need for the freedom to determine her own life. *L*   MRS

TROLLOPE's last completed novel, *An Old Man's Love*, appeared posthumously in 1884. As in *The Fixed Period* (1882) and *Mr Scarborough's Family* (1883), the ageing Trollope studies an ageing man reluctant to cease participation in life. In all three novels there are tensions between legalities and emotion, the letter of the law and its spirit.

Mr William Whittlestaff, 50, the 'old man' of the title, and young John Gordon are rivals for Mary Lawrie. Whittlestaff has given Mary a home after her father, his old friend, has left her penniless at 25. He treats Mary as his daughter, and makes her mistress of his house, without fully admitting to himself that he may ask her to be his wife. He hesitates for months before proposing. When he does so, she accepts out of a sense of duty and obligation. Earlier she had met and fallen in love with Gordon, then poor, but he had 'passed on his way without speaking' (III) and she has heard nothing of him for three years.

Whittlestaff's proposal is his last bid for happiness. As a young man he was disappointed in love, in his hopes for a university fellowship, and in his hope for recognition as a poet. Accustomed to disappointment, accepting it as his lot, he is delighted when Mary accepts him, though he senses that she is motivated by gratitude rather than love.

Trollope's plot hinges on a coincidence. Gordon has made a fortune in the Kimberley diamond mines. He arrives to claim Mary a few hours after she has agreed to marry Whittlestaff. Had Gordon arrived a day sooner, she would gladly have accepted him. But now she considers herself bound to keep her promise to Whittlestaff. He considers himself entitled to Mary because she accepted him first, and knows she will not break her word. Gordon believes that he and Mary had a prior if unspoken understanding.

Trollope's interest is in Whittlestaff's conflict with himself. To free Mary from her promise is to relinquish his last chance at happiness. To insist on his prior right is alien to his temperament, and he realizes that Mary's happiness depends on marrying Gordon. Trollope portrays his inner struggle believably and sympathetically, as he urges himself to hold Mary to her word, and at the same time disdains both his insistence that she do so, and his recognition that he should give her up.

Whittlestaff's housekeeper, Mrs Baggett, urges him to insist on his rights, and scorns his finer feelings. At the same time she insists to Mary that she is obliged to marry him, while perversely announcing that she will leave the house rather than accept Mary as her mistress. A loyal but demanding servant, her dependency is a kind of power.

Whittlestaff is aided in releasing Mary by his reading of Trollope's beloved Horace, whose poems advise accepting limited pleasures and expectations, and avoiding aggression. He finally relinquishes Mary in an affecting scene which allows him to be at once generous and resentful. He invites Gordon to a meeting, treats him rudely, suggests that Gordon does not really love Mary and will mistreat her, implies that diamond mining is a dirty and dishonourable business, then abruptly abandons his claim to Mary and hurries away to his hotel, where he 'shut himself up in his own bedroom,—and when there, he sobbed, alas! like a child' (XXII). There is further poignancy when Gordon accepts Whittlestaff's sacrifice as a matter of course. Whittlestaff considers some grandly romantic gesture, such as giving his house and fortune to the young couple and going himself to the diamond fields. But he returns to his old reclusive life. He attends Mary's wedding 'moody and silent' but finally sends Gordon his 'love', adding, 'I shall never cease to regret all that I have lost' (XXIV).

Contemporary reviewers responded tepidly to *An Old Man's Love*. C. E. Dawkins (*Academy*) called it 'slighter than his best work, but there is no falling off in the vigour and sincerity of the style'. *Saturday Review* spoke of 'a not unfitting finale to an almost unparalleled series of works in fiction' (Smalley 520–1). The most extended modern commentaries are in Robert Tracy, *Trollope's Later Novels* (1978), and John Sutherland's introduction to the Oxford World's Classics edition (1991). The manuscript is in the Robert H. Taylor Collection at Princeton University.   RT

O'Mahony, Rachel, daughter of Gerald O'Mahony, an Irish-American political agitator, and fiancée of Frank Jones, English heir of an Irish estate, who successfully supports herself and her father as a singer on the London stage. Complex, self-aware, and often contradictory, she is fearless yet vulnerable; tolerant of her father's championing of the Irish underdog, yet vehemently anti-Semitic; affectionate but unsentimental. As a stage performer, she represents a new conceptualization of the fictional heroine, but the promise of independent female life is curtailed when losing her voice redirects her energies into a conventional end: marriage with an utterly conventional man. *L*   MRS

O'Malley, Mr, lawyer from Dublin who defends Thady Macdermot, on trial for the murder of Myles Ussher. Concerned to establish the truth about the circumstances of Ussher's death, he pieces together a narrative of events that vindicates Thady of premeditated murder, but the death of his material witness, Feemy Macdermot, renders it unreliable in a court of law. *MB*   MRS

O'Meagher, Mr, MP for Athlone who, having spent 'three glorious weeks in New York' (XI), returns to Ireland inflaming his constituents with ideas about the evils of rent, underlining Trollope's belief that the political agitation was provoked by American money and influence. *L*   MRS

Omnium, Duchess of. See PALLISER, LADY GLENCORA.

Omnium, Duke of (the old Duke). As his name, the Duke of 'All', suggests, the Old Duke is considered to be the highest of all English nobles, his private fortune exceeding even the Queen's. Although the Duke is famous for his wealth, political liberalism, and alleged debaucheries, he gains greatest recognition for his lordly manner. As Lady Glencora expresses it: 'he was too magnificent to care about anything . . . his magnificence was incompatible with ordinary interests' (*PR* XXVI). The old Duke makes appearances in *Doctor Thorne, Framley Parsonage,* and *The Small House at Allington,* but he is in these novels characterized by magnificent remoteness. The Palliser series offers a more intimate portrait as the ageing Duke interacts with Lady Glencora and his beloved Mme Max Goesler. Though the Palliser novels show the Duke in his dotage, spoiled and childish, the more human scale of his interests and activities—falling in love with Mme Max in *Phineas Finn,* avidly interested in the scandal surrounding Lady Eustace's jewels in *The Eustace Diamonds,* and his pathetic death in *Phineas Redux*—creates a sympathy for the Duke that is not part of the earlier novels. *CYFH*   JMR

Omnium, Duke of (the young Duke). See PALLISER, PLANTAGENET.

'On Anonymous Literature' (article). Publishing unsigned articles is a bad practice. Editorials on political issues might be exempted; most authors should be held responsible for their work. Some writers now allegedly do not read the books they review. *Fortnightly Review* (July 1865), 491–8.   AKL

O'Neill, Henry Nelson (1817–80), historical and literary genre painter best known for *Eastward Ho* (1857) and *Home Again* (1859); illustrator of Milton's poems; lecturer on art at the Royal Academy. O'Neill painted Trollope's portrait, now in the smoking room of the Garrick Club. O'Neill's essay 'Taste' appeared in the first issue of *Saint Pauls* (October 1867). O'Neill's *Satirical Dialogues: Dedicated to Anthony Trollope* (1870) includes a dialogue between Author and Painter, which gives a fair impression of Trollope's views on topics such as marriage, town and country life, and painting versus literature. O'Neill tried to reconcile Trollope and Charles

*Reade in 1872 over Reade's unauthorized stage version of *Ralph the Heir*. Trollope wrote O'Neill's obituary in *The Times* (March 1880).

RCT

'On English Prose Fiction as a Rational Amusement' (lecture). The novelist's profession is frequently attacked unfairly. A history of genre is helpful to understand public attitudes. English tradition begins with Lyly's *Euphues* and Sidney's *Arcadia* (16th century) and continues to the present. Because novels depend on their own times and customs, they are often ephemeral; this is as it should be. Some have been dull (Aphra Behn's); some coarse (Fielding's), or coarser (Smollett's). Some have been simple and honest (Goldsmith's), some less strong (Edgeworth's) than others (Austen's). With the novels of Scott, prose fiction became solidly wholesome, instructive, and entertaining, more realistic than romantic. Scott's and Thackeray's works are models of the best. Everyone in England now reads novels, so it is foolish to castigate them all—better to discriminate, enjoy the best, and leave the wildly sensational or scandalous alone. Young women should not be more protected from reading materials than are young men. Truth to nature is the central requirement for good fiction, and genuine emotion, rather than sentimental cliché, is to be looked for. The recent fashion for the sensational novel need not alarm—that which is true cannot be dangerously sensational. While some authors pander to the public curiosity for scandal and lurid details, and in doing so, most modern fiction writers are not of this sort. Much admirable fiction is available, and it accomplishes good work. *Four Lectures*, 91–139.

AKL

Ongar, Lady Julia (née **Brabazon**). Younger daughter of impoverished Lord Brabazon, she 'sold herself' to the debauched Lord Ongar, who drank himself to death in the first year of the marriage. After her return to England she renews her feeling for Harry Clavering, but fails to capture him. Like her sister Lady Clavering, she isolates herself from the human contact she craves by a worldly match. Though her appearance is statuesque, and her showy speech can make her sound insincere, her deeper instincts are selfless. *C*

PJT

Ongar, Lord, rich disreputable nobleman married to Lady Ongar. Though only 36 years old, he has already suffered an attack of delirium tremens. He remains insolent and foul-tempered to the last, drinks nothing but brandy, and dies after just over a year of a marriage, events of which are recalled by his wife in lurid whispers. *C*   PJT

Ongar Park, secondary seat of Lord Ongar (after Courton Castle), lying among the Surrey hills. The house is compact but beautifully appointed, and the grounds imposing, with a choice home farm. Lady Ongar takes possession of the estate after her husband's death, but finds her isolation there insupportable and eventually returns it to the family. *C*   PJT

'On Reading' (lecture). Reading is an acquired, very rewarding pastime; if not taken up in youth, it is not enjoyed later. Novels should be part, but not all of the reading diet. Poetry and instructive books are the best; the works of Scott, Thackeray, and Dickens are worthwhile. Books, unlike museums and art galleries, are portable. *The Times* (4 March 1876), 11; (29 November 1876), 6.

AKL

'On Securing an International Law of Copyright'. Trollope's paper was read on his behalf at the Congress of the National Association for the Promotion of Social Science at Manchester on 4 October 1866. This vehement defence of authors' rights, prompted by his disgust at American literary piracy, followed his open letter to James Russell Lowell (*Letters* 1, 193–8) published in the *Athenaeum* (6 September 1862). See also 'REJOINDER TO MR HARPER'; COPYRIGHTS, HALF-PROFITS, ROYALTIES.   RCT

Onslow, Herbert, hard-working English suitor to Isa Heine. He chafes at the delay in their marriage, which stimulates Isa into getting her uncle's permission for an early wedding. 'Heine' *TAC2*   GRH

'On Sovereignty' (article). Constitutional monarchy, such as exists in England, is superior to the 'autocratic sovereignty' of France and 'elected sovereignty' of the United States in its ability to respond to the will of the governed and the exigencies of the times. *Saint Pauls* (October 1867), 76–91.   AKL

Optimist, Mr, industrious chairman of the Board of Commissioners of the General Committee Office. Supported by the *Jupiter*, Mr Optimist has honesty and energy, but lacks strength of purpose. *SHA*   NCS

Oriel, Caleb, high-church rector of Greshamsbury. Dark-haired, good-looking, with £30,000 and good family, he delights in Anglican formalities. Not given to marriage, he escapes Miss Gushing's attentions but eventually becomes less rigorous and marries Beatrice Gresham. Serves on the clerical commission in *The Last Chronicle of Barset*. *DT*   NCS

Oriel, Patience, beautiful, wealthy sister of Revd Caleb Oriel of Greshamsbury. She befriends

Mary Thorne and Beatrice Gresham, quietly advancing the latter as a wife for her brother, and eventually serves as bridesmaid for both. *DT*

NCS

Orley Farm (*see page 407*)

Orley Farm, home of Lady Mason and her son Lucius Mason, about 25 miles (40 km) from London. The codicil to Sir Joseph Mason's will, leaving the property to Lucius, forms the dispute of the 'Great Orley Farm Case' and the trial of Lady Mason twenty years later. The original for the house is Trollope's boyhood home at Harrow, which formed the basis for Millais's illustrations of the house for the serial. *OF*　　　MT

Orme, Edith, widow of Sir Peregrine Orme's only child and mother of Peregrine Orme. Mrs Orme lives with her father-in-law at the Cleeve, where she remains a widow twenty years after her husband's death. She idolizes her carefree and somewhat reckless son Perry, and is a dedicated friend to her neighbour Lady Mason in the second trial. With great compassion, Mrs Orme tells Lucius Mason the story of his mother's forgery, in order to spare Lady Mason from having to confess to her son. *OF*　　　MT

Orme, Peregrine (Perry), son of Edith Orme and grandson of Sir Peregrine Orme. An immature young man, sent down from Oxford for juvenile pranks, Perry is the complete opposite of his friend and contemporary, serious-minded Lucius Mason. Perry gambles, accumulates bills, and is inclined to attend cockfights—all of which suggest to Sir Peregrine behaviour unbecoming a gentleman. He unsuccessfully woos Madeline Staveley. *OF*　　　MT

Orme, Sir Peregrine, squire of the Cleeve near Hamworth, and grandfather of Peregrine Orme. Sir Peregrine is the quintessential Trollopian gentleman who represents chivalric values which are quickly fading in mid-Victorian Britain. He gallantly remains loyal to his friend and neighbour Lady Mason, a woman in distress, and offers to marry her. 'He was generous, quick tempered and opinionated' (III) but wholly honourable, trusting, and trustworthy. *OF*　　　MT

Osborne, Colonel Frederic, bachelor, member of Parliament, and friend of Sir Marmaduke Rowley. 'He was fond of intimacies with married ladies, and perhaps was not averse to the excitement of marital hostility' (I). This 'ancient Lothario' (I) feigns innocence but knows full well the consequences of his continuing attentions to Mrs Trevelyan. He tells her father: 'if it hadn't been me, it would have been some one else' (LXIV). *HKWR*　　　RC

Ostend, Belgian port to which Gertrude Tringle and Captain Benjamin Batsby idiotically elope. *AA*　　　WK

'Our Rulers, as Described by One of Themselves' (review). Lord Campbell's recent biographies of Lords Eldon, Lyndhurst, and Brougham are truly shocking. Campbell not only details the most venal and dishonest behaviour by these three subjects, he does not condemn them. If they did behave and believe as he reports (he worked with all of them), they should be publicly punished and disgraced. It is difficult to believe that they were as described; but more difficult to observe the tolerance of this. *Saint Pauls*, November 1870, 167–76.　　　AKL

Outerman, Nathaniel, London tailor to whom Charley Tudor owes money. Outerman sues Charley for the sum owed, thus causing Charley's eventual arrest and brief imprisonment. Harry Norman pays off the debt to Outerman. *TC*　　　MT

Outhouse, Mary, clergyman's wife and sister of Sir Marmaduke Rowley. She and her husband dutifully but reluctantly shelter their niece Emily Trevelyan, her son, and her sister. 'They would think no evil, they said; but the very idea of a married woman with a lover was dreadful to them' (XXIX). *HKWR*　　　RC

Outhouse, Oliphant, rector of St Diddulph's-in-the-East, a poor working-class parish outside London. Dedicated to his work among the poor, he regrets but endures the expense and trouble engendered by his wife's strong-willed nieces Emily and Nora Rowley, by their suitors, and by Emily's husband Louis Trevelyan and his agent (Bozzle). *HKWR*　　　RC

Ouvry, Frederic (1814–81), Dickens's lawyer. A treasurer of the Royal Literary Fund, he conducted the annual audit with Trollope in 1878.

RCT

Oval, Sir Kennington, aristocratic member of the English cricket team which travels to Britannula for a match. His pursuit of Eva Crasweller hastens Jack Neverbend's declaration of love for her. It is Oval's telegram to his uncle, the Duke of Hatfield, which prompts the English to reannex Britannula in order to overrule its 'Fixed Period' policy. *FixP*　　　SRB

Owen, Robert (1771–1858), Utopian socialist and philanthropist, whose radical ideas on the need for cultural transformation, outlined in *New Moral World* (1834) and numerous tracts, inspired Trollope's mother to visit the Nashoba

(*cont. on page 411*)

Illustrations of hunting scenes in the fiction are few considering Trollope's passion for the sport. 'Monkton Grange' in *Orley Farm* (XXVIII) by Millais captures the bustle of the occasion with horses, dogs, and carriages on a hunting morning. 'Edgehill hunt' by H. K. Browne for *Can You Forgive Her?* (XVII) is another spirited rendering.

TROLLOPE's eleventh novel is about truth, a moral touchstone throughout Trollope's works. But here both plot and character are centred on issues of truth and deceit. Lady Mason has committed forgery and perjury. Her trials for these offences involve a host of lawyers through whom Trollope elaborates a general critique of the legal profession, especially the view that 'no amount of eloquence will make an English lawyer think that loyalty to truth should come before loyalty to his client' (XVII). His scruffy but brilliantly realized Old Bailey barrister, Mr Chaffanbrass, makes his second appearance: 'if any man in England could secure the acquittal of a guilty person under extraordinary circumstances, it would be Mr Chaffanbrass' (XXXIV).

Sir Joseph Mason of Groby Park, Yorkshire, dies. He leaves a young widow, Lady Mason, and her infant son Lucius, and from an earlier marriage he leaves three daughters and a now grown son, Joseph. Joseph expects to inherit Orley Farm along with Groby Park, but a codicil to Sir Joseph's will leaves the farm to Lucius. Joseph disputes the codicil, which was witnessed by Lady Mason and others, but a trial acquits her of forgery. Another witness to the codicil, Miriam Usbech, marries Samuel Dockwrath, an unscrupulous solicitor who rents two fields from Lady Mason. Aggrieved when they are reclaimed from him upon Lucius's coming of age, he maliciously seeks out new evidence, approaches Joseph and his solicitors, Round & Crook, and stirs them up to a new trial, this time for perjury. Contrary to legal etiquette, Lady Mason, instead of consulting a solicitor, seeks advice directly from the barrister Mr Furnival. Furnival overlooks the irregularity because, at age 55, a dangerous age for Trollope's men, he is susceptible to attractive women, successful in his profession but 'obtaining for himself among other successes the character of a Lothario' (X). 'Comely in the eyes of the lawyer' (XXV), Lady Mason plays upon Furnival's susceptibilities and, although he suspects her guilt, persuades him to organize her defence. Mrs Furnival is deeply jealous of their relationship.

Sir Peregrine Orme, a fine, white-haired English gentleman, loves Lady Mason and seeks to protect her. He proposes marriage, considering that his position will be serviceable to her. When he tells Furnival, who has come to see him about the case, Furnival is bitter and jealous, though he would be angry to be told so. 'Though he believed her to have been guilty of this thing, though he believed her to be now guilty of the worse offence of dragging the baronet to his ruin, still he was jealous of her regard' (XL). Lady Mason, aware of the scandal surrounding her, has scruples but accepts Sir Peregrine. As preparations for the trial proceed, at the mid-point of the novel, Lady Mason confesses her guilt to him.

In the meantime, though with distaste, Furnival approaches Chaffanbrass to take the case, and Chaffanbrass suggests Solomon Aram as an appropriate solicitor. Neither doubts that Lady Mason is guilty. Furnival, through his clerk Crabwitz, unsuccessfully tries to bribe Dockwrath to get the case dropped. Also wishing to avoid a trial, Sir Peregrine thinks of getting Round to drop the case if Lady Mason gives up the property, but Sir Peregrine with his exceptionally fine scruples frets about aiding a criminal in her escape.

In a sub-plot, the young barrister Felix Graham toys with moulding Mary Snow, a drunken engraver's daughter, to be his wife. But he gives up that plan upon falling in love with Madeline Staveley, the daughter of Judge Staveley, an admirable and much respected jurist. (Felix arranges a marriage between Mary and an apothecary.) Felix has very high-minded opinions—rather like Trollope's—about the roles of lawyers. Though he becomes part of the defence team acting for Lady Mason, he is horror-stricken by his alliance with Chaffanbrass, 'as though he had been asked to league himself with all that was most disgraceful in the profession;—as indeed perhaps he had been' (XLVIII). He spends much of the trial preoccupied with 'the absolute truth in this affair', sharing with Trollope the notion that with good intent such absolute truth is attainable (LXVIII). Chaffanbrass watches him with interest, having earlier decided that Graham does not understand a barrister's duty to his client, and that if his heart changed toward the client he would drop the case. Mainly through Chaffanbrass's efforts, Lady Mason is pronounced not guilty. Nevertheless, arrangements are made to return the property to Joseph Mason. Sir Peregrine, still in love with Lady Mason, broods about marrying her, but in consultation with his daughter-in-law Mrs Orme agrees that, if he did, 'he would offend all social laws' (LXXIX). Lady Mason, however, releases him from his offer of marriage. She goes to live in Germany and Lucius emigrates to Australia.

With some reservations, Trollope was very pleased with *Orley Farm*, saying in *An Autobiography*: 'The plot of *Orley Farm* is probably the best I have ever made; but it has the fault of declaring itself, and thus coming to an end too early in the book. When Lady Mason tells Sir Peregrine that she did forge the will, the plot of *Orley Farm* has unravelled itself;—and this she does in the middle of the tale' (*Auto* IX). In the novel, Trollope indulges in one of those explanations to the reader that Henry James deplored as lessening the illusion of reality. 'I venture to think,' says Trollope, 'I may almost say to hope, that Lady Mason's confession at the end of the last chapter will not have taken anybody by surprise. If such surprise be felt I must have told my tale badly' (XLV). Here as elsewhere, Trollope is more interested in *how* things happen than in creating suspense about *what* happens. His emphasis is reflective and psychological. Nevertheless, both Lady Mason and the narrator are more complicated than Trollope's affectation of a straightforward, cards-on-the-table manner would suggest.

Lady Mason is intriguing in the ambiguity of her sexual consciousness. A widow with a grown son, she is concerned to maintain an air of innocence, that of a dignified and helpless woman beset by the machinations of Dockwrath and Joseph Mason, and as such appealing both to Sir Peregrine and to the much more worldly Mr Furnival. Many readers have been attracted by her pathos, and Trollope allows her a good deal of tearful writhing on the ground. Less attention has been paid to her manipulative exploitation of sexual appeal. The narrator at once foregrounds and repudiates her seductiveness, creating, as it were, two Lady Masons, one for one type of reader, one for another. 'Women,' he says, 'for the most part are prone to love-making—as nature has intended that they should be; but there are women from whom all such follies seem to be as distant as skittles and beer are distant from the dignity of the Lord Chancellor. Such a woman was Lady Mason' (II). But in her consultations with both Sir Peregrine and Mr Furnival she deftly deploys her sexuality. Even her pathos has an erotic edge, as Sir Peregrine discovers: 'there was a soft meekness about her, an air of feminine dependence, a proneness to lean and almost to cling as she leaned, which might have been felt as irresistible by any man' (XXVI). She summons the barrister all the way from a meeting in Birmingham, with an intriguing air of secrecy which Furnival finds himself having to maintain before his wife. The narrator underlines the situation with tongue-in-cheek coyness: 'this deceit was practised, not as between husband and wife with reference to an assignation with a lady, but between the lawyer and the outer world with reference to a private meeting with a client. But then it is sometimes so difficult to make wives look at such matters in the right light' (XI). For her meeting with him, Lady Mason takes pains with her dress, holds his hand frequently and lingeringly, and weeps fetchingly (though she meets her son Lucius minutes later with no signs of sorrow or tears). In short, she instinctively knows how to wind Furnival around her finger. The scene, in fact, is essentially comic. Using a familiar Victorian trope, Trollope tells us: 'Lady Mason was rich with female charms, and she used them partly with the innocence of the dove, but partly also with the wisdom of the serpent. . . . She did wish to bind these men to her by a strong attachment; but she would have stayed this feeling at a certain point had it been possible for her so to manage it' (XXXV). It is as though she cannot help it—she automatically puts eros at the service of survival. In a second interview she cranks up her performance to an even greater degree of seductiveness: 'she looked at him with eyes that would almost have melted his wife' (XLI), artfully telling Furnival of her engagement to Sir Peregrine in such a way that he is invited to think it forced on her. The sexual comedy is fully acted out, but with disclaimers—Lady Mason is only partly conscious of what she is doing, and the narrator affects coy disbelief: 'That Mr Furnival liked his client because she was good looking may be true. I like my horse, my picture, the view from my study window for the same reason. I am inclined to think that there was nothing more in it than that' (XIII). Throughout, the narrator carefully hedges: 'such follies *seem* to be as distant', 'I am *inclined* to think'. The play between conscious and subconscious in Lady Mason provides subtle characterization; the narrator's tension between a wish to believe in her pathetic simplicity, while comically demonstrating her wiles, provides a more complex narrative stance than Trollope is often credited with. Nevertheless, though Trollope indulges in subtle humour, for many readers *Orley Farm* is essentially tragic, a searching exploration of Lady Mason's anguish, guilt, and pathos.

Trollope's narratorial stance towards lawyers is less subtle, and his treatment of law drew considerable hostility from reviewers. His targets were, first, the disposition, as he saw it, of lawyers to put their clients' interests before concern for the truth; and, secondly, the undignified badgering of witnesses in cross-examination. Chaffanbrass, as he had in *The Three Clerks*, embodies all the qualities that Trollope protests against. All the lawyers, except the rather priggish Felix Graham and venerable Judge Staveley, provoke Trollope's exasperation. Of the defence team he says, 'These were five lawyers concerned, not one of whom gave to the course of justice credit that it would ascertain the truth, and not one of whom wished that the truth should be ascertained. . . . I cannot understand how any gentleman can be willing to use his intellect for the propagation of untruth, and to be paid for so using it' (LVI). John Kenneby, cross-examined in both trials, sees himself as a martyr to legal bullying. And the narrator waxes vehement about it: 'To stand in a box, to be bawled after by the police, to be scowled at and scolded by the judge, to be browbeaten and accused falsely by the barristers, and then to be condemned as perjurers by the jury,—that is the fate of the one person who during the whole trial is perhaps entitled to the greatest respect, and is certainly entitled to the most public gratitude' (LXXV). Cross-examination remained a bugbear with Trollope, stemming, perhaps, from an occasion on which he testified during two trials for theft from the Post Office in Ireland, and where he indulged in verbal fencing with the eminent advocate Sir Isaac *Butt (reported in the *Tralee Chronicle*, 31 March 1849 and the *Kerry Evening Post*, 28 July 1849). Old Bailey lawyers like Chaffanbrass were famed for their ferocity in cross-examination, which Trollope chose to see as mere aggressive bamboozlement.

E. S. *Dallas in *The Times* (26 December 1862) expressed astonishment at Trollope's notions about the administration of law and the behaviour of barristers. The *Saturday Review* (11 October 1862) affected to be almost ashamed to have to explain the morality of advocacy yet again. The *National Review* (January 1863, 176–7) declared: 'Some of the details of the trial, especially the cross-examination by the counsel for the defence, are so ludicrously unlike real life, that it is evident Mr Trollope's visits to a court of justice have been few and far between, and have left on his mind only a vague and indistinct impression, which nothing but the haze in which it is involved preserves from instant exposure' (Smalley 176–7). The *London Review* (8 November 1862) detailed Trollope's errors, observing correctly that there is 'a code of professional morals amongst barristers, and that this code condemns in the strongest way the very practices which Mr Trollope asserts to be characteristic of the profession and to be justified by its members' (344–5). And the matter did not rest there—Sir Francis Newbolt in '*Reg. v. Mason*', *Nineteenth Century* (February 1924), 227–36, amusingly takes the whole tissue of errors in the trial apart in an imaginary address to the court by a bemused and despondent judge.

Despite such critical displeasure about his treatment of law, often over technicalities, Trollope was seriously interested in general questions of legal theory and reform. The law reform conference at Birmingham, attended by Furnival and Chaffanbrass in chapter XVII, is based on discussions of reform in the criminal law at the first congress of Brougham's National Association for the Promotion of Social Science in Birmingham in 1857, and would thus have had an air of topicality for contemporary readers. And the spate of hostility to Trollope's ideas about law and legal procedure may, indeed, have been beneficial. Thereafter, Trollope took pains to get the details right, as when he consulted his friend Charles *Merewether QC about heirlooms for Thomas 'Turtle' Dove's opinion in *The Eustace Diamonds*. As he became famous himself, he had a coterie of famous and distinguished lawyers with whom he could discuss legal niceties. Chaffanbrass remains the spirited, irreverent defence lawyer to the end, but in *Phineas Redux*, where Phineas Finn is tried for murder, we see things more from Chaffanbrass's side, and tellingly. Reviewers were, of course, interested in more than the law in *Orley Farm*. On the whole, response was very favourable. Trollope's friends considered it his best book. And Trollope himself was proud of it.

He was especially pleased, too, with John Everett Millais's illustrations for the novel, two per number, 40 altogether. Trollope advised Millais to base his illustration of Orley Farm itself on Julian Hill near Harrow, previously owned by Trollope's father.

The novel appeared in twenty monthly parts, from March 1861 to October 1862, and in two volumes in 1862. The manuscript is in the Carl H. Pforzheimer Library.

RDM

Fisichelli, Glynn-Ellen, 'The Language of Law and Love: Anthony Trollope's *Orley Farm*', *Journal of English Literary History*, 61 (1994), 635–53.

McMaster, R. D., *Trollope and the Law* (1986).

Trollope, Anthony, *Orley Farm*, ed. David Skilton (1985).

community in Tennessee. Mrs Trollope sailed for America in a group including Owen's son, Robert Dale Owen. Despite being appalled by the poverty at Nashoba, she sent her son Henry to Owen's New Harmony settlement, where he stayed a month before rejoining his mother in Cincinnati, Ohio. RCT

Owen, William, minor canon of Hereford Cathedral, but, as grandson of a Pembroke innkeeper, considered unworthy of the Lady of Llanfeare. When she returns to Hereford, his manly wooing wins her heart though she refuses to marry and bring him to penury. When her fortune is restored, it is she who sweeps aside his scruples. *CH* AWJ

Oxfordshire, county where George Vavasor keeps horses and rides with the Edgehill hunt. See ROEBURY. Lufton Park is also in the county. *CYFH, FP* JMR

Oxford University. New College, via the traditional Winchester route, was Thomas Anthony Trollope's wish for his sons. Only Tom, the eldest, went to Oxford, emerging with a third-class degree granted in 1835. The nearest Anthony came was a scholarship at Trinity he tried for unsuccessfully. 'And very fortunate it was,' he wrote, since poverty would have guaranteed future 'debt and ignominy' (*Auto* I). Respecting his father's memory, perhaps, he had Oxford educate at least 45 of his characters. Lazarus College was invented for Francis Arabin (also a Balliol man), Tom Staples, and Josiah Crawley, where Dr Gwynne was Master (*W, BT, LCB*). Dr Grantly was also an Oxford man. Christ Church graduates include the Duke of Mayfair and Dr Mainwaring (*AS*), Peregrine Orme (*OF*), and both Lord Silverbridge and Frank Tregear (*DC*). Dr Wortle had been a fellow of Exeter College (*DWS* I). In the same novel Lord Carstairs is destined for Christ Church. Lord Hampstead left Oxford without taking a degree (*MF* I). RCT

Oxney Colne, Revd Woolsworthy's parish in Devon. 'Colne' *TAC2* GRH

P

Pabsby, Mr, Wesleyan minister at Percycross who reportedly has political influence over his flock. He is canvassed by Sir Thomas Underwood, but does not vote for him. Pabsby has a voice made up of 'pretence, politeness and saliva' (XX). *RH*   ALS

Packer, steward of Lord Trowbridge eager in pursuing the feud between the Marquis and the vicar. *IMP*   RCT

Palliser, Adelaide (later **Maule**), portionless cousin of the young Duke of Omnium. Adelaide Palliser is beautiful, spirited, aristocratic, and an avid hunter. Though without family money, she is heir to her family's stubborn streak and shows greater strength of character than her lover Gerard Maule. Miss Palliser is ultimately enabled to marry her fiancé with financial help from the Duchess of Omnium. *PR, DC*   JMR

Palliser, Lord Gerald, second son of the Duke of Omnium, sent down from Oxford for attending the Derby. Lord Silverbridge suggests he become an attaché. The Duke despairs at the thought of the exam, but Lord Gerald evidently passes it since he figures in Foreign Office gossip in *The American Senator*. *DC*   MG

Palliser, Lady Glencora (née **M'Cluskie**). 'Lady Glen', as she is affectionately known, is the reigning queen of the Palliser series, as Mrs Proudie is the female potentate who strides through the Barsetshire series; and the two of them allow Trollope to explore the issue of women and power in the private and public spheres. An heiress pushed into a marriage of interest to the heir

of the Duke of Omnium, Glencora appears in *Can You Forgive Her?* as a young wife yoked to a dull, uncongenial husband, and hankering after her lost love, the handsome ne'er-do-well Burgo Fitzgerald. But once she has put that waft of romance behind her, she comes to interest herself intensely in her husband's political career, to have her finger in many pies, and to wield enormous personal power as hostess and wife. 'They should have made me Prime Minister,' she declares (*PM* LVI); and in many ways she would have made a better one than her husband, the scrupulous Plantagenet Palliser.

While the taciturn Palliser requires the narrator's commentary to convey his inward thoughts, Glencora dramatizes herself by her speech. 'I'm one of those who likes talking,' she characterizes herself (*CYFH* XXII). She is defined by her talk, which is engagingly frank and vivid. Whether she is scandalizing her husband by her use of slang or putting an eminent minister in his place, she never minces words. 'She says exactly what she thinks at the time', says Violet Effingham, 'and she is always as good as her word' (*PR* LXIX). It is a rare tribute, and deserved.

Once she has settled to her roles as minister's wife, hostess, and duchess, she relishes her position of influence. People are her material, and she exerts herself to make something of them and to shape their lives. When a young engaged couple fall out, she undertakes to put everything right: 'If it's the kind of thing that ought to be', she says, 'I'd manage it in a week' (*PR* LXIX); and she does. She choreographs the union of Phineas Finn with Marie Goesler, and plays goddess in her domains at Matching and Gatherum Castle. When she makes mistakes—and she does—she is ready to bear responsibility for them. 'My back is broad enough,' she says cheerfully, while the scrupulous Duke agonizes (*PM* LI).

She enjoys power, and would like more of it than her society permits. When the Duke becomes Prime Minister, she is triumphant, and at once resolves 'to put the Queen down', and 'to make Buckingham Palace second-rate' (*PM* VI). She launches social manœuvres on a grand scale, and is both her husband's most tireless supporter and his chief rival for prestige and influence. As the Duke of St Bungay notes, 'though she had failed to love the man, she had given her whole heart to the Prime Minister' (*PM* LXVI). An ill-assorted couple launched in a loveless match of interest, Glencora and Plantagenet Palliser yet make a success of their marriage. As Trollope believed, this pair, along with Josiah Crawley, were his best claim to fame (*Auto* XX).   JM

Palliser, Jeffrey, cousin to Plantagenet Palliser and next in line of succession to the dukedom of Omnium should Plantagenet fail to father an heir of his own. An appealing young man with a small income, Jeffrey Palliser strikes up a warm friendship with Alice Vavasor while both are staying at Matching, but Alice declines to encourage him. *CYFH*   JMR

Palliser, Lady Mary, daughter of the Duke and Duchess of Omnium. Observing Lady Mary's struggle with the Duke over her engagement with Frank Tregear, one clearly sees in her both the Duchess's courage and the Duke's nobility. Unlike her mother, Lady Mary is finally allowed to marry the man she loves, proving that a young woman may act with strength and intelligence to help shape her own fate. *DC*   JMR

Palliser, Plantagenet (Duke of Omnium). Nephew of the old Duke and later himself Duke and Prime Minister, he is the male character on whom Trollope expended most pains through a long series of novels. He appears first in *The Small House at Allington*, where he pays rather perfunctory attentions to a married woman, the beautiful Lady Dumbello; but at the end of that novel he enters into an arranged marriage with Lady Glencora, who shares the spotlight with him through most of the Palliser novels. *Can You Forgive Her?* shows their early married years, when she finds her marriage unfulfilling, and hankers after her lost love Burgo Fitzgerald; and there he makes his gesture of sacrificing his chance to become Chancellor of the Exchequer in order to pay full attention to his wife's needs. In *Phineas Redux* he becomes Duke of Omnium—much to his regret, since he regards the chancellorship as far more desirable than the dukedom. In *The Prime Minister* he heads a coalition ministry, and tastes the attractions and pains of leadership. And in *The Duke's Children* we see him also in his role as father, when, bereft of Glencora, he has to cope with the ill-advised loves—as he considers them—of his daughter and two sons.

'A tall thin man' (*CYFH* XXII), he is taciturn, agonizingly uncommunicative in personal and social matters, and given to brooding. While he can hold forth while on his legs in the House, he has no small talk, and he is cripplingly aware of his own 'inaptitude for society' (*DC* XLV). But whatever his social failings, we are left in no doubt of his being a man of strict principle, and dedicated to the good of his country and the welfare of his family. 'To endeavour to be just was the study of his life' (*DC* VII). But Trollope as always is astute in detecting too much of a good thing: 'A little too conscientious, a little too scrupulous', as even his best friend characterizes him,

he is 'hardly fitted to be head of a ministry' (*PM* LXXVIII, XXVII). His liberal political principle, of a gradual levelling of power and lessening of differences between class and class, matches Trollope's own (*PM* LXVIII; *Auto* XVI); but he is not allowed to accomplish much, for all his capacity and dedication. His scheme to convert English coinage to a decimal system is never realized; and as Prime Minister he is labelled quixotic, and he leaves office a discontented man.

Palliser is a great creation as a character outwardly dull who is made fascinating by the exploration of his inner life. The relation of this thin-skinned, hypersensitive man to his extrovert wife Lady Glencora supplies some of the best reading in Trollope's fiction; and by his own account Trollope had put his best efforts into the realization of the character he called 'a perfect gentleman' (*Auto* XX).   JM

Palliser series. There are six Palliser novels connected by their political characters and concerns. They are: *Can You Forgive Her?* (1865), *Phineas Finn* (1869), *The Eustace Diamonds* (1873), *Phineas Redux* (1874), *The Prime Minister* (1876), and *The Duke's Children* (1880). Trollope had doubts about including *The Eustace Diamonds*, since it is the least politically oriented. Michael Sadleir grouped them as novels of Parliamentary Life and, with the exception of *The Eustace Diamonds*, their principal concerns lie with the corridors of power at Westminster, although their geographical reach extends far beyond London to the north of England, Scotland, and Europe. Their intellectual range is also wide, focusing on significant clashes of conservative and liberal policies in the great era of Victorian progress during the 1860s and 1870s. Thus the Palliser novels cast a far wider net than the 'Barsetshire Chronicles', and offer particular rewards for the more sophisticated reader. The canvas is crowded with a vast social range from aristocrat to artisan, but with the usual emphasis on middle class, landed gentry, and new mercantile forces. The subject matter, too, is wide-ranging, rooted in the political battles of Conservatives and Liberals over vital issues such as emancipation, Ireland, international affairs, colonialism, and commerce. At the centre of the series are the lives of Plantagenet Palliser, who becomes Duke of Omnium, and his wife Lady Glencora. Trollope, 'debarred' (as he put it) 'from expressing my opinions in the House of Commons' (*Auto* XVII), said that these two 'have served me as safety-valves by which to deliver my soul' (*Auto* X). As in Barsetshire the Palliser world is caught up in the turmoil of old order and new. And just as the Barset novels intertwine domestic and social affairs with political actions, so the Palliser novels engage intimate personal relationships as well as professional ones with astonishing truth of vision. This is achieved chiefly by the grip Trollope maintains on the time frame and chronology of events and by the 'progression in character' Trollope observes in Phineas Finn and the other leading characters (*Auto* XVII). Nowhere is this more poignant and subtle than in the portrayal of Glencora and Plantagenet, from the early days of their troubled marriage to his pain after her death and further trials in relations with his children. The series has grown remarkably in critical stature, and is now judged by many critics to be the pinnacle of Trollope's art.   RCT

Pall Mall Gazette, an evening paper with a literary emphasis, founded in 1865 by the publisher George *Smith. Ten years earlier, Smith had launched the *Cornhill Magazine*, edited by Thackeray, and Thackeray had enlisted Trollope as a contributor, thereby initiating Trollope's long association with Smith. The *Pall Mall Gazette*, which was usually referred to as the *PMG*, took its name from the fictitious journal in Thackeray's *Pendennis*. Frederick *Greenwood, who after Thackeray's retirement from the *Cornhill* in 1862 served until 1868 as joint editor, with G. H. *Lewes, of that periodical, was also Smith's choice to edit the *PMG* for its first fifteen years; Greenwood was later offended by Trollope's account in chapter XI of *An Autobiography*, which credits 'the unassisted energy and resources of George Smith' in making the *PMG* a success. Trollope also asserted that 'I have met at a Pall Mall dinner a crowd of guests who would have filled the House of Commons more respectably than I have seen it filled even on important occasions'; these contributors included G. H. Lewes and Matthew Arnold, but Trollope named 'Jacob Omnium' and Fitzjames Stephen as the strongest members of the group. Trollope regarded himself as 'a permanent member of the staff' from 1865 to 1868. During this period he contributed over 70 pieces to the *PMG*; as he remarks in *An Autobiography*, 'my work was very various'. The first issue, which appeared on 7 February, included an anonymous note by Trollope on Napoleon III's *History of Julius Caesar*, and his signed 'Letter' on the American Civil War. Trollope's eight 'Hunting Sketches' began in the third issue. Hunting, like the American War, was a topic on which, to use Trollope's phrase, his feelings were 'very keen', but this was not true of all his work: asked by Smith to attend the entire season of the May meetings of the evangelicals in Exeter Hall, Trollope was able to complete only one paper, 'The

Zulu in London', which was published in the issue of 10 May 1865. His eight 'Travelling Sketches' appeared from August to September 1865, and the ten-part 'Clergymen of the Church of England' from November 1865 to January 1866. The 'Hunting Sketches', 'Travelling Sketches', and 'Clergymen of the Church of England' were each collected and reprinted in volume form by Smith. Trollope's other contributions included essays on 'The Brazilian Question', 'The Public School's Calendar for 1865', 'The Election of M. Prevost-Paradol', and 'Bazaars for Charity'. Trollope asserted in *An Autobiography* that his work on the *PMG* taught him he was 'unfit for work on a newspaper': he was unhappy to have his work edited, and he wanted to select his own subjects. He also felt that the payments from Smith were not commensurate with the time he expended. Thus, 'as a permanent member of a staff I was of no use, and after two or three years I dropped out of the work'. In 1879, Trollope's *Thackeray* was published in the series 'English Men of Letters', which was edited by John *Morley for Macmillan. Reviews of *Thackeray* were mixed, but the anonymous review in the *PMG* was particularly harsh, asserting that Morley should never have assigned the task to one so incapable of appreciating Thackeray. In 1880, Smith gave the *PMG* to his son-in-law Henry Yates Thompson; Greenwood was replaced as editor by John Morley; and Trollope promptly contributed the series of eleven essays on 'London Tradesmen' which appeared from 10 July to 7 September. In 1891, Trollope was sufficiently pleased with the *PMG*'s reviews of the *Life of Cicero* and *Dr Wortle's School* that he sent copies to his son Henry.   PTS

Palmerston, Henry John Temple, 3rd Viscount (1784–1865), distinguished statesman, one of Trollope's heroes among national leaders; served as Foreign Secretary (1830–41); Prime Minister (1855–7, 1857–8, 1859–65). Trollope admired him for integrity, hard work, and passion for his country. His liberalism of conservative stamp thoroughly suited Trollope, who defended his policies stoutly into old age (*I & R* 225–6). Events associated with his periods in office form the background for several Palliser novels. Lord *Brock (notably in *FP, CYFH*) has been thought modelled on the statesman. Brock's use of 'drawing-room influences' in his career are a possible link with Lady Palmerston's receptions. Brock is associated with the successful ending of the Crimean War and the Indian Mutiny, as was Palmerston. See also Trollope's *Lord Palmerston*.   RCT

Panama City, where the ways of the travellers Emily Viner and Ralph Forrest finally part. 'Panama' *LS*   GRH

'Panjandrum, The', first published in *Saint Pauls*, January–February 1870 (reprinted in *ET*). 'Just thirty years' ago the editor and five friends resolved to launch a magazine called 'The Panjandrum'. His collaborators were Mr St Quinten ('an ogre'), his amiable wife Sophronia, the philosophical Churchill Smith, the Irish barrister Patrick Regan ('my dearest friend'), and another lawyer, Jack Hallam. The new venture is fraught with difficulties which come to a head when the editor, after a walk in Regent's Park, has the idea for a novel. The journal founders on whether fiction is admissible. The novel is published in another magazine.   JS

Paradise Row, a street in Holloway, suburban London, where lower-middle-class neighbours spy on one another and gossip about their affairs. Clara Demijohn particularly monitors the doings of Marion Fay, Lord Hampstead, and Mary and George Roden. The local pub is the Duchess of Edinburgh. *MF*   SRB

parents and children. The details of Trollope's childhood in *An Autobiography*—the tutoring at his father's hand, the humiliations of being a day-boy at Harrow, the sense of abandonment when his mother went to America with his brothers and sisters—suggest a blighted early life which is somewhat at odds with the reminiscences from family friends that Mrs Trollope was known for her lively parties, picnics, games of charades, and entertaining conversation. She perhaps inspired the Staveley Christmas party games (*OF* XXII). Looking for evidence about Trollope as a parent himself is equally speculative. However, the eagerness with which he and Rose made their niece Edith part of their family when his sister Cecilia died, and their sadness at parting with her a year later, suggest that they enjoyed their small children.

Though there are comparatively few small children in his novels, his descriptions of child-rearing are astute, sharply observed, and often very entertaining. Trollope dismisses Lady Arabella's talents for mothering sarcastically with 'Lady Arabella could not suckle the young heir herself. Ladies Arabella never can. They are gifted with the powers of being mothers, but not nursing mothers. Nature gives them bosoms for show, but not for use' (*DT*, II), and Frank Gresham was followed into the nursery by nine costive little girls who fared no better. At the latter end of his writing career, Mary Lovelace, the granddaughter of a stable-keeper, breast-feeds

the future Marquis of Brotherton (*IHP*); Trollope seems to be making a point about the vigour of yeoman stock compared with the effete aristocracy.

Trollope's fictional fathers can be closely involved with their offspring. John Caldigate prides himself on his skills as a nurse for his baby son (*JC* XXV). Henry Grantly pushes the pram (*LCB* VI). Depiction of the Burtons in *The Claverings* parenting their three well-spaced children is finely done—the conversation of a 7-year-old; the extra licence given to a 3-year-old; and a firm line about bed-times. Florian Jones's tragedy in *The Landleaguers* is a commentary on the problems that arise when a father's preoccupation with his own grief at the loss of his wife causes him to neglect the parenting of his 10-year-old. Trollope puts some of his most careful writing into his descriptions of the three Grantly sons (*W* VIII), where he contrives to lampoon three bishops of the day, translate adult traits into boyish manners, and expose the subtle gap between a parent's estimation and objective observation. Trollope knows the pleasure of having fun with children. Lord Hampstead (*MF* III) throws his little half-brothers into the air and catches them. Mary Lowther (*VB* II) plays ball with the Fenwick children and falls in the river. Even Adolphus Crosbie shows some skill at playing with the Gazebee offspring (*SHA* XXXV). Dr and Mrs Wortle (*DWS*) know about the importance of good wholesome food, and the interest and concern of an adult who takes pleasure in a child's company. One could conjecture that Trollope's experience as a father of boys made him sharper in his portrayal of boys than girls, since his description of Marion Staveley (*OF* XXII), though full of warmth and affection, is somewhat sugary and sentimental, as are the passages between Septimus Harding and his granddaughter Posy (*LCB*).

Death regularly visits the parents of children. Families were large, and Trollope was writing at a time when contraceptive knowledge was only just becoming widespread. Women often died in childbirth, and children died in infancy. The Grantlys lose Samuel and Florinda, and of Mr Wharton's six children, only two survive to adulthood (*PM* II). Mr Caldigate (*JC*) loses four daughters and a wife in quick succession. While his determination to keep his feelings under wraps earns him the respect of his neighbours, it contributes to the poor understanding between him and his surviving son for the next few years.

Trollope's finest explorations of the primary relationships in infancy occur in *He Knew He Was Right*. The Trevelyans part when Louey is about nine months old. For the next three months he lives with his mother in the country and then in London with her aunt and uncle, until he is abducted by his father and taken to Italy. Six months later, a bewildered and withdrawn Louey is returned to his mother's custody. Trollope shows us, in painful detail, the effect on a small child of so many separations and losses. 'He was cowed and overcome by the terrible melancholy of his whole life.' Trevelyan thinks Emily has fostered dislike of his father in him. Trollope comments, 'When age is counted in months, almost anything may be forgotten in six weeks' (XXXII). He recognizes a mother's need for physical contact with her baby, and its importance for the healthy development of closeness between them. 'It seemed to her that she had not seen her boy until she had kissed his limbs, and had her hand upon his smooth back' (LXVII). These insights are strikingly modern, and their logic exposes the false premiss of the implementation of custody laws of the time. (See also MARRIAGE AND DIVORCE.)

Trollope was a generous father to his sons as they grew up, and there is a great deal more material in the novels for a study of parents relating to their children as young adults. Trollope says, in *The Way We Live Now*, that every vice might be forgiven in a man and in a son, though every virtue was expected from a woman, and especially from a daughter (II), and evidence of this is a regular theme. Young men, particularly those not required to earn their own bread, regularly get into 'scrapes', squandering vast amounts of money. John Caldigate's gambling debts led his father to disinherit him, but forcing him out to make his own fortune promoted his development into a self-sufficient independent man. Young men in Trollope's aristocratic circles are less promising, as mothers indulge reprobate sons, and heirs go to court with their fathers over their property rights. *The Duke's Children* is devoted entirely to an exploration of a father's struggle to establish closeness with children who have grown apart from him. In *Phineas Finn*, Silverbridge as a toddler says, 'Papa is very well, but he almost never comes home' (LX). After Glencora's death, Plantagenet realizes that the cost of this is to be measured in more than his son's huge gambling debts. He has to learn how to be physically close to his children, and the text suggests that, having struggled to make the first move in stroking his son's hair (XXVI), it becomes easier to embrace him in forgiveness after he has paid off Major Tifto. His relationship with his daughter finds a similar epiphany. It is worth noting that ordinary men and women do rather better at parenting their sons and daughters.

'The principal duty which a parent owes to a child is to make him happy' (*DT* III). Where Trollope is making a point about parenting, it is clear that he thinks parents should be actively involved, that their involvement should include playing games and having fun, and that this sort of involvement leads to children growing into well-balanced young people who get on well with their parents. People who have close and loving marriages make good parents, and having children is the ultimate blessing. MM

Parker, Sextus (Sexty), City man engaged in risky commodities speculations with Ferdinand Lopez. An otherwise honest businessman, Sexty Parker's weak spirit and underlying greed give Lopez the opportunity to dupe the man. Encouraged by a little brandy and water, Parker allows himself to be led by Lopez, and though Mrs Parker cautions her husband against the partnership, the Parkers' small capital falls prey to Lopez's get-rich-quick schemes. *PM*   JMR

Parker, Mrs Sextus, wife of Ferdinand Lopez's business partner. Clear-sighted and courageous, Mrs Parker tries unsuccessfully to caution Emily about her husband's business. Though Lopez makes much of her vulgarity, the kind and honest Mrs Parker is a far better person than Lopez, who ultimately ruins her family. *PM*   JMR

Parnell, Charles Stewart (1846–91), leader of the Irish Home Rule party in the House of Commons, regarded by Trollope as little better than an associate of Irish assassins. Parnell was imprisoned in 1881 for making incendiary speeches, but released in 1882 after an accommodation with Gladstone's government. When Trollope visited Ireland in 1882 to do research for *The Landleaguers*, his judgement on Irish politics was already set. As early as 1876 in *The Prime Minister*, Trollope had his narrator remark that 'For the moment there was not even a necessity to pretend that Home Rule was anything but an absurdity from beginning to end' (XII). Parnell's Land League being open to the extremist Fenians was another damning circumstance for Trollope. RCT

Parrish, Morris Longstreth (1867–1944), bibliographer, bibliophile, whose Trollopiana, including the manuscript of Trollope's *Life of Cicero*, 85 volumes from Trollope's library, and other manuscripts, letters, printed books, and memorabilia, comprise the Parrish Collection, University of Princeton. These, together with the Robert H. Taylor Collection, have been vital sources for scholars of Victorian fiction. Parrish edited *Four Lectures* (1938) comprising 'The Civil Service as a Profession' (1861); 'The Present Condition of the Northern United States of the American Union' (1862/3); 'The Higher Education of Women' (1868); 'On English Prose Fiction as a Rational Amusement' (1870). RCT

Parry, Justice, Catholic judge who is to preside over the trial of Landleaguer Pat Carroll; despite sympathizing with Home Rule sentiments in the past, he does not intend to let personal views influence his ruling. *L* MRS

'Parson's Daughter of Oxney Colne, The', first published in the *London Review*, March 1861 (reprinted in *TAC*2). Patience ('Patty') Woolsworthy lives in Oxney Colne, in Devon, with her widowed father the Revd Saul Woolsworthy. Through a neighbour, Miss Le Smyrger, Patience is introduced to Captain John Broughton, a rising man in London. They fall in love and engage themselves to marry. But he loses his enthusiasm for the match, thinking it will not aid his career. Patience nobly breaks off the relationship, to take care of her father and do good works in the parish. She will be a parson's daughter forever. JS

Patagonia, an isolated but important diplomatic posting in South America assigned to John Morton, and after his death to Mounser Green. *AS* MG

Pateroff, Count Édouard, an Anglicized Pole of 'altogether uncertain' years, blond, dapper, and ostentatiously sophisticated. Having misled his old friend Lord Ongar into thinking that his wife had 'misconducted herself' with him, he follows the widowed Lady Ongar to England, laying siege to her hand and character with cat-like softness. *C* PJT

Patterson, Sir William, Whig barrister and Solicitor-General. He works to settle the suit *Lovel v. Murray and Another* by arranging a marriage between his client, Frederic Lovel, and Lady Anna. Though widely respected, he is criticized for his role as mediator, as opposed to litigator, in this case. Humanity and common sense lead him to accept both the division of the Lovel estate and the marriage of Lady Anna to Daniel Thwaite. *LA* RC

Payn, James (1830–96), popular novelist and essayist; contributor to *Household Words* under Dickens's editorship; reader to Smith, Elder & Co. (1874); editor of *Chambers's Journal* (1859–74) and *Cornhill Magazine* (1883–96). As an editor himself, Payn considered *An Editor's Tales* (1870) 'as convincing a proof of the genius of the author as anything he ever wrote. I once expressed this opinion to Trollope, "who assented to my view of the matter, but added, with a grim smile, that he doubted whether anybody had ever read the book except myself" ' (quoted *I & R* 141). Payn left memories of Trollope in *Some Literary Recollections* (1884), calling him 'the least literary man of letters I ever met', although amongst the most 'large hearted'. He felt that Trollope's prosaic approach to literary labour described in *An Autobiography* damaged his reputation; none the less Trollope was among the great triumvirate of modern novelists (*I & R* 141). RCT

Peacocke, Ella, daughter of a Louisiana planter named Beaufort. Believing her husband (Ferdinand Lefroy) dead, she marries Henry Peacocke. Upon learning that her first husband is alive, she leaves for England, pretends to be Mr Peacocke's legal wife, and works as a matron at Bowick School. When proof of her first husband's death is finally obtained, she is 'married for the third time, and for the second time to the same husband!' (5. XI). *DWS* RC

Peacocke, Henry, Oxford classicist and clergyman hired by Dr Wortle as an assistant teacher and curate. He had previously been Vice-President of the College at Missouri. He continues to live with his American wife (Ella) after learning that her first husband (Ferdinand Lefroy), thought to be dead, is in fact living. After returning to America and learning of Lefroy's subsequent death, he remarries Ella and rejoins the Bowick School. *DWS* RC

Peel, Sir Robert (1788–1850), Tory Prime Minister (1834–5; 1841–6); introduced income tax (1842) and the beginnings of the police force (1815); responsible for repeal of Corn Laws (1846). In his younger days Trollope was highly critical of Peel, relating the decline in public life in the 1840s to his leadership and administrations. He at first strongly objected to removing trade protection, but later saw Peel's policies on this issue as demanded by the times, noting in *An Autobiography* that great action defined a leader, 'as when Peel gave up the Corn Laws' (XX). Expediency, staying in power by stealing the other party's policies, Trollope found his grave flaw, and he roundly criticized the statesman in *The New Zealander*. In *The Three Clerks* Alaric Tudor's moral descent is almost blamed on Peel. 'He [Peel] has taught us as a great lesson, that a man who has before him a mighty object may dispense with those old-fashioned rules of truth to his neighbours and honesty to his own principles, which should guide us in ordinary life' (XXIX). But when he came to write *Lord Palmerston* Trollope called Peel a great man. RCT

Pegwell Bay, small seaside resort to which Zachary Fay brings his ailing daughter Marion. Her gentle farewell to Lord Hampstead and her ensuing death take place here; Hampstead sees a vision of her when he visits the grave a month later. *MF*   SRB

Penge, Caroline, cool, well-born, wealthy, and well-behaved 28-year-old woman who marries Lord Rufford with the aid of his sister and her friend, Lady Penwether. She will love her husband 'as she loves everything that is her own' (LXXIV). *AS*   MG

Penrith. There is a path to this Westmorland town from Thwaite Hall. 'Mistletoe' *TAC2*
                                                        GRH

Penwether, Lady Eleanor, the sister of Lord Rufford, who warns him of the danger represented by Arabella Trefoil to no avail. Conscious of her brother's frailties and the dignity of the family, she finally succeeds in wedding him safely to her friend Caroline Penge. *AS*   MG

Penwether, Sir George, well-liked, respected, wise brother-in-law of Lord Rufford. Despite differences of age and temperament, they are attached to one another and Lord Rufford confides in Sir George and follows his advice respecting Arabella Trefoil. *AS*   MG

Pepé, Carlo, Venetian lawyer who, having brought von Vincke to his house, then objects for political reasons to the latter's courtship of his sister, though he is reconciled to it after the war. 'Austrian' *LS*   GRH

Pepé, Nina, Venetian girl who loves von Vincke, and journeys to Verona to see him when he is wounded to reassure him of her love. 'Austrian' *LS*   GRH

Pepé, Signora, Venetian patriot strongly opposed to the Austrian occupation, but reconciled finally to her daughter's love for von Vincke. 'Austrian' *LS*   GRH

Pepper, Fred, a 'young man' of about 45, resident at the Moonbeam and a regular hunter with the B&B (Berkshire and Buckinghamshire Hunt). He has 'sold out and promised his family that he would go to Australia', but is determined to enjoy one more season hunting. *RH*   ALS

Peppercorn, Mr. A brewer ambitious for his daughter Polly, he ultimately gives way and lets her marry the rising maltster Jack Hollycombe. 'Plumplington'   GRH

Peppercorn, Polly, spirited friend of Emily Greenmantle. She decides to lay by her best silk and dress poorly to irritate her father so that he will no longer resist her plan to marry Jack Hollycombe. 'Plumplington'   GRH

Peppermint, Mr, Charley Tudor's rival in love for Norah Geraghty. A widower with three children in search of a suitable mother, Mr Peppermint makes Charley Tudor jealous by proposing marriage. Norah prefers Charley but settles for the safer option and marries Peppermint. *TC*
                                                         MT

Percy, Lord Alfred, 15-year-old naval lad on the *John Bright* which takes President Neverbend to exile in England. Percy's simplistic arguments against euthanasia, using his grandfather, the good and popular Duke of Northumberland, as an example, force Neverbend to reflect on general condemnation of his policy. *FixP*   SRB

Percycross, properly known as Percy St Cross, the borough for which Sir George Underwood stands as Conservative candidate. It retained its two members following the Reform Bill, but is disenfranchised following the discovery of widespread corruption. The account of the election is evidently based on Trollope's experience at Beverley. *RH*   ALS

periodicals. The 1860s saw a vast expansion of periodicals as outlets for novelists and providers of information about science, travel, and culture. Trollope's arrival on the literary scene with the launching of *Cornhill Magazine* (January 1860) was extremely fortunate. *Temple Bar*, *Good Words*, and *London Review* started up in the same year, followed by *Public Opinion* (1861). *Macmillan's* had begun (1859) as had *Tinsley's Magazine*, *Once a Week*, and *All the Year Round*. *Dublin University Magazine*, founded in 1833, increased its circulation under Sheridan Le Fanu from 1861. Another journal of early origin, *Blackwood's Magazine*, held its own, major novelists such as George Eliot and Trollope (with five novels) appearing in its pages. *Argosy* entered the market in 1865, its owner, Alexander Strahan, taking three of Trollope's short stories. The *Graphic*, which paid well, published three Trollope novels and one short story. Its rival, the *Illustrated London News*, begun in 1842, ran a Trollope story in 1861. Rivalry for market share was intense between such competitors as the *Saturday Review*, begun in 1855, and the *Spectator*. From *Cornhill's* huge early circulation of around 100,000 copies, sales fell steadily to just over one-quarter of that number by 1868. Price reductions, more pages, better technology further cut into profits. Trollope shrewdly studied the market and was centrally involved with *Fortnightly Review* (January 1865) and *Saint Pauls* (October 1867), which he edited until 1870. The advent of personality journalism in the 1870s was a development of which Trollope heartily disapproved. *Yates started the *World* in

1871, at one point offering to feature Trollope as one of his 'Celebrities at Home'. Trollope declined. *Truth*, a sixpenny weekly, started in 1877 by Henry Labouchere, specialized in gossip about the rich and famous. Trollope commented on it and its kind that 'such periodicals can only live by being rascally, it is useless to hope that they will cease to be so' (*Letters* 2, 706).   RCT

Perivale, located in Somerset, 'the dullest little town in England' (I). *BE*   WK

Persiflage, Lady Geraldine, sociable young wife of Lord Persiflage. Much more tolerant than her sister, the Marchioness of Kingsbury, to the latter's stepchildren, she advocates acceptance rather than cold disapproval. She and her daughter Lady Amaldina embody social grace and worldly understanding. *MF*   SRB

Persiflage, Lord, gifted diplomat and successful if relaxed Secretary of State. Worldly minded and generous, he makes social and political efforts to ease reconciliation within the family of his sister-in-law the Marchioness of Kingsbury. *MF*   SRB

Persse, Mr, hunting man who volunteers to approach Tom Daly to plead that no violence be used against disrupters of the fox coverts. *L*   MRS

Petrarch (1304–74), Italian poet and scholar whose famous sonnet sequence to his unattainable Laura inspired the English sonneteers. Trollope praised 'his great labors to promote the study of ancient literature' (*Letters* 2, 1028).   RCT

Petrie, Wallachia, American poet known as 'the Republican Browning' (LV). She is an outspoken feminist and democrat, whose rhetorical fervour and florid oratory are irrepressible. She opposes Caroline Spalding's marriage, having hoped that her friend 'would through life have borne arms along with her in that contest which she was determined to wage' (LXXVII)—a battle against men, rank, and riches. *HKWR*   RC

Phillpotts, Henry (1778–1869), Bishop of Exeter, well known for his controversial high-church views, satirized in *The Warden* as Archdeacon Grantly's second son Henry. The Bishop's combative approach to the poor law, government action over the Peterloo massacre (1817), and especially Catholic emancipation, which he vehemently opposed, earned him a reputation ripe for comic purposes. Grantly's other two sons were jokes directed at Charles James *Blomfield (1787–1857), Bishop of London, and Samuel *Wilberforce (1805–73), Bishop of Oxford.   RCT

Phineas Finn (*see next page*)

Phineas Redux (*see page 424*)

Pickering, Fred. Naive and starry-eyed about authorship, Fred tries to support himself and his family in London by writing; facing the poorhouse, he returns to the Manchester attorney's office he had quitted. 'Pickering' *LS*   GRH

Pickering, Mary. More sensible and far-sighted than her husband, she 'consented to be as imprudent as himself', but in the end urges him to write to his father for help. 'Pickering' *LS*   GRH

Pickering Park, property in Sussex belonging to the Longestaffes, which they sell to Augustus Melmotte. Melmotte immediately mortgages the property, but his forgery regarding the title deeds ultimately brings about his downfall. *WWLN*   SRB

Pie, Sir Omicron, distinguished London physician called to Barchester to attend both the Bishop and the Dean in their final illnesses. Their remaining alive for several days adds to Sir Omicron's considerable reputation for omniscience, much to the dismay of the local doctors. *BT, DT, PM, SHA, B.*   NCS

Pigott, Edward Frederick Smythe (1824–95), lawyer and journalist for the *Daily News*; examiner of plays in the Lord Chamberlain's Department (1874–95). Pigott accompanied Trollope to Vienna in 1865 when he was seeing his younger son Fred start for Australia. He provided Trollope with an article on yachting for *Saint Pauls* in May 1868.   RCT

Pike, Matthew, Peter Prosper's discreet butler, a wheezing old man who had been at Buston Hall for over twenty years. It is his particular duty to prevent unwanted visitors from seeing Mr Prosper. *MSF*   MT

Pile, Mr, a Percycross bootmaker and 'a sort of father of the borough in the way of Conservatives' (XX). 'Not a pure-minded politician', one whose penchant for bribery in elections causes problems for Sir Thomas Underwood. *RH*   ALS

Pipkin, Mrs, kind-hearted landlady in the Islington district of London. Her boarders include the somewhat rebellious Ruby Ruggles, whom Mrs Pipkin admonishes, and Winifred Hurtle, for whose ladylike graces and assured business Mrs Pipkin is very grateful. *WWLN*   SRB

Plaistow Hall, Tudor mansion in Norfolk, home of Will and Mary Belton. *BE*   WK

'Nature had been very good to [Phineas Finn]', the narrator tells us, 'making him comely within and without' (XL). Although his success largely arises from his handsome appearance this fortunate Irishman is also a decent man with a conscience, even if he somewhat lacks self-knowledge. He always has an eye to the main chance, and his political ascent is inextricably bound to his success with women, but he is engagingly naive about using the influence that his good looks obtain for him, and he acts, by his own lights, scrupulously.

Phineas Finn appeared serially from 1866 to 1867 in Trollope's journal *Saint Pauls Magazine*. It is the second novel in the Palliser series, following on *Can You Forgive Her?* of 1864–5; but it may be said to be the first really 'political' novel of the series. Trollope is more interested in political process than in political causes; but the causes are prominent too. Events cover the years leading up to the Second Reform Bill of 1867, and though Trollope rearranges political events and personages to suit his own fictional purposes, the historical parallels are quite recognizable, and were swiftly identified.

At the beginning of the novel Phineas is a promising young Irishman in his early twenties, a doctor's son from Killaloe in Co. Clare, who has come to London intending to become a barrister. Quite unexpectedly, he is offered the chance of standing for election as a Liberal in his home constituency of Loughshane. Against the advice of Mr Low, the barrister who is preparing him for a profession in law, but with the cautious support of his father, Phineas stands and is elected, becoming indeed a member of Parliament, but—in the days before pay for MPs—a very impecunious one. His hope is to work himself into a salaried position in the government; but such a position is contingent not only on the success of his party, and his continuing to win a seat, but on his voting with his party at all times. And for a radical Liberal who treasures his independence, such conditions make for a precarious career.

As a young MP, Phineas is taken up by the intelligent and influential Lady Laura Standish, who is, as he well knows, 'related to almost everybody who was anybody among the high Whigs' (V). Keenly interested in politics, she feels that 'a woman's life is only half a life, as she cannot have a seat in Parliament' (VI). Phineas becomes her cause, and her means of indirect participation. She makes sure he meets the right people, and gets him invited to Loughlinter along with the Prime Minister and cabinet ministers. Not unaware of her useful political influence, Phineas proposes to her. But she has already made a more prudent engagement to the proprietor of Loughlinter, Robert Kennedy. Although she has made a calculated decision, her marriage is a terrible mistake, and she spends much of the novel regretting her lost chance at happiness with Phineas. She finally separates from her husband. It is through Lady Laura's influence that Phineas gets elected to her father's pocket borough of Loughton.

With remarkable tactlessness, Phineas then makes her his confidante in his court-ship of the lively heiress Violet Effingham, who turns him down in favour of Lady Laura's choleric brother Lord Chiltern. Although Phineas considers 'his back was broken' by this blow, he swiftly finds comfort by confiding his woes to the rich and attractive Mme Max Goesler.

His political career advances alongside his love life. When he loses favour at Lough-shane, he secures a seat at Loughton; when he duels with his patron's son Lord

Chiltern he loses Loughton, but Loughshane miraculously welcomes him back. He becomes an Under-Secretary, and then a Secretary for the Colonies, only one step down from the cabinet, thus fulfilling his ambition for a salaried position in the government. While he avoids the extreme of radicalism represented by the demagogue Turnbull, under the influence of another radical, Mr Monk, Phineas imprudently commits himself at the hustings to the cause of Irish tenant right, a move to increase the franchise. This becomes his downfall. To honour his promise to his constituents, he is obliged to vote against his party, and hence to resign his position on the Treasury Bench, and his salary.

By way of burning his bridges thoroughly, it seems, he engages himself to Mary Flood Jones, the adoring girl back home in Killaloe who would take him on any terms. This commitment too comes back to haunt him, and he is tempted to abandon Mary as he is tempted to renege on his promises to his constituency on Irish tenant right. Mme Max Goesler, who has turned down the hugely powerful Duke of Omnium because she would rather take 'a leap in the dark' with the handsome Irishman (LX), invites him to her home in Mayfair, and offers him her hand and all she has. Her wealth would make him independent of party position, as he has always wanted to be, and her beauty and intelligence sorely tempt him. But he stays true to Mary and his principles, and throws up his career to become a poor-law inspector in Cork. And so *Phineas Finn* ends, although Trollope already had a *Phineas Redux* in mind, in which Phineas is to return to his parliamentary career and to ladies more fascinating than Mary Flood Jones.

'If I wrote politics for my own sake', Trollope explained in *An Autobiography*, 'I must put in love and intrigue . . . for the sake of my readers' (XVII). This sounds like a rather crude formula; but in fact he integrates the politics very artfully with the love. The issue of independence is to the fore in both. Just as Phineas, having no independent income, delimits his freedom by putting his vote at the service of the government, whether he believes in the measure or not, so Lady Laura, having no access to a career in Parliament, sacrifices her independence to attain second-hand influence, and finds that an undertaking to love, honour, and obey a martinet like Kennedy becomes intolerable slavery. Both have been 'paired off', in parliamentary phrase (II), and find themselves shackled to uncongenial partners. The loss of independence galls both the wife and the salaried employee. Mr Low calls Phineas's contractual commitment to party politics 'at the best slavery and degradation' (V). Phineas resents being compelled to subsume his 'convictions' just as Lady Laura resents the annihilation of personality required by 'her lord and master' (XXIII). The loss of independence in marriage troubles Violet Effingham too: in accepting her turbulent and unmanageable suitor, she recalls that when they are married, 'I shall be bound to do your bidding . . . My wonder is that any girl can ever accept any man' (LII). The same imagery of marriage and bondage is employed on a national scale: Ireland in the Union with England is 'the bride . . . bound in compulsory wedlock' (LVII). The compromise in individual identity when subsumed in a larger unit is constantly before us in personal relations as in national politics.

The principal political issue of the day, as in the decade of the 1860s when Trollope was writing, was that of parliamentary reform. Disappointment after the First Reform Bill of 1832 had led to Chartism, and several points of the old Charter of the 1840s are at issue in *Phineas Finn*: the cause of the ballot—a principle that Trollope loathed

(*Auto* XVI)—is espoused by Turnbull, who is hostilely presented as a demagogue. The move towards equal electoral districts is included in the Liberal programme of re-distribution. Payment for MPs is a plea implicit in Phineas's whole predicament as an able and principled man who could be of use to the nation if only he did not have to sell his vote for a seat on the Treasury Bench. And the extension of the franchise is the cause over which Phineas must sacrifice his career. These issues are debated among politicians who were recognizable by their positions if not by their personalities: Trollope's Lord De Terrier is Derby, his Mildmay is Russell; Daubeny is Disraeli, Gresham is Gladstone.

For all this demonstrated familiarity with the men and measures of the day, Trollope has been criticized for a lack of real political commitment in these so-called political novels. 'It is all concerning nothing at all,' complained Hugh Walpole (*Anthony Trollope* (1928), 106). And Bradford Booth concedes, 'of political philosophy there is virtually none' (*Anthony Trollope* (1958), 87). On the other hand, John Halperin suggests this may be the best political novel in English. Trollope is certainly more interested in men than in measures, as a novelist should be. But he does find ways to incorporate his political principles. So far as his philosophy is articulated, it is put in the mouth of Lady Glencora, now much more deeply engaged in politics than when she appeared in *Can You Forgive Her?* 'Making men and women all equal . . . That I take to be the gist of our political theory.' (Such a programme, indeed, in its inclusion of 'women', goes well beyond the programme of the Charter, which advocated only manhood suffrage.) The surrounding Liberals are shocked at her outspokenness. 'Lady Glencora's politics were too fast and furious for [Mr Kennedy]', we hear; and even the advanced Mr Monk concedes, 'equality is an ugly word and shouldn't be used . . . But the wish of every honest man should be to assist in lifting up those below him, till they be something nearer his own level than he finds them' (XIV). The principle is Trollope's own, both as he lays out his philosophy in *An Autobiography*, and as he develops it through Plantagenet Palliser later in the series.

It is perhaps the rich irony in Trollope's presentation of the political issues of his day that has caused critics to complain of his lack of commitment. He relishes the situation of the highly privileged Whig aristocracy—such figures as the Pallisers, the Duke of St Bungay, and Lord Brentford—as obliged to follow through a programme of action that will deprive them of those privileges. Lord Brentford, for instance, has a pocket borough that is virtually in his gift, which he would like to keep in reserve in case his son should enter politics. 'The use of a little borough of his own . . . is a convenience to a great peer'—even to a pro-reform one, the narrator notes archly (XXVII). And when he must vote to abolish this convenience, Brentford lays himself open to the sneers of his Tory opponents. Lord Tulla, never one for political correctness, rejoices, 'There's nobody on earth I pity so much as a radical peer who is obliged to work like a nigger with a spade to shovel away the ground from under his own feet' (L).

There is more than a suggestion, moreover, that the best government is no government, or at least minimal government. Lord Brentford takes the charge that his is a 'fainéant government' as a compliment. 'It has been the great fault of our politicians that they have all wanted to do something', he maintains (XIII). Change will come and may be assisted, but the brakes on the vehicle are just as important as the accelerator.

A great deal of parliamentary process, as we learn along with Phineas, is a matter of going through the motions.

There are power dynamics among the women as among the men, and Trollope as always is intrigued by the indirection that is forced upon the woman who wants to make her way in the world. Each of Phineas's possible wives has her other man whom she balances against him, weighing advantages for herself in the choice. The greatest psychological study, as Trollope was well aware, is Lady Laura (*Auto* XVII). Phineas sees her as 'a woman who looked at the world almost as a man looked at it,—as an oyster to be opened with such weapon as she could find ready to her hand' (XIV). She sees marriage to Mr Kennedy as her chance to advance her own interests, but finds herself utterly stymied and defeated: as Kennedy's wife she is the object and not the subject of power. Trollope makes it clear, from her 'headache' and revulsion from 'certain homely duties', that Kennedy is sexually repulsive to her (XXXII); and her very home 'is like a prison' (LVI).

The spirited Violet Effingham, as an heiress, might be expected to have a good chance at independence, but as a woman she cannot respectably live alone; she must live with her bullying aunt Lady Baldock, until she can be acceptably married and submit herself to other authority. The widow Mme Max Goesler, we hear, 'was highly ambitious, and she played her game with great skill and great caution' (LVII). As a Jewess (probably) and the widow of a Viennese banker, she has manifold social disadvantages to overcome in the society to which she aspires. And she achieves the highest pinnacle of social success for a woman: a proposal of marriage from the fabulously powerful and exclusive Duke of Omnium. Having achieved the proposal she has angled for, however, she gains a more satisfying power from refusing it.

Although the narrative is largely set in the corridors of power, the common man with his concerns is briefly given a voice by Mr Bunce, Phineas's landlord, a law scrivener, whose vote to power, such as it is, is through a trade union, and the mob that follows Turnbull. But Bunce, though he talks big, is subject to authority, and for his mildly revolutionary principles he is detained by the police and even lectured by his wife. Like the ambitious politician and the woman in search of influence, he must settle for severe curtailment of his independence.

Trollope started *Phineas Finn, the Irish Member* on 17 November 1866, and completed it on 15 May 1867. It ran serially from October 1867 to May 1869, through twenty issues of *Saint Pauls Magazine*, of which Trollope had just become editor. Much to his satisfaction—and probably partly because this time he was both author and editor, and so could bring greater powers of persuasion to bear—Millais agreed to be the illustrator, and Millais's work as usual was a good match with Trollope's command of realistic detail. Millais provided an illustration for each number. The novel was published in book form by James Virtue, the printer who was also the proprietor of *Saint Pauls*. The manuscript is in the Beinecke Library, Yale University.   JM

Halperin, John, *Trollope and Politics* (1977).
Polhemus, Robert M., 'The Mirror of Desire: Anthony Trollope's *Phineas Finn/Phineas Redux*', in *Gothic Faith: Being in Love from Jane Austen to D. H. Lawrence* (1990).

T HE hero of *Phineas Finn* (1866–7) had had the proverbial luck of the Irish: constituencies; beautiful influential women courted his favours, sent him to Parliament, and pampered him when he was there; and the happy consonance of his political and personal desires, almost to the end, made him professionally and amatorily successful. But the same hero, brought before the public again in *Phineas Redux* of 1873–4, is judged by his peers to be one 'more ill-used by Fate than had been any man since Fate first began to be unjust' (LII).

At the end of *Phineas Finn*, when Phineas simultaneously renounced his place in the government, his seat in Parliament, and his tender relations with powerful women, Trollope had married him off to the sweet girl back home. In bringing his hero back to politics and the ladies, he faced the 'unpleasant and awkward necessity' (*Auto* XVII) of getting rid of the girl. He did so cleanly. Phineas returns to London and his old lodgings in mourning for his wife, who has died in childbirth. And the novel continues in sombre vein, with a hero who constantly broods on the painful contrast between the difficulties of his current campaigns and the zest and success of his former ones. 'Loughton and Loughshane were gone', he reflects of his earlier constituencies, 'with so many other comfortable things of the old days' (IV).

In the interval between the two novels, Trollope himself had gone through his disastrous campaign at Beverley, and his experience there had undoubtedly tarnished his optimism about politics and electoral process. When Phineas returns to politics, like his creator he experiences 'the miseries and occasional hopelessness of a contested election' (IV). Things turn ugly. He loses to the Conservative candidate, the utterly incompetent Browborough, and finally gets his seat only by proving bribery against the other side.

His friends welcome him back, and Lady Laura Kennedy, now separated from her dourly Calvinistic husband, persuades him to visit her in Dresden, when she compulsively tells him of her 'strong, unalterable, unquenchable love' for him (XII). Previously her eager partisanship had advanced his political career; but now her devotion is both an emotional burden to him and a real political disadvantage. Her husband Robert Kennedy accuses him of adultery, and shoots a pistol at him. Quintus Slide, the meretricious columnist of the *People's Banner*, exaggerates and publicizes Phineas's role in the Kennedy marriage, and does him severe damage. And the eager defence mounted for him by Lady Glencora Palliser and the widow Marie Goesler only makes things worse. Gresham, his party leader, senses 'some woman's fingers in the pie', and withholds the position in the government that Phineas sorely needs (XL).

In the larger political scene, the Conservative leader Daubeny (Disraeli) performs a feat of juggling when he steals the Liberal cause of disestablishing the Church of England and makes it part of the programme of his minority government. The Liberals, though they favour the measure, regard it as a monstrous birth as produced by Conservatives; and the Conservatives, though traditionally supporters of the Church, are obliged to vote for its disestablishment. 'It is no good any longer having any opinion upon anything,' members of Parliament lament in their clubs (XXXIV).

Phineas's rivalry with the political hack Bonteen, which culminates in a row at the Universe Club, also takes a disastrous turn when Bonteen is clubbed down in an alley: Phineas is arrested on strong circumstantial evidence, and put on trial for murder.

While Phineas is going through his valley of the shadow of death, London and the political world seem to enjoy a festival of gossip and excitement. People are titillated by a trial at which one MP is supposed to have murdered another, and the witnesses include the Prime Minister, several cabinet ministers, and the Duke and Duchess of Omnium. Although his friends rally round him and make sure he has the best defence that Omnium money can buy, delicacies to eat, and good books to read in jail, Phineas finds himself agonizingly out of sympathy with everyone, and appalled that anyone who knows him could for a moment believe him capable of the deed he is accused of.

While Lady Laura hopes to pick up the pieces after the trial, Marie Goesler exerts herself to find evidence that will incriminate the other suspect and so clear Phineas's name. The evidence, along with the exertions of Mr Chaffanbrass, barrister for the defence, bring the trial to a dramatic conclusion and a dismissal of the charges.

Though he is resoundingly re-elected for Tankerville, and offered his old and once coveted place as Secretary for the Colonies, Phineas cannot participate in the triumph of his supporters, and suffers something like a nervous breakdown. He turns down the position on the Treasury Bench, and is ready to retire from politics again, as he had at the end of *Phineas Finn*. But at last he proposes to Marie Goesler, and she accepts him joyfully. Her money will allow him to be independent of the worst of party politics, and to vote with his conscience. Lady Laura, bereft and bitter at her joyless lot, is left to solitude.

There are some subsidiary plot-lines. In this novel the old Duke of Omnium dies, and Plantagenet Palliser and Lady Glen become Duke and Duchess. In ascending to the House of Lords, Palliser must abandon his treasured duties as Chancellor of the Exchequer, and his incomplete project to convert the twelve-penny shilling into a decimal system. Marie Goesler refuses a substantial legacy from the old Duke, which finally forms a dowry for Adelaide Palliser in her marriage to the lacklustre Gerard Maule, the 'young love' interest of the novel. In a parodic parallel of politics with hunting, Trollope shows Lord Chiltern, now master of the Brake Hounds, just as outraged about the poisoning of foxes in Trumpeton Wood as the politicians are about *their* sport of church disestablishment.

Perhaps the most consciously developed theme in *Phineas Redux* is what Trollope called 'the state of progressive change' (*Auto* XVII). In linking his six Palliser novels together Trollope achieves a breadth of canvas and an expanse of time that allow for a long evolution in individual character. Phineas, so unselfconsciously keen and energetic in the first novel, in this one goes through a crisis of self-consciousness that comes near to destroying him. And by the time he has suffered his ordeal at the trial, the whole world bears a different significance in his eyes. 'During the last few months a change had crept across his dream,' the narrator explains. 'He had seen a man whom he despised promoted, and the place to which the man had been exalted had at once become contemptible in his eyes' (LXVII). The charming, uncalculating Irishman now feels consciousness a burden: 'I am conscious of a certain incapability of getting rid of myself,' he admits. He has become a subject for the psychiatrist (LXVII).

Trollope, who is always concerned with what constitutes 'manliness', ponders the newly sensitive Phineas's sexual identity. Always finding it easier to get along with women than with men, Phineas accepts Lady Laura's judgement that he has 'enough of the feminine side of a man's character' (V). Later, after the trial, he is prone to weeping, and calls himself 'unmanned' and 'womanly' (LXVII). But although some characters blame Phineas for his lack of manliness, Trollope makes it clear that Phineas is the greater for his acquired sensitivity. The sturdy huntsman Lord Chiltern is the contrast: 'The balance which regulated [Lord Chiltern's] conduct was firmly set, and went well. The clock never stopped, and wanted little looking after. But the works were somewhat rough, and the seconds were not scored' (LXVIII). The clock of Phineas's temperament, to follow the metaphor, if more fragile, is a finer instrument, and the seconds are scored. Trollope must frequently have been assessing his own internal mechanism in the same terms. His social world took him for a Chiltern, solid, loud, outspoken; he knew himself to be a Phineas, prone to internal agonies, but registering fine distinctions to the last delicate nuance.

The people around Phineas change too. Kennedy, who is aligned with Phineas in that he courted and won the woman young Phineas would have liked to marry, deteriorates into brooding obsession and madness. And Lady Laura, once so eagerly participating in the world's doings, becomes like Phineas unable to take any interest in anything beyond herself. 'I hardly care who is in or out', she admits; 'and yet never was a human being more weary of herself' (LXX).

Change and disenchantment reign in the political scene too, with a weary sense that things are not as good as they used to be. Disraeli's political opportunism, most obvious in his 'stealing the Whigs thunder' by introducing the Second Reform Bill of 1867, was thoroughly distasteful to Trollope, and he shows it as callous political cynicism. Trollope satirically represents the Conservative line of thinking about household suffrage and the growth of democracy: 'As poor old England must go the dogs'—so the Conservatives view the growth of democracy—'as the doom has been pronounced against the country that it should be ruled by the folly of the many foolish, and not by the wisdom of the few wise, why should the few wise remain out in the cold?' (VIII). That is, they bring in a measure they do not believe in as a means of staying in office. This is cynicism institutionalized, and on a grand scale. And when Trollope's Daubeny, whom he characterizes as a conjurer, practises his prestidigitation on the issue of church disestablishment, both parties are as a matter of course called on to vote against their consciences and their traditional political and religious allegiances. Every MP is forced to reflect that 'It is not now as it hath been of yore.'

When Phineas faces the possibility of hanging, the barrister Mr Low responds piously, 'May God, in His mercy, forbid.' 'No', counters Phineas; '*not* in His mercy; in His justice' (LV). Point well taken: Phineas, after all, is innocent. But the brief exchange is central to Trollope's concern in this novel not just with the flaws in the legal system, but with the huge disproportion of cause and effect, and the uneven and arbitrary distribution of rewards and punishments. This is the vision of Ecclesiastes, a world in which the race is not to the swift, nor the battle to the strong.

There is no match, the novel suggests, between deserts and rewards, guilt and punishment. The whole system of values is vitiated, and priorities are reversed or falsified. The old Duke of Omnium, a libertine who has done absolutely nothing with his enormous wealth and power, is viewed as more admirable than the young Duke, a morally scrupulous man who works day and night for the good of the nation. Social prestige attaches to murder: Phineas's acquaintance rather hope he is found guilty, for 'to have known a murdered man is something, but to have been intimate with a murderer is certainly much more' (L). Though Phineas was unable to achieve political advancement for his real competence, after the trial he is re-elected by acclaim and courted by his party for no better reason, as he sees it, than 'because I didn't knock poor Mr Bonteen on the head' (LXX).

In human relations, too, there is a painful discontinuity. To Lady Laura, Phineas is all-important, and her whole life is arranged around first repressing and then finding a way to express and realize her love; to him she is nothing more than the woman he has almost forgotten he once loved. And in the sub-plot, when Adelaide Palliser prefers the indolent Gerard Maule to himself, the energetic Mr Spooner fumes over women's criteria for selection: 'Because a man greases his whiskers, and colours his hair, and paints his eyebrows, and wears kid gloves, by George, they'll go through fire and water after him' (XXIX). This is the comic dimension of a more serious questioning of human values. 'What does it matter who sits in Parliament?' asks Phineas in his disillusion. 'The fight goes on just the same. The same falsehoods are acted. . . . The same mock truths are spoken. The same wrong reasons are given' (LXVIII). Although Trollope supplies a happy ending in which Phineas achieves his long-delayed success in love and politics, still *Phineas Redux* is one of his darker novels, and one in which Trollope often sounds like the later Hardy.

Trollope wrote *Phineas Redux* in 23 weeks, from 23 October 1870 to 29 March 1871. He composed it in the same format as *Phineas Finn*, to run in twenty numbers of four chapters each, and probably originally hoped that *Redux* too would appear in *Saint Pauls*. His working calendar shows, though, that he made the structure adaptable to 26 parts of three chapters each (with an extra chapter each for the final two parts). He was always ingenious at such arrangements. As things turned out, in the interval between *Finn* and *Redux* he gave up the editorship of *Saint Pauls*, and *Phineas Redux* was set aside. In June 1872, when he was in New Zealand, Arthur *Locker of the *Graphic* wrote to him with a request for a novel. 'I should not trouble you during your antipodal tour', Locker explained, 'only that I know you are a man of such unflagging industry that probably you will write a tale on the homeward voyage.' Locker must have been stunned to receive Trollope's reply from Wellington: 'I have a novel already written called Phineas Redux, a sequel to one written by me called P. Finn; & of the same length. My price for the copyright would be £2,500' (*Letters* 2, 565, 569). The contract was forthcoming, and *Phineas Redux* ran in 26 weekly parts in the *Graphic* from 19 July 1873 to 10 January 1874. Trollope's ingenuity in preparing his serial for two possible formats had paid off. In book form *Phineas Redux* was published by Chapman & Hall in December 1873, with an 1874 imprint.

An examination of the manuscript in the Beinecke Library at Yale clears up one anomaly. 'Lough Linter', as the Kennedy estate is named in the first and subsequent editions, is a form produced by the compositors. Trollope had throughout written 'Loughlinter', as in *Phineas Finn*.

Locker had used the *Graphic*'s reputation for excellent illustration as a means to lure Trollope to his journal. Frank Holl's very sombre illustrations have the advantage of matching the often grim and disenchanted tone of this novel.   JM

Hall, N. John, *Trollope: A Biography* (1991).
Kincaid, James R., *The Novels of Anthony Trollope* (1977).

Planken, Fritz, attractive young man and excellent dancer who pays Lotta Schmidt marked attentions, but fails to win her. 'Schmidt' *LS*
GRH

Plomacy, Mr, venerable steward of Ullathorne Court for over 50 years. Having delivered secret letters during the French Revolution, he became noted for his political enterprise and discretion, talents now required in sorting the guests to the Ullathorne fête into locations appropriate to their stations. *BT*
NCS

Plum-cum-Pippins, church of Revd Augustus Smirkie, near Cambridge. *JC*
SRB

Plume, Auguste, loyal lieutenant of the 'Mad Captain' Adolphe Denot, originally a baker in Laval and later assistant in the employ of Chapeau, now a barber in Paris. *LV*
GRH

Plumplington, small town in Barsetshire. 'Plumplington'
GRH

Plumstead Episcopi, Barchester parish of Archdeacon Theophilus Grantly. Comfortable and well furnished, the rectory nevertheless has a heavy, dull air about it. The church, with beautiful stonework and perfect colour, is kept in excellent repair. Appears throughout the Barsetshire novels. *W*
NCS

Plumstock, parish in Cheshire of which Revd Granger was rector. 'Widow' *LS*
GRH

Poe, Edgar Allan (1809–49), American writer and critic who, along with *Hawthorne, helped establish the short story in England. Trollope's attention to short stories after 1859 may have owed something to the popularity of the form. He responded to an article on 'The Imaginative Literature of America' by his friend Lady Pollock in the *Contemporary Review* by claiming greater power for Poe than was suggested in her essay (*Letters* 2, 596).
RCT

poetry, contemporary. Trollope—who, as *An Autobiography* claims, felt poetry composition not to be 'within my grasp' (III)—does not seem to have been especially responsive to contemporary poetry; or, at least, his veneration of those poets he deemed great was offset by his mistrust of would-be poets (although in later life he was encouraging to young poets such as H. Austin *Dobson and Frederick *Locker-Lampson). In his 'Introduction' to *Saint Pauls*, for example, Trollope the editor actively discourages young poets from submitting work to the magazine, arguing that poetic language inherently risks obfuscating that which it wishes to represent or communicate: '[T]he young poet becomes enamoured of the sound and melody of his own lines, and cannot judge of them with that severity

against himself which is within the compass of the writer of prose. . . . [T]he poet, though he may have succeeded in putting good thought into faultless verse, may have missed, and, alas! so often does miss, that power of expression which will enable others to enjoy his music with him' (*Saint Pauls* (October 1867), 1–7). Trollope's stress on linguistic clarity and 'power of expression' indicates how he judges poetry from a novelist's perspective, believing that 'a plain narrative, whether in verse or prose, is everything' (*Fortnightly Review* (1 October 1865), 129–46). Consequently, whenever he critiques his poetic contemporaries, both his praise and his censure are clearly measurable against his own prescription for successful novel-writing, that the 'language used should be as ready and as efficient a conductor of the mind of the writer to the mind of the reader as is the electric spark which passes from one battery to another battery' (*Auto* XII). For example, in an essay on Longfellow, Trollope applauds the poet for 'a clearness in his mode of telling his story, and . . . a purity and pathos in his manner of telling it, which will ensure him against oblivion' (*North American Review* (April 1881), 383–406). By contrast, he criticizes Robert *Browning because 'with him thought and reasoning are so apt to overlay the passion and action of his personages, as to rob him of the advantages of clear narrative' (*Fortnightly Review* (1 October 1865), 129–46). In his social commentary *The New Zealander*, Trollope includes the names of two contemporary poets in his list of eighteen giants of English literature: Alfred *Tennyson and the now-forgotten Sir Henry *Taylor. He commends the former for his 'mysterious, heavenly melody' and the 'poetic electricity, felt but indefinable, with which Tennyson touches, and but touches, the chords of the heart'; while Taylor's *Philip Van Artevelde*, a massive 'Dramatic Romance in Two Parts' (1834), he calls 'one, long, sustained and precious song' (*NZ* XII). Trollope wrote a long and appreciative review of Taylor's *Collected Poems*, and regarded *Philip Van Artevelde* especially highly; but here again his approval comes from a novelist's perspective: for Trollope, Taylor possesses 'as complete a power of impersonation in dialogue as has ever been exhibited by a dramatic writer' (*Fortnightly Review* (1 October 1865), 129–46). Taylor is the contemporary poet that Trollope alludes to most in his fiction (with Tennyson a close second). Trollope's narrators' frequent observation that women 'grow on the sunny side of the wall' is from *Philip Van Artevelde* (I. i. 2), as is the quotation invariably put in the mouths of Trollope's young women when they feel guilty about rejecting an unwelcome lover's advances: 'Alas! I do not have the wit | From such a sharp and waspish word as "No" | To pluck the sting' (I. i. 2). See also, in *Barchester Towers*, Mr Arabin's meditation on a long passage from the poem (XXX). Turning to other contemporary poems that feature prominently in Trollope's fiction, one should note: the sustained thematic treatment of Longfellow's mystical parable of self-help 'Excelsior' (in his *Miscellaneous Poems*, 1841–6) throughout *The Three Clerks*; the comic mingling (and mangling) of Thomas Hood's 'The Bridge of Sighs' (1844) with Hamlet's famous soliloquy in *The Struggles of Brown, Jones, and Robinson* (VIII); and a number of allusions to *The Loving Ballad of Lord Bateman* (1839) a piece of doggerel by Thackeray (with illustrations by Cruikshank and mock-learned footnotes by Dickens); for instance, the ballad is alluded to by Lady Glencora (*CYFH* XLVIII), translated into Greek by Josiah Crawley (*LCB* IV), and translated into Latin by Pat Regan in the short story 'The Panjandrum' (*ET*). Trollope's programme of reading aloud to his family included: Elizabeth Barrett Browning's *Aurora Leigh* (1857), Browning's *The Ring and the Book* (1868); Longfellow's *Hiawatha* (1855); and Tennyson's *Idylls of the King* (1859). Here again, one discerns a marked preference for narrative poetry (Hall 418).   HO

poetry, early 19th-century. Trollope was very well acquainted with the work of certain poets of the early 19th century, familiarizing himself, as a young man, with the writings of Lord Byron and Sir Walter Scott (*Auto* III); and his writings abound with allusions to Byron, Scott, and Thomas Moore. (Allusions to Wordsworth and Coleridge, by contrast, are very rare indeed; allusions to Shelley, Keats, and Robert Southey marginally less so.) Despite such familiarity, one can detect a profound ambivalence in Trollope's attitude to these writers. On the one hand, as *The New Zealander* reveals, he included Byron, Scott, and Southey in his list of the eighteen giants of English literature (XII). On the other, his treatment of Romantic writers in his fiction more often than not equates their poetry with falsity of sentiment, and emotional immaturity. The best example of this is Lizzie Eustace's constant recourse to Byron and Shelley in order to give her tawdry deceptions and self-deceptions a surface glamour. Her half-hearted attempts at memorizing Shelley's *Queen Mab* (1813) (*ED* XXI), and her determined search for a 'Giaour' or a 'Corsair' (after Byron's two narrative poems of, respectively, 1813 and 1814), are both held up as instances of her insincerity and her lack of grasp on reality. Similarly, Phineas Finn and Lady Laura argue over who was the more 'false',

Moore or Byron, while both are disguising their true feelings for one another (*PF* XIV); and the crass Lord Popplecourt's liking for Moore's *Irish Melodies* (1807) is an implicit indication of his unsuitability as a lover for Lady Mary Palliser, whose preference is for Tennyson and Shakespeare (*DC* XLVI). In *Lady Anna*, an entire chapter is given over to the tailor Daniel Thwaite's encounter with the 'Keswick Poet', a barely disguised portrait of Southey, in which Thwaite is surprised by the conservatism of the old radical. Trollope here deploys a standard Victorian criticism of Southey: that his position as Poet Laureate, and the Toryism of his later years, sit oddly with the Jacobin sentiments of his youth. Again, there is an implicit charge of falsity laid against the poet; even as Thwaite seeks approval for his desire to marry into the aristocracy, the poet observes: '[T]he love of which we poets sing is not the love of the outer world. It is more ecstatic, but far less serviceable. . . . We tell of a constancy in love which is hardly compatible with the usages of this as yet imperfect world' (*LA* XXVII). Even so, Trollope's novels, through repeated allusions and quotations, presume a broad knowledge of many poetical works from the period: chief of these are Byron's *Childe Harold* (1812–18) and *Don Juan* (1819–24), Moore's *Lalla Rookh* (1817), and Scott's *Marmion* (1808).   HO

poetry, Elizabethan. Apart from Shakespeare, Trollope's knowledge of Elizabethan literature is not readily inferred from his writings. We know from Hall ('Trollope's Reading Aloud', *Letters*, appendix C, 2, 1033–4) that Spenser's *Faerie Queene* was one of the narrative poems that the novelist read to his family (posterity has not recorded the extent of their gratitude); however, allusions to Elizabethan poetry other than Shakespeare are infrequent in Trollope's fiction. ''Tis merry in hall | when beards wag all', from Thomas Tusser's *Five Hundreth Pointes of Good Husbandrie* (1573, 1580), is quoted a number of times, but as the phrase was semi-proverbial in the Victorian period, it is hard to determine whether Trollope was quoting it knowingly or not.   HO

poetry, 17th-century. The 17th-century poet that Trollope regarded most highly was John *Milton. No other poet of the 17th century is much mentioned; however, there are a number of quotations which occur comparatively frequently, chief among these being: 'Lovely Thais sits beside thee, | Take the good the gods provide thee', from Dryden's 'Alexander's Feast' (1697).   HO

Poitevins, the royalist club in Paris of which Lescure, De Larochejaquelin, and Denot are members. *LV*   GRH

Poitou, royalist province, its capital town Poitiers, which fosters the start of the Vendean rebellion. *LV*   GRH

political issues in Trollope's fiction. Stendhal said politics in a work of literature is like a pistol shot at a concert, loud and vulgar and impossible to ignore; but for Trollope politics is not (necessarily) a vulgar or arcane element of the human experience. Trollope's subject is always people living together, and therefore his novels are always in some sense political, though he is well-known for his study of professional political life in the Palliser series.

Politics in fact figures in Trollope's novels in three ways. First, as identifiable national or international political events or conflicts, usually in the background, providing context for character and theme, like the American Civil War in *Dr Wortle's School*, or even the battle over electoral reform in *Phineas Finn*. Trollope's novels rarely foreground politics in this sense, and even in the Palliser or parliamentary novels, political plots do not usually predominate. Second, politics appears in the form of political issues, like colonial dependence or women's rights to education and the vote, issues which may have larger constitutional or parliamentary aspects, but which also affect lives very concretely in the novels. These kinds of political issues appear throughout Trollope, in the Irish novels, or in those novels which focus on challenges to traditional privileges of gender (*HKWR* or *KD*), of church institutions (*W*), or of class (*DT*).

But politics is most widely important in Trollope in the third sense, the one in which, as Robert Tracy says, '*political* and *social* are almost interchangeable terms' (*Trollope's Later Novels* (1978), 85). Even party politics in the Palliser novels are mostly a matter of personalities and local loyalties, not grand theories. The great issues of Victorian Britain for Trollope were challenges to traditional social arrangements, and he investigates those challenges in most of his novels. He was not interested in other major paradigm shifts of the 19th century, in Darwin or palaeontology or the new biblical criticism. The changes that mattered for Trollope were deeply social, and therefore political, because they were about the shape and exercise of power.

Some characters in Trollope's novels know this truth, and think about it, as did their creator, and so Trollope's politics can also be ideas about politics. Institutional politics, whether in Parliament or the Post Office, is often a game in Trollope,

but this realism (or cynicism) does not mean Trollope or his characters have no political notions, nor that those notions are insignificant.

Trollope's own political ideas, whose direct expression is scattered across his non-fiction, do not exactly add up to a consistent 'political theory', whatever Trollope claimed in *An Autobiography* for his stance as an 'advanced, but still conservative liberal' (XVI). But there is a deep structure in Trollope's political writings which illuminates his novels. His political allegiance was divided between traditions of privilege and a movement towards greater social justice, or between Cicero and Caesar. Significantly, each Roman was the subject of a book by Trollope. In his *Commentaries of Caesar*, Trollope saw Caesar as initially a necessary historical and moral force: 'The wolf, though he be a ravenous wolf, brings with him energy and knowledge' (II). This energy has uncomfortable consequences, however. 'The pain of history consists of the injustice of the wolf towards the lamb; joined to the conviction that thus, and not otherwise, could the lamb be brought to better than a sheepish mode of existence' (*CC* IV). Ten years later, in 1880, Trollope identified closely with the figure of Cicero, who in Trollope's eyes defended a corrupt Roman republic because of what he 'fancied it had been': 'I cannot but think that, had I been a Roman of those days, I should have preferred Cicero, with his memories of the past, to Caesar, with his ambition for the future' (*LC* I).

To be caught between Caesar and Cicero is Trollope's political quandary in miniature, and his thoughtful political figures, like Phineas Finn and Frank Tregear, recognize the dilemma, even if they are politically committed to one side or the other. With some obvious exceptions, like the ballot, Trollope's own commitments were pretty consistently liberal, as his praise of American egalitarianism, especially in matters of education, demonstrated. But he never lost his sense of the cost of change. Perhaps the schoolboy humiliated at Harrow wanted to retain a vision of a world of privilege, courtesy, grace, and ritual to which he might someday belong before it disappeared, that world which the American Senator Elias Gotobed, however unwillingly, found so attractive.

The arena of professional politics, that first circle of politics outlined above, is, in one of the great ironies of Trollope's work, the arena where political ideas matter least. The battle over reform of the franchise in *Phineas Finn*, for example, modelled on the agitation for the Second Reform Bill between 1865 and 1867, tangles political ideologies. Phineas faces the loss of his seat, a pocket borough, if reform is successful, and fights to have it protected. The Liberal government faces a temporary partnership of the radical Turnbull and the Tory Daubeny, both of whom vote to abolish Phineas's rotten borough. Daubeny's 'beautiful speech about the seven [rotten] boroughs;—the seven sins, and seven stars, and seven churches, and seven lamps' is in fact an opportunistic attack on the party of reform, which itself is caught defending the privilege it seeks to abolish (XLVII). Phineas shocks the Liberal party hack Barrington Erle by proposing the value of political beliefs for a member of Parliament: 'But what is a man to do, Barrington? He can't smother his convictions.' Erle's reply is Trollopian wit at its best:

'Convictions! There is nothing on earth that I'm so much afraid of in a young member of Parliament as convictions. There are ever so many rocks against which men get broken. One man can't keep his temper. Another can't hold his tongue. A third can't say a word unless he has been priming himself half a session. A fourth is always thinking of himself, and wanting more than he can get. A fifth is idle, and won't be there when he's wanted. A sixth is always in the way. A seventh lies so that you can never trust him. I've had to do with them all, but a fellow with convictions is the worst of all' (LXVII).

Erle, like Daubeny, thinks in sevens, but the man of convictions is completely outside the pale, beneath even the liar. For Erle, politics is simply our men versus their men. Oddly enough, a much more likeable character, Palliser's son Silverbridge, comes to similar conclusions in *The Duke's Children*, when he first declares himself a Conservative, is elected to Parliament as such, and then decides to cross the aisle to the Liberals, explaining to his Tory friend Tregear, 'After all it is not very important. . . . I don't think it matters on which side you sit' (LXXVI).

Principles do figure in this arena of practical politics, even if only for the Barrington Erles to rail against. Phineas resigns his office and his seat in Parliament at the end of *Phineas Finn* because he believes in protecting Irish tenants' rights, and yet this campaign has come to be supported by Tories who despise it, and opposed by a Liberal government which ought to promote it. Amidst the contradictions of parliamentary life, however, a slippery slope leads from principle to the quixotic to the useless and over-scrupulous.

Indeed, in Trollope's world of active politics, too much integrity threatens failure as certainly as, in its own way, too little integrity. The over-fine conscience faces two kinds of threats: one, the compromises necessary to act politically with others of perhaps somewhat different beliefs; and two, the intellectual resignation necessary to choose an action on issues about which one genuinely sees the force of contrary arguments. The 'independent' citizen may suffer from both kinds of compromise, as does Trollope's most complex political figure, Plantagenet Palliser. Trollope had thought much about the uselessness of over-fine scruples and intellect, partly because these were key themes of a book by his close friend and member of Parliament Charles *Buxton. The book, *Ideas of the Day on Policy* (1865), is a curious, bravely even-handed inventory of the primary 'ideas' about each important issue of 1865. Buxton concludes about the dangers of such intellectual open-mindedness, 'The continual endeavour to look at both sides of each question . . . might easily give the habit of wavering that would be fatal to success and utility. Such a man might sink at last into that mood, wherein the poisonous sentiment grows rank, that "There's nothing true, and it's no matter" ' (*Ideas of the Day*, 10–11). Trollope's review of his friend's book in the *Fortnightly* entered deeply into the experience of failure of the 'impracticable man' who may seem 'a black sheep not only to others, but to himself', because he is doomed to 'vacillate with a pendulous motion that has in it more of honesty than doubt' (*Fortnightly Review* (15 January 1866), 650). Trollope could as well be describing the Palliser who leads a coalition government in *The Prime Minister* for three years, and achieves triumphs of inaction.

What many contemporary readers remembered about the world of professional politics in Trollope was the clash of personalities familiar from the newspapers and history books. The political drama, on and off the parliamentary stage, seemed to have a cast of characters, from radical manufacturer Turnbull, to the elderly statesman De Terrier, the wily Conservative leader Daubeny, and the Liberal Gresham, that required only minimal translation into their historical counterparts Bright, Derby, Disraeli, or Gladstone. (See POLITICIANS AS CHARACTERS IN TROLLOPE'S NOVELS.) But beyond their *roman-à-clef* reception, Trollope's political stories seemed 'real' in their portrait of shifting alliances, betrayals, inflated self-importance, and rhetorical bombast in Britain's most powerful political circles, and real in the way they drew links between the public and the private, between the salons of powerful women like Lady Glencora and the exercise of power, and between perceptions of reality and representations in media organs like Quintus Slide's *People's Banner*.

As Trollope's age recedes into history, the deeper conflicts about power and privilege behind the salons and the personalities have taken centre stage for most students of Trollope. His most characteristic effect is his Buxton-like ability to look at all sides of these conflicts, especially because in his fiction Trollope always took pleasure from entering into multiple points of view. As Ruth apRoberts puts it, 'It is Trollope's art to be advocate for each one of his characters; he makes the best case possible for one, and then juxtaposes this with the demands of the other, defended with a similar passionate sympathy' (*Trollope: Artist and Moralist* (1971), 53).

One fundamental question about power and class in Trollope's fiction is, who or what is a gentleman? The question is so important because it spotlights quintessentially Victorian issues of class boundaries and class mobility. Sometimes 'gentleman' in Trollope is a moral concept, and sometimes it is a social category. Aristocratic or gentry lineage may increase the likelihood that a character will be a gentleman in the ethical sense, but it is no guarantee, as Lord Rufford in *The American Senator* demonstrates. Furthermore, is it enough to be a gentleman, and enough for what? When his daughter Mary wishes to marry the commoner Tregear, whom she calls 'a gentleman', Plantagenet Palliser protests in *The Duke's Children*, 'There is not a clerk in one of our public offices who does not consider himself to be a gentleman. . . . The word is too vague to carry with it any meaning that ought to be serviceable to you in thinking of such a matter.' To which Mary replies, 'I do not know any other way of dividing people' (VIII). To be a gentleman is and is not enough for the Pallisers.

Trollope's characteristic tension between old and new is well illustrated by the intense debate over class between Daniel Thwaite and Sir William Patterson in chapter XLVII of *Lady Anna*. Sir William praises Daniel's innate qualities, as if being born a tailor were a kind of mistake, or a test of Daniel's gentlemanly essence. 'By your good fortune and merit, if you will allow me to say so, you have travelled from one pole very far towards the other.' But Daniel will not be flattered or seduced. 'I like my own pole a deal the best, Sir William,' and when Sir William advises him, 'Do not allow yourself to despise that condition of society which it is the ambition of all men to enter,' Daniel replies, 'It is not my ambition.' Sir William then appeals to a meritocratic notion of class. 'Lords have been made lords in nine cases out of ten for good work done by them for the benefit of their country,' but again Daniel resists. 'Why should the children of lords be such to the tenth and twentieth generation?' So far all the best lines in the debate are Daniel's.

But Sir William's trump card for class hierarchy and the gentleman is a gender card. Daniel should accept 'the position which your wife's wealth and your own acquirements will give you', because 'it will show a higher manliness in you'. And Daniel is persuaded: 'He began to believe that it would be more manly to do as he was advised.' Daniel acquiesces to social convention in the name of an ethical ideal which transcends class (if not gender), and yet epitomizes the old virtues of Sir William's élite. So Trollope gets to have his class politics both ways: he honours Daniel's pride as a working man, yet Daniel somehow fulfils that pride by rising in class identity; and Trollope allows his tailor a place within the privileged which he also owes to good luck and to the wisdom of the privileged to admit him. These contradictions about class are exactly the work of an 'advanced, but still conservative liberal'. Social convention and moral judgement work together to critique both radical notions of simple equality and the deeper injustices of class privilege.

'Equality' as a political goal is in Trollope's fiction a dangerous dream, and also a kind of moral ideal. These conflicting elements shape the contrast between the young Duke, Plantagenet Palliser, and the old Duke, St Bungay, in *The Prime Minister*. Palliser admits, 'Equality would be a heaven, if we could attain it. How can we to whom so much has been given dare to think otherwise'; and a few pages later the narrator interprets St Bungay's thoughts, occasioned by a new reform of the franchise, 'There must surely have been a shade of melancholy on that old man's mind as, year after year, he assisted in pulling down institutions which he in truth regarded as the safeguards of the nation;—but which he knew that, as a Liberal, he was bound to assist in destroying!' (LXVIII). Reform of the franchise is a political and ethical good in Trollope's fiction, and yet the old system of patronage has its benefits too, as Trollope shows when Phineas is given a seat in Parliament in *Phineas Finn*.

Other issues of social justice are also complicated in Trollope's fiction. Women's rights, for example, are the target of satire in *He Knew He Was Right* and *Is He Popenjoy?* Trollope's narrator said of the feminist Wallachia Petrie that she had not learned 'to read human nature aright' (*HKWR*, LXXXI). And Trollope gave a lecture in his various tours around provincial England in the 1860s and 1870s called 'The *Higher Education of Women' in which, while endorsing greater access to schooling, he argued for 'natural' boundaries for women's lives. Trollope did not like the campaign for women's suffrage. Yet in his novels Trollope renders women's experiences of disadvantage and vindictive male power with profound feeling. *He Knew He Was Right* does caricature Wallachia Petrie, but in Louis Trevelyan it also draws a devastating picture of male obsession with mastery over women. Equally importantly, Trollope creates intelligent, powerful women whose ability to act in the world is limited by convention and other people's assumptions, limits to which they in the Trollopian way often accede. Caroline Spalding, in the same *He Knew He Was Right*, and Isabel Boncassen in *The Duke's Children*, and Glencora throughout the Palliser series are examples of these Trollopian women.

To understand Trollope's politics, readers always need to distinguish between Trollope's narrator and his characters. Trollope for example has often been accused of some degree of anti-Semitism. One of Trollope's special talents as a storyteller is his ability to enter various minds and present them fully, with judgement sometimes suggested only indirectly. So Trollope gives his readers sympathetically specific accounts of characters with 'liberal' and 'conservative' views. He also relays to readers the operations of minds engaging in anti-Semitic judgements, when for example Georgiana Longestaffe thinks, in *The Way We Live Now*, 'She could have plucked up courage to face the world as the Jew's wife, but not as the young woman who had wanted to marry the Jew and had failed' (LXXIX). But it becomes clear how cruel Georgiana's thoughts are 'even' to Trollope when the reader sets her words beside the warm and deeply insightful letters of 'the Jew' who has proposed to her. Understanding politics in these novels requires an eye for literary and dramatic structure.

Political issues loom large, then, in Trollope's fiction. Interpreting them, and Trollope's interpretation of them, is not easy, because art reshapes the historical realities of Trollope's time and the views Trollope expressed in his own voice outside his novels. Trollope's art as a political novelist was to weave a rich tapestry of political consciousnesses, of people wrestling with enormously complex experiences and issues of privilege, power, and justice that were specifically, but not only, Victorian.   GB

Butte, George, 'Trollope's Duke of Omnium and "The Pain of History": A Study of the Novelist's Politics', *Victorian Studies* (winter 1981), 209–27.
Halperin, John, *Trollope and Politics* (1977).
Tracy, Robert, *Trollope's Later Novels* (1978).

politicians as characters in Trollope's novels. Trollope was deeply interested in politics, and so politicians figure both as protagonists (Phineas Finn, Plantagenet Palliser) and as minor characters in many of his novels. Even if Trollope's more profound political interests focused

on abiding problems of power and privilege, of hierarchy and community, he was nevertheless fascinated by the complexities of parliamentary politics, especially in the novels written in the turbulent decades of the 1860s and 1870s.

Politicians appear as several kinds of characters in Trollope. They are major and minor figures in their novels; and they are, arguably, more or less fictional. The minor figures who might be versions of famous Victorian politicians have occasioned the most disagreement among historical scholars. Certainly by the publication of *Phineas Finn* (serialized between October 1867 and May 1869) many contemporary readers approached each of Trollope's political novels as a *roman-à-clef*. National political figures had appeared around the edges of Trollope's novels almost from the beginning, as in *Framley Parsonage*'s Prime Ministers Brock and De Terrier. But political activity looms larger as Trollope's novels (and his readers) move through the Second Reform Bill crisis, and *Phineas Finn* was roundly condemned by a leader in the *Daily Telegraph* (31 March 1869) for drawing only slightly veiled portraits of living politicians with a 'malignant' touch. Trollope responded immediately, denying emphatically any such intentions. One accusation of the *Daily Telegraph* clearly touched a nerve in Trollope, because he quotes it in a letter: 'Is it gentlemanlike to paint portraits thus?' Trollope agrees that to do so is 'neither gentlemanlike nor right', and asserts his intention to draw characters so that 'no likeness should be found in our own political circles' (*Letters* 1, 468).

Trollope critics have read his self-defence as disingenuous, even a conscious lie, as self-deception, or in some sense true. The *Daily Telegraph*'s particular topic was the character of the radical manufacturer Turnbull, who seemed to resemble John Bright. Turnbull's character is dissimilar from Bright's in some ways: for example, he refuses on principle to join a government, whereas Bright was a member of several cabinets, and was head of the Board of Trade when Trollope wrote his letter. But the similarities are also significant: Turnbull's 'free trade in everything except malt', for instance, might remind Trollope's reader of Bright the Quaker and temperance campaigner (A. O. J. Cockshut, *Anthony Trollope* (1955), 244).

A similar pattern of differences within resemblances marks the other topical portraits. Mildmay and Brock and De Terrier are similar to Palmerston and Russell and Derby, and yet discrepancies crop up, especially when readers fit Trollope's plots into history. In *Phineas Finn*, for example, reform is accomplished by a Liberal, not a Conservative government. The characters who most seem to point outside the novels to history are the Liberal and Conservative Prime Ministers Gresham and Daubeny. Trollope's names are too similar to Gladstone and Disraeli for a reader to find 'no likeness' in them.

The Daubeny–Disraeli link is the closest of Trollope's apparently topical politicians. Trollope deeply distrusted Disraeli, as his essays for *Saint Pauls* and *An Autobiography* attest. Daubeny has the same traits Trollope saw in Disraeli: absence of principle, wily charm, and a capacity for machiavellian manœuvring. The Daubeny of *Phineas Redux*, who proposes to disestablish the Church, is the Disraeli Trollope saw in the Second Reform Bill crisis: a Conservative willing to out-Liberal the Liberals to gain power. Trollope's narrator speaks of him in *Phineas Redux* as 'this audacious Cagliostro among statesmen, this destructive leader of all declared Conservatives' (XIII). Still, it is worth remembering that a similarity is not an identity. *Could* Disraeli have really proposed to disestablish the English Church? Not all observers think Disraeli was that unprincipled.

Quarrelling over the degree of reference to specific historical figures in Trollope's politicians can obscure the larger point. Unless a reader approaches Trollope's fiction *for* historical information, the novels function as witty, formally sophisticated narratives about political and social conflict. Of course they draw on people and issues of Trollope's day. All of his politicians are to some degree composites, and some are closer to a particular original than others. Tracing Trollope's sources, and linking his stories to events of the 1860s and 1870s, have one valuable result: they remove any doubts about Trollope's understanding of professional politics and his substantial political intelligence.

Other minor characters are historical in only a general sense, and are some of Trollope's best creations: lesser members of Parliament, the party hacks, the hangers-on, the election agents, the newspaper people. In Barrington Erle, Mr Ratler and Mr Roby, Mr Trigger, and Quintus Slide, for example, Trollope vividly creates the network of auxiliary relations radiating out from the centre of power. Most of these characters and their mini-plots are comic examples of Trollope's prevalent sense that politics is a game, most of whose players (and certainly the minor ones) have no principled stake in the game's outcomes. The comedy can be more or less humorous, of course. Early in *Phineas Finn* Mr Ratler is sure that Sir Everard Powell is dead: 'And then he rubbed his hands, and looked as though he was delighted. And he was delighted—not because his old friend Sir Everard was dead, but by the

excitement of the tragedy' (VIII). But by the second volume of *Phineas Redux*, the rumour mill's effects are much more painful.

The last group of politicians is the group of major characters, who also may be more or less fictional. Despite links to particular historical figures, however, these figures are generally more fictional, because of the richness of their inner lives. Generally their political and private lives are paralleled and compared, as Trollope develops his complex narratives. Politics and romance, politics and marriage, politics and children: these topics propel the stories of Phineas Finn and Marie Goesler, and of Plantagenet Palliser, Glencora, and their children.   GB

Cockshut, Anthony, 'The Political Novels and History', in *Anthony Trollope* (1955).
Dinwiddy, J. R., 'Who's Who in Trollope's Political Novels', *NCF* (June 1967), 31–47.
Halperin, John, *Trollope and Politics* (1977).

politics, Trollope and. Trollope was keenly interested in politics throughout his life, as a sharp observer of political affairs, as a friend to politicians, as a political journalist, and as a candidate for Parliament in 1868. The subject of his political interests ranged from the specifics of party conflict, to parliamentary campaigns for (and against) the ballot or Irish tenants' rights or reform of the civil service, to broader 'condition of England' questions such as the role of tradition and the aristocracy, and such philosophical issues as the merits of Carlylism and Caesarism. Trollope's years at the Post Office immersed him in other kinds of politics, both institutional and international, as he came to travel the world to negotiate postal agreements.

Trollope's political experiences and beliefs point toward two fundamental conflicts, between the ideal and the useful, and between change and tradition. The quarrel among Trollope's critics over his relative conservatism or liberalism hinges on their reading of his struggle with these conflicts. Trollope claimed to be 'rational' in his politics, but his special talent, in fiction as well as politics, was his feeling for the irrational (*Auto* XVI). His characteristic political heroes, from Cicero to Plantagenet Palliser to his close friend Charles *Buxton, were often nearly paralysed between the demands of the old and the new, of tradition and the need for new kinds of social justice. They also suffered from the need to act on ideals in a very imperfect world.

Trollope's most vivid political experience immersed him in that imperfect world, where political ideals almost seemed an illusion. This experience was his campaign to be elected member of Parliament for Beverley, capital of the West Riding of Yorkshire, in October 1868. Trollope's motives for this effort reflect his archetypal conflict between the ideal and the real. He certainly believed in the value of political dedication: 'to serve one's country without pay is the grandest work that a man can do'; but Trollope's 'ambition' was also coloured by pride and more mortal expectations of status conferred. A fundamental motive, he confessed, was a 'jeer' at his expense, levelled some 35 years earlier by an uncle who responded to the young Trollope's dream of parliamentary service, 'Few clerks in the Post Office had become Members of Parliament' (*Auto* XVI). How Trollopian is this coexistence of motives, the yearning for class validation and the desire to be of service.

The story of Trollope's campaign for office at Beverley is full of sad and comic ironies. Trollope originally volunteered in 1867 to stand as a Liberal for a safe Conservative seat in Essex, so that the Conservatives would be required to spend some money on their member. Trollope was to spend some £2,000, 'absolutely in vain', he said (*Auto* XVI). In the event there was no dissolution of Parliament in 1867, and no election; but under a redistribution of seats, Essex had a new, apparently Liberal division, for which Trollope thought he had earned the right to be candidate. But this plum was too attractive to give to a novice, and a seasoned Liberal politician became the candidate (and was elected) for South Essex when the anticipated election did occur, in 1868. Trollope had received a vivid lesson in party politics.

Trollope was then resigned to playing the same role at Beverley, of dutiful party servant with little hope of success. He recounts the words of his election agent: ' "O no!" continued he, with good-humoured raillery, "You won't get in. I don't suppose you really expect it. But there is a fine career open to you. You will spend £1,000, and lose the election. Then you will petition, and spend another £1,000. You will throw out the elected members. There will be a commission, and the borough will be disenfranchised. For a beginner such as you are, that will be a great success" ' (*Auto* XVI). In fact the agent, W. S. Hind, was correct; the borough of some 2,100 electors was thoroughly rotten, with some 800 to 1,000 bribes of fifteen to twenty shillings changing hands. Trollope's victory, when Beverley was disenfranchised in 1869, after about 600 years of parliamentary representation, was not as quixotic as some of Plantagenet Palliser's, and Trollope admitted this outcome 'was to a certain extent a satisfaction' (*Auto* XVI). But Trollope's two weeks as a candidate in Beverley were still miserable, 'the most wretched fortnight of my manhood' (*Auto* XVI). He despised the experience in almost every way. He was cold and wet, walking through the grey October streets, talking to voters who knew him not, and cared even less for what he had to say. Politics here was not about ideas or policies, or even Trollope's possibilities as a representative. Politics was local with a vengeance. 'I had been brought to Beverley to either beat Sir Henry Edwards,—which, however, no one probably thought to be feasible,—or to cause him the greatest amount of trouble, inconvenience, and expense' (*Auto* XVI).

Trollope campaigned as a Liberal and a loyal follower of Gladstone, especially over disestablishment of the Irish (Protestant) Church, which he called 'that monstrous anomaly' (John Halperin, *Trollope and Politics* (1977), 120). But Trollope staked out his own line too, both to the left of the Liberals and to the right. On education he called for new, almost 'American' rights: 'I do not desire to Americanize our English institutions; but I do want to see a system of education established by which every man, woman, and child, and the poorest of the land, may be benefited by it' (from the *Beverley Recorder*, cited by Halperin, 121). Yet Trollope opposed his party on the ballot, and on regulation of public drinking, the two issues of most interest to Beverley Liberals. Trollope found his own voice and maintained a significant integrity in the trenches.

Two specific ironies about Trollope's Beverley experience are significant. According to N. John Hall, the Liberal side was in fact the more popular, and Trollope probably would have won if the ballot had been secret, so that the electors who had already taken bribes would have been able to vote their convictions anyway (Hall 326). The first irony is that Trollope was more popular than he thought, and the second is that he had always opposed the secret ballot, which was to take effect in 1872.

Trollope's experience at Beverley darkened his political outlook, but did not alter its fundamental paradoxes and ironies. His contradictory liberalism gained a deeper sense of the intransigence of those conflicts between tradition and change, and between different understandings of the social good. Trollope also came to see 'real' politics as the action of political parties with only a veneer of ideological principle. Furthermore, he had always suspected that a subtle ethical sensibility was ill suited to the rough and tumble business of the world, whether it was Mr Harding's management of a clerical institution or Plantagenet Palliser's management of the national treasury, and Beverley confirmed those suspicions. In the 1870s Trollope's fiction emphasized experiences of paralysis between conflicting social values and institutions, as in the coalition government of *The Prime Minister*, and Lady

Lovel's self-punishing opposition to her daughter's marriage in *Lady Anna*.

Trollope's other encounters with politics might seem more tangential than Beverley, but they probably taught him more. His peripatetic life with the Post Office thrust him into a wide array of political environments, from Ireland in the 1840s, to the United States during the Civil War, to the West Indies and South Africa. The Post Office itself taught him about institutional politics, as he ascended through its ranks to lose at the end when, as in South Essex, he was passed over for the reward (the assistant secretaryship) he thought he had earned. The Post Office also placed him on the stage of international diplomacy, in a modest way, as he negotiated not only postal treaties, but in 1868 was asked to work with the Americans on international copyright during his months in Washington.

Trollope then was a public man in arenas far removed, or at least removed, from his novels. His life as a journalist, for example, also connected him to a world of political ideas and influence. Writing is a kind of political action, and Trollope often sought out opportunities to speak about issues of the day, as in 1850 when he proposed to the *Examiner* that he publish several articles based on his years in Ireland about the conditions which the New Poor Law and the Encumbered Estates Bill sought to address. Later, as one of the founders of the important *Fortnightly*, and at his own less successful monthly magazine, *Saint Pauls*, Trollope continued to write about current issues. He even took to the lecture circuit around the country in the 1860s and 1870s, discussing the American Civil War, higher education for women, and 'Politics as a Daily Study for the Common People'.

Characterizing the political outlook of this multi-faceted man, with such a wide-ranging career, is not easy. In *An Autobiography* Trollope described himself as 'an advanced, but still a conservative liberal', and it is this position which he considered 'not only as a possible but a rational and consistent phase of political existence' (XVI). The complications of 'advanced, but still conservative' apply to most aspects of Trollope's Gladstonian liberalism. With characteristic generosity he admitted, for example, to a Tory as well as a Liberal idealism: 'The Tory would always wish to be bountiful to those below him; whereas the Liberal would fain give nothing in bounty, but would enable him who wants to earn all in justice' (*Saint Pauls* (October 1867), 541–2). Trollope supported electoral reform, for example, and criticized Carlyle's polemics against the Second Reform Bill, and yet honoured the political aristocracy of both Whigs and Tories. He disliked

Disraeli deeply for what to Trollope was a lack of principle which dishonoured a noble Conservative tradition. Trollope was pleased to see Beverley disenfranchised, but also felt the tradition of influence of the dukes of Omnium at Silverbridge was not pernicious. Trollope had a sympathy unusual in Victorian England for the disempowered in Ireland, and he supported measures of relief (a bill in Parliament in 1850 to redistribute property of incompetent landlords) and the disestablishment of the Irish Church. Yet he could not move beyond the givens of an essentially colonial framework.

Issues of privilege always brought to the surface Trollope's contradictory commitments. Aristocratic class traditions appealed deeply to Trollope, and yet he knew the costs of maintaining those traditions, not only because, as Plantagenet Palliser said in *The Prime Minister*, 'We know that power does corrupt, and that we cannot trust kings to have loving hearts, and clear intellects, and noble instincts', but also because the ancient class dispensations ignored the virtues and claims of ordinary people (LXVIII). In the conclusion of *North America* Trollope imagined eloquently what life free of those class concepts must feel like to an immigrant: '[The American] assumes a dignity which he never has known before. . . . It seems to me that such a man must feel himself half a god, if he has the power of comparing what he is with what he was. . . . they do not crouch to the ground for halfpence. If poor, they are not abject in their poverty. They read and write. They walk like human beings made in God's form' (*NA* 2, XVI).

Other challenges to privilege also left Trollope with divided feelings. He did not like the women's suffrage movement, yet he strongly supported greater access to education (including higher education) for women. He supported reform of the franchise, but disliked the secret ballot intensely, believing in an ideal republic in which any honourable British man would be proud to declare his vote publicly. But the contradictions of Trollope's 'advanced, yet conservative liberalism' are deeply consistent with the temperament of Trollope the novelist, drawn to political paradoxes large and small in characters, social classes, and political institutions.   GB

Hall, N. John, *Trollope: A Biography* (1991).
Halperin, John, *Trollope and Politics* (1977).
Letwin, Shirley, *The Gentleman in Trollope: Individuality and Moral Conduct* (1982).

'Politics as a Daily Study for Common People' (lecture). 'Common people' includes everyone except professional politicians. The more politically knowledgeable people are, the better public life becomes; the study should be as popular as novel-reading, among both men and women. Valid opinions, good decisions depend on citizens' knowledge. *Leeds Mercury* (19 February 1864), 3. AKL

Pollington, small town in Essex where the Shand family lives and where John Caldigate prepares for his journey to Australia with his friend Dick Shand. *JC* SRB

Pollock, Lady Juliet Creed (d. 1899), wife of Sir William Pollock; wrote children's stories and a biography of Charles Macready. In *An Autobiography*, Trollope lists her among regular writers for *Saint Pauls* (XV). Her articles included 'Fashion in Poetry' (March 1868), 'Jane Austen' (March 1870), 'M. Victor Hugo's England' (July 1869), a lengthy review of Hugo's *L'Homme qui rit* that castigated the French author and his work, doubtless to Trollope's delight. Lady Pollock told Henry Taylor in 1869 how Trollope, fresh from reading Gerald Griffin's murder story *The Collegians* (1829), met a priest in Killarney whose cousin was the murderer on whom that story was based; 'and I stood on the steps of the scaffold when he was hung'. From his telling of the incident, reported Lady Pollock, it was clear it had proved 'a painful moment' (*I & R* 92). RCT

Pollock, Mr, rider at the Edgehill hunt described as a 'heavy-weight sporting literary gentleman'. Pollock's lifestyle—staying up late to write and rising early for the hunt—as well as his name suggest that this character is modelled after Trollope himself. *CYFH* JMR

Pollock, Walter Herries (1850–1926), miscellaneous writer and critic, editor of the *Saturday Review* (1883–94); son of Lord and Lady Pollock, close friends of the Trollopes; one of several young writers Trollope encouraged. His memorial to Trollope in *Harper's New Monthly Magazine* (May 1883) emphasized Trollope's modesty and geniality, his wide-ranging intellect and strong passions, and his inventiveness and sensitivity as an author. Towards those younger than himself, he noted that Trollope showed no superiority, but spoke 'as between comrade and comrade' (*I & R* 198). When Pollock married, Trollope sent him a batch of Elizabethan plays, saying; 'When you have read them all and thoroughly digested them, so as to be able to answer satisfactorily all questions as to plot, language, character, and customs, I will send you some more' (*Letters* 2, 677). RCT

Pollock, Sir William Frederick (1815–88), called to the bar (1838); Queen's Remembrancer (1874–86); translator of Dante's *Divine Comedy*

(1854); author of *Personal Remembrances* (1887) which frequently mentions Trollope, friend and neighbour at Montagu Square, London. Visiting him in January 1867 Trollope came down to breakfast cheerily after work on the current novel (*PF*) and declared: 'I have just been making my twenty-seventh proposal of marriage' (*Chron* 67–8). Pollock was among those who helped Trollope when legal points needed clarifying for a story. In his memoirs Pollock described Trollope's methodical way of writing novels, adding that his manuscripts were 'entirely free from alterations or additions'. Asked to correct proofs of *The Golden Lion of Granpère*, he found 'there was really nothing for me to do'. Trollope's writing, he claimed, flowed effortlessly from his pen 'like clear liquor from a tap' (*I & R* 91). When Trollope suffered his fatal stroke in 1883, Pollock enquired after him daily. RCT

Polpenno, Frank Tregear's home borough for which he successfully stands as a Conservative parliamentary candidate. *DC* JMR

Polwenning, seat of Frank Tregear's father, close to the borough of Polpenno. *DC* JMR

Polyeuka mine, gold mine in New South Wales owned by Timothy Crinkett and John Caldigate, and from which Caldigate made his fortune. *JC* SRB

Pomfret, John, narrator, now happily married to Maria Daguilar. Pomfret tells how on the way to Seville to propose to her he and his friend unwittingly insulted the Marquis d'Almavivas. 'Bull' *TAC1* GRH

Pook, Mr, trainer who looks after Lord Silverbridge's racehorse Prime Minister. Mr Pook is an honest man, innocent of the plot to lame the horse before the St Leger. *DC* JMR

Pope, Agnes, servant of Farmer Trumbull, believed to have revealed whereabouts of her master's money to his murderer. *VB* RCT

Pope, Alexander (1688–1744), poet and critic famed for satiric works such as *The Rape of the Lock* (1714) and *The Dunciad* (1728). Trollope was fond of quoting 'Whatever is, is right' from *Essay on Man* (1732–4). A favourite expression 'leather and prunella' from that work occurs in *Phineas Finn, He Knew He Was Right, The Way We Live Now,* and *Kept in the Dark*. In *The New Zealander* Trollope listed Pope among eighteen major figures of English literature. An unusually lengthy entry in his Commonplace Book (1834) attacked Pope's 'presumption' in *The Essay on Man* in trying to justify the ways of God to man, but apologized for 'pitching on so beautiful—so popular—so deep—and so powerful a poem as this' (*Letters* 2, 1026). Pope's translation of the *Iliad* and the *Odyssey* formed part of Trollope's evening readings to his family.   RCT

Popenjoy, Lord, son of Frederick Augustus, Marquis of Brotherton, and the Italian Marchioness. The legitimacy of this infant provides the novel's title and his death renders the unanswered question moot. His existence serves as a litmus test for the other characters' sensibilities. Only his father and Lady George Germain express any regret at his death. *IHP*   MG

Popenjoy, Lord Frederick Augustus Tallowax. Born after the death of his uncle Frederick Augustus and his cousin Lord Popenjoy, he is an undisputed Lord Popenjoy. The birth of this heir to the Brotherton titles and estates fulfils the ambitions of both his maternal and paternal relatives. *IHP*   MG

Popham Villa, Fulham villa of the Underwoods. 'Unpretentious, containing two sitting-rooms besides a small side closet . . . the drawing-room . . . opening on to the lawn . . . giving a near view of the bright river as it flowed by, with just a glimpse of the bridge' (II). *RH*
    ALS

Poppins, Polly, formerly Miss Twizzle, sharp-tongued friend of Maryanne Brown who marries Thomas Poppins and tries to keep him in order. *SBJR*   RCT

Poppins, Thomas, friend and confidant of George Robinson despite being opposed to the ways of commerce. *SBJR*   RCT

Popplecourt, Lord, nobleman selected by the Duke of Omnium to wed his daughter Lady Mary Palliser. Though young Lord Popplecourt is dim-witted, he is sharp enough to see that Lady Mary loves another and wisely declines to struggle for the prize of her heart. *DC*   JMR

Porlock, Lord, often-mentioned but seldom seen eldest son of Earl De Courcy, whom he hates and never meets, and the Countess De Courcy, who regards him as her favourite. A slight, sickly, worn-out looking man with something of his father's hardness but none of his ferocity, he nevertheless sues his father over his allowance, and marries to produce an heir and spite his ne'er-do-well brothers. *SHA, DT* NCS

Porter, Mrs Mary (née **Blackwood**), author of *Annals of a Publishing House* (1898), a loyal account of the Blackwood firm by the daughter of John Blackwood, Trollope's closest friend among publishers. Mrs Porter's recollections of many unforgettable visits emphasize Trollope's geniality. She also stressed that his playfulness included assaults on cherished articles of Blackwood faith, such as devotion to the Queen. Other topics for teasing his host included the Conservative Party and Disraeli. Trollope delighted in 'his blasphemies against the "Blackwood faith" ' (*I & R* 95).   RCT

Port Glasgow, small Scottish town, represented in Parliament by the Honourable Septimus Traffick. *AA*   WK

portraits and photographs. The only picture of Trollope in youth is an undistinguished work by *Hervieu, painted in 1832 when Anthony was 17. It is in the National Portrait Gallery, as is the major portrait, a sepia sketch commissioned by the publisher George *Smith. The artist, Samuel Laurence, found his subject difficult to draw, but the result Trollope declared 'done to the life, in a wonderfully vigorous manner' . . . & not a bit more solid than the original' (*Letters* 1, 285). A portrait by Henry *O'Neill is in the Garrick Club. O'Neill's painting *Forty-three Members in the Billiard Room of the Garrick Club*, executed in 1869, shows Trollope in the top row fourth from the left. A drawing by T. Walter Wilson, 'A Memorable Whist Party at the Athenaeum', depicts Trollope with three friends at cards. Millais made a pencil sketch of the author in 1878. He is shown in several sketches by Jemima Blackburn in *How the 'Mastiffs' Went to Iceland* (1878).

Trollope wrote in 1876, 'I *hate* sitting for a photograph'; two years later, he said, 'I do not like photographs, and dislike my own worse than all others.' Earlier he had said, 'Some people wont [*sic*] come out well. Mine are always wretched.' The long time holding a pose required by the new process was agony, and explains the strained, irritable look in most pictures. Of one by Herbert Watkins of Regent Street, taken in April 1860, he commented 'It looks uncommon feirce [*sic*], as that of a dog about to bite; but that I fear is the nature of the animal portrayed' (*Letters* 1, 101). One of the earliest photographs shows him standing hatless in long black coat and pepper and salt trousers. At about age 40 he is already very bald (see p. 539). Another photograph, taken in Florence, shows him with his brother Tom, who is gazing intently at him with a somewhat incredulous air. Sending a copy to a relative, in June 1864, Trollope commented, 'You will perceive that my brother is pitching into me. He always did' (*Letters* 1, 268) (see p. 555). Elliott & Fry's portrait (*c*.1867), taken in the company's Baker Street studio, shows him seated and looking thoughtful. The following year Napoleon Sarony of New York has him in characteristic pose, full-length with hands on hips frowning with concentration (see p. 598). Julia Cameron's artistry with the camera caught him effectively in October 1864. Another expressive head and shoulders (1877) has a softness in the eyes not usually conveyed. He was photographed by the Stereoscopic Co. of Regent Street, Lock & Whitfield, and others (see *Letters* 2, 682; 2, 786; 2, 675; 1, 101). A study of contemporary writers, which included Trollope with Carlyle, Thackeray, Collins, Dickens, and others, was made in 1876, reprinted in Greville MacDonald, *George MacDonald and his Wife* (1924). A late photograph shows him with a small cheroot in his mouth, his beard now white and fuller than ever. His son Harry thought it perfectly conveyed his father. Another atmospheric full-length study shows him in light flat hat and leaning on a cane with the look of a mariner uncomfortably ashore, an impression heightened by voluminous bell-bottomed trousers. The pictures overall justify many descriptions of the novelist looking like a country squire or farmer. One of the best photographic portraits appeared in the collection 'Men of Mark' 3rd series (1878) and is often reproduced. Many of the photographs are in the Morris L. Parrish Collection at Princeton.   RCT

Portray Castle, the magnificent if somewhat modern Scottish retreat belonging to the Eustace family. After her husband dies, Lizzie Eustace is left with a life interest in the place. She pretends to read Shelley near the seashore and entertains her dubiously respectable friends. *ED*   JMR

Portsmouth, port city in Hampshire; birthplace of Mrs Baggett, whose husband still resides there. *OML*   RC

Possitt, Mr, young, ingratiating low-church curate at Perivale. Every Sunday between services, he dines at the home of Mrs Winterfield, who always gives him 'two glasses of her best port wine to support him' (VIII). He is deprived of this invigoration when Mrs Winterfield dies. *BE*   WK

Postal Museum, National. Trollope's thirty-three years' devoted service is celebrated at the museum in the former London Chief Post Office in King Edward Street, EC1A 1LP, near St Paul's Cathedral. The exhibit focuses on what Trollope recalled with pride in *An Autobiography* as the chief pleasures in his official life: 'That the public in little villages should be enabled to buy postage-stamps; that they should have their letters delivered free and at an early hour; that pillar letter-boxes should be put up for them', and that letter-carriers should earn their pay and that their working conditions should be improved (XV). The museum displays the portable desk Trollope used on his journeys around Britain, and the signature stamp he had made to save writing his name on every document. There are also several examples of the kind of pillar box Trollope recommended in November 1851 for trial use in the Channel Islands. In a report to his superior George Creswell, Surveyor of the Western District, on England, Trollope suggested that St Helier, Jersey, would be most suitable, since postage stamps were readily available throughout the town; 'all that is wanted is a safe receptacle for letters'. He thought iron posts could be placed at street corners or, better still, iron letter boxes about five feet from the ground where suitable permanently built walls could be found. The free-standing box adopted was at first hexagonal, coloured green. Four prototypes were tried out in Jersey and three more in St Peter Port, Guernsey, one of which is in Union Street. Another box of the earliest type stands at Barnes Cross, Sherborne, Dorset, and is still in use. Jemima Stanbury, in *He Knew He Was Right*, carried her letters to Exeter's chief post office. 'As for the iron pillar boxes which had been erected . . . she had not the faintest belief that any letter put into them would ever reach its destination' (VIII). Frank Greystock posts his letter proposing marriage to Lucy Morris in a pillar box in Fleet Street. Trollope observes that it remains there over Sunday, but that it appears on Monday's breakfast table, thanks to the 'accuracy in the performance of its duties for which [the Post Office] is conspicuous among all offices' (XV). Trollope is also drawing on fond memories when he has Mrs Crump, the postmistress at Allington, angry at being inspected and threatened with dismissal. 'Discharged the sarvice! Tuppence farden a day. So I told 'un to discharge hisself, and all the old bundles and things upon his shoulders. Letters indeed!' (*SHA* LX).   RCT

Postlecott, Mr, clerk who is fifth on the list for compulsory euthanasia. His melancholy dread of the event is enhanced by the responses of the four before him: Crasweller's stoical reluctance, Barne's mental breakdown, Tallowax's threats of violent resistance, and Exor's insistence on legal revision. *FixP*   SRB

Postlethwaite, Matilda, one of the Shand daughters who comments on John Caldigate's ability to love several young women all at the same time. *JC*   SRB

Pott, Mr, unremarkable young gentleman of fortune 'against whom very little can be alleged' (IX). Under the charge of his tutor, the clergyman Mr Cruse, he joins Miss Todd's picnic to the Valley of Jehoshaphat while on the Jerusalem leg of his 'grand tour'. *B*   MRS

Among Trollope's best-known services to the Post Office was his role in establishing pillar letter boxes. Experimental ones like this were tried in the Channel Islands in 1852 and rapidly transformed the letter-delivery system throughout the country.

Pottery Hamlets, 'radical' borough, possibly intended to portray London's 'Tower Hamlets'. The subject of some confusion, Pottery Hamlets is one of two boroughs supposed to be represented in Parliament by Joshua Monk, the other being West Bromwich. *PF*　　　　JMR

Pountney, Major, guest at Gatherum Castle who proposes himself to the Duke of Omnium as a parliamentary candidate for the borough of Silverbridge, much to the Duke's discomfiture. The Major's impertinence results in his being expelled from the house and hails the end of the Duchess's hospitality at Gatherum. *PM*　　JMR

poverty was still viewed by many Victorians as part of God's plan: 'The poor are always with us,' says the Bible. In recognition of this a national welfare provision called the poor law had been in existence since Elizabethan times. A local tax, the poor rate, was levied on all land, and its proceeds were devoted to relieving the poor. Until 1834 this had been a local responsibility, independently administered at the parish level. A popular form of assistance in agricultural areas was outdoor relief, in which payments from the poor law became subsidies for low wages. In response to complaints by economists and others that such practices distorted the labour market and muddied the crucial distinction between the able-bodied poor and those who were poor through disability, old age, or orphanhood, Parliament drastically overhauled the system in 1834.

The New Poor Law consolidated the parishes into unions, centralized administration, and made the rules and standards of relief uniform throughout the country. Most controversially, it decreed that the able-bodied poor could receive assistance only by entering the workhouse, a grim institution purposefully made unpleasant to save money by deterring all but the most desperate paupers. Once entered, it was very hard to leave, hence its popular name, the 'Bastille'. The new system was not fully implemented due to local resistance, particularly in the industrial north, where cyclical unemployment was a problem. Nevertheless it did succeed in branding fear of the workhouse, the ultimate humiliation, on the minds of the working classes. Trollope's early lodgings in London overlooked Marylebone Workhouse, described as 'that black building' in *The Claverings* (XLVI). The New Poor Law was extended to Ireland, against expert advice, in 1838; and the irrelevance of its ban on outdoor relief was tragically demonstrated during the Irish famine, as depicted in *Castle Richmond*. Unlike his mother, Trollope defended the New Poor Law even as it applied to Ireland. Ever suspicious of sentimentalism towards poverty, he respected

its hard-nosed economics and bureaucratic efficiency. Though he was doubtful about philanthropy, particularly in its religious guise, voluntary and private charity played an important role in reinforcing and humanizing poor relief.

The standard of living in Britain was higher than that of any other country, except the United States, yet between 20 and 30 per cent of its population struggled to find life's basic necessities, and perhaps a third of these failed altogether. Low pay, irregular employment, and ill health were the chief causes of poverty, though alcohol and improvidence were important contributors. At any time an unfavourable turn of circumstance could knock the unskilled workers off a precarious existence and into destitution. Most of them would know desperate poverty at one or more times in their lives, and particularly in old age, if they made it that far. The task of devising strategies for survival fell heaviest on women as household managers.

Trollope did not dwell much on the working poor, though rustic poverty is depicted in the Brattle family of *The Vicar of Bullhampton*. It was relative poverty that attracted his notice: 'the poverty of the normal poor', he argued feelingly in *The Last Chronicle of Barset*, did not approach the 'peculiar bitterness' of being poor gentry (IX).　　　　　　　　　　　　　　CK

Henriques, U. R., *Before the Welfare State* (1979).
Himmelfarb, G., *Poverty and Compassion: The Moral Imagination of the Late Victorians* (1991).

Powell, Lord David, younger brother of the Marquis of Llwddythlw who undertakes an administrative task in order that his brother will have time to marry Lady Amaldina Hauteville. *MF*　　　　　　　　　　　　　　　　SRB

Powell, Dr, Carmarthen physician, co-executor of Indefer Jones's penultimate will. *CH*　　AWJ

Powers, Hiram (1805–73), American sculptor best known in England for the *Greek Slave*, exhibited at the Great Exhibition (1851). In 1827 Powers had been befriended by Mrs Trollope in Cincinnati, where he constructed a series of artistic tableaux complete with sound-effects, one of which was a representation of Dante's 'The Infernal Regions', for Joseph Dorfeuille's Western Museum. Unlike Mrs Trollope's ill-fated Cincinnati Bazaar, this venture made some profit.　　RCT

Prague. Brooded over by its half-empty castle, Austrian regent, and military police, its geography symbolizes competing ambitions and ancient divisions between Christians and Jews. New Town's straight thoroughfares contrast with narrow alleys in the Jewish Quarter and secluded courtyards in the Kleinseite. All are linked by the Charles Bridge, site of Nina Balatka's suicide attempt (*NB*). It is also home to the wife Mr Emilius prefers to forget (*ED*). AWJ

Pratt, Fowler, London intimate of Adolphus Crosbie and Onesiphorus Dunn. An inoffensive and useless bachelor of moderate private means, he talks to Crosbie about Lily Dale and is the unconscious means of bringing the former lovers face to face in London. *SHA, LCB* NCS

Prendergast, Mr, lawyer and family friend who restores the Fitzgeralds to their lands and title. Regarded as 'cold, almost unfeeling', but absolutely 'honest and just' (IX), his concern to institute proper legal rights at Castle Richmond is nevertheless complicated by the same love of power that fuels the hunter when he 'beheads and betails' his prey (XXXIX). *CR* MRS

Pre-Raphaelites. In *The Warden* Trollope praised the Pre-Raphaelites for their 'finish and peculiar manner' but found fault with their posing of subjects; he specifically abused a painting by John Everett *Millais of 'a devotional lady looking intently at a lily as no lady ever looked before' (XIV). This criticism of the artist who eventually became his chief illustrator and intimate friend must have proved doubly embarrassing in that it also mistakenly attributes Charles Collins's *Convent Thoughts* (1851) to Millais. Millais may have influenced Trollope's (later) opinion that Raphael, though a 'wonderful' artist, 'prepared absolute ruin for all who were to come after him. . . . Raphael's grace had been the grace of fiction, and not the grace of nature. The artists of Italy were stricken with wonder, and followed the falsehood faithfully, without attaining the grace' ('The National Gallery', *St James's Magazine*, September 1861). See ART AND ARTISTS.
NJH

'Present Condition of the Northern States of the American Union, The' (lecture). The British undoubtedly have a tendency to side with the 'chivalrous' South compared to the 'arrogant' North. Current evidence shows that might and right are with the North. The South's economy is not viable; it is totally dependent on one crop, and without educational resources to diversify or industrialize. Under the US constitution, the South has no right to secede. Slavery is morally indefensible and bound to be abolished. Principle and practicality both favour a Northern victory. *Four Lectures*, 31–48. AKL

'President Johnson's Last Message' (article). The final public statement by a President neither elected nor admired is a noteworthy occasion. Johnson climbed from Southern obscur-

ity to compromise vice-presidency, to unforeseen prominence upon Lincoln's death. He was ill prepared and unequal to the admittedly hopeless tasks that fell to him. Despite personal courage, his failures in dealing with Congress will be remembered. *Saint Pauls* (March 1869), 663–75.
AKL

'President Lincoln' (letter). The writer learned about the assassination disjointedly in Paris, and is terribly grieved. Moderation was Lincoln's greatness; the new President's ability seems doubtful. Let us hope he will prove nobler in office than expected, as did Lincoln. Johnson must soften toward the Southerners. *Pall Mall Gazette* (5 May 1865), 4. AKL

Prettyman, Annabella and **Anne,** spinster sisters who run a girls' school in Silverbridge and employ Grace Crawley as a teacher. Thin, small, and sickly, Annabella is reputed to know more than any other woman in Barsetshire. Anne, the younger, is fat, fresh, fair, kind, and sociable. Both attempt to further the affair of Grace and Major Henry Grantly. *LCB* NCS

Price, Mr, a rich farmer, tenant of Cross Hall, who willingly relinquishes his house to accommodate the Dowager Marchioness and her daughters despite his lease and despite the displeasure of his landlord the Marquis of Brotherton. *IHP* MG

Price, Mrs Minnie, attractive young widow travelling from Suez to Southampton on the *Cagliari* who flirts with Arthur Wilkinson until he prudently withdraws from the game. *B*
MRS

Prime, Dorothea (née **Ray**), evangelical zealot and widowed sister of Rachel Ray. A dour young woman who 'had taught herself to believe that cheerfulness was a sin' (I), Dorothea moves out of the family cottage when Rachel continues to see Luke Rowan. She aligns herself with the women of the Dorcas Society and the local evangelical preacher, Mr Prong. *RR* MT

Prime Minister, The (see opposite)

Pritchett, Samuel, Mr Bertram's lugubrious 'man of business' (VI) who, long acquainted with his patron's money, feels a personal interest in its disposal, unwilling to see it go to others. He urges George Bertram to attend to his uncle and his 'half-a-million' (XLI), but Bertram reckons his solicitude has 'a graveyard touch' (XII). *B*
MRS

Proctor, Anne (née **Skepper**) (1799–1888), widow of the poet Bryan Waller Proctor ('Barry Cornwall') and mother of Adelaide Anne Proctor,

(*cont. on page 447*)

THE fifth of Trollope's six Palliser or parliamentary novels, published in 1876. It is the darkest of the series in tone and outcomes, and in some ways the most controversial.

The story of *The Prime Minister* promises, from the novel's title, to concentrate on the character and political career of Plantagenet Palliser, who has finally become the Duke of Omnium, after the death of the old Duke in the previous Palliser novel, *Phineas Redux*. But well over half the novel tells instead the story of the Whartons and Ferdinand Lopez, leaving something over one-third for the Duke, his wife Lady Glencora, and their milieu, and a much smaller portion for the overlapping of the two plot worlds. Trollope interweaves his two major stories, however, throughout the narrative, so that his reader is never more than a few chapters away from the other tale, and the events and metaphors in each always echo or contrast with the other's.

The Wharton story focuses on the effect of Ferdinand Lopez's intrusion into the London world of Abel Wharton QC and his children Everett and Emily. Lopez, at 33 a City man with a reputation for cleverness and skill at speculation, seems to Wharton an interloper, born of a Portuguese father, educated indeed at 'a good English private school', but then abroad at a German university; he lives with no detectable family connections, in a London flat which 'among all his friends no one was known to have entered' (I). Lopez wants to marry Emily, and Trollope tells us he truly loves her, as she does him. For Emily's father, Lopez's proposal is a kind of violation of caste boundaries, as he admits to the lover: 'Lopez is at any rate a bad name to go to a Protestant church with' (III). None the less, Emily's devotion wins over her father, and she marries Lopez, not the suitor her family prefers, Arthur Fletcher.

Lopez's other goal in the first half of the novel is to be elected to Parliament, since Lady Glencora has adopted him as a protégé, and promises to promote his candidacy for the borough of Silverbridge, once a secure seat for the Omnium interest. But Lopez loses to his Conservative rival, the same Arthur Fletcher who had wanted to marry Emily. The election loss hurts Lopez in a couple of ways: he loves power, and he had borrowed money for the election, counting on his success to lift his other speculations. Lopez's losses are so great that, at the end of the first half of the novel, he and Emily move into her father's London house eight months after their marriage.

The second half of the novel chronicles the darkening of Emily's marriage, in Ferdinand's abuse of her, his sacrifice of a vulnerable (and too gullible) business partner Sexty Parker, and his increasingly desperate schemes for recovery. Trapped by forces outside and inside him, his final solution is suicide, by throwing himself in front of a train at Tenway Junction. In the last quarter of the novel, Emily bears a child that dies, descends into a kind of proud, self-punishing despair at her shame, recovers, and finally marries Arthur Fletcher.

The Palliser story, which begins in chapter VI, follows the political career of the Duke and his wife as he is asked, amidst a stalemate between Conservatives and Liberals, to form a coalition government. What follows is a study of the Palliser marriage as well as a study of British politics. The Duke is uncertain about his fitness for leadership, but his sense of duty and deep idealism lead him to agree to become Prime Minister. He confesses to his wife, 'It may be that I must try—and it may be that I must break my heart because I fail' (VI). In contrast, Lady Glencora throws herself with pleasure into the exercise of power, planning elaborate entertainments and country house parties to wield political influence. The scale of Glencora's efforts at entertainment and influence offends her husband as vulgar, as characteristic of new money rather than an old dynasty. For two months in the autumn, Lady Glencora entertains at Gatherum, with a minimum of 40 guests at any moment; amidst political figures large and small, from Sir Orlando Drought and Sir Timothy Beeswax to hangers-on like Mr Rattler, she meets Ferdinand Lopez, and is attracted to him and his wit.

The by-election at Silverbridge, the borough attached to Gatherum Castle, produces only embarrassment for both the Duke's government and marriage. Palliser opposes his wife's plans to influence the election, but she continues to encourage Lopez. When Palliser publicly disavows these efforts to influence the borough, Lopez's loss is inevitable. In his fury at what he sees as their betrayal, Lopez demands £500 from the Pallisers, and the Duke sadly pays, seeing Lopez as genuinely misused. However, the press hears of the affair, a question is asked in the House of Commons, and Phineas Finn rescues both the Duke and the Duchess by an appeal to a traditional code of honour: of the man asking who compromised Palliser, Phineas says, 'He . . . is only anxious to inflict an unmanly wound in order that he may be gratified by seeing the pain which he inflicts' (LVII). The pain which Palliser and his wife experience is none the less deep, as they measure the fissures in their marriage. It is shortly after Phineas's explanation in Parliament, during the deepest estrangement between the Pallisers, that Lopez commits suicide.

The coalition government's three years in power are marked by no major initiatives, and paralysis finally gives way to life, and a new ministry under the Liberal leader Mr Gresham. Similarly, Emily's paralysis gives way to a new beginning as Mrs Fletcher, whom Lady Glencora promises her husband to visit, in the novel's final, downbeat scene.

The Prime Minister's rich themes radiate outward from its core organizing metaphors, in marriage as an image for politics, and politics as an image for marriage. Both images provide a focus for Trollope's profound study of the nature of power and community. Each topic, politics and marriage, is essential to the other, as each of Trollope's two plot strands is a frame for the other.

In this novel about a coalition government, politics as marriage is an image that emphasizes compromise leading to paralysis. The willingness of the Duke's government to include such diverse elements as the Conservative Beeswax and the Liberal Finn, or to allow the candidacy of a parvenu like Lopez, is a symptom of both its virtues and its weaknesses. For the most part, politics in this novel are not about ideas or political programmes, but about social groups, political parties as sources of influence, class, and economic privilege. Glencora describes this world to Mrs Finn: 'I don't care a straw whether [the coalition] run to Radicalism or Toryism. . . . I don't think it makes any difference as to what sort of laws are passed. But among ourselves, in our set, it makes a deal of difference who gets the garters, and the counties, who are made barons and then earls, and whose name stands at the head of everything' (VI). *The Prime Minister* has often been praised precisely for its portrait of politics as process, as a game in which the prize, Parliament, 'appears . . . as interesting, magnificent, desirable, and fundamentally futile' (A. O. J. Cockshut, *Anthony Trollope* (1955), 96).

Philosophical convictions about politics are largely absent in all of the Palliser novels. *The Prime Minister* is unusual in that one full-scale conversation about political principles does occur, towards the end of the novel, in chapter LXVIII ('The Prime Minister's Political Creed'). The Duke of Omnium's conservative liberalism reflects the same refinement of conscience and the same anguish over the conflict between tradition and reform that characterize his political life generally. It also happens to reflect, sometimes in the same words, Trollope's own conservative liberalism as articulated in *An Autobiography*, where he calls himself 'an advanced, but still a conservative liberal' (XVI). The Conservative, Palliser says, seeks 'to maintain the differences and distances which separate the highly placed from their lower brethren', but the Liberal seeks to lessen those distances (LXVIII), and Trollope uses the same terms. Both attend to the reality of human suffering in a hierarchical social order. Palliser says, 'How can you look at the bowed back and bent legs and abject face of that poor ploughman, who winter and summer has to drag his rheumatic limbs to his work, while you go a-hunting or sit in pride of place among the foremost few of your country, and say that it all is as it ought to be?' (LXVIII). And Trollope writes in his own voice, 'I . . . cannot look upon the inane, unintellectual, and toil-bound life of those who cannot even feed themselves sufficiently by their sweat, without some feeling of injustice, some sting of pain' (*Auto* XVI).

But the Duke's behaviour is by no means always consistent with his social conscience, and Trollope is as interested in his characters' political inconsistencies as in their other contradictions. Palliser may believe in 'lessening' the distance between classes, but he feels acutely any diminution of respect for his position. Hence his distress at Glencora's 'vulgar' display in the entertainment at Gatherum, the 'assumed and preposterous grandeur that was as much within the reach of some rich swindler or of some prosperous haberdasher as of himself' (XIX). And hence his discomfort at the opportunistic attacks of Slide, editor of the *People's Banner*, who might reasonably claim to attend to the interests of that ploughman more consistently than the Duke does.

Marriage as politics is the mirror theme to politics as marriage. Trollope's double plot structure compares the coalitions of his two marriages, their compromises, failures, and successes. In a sense the Palliser marriage is a success, yet it began with failure, in *Can You Forgive Her?*, when Glencora confessed, 'I shall never make you happy. You have never loved me, nor I you. We have never loved each other for a single moment' (LVIII). Glencora's thoughts in *The Prime Minister* echo her earlier words: 'She revered, admired, and almost loved him' (XVIII). At the most painful moment of crisis in their marriage in *The Prime Minister*, Palliser pleads, 'Cora, do not separate yourself from me' (XXXII). In some ways, in his vulnerability, his near-paralysis, and his 'thin skin' before others' judgments, Palliser is feminized, and mirrors Emily Lopez. Critics have differed in their judgements about the marriage, from those arguing its failure (Robert M. Polhemus, *The Changing World of Anthony Trollope* (1968), 214) to those who see a kind of happiness: 'With the best will in the world and with by now a love for one another as convincingly portrayed as any in the English novel, they can manage only a very imperfect union' (James R. Kincaid, *The Novels of Anthony Trollope* (1977), 224).

These imperfections pale beside those of the Lopez marriage, which is one of the most troubling studies of marital pain and failure in English literature. Emily's attraction to Ferdinand is overpowering, linked in obscure ways to rebellion and a wilful masochism. The brilliance of Trollope's characterization is to connect Emily's love for

Ferdinand to that quality which also makes her an ideal Victorian girl, 'that feminine sweetness which has its most frequent foundation in self-denial' (V). Yet the abuse which her marriage brings her, and her husband's suicide, are in Emily's view a fit punishment for her 'perverse self-will' (LXXIV). Lopez can both cherish and degrade Emily's sweetness, as she does herself, in her behaviours which veer from passivity to stubborn independence. Trollope's study of contradictions in Emily and her marriage is one of the triumphs of his fiction.

In style *The Prime Minister* is one of Trollope's most polished, subtle novels. His narrator perfects here his ability to enter into many minds and represent to his audience their troubled and troubling consciousnesses. Whether that mind is Lady Glencora's, pondering her relation to Palliser and what she understands of his feelings about her, or Ferdinand Lopez's, Trollope's storyteller is always the attentive listener. Even Lopez is, at the moment of his suicide, 'our friend', a phrase the narrator utters without irony (LX). This translation of complex feelings from a position slightly outside the character is one of Trollope's greatest strengths, because it enters so deeply into a character, yet preserves by implication an external point of view. Sometimes Trollope's strategy has made trouble for later readers, as in his account of Mr Wharton's anti-Semitic reflections. 'And he tried to be fair on the subject. It might be that it was a prejudice. . . . Others would not suspect a man of being of Jewish blood because he was swarthy, or even object to him if he were a Jew by descent' (XIII). Is Trollope's summary an implicit endorsement of Wharton's prejudices, or is his distance an adequate judgement? Readers have argued both views. The debate is at the least a tribute to the complexity of this novel.

The Prime Minister was not always regarded so highly. James Kincaid has spoken of it as 'Trollope's most important novel' (216), but when first published it was thoroughly panned. Trollope wrote the novel between April and September 1874, and published it in eight hefty monthly parts (as Eliot's *Middlemarch* was) from November 1875 to June 1876. It appeared in hardback as four volumes in May 1876, and received perhaps the worst reviews of any Trollope novel. The *Saturday Review* critic wrote, for example, that 'to whatever part of the novel he may turn, the reader of *The Prime Minister* is unable to escape the all-pervading sense of artistic vulgarity', and the *Spectator*'s reviewer was 'half-inclined to believe that Mr Trollope's power itself had declined' (Smalley 426, 422). These reviews saddened Trollope, especially the *Spectator*'s, whose author Trollope incorrectly thought was his friend R. H. *Hutton (it was Meredith White *Townsend). But the deeper reason for his despondency was the intensity of his investment in these characters and their story. Most readers disliked the Lopez 'sub-plot', and sometimes even regarded the Palliser story primarily as a *roman-à-clef*, with Daubeny as stand-in for Disraeli, Gresham for Gladstone, and so on.

At least one contemporary reader had a different opinion. Tolstoy wrote to his brother in 1877 that he thought *The Prime Minister* was a 'splendid' book (N. John Hall, *NCF* (September 1976), 215). Readers have noted the similarity between Lopez's suicide and Anna Karenina's, who also threw herself in front of a train; but although Tolstoy's novel was being serialized 1875–7, Tolstoy included Anna's suicide in early drafts of the novel in 1873, drawing on the similar suicide of a neighbour's mistress (Hall, *NCF* 215). Still, modern readers have become more sympathetic to the later, more pessimistic Trollope and, since the Second World War, with the broader re-evaluation of Trollope, *The Prime Minister* has been reread warmly, and is now commonly regarded as one of his most significant novels. The manuscript is in the Arents Collection, New York Public Library. **GB**

Cockshut, A. O. J., *Anthony Trollope* (1955).
Kincaid, James, *The Novels of Anthony Trollope* (1977).
Polhemus, Robert, *The Changing World of Anthony Trollope* (1968).

poet. A distinguished hostess in literary London, she first met Trollope in September 1867 at Bulwer-Lytton's. 'I found Trollope very pleasant,' she wrote to Lord Houghton (*Letters* 2, 769 n.). RCT

Prodgers, Mr, detective searching for Mountjoy Scarborough. The moneylender Mr Tyrrwhit provides funds for Prodgers to search for the debt-ridden Mountjoy. *MSF* MT

projected or unpublished works by Trollope. In addition to the ambitious *'History of World Literature' and a *'History of English Prose Fiction', Trollope wrote part of a guidebook to Ireland, which he tried to sell to John Murray in 1850. Ten years later he proposed a book on India for George *Smith. Other nonfiction plans included articles on America for *Cornhill Magazine* (1861); a series of 'Imaginary Meditations' for *Pall Mall Gazette* (1865), only one of which was published; and also in 1865 he offered to review Froude's *Reign of Elizabeth*; for the same journal during 1865–6, he suggested articles on church endowments, on church preferments, on ladies and parsons hunting, and on America (1868), including a ballad on New York women which he decided was too spiteful to print. For *Harper's Magazine* (1875) he intended an article on Australia, and for *Good Words* (1877) on telegraph boys. Unrealized fictional schemes included a story on Italy (1860) for *Cornhill*, and for the same journal, some observations on current attacks on the morality of fiction; a story for *Routledge's Christmas Annual* (1869), a series of stories for *Bow Bells* (1881); and one for a German paper (1881). The item scholars regret is an article on the third number of *Little Dorrit*, now lost, for the *Athenaeum* in 1856. See Bradford Booth, 'Trollope and *Little Dorrit*', *NCF* (March 1948), 237–40, and *Letters* 2, 1079. RCT

Prong, Samuel, zealous evangelical vicar in Baslehurst. Mr Prong is a severe, proud, and intolerant low churchman, on whom Trollope pours scorn. It is noted that 'sometimes he forgot his "h's" ' (IV), and, even worse for an English clergyman, 'he was not a gentleman' (VI). He proposes to Rachel Ray's sister Dorothea Prime, partly in an effort to get at her private income, but is thwarted by Dorothea's strong independence. *RR* MT

property and inheritance. The ownership and transmission of property furnished Trollope with an enormous variety of potential plot devices, and he made use of most of them, from the disintegrating Macdermot estate, at the start of his career (*MB*, 1847), to John Scarborough's finagling with his two marriage certificates, near the end of it (*MSF*, 1882–3). Wills, those favourites of sensational fiction, are instrumental in several novels. In *Orley Farm*, Lady Mason has forged a codicil to her husband's will; she is tried twice for the crime and acquitted both times, though the reader knows from early on that she is guilty. In *Cousin Henry*, pathetic Henry Jones comes upon his uncle's last true will, hidden in a copy of Jeremy Taylor's sermons; it supersedes the will that is believed to be current, and it disinherits Henry. He spends most of the novel feebly attempting to hide his guilty knowledge, but in the end the fraud is exposed.

Sometimes, inheritance is complicated by problems of legitimacy. In *Ralph the Heir*, Gregory Newton almost succeeds in bestowing Newton Priory on his illegitimate son Ralph, rather than his legitimate heir, his nephew, also named Ralph. At the last minute, Gregory is killed in a hunting accident, and the proper Ralph inherits. In *Is He Popenjoy?*, the question is whether the infant son of the dissolute Marquis of Brotherton is the legitimate heir of Manor Cross. Accident solves this problem, too, when the baby dies and the Marquis shortly after him; the estate goes to the Marquis's younger brother, Lord George Germain, whose newborn son becomes his unquestionable heir. *Mr Scarborough's Family* rings further changes on this theme. Rather implausibly, John Scarborough married his wife twice and has two marriage certificates; according to the earlier, his elder son, the spendthrift Mountjoy, is legitimate, while according to the later he is not, and the younger son, the prudent but hateful Augustus, will inherit. Mountjoy eventually proves himself the better man, and the estate goes to him—whereupon he rushes off to Monte Carlo.

While few of Trollope's novels rely so heavily on property and inheritance, nearly all employ such matters to some extent. In *The Warden*, for example, the will at issue is that of John Hiram, who died in 1434. His long-distance heir, the Revd Septimus Harding, is accused of mismanaging Hiram's bequest, and a *cause célèbre* results. In *The Belton Estate*, Bernard Amedroz cannot leave Belton Castle to his daughter Clara, because it is entailed on a distant cousin, Will Belton. When Bernard dies, Clara faces homelessness. Entail—an arrangement that bestows an estate on the next male in line, regardless of the current holder's wishes—also figures in *Ralph the Heir* and *Lady Anna*. In *The Eustace Diamonds*, the intrigue centres on the legal status of the eponymous necklace. Lizzie Eustace claims that her husband gave it to her before he died, and that it is therefore her own; the Eustace family contends that the necklace is an heirloom and cannot be given away. The conflict is never resolved.

Property and inheritance were crucial concerns in the upper-middle-class and aristocratic Victorian world, and when Trollope portrays that world he naturally enough focuses on them. He exhibits a thorough knowledge of legal technicalities, though on at least two occasions (*The Eustace Diamonds* and *Cousin Henry*), he consulted experts to make sure he had the nuances right. Yet Trollope is never interested in technicalities for their own sake. The orderly transmission of property from one generation to the next represents for him, as it does for Jane Austen, the continuance of all that is good in England. Trollope reveres men who improve their estates in order to pass them on; he despises upstarts, like Melmotte in *The Way We Live Now*, whose wealth is based on nothing tangible and might evaporate at any moment.

The inheritance of property is crucial to the relations between parents and children, as well as to those between prospective husbands and wives. Property rarely determines the outcome of a Trollopian courtship—only love does that—but it is often the gauge of a suitor's worthiness. The inheritance of property distinguishes the landowning classes from those that work for wages. In general, Trollope values that distinction and wishes to preserve it, though he makes exceptions in a few cases, when individual excellence qualifies a young woman to rise above her station. Mary Masters in *The American Senator* is only a provincial lawyer's daughter, but she will make a far better wife for the heir of Bragton than the tawdry though well-born Arabella Trefoil would do. Isabel Boncassen in *The Duke's Children* is an American, of all things, yet she,

not Lady Mabel Grex, marries Lord Silverbridge at the end of the Palliser series.

Primarily, however, Trollope uses property and inheritance to test his characters, to make them reveal themselves. The letter of John Hiram's will is finally of no importance in *The Warden*; what matters is how Mr Harding conducts himself under the stress of the controversy. Similarly, it makes little difference to whom, if anyone, the Eustace diamonds belong. The struggle over them gives Lizzie the chance to display her fascinating mendacity, and it allows the other characters to show their true natures as they respond to her. Trollope maintained that 'the highest merit which a novel can have consists in perfect delineation of character, rather than in plot' (*Auto* IX). He left the devising of intricate plots to Wilkie Collins and the other sensationalists, for whom the forging of a will constituted an event of supreme interest in its own right. Lady Mason confesses her forgery in chapter XLIV of *Orley Farm*, just over halfway through the novel; mere plot interest may suffer from this early revelation, but the portrait of Lady Mason's character is deepened by it. And that, in all his novels, is Trollope's principal aim.   WK

Prosper, Peter, Harry Annesley's uncle and the owner of Buston Hall. Prosper names Harry Annesley as his heir, only to disinherit him after incorrectly believing malicious gossip. Foolish Prosper unsuccessfully woos Matilda Thoroughbung, the local brewer's spinster daughter. *MSF MT*

Proudie, Mrs. Mrs Proudie (she has no Christian name) is the Sabbatarian wife of Bishop Proudie, and, as niece of a Scottish earl, has the energy, self-confidence, money, and social position which he lacks, as the mere nephew of an Irish baron on his mother's side. When she first appears in *Barchester Towers*, they have three grown daughters, and a number of sons away at school. She is severe to all around her on religious and particularly sabbath observance, and to her servants very repressive on sexual matters, threatening with damnation all who deviate from her line. A domineering character, she is 'habitually authoritative to all, but to her poor husband . . . despotic' (*BT* III). She interferes directly in diocesan affairs, usurping her husband's authority most egregiously in the matter of the wardenship in *Barchester Towers* and, in *The Last Chronicle of Barset*, in the proceedings against Josiah Crawley, who silences her with a memorable, 'Peace, woman . . . the distaff were more fitting for you' (*LCB* XVIII). She is a minor character in *Doctor Thorne* and *The Small House at Allington*, but is always a major structuring

A striking portrayal of Mrs Proudie and the bishop for *The Last Chronicle of Barset*. The illustration by G. H. Thomas bears the caption '"A convicted thief," repeated Mrs. Proudie' (XI). Trollope was not entirely happy with the picture—'Not quite my Mrs. Proudie' he commented—but he found the drawing of the bishop 'very good'.

force in the fictional world, in polar opposition to Archdeacon Grantly. Indeed Trollope suggests that *Framley Parsonage* is largely organized around 'my old friends Mrs Proudie and the Archdeacon' (*Auto* VIII). The author sums up her character: 'It was not only that she was a tyrant, a bully, a would-be priestess, a very vulgar woman, and one who would send headlong to the nethermost pit all who disagreed with her;— but that at the same time she was conscientious, by no means a hypocrite, really believing in the brimstone which she threatened, and anxious to save the souls around her from its horrors' (*Auto* XV). Her death comes when her husband finally tells her that she has made his life miserable: 'she loved him still; but she knew now . . . that by him she was hated!' She suffers a heart attack, and such is her power as a character that she remains upright and staring, even in death (*LCB* LXVI). Trollope tells us that he killed her off 'with many misgivings' because he overheard two clergymen object to his habit of reintroducing characters. 'I acknowledged myself to be the culprit. "As to Mrs Proudie," I said, "I will go home and kill her before the week is over." And so I did. . . . I have sometimes regretted the deed, so great was my delight in writing about Mrs Proudie, so thorough was my knowledge of all the little shades of her character. . . . I have never dissevered myself from Mrs Proudie, and still live much in company with her ghost' (*Auto* XV). She is a triumphantly successful comic character, even today when as 'a would-be priestess' she is objectionable because she is a bully and because she assumes the power of a position she does not fill, and not because she steps out of her place as a woman.   DS

Proudie, Olivia, eldest daughter of Bishop and Mrs Proudie of Barchester. A spirited girl, she nurses a justified hatred of Mr Slope after he withdraws a declaration of affection on discovering her lack of dowry. In *Framley Parsonage* she marries the widowed Revd Tobias Tickler. *BT*
NCS

Proudie, Thomas. Thomas Proudie, the henpecked Bishop appointed in *Barchester Towers*, is important in *Framley Parsonage* and *The Last Chronicle of Barset*, appears briefly in *Doctor Thorne* and *The Small House at Allington*, and is mentioned in *The Claverings* and *He Knew He Was Right*. Belonging to the broad-church tendency, between the High Church of Grantly and evangelicalism of Mrs Proudie, he has 'adapted himself' to Whig views 'on most theological and religious subjects', tolerating Roman Catholicism and Presbyterianism equally, assisting liberal religious reforms in Ireland, and sitting on the

commission which recommended the admission to Oxford and Cambridge of undergraduates not belonging to the Church of England. He is not 'a man of great mental powers, or even of much capacity for business', since the work is done by others, but he is known in the newspapers, and is rewarded when Barchester falls vacant (*BT* III). He is 'comparatively young' and very ambitious, thinking in terms of Canterbury and York, and so not wanting 'to bury himself in Barchester'. He is 'about five feet four', 'a good looking man; spruce and dapper, and very tidy', who tries to conceal 'an air of insignificance'. The Bishop's stipend has gone down from £9,000 to £5,000, on which he struggles to support a large family, including three daughters and a wife with fashionable pretensions. He would not have been made bishop without his wife's money and energy, and indeed many of his acts are controlled by her, including the appointment and dismissal of Slope, and some of his conduct of the case against Crawley in *The Last Chronicle of Barset*. He rarely defies his wife, but finally tells her she has made his life miserable, whereupon she has a heart attack and dies, leaving the Bishop 'praying that God might save him from being glad that his wife was dead' (*LCB* LXVI–LXVII).   DS

Pryor, Bessy, adopted daughter of Mrs Miles. Bessy's love for her comes into conflict with her love for the son Philip, but she sticks to principle and the young defeat the old. 'Launay' *WFF*
GRH

Pryor, John, reserved Englishman, somewhat older than Ophelia Gledd, who, slightly surprisingly, marries her. 'Gledd' *LS*   GRH

'Public Schools' (article). Fondly remembered tradition will not serve as well in education as new buildings, more teachers, better management, innovative teaching methods, and less restrictive admissions. Those involved in the process and problems should be involved in any reform planning. *Fortnightly Review* (1 October 1865), 476–87.   AKL

'Public School's Calendar for 1865, The' (review). Time and progress have forced changes in public schools as in other things. Everything is now ordered by competition, not family or birthplace—a just, but major, change. The education nurtures conservative tastes and liberal actions. Society's good manners are chiefly due to public-school education. *Pall Mall Gazette* (2 March 1865), 6.   AKL

public service of Anthony Trollope. Trollope's public service included 33 years in the employ of the Post Office and the creation of a character through whom he had a fifteen-year vicarious career in politics in the Palliser novels. In Plantagenet, the antithesis of worldliness and ambition, Trollope stressed the importance of integrity and self-sacrifice in public service.

In the 1860s Trollope served as an after-dinner speaker at fund-raising dinners, organized a lecture series for the Post Office Library and Literary Association, campaigned for an international copyright law, and became a lifelong, active member of the Royal Literary Fund, a charity for indigent writers and their families. Later he served on the council of the Metropolitan Free Libraries Association.

Trollope attempted to enhance the image of the public service in an explanatory lecture given first in 1861, 'The *Civil Service as a Profession', published in the Cornhill (February 1861, 214–28). He insisted that public service was as respectable if not always as remunerative a career as others for which more education was required at the entry level, such as law, medicine, teaching, or the clergy.

In 1853 Sir Charles *Trevelyan and Sir Stafford *Northcote conducted an inquiry into the efficiency and economy of the civil service. Their report, placed before Parliament in 1854, contended that incompetence and inertia were the natural consequences of admission by political patronage and promotion by seniority. Their recommendations to abolish patronage and fill positions by competence demonstrated in examinations were adopted.

Trollope contended that competitive examinations could not be relied on as a means of identifying the most suitable applicants. Such a system, he argued in An Autobiography, placed too much emphasis on acquired information and not enough on birth and rank. All it would do, he insisted, was identify the most ambitious— those who had crammed the hardest in preparation for the examinations.

Always resistant to systems and purported efficiencies, Trollope parodied Sir Charles, their chief proponent, in the character of Sir Gregory Hardlines in The Three Clerks. The hero proves to be not his favourite, the ambitious Alaric Tudor, who beats the competition to become a senior clerk at six times his previous salary, but his cousin Charley Tudor, a slow starter who shines when given a challenge. Charley, whose early career resembles Trollope's as described in An Autobiography, proves not only willing to work but reliable, useful, and honest; Alaric's ambition, which prompts him to 'borrow' money in order to buy shares in a mine that he is supposed to be impartially inspecting, lands him in prison.

Trollope insisted in his lecture, given several times in the 1860s, that civil servants had as much right as anyone else to the vote. However, as he makes plain in The Three Clerks, he did not believe that an employee of the public service should be able to stand for Parliament, and his own bid for election in 1868 came a year after his retirement from the Post Office. See also GOVERNMENT OFFICIALS AS CHARACTERS; POLITICIANS AS CHARACTERS.   JK

publishers and publishing. Trollope was undoubtedly exaggerating when he wrote to Edward Chapman, of Chapman & Hall, 'Ah—I wish Providence had made me a publisher' (Letters 1, 81). Still, he was exceptionally well informed concerning the business of publishing, which expanded rapidly during the mid-19th century. As early as 1835, Trollope began acting as his mother's agent with such publishers as Henry Colburn, John Murray, and Richard Bentley. Frances Trollope asked Murray if he might employ Anthony part-time, perhaps as a proofreader; Anthony asked Bentley to assist him in placing his own work in periodicals. Neither request was successful. Frances did, however, persuade Thomas Newby to publish Anthony's first novel, The Macdermots of Ballycloran, on the 'half-profits' system. Newby produced a shoddy three-volume edition, and even though he advertised the book as being by Mrs Trollope, there were no profits to be shared. Trollope disliked the half-profits system, reasoning that a publisher would be more motivated 'to push a work' that had been purchased outright, but he did not yet have the reputation to insist on such an arrangement: his next two novels—The Kellys and the O'Kellys and La Vendée, published by Colburn— were both unprofitable. The Warden and Barchester Towers, however, which appeared under the more prestigious imprint of Longman & Co., were moderately successful, and Trollope tried to persuade William Longman to purchase The Three Clerks for 'a lump sum down' (Auto VI). Longman declined, but Richard Bentley agreed to purchase the copyright for £250. When Bentley hesitated over how much to offer for Trollope's next novel, Trollope moved on to Chapman & Hall, who purchased Doctor Thorne for £400. It was the beginning of a long association: by the time of Trollope's death, Chapman & Hall had published 22 of his novels, 2 collections of his short stories, and 8 volumes of his non-fiction.

Despite his enduring relationship with Chapman & Hall, from 1860 on Trollope had dealings with several other publishers. These arrangements almost invariably resulted from the serial publication of his novels. In 1859–60, George Smith, of Smith, Elder & Co., paid Trollope

£1,000 for the copyright of a novel to be serialized in his new magazine, the *Cornhill*. Both the novel—*Framley Parsonage*—and the magazine attracted an enthusiastic readership, and Trollope contributed three more novels to the *Cornhill* in as many years. Trollope recalled in *An Autobiography* that for *The Claverings*, the last of his novels to appear in the *Cornhill*, he received £2,800, 'the highest rate of pay that was ever accorded to me' (XI).

Although seven of Trollope's first eight novels were published originally in the standard three-volume format (the exception being *The Warden*, published in one volume), most of the novels from *Framley Parsonage* on were published in parts before being reissued in volume form. During the same years that George Smith was serializing Trollope's novels in the *Cornhill*, Frederic *Chapman published three novels (*Orley Farm*, *Rachel Ray*, and *Can You Forgive Her?*) in separate monthly parts. In 1865, Trollope and Chapman were among the founders of the *Fortnightly Review*. *The Belton Estate* commenced serialization in the first issue; *The Eustace Diamonds* and *Lady Anna* also appeared in the *Fortnightly*, and were subsequently published in volume form by Chapman & Hall. In the same way, Trollope sold the copyrights to novels that were serialized in *Blackwood's Edinburgh Magazine* or *Macmillan's Magazine* before being republished, in volume form, by the firms that owned these periodicals.

Frederic Chapman, George *Smith, and John *Blackwood became close friends of Trollope's, as did James *Virtue, a printer and publisher who had been involved in the founding of the *Fortnightly Review*. In 1866, Virtue persuaded Trollope to serve for a time as editor of his new periodical, *Saint Pauls Magazine*. *Phineas Finn*, which appeared in the first volume of *Saint Pauls*, was then published in volume form by Virtue, who also purchased the copyrights to *He Knew He Was Right* and *Ralph the Heir*. After Virtue transferred *Saint Pauls Magazine* to the publisher Alexander *Strahan, whose firm was financially intertwined with Virtue's printing and publishing business, the novels Virtue had purchased were published in parts and in volume form under Strahan's imprint. Trollope had known Strahan for several years, but their relationship was sometimes vexed: in 1862, Strahan offered Trollope £1,000 for a novel to be serialized in another of his periodicals, *Good Words*. But the novel that Trollope delivered—*Rachel Ray*—was rejected as being inappropriate for the Christian evangelicals who constituted the readership of *Good Words*. Trollope demanded and received half payment from Strahan, and then sold *Rachel Ray* to Chapman & Hall. Trollope continued to

sell stories to Strahan for publication in his various periodicals, which led to another disagreement when Strahan proposed, in 1867, to republish in two volumes a group of stories that Trollope insisted would give 'adequate measure' only if published in a single volume. In 1869, Strahan was in financial difficulties, and could not afford to keep Trollope on as editor of *Saint Pauls*.

Trollope's close association with the *Cornhill* had necessarily ended when he assumed the editorship of a rival magazine; the last of his novels to be published by Smith, Elder was *The Last Chronicle of Barset*. In contrast, he was becoming more closely connected to Chapman & Hall. In 1869, Trollope invested £10,000 to buy a one-third partnership for his son Harry, and although Harry remained with the firm only until 1872, in the 1870s most of Trollope's novels were published by Chapman & Hall, after appearing initially in periodicals or in parts. Trollope recorded in *An Autobiography* that in the late 1870s he 'encountered a diminution' in the price he was paid for his fiction (IX). Super suggests that part of the problem may have been Trollope's commitment to Chapman & Hall, which was encountering financial difficulties (Super 381). When the firm was converted to a limited liability company in 1880, Trollope became a shareholder. He also served as one of the three directors, a position that entailed two five-hour meetings a week: 'That I am half ruined is nothing to the trouble and annoyance and shame of such an employment', he complained (*Letters* 2, 867). It was probably as a result of the firm's problems that, in the 1880s, Trollope's novels were published by other firms, particularly Chatto & Windus.

Due to the inadequate copyright protection afforded British novelists under American law, Trollope also experienced difficulties with American publishing firms. In the 1860s, Trollope sold stories to *Harper's New Monthly Magazine*, but failed in his attempts to persuade the American publishing firm to pay a fair price for the right to republish in volume form the novels already published in England. In 1876–7, Trollope was a member of the Royal Commission on Copyright. He devoted several pages of *An Autobiography* to his attempts to overcome American opposition to an international copyright (XVII).   PTS

Hamer, Mary, *Writing by Numbers: Trollope's Serial Fiction* (1987).

Srebrnik, Patricia Thomas, *Alexander Strahan, Victorian Publisher* (1986).

Pucker, Miss, spinster, low-church member, and friend of Dorothea Prime. A sour evangelical, her disfiguring squint signals Trollope's gen-

ANTONIUS TROLLOPIUS.

AUTHOR OF THE LAST CHRONICLES OF CICERO.

"O Rare for Antony!"—SHAKSPEARE.

At the height of his celebrity, despite diminishing sales of his novels, Trollope was a favourite subject for *Punch* parodies and cartoons. Linley Sambourne took aim at Trollope's interests in classical literature in 'Fancy Portraits' in February 1881, with 'Antonius Trollopius, Author of The Last Chronicle of Cicero'.

eral disapproval of her intolerance of young love. She first spreads rumours about Rachel Ray and Luke Rowan, and she takes in Dorothea when she leaves Bragg's End. *RR*   MT

Puddicombe, Mr, exemplary vicar of the parish next to Bowick. He provides direct and difficult counsel to Dr Wortle. Neither intellectual nor witty, but thoroughly rational and principled, he compares Dr Wortle's situation to a person trying to hide a muddy boot: 'The dirt, when it is rubbed and smudged and scraped, is more palpably dirt than the honest mud' (5. I). *DWS*   RC

Puddingdale, parish of Revd Mr Quiverful, four miles (6 km) from Barchester, worth £400. Offered as a curacy to Mr Slope by Mrs Proudie in a final gesture of contempt. *BT, W, LCB*
                              NCS

Puddlebrane, Mr, English cricketer in the match against Britannula. He is one of many who abhor Britannula's 'Fixed Period' policy of enforced euthanasia, arguing especially against cremation. *FixP*   SRB

Puddleham, Mr, Dissenting minister who considers it his duty to attack the Church of England. Toady to the Marquis of Trowbridge, Puddleham gains the latter's support in building an offensive chapel next door to the vicarage but Fenwick, the vicar, refuses to be offended by Puddleham's quarrelsome, sour disposition. *VB*
                              SRB

Puffle, Miss, middle-aged woman of fortune to whom Peter Prosper briefly considers offering his hand. Prosper believes Miss Puffle to be 'superior to Miss Thoroughbung in many ways' (XXVII), but she goes off with Farmer Tazlehurst's son, scuppering his plans to get at her wealth. *MSF*
                              MT

Puffle, Mrs, pretty sister-in-law of the pseudonymous 'Josephine' who mediates between her and Jonathan Brown. 'Montmorenci' *ET*   GRH

Punch. In 1841, Ebenezer Landells, Henry Mayhew, and Mark Lemon began this weekly publication, also known as the *London Charivari*. *Punch* was descended from a long line of humour magazines, including Defoe's 17th-century *Review* and the later *Tatler* and *Spectator*. All combined wit with social and political purposes. *Punch* too was a humorous magazine with a

strong social purpose, beginning as a champion of the poor.

Lemon, a playwright and magazine writer, was the editor of the *London Journal, Family Herald, Once a Week,* and the *Field.* He became the first editor of *Punch* with assistance from Mayhew, a journalist who had helped Gilbert à Beckett with *Figaro in London,* another precursor of *Punch.* They owned shares equally along with Joseph Last, the printer, and Landells, a wood engraver. The name for the magazine was suggested by Douglas Jerrold's *Punch in London,* an 1832 rival of *Figaro in London. Punch* had enormous influence on later humorous magazines which shared its desire to reform.

Its excellent caricatures were well known. In 1880 Trollope published his *Life of Cicero* in which he drew frequent comparisons between life in Cicero's time and in his own. *Punch* used this theme for a cartoon showing Trollope placing a top hat on Cicero's bust (see CARTOONS AND PARODIES, and p. 453). Trollope had already been noticed by *Punch* in 1871, in a cartoon in which an elderly woman embraces a young man who had married her for money. He objects to her attentions in public, but she, being 'up in Mr Anthony Trollope', asks why a woman should not glory in her love. In June 1874, another cartoon showed Revd Duodecimus Lazarus Quiverful of Barchester pushing a carriage full of sleeping children, and in August a cartoon satirized bad table manners under the heading 'The Way We Live Now'.   JWM

Puritan Grange, large red-brick house in the village of Chesterton, near Cambridge. As the aptly named home of the Bolton family, it represents Mary Bolton's puritanical strictness. Hester's parents lure and imprison her here after her husband John Caldigate is accused of bigamy. *JC*   SRB

Pycroft Common, small hamlet near Bullhampton, home of Mrs Burrows. She shelters Carry Brattle here briefly, and the evidence against the murderers of Farmer Trumbull is buried in her garden. *VB*   SRB

Pyramids, tourist destination outside Cairo where Jefferson Ingram proposes to Fanny Damer. 'Pyramids' *TAC1*   GRH

Pyrenees. The baths at Vernet lie in a secluded valley. 'Bauche' *TAC1*   GRH

Quain, Sir Richard (1816–98), Physician Extraordinary to Queen Victoria (1890); editor of the *Dictionary of Medicine* (1882); Trollope's London physician and fellow member of the Garrick and Cosmopolitan clubs. As a chest specialist, he was called in regarding Trollope's chronic shortness of breath. After Trollope's death, he confided to T. H. Escott that Trollope's extreme sensitivity to the opinion of others produced in him 'a genial air of grievance against the world in general, and those who personally valued him in particular' (quoted *I & R* 119). RCT

Quaverdale, Mr, literary hack and friend of Harry Annesley. A writer for *The Coming Hour,* Quaverdale 'made his five or six hundred a year in a rattling, loose, uncertain sort of fashion, and was,—so thought Harry Annesley,—the dirtiest man of his acquaintance' (XXII). *MSF* MT

Quickenham, Richard, successful, hard-working barrister, brother-in-law to the Fenwicks. He discovers illegalities in the erection of a Methodist chapel on vicarage land and thus provides the impetus for its removal, much to the chagrin of Mr Puddleham and the Marquis of Trowbridge. *VB* SRB

Quin, Lady Mary, daughter of the Earl of Kilfenora whose hospitality and charms have little effect on Fred Neville. So her letters to his aunt, in which she relays gossip about the O'Hara ladies, are not entirely disinterested. *EE* AWJ

Quin Castle, about three miles (5 km) from the coast in Co. Clare; home of the Earl of Kilfenora and his daughters. *EE* AWJ

Quiverful, Letitia, long-suffering, plain-speaking wife of Revd Quiverful of Puddingdale.

Pleading their fourteen children, she enlists Mrs Proudie's aid in gaining her husband's appointment as warden of Hiram's Hospital, thus precipitating a major conflict between her patron and Mr Slope. *BT, LCB* NCS

Quiverful, Mr, rector of Puddingdale whose large family (twelve children in *W,* fourteen in *BT*) stretches his modest income to the breaking point. Honest, painstaking, and drudging, he sides with Mr Slope in hopes of appointment to the lucrative wardenship of Hiram's Hospital, though he has no desire to hurt his friend Mr Harding. A member of the clerical commission in *The Last Chronicle of Barset. BT* NCS

R

race and racism. Although Britain ruled millions of coloured people throughout the most extensive empire ever known, the British were proud that theirs was the first European empire to abolish slavery (1833). Black American antislavery lecturers visiting the country before the Civil War often commented on the dignity and respect with which they were treated in Britain, respect that was accorded to their education and perceived social status as black gentlemen. Britain's own coloured population, concentrated in port cities, was very small and largely working class. Its members were apparently treated by fellow white workers without prejudice and intermarriage was common. The idea of racial equality had little purchase in a country where inequality was the central principle of the social system. The famous motto of the abolitionists—'Am I not a man, and a brother?' put in the mouth of a black slave—meant above all spiritual equality to a movement essentially driven by religious conscience.

Victorian Britain became more racist, however. This was partly the result of intellectual developments such as the efforts of scientists to give a physical definition of race. The old debate between polygenists, believers in the separate creation of several distinct human races, and the monogenists, who believed in a single origin for all races, was made irrelevant by Darwin's evolutionary theories which sidetracked the issue of creation by giving all races a shared primitive ancestry. However, evolution opened the door to more deterministic theories which tied race to environment and encouraged stereotypical attitudes recognizing little or no difference among the individual members of another race: 'they' were all the same. It also facilitated the assumption that scientific and technological superiority, such as Europe and especially Britain undoubtedly enjoyed in the 19th century, especially in weaponry, was the prime indicator of racial superiority. Such developments made it possible for a working-class Briton to look down upon all coloured people regardless of social or intellectual status. Demeaning racial stereotypes were increasingly promoted in the popular press, in children's literature, in advertising (notoriously in advertisements for soap) and in mass entertainment, where the craze for minstrel shows made blacks figures of fun.

Early Victorian philanthropy was often committed, however complacently and ethnocentrically, to the doctrine of improvement by which former slaves and other coloured people could be transformed by Christianity and capitalism into grateful, docile black Englishmen. The horrors of the Indian Mutiny of 1857, the Jamaica rebellion of 1865, the Maori Wars, the American Civil War, and Reconstruction all cast doubt on such sentimental notions and marked a distinct hardening of racist attitudes in Britain by evoking visions of ineradicable primitive savagery. As Trollope's disparaging remarks about blacks in *The West Indies and the Spanish Main* and *North America* make clear, he was no believer in racial equality, such believers being very uncommon in his time. However, like many liberals, Trollope criticized the increasing racial arrogance of late Victorian imperialism, fearing that it might eventually exterminate the aboriginal peoples of America, Australia, and Africa which, however inferior in the racial hierarchy, according to his view, still had the right to exist—a right many of the more full-blooded imperialists dismissed contemptuously. CK

Bolt, Christine, *Victorian Attitudes to Race* (1971).
Lorimer, Douglas, *Colour, Class and the Victorians* (1978).

Rachel Ray (see opposite)

radicalism was the political denomination of some hundred largely middle-class MPs after 1832, usually representing newly enfranchised towns. They were hostile to aristocratic values and the power of the landed interest, the established Church (most were Nonconformists), the universities, and the military. Their politics tended to be negative, moralistic, and pressure group oriented, focusing on the single issue or obstacle blocking the path of virtue. The Anti-
(*cont. on page 458*)

THOUGH modest in scale and in social setting, some of its dialogue has the reson-
ance of drama, and *Rachel Ray* is one of Trollope's wittiest novels. The battle of
wills between an evangelical clergyman, Mr Prong, and Mrs Prime, the widow who
has agreed to marry him, is only thinly disguised by piety. Mr Prong is taken aback
when Mrs Prime asks how he is going to vote in the forthcoming election: 'Judge not,
lest ye be judged, Dorothea; remember that.' 'That doesn't mean, Mr Prong, that we
are not to have our opinions, and that we are not to warn those that are near us when
we see them walking in the wrong path.' (XXIV)

The story is set in Devon, among the community of Baslehurst, where the biggest
business, in which the hero has an interest in learning the trade, is Bungall & Tappitt's
Cider Brewery. Like the naming of Samuel Prong, the earnest and hard-working clergyman, this title offers the reader a playful invitation, indicating high spirits on the
part of the writer, who was consciously baiting Norman Macleod, the clergyman who
had commissioned this work.

Mr Prong wants to marry Dorothea Prime, a widow, for her small independent
income but he does not bargain for the independence of mind that income brings.
Satirizing piety when it is found together with greed is easy: Trollope does something
more interesting here when he suggests that puritan seriousness about money might
keep a certain realism alive and provide a defence, particularly for women, against
cant.

Not that the character of Dorothea or an evangelical interpretation of behaviour are
endorsed: she calls her younger sister Rachel Ray, the story's heroine, a castaway for
inadvertently spending a few unaccompanied moments with a young man. She moves
out of the house that she shared with her mother and sister to live with her sharp-
tongued friend Miss Pucker, who runs the Dorcas Society, where pious women meet
to sew for charity. Similarly, it is the undue respect that she has for the opinion of Dr
Comfort, the parson, that causes Mrs Ray to instruct Rachel to respond coldly to her
lover Luke Rowan and nearly succeeds in destroying her happiness. Only the intervention of two married women, Mrs Cornbury and Mrs Stuart, who take firm secular
action, speaking plainly to Luke and arranging for the young couple to meet in
privacy, permits them to repair the mistake.

Rachel is established as a vigorous, physically energetic woman, and it is implied
that her instinctive vitality is what enables her to remain oriented in this world of
exaggerated prohibition. She admits that she has spent time walking under the elms in
the churchyard with the young man from the brewery and is prepared to do it again.
When she is invited to a party at the Tappitts, where there will be dancing, and she will
meet Luke, she is mutinous until she gets permission to go. After reading this novel
George *Eliot concluded that it did people good, made them healthier, to read Trollope's books.

Eliot, who had just published *Romola* when *Rachel Ray* came out, wrote to Trollope
praising his novel for its fine construction, but in general critics, from the *Athenaeum*
to *The Times*, were more struck by the continuing proof of the novelist's power to
inhabit the inner life of women. The *Saturday Review* seemed to feel that this did not
necessarily make for substantial reading and that Trollope was telling the world more
than it had ever wanted to know about girls (Smalley, 180–91).

The novel was written between 3 March and 29 June 1863 and was due to start publication while *The Small House at Allington* was still coming out in the *Cornhill*. Norman *Macleod, one of Queen Victoria's Scottish chaplains, and a well-known liberal clergyman in his own right, had approached Trollope to write a serial specially for *Good Words*, the high-circulation evangelical magazine of which he was editor. Macleod, who was already a friend of Trollope's, cherished the idea that his readership might bring out what was finest in the novelist.

The magazine's publisher, Alexander *Strahan, was prepared to offer £1,000 for a short work, the length of two volumes. But when Macleod saw most of the novel at the proof stage, in May 1863, he registered that Trollope had mischievously posed a challenge specifically aimed at evangelical readers. The story invited a questioning of the assumptions and the pieties used to frame behaviour in a provincial evangelical community. *Good Words* was already under attack from another evangelical magazine for commissioning Trollope in the first place, dismissing him as a sensation writer, unfit to appear in a religious-minded periodical. Macleod decided to withdraw from the arrangement. He offered apologies and compensation from Strahan, his publisher, of £500, both of which Trollope accepted.

It had already been agreed by a contract of 26 January 1862 that for a payment of £500 Chapman & Hall should handle the publication of *Rachel Ray* in volume form. Once serial publication was cancelled, on 10 June Chapman & Hall signed a new contract, agreeing simply to double their print run and their payment. Trollope got £1,000 and 3,000 copies were printed.

Although the novel was apparently reprinted six times in its original two-volume form, between October 1863 and May 1864, Sadleir's *Bibliography* (52–3, 277–9) argues that these 'editions' were all taken from the original printing. When the cheap one-volume issue appeared in 1864 it carried a frontispiece by Millais not previously published. By 1866 *Rachel Ray* was available in cloth at half a crown and at two shillings as a 'yellowback'. The manuscript is in the Arents Collection, New York Public Library.   MH

Hall, N. J., *Trollope: A Biography* (1991).

Corn Law League epitomized the middle-class radical political style. Because of their different enthusiasms and a certain stiff-necked individualism, they never formed a coherent party but generally—though often uneasily—they supported the Whigs. They were considerably more comfortable in the Liberal Party which evolved from the Whigs after 1860, but Trollope, an 'advanced but still conservative liberal' (*Auto* XVI), was none too comfortable with them.

Radicalism had no clearly articulated ideology but was strongly anti-socialist, and suspicious of state intervention. Among its varieties were philosophic radicalism, inspired by Jeremy Bentham and more statist than others, the Manchester School of Peace and Free Trade zealots led by Richard Cobden and John Bright—epitomized by Mr Turnbull in *Phineas Finn* (XVIII)—and, from the 1860s, the academic radicals, 'insiders'

such as Thomas *Hughes who wished to open the establishment to outsiders. Distinct from these, and viewing them with mixed suspicion and respect, were working-class radicals like the bootmaker Ontario Moggs in *Ralph the Heir*, who aimed at manhood suffrage and more—a prospect which made most middle-class radicals uneasy.   CK

Adelman, Paul, *Victorian Radicalism: The Middle Class Experience 1830–1914* (1984).

railway bookstalls. W. H. Smith opened the first such outlet offering cheap reprints of popular fiction at Euston station in 1848. Other London stations quickly followed suit. In *The Small House at Allington*, Johnny Eames thrashed Adolphus Crosbie at Paddington, laying 'his foe prostrate among the newspapers in Smith's book-stall' (XXXIV). Eventually Smith's network covered the country. Several publishers targeted these bookstalls with extensive series. Chapman & Hall's 'Select Library of Fiction' was one; Trollope's novels were republished by this means.

TB

Ralph the Heir (*see next page*)

Rapinski, jeweller in Prague's Old Town square (Grosser Ring). He lends Nina money on deposit of the treasured necklace that belonged to her dead mother. As a sign of love, Trendellsohn redeems it for her. *NB*   AWJ

Ratler, Mr (sometimes **Rattler**), minor Liberal parliamentary official appearing frequently in the Palliser novels. Though Mr Ratler is not a great political light, he has good sense and does his work conscientiously. He helps Phineas Finn find his footing at the outset of the young man's parliamentary career. *PF*   JMR

Ray, Mrs, widowed mother of Rachel Ray and Dorothea Prime. An essentially weak character, Mrs Ray is a woman 'who cannot grow alone as standard trees' (I) but needs the endless support of others to lean on. Her chief fault is her indecisiveness and lack of confidence about her own moral understanding, as when she prevents Rachel from seeing her lover Luke, against her better wishes. *RR*   MT

Ray, Rachel, young heroine who loves Luke Rowan. Living with her widowed mother and sister in a small cottage with little money, Rachel is devoted to making the home as cheerful and pleasant as possible, and to making her mother happy, but 'the days of . . . rebellion were coming' (I). Rachel is one of Trollope's young heroines with pluck, and her own independent thinking in wishing to continue seeing Luke leads to a split in the family, and the central tension in the novel. Naturally, Rachel's behaviour is beyond reproach, and although the evangelicals, including her sister, condemn her wrongly, Rachel marries her successful lover. *RR*   MT

Reade, Charles (1814–80), novelist and playwright, whose interests in both forms led to several adaptations from book to stage. Social problem novels like *It Is Never Too Late to Mend* (1856) and, on a historical theme, *The Cloister and the Hearth* (1861) made his name. In 1860 he wrote a book defending authors' rights to their materials, *The Eighth Commandment*. This did not stop him making a play out of Trollope's *Ralph the Heir* called *Shilly-Shally* (1872) without the author's prior permission. Trollope angrily wrote to George Smith, *Pall Mall Gazette* (16 June 1872), and the *Daily Telegraph* (1 June 1872) about what he considered plagiarism. Fellow whist-players hitherto, they glowered wordless across a

table at the Garrick for many months. Relations were re-established eventually, Reade serving as steward at a Royal Literary Fund dinner in 1878. Still sore when he wrote *An Autobiography*, Trollope wrote a stinging comment about taking another's words and passing them off as his own (XIII).   RCT

'Real State of Ireland, The'. See 'LETTERS TO THE *EXAMINER*'.

Reckenthorpe, Frank, fighter for the North in the Civil War and rival of his brother Tom for Ada Forster; they are reconciled after Tom is badly wounded. 'Generals' *LS*   GRH

Reckenthorpe, Major. Father of the divided brothers, he suffers greatly because of the Civil War and their differences. 'Generals' *LS*   GRH

Reckenthorpe, Tom. Engaged to Ada Forster, proud of his Southern loyalties, fights with distinction but drops his gun when he faces his brother on the battlefield; he is badly wounded, and the brothers are reconciled. 'Generals' *LS*
GRH

Reddypalm, Mr, owner of the Brown Bear pub in Barchester. A man of humble desires who only asks that his bills be paid, he finally delivers the votes that ensure Sir Roger Scatcherd's victory. However, payment of an old account by Sir Roger's agent leads to the election being overturned. *DT*   NCS

red house, an actual building on Nuremberg's Shütt island, described picturesquely as the Tressels' ancestral home. *LT*   AWJ

***'Red Shirt, The* by Albert Mario: Critical Notice'** (review). This quite improbable narrative purports to be an account of a follower of Garibaldi. While it is an eloquent expression of admiration for Garibaldi, it will not survive as good history. *Fortnightly Review*, February 1866, 775–7.   AKL

Reeve, Henry (1813–95), civil servant, Registrar to the Judicial Committee of the Privy Council (1843–87); expert on foreign affairs for *The Times* (1840–55); edited *Greville Memoirs* (1874); member of the Royal Literary Fund; editor of the *Edinburgh Review* (1855–95). His doubling of careers exemplified Trollope's point that a 'government clerk, who is not wedded to pleasure, may follow any pursuit without detriment to his public utility' (*Letters* 1, 118).   RCT

Reform Act. The Reform Act of 1867, or Second Reform Act, was the seemingly inevitable sequel to the First Reform Act of 1832, which substantially enfranchised the urban middle class. The

(*cont. on page 463*)

Ralph the Heir

TROLLOPE's twenty-sixth novel was written between 4 April and 7 August 1869, though the novelist had mentioned the prospect of a new novel to run serially in *Saint Pauls* in a letter of 14 December 1868 to James Virtue, the magazine's proprietor. He began *Ralph the Heir* at a spirited pace, writing eight pages on the first day and another twelve two days later. He then fell 'very ill' and did not continue until 16 April when he completed the first number. When he finished the manuscript of the novel on 7 August he inscribed his writing calendar with the words: 'Finitum est opus et propositum in partibus duodeviginti intra dies septem octo-decies repetitas' (The work is finished and published in eighteen parts within seven days eighteen times repeated [= within eighteen weeks]). According to an agreement with Virtue of 13 April 1869, the publisher agreed to pay Trollope £2,520 for a serial in eighteen parts, but insisted that he should be free to publish the novel other than in *Saint Pauls* should he dispose of the magazine (of which the novelist was still editor). He did indeed dispose of both the magazine and the copyright of the novel to James Strahan (in whose business he owned a controlling interest) in May 1869. *Ralph the Heir* was eventually published in nineteen, rather than the planned eighteen, monthly parts, priced at sixpence, between January 1870 and July 1871. All except the final number contained a full-page illustration by Francis Arthur *Fraser. Strahan reused the sheets of the unsold monthly parts as a 'free supplement' sewn into the back of issues of *Saint Pauls* during the same period (though the illustrations were dropped in the 'supplement' after the eleventh part). Strahan in turn sold the rights to Hurst & Blackett who brought out a three-volume edition, without illustrations, on 6 April 1871, but published a single-volume edition of his own in June or July containing only eleven of the original plates. In the following year Routledge issued a cheap (six-shilling) one-volume edition with all the illustrations.

Despite the fact that Trollope used the composition of *Ralph the Heir* to work out some of his recent political frustration and to take his revenge on Beverley and its electoral corruptions, he seems to have regarded the novel with some distaste. 'I have always thought it one of the worst novels I have written', he commented in *An Autobiography*, 'and almost to have justified that dictum that a novelist after fifty should not write love stories' (XIX). He insisted in particular that his central male lovers were failures, finding that Ralph (the heir) 'has not much life about him; while Ralph who is not the heir, but is intended to be the real hero, has none'. Trollope did, however, concede that 'that part which appertains to politics and which recounts the electioneering experiences of the candidates at Percycross is well enough', adding that 'Percycross and Beverley were, of course, one and the same place'. The novel's first reviewers certainly liked it well enough. An anonymous critic in *The Times* noted of the electioneering scenes and of the Neefit courtship that 'probably no man alive, now that Charles Dickens has departed, can write on such subjects so humorously and so truthfully' (April 1871), and the *Athenaeum*, the *Spectator*, and (less enthusiastically) the *Examiner* also agreed in praising the novel's impression of 'truth'. Even the *Saturday Review*, often no friend to Trollope, found the novel 'a marvel of freshness' (Smalley, 346–54).

As *An Autobiography* also reminds readers, *Ralph the Heir* had been dramatized, without prior authorial permission, by Charles *Reade in 1872 (though Trollope preferred to describe the process as Reade 'taking a plot and making on it a play'). Reade's play, *Shilly-Shally*, had opened at the Gaiety Theatre on 1 April 1872. Trollope belatedly received the letter announcing Reade's intentions (dated 7 March) when he was in Australia and was vexed that his name might have appeared on a London play-bill as a joint author with Reade. In May 1872 he wrote a letter to the editor of the *Pall Mall Gazette* complaining that he 'ought not to be placed in jeopardy without my own consent'. He also wrote to the editor of the *Daily Telegraph* in June insisting that he was 'in no way responsible for the play', that his plot had been 'adopted' without his knowledge, and that as he claimed 'no share in the dramatic merits of the piece' so neither was he responsible for its faults. He remained estranged from Reade until 1877.

The main plot-line of *Ralph the Heir* hinges on the problem of inheritance in an old, landowning family in Hampshire. The two central male characters are confusingly both named Ralph Newton. They are cousins, one legitimate, the other illegitimate. The legitimate Ralph, 'the heir', is the nephew of Gregory Newton of Newton Priory. The Newton estate has been entailed by the cousins' grandfather on the male heir of the family in the second generation and is thus to come to this first Ralph. Gregory Newton's illegitimate son Ralph is the product of a liaison with a German lady who died before a marriage could be formalized. Being anxious that Newton Priory should be inherited by the worthy, country-based, bastard son to whom he is passionately attached, Squire Newton persuades his profligate nephew to sell him the reversion of the estate for £50,000, but the old man is unexpectedly killed in a hunting accident before negotiations have been completed. The virtuous, intelligent, but illegitimate Ralph does, however, receive £40,000 under the terms of his father's will and finally purchases an estate in Norfolk. To confuse matters further for those readers not attuned to the complexities of inherited nomenclature and the use of namesakes in county families, Ralph 'the heir' has a younger brother, another Gregory, who is the rector of the family living of Newton Peele. The legitimate Ralph is an easygoing, lackadaisical young man much given to hunting, 'unsteady, extravagant and idle'. Though based in London at the beginning of the novel, Ralph regularly escapes down to the Moonbeam where he stables his horses and hunts with the Berkshire and Buckinghamshire (the 'B&B'). This Ralph is also heavily in debt to the obliging Conduit Street breeches-maker Thomas Neefit. The prosperous, pushy, and ambitious Neefit is determined that his daughter Maryanne (Polly) should marry a gentleman and thus assure the family's social rise. In order to assist his campaign he offers to cancel the existing debts and to give the prospective bridegroom £20,000 should Ralph agree to an engagement to Polly. She, however, will have none of the scheme, preferring, with her mother's support, the offer of marriage from a very different suitor, the radically minded and decidedly ungentlemanly Ontario Moggs, the son of a London bootmaker. When Ralph inherits the Newton estate from his uncle and transfers his suit from the unenthusiastic Polly to Augusta Eardham (the daughter of a Berkshire baronet), Neefit clumsily attempts to threaten him but is eventually persuaded to accept the status quo. When Ralph marries Augusta Eardham, his former guardian, Sir Thomas Underwood, shrewdly comments: 'I think he will be happy;—what people call happy. He is not gifted,—or cursed, as it may be,—with fine feelings, and is what perhaps may be called thick skinned; but he will love his own wife and children . . . I shouldn't wonder if he becomes a prosperous and most respectable country gentleman, and quite a model to his neighbours' (LVI).

Ralph the Heir

The second line of the plot is concerned with the Underwood family, and especially with the widowed Sir Thomas, a reclusive Chancery barrister, former MP and sometime Solicitor-General in a Conservative administration. In his working calendar Trollope had given the new novel the provisional title 'Underwood', suggesting that in his original conception of his story this somewhat morbid barrister with political ambitions was to have been his central character. Since his defeat in the election which followed the fall of the government in which he had served, Sir Thomas has returned to his legal career, spending most of his week in his lonely chambers in Southampton Buildings, and only occasionally visiting his two daughters, Patience and Clarissa, at the family home on the banks of the river Thames, Popham Villa, Fulham. Here the Underwoods are joined by Sir Thomas's new ward, his orphaned niece Mary Bonner, who has been brought up in Jamaica. The younger daughter, Clarissa Underwood, believes herself to be in love with Ralph 'the heir' until he abruptly transfers his attentions to her cousin Mary and then, under obligation, to Polly Neefit. When Mary finally agrees to marry the illegitimate Ralph and becomes mistress of Beamingham Hall, Norfolk, Clarissa accepts an offer of marriage from the Revd Gregory Newton, who has long been attached to her but who had appeared to be romantically overshadowed by his brother.

It was, however, Sir Thomas Underwood's attempt to forge a second parliamentary career for himself which evidently most interested Trollope in planning his novel. In chapter XX Sir Thomas receives an invitation to stand as one of the two Conservative candidates in the election at Percycross. The sitting Conservative member, Mr Griffenbottom, has formerly assured his election to Parliament by being 'very generous with his purse'. The scenes concerned with the unhappy Percycross election campaign and the account of the electoral corruption of that borough have both a detailed comic vividness and a compelling seriousness which set them aside from the elections which figure in *The Three Clerks*, *Doctor Thorne*, *Can You Forgive Her?*, and *Rachel Ray*. Percycross had heretofore returned one Conservative and one radical member, but the invitation to Sir Thomas is set to undermine the existing working balance in the borough's politics. Against the two Conservatives stand two radicals, the well-established sitting member, Mr Westmacott, and *his* running mate, Polly Neefit's sweetheart Ontario Moggs, the bootmaker's son who holds 'horrible ideas about co-operative associations, the rights of labour, and the welfare of the masses' (VIII), and who has already made a career for himself addressing political meetings of like-minded artisans in the front parlour of the Cheshire Cheese in London. It is not, however, on political programmes or on the niceties of contemporary political debate that Trollope chooses to dwell. His chief narrative concern is with exposing the sordid venality of the Percycross campaign, the disruptive public violence of the hustings (during which Sir Thomas has his arm broken by a stone), and with the growing disillusion and incomprehension of the honourable but fatally indolent Underwood. Despite the obvious differences between the character and the politics of the fictional Sir Thomas and those of Trollope himself, the former's jaded disillusion clearly parallels that of his creator. Underwood too is warned by a 'learned pundit', in words which echo those of *An Autobiography*, that he is likely to waste his money and lose the election and that the victors will be unseated by petition and the borough disfranchised. The corrupt Griffenbottom bears more than a passing resemblance to Sir Henry Edwards, as does the Tory agent, Mr Trigger, to Sir Henry's agent at Beverley.

Although, unlike Trollope at Beverley, Underwood wins his seat at Percycross, he is later obliged to surrender it in humiliating circumstances and is driven to express a painful disillusion: 'What excuse had he for placing himself in contact with such filth? Of what childishness had he not been the victim when he allowed himself to dream that he, a pure and scrupulous man, could go among such impurity as he had found at Percycross, and come out, still clean and yet triumphant?' (XL). Later in the novel the narrator generalizes as Sir Thomas's thoughts become yet more gloomy: 'There come upon us all as we grow up in years, hours in which it is impossible to keep down the conviction that everything is vanity, that the life past has been vain from folly, and that the life to come must be vain from impotence . . . Was not life becoming to him vainer and still vainer every day? He had promised himself once that books should be the solace of his age, and he was beginning to hate his books, because he knew that he did no more than trifle with them. He had found himself driven to attempt to escape from them back into public life; but had failed, and had been inexpressibly dismayed in the failure. While failing, he had promised himself that he would rush at his work on his return to privacy and to quiet; but he was still as the shivering coward, who stands upon the brink, and cannot plunge in among the bathers' (LI). Though he self-evidently lacks his creator's energy, the defeated Sir Thomas does genuinely attempt to act and to find some solace in literature. Having retired to his solitary life in his chambers he resumes the 'very great piece of work' on which he has been engaged since he was called to the bar but of which he has not written a single word, a Life of that corrupt Chancery lawyer and eminently corruptible public servant Francis Bacon. The novel ends with the perhaps vain, but certainly pious, hope 'that the great Life of Bacon may yet be written' (LVIII). The manuscript is in the Houghton Library, Harvard.   ALS

next step was the working class, but how many? and when would it be 'safe'? The moment seemed to be ripening in the prosperous 1860s. The extra-parliamentary Reform Union and Reform League mobilized respectable support and Palmerston's death in 1865 removed a parliamentary obstacle. Earl *Russell, chief author of the 1832 Act, now became Prime Minister and, with the support of his heir apparent *Gladstone, a recent and ardent convert to reform, seized the opportunity to add to his record as a reformer. However, the Conservative opposition, supported by anti-reform liberals, defeated Russell's cautious reform bill in June 1866, causing his government to fall.

The moving spirit in the new government of Lord Derby was *Disraeli, who smelled an opportunity to 'steal the Whig's clothes' and create new supporters for the Conservative Party among the deferential working class with a reform bill of his own. Improvising desperately and facing down the hostility of Conservative colleagues he kept the minority government in office by introducing a hastily devised reform bill and then accepting practically every radical amendment made to it. (One amendment however was far too radical for the House—that of John Stuart *Mill to extend the franchise to women.) Outside pressure, including threats of working-class violence—not perhaps altogether serious—helped Disraeli to persuade his party of the necessity for an extensive measure. The final outcome was a bill far more radical than Russell's 1866 bill. Extending the franchise to all urban householders, it doubled the electorate, nearly half of which was now working class, and further diminished the number of small borough seats controlled by patronage. *Phineas Finn* was written in the midst of these events and engages them closely.   CK

Smith, F. B., *The Making of the Second Reform Bill* (1966).

Regan, Patrick, Irish barrister with a poetic bent who became 'Attorney-General at one of the Turtle Islands'. 'Panjandrum' *ET*   GRH

regional novels. By the middle of the 19th century English novel-readers and English publishers disliked what they perceived as the insistent grimness of many Irish tales. The famine and Fenianism exacerbated this distaste for Ireland as a setting. Scotland's popularity as a regional setting found no successor to Sir Walter *Scott. Mainstream Victorian novels are often urban rather than rural or regional, but Trollope ploughed a lone and characteristic furrow. His 'regional' works fall into two distinct categories: the Irish novels combine well-observed local colour with observation upon contemporary events; the Barsetshire novels create a new English shire and are less directly bound to grim contemporaneity.

Trollope wrote perceptively and compassionately about Ireland. Because he knew and liked them he took the Irish seriously at a time when the English stage produced only stereotyped comic micks, and when the Anglo-Irish novelist Charles *Lever was traduced by his nationalist countrymen (however unfairly) for what they saw as patronizing accounts of Irish life. Trollope avoids both the unremitting grimness which made Carleton, for instance, unpopular with English readers, and the cavalier insouciance of Lever.

The early Irish novels are sympathetic not only to the Irish poor, but to the priests of the Catholic religion. *The Macdermots of Ballycloran* gives an uncompromising account of the squalor and hopelessness of the decayed local squirearchy in Co. Leitrim. Yet it is relieved by scenes of local life and scenery. The later Irish novels preach, at chapter length, material which would be more appropriate to pamphlets on famine relief or the Land League. But the pictures of Irish people and places remain sharp, poignant, and original. No other English novelist between 1840 and 1885 equals the honesty, experience, or skill with which Trollope describes the people, places, and problems of his adopted and much-loved second home.

Trollope is best remembered for the creation of his own highly imaginative kind of regional novel. The story of the genesis of Barsetshire is familiar enough: Trollope's Post Office forays through the south-western counties of England inspired the conflation of Salisbury and Winchester into his imaginary ecclesiastical city and shire. Trollope boasted of 'the new shire which I had added to the English counties. . . . there has been no name given to a fictitious site which does not represent . . . a spot of which I know all the accessories, as though I had lived and wandered there' (*Auto* IV). The settings grow organically richer, more convincing, as the series progresses. Although Trollope is usually perceived as an author more proficient in describing people than places, and although he never creates scenery

which asserts a symbolic presence as it does in Hardy, yet by the conclusion of the Barsetshire novels the organic consistency of his 'dear county' presents a convincing and consistent imaginative world.   TB

Cronin, J., 'Trollope and the Matter of Ireland', in T. Bareham (ed.), *Anthony Trollope* (1980).
Knox, R., *Literary Distractions* (1958).
Pollard, A., *Anthony Trollope* (1978).

'Rejoinder to Mr Harper' (letter). Regarding Mr Harper's defence of his publication of *North America* without permission (*Athenaeum* 18 October), some of his statements are incorrect. His argument that any publishing is risky, and the first publisher on the scene is entitled to the profits, is itself an argument for the necessity of an international copyright law. *Athenaeum* (25 October 1862), 529–30.   AKL

'Relics of General Chassé: A Tale of Antwerp', first printed in *Harper's New Monthly Magazine*, February 1860 (reprinted in *TAC1*); Trollope's first published short story. Visiting a museum devoted to the memory of the Dutch general who defended the city of Antwerp during its siege in 1832, the Revd Augustus Horne and the narrator are taken by the great soldier's breeches. Horne tries them on, only to be surprised by a troupe of English ladies. He hides himself, while they cut strips from his trousers ('unmentionables') for their patchwork boxes. After some jocular embarrassment, all ends well.   JS

religious faith and worship. In the 19th century religious faith came under increasing challenge from both textual scholarship, which questioned the authority of Scripture, and science, which raised doubts about man's divine origin. Trollope's faith was unshaken by this climate of scepticism, and he remained a devout Christian, a lifelong regular worshipper, and assiduous in his private prayers. He believed in a merciful God, lived as a Christian gentleman, and, as he told his friend George *Rusden, he looked forward to an everlasting reward for the quality of his earthly life.

Trollope's spiritual hero is Mr Harding, a high churchman and utterly different in temperament from himself, the moral centre of *The Warden* and *Barchester Towers*. In his dignified and gracious life are united the fundamental Christian values of humility, charity, faith in a beneficent God, delight in his world, and gratitude for his many blessings. Mr Harding's acute conscience compels him to resign the wardenship of Hiram's Hospital, and later his innate humility and respect for the offices of the Church lead him to refuse appointment as Dean of Barchester. His simple faith is summed up in *The Warden* on the occasion of his farewell to the bedesmen of Hiram's Hospital: 'I hope you may live contented, and die trusting in the Lord Jesus Christ, and thankful to Almighty God for the good things he has given you' (XX). And for Trollope not least among Mr Harding's qualities is his devotion to church music and to the improvement, during his time as precentor, of the cathedral choir.

Although frequent biblical quotations, and occasional references to biblical incidents, occur in his fiction, religious faith is rarely a subject. But it does find expression in his non-fictional writings. In *Clergymen of the Church of England* and *The Life of Cicero* he asserts the divinity of Christ, and argues for the fundamental importance of religious faith in human experience.

Trollope's attitude to reform within his own Church was quite liberal, accepting the phasing out of the Athanasian Creed, and defending Bishop Colenso's questioning of the literal accuracy of the Scriptures, while retaining a core belief in the essentials of Christian doctrine. But his instincts were high church. He was sympathetic to the influential Oxford Movement, begun in the 1840s, with its spiritual energy, its emphasis on the sacraments and liturgical ritual, and its concern for the integrity of the Church. Essentially, for Trollope the Church of England was the Church of gentlemen, such as the Barsetshire clergymen Archdeacon Grantly and Mr Harding.

As one would expect from a man whose friends included prominent Catholics and Jews, Trollope was tolerant of other faiths. He admired the fact that, in spite of its authoritarianism, Roman Catholicism so directly addressed human nature. Trollope also writes with sympathy of the Irish Catholic poor in novels such as *The Macdermots of Ballycloran*. His worthy priests include its gentlemanly Father John McGrath, and also the liberal Catholic priest Father Gondin in *The Golden Lion of Granpère*. Trollope's understanding of the ghetto mentality of European Jews is evident in *Nina Balatka*. He ridicules anti-Semitism in *The Way We Live Now*, by presenting the Jewish banker Mr Brehgert as a gentleman, whose code of conduct is based on religious faith. Trollope's tolerance did not encompass evangelicalism, however, which he associated with cant, and which he took to task many times, as in Mrs Proudie and the Bishop's chaplain Mr Slope in *Barchester Towers*, or Mr Stumfold and his curate Mr Maguire in *Miss Mackenzie*.

Trollope was interested in ecclesiastical rather than theological aspects of religious faith in his fiction, relishing the drama of the battle between High Church and evangelicals in Barsetshire. But unusually, in *Linda Tressel* he explores the psychology of religious fanaticism in Linda's aunt Charlotte Staubach, an Anabaptist, who wants to crush her niece's capacity for enjoyment. *The Bertrams* is notable for its inclusion of a visit to Palestine; for a serious debate between George Bertram and his friend the clergyman Arthur Wilkinson, about scientific materialism and religious belief; and for its treatment of Bertram's sceptical book *The Romance of Scripture*, which challenges the literal interpretation of certain biblical passages.

Worship is mentioned rarely, but part of the ecclesiastical war in *Barchester Towers* is carried forward by Mr Slope's onslaught on the high-church tradition of cathedral music, and Trollope's clear preference emerges for the ritualism and dignity of the high-church liturgy.   GH

Rerechild, Mr, one of five Barchester doctors, with slightly more modern views of medicine. He treats baby Johnny Bold and assists Dr Fillgrave with the dying Dean. He also ministers to Sir Roger Scatcherd in *Doctor Thorne*. BT   NCS

'*Resources and Prosperity of America* by M. Peto' (review). This is a voluminous book of facts, statistics, and data about America's agriculture, minerals, and commerce. Credit is given to a people full of energy and industry. Curiously there is no treatment of the outstanding public education system. It is dull but informative. *Fortnightly Review* (15 May 1866), 126–8.   AKL

'Returning Home', first serialized in *Public Opinion*, 30 November and 7 December 1861 (reprinted in *TAC2*). Harry and Fanny Arkwright, a young British couple with a baby, prepare to make the arduous journey home to England from San Jose in Costa Rica. At her irrational insistence they take the most difficult route, by mule through the forests and boat along the Serapiqui river. Assisted by her brother Abel, they finally reach the embarkation point on the river, which has been swollen by rains. Fanny's canoe capsizes and she drowns. Arkwright returns to San Jose, unable to face his wife's mother in England.   JS

Revoke, Lady Ruth, ardent whist-player whose passion for winning leads to a hysterical fit. B   MRS

Rewble, Harriet, one of the Shand daughters who is married to a curate and assumes a self-righteous demeanour regarding Hester Caldigate's ambiguous position during John Caldigate's bigamy trial. JC   SRB

Reynolds, Joe, tenant of the Macdermots, and brother of Pat and Tim Reynolds, both imprisoned by the activities of Myles Ussher. Marked by the authorities as a leader of local Ribbonmen, he not only induces an intoxicated Thady Macdermot to join them against Hyacinth Keegan and Myles Ussher, but assaults Keegan, hacking off his foot with an axe. When Thady is led to execution at Carrick jail, Reynolds ensures, in concert with the priests, that there are no public witnesses to the hanging. *MB*   MRS

Reynolds, Tim, tenant of the Macdermots, and brother of Ribbonman Joe Reynolds, who, though technically innocent of distilling illicit whiskey, is caught in a raid by Myles Ussher, and, unable to pay a fine of £10, sentenced to an indefinite period of imprisonment at Ballinamore jail. *MB*   MRS

Richard, Herbert Fitzgerald's loyal Irish servant who welcomes his master's return to Castle Richmond. *CR*   MRS

Richardson, Samuel (1689–1761), famous for *Pamela: or Virtue Rewarded* (1741) and *Clarissa* (1748). Trollope never reconciled himself to the epistolary form, which seemed 'awkward and tedious' (*Letters* 1, 444). He reviewed an abridged *Clarissa* by E. S. Dallas critically in *Saint Pauls* (November 1868). He found the use of letters an 'impossible' narrative device and declared the main characters untrue to nature. Also objecting to the length of Richardson's novel, he doubted Dallas's abridgement did much to improve upon the original.   RCT

Richmond, location of Fawn Court. *ED*   JMR

Ricketts, Mr, Apjohn's confidential clerk who terrorizes Henry Jones with gleeful accounts of Mr Cheekey's ferocity as a cross-examining lawyer. *CH*   AWJ

'Ride across Palestine, A' (originally 'The Banks of the Jordan'), first serialized in the *London Review*, 5, 12, 19 January 1861 (reprinted in *TAC2*). 'Jones', as the narrator calls himself, is asked by a 'John Smith' if he may accompany him on a journey by horse across the Holy Land. They set off together and see the Dead Sea, Jerusalem, the Jordan. At Jaffa, Jones (a happily married man) is confronted by an angry Sir William Weston, who informs him that 'John Smith' is in fact his niece Julia. After all is explained, Jones bids farewell to his erstwhile companion, who thanks him tenderly.   JS

'Right of Secession, The' (letter). A response to the recent claim that secession in the USA must be a right, because it was threatened by the Northerners in the past: this is analogous to the threatened break with Britain by the Irish leader O'Connell. Both countries allow latitude in speech; only deeds are prosecutable, as with Smith O'Brien here and the confederacy there. There is no provision for secession in the constitution, so it must be rebellion. *Pall Mall Gazette* (2 June 1865), 4.   AKL

Ring, Abel. Partner and brother-in-law to Harry Arkwright in Costa Rica, he sees his sister drown. 'Returning' *TAC2*   GRH

Ringwood, Trollope's groom-cum-manservant who joined the household after Barney, Trollope's servant of many years, returned to Ireland. He was paid 22 shillings a week. He was frequently observed in the local inn: Trollope noted, 'he does not become drunk, but is exactly like an owl' (*Letters* 2, 871).   RCT

Roanoke, Lucinda, stately, beautiful, and forbidding niece of Jane Carbuncle, who enters into a disastrous engagement with Sir Griffin Tewett. Much against her will, Lucinda is dragged into the marriage market by the scheming Mrs Carbuncle, who is anxious that her niece find a proper establishment before exhausting her limited funds. After lapsing into near-madness at the prospect of marrying the sadistic Sir Griffin, Lucinda refuses to go to the church on the day set for the wedding. *ED*   JMR

Robarts, Dr, Exeter physician whose lucrative practice enables him to maintain and educate seven children. He encourages the friendship of his eldest son Mark with young Lord Lufton, which leads to Mark's appointment as rector of Framley Parsonage. A generous man of whom it was said his life had been good and prosperous and his will just. *FP*   NCS

Robarts, Fanny (née **Mansell**), a large woman, with copious brown hair and distinctive brown eyes. A friend of Justinia Lufton, she marries Mark Robarts. Gentle, tender, and loyal, she defends her husband's vices to his patron, Lady Lufton, and supports him when his imprudence leads to the seizure of their property. She sympathizes with the tribulations of her sister-in-law Lucy, and takes in the children of Revd Josiah Crawley when their mother contracts typhus. *FP, LCB*   NCS

Robarts, Gerald, second son of Dr Robarts of Exeter, brother of Revd Mark Robarts. Officer in a crack regiment, he becomes a captain in Crimea. *FP*   NCS

Robarts, Jane, third daughter of Dr Robarts of Exeter, after whose death she goes to her sister and brother-in-law, Squire Crowdy of Devon, whose neighbour reportedly seeks a wife. *FP* NCS

Robarts, John (Jack), youngest son of Dr Robarts of Exeter, and assistant private secretary to the Minister of the Petty Bag Office. Five months short of his majority when his father dies, he cannot claim his legacy, which might help pay his brother Mark's debts. A well-built, pleasant young fellow, he thrives when promoted to private secretary, displaying his new clothes and natty umbrella. *FP* NCS

Robarts, Lucy, youngest daughter of Dr Robarts of Exeter. At 19, she comes to live with her brother Mark at Framley Parsonage. Smaller and plainer than her sisters, she has fine eyes and a reputation for cleverness. Too proud to accept Lord Lufton's proposal and the concomitant displeasure of his mother Lady Lufton, Lucy lies to her suitor and then avoids him. Undemonstrative and contented, she proves her generosity and courage in nursing Mrs Josiah Crawley through an episode of typhoid fever. Also appears as the younger Lady Lufton in *The Last Chronicle of Barset. FP* NCS

Robarts, Mark, vicar of Framley in Barsetshire, and eldest son of Dr Robarts of Exeter. After receiving his living from Lady Lufton, he falls in with a disreputable group of politicians led by Nathaniel Sowerby, who entangles him financially. Tall, manly, and fair-haired, fond of pleasure and high society, the young minister takes up fox-hunting and expensive social activities, to the despair of his devoted wife and Lady Lufton. He succeeds Dr Vesey Stanhope as prebendary of Barchester, but his debts fall due. His sister Lucy's love for his friend Lord Lufton further complicates his life, since it antagonizes Lady Lufton. In *The Last Chronicle of Barset* he aids Revd Josiah Crawley. *FP* NCS

Robespierre, Maximilian (based on historical figure). Pre-eminent in power at the time; ruled by cool rationalism, he determines to put down the Vendean revolt, sparing nobody in the process, and, when Eleanor Duplay begs him to be merciful, becomes suspicious of her. *LV* GRH

Robinson, Ellen Lawless (née **Ternan**) (1839–1914), sister of Thomas Adolphus Trollope's second wife Frances. A member of the Ternan acting family, she had been Dickens's mistress. In 1876 she married the Revd George Wharton Robinson, joint principal of Margate High School. Trollope's grandson later attended the school. On sports day in July 1878, Trollope gave out the prizes. He told the pupils, 'I went to school when I was seven, and I left school when I was nineteen . . . and in all those years I don't think I ever saw a prize, and I'm sure I never got one!' (*Chron* 127). In this instance Trollope was perhaps disingenuous; he won an essay prize while at Harrow. RCT

Robinson, George, junior partner of the firm, who brings ruin upon the haberdashery business by lavishly worded advertisements. When bankruptcy is declared he advertises it with bills: 'Ruin! . . . Wasteful and Impetuous Sale', to bring in customers (XXII). *SBJR* HO

Robinson, Revd George Wharton, husband of Ellen Lawless Ternan, Dickens's mistress and sister of T. A. Trollope's second wife Frances; joint principal of the High School, Margate, attended by Frank Trollope, Trollope's grandson. RCT

Robinson, Jemima, friend of Mary Tomkins who urges her to choose from her two suitors, preferably John Thomas. 'Never' RCT

Robinson, John, friend of George Walker who takes his family to Suez. 'Walker' *TAC2* GRH

Robinson, Mr, narrator travelling in northern Italy who befriends the Greenes, comes under suspicion when their box of valuables is lost, and parts from them thankfully. 'Money' *TAC2* GRH

Roby, Harriet, sister-in-law of Abel Wharton and frequent companion of his daughter Emily. A lady of doubtful judgement and dubious character, Mrs Roby is attracted to Ferdinand Lopez's polished manners and dark good looks. She does everything in her power to forward the match between him and her niece Emily. *PM* JMR

Roby, Richard, husband of Harriet Roby, brother-in-law of Abel Wharton, and younger brother of the Roby who serves as Secretary of the Admiralty. Avidly interested in sporting activities and somewhat of a braggart, Dick Roby attempts to meet the genteel expectations of his wife's family, but with indifferent success. *PM* JMR

Roby, Thomas, Conservative Whip, Patronage Secretary, and, eventually, Secretary of the Admiralty. A relation by marriage of the Whartons of *The Prime Minister*, Mr Roby is a useful man, though perhaps not so good-natured as his Liberal counterpart Mr Ratler. *PF, PR, DC* JMR

Roden, George, postal clerk with radical political opinions who challenges the meaning of nobility in *Marion Fay*. He and Lady Frances Trafford fall in love, partly as a result of her democratic principles but also because she believes him to be a gentleman in bearing and education. When it is discovered that George is actually the son of an Italian duke of the historic di Crinola family, English society tries hard, against George's wishes, to grant him income and privileges due to his station. *MF*   SRB

Roden, Mary, decent, quiet-living mother of George. She keeps secret from him the fact that his father was an Italian duke until the latter's death clears her own name. She is also a kind and supportive friend to Zachary and Marion Fay in their troubles regarding Marion's aristocratic lover Lord Hampstead and Marion's final illness. *MF*   SRB

Roebury, popular hunting territory frequented by George Vavasor, Pollock, and other metropolitan sportsmen. *CYFH*   JMR

Rolland, Mr, Bishop of Broughton, a good man, but also a pragmatic one, placing his own professional interests and the welfare of his family before a disinterested sense of duty. Mildly jealous of and occasionally antagonistic to Dr Wortle, the Bishop is drawn into the controversy surrounding the Peacockes. *DWS*   RC

roman-à-clef, a novel attributing fictitious entities to recognizable real-life originals. *The Warden* is based upon two real cases involving misappropriation of ecclesiastical funds; Mr Popular Sentiment and Dr Pessimist Anticant are customarily identified with Dickens and Carlyle respectively; the magisterial interference of the *Jupiter* embodies Trollope's critique of *The Times*. In the Palliser novels no such regular attributions should be made. Mr Gresham is not simply or even principally Mr Gladstone, nor Mr Daubeny Disraeli. Such forced parallels weaken the originality of Trollope's perceptions.   TB
  Cockshut, A. O. J., appendix to *Anthony Trollope* (1955).

Roman Catholic Church. Trollope was friendly with prominent Roman Catholics, including Cardinal *Manning, but he first came to know Catholics intimately during his tour of duty for the Post Office in Ireland. Trollope recognized affinities between his own high-church wing of the Church of England and Roman Catholicism, though he could not accept Catholic doctrine. And although his respect for Roman Catholicism as a sympathetic and humane creed was considerable, as he points out in *North America*, he felt that their unquestioning obedience, though admirable, was almost child-like.

His religious tolerance extended even to fanatics, such as Father George Bampfield, a local clergyman who had converted to Rome, and who was staying with the Trollopes during a period of hardship. A good man and a gentleman, he nevertheless made an unfortunate attempt to convert his host. This episode is fictionalized in *The Way We Live Now*, with Roger Carbury as the unfortunate victim of Father Barham's missionary zeal. In Trollope's working papers for the novel, Bampfield is denoted as 'Pervert. Waltham Priest'.

Catholicism is dealt with, of course, in the Irish novels. *The Macdermots of Ballycloran* reveals Trollope's sympathy for the suffering of rural Irish Catholics, such as the Macdermots, small gentry in the process of being ruined by debt. Unusually, the novel's hero is a Roman Catholic priest, Father John McGrath, a moral man with a liberal attitude towards other faiths. By contrast, Father Marty, in *An Eye for an Eye*, which is set in the west of Ireland, is an ambivalent figure, who, although a worthy man, was educated in France and belongs to the literary tradition of wily Catholics who trap young Protestant aristocrats into marriage. In the late Irish novel *The Landleaguers*, Trollope's historical sense is again in play, as the youngest of the novel's three priests has become implicated in terrorism. Such involvement of the Church in political violence is deplored.

Roman Catholics are portrayed from various perspectives in those novels with a European setting. In *Nina Balatka* the warm humanity of the priest, Father Jerome, is contrasted with the fanaticism of Nina's aunt. Conversely, the Calvinism of Linda Tressel's aunt Charlotte Staubach appears extreme set beside the kindness of the Catholic servant Tetchen. The problem of Protestant–Catholic marriages occupies *The Golden Lion of Granpère*, and the priest in this novel, Father Gondin, who resists the impulse to proselytize, represents the kind of religious liberalism Trollope approved of.

The only really prominent Roman Catholic layman in Trollope is Phineas Finn, whose career is followed in *Phineas Finn* and *Phineas Redux*. From the outset, Trollope emphasizes the freedom from religious bigotry of middle-class Roman Catholics. Finn is the product of a marriage of Protestant and Catholic, and although brought up a Catholic, he attends the Protestant Trinity College, Dublin. And indeed, his religious convictions are of less consequence than his situation as an Irish Catholic interloper in English society.   GH

Rome, favourite dwelling place of expatriate aspiring artists. 'Talboys' *TAC2*   GRH

Rooney, Terry, Barry Lynch's manservant, cowed along with the other household servants by his master's anger, and made fearful for the safety of Anty Lynch. *KOK*   MRS

Roper, Amelia, daughter of Mrs Roper of Burton Crescent. A clever, dark-haired, mischievous, and practical 30-year-old former 'first young lady at a millinery establishment in Manchester' (IV), she sets out to trap Johnny Eames into marriage, but finally settles for his friend Joseph Cradell. *SHA, LCB*   NCS

Roper, Mrs, landlady of the boarding house in Burton Crescent where Johnny Eames lodges. Known as 'Mother Roper', she runs her barely respectable house kindly but ineffectively, troubled by the non-paying Lupexes and saved only by her cousin, the elderly Miss Spruce. *SHA*   NCS

Rosebank, formerly Barleystubb Farm near Barchester, home of the Lookalofts. Wishing to raise her status, Mrs Lookaloft has a pianoforte in the drawing room and other finery to ape the upper class. *BT*   NCS

Ross, Dick, impoverished bachelor confidant of Sir Francis Geraldine who finally becomes so repelled by the Baronet's attitudes toward women in general and Cecilia Western in particular that he gives up the nobleman's bounty. *KD*   NCS

Rossiter, Major John. Deputy Inspector General of the Cavalry, he is tempted to marry Georgiana Wanless, but he chooses his childhood sweetheart Alice Dugdale in the end. 'Dugdale' *WFF*   GRH

Rossiter, Mr, rector who wants his son Major Rossiter to marry Alice Dugdale. 'Dugdale' *WFF*   GRH

Rossiter, Mrs. Unlike her husband she is ambitious for her son to marry Georgiana Wanless. 'Dugdale' *WFF*   GRH

Rothschild, Baron Meyer Amschel de (1818–74), Liberal MP for Hythe, 1859–74; art collector; sportsman and hunter who kept deerhounds at Leighton Buzzard in Bedfordshire. Returning from Australia in December 1872 with renewed zest for hunting, Trollope 'became one of that numerous herd of sportsmen who rode with the "Baron" ' (*Auto* XIX).   RCT

Round, Matthew (Mat), son of Richard Round and an attorney for Joseph Mason. A partner in the firm of Round & Crook of Bedford Row, Matthew Round is as trustworthy as his father and works for Mason during the trial of Lady Mason. *OF*   MT

Round, Richard, attorney for Joseph Mason at both Orley Farm trials and one of the senior partners in the firm of Round & Crook, Bedford Row. He is respectable and honest, and when Joseph Mason insists on wishing to punish Lady Mason after the second trial, he ejects him from his offices. *OF*   MT

Rowan, Luke, young man who inherits an interest in the Bungall & Tappitt Brewery and who eventually marries Rachel Ray. Luke is one of Trollope's affable and ambitious young heroes, ripe for marriage. He enters Baslehurst with 'newfangled ways' (X), intent on brewing good beer in a region known for bad beer and cider. He has to contend with old-fashioned business practices at the brewery and with gossiping townspeople in his love life, but he triumphs in the end. *RR*   MT

Rowan, Mary, Luke Rowan's younger sister. The Tappitt girls hope to take Mary under their wing when the Rowans come to visit. Mary 'was by no means stately' and was 'very willing to be pleased, with pleasant round eager eyes, and a kindly voice' (VI). *RR*   MT

Rowan, Mrs, Luke Rowan's mother who comes to stay with the Tappitts in Baslehurst. A loving but protective mother, she initially tries to put a stop to Luke's courtship of Rachel Ray. She aligns herself with Mrs Tappitt at first, but in a memorable scene in Mrs Ray's parlour, the maternal alliance comes unstuck, and Mrs Rowan later welcomes Rachel into her family. *RR*   MT

Rowley, Lady Bessie, wife of Sir Marmaduke. She recognizes that her daughter should not see Colonel Osborne but defends Emily's conduct. Her effort to reconcile the spouses is repulsed by Louis Trevelyan. Although supportive of her husband, she is less irascible and more ready to accept Hugh Stanbury as a prospective son-in-law. *HKWR*   RC

Rowley, Emily. See TREVELYAN, EMILY.

Rowley, Sir Marmaduke, British Governor of the Mandarin Islands. An indolent administrator, he has saved nothing to provide for his eight daughters. His irascible treatment of his son-in-law Louis Trevelyan, and his daughter Nora's suitor Hugh Stanbury suggests that this 'vehement man' (LXI) is no more adept at ruling his house than the British colony. *HKWR*   RC

Rowley, Nora, second of Sir Marmaduke's eight daughters. She leaves her family in the Mandarin Islands to live with her married elder sister Emily Trevelyan in England. She rejects the proposal of a wealthy aristocrat (Charles Glascock) in the hope of marrying a poor journalist

(Hugh Stanbury). Their prospective middle-class life together is represented by 'an emblematic beef-steak' (XCVI)—their substantial but modest daily fare. *HKWR*   RC

Royal Academy of Arts. The Royal Academy was the summit of the artistic establishment and never more influential than in the mid-Victorian period. Its self-elected members, mostly painters, were the arbiters of popular taste. Attending its summer exhibition, especially the exclusive Private View, which Trollope did regularly, was an essential ritual of the season. W. P. Frith's painting *The Private View of the Royal Academy, 1881* superbly captures its ambience, depicting a group of eminent Victorians including Browning, Gladstone, and Huxley, with Oscar Wilde at one side gazing aesthetically upwards and Trollope on the other formally dressed with eyes intent on the work at hand. Trollope was several times a guest speaker at anniversary banquets. At a function prior to the opening of the exhibition to the public on 4 May 1867, he responded to a warm tribute from the President, Sir Francis Grant, who had said that Trollope's novels appealed so strongly to artists because they were so graphic and faithful to nature. A few days before leaving for Australia in May 1871, Trollope again spoke at the Royal Academy banquet. In fiction Trollope shows Ralph Newton 'Among the Pictures' at the Academy (*RH* XLIX).   CK

Hutchinson, Sydney C., *History of the Royal Academy 1760–1968* (1968).

'Royal Geographical Society Address' (response to report). As a recent traveller to the Transvaal, the speaker finds the preceding account over-optimistic. Since the British takeover, the native (African) population has increased, while the numbers of Europeans have not—very unlike the experience in other colonies, e.g. Melbourne. The Transvaal cannot economically support a British labourer at the level of other colonies. *The Times* (16 January 1878), 6.   AKL

Royal Literary Fund. The Literary Fund was constituted in 1788 on the initiative of the Revd David Williams, with the intention of relieving the financial difficulties of distressed authors. Its first formal committee meeting was held in May 1790. It was only in 1842, thanks to the interest of Prince Albert, that the Fund added Royal to its title. Its main social and fund-raising event, an annual anniversary dinner, was first held in May 1792. In 1839 Dickens was elected to the committee intent on reforming the Fund's constitution (he disliked the idea of its being petitioned by needy authors and sought a greater stress on the 'professional' status of writers). His attempts at reform were thwarted over a period of some

twenty years. In 1859 Thackeray alluded at the anniversary dinner to the problems Dickens had caused to the reputation of the Fund and to his own support for it ('I do not know for what earthly reason people are perpetually flinging mud at us. It was not as a literary man . . . that I came here, but as a supporter, as an admirer, and a cordial friend of this Society'). It was doubtless Thackeray's example of public support for the Fund's work that attracted Trollope. Trollope, who was introduced to the Fund by Robert *Bell in 1861 (subscribing ten guineas), was elected to the committee in March 1864. He was to pay tribute to the deceased Thackeray at that year's anniversary dinner ('I do not think that we yet know how great a man that was'). Significantly, when he spoke at the dinner of 1871, there was no allusion to Dickens's death. He also spoke at the anniversary dinners of 1861, 1863, 1866, 1867 and 1869. In 1866 he persuaded his friend Charles Merivale to join him as a member of the committee (*Letters* 1, 132 n.). Trollope, who had written to the committee in support of Sophia Coulton in 1863 (*Letters* 1, 239), was to serve actively as the Fund's treasurer from 1869 to his death. During his time as treasurer he supported grants for, amongst others, the widows of Mark *Lemon (*Letters* 1, 525) and Shirley *Brooks (*Letters* 2, 619); Helen Crickmaur ('a dear old lady . . . now I fear almost starving instead of living' (*Letters* 2, 707); Isabella (Mrs Linnaeus) Banks (*Letters* 2, 801–2); and Ann Rowe, the widow of a former contributor to *Saint Pauls* (*Letters* 2, 1018). He was also to oversee the increase in the maximum grant from £50 to £100. In *An Autobiography* he refers to his 'great affection' for the Fund and expresses 'convictions' of his own: 'The experience I have acquired by being active in its cause forbids me to advise any young man or woman to enter boldly on a literary career in search of bread . . . the author's poverty is, I think, harder to be borne than any other poverty . . . The more absolutely he fails, the higher it is probable, he will reckon his own merits' (XI).

ALS

Booth, Bradford, 'Trollope and the Royal Literary Fund', *NCF* (December 1952), 208–16.
Cross, Nigel, *The Royal Literary Fund 1790–1918* (1984).
Super, Robert H., 'Trollope at the Royal Literary Fund', *NCF* (December 1982), 316–28.

Royal Literary Fund addresses (speeches).

1. 15 May 1861. Literature promises to become a profession equal in status and earnings to law or medicine.

2. 13 May 1863. Novels are useful and ornamental to civilization; they teach ladies to be women and men to be gentlemen.

3. 18 May 1864. Let us single out for honour Mr Thackeray, who has recently died, as the greatest and kindest of English authors.

4. 2 May 1866. A pioneer of civilization goes out into the wilds, eats horses, has a bad time of it, returns, writes a book, has a good time. Sir Samuel Baker, tonight's speaker, is such a pioneer.

5. 15 May 1867. Poetry is a higher art form than fiction. We honour Balzac, an outstanding stylist, an example for many of us, and also Robert Bell, a very valuable member of this organization, recently deceased.

6. 5 May 1869. Thousands now earn their livings by writing; few physical facilities are needed, but much mental effort and considerable risk; all aspirants deserve encouragement.

7. 17 May 1871. Thanks to all who support the Fund; we see too often the injustice of fortune, as many good authors fail and bad ones succeed. Nos. 1, 3, 4, 6, 7 above: *NCF* (December 1952), 208–16. Nos. 2, 5: *NCF* (December 1982), 316–28.

AKL

Rubb, Samuel, business partner of Tom Mackenzie. Despite being a socially forward tradesman, he wins Margaret Mackenzie's interest for a time. Generally honest and well-meaning, he unscrupulously uses Margaret's loan to the company but falls in love with her and tries to make amends. He proposes, unsuccessfully. *MM*

SRB

Ruddles, Mr, Phineas Finn's election manager at Tankerville. Keeping close track of local political sentiment, the worldly-wise Mr Ruddles proposes that Phineas speak against church endowments. Ruddles also observes election bribery by Phineas's opponent. *PR* 　　JMR

Rudham Park, country house of Mr De Baron, the only place where the Marquis of Brotherton is welcome. *IHP* 　　MG

Rufford, small agricultural county, the location of Rufford Hall and most of Dillsborough. Rufford is also the name of the county seat. *AS*

MG

Rufford, Lord, handsome, rich, popular, cheerful peer dedicated to hunting and shooting. He has his coverts poisoned by Mr Scrobby, is sued by Dan Goarly, is studied by Elias Gotobed, is pursued by Arabella Trefoil, and marries Caroline Penge out of weariness. Gotobed is appalled by his ignorance and charmed by his hospitality and manners. He enjoys his dangerous game with Arabella and, finding himself tamed by his wife, regrets his choice. *AS* 　　MG

Rufford Hall, elegant country home of Lord Rufford, which Arabella Trefoil covets more than she covets its owner, whom she pursues with matrimonial intent. *AS* 　　MG

Ruggles, Daniel, rough, miserly tenant farmer, grandfather and guardian to Ruby. When he beats her for refusing to marry John Crumb, she runs away and he slips into increasing drunkenness. He reluctantly forgives her when she returns to marry Crumb. *WWLN* 　　SRB

Ruggles, Mr, friend of President Neverbend and lukewarm supporter of the 'Fixed Period' policy of compulsory euthanasia. His wise counsel about Eva Crasweller's emotional appeal for her father, the first victim, alarms Neverbend with the possibility of general rebellion against the policy. *FixP* 　　SRB

Ruggles, Ruby, pretty farmer's daughter who aspires above her position when she scorns the love of the solid miller John Crumb and pursues the reckless Felix Carbury to London. Clever and impudent, she is not without principle, but naivety nearly leads to her downfall until Crumb beats Felix and Ruby is persuaded to marry the miller. *WWLN* 　　SRB

Rummelsburg, town in Prussia (now Poland) where John Scarborough first marries his wife. In an effort to keep his marriage as untraceable as possible, Scarborough marries in this remote town in Pomerania as part of his scheme to defy the law of entail. *MSF* 　　MT

Runce, John, salt-of-the-earth English hunting farmer. Horrified by the anti-English opinions expressed by Elias Gotobed at Lord Rufford's hunt breakfast, he gathers up his meal and moves away. *AS* 　　MG

Runciman, Mr, proprietor of the Bush in Dillsborough. A canny businessman, he hosts the Dillsborough Club for the revenue it provides and for his own enjoyment. He is a good friend when Lawrence Twentyman needs one and, among other things, warns him of the perils of drink. *AS* 　　MG

Rusden, George William (1819–1903), Australian author of works on education and history, who became Trollope's close friend. Rusden was Clerk of the Legislative Council (1856–81) in Melbourne and active on behalf of National Schools. Before meeting Trollope, he had dedicated his pamphlet *The Discovery, Survey and Settlement of Port Phillip* (1871) to him. Trollope read it while staying with his son Fred at Mortray station in Australia. Trollope disagreed with Rusden on issues such as the separation of the colonies, but found him well informed. When *Australia and*

Ruskin, John

New Zealand was published, Trollope sent a copy to Rusden, stating, 'I care more for your criticism on it than for that of any other colonist' (*Letters* 2, 580). Trollope also got Rusden elected *in absentia* to the Garrick, and encouraged him to write a history of Australia and New Zealand. He arranged for Rusden to come to England and for Chapman & Hall to publish the volumes. His letters to Rusden over many years 'are among the few truly personal ones he wrote' (Hall 376). Rusden was one of the mourners at Trollope's funeral.   RCT

Ruskin, John (1819–1900), aesthetic and social critic famous for the five volumes of *Modern Painters* (1834–60) and other books interpreting the art of his time, and for promoting work of contemporary artists, particularly the Pre-Raphaelites. In relating art to the monetary culture of greed, in the manner of Carlyle, he drew opposition. Trollope grew increasingly irritated by lofty moralizing about the function of art and the pessimism embodied in it. He sharply criticized Ruskin's *Sesame and Lilies* in the *Fortnightly Review* (July 1865), provoking a wrathful outburst from Carlyle.   RCT

'Ruskin's *Sesame and Lilies*, by John Ruskin: Notices of New Books' (review). This work is sadly inferior to Ruskin's earlier works on art; he tries to preach here on social/economic matters that he is not expert nor convincing about. *Fortnightly Review* (15 July 1865), 633–5.
AKL

'Ruskin's *The Crown of Wild Olive*. Three Lectures on Work, Traffic, and War. By John Ruskin: Critical Notice' (review). These lectures, published with a 'fantastic' title, are very disappointing. Mr Ruskin should return to considering and writing on art appreciation, his forte. These lectures are pedantic and illogical. *Fortnightly Review* (15 June 1866), 381–4.
AKL

Russell, Lord John (1792–1878), 1st Earl Russell; came to prominence in 1830s as proponent of First Reform Bill; Foreign Secretary under Palmerston (1859–65); Prime Minister (1846–52, 1865–6). Trollope endorsed many of his policies and political attitudes 'and sometimes used his name to represent what he most admired in a statesman—nobility, honesty, and candor' (John Halperin, *Trollope and Politics* (1977), 218). Critics have seen parallels with William Mildmay in the Palliser novels, particularly in *Phineas Finn* and *Phineas Redux*. Trollope has Mildmay's terms of office roughly parallel Russell's, and draws on the statesman's conservative liberalism, his old-fashioned gradualist principles over reform of

education and enfranchisement. Trollope's acceptance among the Russell family through Lady Stanley of Alderley widened his appreciation of old Whig aristocracy and values. In early life he supported Russell's policies in Ireland with letters to the *Examiner* about the famine (1849–50). He met Russell in 1866, possibly to try to influence him to change the law preventing civil service employees from voting. In 1864 the statesman proposed the toast to literature coupled with Trollope's name at the Royal Literary Fund dinner. Trollope wrote about him in '*What It is to Be a Statesman*' (*Pall Mall Gazette*, July 1866).   RCT

Russell, Sir William Howard (1820–1907), foreign correspondent for *The Times*, famed for coverage of the Crimean War and American Civil War. He was a close Garrick Club friend of Trollope's, recalled as 'Billy', equalled only by Lever for 'quickness and continuance of witty speech' (*Auto* IX). Shirley *Brooks noted at a gathering after Trollope's return from Australia (1873): 'When we were at cards we heard Anthony's thunder, and then a wild Banshee cry from the Irishman, till we threatened them with the police. Then Anthony said we were conventional tyrants, and Russell said in a weeping voice that Ireland was accustomed to be trampled on' (*I & R* 102–3).   RCT

Russia. To a 19th-century Englishman Russia was a land of mystery and danger. Ruled by an autocratic tsar, the 'Russian Bear' sprawled from Poland, deep in central Europe, through all of eastern Europe, and across northern Asia to the Pacific. As the Russians pressed southwards in Asia, their interests came into conflict with those of the British, from Persia to China. British foreign policy, especially towards the Mediterranean and the Middle East, became preoccupied with Russia, and preserving the decadent Ottoman Empire was one of its props. Britain felt it had to prevent Russia from gaining control of Istanbul and the Dardanelles to keep the Russians out of the Mediterranean; the protection of British routes to India was of paramount concern.

Between 1815 and 1914, the only war fought by Britain in Europe was against Russia—the Crimean War of 1854–6. An inglorious episode in British military history, despite the exploits of the 'thin red line' and Tennyson's celebration of 'The Charge of the Light Brigade', the war was an attempt to deflect Russian advances in the Balkans. Britain and Russia came near clashing in 1878, again over the Balkans, and in the ensuing tension and Russophobia, the term 'jingoism' was coined from a popular anti-Russian music-hall song. In 1886, the British Parliament voted credits and threatened war to protect its central Asian buffer state, Afghanistan, from Russian encroachment; the Russians backed down and negotiated a border settlement. Despite such rivalries, in 1907 both countries and France became parts of the Triple Entente. Russian novelists respected Trollope's work. Tolstoy praised *The Bertrams* and *The Prime Minister*, and noted, 'Trollope kills me with his virtuosity' (quoted Hall 401 n). The novelists never met. Turgenev, however, was welcomed by Trollope, who helped him obtain membership to the Athenaeum during his visit to London in 1871.   LK

Chamberlain, M. E., *'Pax Britannica'? British Foreign Policy 1789–1914* (1988).

Russian literature. The outpouring of great Russian novels in the 19th century was available in translations and Trollope was familiar with works by Tolstoy and Turgenev, although his library catalogue lists none of their works. Trollope never met Tolstoy, who admired his novels.

The two writers almost simultaneously included suicide on a railway track in their works: Trollope's Lopez in *The Prime Minister* (LX) and Tolstoy's Anna Karenina. During Turgenev's visit to England in 1871 Trollope met him at a luncheon given by George Eliot and G. H. Lewes in April at their house, the Priory, Regent's Park. Other guests included Browning, Burne-Jones, and Louis Viardot. Lady Castleton, who was also present, remarked to Lewes later about the variety of genius gathered together on the occasion. In October 1881, Trollope again met Turgenev, at a dinner in London given by the Russian author's English translator William Ralston. Turgenev died nine months after Trollope and the *Saturday Review* made comparisons between the two novelists, who resembled each other physically as well as in their fiction: 'in both cases numberless fine details go to make up a singularly living presentment of character, whether in the principal or in the subordinate personages introduced' (8 September 1883, quoted Super 423).   RCT

S

terprise was spreading into public life, and the danger of people becoming desensitized to it. That theme, announced in his early fiction, has its most trenchant statement in *The Way We Live Now*. Sadleir was one source for Melmotte.

RCT

Sadleir, Michael (1888–1957), novelist, bibliographer, whose *Excursions in Victorian Bibliography* (1922) blazed a trail in studies of Victorian writers. His *Trollope: A Commentary* (1927) and *Trollope: A Bibliography* (1928) pioneered serious study of the novelist and his works. Sadleir's best-known novel was *Fanny by Gaslight* (1940).

RCT

'St Albans Raiders, The' (article). Canada's decision to refuse the extradition of the men who ravaged St Albans, Vermont, and fled across the border violates both treaty and common sense. The argument that the raiders were Confederate soldiers at war is not supported by the evidence. *Pall Mall Gazette* (17 June 1865), 10–11.   AKL

St Bungay, Duchess of, spoiled and oversensitive wife of the Duke of St Bungay. The Duchess is not very clever and is apt to become an object of ridicule for quicker-witted ladies. Deeply resenting the fun had at her expense, she insists that her great husband protect her from such indignities. *CYFH*   JMR

St Bungay, Duke of, one of the principal political characters of the Palliser novels. Though he holds offices in various parliamentary ministries in the Palliser novels, the Duke's 'behind the scenes' activities as architect of Liberal ministries and counsellor to Liberal prime ministers are more important than any official position. Most significant, perhaps, is the Duke's role as friend and mentor to the young Duke of Omnium, to whom he first offers the position of Chancellor of the Exchequer (in *CYFH*). This role becomes more challenging, however, in *The Prime Minister*, where he attempts to support and encourage his friend, despite misgivings that the young Duke is simply too thin-skinned to be Prime Minister. *PF, ED, PR, DC*.   JMR

St Cuthbert's, tiny Barchester parish whose singular Gothic church is no bigger than an ordinary room. Septimus Harding becomes its rector. *W*   NCS

St Cuthbert's, one of the grandest boys' schools in England. Harry Clavering teaches there briefly, having been chosen from a field of 100 candidates. *C*   PJT

St Diddulph's-in-the-East, poor parish in the east end of London, overseen by Revd Outhouse

Sabbatarianism. Deriving its authority from the Lord's Day Observance Act in the previous century, this strict code of religiously sanctioned behaviour was a focus of national debate during the Victorian period. In *Barchester Towers* the battle between the evangelicals and the high-church party includes the new 'Sabbath schools' and the abolition of both Sunday train services and letter deliveries, the proposed curtailment of which is vehemently opposed by Archdeacon Grantly in *The Last Chronicle of Barset*.

Trollope hated evangelical cant about the 'sabbath', and, as he makes clear in *The New Zealander*, regarded Sunday as a source of individual comfort. Trollope himself occasionally used the day for writing, and he found repellent the idea of even devout worshippers being denied the simple pleasures of reading, music, or letter-writing by small groups of religious bigots.

His experience of evangelicalism in Cheltenham, where the vicar had sought to suspend the Sunday post, is employed in the similarly restrictive society of Littlebath in *Miss Mackenzie*. Another example of sabbath observance occurs in *Phineas Finn*, in the gloomy household of the Scottish Calvinist Robert Kennedy, Lady Laura's husband, who frowns on her desire to read a novel.   GH

Sadleir, John (1814–56), notorious banker who dealt fraudulently in railway shares and other swindles; elected MP (1847, 1853); committed suicide in February 1856. Trollope cited Sadleir in *The New Zealander* and *The Three Clerks* as a symbol of the way dishonesty in commercial en-

and populated largely by the working classes, especially dock labourers. *HKWR*   RC

St Ewold's, Barsetshire living worth some £300 a mile outside Barchester, in the preferment of Archdeacon Grantly. Containing a picturesque church, parsonage, and legend, the living is presented to Francis Arabin. *BT*   NCS

Saint-Florent, small town, scene of the first royalist resistance. *LV*   GRH

St George, Lord, level-headed son of the ostentatious Marquis of Trowbridge. He acts as peacemaker between his father and the fiery vicar of Bullhampton, thus cleverly cheating them both of their grievance by forcing a reconciliation. *VB*   SRB

St Laud, church near Échanbroignes from which Father Jerome is excluded by the revolutionary Directorate. *LV*   GRH

Saint-Laurent-sur-Sèvre. Agatha de Larochejaquelin nurses the dying Cathelineau there in the hospital she helped to establish. *LV*   GRH

St Louis, mid-western American city and site of the College at Missouri, where Mr Peacocke serves as Vice-President. *DWS*   RC

Saint Pauls Magazine. In October 1867, James Sprent *Virtue, successful printer and publisher, began this 128-page, monthly, shilling magazine, edited by Anthony Trollope. Virtue and Trollope had known each other from their work on the *Fortnightly Review*, Virtue as printer and Trollope as a founder and a proprietor.

In the autumn of 1866, Virtue had suggested they take over the *Argosy*, a monthly, sixpenny magazine, with Trollope as editor. Virtue was following the practice of having a well-known novelist's name on the title-page, some of them editors in name only: Thackeray was editor of the *Cornhill*; Dickens of *Bentley's Miscellany*, *Household Words*, then *All the Year Round*; Edmund Yates of *Tinsley's Magazine*; W. Harrison Ainsworth of *Ainsworth's Magazine*. Virtue was continuing the family business begun by his father George, who had come from Scotland and become a bookseller, then a publisher of popular fiction, travel, and art books. After purchasing the *Art Journal*, he had become a printer as well. When he retired, he gave the business to James, who in 1866 became involved with Strahan & Co., publishers. Alexander Strahan's business was in dire need of cash. He had already borrowed from Spalding & Hodge, his paper suppliers, and had obtained an additional £15,000 from them and £10,000 from J. S. Virtue & Co. The loans were secured with copyrights to Strahan's periodicals, *Good Words*, *Sunday Magazine*, *Contem-*

porary Review, and *Argosy*, with Virtue to print and bind them. Virtue suggested taking over the *Argosy* to relieve Strahan of part of his debt, but later dropped the idea and proposed to Trollope that they start a new magazine.

Trollope rejected Virtue's suggestion of using his name in the title of the magazine. Instead, the name they selected followed the practice of naming periodicals after London landmarks, like the *Cornhill*, *Temple Bar*, and *Belgravia*. Virtue's business was close to St Paul's Cathedral. Trollope was to serve as editor for two years for £1,000 per year, paying £250 out of that for a sub-editor. Advertisements for the new magazine displayed Trollope's name prominently with that of the illustrator, John *Millais. Trollope designed the plan for the magazine. *Saint Pauls*, unlike other shilling magazines, would include politics, foreign and domestic, with a Liberal bias. There would be little reviewing. Trollope was to provide the first novel, *Phineas Finn*, with a second novel by another author to be paid less than Trollope. Trollope would comment on Parliament when it was in session. He would pay contributors well, twenty shillings a page. Trollope asked his friend Robert Bell to be sub-editor, but he was too ill to accept. He then asked Edward Dicey, a fellow member of the Garrick Club and foreign correspondent for the *Daily Telegraph*, who accepted.

Trollope turned to people he knew for contributions, including his brother Tom and wife Fanny, to write about Italy. Austen Henry Layard, Under-Secretary for Foreign Affairs in the Whig ministries of Palmerston and Russell and British minister at Madrid, agreed to write on foreign affairs. George J. Goschen would write on politics; he had been in Russell's cabinet, then later in Gladstone's cabinet as President of the Poor Law Board. Francis Lawley, a friend of Dicey's on the *Daily Telegraph*, would write on horse racing, and Henry Nelson O'Neill, the painter, agreed to write on art. Many contributors also contributed to the *Cornhill* and *Fortnightly Review*. Although Trollope had insisted that all articles in the *Fortnightly* be signed, he abandoned this idea in *Saint Pauls*.

Trollope determined that the salary Virtue was paying him was sufficient to allow him to resign from the Post Office early, forfeiting his pension. He did so in October 1867, when the first number appeared. In his 'Introduction', Trollope described how *Saint Pauls* fitted the current periodical scene. Some publications, like the *Cornhill*, sought to amuse rather than to instruct. Others chose to be instructive and grave (a reference to the *Fortnightly*). *Saint Pauls* would strive to unite the two extremes, presenting serious topics along with entertaining ones.

The first number received good reviews, the *Bookseller* saying it would be one of the most successful of modern literary ventures distinguishing itself by the solidity of its articles. Later numbers contained poetry, frequently from a young poet, Austin Dobson. Trollope was an active, involved editor, reading every submission, writing explanations on rejected articles, soliciting articles from prospective contributors, and conferring with Virtue about rates of pay. He was also the most frequent contributor to the first twenty numbers, with articles on hunting, Gladstone, the Irish Church, crime in London, American politics, Carlyle, and a defence of President Andrew Johnson, along with fiction— *Ralph the Heir* (January 1870–July 1871) and six short stories.

In spite of his and Virtue's efforts, the magazine never reached the circulation of 25,000 that Virtue had optimistically proposed as necessary for the magazine to pay. It peaked around 10,000. Virtue decided to sell, and approached Chapman & Hall, who were interested at first, but then declined. By this time, Virtue largely owned Strahan's business because of long-standing debts, so he decided to transfer the magazine to him for managerial purposes, hoping Strahan's experience with periodicals might make *Saint Pauls* profitable. Virtue retained financial control. Although his term as editor was planned to last only until September 1869, Trollope stayed on until July 1870, although by January 1870 Strahan had informed him that he had decided to take over all editorial decisions to save money. After Trollope left, Strahan changed the magazine's character, making it far lighter, decreasing the number of pages, and eliminating the illustrations. By March 1872, Strahan's creditors forced him to give up his association with Strahan & Co.; he then took *Saint Pauls* to Henry S. King, who continued publishing it until March 1874.

JWM

Srebrnik, Patricia T., *Alexander Strahan, Victorian Publisher* (1986).

St Peter's-cum-Pupkin, Exeter parish of which Mr Gibson is the rector. *HKWR*   RC

St Quinten, Mrs. The only woman author among six friends planning a magazine, ruthlessly humiliated by her cousin Churchill Smith for her pretentious writing. 'Panjandrum' *ET*
                                        GRH

Sala, George Augustus (1828–96), journalist and editor, and, like Trollope, associated with the Royal Literary Fund. Sala wrote regularly for Dickens's journals, and founded *Temple Bar*

(1860), of which nominal editorship was offered to Trollope (the actual work to be done by Edmund *Yates). Trollope declined this 'mock Editorship' (*Letters* 1, 157 n.). Sala's memoirs, *Things I Have Seen and People I Have Known* (1894), declared that Trollope 'had nothing of the bear but his skin', but added, that 'ursine envelope was assuredly of the most grisly texture' (*I & R* 68). Trollope described Sala as a man 'who, had he given himself fair play, would have risen to higher eminence than that of being the best writer in his day of sensational leading articles' (*Auto* VIII).   RCT

Salisbury, county town and location of business, trade, banking, and clubs in *The Vicar of Bullhampton*. The Revd Chamberlaine is a prebendary of the cathedral here. It is also the site of the Three Honest Men, an inn where Sam and Carry Brattle stay briefly, and Mrs Stiggs's boarding house, Carry's residence while awaiting Sam's trial. *VB*   SRB

Salisbury,   Robert   Arthur   Talbot Gascoyne-Cecil,   3rd   Marquess   of (1830–1903), succeeded Disraeli as Tory leader in 1867. In 1897, on Alfred Austin's application, his government granted Rose Trollope a Civil List pension of £100 a year 'in consideration of the distinguished literary merits of her husband, . . . and of her straitened circumstances' (Super 436).
                                        RCT

Sally, antiquated servant at Dunmore Inn who quaffs sweetened tea by the pint. *KOK*   MRS

Sally, Aunt, outspoken woman who condemns Miss Grogram for cutting up the 'relics'. 'Chassé' *TAC1*   GRH

Sambourne, Edward Linley (1844–1910), artist and book-illustrator; began drawing for *Punch* (1867) and became its chief cartoonist (1901). In a series, 'Fancy Portraits', he depicted Trollope as 'Antonius Trollopius, Author of The Last Chronicle of Cicero, "O Rare for Anthony!" SHAKESPEARE' (*Punch*, 5 February 1881; see p. 453). A copy in Linley Sambourne House, 18 Stafford Terrace, London. Sambourne also drew several cartoons to accompany Francis *Burnand's parody of a Trollope novel in *Punch* between May and October 1880.   RCT

San Francisco, city in California where Ferdinand Lefroy dies and is buried. *DWS*   RC

Sand, George (1804–76), pseudonym of Amandine-Aurore Lucille Dupin, baronne Dudevant, novelist, essayist, bohemian, and champion of women's rights and republicanism. In Paris (1835) Trollope's mother, a great admirer, became acquainted with her. Trollope's critique of Sand's *L'Uscoque* (1838) went against popular reaction by viewing it as a morally sound novel; it 'makes vice ugly & virtue beautiful' (*Letters* 2, 1025). In *Partial Portraits* (1888) Henry James claimed that Trollope's narrative pace outmatched 'even that of the wonderful Madame Sand' (Smalley 526).

RCT

Santerre, Antoine-Joseph (based on historical figure). One of the Commissioners sent to reduce the Vendeans, he captures Durbellière, rather despises Denot, spares the household, is himself captured, and behaves throughout with dignity. *LV* GRH

Saratoga Springs, resort in New York State, where the Bell family take summer boarders. 'Bell' *TAC1* GRH

Sarony, Napoleon (1821–96), celebrated New York photographer who took pictures of Trollope and Kate Field in June 1868. Trollope, who loathed being photographed, referred to him as 'that horrid little Silenus' (*Letters* 1, 433). He received a photograph of Kate from that sitting: 'I have got your section framed down to the mere hat and eyes and nose. It is all I have of you except a smudged (but originally very pretty) portrait taken from a picture' (*Letters* 2, 437).

RCT

Saturday Review. In 1855, John Douglas Cook, a Scottish Episcopalian, became editor, and joint proprietor with Anthony Beresford Hope, of the *Saturday Review.* Cook edited it for thirteen years. Beginning as a 24-page, weekly journal, containing little of literary value except a few reviews, it was a high-church, conservative publication which frequently attacked popular phenomena, particularly Dickens. John Bright the MP called it the 'Saturday Reviler'. In the late 1850s, the *Saturday Review* took it upon itself to criticize Victorians for pursuing novels merely for amusement, accusing them of taking more trouble in their idling than most nations did in their working.

By 1860 the reviews had become long and important. John St Loe Strachey became a frequent contributor in the 1880s and proprietor and editor in 1898. By 1890 almost half its 30 pages were occupied with critical articles. In later numbers it became a miscellaneous publication with sections on general interest, reviews of fiction, theatrical criticism, art, and poetry with an impressive list of contributors including George Bernard Shaw, H. G. Wells, Aubrey Beardsley, Arthur Symons, and Max Beerbohm, who was discovered by Frank Harris while he was editor between 1894 and 1898.

It reviewed more than 50 of Trollope's works, beginning in 1857 and continuing until his death.

The weekly noted much about the topics of his novels, his strengths and, particularly, weaknesses, his manner of working, even his choice of characters. *Barchester Towers*, it declared, had raised Trollope into a very considerable position among novelists of the present day.

In *The Three Clerks*, it asserted that Trollope had created characters that almost rivalled Thackeray's, but it urged Trollope to clean up errors caused by his rapid writing. It also pointed out a legal error and suggested he seek out the advice of a lawyer next time. In his next novel, *Doctor Thorne*, Trollope alluded to the reviewer's advice, saying he could not afford a barrister.

More than one issue praised *The West Indies and the Spanish Main*, saying that Trollope was clever in introducing people to an area they did not know much about.

After *Framley Parsonage* began in the *Cornhill*, the *Review* said that Trollope would make the fortunes of the circulation libraries and that no girl could pretend to be literary unless she knew the latest about Lucy Robarts's heart. Referring to *Orley Farm* it stated that he wrote the best descriptions of English family life, and in praising *The Small House at Allington*, compared Trollope with Jane Austen in his handling of love affairs.

The *Saturday Review* was one of several publications that criticized Trollope for reusing old characters, which may have contributed to his decision to kill Mrs Proudie in *The Last Chronicle of Barset*. It also criticized Trollope for his heavy satire in *The Way We Live Now*. Another negative review suggested that the characters and incidents in *The Struggles of Brown, Jones, and Robinson* were vulgar and stupid. Not surprisingly, this journal of high-church sympathies did not like *Sir Harry Hotspur of Humblethwaite* because of its unsympathetic treatment of the aristocracy. And, as a strong supporter of the American South during the Civil War, it also disliked Trollope's *North America*.

Trollope and the *Saturday Review* occasionally tangled over an issue. Norman Macleod, a liberal minister of the Church of Scotland, had made an address against the rigorous restraints on Christians' observance of the sabbath, which was then printed as a pamphlet. Trollope supported his point of view in an article, 'The Fourth Commandment', in the *Fortnightly Review*. The *Saturday Review* then criticized Trollope for commenting on areas in which his opinion was of no importance, saying it did not find faults with his opinions, but wondered why novel-writing was not enough for him. Trollope responded in the *Pall Mall Gazette* saying he would spend his time doing as he saw fit in spite of the *Saturday Review*.

There was a similar skirmish over a letter Trollope had written to *The Times* about his experiences on a train trip from London to Basle. He had been charged more than the advertised rate of 124 francs; 56 pounds of luggage was to be allowed for free, but Trollope was charged for each pound; he had been told they would not have to change trains, but they did; and there was no way to get refreshments for more than fifteen hours during the trip. In addition, one of the conductors dropped Trollope's tickets down the window frame and made him pay to replace them. The *Saturday Review* criticized Trollope for his ignorance as a traveller. Trollope responded that even if he possessed the omniscience of the *Saturday Review*, he could not have corrected these problems. (See HOLIDAYS ABROAD.)

In a tribute after his death, these minor vexations were forgotten, however: the *Saturday Review* said Trollope's characters would cause him to be remembered as one of the very finest English novelists. JWM

Saul, Samuel, Revd Henry Clavering's curate at Clavering. Though rusty in appearance and with no income beyond his curacy, his Tractarian enthusiasm and his dedication as a lover ensure he is taken seriously as a suitor for Fanny Clavering's hand. At the end of the novel he becomes rector of Clavering. *C* PJT

Saulsby Castle, country residence of Lord Brentford and his family. The heir, Lord Chiltern, dislikes and avoids the place. Nearby Saulsby Wood is the scene of childhood adventures of Violet Effingham and Lord Chiltern as well as of Phineas Finn's marriage proposal to Violet Effingham. *PF, PR* JMR

Saumur, large fortified town taken by the Vendeans, their first major success. *LV* GRH

Sawyer, Dr, surgeon who treats Adelaide Houghton at Manor Cross when she dislocates her shoulder hunting. Trollope remarks there is always a doctor in the field, and professes to believe this dispensation 'arises from the general fitness of things' (VIII). *IHP* MG

Scandinavia and Iceland. Trollope's trip to Iceland was a pleasure trip on the yacht *Mastiff* in 1878, and resulted in the privately printed entertainment **How the 'Mastiffs' Went to Iceland*. On the way he visited the Danish colony of the Faeroe Islands. At the time of his journey, Norway and Sweden were joined in an unpopular union which was dissolved in 1905, and Denmark, which had been forced to give up Norway in 1814, still controlled the former Norwegian

colonies of Iceland, Greenland, and the Faeroes. Trollope concentrated on the social aspects of his visit to Reykjavik, the capital of Iceland. He said nothing to suggest the political tension that must have existed among his hosts.

Iceland was first settled by Vikings from Norway in the 9th century, and in the next century became a republic with its own parliament, the Althing. In the 13th century it came under the Norwegian crown in a personal union, and in the 14th, both Norway and Iceland passed under Danish control. Iceland gradually lost its political autonomy, a process which was deeply resented, especially since the economy was dominated by the Danes. In the course of the 19th century, the Icelanders increasingly pressed for a restoration of rights; the Althing was re-established in 1843, and in 1874 Iceland was given limited home rule. Early in the 20th century Iceland gained complete home rule, and in 1944 broke all ties with Denmark, becoming an independent republic.

Yachting trips to view spectacular fiords in Norway and thermal pools in Iceland were popular alternatives to destinations in the Mediterranean. Trollope referred to a previous journey by Lord Dufferin in 1856, and the explorer/ethnographer Richard Burton published *Ultima Thule* in two volumes in 1875. *How the 'Mastiffs' went to Iceland* was translated and published in Icelandic. LK

Scarborough, Augustus, lawyer and younger son of John Scarborough. Briefly heir to Tretton Park, Augustus is a self-interested, calculating, mercenary young man who is able to talk 'of the misdoings of the one parent and the other with the most perfect *sang froid*' (V). Augustus is disinherited after his father realizes he anxiously awaits his death. *MSF* MT

Scarborough, John, head of the Scarborough family, owner of Tretton Park, and brother of Mrs Mountjoy. A complex character, Mr Scarborough tries to defy the law of entail which he sees as unjust. 'He had never been selfish, thinking always of others rather than of himself. Supremely indifferent he had been to the opinion of the world around him, but he had never run counter to his own conscience. For the conventionalities of the law he entertained a supreme contempt, but he did wish so to arrange matters with which he was himself concerned as to do what justice demanded' (LVIII). *MSF* MT

Scarborough, Martha, unmarried sister of John Scarborough who lives at Tretton Park. She is one of the family members 'most anxious to assure the marriage of Florence and the captain' (VII). *MSF* MT

Scarborough, Captain Mountjoy, elder son of John Scarborough and a compulsive gambler. Mountjoy is supposedly a bastard son and so cannot inherit Tretton Park, but this is all part of his father's scheme to keep his fortune out of the hands of the moneylenders, who own Mountjoy's future. Although Mountjoy is addicted to gambling and has squandered his fortune, he is redeemed by a goodness which his cold brother lacks. Mr Scarborough reinstates Mountjoy as heir, but there is no guarantee that Tretton Park will finally be safe from creditors. *MSF*   MT

Scarrowby. Located in Durham, the secondary estate of the Hotspurs had been in the family for over 150 years. *SHH*   MG

Scatcherd, Lady. Devoted working-class wife of Roger Scatcherd, she serves as wet-nurse to Frank Gresham. Never comfortable as a baronet's wife, she remains the staunch friend of Dr Thomas Thorne and welcomes his niece Mary to her lavish home. After the deaths of her husband and son, she retreats to a small Greshamsbury cottage. *DT, FP*   NCS

Scatcherd, Sir Louis Philippe, alcoholic son of Sir Roger Scatcherd. Sickly, dissipated, obstreperous, and irredeemable, he treats everyone as his inferior. He annoys Dr Thorne, the executor of his father's will, threatens to foreclose on the Greshamsbury estate, and proposes marriage to Mary Thorne. *DT*   NCS

Scatcherd, Sir Roger, journeyman Barchester stonemason who becomes a baronet worth £300,000. In a drunken rage, he kills his sister's seducer and serves six months for manslaughter, after which he becomes a contractor for government projects. Always a heavy drinker and compulsive worker, he becomes a national hero, is knighted, and wins parliamentary election for Barchester as a radical, serving in the House for two months before the election is overturned. He retires broken-hearted, though his obituary stresses his material success. *DT*   NCS

Schlegel, Augustus Wilhelm von (1767–1845). His *A Course of Lectures on Dramatic Art and Literature* (trans. 1815) was a major resource for Trollope's reading and literary annotations for his Commonplace Book (1825–40).
      RCT

Schlessen, Fritz, lawyer adviser to Frau Frohmann who wants her to raise her prices and to provide the 'mitgift' (dowry) for Malchen before they marry. 'Frohmann' *WFF*   GRH

Schmidt, Lotta, independent-minded Viennese girl who, despite the blandishments of the more glamorous Fritz Planken, chooses her middleaged suitor, the shy, talented musician Herr Crippel. 'Schmidt' *LS*   GRH

scientific enquiry became increasingly specialized and professionalized during Trollope's lifetime, and the very words science and scientist entered the language in their modern sense. In Trollope's youth science still belonged to a common context and scientists like the chemistphysicist Michael Faraday felt it their duty to be intelligible to the educated lay public. Geology had the greatest visibility, quite literally: new railway cuttings exposed the earth's stratigraphy to the casual traveller; dinosaurs captured the public imagination, and fossil hunting became a popular hobby. Debates among geologists over the age of the earth which rumbled through widely read journals like the *Quarterly Review* and *Edinburgh Review* were resonant to any reader of the Old Testament. The concept of biological evolution dramatically formulated by Darwin's *Origin of Species* (1859) raised even greater problems for biblical literalists. Liberal intellectuals like Trollope generally took the side of science in such matters—for instance against the fundamentalist persecutors of *Colenso, the Bishop of Natal, who, in translating the Book of Genesis for Zulus, found himself unable to give orthodox answers to their astute questions about its story.

The scientistic ideology of Auguste Comte, with which the *Fortnightly Review* was strongly associated, claimed to offer a comprehensive overview of scientific enquiry which appealed to many non-scientific intellectuals, and some social scientists, but natural scientists like T. H. Huxley generally scorned its pretensions. Though connected with such circles Trollope was not intellectually at home among them, his voice reportedly drowning out Huxley's at a fashionable intellectual dinner party. Many people would have accepted enthusiastically the Astronomer Royal's invitation to visit his observatory which Trollope declined, remarking that he cared little for stars. Astronomical discoveries caught the public attention with the predicted return of Halley's comet in 1834 and the development of increasingly powerful telescopes capable of resolving nebulae and encouraging speculation about other galaxies and their creation.

The common context of science and general culture was dissolving during Trollope's adulthood. Though as editor of *Saint Pauls* he turned down an article on Darwin, claiming to be 'afraid of the subject' (*Letters* 1, 447) through ignorance, biology and astronomy were still at least accessible to the non-expert. Very different was the contemporary work of James Clerk Maxwell, whose unified field equations laid the foundations for modern physics and were beyond the comprehension of many of his own colleagues. The founding of the journal *Nature* in 1869 symbolically inaugurated the dominance among scientists of discourse inaccessible to lay people.

Daily mid-Victorian life was not dramatically impacted by new scientific discoveries. The steam technology increasingly dominant in transportation represented old science. Newer scientific discoveries were laying the groundwork for remarkable changes that would arrive shortly after Trollope's death, above all as electricity moved from the laboratory to the street. Medicine was on the threshold of important advances drawing on chemistry (new drugs) and physics (X-rays). In Trollope's own day science's most notable new impact was on communications, with telegraphy and photography. Ominously, however, some of the most significant scientific research had great implications for warfare—the metallurgy of armour plate and the chemistry of high explosives.   CK

Gillispie, Charles C., *Genesis and Geology* (1959).
Yeo, Richard, *Defining Science: William Whewell, Natural Knowledge and Public Debate in Early Victorian Britain* (1993).

Scotland. Trollope's liking for Scotland began with postal work in Glasgow first in 1854 then in 1859, a holiday with Rose sandwiched in during the summer. In later years the Trollopes were often guests of John *Blackwood at Strathtyrum, St Andrews, and on a rare occasion Trollope took a grouse-shooting holiday in Inverness (June 1873). Trollope liked Scottish folk, with the exception of the more inflexible Presbyterians, the most notable in his fiction being Robert Kennedy, millionaire MP and owner of Loughlinter, Perthshire, a paradise of lough and mountain (*PF* XIV) where he dies melancholy mad (*PR* LII). Other Scots characters and locales include Portray Castle in *The Eustace Diamonds* in which Lizzie Eustace had a life interest (XXI), and the estates of Crummie-Toddie some twelve miles (19 km) from Killancodlem, Perthshire, where the shooting was leased by Lord Popplecourt and Reginald Dobbs in *The Duke's Children* (XXXVIII–XL, XLII). Lady Bertha Grant in *Kept in the Dark* has a home in Perth (VIII), and Captain Jonathan Stubbs in *Ayala's Angel* keeps Drumcaller, a small place near Glenbogie.   RCT

Scott, Captain Valentine, brother of Undecimus Scott and second husband of widowed Mrs Golightly. With the help of Undy, Captain Scott tries to bribe Alaric Tudor to use Clementina Golightly's trust money to purchase stocks for him.

Captain Scott is another useless bad seed in the Scott family. *TC*   MT

Scott, Mrs Valentine, wife of Captain Scott and mother of Clementina Golightly. As a widow, Mrs Golightly married the poor Captain Scott in order to be associated with his aristocratic family. She aspires to the highest social circles and patronizes those she deems inferior, such as Gertrude Woodward. *TC*   MT

Scott, Sir Walter (1771–1832). Trollope was a child when the great Waverley novels appeared, and in *An Autobiography* he lists Scott among the classics he appreciated in his boyhood. He ranked Scott almost as highly as his favourite Thackeray, considering *Ivanhoe*, with its 'almost perfect' plot (*Auto* VII), inferior only to *Henry Esmond* and *Pride and Prejudice* among all English novels (*Auto* III). In addition to relishing his powers of characterization, Trollope esteemed Scott's 'infinite imagination' (*Letters* 2, 660), admiring his craft in dovetailing apparently sensational scenes, such as Rebecca with Ivanhoe in the castle, or Burley in the cave with Morton, with the wider artistic purpose of the novel (*Auto* XII). He found Scott's better books impossible to skip (B. Booth, *Anthony Trollope* (1958), 146). Another of Scott's strengths for Trollope was the part played by his 'correct morality' (*Auto* XII) in domesticating fiction for a family readership, after the robustness of the 18th-century masters. Trollope, who never enjoyed research, appreciated the bird-like speed with which Sir Walter gathered his sources. 'I doubt whether Scott prepared himself [for the writing of *Ivanhoe*] by reading many memoirs of John's reign', he told an apprentice historical novelist (*Letters* 2, 908). He nevertheless marvelled at the number of books Scott must have used for his *Life of Napoleon* when performing the quieter scholarly tasks necessary to the composition of *Commentaries of Caesar* (*Letters* 2, 514). He was confident that the Victorian passion for lake and mountain scenery owed much to Scott (M. L. Parrish (ed.), *Four Lectures* (1938), 114).

Though Trollope usually uses present-day settings, is 'realistic' where, he believed, Scott depended on 'incidents' for his effects (*Letters* 1, 390), and resists Scott's 18th-century tendency to choose as hero and heroine 'pattern people no-one cares a farthing about' (*The Miscellaneous Prose-Works of Sir Walter Scott* (1834), 19, 28), Trollope's early work is influenced by Scott. Trollope's confidence and authority in unfolding the Irish materials of his first two novels to a cosmopolitan audience owes more to Scott than to his Irish contemporary Maria Edgeworth, while Trollope's historical novel *La Vendée* is not only modelled on the Waverleys, but was actually based on *Memoirs of the Countess de Larochejacquelin* that Sir Walter had himself translated. In later years Trollope's short fiction, especially when unpacking an unfamiliar setting, shows marks of the anecdotal form Scott favoured in the short story, while his flowery squib 'The Gentle Euphemia' traces its cod medievalism back to Scott, and Anthony Allan-a-dale, who features in one of Charley Tudor's *Daily Delight* articles in *The Three Clerks* (XIX), is named after a character from Edmund of Winston's song in *Rokeby*. Though Trollope was not above confusing the characters of one Waverley with those of another (*Letters* 2, 605), his references assume comfortable familiarity on his reader's part. He is fond of citing Scott's characters as archetypes: for example, Caleb Balderstone as loyal servant, Dominie Sampson as conscientious schoolmaster, Di Vernon as spirited tomboy. Quotations from Scott's narrative poems are mainly decorative. Lochinvar's appearance in *Marmion* is a favourite source of these, and the tag 'Love shall still be lord of all' from *The Lay of the Last Minstrel* is also used frequently. (Scott references occur in *TC* XXXIII, *HKWR* LXX, *PR* LXI, *ED* XXXV, *GLG* XI, *AA* XIV, *DWS* I, III.)

Trollope had his reservations about Scott. He complains that, for all their strengths, there is 'an infinity of padding' in the Waverleys, and much 'very lax work' (*Letters* 2, 660). Visiting St Andrews in 1868, Trollope brassily denounced Scott's fiction, objecting that the books would be too 'dull' for the tastes of the present day, and Jeanie Deans of *Heart of Midlothian* (praised as a perfect heroine in *RH* LVI) the only tolerable leading lady (A. K. H. Boyd, *Twenty-Five Years of St Andrews* (1892), 1, 101). But he was probably teasing his Scottish auditors. The plaudits in *An Autobiography* suggest he continued to admire the '20-horse-power' of Scott's 'vivacity' (*Letters* 2, 660), and even empathized with it, contemplating with compunction the earlier novelist's furious sponsored write against debt and time. 'The writing of a novel', he says, 'is a task that may be supposed to demand a spirit fairly at ease. The work of doing it with a troubled spirit killed Sir Walter Scott' (*Auto* II). PJT

Scott, Undecimus (Undy), son of Lord Gaberlunzie, MP for Tillietudlem, and stockjobber. Villain of the novel, Undy Scott is a good-humoured parasite who feeds off the vulnerability of those around him. He leads Charley down the slippery slope by luring him into stock speculation and by bribing him. He is 'the incarnation of evil, which it is always necessary that the novelist should have personified in one of his char-

acters to enable him to bring about his misfortunes, his tragedies, and various requisite tragedies' (XLIV). *TC* MT

Scrobby, Mr, successful tradesman unable to make the transition to a more genteel station. In an act of revenge against his former landlord Lord Rufford, he has Goarly plant poisoned herring in Dillsborough Woods. He is sentenced to twelve months' hard labour. *AS* MG

Scroome, Josiah. The Congressman from Mickewa is the recipient of two long letters from his close friend Elias Gotobed detailing the American Senator's travails in England. *AS* MG

Scroope, Earl of, broken by his daughter's death in childbirth and his son's dissolute self-destruction, he is relieved to discover that his nephew will, by all appearances, live true to the family's motto: *Sans reproche*. Though he would like him to marry and resign from the army, he will not press his heir on either point, hoping to avoid fresh disappointments. However, Fred Neville is impressed by his uncle's sense of honour and despite his Irish adventures promises that he will never make Kate O'Hara a countess. *EE* AWJ

Scroope, Lady Mary (née **Wycombe**). Born to the noblest of families and devoted to religion, the Countess despairs at the thought that Fred Neville might marry an ill-born Catholic. Having wrestled with her conscience, she implores him to break his word to the girl he seduced, preferring that betrayal to still greater dishonour. This request haunts her after Fred's death. Feeling responsible for his tragedy, she lives in seclusion for the rest of her days. *EE* AWJ

Scroope Manor, Dorset residence of the earls of Scroope, an Elizabethan building whose old-fashioned quietude proclaims the 12th Earl's conservatism and his servants' and tenants' good fortune. 'Marlbro' school', attached to the estate, suggests that Trollope modelled this locale on the Seymours' Wiltshire mansion, site of the actual College. *EE* AWJ

Scruby, George, huntsman of the Brotherton Hunt which meets at Cross Hall Gate. *IHP* MG

Scruby, Mr, George Vavasor's indifferently honest parliamentary agent. Mr Scruby develops the campaign strategy that wins George his seat in Parliament, but Scruby later neglects George's cause when he suspects that his client will have difficulty raising the funds to make payment. *CYFH* JMR

Scudamore, Frank Ives (1823–84), Post Office administrator; organizer of the Post Office Savings Bank; promoted Assistant Secretary over Trollope's head (though his junior by six years) in 1864. Trollope acknowledged him 'a great accountant' (*Auto* XV), but admitted resentment. He later reflected that this disappointment had given him time to write and hunt. When Trollope retired, Scudamore at the farewell dinner acknowledged that his great literary achievements had been accomplished without detriment to Post Office work. Several years later in *The Way We Live Now*, Trollope alluded to Scudamore's expansion of the telegraph service, for which he had diverted Savings Bank funds without proper authorization. When Marie Melmotte's attempt to elope with Felix Carbury was foiled by a telegram, she 'would certainly have gladly hanged Mr Scudamore'. Moreover, the narrator coyly wondered 'whether the gentleman who spent all the public money without authority ought not to have been punished with special severity in that they [telegrams] had injured humanity, rather than pardoned because of the good they had produced' (XLIX). RCT

Scuttle, Jem, former post-boy at the Dragon of Wantly in Barchester who has emigrated to New Zealand with Anne, the under-chambermaid. He had supposedly given Mr Soames's lost cheque to Dan Stringer. *LCB* NCS

sea-bathing. Growth of the railway system, crowding in cities, greater middle-class prosperity, and better working hours made weekend excursions and summer holidays a British institution in Trollope's lifetime. Frith's paintings *Ramsgate Sands* (1854) and *The Railway Station* (1862) were huge successes with the public. Trollope loved his holidays. He courted Rose at a resort, Kingstown, near Dublin (August 1842). As his Post Office responsibilities increased, his journeys included holidays at the seaside and took him to more exotic locations. He liked swimming, preferably in the nude, declaring, 'I love to jump into the deep clear sea from off a rock, and I love to be hampered by no outward impediments as I do so' (*NA* 1, II). On his West Indies tour (1859) he swam from the ship despite the sharks (Mullen 335). In Holland he had to use the cramped bathing machines and rented a costume that was too small. Embarrassed, he swam quickly out to sea ('My Tour in Holland', *Cornhill*, November 1862). RCT

Seeley, Sir John Robert (1834–95), historian and essayist, notorious author of *Ecce Homo*, published anonymously in 1865, which Trollope read. Seeley's attempt to create a 'historic Jesus' without considering his divine nature caused controversy, but, unlike many of his contemporaries, Trollope did not condemn the book, thereby showing his intellectual curiosity and tolerance towards 'irreligious' ideas, while maintaining his broad Christian faith. RCT

Seely, Mr, John Caldigate's gloomy, oppressive lawyer who believes his client is guilty of bigamy but who prides himself on his neutral stance. He nearly gives up the case when Caldigate appears to bribe his accusers. *JC* SRB

self-help, a phrase popularized by the bestselling 1859 book of that title by Samuel Smiles. The phrase comes from Thomas Carlyle, as did much of the message, though Smiles's facile pen made the Carlylean gospel of work banal, if more accessible. Other works by Victorian Britain's leading purveyor of success literature included *Thrift* (1875), *Duty* (1880), *Character* (1871), and especially *Lives of the Engineers* (1861–2). Paragons of upward mobility like the railway builder George Stephenson, the canal builder James Brindley, and the bridge builder John Rennie were at once celebrated for their genius and held up as examples of what adherence to the ordinary copybook maxims of self-help could lead to. Sir Roger Scatcherd in *Doctor Thorne* had real counterparts in railway contractors like Thomas Brassey. Many died young, burnt out by overwork, but Scatcherd mocks these heroes by rising from nowhere and performing prodigies while being an alcoholic. Smiles's hagiographical approach to his heroes involved suppressing certain unedifying details, though perhaps his most interesting distortion was his insistence on their lack of education and of theoretical or scientific knowledge: sturdy British empiricism and rule of thumb were all-conquering in his version of industrialism.

Ideology apart, the reality of Victorian self-help placed much emphasis on adult education. Trollope was familiar with the world of intellectual improvement, lecturing at many of the mechanics' institutes, athenaeums, and literary and scientific societies that dotted the country. Their libraries and soirées were alternatives to the gin palaces, music halls, and worse that tempted him as a young man alone in London. Self-help meant social mobility, however, which raised problems for Smiles, as for Trollope. Despite his reputation, Smiles was no apologist for rampant individualism and social striving. The main thing for him was character development rather than material gain. According to his creed even a manual labourer could be a gentleman if he belonged to the 'aristocracy of character'.

Trollope essentially subscribed to such principles.

Self-help meant mutual improvement and was very much a collective endeavour in Victorian Britain, which created an extensive network of voluntary organizations dedicated to practical social betterment without charitable or government assistance. Among these were thousands of friendly societies, burial societies, building societies, and cooperative societies which offered modest protection against life's vicissitudes. They provided the sense of independence and self-respect that was so essential to the working-class culture of respectability.   CK

Briggs, Asa, 'Samuel Smiles and the Gospel of Work', in *Victorian People* (1955).
Gosden, P. H. J. H., *Self-Help: Voluntary Associations in Nineteenth-Century Britain* (1973).

sensation fiction. Popular in the 1860s, the sensation novel may have been an attempt to domesticate and Victorianize the Gothic horror novel. The taste for stage melodrama which flourished at the same time demonstrates how this transient vogue took mid-Victorian society by storm. Derangement, horror, mystery, and lurid marital problems underpin many of the plots of both genres. Most contemporary reviewers detested sensation fiction; the Archbishop of York even preached against it. Some of this unease may rest in a dim perception that these fictions shadowed the 'other' life of the Victorians, with its child abuse, illicit sex, violent crime, and the fearful degradations inherent in greedy industrialization.

Most sensation novels were heavily plot-oriented. It was the genius of Wilkie *Collins, and principally of Dickens, to perceive how this taste for the lurid and the prurient could be made to serve a higher purpose. Through its marital secret, its long-running serialized suspense, and its juxtaposition of great wealth with abominable poverty, *Bleak House* (1853), for instance, prefigures as it transcends the pot-boiler norm of sensation fiction. In the hands of Wilkie Collins the 'novel with a secret' developed into the detective novel. Edgar Allan Poe helped to give poignant savour to this fusion of mystery, perversion, and preoccupation with crime.

No major Victorian novelist was further from the sensationalists in his regular practice than Anthony Trollope. His representative strength lies in giving an imaginative distinction to well-observed normality. The quiet world of Barsetshire is at the other end of the spectrum from the highly charged emotionalism of Dickens, whose style (which Trollope found sensational) is satirized in *The Warden* under the guise of Mr Popu-

lar Sentiment. Praising *The Duke's Children* in August 1880 the *Nation* (New York) emphasized 'the usual quiet key which all readers of his books know so well, and which is maintained with the hand of a master' and praises Trollope as 'the last of the realists. . . . He paints the world as he sees it, but he sees it with just that amount of artistic vision which saves his picture from having the dull flatness of every-day life, and yet never makes the light and shade any lighter or darker than everybody feels to be within the bounds of naturalness' (Smalley 473).

This capacity to illuminate the ordinary customarily informs his best character studies—his 'complete appreciation of the usual', his 'great apprehension of the real', as Henry James called it. There are virtually no out-and-out villains in Trollope; he seldom attempts the grotesques or the eccentrics in which Dickens excels. Nor does he choose, often, to plumb the crooked recesses of emotional torment or violent crime. His heroines are strongly and warmly drawn, but few disgrace themselves or carry guilty secrets nor, save in the case of Lily Dale, do they surprise us by wilful unpredictability.

Occasionally Trollope *will* produce surprises. *He Knew He Was Right* explores the obstinate monomania of Louis Trevelyan in believing his wife guilty of a most improbable marital impropriety. The subject is close to the kind which characterizes sensation fiction. But the strength of Trollope's account lies precisely in its unsensational approach to this extraordinary monomania. And in *The Last Chronicle of Barset* the Revd Josiah Crawley represents Trollope's masterpiece of tragic characterization, again, not by exaggerating Crawley's derangement, nor by sentimentalizing his self-inflicted mental anguish, but by totally convincing and deeply sympathetic insistence on the foolish, stubborn, heroic integrity which drives the man towards self-destruction.

Just once or twice Trollope acknowledges the rival presence of sensation fiction—at its height exactly during the decade of his own greatest popularity—by borrowing its plots or methodology. *The Eustace Diamonds* flirts parodically with the mystery of the purloined jewel in Wilkie Collins's *The Moonstone*, though Trollope de-mystifies and de-sensationalizes Collins's material. Typically the lost diamond itself is the least important and memorable element of Trollope's book, which is a marvellous tragi-comic study of Lizzie Eustace's social ambitions and self-delusions. And though *Orley Farm* takes us into a world of forged wills, family mystery, and highly charged lawsuits—the typical stuff of sensation fiction—Trollope studiously avoids letting his novel become emotionally highly charged. It is memorably leavened by the presence of some of Trollope's finest comic writing and some of his warmest social pictures. TB

Pykett, L., *The Sensation Novel* (1994).
Rance, N., *Wilkie Collins and Other Sensation Novelists* (1991).

Sentiment, Mr Popular, popular novelist, the most powerful and effective of all contemporary reformers. His novel *The Almshouse* takes up in typical glaring exaggeration the cause of Hiram's Hospital. Trollope's brief but potent comment on Charles Dickens's methods of characterization and social reform. *W* NCS

serialization. The publication of fiction in instalments prior to the appearance of the completed story had been practised in the 18th century, when such numbered parts were known as 'number books'. But in the early years of the 19th century the custom fell out of favour. It was the appearance of Dickens's *The Pickwick Papers*, published by Chapman & Hall and running through twenty one-shilling, monthly parts from April 1836 to November 1837, which gave a new life to serial or episode publication. Once *The Pickwick Papers* had established its popularity, the monthly sales picked up from 500 copies of part 2 until part 15 achieved the extraordinary total of 40,000 copies.

Like all novels issued in parts, *Pickwick* was issued as a complete volume at the end of the serial run, thus hugely augmenting the total sales. Dickens continued to employ this method of publishing his work, and it proved uniquely successful for him.

The monthly parts for these serials appeared in paper wrappers of a characteristic colour (Dickens's wrappers were green, Lever's were always pink) and they customarily identified themselves by a striking and vigorous woodcut cover design. The illustrations which accompanied the first issue in volume form were distributed throughout the serialized text.

First editions in book form sometimes used up unsold sheets from the parts issue. Where first editions are bound from parts this can be identified by the stab-holes which served to assist the loose sewing-up of the sheets into their parts form. Some collectors prefer such copies bound from the parts.

Following Dickens's successful example, Trollope, Thackeray, Ainsworth, and Lever all issued novels in serial episodes. There were variations on the monthly shilling numbers. *He Knew He Was Right* first appeared in 32 sixpenny numbers, weekly, from 17 October 1868 to 22 May 1869. Then, starting in November 1869, a monthly series of bound parts was initiated. Both these preceded the one-volume first edition in 1869. Lever went one stage further. Several of his early novels appeared simultaneously in monthly parts and concurrently as serials in the *Dublin University Magazine*.

Despite these expedients to maximize the number of bites author and publisher might take at the cherry, nobody but Dickens could sustain this method of publication where the author was thinking out and planning his story in monthly chunks, and in some cases might be working on two or more serials simultaneously. When Trollope says that a writer must learn the tricks of his trade before he can make money, the techniques and pressures of writing for serialization are among the 'tricks' he has in mind.

The practice of monthly or weekly serialization declined after the 1860s—though Trollope continued sometimes to use it. Serialization in magazines became the more commonly accepted practice, where the book was not scheduled simply for immediate issue in volume form. The *Cornhill Magazine* carried *Framley Parsonage* as its main serial from January 1860 through to April 1861, but improved technology which had reduced production costs meant that the magazine could afford also to carry Thackeray's *Lovel the Widower* and *The Adventures of Philip* at the same time.

Critics sometimes complained of the effects which serial writing had on the author: 'The habit of writing a story in periodical instalments is almost always fatal to that coherence and proportion without which no work can lay claim to any really artistic merit,' pontificated the *Westminster Review* of *Framley Parsonage* in July 1861 (Smalley 133). At best the method gets damned with faint praise; the *Saturday Review* for 19 August 1865 observed, with reference to *Can You Forgive Her?*: 'Mr Trollope is right in publishing his book in monthly parts. A little of it once a month is just what everybody would like, and the story is far from being so fearfully absorbing that the break would leave us in too painful suspense' (Smalley 242). Conversely, *Public Opinion*, 12 June 1869, found the course of events in *He Knew He Was Right* so absorbing that it sympathized with avid readers who were forced to wait, week by week, to find out what happened next! Thirty-two of Trollope's novels made their first appearance either in weekly or monthly numbers, or as magazine serials. From *Framley Parsonage* onwards it was the exception for the volume form to appear without prior episodic appearance. Eleven different magazines or newspapers carried serialized Trollope at different times. TB

servants as characters. When Trollope was writing, one in every ten of the female population was in service; a major section of the economy depended upon this two-way relationship. To have a servant was to allow a stranger to be privy to the most private areas of domestic life. There are some fortunate people, says Trollope in *The Eustace Diamonds* (XXI), whose servants are loyal and faithful, who have become part of the family, rather like Mrs Toff in *Is He Popenjoy?* Such is not Lizzie Eustace's lot, since her maid Patience Crabstick's belief that her mistress is no better than she should be justifies the deal with the housebreakers, and the theft of the diamonds (*ED* LVIII). Loyal and supportive servants 'are plants that grow slowly' (XXI), and Trollope knows the worth of such people.

He says in *Castle Richmond* that, contrary to popular prejudice, he never had an Irish servant who was faithless, dishonest, or intemperate. As a bachelor in Banagher he had employed a groom, *Barney, who stayed with him till old age. Barney was paid an extra £5 a year to wake him early, and tales about him became part of the Trollope family mythology. The Trollope family did not always have such luck with their servants. A running joke through his correspondence is the trouble they had with cooks; one drank, another went blind—not that that seemed to make any difference, he wrote (Glendinning 270).

Perhaps he drew on such experiences when he created servants who regularly provide a comic thread. Following the convention of the lower orders providing comic relief, a contemporary reviewer of *The Way We Live Now* criticized Trollope for not making Mrs Pipkin, a working-class mother struggling to maintain respectability while earning her bread, comic enough. It was not a crime he was often guilty of. Trollope's servants speak in the vernacular, talking and acting with directness denied to those aspiring to refinement. Mrs Baker, the Stavely family nurse, says of Madeleine, 'none of 'em aint kinderhearteder' (*OF* XXXI); Bridget, Dr Thorne's maid, hits Louis Scatcherd's man with her rolling pin when he tries to take liberties (*DT* XXXIV).

That servants are subject to a different code of behaviour is regularly pursued. Lucy Morris jokes that she will not be allowed 'followers' when she is in Lady Linlithgow's employ (*ED* XXXIII). Martha, Jemima Stanbury's maid, puts it rather more bluntly when she reflects on the licence given to young ladies, when such behaviour would have a young working woman turned out onto the street without a reference (*HKWR* LXXII). Martha's position as employee and confidante is carefully explored. She has been with Miss Stanbury for twenty years; she has great

gifts, we hear. She was never ill, and she really liked having sermons read to her (VII). Both are sharp about money, and invest it, misguidedly, with the power to control. They both prefer gossip with an edge of malice, as they exchange titbits about the French girls, and they speak their minds to each other. The closely tracked conversation when Martha is sent to buy a shoulder of lamb (LXVI) shows the degree to which Martha has the measure of her employer, and the trust which is invested in her—in spite of being called a fool. Indeed, she is the only character in the book who can confront Miss Stanbury with the impact of her actions, while keeping her goodwill.

The despotic behaviour of Hopkins, the gardener (*SHA*), mirrors Squire Dale's conviction that his views should hold sway. Now over 60, he has spent his whole life on the Allington estate. He has a primeval relationship with his job; the cutting of the asparagus and the cherishing of the grapes are more important than being paid. The episode with the manure, when Hopkins bests his employer till Squire Dale has to apologize for sacking him, is packed with ironic burlesque, parodying Hopkins's relationship with the soil, and the convention of romantic comedy which demands a happy ending for a heroine, thwarted by Lily (LX). There is a bucolic dignity to his relationship with Bell and Lily, 'the two young ladies he did love, and snubbed in a peremptory way' (II). He 'Thees' and 'My darlings' Lily, and his vox populi disparagement of Crosbie passes unchecked when he expresses murderous intent (XXXI), and when he wishes he could celebrate her marriage to Johnny Eames (XL).

Passages like these suggest that the role of servant-characters like Martha and Hopkins is rather like that of the Shakespearian fool. They speak the truth in a direct manner which goes straight to the beliefs and wishes of the audience, their homespun wisdom making their own commentary and parody of the main plots.   MM

Sevenkings, Ezekiel, American poet from the far west invited to lunch by Elias Gotobed, the American ambassador in London. *DC*   RCT

Seville, Spanish city where John Pomfret visits Maria Daguilar. 'Bull' *TAC1*   GRH

Seward, Fanny, daughter of William Henry Seward, American Secretary of State, who met Trollope at dinner in December 1861 when she was 17. She noted in her diary that he was decidedly common, 'a great homely, red, stupid-faced Englishman, with a disgusting beard of iron grey'. Since conversation at table had covered the international incident of the Slidell and Mason affair (described below), doubtless Trollope had been more vociferous than usual (*I & R*, 81 n.). RCT

Seward, William Henry (1801–72), American Secretary of State during and after the Civil War (1861–70); dined with Trollope on 27 December 1861, the day on which the threat of war between Britain and America was finally defused. On 8 November, the British ship *Trent* had been boarded by American forces under Captain Charles Wilkes, and two Confederate diplomats under British protection, James Murray Mason and John Slidell, were taken prisoners. Seward favoured returning the men to the British, and this was the day when Lincoln accepted Seward's position (*Auto* IX). RCT

Sewell, Revd James Edward (1810–1903), Warden of New College, Oxford (1860–1903). The Sewell family played a prominent role in high-church activities in Oxford, which Trollope appreciated. According to his first biographer, Trollope called *The Warden* 'an idealized photograph, whose chief features were, by an eclectic process, taken from more than one member of the Sewell family' (T. H. S. Escott, *Anthony Trollope* (1913), 107). RCT

Sewell, Mary (1797–1884), minor author interested in philanthropic movements, notable for *The Rose of Cheriton*, verse essays Trollope reviewed for the *Fortnightly Review* (February 1867). Trollope cared little for pietistic literature, especially when it preached that major social problems could be remedied by closing down beer-shops. He pointed to the failure of prohibition in some American states and argued that education, rather than legislation, was the answer to alcohol problems. RCT

sexuality. The conventions of Victorian public discourse did not permit the direct portrayal of sexual feelings or acts in fiction. Yet Trollope's characters are by no means ethereal beings; their sexuality, though always implied, is always plain. Trollope often used oblique or symbolic means to suggest physical passion roiling beneath a decorous surface. As Victoria Glendinning points out (465), when Trollope's young lovers meet on bridges or by fast-moving streams, the water's power and fluidity plainly mirror the force of unspoken sexual desire. Trollopian lovers have a habit of visiting such places, which can be frightening as well as exhilarating. As Mary Belton says in *The Belton Estate*, falling in love 'is something like jumping into a river'. The jump is voluntary, but 'the person can't help . . . being in when the plunge has once been made' (XIII).

Trollope's trademark hunting scenes also often contain a sexual element, as young men and women pursue the fox (and one another) across the countryside. The combination of strenuous physical exercise, the close proximity of the opposite sex, and the constant threat of injury makes a heady experience, especially for Trollope's young women. 'This was to live', as Lizzie Eustace discovers her second time out. 'There was, however, just enough of fear to make the blood run quickly to her heart' (*ED* XXXVIII).

The vast majority of Trollope's characters are robustly heterosexual, including his young women, whose unabashed acknowledgement of physical attraction to their chosen men struck some early reviewers as coarse. But for Trollope it is simply natural. He makes rather laborious fun of women—notably the Americans Wallachia Petrie in *He Knew He Was Right* and Olivia Q. Fleabody in *Is He Popenjoy?*—who deny their true natures and seek to transform sexuality into a political issue.

Most of Trollope's men are equally straightforward in their heterosexuality; he treats the exceptions as ludicrous, sinister, or sad. Greasy Obadiah Slope in *Barchester Towers* tries to be robust, in his devious way, but most women find him physically repellent. The obvious sadism of Sir Griffin Tewett in *The Eustace Diamonds* is frustrated when his intended slave, Lucinda Roanoke, recoils into madness. In *Castle Richmond*—Trollope's sole portrayal of what might be construed as male homosexual desire—Owen Fitzgerald's ardent love for the young Earl of Desmond leaves Owen, at the end, wandering the world alone.

Trollope was undoubtedly aware of deviations from the genitally focused, heterosexual norm that prevails in his fiction. But like his contemporaries, he did not regard sexuality of any stripe as an independent feature of human character that could be analysed apart from one's whole personality. Certainly he did not consider sexuality to be definitive of one's nature and destiny, as post-Freudian Western culture has taught itself to do. That sane view, rather than Victorian prudery or hypocrisy, accounts for the absence from Trollope's fiction of this quintessentially modern topic of discussion. WK

Seymour, Henry Danby (1820–77), Liberal MP for Poole (1850–68) and, along with Trollope and others, one of the original proprietors of the *Fortnightly Review* (May 1865). In November 1864 George Meredith had written to Chapman that Seymour hoped he would have *de facto* running of the magazine, but the more experienced and distinguished G. H. *Lewes became editor. RCT

Shakespeare, William (1564–1616). As *An Autobiography* records, Trollope familiarized himself with Shakespeare's writings as a young man (*Auto* III), and talked about him in conventionally hyperbolic terms, referring to him in *The New Zealander*, for instance, as 'that name of which all Englishmen are so immeasurably the proudest' (XI). We know from the copious annotations that Trollope made on his collection of Elizabethan and Jacobean drama many of Trollope's views of individual plays. Thus, for instance, *Macbeth* is 'on the whole the finest play of Shakespeare', while there is 'nothing, perhaps, in the whole range of poetry to exceed the finest passages of Lear'. *As You Like It* is 'the prettiest comedy that was ever written in any language', and *Hamlet* is 'the greatest work of man' (quoted Hall 416; Hall also details some of Trollope's minor reservations about Shakespeare). The proliferation of Shakespearian allusions and quotations in Trollope's writings reflects not only his own knowledge of the playwright's works, but also his presumption that his readers will share such knowledge, using it as a cultural lingua franca. Most of the Shakespearian allusions are to *Hamlet* and *Macbeth*, and there are certain lines and passages from both plays that the novelist deploys repeatedly. See for instance: 'The labour we delight in physics pain' (*Macbeth*, II. ii. 47, in: *FP* III; *HKWR* XLII; *LCB* IX; *OF* XIII; *TC* XL), 'shut up | In measureless content' (*Macbeth*, II. i. 16–7, in: *BE* X; *OF* XXIV); various lines from Hamlet's famous meditation on suicide (*Hamlet*, III. i. 56–88, in: *B* XLVI; *BT* XLIX; *CH* II; *KD* XVII; *LCB* XIX; *MSF* XVI; *PM* LXII; *PR* I; *RH* LI; *SBJR* VIII ff.; *VB* LII); 'Woo't drink up Esil? eat a crocodile?' (*Hamlet*, V. i. 299, in: *BE* XX; *HKWR* LXXVIII; *PR* LXV; *SBJR* XIX). Of course, this most restrictive of lists cannot possibly do justice to the sheer range of Shakespearian allusions and quotations on offer in Trollope's fiction. However, one may safely generalize that in most cases it is difficult to infer any strong thematic reason for the deployment of a given allusion in a given novel. A major exception might be *He Knew He Was Right*, in which the monomaniacal jealousy of Louis Trevelyan, giving rise to false but obsessive fantasies about his wife's infidelity, constantly invites comparison with *Othello*; while *The Struggles of Brown, Jones, and Robinson* bathetically invokes *King Lear* and *Hamlet*, in order to ridicule the disparity between George Robinson's lofty ambitions, and the tawdry reality of his existence. *Ralph the Heir* might also be seen as a curious inversion of *King Lear*, in which the structure of Shakespeare's play is taken and turned upside down: Lear and his three daughters parallel Sir Thomas Underwood, his two daughters, and—a surrogate daughter—his niece Mary Bonner; Gloucester, his illegitimate son Edmund, and his legitimate son and heir Edgar parallel Squire Newton, his illegitimate son Ralph, and his nephew and heir, also Ralph. However, whereas Lear wants—broadly speaking—to renounce his throne and live with his daughters, Sir Thomas Underwood actively shuns spending time with his two daughters and niece, and is desperate to re-enter public life. Similarly, in the parallel plot, whereas illegitimate Edmund is evil, illegitimate Ralph is goodness itself; and whereas the legitimate Edgar is Gloucester's favourite and chosen heir, Ralph the Heir is despised by Squire Newton as an irredeemable scapegrace, and the squire is desperate to buy back Ralph the Heir's entitlement to the family property. One cannot push the parallels too far, but the novel does seem to represent one of the clearest examples in Trollope's fiction of a deliberately allusive formal structure. HO

'Shakespeare Foundation Schools' (article). This article in the *London Telegraph* describes a public meeting at the New Adelphi Theatre on 11 May 1864 presided over by Dickens, regarding the establishment of a public school for children of actors, on the property of the Shakespeare Foundation. Anthony Trollope proposed the following resolution: 'That the schools shall be called the "Shakespeare Foundation Schools", and shall be devoted to the sound and liberal education of pupils of both sexes, and not be restricted to any profession or class; that there shall be a certain number of "foundation scholars", so many girls and so many boys, according to the wealth of the endowment; that these foundation scholars shall receive their education gratuitously, and shall always be the children of actors, actresses, or dramatic writers.' (The motion passed.) This is the only mention of Trollope at the meeting. *London Telegraph* (12 May 1864), 5. AKL

Shand, Alexander Innes (1832–1907), journalist and critic; fellow member of the Athenaeum Club (on Trollope's nomination, February 1871). Shand wrote 'Mr Anthony Trollope's Novels', for the *Edinburgh Review* (October 1877), a slightly patronizing estimate of the novelist's work from *The Warden* to *The American Senator*. 'His talent is emphatically of the serviceable order, and wears wonderfully well' (Smalley 439). Perhaps Trollope smarted a little. Shand is thought to be the original for Alfred Booker, a newspaper editor in *The Way We Live Now*, whom Lady Carbury courts for favourable reviews. In his memoranda for the novel, Trollope wrote 'Shand' against the name of that character. The title of

Shand, Dr

one of Lady Carbury's novels, *The Wheel of Fortune*, suggests Shand's novel *Fortune's Wheel* (1886) (Glendinning 371).   RCT

Shand, Dr, successful country doctor and father of a large, generous-minded family. His son Dick seeks gold in Australia with John Caldigate. *JC*
                                                    SRB

Shand, Maria, sister of Dick, the adventurer who travels to Australia with John Caldigate. Caldigate's flirtations and farewell kiss to Maria give her hope, but even when he marries Hester Bolton upon his return to England, Maria maintains her good opinion of him. *JC*   SRB

Shand, Richard (Dick), college friend of John Caldigate's who goes with him to seek gold in Australia. Although they strike gold, Dick loses his way through drinking and becomes a vagrant shepherd. He disappears for some years but returns to England and gives evidence that Caldigate is not guilty of bigamy. *JC*   SRB

Shandy Hall, home of the Leslies near Newcastle in Jamaica. 'Jack' *TAC1*   GRH

Shap, village near Vavasor Hall notable for its railway station and small inn. *CYFH*   JMR

Sharp, Mr, legal adviser to the editor who suggests a payment of £10 to placate Mrs Brumby. 'Brumby' *ET*   GRH

Sheep's Acre Farm, farm belonging to Bishop Yeld and Roger Carbury but leased to Daniel Ruggles. *WWLN*   SRB

Shelley, Mary (1797–1851), daughter of feminist Mary Wollstonecraft and radical philosopher William Godwin, wife of poet Percy Bysshe Shelley, and author of *Frankenstein, or the Modern Prometheus* (1817). She was part of a radical Anglo-French network in Paris that included Mrs Trollope, with whom she stayed in 1827 and was invited to join the Nashoba commune venture Fanny Wright had designed. She declined.
                                                    RCT

Shelley, Percy Bysshe (1792–1822), poet and essayist, best known for *Prometheus Unbound* (1820), and *A Defence of Poetry* (1821), listed by Trollope among his 'giants' of English literature. Shelley's 'Queen Mab' was among Lady Eustace's favourite reading (*ED* XXI). During March 1877, Trollope read *The Revolt of Islam* to his family (*Letters* 2, 1033).   RCT

Sheridan, Richard Brinsley (1751–1816), Irish dramatist famous for sparkling comedies such as *The Rivals* (1775) and *The School for Scandal* (1777). Sheridan's humiliation at Harrow as a poor player's son resembled Trollope's. Although he left no criticism of Sheridan's plays, Trollope referred to them occasionally. On the effect of novels on immature minds he cited Sir Anthony Absolute to Mrs Malaprop (*Auto* XII). In *Thackeray*, he differentiated Thackeray's use of malapropisms from the playwright's (IX). When Strahan envisaged *Lotta Schmidt and Other Stories* in two volumes, Trollope vehemently protested at 'a poor rill of type meandering thro' a desert of margin', recalling *School for Scandal*, I, i (*Letters* 1, 372).   RCT

shooting season, the season for the exclusive and expensive sport of shooting game birds, particularly grouse, on the moors of Scotland. It began on 12 August as the London season ended, Parliament recessed, and fashionable society took to its country houses. As Trollope noted in *The Prime Minister*, 'Men do not really like leaving London before the grouse calls them—the grouse, or rather the fashion of the grouse' (XLI). Though not keen on the sport himself Trollope recognized its social and even political importance. Many large landowners raised game for sport: shooting party invitations were much sought after, even those of the tedious Robert Kennedy in *Phineas Finn*. To be a good shot, as was Phineas Finn, was a considerable social asset, and gifts of game were prestigious social currency.   CK
   Ruffer, Jonathan G., *The Big Shots* (1977).

short stories, Trollope's. Trollope took up short stories relatively late in his career, although once embarked he was typically industrious, producing some 42 between 1859 and his death (his last completed work of fiction was a short story, 'Not if I Know It'). The immediate stimulus for venturing into this new field was his trip to the West Indies in 1858–9, and his stopover in the USA on the return leg. Trollope was evidently struck while in New York by *Harper's New Monthly Magazine*, and the lucrative outlet for short fiction it provided writers like himself. It so happened that an equivalent to *Harper's* was being launched in London, the *Cornhill Magazine*, edited by W. M. Thackeray. Trollope's first intention was to thematize his short stories around his traveller's experiences; place them multiply in British or American journals; and collect them together in volume form as 'Tales of All Nations'. His first effort was the farcical 'Relics of General Chassé: A Tale of Antwerp', published in *Harper's*, February 1860. The relationship with the American magazine broke down with the fourth story, 'La Mère Bauche', whose grimness was probably not to its taste. Thereafter Trollope published a batch of his short stories in Cassell's *Illustrated Family Paper*. His first series of *Tales of All Countries* (collecting his short stories to date) came out in 1860, featuring settings as far flung as Spain, Jamaica, New England, Egypt, Ireland, and France. The tone is predominantly comic and frequently self-mocking (see, for example, the farcical 'The O'Conors of Castle Conor'). Trollope found another temporary berth as a short story writer with the *London Review*, before they took exception to his 1861 tale 'A Ride across Palestine', with its suggestive transvestite plot. Sexual frankness also led to *Cornhill* rejecting 'Mrs General Talboys'; a breach with Thackeray was narrowly avoided. A second series of *Tales of All Countries* came out in 1863. Again the settings of the collected stories were extraordinarily diverse. The overall tone of the book was more sombre, stories like 'Returning Home' (1861) being frankly tragic and 'Aaron Trow' (1861) startlingly violent. But Trollope was demonstrably refining his technique in the short form (particularly in the handling of dialogue and narrative surprise). He wrote relatively few short stories between 1861 and 1866. Of especial interest are his tales of the American Civil War, 'The Widow's Mite', 'The Two Generals', and 'Miss Ophelia Gledd' (all 1863). In the last-named he is thought to have given a pen-portrait of his young American friend Kate Field. 'Malachi's Cove' (1864) is a full-blooded Cornish melodrama. In the second half of his writing career, Trollope's short stories are more heterogeneous and less traveller's tales. A relationship with the *Argosy* magazine in 1866 produced the Viennese love story 'Lotta Schmidt', the title piece in his third collection *Lotta Schmidt and Other Stories* (1867). The magazine also published one of Trollope's powerful studies of the perils of authorship, 'The Adventures of Fred Pickering' (1866). Trollope's most coherent sequence of short stories arises from his tenure as editor of *Saint Pauls Magazine* (1867–70). *An Editor's Tales* (1870) show the author at his most mellow, self-ironizing, and lovable. Particularly noteworthy are the pathetic-comic 'The Turkish Bath' (1869; the only portrait we have of Trollope in the nude), the poignantly erotic 'Mary Gresley' (1869), the uproariously funny 'Josephine de Montmorenci' (1869), the reminiscential 'The Panjandrum' (1870), and the heart-rending 'The Spotted Dog' (1870; another lament on the woes of authorship). Between 1870 and his death in 1882, Trollope produced sufficient stories, of somewhat mixed quality, to fill another book, *Why Frau Frohmann Raised her Prices and Other Stories* (1882). The title story, set in a hotel in the Tyrol, is a revealing illustration of the author's economic theories. Also revealing, as the only fiction Trollope wrote with the Post Office as its

subject, is 'The Telegraph Girl' (1877). Trollope used the long-short story for the last of his 'Barsetshire Chronicles', the good-natured 'The Two Heroines of Plumpington' (published posthumously in *Good Words*, 1882). Trollope wrote his short stories for relatively small sums of money: often during his holidays, or in breaks from more demanding literary tasks. He never lavished as much care on these 'by-jobs' as on his full-length novels. But taken altogether the short stories display to advantage all his authorial skills and some facets of his genius (a talent for the macabre, sharp pathos, knockabout farce, exotic location) not readily found in the major novels. JS

Shropshire, location of Trafford Park, the grand seat of the Marquis of Kingsbury, and of Hartletop, estate of the Marquis of Hartletop. *MF, SHA* SRB

Sichel, Walter (1885–1933), author of studies on Bolingbroke, Disraeli, Sheridan, and Sterne. His memoir, *The Sands of Time* (1923), described Trollope as 'outwardly a curmudgeon, inwardly the soul of good-fellowship . . . I had cut myself shaving, and he took care to tell me so at the outset' (*I & R* 142). RCT

Siena. Northern Italian hill town. Emily Trevelyan takes lodgings here to care for her child and ailing husband at Casalunga, which is seven miles (11 km) outside of town. *HKWR* RC

Silverbridge, West Barsetshire borough represented in Parliament by Plantagenet Palliser. *SHA* NCS

Silverbridge, main railroad town in northern Barsetshire, 20 miles (32 km) by road and 40 miles (64 km) by rail from Barchester. Revd Josiah Crawley is brought there to face charges of theft. *LCB* NCS

Silverbridge, Lord (Palliser), eldest son of the young Duke of Omnium. Lord Silverbridge's early career alarms his father: a youthful prank gets him expelled from Oxford, he turns against family precedent and becomes a Conservative, and he loses more than £70,000 betting on a horse. Despite these follies, however, Lord Silverbridge matures quickly as his love for Isabel Boncassen deepens. Initially grieved that his son would marry an American of low birth, the Duke is reconciled to the marriage by Lord Silverbridge's growing manliness. *DC* JMR

silver fork fiction has its origins in the 18th-century novel of manners, in Goldsmith's and Sheridan's revival of comedy of manners, and in the closely observed social pictures of Fanny Burney, Jane Austen, and Maria Edgeworth. The term was coined by Theodore Hook (1788–1841), who expressed a fascination that the upper classes ate their fish with a silver fork. It reflects post-Regency fascination with high life, and depicts (often uncritically) the society of the idle, rich, and privileged. Bulwer-Lytton (1803–73) had the first and most enduring success of the genre with *Pelham* (1828). By far the best novel deriving from the silver fork school is Thackeray's *Vanity Fair* (1847–8), though it transcends and surpasses the routine performances of his contemporaries.

The society depicted in Trollope's richly perceptive social comedy frequently touches on silver forkery, but he exposes exactly the people—like Adolphus Crosbie and the De Courcy family in *The Small House at Allington*—who form the uncritical centre of 'straight' silver fork fiction. Indeed, one of Trollope's most endearing achievements is the perception with which he lays bare social pretence and silly preoccupation with trivia. He excels at characters who possess a self-satisfied appreciation of their own social worth and manners at whatever level of society. He deflates these pretences equally perceptively in the minor aristocracy, the self-satisfied middle classes, and the sleazy social world of Mr Kantwise, the commercial traveller in *Orley Farm*. This social awareness was probably sharpened by Trollope's early years in London as recalled in *The Three Clerks*. TB

Aldburgham, A., *Silver Fork Society* (1983).
Rosa, M. W., *The Silver Fork School* (1964).

Simpkinson, Cornet. He offends Fred Neville by drinking to Kate O'Hara, but redeems himself by delivering news of Fred's peerage. Much to his disappointment, nothing comes of that favour. *EE*   AWJ

Sing Sing (John), Chinese cook who, not being much trusted at Gangoil, repays this lack of faith by joining the Brownbies at Boolabong when it appears Gangoil may go up in flames. *HHG*   MRS

Sir Harry Hotspur of Humblethwaite (*see opposite*)

Slide, Quintus, slanderous editor of the *People's Banner*. As his name suggests, Slide is a slippery character. Though he pretends to perform an important social service, Slide uses his newspaper as a platform to flatter his friends and to abuse those who displease him. At one time, Slide even attempts to print a crazed letter written by the estranged husband of Lady Laura Kennedy. Initially a radical, Slide becomes a Conservative, reversing the entire political policy of his paper in order to give vent to his wrath against his nemesis, Phineas Finn. *PF, PR, PM*   JMR

Slope, Revd Obadiah. Obadiah Slope is the evangelical domestic chaplain to Bishop Proudie in *Barchester Towers* and a special protégé of the Bishop's wife, with ambitions to rule the diocese. As a sectarian controversialist in the national press, he has crossed swords with Francis Arabin. He has earlier successfully wooed Olivia Proudie, but has given her up because her father was not rich, and subsequently attempted to rekindle the flame on the latter's preferment. His first act in Barchester is to preach a sermon in the cathedral deliberately offensive to the majority of the clergy. In affairs of the heart he switches his attention to Eleanor Bold and her income, to the consternation of Archdeacon Grantly's party, and on the death of Dr Trefoil persuades Tom Towers of the *Jupiter* to propose him, unsuccessfully, as dean. He becomes entrapped by the Signora Neroni's sexual charms, to the horror of Mrs Proudie, who expels him from Barchester. He returns to London, marrying a rich widow and obtaining a living near the New Road. He is said to be lineally descended from Dr Slop, 'who assisted at the birth of Mr T. Shandy', and has 'added an "e" to his name, for the sake of euphony, as other great men have done before him'—a joke on Trollope/trollop (*BT* IV). The Christian name, Obadiah, derives from a servant of Tristram Shandy's father. Slope is presented negatively throughout, the fact of having been a sizar at Cambridge being held as a social disgrace, his family's conversion from Roman Catholicism contributing to the impression of hypocrisy, and his personal appearance—red hair, red face, thin bloodless lips, prominent pale brown eyes, and a spongy red nose, sweaty palms, and (cut from the manuscript at Longman's request) bad breath—completing his unattractiveness. DS

Small House at Allington, The (*see page 493*)

Small, William (1843–1929), watercolourist and illustrator. He contributed 26 'splendid' illustrations for *Marion Fay* (Super 404), serialized in the *Graphic* (3 December–3 June 1882). The pictures were dropped for the book edition.

Smalley, George Washburn (1833–1916), American journalist; chief of the *New York Tribune*'s European staff (1867–95) and a literary ambassador between the two countries; author of *Studies of Men* (1895) and many other collections. When Smalley enthusiastically reviewed Trollope's *South Africa* for the *Tribune* (March 1878), as 'the best existing book on its subject for the general reader', Trollope replied, 'It was by far the pleasantest [review] that I have

(*cont. on page 498*)

TROLLOPE's twenty-fifth novel has been called his 'saddest story' by one modern critic (Hall 359), while another comments that the novel reverses 'a traditional comic situation wherein a young and spirited heroine holding to the values of the heart stands against the prudent and restrictive maxims of her elders' and finds happiness by doing so (James R. Kincaid, *The Novels of Anthony Trollope* (1977), 146). This grim tale of hope abridged, deferred, and finally lost, with its relentless downward momentum, does indeed frustrate the longing for fulfilment which it initially raises.

When the story opens, Sir Harry Hotspur, a wealthy, elderly, and honourable baronet, has just lost his only son. Sir Harry and his wife have one remaining child, Emily, a lovely girl of great integrity. Though Sir Harry's title must now pass to a cousin, George Hotspur, his estates are unentailed. Soon Sir Harry decides to leave the property to Emily, but in his immense pride of family he longs to keep the estates and title together. And so he fantasizes a marriage between Emily and her cousin, although he knows George to be a dissipated youth. He invites George to visit Humblethwaite.

It is the novel's premiss that, at the time of this visit, George's debaucheries have not yet damaged his beauty or charm, but have none the less carried him past the point where redemption is still possible. Not only is George an incipient alcoholic, but, under the stress of mounting debt, he has engaged in dishonest practices that would preclude his acceptance in decent society if they were exposed. George, who must lie to hide his past iniquities and devise new swindles to supply his immediate wants, is slipping down a precipitous moral slope.

Sir Harry has heard rumours concerning George's worst deeds, but is not sure they are true; therefore, he cannot decide how to treat his cousin. He suspects that George is no fit husband for Emily, and yet the notion of a family marriage so allures him that he vacillates, allowing George to meet Emily repeatedly. Finally George proposes to Emily and is accepted. Horrified, Sir Harry asks his lawyer to investigate. Almost everything comes out, and Sir Harry forbids the marriage. But Emily stands firm, arguing that it is her Christian duty to reclaim this prodigal. Emily is so ignorant of vice that she cannot comprehend the depths to which a man like George might descend.

But she soon learns. Vacillating once again, Sir Harry agrees to join Emily in an attempt to reform George. If the attempt succeeds, he will permit the marriage. No sooner does Sir Harry make this concession than he learns of George's involvement in a card-sharping scheme far more dishonourable than his previous villainies. Sir Harry's indecision finally ends, as he concludes that it would be better for Emily to die than to marry her cousin. Realizing this, George writes a callous letter renouncing Emily in exchange for Sir Harry's promise to pay his debts. But Emily still hopes for a miraculous conversion that will restore George to her. When she hears that he has married his mistress, she dies. Her heartbroken father leaves his estates to a wealthy relation who neither needs nor wants them.

Sir Harry Hotspur received excellent reviews. The *Athenaeum* and the *Spectator* judged it to be among the most successful of Trollope's shorter fictions. The *Spectator*'s R. H. Hutton argued that the book's distinction springs from the fidelity with which it traces 'the conflict of feelings in the mind of a high-minded, but proud man', whose duty to his station 'comes into direct collision with his duty to his daughter'

(Smalley 341). But the reviewer for *The Times* argued that what makes the novel exceptional is its bold portrayal of vice. Comparing *Sir Harry Hotspur* to Trollope's previous novel, *The Vicar of Bullhampton*, which told a fallen woman's story in extremely polite terms, this reviewer called *The Vicar of Bullhampton* 'safe reading for ladies' schools', but for that very reason, uninteresting to a general audience. *Sir Harry Hotspur*, however, is certainly not dull; indeed, the description of its reprobate villain's debaucheries is marked by such 'frankness and vigour' as to unfit the book 'for the perusal of the young' (Smalley 339).

Most 20th-century criticism of the novel has tended to follow Hutton in focusing upon Sir Harry's conflict between his duty to the estate and his duty to his daughter as a human being. Some critics have judged Sir Harry harshly for the way he handles this dilemma; thus P. D. Edwards argues that Emily's death 'is a judgment on the aristocratic pride of her father' (*Anthony Trollope* (1977), 125). Others, like Robert Tracy, are kinder to Sir Harry, whom Tracy believes to be a good man destroyed by nothing more culpable than an 'excessive devotion to duty' (*Trollope's Later Novels* (1978), 111). Recent criticism has not, however, picked up on *The Times* reviewer's suggestion that this novel and its predecessor might be viewed as contrasting treatments of vice. And yet this remark offers a promising approach.

In *The Vicar of Bullhampton*, Carry Brattle's illicit affair with a man above her station takes place offstage. Clearly Trollope feared that his readers might lose sympathy with the girl if he described her seduction in detail. When we meet Carry, she is already trying to return to the paths of virtue, but the harsh attitudes of her family and friends make this very difficult. Discussing the novel, Trollope protested eloquently against the Victorian double standard of sexual morality: 'No fault among us is punished so heavily as that fault, often so light in itself but so terrible in its consequences to the less faulty of the two offenders, by which a woman falls. All her own sex is against her, and all those of the other sex in whose veins runs the blood which she is thought to have contaminated' (*Auto* XVIII). Trollope began work on *Sir Harry Hotspur* immediately upon finishing *The Vicar of Bullhampton*. The earlier novel politely shows that it is almost impossible for a girl to erase the consequences of a single indiscretion, while the later work graphically portrays a young man whose vices are almost endlessly forgiven, because of his sex and the social position for which it qualifies him. The symmetry is striking.

In justifying her loyalty to George, Emily often claims that Christianity commands of its adherents that they try to reclaim even the blackest sinners. Yet it is clear that she draws a dramatic distinction between female and male sinners, judging the former harshly, but excusing the latter on the ground that society encourages their vices. This suggests that one of the unfortunate consequences of the double standard is the way it makes vice an integral part of the definition of masculinity. Men's vices then become attractive to women, even conscientious, religious women like Emily. The narrator of *Sir Harry Hotspur* wryly asks, concerning 'a male sheep with a fleece as white as that of a ewe lamb, is he not considered to be, among muttons, somewhat insipid? It was this taste of which Pope was conscious when he declared that every woman was at heart a rake' (V).

Unlike his daughter, Sir Harry knows that George's conduct has crossed the line which, for most people, separates the flavourfully masculine from the downright dishonourable. And yet he joins his daughter in one last scheme to reclaim this appalling debauchee, simply because the laws of primogeniture have conferred such great importance upon him. The comments on *The Vicar of Bullhampton* quoted above show Trollope to be well aware of the role that British customs for transmitting property played in the severe punishments visited upon fallen women. In *Sir Harry Hotspur*, he shows himself equally aware of the way those arrangements could procure lenient treatment for an utterly worthless man.

The explicit description of George's sins that is so striking a feature of this novel, then, may be the fruit of Trollope's hope that he can convince its readers to deny George the unmerited sympathy that he receives from its characters. Because Victorian readers shared the tolerant attitudes toward male vice which *Sir Harry Hotspur* analyses and laments, Trollope knew that he must make George's vices shocking indeed to accomplish this aim.

Trollope began writing *Sir Harry Hotspur* in November 1868. He sold the entire copyright to Alexander Macmillan for £750. From May to December 1870, the story was serialized in *Macmillan's Magazine*, where it was not especially successful. Macmillan then sold the book-rights, for a nine-month period, to Hurst & Blackett, who published the novel, in one volume, in November 1870. Hurst & Blackett had originally wanted to publish the novel in two volumes, but Trollope vigorously objected that it was too short for such treatment, and he ultimately prevailed. The manuscript of *Sir Harry Hotspur* is in the Beinecke Library, Yale University.   JN

Edwards, P. D. *Anthony Trollope* (1977).
Kincaid, James, *The Novels of Anthony Trollope* (1977).
Tracy, Robert, *Trollope's Later Novels* (1978).

Small House at Allington, The

ALTHOUGH Trollope himself at times did not think of it as part of the series, *The Small House at Allington* is considered the fifth Barsetshire novel. Allington is not, strictly, in Barsetshire but in the next county. And there are no major roles for clergymen: Mr Boyce, the rector of Allington, is barely present. But Bishop Proudie, the Grantlys, and Mr Harding, all from *Barchester Towers*, make appearances, however brief, and the De Courcys, from *Doctor Thorne*, are elaborately developed. Then, looking forward, the Lily Dale–Johnny Eames–Adolphus Crosbie story continues as a major component of the later novel, *The Last Chronicle of Barset*. Since writing *Framley Parsonage*, Trollope had been ranging far afield, from *North America* to *Tales of All Countries*, from the legal matters of *Orley Farm* to the humble country people of *Rachel Ray*. In *The Small House at Allington* he is returning to the country gentry, and developing also the London life he had broached in *Framley Parsonage*.

The Great House at Allington has been the property of the Dale family for generations. In his youth the present squire was disappointed both in love and in politics, and has remained single and somewhat morose. A younger brother had eloped with the penniless daughter of the local aristocrat, Lord De Guest, and Bernard, the son of this union, is heir presumptive. He holds a commission in the Engineers and lives mostly in London. Another younger brother of the squire had died young leaving a widow with two daughters, and the squire, apparently more out of duty than love, had installed them in the Small House, close by. It shares a garden with the Great House—and a gardener, the aged and talkative Hopkins. The daughters, Bell and Lily, are the 'two pearls of Allington'. Bernard brings to Allington a London friend, Adolphus Crosbie, a clerk at the General Committee Office—a 'mere' clerk, says Lily, but also something of a 'swell', living a fashionable city life. In appearance he is an Apollo, Lily grants, and he has considerable culture and wit. The four young people abandon themselves to croquet and badinage, and something very close to a roll in the hay—at least Bernard covers Lily with hay, and Lily does the same to Crosbie. At first Crosbie is attracted to Bell, who is the more beautiful, but Lily is captivatingly playful, and when she falls in love with Crosbie, he proposes. Lily accepts, joyfully resigning her life and love to him, and he is enchanted by her passion.

Crosbie had lightly assumed that Lily's uncle the squire would be giving her some fortune, and Bernard thinks it may be so. But Crosbie, when he is not in Lily's charming presence, becomes anxious and confronts the squire, who assures him there will be no money settled on Lily. From this point on, Crosbie becomes increasingly regretful about the engagement. His income of £800 has been just enough to give him that free social life he loves, and he plumes himself on his aristocratic friends. He had pressed Lily for an early wedding, but now tries to explain that it must be postponed. Lily, oppressed by Crosbie's anxieties about money, offers to release him from the engagement. But although he has been longing to be released and to resume his bachelor life as a 'swell', Lily's generosity and devotion are so disarming, he swears he will never break it off, believing this when he swears it. But now he has received an invitation to Courcy Castle in Barchester, which he accepts by cutting short his sojourn at Allington.

Lily has already had a long-term admirer, neighbour Johnny Eames, immature (or 'hobbledehoy') but worthy, who loathes Crosbie. He has recently gone away to London to a modest clerkship in the Income Tax Office. In London he and his fellow clerk Cradell board at the humble house of Mrs Roper. Also in the house live Mr Lupex, a low theatre scene-painter who drinks, and his flirtatious wife. Cradell flirts dangerously with Mrs Lupex, and Amelia, the daughter of the house, makes a play for Johnny. Although he rather dislikes her, he nevertheless proves susceptible to her advances, and makes regrettable concessions, although he has sworn to love no one but Lily Dale.

Now we see Adolphus Crosbie leading the high life among the aristocratic De Courcys, a family which is wonderfully dysfunctional. The Earl is an old roué now confined by old age and gout to his own hearth and his long-suffering Countess, who had found his absence a blessing. He has made an enemy of his heir Lord Porlock by cheating him of money. Porlock fears he will eventually kill the Countess. The other sons are objectionable in various ways: Lord George has married a woman for money and has become miserly; Lord John is a sponger and ne'er-do-well. When Lord George's wife becomes pregnant, Porlock marries his mistress to spite his brother's heir. The daughter Amelia has married beneath her to lawyer Mortimer Gazebee, and the other daughters are ageing and single. Of these, the Lady Alexandrina has had something of a friendship with Crosbie and is desperate to marry. The Dales' neighbour and connection Lady Julia De Guest is a member of the party at Courcy Castle, and is making it well known that Crosbie is engaged to Lily Dale. But for Crosbie the idea of an aristocratic connection is too seductive, and he actually proposes to the

Lady Alexandrina and is accepted. Almost immediately he regrets it. He is clasped irretrievably to the bosom of this terrible family. The Countess, very careful to secure the marriage, offers to write to Lily's mother explaining how the engagement to Lily was a mere passing fancy; ostensibly it is a friendly offer, but actually it is a kind of blackmail. Crosbie winces. It is now impossible for him to escape. He writes some weaselly letters to Lily that puzzle her, and then at last breaks the engagement, saying that he could not have made her happy. Mrs Dale exclaims, 'It will kill her' (XXX). It certainly kills something in her. Her devastation is proportionate to her utter devotion. Everyone is appalled at Crosbie's villainy, but Lily refuses to hate him.

Johnny Eames, at home on holiday, though fearing breach-of-promise threats from Amelia Roper in London, gets his courage up to declare his love for Lily, who assures him of her faithful love for him—as a brother. Walking home along the fields, he finds his neighbour Lord De Guest threatened by an enraged bull, and Johnny courageously leaps the fence and saves him. The Earl is much moved by this act, and thereupon becomes Johnny's patron and supporter. Returning to London, Johnny encounters Crosbie and on the train platform gives him a thorough thrashing. When news of this gets about, both the Earl and his sister Lady Julia are more than ever devoted to Johnny, and resolve to support his suit to Lily. The squire, outraged at the betrayal of his niece, goes to accost Crosbie in London at his club, but Crosbie puts him off with an intermediary, thus proving himself, says the squire, a coward as well as a scoundrel. Crosbie has been promoted to a secretaryship at his office, and in other circumstances would have been glad of the increase in income, but now all is turned to ashes. He must submit to the disadvantageous financial arrangements made by his brother-in-law lawyer Gazebee, and undergo the wedding made shabby by the Earl's penury. There is a miserable honeymoon in economical Folkestone, a return to London to a damp house in a none-too-fashionable quarter, and the loss of friends and club life. The jilting of Lily Dale has brought on him a terrible punishment.

The squire, although crusty and curt on the exterior, nevertheless has a warm affection for the girls, and urges his nephew to marry Bell, the elder of the two. Bernard courts Bell, rather perfunctorily, but when she refuses him becomes much keener for the match. The squire presses Mrs Dale to persuade Bell to this advantageous alliance, but Mrs Dale rebuffs him, saying the decision must be entirely Bell's. Bell has another suitor, the young local doctor Crofts, but Crofts feels he is too poor yet in his profession to propose marriage. An older local doctor has offended Earl De Guest and so he calls in Dr Crofts, and takes a liking to him. His more-or-less chronic condition requires, he feels, frequent consultation, and we gather Dr Crofts is on the way to an increased income. Earl De Guest and his sister are strong supporters of Johnny's suit to Lily, and the Earl plans to settle money on Johnny to make the marriage comfortable. He enlists the squire in the cause, who promises to settle a certain generous sum on Lily. Meantime, poor Lily, 'the wounded fawn', has become gravely ill with scarlatina. Consequently Dr Crofts is much at the house, and even after Lily is recovering persists in making house calls. Bell is a woman who thinks for herself, and she has rather despised Crofts for thinking he could not subject a wife to poverty; women, she believes, can stand much more than men. But when she begins to soften toward him, a word from Lily encourages Crofts to try again, and at last Bell comes to realize that in this man there is an inestimable worth. In a way, the diametric contrast to Crosbie's faithlessness acts as a catalyst to her love.

The squire persists in pressing Bernard's suit with Mrs Dale, and now presses her also with Eames's suit for Lily. The two girls resent the squire's bullying of their mother, and persuade her they must give up the squire's charity, and take humble lodgings in the village. But Bell's acceptance of Dr Crofts finishes Bernard's hopes and the squire's hopes for him. Bernard takes an assignment abroad. The family of the Small House are packing up the household for the move to the village, when various factors make the move seem impractical. For there will be only Lily and her mother now; the gardener Hopkins, a devotee of Lily's, is opposed to the move. He tells them it will be the death of the squire. And Lily and her mother, now persuaded of the squire's true warm heart, consent to remain, and go about unpacking. The squire decides to make equal generous settlements on both girls. Johnny Eames once more proposes to Lily, and is definitively refused at last. 'I should be disgraced in my own eyes if I admitted the love of another man' (LIV), she says. There is a kind of triumph by both girls in that each achieves self-determination. Johnny Eames makes the decision to move out of the Roper establishment, cutting himself off from the deplorable society there. With the money settled on him by the Earl De Guest, he can afford better accommodation, and gains respect at his office. His friend Cradell finally deserts the dangerous Mrs Lupex, and marries Johnny's cast-off friend Amelia Roper. Crosbie seems adequately punished. His marriage is short-lived: the Countess, his mother-in-law, can stand her unpleasant husband no longer, and departs to live cheaply in Baden-Baden, and the Lady Alexandrina joins her. It is a Victorian substitute for divorce. Crosbie is left with diminished resources, a limited social life, and the comforts of the efficiency in his secretaryship.

If *The Small House* is not strictly a Barchester novel, it certainly has its links. In chapter XVI Trollope seems at pains to enforce the connection: Crosbie on his journey to Courcy Castle visits Barchester and drops in on the cathedral service, where he hears Mr Harding chant the Litany. Afterwards he falls into conversation with him, realizing he is the grandfather of his noble acquaintance Lady Dumbello. The chapter is quite superfluous, although it shows Crosbie capable of appreciating pure virtue, which capacity is what makes his own villainy so reprehensible to himself.

This novel also has links with the Palliser novels to come. In it we encounter Plantagenet Palliser for the first time. His very first remark suggests the man to be portrayed later: the company at Courcy Castle has heard how Johnny Eames rescued Earl De Guest, and De Courcy is indulging in savage hilarity at the idea of his fellow Earl being tossed by a bull. 'I don't see anything to laugh at,' says Plantagenet. His main activity in this novel is a flirtation with Lady Dumbello, a tepid affair consisting of remarks about the weather, and faint smiles; but society loves to gossip, and it is predicted that Palliser will be running away with Griselda before spring. When the Duke hears the gossip he has his man of business warn Plantagenet against the affair, under threat of disinheritance. Plantagenet feels defiant, and goes so far as to ask Lady Dumbello if he may call on her in London. Her parents the Grantlys have word of the gossip, and Mrs Grantly writes a diplomatic letter of warning to her. Griselda shows this to her husband, complaining of the viciousness of gossip, and all is made serene. The ambiguities of the clerical life are nicely balanced when Trollope comments that Mrs Grantly trusted her daughter; she 'had herself so successfully served God and Mammon together, that her child might go forth and enjoy all worldly things without risk to things heavenly' (LV). In fact, the affair came to nothing because neither knew quite how to proceed. In this same chapter, Trollope suggests what is to become of Plantagenet, how he was introduced to the heiress Lady Glencora M'Cluskie, who, although attracted to Burgo Fitzgerald, accepted Plantagenet's proposal, much to the satisfaction of her own family and of the Duke and Mr Fothergill. It seems that Trollope was envisaging the series to come.

The *Small House at Allington* is remarkable for the charming wit of the three Dale women, Lily especially. It is rich in authorial comment, too, in Rochefoucauldian mode. The Countess, for instance, with her handful of ageing unmarried daughters, enjoyed hearing of girls' losing their fiancés: 'She did not know she liked it, but she did' (XVII). And there is some amusing literary chat. Lily refers to Thackeray when she makes a joke about 'that bad man' who attacks mothers-in-law. Lily and Bell argue about novels: Lily wants them 'sweet', or wish-fulfilling, but Bell wants them with real life, now that we cannot have heroic novels like *The Heart of Midlothian*. Then Lily grows impatient with novels, and thinks of rereading *Pilgrim's Progress*, saying, 'I can never understand it, but I rather think that makes it nicer.' But Bell, who seems to speak for Trollope, thinks books should be 'clear as running water'.

Readers have recognized autobiographical elements in this novel, especially in the person of Johnny Eames. Earlier, Trollope had created a similarly autobiographical character in Charley Tudor of *The Three Clerks*. And he had himself undergone the kind of persecution Johnny receives from Amelia Roper (*Auto* III). There is fine satire of bureaucratic types such as Johnny's chief Sir Raffle Buffle, or old 'Huffle Scuffle' as the young clerks call him. And as in other novels, Trollope throws in knowing details about the Post Office, here in the person of Mrs Crump, the bad-tempered post-mistress.

The Small House at Allington from the first has engaged readers in a particular way. They would take sides personally, contemporary reviewers remarked, hoping Crosbie would give up Lady Alexandrina, begging Trollope to let Lily Dale marry Johnny Eames, and so forth. It elicited perceptive comment from one of Trollope's best con-temporary critics, Richard Holt *Hutton, on Trollope's grasp of the 'social strategies', the 'moral "hooks and eyes" of life'. The characterization of Crosbie was much ad-mired, how Trollope 'has kept the reader in charity with him, in spite of all his sins' (Smalley 194). Lily Dale above all captivated the public, although Trollope himself felt 'she is somewhat of a female prig' (*Auto* X), and some readers have found her tire-somely stubborn. A feminist view sees her as something of a new woman, rejecting marriage in favour of useful life in a larger community (Judith Weissman, 'Old Maids Have Friends', *Women and Literature* (1977), 15–25). And, perhaps inevitably in our permissive age, it has been taken as a story of illicit sex. Margaret Markwick argues that Trollope intends us to understand that Lily has lost her virginity to Crosbie (*Trollope and Women*, 1997). Lily is unquestionably passionate—one of the impressive things about the book is how Trollope communicates that—but she is also very wise and virtuous; it is the completeness of her emotional surrender that has made her so vulnerable. Some critics object, not without cause, to the Roper boarding-house scenes as inferior, but as usual with Trollope sub-plots have a way of relating to the main. The whole Roper ambience contrasts in its moral shabbiness with the genuine-ness of Allington, and of course it reveals real—if understandable—weakness on Johnny's part, which partly justifies Lily's rejection.

Mary Hamer observes Trollope's increasing power in this novel, in 'a bolder use of dialogue and direct speech' (*Writing by Numbers* (1987), 113). Juliet McMaster has viewed it as variations on the theme of perversity: Crosbie seeks out destruction with Alexandrina, Eames with Amelia, Lily with Crosbie, and Lily rejects her own best good in rejecting Eames (*Trollope's Palliser Novels*, 1978). This interpretation is valuable for Trollope's whole *œuvre*: what he calls 'the cross-grainedness of men' (*LCB* LVIII) is his recurrent concern. And so this engaging novel keeps its appeal: a prime minister of our time, John Major, chose it as his favourite book, on the BBC's *Desert Island Discs* programme.

The Small House at Allington was composed 1862–3, sold to Smith, Elder for £2,500, and came out in twenty parts, September 1862 to April 1864, in the *Cornhill*, illustrated by Millais. It was published in two volumes in 1864. The manuscript is in the Hunting-ton Library.   R apR

Hamer, Mary, *Writing by Numbers: Trollope's Serial Fiction* (1987).
McMaster, Juliet, *Trollope's Palliser Novels: Theme and Pattern* (1978).
Markwick, Margaret, *Trollope and Women* (1997).

read' (*Letters* 2, 763). Smalley helped negotiate publication of *Ayala's Angel* in the *Cincinnati Commercial* (November 1880–July 1881). Early on he called at Montagu Square towards noon and found Trollope still breakfasting. Trollope invited him to join him but Smalley declined, having already eaten. At this Trollope roared, 'do you mean to say you are not man enough to eat two breakfasts?' In 'English Men of Letters', for *McClure's Magazine* (January 1903), Smalley viewed Trollope as a model country squire, red-faced, hearty, and a great outdoors man. His literary strength lay principally in attention to detail. Trollope not only knew every inch of London, but 'for all social and personal traits [Trollope] had a microscopic eye' (*I & R* 153).   RCT

Smiler, Mr, notorious thief involved in the attempted theft of the Eustace diamonds at Carlisle. *ED*   JMR

Smiley, Maria, widowed friend of Mrs Moulder. Mrs Smiley is a 'firm set, healthy-looking woman of—about forty' (XLIII), with a fortune of £200 a year, in search of a second husband. Mrs Moulder arranges the union between her brother John Kenneby and Mrs Smiley. *OF*
                                                    MT

Smirkie, Revd Augustus, rector of Plum-cum-Pippins, a widower with five children. He marries Julia Babington and self-righteously congratulates her on escaping a bigamous marriage to John Caldigate. His verbal persecution of the latter goads his otherwise genial father-in-law into a spirited defence of Caldigate. *JC*   SRB

Smith, Barney. Charged with making illicit whiskey in the vicinity of Mohill, and unable to pay his fine, he is sentenced to an indefinite period of imprisonment in Ballinamore jail. *MB*
                                                    MRS

Smith, Churchill, one of the six collaborators in a reforming periodical. High-minded and conceited, he calls Mrs St Quinten's article 'utter nonsense', and throws it in the fire. 'Panjandrum' *ET*   GRH

Smith, Elder & Co., agents and suppliers to the British army who also held banking and shipping interests, plus a well-known publishing company that, after the death of Thackeray, adopted Trollope as one of its leading authors. The company of Smith, Elder was responsible for publishing some of the most prominent writers of the day, including Charlotte Brontë, Thackeray, and Ruskin. It was also the proprietor of the *Cornhill Magazine*, a monthly publication which gave Trollope his first chance at serial publication with *Framley Parsonage*, the greatest circulation ever achieved by a Trollope novel—109,274 copies for the first number (Super 107, 112). The company also published Trollope's final Barsetshire novel, *The Last Chronicle of Barset*.   RCT

Smith, Mrs Euphemia, outspoken, unconventional woman whose shipboard romance with John Caldigate leads to their living together in Australia. Known at times as Mlle Cettini, a singer and dancer, she also makes money in various gold enterprises. After Caldigate returns to England and marries Hester Bolton, she falsely accuses him of bigamy in order to extort money from him. She is ultimately imprisoned for three years for perjury. *JC*   SRB

Representations of the saintly Mr Harding are few among illustrations. In *The Small House at Allington* Millais has perfectly captured the 'little, withered, shambling man . . . with uncertain, doubtful step' (XVI) watched by Adolphus Crosbie; several critics have commented on the neat juxtaposition between moral touchstone and cynical worldliness in this pairing.

Smith, George (1824–1901). Smith's Scots-born father established a partnership with Alexander Elder to found the house of Smith, Elder & Co. (1816–1917). Smith, with uncanny flair and sound business sense, attracted major novelists from 1847 after Charlotte Brontë's *Jane Eyre*. He began *Cornhill Magazine* with Thackeray as nominal editor (1859), *Pall Mall Gazette* (1865), and the *Dictionary of National Biography* (1882). His business ventures included banking, shipping, and selling the mineral water Apollinaris. Reaching out to Trollope via Thackeray he secured what he wanted to launch *Cornhill*, 'an English tale, on English life, with a clerical flavour' (*Auto* VIII). He got *Framley Parsonage* and Trollope's writing career took off. Their friendship grew. After the success of *Framley Parsonage* Smith gave Trollope a surprise present of a travel bag which elicited this comment: 'No one is more accessible to a present than I am. I gloat over it like a child, and comfort myself in school hours by thinking how nice it will be to go back to it in play time' (quoted R. C. Terry, *Anthony Trollope* (1977), 45–6). Smith commissioned and gave him his portrait by Samuel *Laurence (1864). He published five Trollope novels, *Framley Parsonage* (1861), *The Struggles of Brown, Jones, and Robinson* (1870), *The Small House at Allington* (1864), *The Last Chronicle of Barset* (1867), *The Claverings* (1867). RCT

Smith, Harold, member of Parliament and part of a fast set led by his wife and Nathaniel Sowerby. A career politician, he is laborious, well informed, and generally honest, but also conceited, long-winded, and pompous. He becomes Minister for the Petty Bag Office in Lord Brock's government for a brief time before its defeat in the House. He becomes a bitter enemy of the journalist Mr Supplehouse. *FP, LCB*   NCS

Smith, Mrs Harold, wife of Harold Smith MP and sister of Nathaniel Sowerby, for whom she tries to arrange marriage with the wealthy Martha Dunstable. Clever, bright, worldly, and disappointed in her husband, the 40-year-old loves her brother more than anyone, eventually arranging for Miss Dunstable to take over his mortgages from the Duke of Omnium. *FP, LCB*   NCS

Smith, Joe, one of three men captured by Myles Ussher's raid on a cabin supposedly used for the illicit distilling of whiskey. Although no poteen is found, he and his companions wind up in Ballinamore jail. *M*   MRS

Smith, Revd Sydney (1771–1845), ordained 1794; canon of St Paul's (1831); prolific writer on social and religious subjects; renowned for his wit. Trollope admired Smith's writings, especially on public schools, American finance, and churches. Smith characterized the public-school regimen as one of 'abuse, neglect, and vice', a description with which Trollope agreed. Trollope also supported Smith's denunciation of American policies regarding interest on debts to foreign investors (*NA* 2, XII). Smith's statement 'that it was impossible to say how much melted butter a gentleman would bear to have poured into his dress-coat pocket' Trollope thoroughly endorsed (*Letters* 2, 997).   RCT

Smith, Sir William (1813–93), lexicographer; editor of the *Quarterly Review* (1867–93); active in the Royal Literary Fund. He and Trollope disagreed about who should chair the Fund's anniversary dinner in February 1879. Trollope offered to resign over the issue (*Letters* 2, 816–17).   RCT

Smith, William Henry (1825–91), head of W. H. Smith's booksellers which spread railway bookstalls throughout Britain. He acquired copyrights to many of Trollope's novels for reissue as cheap 'yellowbacks', so-called for their covers. These began to appear from 1865, under the Chapman & Hall imprint as part of the 'Select Library of Fiction'. Thanks to this move, Trollope's income from writing rose from £5,866 to £6,291 (Super 182). In 1881, when William Smith sold his interest in the series of more than 400 'Select' titles, it included 27 of Trollope's novels and short story collections. Smith had also developed a circulating library, and in 1859 contributed to the opening of the Post Office Library and Literary Association with a donation of 300 volumes (Glendinning 245 n.). But more importantly, he secured enormous profits for his firm by establishing a railway bookstall monopoly. During the fight between Johnny Eames and Adolphus Crosbie in *The Small House at Allington*, Trollope has Eames fall 'into the yellow shilling-novel depot' in the fury of his energy (XXXIV).   RCT

Smithfield, London's historic meat market. Mr Brown wishes to set up a haberdashery business in the area. *SBJR*   HO

smoking. Trollope was a heavy smoker. Cigars became an obsession after his visit to Cuba in 1859. Thereafter he imported them by the thousand from Havana. At Waltham he stored them carefully in specially made cabinets, keeping track of ventilation and moisture, and making sure that cigars were smoked according to age by moving pegs along the cabinets. He kept his friends supplied. To George Eliot in August 1866 he suggested that Lewes might like some of his new batch of 8,000 from Cuba (*Letters* 1, 346–7).

George Smith, head of the Smith, Elder publishing house, portrait by G. F. Watts.
Launching *Cornhill Magazine* in 1860, Smith urged Trollope to contribute 'an English tale,
on English life, with a clerical flavour'. Trollope produced *Framley Parsonage*. Smith also
endeared himself to Trollope by bringing him and Thackeray together at regular Cornhill
dinners.

He smoked about four a day. Smoking was another social activity. 'A man enjoys the tobacco doubly when another is enjoying it with him' ('Palestine'). When Sir Leslie *Ward ('Spy') cartooned him for *Vanity Fair* (April 1873) he put a cigar in his hand. As cigar prices went up, Trollope threatened to take up pipe-smoking. In December 1872 he wrote, 'If I can not smoke a small cigar under eight pence, I will not smoke them at all' (*Letters* 2, 573). To A. Arthur Reade, seeking information for his book *Study and Stimulants* (1883), he wrote in February 1882, 'I have been a smoker nearly all my life. Five years ago I found it certainly was hurting me, causing my hand to shake, and producing somnolence. I gave it up for two years' (*Letters* 2, 946). He was now down to '3 small cigars (very small) and so far as I can tell without ill effect. I am 67' (*Letters* 2, 946). At Waltham House smoking went on in the garden or in an outhouse, perhaps under Rose's mandate. At Montagu Square smoking took place in the library. Clubs offered more freedom for smokers. Trollope's fiction shows a developing taste for cigarette-smoking. In *Phineas Redux* (1874) the indolent Maurice Maule puffs away at his cigarette (XXI). The obnoxious Marquis of Brotherton in *Is He Popenjoy?* (1878) is a smoker, as is Lord Rufford in *Ayala's Angel*, who has given up cigars for two cigarettes a day (XXIII). In *He Knew He Was Right* (1869) the journalist Hugh Stanbury puffs his pipe on a bus as he makes up his mind to pop the question to Nora Rowley (XXXIII). RCT

Smollett, Tobias (1721–71), Scottish novelist, editor of the *Critical Review* (1756–63) and other periodicals, translator of Cervantes's *Don Quixote*, best known for picaresque novels such as *The Adventures of Roderick Random* (1748). Trollope scattered references to his works in letters, but left no commentary on the novels. RCT

Smyth, Eleanor, daughter of Sir Rowland Hill, originator of the penny post, and author of *Rowland Hill: The Story of a Great Reform, Told by his Daughter* (1907). Her account of Trollope, considering his implacable opposition to her father, was charitable: on one visit 'somehow our rooms seemed too small for his large vigorous frame.' He was like 'Dickens's Mr Boythorn, minus the canary, and gave us the impression that the one slightly built chair on which he rashly seated himself during a great part of the interview, must infallibly end in collapse, and sooner rather than later' (*I & R*, 54). RCT

Snape, Thomas, head of the clerks' room at the Internal Navigation Office. 'Poor Mr Snape had selected for his own peculiar walk in life a character for evangelical piety' (II) and is harsh to the clerks below him. In return, the clerks abuse his religious sentiment with all manner of blasphemy. *TC* MT

Snapper, Mr, chaplain to Bishop Proudie of Barchester. Relatively neutral in dealing with the Proudies, he takes over much of the Bishop's correspondence after Mrs Proudie's death. In the continuing battle over Hogglestock parish, Mr Snapper preaches there when Mr Thumble refuses. *LCB* NCS

Snow, Mary, daughter of a dissolute father, and the woman Felix Graham hopes to wed. In an act of 'quixotic chivalry' (XXXIII), Felix wishes to rescue Mary from her poverty and mould her into the perfect wife. He fails, and she marries the druggist Albert Fitzallen. *OF* MT

Snow Hill, street running from Newgate Street to Holborn, main highway to the west. Mr Jones was employed here before rising to window-dresser of the haberdashery store at Bishopsgate Street. *SBJR* HO

Soames, Mr, business manager of Lord Lufton in Barsetshire. Convinced that Revd Josiah Crawley has misappropriated a £20 cheque that he has lost, he institutes charges of theft that become the talk of Silverbridge and disrupt the lives of the Grantlys and the Crawleys. *LCB* NCS

Socani, Mme, opera singer and reputed mistress of Mahomet M. Moss, who earns the enmity of Rachel O'Mahony for spreading rumours implicating her rival in illicit sexual liaisons. *L* MRS

Somers, Mr, busy Irish agent respected for his management of Sir Thomas Fitzgerald's estate, and his work on the famine relief committee. Directly affected by the prospect of Castle Richmond changing hands, and proud and 'true as steel' (XII), he refuses to be obsequious to its new lord, Owen Fitzgerald, though as a practical man in need of income, he makes a friendly if unsuccessful overture. *CR* MRS

Somerset, one of Trollope's best-loved counties. The setting for Ullathorne Court in *Barchester Towers* is based on Montacute House. In *The Belton Estate* 'somewhat off the high road from Minehead to Taunton, and about five miles from the sea' (I) is Belton Castle. Much action in *The Bertrams* and *Miss Mackenzie* revolves around the Paragon in Littlebath, assumed by W. G. and J. T. Gerould in their *A Guide to Trollope* (1948) to be Bath. Super suggests it is a likelier pseudonym for Cheltenham. 'The Lady of Launay' is set in Somerset. At the end of his life Trollope insisted to

E. A. *Freeman that Barsetshire was Somerset.

MRS

Souchey, though loyal servant to the Balatkas, is susceptible to Lotta's charms: her nest-egg and the leftovers she serves him at the Zamenoys. Christian prejudice ultimately brings him into the plot against Nina and her Jewish lover. After witnessing Nina's suicide attempt, he rejects Lotta, despite her cleverness and florins. *NB*

AWJ

South Africa. Trollope's decision to go to South Africa was precipitated by the entry of Sir Theophilus Shepstone into Pretoria, capital of the Transvaal, in April 1877, when, accompanied by 25 mounted policemen, he annexed the Boer province. On 29 June 1877 Trollope embarked for Capetown, having negotiated an agreement with Chapman & Hall to write a travel book for £850 and also to provide fifteen letters to provincial newspapers for £175. He arrived at Capetown on 22 July, having completed *John Caldigate* the previous day. The time was ripe for a visit and evaluation, for Lord Carnarvon's scheme of South African Confederation was being debated in the House of Commons (it became law on 13 August 1877). Trollope was fascinated by the mix of British colonists, Boers and natives, particularly the Zulus and their charismatic chief *Cetywayo, who was not defeated by the British until 1879.

In his introduction to *South Africa* Trollope asserts of the indigenous people that 'Work alone will civilize him' (1, I). His historical summaries cover Dutch and English history (II–III), and he gives a particularly lively, independent, and idiosyncratic account of Capetown. He stayed a fortnight, visiting the libraries, the botanical gardens, and of course the Post Office, where he noted with amusement that any professional advice he gave was, as ever, ignored (V). His insights into the government of the Cape Colony are probing and forceful, and there is a superb cameo of a Cape politician, Saul Solomon, who 'has never been in the government and rarely in opposition' (VI), but who commands the respect of all, a diminutive man of the utmost integrity. His exploration of the western province includes a brief appraisal of ostrich-farming, mainly in the Karoo, and then he visits Oudtshoorn 'chiefly to see the Kango Caves' (VII), where he is fascinated by the 'wonderful forms and vagaries of the stalactites'. Various incidents are vividly described: a brief encounter with two klipspringers (IX), a wonderfully relaxed moment watching children playing kiss-in-the-ring in a little park

in Port Elizabeth (X), after which he returns sadly to his club.

Moments of poignancy and humour irradiate the narrative. It takes eleven hours to get to Grahamstown by Cobb's omnibus. He inspects another ostrich farm, delighting in breeding and sale statistics, and, travelling on 'a hired Cape cart', attends a conference of Kafir chiefs, one Siwani telling him that it would be best if the British all went away (XI). He journeys to East London by railway, visits Kafir schools, and pronounces on the refusal of white labourers to work on an equal footing with Kafirs (XII). His visit to Natal is prefaced by a history of the province, including the sufferings of the Dutch and the mark made on contemporary history by the Zulu leader *Langalibalele. He is entertained by Bishop Colenso, to whose controversial views about the literal truth of the Bible he was sympathetic. In Durban he stays at that colonial institution the club (XV), then takes a Cobb's coach to Pieter Maritzburg, enjoying the comedy when a fellow passenger insists on bringing a 45-pound fish on board, and rather admiring the man's pertinacity. Chapter XVII deals with the history of the Zulus in Natal, notes the predominance of natives in Pieter Maritzburg ('I liked the Zulu of the Natal capital very thoroughly'), and leads naturally into the history of Langalibalele (XVIII), who refused to attend when summoned to the British presence, stripping the messenger of his jazy or greatcoat, and as a result was imprisoned on Robben Island.

Part 2 opens with the visit to the Transvaal, now a British colony. Trollope travels 30 miles (50 km) a day on horseback, visits the homes of Dutch Boers, who often lived in poor conditions in houses with earthen floors, before reaching Pretoria. Trollope presents a sketch of Transvaal history in 2, II, including a summary of ex-President Burgers's troubles with the indigenous population as well as the British, and exacerbated by lack of funds. *Shepstone's 'high-handed' deed is fully examined, Burgers even confiding to Trollope that this 'wrong' action might benefit Dutch, British, and natives alike, and Trollope comes down on Shepstone's side (III). Pretoria he finds 'picturesque and promising' (IV), and while there he rides out to see the 'Zoutpan' or saltpan, and sleeps in the veld. The impact of the discovery of gold and the need for a railway are discussed in chapter V, and he notes that the Transvaal is the 'corn chamber' of the colony. From Pretoria he visits the diamond mines (VI) by cart, is moved by the suffering of the horses (on one day they travel 50 miles (80 km)), and gives a brief account of the development of the diamond industry in Griqualand

West (VII), expanded in 'The Story of the Diamond Fields' (VIII). He next goes to Barkly, another important diamond centre, and then Kimberley (IX). Graphic descriptions of frenzied greed are complemented by statements of Trollopian creed—'Who can doubt but that work is the great civilizer of the world?' and, almost immediately afterwards, the assertion that the work ethic in Kimberley has been instrumental in the civilizing of the natives, though he does acknowledge the 'stain' attached to diamonds. An account of the Orange Free State includes the defeat of the Basutos and their appeal to the British. Later, touring the state, he records whites and natives, employers and employed, working side by side. He praises the courtesy of the local Boers and finds the capital, Bloemfontein, 'more English than Dutch' (XI), a 'pleasant little town', recommended for those with chest troubles (XII). Next he encounters the Bechuanas and gives a vivid sketch of their chief Sapena, 'dressed like a European' (XIII). Much space in chapter XIV is given to Kreli and his Kafirs, with an emphasis on polygamous practices, customs, and laws (XIV) and following this the cannibalism of the Basutos (XV). The conclusion is noteworthy for the independence of its assertion that the Dutch Boer is a gentleman and for Trollope's disarming admission that he has written the book in a hurry. His overall view is predictable and somewhat shallow: though he asserts that 'South Africa is a black country and not a white one' (XVII), he maintains that 'the coloured man has been benefitted by our coming'. The chapter on 'Zululand' (XI) was inserted in the abridged (fourth) edition of 1879, at the time of the Zulu War, and its explanation of events underlines Trollope's pro-Zulu stance and his criticism of Sir Bartle *Frere, Governor of the Cape and High Commissioner of South African Affairs. Frere asserted that Zulu promises had not been kept and that savagery under Cetywayo had worsened. Trollope takes issue with this and points out that no missionaries, for instance, have been killed; although we, the British, claim that we want no more expansion, annexation still continues; he deplores Frere's ultimatum which ordered, among other things, the disbandment of the Zulu army. British forces had entered Zululand on 11 January 1879, to Trollope's disgust: Natal, he believes, is not seriously at risk because of the Zulus, but he fears that Zululand will 'be overrun by hostile Britons'. *South Africa* reflects Trollope's wide tolerance, his capacity to combine formal evaluations (and subjective ones) with delightfully anecdotal narrative. He is rarely dogmatic; his views form, develop, and change as he probes and investigates, and his comments are spiced

with humour, a certain delight in controversy, a zest for exploration before he is too old. His stamina, on horseback or by cart, by coach or rail or sea, is prodigious. The quest for experience is undiminished. He records the grace of the Zulus, the lure of diamonds and gold, the decimating effects of the tsetse fly on the Limpopo river, racial characteristics, British acquisitiveness, statistics. The whole narrative is warm with immediacy, from the minutest detail to the spatial overview. *South Africa* was written 23 July 1877–2 January 1878 and published in two volumes in February 1878, with three editions in that year and a fourth abridged edition in 1879. The manuscript is at the Huntington Library, San Marino, California. Reviews in England were generally favourable, like those in *The Times* and the *Saturday Review*. The fifteen letters (see above) were published in the *Cape Times*: their tone and inaccuracies provoked much criticism in South Africa and in part mirrored reception of the book there. See also 'LETTERS FROM SOUTH AFRICA'. GRH

Trollope, Anthony, *South Africa*, ed. J. H. Davidson (1973). A reprint of the 1878 edition. Introduction, notes, appendixes.

South America. Trollope visited South America during his postal tour of the Caribbean in 1858–9. Almost all areas of South America had broken free from European colonial control during and after the Napoleonic Wars (mainly 1810–25) except for the small British, Dutch, and French colonies in the Guianas. Trollope was impressed by Demerara (British Guiana) because the planters had maintained sugar production by importing 'coolie' labour from Asia, but he was scathing about the republic of New Granada (now Colombia) which he considered unprogressive. Only the Isthmus of Panama, belonging to New Granada, interested him, because of canal potential. LK

Sowerby, Nathaniel, Whig MP for West Barsetshire for 25 years under the patronage of the Duke of Omnium. A poor man, his great estate of Chaldicotes heavily mortgaged, the unprincipled Sowerby spends money on elections and gambling, surviving by borrowing from friends. Bald, 50, clever, and pleasant, he eventually turns Lord Lufton and Mark Robarts against him, loses his lands to Martha Dunstable and his seat to Lord Dumbello, though he does suffer some pangs of conscience over the Robarts affair. *FP, LCB* NCS

Spalding, Caroline, elder daughter of a Boston lawyer and niece of Sir Jonas Spalding. Despite her reservations about the damage an American wife might cause to an English lord and against the wishes of Wallachia Petrie, she accepts the proposal of Charles Glascock. She is Nora Rowley's friend and has no jealousy of the woman to whom her husband first proposed marriage. *HKWR*   RC

Spalding, Jonas, uncle of Caroline and Olivia Spalding and American ambassador to Italy who hails from Nubbly Creek, Illinois. He is given to sententious sermonizing on the virtues of American democracy and the vices of the English aristocracy—at the same time that he strives 'to be as English as possible' (XLVI). *HKWR*   RC

Spalding, Olivia (Livy), younger daughter of a Boston lawyer and niece of the American ambassador in Florence, Sir Jonas Spalding. She and her sister are from Providence, Rhode Island. *HKWR*   RC

Spanish Town, town in Jamaica, home of Sarah Jack, and where the House of Assembly meets, but dull, 'a city of the very dead'. 'Jack' *TAC1*   GRH

Sparkes, Mrs Conway, fashionable poet invited as part of a large gathering at Matching. Mrs Sparkes, a 'very clever . . . [though] not perhaps very good-natured' woman (XXIII), uses her wit to persecute the foolish Duchess of St Bungay, much to the discomfort of Lady Glencora. *CYFH*   JMR

spas or watering places such as the eponymous Spa in Belgium and Ems, Marienbad, Hamburg, and Baden in Germany were fashionable resorts where society recovered from the season by drinking and bathing in natural mineral waters. The gaming tables were an attraction for the faster set and Lady Glencora Palliser annoys her husband in *Can You Forgive Her?* by succumbing to the urge to gamble at Baden (LXVIII). Trollope liked visiting the German spas as well as the quieter French ones like Aix-les-Bains in the French Alps. Among English spa towns Cheltenham, popular among genteel widows and retirees, probably features as Littlebath in *The Bertrams* and *Miss Mackenzie*.   CK
  Sproule, Anna, *The Social Calendar* (1978).

Spectator. This weekly journal of news, politics, literature, and science was begun in 1828 by Robert Stephen Rintoul, who had been printer and editor of the *Dundee Advertiser* from 1811 to 1825 before coming to London in 1826. Published on Saturday and selling for one shilling, the *Spectator*'s early numbers contained 24 pages, mainly a mixture of politics, literature, and science. Rintoul attempted to promote social and civil reforms regardless of party. He maintained that his readers liked to listen to all sides of a controversy,

provided the argument was presented in an evenhanded way. Rintoul remained proprietor, with editorial assistance from Thornton Hunt, until his death in 1858.
  Richard Holt *Hutton, editor and theologian, in partnership with Meredith *Townsend, journalist, took over the journal. They expanded it to 32 pages, the last six being advertisements, and put far more emphasis on literature, including strongly opinionated reviews and early recognition of such writers as Samuel Butler, R. L. Stevenson, George Moore, and Thomas Hardy. Contributors included Thomas Carlyle, Leigh Hunt, Thomas Hughes, Edmund Gosse, Julian Hawthorne, George Saintsbury, John Morley, and Margaret Oliphant.
  J. St Loe Strachey began reviewing for the *Spectator* in 1885, then became editor and proprietor in 1895. Under his direction, the journal doubled in circulation and prospered.
  The *Spectator* reviewed most of Trollope's works, generally positively, the reviews frequently being written by R. H. Hutton who respected Trollope's talents. When Trollope published *Nina Balatka* anonymously, an unsigned review, probably by R. H. Hutton, noted a phrase frequently used by Trollope, 'made his way', and thus identified him as the author. Of the *Tales of All Countries*, the journal claimed they approached Pickwick itself in their comic scenes. A review of *The American Senator* said the Senator was the best part of the book and regretted he was not more prominent. In *The Macdermots of Ballycloran*, a reviewer noted Trollope's greatest skill as the creation of natural characters, human in their vices. Assessing *The Warden* Trollope's keen observation of public affairs and great cleverness was admired, but the reviewer wondered if he had drawn any conclusions about the matters he was writing about. *The Prime Minister* prompted the question of whether Trollope's powers had declined. The article upset Trollope, especially since he thought it had been written by Hutton, whom he had always liked. (In fact it had not.) The *Spectator* considered *The West Indies and the Spanish Main* an official report disguised as a novel. *The Small House at Allington* won great praise for Trollope's ability to understand humanity. Alongside it, *Phineas Finn*, though not one of Trollope's lesser works, did not measure up. When Trollope announced that *The Last Chronicle of Barset* was the end of the series, the reviewer said this news was depressing, as if he would never get to see a good friend again. The verdict on *The Duke's Children* was that although it was probably not Trollope at his best, it was thoroughly readable. The review of *Australia and New Zealand* showed insight when

it suggested that Trollope conveyed a sense of boredom and weariness: he had commented in a letter at that time that eighteen months was too long to be away from home.

The *Spectator* did not like *The Way We Live Now*, in which Trollope had made the same mistake he had made in *The Struggles of Brown, Jones, and Robinson*, which it had called a disagreeable novel. In both he had immersed his characters in a sordid atmosphere without relief or pleasantness. It complained that even the subordinate comic characters were disagreeable.

Of *Saint Pauls'* first number, Hutton wrote a long, non-committal review saying that it was a readable magazine with nothing to offend, but that it was tame, with little vivacity, in fact colourless. Hutton, who knew Trollope so well, was able to discern that Trollope had written the article 'On Sovereignty' and said that in picking his writers, he had trusted too much to men who had made their reputations already, but who had lost their zeal.

In reviewing *Cousin Henry*, Julian Hawthorne, son of Nathaniel Hawthorne, praised Trollope's episodes and sentences, saying they moved without a hitch or creak, so the reader never had to read a paragraph twice, but was never sorry to have read it once.

The Duke's Children found favour: no other novelist had such a comprehension of British aristocracy, and it praised his creation of the American Isabel Boncassen, saying even Americans would have no criticism of her.

In its review of *An Autobiography*, the *Spectator's* final judgement of Trollope was as a man of genius, energy, and ability.   JWM

Spenser, Edmund (?1552–99), Elizabethan poet whose *The Faerie Queene* (1589, 1596) Trollope read aloud to his family November–December 1876. The poem figures in Lizzie Eustace's unfulfilled reading plans (*ED* XXII). His often-used tag 'Love shall be lord of all' (*SBJR* XVI; *OF* XXV; *C* XLVIII) was originally from Spenser's 'Colin Clout's Come Home Again', although another source for the line, equally familiar, would have been Scott's *The Lay of the Last Minstrel* (1805) (VI. xi).   RCT

Sperl's dancing saloon, 'Great institution at Vienna'. Although it is open on Sundays and stays open late, there is nothing to offend. 'Schmidt' *LS*   RCT

Spicer, Mr, a Percycross mustard-maker who controls the votes of his employees. He suggests to Sir Thomas Underwood that once in Parliament he should concern himself with government mustard contracts. *RH*   ALS

Spinney Lane, down-at-heel east London residence of Mrs Mary Swan, Matthew Mollet's legitimate wife. *CR*   MRS

Spiveycomb, Mr, paper-maker who supports the Conservatives at Percycross largely because contracts are put his way by Trigger, the local party agent. *RH*   ALS

Spondi, Signorina Camilla, mistress of dissolute Earl Lovel to whom he tried to leave his fortune, claiming that he had married her in Italy prior to marrying Countess Lovel. *LA*   RCT

Spooner, Miss, spinster neighbour of the Underwoods at Popham Villa, Fulham. Clarissa Underwood maintains that she 'lives upon her grievances' (LVII). *RH*   ALS

Spooner, Mrs, somewhat vulgar wife of Thomas Platter Spooner. An attentive wife but even more attentive hunter, Mrs Spooner bullies her husband, but her matronly warmth takes some of the sting from her otherwise dictatorial manner. *DC*   JMR

Spooner, Ned, much cleverer cousin and companion of Thomas Spooner, who manages most of the Spoon Hall business while his cousin hunts. Penniless himself, Ned sometimes suffers from his wealthy cousin's temper, especially during Thomas Spooner's unsuccessful courtship of Adelaide Palliser. *PR*   JMR

Spooner, Thomas Platter, avid hunter with the Brake hounds. Thomas Spooner is of an old family, has good property, and once stood as High Sheriff for his county. He endures a brief but hopeless passion for Adelaide Palliser, determining to remain a bachelor when she pointedly refuses him. In his later years he is somewhat cowed by a domineering wife. *PR, DC*   JMR

'Spotted Dog, The', first serialized in *Saint Pauls*, March–April 1870 (reprinted in *ET*). The editor receives a request for literary employment from Julius Mackenzie, whose postal address is the public house the Spotted Dog, in east London. It emerges that Mackenzie is a scholar of good breeding. He has ruined himself by marrying a woman beneath him, who has taken to drink. The sympathetic editor finds Mackenzie work indexing a work on Greek metrics. But, after a drunken orgy, Mrs Mackenzie burns the manuscript. Her husband cuts his throat. His body is laid out at the Spotted Dog.   JS

Sprout, Mr, Silverbridge cobbler with political interests. A Conservative, Mr Sprout is one of a small delegation which assists Lord Silverbridge's candidacy at the start of his parliamentary career. Sprout's 'cork soles' are recommended to the

Duke of Omnium by Lady Rosina De Courcy. *PR, DC*   JMR

Spruce, Sally. Maiden cousin of Mrs Roper, she has lodged in Burton Crescent for twelve years. She repeatedly comments, 'I'm only an old woman', after witnessing disreputable actions of other lodgers, but finally despairs at the lack of respectability and threatens to move. *SHA*
                                                      NCS

Sprugeon, Mr, ironmonger at Silverbridge to whom the Duchess of Omnium makes it known that Ferdinand Lopez has the 'interest' of Gatherum Castle in an upcoming contest for the borough. *PM*   JMR

Squercum, Mr, provoking, unconventional lawyer employed by Dolly Longestaffe to ferret out Augustus Melmotte's illegal negotiations in the sale of Longestaffe property. Squercum is motivated by 'pure ambition' to expose and destroy the grand swindler Melmotte. He succeeds. *WWLN*   SRB

Stackpoole, Mr, acquaintance of Sir Harry Hotspur and George Hotspur who unintentionally exposes to Emily Hotspur George's lie about not attending the meet at Goodwood. *SHH*
                                                      MG

Staines, electoral district for which Samuel Cohenlupe is member of Parliament. *WWLN*
                                                      SRB

Stalham, Sir Harry Albury's luxurious country house in the county of Rufford. *AA*   WK

Stanbury, Dorothy, pliant and good-natured younger daughter of Revd and Mrs Stanbury. She agrees to live with and becomes a favourite of her quarrelsome aunt Miss Stanbury. Rejecting the offer of a husband (Mr Gibson) and an income (£2,000), she withstands her aunt's displeasure and finally wins approval of her engagement to Brooke Burgess. In the process, she is transformed from a timid and quiet to an independent and witty woman. *HKWR*   RC

Stanbury, Hugh, poor son of a clergyman sent to Oxford by his aunt. This 'briefless barrister' (IV) gives up an unsuccessful legal career in order to work for a penny newspaper, the *Daily Record*, a career change that, combined with his mild bohemianism and iconoclastic thinking, leads Miss Stanbury to disinherit him. He becomes engaged to Nora Rowley over the objections of her parents. He brings the Trevelyans back from Casalunga to England. *HKWR*   RC

Stanbury, Jemima, unmarried sister of the vicar of Nuncombe Putney. 'The Juno of the Close' (XLVII) is an imperious woman with

fiercely held conservative sentiments. 'All change was to her hateful and unnecessary' (VII). Having inherited considerable wealth from the elder Brooke Burgess, she is alienated from both the Burgess and Stanbury families. Dorothy Stanbury, however, provides love and companionship for the first time in her aunt's life. She settles down with Dorothy and her husband (the younger Brooke Burgess), having secured their financial future. Her character is drawn from memories of Trollope's cousin Fanny *Bent. *HKWR*   RC

Stanbury, Mrs, widow of the vicar of Nuncombe Putney and Miss Stanbury's sister-in-law. She lives in poverty with her two daughters, generally submitting to the authority of the elder, Priscilla. After the younger's (Dorothy's) marriage, she lives in Laburnum Cottage, which has been much improved thanks to her son Hugh's increasing income. *HKWR*   RC

Stanbury, Priscilla, elder daughter of Revd and Mrs Stanbury. Stoic by nature, she is a confirmed and mildly misanthropic spinster, who lives with and generally rules over her mother and younger sister. Both loving and strong-willed, she staunchly supports her siblings' efforts at independence from their domineering aunt. *HKWR*   RC

Standish, Lady Laura. See KENNEDY, LADY LAURA.

Standish, Oswald (Lord Chiltern). A red-haired, red-faced man with a violent temper, Chiltern appears to be one of Trollope's familiar Byronic figures. A man may, however, not be as bad as his reputation paints him. He has been sent down from Oxford, he has lost a fortune on horses, he has quarrelled seriously with his father Lord Brentford, but many of the stories circulated about him are apocryphal. Often referred to as 'savage', he is aptly compared by Violet Effingham to a griffin or a lion. His family would forgive all if Violet would marry him, and he loves her desperately, but she refuses him over and over. He rides a wild horse called Bonebreaker that no one else can control and he fights a duel with his friend Phineas Finn over Violet. Incapable of holding a grudge, he reconciles with Phineas. Violet eventually admits she loves him and they marry. In *Phineas Redux* Chiltern has become the master of the hounds for the Brake Hunt. Although happily domesticated, he retains his griffin, or lion, nature. Perhaps based on Lord Hartington, he also appears briefly in *The Eustace Diamonds*, *The Prime Minister*, and *The Duke's Children*. *PF*   MG

Stanhope, Charlotte, eldest daughter of Dr Vesey Stanhope. A fine young woman about 35, she has taken over the domestic arrangements of her unstable family. She befriends Eleanor Bold in hopes of marrying her to her impecunious brother Bertie. *BT*   NCS

Stanhope, Ethelbert (Bertie), impoverished, handsome, unprincipled, but engaging artist son of Dr Vesey Stanhope. Educated at Eton, Cambridge, and Leipsic (Leipzig), Bertie attempts law, painting, Catholicism, Judaism, and sculpture. At his sister's instigation but without much enthusiasm he pursues the widow Eleanor Bold to improve his fortune, accepting his rejection philosophically. His caricatures of Barchester personages suggest his satiric capabilities. *BT*
                                                        NCS

Stanhope, Madeline. See NERONI, SIGNORA MADELINE.

Stanhope, Mrs, handsome 55-year-old wife of Dr Vesey Stanhope, prebendary of Barchester. Her only purpose in life is to dress exceedingly well, and she thereby keeps herself aloof from the tribulations of the rest of her family. *BT*   NCS

Stanhope, Philip Henry, Earl (1805–75), 5th Earl (1855); pioneered building of London's National Portrait Gallery; elected Conservative MP (1830); President of the Royal Literary Fund (1863–75). He introduced Trollope into social and literary circles and became his friend. Trollope's friendships among the aristocracy are well described in *An Autobiography*, the intimacy coming first from the higher rank, and 'if the intimacy be ever fixed, then that rank should be held of no account' (XIV). That principle served him well. Stanhope helped elect Trollope to the Athenaeum Club (1864). As President of the Literary Fund, Stanhope at the 1867 annual dinner commended Trollope's fiction. He presented Trollope to the Prince of Wales at a levee in March 1868, public recognition Trollope highly prized.   RCT

Stanhope, Dr Vesey, minister of three Barsetshire parishes, Crabtree Canonicorum, Stogpingum, and Eiderdown, who resides in Italy. The good-looking, sixtyish gentleman enjoys food and wine, collects butterflies, and rants about his children's bills. Called home by Bishop Proudie, he brings his feckless family who upset Barchester's staid traditions. He is reported to have died of apoplexy at his Lake Como villa (*DT*) after having fled creditors in England (*FP*). *BT, W*
                                                        NCS

Stanley, Arthur Penrhyn (1815–81), canon of Canterbury (1851); Dean of Westminster from 1864; liberal Anglican theologian dedicated to ecumenical reform and free enquiry into Bible studies; fellow member of the Athenaeum Club and colleague on the Royal Literary Fund Committee which Trollope joined in 1864. Stanley presided at the Fund's anniversary dinner in May 1878.   RCT

Stanley, Henrietta Maria (Lady Stanley of Alderley) (1807–95), wife of Lord Stanley, Baron of Alderley; promoter of women's education; society hostess who rendered useful service to the Whig Party. Trollope was her guest at least six times.   RCT

Stanley of Alderley, Edward John, Baron (1802–69), Postmaster General (1860–6). When Trollope was elected to the Cosmopolitan Club in 1861, he came into the presence of notable Liberal politicians such as Stanley, who 'used to whisper the secrets of Parliament with free tongues' (*Auto* IX). As Postmaster General, Stanley was generally supportive of Trollope in his opposition to Rowland *Hill, as in his maintaining of the committee inquiring into complaints over pay and working conditions despite Hill's call for its suspension. When Trollope published his lecture 'The Civil Service as a Profession' (1861), he circumvented complaint from Hill by showing Stanley the article in proof. When Hill demanded his dismissal, Trollope smugly commented that Stanley had only laughed: 'I knew myself to be too good to be treated in that fashion' (*Auto* VIII). Trollope's application for seven months' leave (1861) to visit America, opposed by Hill, was granted by Stanley, another victory Trollope recalled happily (*Auto* IX). When Stanley rebuked him for his conduct in a pay dispute (1864), the dressing down came more from John *Tilley, Permanent Secretary, than from Stanley (R. H. Super, *Trollope in the Post Office* (1981), 66).   RCT

Stantiloup, Juliana, mother of a former pupil in Bowick School, whose disagreement over billing practices escalates into a bitter feud with Dr Wortle. Her malicious gossip and false rumours concerning the Peacockes very nearly lead to the closing of the school. *DWS*   RC

Staple, Tom, Oxford don recruited for the Grantly cause in the move to have Mr Harding made dean of the cathedral. *BT*   RCT

Stapledean, Marquis of, gloomy patron of the living at Hurst Staple who perversely stipulates that Arthur Wilkinson turn over the majority of his clerical income to his mother, then harshly berates her for insisting on her right to dominate the living. *B*   MRS

Startup Farm, large farm near Salisbury where George Brattle lives. His wife refuses to take in his fallen sister Carry here. *VB*   SRB

Staubach, Charlotte, an Anabaptist who believes that women's susceptibility to worldly pleasure must be 'crushed' by self-denial. Loving the orphaned niece whom she has tended since early childhood, she feels Linda needs the guidance of a middle-aged husband. Facing rebellion, she battles to redeem that 'castaway' with tearful prayer and admonition, convinced that faith can move mountains. Thus her relentless virtue crushes the soul she loves. *LT*   AWJ

Staveley, Augustus, son of Judge Staveley and friend of Felix Graham, 'who had nearly succeeded in getting the Newdigate, and was now a member of the Middle Temple' (XVIII). But he is a young man for whom life has been too easy. *OF*   MT

Staveley, Lady Isabella, wife of Judge Staveley of Noningsby. 'Lady Staveley was a good, motherly, warm-hearted woman, who thought a great deal about her flowers and fruit' but 'she thought most of all of her husband' (XIX). *OF*   MT

Staveley, Judge, respected judge who lives at Noningsby, near Alston. Judge Staveley 'was one of the best men in the world, revered on the bench, and loved by all men' (XVIII). Judge Staveley is a moderate man who advises young Felix not to be hasty in judging others. Unlike the other judge, Baron Maltby, Staveley accepts that legal reform may be necessary. *OF*   MT

Staveley, Madeline, daughter of Judge and Lady Isabella Staveley. The narrator informs us that Madeline is to be 'the most interesting personage in this story' (XIX). A young woman of 19, Madeline is an imperfect but expressive beauty who 'smiled with her whole face' (XIX). She is courted by Perry Orme but eventually marries idealistic Felix Graham. *OF*   MT

Steele, Anna Caroline (née **Wood**) (d. 1914), daughter of Trollope's friends Sir John Page Wood and Emma Wood; minor author, noted for *Gardenhurst* (1867). For ten years thereafter she and Trollope kept up a regular correspondence, mildly flirtatious and genuinely affectionate, covering politics, literature, and hunting. After his loss in the Beverley elections, his first news was that he was once again riding, the Beverley experience itself 'water off a duck's back' (*Letters* 1, 454). Three months later, Trollope invited her: 'I'll mount you, & take you out, and find you in everything except whip & spurs,—including sherry, sandwiches, & small talk' (*Letters* 1, 463).

In May 1870, the subject was fallen women, among 'the most terrible sufferers of this age' who often came to their misery 'almost without fault at all' (*Letters* 1, 522). Trollope also encouraged Mrs Steele's literary efforts.   RCT

Stein, Annot. Daughter of Michael the blacksmith, she accepts Chapeau's attentions, and, despite opposition, wins her father's consent (she has money of her own) and goes to Paris after the war where her husband becomes a barber. *LV*   GRH

Stein, Michael. Taciturn blacksmith of Échanbroignes who intends to keep his two sons Jean and Peter out of the Vendean conflict. His attempts to break his daughter's relationship with Chapeau are equally unsuccessful. *LV*   GRH

Steinmarc, Peter. Self-satisfied and acquisitive, he cannot imagine the depth of Linda's horror when he seeks to be her husband. Driven to possess the red house and outmatch his disreputable young cousin, his vindictive pride speaks louder than Linda's stubborn rejection or frantic threat to make life miserable after their wedding. *LT*   AWJ

Stemm, Joseph, Sir Thomas Underwood's clerk at his chambers at Southampton Buildings. 'Hardly more than five feet high, and . . . a wizened dry old man, with a very old yellow wig. He delighted in scolding all the world, and his special delight was in scolding his master' (X). *RH*   ALS

Stephen, Sir James Fitzjames (1829–94), renowned judge; prolific commentator on criminal law and law of evidence; prominent among those writing for the *Pall Mall Gazette*. In March 1865, Stephen wrote two letters to the *Pall Mall*, one signed 'Homo Sum', which took issue with Trollope for coming down against parsons hunting, and the other, signed 'Thalestris', supporting Trollope's opinion in favour of women hunting (*Letters* 1, 296 n.). Trollope insisted on his inclusion on the Copyright Commission for his legal expertise (*Letters* 2, 722).   RCT

Stephen, Sir Leslie (1832–1904), prolific essayist on philosophy, religion, and literature; later editor of *Dictionary of National Biography*; married to Harriet ('Minnie') Thackeray, who died in 1875; then to Julia Duckworth; their children were Virginia (Woolf) and Vanessa (Bell). Editor of *Cornhill* (1871–82), Stephen contributed to *Saint Pauls* 'About Rowing' (December 1867), 'Alpine Climbing' (January 1868), and 'Anonymous Journalism' (May 1868). As widower of Thackeray's elder daughter he agreed that Trollope should write the 'English Men of Letters' volume on his late father-in-law. RCT

Sterling, Captain Edward (1773–1847), assistant editor of *The Times* (1815–40), byline 'Vetus', then 'Magus', noted for his aggressive style. Sterling coined the term 'thunderer' for the paper. Memories of the forceful journalism developed by *The Times* and of Sterling's contribution influenced Trollope's portrayal of press men, at their worst in Quintus Slide in the Phineas novels and *The Prime Minister*. In *John Sterling*, *Carlyle claimed that Edward Sterling, 'more than any other man or circumstance, *was* the *Times* Newspaper, and thundered through it to the shaking of the spheres' (R. C. Terry, *Anthony Trollope* (1977), 217, 279; *Brewer's Dictionary of Phrase and Fable* (1959), 1101). RCT

Stevenage, Duchess of, leader of London society, and sister of Lord Alfred Grendall who has been financially rescued by Augustus Melmotte. Her attendance at Mme Melmotte's grand ball in Grosvenor Square sets the precedent for Melmotte's social acceptance. *WWLN* SRB

Stevenson, R. L. (1850–94), Scots novelist, poet, essayist, and travel writer, best known for *Treasure Island* (1883) and *The Strange Case of Dr Jekyll and Mr Hyde* (1886). One of the few younger novelists who appreciated Trollope, Stevenson wrote to his parents in 1877, 'Do you know who is my favourite author just now? How are the mighty fallen! Anthony Trollope. I batten on him; he is so nearly wearying you, and yet he never does.' Trollope 'might have written a fine book; he has preferred to write many readable ones' (quoted Super 377). RCT

Stickatit, George, successful junior partner in the legal firm Dry & Stickatit, named executor along with George Bertram of the senior Mr Bertram's estate. *B* MRS

Stiggs, Mrs, decent, hard-working landlady of Trotter's Buildings who shelters Carry Brattle at Frank Fenwick's expense while he tries to reconcile her father to her and while she awaits her brother Sam's trial for murder *VB* SRB

Stistick, Mr, MP for Peterloo who dines at Lord and Lady Harcourt's Eaton Square home, where he pontificates endlessly about parliamentary blue books and other statistical matters. *B* MRS

Stistick, Mrs, guest at Lord and Lady Harcourt's Eaton Square home. Having respectably raised seven children, she has sunk into a tranquil state whereby conversation and other acts of effort are no longer welcome. 'To sit easily on a sofa and listen to the buzz of voices' (XXXIII)

encapsulates the limits of her social activity. *B* MRS

Stobe, Herr. He dislikes Valcarm, his co-worker at Sach breweries, so accepts Steinmarc's bribes to watch that ne'er-do-well's activities. Thus the news gets out about Valcarm's romantic leap across the river to the red house. *LT* AWJ

Stobel, Carl, diamond-cutter engaged to Marie Weber, Lotta Schmidt's friend. They marry a week before Lotta. 'Schmidt' *LS* GRH

Stofflet, Jean Nicolas (based on historical figure), one of the Vendean leaders in the early part of the campaign, killed at Angers. *LV* GRH

Stogpingum, Barsetshire parish of the absentee Dr Vesey Stanhope, joined with the parish of Eiderdown to form Stoke Pinquium. *BT, W* NCS

Stokes, Mr. When the old-fashioned family solicitor is informed of the proposed enquiry into the legitimacy of Lord Popenjoy by Lord George Germain and the Dean of Brotherton, he points out that he represents the Marquis of Brotherton. He provides a sharp contrast to the Dean's more modern lawyer, Mr Battle. *IHP* MG

Stone, Marcus (1840–1921), historical and genre painter; Associate of the Royal Academy (1877); illustrator of Dickens's *Our Mutual Friend* (1865) and Trollope's *He Knew He Was Right*. Stone's illustrations for Trollope were, in detail and intensity, second only to Millais's (N. John Hall, *Trollope and his Illustrators* (1980), 124). He received £500 for the pictures accompanying each weekly number. In *Boz Club Papers* (1906) Stone recalled difficulty getting started from only two numbers: 'I found two young ladies whom I had to draw, two of the principal characters in the book, of whose appearance there was not the least description. I applied to Anthony Trollope and said, "Is Julia dark and Clara fair? How am I to distinguish one from the other?", and he replied, "I do not know; do what you like." ' Stone concluded that Trollope's characters, unlike Dickens's, 'were in no way alive to [him]' (*I & R* 125). RCT

Stowe, Harriet Beecher (1811–96), American writer, honoured by Queen Victoria in 1853. Although admired by society, her achievement was disputed by several writers, including Trollope, who found her novels 'falsely sensational and therefore abominable' (*Letters* 2, 596). After the success of *Uncle Tom's Cabin* (1852) Beecher Stowe, like Trollope, was published in the *Cornhill Magazine* (Super 112). In 1862, George Smith advised Trollope to change the title of a yet-unwritten work, 'The Two Pearls of Allington', because Beecher Stowe's novel *The Pearl of Orr's Island* was currently being serialized in England. Trollope reluctantly agreed, and the work appeared as *The Small House at Allington*. When in 1869 Beecher Stowe published 'The True Story of Lady Byron's Life' in September issues of *Atlantic Monthly* and *Macmillan's*, an account which accused Byron of incest with his half-sister Augusta, Trollope wrote to Alfred *Austin, 'no more outrageous piece of calumny,—in the real sense of the word, was ever published; or as, I think, with lower motives' (*Letters* 1, 482). RCT

Stowte, Caroline and **Sophie,** proud daughters of Lord Trowbridge who patronize the local folk and consider the vicar something of an infidel. *IMP* RCT

Strahan, Alexander (1833–1918), Scots businessman; publisher of *Good Words, Argosy, Contemporary Review,* and Trollope's *Lotta Schmidt and Other Stories, He Knew He Was Right, An Editor's Tales,* and part-issue and first illustrated edition of *Ralph the Heir* (*Letters* 1, 178 n.). In May 1870, he acquired *Saint Pauls* magazine, then in financial straits: under his direction it survived another four years until March 1874 (*Letters* 1, 495 n.). RCT

Strathbogy, Scottish borough which Alaric Tudor hopes to represent as MP. Strathbogy is located on the estate of Lord Gaberlunzie, Undy Scott's father. Undy suggests that the seat can be Alaric's if he is willing to help Undy financially. *TC* MT

Stratton, a cheap and cheerful country town, some twenty miles (32 km) from Clavering, home of Mr Burton of Burton & Beilby. *C* PJT

street musicians, especially Italian barrel organists and itinerant German brass bands, were a ubiquitous and controversial feature of Victorian cities. Many intellectuals, including Trollope, Dickens, and Tennyson, decried them as a maddening addition to the cacophony of urban life and sought legislation to control them. Trollope's outburst over the din of a German band playing outside Garlant's Hotel, Suffolk Street, on 3 November 1882 is thought to have contributed to his collapse that day with a stroke. CK

Sponza, Lucio, *Italian Immigrants in Nineteenth Century Britain: Realities and Images* (1988).

Stringer, Daniel, cousin of the landlord of the Dragon of Wantly in Barchester and clerk in the bar. A shabby, disreputable man with a red nose, he obtained Mr Soames's famous cheque, thought stolen by Revd Josiah Crawley, and gave it to Mrs Arabin for rent. A self-appointed member of the Proudie faction, he escapes to London. *LCB* NCS

Stringer, John, proprietor and former owner of the Dragon of Wantly in Barchester. Suffering from gout and generally forlorn, he disappears shortly after the matter of Revd Josiah Crawley's cheque is cleared up. *LCB* NCS

Struggles of Brown, Jones, and Robinson, The (*see next page*)

Stuart, Jack, owner of a small yacht, not much more than a river-boat, good enough for inshore work, but out of place on a long fishing trip to Norway. The yacht founders off Heligoland, drowning Sir Hugh and Archibald Clavering and others who took to the lifeboat; Stuart himself, who remained on board, is saved. *C* PJT

Stuart-Wortley, Charles Beilby (1851–1926), later Lord Stuart. Engaged to Trollope's niece Beatrice (Bice) in 1879; married at the British Embassy in Paris (1880), 'Uncle Tony' being one of the witnesses. Beatrice died of puerperal fever in July 1881, eleven days after the birth of a daughter. At Trollope's funeral on 6 December 1882, Charles Stuart-Wortley was among mourners who accompanied the hearse. RCT

Stubber, Captain, along with Abraham Hart one of George Hotspur's disreputable creditors. He wants his money, but, a malignant man, he would be as pleased to harm George. He is the only character in the novel described as worse than George and is the only man George truly hates. *SHH* MG

Stubbs, Colonel Jonathan, nephew of the Marchesa Baldoni, at 28 'supposed to be the youngest Colonel in the British army' (XVI). Red-haired, with a bristly beard, he initially strikes Ayala Dormer as impossibly ugly. But by degrees she discovers that he is her Angel of Light. *AA* WK

Stumfold, Mr, evangelical clergyman who denounces most pleasures but is jovial and friendly. With a devoted following at Littlebath, he is popular with the ladies for his mild liberties with the gospel, but also for his clerical zeal and industriousness. His overbearing wife supervises the behaviour of their followers. *MM* SRB

Stumfold, Mrs, stern and commanding wife of the Revd Stumfold of Littlebath, with a high opinion of herself and of her husband's position. Hypocritical and martyred in her behaviour towards her aged father, she also dictates to her husband's parishioners, interfering especially in the lives of Mary Baker and Margaret Mackenzie. *MM* SRB

Struggles of Brown, Jones, and Robinson, The: by One of the Firm

ONE of Trollope's lesser-known novels, *The Struggles of Brown, Jones, and Robinson* is a broad satire on trade and advertising. It tells how the bill-sticker George Robinson ingratiates himself into a London haberdashery business, owned by the old-fashioned Mr Brown, and proceeds to ruin it by his grandiose schemes, fraudulent advertisements, and fervent belief in the power of 'credit'. The firm's ruin is compounded by the greed of Brown's two daughters, and the dishonesty of the second partner, Mr Jones. Despite bringing the firm to bankruptcy, the irrepressible Robinson remains seduced by dreams of higher things, and the novel ends with his succumbing, Dick Whittington-like, to fantasies of a career in politics: '[H]e knew that the bells of Edmonton were ringing . . . The words could not be mistaken. "Turn again, Robinson, Member of Parliament." Then he did turn, and walked back to London with a trusting heart' (XXIV). The novel is unusual for Trollope, in that the third-person narrative purports to have been written by Robinson himself, and much of the humour lies in the bathetic disparity between Robinson's high-flown language and the prosaic—and downright criminal—events he describes. Possibly because it is so radically 'un-Trollopian', it has conventionally been regarded as Trollope's worst novel, although its chronic irreverence and deliberate tastelessness are often hilarious. Trollope wrote the novel in two separate bursts of activity, separated by nearly four years: between 24 August and 7 September 1857, and between 23 June and 3 August 1861. The novel was published in the *Cornhill Magazine* in eight monthly instalments, from August 1861 to March 1862. It was eventually released in a single-volume format by Smith, Elder in 1870 (although Harper & Brothers of New York published a pirated edition in April 1862). Smith, Elder gave £600 for the copyright; in *An Autobiography*, Trollope noted that '*Brown, Jones and Robinson* was the hardest bargain I ever sold to a publisher' (*Auto* IX). The manuscript has not survived.   HO

Sturt, Mrs, neighbour of the Ray family at Bragg's End. A kindly and plain-speaking farmer's wife, she is protective of Rachel Ray, and arranges for Luke Rowan and Rachel to declare their love once and for all. Her simple rural values are in contrast to the pretensions of the Tappitt family and other Baslehurst townspeople. *RR*   MT

Suez, visited by George Walker for his health. 'Walker' *TAC2*   GRH

Suffolk, location of Lord Popplecourt's family seat, Popplecourt, in *The Duke's Children*; Babington House in *John Caldigate*; Carbury Hall, Caversham, and Toodlum in *The Way We Live Now*.   JMR

suffrage. The qualification to vote in parliamentary elections between 1832 and 1867 was held by about one in five adult Englishmen, one in eight Scotsmen, and one in twenty Irishmen. Since the franchise was property-based, these figures reflect the disparities of prosperity within the United Kingdom. The borough franchise qualification was owning or renting property worth at least £10 per year. At this level most of the middle class was enfranchised and in some industrial towns, and in London, some of the more prosperous working class. In counties the qualification was outright ownership of land worth at least £2, seemingly low, but landownership of any extent was largely confined to the well off. Inclusion on the electoral roll was not automatic, and the complexities of registration were an important incentive to greater party organization. Since most constituencies had two members, each voter had that many votes. He could either vote for two candidates, or 'plump' for one, leaving his other vote unused.

Voting was open until the Ballot Act of 1872. It was felt by many, including Trollope, that voting was a public act, an argument with some force when most had no vote. If those who did were in a sense representing them, the unenfranchised were at least entitled to know the political judgements of their 'betters'. Knowing the votes of shopkeepers, unenfranchised customers could patronize those whose politics they agreed with, a practice called 'strict dealing'. The strongest argument in favour of the ballot was that it would end vote-buying and intimidation. The former, and less so the latter, were widespread, particularly in smaller boroughs. Due in large part to the expense of contests, 45 per cent of seats were uncontested between 1832 and 1865. Extension of the franchise was considered an inevitable process by most Victorians. The question was—how far? and how fast? Here as elsewhere, Trollope's creed was cautious gradualism.　　　　CK

Gash, Norman, *Politics in the Age of Peel* (1953).

Sullivan, Sir Arthur (1842–1900), composer, collaborator with W. S. Gilbert, of comic operas such as *HMS Pinafore* (1878) and *Patience* (1881), in which Trollope is mentioned; member of the Garrick Club. When Sullivan needed an oboist Trollope recommended an American, Miss Jeanie Dulany (*Letters* 2, 680 n.). Trollope remarked that his niece Bice's singing had greatly impressed Sullivan, who had said that he knew 'nothing in private life like her voice' (*Letters* 2, 687). When Millais hosted a party in May 1881, Sullivan won £6 from Trollope at cards (*I & R* 151 n.).　　RCT

Sumner, Charles (1811–74), American Senator who opposed releasing two prisoners seized from the British ship *Trent* by American forces under Captain Charles Wilkie. He met Trollope during his American tour of 1861–2 (*Letters* 1, 164–5 n.). Trollope heard Sumner's speech to Congress on the *Trent* affair, opposing the prisoners' release, and was not impressed, fearing the American action would lead to war. Trollope dined with Sumner on two occasions, first at the home of Dr Samuel Kirkland Lothrop, in Boston on 6 September 1861, second at the home of American Secretary of State, William Seward, who supported releasing the prisoners.　　RCT

Supplehouse, Mr, MP and journalist, one of Nathaniel Sowerby's coterie. Supported by the *Jupiter* as the nation's saviour, he finds his talents under-utilized, however, and, as an 'Enceladus of the press', writes articles critical of his party and, especially, of Harold Smith who becomes his mortal enemy. *FP*　　NCS

Surbiton Cottage, pretty, secluded, and modest home of the Woodwards on the outskirts of Hampton. *TC*　　MT

Surrey. Fawn Court where Lucy Morris was governess (*ED*) is in the county, as is Ongar Park in *The Claverings*, 'supposed to be the most delightful small country-seat anywhere within thirty miles of London' (III). In *The Duke's Children* Mr and Mrs Finn have property in Surrey. The county's most celebrated residence is the Horns, Lady Glencora Palliser's wedding gift from the old Duke of Omnium, often mentioned in the Palliser novels.　　RCT

Sussex, in *Ayala's Angel* the setting for Sir Thomas Tringle's country home, Merle Park, where the hunting is poor (XLVII). Pickering Park, the large estate owned by the Longestaffes and dubiously acquired by Augustus Melmotte in *The Way We Live Now*, is also in Sussex.　　RCT

Swift, Jonathan (1667–1745), essayist, poet, and satirist, best known for *Gulliver's Travels* (1726); included by Trollope in his eighteen 'giants' of English literature. Although Trollope had none of the savage rage of the true satirist he did see his novel *The American Senator* as Swiftian, 'not to deal out impartial justice to the world; but to pick out the evil things' (*Letters* 2, 702).　　RCT

Synge, William Webb Follett (1826–91), diplomat in Washington, Central America, and Cuba; author and contributor to *Punch* and *Saturday Review*; met Trollope in Costa Rica in 1859. In *The West Indies and the Spanish Main*, Trollope described Synge as 'a very prince of good fellows', equally at home with Foreign Office protocol and the mules and straw hats of Costa Rica—in all, 'as pleasant a companion as a man would wish to meet on the western, or indeed on any other side of the Atlantic' (quoted *Letters* 1, 182 n.). The two became 'fast friends', according to Trollope's granddaughter Muriel Trollope (*I & R* 244). In 1862, Thackeray and Trollope came to Synge's assistance, lending him £900 apiece. Trollope's account of this event in *Thackeray* mentions Thackeray's generosity, but remains silent about his own. Synge's two sons spent time with the Trollopes at Waltham.　　RCT

Tagmaggert, Lady Emily, youngest daughter of the Earl of Mull; she marries Captain Frederic Aylmer. Lady Emily is over 40 and plain, with a red nose. 'I cannot conceive why any man should marry such a woman as that,' says Clara Belton, née Amedroz (XXXII). *BE*   WK

Talbot, John, friend of Dr Wortle since their days at Oxford. He leaves his son at the school despite the scandal, and describes Dr Wortle's chief antagonist, Mrs Stantiloup, as 'Old Mother Shipton' (4. XII). Of all of the parents, he alone receives a full account of the Peacockes' history from Dr Wortle. *DWS*   RC

Talboys, Arabella, apparently emancipated woman, but actually 'of rigid propriety', her views lead Charles O'Brien to suggest an elopement. 'Talboys' *TAC2*   GRH

Tales of All Countries: First Series, one volume, Chapman & Hall, 1861. Trollope's first volume of collected short stories mainly contains works first published in magazines between July 1859 and November 1860. As the title indicates, the stories were intended to reflect the author's extensive travels at the period.   JS

Tales of All Countries: Second Series, one volume, Chapman & Hall, 1863. Trollope's second volume of collected short stories mainly contains works published in magazines between January and December 1861. As in the first series, the settings are mainly foreign.   JS

Tallowax, Miss. The amiable, vulgar, shrewd, and rich great-aunt of Lady George Germain is impressed by her visit to Manor Cross, but she none the less clearly sees the narrowness of life there. She becomes the godmother of Lord Popenjoy with a gift of £20,000. *IHP*   MG

Tallowax, Mr, maternal grandfather of Lady George Germain. By leaving her the considerable fortune he made as a wax-chandler, his death paves the way for Mary Lovelace to marry Lord George. *IHP*   MG

Tally-Ho Lodge, lodge for the Runnymede Hunt and primary residence of Major Tifto, MFH. *DC*   JMR

Tankerville, corrupt borough ordinarily represented in Parliament by Mr Browborough. Phineas Finn wins the seat after a close contest with Browborough and a subsequent parliamentary investigation exposing Browborough's bribing of voters. It is the first seat held by Phineas after the death of his Irish wife. *PR*   JMR

Tappitt, Margaret, wife of Thomas Tappitt, mother of three marriageable daughters, and aspiring middle-class hostess in Baslehurst. Mrs Tappitt welcomes Luke Rowan into her home with an eye to marrying off one of her daughters. She throws a memorable ball in an effort to impress Luke's London family, but all her designs are wasted since Luke loves Rachel Ray. A crafty manipulator and one of Trollope's viragos, she is defeated by young love in the end. *RR*   MT

Tappitt, Thomas, head of the Bungall & Tappitt Brewery in Baslehurst, and father of three daughters in want of a husband. Mr Tappitt is appalled by Luke Rowan's wish to brew better beer, and he recklessly seeks to prevent Luke from founding a rival brewery in town. Mr Tappitt drinks too much and foolishly gets entangled with the shady lawyers Sharpit & Longfite. Tappitt is ruled at home by the iron hand of his wife. *RR*   MT

Tappitt family, aspiring middle-class commercial family connected to the brewery in Baslehurst. Old Mr Tappitt resents young Luke Rowan's partnership in the brewery, while Mrs Tappitt looks upon Luke as an eligible bachelor for one of her three daughters, Augusta, Martha, and Cherry. The Tappitts close ranks against Rachel Ray when they learn that Luke favours her, and Mr Tappitt rails against Luke's new ideas for his business. Confounded on every front, the family eventually retire to Torquay. *RR*   MT

Tauchnitz, Christian Bernhard von (1816–95), Baron Tauchnitz of Leipzig, publisher from 1841 of foreign editions of English books. Tauchnitz found a lucrative market producing English-language books in compact format for travellers abroad. Trollope liked his 'Collection of British Authors' and told him in December 1872, 'I am so fond of your series that I regret to have a work of mine omitted from it' (*Letters* 2, 572). Tauchnitz published fifteen of Trollope's novels, two travel books, *An Autobiography*, and a book of short stories.   RCT

Taunton, county town of Somerset, twenty miles (32 km) from Belton Castle. *BE*   WK

Tavistock, town in Devon where Alaric Tudor and Fidus Neverbend are sent to investigate a dispute over mining boundaries. It is here that Undy Scott first tempts Alaric into reckless speculation and deceit. *TC*   MT

Taylor, Sir Charles (1817–76), close Garrick friend of Trollope's and a man rather like Trollope himself: 'rough of tongue, brusque in manners, odious to those who dislike him, somewhat inclined to tyranny, he is the prince of friends, honest as the sun, and as open-hearted as Charity itself' (*Auto* VIII). Taylor asked Trollope's help in preparing for publication his brother-in-law's *The Life and Times of Lord Brougham* (1871). The time and effort involved was prodigious, another reminder of the energy Trollope devoted to others' interests.   RCT

Taylor, Miss E., amateur artist, based at St Leonards, possibly a friend of Trollope's, brought in to illustrate the last ten numbers of *Can You Forgive Her?* She did twenty drawings, one of them a vigorous scene of the House of Commons in session and a striking 'Lady Glencora' (N. John Hall, *Trollope and his Illustrators* (1980), 98–101).   RCT

Taylor, Sir Henry (1800–86), civil servant in Colonial Service (1824–72); dramatist whose *Philip Van Artevelde* (1834) was Trollope's favourite contemporary play. He listed Taylor among his eighteen 'giants' of English literature in *The New Zealander*. Taylor gave him a present of his three-volume *Poetical Works* (1864) of which Trollope wrote a warm review in *Fortnightly* (June 1865), perhaps unmindful of his golden rule that 'there should be no intercourse at all between an author and his critic' (*Auto* XIV).   RCT

Taylor, Robert H. (1909–85), bibliophile and founder of an extensive collection of Trollope manuscript material and letters housed in Princeton University.   RCT

Taylor, Tom (1817–80), civil servant in the Board of Health and later the Sanitary Department; playwright famous for *The Ticket-of-Leave Man* (1863) which Trollope knew well; editor of *Punch* (1874–80) after Shirley *Brooks. Taylor

was among those supporting Trollope's election to the Garrick. Trollope joined Taylor, Millais, and Frith in setting up a fund for Brooks's widow and sons. Always the willing work-horse, Trollope was treasurer, which involved much correspondence over several months. £2,000 was raised.   RCT

'Telegraph Girl, The', first published in *Good Cheer*, December 1877 (reprinted in *WFF*); Trollope's only story about the Post Office. Two young girls employed at the Telegraph Office in London decide to lodge together in Clerkenwell. The elder of the two, Lucy Graham, is strong and independent; Sophy Wilson is prettier, but flighty and frail. A widowed printer, Abraham Hall, pays court to Sophy. But, gradually, he falls in love with Lucy. Finally, when Sophy accepts another, Abraham proposes to Lucy. He has been offered a promotion in Gloucestershire, and Lucy follows him to become 'as good a wife as ever blessed a man's household'.   JS

Tempest, Revd Dr Mortimer, Elderly rector and magistrate of Silverbridge, and Rural Dean of Barchester. Considered hard and unfeeling, but practical and just, he helps commit Josiah Crawley to trial; later, he presides over the Bishop's ecclesiastical commission to consider the case. His refusal to discuss the issue with Mrs Proudie prompts the Bishop to articulate his feelings to his wife. *LCB, DC*   NCS

Temple Bar. In December 1860, John Maxwell, publisher, began a monthly, shilling magazine, *Temple Bar*. Maxwell had founded *Town Talk* in 1858; he also founded *St James's Magazine* in 1861, and *Belgravia* in 1866. *Temple Bar* had a strong start with a circulation of 30,000. This dropped to 11,000 by 1866 then levelled off at 13,000 by 1870. The name reflected the practice adopted by several magazines of using London place names—the *Cornhill*, *St James's*, and later *Saint Pauls*. Containing 150 pages, *Temple Bar* was larger than the first shilling magazine, *Macmillan's* (80 pages), or the *Cornhill Magazine*, and later *Saint Pauls Magazine* (both 128 pages). From the beginning it was edited by George Augustus Henry *Sala, foreign correspondent for the *Daily Telegraph*. Edmund *Yates, a journalist and novelist who, like Sala, wrote for Dickens's publications, was his sub-editor.

Maxwell set out to rival the *Cornhill* with serious, unsigned articles and fiction, but by 1862 his magazine had fallen into a more popular mode, with sensational fiction by writers like Mary Elizabeth *Braddon, who eventually became editor and principal novelist of *Belgravia*.

Tennyson, Alfred

By 1864 *Temple Bar* included two serials, stories, poetry, and articles such as biographies, travel pieces, and reviews, but no politics. Articles were written for the poorly educated middle-class reader who read for entertainment; the readers of *St James's*, *Argosy*, *Victoria Magazine*, *Belgravia*, and *Tinsley's*. *Cornhill* and *Saint Pauls* were in a different class.

By 1861, Trollope's success with *Framley Parsonage* in the *Cornhill* led to invitations from other magazines. Maxwell asked an old friend of the Trollope family, M. de Fauche, to offer Trollope nominal editorship of *Temple Bar*, taking over from Sala at a salary of £1,000 per year for three or five years. Yates would still do all the real work, but Trollope's name would be on the title-page. Trollope responded that his hands were full and that he would not be an editor in name only. Sala remained in the post until 1863, when he left to cover the American Civil War. Yates followed him as editor.

Trollope's only contribution to the magazine was *The American Senator*, which ran from May 1876 to July 1877 under the editorship of George Bentley. Richard Bentley & Sons had bought *Temple Bar* in 1866.   JWM

Tennyson, Alfred (1809–92), 1st Baron Tennyson; Poet Laureate, author of *In Memoriam* (1850) and *Idylls of the King* (1859). Trollope came into contact with him through Lord Houghton's dinners in London and occasionally at the Cosmopolitan Club. Of dissimilar temperaments, they were never good friends. Trollope enjoyed reading his poetry aloud in the family circle (1876–8) but took exception to 'The Two Voices' (*Poems*, 1833): 'There is nothing to fear in death,—if you be wise. There is so much to fear in life, whether you be wise or foolish' (*Letters* 2, 942). Trollope occasionally used a Tennyson line, most effectively in *The Eustace Diamonds* (XIII) with 'Doänt thou marry for munny, but goä wheer munny is' ('Northern Farmer "New Style" '). Although he listed Tennyson among his 'giants' in *The New Zealander*, Trollope did not care for the lofty utterances of the great poets of his own day. For his part Tennyson discounted the popular writers, observing to William *Allingham (1885) of Trollope's novels 'so dull—so prosaic; never a touch of poetry' (quoted R. C. Terry, *Anthony Trollope* (1977), 88).   RCT

Tenway Junction, busy railway station just outside metropolitan London. As its name suggests, the station is a hub for trains headed in all directions. It is the site of Ferdinand Lopez's dramatic suicide. *PM*   JMR

Ternan, Ellen. See ROBINSON, ELLEN LAWLESS.

Tetchen. Disdaining Madame Staubach's Calvinism and Steinmarc's contemptible ambitions, the Tressels' elderly retainer arranges ways for Valcarm to lay romantic siege to Linda and cannot understand why that should distress her adored young mistress. *LT*   AWJ

Tewett, Sir Griffin, quarrelsome baronet, mean with money though heir to a large property; embroiled in legal battles with almost all his family. Sir Griffin's engagement with Miss Roanoke is highly combative, his love for her being mixed with 'a good deal of hatred' (XLI). *ED*
          JMR

Thackeray. Trollope's 1879 book on Thackeray in the Macmillan series, 'English Men of Letters', is notable for what it reveals both of his view of the novelist he most admired and of his own critical principles. It is a curiously ambivalent book, however: the personal affection for his subject coexists with a perceptible irritation, and the disciple's professional admiration for the master is heavily qualified by a sometimes ungenerous insistence on the flaws in Thackeray's works and working habits.

Trollope was hampered in his task by the fact that Thackeray had insisted that no biography should be written. Nevertheless, as a friend and associate of Thackeray's, he had received the blessing of Thackeray's daughter *Anne and of Leslie Stephen, the widower of the younger daughter. John *Morley, general editor of the series, had also urged Trollope to 'give as much as ever you can in the personal vein, by way of background to the critical and descriptive' (*Letters* 2, 813). But Trollope seems to have been so anxious not to supply the kind of 'fulsome' picture Thackeray objected to that he erred in the other direction. Moreover, as the reviewers were quick to notice, he focused on those faults of Thackeray that would show up his own virtues by contrast.

In *An Autobiography*—already written though not published—Trollope had not hesitated to call Thackeray 'the first' of English novelists of his day (XIII), and in his obituary of Thackeray for the *Cornhill* he unequivocally placed *Henry Esmond* as 'the first and finest novel in the English language', and Colonel Newcome as 'the first single character in English fiction' (February 1864, 136). But in *Thackeray* he pointedly avoids such ranking, and concentrates on shortcomings instead. It is difficult not to hear an implied contrast with his own superior practice in much of what he says of Thackeray's faults. 'It was his nature to be idle,—to put off his work' (I)— '[unlike me]' seems to be the secret implication. Or again, Thackeray could not have combined a job in the Post Office with writing novels, unless like Trollope he could 'have risen at five, and have sat at his private desk for three hours before he began his official routine' (I). The Thackeray who emerges sometimes seems like the antithesis of the more admirable narrator: he 'was not a good editor'; he had 'no great power of conversation'; he was 'too desultory for regular work'. 'Unsteadfast, idle, changeable of purpose, aware of his own intellect but not trusting it, no man ever failed more generally than he to put his best foot foremost' (I).

On the other hand, Trollope stresses the personal appeal that goes with these professional faults: the modesty, the self-doubt, the agonized sense of failure. Taking a cue from Thackeray's famous self-portrait as the fool who removes a laughing mask to reveal a worried face, Trollope emphasizes the 'continual playfulness . . . lying over a melancholy which was as continual' (I). Some of his best creations, Trollope suggests, were those that came without effort, the 'pearls' that he dropped carelessly without counting their value: the sketches, the impromptu verses, the playful sallies. The critical insight that Thackeray was at his most brilliant when he was most careless is one that has been developed by a modern critic like John Sutherland in *Thackeray at Work* (1973), though Sutherland does not castigate Thackeray's idleness as Trollope does. Thackeray's artistic largesse in dropping his pearls is matched by his practical generosity. Trollope tells an anecdote of approaching Thackeray with a tale of distress about a mutual acquaintance (W. Synge) in sore need of £2,000; after some initial indignation, 'there came over his face a peculiar smile, and a wink in his eye. . . . "I'll go half", he said, "if anybody will do the rest". And he did go half' (I). Trollope does not mention that he himself went the other half. The anecdote links the two novelists, and ends the biographical section of the book, after the fault-finding, on a note of tenderness for this 'most soft-hearted of human beings, who went about the world dropping pearls, doing good, and never willfully inflicting a wound' (I).

Trollope's judgements on Thackeray's works seem rather eccentric today. He admired *Henry Esmond* as by far the best of all his work. (His working calendar shows that he reread *Esmond* while writing the book.) He praises the characterization of Rachel and Beatrix Esmond, and of the hero, because (like Trollope's own Palliser) 'he is a gentleman from the crown of his head to the sole of his foot' (V). He admires the period flavour of the prose, and the power of the love scenes. In his view, this is the one novel on which Thackeray really expended that 'elbow-grease of the mind', the hard preliminary creative thinking, that he felt Thackeray usually skimped on. Surprisingly, Trollope has scant praise for *Vanity Fair*, the novel most critics consider to be his masterpiece, though he had been haunted by the notion that his own Lizzie Eustace of *The Eustace Diamonds* would be taken as a second Becky Sharp. He is impatient with the Thackerayan trademark of intimacy with his reader, the 'sort of confidential talk between writer and reader' that Thackeray defined in his preface to *Pendennis*. Trollope finds this 'affected familiarity' undignified (IX). Next after *Esmond* Trollope places *Barry Lyndon*—again an unusual choice; he likes *The Newcomes* for Colonel Newcome, who again is a complete 'gentleman': but *The Virginians* is marred by 'that propensity to wandering which came to Thackeray because of his idleness' (V). And he has a developed taste for the ballads and burlesques, especially *Rebecca and Rowena*, which he calls the best burlesque in the language. (Scott's novels, particularly *Ivanhoe*, often serve as an implicit yardstick for fictional performance.)

Trollope's position on many issues, at this stage of his career, was somewhat reactionary; and he is impatient with Thackeray's political and moral stances. He objects to the irreverent treatment of royalty in the lectures on *The Four Georges*, he criticizes Thackeray for his satirist's propensity to find fault with everything, he is uneasy with his sceptical stance on the domestic virtues. (If he praises the characterization of Amelia, it is because he misses the irony in the presentation of this Angel in the House.) It is Thackeray's position that 'one is bound to speak the truth as far as one knows it, . . . and a deal of disagreeable matter must come out in the course of such an undertaking' (*Vanity Fair*, VIII). It is Trollope's position that Thackeray was rather too fond of the disagreeable matter, and served up rather too much truth.

We learn most about Trollope's own critical principles in the final chapter, on 'Thackeray's style and manner of work'. He defines Thackeray's manner as mainly 'realistic', and he presents realism as the golden mean between the 'ludicrous' and the 'sublime'. At the ludicrous Thackeray also excels, especially in that branch of it called parody. But though parody is a dangerous mode, in Thackeray's hands it does no damage to the original. Good style should be 'easy, lucid, and of course grammatical' (and Trollope carefully defines his terms); and Thackeray passes that test, although there is a little too much personal flavour of Thackeray in his prose: 'I hold that gentleman to be the best dressed whose dress no one observes,' says Trollope characteristically, suggesting his own ideal of an invisible style (IX). As to the *matter*—by which Trollope means the moral tendency of the fiction—Thackeray receives full praise. The novel being the day's most effective conduct book, it behoves the novelist to look to his moral teaching; and though Thackeray has been accused of making his rascals and sinners too attractive, he always supplies enough moral definition that no attentive reader will want to be like Barry Lyndon, or Becky, or Beatrix. To the recurring question of whether Thackeray was a cynic, Trollope answers no, because of his gentle heart; but he *did* 'allow his intellect to be too thoroughly saturated with the aspect of the ill side of things' (IX). Trollope was typical of his period in harbouring strong reservations about satire.

Trollope wrote *Thackeray* in seven weeks, between 1 February and 24 March 1879, taking time off writing to reread *Henry Esmond*, from which he quotes frequently. The reviews of his book on the author he purported most to admire were as contradictory as the attitudes contained in it. T. H. Escott called it 'hero worship', while A. G. Sedgewick characterized it as 'malicious'. A review in the *Pall Mall Gazette* (the journal that owed its name and its inspiration to the one Thackeray invented in *Pendennis*) sneered at Trollope's characteristic specificity about literary earnings. And the book caused a temporary falling-out with Anne Thackeray. If in *An Autobiography* Trollope had largely acknowledged the lesson of the master, in *Thackeray* he takes pains to acknowledge his idol's feet of clay.　　JM

Thackeray, Anne Isabella (Annie)

(1837–1919), Thackeray's elder daughter; married Sir Richmond Ritchie (1877); author of several novels, the best known being *Old Kensington* (1873). Trollope included her in his survey of contemporary novelists, commending her charming characters but taxing her with a certain weakness in her writing (*Auto* XIII). An estrangement between them occurred when Trollope wrote his memoir of her father but was healed in 1882. Annie noted that Trollope had called and, standing by the fireplace, 'very big and kind [he] made it up . . . I said I'm so sorry I quarrelled with you. He said so am I my dear. I never saw dear Mr Trollope again' (quoted *Letters* 2, 947).　　RCT

Thackeray, Harriet Marian (Minnie)

(1840–75), younger daughter of Thackeray; first wife of Leslie Stephen. Trollope was very fond of her and her sister Annie. After Harriet's sudden death, Trollope told a friend that he was trying to write to Annie 'but postponing it from hour to hour because the task is so frightful' (*Letters* 2, 672).　　RCT

Thackeray, William Makepeace (1811–63),

author and illustrator, and editor of the *Cornhill Magazine*, in which Trollope published *Framley Parsonage* and *The Small House at Allington*. According to one view of Trollope's career, at least, Thackeray was the making of him, by launching a still relatively obscure novelist before the public as the principal writer of the great literary success of the day, the *Cornhill Magazine*. When the two novelists first had personal contact, in 1859, Thackeray was at the height of his fame, though declining in creative power, while Trollope was just on the way up. Thackeray's invitation to join the *Cornhill* team made a huge difference, and Trollope was lastingly appreciative. At the same time, though, he was perceptibly envious of a reputation that he felt was not as hard-earned as his own.

William Makepeace Thackeray was born in Calcutta in 1811, son of Richmond Thackeray, an employee of the East India Company; and, as was usual with the children of Anglo-Indians, at 6 was sent to school in England, and to stay with relatives. He attended the Charterhouse school, which figures in his novels as Greyfriars. He left Cambridge without a degree in 1830, and lost his patrimony by a combination of gambling and ill-advised investments. Faced in his early twenties with the unexpected task of earning his own living, he tried various careers: he dabbled in the law, and he tried to become an artist. As part of this enterprise, he applied to become the illustrator of *Pickwick Papers* (1836–7); but the young Dickens, already launched in his rocket-like career, turned him down—the first of many unfortunate incidents that plagued the relations of the two great novelists of the age. Although, like his own artist hero Clive Newcome, Thackeray could never have become a successful painter of serious subjects, his comic graphic work has lasting appeal, and he is still the best illustrator of his own novels.

In the mid-1830s, when he was working as a journalist in Paris, he fell in love with Isabella Shawe, and, without much to support them, in 1836 the two were married. Back in London, during the young couple's hand-to-mouth existence while Thackeray was trying to establish himself in a literary career, Isabella became unbalanced, attempted suicide, and was ultimately permanently confined as insane. Thackeray became, in effect, the single parent of two young daughters, Anne and Harriet—though his mother, who remained jealously devoted to him, helped him in their care. He formed an intense friendship with a married woman, Jane Brookfield, but her husband became jealous, and in 1851 the relationship was ended.

W. M. Thackeray, portrait by Samuel Laurence (1864). Long an admirer of Thackeray's work, Trollope became a close friend when Thackeray welcomed him as a colleague in George Smith's new periodical *Cornhill Magazine*. After Thackeray's death in 1863 Trollope wrote a loving tribute. In *An Autobiography* he named Thackeray the first among contemporary novelists (XIII).

Thackeray, William Makepeace

His early work for *Fraser's Magazine*, such as *The Yellowplush Papers* (1837–40), *Catherine* (1839–40), and *Barry Lyndon* (1844), is sharply satiric. Much of it was written under pseudonyms, so that although his talent was recognized by those in the know, he failed to build a reputation and a name. More congenial to him than *Fraser's* was the newly formed comic weekly *Punch*, of which Thackeray became a mainstay. In the *Punch* work *The Snobs of England, by One of Themselves* (1846–7)—a characteristic title—and *Punch's Prize Novelists* (1847), a series of parodies of contemporary novelists, Thackeray was developing the social vision and the stylistic versatility that were to inform his major works.

He made his name with *Vanity Fair*, which emerged from 1847 to 1848 in the yellow-covered monthly numbers that became his 'jaundiced livery'. The lively unscrupulous adventuress Becky Sharp, and her foil, the clingingly tender Amelia Sedley, are among the most famous characters in fiction. *Pendennis* (1848–50), a novel about a novelist, ran concurrently with *David Copperfield*. *Henry Esmond* (1852), which Thackeray published not serially but in three volumes, allowed him to explore the manners and morals of his favourite 18th century, as did its sequel, *The Virginians* (1857–9), and the two series of lectures which he delivered in America, *The English Humourists* (1853) and *The Four Georges* (1856). *The Newcomes* (1853–5), with an artist hero, is an anatomy of the 'respectable' classes. Thackeray was always delighted by children, and *The Rose and the Ring*, his Christmas book for 1855, has become a classic Victorian fairy tale.

The so-called 'Garrick Club Affair' of 1858, a dispute over some malicious gossip published by a young journalist called Edmund *Yates, caused more bad blood between him and Dickens, the two novelists who were now recognized as being rivals 'at the top of the tree'.

In 1859, at the invitation of 'the prince of publishers', George *Smith, Thackeray became editor of the *Cornhill Magazine*, the enterprise that brought him into relation with Trollope. His own novels of this time, *Lovel the Widower* (1860) and *Philip* (1861–2), show his creative energy was flagging, though he could still deliver his satiric bite, and the combination of cynicism with tenderness for which he was famous. He died at 52 on 23 December 1863. 'I have not the heart to wish any one a Merry Christmas,' Trollope wrote on Christmas Day (*Letters* 1, 244).

In 1859 Trollope had published nine novels and a travel book, and though he was improving the prices he was paid for them—a matter he always cared about—he had not as yet commanded high figures. For *The Warden* and *Barchester Towers*

combined, by his own account, he earned some £727, for *The Three Clerks* only £250. When the offer came from George Smith of £1,000, and the invitation from Thackeray to provide the leading novel for the much-heralded *Cornhill*, he was understandably elated. He offered an Irish story, but was told that an English story, preferably about clergymen, would be more acceptable. 'The details' of the offer, as he euphemistically called the money, 'were so interesting that had a couple of archbishops been demanded, I should have provided them' (*T* I). *Framley Parsonage*, with illustrations by Millais, came first in the journal (Thackeray himself having failed to get his own *Philip* ready in time), and was 'received with greater favour', Trollope wrote, than any previous or subsequent novel of his (*T* I). Thus established among the distinguished contributors to the *Cornhill*, Trollope's prices thereafter leaped into the range of £2,000 or more for a full-sized novel.

If Thackeray and the *Cornhill* were not the making of Trollope, then they clearly contributed notably to his success and long-term reputation. And Trollope felt a warm professional gratitude to Thackeray, which he manifested in several ways. At Thackeray's death he promptly offered to supply the obituary, 'as a work of love' (*Letters* 1, 224), and he busied himself to ensure there was a suitable memorial to Thackeray in Westminster Abbey; in *An Autobiography* he named Thackeray as the foremost novelist of the time; and he wrote the *Thackeray* volume for the Macmillan series on 'English Men of Letters'.

However, the relation of the two novelists was not without its problems. When Trollope finally got to meet his literary hero, at a dinner at Smith's house, Thackeray slighted him (they were introduced at a moment when Thackeray, already in uncertain health, suffered a spasm of pain), and Trollope was very angry. Later Thackeray rejected a story of Trollope's, 'Mrs General Talboys', on moral grounds, and though Trollope responded in good part, the rejection rankled, as his account of the incident shows. On another occasion Trollope inadvertently embarrassed Thackeray and Smith by gossiping about the *Cornhill* dinners to Thackeray's old enemy Edmund Yates.

But deeper than these passing misunderstandings seems to have been a certain irritation on Trollope's part that Thackeray had won easily what he himself had worked for much harder. Though he habitually deferred to the great man, and admitted his own inferior stature, there is an undercurrent of exasperation in his commentary on him. 'He was but four years my senior in life, but he was at the top of the tree, while I was at the bottom' (*Auto* VIII). And in *Thackeray* he conducts some running battles with his admired subject even while he praises him. He criticized him for his lack of dignity in narration, his satiric vision, and especially his 'idleness'.

Like Trollope himself, Thackeray had at different times aspired to an alternative career, as civil servant and member of Parliament, as well as editor. Trollope seems most irritated of all at Thackeray's application in 1858 for a senior position in his own bastion of the Post Office. Thackeray was totally unfitted for such a position, Trollope insists, by temperament and habits as well as inexperience. The gist of his objections seems to be his sense that Thackeray was lazy and undisciplined, and incapable of the kind of methodical organization that had enabled Trollope himself to make a success of two careers. 'Of all men Thackeray was the last to bear the wearisome perseverance of such a life' (*T* I). Trollope's *Thackeray*, in fact, often reads like the ant's commentary on the grasshopper. (In the event, that particular Post Office appointment went to John Tilley, Trollope's close friend and brother-in-law.)

The audible tone of rivalry aside, Trollope's writings about Thackeray show more than admiration for a great writer; they show deep personal affection, and a sympathetic understanding of Thackeray's habitual self-doubt, if not an appreciation of his satire and his habitually ironic stance. JM

Thakombau, King of Fiji, first among native chieftains; elected President (1865); crowned King (1868); ceded the islands to British rule in person of Sir Hercules Robinson, Governor of New South Wales, and friend of Trollope's (1874). Trollope had strong doubts about the wisdom of Britain's annexations both there and in New Guinea. See *The Tireless Traveller*, ed. B. Booth (1941), 182–90. RCT

theatre, Victorian. (See also ACTING AND ACTORS.) At Victoria's accession, drama was subservient to theatrical display since the two patent houses, Covent Garden and Drury Lane, lured audiences to their cavernous auditoria with sumptuous and lengthy entertainments. By 1850, when Trollope wrote his first play, having failed to make his name as a novelist, the theatre had achieved a certain cachet. In reaction to mere spectacle, the actor William Charles Macready gathered together a number of writers whose mission was to make dramatic literature equal to the other arts. They adopted a neo-Elizabethan grandeur, hoping to create a second Golden Age of British Drama. Their leader was Edward Bulwer whose *Richelieu* (1839) and *The Lady of Lyons* (1838), though hardly golden, continued to be produced till the turn of the century. British drama gained further prestige after 1848 when the Queen and Prince Albert gave it their conscious support (with command performances in London and Windsor) after demonstrators protested a French company's arrival at Drury Lane.

So Trollope aimed high when he modelled *The Noble Jilt* after Bulwer's successes and chose a subject (revolutionary uprising) of some topicality in riot-torn Europe. His blank-verse arias are technically proficient, but he fails to organize them emotionally. Audiences expected to be swept away by noble ideals tempered by reassuring touches of domestic pathos. Trollope's heroine pits one against the other, and that effect grows still more disconcerting when the villain's cynicism and the citizens' foolishness (shades of Dogberry and watchmen) show the ideals she espouses are far from noble. It was precisely that confusion of sympathies which caught the eye of George Bartley when Trollope sought his advice. Nor could Bartley (as a former actor-manager) commend a villain who was in most respects heroic and a hero who had so little to do (*Auto* V). Victorian actors liked to be admired, stage-centre.

Trollope's second play also failed to meet the theatre's demands. Yet Act I of *Did He Steal It?* (1869) has many of the qualities of Tom Robertson's cup-and-saucer dramas which the Bancrofts made fashionable at the Prince of Wales's in the 1860s. Those plays reversed the formula by creating a domestic charm that admitted moments of bright-eyed heroism. They required a less declamatory style, based on everyday rhythms and short exchanges of conversation. Realistic scenery and the interplay between actors created an illusion of actuality, though characters were still drawn to type and their values remained idealistic. The opening episode between Grace Crawley and her mother perfectly reflects this genre in the way Grace tremulously breaks the news of Oakley's proposal and (to little hand-taps of comfort and encouragement from mother) bravely maintains how wrong it would be to consider him while her father's good name remains in question. Then Toogood's arrival offers just the sort of cheery eccentricity audiences delighted in, and the sequence concludes with low-keyed emotion between the Crawleys as he hints at suicide. A writer of genuinely theatrical instincts would end this in suspense, but Trollope resolves things as the curtain falls. The rest of the play is similarly undramatic. Its crises are either wrongly placed or understated; the characters' entries and exits seem arbitrary; Act

III is anticlimactic. Again there are no sustained acting parts, and the script was rejected.

Trollope's third brush with the theatre was less intentional and more painful. In 1872, Charles *Reade, the successful novelist and playwright, adapted *Ralph the Heir* for the stage. Such an arrangement was quite usual under the copyright laws; indeed, managers were particularly fond of plays 'adapted from the French', diluted to London's high standards of bashfulness at minimum cost and without fees to the original author. Novels were also a source of plunder. Having suffered from that himself, Reade determined to acknowledge Trollope's contribution and, unable to consult his friend personally since the Trollopes were in Australia, wrote to tell him so. By the time he received that letter, *Shilly-Shally* had closed at the Gaiety, but Trollope was furious. Had Reade asked permission before adapting the novel, he would 'have taken it as a compliment', but to use his name without consultation 'was utterly unjustified' (*Letters* 2, 583). Trollope fired off disclaimers to the British press and, though insisting he had no wish to quarrel, the affair escalated into a bitterness that lasted some five years. Hot-tempered and punctilious about conduct between gentlemen, he was usually quick to forgive. Given his past efforts, perhaps what rankled was Reade's (unknowingly) patronizing assurance that their collaboration 'will open the theatre to you, should you at any time feel disposed to enter it relying on your talent only' (*Letters* 2, 558).

Despite his lack of practical success, Trollope was an avid student of drama. What plays he saw as a postal clerk remains unknown, since he destroyed his youthful journals (*Auto* III). Considering his hand-to-mouth existence, he cannot have seen many except when he lived with his mother (1839–40). However, in struggling to organize his frustrated energies, he also kept a Commonplace Book (*Letters* 2, 1021–8) where he lists five plays that exemplify 'Excellencies and defects of the modern English' stage: Fanny Kemble's *Francis I* (1832), Sheridan Knowles's *The Hunchback* (1832), Henry Taylor's *Philip Van Artevelde* (1834), Joanna Bailey's *Henriquez* (1812), and Thomas Talfourd's *Ion* (1836). These plays represent the literary theatre Macready hoped for: *The Hunchback* and *Ion* were part of his repertoire at Covent Garden. Taylor's verse drama went unproduced until 1847 (by Macready at the Princess's where it failed badly), but that text made a lasting impression on Trollope who, in his maturity, thought it 'the best poem of these days' (*Letters* 1, 118) and quoted its hero in his final novel (*L* XXXII). It may also have stirred youthful ambition since the Commonplace Book shows him

contemplating a 'dramatic poem' on Henry IV. Admitting it 'would be a dangerous job' to compete with Shakespeare, he felt this play could express a 'prevailing sentiment' of Liberty: 'A good character might be made of a London citizen—averse to Richard's profligacy—but equally averse to the growth of Henry's power.' Those ideas evaporated: 'drama . . . I believed to be above me . . . yet no day was passed without thoughts of . . . the disgrace of postponing it' (*Auto* III). When he eventually wrote *The Noble Jilt*, Taylor's poem about a Flemish patriot must have influenced his choice of subject. As for less elevated theatre in those disreputable years, the Commonplace Book offers one faint clue when Trollope earnestly considers the destructive influence of attractive rogues like Jack Sheppard. Harrison Ainsworth's novel (1839) had proved so popular that it was quickly dramatized and, 30 years later, Trollope recalled the 'immense deal of mischief' its vivid episodes and 'excellent acting' did to an impressionable mind ('Formosa').

By the time Trollope returned permanently to England, the royal patent had been long abolished (1843): Covent Garden was an opera house and Drury Lane presented pantomime and melodrama. New theatres, in increasing numbers, became intimate and genteel. In 1862 Trollope was elected to the Garrick, a club where liberal-minded aristocrats might meet writers, painters, actors on equal terms. He felt easy in that atmosphere, and his letters trace a continued interest in the theatre's changing fashions (as do his two playscripts) and an acquaintance with Tom Taylor's *Ticket-of-Leave Man* (*Letters* 1, 263), H. J. Byron's burlesqued *Orpheus and Eurydice* and Augustin Daly's *Leah* (2, 1007), W. G. Wills's *Charles I* (2, 577–8), Wilkie Collins's *New Magdalene* (2, 589). When Kate Field appeared in *Extremes Meet* (adapted from the French), Trollope 'liked it very much' (2, 714).

In 1869, Boucicault's *Formosa* caused a furore at Drury Lane with its spectacular depiction of an Oxford–Cambridge boat race and, more scandalously, the machinations of a prostitute. Trollope took issue in *Saint Pauls* with that uproar. He had no wish to keep audiences in ignorance—'lock and key . . . can never establish virtue'—but did object to the triumph of sin. With his own Carry Brattle in mind (*VB*), he insisted that 'the career of an English prostitute is the most miserable': an accurate portrayal might make men more circumspect and women more charitable.

The Victorian theatre was always vulnerable to middle-class suspicion. Trollope's novels reflect that prejudice in Lupex, the drunken scene-painter of *The Small House at Allington*, and Euphemia Smith who, under her stage-name of Mlle Cettini, returns from Australia to muddy the fortunes of John Caldigate. Rachel O'Mahony in *The Landleaguers* is more complex. Her fantastical career parallels the topsy-turvy politics of contemporary Ireland. Her Jewish name and its echo of the panther-like actress 'Rachel' signify a subversive world in which a woman, as wealthy diva, controls her father and endangers her fiancé. But Frank Jones is a gentleman, and Rachel must resist the theatre's gaslight. When her voice fails, she happily accepts domestic poverty.

Visits to the theatre are often pointers to character or social milieu. The way Toogood's daughter clamours for pantomime tickets shows how his children 'have it pretty much their own way' (*LCB* XXXII). Lucy Graham, 'The Telegraph Girl', enjoyed '*Hamlet* at the Lyceum, or *Lord Dundreary* at the Haymarket' where her brother used to take her but would not go to any theatre alone and would certainly not join her co-workers at a music hall. When Mrs Carbuncle goes to the theatre (*ED* LII), she sees *The Noble Jilt*, about which the critics are entirely contradictory. Had that script actually been produced, Trollope would have had to face those biased judgements, the vanities of actor-managers, the audiences' preference for character-types and emotional thrills: dolls and declamation.   AWJ

Jenkins, Anthony, *The Making of Victorian Drama* (1991).

Thirkell, Angela Mackail (1890–1961), author of popular novels reflecting English county life from about 1932 in nostalgic scenes among landed gentry and distressed gentlefolk in peace and wartime amid social changes. Twenty-three of her novels are placed in her version of Barsetshire, with towns and villages familiar to Trollopians, families and names from Trollope, and in-jokes such as Tom Grantly working for the Bureau of Red Tape and Sealing Wax. See Laura Roberts Collins, *English Country Life in the Barsetshire Novels of Angela Thirkell* (1994).   RCT

Thomas, George Housman (1824–68), engraver, illustrator and artist, known for sketches for *Illustrated London News*. Queen Victoria commissioned him to picture major events in her reign (1855–68). Thomas produced fine illustrations for Wilkie Collins's *Armadale* (1866). When Millais declined to illustrate *The Last Chronicle of Barset*, Thomas was given the job. He produced 32 plates and vignettes as the book appeared (December 1866–July 1867) which went into the edition (1867). See N. John Hall, *Trollope and his Illustrators* (1980), 114–23.   RCT

Thomas, John, Post Office clerk who rises to the rank of Postmaster General, but who fails to win Mary Tompkins. 'Never'   GRH

Thomas, Mrs, woman who keeps a small school and takes Mary Snow as her pupil with a 'duty to inculcate in her pupil love and gratitude' toward Felix Graham (XXXIII). *OF*   MT

Thompson, Fanny, prudent young widow in Le Puy for her elder daughter's education. She finally accepts the proposal of M. Lacordaire, although he is only a tailor. 'Polignac' *TAC1*   GRH

Thompson, Sir Henry (1820–1904), 1st Baronet (1899); Emeritus Professor of Clinical Surgery, University College Hospital, London. An advocate for cremation, he held a meeting of prominent people, Trollope among them, in January 1874, out of which emerged the Cremation Society of England (1874). Thompson became its President. Cremation became legal in 1884. Trollope's *The Fixed Period* (1882) supports the practice, though with somewhat equivocal argument.   RCT

Thompson, Jane, younger sister of Mrs Brown who is engaged to the unfortunate Mr Jones. 'Thompson' *WFF*   GRH

Thompson, Lilian, 15-year-old elder daughter of Fanny Thompson at school in Le Puy. 'Polignac' *TAC1*   GRH

Thompson, Mimmy, 13-year-old daughter of Fanny. Pretty and playful, she forwards her mother's romance with M. Lacordaire. 'Polignac' *TAC1*   GRH

Thompson, Mr, Silverbridge Superintendent of Police who sympathetically escorts Revd Josiah Crawley and his wife to appear before the magistrates over the matter of a stolen cheque. *LCB*   NCS

Thompson Hall, family home at Stratford-le-Bow where Mrs Brown longs to spend Christmas. 'Thompson' *WFF*   GRH

Thomson, James (1700–1748), poet famed for *The Seasons* (1726–30), which Trollope read aloud to his family in February 1877. He listed Thomson among his eighteen 'giants' of English literature in *The New Zealander*.   RCT

Thomson, William (1819–90), entered the Church (1843); Archbishop of York from 1862 until his death. Addressing Huddersfield Church Institute (October 1864) he attacked the immorality of current fiction, his speech widely reported in the press. A *Times* leading article (3 November) supported the prelate, reversing itself one day later. Trollope's lecture 'On English Prose Fiction as a Rational Amusement' (1870) is a counterblast with direct reference to Thomson. 'A bishop gets up now and then to lecture against novels . . . Sometimes we have novels attacked in sermons' (*Four Lectures*, 95–6).   RCT

Thorne, Henry, wild younger brother of Thomas Thorne who consorts with the Barchester working class. He seduces Mary Scatcherd, fathering her illegitimate daughter, and is killed by her brother Roger. *DT*   NCS

Thorne, Mrs Martha (née **Dunstable**), 30-year-old heiress of the 'Ointment of Lebanon', worth a fortune from sale of a patent medicine, and thus an attractive marriage target. Intelligent, perceptive, witty, and strong-willed, she knows her position and her adversaries. She appropriately deflects proposals from Gustavus Moffat, George De Courcy, and Frank Gresham, becoming good friends with the latter and advising him to remain true to Mary Thorne. In *Framley Parsonage* she avoids the addresses of Nathaniel Sowerby and Mr Supplehouse, and marries Dr Thomas Thorne; in *The Last Chronicle of Barset*, she encourages the suit of Johnny Eames. *DT*   NCS

Thorne, Mary, illegitimate niece of Dr Thomas Thorne of Greshamsbury. Permitted, despite her unknown antecedents, to share the education of the Gresham girls, she demonstrates independence and moral sense. Proud, generous, intelligent, and spirited, with animation transcending conventional beauty, she devotes herself to her uncle, tempers the impetuosity of her lover Frank Gresham, and accepts the unfair treatment of his mother Lady Arabella. Avoiding the attentions of Sir Louis Philippe Scatcherd, she finally becomes a great heiress. *DT*   NCS

Thorne, Mrs Maude (née **Hippesley**), daughter of Dean Hippesley of Exeter, niece of Sir Francis Geraldine, and the most cherished of Cecilia Western's friends. She exhibits common sense toward her friend and her uncle, and about marriage in general. *KD*   NCS

Thorne, Monica, spinster sister of Squire Thorne of Ullathorne and a 'pure Druidess'. Ten years older than her brother, she caricatures all his foibles. Living according to the modes and culture of the century before, she organizes the great fête at Ullathorne and attempts to make a match between Eleanor Bold and Mr Arabin. *BT*   NCS

Thorne, Dr Thomas, Greshamsbury doctor, formerly of Barchester, and second cousin to Squire Thorne of Ullathorne. A kind, proud,

skilled physician, he raises his brother's illegitimate daughter as his niece. He ministers to Lady Arabella Gresham, despite her arrogant tantrums, and serves her husband, Squire Gresham, as friend and financial adviser. Friend and doctor to the Scatcherds, he tries unsuccessfully to save Sir Roger and his son from alcoholism. He refuses to interfere in the affair between his niece and Frank Gresham, though he finally becomes the means by which she attains her inheritance. In *Framley Parsonage*, he marries the great heiress Martha Dunstable. *DT*, *LCB*   NCS

Thorne, Wilfred, squire of Ullathorne, a contemporary representation of Feeling's Squire Western. Proficient in 18th-century literature and genealogy, an unflinching conservative, and a sportsman, he falls under the spell of Signora Madeline Neroni though is less enchanted by her daughter. *BT*, *DT*, *FP*, *LCB*   NCS

Thoroughbung, Joshua, young brewer in Buntingford who marries Mary Annesley. A keen huntsman, Mr Thoroughbung is triumphant at the Cumberlow Green meet. Harry Annesley is fond of his good-natured future brother-in-law. *MSF*   MT

Thoroughbung, Matilda, middle-aged single woman whom Peter Prosper hopes to marry. 'Miss Thoroughbung was fat, fair, and forty to the letter, and she had a just measure of her own good looks, of which she was not unconscious. But she was specially conscious of twenty-five thousand pounds, the possession of which had hitherto stood in the way of her search for a husband' (XXVI). She refuses to relinquish her financial independence to marry the foolish Prosper. *MSF*   MT

Three Clerks, The (*see next page*)

Thumble, Caleb, itinerant Barchester clergyman who exists on crumbs of patronage from Mrs Proudie. A little man, about 40, humble to his superiors and condescending to his inferiors, he is sent by Mrs Proudie to relieve Revd Josiah Crawley of his parish duties and later appointed to the clerical commission investigating the disgraced clergyman. *LCB*   NCS

Thwaite, Daniel, like his father (Thomas) a tailor and political idealist. He 'hated the domination of others, but was prone to domineer himself' (XXI). His love for Lady Anna is uninfluenced by her inherited title and wealth. Although willing to give up his beloved should she request it, he resists all attempts by the

(*cont. on page 527*)

WHEN Trollope wrote this novel, he was recalling his life as a junior Post Office clerk in London. Two strands of narrative are interwoven: the romantic entanglement of the three clerks of the title with the three daughters of a clergyman's widow, and their contrasted careers in the civil service. Henry Norman, reserved and moralistic, and his friend Alaric Tudor, intelligent, charismatic, and nakedly ambitious, are clerks in the prestigious Weights and Measures; while Alaric's young cousin Charley Tudor, a good-natured scamp, has a post in the notorious Internal Navigation. Through Norman's family connection, they spend their weekends at the widowed Bessie Woodward's cottage at Hampton, in the company of the somewhat worldly eldest daughter Gertrude; the affectionate Linda; and Katie, who is little more than a girl.

The romantic and the professional are linked through the theme of competition. Henry Norman is doubly wounded by Alaric Tudor's success in marrying Gertrude, who will inherit from Uncle Bat, and in triumphing in the civil service examinations. Alaric Tudor's career founders in corruption. He is manipulated by Undy Scott, a rapacious, upper-class stockjobber, into the fraudulent conversion of his ward's fortune, and finds himself on trial at the Old Bailey. Gertrude stands by him, and after a short term of imprisonment he emigrates with his young family to Australia, where he is last heard of working as a humble bank clerk. Henry and Linda accommodate themselves to disappointment, and find happiness with each other. On his marriage and inheritance, Henry Norman resigns from the civil service, ensuring that his post will go to Charley Tudor. The relationship between Katie and the scapegrace is a convincing presentation of first love, with its beginnings in an act of rescue on the Thames. Katie's recovery from a lengthy illness and Charley's moral reformation coincide with his promotion to the illustrious Weights and Measures, and after their marriage he continues his second career as a writer of popular fiction.

The Three Clerks draws heavily on Trollope's own experience. There are Alaric Tudor's early family bereavements, his period as an assistant in a school in Brussels, and the way that family influence gets Alaric his appointment. But the parallels are closer in Trollope's treatment of Charley Tudor, which includes several echoes of his early life. There is the exact correspondence of the farcical examination of his clerical competence by the writing out of pages of Gibbon's *Decline and Fall*, of which no official notice is taken thereafter. In *An Autobiography* Trollope records how difficult it was for a young man to live on £90 a year (Charley's salary); and Charley's arrest for debt to a tailor mirrors almost exactly Trollope's own youthful dealings with a London tailor, which led him into the clutches of a moneylender. Mrs Davis's comic pursuit of Charley, in her role as surrogate mother to her barmaid Norah Geraghty, into the offices of the Internal Navigation was written directly from Trollope's similar embarrassment at the hands of an outraged mother. However, these episodes do not read like interpolations; rather they give the novel detailed physical and psychological specificity.

Another influence was Dickens. On the opening page of *The Three Clerks* Trollope defends the reputation of the Weights and Measures in direct opposition to Dickens's satire on the civil service in his Circumlocution Office in *Little Dorrit*, which had been serialized between 1855 and 1857, at the time when Trollope held the rank of surveyor in the Post Office. Trollope's attitude to the civil service was conservative, and although in the novel he admits realistically to deficiencies in the Internal Navigation, he supports the service staunchly. However, his hobby-horse was the competitive examinations, introduced as a result of the 1853 *Northcote–*Trevelyan Report. He was against a meritocratic system on the grounds that it encourages careerists, such as Alaric Tudor, in preference to gentlemen like Henry Norman.

Dickens is also referred to explicitly later in the novel, when Trollope compares the villainy of Undy Scott and Bill Sikes, arguing that while the crimes of Dickens's underworld criminal proceed from social deprivation, for the likes of Scott, with all his advantages, there could be no excuse. The influence of Dickens may be seen too in the creation of the bluff Captain Cuttwater, and in the symbolic use of landscape and milieux, such as the Wheal Mary Jane mine, and the river Thames; and also in the uncharacteristically tight narrative pattern. A further, unconscious, influence on the themes and unusual structuring of *The Three Clerks* may have been Trollope's reading of the satiric city comedy *Eastward Ho!*, by Jonson, Chapman, and Marston.

The Three Clerks anticipates *The Way We Live Now* in the range of the novelist's targets, but central is the City, and in particular speculation. There is Undy Scott's endeavour to manipulate share prices through the corruption of public officials such as Alaric Tudor, but there is the more legitimate flotation of the Limehouse and Rotherhithe Bridge venture, which everyone, including the parliamentary committee that examines it, knows is merely a pretext for speculation on the company's share price. The operation of the law also scandalized Trollope, and his anger is directed at its adversarial nature, a theme he returns to in *Orley Farm*. The lawyer who attracts Trollope's disgust in that novel is introduced for the first time in *The Three Clerks*, the great defence attorney Mr Chaffanbrass. Trollope's rage at Chaffanbrass's badgering honest witnesses into confusion, and seeking to secure the freedom of the guilty in pursuit of his professional fee, is balanced by his fascination with the nature of the man. Mr Chaffanbrass is one of Trollope's great characters: dirty, unkempt, wig awry; but a true ham, confident of his forensic skill and of his ability to hold the court with his charismatic power; at home, ironically, he is domesticated and henpecked. The climactic scene at the Old Bailey when Undy Scott is cross-examined, is superbly achieved.

At the moral centre of *The Three Clerks* is Mrs Woodward, Trollope's favourite character; independent, living on terms almost of equality with her daughters, protective of them, and emotionally vulnerable. Her judgement turns out to be the truest. She is uncomfortable with Alaric Tudor, and not on terms of complete intimacy with Gertrude. Charley Tudor gains her sympathy, love, and forbearance, but not at the expense of Katie's happiness, which requires her vigilance. Henry Norman is her favourite, though his virtues emerge only slowly, in an increasingly convincing characterization. He recognizes his own intellectual limitations and admires his successful rival; is an agent of Charley's redemption; and finally extends financial support to the floundering Alaric Tudor. But honest, true, and generous though he is, he remains something of a prig, lacking in romantic energy, and unable to forgive Alaric for winning Gertrude.

Stylistically, *The Three Clerks* depends on Trollope's unusual employment of parody. It parodies the form of the 'Excelsior' myth, as we are insistently reminded, and also the sentimental love story. Like Trollope, Charley Tudor the clerk wishes to pursue a second literary career, and he reads his romantic tale 'Crinoline and Macassar' to the assembled company at Surbiton Cottage. Essentially it parodies works that depend on plot, sensation, moralizing, and tragic effects, emphasizing by contrast the disturbing, shifting realities of the larger world of *The Three Clerks*. And there is also an element of comic self-parody in the figure of the aspiring author.

The Three Clerks was written between 15 February 1857 and 18 August 1857. This was the second novel for which Trollope produced a work schedule, and he managed on average between 24 and 27 sheets per day, though he notes that he took one month off with a 'Bad foot'. The novel was published by his mother's publisher Richard Bentley, in three volumes, in December 1857, for which he received £250. During 1855 and 1856 Trollope was working on a non-fictional work, *The New Zealander*, in which he examines mid-Victorian society; but a chapter which did not survive may have been used instead in the first edition of *The Three Clerks*, under the title 'The Civil Service', which gives his views at length and in detail. When the novel went into a second edition in January 1859, this intrusive chapter XII of the original volume 2 was dropped. After some discussion, in the 1860 edition the 'Crinoline and Macassar' chapters were retained.

The novel's reception was somewhat varied. His friends the Brownings both enjoyed it, and Thackeray praised it highly, subsequently inviting him to contribute to the *Cornhill*. Some reviewers were surprised by Trollope's departure from the style of *The Warden* and *Barchester Towers*, while *The Times* called it 'a really brilliant tale of official life' (23 May 1859, 12). The manuscript is not extant.   GH

Countess, the Lovels, and their legal representatives to prevent his marriage. After marrying, he and Lady Anna emigrate to the Antipodes. *LA*
RC

Thwaite, Thomas, tailor of radical political sentiments who befriends the Murrays. He despises Earl Lovel and spends much of his income defending Josephine and her daughter Anna. He nevertheless encourages his son to respect the class differences between themselves and the Murrays/Lovels. *LA*   RC

Thwaite Hall, Garrow residence in Westmorland. 'Mistletoe' *TAC2*   GRH

Tichborne case (1873–4), one of the age's sensational soap opera mysteries. Edward Fitzgerald claimed that it fascinated him almost as much as *The Eustace Diamonds* and Trollope on board ship to Australia had to borrow a newspaper to follow the case. Spin-offs included comic songs, burlesques, and a model in Madame Tussaud's. The affair concerned an ancient baronetcy and Hampshire estates of Sir Roger Charles Tichborne (1829–54?), who had disappeared. About ten years later Arthur Orton, son of a Wapping butcher, appeared in Wagga Wagga, Australia, claiming to be the missing heir. He was tried for perjury in one of the longest trials in English history and jailed for fourteen years. Charles

*Reade used the Tichborne case for his novel *A Wandering Heir* (1872). Trollope had fun with it in *John Caldigate*, having his hero pass through Wagga Wagga. Recalling Orton's run for the big prize he has Euphemia Smith, seeing her hopes for a fortune evaporate, say, 'I'd sooner have fourteen years for perjury, like the Claimant' (LV). Loans to Orton were reportedly £20,000, the sum Caldigate paid to the importunate Crinkett. Reference is also made to the case in *The Way We Live Now* (LXXVIII). In *An Old Man's Love* there is a pub called the Claimant's Arms.
RCT

Tickle, Jemima, spinster companion of Matilda Thoroughbung and about twenty years her senior. Her remaining in the household is a condition Matilda imposes on her suitor Peter Prosper. *MSF*   MT

Tickler, Tobias, 43-year-old widowed preacher of Trinity Church, Bethnal Green, with three children, who marries Olivia Proudie. *FP*   NCS

Tierney, Mat, sporting associate of Lord Ballindine, who broaches the news that Fanny Wyndham has broken her engagement with Lord Ballindine. He is later used by Lord Kilcullen, who hopes his jovial presence at Grey Abbey will buffer him against his father's eloquence. *KOK*
MRS

Tifto, Major, member of the Beargarden Club, master of the Runnymede hounds, and dishonest sporting companion of Lord Silverbridge. During Lord Silverbridge's sporting days, the dubiously respectable Major Tifto seems a fit companion, but as Silverbridge matures, entering politics and leaving the turf behind, the Major's friendship becomes increasingly burdensome. Tifto ultimately destroys his position by deliberately laming Prime Minister, the horse that he and Lord Silverbridge intended to run at the St Leger. *DC*
JMR

Tilley, Arthur Augustus (1851–1942), son of Sir John Tilley by his second wife Mary Anne Partington; admitted to the bar (1876) and made fellow of King's College, Cambridge, the same year. Trollope wrote to him (December 1881) of *Barchester Towers*, 'There is not a passage in it I do not remember' (*Letters* 2, 933). RCT

Tilley, Sir John (1813–98), Post Office employee, surveyor (1838); Assistant Secretary (1848); Secretary (1864–80); married Trollope's sister Cecilia (1839). After her death (1849) he married Mary Anne Partington, who died about a year later, three weeks after the birth of their son Arthur. Tilley married once again; his third wife Susannah Montgomerie died in 1880. Tilley and Trollope were close friends. Tilley was godfather to Fred Trollope and helped with the practical details of publishing *Barchester Towers*. Proximity in their official lives caused strains, aggravated by the paranoia of Rowland *Hill, Secretary. They clashed over a pay demand for surveyors (1864), Trollope clinging like a terrier as usual to the bone of contention. In a letter to the Postmaster General, Lord *Stanley, he cast Tilley as 'very like Bumble' and the surveyors as charity boys asking for more (*Letters* 1, 281). Yet they remained friends. Tilley, an austere, reserved man, enjoyed his brother-in-law's robust energy, sometimes vacationing with the family. When Trollope retired, Tilley's response was copied into *An Autobiography* (XV). Trollope was dining with the Tilleys when his fatal stroke occurred. RCT

Tillietudlem, Scottish borough represented variously by Undy Scott and Mr M'Buffer. *TC*
MT

Time. Edmund *Yates edited this magazine, in which T. H. S. *Escott published 'A Novelist of the Day', an interview with Trollope, in 1879. Escott asserted that Trollope had enriched English letters with novels that would become 19th-century classics. He later became editor of the *Fortnightly Review* 1882–6; Trollope was partly responsible for the appointment. Escott became Trollope's first biographer. JWM

Times, The. Founded in 1785, *The Times* became within its first quarter-century the most influential newspaper in the world. John Thadeus *Delane, who edited *The Times* from 1841 to 1877, believed that 'whatever passed into its keeping becomes a part of the knowledge and the history of our times'. Trollope's attitude toward *The Times* was ambivalent. Although 'moved . . . very much' in 1848 to learn that *The Kellys and the O'Kellys* was to be 'noticed in that most influential of "organs" ', he was displeased that the notice had been arranged by a friend who had been 'dining at some club with a man high in authority among the gods of *The Times*'. The notice also proved a disappointment in its comparison of *The Kellys and the O'Kellys* with 'legs of mutton . . . substantial, but a little coarse' (*Auto* IV). However, as Trollope remarked in *The New Zealander*, he regarded it as 'his duty as an Englishman' to read *The Times*, and what he read there often prompted him to take up his pen. Angered, in 1849, by a series of letters in *The Times* charging that the government had not done enough to relieve the famine in Ireland, he responded with a series of letters in defence, published in the *Examiner*. The plot of *The Warden* is to some extent based on reports in *The Times*, from 1849 on, concerning the distribution of the endowments of the Rochester Cathedral School. In *The Warden*, the fictitious paper that orchestrates public outrage is named the *Jupiter*, and is described as 'Mount Olympus—that high abode of all the powers of type, that favoured seat of the great goddess Pica . . . from whence, with ceaseless hum of steam and never-ending flow of Castalian ink, issue forth eighty ['fifty' in earlier World's Classics editions] thousand nightly edicts for the governance of a subject nation' (XIV). The thunderous leading articles of the *Jupiter* are written by Tom Towers, who reappears in *Barchester Towers* and *Framley Parsonage*. In a generally favourable review of *The Warden* and *Barchester Towers*, *The Times* rebuked Trollope for satirizing actual individuals. Trollope acknowledged that the *Jupiter* was a parody of *The Times*, but denied that the character of Tom Towers was based on Delane or anyone else connected with it. In 1859, *The Times* published a laudatory overview of Trollope's fiction; in 1860, it strongly endorsed the controversial opinions expressed by Trollope in *The West Indies and the Spanish Main*. Trollope acknowledged that these articles significantly advanced his career, even though, when approached by their author, E. S. *Dallas, Trollope denied that he owed Dallas any personal obligation (*Auto* VII). Several more notices of Trollope's work, most of them by Dallas, appeared in the 1860s; in the early 1870s, Trollope's books were usually reviewed in *The Times* by either F. N. Broome or George Dasent. Most of these reviews were more favourable than not: for example, in its review of *Orley Farm*, *The Times* praised its 'tragic force', even while protesting Trollope's strictures against lawyers and law courts. In 1871, the paper declined Trollope's offer to contribute a series of travel letters from Australia: Mowbray Morris, manager of *The Times*, wrote that the paper could not afford Trollope 'ample space and verge enough to develop your subject in such a manner as to do justice to your own style and mode of treatment', and the letters, signed 'Antipodean', appeared instead in the *Daily Telegraph*. Trollope had satirically asserted, in *The New Zealander*, that the 'threat' of writing a letter to *The Times* had become 'the common and immediate resource of impotent anger', and indeed, in 1874, when Trollope believed he had been overcharged during a European railway journey, he was recompensed after airing his complaints in three indignant letters published in *The Times*. By then, *The Times* had come to concur in Trollope's increasingly dark view of English society: although most other periodicals responded with anger to *The Way We Live Now*, the review by Lady Barker, the wife of F. N. Broome, defended the novel as 'only too faithful a portraiture of the manners and customs of the English at the latter part of this 19th century'. It has been suggested that one character in *The Way We Live Now*—Mr Booker, editor of the fictitious *Literary Chronicle*—was based on Alexander Innes *Shand, who in 1877 contributed a laudatory discussion of Trollope's novels to the *Edinburgh Review*. From 1876 on, Shand also wrote the unsigned notices of Trollope's books that continued to appear regularly in *The Times*. In the late 1870s, however, the paper agreed, along with most other periodicals, that such novels as *The American Senator*, *Is He Popenjoy?*, *Cousin Henry*, and *The Fixed Period* were inferior to the earlier fiction. Already, in the unpublished manuscript of *An Autobiography*, Trollope had described *The Times*, along with the *Saturday Review* and the *Spectator*, as having the critical 'weight' to determine reputations (*Auto* X), and certainly *The Times* was influential in assessing Trollope's career. The day after Trollope's death, *The Times* published an unsigned essay, actually written by Mrs Humphry Ward, which denied that Trollope could be included in the first rank of novelists; rather, it assigned him, along with Jane Austen, to 'the head of the second order'. Ten months later, in two articles by Shand, *The Times* enthusiastically welcomed *An Autobiography*, which it described as 'extremely frank' and even 'sensational'. By the time Rose

Trollope died in 1917, *The Times* could confidently assert that Trollope's widow had 'lived long enough to see his reputation . . . perhaps even more securely established than at the height of his popularity during his lifetime'.   PTS

Tinsley, William (1831–1902), partner in Tinsley Brothers, publishers, founders of *Tinsley's Magazine* (1867). They published *The Golden Lion of Granpère*.   RCT

Tintagel. Between this Cornish town and Bossiney Mally Trenglos and her grandfather live. 'Malachi' *LS*   GRH

'Tireless Traveller, The' (twenty-article series).

1. Rome. The Italian government must conquer its deficit, balance income and expense, to flourish. Crime thrives, due to insufficient police and inadequate verdicts. The government has put down the Church, and created resentment and lack of support.

2. Aden. The trip through the Red Sea is hot and tedious. The costs of Suez are enormous—travellers, not investors, will profit. Aden is remarkable for its scenery and the racial mixture of the inhabitants.

3. Colombo. Galle (pop. 47,000), a major port of Ceylon, is a stopping-off point for travellers to the Orient; one's laundry is done in six hours. It is 72 miles from the capital, Colombo, and marked by heat, hawkers of jewellery 'bargains', and many races (Arabic, black, Tamil, Sinhalese) and religions (Muhammadan, Hindu, Buddhist, Christian).

4. Colombo. Ceylon railways and roads are very good; there is documented history of the country to 500 BC. There is a sacred Bo tree here, and ruins of ancient temples. Coloured people outnumber whites 100 to 1, creating difficulties. Universal suffrage is an impractical ideal; it would cause white desertion, and the renewed misery of the coloureds. The lawyers are dishonest and exploitative.

5. Colombo. Kandy, in the north, is a clean and pretty place (pop. 17,000). It could be Eden; there is a beautiful 200-acre public park. A great Buddhist temple with a 'tooth of Buddha' is here (not open to the public). The tooth (wrapped in cloth and a silver case) is undoubtedly false; Portuguese Christians destroyed the original as an idol. The temperature is perhaps more moderate than in the south, but it is still hot.

6. Point de Galle. Coffee is the mainstay of the Ceylon economy; the increasing price encourages the cutting of forests for new plantations. There are many stories about the decline of elephants

due to development. Tea is beginning to be a significant product.

7. Melbourne. Western Australia ('Swan River') is not well known; the land is poor. The agreement to accept British convicts was humiliating (it is no longer done), but probably saved the economy. It is regarded in other areas as disreputable. Living is difficult here. There are many aborigines here—ugly but good-natured people—there is no hope of civilizing them.

8. Melbourne. The writer has been frequently criticized by the inhabitants for a book published three years ago; nothing but praise was wanted. The best 'colonies' are places for the labouring classes to thrive with reasonable effort. Rich people can get along anywhere. The Australian colonies are proving successful as a place for honest immigrants.

9. Melbourne. Much Australian wealth comes from gold in Victoria. The costs and risks of mining are high; many have lost everything, even their lives; these facts are not proving a deterrent. As this source of wealth decreases, other economic bases are needed.

10. Melbourne. There is twice Montreal's population here already—an amazingly fast growth. Wages are good; there are virtually no street beggars; the cost of living is a bit high, but schools are free for all children. There are fewer social distinctions than in England.

11. Sydney. The proposal to annex New Guinea is a bad idea; the population is savage; there is no motivation for the English to settle there. There is no possible livelihood for the working classes.

12. Sydney. There is civic rivalry between Sydney and Melbourne. Sydney is the most attractive of large cities. The land is poor, but adequate for the thriving wool business. The taint of the criminal past is all but gone.

13. Sydney. Local gold production is so expensive as not to be profitable. The sheep/wool business is much more economical. There are many very rich sheep breeders ('squatters') here—the country gentlemen of Australia. They generally begin by leasing land, buying as their income permits. Fire is the greatest danger, as summers are extremely hot and dry. The great distances between homesteads require the maintenance of large stores of staples.

14. Sydney. Rural labourers can earn adequate money but the work is tedious and isolated. Food and quarters are provided, so virtually all earnings are savable. No alcohol is allowed during work periods; but binge drinking between jobs is common.

15. Sydney. Colonial administrators know land is the best inducement for responsible settlers; this fact has caused difficulties here. Long-term

leases are always subject to buyouts by 'freeholders', who can break up large tracts. Limits on the size of purchases are also problematic.

16. Sydney. Tasmania (once Botany Bay and Van Diemen's Land) still lives under the shadow of the criminal past. South Australia is a major sheep/wool producer; it is also good land for wheat. The present farming methods exhaust the soil within years. Much copper is mined here. Adelaide is one of the pleasantest towns in Australia. Queensland is an enterprising, wealthy colony of loud-mouthed people. There are many Chinese immigrants here; they work hard and do not mind the heat. South Sea Islanders are imported for sugar plantation work, which is not suitable for white men.

17. Sydney. Fiji's annexation is the source of some dispute; England has enough colonies for its needs; more would be burdensome. Fiji is a less promising colony than New Zealand was. The Fiji natives are of two sorts: blacks with 'crisp' hair, as in Australia, and Polynesian people with 'lank' hair, as in the islands east of Fiji. The current Fiji King sent a war-club as a gift to Queen Victoria; he has acknowledged Fiji must yield or be defeated and absorbed.

18. Sydney. Some control is needed for English subjects, 'gone half-wild' by long absence from home. They retain enough of civilization to work at converting the natives, but lack discipline. England is now poised to annex New Guinea, but must not take on too much. Exploiters come with the settlers, and treat the natives basely. Some argue annexation could lead to the protection of minorities. The polarization of the natives and the British government must be stopped.

19. San Francisco. New mail routes are being developed between Sydney and the south-west. Doubtless cheaper, faster routes will be found. Honolulu is remarkably superior to other savage-ruled towns. The present government system works well.

20. New York. San Francisco is not a very interesting city; the stock market is the liveliest place. The dependence on personal trust in business matters is truly astonishing. The trip to Yosemite valley was tedious, but the scenery there was worth the trip. The train trip eastward across the nation was very pleasant except for the lack of bathing facilities. *Pall Mall Gazette* (3 August–6 September 1865); reprinted 1866.

AKL

Todd, Miss Sally, jovial friend and feisty travelling companion of Miss Baker and Caroline Waddington, and one of the Littlebath ladies courted by Sir Lionel. Said to be modelled on the

Victorian feminist Frances Power Cobbe, Miss Todd is endowed with 'commanding genius and great power of will', and is most amenable when 'allowed to do exactly what she liked' (XXII). She proves an equal match for her insincere suitor, answering his feigned tenderness 'with terrible loudness, with a shaking of her sides' (XXXI). *B*
MRS

Toff, Mrs. An old family retainer, the head housekeeper of Manor Cross is turned out by the Marquis of Brotherton when he tires of her reports on his life to his mother and sisters. She is taken in at Cross Hall. *IHP*
MG

Toffy, Mr. Head constable in the investigation of Farmer Trumbull's murder, he derides the inefficiency of other police officers. Highly suspicious of Sam Brattle and often baffled in his enquiries, he eventually brings the real offenders to justice. *VB*
SRB

Tolstoy, Count Leo Nikolayevich (1828–1910), Russian novelist, essayist, moral philosopher. While writing *War and Peace* in 1865 he noted in his diary, 'Read Trollope [*The Bertrams*]. If only there was not diffuseness. Excellent.' Shortly afterwards he noted, 'Trollope kills me with his virtuosity. I console myself that he has his skill and I have mine' (quoted Hall 401 n.). He also admired *The Prime Minister*. Tolstoy owned eleven of Trollope's books in *Tauchnitz editions.
RCT

Tombe, Mr, John Grey's lawyer. He helps arrange the financial ruse wherein George Vavasor accepts funds from Mr Grey's account rather than from his cousin Alice's to aid him in his parliamentary aspirations. When confronted by George Vavasor, the lawyer cleverly avoids telling him anything about the arrangement. *CYFH*
JMR

Tomkins, Mary. Wooed by two lovers she refuses both, despite urgings of her friends, and then embroiders her gown 'Old Maid'; she is a burlesque character recalling Lily Dale. 'Never'
RCT

Tomlinson, Mary (née **Scatcherd**), Barchester apprentice bonnet-maker and sister of Roger Scatcherd. Seduced by Henry Thorne, she gives up her daughter Mary to marry a hardware dealer and emigrate to America. *DT*   NCS

Toneroe, farm in Co. Mayo leased by Martin Kelly from Lord Ballindine. *KOK*   MRS

Toodlum, country home of George Whitstable, which qualifies him to become the successful suitor of Sophia Longestaffe. *WWLN*   SRB

Toogood, Mrs Maria, wife of London lawyer Thomas Toogood and concerned mother of twelve living children who call her 'Thais'. *LCB*
NCS

Toogood, Thomas, good-hearted and affable London lawyer, first cousin of Mary Crawley and uncle of John Eames. A cheery-looking man of 50 with grizzled hair and large whiskers, partner in the successful and respected firm of Crump & Toogood, he makes considerable effort out of his own pocket to aid Revd Josiah Crawley and eventually solve the mystery of the stolen cheque. *LCB*
NCS

Tookey, Fitzwalker, lawyer who becomes a diamond speculator. Having made and lost several fortunes in South Africa, he is John Gordon's partner in the Stick-in-the-Mud claim. He reputedly purchased his second wife, Matilda, from her husband. Their union yields three neglected children and is marred by alcohol and violence. *OML*
RC

Tookey, Matilda, wife of Fitzwalker Tookey, allegedly purchased from her previous husband with diamonds. She deserts Tookey for a man named Atkinson, but returns when the latter is imprisoned in Cape Town. The couple plans to return from England to the diamond fields and their three children in South Africa. *OML*   RC

Towers, Tom, influential journalist of the London newspaper the *Jupiter* and intimate friend of John Bold, who thinks him the author of the paper's attack on Mr Harding. Bold visits the young sybarite at his Temple chambers and learns of attacks by Dr Pessimist Anticant and Mr Popular Sentiment. Towers keeps in the background, but considers himself Europe's most powerful man because of the *Jupiter*. Also a friend of Obadiah Slope in *Barchester Towers*, Towers devises, on a slow news day, an editorial supporting Mr Slope's candidacy for dean of Barchester. In *Framley Parsonage* he surprisingly attends Martha Dunstable's London gala. *W*
NCS

Townsend, Revd Aeneas, shabbily dressed Protestant vicar in the Catholic parish of Drumbarrow, regarded by some as 'a good man, but a bad clergyman' (X) on account of his extreme hatred of Catholicism. His prejudices are put to the test when relief work for the Irish famine forces him to team up with the priest, Father Bernard. As he comes to recognize the priest's contributions, animosity yields to friendship. *CR*
MRS

Townsend, Meredith White (1831–1911), co-editor with R. H. *Hutton of the *Spectator*

from 1860. He wrote an unfavourable review of *The Prime Minister* (July 1876) which wounded Trollope, thinking it the work of Hutton whose opinion he respected. Townsend was usually hard on Trollope. Reviewing *The Way We Live Now* (June 1875) he found its atmosphere sordid and its characters uniformly unpleasant, from Roger Carbury, 'an overbearing prig', to Melmotte, 'a mere brute' (Smalley 397–400). RCT

Townsend, Mrs, friend of Letty Fitzgerald, and wife of the vicar of Drumbarrow, whose anti-Catholic rhetoric is even more extreme than her husband's. *CR* MRS

Tozer, Tom, younger brother of the infamous Tozer clan of London bill-discounters, also known as Mr Austen, junior, for respectability. A bull-necked, beetle-browed rogue, Tozer and his brother harass Nathaniel Sowerby and Sowerby's victims, including Mark Robarts, to collect on notes they have acquired. *FP* NCS

tradesmen as characters. In *Orley Farm* Trollope reveals his familiarity with the special arrangements available for commercial travellers at hotels, and his series of essays entitled *London Tradesmen* displays extraordinarily detailed knowledge of a variety of trades. The first essay is called 'The Tailor', and tailors appear frequently in his novels. In *The Three Clerks* Charley Tudor's inability to settle his tailor's account echoes Trollope's own debt to a tailor, incurred while a young clerk in London.

Drawing on Francis Place, the famous 'Radical Tailor of Charing Cross', Trollope associates the trade with revolutionary politics, most obviously in Daniel Thwaite in *Lady Anna*, who wishes to marry his childhood friend, Lady Anna Lovel, against the fanatical opposition of her mother the Countess. Daniel Thwaite's actual trade is avoided to a large degree, and Trollope solves the problem of introducing a committed radical into society by having the couple emigrate to Australia.

Elsewhere tailors are used as fictional shorthand for political danger. The Baslehurst Liberal candidate standing for Parliament in *Rachel Ray* is described as a 'Jew tailor from London' (XXIV). In *Doctor Thorne*, when Moffat, the son of a tailor, puts up as a candidate in Barchester, the opposition taunt him with his background in trade; while a caricature of a radical tailor is put into the Marquis of Kingsbury's pocket borough in *Marion Fay*.

Social discrimination within trades interested Trollope. The aptly named Neefit, the breeches-maker in *Ralph the Heir*, prides himself on serving the hunting fraternity, but he is sometimes tempted by his gentlemen's unpaid bills to swallow his pride and descend to the level of a mere tailor. This pride encompasses matters of social class generally. Neefit is portrayed as a social climber, who fails to purchase gentility by persuading the heir, Ralph Newton, to marry his daughter Polly. This association of land and trade is usually more successful, as it is in *Doctor Thorne*, where money demolishes scruples and Squire Gresham does not withhold his consent to his daughter Augusta's marriage with the tailor's son, Moffat.

The social aspiration of tradesmen is frequently a source of comedy. In *Miss Mackenzie*, Mr Rubb's mimicking of gentility fails absurdly. His cheap romanticism and lapses of taste (excessive compliments and yellow gloves) do not deceive Miss Mackenzie as to his proper social sphere. A more extensively drawn comic figure is the bootmaker Ontario Moggs in *Ralph the Heir*, who stands for election for Percycross as a radical, with the slogan 'the rights of labour'. Ironically his speeches are warmly received by the town's workmen because they are perceived as coming from a capitalist with radical sympathies. Lacking the self-awareness of a gentleman, Moggs is living in a dream world, and never escapes caricature.

Wherever possible the brewing trade assumed middle-class status, hunting with the landed gentry when permitted, as Ned and Frank Botsey, the Norrington brewers, do in *The American Senator*. Or it sought to consolidate the social ground gained, as in *Mr Scarborough's Family*, where a minor character, Joe Thoroughbung who belongs to a wealthy brewing family, hunts with the gentry of the Essex (Trollope's own hunt), and marries a rector's daughter.

Regarded as not quite gentlemen by Victorian society, the brewers' ambivalent social position is explored most thoroughly in that very class-conscious novel *Rachel Ray*. Tappitt (Trollope could not resist a pun, and the brewery is called Bungall & Tappitt), for whom business is competition, profit, and status, is contrasted with Luke Rowan, who intends to descend from a gentleman (he has a professional background in the law) to a brewer. Although Luke challenges his mother to define the term 'gentleman', Trollope seems to be arguing that he is a gentleman brewer partly because of his social background, and ownership of the brewery, but partly also because he takes genuine pride in the craft.

Apart from *moneylenders, of whom there are several in Trollope, among them Samuel Hart in *Mr Scarborough's Family*, Jabesh M'Ruen in *The Three Clerks*, and Mr Clarkson in *Phineas Finn*, Trollope reserved his particular venom for commercial travellers. In *Orley Farm* he savagely criticizes salesmen such as Moulder, who travels for Hubbles & Grease, dealers in tea, coffee, and brandy, and Kantwise, who sells metallic furniture, for their duplicity, materialism, and vulgarity. And with satirical scorn, he reduces the legal profession to the level of trade, when Moulder approvingly equates his salesmanship for Hubbles & Grease with the attorney Mr Chaffanbrass's advocacy on behalf of Lady Mason.   GH

Traffick, Augusta (née **Tringle**), self-important, bossy elder daughter of Sir Thomas and Lady Tringle. At age 24, she marries the considerably older Septimus Traffick MP, an accomplishment that must, she thinks, spark envy in the likes of penniless Ayala Dormer. Instead, Ayala is mildly appalled. *AA*   WK

Traffick, Septimus, second son of Lord Boardotrade, member of Parliament for Port Glasgow. Forty-five years old, he is 'somewhat bald, somewhat grey, somewhat fat' (V), and wholly devoted to saving every penny of the £120,000 Augusta Tringle brings with her on their marriage. *AA*   WK

Trafford, Lady Frances (Fanny), strong-minded, spirited daughter of the Marquis of Kingsbury. Her love for the postal clerk George Roden proves her democratic principles. She determines to marry him despite her family's objection, including that of her brother Lord Hampstead who is a close friend of Roden. Social obstacles are removed when it is eventually discovered that Roden is the Duca di Crinola. *MF*   SRB

Trafford, Lord Augustus, Lord Frederic, and **Lord Gregory,** the three sons of the Marquis and Marchioness of Kingsbury. Flaxen-haired, boisterous, and born 'absolutely in the purple', they love 'Jack', their elder brother Lord Hampstead, but the Marchioness hates him for standing in Frederic's way. Presumably, however, Frederic will become heir when Hampstead, at the end of the novel, chooses a solitary life after the death of his love, Marion Fay. *MF*   SRB

Trafford Park, grand estate in Shropshire of the Marquis of Kingsbury. The atmosphere is generally very disagreeable because of family squabbles between the Marquis and his chaplain Mr Greenwood, and between the Marchioness and her stepchildren Lord Hampstead and Lady Frances. *MF*   SRB

transportation and travel. Trollope was always a traveller. His childhood moves were thrust upon him—from Harrow, to Sunbury, to Winchester, back to Harrow, then in young manhood to Brussels, to Bruges, to London before the major move to Ireland. This conditioning became a lifetime habit, an indulgence, a professional discipline, with holidays fuelling fiction, Post Office journeys practical decisions, travel books, more fiction. The restless, zestful pattern began with the Tramp Society—'we wandered on foot about the counties adjacent to London. Southampton was the furthest point we ever reached: but Buckinghamshire and Hertfordshire were most dear to us' (*Auto* III). Next came riding throughout Ireland on horseback and in jaunting-cars, then return to England and professional dedication to his tasks in the south-western counties, where he went almost everywhere on horseback, averaging 40 miles (64 km) a day. European excursions followed, at first in the carriage/diligence, then on the faster and more comfortable railway; the 'new' telegraph was used to reserve hotel rooms. Several of his travel experiences are mentioned in *An Autobiography*. On a visit to Verona, for example, Trollope, Rose, and brother Tom were greeted at the station 'by a glorious personage dressed like a beau for a ball', with three carriages and much ceremony. It was the first time the hotelier had ever received a telegram (VI).

Journeys grew longer, itineraries more complex. By the time he visited the Middle East to negotiate a postal treaty with Egypt, the importance of the steamship is shown in his recognition of the P. & O. Company's role in the more efficient carrying of mail, but Trollope the traveller had to experience the sheer physicality of life in the area, the sores from a Turkish saddle, the ascent of the pyramid, the touristy wanderings on foot and mule contrasting with 'the accustomed haste and comfort of a railway'. On the visit to the West Indies and Central America (1859), he went to Cuba in a 'wretched sailing vessel', explored Mount Irazu in Costa Rica, went down the Serapiqui by canoe, and took a sailing vessel from Bermuda to New York. His exploration of the United States and Canada in 1861–2 included an evaluation of travel in railway cars and an ascent of Mount Washington on a pony. He enjoyed the steam boats on the Mississippi and, with reservations, the street cars in New York. In Canada he and Rose 'went with the mails on a pair-horse waggon'. The North American experience was for him partly a celebration of the New World's technological advances. In Australia and New Zealand (1871–2) he got plenty of riding on the sheep stations, but also travelled over the bush roads by Cobb's coaches and noted the widespread use of horse-drawn light buggies, though he himself found travelling on horseback 'the pleasantest mode'.

He was fascinated by the telegraph, undertaken for the whole colony by South Australia (1871–2), with the submarine line to Java, Singapore, and 'home to Europe' being 'in other hands'. Although he walked much in New Zealand, he also appreciated the 'well appointed coaches'. In 1877 came his last major, perhaps most ambitious journey, to South Africa. He went to Pieter Maritzburg on a coach which had a back carriage of 'the waggonette fashion' and observed with amusement the difficulties caused by a passenger carrying a very large and smelly fish. Trollope rode out to English and Boer farms on his own, but unflagging interest in the postal service also prompted him to go by mail cart from Pieter Maritzburg to Newcastle: it 'took two and a half days on the journey, and was on the whole comfortable enough'—this from a man who weighed sixteen stone (100 kg) and had less than three years to live!

In England as an adult, he had witnessed major changes in transportation. Carriages ranging from the phaeton and brougham to the post-chaise and dog-cart continued to be the emblem of status. Trollope owned a brougham in later years. Carriages could be rented from livery stables, but to hire one—witness Lady Alexandrina De Courcy's horror in *The Small House at Allington*—was a sign of social inferiority. Trollope began to travel more often on trains than by coach or horseback, and devised his own writing support (see POSTAL MUSEUM, NATIONAL) on which he could work as well as at a desk; on ocean steamships a similar device was often set up for him. His fiction registers the change after the introduction of the railways in the 1830s, with Paddington, Victoria, and Waterloo often mentioned, as is the underground in the 1860s and 1870s. His letters to the *Liverpool Mercury* in 1875, published by Bradford Booth as *The *Tireless Traveller* (1941), were sent by telegraph, the latter's widespread use probably established by the Crimean War. Always travelling, always working, always communicating, he took holidays with Rose, if the word 'holiday' could be accurately applied to the determined researcher of fact and the inspired delver for fiction. The later years, the postal professionalism over, were frenetic with journeys, with the second familial visit to Australia taking in, for example, Ceylon, and then the annual Swiss (and sometimes French) trip with Rose and Florence Bland, his niece/amanuensis. The latter accompanied him to Ireland—this after a stay in Florence—on his very last journey (May–June 1882) to undertake research for *The Landleaguers*. Living through a period of phenomenal change, Trollope recorded it all, up-to-the-minute, enthusiastic, forward-looking. The writer of fiction is also a major commentator on the facts of his society, its technological advances part of his creative experience, his professional decisiveness, his mirroring of progress. See also HOLIDAYS ABROAD; 'TRAVELLING SKETCHES'. GRH

'Transvaal 2' (letter). Please correct yesterday's account of the address, the report of the 'European' population in Transvaal; the word used was 'British'. *The Times* (17 January 1878), 10. AKL

'Travelling Sketches' (eight-article series).

1. 'The family that goes abroad because it's the thing to do.' A late summer trip, even to Margate, is now part of family routines. Unfortunately often the family has no plan or goal or only a vague 'educational' aim. Fathers suffer much, carry the parcels, and pay for all; mothers worry, and behave crossly; daughters begin joyfully, try everything, look at everything, and become exhausted. The main pleasure too often is returning home. The learning is superficial but probably good.

2. 'The man who travels alone.' The bachelor with few internal resources, travelling alone, generally has a bad time of it. He frequently becomes a nuisance trying to join other travellers who do not wish additional company.

3. 'The unprotected female tourist.' This is an admirable woman, who generally knows what she is about, and can make conversation easily. She has a good time and learns much whether by herself or with others. She is alert to social possibilities but not dependent on them. Men find her conversation fascinating, but her independence frightening.

4. 'The united Englishmen who travel for fun.' Groups of young men are less serious about their travel than people of other ages or nationalities. Casual, sometimes rough, not intentionally rude, they are essentially gentlemen in the making. They cause little harm, though ruining their clothes; they gain some sense of self and the world from travels. They remind their elders of their earlier, lighthearted selves.

5. 'The art tourist.' This person is earnest, persevering almost beyond reason; he rushes from museum to gallery, memorizing and concentrating without seeming to enjoy anything. He mistakes knowing for understanding. He rarely bothers others, but becomes narrow and unappreciative of beauty.

6. 'The tourist in search of knowledge.' He is determined to make something of the trip, and of himself, in the process. He is diligent but boring, evaluating all that he sees—what good has this done to anyone? How much? How many? He knows the facts and figures and statistics of every

place. Women in this group are less annoying than men; they read by themselves, and ask questions softly.

7. 'The Alpine Club man.' This rugged outdoorsman knows how to hike and climb, and takes ropes and blankets. Accidents occasionally happen, sometimes fatal. Some excitement of the adventure comes from the peril. He lives for the joy; defeat leads to another effort; this attitude is admirable.

8. 'The tourists who don't like their travels.' Some want to have done things, but take no pleasure in the doing. Frequent causes of unhappiness are unfamiliarity with languages and over-ambitious schedules. Driven by guidebooks, racing against the calendar wears one out. While ignorance of French is acceptable, it is disgraceful (and foolish) to pretend fluency. Language proficiency is good; honesty is better. Mountains, valleys, and museums do not require another tongue. *Pall Mall Gazette* (3 August–6 September 1865); reprinted as *Travelling Sketches* (1866).

AKL

Trefoil, Arabella, stately, graceful, scheming woman who has become shopworn from her years on the marriage market. A cold fish who wants status, not love, from a man, she works hard at husband-hunting, showing great pluck despite her unhappiness. She tries to snare Lord Rufford while engaged to John Morton. Because Morton is the only man who never betrayed her, she confesses her betrayal to him on his deathbed. His legacy enables her to marry Mounser Green. He is far below her but the marriage frees her from having to appear 'gay in order that men might be attracted' (LXXVI). *AS*   MG

Trefoil, Lady Augustus, daughter of a banker married to the younger brother of the Duke of Mayfair. She abets her daughter Arabella in her matrimonial pursuits but her unlikeable personality is also a hindrance. She cannot understand her daughter's good nature and scruples. *AS*
MG

Trefoil, Lord Augustus. Younger brother of the Duke of Mayfair, his only interest in life is whist. Having spent her fortune, he no longer lives with Lady Augustus. When he is forced into a reluctant confrontation with Lord Rufford on his daughter Arabella's behalf, he proves his oft-stated uselessness. *AS*   MG

Trefoil, Dr, elderly, inoffensive, and ineffective 80-year-old Dean of Barchester, whose death of apoplexy leads to another conflict between the Grantly and Slope factions over the deanship. *BT*
NCS

Trefoil, Miss, spinster daughter of Dean Trefoil of Barchester, learned in stones, ferns, plants, and vermin. *BT*   NCS

Tregear, Francis (Frank), Lady Mary Palliser's determined suitor. The second son of Squire Tregear of Polwenning, Conservative Frank Tregear successfully stands for his family's home borough of Polpenno. Though the young Duke of Omnium is suspicious of the penniless Tregear's interest in Lady Mary, the young man's intelligence and spirit, and his successful stand for Polpenno, eventually win him the Duke's respect as well as the hand and fortune of his daughter. *DC*   JMR

Tregothnan Hall, Mudbury Docimer's country house, two miles (3 km) from Penzance. *AA*
WK

Tremenhere, Mary, pretty, flighty girl who jilts George Western and marries the younger and richer Captain Walter Geraldine. *KD*   NCS

Trendellsohn, Anton, the one man in Prague who could lead his people out of social isolation into the freedom Jews enjoy in western Europe. Anti-Semitism makes him reserved and suspicious, yet he responds to Nina's gentle sympathy. Persuaded by the Zamenoys to doubt her, he tests her loyalty. When he finds what he thinks is proof of her betrayal, he retreats in cold bewilderment, only to discover she loves him more than life itself. *NB*   AWJ

Trendellsohn, Stephen. Despite his love for Anton and his kindness to Nina, he cannot accept his son's marriage to the Gentile. Bound by racial tradition, he is scrupulously fair, allowing Anton the fruits of his labours in the family business when the pair leave for a better life in Frankfort. *NB*   AWJ

Trenglos, Mahala (Mally), wild 'mermaid' of a girl who works tirelessly gathering seaweed to support her grandfather, saves Barty Gunliffe's life, and later marries him. 'Malachi' *LS*   GRH

Trenglos, Malachi (old Glos), seaweed gatherer, in old age and poor health dependent on his granddaughter Mally. 'Malachi' *LS*   GRH

Tressel, Linda. Taught to resist worldly temptation, she means to live virtuously. But when her aunt insists she marry Steinmarc for her soul's welfare, she cannot suppress her disgust. Their unrelenting campaign drives her to Valcarm, but escape to Augsburg shatters that romance. Convinced of her sinfulness, she sinks to near-madness as she struggles between obedience to the aunt she loves and repulsion for her loathsome suitor. She breaks free, but never recovers her health and spirit. *LT*   AWJ

Tretton Park, John Scarborough's estate in Hertfordshire, an essentially industrial estate, in which a town and pottery works have been established. *MSF*   MT

Trevelyan, Sir Charles Edward (1807–86), Assistant Secretary to the Treasury (1840–59). With Sir Stafford Northcote and advice from Benjamin Jowett he produced 'Organization of the Permanent Civil Service' (November 1853), recommending competitive examinations for entrants. Trollope satirized him in *The Three Clerks* (XI) as Sir Gregory Hardlines, which became his family's name for him. Later Trevelyan became a friend of Trollope's and contributed 'Army Reform' to *Saint Pauls* (May 1869). He joined Trollope and others at a special meeting in John Murray's office (February 1870) to debate the Anglo-American copyright problem.   RCT

Trevelyan, Emily (née **Rowley**), eldest daughter of Sir Marmaduke Rowley and wife of Louis Trevelyan. Strong and self-willed, she resents her husband's suspicions concerning her friendship with Colonel Osborne. Despite their continuing love and shared knowledge that she has not been unfaithful to him, neither will compromise. Their minor quarrel escalates until she is separated, first from him and then from her son. She returns to her husband only when mental and physical decline have brought him to death's door; she confesses wrongdoing only to placate a dying man. *HKWR*   RC

Trevelyan, Louey, son of Emily and Louis Trevelyan. He becomes a silent and morose child. As a result of his parents' dispute, he is taken by his mother to Clock House and to St Diddulph's-in-the-East; and by his father to River's Cottage and to Casalunga. After his father's death, he remains in Twickenham with his mother. *HKWR*
                                                        RC

Trevelyan, Louis. A young man with a substantial fortune and no living relatives who looks like the perfect son-in-law. When he marries Emily Rowley, at the start of *He Knew He Was Right*, he appears set to be a model of success: an intellectual, he could have been a fellow of his Cambridge college but instead chose to occupy the time until he felt ready to go into Parliament by a life of gentlemanly study; a man about town, he has the knack of never seeming too bookish.

It is marriage that tests out Trevelyan and the world of ideas that he represents, until what seemed like a mere flaw, a certain wilfulness in his disposition, produces a crisis in which his sanity and his life are lost. He cannot tolerate what he takes as his wife's refusal to obey him when he forbids her to receive the visits of Col-

onel Osborne, an old roué but a friend of her father's. Sexual jealousy is only the ostensible excuse for Trevelyan's wish to absorb all his wife's attention. Emily Trevelyan resists the feeling of shame that he tries to impose on her, a resistance that he insists on interpreting as rebellion. With few close friends, Trevelyan seems insensitive to the ordinary decencies, perhaps because these are learned through intimacy rather than taught as abstractions. He takes a series of ill-advised decisions, sending his wife away and setting a detective to spy on her, then snatching back his son and removing him to an isolated farmhouse in Italy. These moves, which bring on his own breakdown and death, act out an alienation that, as the novel suggests, underlay this ideal example of Victorian masculinity from the start.   MH

Tribbledale, Daniel, clerk who languishes for the love of Clara Demijohn when she decides to marry Samuel Crocker instead. Tribbledale's 'poetical soul' and slightly higher income triumph in the end, and he wins Clara. *MF*   SRB

Trigger, Mr, Mr Griffenbottom's 'confidential agent' for the election at Percycross who also manages Sir Thomas Underwood's campaign. His underhand financial deals, sweeteners, and bribes ultimately cause the borough to be disenfranchised. *RH*   ALS

Tringle, Lady Emmeline (née **Dosett**), wife of Sir Thomas Tringle and mother of Tom, Augusta, and Gertrude Tringle. A kind-hearted woman who wishes everyone well, Lady Tringle suffers great inconvenience from Tom's love for Ayala Dormer, Gertrude's infatuation with Frank Houston, and Augusta's marriage to the freeloading Septimus Traffick. *AA*   WK

Tringle, Gertrude, foolish younger daughter of Sir Thomas and Lady Tringle. Thwarted in her desire to marry Frank Houston, she elopes to Ostend with the equally dim-witted Captain Benjamin Batsby. Thwarted again, she finally marries the Captain, in a double wedding with Lucy Dormer and Isadore Hamel. *AA*   WK

Tringle, Sir Thomas, Baronet, husband of Lady Emmeline Tringle, and uncle of Lucy and Ayala Dormer, a partner in Travers & Treason, Lombard Street. Extremely wealthy, with country houses in Scotland and Sussex and a mansion in Queen's Gate, London, Sir Thomas is nevertheless a sympathetic figure, much troubled by the romantic foolishness of his son Tom and daughter Gertrude, as well as the sponging habits of his son-in-law Septimus Traffick. *AA*   WK

Tringle, Tom, son of Sir Thomas and Lady Tringle, a 'stout and awkward looking' young

Marcus Stone's illustrations for *He Knew He Was Right* are effective, atmospheric accompaniment to the novel, as this drawing 'Trevelyan at Casalunga' proves. Stone has caught the solitary man brooding over his wrongs amidst the arid landscape of his Italian retreat: 'its look of desolation was extreme' (LXXVIII).

man who is also 'good-natured and true' (V), despite his fondness for wearing flashy jewellery. When Tom's sincere love for Ayala Dormer proves hopeless, his despair leads to drunkenness and assault of a police officer. In the end, Sir Thomas packs Tom off to America, where his complete recovery and eventual marriage are expected. *AA*   WK

Trollope, Anthony (1815–82). Four major biographies up to the 1960s, led by Michael Sadleir's pioneering *Trollope: A Commentary* (1927), laboured under the shadow of *An Autobiography* (1883), a work which for all its plain speaking was a masterpiece of the disguise and concealment essential to any writer. Four major biographies of the modern period have read between the lines more subtly, uncovered more documented information, and enabled us to see him more clearly as man and artist. We know more about his parents, his wife, his family, his social life, his Post Office career, and his emergence as a great novelist. More than ever before we can appreciate his place in Victorian culture.

Anthony Trollope was born on 24 April 1815 at 16 Keppel Street, Bloomsbury, the fifth child of Thomas Anthony, a barrister, and Frances Milton, a clergyman's daughter. They married on 23 May 1809, when Frances (Fanny) was 30 and her husband 35. The Trollopes had seven children between 1810 and 1818, only three of whom reached adulthood. Their first child, Thomas Adolphus, was named to honour a wealthy kinsman, Adolphus Meetkerke, in whom lay expectations of fortune. Meetkerke owned a large estate in Hertfordshire called Julians.

The Trollopes came of a long line of clergymen, naval and army officers, and country gentry. Thomas Anthony's first cousin, Sir John Trollope, was the 6th Baronet, of Casewick, near Stamford, Lincolnshire, and the Trollope lineage could be traced back to the 1300s. A legend linked the family name to an ancestor credited with slaying three wolves thereby acquiring the name 'trois loups'. Unwisely, Anthony told this tale at school and was ragged unmercifully for it. 'It is the nature of boys to be cruel,' he laconically observed, long after the event (*Auto* I). But lineage mattered among the Trollopes. Thomas Anthony maintained a liveried footman at Keppel Street; his successful son had the family crest of leaping stags engraved on his notepaper. Birth and pedigree were to be major fictional concerns, to which events in childhood added a deeper theme: loss of place and fortune occasioned by mischance and character flaw.

The circumstances of Anthony's childhood, arising from his father's not becoming Meet-

kerke's heir and what followed when he abandoned law to farm in Harrow, are told with painful clarity in the autobiography. The narrative conveys a strong sense of loneliness and psychological trauma caused by separation from his mother and by uneasy existence with his choleric father, causing self-doubt, which haunted his life. But what in some cases might cripple an individual drove Anthony to triumph over adversity, to succeed as a civil servant, and to become a novelist second only to Dickens in popular appeal. In many ways his life story is the archetypal Victorian success story of an individual's struggle to establish identity and to live well.

The wretchedness began with his first period at Harrow School in 1823, when he was about 8. Being a day-boy carried a social stigma, and resulted in a 'daily purgatory' from his schoolmates as he trotted from home to school. In 1825 he was switched to a private school at Sunbury of which his main memory was being accused of some misconduct (presumably sexual) with three other boys of which he was totally innocent. The injustice is a central episode in the narrative of his early life which demands attention. As he wryly notes, none of the 'curled darlings' would have chosen him to share their wickedness to begin with. What wounded him was not so much his own quite unfair victimization but the dishonesty made apparent by the craven silence of the boys. Sticking to the truth in face of ambiguous sets of experiences and pressures became major issues of his fiction.

In the spring of 1827, just before his twelfth birthday, he joined Tom at Winchester, where regular thrashings from his elder brother added to the other scourges of public-school existence. Home life was largely non-existent at this period. For nearly four years from the summer of 1827 Anthony, in the years of puberty between 12 and 16, was without his mother's mediating presence in the home. She was travelling in America, creating her own life, at one point attempting to repair the family fortunes by opening a bazaar in Cincinnati selling British-made trinkets, sent by her bemused husband, who followed her to America in September 1828. For over six months Anthony was without both parents and endured awful loneliness: 'I had no friend to whom I could pour out my sorrows . . . how well I remember all the agonies of my young heart; how I considered whether I could not find my way up to the top of that college tower, and from thence put an end to everything?' (*Auto* I).

In 1829 another move, to a dilapidated farmhouse in Harrow Weald, meant further strain for Anthony, shunted back to Harrow School, once again a social pariah, and facing a daily trek of

Trollope was about 40 years old when this photograph was taken, not yet known as a novelist but a valued official of the Post Office. Already he is very bald and sports a huge beard approaching its full pepper-and-salt magnificence.

twelve miles (20 km) to and from school—'dreadful walks'—he recalled, which made this final phase of his schooling the worst period of his young life. At home, his father, dependent on calomel to relieve blinding headaches, was increasingly prone to outbursts of violence. In the midst of this turmoil Trollope began making up stories, stretching his imagination to create 'castles in the air', in which he could make friends, control events, and resolve the muddle of real life. From the age of 12 he kept a diary, he told his friend and first biographer, T. H. S. *Escott. At 15 and for ten years he kept a journal. Such activities relieved his isolation, and, more significantly, began a process of developing observation and expression through the written word.

When *An Autobiography* appeared, some contemporaries—his brother among them—felt that Trollope had drawn too dark a picture of his childhood. Escott noted Trollope's own admission about the diary as 'a friendless little chap's exaggerations of his woes' (T. H. S. Escott, *Anthony Trollope* (1913), 16). This may well be so, but does not affect the impression modern readers have of psychological burdens Trollope carried all his life. Certainly there were happy times and modest successes in the early years, signs of scholarly abilities, which are downplayed if not forgotten altogether. The persuasive rhetoric of *An Autobiography*, with its focus on idleness and want of 'moral courage' (*Auto* I), tends to obscure the narrative's 'novelistic' Copperfield theme of triumph over adversity. Whether Trollope exaggerated or not is immaterial. The modern reader will recognize that the tension of his chronically disordered home life was one catalyst of his art. It inspired a desire for order and a balanced mind while recognizing that self-fulfilment was hardly won and precariously held in the face of inconsistency and misadventure. Events in the next phase of his growth to maturity validated these intimations of what was to work for, endure, or overcome.

Attempts to enter university failed, and Trollope, now 19, had to find a career. Family circumstances, briefly improved by the success of Fanny Trollope's *The Domestic Manners of the Americans* (1832), now plunged towards catastrophe. Thomas Anthony's ruin, through the disastrous farming venture, and errors surrounding the marriage settlement and deeds of the Keppel Street house, led to sudden ignominious flight to Bruges in April 1834, and the utter collapse of his health. Two of the children, Henry and Emily, were in the grip of consumption. Henry died in December, and Emily less than two months later. Although he avoided that particular Victorian scourge, Anthony was seriously ill twice in the

formative years, once in 1834 and again in 1840. While Frances Trollope coped with her sick family, writing late into the night to keep some money coming in, it was vital for Anthony to find work. Briefly it seemed that he might be commissioned in an Austrian cavalry regiment, but his mother's influence brought an opening in the General Post Office. On 4 November 1834, Trollope became a junior clerk at St Martin's-le-Grand at a salary of £90 a year.

For almost seven years in London, by his own admission, he was aimless, uncommitted, and far from industrious, at odds with his boss, W. L. *Maberly, and frequently on the carpet. He became seriously in debt, and was once involved in an embarrassing sexual entanglement. Something of his hobbledehoy existence was recreated in *The Three Clerks* and *The Small House at Allington*. In *An Autobiography* he accuses himself of self-indulgence and idleness. Readers are not taken in by this. If his official life was unfocused, his personal life and cultural horizons were broadened by exposure to London itself. Soon after his appointment he began keeping a 'Commonplace Book' making notes on his omnivorous reading. This indicates growing self-discipline. On 5 October 1837, sponsored by his friend John Merivale, he applied for a reader's ticket to the British Museum Reading Room. Some 39 years later he requested a ticket for his elder son, who, he suggested, shared his love of books. Such endeavours, combined with writing official reports, and occasionally acting for his mother with publishers, steered him towards his future vocation. But the lengthy process and uncertainty of the goal frustrated him, and he was constantly goading his superiors in the Post Office, beset by duns, twice taken up for debt, and once harried by a woman in the office demanding, 'Anthony Trollope, when are you going to marry my daughter?' (*Auto* III).

An opportunity to wipe the slate clean occurred when he became surveyor's clerk in the Central District of Ireland. He arrived in Banagher, Co. Offaly, on 19 September 1841, and his life changed. He began to take official work seriously. He met and married Rose Heseltine. They had two sons, Henry Merivale (b. 1846) and Frederic James Anthony (b. 1847). And in July 1845 he completed his first novel, *The Macdermots of Ballycloran*, which had originated two years previously when his imagination had been stirred by a ruined house at Drumsna, Co. Leitrim. *The Macdermots* and several more works were failures. As the Great Exhibition of 1851 approached, he wrote to his mother that he intended to exhibit four three-volume novels—'all failures—

which I look on as a great proof of industry at any rate' (*Letters* 1, 22).

A long apprenticeship to writing ensued, while increasing official responsibilities demanded more of his time and energy, but a turning point came in early summer of 1852, when the idea for *The Warden* came to him as he wandered in the vicinity of Salisbury Cathedral 'whence came that series of novels of which Barchester, with its bishops, deans, and archdeacons, was the central site' (*Auto* V). Publication of *Barchester Towers* in May 1857 brought intimations of future success. To make the most of his time and eradicate poor work habits he evolved a programme from which he hardly deviated until late in life. On train journeys for the Post Office he made a portable tablet for his manuscript (see POSTAL MUSEUM, NATIONAL). He kept a diary recording the number of pages written each day. At home he rose at 5.30, setting himself to produce, with his watch in front of him, 250 words (one page of his racing hand) every quarter of an hour for about three hours. He could produce on average about 40 pages of copy at a sitting, although the figure could sometimes fall to 20 (see WORKING HABITS OF TROLLOPE).

Literary prestige came at a time roughly parallel with success as a public servant. From 1851, when his reports from the Channel Islands led to the use of roadside pillar letter boxes, he was increasingly entrusted with missions throughout Britain. In July 1855, his testimony before a parliamentary committee earned commendation. In 1857, the year *Barchester Towers* appeared, his 'History of the Post Office in Ireland' was part of the Postmaster General's annual report. Official missions of greater responsibility followed, to the Middle East in 1858, and the West Indies in 1859, the latter resulting in his first travel book. The miseries of school and the frustrations of early manhood in London were behind him. Hailed by E. S. *Dallas in *The Times* as the star of Mudie's Circulating Library, he could now address those ghosts of his childhood, his dread of poverty, his longing for friendship, and recognition from the outside world of his identity and worth.

The security Rose inspired, and the centring of his life in home and family, is now recognized as the springboard of his public career and mature art. It is significant that in one wing of his beloved Waltham House, Hertfordshire, he conducted meetings of Post Office colleagues, while in another he pursued his writing and private life. Besides running a household with five servants, Rose read and copied out his manuscripts. To what extent she influenced the writing process is impossible to determine, and comparatively little is known of her, although recent biographers have brought her out of the shadows. Undoubtedly she had a strong character and the couple were good companions.

In the early 1860s Trollope consolidated his twin careers. Granted leave from the Post Office, he travelled to the United States between August 1861 and March 1862, meeting distinguished politicians, writers, and publishers, and producing a second travel book, *North America* (1862). In the mid-1860s Trollope extended his activities in journalism, notably in the promoting and organization of the *Pall Mall Gazette* and the *Fortnightly Review*. His public service also increased, with lecturing and committee work for the Royal Literary Fund. His rise in literary terms was phenomenal. 1859/60 was a crucial year, when *Thackeray invited Trollope to write for George *Smith's new journal, *Cornhill Magazine*. Here his fourth Barsetshire novel, *Framley Parsonage*, was serialized. On its publication in book form the *London Review* commented: 'Mr Trollope has now got his foot fairly in the stirrup.' Publication of *Orley Farm* (1861/2), the first of his novels issued in parts, prompted the *Saturday Review*'s comment that no one had ever drawn English families better, a sentiment echoed by the *Reader* when *The Small House at Allington* appeared (1863/4). His income from fiction rose swiftly in the 1860s. For *Orley Farm* he received £3,135; for *Can You Forgive Her?* (1864/5) £3,525. Figures over the £3,000 mark were achieved for *The Last Chronicle* (1867), *Phineas Finn*, and *He Knew He Was Right* (both 1869). The sums were proudly set down at the end of *An Autobiography*.

Trollope's need for the approval of his peers was satisfied by membership of several clubs, first the Cosmopolitan, to which he was elected in 1861. In this haunt of politicians and editors amidst the late evening cigars and gossip he found material for the political and social themes which broaden the scope of later fiction. His second and favourite club was the Garrick, to which he was elected the following year. Here among actors and writers he found the popularity he craved. Thackeray, who seconded his nomination, was its presiding genius, and soon Trollope was roaring amidst the whist-players. In 1864 Trollope was accepted by his third club, the Athenaeum, where among its distinguished churchmen, he wrote regularly in the long drawing-room, and was supposed to have decided the fate of Mrs Proudie. Seeing his son Harry elected in 1882 was a great joy in the last year of Trollope's life. Several other clubs played a part in Trollope's social round, the Arts, the Civil Service, and the Turf. At a meeting of the Alpine Club in June 1862, he declined membership in an after-dinner speech, claiming that time and flesh were against him. The Reform invited him to join in 1874 and he was late in life sought by the United Services Club (see LONDON: CLUBS). His public service roles expanded too, with lecturing and committee work for the *Royal Literary Fund, which involved much letter-writing and consultation. The year 1867 saw publication of *The Last Chronicle of Barset*, for many readers, and for Trollope himself, the pinnacle of his literary endeavours to date. He had by now published nineteen novels, two travel books, three volumes of short stories, three collections of essays, and many articles.

Comfortably off, well established in his twin careers, he could organize his life efficiently, keeping to his obsessive writing schedules, meeting requirements of his office superiors, and taking Rose for holidays in Europe. During a visit to Italy in the autumn of 1860, Trollope met Kate *Field, an American, whose personality and independent spirit captivated him. With some 23 years' difference between them, it was possible for Trollope to play flirtatious uncle without too much of a problem for Rose, and next to Rose she was undoubtedly his closest female friend, influencing his depiction of several spirited American women in his fiction.

The male friendship Trollope had longed for was found on the hunting field as well as the club. Hunting, which he had taken up seriously in Ireland, remained his favourite sport for the rest of his life. From Waltham he rode with the Essex hounds, but would willingly send horses to other counties when opportunity arose. He wrote articles about hunting, and frequently included hunting scenes in his novels. He rode fearlessly despite poor eyesight, in January 1875 taking a fall that could have been fatal. He had finally to dispose of his horses three years later (see HUNTING).

These varied activities and relationships filled his need for outside approval, but family ties were his anchor: Rose and his comfortable house, and close relations with his sons. Henry was a confidant close at hand, steadily becoming more interested in literary affairs. Fred, who had been in Australia since 1865, returned for a visit in December 1868. The focus of Trollope's second visit to Australia in 1875 was to spend time with Fred at his sheep station. Now 60, Trollope was in his prime, successful public man and author, and, according to many accounts, the epitome of John Bull. He had the physique to match. At five feet ten inches he weighed fifteen stone (95 kg), and dieting did not prevail. The pleasures of the table and convivial society were always dear to him. He loved fine food, wine, and cigars.

The public persona was firmly established, giving rise to scores of anecdotes and some misunderstandings. Ever since Ireland he had been loud, boisterous, and hyperactive. In conversation he had developed a Johnsonian relish for tossing and goring. If he overdid the bluster it was often with a secret pleasure in disturbing the peace or teasing the over-serious, as when he offended an earnest clergyman up at John Blackwood's place in Scotland by his unkempt appearance, coarse language, and unruly antics on the golf course. Frederic Harrison's observation of the novelist at one of George Eliot's austere Sunday gatherings perfectly captures that combination of bluff integrity and showing off. Talking of his fictional production line, Trollope savoured the reactions to a tale told many times. Eliot blanched. There were days when she could barely write a line. Trollope immediately discounted his work as mechanical—sheer industry: 'It's not the head that does it—it's the cobbler's wax on the seat and the sticking to my chair!' Unable to resist an extra frisson, Harrison added that Trollope accompanied his explanation 'with an inelegant vigour of gesture that sent a thrill of horror through the polite circle there assembled' (*Studies in Early Victorian Literature* (1895), 203).

Trollope could be crude and he was certainly loud, but those who knew him well saw a gentle side, a man ready to listen and a genuinely kindly personality. In small homely gatherings, friends like the Revd W. Lucas *Collins found a much quieter man. He recalled, after Trollope's death, the author at Waltham 'very happy . . . amongst his cows, and roses, and strawberries . . . delighted to welcome at his quiet dinner-table some half-dozen of intimate friends'. In the garden on warm summer's evenings, 'wines and fruit were laid out under the fine old cedar tree and many a good story was told while the tobacco smoke went curling up into the soft twilight' (*I & R* 161) (see HOMES). Many agreed with G. A. Sala's comment that his bearish demeanour was only skin-deep (*I & R* 68). But others were baffled, as W. P. Frith put it, at the disparity between books 'full of gentleness, grace and refinement', and a man 'loud, stormy and contentious'. For all writers concealment is important.

The late 1860s were a transitional phase, as old insecurities resurfaced. Experimenting with writing three novels anonymously seems to express as much a need to re-establish an identity or prove himself as a writer without the magic name, as to get around the charge that he brought his wares to market too often. The year 1867 marks a turning point: Trollope resigned from the Post Office, disappointed at not gaining the advancement he felt he deserved, although the official reason was extra work from accepting editorship of the new *Saint Pauls Magazine*, an unwise step since he never felt comfortable in the role. Perhaps this move, too, has an element of identity crisis. Trollope chafed under his responsibilities, the magazine scarcely prospered, and he was relieved to escape from it in June 1870. However, the more serious and psychologically damaging change was running for Parliament in the election of 1868, contesting Beverley, Yorkshire, for the Liberals. 'I let that run like water off a duck's back', he said to a friend (*Letters* 1, 454), but *An Autobiography* tells a different tale of mortification and disillusionment. The miseries of canvassing, described in *An Autobiography*, are part of his novel *Ralph the Heir* (1870/1). On election day, 17 November 1868, Trollope came bottom of the poll.

Characteristically, though, the experience was put to good use in the broader social analysis of later fiction. That sense of 'alienation from one's better self' perceived in youth, as Victoria Glendinning has described it, was sharper than ever, resulting in greater subtleties of motivation and division in his fictional characters. A last task for his old masters took him to the United States to improve sea passage for the mail between London and New York (April–July 1868). The mission, which lasted 111 days, was only partially successful. This was a blow to his professional self-esteem, since he had negotiated Post Office affairs so well in the past. While in America he had another task to perform involving his personal crusade for an international copyright agreement. The mandate came from the Foreign Office, and in order to act for his country he had been presented at court. The grand ceremony at St James's Palace was conducted by the Prince of Wales on St Patrick's Day, 17 March 1868. The mission, however, was another disappointment.

A gradual decline in literary reputation marks the next phase of Trollope's life, although during the 1870s he did some of his finest work, four Palliser novels, *The Way We Live Now* (1875), and two major travel books, *Australia and New Zealand* (1873) and *South Africa* (1878). The travelling, always undertaken with such gusto, had become more exacting, but he drove himself hard with all his old curiosity, making two journeys to Australia in the 1870s and a third exhausting tour of South Africa (1877). On such trips his notebooks had to be filled, his writing schedule maintained, in addition to a full timetable of speaking engagements and public appearances. Although not outstanding as a speaker, he appeared often on public platforms promoting cultural and educational causes, such as libraries, theatres, and art galleries (see LECTURES AND SPEECHES). International affairs, largely stemming from his study of British imperi-

alism and colonialism, also occupied his time, and there were always duties for the Royal Literary Fund, of which he was a member for eighteen years. From 1880 he served on the board of Chapman & Hall after it had become a limited company. He found the work tedious in the extreme, but personal interests were involved; in 1869 he had put £10,000 into the firm to give Henry a partnership. Nothing speaks more eloquently than this period of Trollope's life to his superb endowment of physical stamina.

But more frequently he began to succumb to those blue devils of his early years, insecurity and uncertainty about his innermost being, and perhaps to feel haunted by memories of his father's chronic depressions and inability to act. The great book to come out of this growing need to wipe the slate clean and somehow validate himself and re-establish identity was *An Autobiography*, written in the mid-1870s. Here is testimony of his longing for friendship in childhood and recognition in early adult life, with the not entirely convinced balance sheet of successes, capped with the disclaimers and modest farewell of the last pages.

In December 1872, the Trollopes moved into central London, making their new home at 39 Montagu Square (Waltham having been abandoned prior to their departure for Australia in 1871). They plunged into decorating and furnishing, Trollope busy with his huge collection of books and the daily routine of writing, clubs, whist, and hunting, the last as much a passion as ever despite longer travelling from London. 'In some coming perfect world', he wrote to Alfred Austin in 1873 when the season ended, 'there will be hunting 12 months in the year' (*Letters* 2, 585). Having to give it up in March 1878 was a great blow.

Trollope was now increasingly troubled by declining health and energy. Mitigating his early rising and writing schedule, and having his niece Florence Bland write to his dictation to counter writer's cramp, he was beset by asthma and early warnings of angina. That his literary output continued more or less on the old basis is astonishing. As he told G. W. Rusden in September 1878, having just finished his eightieth tale: 'I doubt whether a greater mass of prose fiction ever came from one pen' (*Letters* 2, 792).

In summer 1880, the Trollopes moved back to the country, choosing Harting Grange, near Petersfield, on the Sussex–Hampshire border. Trollope got to work on the property with typical zest: 'I am as busy as would be one thirty years younger', he wrote, 'in cutting out dead boughs, and putting a paling here and a little gate there' (*Letters* 2, 887–8). Indoors he had his precious library to rearrange. Reading had been a passion all his life. In his early twenties he had embarked on a history of world literature for which the outline still exists. In 1866 he had begun a 'History of English Prose Fiction'. Continuing interests—European holidays, the garden, dining with friends, work for the Free Libraries Association, Royal Literary Fund, and Chapman & Hall—showed his appetite for activity. Some five years before he died he wrote to Austin: 'I observe when people of my age are spoken of, they are described as effete and moribund, just burning down the last half inch of the candle in the socket. I feel as though I should still like to make a "flare up" with my half inch' (*Letters* 2, 702). He might indeed have made his 'flare up' in high political circles, for in 1881 there was talk of a place in the House of Lords, but word got about that Trollope was too noisy.

There was plenty of other work for a still powerful man. If he was more cautious alighting from a train before it had stopped, he continued to ask a great deal of his mind and body. With *Mr Scarborough's Family*, written March–October 1881, he made something of a literary 'flare up', but he did not live to see the favourable reviews in several journals. Around Harting his presence was strongly felt. The local parson recalled him out riding in the parish, attending school management meetings, promoting lectures, and attending Holy Communion, 'an alert and reverent and audible worshipper' (*I & R* 237). Determined to have his final say on Ireland in a period of acute social unrest, he embarked on *The Landleaguers*, making two arduous trips to the country which had played such a role in his formative years.

Heart disease, looming for several years, now worsened, but he was obsessed with the new book, crossing to Ireland in May 1882. Despite medical advice he was not to be dissuaded from an exhausting itinerary. Briefly home to welcome his brother to Harting, he set off again to Ireland to gather more material for his novel. Now severe asthma attacks were more frequent, and, home by mid-September, he was uncomfortable with the dampness for which Harting was blamed, so began searching for London accommodation.

Few suspected the end was so close. In late October he visited E. A Freeman in Somerset. They took walks around Glastonbury and Wells and had their usual arguments, one of which centred on where Barchester and the beloved county existed. 'Barset was Somerset,' Trollope insisted, and 'Barchester was Winchester, not Wells'. He dined at the Garrick with Browning on 1 November, and with the Macmillans at Tooting on the 2nd, where he talked as heartily as

usual. The next day he was with the Tilleys for dinner, thoroughly enjoying after the meal the reading aloud of F. Anstey's popular novel *Vice Versa*. In the midst of the general laughter he suffered a stroke. A carriage took him to his hotel, but he had to be moved to a nursing home at 34 Welbeck Street.

The Times published thirteen bulletins as he lingered, paralysed and without power of speech, until his death on 6 December. Burial was at Kensal Green on 9 December. The inscription on his grave read 'He was a loving husband and a loving father and a true friend.'

At the time of his death three novels were not yet in book form, plus *An Autobiography*, which Henry saw through the press. In all Trollope had written 47 novels, 43 short stories, 5 travel books, 3 biographical studies, 1 classical commentary, and a vast amount of essays and reviews. It was a feat of industry few could match. A fair proportion of this had been accomplished while he was serving as a public servant. He left behind him in that sphere, as in the literary, the highest standard of probity, dedication, and devotion to human welfare and happiness.

Trollope's place among the great writers was acknowledged in 1991 with a memorial in Poets' Corner in Westminster Abbey.   RCT

Trollope, Beatrice (Bice) (1853–81). Only child of Thomas Adolphus Trollope and his first wife Theodosia, she was noted among the British community in Florence for her precocious talent as a singer. After her mother's death (1865) she lived with her Uncle Anthony and Aunt Rose at Waltham, where Frances Eleanor Ternan became her music teacher, returned with her to Florence, and married Tom (1866). A difficult child, Bice was sent to school in Brighton, and thereafter shuttled among friends and relatives, constantly at odds with her father over money matters (see *Letters* 2, 797–8). She married Charles Stuart-Wortley in Paris (1880) with Anthony and Rose present, her devoted uncle having supervised arrangements. She gave birth to a daughter in the following year, but died within two weeks. Saddened but clear-eyed as to his niece's character, Anthony wrote: 'The fault was my brothers [*sic*] in allowing her to have her own way, till her own way ceased to please her' (*Letters* 2, 919). See GARROW, THEODOSIA.   RCT

Trollope, Frances (née **Milton**) (1779–1863), Anthony's mother, herself a celebrated novelist and travel writer during the 1830s and 1840s. Known to her family as 'Fanny', she was the third daughter of the Revd William Milton and his wife Mary, née Gresley. Her father, the son of a Bristol saddler, held the living of Heckfield in

Trollope's mother, Frances, a famous novelist in her own right whose dedication and industry inspired her more talented son to embark upon a literary career. The portrait by Hervieu, *c.*1832, is in London's National Portrait Gallery.

Hampshire but at the time resided at Stapleton, a few miles north-east of Bristol. Her mother's family claimed Norman ancestry, leading her children to jest about 'the illustrious Norman blood that runs in our veins'. The children were brought up in Bristol, where their mother died in 1784. When Fanny was 22 her father, now remarried, decided to take up residence at Heckfield again, after an interval of 26 years. Fanny and her elder sister Mary remained there only eighteen months before moving to London to keep house for their brother Henry, who had become a clerk at the War Office after leaving Oxford. Their house was at 27 Keppel Street, Bloomsbury. Thomas Anthony Trollope, a barrister and a friend of Henry Milton's, lived at 16 Keppel Street. He proposed to Fanny, by letter, on 1 November 1808, and they were married six months later, on 23 May 1809, Thomas Anthony's thirty-fifth birthday. Fanny had turned 30 two months earlier. The letters they exchanged before and immediately after their marriage leave no doubt that theirs was a love-match. For the first seven years of their marriage they lived in Thomas Anthony's house at 16 Keppel Street, where four sons and a daughter were born to them: Thomas Adolphus (1810–92), Henry (1811–34), Arthur William (1812–24), Emily (born and died 1813), and Anthony (1815–82). Two more daughters, Cecilia (1816–49) and a second Emily (1818–36), were born after the family moved to Harrow early in 1816.

At Keppel Street the Trollopes enjoyed a comfortable social life, surrounding themselves with lively and interesting friends, including Italian and French exiles. Fanny, always gregarious, and proficient in French, Italian, and Latin, was free to indulge her lifelong weakness for 'clever', unconventional people. Financial losses and enforced economies, occasioned largely by her husband's folly, brought the family to the Harrow farmhouse Julian Hill, which later served as the model for Anthony's *Orley Farm*.

Again, and for the next seven or eight years, Fanny gathered a happy social circle round herself and her children, which provided some of the most abiding friendships of their lives: for example, with her neighbour Colonel Grant and his family, the Drurys of Harrow School, and their relatives the Merivales. Fanny taught her two eldest sons French and Italian, devised charades, and staged plays. In the meantime, however, both the family's financial situation and her husband's mental and physical health continued to deteriorate. The tortures her sons Thomas Adolphus and Anthony suffered as a result of their father's bad temper, pedagogical fanaticism, and killjoy gloom are feelingly recalled in their respective autobiographies (*What I Remember* and *An Autobiography*); what Fanny herself had to endure can only be imagined, although traces of it found their way into at least one of her novels, *One Fault* (1840), which may have helped inspire her son Anthony's great study of a blighted marriage in *He Knew He Was Right*. By early 1827, Julian Hill in turn had to be let, and the family moved to a decrepit house on a farm that Thomas Anthony had rented at Harrow Weald. Of Fanny's four sons, Arthur, who had always been sickly, had died in 1824, Henry had recently left Winchester and was now in Paris improving his French, and Thomas Adolphus was still at Winchester, where Anthony had just started. Fanny and her two daughters remained with Thomas Anthony at Harrow Weald. But not for long. In September 1827, on a visit to Henry in Paris, Fanny renewed her acquaintance with another Fanny, Frances Wright, a wealthy Scottish woman fifteen years her junior, who was a ward of the marquis de Lafayette and whom she had first met in Paris in 1821; Wright had later visited her at Harrow and in 1823 had introduced her and Thomas Anthony to Lafayette in Paris. In 1827 Wright had recently returned from America, where she had established a community for freed slaves at Nashoba, Tennessee. Less than two months later, on 4 November, Fanny herself set sail with Wright to join the community. She was accompanied by three of her children, Henry, Cecilia, and Emily, and a young French artist, Auguste Hervieu.

For a woman of 48 it appeared to most of her friends an act of preposterous folly, and its immediate consequences proved disastrous both for what remained of her family's capital, and for her son Anthony (who was left at home alone with his father and eventually had to leave Winchester and return as a day-boy to Harrow). For Fanny herself, as she admitted, Nashoba offered a welcome alternative to continued immurement with her husband at Harrow Weald; but it also seemed to promise employment for Henry, as a teacher, and she and her daughters could expect to live much more cheaply there than in England. She would, in addition, be serving a cause in which she passionately believed: her abhorrence of slavery was later expressed in one of her most popular and influential novels, *Jonathan Jefferson Whitlaw* (1836). And at the back of her mind must always have been the idea that, if all else failed, her travel diary of her American adventures might make a publishable, even profitable book. In the event, the three and a half years she spent in America proved a farcical, almost nightmarish disappointment of all her hopes except the last. Nashoba was found to be an inhospitable wilderness, from which even Frances Wright herself quickly fled, resettling her freed slaves in Haiti. Henry obtained no suitable employment either at Nashoba or at New Harmony, Robert Owen's socialist utopia in Indiana, to which Fanny sent him after Nashoba. And when Fanny, with optimism still undimmed, persuaded her husband to sink $6,000—perhaps the remainder of her fortune—in a 'bazaar', or shopping-centre-cum-cultural-centre, at Cincinnati, Ohio, it failed so abysmally as to earn the sardonic nickname 'Trollope's Folly'. Before and after joining her briefly in Cincinnati, and giving the madcap project his blessing, Thomas Anthony at times left her with insufficient money to support herself and her three children, so that she had to depend on Hervieu's earnings as art-teacher and painter.

Fanny arrived back in England on 5 August 1831, having stayed with an old friend, Anna Maria Stone, at Stonington, Virginia, and visited the Niagara Falls before leaving America. Her book, *Domestic Manners of the Americans*, was published the following year, when she was 53. It made her an instant celebrity, not only in England and America but throughout western Europe. During the next three years she continued to 'write, write, write', even after the family had to flee from Harrow to Bruges to escape its creditors, and even as she nursed her husband and two of her surviving children, Henry and Emily, on their deathbeds. Without the proceeds of her pen they would have died almost in poverty. *Domestic Manners of the Americans*, with its remorseless accumulation of examples of boorishness, crude egalitarianism, laughable chauvinism, and lack of civilized amenities, offended many liberally inclined readers in England, and most Americans. But Mark Twain later praised it for its 'truth' and plain speaking, and the reputation it won Fanny for sharpness of observation, mordancy of phrase, and bluntness often tipping over into 'vulgarity' launched her on a highly successful literary career that lasted until she was nearer 80 than 70. The first of her 35 novels (all in three volumes) was published the year after *Domestic Manners of the Americans*, which was also followed by another five travel books (all in two volumes). From 1838 she was prosperous enough to be able to employ her eldest son Thomas Adolphus as her 'companion and squire'. In 1842 she built a house near Penrith, Carlton Hill, which she and Tom stayed in for only a year before tiring of rustic life. For the remaining twenty years of her life she lived chiefly in Florence, from 1850 in a house usually known as the Villino Trollope which she shared with Tom, his first wife, and his father-in-law.

Her circle there included many leading expatriate writers and artists, but Elizabeth Barrett Browning 'shrank away from it' as too 'heterogeneous'. (Even Mary Russell Mitford, to whom Browning confided this information, felt constrained to acknowledge Fanny's 'terrible coarseness', although she had known her as a girl at Heckfield and thought her 'a most elegant and agreeable woman . . . wonderful for energy of body and mind'.) Fanny died on 6 October 1863, but her mind had begun to fail several years earlier and she probably remained unaware that her son Anthony's literary fame was already eclipsing hers.

Anthony's disparaging comments on his mother's conversion to Toryism struck his brother Tom as 'mistaken' (*What I Remember* (1887), 2, 332–7), and Tom would equally have thought Anthony's concluding assessment of her in *An Autobiography* (II) a little lukewarm: 'She was an unselfish, affectionate, and most industrious woman, with great capacity for enjoyment and high physical gifts. She was endowed, too, with much creative power, with considerable humour, and a genuine feeling for romance. But she was neither clear-sighted nor accurate; and in her attempts to describe morals, manners, and even facts, was unable to avoid the pitfalls of exaggeration.' On the part of a son it is hardly an over-generous assessment, though patently an honest and not unfair one. But it would have been surprising if Anthony had not seen his mother's faults, both as woman and as novelist, more clearly than Tom. He had been deprived of maternal comfort for three and a half painful and humiliating years during his adolescence—when she was in America—and though she had greeted him upon her return with unfeigned, no doubt guilty effusiveness, he was the first of the children to be put to work and was never rescued from his drudgery by his mother as Tom soon was. It is a measure of his moral strength that he largely transcended, or at least kept to himself, the resentment he must have felt. In most respects, in fact, his mother's influence on him and his feelings towards her were clearly positive and creative. She is the obvious model for the impressively forthright, strong-minded women who dominate his fiction, and for the direct, natural, unornamented prose style, avoiding mealy-mouthed euphemisms, which makes his novels so accessible to readers even a century after his death. That her own novels, in contrast, hardly outlived her can probably be attributed in part to their heavy reliance on the kind of broad comedy that was so popular in the 1820s and 1830s, but much less so in the mid-Victorian period—in novels if not on stage—and in part to their predilection for fashionable topics, often treated in a fashionably partisan, even polemical spirit. In Anthony's œuvre there are no parallels to her anti-slavery novel *The Life and Adventures of John Jefferson Whitlaw*, her 'industrial novel' *The Life and Adventures of Michael Armstrong, the Factory Boy* (1840), or her 'condition-of-England novel' *Jessie Phillips: A Tale of the Present Day* (1843): all serious, even earnest novels, still interesting historically but hardly entertaining. In the most frequently cited cases where his novels do appear to borrow characters or subjects from hers, he is hardly seen at his best: for example, in his grotesque caricatures of 'evangelical' clergymen inspired, at least to some extent, by his mother's *The Vicar of Wrexhill* (1837), and in comic subplots such as the one centring on the Widow Greenow in *Can You Forgive Her?*, which certainly owes much to his mother's most amusing novel, *The Widow Barnaby* (1839), and its sequels *The Widow Married* (1840) and *The Barnabys in America* (1843). The most famous exponents of 'petticoat government' in his novels, Mrs Proudie and Lady Glencora Palliser (the latter of whom may have been modelled more on Fanny herself than on any of her fictional creatures), become far more complex, believable, and interesting than any of the characters in Fanny's novel *Petticoat Government* (1850). Her most valuable legacy to Anthony was not what she wrote but the energy, determination, and fortitude she brought to the task of writing, the example she afforded him of what a writer could achieve by unremitting, seemingly mechanical toil, regardless of distractions, at whatever hour of the day or night.   PE

Johnston, Johanna, *The Life, Manners, and Travels of Fanny Trollope* (1979).
Trollope, Anthony, *An Autobiography* (1883).
Trollope, Frances Eleanor, *Frances Trollope: Her Life and Literary Work*, 2 vols. (1895).

Trollope, Frances Eleanor (Fanny) (née Ternan), (?1834–1913),

Member of an acting family led by her widowed mother, also Frances Eleanor, well known in London theatre. Fanny was one of three daughters, of whom the youngest, Ellen, became Dickens's mistress. Fanny went to Florence, with financial help from Dickens and assistance from Trollope, to study singing. In Paris (October 1868) she married Thomas Adolphus, Anthony being one of the witnesses. Like all Trollopes, Fanny wrote fiction, such as *The Sacristan's Household*, serialized in *Saint Pauls* (July 1868–June 1869); *Anne Furness*, serialized in *Fortnightly* (July 1870–August 1871). Trollope held a watching brief (*Letters* 2, 543). Her major contribution to the family œuvre was her memoir of Anthony's mother, *Frances Trollope: Her Life and Literary Work* (1895).   RCT

Trollope, Frederic James Anthony

(1847–1910), Trollope's younger son, born at Clonmel, Ireland, on 27 September 1847. After boarding for a year (1858–9) at St Columba's College, Rathfarnham, near Dublin, he attended St Andrew's College, Bradfield, a small new public school which had Gladstone as a member of its council, from the beginning of 1860 to 1865. There his Irish brogue earned him the nickname 'Paddy Minor', his elder brother Henry being 'Paddy Major'. He won an epic fist-fight against a bully bigger and stronger than himself, recalling his father's similar feat at Harrow (of which he was told, years later, by a former fag of his father's who like Fred himself had settled in Australia). In general he distinguished himself more as an athlete than as a scholar. When he left Bradfield, just before turning 18, his parents agreed to allow him to try his luck as a sheep farmer in Australia. They and his elder brother Harry accompanied him on a continental holiday before he set sail for Melbourne, where he arrived on 17 December 1865. For three years he worked on sheep stations in the Riverina district of New South Wales and the Western District of Victoria. Then, as previously agreed with his parents, he returned to England in the winter of 1868–9. He enjoyed the hunting there, but remained determined to settle in Australia. Soon after arriving back in Melbourne on 12 July 1869, he bought a small sheep station called Mortray, near Grenfell in New South Wales. By the time his parents came to see him in the second half of 1871, Mortray carried 10,000 sheep on 27,500 acres (11,140 ha). Trollope, who stayed with Fred from 20 October to about 12 November 1871, and again for several days in June 1872, described Mortray in chapter XX of *Australia and New Zealand*, 'Station Life in the Bush'. He also used Fred as the model for the hero of his novel *Harry Heathcote of Gangoil* (1873), written after his return to England: it shows a young squatter struggling for survival against the natural hazards of drought and bushfires, who exacerbates his problems by a 'too imperious, too masterful' demeanour towards his neighbours and employees, and a refusal to compromise with the egalitarian spirit of the bush. Harry Heathcote emigrated to Australia for the same reason as Fred: because 'Boys less than himself in stature got above him at school, and he had not liked it'. The same age as Fred was in 1871, Heathcote has a wife, and two babies the same ages as those Fred had by the time the novel was published. He is a magistrate, as Fred became in September 1872—thanks to a request made by his father to Henry Parkes, a leading colonial politician. (*HHG* I; *Letters* 2, 566). Although they were in Australia at the time,

Trollope and his wife were not present at Fred's wedding on 14 December 1871, evidently because Trollope had prior engagements in Melbourne. Fred's bride was Susannah Farrand, the daughter of the police magistrate at Forbes, not far from Mortray. According to family tradition, Trollope was very fond of his daughter-in-law but his wife patronized her. The couple eventually had eight children.

Trollope saw Fred for the last time when he visited Australia again in 1875, and it was decided that Mortray would have to be sold following a succession of bad seasons. Though he lost £4,600 of the £6,000 he had advanced Fred for the purchase of the property, he assured his elder son Harry that Fred was in no way to blame (*Letters* 2, 677–9). Soon after, Fred bought another, presumably cheaper sheep station further inland, Borroondara East, near Cobar, but said later that he was prevented from working it by ill health. His father probably lent him more money, in addition to acting as guarantor for the last £750 of the purchase price. On 19 September 1876, Fred was appointed an Inspector of Conditional Purchases in the New South Wales Land Department; he continued to work for the Department until just before his death, rising to the status of chairman of various local Land Boards at a salary of £750 a year. He was posted initially to Inverell, and subsequently to Grafton, Wilcannia, and Hay. He became a leading citizen in each place, and the judicial fairness he displayed in his work appears to have been highly admired. At Wilcannia, where he served from 1885 to 1887, Charles Dickens's son Edward Bulwer Lytton ('Plorn') was a fellow-magistrate, parochial councillor, and member of the cricket club, and Fred was a member of the Athenaeum Committee; Plorn later became MP for the district. Like his father in the Post Office, Fred complained constantly, at times publicly, about the arbitrariness and incompetence of his official superiors. Both he and his wife, who was a diabetic, suffered acutely from the summer heat in all the places he was posted to: the hotness of Hay, where they lived from 1891 to 1903, had already passed into colonial folklore. For the last two years of his life he was on leave of absence from the Land Department on the grounds of ill health. His wife died in 1909, and he on 31 May 1910, at the age of 62.

For at least seven years after his father's death, he wrote regularly to his mother and occasionally to his elder brother, but he did not see them again until 1903, when he spent several months in England on leave of absence. His mother sometimes sent him small sums of money. He named the house in Sydney that he and his fam-

ily occupied in 1883–4 and from 1903 to 1910 'Clavering Cottage', though his favourite Trollope novel was *Orley Farm*. All of Trollope's surviving descendants are descended from Fred. Two of his sons eventually succeeded to the family baronetcy. The present baronet, Sir Anthony Trollope, is his great-grandson and lives near Sydney.   PE

Edwards, P. D., *Anthony Trollope's Son in Australia: The Life and Letters of F. J. A. Trollope (1847–1910)* (1982).

Glendinning, Victoria, *Anthony Trollope* (1992).

Hall, N. John, *Trollope: A Biography* (1991).

Trollope, Henry Merivale (1846–1926), Trollope's elder son. Born at Clonmel, Ireland, on 13 March 1846 and baptized at St Mary's Church there, he was named after Trollope's brother Henry and his old friend John Merivale, who was one of the boy's godparents along with his grandmother Frances Trollope, and his uncle Thomas Adolphus Trollope. To his family he was always 'Harry'. When he was 6, his father described him and his younger brother Fred as 'very nice boys—very different in disposition but neither with anything that I could wish altered' (*Letters* 1, 31). From March 1858 to 1859 he attended St Columba's College outside Dublin and then, after his parents' move to Waltham Cross towards the end of 1859, St Andrew's College, Bradfield, a new school cheaper than the most famous public schools, and with a higher ratio of staff to students. After leaving Bradfield in 1863, Harry spent eight months in Florence with his uncle Thomas Adolphus; his grandmother Frances Trollope died while he was there. By May 1864 he was back in England, and Trollope sought Lord Houghton's help in obtaining him an appointment in the Foreign Office. When nothing came of this he began reading law with Montague Hughes Cookson at Lincoln's Inn. In 1867 he purchased a commission as cornet in the Mounted Yeomanry (*Letters* 1, 393), but he quickly returned to his legal studies and was called to the bar in June 1869, though he never practised as a barrister. Two months later, on 30 August, Trollope bought him a one-third partnership in Chapman & Hall, the publishers of many of his own books, for £10,000. Trollope may have hoped that Harry would follow in the family tradition and become a novelist himself (see *The Notebooks of Henry James*, ed. F. O. Matthiessen and Kenneth B. Murdock (1961), 10, 93); but eighteen years were to elapse before his only published novel appeared (*My Own Love-Story*, 2 vols., 1887), and it displays no sign whatever of the family talent.

The initial enthusiasm that Trollope reported Harry as showing for his work as a publisher (*Letters* 1, 483–4) apparently waned during his parents' nineteen-month-long trip to Australia and New Zealand in 1871–2. There are hints that he had quarrelled with his partner Frederic Chapman by the time they got back, just before Christmas 1872. He had also fallen in love with and wanted to marry a woman variously described as a French actress and a 'woman of the town'. Within a few days his father bundled him off to Australia, to cool down on his younger brother's sheep station in New South Wales. He arrived in Sydney on 21 February and left for home on 12 July 1873. Either while he was away or after his return he left Chapman & Hall, ostensibly to devote himself to literature, the family profession. Thereafter he lived mainly on the Continent until his father's death in December 1882. But during Trollope's absence in South Africa in 1877, Harry attended to his business affairs in London, and just before Trollope's death they shared digs at Garlant's Hotel in Suffolk Street. In 1878 he was entrusted with his most important commission, that of seeing his father's autobiography through the press after his death.

His own literary career never flourished. He was paid £50 to ghost-write a life of Charles Bianconi, but it was published (in 1878) without his name on the title-page. Apart from his novel, the only books he produced were the volume on Corneille and Racine for Blackwood's series 'Foreign Classics for English Readers' (1881) and a life of Molière (1905). He also translated two works from the French, G. Letourneau's *Sociology Based upon Ethnology* (1881) and Count d'Haussonville's *The Salon of Madame Necker* (1882), had a couple of articles published in monthly magazines, and wrote or contributed to *Dickens's Dictionary of Paris, 1882: An Unconventional Handbook* (though again his name did not appear on the title-page) and an untraced guidebook to Normandy and Brittany. On his father's initiative, he had been elected to the Garrick Club around the time he joined Chapman & Hall, and in 1882 he became a member of the Athenaeum. As long as Trollope was alive he had the benefit of his advice and of his influence with publishers. Generally, however, he must have been as much embarrassed as encouraged by his father's regular requests for progress reports on projects that typically progressed all too slowly. It took him four years to complete the book on Corneille and Racine, and Margaret Oliphant, the editor of the Foreign Classics series, did not like it when it was delivered. Admittedly, she had not wanted him to do the book in the first place, but given that she was a noted admirer of his father, publicly at least, this can hardly account, on its own, for the brutally unflattering picture she painted of Harry in a letter to William Black-

wood: she thought he looked 'extremely *queer*' and 'anything but prepossessing', altogether 'a very odd creature to follow upon two generations of literature' (quoted in *Letters* 2, 856 n.). Whether he perceived it himself or not, his father's fame and affectionate solicitude for him clearly made it harder rather than easier for him to establish a literary career of his own. Trollope movingly expressed his love for Harry in the letter committing *An Autobiography* to his care and in another letter dated 21 December 1880 (*Letters* 2, 685–6, 886), but in Harry's youth he had evidently been a rather irritable and peremptory father, often too busy to take much notice of him. Harry put a great deal of effort into the preparation of *An Autobiography* for publication, making a copy of it and in the process apparently perpetrating many errors, or causing the printer to perpetrate them. He also wrote a brief, dignified preface, which his father would have approved of, and made a few minor deletions, such as his father had foreseen might prove advisable.

In 1884, a little over a year after his father's death, Harry married Ada Strickland, whom he had known for some time as a former schoolfriend of his cousin Florence Bland's. He and Ada had two children, Muriel Rose (1885–1953) and Thomas Anthony (1893–1931), neither of whom married. Harry continued to spend much of his time on the Continent, and kept in close touch with his uncle and godfather Thomas Adolphus. His father would almost certainly have been dismayed at the rather extreme and cantankerous Toryism that both Harry and his brother Frederic openly professed after his death, perhaps taking their lead from their uncle. Much of the money Harry and his mother inherited from Trollope was invested in Chapman & Hall and was lost when the firm collapsed in 1887. But Harry was apparently able to maintain a gentlemanly and leisurely style of life until his death at the age of 80, on 24 March 1926. His mother, who survived until she was 96, lived with him in his house at Minchinhampton, near Stroud, for some years before her death there in 1917. After his death his daughter Muriel continued to reside at Minchinhampton, in the 'Small House at Forwood'.   PE

Glendinning, Victoria, *Anthony Trollope* (1992).

Hall, N. John, *Trollope: A Biography* (1991).

Mullen, Richard, *Anthony Trollope: A Victorian in his World* (1990).

Trollope, Joanna (1943–), belongs to a branch of the family, the 'Westminster Trollopes', who descend from one of Anthony's great-uncles. Since novels like *The Rector's Wife* (1991) and *The Choir* (1992) explore personal and political conflict below an apparently secure ecclesiastical façade, they have been determinedly compared to Barchester. However, she has a personal fascination with middle-class village life where local incidents seem hugely important, 'like a skyscraper in a desert', and sees a more accurate parallel in a mutual interest in 'the human heart'. Romances like the prize-winning *Parson Harding's Daughter* (1979), which, despite its title, has nothing to do with *The Warden*, mask those connections under the pen-name Caroline Harvey.

AWJ

Trollope, Rose (née **Heseltine**) (1820–1917). She married Trollope 11 June 1844. Until recent years it was assumed that there was little to be found out about her, but the efforts of Trollope's recent biographers, particularly Victoria Glendinning, have shown that to be mistaken. Rose was a girl of 23, five years his junior, on holiday with her family at Kingstown (now known as Dun Laoghaire) in Ireland when she met Trollope. Less than two months later they were engaged. The marriage, which developed into a strong partnership, and the path taken by her husband's career, gave her independent spirit with its passion for reading and travel the scope it required.

Born on 13 December in Rotherham, to Martha Heseltine and Edward J. Heseltine, a bank manager, the third of four daughters, Rose grew up in a household of women. Eliza Ann was 7 when she was born, while Mary Jane was 5: the two living-in servants were women. Her position in this family offers a clue to her later personality, for the accounts given of her by contemporaries are often generalized or confined to observing her taste for personal elegance. As the next to youngest child in a family of four, Rose would have had to fight for attention, yet she had the support of growing up in the company of women, while being able to impose herself as an authority on Isabella, the one child younger than herself. It was a start that seems to have given her confidence in herself, even a certain daring. There is a story that when they were young she and her sisters once sewed lace around the bottoms of her father's trousers when he was asleep.

She was baptized as a Unitarian in Rotherham Unitarian Chapel: she does not appear to have actively kept up that faith in later life, though her early teaching may have helped her to keep her independence of mind, since Unitarians did not demand orthodoxy of belief. Her family lived over the Joint Union Stock Bank, where her father was manager, in the High Street of Rotherham, Yorkshire. These free quarters and a salary of about £300 a year were all that her father's job brought them: he was respected locally, and known as a director of the tiny Sheffield and Rotherham Railway, but the family had no pretensions to class or style. In 1842, the year before Rose became engaged, her mother had died from injuries she suffered in a railway accident. Her two older sisters were already married. Rose and Isabella, the youngest, were visiting Ireland with their father when they met Anthony, who may have had an introduction to them through a fellow clerk.

Anthony's family accepted Rose with better grace than might have been expected: finding out what a keen reader she was pleased Anthony's mother. For her own part, Rose seems to have transferred all her loyalty to her new family, keeping in touch only with her younger sister. Her mother-in-law referred to her after visiting the couple at Mallow in 1848 as Anthony's excellent little wife. It soon became clear that she brought out the best in Trollope, for even before the marriage, with her support, he was able to overcome the inhibitions that had hindered him from getting down to writing the novel that he had longed for years to produce. Rose read *The Macdermots of Ballycloran*, when it was completed a few months after their wedding in 1844, as she was to read all his later works, before anyone else. From then on he would give her his manuscripts to copy out, trusting her to read carefully for the sense and to make minor corrections. The telling details in the accounts of women's dresses in his novels are usually credited to Rose too. He relied on her, with her Mudie's subscription, to keep him up to date with what other novelists were publishing. Until her niece Florence Bland became his amanuensis towards the end of his life, Anthony was always writing with his wife as first reader in mind.

Rose proved herself efficient and adaptable in practical matters, settling down to life in Ireland with a will. Her enthusiasm for Glengarriff, a local beauty spot that they visited from Mallow, blinded her at the time to the many discomforts her more exacting mother-in-law pointed out. Looking back, for the benefit of Frances Trollope's biographer, Rose was amused and could see that she might have been more discriminating. Mountainous scenery always delighted the couple.

Her husband's work as a Post Office official took him away from home a great deal, as it would for many years to come: when she was first in Ireland she travelled about with him when she could, only settling back down in Clonmel, their first home, a week before her son

The only photograph in existence of Trollope's wife Rose. Seemingly content with her domestic role, she remains an enigmatic figure, although her advice and counsel undoubtedly influenced Trollope's depiction of love and marriage. The couple were devoted.

Henry Merivale was born in 1846. A second son, Frederic James Anthony, followed a year later.

When he chose a bride from outside Ireland, offence was taken against Anthony, or at least he felt it to be so, and their social life was restricted. In 1849 Rose took in the youngest child of her dying sister-in-law Cecilia, the 2-year-old Edith Tilley, making herself responsible for the care of three children under the age of 3. There could have been no question, in the modest circumstances of their Irish beginnings, of palming the work off on experienced nursemaids. Though Rose never gave birth to a daughter of her own, she offered a home more than once to daughters who had lost their mother. When her sister Isabella died in 1863, she took in Isabella's 8-year-old daughter Florence Bland: the two were still living together when Florence died in 1908. She also comforted Bice, the daughter of Thomas Adolphus, in 1869 when her mother died, and gave her a base in England; later when the 15-year-old Bice developed mumps Rose stayed at home to nurse her. If she would have liked a daughter of her own, it may also be the case that two pregnancies were enough for her and that she chose to limit the size of her family.

'Dearest Love' began Anthony always, when he was writing his many letters to her. Though they were often kept apart by his work throughout the marriage, he could be counted on to write regularly and with affection, enquiring and giving instructions about matters of common concern. But no love letters that passed between them have survived. The buoyant teasing note struck by some of the happily married women characters he created is as good a clue as we have to Anthony's experience of Rose.

Biographers have speculated that Trollope's delight in the young American woman Kate Field, who filled an important place in his affections from the time he met her in Boston in 1860, may have caused disturbance in the marriage, but a surviving letter from Rose to Kate, dated December 1862, seems to indicate that Rose determined to accept and incorporate this friendship rather than struggle against it.

There certainly seems no need to conclude that Rose was lacking in vitality or fire. One of the details repeatedly remarked about her was her taste for clothes: she took a pride in her appearance and was once said to have beautiful feet. Hostile note was taken by a younger woman, Lady Rose Fane, when she presented herself one evening at the age of 43 with a rose tucked into her prematurely white hair instead of covering it with the conventional cap. Only a woman with a strong sense of her own body makes moves which provoke this kind of criticism.

In conversation she seems often to have been reticent by design. Of course, socially, Rose had been translated out of her original sphere by her marriage. During the early years together in Ireland, their life was humble enough, moving from modest lodgings in Clonmel to a little house in Mallow, but during the four years before they left the country in 1859, Rose was mistress of a handsome semi-detached house, 5 Seaview Terrace, in Donnybrook, outside Dublin. Waltham House in Essex, which they leased on their return to England, was positively grand, and they held at least one ball there during the eleven years they lived in Essex before moving into London in 1871. They were invited on visits, by Sir Arthur Annesley to Bletchingdon Park, and by Lord Houghton to Fryston in Yorkshire, and to other country houses owned by members of the aristocracy. Rose responded with composure to this promotion, learning to spend money and choose furnishings and to draw up menus for her guests. In 1861 Trollope asked George Smith to get his wife to send Rose a recipe she had asked for. The most striking evidence of the development she owed to her marriage was the part she took in assisting Anthony in his work, and the respect he himself displayed for her literary judgement. He said he had never known her wrong about a book. Hearing that their eldest son Harry was planning to write a life of Bianconi in 1877, his father advised him to show the work to his mother when it was done and to take note of her advice.

Harry and Fred had been sent away to school from before the time they were 12, but it still cost Rose a good deal when Fred went off to Australia as a young man. In spite of the distances involved, she later became an active grandmother, and when Fred's son Frank came to school in England wrote earnestly, if not always tactfully, to discuss his progress with his parents. She made use of every connection to advance Fred and his children.

In the days of Trollope's fame, Rose seems to have provoked little comment from those who got to know the couple. G. H. Lewes said that she did not make much impression on him either way. This may have been the result of a deliberate reticence on her part. She did not always approve of the ways of the world in which they moved: though her husband visited the irregular ménage of George Eliot and G. H. Lewes, she never did so herself. When Trollope was away she dined out and went abroad without him and she toyed with membership of a women-only club.

Tantalizingly few traces of her own work have survived: she was a skilled needlewoman, winning a bronze medal in the Great Exhibition of 1851 for a screen embroidered with the Trollope

Trollope, Thomas Adolphus

family crest, and a keen gardener. In F. E. Trollope's *Frances Trollope: Her Life and Literary Work* (1895), however, her memories of her mother-in-law in old age are preserved. *Blackwood's* turned down the one story that she tried to publish, after Trollope was dead and she herself was nearly 70.

After Trollope's death in 1882, Rose sent off his clothes to Fred and sold North End House, their last home in the country, chosen when they had moved out of London because Trollope was having difficulties with his breathing. She moved to 6 Cheyne Gardens with Florence Bland. Under Trollope's will she received a lifetime interest in the trust set up after the sale of his real and leasehold estate but in spite of this her circumstances became straitened by 1897, when she was awarded a Civil List pension of £100 a year. At 83 she was observed to be full of spirit and life and in her nineties she was still reading several books a week. Florence died before her and the last years of her life were spent in the home of her son Harry.
MH

Glendinning, V., *Anthony Trollope* (1992).
Hall, N. J., *Trollope: A Biography* (1991).
Mullen, R., *Anthony Trollope: A Victorian in his World* (1990).

Trollope, Thomas Adolphus (1810–92). Anthony's eldest brother Tom was born at 16 Keppel Street, London, on 29 April 1810. He was Frances Trollope's favourite son, and escaped most of the neglect and trauma which characterized Anthony's upbringing. His education was patchy and sporadic, perhaps accounting for the diverse but unrigorous enthusiasms which characterize his adult work. His was a naturally calm and contented nature—a singular merit amidst the disruptions of his early years. Tom was sent to Harrow in 1818 and was subjected, unruffled, to the same snobbish reception which antagonized Anthony when he went to the school.

In line with family tradition Tom transferred in 1820 to Winchester, where he prospered, becoming a prefect, but without distinguishing himself academically. *An Autobiography* tells how Anthony was horribly bullied by the elder brother he so much aspired to follow to Winchester. L. P. and R. P. Stebbins describe Tom as 'of the stuff which enables English boys to be happy at public school' (*The Trollopes* (1945), 21) and he faced with equanimity experiences which rendered Anthony nearly suicidal. Nor did Tom suffer Anthony's anguish amidst the humiliations involved in the family's debts and dislocations; partly because these occurred at a time when he was old enough to cope with them; partly because both parents better cushioned him from

their effect; and undoubtedly in some measure because he was less sensitive about such things.

In 1828 he finished at Winchester, just in time to accompany his father to America to lend support to Frances Trollope's unavailing efforts at redeeming the family fortunes. Tom had left Winchester as holder of two school exhibitions, which he hoped to use at New College, Oxford. Having waited two years for a vacancy, however, he was forced to settle for St Albania's Hall. Even here his desultory studies were threatened by a quarrel between his father and the college authorities over payment of fees, and Tom transferred to Magdalen Hall—'a recognized asylum for destitute misfits', as the Stebbinses describe it (44). Not even this disconcerted him. By temperament he was charming and kindly, certainly not ungifted, but always ready to pursue idiosyncratic byways of scholarship. The dilettantism which characterized his adult work was already in evidence: any book was of interest so long as it was not directly urged on him by the task actually in hand.

He graduated with fourth-class honours in May 1834, without firm job prospects. Thus he was still, aged 24, entirely dependent upon parental assistance. Sporadic private tutorial work followed, and in February 1835 he was offered a mastership at King Edward's Grammar School, Birmingham. Pending the commencement of this post he accompanied his mother on the trip she took up the river Danube in July 1836. Tom seems to have been completely unfazed by the hazards of travelling rough. Like his mother he was a natural and ardent wanderer.

His time in Birmingham was brief. He seems to have had no natural aptitude for schoolmastering, and reportedly antagonized staff and pupils alike, both by his unprofessional casualness and by the covert snobbery with which he treated grammar school life. He began writing travel journalism, and making plans to settle as his mother's travelling companion and man of business. They remained inseparable for the rest of Frances Trollope's life. This closeness to his mother is one of the marked differences between Tom and Anthony. By 1839 he was in Brittany researching his first travel book *A Summer in Western France* (1841), an entirely characteristic work; its praises are all reserved for out-of-the-way spots and unfashionable byways. Finally abandoning his schoolmastering, he went with his mother first to France, then to Italy.

Anthony was now settled in Ireland. Tom visited him and was delighted by the free and easy manners of the people, and by the unlimited opportunities for wild rambling. This visit marks the rapprochement which henceforward led An-

Trollope with his elder brother, Thomas Adolphus, c.1860, both looking very severe. Sending a copy of the picture to a relative, Trollope commented 'Here you have my brother and self. You will perceive that my brother is pitching into me. He always did.'

thony, despite the schoolboy bullying, to feel so warmly for his elder brother.

By 1846 Tom was established in Florence, where he quickly asserted himself as one of the most popular and influential members of the English community. He became steeped in Italian history, an ardent supporter of moves for Italian emancipation, and the respected correspondent upon Florentine affairs for several British newspapers and magazines. He was intimate with all the literary figures who frequented Florence at this time; George Eliot, the Brownings, Dickens, Lever, Landor, Alfred Austin, Harriet Beecher Stowe, Emerson. His antiquarian interests were manifested in his house, the Villino Trollope, where he collected art and antiques, and established a library of some 14,000 volumes. Visitors were amazed, both at the extent of Tom's collection, and at the precarious financial basis on which it was founded. Tom was always prepared to live hand to mouth in order to sustain his extraordinary ménage. Anthony's American friend Kate Field wrote of the Villino Trollope how 'under its stately colonnades Italian radicals argued with double firsts from Oxford, and the poets of the new Italy . . . exchanged courtesies and sipped the famous Trollopian lemonade' (Stebbins and Stebbins 183).

In April 1848, 'dear old Tom', as the entire Anglo-Italian community knew him, married Theodosia Garrow, and their only daughter Beatrice (Bice) was born in 1853. Tom's earlier writings tend to be conservative in temper, probably echoing his mother's tone, but Theo changed him, and most of the historical material he wrote after this time evinces a characteristically cautious liberalism. Articles for the *Athenaeum* in 1848 show him as a shrewd observer, and fierce antagonist of what he saw as papal abuse of arbitrary authority. He attributed much of the repression in Italy's history to the dominance of the Catholic hierarchy, and both his fiction and his antiquarian works emphasize this, with an enthusiasm sometimes more fervent than balanced. A steady stream of literary work followed over the next two decades—never quite at brother Anthony's prolific rate, but still remarkable.

In 1862 the King of Italy made Tom a knight of the Order of St Maurice and St Lazarus for services to Italian liberalism. Theodosia died of consumption in 1865, and he sold the Villino Trollope. In 1866 Frances Ternan, the sister of Dickens's mistress Ellen, became Tom's second wife. Political upheavals in Florence, consequent upon the Franco-Prussian War in the early 1870s, caused Tom to lose over £10,000 and his library was broken up and sold along with the villa, Ri-

corboli, which had replaced the Villino Trollope. Even this catastrophe he survived with equanimity, moving to Rome as correspondent for the London *Standard*. Though now more than 60 years old, nearly deaf, and suffering from sciatica, the prolific output of novels and socio-historical commentaries continued, as it would right up to 1886, when he resigned from the *Standard*, and returned to England. His last years were occupied with his autobiography, *What I Remember*. He died on 11 November 1892.

Tom Trollope wrote some fourteen novels, five travel books, three volumes of short stories, four books on Italian politics, and seven historical works, an autobiography and a stream of articles. His style is equable but sometimes overbearingly magisterial. Divergent interests preclude his stories from sustaining consistent objectives. His novels are patchy because his strength in description is not matched by, or in tandem with, psychological depth of characterization. Because his heart is not really in novel-writing he does not always seem to know how to conduct his plots in relationship to the characters he creates, and veers between naturalism and sensationalism, especially where an anticlerical story line encourages his penchant for a rather feeble late Gothicism.

Tom himself averred that he wrote fiction for money and history for joy. *Beppo the Conscript* (1864), for instance, was written in 23 days to defray the expenses of Theodosia's final illness. *La Beata* (1861) and *Marietta* (1862) are among his more accomplished novels. *Paul the Pope and Paul the Friar* (1861) elicits praise as exemplifying 'his rich gifts of narrative, description and psychological insight' (Stebbins and Stebbins 182). In his own estimation, *The History of the Commonwealth of Florence* (1865) was his magnum opus. *The Girlhood of Catherine of Medici* (1856), and *Filippo Strozzi* (1860) also command respect as popular and accessible accounts of Italian history.

Though it was regarded as authoritative at the time, none of his historical writing is now consulted. He suffers from attempting the dual functions of journalistic reportage, which he does very well, and philosophical rationalizing, which is often inadequately underpinned by theory or general principles. His instinctively tolerant attitude is sometimes overtaken by his vehement anti-Catholicism.   TB

Poston, Lawrence, III, 'Thomas Adolphus Trollope: A Victorian Anglo-Florentine', *Bulletin of the John Rylands Library*, 55 1 (1966).

Stebbins, L. P., and Stebbins, R. P., *The Trollopes: The Chronicle of a Writing Family* (1945).

Trollope, T. A., *What I Remember*, 3 vols. (1887–9).

Trollope, Thomas Anthony (1774–1835). Anthony Trollope's father was the only son of the Revd Anthony Trollope and his wife Penelope (née Meetkerke). His father, the fifth son of Sir Thomas Trollope, 4th Baronet, of Casewick in Lincolnshire, was rector of Cottered St Mary, Hertfordshire. Thomas Anthony was elected a scholar at Winchester in 1785, entered New College, Oxford in 1794, was elected a fellow of the college in 1796, and graduated BCL in 1801. After being admitted to the Middle Temple in 1799, he was called to the bar in 1804. In 1806 he established himself as a Chancery Court barrister, with chambers at 23 Old Square, Lincoln's Inn. When he married Frances (Fanny) Milton, on his thirty-fifth birthday, 23 May 1809, he was earning £700 a year at the bar and owned property valued at £6,000, including the house at 16 Keppel Street, Bloomsbury, in which he was living prior to his marriage and which became his and Fanny's home for the first six years of their life together. Anthony, born on 24 April 1815, was the fourth of their six children. In 1813 Thomas Anthony took a 21-year lease on Illots Farm, Harrow, owned by Lord Northwick, and the family went to live there just after Anthony's birth. Two years later, in 1818, they moved into a new house, Julians, which Thomas Anthony had built on the farm at a cost of over £3,000. At the time he was heir apparent to his mother's brother Adolphus Meetkerke, a wealthy squire whose estate was also called Julians, but after the death of his first wife in 1817, Meetkerke remarried and in his old age begot six children of his own, including a new heir. In the meantime, Thomas Anthony's income from his legal practice had been steadily shrinking, chiefly because of his habit of treating the clients and solicitors who came to him for advice as ignorant fools; and the farm had not paid. The family had to let the new house little more than a year after moving into it and return to the old farmhouse, which they enlarged at a cost of more than £500 and bravely renamed Julian Hill.

After the first relatively happy years of his married life, Thomas Anthony became increasingly gloomy and cantankerous. Tom, his eldest son, attributed his appalling temper to the copious drafts of calomel (mercury chloride) which he took for the 'sick headaches' that afflicted him all his adult life.

Early in 1827, Julian Hill in turn had to be given up, and the family moved into a more modest farmhouse at Harrow Weald: Tom denied that it was as 'tumble-down' as Anthony made it out to be in *An Autobiography*. In November of the same year, Fanny and three of the other children—Henry, Cecilia, and Emily— accompanied Fanny's friend Frances Wright to America, leaving Thomas Anthony alone at Harrow Weald, except when Anthony was home on holidays from Winchester. It was intended that Fanny would find employment for Henry and some kind of business opportunity for herself and her husband, who would then join her in America. On the fiasco that ensued, see TROLLOPE, FRANCES. Thomas Anthony travelled to America in September 1828, and spent several months with Fanny. Initially he had been sceptical about her 'bazaar' at Cincinnati, subsequently known as 'Trollope's Folly', but following his return to England he squandered money on unsuitable stock for it. During her absence he finally abandoned his legal practice and, in what Anthony described as 'the last step preparatory to his final ruin', took a second farm. Anthony thought it 'odd' that a highly educated and very clever man should have persisted so obstinately in the belief that he could make money out of farming without any 'special education or apprenticeship' to it, and now without any capital (*Auto* I). In 1830, no longer able to pay Anthony's bills at Winchester, Thomas Anthony had to withdraw him from the school and send him back to Harrow as a day-boy (exempt from fees). While she remained in America, Fanny sometimes had to depend on financial assistance from the French artist Auguste Hervieu who was travelling with her. When she was ready to return to England, in the summer of 1831, she had to shame her husband into sending the £80 required for her, Henry's, and the two girls' fares by threatening to ask his relatives for it.

Both the family's financial situation and Thomas Anthony's mental and physical health continued to worsen, notwithstanding the spectacular success of Fanny's *Domestic Manners of the Americans* (1832) and the other books that followed it. In 1834 he too made his debut as an author, when John Murray published, by subscription, the first volume—down to the letter 'D'—of a projected *Encyclopaedia Ecclesiastica* which he had been toiling away at for many years. But in the same year the family was forced to flee to Bruges to escape his creditors, and although he kept working on the remaining volumes until the time of his death, none of them was completed. Anthony, now 19, saw him for the last time towards the end of October 1834, a year before his death on 23 October 1835, apparently from some new illness or sudden development of his old one. According to Anthony, he had spent nearly half his time in bed with sick headaches for the last ten years of his life (*Auto* I). He was buried in the cemetery outside Catherine's Gate, Bruges, close to his second son Henry, who had died on 23 December 1834. (Another son, Arthur, and two daughters both named Emily had died years earlier.)

As described by Anthony, the period when he was left alone with his father at Harrow Weald during his mother's absence in America was one of almost unrelieved misery and humiliating scarcity of money. His memories of his father, like his eldest brother Thomas Adolphus's, were dominated by the fearsome pertinacity with which he tried to drum some knowledge of the classical languages into them and to keep them constantly at their books: 'From my very babyhood, before [my] first days at Harrow, I had had to take my place alongside of him as he shaved at six o'clock in the morning, and say my early rules from the Latin Grammar, or repeat the Greek alphabet; and was obliged at these early lessons to hold my head inclined towards him, so that in the event of guilty fault, he might be able to pull my hair without stopping his razor or dropping his shaving-brush. No father was ever more anxious for the education of his children, though I think none ever knew less how to go about the work. Of amusement, as far as I can remember, he never recognized the need. He allowed himself no distraction, and did not seem to think that it was necessary to a child. I cannot bethink me of aught that he ever did for my gratification; but for my welfare,—for the welfare of us all,—he was willing to make any sacrifice.' He did not beat his sons, but once, in a fit of rage, he knocked Anthony down with his 'great folio Bible' (*Auto* I). His wife admitted that escaping his company was one of her motives for going to America and lingering there as long as she could. Anthony, writing at the age of 60, remembered him as a sad, even tragic figure: 'He was a man, finely educated, of great parts, with immense capacity for work, physically strong very much beyond the average of men, addicted to no vices, carried off by no pleasures, affectionate by nature, most anxious for the welfare of his children, born to fair fortunes,—who, when he started in the world, may be said to have had everything at his feet. But everything went wrong with him. The touch of his hand seemed to create failure. He embarked in one hopeless enterprise after another, spending on each all the money he could at the time command. But the worse [*sic*] curse to him of all was a temper so irritable that even those whom he loved the best could not endure it. We were all estranged from him, and yet I believe that he would have given his heart's blood for any of us. His life as I knew it was one long tragedy' (*Auto* II).

Thomas Anthony has often been seen as a model for Anthony's best-known tragic charac-

ter, Josiah Crawley in *The Last Chronicle of Barset*. His isolation and sense of failure are reflected also in characters such as Louis Trevelyan (in *He Knew He Was Right*) and Sir Thomas Underwood (in *Ralph the Heir*). His love–hate relationship with his sons is replicated in many of the father–son relationships in Anthony's novels; and the incompatibility between him and his wife clearly helped inspire the great saga of marital tension and misunderstanding that is unfolded in Anthony's Palliser novels. PE

Hall, N. John, *Trollope: A Biography* (1991).
Trollope, Anthony, *An Autobiography* (1883).
Trollope, Thomas Adolphus, *What I Remember*, 2 vols. (1887).

Trollope Society. A Trollope Society flourished briefly in the United States during the 1940s under the leadership of A. E. Newton, Morris L. Parrish, and Henry S. Drinker. Along with it came the *Trollopian*, which was announced in summer 1945 as a journal devoted to studies in Anthony Trollope and his contemporaries. This became *Nineteenth Century Fiction* (now *Nineteenth Century Literature*). The aim of the society was to secure publication of a complete edition of Trollope's works, but the project foundered, and with the deaths of Newton and Parrish the society ceased; its papers and records were destroyed. In 1987 the Trollope Society was reborn in London. At that time there was still no complete edition of the novels and no memorial to Trollope in Westminster Abbey. Ten years later, the memorial in Poets' Corner was unveiled by Prime Minister John Major. An edition was put in hand in collaboration with the Folio Society, producing since 1989 four titles a year. The Trollope Society operates from 9a North Street, London SW4 0HN, and the Mercantile Library, 17 East 47th Street, New York NY 10017. Both groups hold annual dinners and lectures, and support a quarterly magazine called *Trollopiana*. RCT

Trow, Aaron. Convicted of killing a constable, Aaron escapes from the Bermuda settlement, terrorizes Anastasia Bergen, and, after a fight with Morton, finally perishes in the sea. 'Trow' *TAC2* GRH

Trowbridge, John Augustus Stowte, Marquis of, landowner in Bullhampton, imperious, conceited, and altogether unendurable. Outraged at the insolence of the vicar Frank Fenwick, he seeks revenge by encouraging his sycophant, Mr Puddleham, to build a Methodist chapel beside the vicarage. He also slanders Fenwick as an infidel and adulterer. *VB* SRB

Photograph of Trollope aged 62, one of the best likenesses of the novelist in his maturity.
The picture by Lock and Whitfield was first shown in *Men of Mark*, third series, 1878.

Trübner, Nicholas (1817–84), author, authority in Oriental studies, publisher, specializing in classics of Victorian fiction others missed, like Charles Reade's *The Cloister and The Hearth* (1861) and Samuel Butler's *Erewhon* (1872). He invited from Trollope, before his second journey to Australia, a series of letters from abroad for publication in provincial newspapers. Trollope agreed on £15 each for twenty letters. These appeared in the *Liverpool Mercury* (3 July–13 November 1875) and were collected in Bradford Booth's *The *Tireless Traveller* (1941). Another arrangement with Trübner involved fifteen letters from South Africa at the miserable rate of £175. They ran in the *Cape Times* (10 November 1877–4 March 1878) and in several British newspapers. Trollope carefully paced himself. By November 1877 he wrote to Henry *Merivale that he had sent his eleventh and done two-thirds of his book (*SA*)—'I never worked harder' (*Letters* 2, 746).
RCT

Trumbull, Farmer, tenant farmer in Bullhampton. He is robbed and murdered, thus sparking the investigation which implicates Sam Brattle, who is eventually cleared when Jack the Grinder is found guilty. *VB*   SRB

Trumpeton Wood, site of a decades-long feud between Lord Chiltern and the duchy of Omnium. A traditional part of the Brake Hunt, Trumpeton Wood is supposed to be a perfect breeding ground for foxes but, due to corrupt management and general neglect, the wood will not produce its quota of foxes, a fact which continually enrages Lord Chiltern. *PR*   JMR

Tuam, home of J. Daly, Barry Lynch's attorney, a small village near Dunmore, Co. Galway. *KOK*
MRS

Tuckerman, Charles Keating (1821–96), American politician; First Minister Resident of the United States in Greece (1868–72); author of *The Greeks of Today* (1872). In *Personal Recollections of Notable People at Home and Abroad* (1895) he said that Trollope's book on America was impartial and unprejudiced. He described Trollope meeting his brother Henry in New York, bursting into his library 'like a rough, shaggy Newfoundland dog about to leap upon him in the exuberance of animal spirits'. Charles Tuckerman met the novelist twice in London. On one occasion the dinner conversation turned to life after death. One diner observed that if heavenly bliss meant being angels singing endless hallelujahs he opted for staying here as long as possible. Trollope had some sympathy for his point, but added, 'if I thought I should never see dear old Thackeray again, I should be a very unhappy man' (*I & R* 78–9).   RCT

Tuckerman, Henry Theodore (1813–71) American poet, critic, essayist; author of *America and her Commentators* (1864), in which he took Trollope to task for some of his comments in *North America* (1862).   RCT

Tudor, Alaric, junior clerk at the Weights and Measures Office, then a commissioner in the civil service. One of the eponymous clerks, Alaric rises rapidly through the ranks of the civil service, becoming a favourite of Sir Gregory Hardlines. Alaric marries Gertrude Woodward and in so doing loses the friendship of Harry Norman. The novel charts the rise and fall of this essentially good young man (his catchphrase is 'Excelsior'), who is tempted by ambition and power and brings disgrace on the Woodward family. *TC*   MT

Tudor, Charley, clerk at the Internal Navigation and cousin of Alaric Tudor. Charley is one of the 'infernal navvies' (II) in the least respectable branch of the civil service. 'A gay-hearted, thoughtless, rollicking young man' (II), Charley soon becomes a hobbledehoy deeply in debt. He comes perilously close to marrying a barmaid, but eventually transforms into a steady and thoughtful young man, largely through the love of Katie Woodward whom he eventually marries. Charley is often said to be loosely based on the young Trollope. *TC*   MT

Tupper, Martin Farquhar (1810–89), versifier, noted for *Proverbial Philosophy* (four series, 1838–67, 1876?), which made him highly popular at home and in America. 'Cuthbert Bede' (see BRADLEY, REVD EDWARD) amused Trollope by showing him a photograph he had bought in Birmingham labelled 'Mr M. F. Tupper' (*I & R* 111).
RCT

Turbury, Dr Trite, London physician consulted by Sir Marmaduke Rowley in hopes of having his son-in-law declared insane. He will do nothing in the case without prior legal action. *HKWR*   RC

Turgenev, Ivan Sergeyevich (1818–83), Russian author of *Torrents of Spring* (1872) and other novels. Trollope met him at the London home of George Eliot and G. H. Lewes in April 1871. Other guests included Browning and Burne-Jones. Turgenev was made an honorary member of the Athenaeum with Trollope's assistance. He also met Turgenev on his later visit to England (October 1881) arranged by William Ralston, Turgenev's English translator. Comparisons were drawn between the work of the two authors. Turgenev died nine months after Trollope.   RCT

'Turkish Bath, The', first published in *Saint Pauls*, October 1869, (reprinted in *ET*). The unnamed editor (evidently Trollope himself) is accosted, while vulnerably naked in a Turkish bath in Jermyn Street, by a garrulous and similarly naked Irishman, who persuades him to look at an article for publication. When the piece finally comes, the editor discovers that it is 'rubbish'. With his clothes on, its author is not at all prepossessing. Investigation reveals that Michael Molloy is insane. The editor visits his home in Hoxton, and talks to his wife, a nurse. Molloy never troubles the editor again.   JS

Turnbull, Mr, member of Parliament for Staleybridge. A thorough independent and radical, somewhat given to demagoguery, Mr Turnbull seems sometimes to think more of his popularity than of his responsibilities as a legislator. Believed by some contemporaries to have been modelled after John Bright, Mr Turnbull causes a political upset by siding with the Conservatives, refusing to vote for a reform bill that he considers too timid. *PF*   JMR

Turnover Park, castle and seat of the Marquis of Trowbridge. *VB*   SRB

Twain, Mark (Samuel Clemens) (1835–1910), American author of *The Adventures of Tom Sawyer* (1873), amongst others. He met Trollope in England (July 1873) at a dinner Trollope hosted honouring his fellow American, the poet Joaquin Miller. Thomas Hughes, the Hon. Frederick Leveson-Gower, and one other guest made up the party. Twain noted that Trollope was 'voluble and animated' but that he and Hughes spoke only to their noble friend, with a deference which made him feel he was at a religious service, Leveson-Gower being 'the acting deity' (*I & R* 156).   RCT

Twentyman, Lawrence, worthy, good-hearted farmer madly in love with Mary Masters. His aggressive masculinity remains attractive, despite his rather flashy dress and swaggering walk, and his only failing is a wish to stand higher with the gentry. An avid hunter, he is involved in the life of Dillsborough generally. He threatens to emigrate when Mary turns him down, but his interest is kindled at the thought of adding Goarly's acres to Chowton Farm. Also appears in *Ayala's Angel* married to Mary's half-sister Kate Masters. *AS*   MG

Twickenham, village where the Trevelyan family, briefly reunited, reside in a cottage on the river Thames. *HKWR*   RC

'Two Generals, The', first published in *Good Words*, December 1863 (reprinted in *LS*). A tale of the American Civil War, set in neutral Kentucky. Major Reckenthorpe has two sons; the elder, Tom, joins the Southern cause. The younger, Frank, fights for the North. The brothers' bitterness is heightened by their both loving the same girl, Ada Forster. The Reckenthorpes are promoted to the rank of general in their respective armies. On the battlefield in Virginia the brothers meet face to face. Tom is wounded, loses a leg, and is taken prisoner. He returns home to Kentucky to find that Ada still loves him.   JS

'Two Heroines of Plumplington, The', first published in *Good Cheer*, December 1882. Trollope's last 'Barsetshire Chronicle', set in 'the little town of Plumplington'. The heroines are Emily Greenmantle, daughter of a bank manager, and Polly Peppercorn, daughter of a foreman at Du Boung's brewery. Emily has a lover, Philip Hughes, a cashier in her father's bank; Polly has a lover, Jack Hollycombe, a dealer in malt. Both fathers disapprove of their daughters' choices on grounds of their different, but equally strong, class snobbery. Through the good offices of Dr Freeborn, and the exercise of the heroines' feminine wiles, both parents are eventually brought round.   JS

Tyrrwhit, Mr, moneylender who pursues Mountjoy Scarborough. Tyrrwhit is believed practically to own Tretton Park, so deeply is Mountjoy indebted, and he tries tirelessly to ensure that he is not outwitted by John Scarborough's trick about the entail. *MSF*   MT

U

Ullathorne Court, three-storey country home of Squire Thorne in the parish of St Ewold's, Barsetshire. A gem of Tudor architecture modelled on Montacute House in Somerset, noted for its enclosed quadrangle, rich tawny colour, and true English hall rather than dining room, it is the setting for both Miss Thorne's *fête-champêtre* and the engagement of Eleanor Bold and Francis Arabin. *BT*   NCS

'Uncontrolled Ruffianism of London, The' (article). Following recent public alarms at the increase of pickpockets and garrotters, a personal survey of friends and acquaintances reveals minimal experience of street crime. The published advice to carry no money (cab fare? Supper?), walk in mid-street (what of the danger of being run over?), and carry a 'huge knob-stick' (an umbrella is more likely to be needed) or loaded revolver (more dangerous to everyone in the vicinity than a possible mad garrotter!) seems questionable. All large cities have some crime; there is no need for hysteria. *Saint Pauls* (January 1868), 419–24.   AKL

Underwood, Clarissa, younger daughter of Sir Thomas Underwood. 'The fact that she was a beauty was acknowledged by all who knew her, and was well known to herself' (II). She believes herself to be in love with Ralph Newton, the heir, until he transfers his attentions to her cousin Mary Bonner, and then to Polly Neefit. She marries Ralph's brother Gregory, the rector of Newton Peele, who has loved her devotedly for many years. *RH*   ALS

Underwood, Patience, Sir Thomas Underwood's elder daughter. 'Certainly not pretty . . . She was clever, and knew herself to be clever. She could read, and understood what she read. She saw the difference between right and wrong, and believed that she saw it clearly' (II). *RH*   ALS

Underwood, Sir Thomas, father of Patience and Clarissa and the former guardian of Ralph Newton (the heir), a 60-year-old widowed barrister who had served briefly as Solicitor-General in a Conservative government but lost his seat on the collapse of the administration. He lives in his chambers at Southampton Buildings, visiting his daughters at Fulham only occasionally. He stands successfully in the Percycross election, but once charges of corruption are laid the borough is disenfranchised. Sir Thomas returns to his legal career and to his long-held project of writing a life of Francis Bacon (not a word of which is written). *RH*   ALS

'Unprotected Female at the Pyramids, An', first serialized in Cassell's *Illustrated Family Paper*, 6 and 13 October 1860 (reprinted in *TAC1*). An exercise in Trollopian misogyny. The narrator finds himself with a party of other European tourists in Cairo. Particularly vexatious is the spinster Miss Sabrina Dawkins—an 'unprotected female'. She attaches herself to the good-natured Damer family during an expedition to the pyramids, and makes every effort to continue in their company on a voyage up the Nile. Meanwhile, young Fanny Damer falls in love with an eligible young American, Mr Jefferson Ingram. The story ends with Miss Dawkins repulsed and the young couple engaged.   JS

Unthank, Jackson, wealthy American friend of Jonas Spalding in Florence, resolved on having a grand collection of pictures for his house in Baltimore 'that no English private collection should in any way come near' (XLVI). *AS*   RCT

urbanization and population. Anthony Trollope was born into a baby boom—during the decade 1811–21 Britain's birth rate peaked. It fell back somewhat in subsequent decades, though remaining high, and crested again at an all-time record during Trollope's last decade. The birth rate then entered a decline that would not be reversed until the post-Second World War baby boom. Trollope therefore lived through a period of dramatic population growth. In 1815 the population of England and Wales was 19.2 million, Scotland's 1.9 million, and Ireland's 6.3 million. By 1881 these figures were 35.2, 3.8, and 5.1 million respectively.

It is generally held that a sustained high birth rate rather than a falling death rate was the chief cause of this growth. The reason for the glaring Irish anomaly was the great famine of the late 1840s, with the catastrophic death toll and the massive emigration that attended it. Britain had a higher marriage rate than most European countries, which meant fewer non-child-bearing spinsters. A typical early 19th-century family had six children, as did Trollope's parents. The death rate did fall, particularly among adults later in the century. Life expectancy around 1850 was 39.9 years for men and 41.9 years for women: by 1900 these figures were 51.5 and 55.4. However the death rate for infants remained shockingly high until the end of the century due to disease. Surviving to age 2 increased one's life expectancy dramatically.

The period was one of soaring urbanization. By 1851 the urban population matched the rural population: by 1881 Britain was two-thirds urban, and only one-third rural. The fastest-growing cities tended to be in the industrial North—cotton textiles centres like Liverpool and Manchester, whose populations rose from 120,000 to 630,000 and 100,000 to 500,000 respectively between 1815 and 1881. Leeds, centre of the woollens industry, and the metal towns Birmingham and Manchester also expanded fivefold. Cardiff, Glasgow, and Belfast, the industrial centres of Wales, Scotland, and Ireland, underwent similar explosive growth. By contrast, in the south of England once-important towns languished, though Bristol managed to triple and Norwich to double in size during Trollope's lifetime. Southern exceptions were Brighton, which grew from 18,000 to 110,000, and above all London, of which Brighton was a satellite holiday town. As the world's largest city, London was in a class utterly apart. No other British city had even a tenth of its population in 1815. By 1881 it had nearly tripled to 3.8 million. Although its manufactures, such as clothing and furniture, were not negligible, it was above all the centre of government, commerce, finance, and fashion. Its metropolitan pull was resented by the proud provincial élites of the new northern cities, but it was inexorable and irresistible. The spread of its mass media, and the communications networks of telegraph and railway, of which London was the hub, further strengthened its gravitational force. The enormous mass of London required its own transportation network. In 1863 its first underground railway was opened, while sixteen other railways delivered the huge suburban population to its centre.

The population growth of these mushrooming cities depended on heavy immigration from the countryside, and especially Ireland. London attracted significant immigration from Europe,

waves of refugees from continental revolutions, political exiles, and, from the 1870s, east European Jewish fleeing from pogroms. Port cities also harboured small but distinctive third world populations associated especially with Britain's cosmopolitan merchant navy. Cities offered opportunities and risks. The death rate in Liverpool and Manchester was double that of the Isle of Wight in the 1840s, but the overall quality of urban life began to improve markedly from the mid-century as governments acted to improve sanitation and housing. Much improved statistical information, resulting from the centralized registration after 1837 of births, deaths, and marriages by the General Register Office, identified and quantified the problems of the cities, galvanizing public concern and government policy. Journalists made a genre of slum exploration stories which played on respectable fears about the city's unknown hordes.

Agricultural counties like Wiltshire, at the heart of Trollope's Barsetshire, where rural unemployment accompanied collapsing grain prices, had virtually static population growth by the 1870s due to the drain of young people who took their energy and fertility to the cities. But the 1870s also marked the start of a fall in the birth rate among the middle classes indicative of birth control, a practice that would trickle down to the working classes by about 1900 and so end Britain's great population explosion. Victorian Britain may have been heavily urbanized, but it did not enjoy city life the way, for instance, the French did. Trollope's nostalgia for rural life, as in *Doctor Thorne* (XV), was widely shared, and contributed then as now to the appeal of his novels. CK

Briggs, Asa, *Victorian Cities* (1963).
Woods, Robert, *The Population of Britain in the Nineteenth Century* (1992).

Uren, J. G., Post Office employee at Falmouth, Cornwall, when Trollope was revising rural posts in the west of England (1851–2). He recalled how Trollope stalked into one office 'booted and spurred', frightening a rural messenger almost out of his wits. At Mousehole, however, he met his match in a formidable postmistress, Miss Elizabeth Trembath, who gave as good as she got. Trollope revelled in the encounter, putting her fiery retorts into the character of Mrs Crump in *The Small House at Allington* (*I & R* 45–7).

RCT

Urmand, Adrian, young, handsome, showy, easily driven, wealthy linen-buyer from Basle. He is encouraged by Michel Voss in his pursuit of Marie Bromar, who first accepts and then rejects him. He comes to terms with his dismissal when a scenic picnic to save face is arranged for him. *GLG*   MG

Ushant, Lady Margaret, great-aunt of Reginald Morton. A gentle woman with old-fashioned ways, Lady Ushant had taken Mary Masters to live with her at Bragton and educated her. Lady Ushant, who had raised Reginald, is delighted when Reginald inherits Bragton and marries Mary. *AS*   MG

Ussher, Captain Myles, handsome 'man of danger' (IV), sub-inspector of the revenue police in Mohill, Co. Leitrim, a Protestant in service of the English authorities, killed by Thady Macdermot when he tries to elope with Feemy Macdermot. Hated by the Irish tenantry for his 'overwhelming contempt of the poor' (IV), and hated by Thady for dishonouring his sister's name, he thematizes the link between sexual and colonial politics. *MB*   MRS

'Usurers and Clerks in Public Offices'. (article). The current rule dismissing public employees discovered dealing with professional moneylenders is foolish. While its intent is to protect employees, it fails; once dismissed, the debtor is in more difficulty than before. Furthermore, civil servants' financial affairs should be their own business. *Pall Mall Gazette* (23 March 1865), 2.   AKL

Utterden, parish near Cambridge which, along with neighbouring Netherden, is largely owned by Daniel Caldigate and is the location of his residence of Folking. *JC*   SRB

Valcarm, Ludovic. He has an unsavoury reputation in Nuremberg for fast living and subversive politics. He moves in and out of prison as audaciously as he invades the red house: a romantic and dangerous threat to Linda's inexperienced heart. Though he persuades her to flee to Augsburg, he scarcely notices her physical and moral discomfort. When he again pursues 'his queen', she has learned her lesson. *LT*   AWJ

Vancouver's Island. Ralph Forrest plans to travel by steamboat via the Isthmus of Panama to this most western part of Canada. 'Panama' *LS*   RCT

Van Siever, Clara, handsome 25-year-old daughter of Mrs Van Siever. Her strong features, independent manner, and lack of feminine softness lead the artist Conway Dalrymple to paint her as Jael, though he later falls in love with her. *LCB*   NCS

Van Siever, Mrs, rich widow of a Dutch merchant, mother of Clara, and partner of Augustus Musselboro and Dobbs Broughton in a money-lending business. Thin but wiry, with long false curls, she dominates and terrorizes her acquaintances with her single-minded devotion to money. *LCB*   NCS

Vavasor, Alice. Tormented by the idea that her fiancé John Grey is too good to become her husband, she jilts Grey and agrees to marry her ungentlemanly cousin George Vavasor. As Alice fends off the various attacks that result from this switch, she shows her mettle; she is strong, virtuous, and uncommonly wilful for a Victorian woman. *CYFH*   JMR

Vavasor, George, dastardly cousin of Alice Vavasor, whose object is purely mercenary when he tempts her into an engagement. Having attacked and killed a burglar in his youth, George is left with an unsightly 'cicatrice' which reddens angrily when he is enraged. This scar, and the violence which begot it, serve as indicators of George's true nature which is ruthlessly selfish and abusive. This is illustrated in the violent way he treats Alice and his sister Kate, in his fantasies of murdering his grandfather, and in his assaults on John Grey. *CYFH*   JMR

Vavasor, John, Alice Vavasor's father, who has a government sinecure and spends time at his club, selfishly refusing to be a real father and companion to his daughter. Though his responsibilities are minimal, Mr Vavasor feels smothered both by his professional and his parental obligations. *CYFH*   JMR

Vavasor, Kate, doting sister of George Vavasor who betrays her cousin Alice in an effort to pro-

mote a marriage between her and George. Appearing to act out of love, Kate is a hypocritical schemer, with cynical views on love and fidelity. When family property is left to her rather than George, he pushes her down and breaks her arm. *CYFH*   JMR

Vavasor, Squire, father of John Vavasor and grandfather of Alice, George, and Kate. The squire, who has a bitter temper and a suspicious nature, quarrels with George, his heir, when George seeks to borrow money against the old man's property. The quarrel grows until George wishes only for the squire's death. *CYFH*   JMR

Vavasor Hall, family residence of the Vavasors, occupied by Squire Vavasor. The small, old-fashioned house is set among the fells where Alice and Kate Vavasor love to walk, but both the Hall and the surrounding land are hateful to the heir apparent, George Vavasor. *CYFH*   JMR

Venice, during the occupation by Austria (1815–66) the site of friction between locals and Austrian regiments. 'Venice' *LS*   GRH

Vernet, French village noted for its hot springs where la Mère Bauche has her inn. 'Bauche' *TAC1*   RCT

Vicar of Bullhampton, The (*see next page*)

Vienna, capital of the Austro-Hungarian monarchy, where Herr Crippel plays violin in the Volksgarten. 'Schmidt' *LS*   GRH

Vigil, Whip, Tory MP, party whip, and member of the Parliamentary Committee on the (*cont. on page 568*)

TROLLOPE's twenty-fourth novel sets out to explore what can be done to set the crooked things of this world straight. It equips one of Trollope's most unalloyed and fully endowed heroes, Revd Frank Fenwick, with everything he needs for the job: worldly wisdom, courage, energy, deep sympathy, and an almost democratic spirit of tolerance. The good-natured vicar is granted an equally capable wife, a hefty bank account, a friendly bishop, considerable authority (as these things go), and what should be manageable problems: a marriage to arrange between a pretty girl without money and a squire with plenty, a rival Nonconformist and obtuse clergyman to play with, a lofty and even stupider marquis to fight with, a murder mystery (not very tangled) to solve, and a bull-headed but honest miller to reunite with his fallen, now repentant daughter and welcome her back to his heart. The only enemies the vicar faces are human obstinacy, self-love, prejudice, cross-grainedness, and dimness. It looks like a set-up for gentle comedy.

Instead, we soon find ourselves in the midst of one of Trollope's darkest novels, where even that most dependable arena of civil life, the dinner party, is made ugly: 'The usual courtesies of society demand that there shall be civility' between host and guest, and yet so very often, even in the midst of these courtesies, 'there is something that tells of hatred, of ridicule, or of scorn!' and 'the guest knows that he is disliked, or the host knows that he is a bore' (VIII). 'Hatred' is a strong word, a word not well suited to what we suppose we will find in one of Trollope's comedies of rural and clerical folly. Perhaps for that reason, this novel, one of his greatest, has never been much read or appreciated. Henry James was one contemporary who read it carefully and with great admiration, praising it as 'a capital example of interest produced by the quietest conceivable means' (*Partial Portraits* (1888), 107). Most reviewers, however, setting the tone for subsequent critics, yawned in its face, content to agree with *The Times* that it was 'a nice, easy, safe reading book for old ladies and young ladies' and to allow the *Saturday Review* to voice the verdict: 'third-rate'.

This was not what Trollope expected, judging by his nervous preface, a preface he wrote and then waved before us, knowing it was a mistake as he did so, that it could not undo what his writing was doing. But he thought he had better set about 'defending myself against a charge which may possibly be made against me by the critics', a charge of being indecorous or worse in dealing directly with the subject of prostitution and dealing sympathetically with it at that. Far from creating a furore, however, Trollope's careful argument for tender mercy toward prostitutes, his telling points about how heavy the punishment was on the woman (for such a minor offence) and how light on the man, and his bold portrayal of the struggling Carry Brattle were all thrown away. Such complaining about women characters as there was from reviewers concerned not Carry but the genteel heroine Mary Lowther, whose dithering caused *The Times* to dub her 'the most provoking' heroine ever, and whose willingness to break engagements caused Mrs Oliphant loudly to sniff.

Nobody cared much, it appears, about Carry or about the novel—one way or another. That is odd, considering its richness and dark power. *The Vicar of Bullhampton* brilliantly subverts the pastoral comedy it sets up for us, forcing us to place our bets on the vicar and then watch helplessly as he fails or achieves only oblique and unsatisfactory partial triumphs. Frank Fenwick is Trollope's most explicitly religious figure, in that he strives to create a kind of relaxed, sweet-hearted Eden right there in

Bullhampton, an Eden which would allow people to live easily, with tolerance and comfort, not bothering their neighbours much and nursing happy and mostly harmless grievances. Fenwick is a kind of compound of Trollopian virtues and is subject to almost no irony at all, quite unusual for a Trollope hero.

But he accomplishes very little indeed. He links all the major plots, one way or another; but those that get solved he does not solve, and those he meddles with are sometimes, happily not quite always, the worse for his meddling. There are really three plot strands, only loosely, if at all, connected, except through the vicar: the love story involving Mary Lowther and the vicar's dear friend Squire Gilmore; the travails of the nearby Brattle family, concerning the fierce miller and his daughter Carry, as well as his son Sam, suspected for a time in the murder of a neighbouring farmer; the comic plot involving Mr Puddleham and the erection of a hideous chapel practically in the vicar's backyard, all because of the absurd interference of the Marquis of Trowbridge, the local landowning peacock and the vicar's favourite target for robust combat.

The last plot comes off reasonably well, not through the vicar's doing, however; with the Brattle family he has only very moderate luck (none at all with old Jacob, the grim patriarch); from arranging the life of Squire Gilmore and Mary Lowther, he and his wife have to retreat in dismay. At one point, a drunken landlady tells the vicar, 'People know what is good for them to do, well enough, without being dictated to by a clergyman!' (LXIII). To his great credit, Fenwick is prone to agree, and finds himself amused by the charge, not angered.

Still, he sets to work not just to heal the meek but to help them inherit the earth. He has great radical political strength, never worrying about doctrinal difficulties: he knows whom he loves and that is enough—enough for him but, as it turns out, not quite enough for all situations. We want this tender-hearted vicar to triumph, but Trollope is much less sentimental than we and knows that crooked things are not going to be made straight by such a soft thing as love, even by such great democratic love as the vicar's. His determination to help Carry is very moving, not least because it is so human: he is driven partly by his own erotic feeling for Carry's 'prettiness', partly by his own romantic castle-building and 'the sweet smiles of affectionate gratitude' he imagines himself receiving later, and partly by a mercy and generosity that force him closer and closer to the most radical New Testament Christianity. He sees how cruel mere justice is, including the justice generally thought of as demanding 'repentance', and he goes about helping Carry by insisting that she is not, in some way, like other women but in *every* way like all of us: 'speak of her as you would any other sister or brother' (XVII). Fenwick's wife considers that she herself might have fallen, had she been so fair as Carry; and at the heart of the novel is an offering not of doctrinal wisdom but of affection. In the end, the comfort and salvation Fenwick offers to her is not God's but his own: 'I love you, Carry, truly.'

But he can never achieve anything like the softening of Carry's father he had planned, nor can he reconcile the son, Sam Brattle, to the beauties of justice. The murder trial winds down without the vicar being able to do much in or for it, and Sam sees clearly at the end that 'there ain't been much justice in it . . . there never ain't much justice'. With his friend the squire he can do even less. He and his wife press Mary Lowther to accept Gilmore, which she does not and then does and then does not, choosing instead the man she has loved all along (and who now can afford to marry). Gilmore goes into some sort of ugly, self-perpetuating sulk, not simply nursing his wounds but letting them define him permanently.

The vicar is left with nothing to do but regret that Mary had ever come to visit and that he had ever tried to matchmake. He does some good things and he is left at the end as admirable as when we first met him, loving friendship, good digestion, and a hearty grievance. We also get the sense, in this unusually erotic novel, that he loves sex, and that the narrator does too. For all its toughness in some areas and its refusal to give in to sentimentality, *The Vicar of Bullhampton* does talk a lot about kissing, rubbing faces 'together like two birds' (XVIII), a sense of attraction so strong 'she could hardly forbear to touch him with her shoulder' (XX). The pastoral is there in the sense that things touch, things bloom; it is just that the blooming is so erratic and so out of control, even of the most attractive and skilled of Trollope's gardeners.

The Vicar of Bullhampton was begun on 15 June 1868, just three days after the completion of *He Knew He Was Right* and while Trollope was in New York. He finished the novel in November of that year, though publication of the first instalment was delayed until June 1869. It had been scheduled for E. S. *Dallas's *Once a Week*, but the desultory habits of Victor *Hugo put Dallas behind schedule and he begged Trollope to allow him to run *The Vicar of Bullhampton* in the inferior *Gentleman's Magazine* instead. Trollope, who did not admire Hugo, was incensed, but finally agreed. The novel ran until 18 May 1870, with book publication in April 1870. It was illustrated by Henry Woods. The manuscript is in the Houghton Library, Harvard.   JRK

apRoberts, Ruth, *Trollope: Artist and Moralist* (1971).
Cadbury, William, 'The Uses of the Village: Form and Theme in Trollope's *The Vicar of Bullhampton*', *NCF* (September 1963), 151–63.
Edwards, P. D., *Anthony Trollope: His Art and Scope* (1978).

Limehouse Bridge. An astute parliamentary insider, Whip Vigil is opposed to the Limehouse project in which Alaric Tudor and Undy Scott have bought extensive shares. *TC*   MT

Vignolles, Captain, professional gambler. A 'small, dry, good-looking little fellow, with a carefully preserved moustache, and a head from the top of which age was beginning to move the hair', Captain Vignolles 'lived by cards, and lived well' (XLI). He fleeces Mountjoy Scarborough. *MSF*   MT

Vincent, Mrs, cousin and friend of Mary Roden whom she supported through the latter's disastrous marriage break-up years earlier. The two women visit regularly. Although more severe in her religious and social tenets, she has remained on friendly terms with the radical young George Roden. *MF*   SRB

Viner, Emily. Dreading marriage to her elderly suitor, she confides in Ralph Forrest but, learning of the man's death, she resolves to return alone to England, refusing Ralph's offer to travel with her. 'Panama' *LS*   GRH

Virgil (70–19 BC), next to Horace, Trollope's most often quoted Latin author. Calling upon the commonly shared classical knowledge amongst educated men Trollope relied on fairly familiar allusion from the *Aeneid*, as in the description of Caroline Waddington in *The Bertrams*, '*Vera incessu patuit Dea*' (IX) (One recognized the goddess by her gait). Mr Gresham's great oration in *Phineas Redux* is introduced 'he uttered that well-worn quotation "[Via prima salutis] *Quod minime reris,—Graiâ pandetur ab urbe*" ' (IX) (The first path to safety—something you least expect—will be opened up from a Greek city). In fact Trollope's classical knowledge extended well beyond the commonplace reference. From 1870 he read Latin authors devotedly, especially when preparing to write his book on Caesar.   RCT

Virtue, James Sprent (1829–92), printer and publisher from 1855. Rather than take over Alexander Strahan's *Argosy* magazine he started his own, inviting Trollope to become editor. *Saint Pauls Magazine* was edited by Trollope from its inception in 1867 until 1870. Virtue was responsible for a 'Spy' cartoon of Trollope in *Vanity Fair*

(April 1873) secretly drafted by Sir Leslie *Ward when he was a house guest. Trollope reprimanded Virtue for this breach of hospitality. *Phineas Finn* (1869) and *He Knew He Was Right* (part-issues 1868–9) appeared under the Virtue imprint. He also printed Trollope's comedy *Did He Steal It?* (privately, 1869) and a catalogue of Trollope's library; and for Chapman & Hall *Lady Anna* (1874), *The American Senator* (1877), and *South Africa* (1878).   RCT

Vivian, Mr, well-mannered, easy-living, and somewhat conceited junior private secretary to Lord Persiflage and also a friend of Lord Hampstead. He works to advance George Roden's social position when the latter turns out to be the Duca di Crinola. *MF*   SRB

von Vincke, Captain Hubert, cultivated Austrian officer who loves Nina Pepé, is seriously wounded, and eventually realizes that her journey to Verona to see him is a renewed declaration of love. 'Venice' *LS*   GRH

Voss, George, as hard-working and obstinate as his father Michel Voss. After an argument with Michel over his love for Marie Bromar, George goes to work for Mme Faragon in Colmar. He eventually gains both Marie and the Hôtel de la Poste. *GLG*   MG

Voss, Josephine, second wife of Michel Voss, stepmother of George Voss, and aunt of Marie Bromar. In all matters she follows the lead of her husband, including trying to convince Marie to marry Adrian Urmand. However, Josephine, unlike Michel, sees that Marie loves George. *GLG*   MG

Voss, Michel, proprietor of the Lion d'Or, father of George, and uncle by marriage of Marie Bromar whom he loves as a daughter. A physically powerful, warm-hearted, but stubborn man of 50, he opposes the marriage of his son and Marie because he did not suggest it. He is furious when Marie adamantly refuses his choice, Adrian Urmand. Distressed by the unhappiness around him, he eventually approves of Marie's choice of husband. *GLG*   MG

Vossner, Herr, accommodating manager of the Beargarden Club. He provides instant loans to the young men who gamble there, but stuns them all by decamping after selling their IOUs to a moneylender. The club breaks down after his departure. *WWLN*   SRB

W

'W. M. Thackeray' (article). With the death in December last of this fine and gentle man, the founder of *Cornhill*, we have lost not only a famous and admired person, but 'The fine grey head, the dear face with its gentle smile, the sweet manly voice . . . it is of those things lost forever that we are now thinking.' Thackeray's kind heart led him to resign editorship of *Cornhill* after two years because he hated saying *no* to so many. He remained connected with this journal; recently his 'Strange to say, on Club Paper' appeared; it ridicules silly gossip about Lord Clyde, with that mingled tenderness toward subject and sarcasm for gossip representative of all his work. Although *Vanity Fair* will endure as his most-remembered work, *Esmond* is perhaps the best English novel; no one has illustrated love with such delicacy. Colonel Newcome (of *The Newcomes*) is the finest character in English fiction—of all fiction save *Don Quixote*. A biography must be written, and carefully, to do him justice. While the burial was simple and the grave plain, in time there must be a bust of Thackeray in Westminster Abbey. *Cornhill* (February 1864), 134–7. See also *THACKERAY*; THACKERAY, WILLIAM MAKEPEACE. AKL

Waddle, Mr, foreman of Neefit's breeches-maker's shop. Neefit's confidant who 'did not understand men as well as his master . . . and . . . knew nothing of his master's ambitious hopes' (V). *RH* ALS

Waddy, Frederick (fl. 1873–8), exhibited pencil drawings in London (1878) and drew for *Portraits of the Day* published by the Tinsley Brothers (1873). Waddy cartooned Trollope for *Once a Week* (June 1872), showing him atop a stack of his novels holding a clergyman puppet. RCT

Wade, George. Afraid of being caught guaranteeing money, he rudely refuses his brother-in-law's request for a signature. 'Not if' RCT

Wales. Although he surveyed six counties for the Post Office and spent family holidays on the south coast, Trollope was not imaginatively attached to the principality; after weeks of rain, he could think of 'nothing worse' to wish any enemy 'than [lifelong] residence in South Wales' (*Letters* 1, 33). His Welsh tenantry in *Cousin Henry*, the sole novel set in Wales, speak exactly like their Barset counterparts, and place names are linguistically inaccurate or comic tongue-twisters, like Lord Llwddythlw, the only Welsh connection in *Marion Fay*. However, the Welsh setting surrounds the dynastic concerns of *Cousin Henry* with comic irony, since Jones is as commonplace as Smith is in England. AWJ

Wales, Prince of (Edward VII) (1841–1910), reigned 1901–10. The Prince presided at the Royal Literary Fund dinner (May 1864) when Trollope responded to the toast to literature. Trollope was formally presented at a levee (March 1868) prior to departure for America on postal business and international copyright. The Prince occasionally dropped in at the Cosmopolitan Club, which Trollope used, but it was coming out of the Turf Club on one occasion that the Prince greeted him without receiving any acknowledgement, the social gaffe being due to Trollope's poor eyesight. It became a joke next time they met (Glendinning 342). In *Phineas Redux* the narrator observes that when the Prince strolled into the Universe Club those 'with royal instincts' gravitated to him (XLVI). Despite this nicely ironic comment, Trollope would probably have been one of them. RCT

Walker, George, elderly Silverbridge attorney who heads the Liberal political interests of the borough. *DC* JMR

Walker, George. Visiting Suez the narrator, a businessman, narrow-minded and pompous, is flattered by Mahmoud al Ackbar, thinking he is his namesake Sir George Walker. 'Walker' *TAC2* GRH

Walker, George, lawyer of the firm of Walker & Winthrop, and one of the leading men of Silverbridge. A short, corpulent, but comely man in his fifties, he prosecutes the case against Revd Josiah Crawley, while expressing sympathy for the clergyman and helping Mr Toogood discover the truth. *LCB*   NCS

Walker, Sir George, the new Lieutenant-Governor of Pegu, for whom George Walker is mistaken. 'Walker' *TAC2*   GRH

Walker, Green, Whig MP for Crewe Junction and friend of Harold Smith. The nephew of the Marchioness of Hartletop, he is considered a young but rising man. *FP*   NCS

Walker, Mr, gentleman of lower social standing than George Hotspur, with whom he plays cards. George wins £300 from him by cheating. Although central to the plot and much discussed, he never appears in the novel. *SHH*   MG

'Walk in a Wood, A' (article). Thinking is the most difficult human activity; because it is an essential one, finding ways of making it 'pleasant, brisk, and exciting as well as salutary' is a great task. Personal experience finds the plotting of stories is best done in small segments. The story develops according to character and event; the outcome is not known until reached. Working out plots, like all real thinking, is best done out of doors, in a certain kind of wood. It must be truly thick, without humans or human signs; no wide avenues, or regular rows of trees; it must be possible to get lost. Very few spots left in England or Scotland are suitable—Devon is the best. Australia has wonderful sites, but it is too distant (as also are New Zealand, South Africa, and California) to be practical. Tuscany has such spots, and Lucca. The Black Forest and the area near Baden are good; Switzerland is possible; there is not much in Belgium. Once in such a spot, one must be alone—even a dog is a distraction. One must sit or walk and think out likely developments, truly see them acting out. Keeping to the task is difficult—the mind wants to wander 'like a pig on way to market', wasting time in remembrance or unuseful tangents. Everyone has an interior Ariel, and must train it. Some may function anywhere—such were Homer, Cicero, Dante, Bacon, and Shakespeare. Others must labour to create plots that illustrate nobility, humour, pathos, but are always true to human experience. Writers are often driven almost to despair by frustration in this attempt; the author advises them to try a walk in a wood to resolve the difficulty. *Good Words*, 20 (1879), 595–600.
                    AKL

Wanless, Georgiana, cold beauty shown off at archery, riding, and tennis to trap Major Rossiter into marriage, but finally attached by her mother to Mr Burmiston, son of a wealthy brewer. 'Dugdale' *WFF*   GRH

Wanless, Lady, scheming mother, dedicated to finding husbands for her well-bred but penniless daughters. Her primary target is Major Rossiter for Georgiana. 'Dugdale' *WFF*   GRH

Wanless, Sir Walter. Desiccated, snobbish baronet, who does little to help his wife and her schemes. 'Dugdale' *WFF*   GRH

Warburton, Mr, the Duke of Omnium's private secretary during the Duke's tenure as Prime Minister. Privy to all the schemes and intrigues by which the Prime Minister is unwillingly surrounded, Mr Warburton's practical service to the tormented Duke does honour to the secretary's sensitivity, insight, and discretion. *PM*   JMR

Ward, Mrs Henrietta Mary Ada (1832–1924), wife of the artist Edward Matthew Ward and a painter herself. In *Memories of Ninety Years* (1924) she gave an example of how Trollope could behave when he lost his temper. On a visit to Lord Cowper's estate, Panshanger, in 1868, she saw from her carriage 'to our intense amusement Anthony Trollope about to have a fight with a broad-shouldered rubicund tradesman. Anthony had divested himself of his coat and was shaking his fists in his opponent's face, as he danced around him.' The outcome was not known, but, she added, the betting was on Trollope (R. C. Terry, *Anthony Trollope* (1977), 21).   RCT

Ward, Sir Leslie ('Spy') (1851–1922), portrait artist of many eminent Victorians. In *Forty Years of 'Spy'* (1915) he described the cartoon he produced for *Vanity Fair*'s 'Men of the Day' series, No. 60 (April 1873). 'I had portrayed Trollope's strange thumb, which he held erect whilst smoking, with his cigar between his first and second fingers, his pockets standing out on either side of his trousers, his coat buttoned once and then parting over a small but comfortable corporation' (*I & R* 176). Ward had done the sketching surreptitiously, and Virtue had not warned Trollope, who was furious when the picture appeared. Ward thought the accompanying text, by 'Jehu Junior' (T. G. Bowles), much more offensive than his drawing.   RCT

Warden, The (*see page 573*)

Ward, Lock & Co., publishing house founded in 1854. A rival of W. H. Smith, Ward, Lock's 'Railway Library' published an edition of *Dr Wortle's School* at two shillings (November 1881). Smith sold his 'Select Library of Fiction' series to the firm (July 1881). To the 27 Trollope books on the list, Ward, Lock added another 3 and an edition of *Australia and New Zealand*.   RCT

Cartoon by 'Spy' (Sir Leslie Ward) for the magazine *Vanity Fair*, April 1873. Trollope was gravely offended since 'Spy' did his preliminary sketches while he and Trollope were guests of the publisher, James Virtue, a sin against the laws of hospitality.

THE Revd Septimus Harding is the quiet-living, music-loving precentor of Barchester Cathedral and Warden of Hiram's Hospital, while at the same time holding the less well-endowed living of Crabtree Parva, where he has installed a curate. He is a widower, and old friend of the Bishop of Barchester, who originally appointed him to the wardenship, and father-in-law to the Bishop's son, Theophilus Grantly, the well-to-do rector of Plumstead Episcopi and Archdeacon of the diocese, and a staunch upholder of clerical privileges. Hiram's Hospital was established centuries ago for the relief of twelve superannuated working men. A radical surgeon, John Bold, has noticed that although Hiram's legacy has greatly increased in value and now gives the Warden a very comfortable house and an income of £800 per annum, the proportion of the trust devoted to charity has declined. Despite his love for Harding's second daughter Eleanor, Bold is spurred on by reforming zeal and by an actual historical case—the far worse scandal of the Hospital of St Cross in Winchester. The mastership of St Cross was enjoyed by the Revd Francis North, 5th Earl of Guilford, a wealthy man in his own right who had been appointed by the Bishop, his father, who in turn had been preferred by his brother, the Prime Minister, Lord North. Guilford also held, with dubious legality, a canonry at Winchester and two parish livings besides. Bold institutes legal proceedings on behalf of the inmates of Hiram's Hospital, and has the matter aired by his journalist friend Tom Towers in the *Jupiter* (fictional equivalent of *The Times*). The Warden suffers greatly from these attacks, while the Archdeacon stoutly defends the Church's temporalities. Harding eludes his overbearing son-in-law and travels to London to see Sir Abraham Haphazard, Attorney-General of the day, and the lawyer engaged by the Archdeacon. Sir Abraham fails to understand that a scrupulous man may feel a conflict between legality and rectitude, and Harding is shown to possess an unusual degree of unworldly virtue. He resigns from the Hospital on conscientious grounds. Although prepared to renounce Bold for her father's sake, Eleanor is able to marry, and Harding is found a suitable though less remunerative living within Barchester, but not before the failure of a proposed compromise whereby Harding would exchange his comfortable post for the small living of Puddingdale. Mr Quiverful, the vicar of Puddingdale, is hard pressed to support his wife and twelve children, and is unable to worry about the source of his income. To the Warden, this arrangement smacks of the sin of trading in holy offices, and he will have none of it. His resignation leaves the old men, to whom he has devoted great love and attention and whose incomes he has personally subsidized, without effective pastoral care. No new arrangement for the hospital is made until *Barchester Towers*.

Harding is an honest, almost saintly man, who, by following tradition unthinkingly, has found himself in a position which meets with disapproval in the new age. The novel contains attacks on *Carlyle as 'Dr Pessimist Anticant', the author of a pamphlet on *Modern Charity*, on *Dickens as 'Mr Popular Sentiment', author of *The Almshouse*, and on *The Times* as the *Jupiter*, all of them indicted for campaigning in cases where they do not know the personalities and motives involved, and for publishing outrageous travesties of the character of Septimus Harding. Church matters are brought to a focus in satires on three contemporary bishops—Charles James Blomfield, Bishop of London, Henry Phillpotts, Bishop of Exeter, and Samuel Wilberforce, Bishop of Oxford—presented as Archdeacon Grantly's sons. These satires seem discordant in tone when judged against the dominant style which Trollope evolves in the later

'Chronicles of Barsetshire' in the 1860s. *The Warden*, however, is a novel that draws attention to its own literary artifices far more than do *Framley Parsonage* or *The Last Chronicle of Barset*, which become the later standard by which Trollope's works of the 1850s are unfairly judged. The satires in *The Warden* are appropriate to that novel's style, and are thematically relevant for those versed in church history, even if commonly judged by others as an excrescence.

Trollope considered that he would have done better to make a straightforward attack on either the misuse of church funds or 'the undeserved severity of the newspapers' towards offenders in such cases. He failed to recognize, however, that his novel had turned out quite unlike the many Victorian novels with a social mission. He had produced a much more complex story of a conscientious individual caught between powerful but mutually irreconcilable demands which threaten to destroy him. The opposition between forces of tradition and reform in this novel accords with the author's later statement of his political position as that of 'an advanced but still a conservative liberal' (*Auto* XVI). In *The Warden* and the subsequent Barsetshire novels, the conservative, traditional elements seem to the later reader to predominate, although modern aspects of the fictional world were more immediately apparent to contemporary readers: it may be difficult to recapture the balance then felt between Barchester as part of the up-to-date political world, and a nostalgia for fading tradition. Like its successors, *The Warden* shows enjoyment of change and some sharp thrusts at old-fashioned high-church complacency, such as the inexcusable pluralism of the Hon. and Revd Dr Vesey Stanhope, who holds the livings of Crabtree Canonicorum, and Eiderdown and Stogpingum, as well as the prebendal stall of Goosegorge, and 'whose hospitable villa on the Lake of Como is so well known to the elite of English travellers' (XIII). The ending of the story is achieved not by the triumph of modern, reforming values, but through Harding's exercise of the age-old virtue of honesty. The world is not made a better place, but Mr Harding's peace of mind is saved, and the new wave of ecclesiastical reform has as yet hardly been felt in Barchester.

This was the fourth of Trollope's novels, the first to be set in England, and the first to introduce his fictional county of Barsetshire, and although the list of characters is short in comparison with that of many of his novels, he introduced a number of characters and situations which would be richly developed in later novels in the series, such as the home life at Plumstead Episcopi and Mrs Grantly's 'curtain lectures' to the Archdeacon, as well as the Stanhopes, Mr Quiverful, and the Archdeacon's children. Although *The Warden* brought the author little payment—'[i]ndeed, as regarded remuneration for the time, stone-breaking would have done better' (*Auto* V)—he began to be acknowledged as a significant new novelist, and as time passed and critics and public looked back at it through the succeeding novels which constitute the 'Chronicles of Barsetshire', it gained in stature. In accordance with the thinking of the day, Trollope and his critics concentrated on the success of the characters he created and was able to carry through subsequent stories, especially Septimus Harding and Theophilus Grantly. Trollope claimed no special acquaintance with clergymen at the time, and attributed his success with these characters to his 'moral consciousness'.

Geraldine Jewsbury (anon.) in the *Athenaeum* (27 January 1855, 107–8) praised the 'clever, spirited, sketchy story', but found it marred by 'too much indifference as to the rights of the case', while the *Spectator* (6 January 1855, 27–8) considered that even though Trollope condemned the abuse, 'the whole tenour of the feeling of the narrative is the other way'. The *Leader* (17 February 1855, 164–5) thought the story was 'based on a good and solid foundation' and was 'an excellent subject for a novel', but objected that the author (or, as we should now say, the narrator) spoke 'far too much in his own person' and apostrophized his characters (Smalley 32–8). E. S. Dallas, who anonymously noticed *The Warden* with *Barchester Towers* in *The Times* (13 August 1857, 5), attacked Trollope for descending to personalities when presenting Tom Towers of the *Jupiter*, leading the author to reply belatedly in *An Autobiography* that at the time he 'had not even heard the name of any gentleman connected with The Times' (*Auto* V).

In *An Autobiography* Trollope relates how he came to conceive the story and setting of *The Warden* while travelling on Post Office business on a special postal mission aimed at 'extending the rural delivery of letters and . . . adjusting the work, which up to that time had been done in a very irregular manner': 'I visited Salisbury and whilst wandering there on a midsummer evening round the purlieus of the cathedral I conceived the story of *The Warden*,—from whence came that series of novels of which Barchester with its bishops, deans, and archdeacon was the central site.' He delayed composition in a way that would later become unthinkable, and 'on the 29th July 1853,—having been then two years without having made any literary effort,—I began *The Warden* at Tenbury in Worcestershire. It was then more than twelve months since I had stood for an hour on the bridge in Salisbury, and had made out to my own satisfaction the spot on which Hiram's hospital should stand. Certainly no other work that I ever did took up so much of my thoughts. On this occasion I did no more than write the first chapter, even if so much. . . . It was not till the end of 1853 that I recommenced it, and it was in the autumn of 1854 that I finished the work. It was only one small volume, and in later days would have been completed in six weeks,—or in two months at the longest if other work had pressed' (*Auto* V).

At the prompting of his old friend John *Merivale, Trollope sent the manuscript to William Longman on 8 October 1854, under the title 'The Precentor', and Longman's reader, J. Cauvin, reported favourably: 'This story takes its rise from the recent exposé of the abuses that have crept into Cathedral and Hospital Trusts. Not a very promising subject, one might infer at first sight! But such is the skill of the author that he has contrived to weave out of his materials a very interesting and amusing tale. . . . The characters are well drawn and happily distinguished; and the whole story is pervaded by a vein of quiet humour and (good-natured) satire, which will make the work acceptable to all Low Church men and dissenters. The description of the *Times*, under the nom de guerre of *Mount Olympus*, I will back against anything of the kind that was ever written for geniality and truth. In one word, the work ought to have a large sale.' (*Letters* 1, 38–9).

The novel was published by Longman on the half-profits system, which yielded Trollope a mere £20 3*s*. 9*d*. The manuscript is lost. Trollope reports that in its original form the novel 'never reached the essential honour of a second edition'. It appeared in 'Tauchnitz's British Authors', and was first published in America in 1862. Since then it has become one of the most reprinted of his novels, with simplified versions for schools and English-language learners alongside single book editions and inclusion in numerous anthologies.

Trollope made minor revisions to *The Warden* for publication in the 'Chronicles of Barsetshire', which came out as a collection for the first time from Smith, Elder & Co. in 1878. He increased the *Jupiter*'s circulation figure in chapter XIV from 5,000 to 8,000, included in chapter XV a quotation from Horace (*Satires* 1. 10. 14), added a short passage elaborating on the Warden's motives in going secretly to London, and inserted footnotes to the description of his trip to London to account for changes that had occurred in the city since 1855.   DS

Watkins, Herbert, photographer of Regent Street, London, who took pictures of Trollope in April 1860. Seeing the result, Trollope said 'It looks uncommon feirce [*sic*], as that of a dog about to bite; but that I fear is the nature of the animal portrayed' (*Letters* 1, 101). Trollope loathed sitting for photographers.   RCT

Watt, Walter, fellow of an Oxford college and one of six collaborators in founding a magazine, 'very far gone in his ideas of reform'. 'Panjandrum' *ET*   GRH

Waugh, Arthur (1866–1943). In *A Hundred Years of Publishing, Being the Story of Chapman and Hall Ltd.* (1930), drawing on the recollections of a long-standing employee, he described Trollope as 'a terror to the staff' who would tramp into the office as soon as it opened, wearing his pink coat, with a sheaf of papers in his pocket, 'and how he would bang on the table with his hunting crop, and swear like a sergeant-major because there was no one in authority yet arrived to receive his hectic instructions' (*I & R* 64).   RCT

Way We Live Now, The (*see opposite*)

Webb, Counsellor, magistrate of Ardum, renowned as 'a good man and a gentleman' (XIX), who urges amelioration of the social and economic conditions that lead to such crimes as illicit distilling of whiskey. When Thady Macdermot is accused of murder, Webb fights a duel with Jonas Brown on his behalf, and visits the Lord-Lieutenant to plead for mercy. *MB*   MRS

Webb, Wickham, literary clubman who tells Fred Pickering that literature is the hardest profession in the world, and advises him to return to his father. 'Pickering' *ET*   GRH

Weber, Marie, Lotta Schmidt's friend, engaged to a diamond-cutter. She tries to assist Lotta in choosing a husband. 'Schmidt' *LS*   GRH

Wednesbury, parliamentary borough held by the Marquis of Kingsbury in his younger radical days, before he returns to Tory convictions. *MF*   SRB

Weiss, Frau. She argues with Frau Frohmann because the Tendel sisters are not paying the increased room rate, but stays none the less. 'Frohmann' *WFF*   GRH

Weiss, Herr, magistrate who brings his family annually to stay at Frau Frohmann's inn but is congenitally mean. 'Frohmann' *WFF*   GRH

West Bromwich, borough in Birmingham represented in Parliament by Joshua Monk. The subject of some confusion, West Bromwich is one of two boroughs supposed to be represented in Parliament by Joshua Monk, the other being Pottery Hamlets. *PF*   JMR

West Cork and Ballydehob Branch Railway, a money-making venture in the form of a railway project in Ireland in which Undy Scott and Alaric Tudor invest. *TC*   MT

Westend, Sir Warwick, member of the Examining Board of the civil service. One of 'the three kings' heading the new exams board, Sir Warwick 'was a man born to grace, if not his country, at any rate his county' (XI). He was based on Sir Stafford Northcote. *TC*   MT

Westerman, François Joseph (based on historical figure), the general deputed to destroy the Vendeans. A German whose mercenaries carry out his commands ruthlessly, he is himself a man of strong courage. He burns Clisson after the de Lescures escape. *LV*   GRH

Western, Cecilia (née **Holt**), beautiful, strong-willed, aesthetic young woman who jilts Sir Francis Geraldine, then marries George Western without revealing her previous engagement. Though innocent of anything save an embarrassed silence, she is deserted by her husband. She refuses his money, but gives her suspicious husband little encouragement or opportunity to learn the truth. As stubborn as Western, she seldom takes advice. Finally, however, she relents, (*cont. on page 582*)

PARTLY modelled on Juvenal's attacks on 2nd-century Rome's amorality, *The Way We Live Now* is Trollope's sustained assault on contemporary mores, 'instigated by what I conceived to be the commercial profligacy of the age' (*Auto* XX). A panorama of London's intersecting financial, political, and social worlds, the novel condemns all three for their mutual abandonment of traditional morality.

Trollope creates two opposing figures to represent traditional values and the new indifference to those values. Roger Carbury, squire of Carbury Manor in Suffolk, is a country gentleman of ancient lineage and unimpeachable morality, firmly rooted in his ancestral estate. His opposite is Augustus Melmotte, a foreigner of undetermined origin, who has recently settled in London. Melmotte is rumoured to be a financial wizard, enormously rich and capable of furthering or thwarting any enterprise. Neither Roger nor Melmotte are fully realized as characters, presumably because for Trollope they are more important as representative types.

Trollope organizes his novel around three families, Carburys, Melmottes, and Longestaffes, whose complex interactions constitute most of the plot. Roger Carbury is head of his family. His widowed aunt Lady Carbury lives in London, where she adds to her income by writing worthless books of pseudo-history, and eventually a bad novel. Her son Sir Felix Carbury is a vacuous wastrel, who has inherited his father's baronetcy without any estate or fortune to maintain the rank; his 'business is to marry an heiress' (II). Urged by his mother, he 'goes in for' marriage with Melmotte's daughter, and joins one of Melmotte's enterprises as a nominal board member. Roger Carbury hopes to marry Lady Carbury's other child, his cousin Hetta (Henrietta), and make her mistress of Carbury Manor, a plan her mother enthusiastically endorses. But Hetta does not love him, preferring instead his younger, more attractive, and less scrupulous friend Paul Montague.

Melmotte claims to be English, not very convincingly, and his wife, 'a Bohemian Jewess', is not the mother of his daughter Marie, the heiress, who is probably illegitimate. He is determined to purchase a titled husband for her, to establish her and to promote his own acceptance in English society despite his murky background.

The third family, the Longestaffes, are neighbours of Robert Carbury in Suffolk. Mr (Adolphus) Longestaffe is squire of Caversham, and short of cash. His wife Lady Pomona has encouraged her daughters to marry money and rank, without much success: Sophia has married a petty squire and Georgiana Longestaffe has spent many London seasons seeking a husband, gradually lowering her expectations from lord to commoner. Adolphus Longestaffe, the only son, known to his friends as Dolly, is lazy, dim-witted, and contrary. When his father wants to sell the estate of Pickering Park to Melmotte, a decision on which father and son must agree, Dolly opposes the sale, then demands half the purchase money, but eventually discovers that Melmotte has forged his signature on a letter of agreement. With that discovery, Melmotte's reputation and power begin to unravel. The three families are closely entwined. Dolly is a friend and companion of Sir Felix Carbury and Paul Montague, and briefly considers entering the contest for Marie Melmotte's hand. Mr Longestaffe rents his London house to the Melmottes, and becomes a board member of Melmotte's projected South Central Pacific and Mexican Railway; Georgiana spends her last London season as an uncomfortable guest of the Melmottes.

Trollope portrayed Melmotte as 'the great speculator who robs everybody' and so exemplifies that 'commercial profligacy' he defines (*Auto* XX) as his chief target in *The Way We Live Now*. But he also aimed at other vices. In Georgiana he depicts 'the intrigues of girls who want to get married', in Dolly and his companions 'the luxury of young men who prefer to remain single', while Lady Carbury, discovered in chapter I writing to various editors in hopes that her book will be favourably reviewed, represents 'the puffing propensities of authors who desire to cheat the public into buying their volumes'. The amorality of the commercial world, which admits and reveres an impostor like Melmotte, is thus extended from the stock market to the marriage market, to the Beargarden Club, where Dolly and his friends have created a club without rules, and to the literary market place. Even the clergy are affected. Both the easygoing Bishop Yeld and Father Barham, the unworldly Catholic priest, admire Melmotte for his contributions to their churches. In the political world, both parties court Melmotte; he is eventually adopted by the Conservatives and elected to Parliament as MP for Westminster, whereupon he is introduced into Parliament by the Conservative leader, unnamed but clearly Benjamin Disraeli, whom Trollope disdained both as statesman and as novelist. These willing admirers and approvers of Melmotte emphasize Trollope's argument that for a criminal upstart to achieve acceptance and even extravagant adulation, it is necessary that those who ought to maintain moral and social standards, by challenging a new arrival about his origins and previous behaviour, ignore this duty. Royalty, nobility, clergy, and gentry eagerly welcome Melmotte as a great man, a Napoleon of finance, even though they suspect his shady past and dislike his uncouth manners.

Melmotte presumably speculates widely, but Trollope focuses on the South Central Pacific and Mexican Railway as typical. Hamilton K. Fisker of San Francisco, like Melmotte an unscrupulous outsider in London, brings Melmotte into the railway project, both men tacitly understanding that the purpose is to sell and speculate with stocks rather than to lay track and run trains. The railway's board of directors consists of Fisker, Sir Felix, Mr Longestaffe, Paul Montague, Lord Nidderdale, Lord Alfred Grendall, and a shady businessman, Mr Cohenlupe. Lord Alfred Grendall is Melmotte's trophy nobleman and flunkey. His son Miles Grendall is Melmotte's secretary and a member of the Beargarden. Lord Nidderdale, son and heir of the Marquis of Auld Reekie, is a member of Parliament, Melmotte's preferred suitor for Marie's hand and fortune, and also a Beargarden regular. Apart from Melmotte, Fisker, and Cohenlupe, none of the directors knows anything about business; they are on the board only to give it an appearance of respectability. A partial exception is Paul Montague, who has lived for a time in San Francisco, where he has been Fisker's partner in several enterprises. He agrees to join the board when he realizes that his capital is tied up in the railway because of decisions Fisker has made. When Montague becomes suspicious that the railway is a sham, he resigns.

While in America, Montague has also become engaged to Mrs (Winifred) Hurtle, the third of the book's trio of outsiders who invade and disturb English life. Mrs Hurtle may or may not be legally divorced; her husband may still be alive; she has shot a man in Oregon. No bashful Trollopian maiden, she follows Montague to London to demand that he fulfil his promise to marry her. Montague is weak in his evasive refusals, despite his clear preference to be rid of her and to marry the more conventional Hetta Carbury. Sexually aggressive, Mrs Hurtle is also the most out-spoken admirer of Melmotte's buccaneering business practices, insisting that men such as he are above the law.

The Beargarden, where idle and generally impecunious young aristocrats gamble for each other's worthless IOUs, serves as a kind of parody of the world of speculative finance. Like the Beargarden gamblers, Melmotte's financial games involve the circu-lating of worthless pieces of paper among those who pretend they have value. Lady Carbury's books extend the parody to the literary world; they are not worth the paper on which they are written. Trollope's attack on 'profligacy' involves an exposure of sham.

Trollope handles his large cast of characters and their interrelationships with con-siderable skill. Melmotte acts as a kind of black hole, drawing them all into his vacuity, though Trollope, with his usual tenderness toward even his rascally characters, allows most of them to escape the final debacle and have a second chance.

The events of the story take place in a fairly brief period, between late February and the beginning of September of a single year, with a few loose ends tied up a little later, in the last few chapters. Trollope sets the story in 1873, though he dates events by an 1872 calendar. The most dramatic action is compressed into an even briefer period, roughly the first three weeks of July, when Melmotte achieves the pinnacle of his greatness and fame, only to fall spectacularly and end as a suicide.

For all his financial sharpness, Melmotte is brought down by the unlikely agency of Dolly Longestaffe, who vehemently denies that he has signed the agreement to sell the Pickering estate to Melmotte. Vastly over-extended, Melmotte has already mortgaged Pickering to keep his enterprises afloat, and is unable to satisfy the Longestaffes with the cash payment they demand. By this time rumours are circulating that Melmotte is insolvent, is a criminal, even that he is about to be arrested.

Suspicions about Melmotte begin to circulate as he is preparing to host a great dinner for the visiting Emperor of China. The guests are to include royalty, the aris-tocracy, members of the government, and representatives of the business world. As the dinner approaches, invitations become objects of desire, and are bargained for like stock certificates. But as the rumours gain hold, the invitations fall in value, and many guests, especially those in politics or business, eventually fail to attend.

Despite this public embarrassment, Melmotte wins the parliamentary seat for West-minster the next day, and is able to take his seat in the House of Commons. There he is generally shunned, even by members of his own party. Rumours continue to under-mine his credit, and Marie, furious because he will not let her marry Sir Felix, refuses to sign a document making over to his use money he had previously settled on her, which he desperately needs. When he forges her name on that document, together with the name of Croll, his confidential clerk, Croll detects the forgery, returns the document to him, and leaves his employment. Unable to pay his creditors, Melmotte makes one last appearance in the House. Drunk when he rises to speak, he cannot think of anything to say, then tumbles and falls over those seated in front of him. This literal fall signals his fall from fortune and eminence. Melmotte returns home, and destroys himself with prussic acid. Ironically, it later appears that many of his enter-prises are valuable. He has lived by rumour, which inflated his reputation, and he dies by rumour, which to some extent exaggerates his crimes.

In the aftermath of Melmotte's death, Cohenlupe flees to the Continent after plundering their joint enterprises. Marie Melmotte marries Hamilton Fisker, and sails to America with him, where he will continue to sell shares in the railway.

In a parody of the collapse of Melmotte's fraudulent empire, the Beargarden also collapses when the steward, Herr Vossner, decamps to the Continent, leaving behind the club's unpaid bills and taking with him the club's remaining funds.

The Longestaffes recover Pickering. While a guest of the Melmottes, Georgiana Longestaffe has recognized that her value on the marriage market is shrinking rapidly, and so has agreed to marry Mr Brehgert, an elderly Jewish widower, demanding from him certain cash guarantees, and his promise to maintain both a country house and a house in London. Brehgert is a decent and honourable man, with no resemblance to some of Trollope's stereotypical Jewish moneylenders; Georgiana is rapacious and a greedy bargainer. Trollope depicts the common anti-Jewish prejudice of Victorian England in the Longestaffe family's hostility to the planned marriage, and dramatizes this hostility when Georgiana purchases for Brehgert an invitation to her friend Lady Monogram's in return for an invitation to the Emperor's dinner. Brehgert is snubbed at Lady Monogram's party, which he soon leaves. When he loses part of his fortune in Melmotte's fall, and explains to Georgiana that he will not be able to afford a London house for two or three years, she breaks off their engagement. On her sister's wedding day she elopes with a curate.

Roger Carbury relinquishes his cousin Hetta to Paul Montague, and decides that their child shall be heir to Carbury Manor. Mrs Hurtle removes herself from England, returning to San Francisco with Fisker and Marie Melmotte. Sir Felix has already bungled his planned elopement with Marie Melmotte, by gambling away at the Beargarden the money she has given him, getting drunk, and so failing to join her at Liverpool as agreed. His plan to seduce Ruby Ruggles, granddaughter of one of Roger Carbury's tenant farmers, ends ignominiously when he is thrashed by her rustic lover John Crumb. Shunned at the Beargarden in that institution's last days, he is finally packed off to straitened exile in Germany in the charge of a clergyman. Lady Carbury agrees to abandon literature and her title for marriage with Mr Broune, a respectable journalist.

Trollope's affection for even the meanest of his creatures does not extend to Sir Felix, but allows Melmotte some measure of dignity at his death. The novelist's attack on the degeneracy of the age is, however, somewhat muted by what follows Melmotte's suicide. Though he is initially portrayed as a symptom of that degeneracy, rather than its instigator, when he is removed from the scene Trollope ends the novel in an optimistic mood. With Melmotte's fall, all the dangerous outsiders leave London: Marie Melmotte and her mother, Fisker, Cohenlupe, Mrs Hurtle. The Beargarden is broken up. Sir Felix goes into exile, and a series of marriages re-establish the proper social and moral order. Lord Nidderdale expresses the new seriousness when he resolves to devote himself to parliamentary business and live economically. Though Roger Carbury has lost Hetta, Trollope implies that now that the disruptive forces have been expelled, Roger's traditional values will prevail.

Trollope's denunciatory mode owes something to his early reading of Carlyle, and especially to Carlyle's 'Hudson's Statue' in *Latter-Day Pamphlets* (1850), which denounces George *Hudson (1800–71) as a 'swollen Gambler'. Known as 'the Railway Napoleon' and 'the Yorkshire Balloon', Hudson, who built some railways and speculated in others, had become a Conservative MP like Melmotte, and like him had entertained royalty and aristocracy at his London mansion before his sudden ruin. Other probable models included Henry Fauntleroy, a banker executed for forgery in 1824; John *Sadleir, who failed when the City lost confidence in him, and committed suicide with prussic acid after ostentatiously showing himself in the City and at his club; and Charles Lefevre, who escaped to Paris with £1 million raised by selling stock in an Atlantic–Pacific railway across Honduras. The Bank of England forgery (1873) involved American criminals who forged signatures on bills of exchange, and bankers too trusting to examine those signatures carefully. Trollope's picture of unbridled and unprincipled speculation is echoed in a *Times* editorial (1875) written by his friend John *Delane and the Revd Thomas Mozley.

Themes of inflation and deflation in *The Way We Live Now* were graphically expressed by the cover design for the novel's publication in parts, drawn by an unidentified J.B. A weeping Father Time sits atop a globe, shielding his eyes from the scenes around him, shown within the frames of five fat money bags. One shows Melmotte, who somewhat resembles Napoleon I; others show a board of directors' meeting, Melmotte conversing with Fisker, Melmotte bowing to the Chinese Emperor. Two side panels depict the imperial banquet and Melmotte electioneering. At the bottom of the cover, three collapsing bags present Melmotte among his enemies, Melmotte bullying his daughter, and finally Melmotte dead with the vial of poison beside him.

Trollope began *The Way We Live Now* on 1 May 1873, stopped at the end of May to spend June writing *Harry Heathcote of Gangoil: A Tale of Australian Bush Life* (1874), then completed *The Way We Live Now* between 3 July and 1 December. The novel appeared in what was already an outmoded method, parts publication, in twenty numbers from February 1874 to September 1875. Forty feeble illustrations by Lionel Grimston *Fawkes, two to each part, also appeared when the complete novel was published in two volumes in July 1875.

Contemporary reviewers were not pleased with *The Way We Live Now*. The *Athenaeum* considered it 'carelessly constructed and carelessly written'. *Spectator* objected to the prevalence of 'detestable' characters, and called Roger Carbury 'an overbearing prig'. The *Examiner* found the characters uninteresting and the whole careless and hasty. Only *The Times* took Trollope's satiric aims seriously. 'A more copious record of disagreeable matters could scarcely be imagined . . . than *The Way We Live Now*,' declared Henry James, writing soon after Trollope's death (Smalley 394–416, 528).

Michael Sadleir began a re-evaluation in *Trollope: A Commentary* (1927), considering it 'of supreme importance', a 'long and trenchant satire', and even wondering 'whether this fierce tremendous book is not the greatest novel Trollope ever wrote' (Sadleir 396–401). A. O. J. Cockshut, more decisively, declared that 'Formally, Trollope came near to writing a masterpiece' (*Anthony Trollope* (1955), 214). Since the 1960s, critics have recognized *The Way We Live Now* as Trollope's most impressive achievement, and a major Victorian novel. The manuscript is in the Pierpont Morgan Library, New York.   RT

apRoberts, Ruth, *Trollope: Artist and Moralist* (1971).
Kincaid, James R., *The Novels of Anthony Trollope* (1977).
Tracy, Robert, *Trollope's Later Novels* (1978).

suggesting his right to be obeyed. At their reconciliation, she owns that she has been wrong to conceal anything, but will not ask his forgiveness, even though he acknowledges his mistake. *KD*

NCS

Western, George, a man of modest private means who marries Cecilia Holt, but is 'kept in the dark' about her previous engagement. Brooding, unhappy, and generally unsatisfied—a distinguished Oxford graduate, a lawyer who had not practised, an MP who found government a waste of time—he is ruled by suspicion, stubbornness, and an unforgiving nature. Morbid jealousy magnifies his wife's secrecy into a plot against his fortune and happiness. Western's character tends toward tragic melancholy, though he finally makes an awkward apology to his wife. *KD*

NCS

West Indies. Trollope was sent by the Post Office to the West Indies in 1859 to improve postal service from that region. The literary result of this journey is a delightful and highly personal travel book, The *West Indies and the Spanish Main*. Of the islands on his itinerary, he gave most attention to the British colonies of Jamaica, Barbados, and Trinidad, and to the Spanish colony of Cuba. He was also much interested in the Isthmus of Panama and in Costa Rica, and discussed at length the possibilities of building a canal there.

The West Indian sugar colonies were the gems of the British colonial system in the 18th century, but were in decline in the 19th, being faced with increasing competition from cheaper producers in the East Indies and more fertile Caribbean islands such as Cuba. Their economic strength had also been weakened by British abolition of their slave trade, effective in 1807, and the abolition of slavery in 1834 at a time when Cuba still retained its slaves. The British colonies Trollope visited had elaborate governmental structures, which he mocked because they were out of all proportion to the resources available to maintain them. Trollope also lamented the seemingly irreversible economic decline of these once proud colonies, where ex-slaves who had the option refused to provide adequate cheap labour for the plantations. The larger colonies, with surplus land on which the black population established a subsistence agriculture, were chronically short of labour, unless they began to import indentured labour from India.

Trollope presented an excellent picture of the social structure of the area, though his judgements on the coloured and black population were affected by the biases that he struggled against, unsuccessfully. To Trollope, the whites were polite, hospitable, and cultured, but unable to shake off visions of their privileged past and initiate progressive economic policies. The coloured people were ambitious and capable to a certain extent, but with an aggressive reach beyond their abilities. The blacks were often rude, more as an assertion of their independence than from malice, supine, lazy, and a drag on the island economies. Apart from the unfairness of some of his judgements, what Trollope missed was the potential explosiveness of this mixture, particularly in Jamaica, where in 1865 a rebellion erupted, leading to a number of casualties, a severe repression, and acts of dubious legality or morality. The result was the dismissal of Governor Edward Eyre, and the eventual replacement of most of the island assemblies with Crown Colony government. In England there was a lengthy and furious debate between the supporters of Eyre and those who wished to prosecute him for his acts. Oddly, despite his knowledge and interest, Trollope appears not to have been involved in the debate.

The West Indies provided Trollope with settings for several short stories: 'Miss Sarah Jack, of Spanish Town, Jamaica', 'The Journey to Panama', 'Returning Home', and 'Aaron Trow'.

LK

Rogozinski, J., *A Brief History of the Caribbean* (1992).

West Indies and the Spanish Main, The. (See also WEST INDIES.) Trollope sailed for the West Indies on 17 November 1858, his second postal mission requiring that he should 'cleanse the Augean stables' (*Auto* VII) of the services in the area. With exemplary professionalism he established local control of the post offices in Jamaica and British Guiana, evaluated the shipping of mail across the Isthmus of Panama to the west coast of America, and urged upon the Spanish possessions of Cuba and Puerto Rico the need 'to reduce their charges for local forwarding of mail sent from the United Kingdom' (Super 103). He checked local postal routes meticulously, as was his standard practice, prescribed economies, and initiated changes. He negotiated the carrying of mail in Panama for an annual fee, and on 16 July 1859, a fortnight after his return, he submitted his report. In it Jamaica was effectively made the centre for mail in the region, while his recommendations aimed to save the packet company some £15,000 per annum. As on the earlier mission to Suez, Trollope had increased efficiency and reduced costs. There was too an expansive integration of his two professions, that of the decisive civil servant and the career writer. Henceforth travel would become more important in his life, feeding into his fiction (four stories resulted from this trip), giving him new areas to explore, observe, absorb, and the freedom to express opinions in his own right.

He arrived at St Thomas, the trading centre for the region, on 2 December, and sailed from there on the *Derwent* to Kingston, Jamaica. He had continued *The Bertrams* on the voyage out and completed it 18 January 1859. He began his travel book on 25 January, even before he had completed the deal with Chapman & Hall to publish it. Comprising twenty-three chapters, *The West Indies and the Spanish Main* begins with an account of his journey. Then chapters II-IX are devoted to Jamaica, with an acerbic account of Kingston, whose ragged, disreputable streets, ugly buildings, and lack of lighting are an 'utter disgrace', redeemed only by hospitality. He is similarly critical of Spanish Town, the seat of government, 'the city of the dead', under a pitiless sun, with pigs roaming everywhere. He admires the scenic beauty of the island, however, which he compares with that of Switzerland. He notes the provision-grounds of the negroes, the mango, breadfruit, and cotton trees, bemoans the constant awkward river crossings, and gives a delightful account (fiction?) of his meeting with a sad coloured woman who confides in him her star-crossed love. He experiences the effects of an earthquake in Port Antonio, appraises the sugar industry, describes the social life of the whites and the poor roads, and ascends the Blue Mountain, giving a humorous and self-mocking account of endurance and near-exhaustion—'Our wit did not flow freely as we descended' (III).

The following chapters, dealing with racial characteristics and problems, reflect Trollope's trenchant and sometimes unpalatable views. Black men, he asserts, have the gloss of religion—psalm-singing—without positive observance; they are idle, lack application, ambition, have no desire for property. Believing emancipation to be right, he is critical of its after-effects, which include squatting and indolence. Work does not have to mean slavery. Those of mixed race are much more socially responsible and active, enter the public service, sometimes as members of Parliament, and, though incurring the jealousy of the whites, are fit 'to undertake the higher as well as the lower paths of human labour' (V). Disliked by the negroes, they tend to ape the whites and send their children to English schools where they acquire English 'tricks and graces'. Trollope's particular bias, common to his time, is expressed in 'the white will order and the black obey' (VI), but he boldly reiterates that emancipation has meant effectively freedom from work. The resultant free trade crippled the

Jamaican sugar planter and encouraged the import of foreign labour from Africa and China. He charts the decline of the sugar industry, and, as he would later do in Bermuda, makes unfavourable comparisons with Cuba, where his limited investigation found the negroes well fed and cared for, despite working a sixteen-hour day. He condemns filibustering, still prevalent in Cuba, and suggests Britain should support the United States' annexation of the island, whose citizens have no say in their country's government. This does not prevent him recording with zest the 'volantes' (carriages) in Havana, the gambling, dancing, window-sitting habits, the public lotteries, and the universal bribery.

Returning from Havana to St Thomas, he travels via Barbados ('an island that pays its way', XI) and Georgetown to Demerara, British Guiana. Demerara is 'the Elysium of the tropics—the West Indian happy valley of Rasselas' (XII). Here the sugar plantations, employing steam power and imported labour, are superior, the government of this fine colony being that of 'a mild despotism tempered by sugar'. In Barbados he notes that every inch of land is used (the negroes, more heavily built here, had to work), but sugar is grown in the old-fashioned way and the soil suffers. He delights in the generous Barbadian hospitality, but records that the Bims (the whites) feel themselves superior to all other islanders, living in 'little England, as it delights to call itself' (XIII).

His eye ever on statistics, in Trinidad Trollope notes that imported coolies have increased exports by two-thirds. He is critical of the Anti-Slavery Society, which should not 'interfere with the labour of the West Indian colonies' (XIV). His journeys in New Granada and the Isthmus of Panama include an account of the disgraceful conditions in the British Consulate at Santa Martha, the difficulties of procuring labour since emancipation, an obligatory piece on Simon Bolivar, and a note that the Panama railway already pays a 12.5 per cent dividend. This is followed by a comical description of the mule ride to San Jose in Costa Rica. He records the 'processioning' of the whole town in Passion week, defines the House of Congress as a farce, and praises the Costa Ricans for their expulsion of the filibusters. As he did in Jamaica, he makes the risky ascent of a mountain, the volcanic Mount Irazu, and then tells the story of the solitary Englishwoman at Cartago whose gold-washing has failed after her husband's disappearance and subsequent murder in San Jose. Another incident, the drowning of a woman who was setting out for England on the Serapiqui river, would later be transformed into the story 'Returning Home'.

Trollope treks through thick forest, along the side of a volcanic mountain, through mud, and then down the Serapiqui river ('I found my bulk and size to be of advantage to me') by canoe to the Atlantic coast at Greytown, the worst place he had ever seen (XX). In the following chapter he surveys railways, canals, transport in Central America. As to the plans of the Frenchman M. Belly for a Panama Canal, he envisages profits for the potentates of Costa Rica and Cuba but considers the venture impractical—M. Belly had not even been to South America.

Finally, before going north to the United States, Trollope visits the Bermudas, notes the fine climate, the doziness of the people (he himself for once experiences lassitude) and focuses on the convict settlement. He observes that there is a determination 'to do well by our rogues' (XXII) and summarizes the various schemes to improve the lot of prisoners, asserting with his usual forthrightness that they represent an uncertain idealism, and that criminals should be punished and employed in useful work. He is appalled by faction killings among them—and the attempted murder of a warder—and feels that their food and clothing, superior to those of British servicemen and labourers, provide too much comfort. A notable story, 'Aaron Trow', derives from this experience.

On 2 June 1859 he sails for New York and visits the falls at Niagara. Initially disappointed, he observes: 'Their charms grow upon one like the conversation of a brilliant man' (XXIII). *The West Indies and the Spanish Main* was not 'the best book that has come from my pen' (*Auto* VII), but it is rich in observation, commentary on people and places, and careful evaluation of practical issues. His forthright views on race mirror contemporary thinking but have their own integrity based on observation. The book is rich too in anecdote, incident, description, as well as humour. Written February–late summer 1859, it was published on 1 November.   GRH

Westmacott, Mr, a radical who contests the Percycross seat with Ontario Moggs. 'Popular throughout the county . . . he was a born gentleman, which is so great a recommendation for a Radical' (XX). *RH*   ALS

Westminster, Hugh Lupus Grosvenor, Duke of (1825–99). He took his seat as 3rd Marquis of Westminster in the House of Lords (1870). As chairman of an all-day conference at St James's Hall, London, on the Eastern Question (December 1876), he was reduced to tugging at Trollope's coat-tails in order to interrupt his speech after repeated soundings of the bell to announce he had reached his time limit. Trollope

merely turned round, said, 'Please leave my coat alone,' and continued (*I & R* 219).   RCT

Westmorland. The Lake District scenery sometimes forms the backdrop for action. In *Can You Forgive Her?* melancholy existence on the Vavasor estate is matched by the 'stern sameness of the everlasting moorland' (XXXI). Castle Grex in *The Duke's Children* has a lake 'not serenely lovely as are some of the lakes in Westmoreland' (XXXVII). Thwaite Hall in 'The Mistletoe Bough' nestles between Ullswater and Penrith. Westmorland also features in *The Bertrams* (Bowes Lodge) and *Marion Fay* (Hauteboy Castle).   MRS

Weston, Julia. Alias John Smith, she travels across Palestine with the narrator, Mr Jones, to escape from her 'intolerable' uncle, secretly becoming attached to her companion. 'Palestine' *TAC2*   GRH

Weston, Sir William, gruff baronet, who separates his disguised niece Julia from Mr Jones, to whom he apologizes half-heartedly for his suspicions. 'Palestine' *TAC2*   GRH

West Point, the military academy in New York State. 'Generals' *LS*   GRH

West Putford, small rural parish in Hampshire, within walking distance of Hurst Staple. It is home to the Revd Mr Gauntlet and his daughter Adela, where she is visited by Arthur Wilkinson. *B*   MRS

Wharton, Abel, well-to-do father of Emily and Everett Wharton. Though Mr Wharton is a successful barrister and a loving father, his conservative prejudices cloud his judgement. Fearful of Ferdinand Lopez's foreign background, Mr Wharton fails to ask practical questions about the man's character or finances, his basic fitness as a husband. When Emily marries Lopez, her father is keenly disappointed, but does what he can to protect her from her husband's villainy. *PM*   JMR

Wharton, Sir Alured, head of the Wharton family. A simple country gentleman of limited means, the staunchly Conservative baronet lives at Wharton Hall, his 'handsome old family place . . . in Herefordshire', caring for his wife and daughters and lamenting the Liberal reforms of the past 25 years. *PM*   JMR

Wharton, Everett, brother of Emily Wharton and heir to the family estate, Wharton Hall. Though his keen pride and somewhat flighty disposition cause some quarrels with his father, Everett is good-hearted and dutiful. He settles down considerably upon becoming heir to Wharton Hall and engaging himself to his cousin Mary Wharton. *PM*   JMR

Wharton, Mary, cheerful and loving cousin, intimate friend, and ultimately sister-in-law of Emily Wharton. The daughter of Sir Alured Wharton, Mary is disappointed by Emily's marriage to Ferdinand Lopez, but the friendship between them is restored after Lopez's death, when Mary agrees to marry Emily's brother Everett. *PM*   JMR

Wharton Hall, seat of the solidly conservative Sir Alured Wharton and his family. *PM*   JMR

'What Does Ireland Want?' (article). The Irish seem to enjoy complaining of their lot but not exerting themselves sufficiently to change it. The Protestant Church has been disestablished in Ireland because of justice, not Irish demands. The Fenian movement, which loudly demands separation from England, is an American project, made up of and funded by Americans; few Irish really support it. Convicted Fenians' release should be considered, not summarily granted. Demand for a Land Bill granting tenants fixity of tenure is clearly unreasonable. It would destroy landholders, and the whole economy. Legislation is needed to make lease-giving attractive to landlords, and improvements attractive to tenants. But no fixity of tenure. *Saint Pauls* (December 1869), 286–309.   AKL

'What Is a Job?' (letter). The Lord Chancellor is expected to exercise patronage for public, not private, welfare. Rumours abound in the Edmunds case; the inquiry is not public. A full exposition is required, even if Lord Westbury, the best law reformer of the age, should be proved guilty. *Pall Mall Gazette* (28 March 1865), 4.
AKL

'What It Is to Be a Statesman' (letter). A recent article in the *Saturday Review* unfairly and meanly criticizes Lord Russell, one of the country's greatest and most generous statesmen. *Pall Mall Gazette* (18 July 1866), 3–4.   AKL

'Whist at our Club' (article). The writer and some friends equally 'well-stricken in years' gather in the afternoons at the club for whist. Card-playing is satisfying and allowed; many former pursuits are now forbidden by doctors or weakness. The lively group startles others with its loudness and mirth; it is frequently requested to be quiet. It has been moved to an upstairs room by the management. The game is boring if it is too sedate. *Blackwood's Edinburgh Magazine* (May 1877), 597–604.   AKL

Whiston, Robert (1808–95). Headmaster of Rochester Cathedral Grammar School (1844–77), he disclosed that the increased income was not being used either to increase free schooling or for scholarships, as required by the terms of the ancient endowment; the cathedral establishment was the obvious beneficiary. *The Times* in 1851–2 gave publicity to the scandal. This was one of several such abuses ventilated during Trollope's gestation of *The Warden* (1855).   RCT

Whitehall Review. This magazine was published in London from 1876 until October 1912. Trollope had written *An Eye for an Eye* in 1870, but was not able to place it with a publisher until it ran in the *Whitehall Review* from 24 August 1878 to 1 February 1879. Chapman & Hall then published it as a two-volume novel in January 1879.   JWM

Whitstable, George, squire of Toodlum, engaged to Sophia Longestaffe. Much despised and maligned by Sophia's sister Georgiana for his dullness, he nevertheless ably fulfils his purpose of providing a respectable marriage and home for Sophia. *WWLN*   SRB

Whittlestaff, William, 50-year-old bachelor of modest but sufficient means. Having failed in his early pursuits—law, literature, and financial speculation—and been jilted by his fiancée (Catherine Bailey), he retires to a solitary life at Croker's Hall. A sensitive and kindly man who often reads Horace for consolation, he reluctantly takes in Mary Lawrie, the penniless daughter of a friend, and gradually falls in love with her. He releases her from their engagement when it is clear that she is in love with John Gordon, thus knowingly sentencing himself to a lonely life 'under the stigma of a second Catherine Bailey' (XV). *OML*   RC

'Whom Shall We Make Leader of the New House of Commons?' (article). The House of Commons leader is more important politically than the Prime Minister. The Liberals must unite, develop a plan, determine on a trustworthy leader, and gather a majority. Compromise is necessary for good to be accomplished. *Saint Pauls* (February 1868), 531–45.   AKL

'Why Frau Frohmann Raised her Prices', first published in *Good Words*, from February to May 1877 (reprinted in *WFF*). Frau Frohmann is proprietor of the Peacock Hotel in Brunnenthal in the Tyrol. It is a matter of great pride to her that over the years she has never raised her prices. In this 'Tory' policy she is supported by her son Peter and the local priest; she is opposed by her daughter Amalia (Malchen) and her lover, the lawyer Fritz Schlessen. Finally the old lady is persuaded to 'swim with the stream' and raise her prices.   JS

Why Frau Frohmann Raised her Prices and Other Stories

Why Frau Frohmann Raised her Prices and Other Stories, one volume, Isbister, 1882; Trollope's last volume of short stories, containing a miscellany of pieces, mainly published in magazines between December 1876 and December 1878. It lacks the coherence of his other three collections. JS

Wickerby, Mr, attorney who defends Phineas Finn during his trial for the murder of Mr Bonteen. Though diligent in Phineas's defence, Mr Wickerby arouses Phineas's resentment by not fully believing in his client's innocence. *PR*
JMR

'Widow's Mite, The', first published in *Good Words,* January 1863 (reprinted in *LS*); a 'social problem' story of the 1860s Lancashire cotton famine, precipitated by the American Civil War. Nora Field, whose family is connected with manufacture, is plighted to marry a wealthy young American, Frederic F. Frew, who is visiting England. Nora nobly intends to donate the value of her wedding outfit for the relief of starving textile workers (her 'mite'), and marry in drab everyday clothes. Frew thinks the gesture absurd. There are arguments between the lovers, but a compromise is eventually reached. JS

Wilberforce, Samuel (1805–73), Bishop of Oxford (1845–69); acquired the sobriquet 'Soapy Sam' for his ingratiating manner. Trollope satirized him in *The Warden,* along with Bishop Charles James *Blomfield of London, and Bishop Henry *Phillpotts of Exeter, as sons of Archdeacon Grantly. When Trollope joined the committee of the Royal Literary Fund (March 1864) Wilberforce was a colleague. RCT

Wilkes, Captain Charles (1798–1877), American naval officer who had Confederate commissioners James Mason and John Slidell seized from the British ship the *Trent,* and detained in Boston harbour (1861), thus precipitating a major international incident. Trollope met Wilkes and was inclined to admire his temerity. He wrote with a great sense of irony about the intricacies of Anglo-American sensibilities in his essay 'The Present Condition of the Northern States of the American Union' (1862–3). RCT

Wilkinson, Arthur (the elder), vicar of Hurst Staple whose family fostered the brilliant young scholar George Bertram. He is disappointed by his own son's fine but unremarkable performance. He is 'a good, kind parent' (II), concerned for the welfare of his family, but when he suddenly dies his insurance policy is insufficient to keep his wife and daughters from poverty. Once this is rectified, however, he is barely missed. *B*
MRS

Wilkinson, Mrs Arthur, comic figure who oversteps her sphere when she starts to wonder 'why she should not be addressed as the Reverend Mrs Wilkinson' (XLII). Like Mrs Proudie, she prepares for the battle to assume personal and ecclesiastical precedence over the reigning vicar of Hurst Staple, her son Arthur Wilkinson, but Lord Stapledean forces her to recognize the absurdity of her position. *B*
MRS

Wilkinson, Revd Arthur (the younger), Oxford graduate, son of the vicar of Hurst Staple, who, despite working hard, never measures up to his foster-brother George Bertram. His lack of early promise is compounded by Lord Stapledean's unreasonable proviso that he remit the majority of his vicar's salary to his mother—thus leaving him unable to support a wife—but he nevertheless wins the enduring love of Adela Gauntlet, and after having his morale raised by Bertram during a trip to Cairo, returns sufficiently emboldened to claim both his ecclesiastical rights and the right to a loving wife. *B*
MRS

Willesden, village about six miles (10 km) outside London. Louis Trevelyan takes Louey there, to River's Cottage, after 'kidnapping' him from his mother. *HKWR*
RC

Wilson, Legge, Liberal member of Parliament, one-time Chancellor of the Exchequer, long-time Secretary of State for India, and friend of Phineas Finn. Mostly peripheral to the plot, Legge Wilson often resurfaces at important moments, for instance, introducing the fabulously wealthy financial speculator Mr Melmotte to the Emperor of China. *PF, ED, PR, WWLN*
JMR

Wilson, Sophy. A superficial girl intent on marriage, employed by the Telegraph Office and helped by Lucy Graham when she becomes ill. She eventually marries a hairdresser. 'Telegraph' *WFF*
GRH

Wiltshire, general setting of *The Vicar of Bullhampton,* including Salisbury, Bullhampton, Heytesbury, and Pycroft Common. SRB

Winchester College. The oldest public school in England, founded in 1382 by William of Wykeham, it maintained its religious traditions and Spartan regime beyond Trollope's schooling there (1827–30). Grimmer for Trollope even than Harrow, its praefectorial system gave licence to bullying. Trollope was subject to his elder brother Tom, as his tutor, who thrashed him regularly. His father's parsimony added to his burdens, leading to a depression painfully recalled in *An Autobiography,* which made him think of climbing the college tower and putting 'an end to everything' (I). None the less he always acknowledged his Winchester schooling and, in July 1879, gave the College a set of the 'Chronicles of Barsetshire'. His knowledge of the city and its environs provided a source for the almshouses of *The Warden*. In *The Bertrams* both Arthur Wilkinson and George Bertram are Wykehamists, as is also Francis Arabin in the Barsetshire novels.

RCT

wine. Trollope appreciated wine and accumulated a substantial cellar. Moving to his last house, North End, Harting, he had iron bins installed to put his wine in order. In January 1882, he wrote to Henry the precise location of two bins to the right of the cellar he was to consider his own, 'Leoville, in the lower, and Becheville in the upper'. They had been brought from Paris. 'It is 1874 wine and will not be fit for use until 1884 at the earliest'. Later that month he wrote, 'John Merivale says that he will have an action against you for recovery of that claret. I held it on trust for my friends, and had no right to make it over secretly to a son' (*Letters* 2, 938, 941). By this time, under doctor's orders, Trollope had largely given up wine for brandy or whisky and mineral water. Early on he had cultivated his taste, and travelling abroad made him a connoisseur, though not a wine snob. His publishers, George Smith and Edward Chapman, sometimes helped with supplies. His favourite claret was Château Léoville; an apostrophe to '64 Léoville occurs in *Ayala's Angel* (V). In *The American Senator* the rector of Dillsborough is disgusted by Senator Gotobed's failure to appreciate his best '57 Mouton (XLII). Wine is also mentioned in *The Prime Minister* (X), and *Mr Scarborough's Family* (XXXVII). RCT

Winterfield, Mrs, widowed sister of Lady Aylmer and unofficial aunt of Clara Amedroz. Mrs Winterfield lives at Perivale, where life is a serious business: 'there was a look of woe about her which seemed ever to be telling of her own sorrows in this world' (I). *BE* WK

Winthrop, Zachary, wealthy bachelor lawyer of Silverbridge, partner of George Walker. Generally considered a fool except by some unmarried ladies, he offers useless advice to Mark Robarts when he is seeking legal help for Josiah Crawley. *LCB* NCS

women's issues. When Trollope began writing novels, England was in the throes of a heated debate concerning 'The Woman Question'. Existing customs and laws were founded upon the widely accepted belief that men and women differed naturally from one another. According to this theory, men were rational, women intuitive; men were speculative and sceptical, women pious and accepting; men were ambitious, women self-sacrificing; men were sexual, women pure.

Woman's nature suited her to a life of subordination in a domestic setting. Her sphere was the home, while man's was the public realm. Her interests were identified with those of the man who headed her family, and because he was the more rational of the two, the law conferred the power of defining their joint interests on him. Thus women's political interests were thought to be adequately protected, even though only males had the vote. On the same grounds, the marriage laws denied wives financial independence, and allowed their husbands to chastise them physically and to control the fate of their children. It was almost impossible for a woman to obtain a divorce. Since the home was her proper sphere, a woman was expected to work, if she needed money, in quasi-domestic occupations like teaching. The universities were closed to women, as were medicine, law, the ministry, and many skilled trades.

In the 1840s, however, a nascent women's movement began to challenge the standard view of female nature in the hope of reforming the laws and customs that it undergirded. The movement enjoyed a measure of success when Parliament passed the Divorce Act of 1857, which provided separated and divorced women certain property rights, and the Married Women's Property Act of 1870, which gave wives limited control over their possessions and earnings. Throughout his writing career, in letters, lectures, journalism, and travel books, as well as fiction, Trollope commented on the continuing debate concerning the role of women in society. But it is not easy to say exactly where he stood on the Woman Question, because he spoke about it in so many different voices.

As N. John Hall notes, Trollope often propounded views on women's rights that differed little from 'the ordinary conservatism common in his day', but he argued such views 'chiefly in his non-fiction' (Hall 339). The most retrograde of his writings on women's issues is the lecture 'The *Higher Education of Women*', which asserts that the necessity for separate spheres 'comes direct from nature,—or, in other words, from the wisdom of an all-wise and all-good Creator'. When we look at Trollope's novels, however, especially his later novels, a different picture emerges.

Although Trollope's narrators often make dismissive comments concerning women's rights, these pronouncements, unlike similar remarks in his non-fiction, are often called into question. The circumstances which evoke them do not support them. What should a woman do with her life? The narrator of *Can You Forgive Her?* answers this question irritably, 'Fall in love, marry the man, have two children, and live happily ever afterwards' (XI). But the female protagonists of the novel find it difficult to follow his advice. One loves a man she cannot marry, another has fallen in love with a man who, she has good reason to fear, may prove a repressive husband, while the third does not love either of her unappealing suitors, a boastful farmer and a feckless conman.

In Trollope's fiction, not only are the narrators' remarks frequently in tension with the stories they tell, but other formal tensions also suggest complex perspectives concerning women's rights. A main plot with conservative implications is balanced against sub-plots of a reformist tendency, or vice versa. Characters who embody ideal femininity prove less attractive than their rebellious, unfeminine foils. Happy endings that do not quite fit conclude darkly ironic stories revealing the powerlessness of Victorian women. Doctrinaire feminists are caricatured in the very novels which describe the plight of women in its most extreme form. Several characters are destroyed by internal inconsistencies in the standard code of feminine behaviour by which they try to live.

The aspects of the Woman Question in which Trollope's novels interest themselves most persistently are restrictions on vocational opportunity, the inequity of the marriage laws, and the double standard of sexual morality. Mme Max Goesler laments that, as a woman, she will never sit in Parliament. And though Dorothy Stanbury is one of the meekest characters in *He Knew He Was Right*, even she complains angrily that a man who is nobody can try to make himself somebody through his work, while a woman has no means of trying. Indeed, in Trollope's later novels, an endless parade of educated, intelligent women are hampered, frustrated, and occasionally destroyed by the absence of any vocational option beyond that of marrying the man and having two children.

The later novels also reveal Trollope's awareness of the danger that England's marriage laws posed for women. When the protagonist of *He Knew He Was Right* decides that his wife must admit wrongdoing in connection with a friendship which she believes to be completely innocent, he is able to expel her from her home and deprive her of her child in an attempt to compel her submission. Though Trollope's male characters often treat their wives affectionately, a series of cruel or neglectful husbands, from Sir Hugh Clavering to Samuel Dockwrath to Robert Kennedy, demonstrate that the marriage laws confer a tyrannical power on husbands which many of them misuse. Such a problem can be solved only by legal reform.

In contrast with the standard Victorian position, Trollope's fiction suggests that many women are highly sexual. In *Can You Forgive Her?*, it is clear that Glencora Palliser yearns for sexual attentions, as well as for love, from her workaholic husband. Only when the threat that she might elope with a lover frightens her husband into spending his evenings with her instead of in Parliament does Glencora conceive a child. Since he took this view of female sexuality, it is not surprising that Trollope found the harsh Victorian double standard of sexual morality monstrously unfair. *The Vicar of Bullhampton* argues passionately that ruined maidens be given a second chance. JN

Barickman, Richard, MacDonald, Susan, and Stark, Myra, *Corrupt Relations: Dickens, Thackeray, Trollope, Collins, and the Victorian Sexual System* (1982).

Morse, Deborah, *Women in Trollope's Palliser Novels* (1987).

Nardin, Jane, *He Knew She Was Right: The Independent Woman in the Novels of Anthony Trollope* (1989).

women writers, contemporary. Trollope was close to three important women writers: his own mother, Frances Trollope (1779–1850), a best-selling author of travel books and novels; George Eliot (1819–80), a novelist, poet, essayist, and translator; and Kate Field (1838–96), an American journalist. After becoming famous as a novelist, Trollope offered advice and practical assistance to many aspiring women artists. Some of these women were family friends; others were strangers who asked his aid, usually by letter. He sent an unsolicited letter of praise to Rhoda *Broughton, a minor novelist who had been criticized for her frank treatment of sexual issues. As an editor, Trollope published fiction, poetry, essays, and journalism written by women, for he believed that women writers could and should work 'at par along side of men' (*Letters* 1, 430). In a collection of stories straightforwardly entitled *An Editor's Tales*, he joked about his penchant for falling in love with aspiring authoresses.

Trollope's letters suggest that he had a harmonious relationship with his mother Frances Trollope, and in *An Autobiography* he speaks approvingly of her industry, generosity, high spirits, and resilience. But he is less complimentary in discussing her books. Concerning her best-known work, *Domestic Manners of the Americans*, Trollope wrote that 'no one could have been worse adapted by nature [than his mother] for the task of learning whether a nation was in a way to thrive. Whatever she saw, she judged, as most women do, from her own standing point. . . . What though people had plenty to eat and clothes to wear, if they put their feet upon the tables and did not reverence their betters?' (II). As a writer, Trollope concluded, his mother had failed to 'avoid the pitfalls of exaggeration' (II). One might hypothesize that the understated style and subtly balanced treatment of moral and social issues which characterize his fiction resulted, in part, from a desire to avoid the pitfalls that had entrapped his mother. In his own travel book on the United States, *North America*, Trollope paid close attention to the political issues Frances Trollope had ignored.

Trollope met G. H. Lewes in 1860. An introduction to his 'wife' George Eliot soon followed. Lewes, unable to divorce his first wife although she had been the mistress of another man for many years, could not marry George Eliot legally. When she met Trollope, Eliot had not yet won acceptance in general society. But her liaison with Lewes did not disturb Trollope, who was later to write sympathetically of similar unions in *The Belton Estate* and *Dr Wortle's School*. The lifelong friendship blossomed quickly—within two years, Eliot referred to Trollope as 'one of the heartiest, most genuine, moral and generous men we know' (Hall 203). Trollope admired Eliot's novels, but with reservations. In *An Autobiography*, he praises her terse and graphic characterization, placing her second among contemporary novelists. But he also notes that 'the nature of [Eliot's] intellect is very far removed indeed from that which is common to the tellers of stories. Her imagination . . . acts in analysing rather than creating' (XIII). Trollope thought that her penchant for philosophy, in combination with her intense desire to produce superior work, resulted in the overstrained style which disfigured her later books. He confided to a friend that he found *Daniel Deronda* 'all wrong in art—Not only is the oil flavoured in every page . . . but with the smell of the oil comes so little of the brilliance which the oil should give!' (*Letters* 2, 689). He consoled himself by remembering how much he admired Eliot's early novels.

While visiting Florence in 1860, Trollope met Kate Field, a beautiful young American who was studying there. Kate was a general favourite of the English community, which included Walter Savage Landor, as well as Robert and Elizabeth Barrett Browning, She was already working as a journalist, publishing accounts of her travels in several American newspapers. Trollope was instantly attracted and formed a semi-romantic, semi-avuncular attachment to Kate that lasted

until his death. As the years passed, Kate often sought Trollope's advice concerning her writing projects. They also corresponded about her second career as a lecturer. In contrast to his generous responses to other aspiring authoresses, Trollope's reactions to Kate's articles and to the manuscripts of her lectures were grouchy and negative. Indeed, no one who learned about Kate Field solely through Trollope's letters would realize that she was a talented and immensely successful woman. Perhaps Trollope resented his emotional dependence on Kate and tried to right the balance by denigrating her literary efforts. Or perhaps her intemperate enthusiasms, so like his mother's, annoyed him when they were recorded in black and white. JN

Wood, Lady Emma Caroline (née **Michell**) (1802–79), mother of Mrs Anna Steele. She began writing fiction in 1866. The Woods and Steeles were close friends of Trollope's and they hunted together in Essex. Trollope sprang to the defence of Lady Wood when her novel *Sorrow on the Sea* (1868) was branded immoral by the *Athenaeum*, causing William Tinsley, its publisher, to withdraw it and refuse payment (*Letters* 1, 450–1). RCT

Wood, Sir Evelyn (1838–1919), distinguished military man who served in the Crimean War; Victoria Cross (1858) for his part in suppressing Indian Mutiny; Adjutant General (1897–1901); Field Marshal (1903). Trollope hunted with Wood in East Anglia. On one outing he was in difficulties, and Wood came to his rescue. ' "For heaven's sake," exclaimed Trollope, "be careful; I am afraid to move lest I should trample on my spectacles which have just fallen off my nose" ' (*I & R* 117). RCT

Wood, Mrs Henry (née **Ellen Price**) (1814–87), author of the best-seller *East Lynne* (1861) and other sensation novels; bought and edited *Argosy* (1867–87). Having taken a stall in a bazaar at St James's Hall (May 1864) to raise funds for London's French Protestant schools, she approached Trollope. Loathing bazaars as fund-raisers, he nonetheless produced a parcel of autographed books. Trollope wrote 'Bazaars for Charity' in *Pall Mall Gazette* (April 1866), and made fun of bazaars in *Miss Mackenzie* (XXVII). RCT

Woods, Henry (1846–1921), artist first in the rustic genre, then in Venetian subjects, having moved to Venice (1876); first exhibited at the Royal Academy in 1869; began his career as an illustrator for the *Graphic* and other magazines.

He did inferior illustrations for *The Vicar of Bullhampton*. RCT

Woodward, Bessie, widow who lives with her daughters Gertrude, Linda, and Katie at Surbiton Cottage, Hampton. Mrs Woodward is a loving, slightly permissive, mother who 'lived on terms almost of equality' (III) with her daughters. Each of her daughters marries one of the three clerks, her own favourite being Harry Norman. *TC*
MT

Woodward, Gertrude, eldest daughter of Bessie Woodward and wife of Alaric Tudor. Gertrude, somewhat despite her mother's private wishes, marries Alaric Tudor, who eventually brings ruin upon the family. Gertrude nobly stands by her disgraced husband, eventually emigrating with him to Australia. *TC* MT

Woodward, Katie, youngest daughter of Bessie Woodward and eventually wife of Charley Tudor. Katie, a girlish teenager through much of the novel, only comes to realize her love for the rakish Charley after he saves her life. She falls seriously ill of heartache when separated from Charley, but her devotion and faith in his ability to reform saves him. *TC* MT

Woodward, Linda, daughter of Bessie Woodward and wife of Harry Norman. Less beautiful than her sister Gertrude, Linda is noted for her softness. She at first loves Alaric Tudor, but eventually marries the steady and trustworthy Harry. *TC* MT

Woolsworthy, Patience (Patty), strong-minded girl who loves Captain Broughton, but, seeing his selfishness and snobbery, breaks the engagement, stays single, and devotes herself to parish work. 'Colne' *TAC2* GRH

Woolsworthy, Saul. An eccentric minister widely known as the 'antiquarian of Dartmoor', he is unselfish over his beloved daughter and accepts her decisions. 'Colne' *TAC2* GRH

Worcestershire, western county of England in which is located Monkhams, the estate of Lord Peterborough, in *He Knew He Was Right*; also Dunripple Park in *The Vicar of Bullhampton*.
RC

working class. While it would be inaccurate to assert that the working class do not feature in Trollope's fiction, nevertheless one does not get from his writings any overwhelming sense of the working classes *as* a class; certainly the urban poor and the social consequences of industrialization are barely mentioned, and any working-class poverty mentioned in Trollope's works tends to be agricultural and rural, such as his portrayal of the bedesmen of Hiram's Hospital in *The Warden*, and the depiction of Mr Crawley's work with the brickmakers of Hogglestock in *The Last Chronicle of Barset*. Nevertheless, such appearances are rare, and even when the working classes feature as main protagonists in Trollope's plots, Trollope resists any attempt at sociological analysis in favour of conventional love complications. Thus, the story of Ruby Ruggles and John Crumb in *The Way We Live Now* rejects—mercifully, one might feel—any Hardyesque discussion of the plight of the agricultural working classes (John Crumb the miller is comfortably off in any case), in favour of a story which owes considerable debts to the conventions of Victorian melodrama, as the doughty Crumb defends Ruby's honour from the unwelcome attentions of the wicked baronet Sir Felix Carbury. Trollope gives much more prominence to the artisan class in his fiction, for example, Daniel Thwaite the tailor in *Lady Anna*, or Ontario Moggs the bootmaker and Neefit the breeches-maker in *Ralph the Heir*. Even so the class of each is merely the obstacle to romantic fulfilment, rather than the focus of interest in its own right. *The Vicar of Bullhampton*'s treatment of Carry Brattle's 'fall' into prostitution might be the closest thing Trollope gets to a social problem novel, and there is a famous brief encounter between Burgo Fitzgerald and a street prostitute in *Can You Forgive Her?* (XXIX), which reveals for a moment in the novel that an underclass even exists. Broadly speaking, Trollope's concerns lie elsewhere. HO

working habits of Trollope. For some time, Trollope was better known for how he wrote than for what he wrote, regarded less as a novelist than as a chugging steam engine of a word-producer, grinding along at so many words per minute. He is, of course, responsible for this caricature, referring in letters to 'my mechanical genius' and, brazenly in *An Autobiography*, to his extraordinarily regular methods of composition. Though contemporaries did not seem to react unfavourably to his way of going at writing as if it were piece-work paid by the yard, later commentators, more ensnared by notions of genius and inspiration, did not look kindly on his view of writing as a craft one mastered—or did not—by hard and steady labour.

Though Trollope loved to compare writers to humble craftsmen who had learned how to make something and, day after day, simply made it, he also made clear in *An Autobiography* that his writing had found its roots not in external habits of puritanical rigour but in cultivating a rich inner life of daydreaming, developed as a systematic escape from the harshness and loneliness of

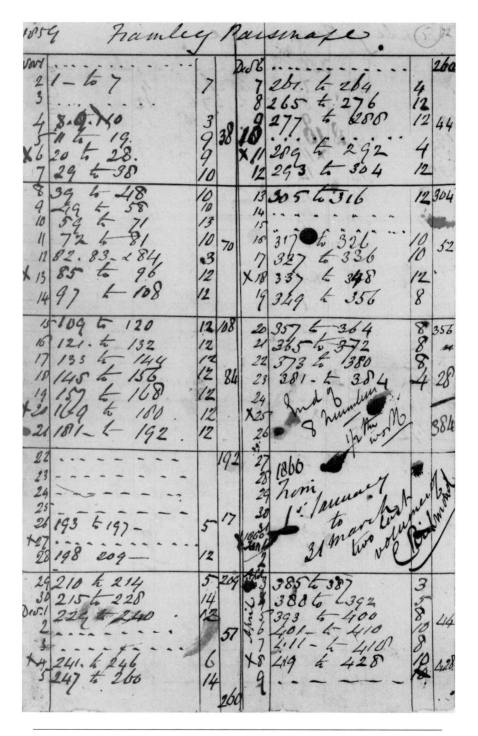

An example of Trollope's meticulous working pattern. The diary for *Framley Parsonage*, 1 November 1859 to 9 April 1860, records dates and number of pages written daily, with daily, weekly, and cumulative page totals. A break in the schedule 1 January to 31 March 1860 indicates time spent writing the last two volumes of *Castle Richmond*.

his sad boyhood. Both family and school offered little but failure and rejection; and, as other boys would not play with him, so he tried to 'form my plays within myself'.

He says he created running stories, going on from day to day, year to year, stories where 'I myself was of course my own hero', but where 'certain proportions, and properties, and unities' were observed. 'Nothing impossible was ever introduced', and he kept even his own character within bounds: never royal, never tall, learned, nor philosophical. 'I was', he admits, 'a very clever person, and beautiful young women used to be fond' (*Auto* III). Still, even in castle-building, Trollope was forming the habits he could exploit as mature novel-writer: the ironic self-awareness, the sense that the castle-building game can only go on if the game has rules, and the absolute psychological dependence on building and maintaining a self by way of stories. Trollope could never have worked so methodically and routinely had his needs not been so absolute and so deep.

But methodical it was, wonderfully so. Once he got into the groove of novel-writing, beginning with *Barchester Towers*, he used lined quarto paper to devise charts, divided into weeks, on which he could record his daily production of pages. There was a good deal of variation from day to day, of course, as even Trollope sometimes had to pause for ill health, family demands, and the stormy world of the Post Office, where he was employed more than full-time. Now and then he would write nothing because he did not feel like it or felt lazy, but so seldom that such days—marked 'Alas!' on his records—are not so easy to find.

Generally, he did what he said, producing an average of about ten pages daily when things were going well, as they mostly were. 'And', he adds, 'as a page is an ambiguous term, my page has been made to contain 250 words; and as words, if not watched, have a tendency to straggle, I have had every word counted as I went' (*Auto* VII). During his years of peak production and before he retired from the Post Office, he paid his groom Barney an extra £5 a year to bring him a cup of coffee at 5 o'clock each morning so that he could be at his desk by 5.30. He then spent 30 minutes going over the work from the day before and then plunged into it: writing with his watch before him, he set a production standard of 250 words every 15 minutes. When he was going at absolute top speed, he could produce a 'four-volume' *Small House* in five months, and in 1864 he managed about eight volumes.

Such regularity may seem both ludicrous and a little frightening in a post-Romantic writerly world that often equates the leisurely with the refined (and thus excuses both). Nabokov says he spent a full month working on a single short paragraph in *Lolita*, clearly expecting us to gasp in admiration; to Trollope, such fiddling would seem preposterous: what was he waiting for, the muse? 'To me', Trollope said, 'it would not be more absurd if the shoemaker were to wait for inspiration, or the tallow-maker for the divine moment of melting.'

Partly, Trollope believed that talk about inspiration was highfalutin nonsense covering sloth; partly, he felt that a laboured approach produced a laboured style. Striving to create effects which were 'natural' and which would work into the mind of the reader without the reader's full awareness of what was being done, Trollope found that revision actually made things worse. He trained himself to write with precise and lucid fluidity, and with remarkable concentration. By such means he could make his writing appear offhand, breezy. Self-conscious writing he regarded as 'artificial', what we would call 'writerly'; and that was certainly a style and a rhetoric he deplored.

It should be said, though, that Trollope never believed he was piping as the linnets sing. He could write each morning and, very often, on trains and on rolling ocean vessels, in hotels and in the midst of hubbub, because he focused so sharply on what he was doing. There was no need, he said, for a writer to sit nibbling his pen if he had been concentrating through the previous day on what he was going to say. By so resolutely and productively keeping his mind on his work when he was not actually working, the writing would come naturally, having been, as it were, pre-formed. Sitting there in the dark, coffee still warm and watch before him, Trollope was very nearly taking dictation from his own mind, copying down work done the day before. His disciplined work habits were generated and made possible by an imagination that never stopped working, building those castles of words.   JRK

Wortle, Dr Jeffrey, rector of Bowick and founder of Bowick School. An 'affectionate tyrant' (1. I) in domestic matters, he runs the school on the same principle of benevolent dictatorship, and brooks interference from neither parents nor clergymen, including superiors. His support of the Peacockes, whose irregular personal situation attracts considerable attention, very nearly leads to the closing of the school. A 'somewhat violent man', he is also 'a man with a kind, tender, affectionate nature' (5. I). *DWS*   RC

Wortle, Mrs Jeffrey, even-tempered and supportive wife of the rector of Bowick. Although she disapproves of the Peacockes' having remained together while not legally married, she publicly defends her husband's position and becomes an admiring and a loyal friend of Mrs Peacocke. *DWS*   RC

Wortle, Mary, only child of Dr and Mrs Wortle, distinguished by a sweet temperament as well as beauty. Courted by Lord Carstairs, she dutifully rejects his offer until it is sanctioned by her parents. *DWS*   RC

Worts, Mr, foreman at the Bungall & Tappitt Brewery in Baslehurst. Worts is 'a heavy, respectable, useful man, educated on the establishment by Bungall and bequeathed by Bungall to Tappitt' (XXIV). Against the wishes of his boss Tappitt, the honest labourer says he will vote for the local squire, Mr Butler Cornbury. *RR*   MT

Wright, Frances (née **Darusmont**) (1795–1852), Scots-born reformer and feminist, much talked of in Trollope's childhood. Having visited America she published *Views of Society and Manners in America* (1821). Captivated by this emancipated spirit, who moved in French intellectual circles, Trollope's mother planned to join her commune in Nashoba, Tennessee (1827), set up in utopian terms to help slaves and integrate black and white citizens, but arrived after the settlement had collapsed.   RCT

Wright, Mr, rector of Belton and Redicote, a bachelor of 70. He 'loved scandal, and was very ill-natured' (II). When rumours arise concerning Mrs Askerton's shady past, Mr Wright enjoys spreading them. Clara Amedroz considers him guilty of 'lying, evil-speaking, and slandering' (II). *BE*   WK

'Writers of Fiction, The' (speech). At the *Royal Literary Fund dinner on 13 May 1863, Trollope responded to the toast proposed by his friend Revd Charles *Merivale. He recalled the bad old days when a novel was looked upon 'as an evil thing'. Now novelists 'are the great instructors of the country'. *NCF* (December 1952), 316–28.   RCT

Wyndham, Fanny, heiress pressured by her guardian Lord Cashel to relinquish her lover Lord Ballindine, a spendthrift. On subsequently inheriting a large fortune, however, she proposes to reconcile with Lord Ballindine, and successfully does so, not only resisting an additional barrage of pressure to marry her guardian's dissipated son Lord Kilcullen, but also defying codes of feminine propriety prohibiting her from asking Lord Ballindine to renew his courtship. *KOK*   MRS

Wyndham, Captain Harry, brother of Fanny Wyndham, a soldier in the Guards whose death makes his sister sole heir of their father's fortune, raising her worth from £20,000 to £100,000. *KOK*   MRS

X, Mr, periodical proprietor. Normally generous, he feels put upon by having to buy off Mrs Brumby. 'Brumby' *ET*   GRH

Y

Yarmouth, small seaside town in Norfolk visited by Arabella Greenow and Kate Vavasor while Widow Greenow is supposed to be in mourning. *CYFH* JMR

Yates, Edmund Hodgson (1831–1894), member of a theatrical family; served in the Post Office (1847–72); drama critic of *Daily News* (1854–60); editor of *Town Talk* (1858), *Temple Bar* (1860), the *World* (1874) and *Time* (1879–84); playwright, novelist, and gossip columnist. Trollope heartily disliked his colleague after an incident at one of George Smith's dinners in July 1860 when he passed on some gossip to Yates involving private conversation of Thackeray, which led to Yates writing up the scene in 'Echoes from the London Clubs' for the *New York Times* (26 May 1860). The *Saturday Review*, scenting blood, took up the story (23 June). Thackeray retaliated with 'On Screens in Dining-Rooms' in *Cornhill* (August 1860). Mortified at his culpability, just when longed-for friendships were beginning, Trollope apologized all round, but he never forgave Yates. The incident reopened the long-standing feud between Thackeray and Dickens, Yates being one of the Dickens circle (*I & R* 68–9). Matters did not improve when Trollope was offered nominal editorship of *Temple Bar* (August 1861), with all the real work to be done by Yates (*Letters* 1, 157). Trollope declined. Yates wanted to feature Trollope in 'Celebrities at Home' for his weekly, the *World*. Trollope, loathing the rise of personality journalism, would have none of it. Considering the enmity between them, Yates's comments on Trollope in *Edmund Yates: His Recollections and Experiences* (1884) are surprisingly moderate. RCT

Yeld, Bishop, popular but incompetent Bishop of Elmham, and neighbour of Roger Carbury. Zealous for good deeds in his parish, he is lax about religious details, especially in contrast to the fervent and antagonistic Catholic priest Father Barham. *WWLN* SRB

yellowbacks, the nickname for cheap reprints of Victorian novels in boards covered with glazed paper, most frequently yellow, with a woodcut cover illustration, customarily printed in three colours. Cheap reprints in boards had been available earlier but the engraver and colour printer Edmund Evans initiated the characteristic yellowback style in 1853. Yellowbacks occasionally carry a frontispiece illustration from the original edition, but seldom any other illustrations. Latterly, alternative bindings in cloth were offered at an enhanced price, and yellowbacks began to appear in diverse and upmarket guises. In the 1870s paperback versions became available.

Several publishers adopted this style for their cheap reprints. From 1848 Routledge's 'Railway Library' appeared thus, and by 1899 when it was terminated, the series ran to over 1,200 titles. In the early 1860s Chapman & Hall began to expand the yellowback 'Select Library of Fiction' which they had initiated in 1857, and they too eventually offered a series list of about 1,000 titles.

Yellowback publishers bought up copyrights (sometimes at job-lot auctions), or made special arrangements with the original publisher. Routledge, for instance, bought all Bulwer-Lytton's copyrights in 1854 with a view to publication in his 'Railway Library'. 'The Select Library of Fiction' appeared under Chapman & Hall's imprint, but the venture was really the work of W. H. *Smith, on behalf of his railway bookstalls, which were a principal outlet for these cheap reprints.

Yellowbacks did much to foster and supply the avid novel-reading habits of the Victorian middle classes. During the 1840s and early 1850s the railway boom increased the volume of travellers and the distance they could go by rail. Reading on the train became the accepted thing: 'A man's seat in a railway carriage is now, or may be, his study,' observed Trollope in 1855, and cheap portable editions of novels were in high demand. Like the circulating library doyen *Mudie, W. H. Smith not only made cheap novels available in attractive and durable form, but he exercised a palpable censorship on the tone and quality of what he published.

Whilst new titles were constantly added to the yellowback series, popular authors like Trollope, Dickens, and Bulwer-Lytton were also continuously reissued. Some Lever titles, for instance, muster fifteen or sixteen separately dated 'new editions' between 1862 and 1880. The author, of course, having ceded his copyright at a much earlier stage, received no direct benefit from these reissues, but they kept him before the reading public and generated expectancy for new works from his pen.

In the early 1880s Chapman & Hall sold the copyrights of their yellowback authors in 'The Select Library of Fiction' to Ward & Lock. Anthony Trollope was deemed to be the most marketable of these and his titles, which had been numbers 85 and upwards, were given pride of place as numbers 1 to 28. TB

Topp, C., *Victorian Yellowbacks and Paperbacks*, vol. 1 (1993).

Yorkshire, county in the north of England where Groby Park is located and one of the primary locations in *Orley Farm*. Yorkshire is also an important location in *The Belton Estate* and *Lady Anna*, and where Matching Priory is located in the Palliser novels. The parish of Kirkby Cliffe is in the West Riding. MT

Young, Anna, companion of Euphemia Smith who returns to England from the Australian gold mines as a witness against John Caldigate in his bigamy trial. Her testimony is questionable. When she and Euphemia quarrel over money given them by Caldigate, she gives evidence against Euphemia, bringing about Caldigate's pardon and Euphemia's imprisonment. *JC*

SRB

Young, Brigham (1801–77), American Mormon, President of the Church of 'Latter Day Saints' after 1847. Travelling across the United States during November 1872, on the way home from Australia, Trollope paused at Salt Lake City to call on 'the great polygamist'. He recounted the story against himself. Young would not let him pass the threshold and insisted that the visitor was a miner. 'I was properly punished, as I had been vain enough to conceive that he would have heard my name' (*Auto* XIX). RCT

'Young Women at the London Telegraph Office, The' (article). Outstanding working conditions are available for young women in the telegraph office of the Post Office. The huge office holds over 800; the work is pleasant, done while seated. Benefits include flexibility in work hours, good pay, job security, medical care, and pensions. There is a dining room on the premises; they may buy a hot meal or bring one to be heated gratis. Here is an example of an outstanding public service facility. *Good Words* (June 1877), 377–84. AKL

Yoxham, Yorkshire rectory and home of Charles Lovel and his family. *LA* RC

Z

Zamenoy, Karil, Nina's 'acutely mercantile' uncle whom she suspects of being instrumental in her father's ruin. A shadowy presence, he remains aloof from his family's plot to separate Nina from her Jewish lover. *NB*   AWJ

Zamenoy, Sophie. Proud of her coach and carpets, though a slatternly housekeeper, Nina's sharp-tongued aunt threatens her with eternal damnation and earthly banishment from Windberg-gasse unless she renounces Anton Trendellsohn. When this fails, she decides that trickery must part her niece from the detested Jews. *NB*   AWJ

Zamenoy, Ziska. Rich, handsome, and pampered, he offers the Trendellsohns title-deeds that are legally theirs provided Anton will relinquish Nina. He would marry her himself, but she hates her unfeeling cousin. So he joins the scheme to ruin her relationship with his rival. *NB*   AWJ

'Zulu in London, The' (pseudonymous letter). 'May Meeting', the conference of Christian clergy in Exeter Hall, was enlightening to this African visitor; a previous sense of tolerance among Christians proved erroneous. The hatred of other beliefs was surprising. Knowledge of the history and customs of the unchurched was called unnecessary. Prayers were offered over the 'ignorant' women (most sewing industriously). Zulu women would not bear such treatment. *Pall Mall Gazette* (10 May 1865), 3–4.   AKL

'Zulu People, The Condition of the' (lecture). Addressing members of Harborne and Edgbaston Institute on 28 October 1879, Trollope posed the question, had Britain done well or ill in respect of the Zulu people? Despite many wars he judged British interference as 'productive alike of good to them and a benefit to us'. As with the Kaffirs the Zulus were advancing in civilization. Trollope warned that fighting might continue against those Zulus close to *Cetywayo, but rulers should 'take care that we did not fight on an idle pretext of mere words (Applause)'. *Birmingham Daily Post* (30 October 1879), col. 2.
RCT

'Zulus and Zululand, The' (lecture). Speaking at an 'inconveniently crowded' Manchester Institute, Nottingham, on 23 October 1879 Trollope described the customs and traditions of the Zulu people to justify their fierce resistance to British rule. On the whole Britain had behaved well, but her record was far from blameless. To applause he declared that colonization had led to destruction of the original inhabitants, that 'in making room for ourselves we had not only banished but exterminated the aboriginal owners of the soil'. That process now proceeded in respect of North American Indians, the Bushmen of Australia, and the Maori of New Zealand. Such a process had not occurred in South Africa where the native population had benefited under British rule. *Nottingham and Midland Counties Daily Express* (24 October 1879), col. 5.   RCT

Trollope in characteristically combative stance, well portrayed by the American photographer, Sarony, and later drawn by R. Birch. The intense scrutiny some found intimidating had something to do with his deafness and short-sightedness. Trollope also found it extremely irritating to hold a long pose for the camera.

CHRONOLOGY

1815	24 April	Born at 16 Keppel Street, Bloomsbury, London.
	? late in year	Family moves to Harrow.
1823	summer	Sent as day-boy to Harrow School.
1825	early in year	Transferred to Arthur Drury's private school at Sunbury.
1827	April	Enters Winchester College.
1830	summer	Removed from Winchester.
1831	January	Sent again to Harrow School.
1834	April	Leaves Harrow. Family's flight to Bruges to escape creditors.
	summer	Becomes for six weeks a classical usher at William Drury's school at Brussels.
	4 November	Appointed junior clerk in the General Post Office, London.
1840	spring–summer	Has serious illness.
1840–1		Plans to write a History of World Literature.
1841	29 July	Appointed surveyor's clerk in Central District of Ireland.
		Begins keeping accounts of official travels.
	15 September	Arrives at Dublin, en route to Banagher, postal headquarters of the Central District.
1843	mid-September	Begins his first novel *The Macdermots of Ballycloran*.
1844	11 June	Marries Rose Heseltine, at Rotherham, Yorkshire.
	27 August	Transferred to Southern District of Ireland as assistant surveyor.
	September	Moves to Cork.
1845	March	Moves to Clonmel, Co. Tipperary.
		Finishes *The Macdermots of Ballycloran*.
1846	13 March	Birth of Henry Merivale Trollope.
?1846–7		Writes *The Kellys and the O'Kellys* (published by Colburn, June 1848).
1847	March	*The Macdermots of Ballycloran* published by Newby.
	27 September	Birth of Frederic James Anthony Trollope.
1848	autumn	Moves to Mallow, Co. Cork.
1848–9		Writes *La Vendée* (published by Colburn, June 1850).
1850		Writes *The Noble Jilt*, play; published 1923.
1851	1 August	Sent to the west of England and Channel Islands on special postal mission. Recommends use of pillar boxes.
	21 December	Returns to Ireland on postal work.
1852	11 March	Continues postal mission in west of England and Wales.
	late May	Conceives, at Salisbury, story of *The Warden*.
1853	19 April–31 May	On leave; holiday abroad with Rose and John Tilley; spends May in Florence with T. A. Trollope.
	29 July	Begins *The Warden*.
	29 August	Appointed acting surveyor of Northern District of Ireland; moves to Belfast.
1854	? autumn	Finishes *The Warden*, sending manuscript to Longman on 8 October (published by Longman, January 1855).
	9 October	Officially appointed surveyor of Northern District.

Chronology

1855	? January	Begins *Barchester Towers*.
	February–March	Writes *The New Zealander*.
	2 April	Longman's reader advises against publication of *The New Zealander*; Trollope revises it through May 1856.
	3 May–13 June	On leave; holiday abroad with Rose; meets Frances Trollope and T. A. Trollope in Venice.
	June	Moves to Donnybrook, near Dublin.
1856	12 May	Resumes *Barchester Towers*.
	9 August–7 September	On leave; holiday abroad with Rose and John Tilley.
	9 November	Finishes *Barchester Towers* (published by Longman, May 1857).
1857	15 February	Begins *The Three Clerks*.
	18 August	Finishes *The Three Clerks* (published by Bentley, November 1857).
	24 August	Begins *The Struggles of Brown, Jones, and Robinson* (breaks off, 7 September).
	5 September	Six weeks' leave; visits with Rose his mother and brother, in Florence.
	20 October	Begins *Doctor Thorne*.
1858	30 January	Leaves from London on postal mission to Egypt.
	10 February	Arrives at Alexandria.
	13–23 March	Visits the Holy Land.
	31 March	Finishes *Doctor Thorne* (published by Chapman & Hall, May 1858).
	1 April	Begins *The Bertrams*.
	4 April–10 May	Returns home via Malta, Gibraltar, and Spain.
	late May–mid-September	Postal duties in Scotland and in north of England.
	? November	Sails from Southampton on postal mission to the West Indies.
	2 December	Arrives at St Thomas; then journeys to Jamaica, Cuba, and other islands of the Caribbean and to Central America.
1859	17 January	Completes *The Bertrams* (published by Chapman & Hall, March 1859).
	25 January–June	Writes *The West Indies and the Spanish Main* (published by Chapman & Hall, October 1859).
	16 May	Starts for home from West Indies visiting New York and Niagara Falls.
	23 June	Sails from New York reaching Liverpool on 3 July.
	4 August	Begins *Castle Richmond*.
	7 September–21 October	Holiday in the south of France with Rose, T. A. Trollope, and John Tilley; writes five short stories later collected in *Tales of All Countries*.
	23 October	Approaches Thackeray, offering short stories for *Cornhill Magazine*.
	26 October	Engaged to write a novel for *Cornhill*, Trollope's first attempt at serial publication.
	2 November	Begins *Framley Parsonage*.
	21 November	Transferred to Eastern District of England; official appointment as Surveyor, 10 January; moves to Waltham House, Waltham Cross, Hertfordshire.
1860	1 January	*Framley Parsonage* serialized in *Cornhill* (until April 1861; book publication by Smith, Elder, April 1861).
	2 January	Continues *Castle Richmond*.

Chronology

	4 January	Gives a lecture on 'The Civil Service as a Profession'.
	? 31 March	Completes *Castle Richmond* (published by Chapman & Hall, May 1860).
	4 July	Begins *Orley Farm*.
	24 September–4 November	On leave; travels abroad with Rose, visiting his mother and T. A. Trollope in Florence, meeting Kate Field.
1861	March	*Orley Farm* begins in twenty monthly parts until October 1862; book publication by Chapman & Hall, Vol. 1, December 1861, and Vol. 2, September 1862.
	20 March	Signs agreement with Chapman & Hall for a book on North America.
	mid-April	Elected to Cosmopolitan Club.
	22 June	Finishes *Orley Farm*.
	24 June	Resumes *The Struggles of Brown, Jones, and Robinson*.
	1 August	*The Struggles of Brown, Jones, and Robinson* serialized in *Cornhill* (1862; book publication by Smith, Elder, November 1870)
	3 August	Completes *The Struggles of Brown, Jones, and Robinson*.
	24 August	Leaves from Liverpool with Rose on his visit to the United States and Canada (Rose returns to England on 27 November).
	5 September	Arrives at Boston.
	16 September	Begins *North America*.
	November	*Tales of All Countries: First Series* published by Chapman & Hall.
1862	12 March	Leaves New York, arrives at Liverpool on 25 March.
	5 April	Elected to the Garrick Club. Thackeray seconds his nomination.
	? 27 April	Finishes *North America* (published by Chapman & Hall, May 1862).
	20 May	Begins *The Small House at Allington*.
	1 September	*The Small House at Allington* serialized in *Cornhill* (until April 1864; book publication by Smith, Elder, March 1864).
	autumn	Extensions built onto Waltham House.
	13–23 September	On leave; visits Holland.
1863	11 February	Finishes *The Small House at Allington*.
	February	*Tales of All Countries: Second Series* published by Chapman & Hall.
	3 March	Begins *Rachel Ray*.
	March	Florence Bland, Trollope's niece, joins household.
	29 June	Finishes *Rachel Ray* (published by Chapman & Hall, October 1863).
	20 July–15 August	On leave; travels to Switzerland, the Rhine and Cologne with Rose, their sons, and their niece Edith Tilley.
	16 August	Begins his first Palliser novel, *Can You Forgive Her?*
	6 October	Death of Trollope's mother.
	30 December	Attends Thackeray's funeral.
1864	1 January	*Can You Forgive Her?* appears in monthly numbers until August 1865; book publication by Chapman & Hall, Vol. 1, September 1864, and Vol. 2, July 1865.
	9 March	Elected to the general committee of the Royal Literary Club.
	12 April	Chosen by committee for membership of the Athenaeum Club.
	28 April	Finishes *Can You Forgive Her?*
	22 May	Begins *Miss Mackenzie*.

Chronology

	18 August	Completes *Miss Mackenzie* (published by Chapman & Hall, February 1865).
	24 August	Begins *The Claverings*.
	3–12 October	On leave; takes Henry to Paris; holiday with Rose on the Isle of Wight.
	autumn	Group led by Trollope begins discussions about starting *Fortnightly Review*.
	31 December	Finishes *The Claverings* (serialized in *Cornhill*, February 1866–May 1867; book publication by Smith, Elder, April 1867).
1865	mid-January	Begins writing articles for *Pall Mall Gazette*.
	30 January	Begins *The Belton Estate*.
	7 February	First issue of the *Pall Mall Gazette*, with two items by Trollope.
	9 February	Contributes first 'Hunting Sketch' to *Pall Mall Gazette* (series finished 20 March; issued in book form by Chapman & Hall, May 1865).
	15–29 April	On leave; goes to Florence, following the death of Theodosia Trollope; returns with his 10-year-old niece Beatrice Trollope to England.
	15 May	First number of *Fortnightly Review* published, containing first instalment of *The Belton Estate* (continuing until 1 January 1866; book publication by Chapman & Hall, December 1865).
	23 May–13 June	On postal business in Scotland and Ireland.
	3 August	First 'Travelling Sketch' appears in *Pall Mall Gazette* (series completed 6 September; issued in book form by Chapman & Hall, February 1866).
	4 September	Finishes *The Belton Estate*.
	16 September–29 October	Travels with Rose and Fred to Koblenz where Henry joins them; Fred continues to Vienna and then Australia.
	3 November	Begins *Nina Balatka*.
	20 November	First 'Clerical Sketch' appears in *Pall Mall Gazette* (series completed 25 January 1866; issued in book form by Chapman & Hall as *Clergymen of the Church of England*, March 1866).
	31 December	Finishes *Nina Balatka* (serialized in *Blackwood's*, July 1866–January 1867; book publication by Blackwood, January 1867).
1866		Writes a few pages of a 'History of English Prose Fiction', then abandons the project.
	21 January	Begins *The Last Chronicle of Barset*, his longest novel to date.
	15 September	Finishes *The Last Chronicle of Barset* (issued by Smith, Elder in weekly numbers, 1 December 1866–6 July 1867; book publication, Vol. 1, March 1867, and Vol. 2, July 1867).
	late September	Holiday with Rose at Bantry Bay, Southern Ireland.
	October	Travels to Paris, where Rose and Henry join him, for T. A. Trollope's marriage to Frances Ternan on 29 October.
	15 November	Invited by James Virtue to edit a new monthly magazine. The title finally chosen was *Saint Pauls*.
	17 November	Begins his twenty-second novel, *Phineas Finn*.
1867	15 May	Finishes *Phineas Finn* (serialized in *Saint Pauls*, October 1867–May 1869; book publication by Virtue, March 1869).
	2 June	Begins *Linda Tressel*.
	10 July	Finishes *Linda Tressel* (serialized in *Blackwood's*, October 1867–May 1868; book publication by Blackwood, May 1868).

Chronology

	18 July–20 August	On leave; goes abroad, Rose joining him in Paris; visits Switzerland.
	August	Third collection of short stories, *Lotta Schmidt*, published by Strahan.
	1 September	Begins *The Golden Lion of Granpère*. Resigns from the civil service.
	1 October	First issue of *Saint Pauls Magazine*.
	22 October	Finishes *The Golden Lion of Granpère* (serialized in *Good Words*, January–August 1872; book publication by Tinsley, May 1872).
	31 October	Farewell dinner after nearly thirty-three years' service in the Post Office.
	13 November	Begins *He Knew He Was Right*.
1868	17 March	Presented at court prior to negotiating a postal convention between England and the United States.
	11 April	Embarks from Liverpool, arriving in New York on 22 April where he meets Dickens about to sail for home.
	12 June	Finishes *He Knew He Was Right* (published by Virtue in weekly numbers, 17 October 1868–22 May 1869; book publication by Strahan, May 1869).
	15 June	In Washington, begins *The Vicar of Bullhampton*.
	15 July	Leaves New York and arrives home on 26 July.
	1 November	Finishes *The Vicar of Bullhampton* (published by Bradbury & Evans in monthly numbers, July 1869–May 1870; book publication, April 1870).
	30 October	Standing for election as Liberal candidate for Beverley, Yorkshire; delivers his first speech to electors.
	17 November	On election day comes last of four candidates.
	27 December	Begins *Sir Harry Hotspur of Humblethwaite*.
	December	Fred returns from Australia for a visit before leaving permanently to settle in Australia (26 April).
1869	30 January	Finishes *Sir Harry Hotspur of Humblethwaite* (serialized in *Macmillan's Magazine*, May–December 1870; book publication by Hurst & Blackett, November 1870).
	? March	Dramatizes *The Last Chronicle of Barset* as *Did He Steal It?* (never performed).
	4 April	Begins *Ralph the Heir*.
	7 August	Finishes *Ralph the Heir* (published by Strahan in monthly numbers and simultaneously as supplement to *Saint Pauls*, January 1870–July 1871; book publication by Hurst & Blackett, April 1871).
	mid-September	Tours Normandy and Brittany with Rose.
	4 December	Begins *The Eustace Diamonds*.
1870	29 January	Begins *The Commentaries of Caesar*.
	January	Under pressure from Strahan, agrees to give up editorship of *Saint Pauls* after the June issue; he stays on until July.
	25 April	Finishes *The Commentaries of Caesar* (published by Blackwood, June 1870).
	June	Fourth collection of short stories, written for *Saint Pauls, An Editor's Tales* published by Strahan.
	25 August	Finishes *The Eustace Diamonds* (serialized in *Fortnightly*, July 1871–February 1873; book publication by Chapman & Hall, October 1872).

Chronology

	13 September	Begins *An Eye for an Eye*.
	10 October	Finishes *An Eye for an Eye* (serialized in *Whitehall Review*, 24 August 1878–1 February 1879; book publication by Chapman & Hall, October 1879).
	23 October	Begins *Phineas Redux*.
1871	1 April	Finishes *Phineas Redux* (serialized in *Graphic*, 19 July 1873–10 January 1874; book publication by Chapman & Hall, December 1873).
	24 May	Having given up Waltham House in April, leaves Liverpool with Rose for Australia, to visit Fred in New South Wales.
	25 May	Begins *Lady Anna*.
	19 July	Finishes *Lady Anna* (serialized in *Fortnightly*, April 1873–April 1874; book publication by Chapman & Hall, March 1874).
	27 July	Arrives in Melbourne to begin an intensive travel schedule to Sydney, New South Wales, and Brisbane, Queensland. Stays with Fred at his sheep station in late October.
	23 October	Begins *Australia and New Zealand*.
1872	April	Charles Reade's *Shilly-Shally*, pirated version of *Ralph the Heir*, put on at Gaiety Theatre, London.
	mid-April	Tours South Australia.
	29 July	Leaves Melbourne for New Zealand.
	3 October	Sails for home, changing ship at Honolulu.
	6 November	Arrives in San Francisco and covers America by train, calling at Salt Lake City.
	December	Arrives home; takes lodgings at 3 Holles Street before moving to his new home at 39 Montagu Square (April).
1873	15 January	Finishes *Australia and New Zealand* (published by Chapman & Hall, February 1873).
	1 May	Begins *The Way We Live Now*.
	1 June	Begins *Harry Heathcote of Gangoil*.
	28 June	Finishes *Harry Heathcote of Gangoil* (published as Christmas number of *Graphic*, 25 December 1873; book publication by Sampson Low, October 1874).
	mid-August–30 August	On holiday with Rose in Killarney.
	22 December	Completes *The Way We Live Now* (published by Chapman & Hall in monthly numbers, February 1874–September 1875; book publication, June 1875).
1874	2 April	Begins *The Prime Minister*.
	23 July–16 September	Holiday with Rose in Switzerland.
	15 September	Finishes *The Prime Minister* (published by Chapman & Hall in monthly numbers, November 1875–June 1876; book publication, June 1876).
	12 October	Begins *Is He Popenjoy?*
1875	1 March	Leaves London, calling at Rome and Naples en route for Australia.
	27 March–12 April	Visits Ceylon.
	3 May	Finishes *Is He Popenjoy?* at sea between Ceylon and Melbourne (serialized in *All the Year Round*, 13 October 1877–13 July 1878; book publication by Chapman & Hall, April 1878).
	4 May	Arrives at Melbourne and travels to Fred's sheep station in New South Wales for a stay of two months.

Chronology

	4 June	Begins *The American Senator*.
	3 July	First of twenty letters, mostly on Australia, published in the *Liverpool Mercury* (continued weekly until 13 November 1875).
	28 August	Sails from Sydney, calling at Auckland and Honolulu, San Francisco, Boston, and New York.
	24 September	Finishes *The American Senator* (serialized in *Temple Bar*, May 1876–July 1877; book publication by Chapman & Hall, June 1877).
	20 October	Sails from New York and begins *An Autobiography*.
	30 October	Reaches Liverpool, having completed thirty-three pages of *An Autobiography* aboard ship.
1876	2 January	Resumes *An Autobiography*, finished 11 April. The manuscript is placed in his safe and Henry is instructed to see it into print after his death.
	March	Gives up hunting.
	2 May	Begins his thirty-ninth novel, *The Duke's Children*.
	8 May	First of forty-eight hearings of Copyright Commission on which he serves.
	end of July–mid-October	Holiday with Rose and Florence Bland in Switzerland.
	29 October	Finishes *The Duke's Children* (serialized in *All the Year Round*, 4 October 1879–14 July 1880; book publication by Chapman & Hall, May 1880).
1877	3 February	Begins *John Caldigate*.
	22 February–12 March	Begins work on two-part article, 'Cicero', for *Fortnightly* (published 1 April, 1 September).
	29 June	Leaves Dartmouth for South Africa, having written thirteen parts of *John Caldigate*.
	21 July	Writes final three parts of *John Caldigate* (serialized in *Blackwood's*, April 1878–June 1879; book publication by Chapman & Hall, May 1879).
	22 July	Arrives at Cape Town; undertakes exhausting travel itinerary in South Africa until mid-December.
	23 July	Begins *South Africa*.
	October	First of fifteen travel letters published in provincial papers.
	11 December	Leaves Cape Town for home, arriving in England on 3 January 1878.
1878	2 January	Finishes *South Africa* (published by Chapman & Hall, February 1878).
	March	Completes arrangements with Chapman & Hall for publication in eight volumes of *The Chronicles of Barsetshire* (November 1878–July 1879).
	25 April	On holiday near Bolton Abbey, Yorkshire, begins *Ayala's Angel*.
	22 June–8 July	Travels to Iceland in yacht *Mastiff*; writes his fifth book of travels, *How the 'Mastiffs' Went to Iceland* (privately printed by Virtue, October 1878).
	late July–30 September	Holiday with Rose and Florence Bland in Switzerland and Germany.
	24 September	Finishes *Ayala's Angel* (published by Chapman & Hall, May 1881).
	26 October	Begins *Cousin Henry*.
	8 December	Finishes *Cousin Henry* (serialized simultaneously in *Manchester Weekly Times* and *North British Weekly Mail*, 8 March–24 May 1879; book publication by Chapman & Hall, October 1879).

	23 December	Begins *Marion Fay* (breaks off after nine days).
1879	1 February	Begins *Thackeray*.
	25 March	Finishes *Thackeray* (published by Macmillan, May 1879).
	8 April	Begins *Dr Wortle's School*, at Lowick Rectory, Northamptonshire.
	29 April	Finishes *Dr Wortle's School* (serialized in *Blackwood's*, May–December 1880; book publication by Chapman & Hall, January 1881).
	August–September	Holiday with Rose and Florence Bland in France, Switzerland, and Germany.
	6 August	Resumes *Marion Fay*.
	21 November	Finishes *Marion Fay* (serialized in *Graphic*, 3 December 1881–3 June 1882; book publication by Chapman & Hall, May 1882).
1880	26 May	Finishes *The Life of Cicero* (published by Chapman & Hall, December 1880).
	6 July	After seven years at 39 Montagu Square, decides to move to North End, South Harting, near Petersfield.
	18 August	Begins *Kept in the Dark*.
	15 December	Finishes *Kept in the Dark* (serialized in *Good Words*, May–December 1882; book publication by Chatto & Windus, October 1882).
	17 December	Begins *The Fixed Period*.
1881	28 February	Finishes *The Fixed Period* (serialized in *Blackwood's*, October 1881–March 1882; book publication by Blackwood, March 1882).
	March	Travels to Rome with Rose and Florence Bland to visit Tom and Fanny Trollope, his last holiday in Europe.
	14 March	Begins *Mr Scarborough's Family*.
	31 October	Finishes *Mr Scarborough's Family* (serialized in *All the Year Round*, 27 May 1882–16 June 1883; book publication by Chatto & Windus, April 1883).
	? November	Begins *Palmerston*.
	December	Fifth volume of short stories, *Why Frau Frohmann Raised her Prices*, published by Isbister.
1882	1 February	Finishes *Palmerston* (published by Isbister, June 1882).
	20 February	Begins *An Old Man's Love*.
	9 May	Finishes *An Old Man's Love* (published by Blackwood, March 1884).
	15 May	Crosses to Dublin with Florence Bland to research material for an Irish novel.
	June	Begins *The Landleaguers*.
	11 August–2 September	Second visit to Dublin for research on his novel.
	2 September	Resumes *The Landleaguers* (left incomplete; serialized in *Life*, 16 November 1882–4 October 1883; book publication by Chatto & Windus, October 1883).
	2 October	Takes rooms at Garlant's Hotel, Suffolk Street.
	3 November	While dining with John Tilley, suffers a stroke.
	6 December	Dies in a nursing home at 34 Welbeck Street.
	9 December	Burial at Kensal Green Cemetery.
1883	October	Publication by Blackwood of *An Autobiography*.

FAMILY TREES

TROLLOPE'S PATERNAL ANCESTRY

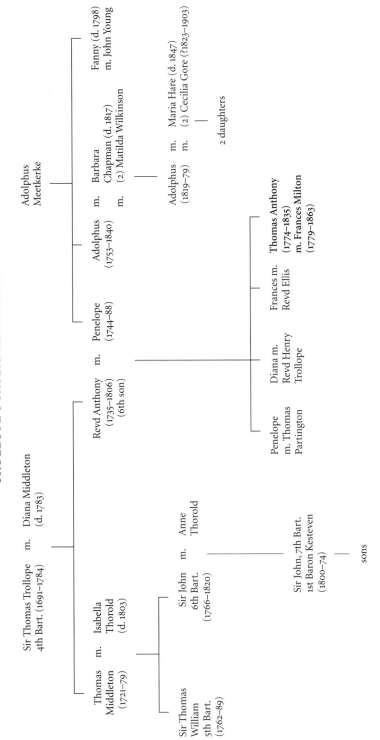

ANCESTRY OF ROSE HESELTINE

MATERNAL ANCESTRY OF TROLLOPE

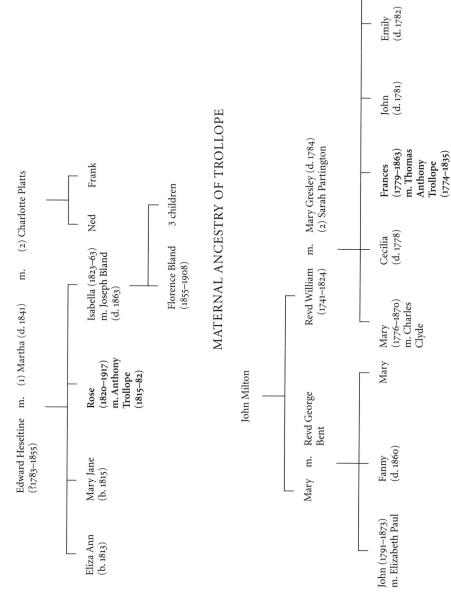

DIRECT FAMILY OF TROLLOPE

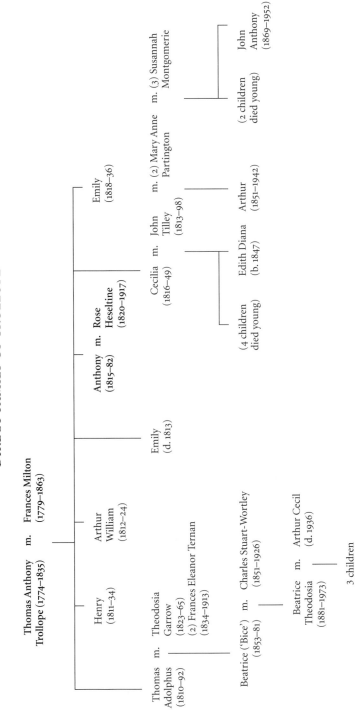

DESCENDANTS OF TROLLOPE

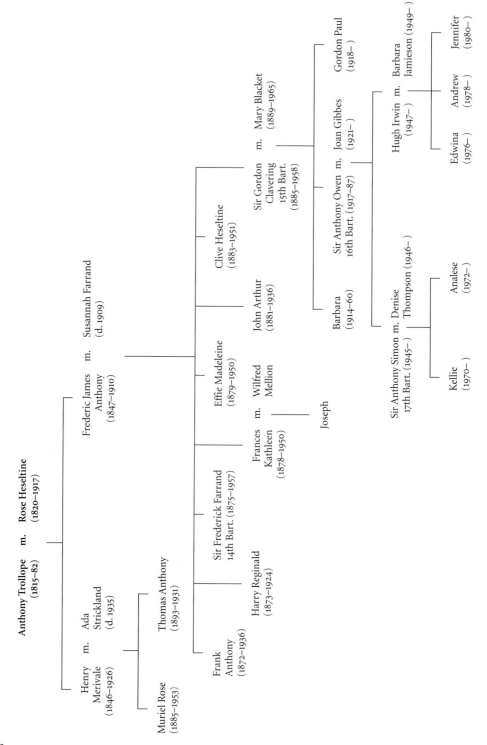

MAPS

BARSETSHIRE
Trollope's almost indecipherable map of the 'dear county', drawn after writing *Framley Parsonage* (*Auto* VIII), was printed by Sadleir in his *Commentary* (1927), and later redrawn with additions by several ardent Trollopians. The version here reproduces only the entries on Trollope's original.

NORTH AMERICA
Following the precedent of his mother's journey and travel book, Trollope embarked on an extensive tour of America, trying hard to interpret its political, social, and cultural institutions for his English readers. *North America* was published in 1862.

IRELAND
As the source of his professional and social maturation, Ireland held a particular attraction for Trollope and he placed five novels there. The map focuses on two major locations, for *The Macdermots of Ballycloran* (1847) and *Castle Richmond* (1860).

SOUTH AFRICA
Trollope's fourth and last travel book, *South Africa* (1878), chronicles the most daunting of his many journeys around the world, but his physical stamina stood up well to an itinerary of gruelling intensity with temperatures in the mid-nineties.

AUSTRALIA AND NEW ZEALAND
Trollope's two journeys to Australia had familial ties, since his younger son, Frederic, had emigrated there in 1865. The first, with Rose, involved a hefty itinerary of six colonies and New Zealand, with heavily documented accounts of history, politics, and social affairs. *Australia and New Zealand* was published in 1873.

WEST INDIES
A journey to the West Indies as a civil servant brought about Trollope's first travel book. My instruction, Trollope noted, was 'to cleanse the Augean stables of our Post Office system there' (*Auto* VI). His duties involved negotiating postal treaties and improving standards of service and management. *The West Indies and the Spanish Main* was published in 1859 to general critical acclaim.

ICELAND
Iceland became a favoured tourist destination in the 1870s as a result of archaeological and linguistic studies. Trollope joined a party of travellers led by John Burns, of the Cunard Steamship Company, whose well-appointed yacht, the *Mastiff*, took them on a holiday trip which resulted in *How the 'Mastiffs' went to Iceland* (1878).

BARSETSHIRE

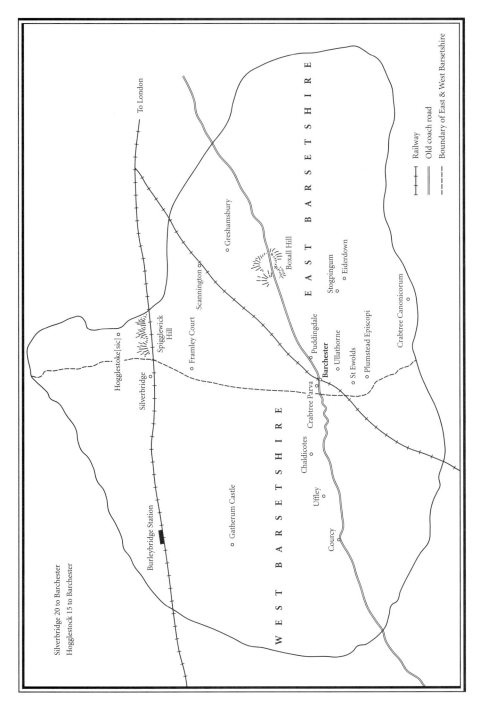

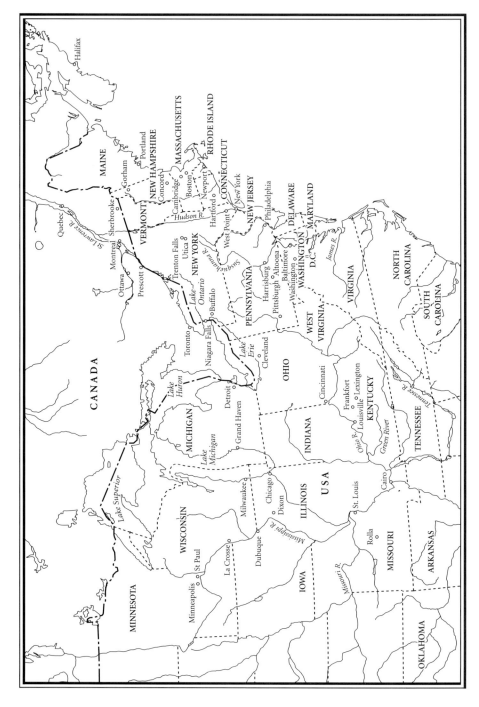

NORTH AMERICA

IRELAND

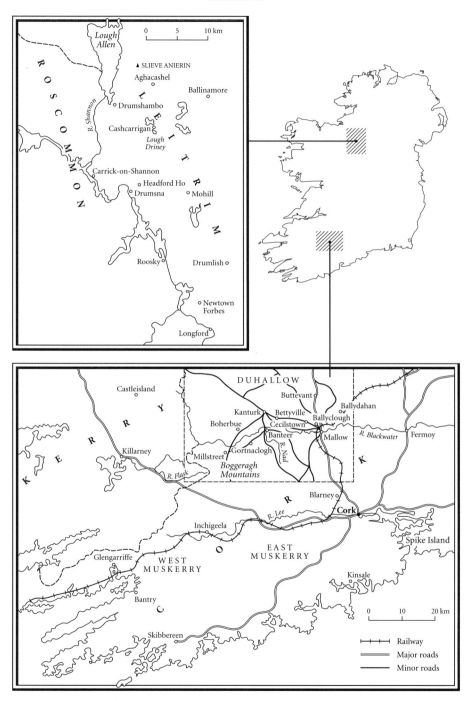

SOUTH AFRICA

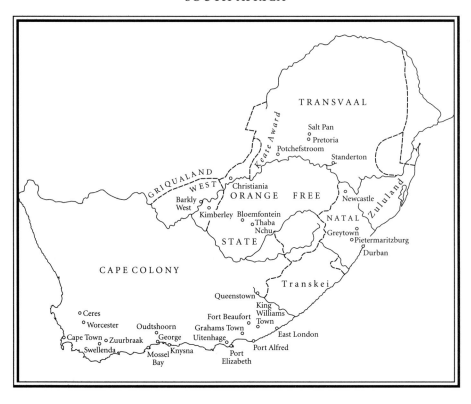

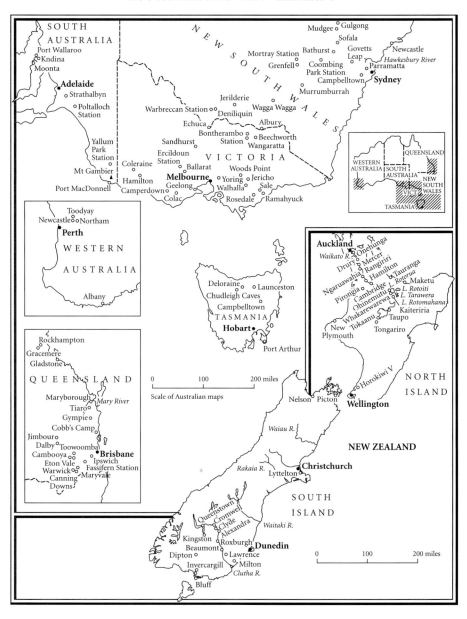

WEST INDIES

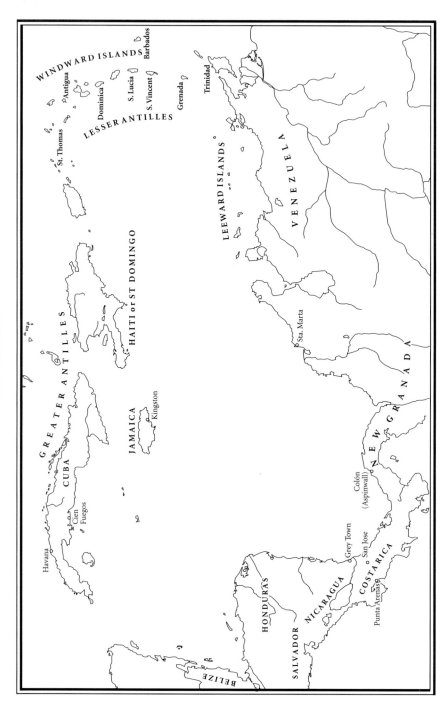

ICELAND

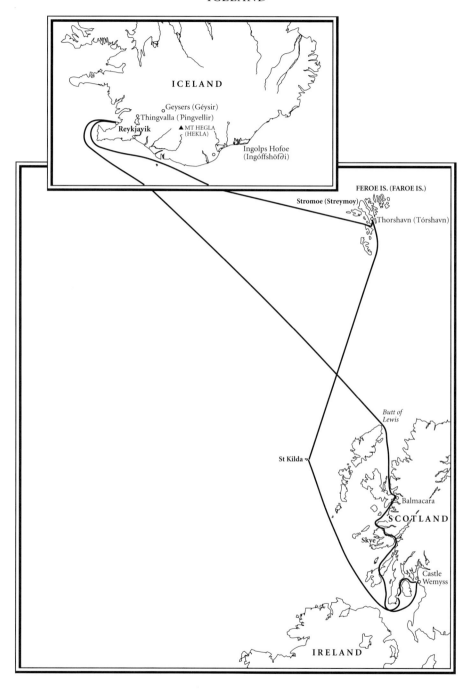

SELECT BIBLIOGRAPHY

apRoberts, Ruth, *Trollope: Artist and Moralist* (1971).
Bareham, Tony (ed.), *Anthony Trollope* (1980).
—— (ed.), *Trollope: The Barsetshire Novels: A Casebook* (1983).
Booth, Bradford A., *Anthony Trollope: Aspects of his Life and Art* (1958).
Clark, John W., *Language and Style of Anthony Trollope* (1975).
Cockshut, A. O. J., *Anthony Trollope: A Critical Study* (1955).
Daniels, Mary L. (ed.), *Trollope-to-Reader: A Topical Guide to Digressions in the Novels of Anthony Trollope* (1983).
Edwards, P. D., *Anthony Trollope: His Art and Scope* (1977).
—— *Anthony Trollope's Son in Australia* (1982).
Epperly, Elizabeth R., *Anthony Trollope's Notes on the Old Drama* (1988).
—— *Patterns of Repetition in Trollope* (1989).
Escott, T. H. S., *Anthony Trollope: His Work, Associates and Literary Originals* (1913).
Gerould, W. G., and Gerould, J. T., *A Guide to Trollope* (1948).
Glendinning, Victoria, *Anthony Trollope* (1993).
Hall, N. John, *The Trollope Critics* (1981).
—— (ed.), *The Letters of Anthony Trollope* (1983).
—— *Trollope and his Illustrators* (1980).
—— *Trollope: A Biography.* Oxford: Clarendon Press (1991).
Halperin, John, *Trollope and Politics: A Study of the Pallisers and Others* (1977).
—— *Trollope Centenary Essays* (1982).
Hamer, Mary, *Writing by Numbers: Trollope's Serial Fiction* (1987).
Harvey, Geoffrey, *The Art of Anthony Trollope* (1980).
Herbert, Christopher, *Trollope and Comic Pleasure* (1987).
James, Henry, *Partial Portraits* (1888).
Kendrick, Walter M., *The Novel-Machine: The Theory and Fiction of Anthony Trollope* (1980).
Kincaid, James R., *The Novels of Anthony Trollope* (1977).
Lansbury, Coral, *The Reasonable Man: Trollope's Legal Fiction* (1981).
Letwin, Shirley Robin, *The Gentleman in Trollope: Individuality and Moral Conduct* (1982).
Lyons, Anne Kearns, *Anthony Trollope: An Annotated Bibliography of Periodical Works by and about Him in the United States and Great Britain to 1900* (1985).
McMaster, Juliet, *Trollope's Palliser Novels: Theme and Pattern* (1978).
McMaster, Rowland, *Trollope and the Law* (1986).
Markwick, Margaret, *Trollope and Women* (1997).
Morse, Deborah Denenholz, *Women in Trollope's Palliser Novels* (1987).
Mullen, Richard, *Anthony Trollope: A Victorian in his World* (1990).
—— and Munson, James, *The Penguin Companion to Trollope* (1996).
Nardin, Jane, *He Knew She Was Right: The Independent Woman in the Novels of Anthony Trollope* (1989).
—— *Trollope and Victorian Moral Philosophy* (1996).
Overton, Bill, *The Unofficial Trollope* (1982).
Polhemus, Robert M., *The Changing World of Anthony Trollope* (1968).
Pollard, Arthur, *Anthony Trollope* (1978).
Pope Hennessy, James, *Anthony Trollope* (1971).
Sadleir, Michael, *Trollope: A Commentary* (1927).
—— *Trollope: A Bibliography* (1928).
Skilton, David, *Anthony Trollope and his Contemporaries* (1972).
Smalley, Donald (ed.), *Trollope: The Critical Heritage* (1969).
Snow, C. P., *Anthony Trollope* (1975).
Srebrnik, Patricia Thomas, *Alexander Strahan, Victorian Publisher* (1986).

Select Bibliography

Stebbins, L. P., and Stebbins, R. P., *The Trollopes: The Chronicle of a Writing Family* (1945).

Stone, Donald D., *The Romantic Impulse in Victorian Fiction* (1980).

Super, R. H., *Trollope in the Post Office* (1981).

—— *The Chronicler of Barsetshire: A Life of Anthony Trollope* (1988).

Swingle, L. J., *Romanticism and Anthony Trollope: A Study in the Continuities of Nineteenth-Century Literary Thought* (1990).

Terry, R. C., *Anthony Trollope: The Artist in Hiding* (1977).

—— *Anthony Trollope: Interviews and Recollections* (1987).

—— *A Trollope Chronology* (1989).

Tracy, Robert, *Trollope's Later Novels* (1978).

Wall, Stephen, *Trollope and Character* (1988).

Walpole, Hugh, *Anthony Trollope* (1928).

Walton, Priscilla, *Patriarchal Desire and Victorian Discourse: A Lacanian Reading of Anthony Trollope's Palliser Novels* (1995).

Wright, Andrew, *Anthony Trollope: Dream and Art* (1983).

PICTURE ACKNOWLEDGEMENTS

frontispiece British Library 24 British Library, Manuscript 56 Scottish National Portrait Gallery
69 British Library 86 Princeton University Library 93 Dickens House Museum, London (with
thanks to Andrew Xavier) 97 The Post Office. Post Office copyright reserved 107 British Library 176
National Portrait Gallery 197 British Library 206 British Library 243 British Library 256
Lowewod Museum, Broxbourne, Herts. (with thanks to Neil Robbins) 263 British Library 291 British
Library 305 British Library 323 British Museum, Department of Prints and Drawings 350
MacMillan Press 368 Princeton University Library 406 British Library 440 Post Office, by courtesy
of H. M. Postmaster General 449 British Library 453 British Library 499 British Library 501
Hulton Getty 519 National Portrait Gallery 537 British Library 539 Hulton Getty 545 National
Portrait Gallery 552 Boston Public Library, Department of Rare Books 555 Bodleian Library, Oxford
559 British Library 572 British Library 591 Bodleian Library, Oxford endpiece Mary Evans